READINGS IN
ORGANIZATIONAL BEHAVIOR
AND HUMAN PERFORMANCE

READINGS IN ORGANIZATIONAL BEHAVIOR AND HUMAN PERFORMANCE

Edited by

W. E. SCOTT, JR.
Graduate School of Business
Indiana University

and

L. L. CUMMINGS
Graduate School of Business
The University of Wisconsin

Revised Edition • 1973

RICHARD D. IRWIN, INC. Homewood, Illinois 60430
IRWIN-DORSEY INTERNATIONAL London, England WC2H 9NJ
IRWIN-DORSEY LIMITED Georgetown, Ontario L7G 4B3

Revised Edition

First Printing, May 1973

ISBN 0-256-01398-5
Library of Congress Catalog Card No. 72-93547

Printed in the United States of America

PREFACE

The primary purpose of the editors in presenting the studies included in this revision is to help the student achieve some understanding of the behavior of individuals and groups in goal-seeking organizations. Our interest has been (1) to emphasize empirically derived knowledge about behavior, (2) to incorporate relevant theory and literature reviews, and (3) to relate this knowledge to the practical problems of the utilization of human effort. Insofar as reliable and generalizable knowledge about any phenomenon helps one to deal with it more effectively, it is possible—indeed, it is our hope—that this book will serve to enhance the leadership potential of those who peruse it.

We have organized the readings to reflect what we consider to be the major categories of concern in organizational behavior and human performance. We begin with a chapter on "Theoretical and Empirical Foundations of Organizational Behavior and Human Performance." Here we attempt to provide the student with an overview of the psychological and social psychological concepts necessary for an understanding of the behavior of people in organizations. Several theoretical models as well as summaries of research findings from the "behavioral basic disciplines" are included as a foundation for some of the more operational and applied materials in later chapters.

In Chapter 2 we move to a consideration of "Dependent Variables in Organizational Behavior and Human Performance." The readings focus on the major criteria by which behavior in organizations could be, and frequently is, evaluated. Such variables as productivity, innovation, and satisfaction, as well as loyalty, turnover, and absenteeism are examined. Both theoretical and empirical literature discussing the nature and interrelationships among these criteria receive attention. Both the multidimensionality and the dynamic nature of behavior in organizations are emphasized.

Chapters 3 through 5 focus on several operational strategies for influencing and changing behavior. In Chapter 3 on "Structural and Environmental Determinants of Behavior in Organizations" we consider three dimensions of the internal environment of the organization as determinants of behavior; (1) the design of both operative and managerial tasks, (2) the design of organizational structures, and (3) the design and administration of the organization's formal reward and penalty system. In the case of each of these dimensions, we attempt to combine trustworthy empirical knowledge and reasonable practicality in the selection of relevant readings.

Chapter 4, "Interpersonal Processes as Determinants of Behavior in Organizations," examines the behavior of people in interaction within operative and managerial groups. Thus, the readings included in this chapter draw heavily upon the literature in social psychology and sociology aimed at the group level of analysis. Articles examining the influence of several group variables on performance and morale are included—for example, group size, structure, ecology, cohesion, and task. A major concern of this chapter centers on the *leadership processes* within groups and on the conditions necessary for effective leadership behavior. The selections included examine the consequences of various leadership behaviors for both organizational goal fulfillment and individual need satisfaction. These readings reflect the major streams of research and theory in the leadership literature.

The concluding chapter, "Behavioral Direction and Change Strategies," focuses on the problems of monitoring, controlling, and changing human behavior in organizations. The readings selected reflect a need for both efficiency and long-run viability in an organization's monitoring and control processes. A diversity of theoretical perspectives and practical tactics are represented on the control, conflict, and change topics. We also examine research data reflecting the effects of various control, conflict, and change tactics.

Thus, in summary, Chapter 1 provides a background in the concepts and variables of the basic disciplines underlying the study of behavior in organizations. Chapter 2 deals with the questions of the criteria of individual and organizational performance and the dependent variables through which modifications in the determinants of behavior can be evaluated. Chapters 3, 4, and 5 focus on the major applied areas in organizational behavior—attempting to draw on three levels of analyses (individual, group, and organizational).

This book is intended primarily for advanced undergraduate and beginning graduate students in all sectors of management and administration as well as organizational behavior, personnel and industrial relations, organizational psychology, and microorganizational theory. The book will probably be most appropriate in courses in the above areas with a two-semester prerequisite in one (or a combination) of the behavioral sciences. The readings have been selected to supplement most of the textbooks presently available in organizational psychology, human relations, and leadership as well as behaviorally oriented texts in personnel and general management. The first edition of the book also has been used successfully in advanced organizational behavior courses in executive education.

We feel that it is appropriate to explicate the viewpoints we, as editors, have attempted to present and lend credence to through our own introductory and integrating comments. Given the present state of our knowledge, we feel that the advancement of knowledge and practice in organizational behavior and human performance requires an eclectic approach. Because of this operating premise, we have selected readings representing varying viewpoints on at least three dimensions:

1. *Theoretical Perspective.* Represented in this book are theoretical positions ranging from highly micro, psychological approaches through social psychological perspectives to more macro, sociological viewpoints.
2. *Methodological Orientation.* Studies are reported utilizing laboratory, quasi-experimental, and field designs. The contents of the readings aim toward providing the student with an opportunity to develop his awareness of the uses of alternative research strategies as well as to provide him with knowledge in several substantive content areas.
3. *Concern with Applications and the "Real World."* An attempt is made to include a mix of selections representing good theory and trustworthy practical knowledge. We also attempt to emphasize the practicality of good theory and the theoretical significance of practical research. In addition, we have explicitly attempted to include materials of relevance across several organizational sectors (both private and public).

A few comments are in order regarding the organization of the book. Each of the chapters is introduced by editorial comment regarding the (1) role of each chapter in the overall mission of the book and (2) the integration of the readings within each chapter; i.e., the relationships among the readings in that specific chapter and the rationale for their selection and sequencing. These editorial comments are intended to aid the reader in integrating the specific authors and ideas into the broader stream of research and theory in organizational behavior and human performance.

Research in the field of organizational behavior and human performance is continuing at an ever-increasing pace. As a consequence, nearly 50 percent of the selections in this revision are new. In order to properly reflect the developments in the field while keeping the book to realistic proportions, we felt it necessary to delete the chapter on knowledge development and a section on environmental stressors. It is not that we consider these topics of no importance. Indeed, we managed to reference and, in some cases, to discuss the deleted materials in the new selections. It was simply that we had to cut some place and the deleted sections seemed to be the most logical in view of the purposes of the book.

We wish to thank several of our colleagues at the University of Wisconsin, Indiana University, the University of British Columbia and elsewhere for their suggestions regarding specific readings and general focus; particularly, Professors John F. Mee, Joseph Reitz, Donald Schwab, Donald Wood, Herbert Heneman III, Vance Mitchell, Dennis Organ, and Merle Ace. Conversations with several colleagues at other institutions have indirectly influenced our thinking regarding the scope and content of such a selection of readings. We specifically wish to thank Professors Allan Filley, Robert House, Lyman Porter, and Victor Vroom.

We are grateful to Miss Gillian Beale, Mrs. Joyce Hein, and Mrs. Barbara Grigsby for their assistance in typing and editing.

April 1973

W. E. SCOTT, JR.
L. L. CUMMINGS

CONTENTS

CHAPTER 1
Theoretical and Empirical Foundations of Organizational Behavior and Human Performance 1

chapter 1

THEORETICAL AND EMPIRICAL FOUNDATIONS OF ORGANIZATIONAL BEHAVIOR AND HUMAN PERFORMANCE

When the puzzled administrator asks "What motivates behavior?" he is usually asking someone to identify the determinants, and in the broad sense, *all* of the determinants of behavior. Scientists actively seeking answers to this very complex question have tended to follow one of two general approaches. Some behavioral scientists have sought to establish lawful relationships between environmental variables and observable behavioral variables, preferring to leave speculations about states and processes within the organism to those so inclined. Another group, noting that behavior is complex and not often related to environmental variables in any simple fashion, has persisted in formulating organismic variables which, along with environmental variables, are believed to determine behavior.

In recent years we have noticed a trend toward the coalescence of the two approaches. In the meantime, it is clear that behavioral scientists, whatever their theoretical preferences, have continued to make significant contributions to our body of knowledge about behavior. Consequently, we have included this chapter of readings in order to provide an overview of their collective efforts. The readings were selected on the premise that an awareness of the different approaches to the problem of understanding behavior and a reasonable grasp of some of the more relevant concepts and findings should serve as a valuable foundation for the study of human behavior in organizations.

We introduce this chapter with a selection from the works of Mark Twain. Among other things, it is a delightfully incisive comment on a very common human frailty. In observing behavior in a complex setting or even, for that matter, under highly controlled laboratory conditions, we often draw erroneous conclusions regarding the determinants of that behavior. Furthermore, we may readily accept an experimental result which is in accord with our preconceived, and possibly erroneous, notions about behavior and reject out of hand an empirical observation which threatens the validity of those notions.

1. ON EXPERIMENTAL DESIGN*

Mark Twain

I constructed four miniature houses of worship—a Mohammedan mosque, a Hindu temple, a Jewish synagogue, a Christian cathedral—and placed them in a row. I then marked 15 ants with red paint and turned them loose. They made several trips to and fro, glancing in at the places of worship, but not entering.

I then turned loose 15 more painted blue; they acted just as the red ones had done. I now gilded 15 and turned them loose. No change in the result; the 45 traveled back and forth in a hurry persistently and continuously visiting each fane, but never entering. This satisfied me that these ants were without religious prejudices—just what I wished; for under no other conditions would my next and greater experiment be valuable. I now placed a small square of white paper within the door of each fane; and upon the mosque paper I put a pinch of putty, upon the temple paper a dab of tar, upon the synagogue paper a trifle of turpentine, and upon the cathedral paper a small cube of sugar.

First I liberated the red ants. They examined and rejected the putty, the tar and the turpentine, and then took to the sugar with zeal and apparent sincere conviction. I next liberated the blue ants, and they did exactly as the red ones had done. The gilded ants followed. The preceding results were precisely repeated. This seemed to prove that ants destitute of religious prejudice will always prefer Christianity to any other creed.

However, to make sure, I removed the ants and put putty in the cathedral and sugar in the mosque. I now liberated the ants in a body, and they rushed tumultuously to the cathedral. I was very much touched and gratified, and went back in the room to write down the event; but when I came back the ants had all apostatized and had gone over to the Mohammedan communion.

I saw that I had been too hasty in my conclusions, and naturally felt rebuked and humbled. With diminished confidence I went on with the test to the finish. I placed the sugar first in one house of worship, then in another, till I had tried them all.

With this result: whatever Church I put the sugar in, that was the one the ants straightway joined. This was true beyond a shadow of doubt, that in religious matters the ant is the opposite of man, for man cares for but one thing; to find the only true Church; whereas the ant hunts for the one with the sugar in it.

Section A

REINFORCEMENT PRINCIPLES AND PROPOSITIONAL CONTROL

The concept of environmental control has been introduced without elaboration. We now turn to clarifying discussions of this all important process.

Michael and Meyerson describe the principles of reinforcement and their implications for counseling and guidance, but their article could just as well be titled, "A Behavioral Approach to Leadership." An organizational leader, responsible for directing behavior, cannot easily modify organismic variables. Therefore, he must resort to environmental change as a means of influencing behavior. Reinforcement principles are singularly useful in this regard because they indicate to the leader how he might proceed in designing or modifying an environment in order to effect specific changes in behavior.

In the next selection, Nord reemphasizes the significance of operant conditioning principles for organizational leaders. Nord feels (and we agree) that this body of knowledge has been somewhat neglected in favor of approaches which emphasize cognitive control of behavior. Such an oversight is understandable but unfortunate. Developed first with animals and then with men, conditioning principles are now recognized as having a wide range of applicability in organizational behavior.

Many reinforcement theorists take the position that reinforcers act directly and automatically to strengthen the behavior upon which they are contingent. Spielberger and DeNike point out, however, that cognitive theorists take issue with the postulate of automaticity. According to the cognitive view, an awareness of the behavior-reinforcer relationship

* Source unknown at this time.

is a necessary prerequisite to performance improvements. Awareness in this case is assumed to be an internal cognitive state inferred from the individual's ability to correctly verbalize the behavior-reinforcer contingency. Spielberger and DeNike list and respond to the behaviorists' criticisms of the cognitive viewpoint and conclude that while not all behavior may be mediated by appropriate cognitions, performance is often facilitated by an awareness of the behavior-reinforcer contingency. Their discussion is confined to verbal operant conditioning but in fact awareness is an issue in the conditioning of all types of human behavior.

In the next selection, Heneman and Schwab critically review expectancy theories which *(a)* emphasize perceptions (an awareness) of behavior-reinforcer contingencies as determinants of behavior and *(b)* have been dominant in the field of organizational behavior. Most expectancy formulations have two basic postulates in common. The first is that behavior (performance) is a function of ability *times* motivation, and the second is that motivation (force to perform or effort) is a function of the individual's belief that a given behavior will be followed by a specific outcome (his expectancy) *times* his evaluation of that outcome. Heneman and Schwab's review indicates that while expectancy explanations are intuitively appealing, they are extremely difficult to test. Perhaps a more fundamental criticism is that with few exceptions, they do not include postulates which relate perceptions of instrumentalities and behavior-outcome relationships to environmental variables. Were it not for the fact that most expectancy theorists go beyond their formulations to suggest ways in which the organizational structure could be modified, the administrator might legitimately inquire as to how he should proceed in constructing a "motivating" environment.

In our view, human behavior can be shaped by reinforcement contingencies in the absence of an awareness of either the contingencies themselves or their behavioral effects. On the other hand, man has learned to observe his own behavior and that of others and to construct rules or propositions which describe the behavior, the setting in which it occurred, and the reinforcing consequences. Such rules (perceptions of contingencies?) when formulated and communicated to oneself or to others serve as discriminative stimuli which tend to evoke the behavior described by the rule. One should be careful not to emphasize propositional control at the expense of actual outcome control, but it is agreed that propositional control combined with reinforcement or actual outcome control can exert a powerful influence over human behavior.

While nearly all extant reinforcement theories have shifted the locus of control from autonomous central agents to the observable environment, the importance of central neural processes heretofore considered under the rubric of motivation is not thereby denied. Berlyne looks back over a decade of motivational theorizing and notes, in particular, the advances that have been made in neurophysiology. Studies of the brain stem reticular formation and the discovery of the pleasure-pain centers in the brain have led to a reconsideration of the role of arousal and affective processes in behavior. Many reinforcement theorists now assume that neural activity is evoked by a reinforcing stimulus and that this underlying activity is necessary to the reinforcement process. Perhaps it is the case that reinforcers evoke activity in the reticular formation and in the pleasure-pain centers and thus produce "emotional" responses as well as consolidating activity in the cortex.

2. A BEHAVIORAL APPROACH TO COUNSELING AND GUIDANCE*

Jack Michael **and** ***Lee Meyerson***†

It is tempting to begin an article of this kind with attention-compelling references to some of the seemingly spectacular results that have been achieved by investigators who have employed procedures derived from what has come to be known as the experimental analysis of behavior. It is fascinating to learn how pigeons were taught to guide a missile (7), how speech was restored in a catatonic patient who had been mute for many years (4), and how some long standing undesirable behavior in mentally retarded and psychotic individuals was changed in a relatively short time (1). Not a great deal is accomplished, however, if the relevance of this work for the educator, the psychologist and the counselor is not per-

* Source: Reprinted from *Harvard Educational Review,* Vol. 32, No. 4 (Fall 1962), pp. 382-402.

† Department of Psychology, Western Michigan University and Arizona State University, respectively.

ceived, and needless harm occurs if the results are dismissed as artificial, impractical experiments by laboratory scientists who "want to treat people like rats and pigeons."

A behavioral approach to counseling and guidance does not consist of a bag of tricks to be applied mechanically for the purpose of coercing unwilling people. It is part of a highly technical system, based on laboratory investigations of the phenomena of conditioning, for describing behavior and specifying the conditions under which it is acquired, maintained, and eliminated.

Much more knowledge of conditioning and its broad field of applicability to human behavior is available today than can be appreciated by those who have only vague recollections of the glandular and motor responses of the dogs studied by Pavlov.

It is the major purpose of this paper to describe, in a didactic way, a portion of the new knowledge that has been obtained. Starting from definitions of specialized concepts and terminology, mastery of which will permit further reading of the technical literature, an overview is given of a descriptive and explanatory system of behavior that has relevance for counseling and guidance. Although application to practical counseling problems is not made in the main body of the paper, no doubt many counselors will perceive the similarity to counseling situations of the behavior processes that are described. A briefer concluding section summarizes some of the theoretical and practical implications of the system for counseling and guidance.

It is necessary to understand at the outset that the familiar characterization of behavior as a function of the interaction of hereditary and environmental variables is accepted, not with the lip service that is sometimes given before fleeing to hypothetical constructs of inner behavioral determiners that are neither heredity nor environment, but with utmost seriousness.

The consequences of this orientation should be made explicit: Inherited genetic and consitutional determiners are not under the control of, or subject to, direct experimentation by behavioral scientists. This means that the only channel open to counselors for influencing human behavior is through changes in the environment. Additionally, certain environmental manipulations, such as separating a person from his frontal lobes or administering drugs that have psychopharmacological effects, are not available to psychologists and educators. The phenomenon with which counselors deal, then, is behavior, and the independent variable which controls behavior must be the environment. A behavioral system attempts to specify, without reference to unobservable, hypothetical inner-determining agents, the conditions and the process by which the environment controls human behavior.

A BEHAVIORAL SYSTEM[1]

Respondent Conditioning

Certain physical events in the environment are related to certain human muscular and glandular activities in a relatively invariable way. A light shined in the eye elicits a constriction of the pupil. An acid solution placed on the tongue elicits secretion by the salivary gland. Such physical events are called stimuli and the muscular and glandular activities are called responses. Some of these stimulus-response relationships or reflexes are present at birth, and in humans most of them are involved in maintaining the internal economy of the body or protecting it against harmful external conditions.

A stimulus which is not a part of a reflex relationship becomes a *conditioned stimulus* for the response by repeated, temporal pairing with an *unconditioned stimulus* which already elicits the response. This new relationship is called a *conditioned reflex;* and the pairing procedure is called *respondent conditioning.*

In general, conditioning does not produce permanent effects. If the conditioned stimulus is presented frequently in the absence of the unconditioned stimulus, a procedure called *extinction,* it loses its eliciting properties.

The procedures for producing conditioning and extinction were first explored systematically by I. P. Pavlov, and respondent conditioning is an area of continued interest and active investigation.

However, if conditioning phenomena were limited in applicability to the transfer of eliciting effects from reflex stimuli to other stimuli, the field would be of little importance in understanding human be-

[1] The principles of the system presented here are based on data reported by a great many people. Most studies within the last 5 years were reported in the *Journal of the Experimental Analysis of Behavior.*

The statements about avoidance are based in large part on work done by Murray Sidman and his associates. Statements about punishment are based primarily on the work of N. H. Azrin and his associates. A more complete treatment of the material basic to this systematic presentation is available in J. G. Holland and B. F. Skinner, *The Analysis of Behavior* (New York: McGraw-Hill, 1961) and in B. F. Skinner's earlier work, *Science and Human Behavior* (New York: Macmillan, 1953). Similar material has been presented in several shorter papers, like the present one, addressed to some special audience. Two of these are especially valuable in their thoroughness and in their detailed discussion of practical applications of research findings. They are C. B. Ferster's Reinforcement and punishment in the control of human behavior by social agencies, *Psychiatric Research Reports,* 1958, *10,* 101–18; and M. Sidman's Operant techniques, in Arthur J. Bachrach (ed.), *Experimental Foundations of Clinical Psychology* (New York: Basic Books, 1962).

havior. Most of the behavior that is of interest to society does not fit the paradigm of the reflex. There is in general no identifiable eliciting stimulus for the broad class of "voluntary" activity called by B. F. Skinner *operant* behavior. The basic operation of respondent conditioning, however, the systematic temporal pairing of stimulus conditions, is of some significance since a portion of almost any kind of stimulus effect can be transferred to a new stimulus by the procedure of pairing the two stimuli.

Operant Conditioning

Whereas for reflexes and conditioned reflexes the event of critical explanatory importance is the eliciting stimulus preceding the response, for a large class of non-reflex behavior the critical events are the environmental consequences of the behavior. Such behavior can be said to "operate" on the environment, in contrast to behavior which is "respondent" to prior eliciting stimuli.

It is convenient to group the kinds of stimulus events which are consequences of acts into three major classes in terms of their effects on operant behavior.

Positive Reinforcers. These stimulus events are defined by the observation that the behavior which preceded them has a higher probability of occurrence under similar conditions in the future. Such events are often called rewards and described as pleasant. Some of these positive reinforcers are of biological significance to the organism such as food, water, sexual contact, and some are of acquired significance such as praise, affection, grades, money.

Negative Reinforcers or Aversive Stimuli. These events are defined by the observation that behavior which preceded their removal is more likely to occur under similar conditions in the future. The common aversive stimuli are those we call painful or unpleasant such as extreme heat or cold, blows on the surface of the body, distortions of certain inner organs as in a stomach ache, very loud sounds or very bright lights. Another class of aversive stimuli are those whose properties are acquired during our lifetimes such as social disapproval, criticism, nagging, threat.

The operation of presenting a positive reinforcer contingent upon a response is called *positive reinforcement.* The operation of removing an aversive stimulus contingent upon a response is called *negative reinforcement.*[2] Both operations are called *operant conditioning* and both increase the future frequency of the response which preceded them.

No Consequence and Neutral Stimuli. Responses continue to occur if they receive either positive or negative reinforcement. They cease if followed by no consequence or by neutral stimuli. The procedure of allowing behavior to occur without reinforcement is called *operant extinction,* and can be contrasted with *respondent extinction* which is the procedure of allowing a conditioned stimulus to occur without pairing it with an unconditioned stimulus.

It should be noted that none of the above statements constitutes postulates, axioms, assumptions or issues of theoretical controversy. The definitions are simply descriptions of observed relationships. Some events serve as reinforcers and some do not. The determination of what constitutes a reinforcer for a particular organism is an empirical problem, although of course, it is often very helpful to have studied biologically similar organisms or those inhabiting similar environments. In the case of humans, the reinforcers of biological significance are apparently very similar to those of other mammals and are fairly well known. On the other hand, the specification of the events of acquired reinforcing value for an individual human requires either a contemporary investigation or considerable knowledge of his environmental history.

Conditioned Reinforcers. Only a small proportion of the important consequences of human behavior are the unconditioned reinforcers attributable to biological characteristics. Other consequences, *conditioned reinforcers,* acquire their reinforcing properties as a function of experience. It appears that an event becomes a conditioned reinforcer in some degree simply by being paired with another reinforcer. However, most of the conditioned reinforcers that are important in human affairs are, in addition, stimuli in the presence of which further behavior is reinforced. In common sense terms, most conditioned reinforcers are means to an end which may be an unconditioned reinforcer or another conditioned reinforcer. For example, a match for a smoker will serve as a reinforcer for the behavior which procured it because it makes possible the further behavior of striking it and lighting the cigarette.

Some conditioned reinforcers are specific to particular unconditioned reinforcers as when signs regarding the serving of food, pictures of food, and menus, function as conditioned reinforcers for humans who are momentarily reinforceable with food. Some conditioned reinforcers, however, because they have been paired with many different unconditioned and conditioned reinforcers and because they have been means to many different ends almost become ends in themselves. Reinforcers that have this property, such as money, social approval, successful manipulation of the physical environment, affection,

[2] Negative reinforcement should not be confused with punishment which is the presentation of an aversive stimulus contingent on a response.

and others are called *generalized conditioned reinforcers.*

Common Sense, Automaticity, and Superstitious Behavior. It may seem that to emphasize the pleasant and unpleasant consequences of acts through "rewards and punishments" is nothing new. The effects described above have long been known and used in an intuitive way, but they also have long been misunderstood. The strengthening effect of a reward is commonly understood in terms of a rational process. It seems only natural that a person will repeat that which he can see will benefit him, and perform again those acts which he believes will terminate unpleasant conditions. However, the effect does not depend on a rational process at all. The foreseeing of consequences or the ability to state the relation between the consequence and the behavior which produced it is unnecessary. Any behavior which is followed by reinforcement—in all of the many species studied, and above all in man—is more likely to occur again in the same or a similar situation. This could be called the *automaticity* of the effect of reinforcement. To increase the occurrence of a particular class of behavior, it is necessary only to ensure that reinforcement occurs relatively soon after the behavior.

The automaticity effect is most dramatically demonstrated in what is called "superstitious behavior." When reinforcement follows behavior, even though the behavior did not produce or in any sense cause the reinforcement, it is called *accidental reinforcement.* Behavior which is developed as a function of accidental reinforcement was whimsically referred to as superstitious behavior in a study with pigeons (8) and the term has become a quasi-technical term in the behavioral field. Humans, probably because of their more complex environment, provide many more examples of superstitious behavior than lower animals. The verbalizations and unique motor activities of gamblers and the unnecessary postures and movements seen in sports activities are examples of the effects of accidental contingencies of reinforcement.

Shaping

Inasmuch as an operant response must first occur before it can be followed by reinforcement, one might suppose that operant conditioning cannot be used to produce new behavior. However, the detailed topography of a response—the particular muscle actions, including force and speed of various muscle components—varies from one occurrence to another. To produce new behavior then, or behavior that has not appeared in the response repetoire before, it is sufficient to selectively reinforce one of the variations in topography which resulted from the previous reinforcement, while allowing the other variations to extinguish. This has the effect of producing a further class of variations from which one may again differentially reinforce some and allow others to extinguish, and so on.

For example, in teaching a child to talk, his efforts to pronounce a particular word will at first be reinforced rather uncritically. Eventually, some of the variations will resemble accepted pronunciation more than others and receive selective reinforcement while other variations are allowed to extinguish. These events have the effect of producing a class of responses which come ever closer to the correct pronunciation than the last reinforced response, and the selective reinforcement can be applied again. This procedure for producing new behavior is called *shaping.* It is essentially the differential reinforcement of successive approximations to some complex form of behavior. It is the technique which animal trainers use to produce unusual and entertaining behaviors in their subjects, and it is the technique whereby humans acquire the complex response topographies of speech, athletic abilities and other motor skills.

Stimulus Control of Operant Behavior

Although the emphasis in describing operant behavior has been on the reinforcement occurring subsequent to the response, stimulus control is implied in the phrase concluding the principle of operant conditioning—if an operant response is followed by reinforcement it is more likely to occur *under similar conditions* in the future. The simplest principle of stimulus control is that the future probability of response is highest when the stimulus conditions resemble most closely those existing at the moment of previous reinforcement. The expression "resemble most closely" must be analyzed in some detail, but first a description is needed of a typical experimental situation in which the effects of stimuli on operant behavior are studied. A lower animal rather than a human is described as the subject in this example because stimulus control in humans is confounded by their extensive training regarding the relevance of certain classes of stimuli (see "discrimination training" below). A food deprived monkey is placed in a small chamber containing a movable foot pedal, and reinforced with food for pressing the pedal. Suppose that the chamber is illuminated by a relatively bright overhead light, a moderately loud tone of 1000 cycles per second plays constantly, and a small transluscent disc above the pedal, at eye level, is illuminated from behind with a bright green light. Although none of these stimulus conditions can be said to elicit the response, they all come to exert some control over its probability, for if any of them is changed, the tendency to respond will be temporarily lowered. Of course, if we continue to reinforce in the presence of the changed stimuli, responding will recover and the class of stimulus conditions controlling the response will be broadened. If, instead of changing only one of the stimulus conditions, we change all of them, the tendency to respond will be very low. In brief, any change from the stimulus conditions that existed at the moment of reinforcement will reduce the tendency to respond, and the greater the change, the greater the reduction.

There is, however, a vagueness in this formulation. How can the extent to which a changed stimulus condition resembles the original one be evaluated? For example, can we predict for a specific monkey whether changing the tone will reduce his tendency to respond more than turning off the overhead light? We cannot. It is an empirical question. To some extent the similarity of different stimulus conditions will depend on the biological characteristics of the species. But in part, as in the case of reinforcers, the importance to the individual organism of the various aspects of the stimulus condition will depend on the previous history of that particular organism.

In the situation described above a change in color on the transluscent disc would not be expected to change the tendency to respond very much because the disc color is only a small part of the total stimulus situation. By skilled use of the procedures of reinforcement and extinction, however, we can bring about the more precise type of stimulus control that is called *discrimination.* If we change the color from green to red, and in the presence of the red disc we do not reinforce the pedal response, it will become less frequent, i.e., extinguish. If we then restore the color and in its presence pedal pressing is again reinforced and so on, alternating the two conditions, the control of the disc color over the pedal response will become quite strong. This procedure is called *discrimination training.* If in the presence of a stimulus a response is reinforced, and in the absence of this stimulus it is extinguished, the stimulus will control the probability of the response in high degree. Such a stimulus is called a *discriminative stimulus.*

Almost all important human behavior is under the control of discriminative stimuli. Although part of the educational process involves extensive shaping, particularly for motor skills, the educator's major efforts are directed toward the development of *discriminative repertoires,* or in common terminology, knowledge. Many details regarding the building of discriminative repertoires have been discovered in the experimental laboratory, and these findings are now beginning to see systematic exploitation in the field of programmed instruction.

The development of effective discriminative repertoires for interpersonal behavior is also a topic of great importance for those dealing with the practical control of behavior, and although the principles of discrimination are the same when the stimuli to be discriminated are the behaviors of other people, the details of application remain to be worked out.

A beginning has been made in applying basic principles of discrimination to verbal behavior, language, and communication. This is presently seen to be a field composed of one discriminative repertoire under the control of the many features of the physical and social environment, with additional repertoires controlled by features of the first (9).

Schedules of Intermittent Reinforcement

Thus far discussion has centered on the role of reinforcement in simply making a response more likely to occur in the future, in shaping up novel topographies or forms of response, and in bringing a response under the control of a particular stimulus condition. But reinforcement does not lose its relevance once an adequate topography has been developed and the behavior is under proper stimulus control. It has additional effects that may be treated according to the schedule by which reinforcement is given.

An important characteristic of much behavior is that it is repeated, either because the appropriate stimulus conditions persist or because they recur. Having learned to ask a parent for a cookie a child can immediately ask for another, and another. This behavior must eventually cease because of temporary changes in the parent's disposition to provide the reinforcer, because the reinforcer loses its effectiveness by satiation, or for other reasons, but there will be other occasions for similar behavior to occur. If every occurrence of such a repeatable response is followed by reinforcement the behavior will continue until other variables exert control. On the other hand, if reinforcement is discontinued altogether the behavior will cease.

Between the extremes of *continuous reinforcement* where every relevant response is reinforced and *extinction* where there is no reinforcement there are many situations where responses are only occasionally reinforced. Such *intermittent reinforcement* might be expected to produce an effect intermediate between continuous reinforcement and extinction, but that is not the case. The situation is much more complex. A schedule of intermittent reinforcement is actually a way of arranging reinforcement contingencies regarding the passage of time, the number of responses, or both. The complexity arises from the varied and intricate ways in which these temporal and number contingencies can be combined and interrelated in natural and laboratory environments, and from the extreme sensitivity of the behavior of organisms to such conditions.

Ratio Reinforcement. There is a large class of schedules involving solely a number contingency, and this is usually specified in terms of the ratio of responses to reinforcements. Industrial piecework pay is an example of ratio reinforcement, as is the payoff schedule provided by the "one-armed bandit" of the gambling house. The principal characteristic of such schedules is that the more rapidly one works the more frequently one is reinforced. Behavior conforms to this kind of requirement by occurring at a high rate. Another feature of this kind of schedule is that very large amounts of work per reinforcement can be tolerated, but to avoid premature extinction the organism must approach such conditions gradually by first being exposed to less stringent requirements. A third feature is that simple ratio reinforcement does not have self-corrective properties. Any temporary reduction in the tendency to respond simply delays the ultimate reinforcement. Vicious circles can easily develop where the less one responds the less one gets, and therefore the less one responds in the future.

Interval Reinforcement. Another class of schedules involves only temporal contingencies. The most commonly studied arrangements are those where the probability of a response being reinforced increases as a simple function of the passage of time, and under these conditions the frequency of responding generally reflects the changing probability of reinforcement. An example from daily life is the behavior of telephoning someone who is not at home. One cannot hasten his return home by rapid re-dialing, as in ratio reinforcement, but the probability of making the connection and completing the call increases as time passes. If the interval varies randomly, response frequency is relatively constant over time. If the interval is constant, responding increases in frequency as the time for reinforcement approaches. In such schedules the rate of responding is directly related to the frequency of reinforcement. Only moderate response rates are generated by interval reinforcement but when the reinforcement is discontinued altogether, responding decreases in frequency very slowly compared with behavior which has been continuously reinforced. Resistance to extinction is high. In contrast to the ratio schedules described earlier, interval schedules in general are self-corrective. Any temporary reduction in response frequency is counteracted by receiving the next reinforcement after fewer unreinforced responses, and this restores the tendency to respond.

Much more complex arrangements of temporal and number contingencies occur in the human physical and social environment, and also in the behavior laboratory. Fortunately the field is somewhat systematized and it is becoming increasingly possible to predict the effects of new arrangements on the basis of what is known about their components.

Intermittent Reinforcement and Motivation. In addition to its general theoretical relevance in illuminating the effects of reinforcement contingencies, intermittent reinforcement is of considerable practical significance because of its relationship to the traditional field of motivation. The well motivated person is one who works at some activity with persistence, even though his reinforcement is long delayed. He is also a person who can put out a very large amount of work with only an occasional reward. It is not evident, however, that these properties are *in* the person or that the behavior cannot be produced by manipulating the environment. Variable interval schedules generate great persistence in the face of non-reinforcement, and ratio schedules produce large amounts of work for the minimum number of reinforcements. Not only good motivation but the pathologically "driven" behavior that is said to characterize the gambler can be generated in the laboratory by programing the same kind of variable ratio schedule that acts on the gambler. Similarly when a child cries and begs his parents with great persistence and intensity to take him with them rather than leave him with a baby sitter, we are likely to say something like "he *wants* very much to go with them." The work on intermittent reinforcement tells us very clearly that just such a performance could be generated by acquiescing to the child's requests after only mildly intense and slightly persistent entreaties at first and then slowly raising the requirement. Whether any particular sample of behavior arose in this way is an empirical question.

Deprivation and Satiation

Not all motivational problems fit the paradigm described above. Deprivation and satiation have two major effects on behavior which cannot at present be reduced to the effects of any of the biological or environmental variables discussed previously.

Food, water, sexual activity, activity in general, and some other similar unconditioned reinforcers will serve as reinforcers only if the organism has been deprived of them. Satiation weakens and deprivation strengthens the effectiveness of these reinforcers. This is one major effect of this variable. In addition, deprivation with respect to a reinforcer results in an increased likelihood of occurrence of all the behavior that has in the past been reinforced with it.

Stated in terms of food, for example, the first effect is that as deprivation time increases, food becomes a more powerful reinforcer. As eating continues, food loses its reinforcing capacity. The second effect is seen in that food-seeking behavior becomes more frequent as time since last eating increases, and less frequent as eating proceeds. This second effect cannot at present be reduced to the first, since the increase in food-seeking behavior can be observed even before reinforcement has been received.

The study of deprivation-satiation variables appears to come closest to the traditional field of motivation, but there are many cases where these variables are *not* relevant but it is common to infer them. For example, one man may show strong persistent behavior directed toward socio-sexual relations with women, and another may show very little such behavior. The customary explanation is in terms of sex drive, with the implication that equivalent periods of deprivation affect the two men differently or that one is more deprived than the other. It is more likely in our culture that differences of this magnitude are due largely to different histories of intermittent reinforcement although again this interpretation would require independent evidence in any particular case. Laboratory studies with lower animals indicate quite clearly that variables such as frequency of reinforcement and kind of schedule can cause variations in frequency and persistence of behavior that are greater than the variations generated by deprivation.

It would also be a mistake to infer a history of specific deprivation from the knowledge that a particular event will function as a reinforcer. In the case of ordinary conditioned reinforcers this mistake would not usually be made—the fact that the sight of a telephone is reinforcing certainly doesn't suggest telephone deprivation, since a telephone is so obviously a means to an end. The generalized conditioned reinforcers, however, of affection, attention, money, because they are means to many different ends, erroneously might be assumed to be subject to the deprivation effect in themselves.

In summary then, deprivation and satiation are critical determiners of the momentary effectiveness of a number of reinforcers, and of the momentary strength of large classes of responses. But to pattern all "motivational" problems on this model would be to neglect other equally if not more important determiners.

Emotion

It is customary to consider emotion as respondent behavior, but operant aspects of emotion can also be specified. Like deprivation, emotional variables affect a large class of operant responses. For example, a person who is ordinarily described as fearful not only shows the respondent effects such as a more rapid heart rate, moist palms and dry throat, but also he shows an increased tendency to engage in all those operant behaviors which have in the past been reinforced by escape from current or similarly difficult situations. Further, those aspects of his repertoire which ordinarily receive positive reinforcement in this situation are weakened. His tendencies to run away, to hide, to seek help from other individuals, are all increased, whereas his tendencies to eat, play, and engage in normal social behaviors are decreased. These phenomena presently are not well understood.

The operations which produce behavioral changes in respondent and operant repertoires under emotion have not yielded to efforts to develop a simple classification scheme. Furthermore, the class of responses which are altered by any particular operation contain such a large component of acquired behaviors that the similarities between different individuals are of little systematic value. However, although an empirical description and ordering of the responses which change with emotion presently are limited, the principles whereby already developed repertoires can be transferred from one stimulus condition to another are somewhat better understood. The operation of temporal pairing is relevant. Any stimulus which is systematically present during an emotional condition will produce some of the respondents and some of the change in the operant repertoire that characterize the emotional condition when it is presented alone. Practical use of principles in this field has been under investigation in the U.S.S.R. ever since the earliest work of Pavlov. More recently, however, a group of British investigators have made very successful deliberate applications of emotional conditioning principles to the treatment of abnormal behavior (3).

Aversive Control

Escape and Avoidance. An evnvironmental arrangement in which an organism's response can terminate an already present aversive stimulus is called an *escape* procedure. It is negative reinforcement, and operant conditioning of the response is the result. When behavior can prevent or delay the onset of the aversive stimulus the procedure is called *avoidance,* and this arrangement also will result in the development and maintenance of operant behavior. Avoidance cannot be considered as a simple case of negative reinforcement, however, since there is often no obvious stimulus termination immediately following the response. Turning off an alarm clock that has already begun to ring is an example of escape behavior, but pushing in the stop before it begins to ring is avoidance.

Examples of this kind of control are easily found in parent-child interactions. Children's cleanliness activities are often maintained as escape behavior where the aversive stimulus is the nagging verbal behavior of a parent. Sometimes these activities constitute avoidance behavior. Here the aversive stimulus is criticism, scolding, or being made to wash over again. Later, when children go to school their studying behavior is often maintained as avoidance behavior, where the aversive stimulus is again criticism, failing grades, or removal of privileges. The distinction between behavior for positive reinforcement and the avoidance paradigm is illustrated in the following not uncommon interchange between parent and child. The child is told to do something and asks "What will I get if I do?" whereupon the parent replies "You'll get something if you don't!"

Laboratory findings with avoidance behavior have indicated several characteristics of this kind of control which are closely related to behavior disorders of many kinds. In the first place, successful avoidance behavior will by its very nature prevent the discovery that the aversive stimulus has been discontinued, and when this is coupled with the extraordinary persistence of such behavior it suffices to explain many human activities that serve no current function.

Another finding relevant to behavior problems is the fact that occasional presentations of the aversive stimulus without respect to the organism's behavior will maintain the avoidance repertoire almost indefinitely. In this way, even though the bad thing that one is avoiding is no longer related to one's behavior, so long as it occurs once-in-a-while the avoidance repertoire may persist.

A final point concerns the conditions under which the escape or avoidance repertoire will occur. In escape behavior the presentation of the aversive stimulus produces immediate strength in the escape repertoire and the escape repertoire is not readily seen in the absence of the aversive stimulus. In avoidance, the presentation of stimuli which have in the past accompanied that or other aversive stimuli strengthen the avoidance repertoire, but an even stronger effect is seen when the aversive stimulus itself is presented momentarily. To maintain behavior in this manner it is necessary to maintain the threat of aversive stimulation.

Punishment. Technically, punishment refers to the operation of presenting an aversive stimulus contingent upon a response, or removing a positive reinforcer contingent upon a response.[3] It is widely used in our culture to reduce the frequency of behavior, and according to "common sense" psychology is often described as opposite in effect from reward. As rewards strengthen behavior, so punishments are believed to weaken it. Considerable experimental evidence is now available regarding the effects of this operation, which turn out to be quite complex.

One kind of complexity arises because whereas the strengthening effects of reinforcement can be studied in isolation, the weakening effects of punishment can only be studied by superimposing them on preceding or ongoing strengthening effects. This is not only a methodological problem. In practical affairs the question of the efficacy of punishment seldom arises except with respect to behavior that has at least moderate probability of occurrence.

It is difficult to generalize about this competition between reinforcement and punishment since the parameters of the positive reinforcement and the aversive stimulus used are critical, as is the availability of alternative responses which are reinforced and/or punished to varying degrees. However, it is probably safe to say that when no other response but the punished one can obtain positive reinforcement, and with positive reinforcers like food, it takes very severe punishment to effectively reduce the frequency of the behavior.

Added to this complication is the fact that an aversive stimulus may have some effects because it is aversive, but it also has other stimulus effects. By the principle of stimulus control mentioned earlier an aversive stimulus can reduce the frequency of responding if the stimulus constitutes a change from the conditions which existed during previous reinforcement, regardless of its aversive characteristics. And since reinforcement often occurs in the same situation as punishment, an aversive stimulus, as a result of some systematic relation to the reinforcement, can acquire even more complex stimulus properties, such as those of a discriminative stimulus, or even a conditioned positive reinforcer.

Finally, there is a complication in interpreting the effects of punishment in human interactions that is brought about by the fact that a person who punishes may for a time be less disposed to provide any ordinary positive reinforcement. If this is the case, punishment systematically precedes a period of extinction. This arrangement results in a reduction in some behavior—but not due to the aversive effects of the punishment. On the other hand, punishers sometimes show a greater disposition to provide positive reinforcement shortly after they have administered punishment. This results in a temporary increase in some kinds of behavior, and, under proper conditions, even a future increase in the punished behavior.

---

[3] Common sense usage often has punishment synonymous with what is referred to here as an aversive stimulus or, even more broadly, as aversive control.

Any stimulus which is paired temporally with an aversive stimulus acquires some of its properties. Such stimuli are called *conditioned aversive stimuli* or conditioned negative reinforcers. Aversive stimuli and conditioned aversive stimuli, in addition to producing the effects described above are also classed as emotional variables, because of their respondent effects and their effects on large classes of operant responses. This emotional effect enters into and further complicates various kinds of aversive control. It also appears to be responsible for various deleterious changes in certain internal organs. Because of this, and for many other reasons, aversive control is in most cases socially undesirable although it is apparently not completely avoidable.

This concludes the presentation of the basic empirical principles of this behavior system. Of course, many details have been omitted, but the major relations have been covered. Further development of this system is proceeding along two lines: workers in experimental laboratories are constantly discovering new details, improving imprecise relations, and sometimes revealing new major principles; others working in applied settings are developing a behavioral technology based on these basic principles.

IMPLICATIONS FOR COUNSELING AND GUIDANCE

General Implications

The behavior system described has the clear implication that observable behavior is the only variable of importance in the counseling and guidance process, and it is the only criterion against which the outcome of the process can be evaluated. Conceptual formulations such as ego-strength, inferiority feelings, or self-concept are not behavior but simply ways of organizing and interpreting observable behavior by referring it to an inner determiner. Such formulations may be incorrect, insufficient, or merely superfluous. They may be harmful or impeding when applied in the sense that they direct attention and effort to irrelevant variables, or they may be unessential "decorations" which do no harm but do not contribute to the counselor's efforts or the learner's behavior.

Almost all approaches to counseling and guidance are in agreement that the goal of counseling is to affect behavior and that behavior is lawful. "Pathological," self-defeating and disorganized behaviors as well as "healthy" behaviors are seen as lawful phenomena whose laws can be discovered. In addition, there appears to be general agreement that the crucial behavior of human beings is learned. Man is not at the mercy of his "unconscious" or his drives; for these entelechies, if they exist, can be expressed in many different ways. The critical questions in counseling and guidance, therefore, seem to relate to how behavior is learned and how it may be unlearned or altered.

It is here that a behavioral approach differs from other approaches in counseling and guidance practice. Present practice is to consider the sociological or psychological category to which a problem may be assigned. Is it an educational, vocational, or social problem, or is it a problem of dependency, self-conflict, or choice anxiety? Alternatively there may be some concern for the locus of the problem: Is it primarily a factual-reality problem whose locus is in the environment or is it primarily an emotional-irreality problem whose locus is in the patient? At least a portion of treatment procedures depends on the answers.

These questions and answers, however, to the extent that they reflect limited concern with the process by which the presenting behavior was learned and what must be done to deal with it, obscure rather than illuminate the problem to be solved. From a behavioral standpoint, the only relevant questions relate to behavior itself. What behavior must be created or maintained and what deficient or inadequate behaviors must be altered? Once these basic questions are answered—and an experienced counselor often can reach a diagnosis in a short time even when the client is unaware of the source of his distress—successful corrective procedures follow the behavioral principles and processes that have been described. Unquestionably, some efforts of guidance workers, counselors, and psychotherapists who use traditional approaches result in great success. They probably do so, however, because of the intuitive use of procedures that may be specified explicitly in behavioral terms.

The entire field of guidance, counseling, and psychotherapy might benefit considerably if all workers considered seriously just one behavioral principle and its corollary, namely, that behavior is controlled by its environmental consequences and that an effective procedure for producing behavioral change is the manipulation of the environment so as to create consequences that will produce the desired behavior. If then, it was desired to create, maintain, strengthen, weaken, alter, or eliminate a particular behavior or set of behaviors, attention would be directed toward the operation of the behavioral determiners outlined in the previous section. One advantage of this kind of formulation is that it is explicit, teachable, and testable. Another advantage is that it tells the counselor what has to be done and allows him to monitor progress within an objective rather than an intuitive framework.

At the beginning of behavioral counseling or psychotherapy, the counselor may have to manipulate the determinants so as to facilitate desired behavior coming under the control of "natural" behavioral consequences in the environment. Some professional workers perceive or create an ethical problem here by asking if it is moral for one person to attempt to control the behavior of another. This question has already been answered in our society and perhaps in all societies. Parents, educators and guidance workers make no bones about their earnest intention to create and maintain the "good" behavior that is valued and approved of by the culture and to eliminate "bad" behavior to the maximum degree of which they are capable. It is not clear that the task of the counselor is, or should be, different.

Advice giving, information giving, interpretation and clarification, training and reconditioning, persuasion, encouragement and moral support, subtle direction toward some things and away from others are all frequently mentioned as currently important tools of counseling and guidance. Even in psychotherapy, "growth-inducing" and uncovering techniques did not come to be preferred to directive and controlling procedures because the therapist could not readily perceive the ineffective behavior of his clients that had to change if better adjustment was to occur. The counseling fashion changed because the crude, directive procedures then available were relatively ineffective except in those fortuitous circumstances where the individual was already under the partial control of some appropriate environmental variable.

A return to inadequate directive procedures is not advocated. Behaviorally oriented counselors agree that telling people what is wrong and what they "should" do is an ineffective procedure. The heart of the behavioral approach in counseling is that the environment must be manipulated so as to allow strong reinforcing consequences to become attached to the behavior that is desired.

This implies, of course, that almost any behavior can be manipulated, and behavior principles do not specify what behavior should be fostered. Certainly the knowledge of how to shape behavior can be misused. However, the ethics of deliberately guiding human beings to personally and socially fulfilling lives may not be a problem for any except a relatively small group of counselors committed to an inner-directed philosophy and seemingly non-directive procedures. For most of those to whom society entrusts the guidance of others, influencing or inducing people to behave in ways that society says are "good" ways is an accepted goal, and the critical question is "How can we 'motivate' a person so that he does behave, 'wants to' behave and 'enjoys' behaving in good ways?"

The principles discovered by researchers in the experimental analysis of behavior offer some direct answers now and some procedures for discovering others.

Specific Implications

There are two major ways in which a behavioral approach to counseling may be useful. One is simply to improve the effectiveness of present counseling efforts. The other is to help build a better world.

Improving Counseling and Guidance. To some degree, behavioral principles, as descriptions of how behavior is created, maintained, altered, or placed under stimulus control are neutral principles. They permit, at least for a time, various theoretical or philosophical views of the *real* nature of the human condition. If, for example, one psychotherapist believes that catharsis is a necessary condition for amelioration or correction of neurotic behavior, while another believes that healthy behavior is best achieved by "accentuating the positive," the same properly applied reinforcement principles will produce catharsis in one patient and healthy talk in the other, or a client can be led from one kind of talk to the other. To the extent that a therapist manipulates the environment so as to facilitate the expression of affect, reduce self-ideal discrepancies, or whatever behavior he believes is necessary for a patient's improvement, he is in control of a powerful tool. If he applies reinforcement principles successfully, it doesn't matter a great deal if the therapist originally believes that he is simply assisting in liberating a primordial, natural force within the person. To the extent that differential results are obtained when he deliberately uses or does not use behavioral techniques, the environmental consequences will shape his behavior also and may even change his theory.

This is not the place for a technical discussion of the origins and treatment of the grossly deviant behavior that is believed to require psychotherapy. It should be mentioned, however, that more than 30 years ago it was demonstrated that phobias, for example, could be induced, generalized, and removed by purely behavioral procedures (5, 12), and in these cases where the origin of the behavior was known, it was superfluous to look for the hidden forces or the "real" meanings which mediated the phobia. Bandura (2) gives an excellent survey of the large amount of more recent experimental and clinical studies using behavioristic psychotherapy. Many kinds of deviant behavior have been treated successfully by direct focusing on the behavior itself.

For problems traditionally assigned to counseling and guidance personnel, the relevance of a behavioral approach is even more clear cut. The great bulk of the problems here do not have disputed ethical implications. In schools, no one questions that it is better for children to learn school subject matter than not to learn it; that it is desirable to get along with other children and with adults without excessive conflicts; that more is to be gained by staying in school than by dropping out; that very early marriage of school children is unwise; that law abiding behavior is better than delinquent behavior. In brief, in great part, the behavior that children "should" engage in is known and agreed upon, and the task of the counselor is to facilitate and strengthen its emergence and maintenance. As in counseling with special populations such as the mentally retarded and the physically handicapped, the problems may be considered straightforward ones of behavioral engineering.

Although there has been little experience with these kinds of problems, it seems reasonable to believe that if a school counselor systematically learned to utilize only a small number of principles such as the behavior-influencing power of positive reinforcement, the undesirable long range consequences of aversive control and some of the details regarding shaping and the development of stimulus control, he could fulfill his job functions with greater efficiency. It is not so much that a behavioral approach would necessarily change a great deal of what the counselor did, but he would know why certain activities such as the recognition of merit are good and other activities such as grading on the curve are not. Knowing the effects of these activities, he might come to manipulate them more effectively. He would also come to ask, in each case of deficient or mal-adaptive behavior, how the behavior was linked to consequences and, instead of measuring abilities or personality, attempt to alter the consequences so as to shape up more desirable behavior.

On the other hand, a counselor who accepted the complete behavioral system and worked within it would tend to ask more radical questions about some present school practices and to initiate more radical changes in counseling functions. For example, in connection with the critical school drop-out problem, he would be less concerned with specifying the characteristics of students who drop out than in studying the kind and frequency of the reinforcements that are available for school learning in comparison with other reinforcers and with the frequency of avoidance and punishing conditions that exist in the classroom. He would experiment with introducing token reinforcers in the classroom dispensable immediately upon the occurrence of a desired response. He would analyze the conditions under which a potential drop-out could be led to emit new responses in a tight, reinforcing feedback loop so as to shape behavior that would ultimately come under the control of the natural reinforcers of the environment. For example, a student might be paid in money for working a teaching machine program in bookkeeping or algebra, or he might be given tokens that would make him eligible for earning money or some other generalized reinforcer. "What!" someone may exclaim, "You propose to pay children for learning what is good for them?" Certainly. Industry does this regularly now. Colleges and universities pay out large amounts of cash to an extent undreamed of a generation ago. We are now paying thousands of students to go to school.

Human beings do not "naturally" like what the experience of the species indicates is necessary or good for them. Drop-out students by their behavior are saying that they are not receiving the "natural" reinforcers of the classroom that influence the school-going behavior of most children, or that these cannot compete in strength with other reinforcers. The task of the counselor is to discover what is reinforcing to potential drop-outs and to make these reinforcers contingent upon school learning. If the drop-out problem is a serious one; if we really believe that our society and economy require an educated population; and if the monetary and social costs of large numbers of uneducated or undereducated persons are great; there should be no hesitancy in taking advantage of scientific principles of learning to apply effective extrinsic reinforcers to help shape desirable behavior. Some problems of juvenile delinquency and its behavioral treatment can be considered in the same way (11)

The social ramifications of this kind of approach are great, and many new kinds of counselor behavior will be required. It is apparent that many aspects of counseling and guidance work that focus on behavior and behavioral change cannot be done effectively in the traditional verbal, face to face, office situation. To a far greater degree than is presently the case, the behavioral counselor must be able to influence the consequences of behavior, as it is emitted, by personal action, by machines, and by enlisting the aid of teachers, parents, and school administrators in creating healthy behavioral environments. The principles for doing this are simple, but the techniques for application are complex, and perhaps progress in appreciable degree may have to wait on the creation of experimental, school behavior laboratories.

Building a Better World. Much, perhaps most, of the present work of counseling and guidance personnel consists of giving information and advice based on the measured characteristics, capacities, interests, and attitudes of the client and helping to resolve the conflicts that arise when there are discrepancies among them, or between any of them and the requirements of the environment.

The recognition of "individual differences" and the development of a technology for measuring them was a tremendous advance in the guidance and control of human behavior at the time these developments occurred. There is danger, however, that the increased precision with which a person can be described at a given moment of time may lead us to neglect or minimize the fact that *what is* is not identical with *what must be.*

Educators and psychologists have always been in the vanguard of those who have striven to push back the boundaries of a personal destiny determined primarily by heredity. It is almost a cliché in the behavioral sciences that inherited genetic and constitutional variables may set limits on the behavior that is possible for a human being, but environmental variables determine the behavior that a person actually engages in. In addition, educational and social experiences have shown that the limiting effects of hereditary variables have always been far slighter than was believed to be true at an earlier time.

This knowledge, of course, has been tempered by the empirical observation that other things equal—in the absence of additional knowledge and a better technology for inducing change—the past is one of the best predictors of the future.

One crucial consequence of the research that has been oriented to a functional analysis of behavior is the explicit notice that other things are no longer equal. An improved understanding of how behavior is formed and maintained, and an improved technology for inducing behavioral change now exist; and we can use this knowledge for the deliberate building of a better world. Skinner (10) has sketched the larger social implications of this revolutionary gain in knowledge. Discussion here will be limited to effects on the concept of "individual differences."

From a behavioral standpoint, most of the variation in behavior that presently is assigned to individual differences reflects the influence of unmanipulated environmental variables. Within wide limits now and even wider limits in the future, as additional knowledge is gained, desired or desirable behavior can be acquired by everyone. A large scale, if brief, foretaste of things to come occurred during World War II when, under less than optimal conditions, Rosie the housewife easily became Rosie the riveter; adolescent college boys became commanders of destroyers; and farm boys became skilled electronic technicians.

Probably few counselors would object to the statement that individual differences arise from the interrelationships among capacity, motivation, and opportunity. The last has a firm footing in the environment, but the first two are often perceived as being somehow *in* the person. It should be evident from the description of principles that this notion is unacceptable in a behavioral system. On the contrary, differences in "intelligence," for example, are reflections of some of the performances that result from differential exposure to learning experiences in a relatively chaotic environment. If intelligence can be analyzed into the behavior that constitutes its component parts, it can be taught in an orderly environment so that almost everyone can reach the same high level of performance. Similarly, motivation can be considered not as an innate function of specific drives but as a function of environmental determiners of which one of the most important is positive reinforcement. Under appropriate environmental conditions, which man can create, almost anyone can be motivated to do anything.

Human beings no longer allow themselves to be pushed around by a chaotic physical environment. We heat cold environments and cool warm ones; we fly into space and dive into the ocean depths; and we rearrange many other features of the physical environment to suit our convenience. The psychological and social environments can be manipulated in similar ways. It is no longer necessary to accept without question what a chaotic "natural" environment offers or what chance provides, but with knowledge now available we can build a better world.

REFERENCES

1. Ayllon, T., and Michael, J. The psychiatric nurse as a behavioral engineer. *Journal of the Experimental Analysis of Behavior,* 1959, *2,* 323–34.
2. Bandura, A. Psychotherapy as a learning process. *Psychological Bulletin,* 1961, *58,* 143–59.
3. Eysenck, H. J. (ed.). *Behavior therapy and the neuroses.* New York: Pergamon Press, 1960.
4. Isaacs, W., Thomas, J., and Goldiamond, I. Application of operant conditioning to reinstate verbal behavior in psychotics. *Journal of Speech and Hearing Disorders,* 1960, *25,* 8–12.
5. Jones, Mary C. The elimination of childrens' fears. *Journal of Experimental Psychology,* 1924, *7,* 382–90.
6. Skinner, B. F., *Cumulative record.* New York: Appleton-Century-Crofts, 1961, pp. 3–36.
7. Skinner, B. F. Pigeons in a pelican. *American Psychologist,* 1960, *15,* 28–37.
8. Skinner, B. F. Superstitution in the pigeon. *Journal of Experimental Psychology,* 1948, *38,* 168–72.
9. Skinner, B. F. *Verbal behavior.* New York: Appleton-Century-Crofts, 1957.
10. Skinner, B. F. *Walden two.* New York: Macmillan, 1948.

11. Slack, C. W. Experimenter-subject psychotherapy: a new method of introducing intensive office treatment for unreachable cases. *Mental Hygiene,* 1960, *44,* 238–56.

12. Watson, J. B. and Rayner, R. Conditioned emotional reactions. *Journal of Experimental Psychology,* 1920, *3,* 1–14.

3. BEYOND THE TEACHING MACHINE: THE NEGLECTED AREA OF OPERANT CONDITIONING IN THE THEORY AND PRACTICE OF MANAGEMENT*

Walter R. Nord†

The work of B. F. Skinner and the operant conditioners has been neglected in management and organizational literature. The present paper is an attempt to eliminate this lacuna. When most students of management and personnel think of Skinner's work, they begin and end with programmed instruction. Skinner's ideas, however, have far greater implications for the design and operation of social systems and organizations than just the teaching machine. These additional ideas could be of great practical value.

While neglecting conditioning, writers in the administrative, management, and personnel literature have given extensive attention to the work of other behavioral scientists. McGregor and Maslow are perhaps the behavioral scientists best known to practitioners and students in the area of business and management. Since the major concern of managers of human resources is the prediction and control of the behavior of organizational participants, it is curious to find that people with such a need are extremely conversant with McGregor and Maslow and totally ignorant of Skinner. This condition is not surprising since leading scholars in the field, of what might be termed the applied behavioral sciences, have turned out book after book, article after article, and anthology after anthology with scarcely a mention of Skinner's contributions to the design of social systems. While many writers who deal with the social psychology of organizations are guilty of the omission, this paper will focus primarily on the popular positions of Douglas McGregor, Abraham Maslow, and Frederick Herzberg to aid in exposition.

Almost every book in the field devotes considerable attention to Maslow and McGregor. These men have certainly contributed ideas which are easily understood and "make sense" to practitioners. Also, many practitioners have implemented some of these ideas successfully. However, the belief in the Maslow-McGregor creed is not based on a great deal of evidence. This conclusion is not mine alone, but in fact closely parallels Maslow's (1965) own thoughts. He wrote:

> After all, if we take the whole thing from McGregor's point of view of a contrast between a Theory X view of human nature, a good deal of the evidence upon which he bases his conclusions comes from my researches and my papers on motivations, self-actualization, et cetera. But I of all people should know just how shaky this foundation is as a final foundation. My work on motivations came from the clinic, from a study of neurotic people. The carry-over of this theory to the industrial situation has some support from industrial studies, but certainly I would like to see a lot more studies of this kind before feeling finally convinced that this carry-over from the study of neurosis to the study of labor in factories is legitimate. The same thing is true of my studies of self-actualizing people—there is only this one study of mine available. There were many things wrong with the sampling, so many in fact that it must be considered to be, in the classical sense anyway, a bad or poor or inadequate experiment. I am quite willing to concede this—as a matter of fact, I am eager to concede it—because I'm a little worried about this stuff which I consider to be tentative being swallowed whole by all sorts of enthusiastic people, who really should be a little more tentative in the way that I am (pp. 55–56).

By contrast, the work of Skinner (1953) and his followers has been supported by millions of observations made on animals at all levels of the phylogenetic scale, including man. Over a wide variety of situations, behavior has been reliably predicted and controlled by operant and classical conditioning techniques.

Why then have the applied behavioral sciences followed the McGregor-Maslow approach and ignored Skinner? Several reasons can be suggested. First is the metaphysical issue. Modern Americans,

---

* Reprinted from *Organizational Behavior and Human Performance,* Vol. 4, No. 4, (November 1969), pp. 375–401.

† School of Business and Public Administration, Washington University, St. Louis, Missouri 63130

The author wishes to acknowledge the helpful comments of Dr. Ann Nord, Dr. Raymond Hilgert, and Mr. Timothy Parker.

especially of the managerial class, prefer to think of themselves and others as being self-actualizing creatures near the top of Maslow's need-hierarchy, rather than as animals being controlled and even "manipulated" by their environment. McGregor (1960) developed his argument in terms of Maslow's hierarchy. Skinner's position is unattractive in the same way the Copernican theory was unattractive. Second, Skinner's work and stimulus-response psychology in general appear too limited to allow application to complex social situations. Certainly, this point has much merit. The application of $S-R$ theory poses a terribly complex engineering problem, perhaps an insoluble one in some areas. Nevertheless, the designs of some experimental social systems, which will be discussed later in this paper, demonstrate the feasibility of the practical application of Skinnerian psychology to systems design. A third possible reason for the acceptance of the McGregor and Maslow school and rejection of Skinner may stem from the fact that the two approaches have considerable, although generally unrecognized overlap. As will be shown below, McGregor gave primary importance to the environment as the determinant of individual behavior. Similarly, although not as directly, so does Maslow's hierarchy of needs. The major issue between Skinner and McGregor-Maslow has to do with their models of man. Skinner focuses on man being totally shaped by his environment. Maslow-McGregor see man as having an essence or intrinsic nature which is only congruent with certain environments. The evidence for any one set of metaphysical assumptions is no better than for almost any other set. Empirically, little has been found which helps in choosing between Skinner's and McGregor's assumptions. Further, since most managers are concerned mainly with behavior, the sets of assumptions are of limited importance. It should be noted, however, that if McGregor's writings were stripped of Maslow's model of man, his conclusions on the descriptive and proscriptive levels would remain unchanged. Such a revision would also make McGregor's ideas almost identical with Skinner's. With more attention to contingencies of reinforcement and a broader view of the possibilities of administering reinforcement, the two sets of ideas as they apply to prediction and control of action would be virtually indistinguishable.

The remainder of this paper will be devoted to three areas. First, the similarities and differences between McGregor and Skinner will be discussed. Then, a summary of the Skinnerian position will be presented. Finally, the potential of the Skinnerian approach for modern organizations will be presented with supporting evidence from social systems in which it has already been applied.

McGREGOR AND SKINNER COMPARED

The importance of environmental factors in determining behavior is the crucial and dominant similarity between Skinner and McGregor. As will be shown below, environmental determination of behavior is central to both men.

McGregor (1960) gave central importance to environmental factors in determining how a person behaves. For example, he saw employee behavior as a consequence of organizational factors which are influenced by managerial strategy. In a sense, Theory *X* management leads to people behaving in a way which confirms Theory *X* assumptions, almost as a self-fulfilling prophecy. In addition, McGregor's statement of Theory *Y* assumptions places stress on "proper conditions," rewards and punishments, and other environmental factors. Further, he recognized the importance of immediate feedback in changing behavior. Also, he noted that failure to achieve results is often due to inappropriate methods of control. These are the very terms a behaviorist such as Skinner uses in discussing human actions. Finally, McGregor (1966) noted stimulus-response psychology as a possible model for considering organizational behavior. However, he discarded the reinforcement approach because it did not permit intrinsic rewards to be dealt with. Such a view not only led him to discard a model which describes, by his own admission, important behaviors, but is based on an incomplete view of reinforcement.

McGregor's basic arguments could have been based on Skinner rather than Maslow. The major difference would be the assumption of fewer givens about human nature. In view of this similarity one need not choose either Skinner or McGregor. Rather, there is considerable overlap in that both focus on changing the environmental conditions to produce changes in behavior. Further, both writers place substantial emphasis on the goals of prediction and control. Both are quite explicit in suggesting that we often get undesired results because we use inappropriate methods of control. In fact, the emphasis that McGregor's (1960) first chapter gives to the role of environment in controlling behavior seems to place him clearly in the behavioral camp.

Certainly there are important differences between Skinner and McGregor as well as the marked similarities noted above. For example, McGregor's (1960) use of Maslow's hierarchy of needs implies a series of inborn needs as a focus of the causal factors of behavior whereas Skinner (1953) views environmental factors as the causes of behavior. This difference does not, however, suggest an unresolvable conflict on the applied level. Skinner too allows for satiation on certain reinforcers which will be subject to species' and individual differences. Proceeding from this premise, Skinner focuses on the environmental control of behavior in a more rigorous and specific fashion than did McGregor. For example, McGregor (1960) advocated an agricultural approach to development which emphasizes the provision of the conditions for behavioral change as a management responsibility. He noted in a general way that features of the organization, such as a boss, will influence behavioral change. He added that the change would not be permanent unless the organizational environment reinforced the desired behavior pattern. Such a general approach is an assumed basis for Skinner, who proceeds to focus on the types of reinforcement, the details of the administration of reinforcement, and the outcomes which can be expected from the administration of various types of reinforcement. Thus, changes in behavior which are predicted and achieved by Skinnerian methods can be viewed as empirical support for the work of McGregor.

There are other commonalities in the thinking of the two men. Both assume that there are a wide number of desirable responses available to a person which he does not make, because the responses are not rewarded in the environment. Both suggest that many undesired responses are repeated because they are rewarded. Both are clearly advocating a search for alternatives to controlling behavior which will be more effective in developing desired responses.

At this same level of analysis, there seems to be one major difference which revolves around the issue of self-control. However, this difference may be more apparent than real. Skinner (1953) wrote "It appears, therefore, that society is responsible for the larger part of the behavior of self-control. If this is correct, little ultimate control remains with the individual (p. 240)." Continuing on self-control, Skinner adds: "But it is also behavior; and we account for it in terms of other variables in the environment and history of the individual. It is these variables which provide the ultimate control (p. 240)."

In apparent contrast, McGregor (1960) stated: "Theory *Y* assumes that people will exercise self-direction and self-control in the achievement of organizational objectives *to the degree that they are committed to those objectives* (p. 56)." Seemingly this statement contradicts Skinner in placing the locus of control inside the individual. However, this conflict is reduced a few sentences later when McGregor (1960) added "Managerial policies and practices materially affect this degree of commitment (p. 56)." Thus, both writers, Skinner far more unequivocally than McGregor, see the external environment as the primary factor in self-control. While McGregor polemicized against control by authority, he was not arguing that man is "free." Perhaps the more humanistic tone of McGregor's writing or his specific attention to managerial problems faced in business is responsible for his high esteem among students of management relative to that accorded Skinner. While metaphorically there is great difference, substantively there is little. It would seem, however, that metaphors have led practitioners and students of applied behavioral science to overlook some valuable data and some creative management possibilities.

One major substantive difference between the two approaches exists: it involves intrinsic rewards. McGregor (1966) saw a dichotomy in the effects of intrinsic and extrinsic rewards, noting research which has shown intrinsic ones to be more effective. He concludes the "mechanical" view (reinforcement theory) is inadequate, because it does not explain the superior outcomes of the use of "intrinsic" over "extrinsic" rewards. Here, as will be discussed in more detail later in connection with Herzberg, the problem is McGregor's failure to consider scheduling of reinforcement. "Intrinsic" rewards in existing organizations may be more effective because they occur on a more appropriate schedule for sustaining behavior than do "extrinsic" rewards. Intrinsic rewards are given by the environment for task completion or a similar achievement, and often occur on a ratio schedule. The implications of this crucial fact will be discussed shortly in considering Skinner's emphasis on the scheduling of rewards. For the present, it is suggested that McGregor gave little attention to reinforcement schedules and made a qualitative distinction between external and internal rewards. He seems to agree with Skinner that achievement, task completion, and control of the environment are reinforcers in themselves. Skinner's work suggests, however, that these rewards have the same consequences as "extrinsic" rewards, if they are given on the same schedule.

By way of summary to this point, it appears that more humanistic social scientists have been preferred by managers to behaviorists such as Skinner in their efforts to improve the management of human resources. Perhaps the oversight has been due to the congruence between their values and the metaphysics of people such as McGregor and Maslow. The differences between McGregor and Skinner do not appear to involve open conflict.

To the extent the two approaches agree, the major criterion in employing them would seem to be the degree to which they aid in predicting and controlling behavior toward organizational goals. The work of Skinner and his followers has much to offer in terms of the above criterion. In particular, McGregor's followers might find Skinner's work an asset in implementing Theory *Y*. The remainder of this paper will develop some of the major points of the Skinnerian approach and seek to explore their potential for industrial use.

CONDITIONING—A SYNTHESIS FOR ORGANIZATIONAL BEHAVIOR

The behavioral psychology of Skinner assumes, like Theory *Y*, that rate of behavior is dependent on the external conditions in which the behavior takes place. Like Theory *X*, it stresses the importance of the administration of rewards and punishments. Unlike Theory *X*, Skinnerian psychology places emphasis on rewards. Like Theory *Y* it emphasizes the role of interdependence between people in a social relationship and thus views the administration of rewards and punishments as an exchange. For those who are unfamiliar with the work of Skinner and his followers, a brief summary follows. Like any summary of an extensive body of work, this review omits a lot of important material. A more detailed, yet simple, introduction to conditioning can be found in Bijou and Baer (1961) and Skinner (1953). Extensions of this work by social exchange theorists such as Homans (1961) suggest that the conditioning model can be extended to a systems approach, contrary to McGregor's (1966) belief.

Generally, conditioned responses can be divided into two classes. Each class is acquired in a different fashion. The first class, generally known as respondent or classically conditioned behavior, describes the responses which are controlled by prior stimulation. These responses, generally thought of as being involuntary or reflexive, are usually made by the "smooth muscles." Common ones are salivation and emotional responses. Initially, the presentation of an unconditioned stimulus will elicit a specific response. For example, food placed on one's tongue will generally cause salivation. If a bell is sounded and then food is placed on the tongue, and this process is repeated several times, the sound of the bell by itself will elicit salivation. By this process, stimuli which previously did not control behavior such as the bell, can become a source of behavior control. Many of our likes and dislikes, our anxieties, our feelings of patriotism, and other emotions can be thought of as such involuntary responses. The implications of emotional responses are of major importance to the management of human resources and more will be said about them later. However, the second class of responses, the operants, are of even greater importance.

The rate of operant responses are influenced by events which follow them. These events are considered to be the consequences of behavior. The responses, generally thought to be voluntary, are usually made by striped muscles. All that is necessary for the development of an operant response is that the desired response has a probability of occurring which is greater than zero for the individual involved. Most rapid conditioning results when the desired response is "reinforced" immediately (preferably about one-half second after the response). In other words, the desired response is followed directly by some consequence. In simple terms, if the outcome is pleasing to the individual, the probability of his repeating the response is apt to be increased. If the consequence is displeasing to the individual, the probability of his repeating the response is apt to be decreased. The process of inducing such change (usually an increase) in the response rate, is called operant conditioning. In general, the frequency of a behavior is said to be a function of its consequences.

The above description of operant conditioning is greatly simplified. The additional considerations which follow will only partially rectify this state. One crucial factor has to do with the frequency with which a given consequence follows a response. There are several possible patterns. Most obviously, the consequence can be continuous (for example, it follows the response every time the response is made). Alternatively a consequence might follow only some of the responses. There are two basic ways in which such partial reinforcement can be administered. First, the consequence can be made contingent on a certain number of responses. Two sub-patterns are possible. Every nth response may be reinforced or an average of $1/n$ of the responses may be reinforced in a random pattern. These two related patterns are called ratio schedules. The former is known as a fixed ratio and the latter is known as a variable ratio. Ratio schedules tend to generate a high rate of response, with the variable ratio schedule leading to a more durable response than both the fixed-ratio and continuous patterns. A second technique of partial reinforcement can be designed where the consequence follows the response only after a certain amount of time has elapsed. The first response made after a specified interval is then reinforced, but all other responses produce neutral stimulus outcomes. This pattern can also be either fixed or variable. Generally, interval schedules develop responses which are quite long lasting when reinforcement is no longer given, but do not yield as rapid a response rate as ratio schedules do. Obviously, mixed patterns of ratio and interval schedules can also be designed.

A second consideration about operant conditioning which deserves brief mention is the concept of a response hierarchy. All the responses which an individual could make under a given set of conditions can be placed in order according to probability that they will be made. In this view, there are two basic strategies for getting an individual to make the desired response. First, one could attempt to reduce the probability of all the more probable responses. Second, one could attempt to increase the probability of the desired response. Of course, some combination of these two approaches may often be used.

Strategies for changing the probability of a response can be implemented by punishment, extinction, and positive reinforcement. Generally punishment and extinction are used to decrease the occurrence of a response whereas positive reinforcement is used to increase its probability. An understanding of these three operations in behavior control is important, not only for knowing how to use them, but chiefly because of their unanticipated consequences or their side-effects.

Punishment is the most widely used technique in our society for behavior control. Perhaps, as Reese (1966) said, the widespread use of punishment is due to the immediate effects it has in stopping or preventing the undesired response. In this sense, the punisher is reinforced for punishing. Also, many of us seem to be influenced by some notion of what Homans (1961) called distributive justice. In order to reestablish what we believe to be equity, we may often be led to punish another person. This ancient assumption of ". . . an eye for an eye . . ." has been widely practiced in man's quest for equity and behavior control.

Whatever the reason for punishing, it can be done in two ways, both of which have unfortunate side-effects. First, punishment can be administered in the form of some aversive stimulus such as physical pain or social disapproval. Secondly, it can be administered by withdrawing a desired stimulus. The immediate effect is often the rapid drop in frequency of the punished response. The full effects, unfortunately, are often not clearly recognized. Many of these consequences are crucial for managers of organizations.

Punishment may be an inefficient technique for controlling behavior for a number of reasons. First, the probability of the response may be reduced only when the threat of punishment is perceived to exist. Thus, when the punishing agent is away, the undesired response may occur at its initial rate. Secondly, punishment only serves to reduce the probability of the one response. This outcome does not necessarily produce the desired response, unless that response is the next most probable one in the response hierarchy. Really, what punishment does is to get the individual to do something other than what he has been punished for. A third effect, is that the punishment may interfere with the response being made under desired circumstances. For example, if an organizational member attempts an innovation which is met with punishment by his superiors because they did not feel he had the authority to take the step, it is quite possible that his creative behavior will be reduced even in those areas where his superiors expect him to innovate.

In addition to these effects there are some other important by-products of punishment. Punishment may result in a person making responses which are incompatible with the punished response. Psychological tension, often manifested in emotional behavior such as fear or anxiety, is often the result. Secondly, punishment may lead to avoidance and dislike of the punishing agent. This effect can be especially important to managers who are attempting to build open, helping relationships with subordinates. The roles of punishing agent and helper are often incompatible. Many line-staff conflicts in organizations undoubtedly can be explained in these terms. Finally, punishment may generate counter-aggression. Either through a modeling effect or a justice effect, the punished person may respond with aggressive responses towards the punishing agent or towards some other stimulus.

The second technique for behavior change, commonly called extinction, also focuses primarily on reducing the probability of a response. Extinction arises from repeated trials where the response is followed by a neutral stimulus. This technique generates fewer by-products than punishment. However, like punishment, it does not lead to the desired response being developed. Furthermore, to the extent that one has built up an expectation of a reward for a certain response, a neutral consequence may be perceived as punishing. Thus, extinction may have some advantages over punishment, but has many of the same limitations.

Positive reinforcement is the final technique for changing behavior. Under conditions of positive reinforcement, the response produces a consequence that results in an increase in the frequency of the response. It is commonly stated that such a consequence is rewarding, pleasing, or drive reducing for the individual. The operant conditioners, however, avoid such inferences and define positive reinforcers, as stimuli which increase the probability of a preceding response. Positive reinforcement is efficient for several reasons. First, it increases the probable occurrence of the desired response. The process involves rewarding approximations to the direct response itself immediately after it is made. The desired behavior is being directly developed as opposed to successive suppression of undesired acts.

Secondly, the adverse emotional responses associated with punishment and extinction are apt to be reduced and in fact favorable emotions may be developed. Since people tend to develop positive affect to others who reward them, the "trainer" is apt to become positively valenced in the eyes of the "learner."

By way of summary, Skinner's (1953) approach suggested that the control of behavior change involves a reduction in the probability of the most prepotent response and/or an increase in the probability of some desired response. Punishment and extinction may be used. These means can only reduce the probability of the unwanted response being made. Also, they may have undesired side-effects. The third technique, positive reinforcement, has the important advantage of developing the desired response rather than merely reducing the chances of an undesired one. Also, positive reinforcement is apt to produce favorable rather than unfavorable "side-effects" on organizational relationships.

This approach seems to suggest that both or neither Theory *X* and Theory *Y* assumptions are useful. This section suggested that conditioning may be both Theory *X* and Theory *Y*. Perhaps since the operant view does not make either set of assumptions, it is neither Theory *X* nor Theory *Y*. Operant conditioning is consistent with Theory *Y* in suggesting that the limits on human beings are a function of the organizational setting, but like Theory *X*, implies something about human nature; namely that deprivation or threat of some sort of deprivation is a precondition for behavior to be controlled. From the managerial perspective, however, the nomonological question is of little significance. The important thing to managers is behavior and the major point of this approach is that behavior is a function of its consequences. Good management is that which leads to the desired behavior by organizational members. Management must see to it that the consequences of behavior are such as to increase the frequency of desired behavior and decrease the frequency of undesired behaviors. The question becomes, how can managers develop a social system which provides the appropriate consequences? In many ways the answer to this question is similar to what Theory *Y* advocates have suggested. However, there are some new possibilities.

APPLICATIONS OF CONDITIONING IN ORGANIZATIONS

The potential uses of the Skinnerian framework for social systems are increasing rapidly. The approach has far more applicability to complex social systems than has often been recognized. McGregor's rejection of the stimulus-response or the reward-punishment approach as inadequate for management because it does not allow for a systems approach is quite inconsistent with this general trend and his own environmentally based approach. Recent work in the field of behavioral control has begun to refute McGregor's position. The Skinnerian view can be and has been used to redesign social systems.

The most complete redesign was envisioned by Skinner (1948) in his novel, *Walden Two*. In this book, Skinner developed a society based on the use of positive reinforcement and experimental ethics geared to the goal of competition of a coordinated social unit with its environment. In other words, the system is designed to reward behaviors which are functional for the whole society. Social change is introduced on the basis of empirical data. As a result of the success of this system, man is enabled to pursue those activities which are rewarding in themselves. Although the book is a novel, it can be a valuable stimulus for thought about the design of social organization.

In addition, Skinner (1954) has taken a fresh look at teaching and learning in conventional educational systems. He noted that the school system depends heavily on aversive control or punishment. The use of low marks and ridicule have merely been substituted for the "stick." The teacher, in Skinner's view, is an out of date reinforcing mechanism. He suggested the need to examine the reinforcers which are available in the system and to apply them in a manner which is consistent with what is known about learning. For example, control over the environment itself may be rewarding. Perhaps grades reinforce the wrong behavior and are administered on a rather poor schedule. It would seem that a search for new reinforcers and better reinforcement schedules is appropriate for all modern organizations.

These speculations suggest the potential for great advances. *Walden Two* is in many ways an ideal society but has been a source of horror to many readers. The thoughts about changes in teaching methods are also a subject of controversy. However, the environment can be designed to aid in the attainment of desired ends. People resist the idea that they can be controlled by their environment. This resistance does not change the fact that they are under such control. Recently, evidence has begun to accumulate that the Skinnerian approach can be employed to design social systems.

Much of this evidence was collected in settings far removed from modern work organizations. The reader's initial response is apt to be, "What relevance do these studies have to my organization?" Obviously, the relationship is not direct. However, if, as the operant approach maintains, the conditioning process describes the acquisition and maintenance of behavior, the same principles can be applied to any social organization. The problem of application becomes merely that of engineering. The gains may well be limited only by an administrator's ingenuity and resources.

Much of the evidence comes from studies of hospitalized mental patients and autistic children, although some has been based on normal lower class children. A few examples from these studies will serve to document the great potential of the conditioning methods for social systems. Allyon and Azrin (1965) observed mental patients' behavior to determine what activities they engaged in when they had a chance. They then made tokens contingent on certain responses such as work on hospital tasks. These tokens could be exchanged for the activities the patients preferred to engage in. The results of this approach were amazing. In one experiment five schizophrenics and three mental defectives served as *Ss*. They did jobs regularly and adequately when tokens were given for the job. Such performance was reported to be in sharp contrast to the erratic and inconsistent behavior characteristic of such patients. When the tokens were no longer contingent on the work, the performance dropped almost to zero. In a second experiment, a whole ward of 44 patients served as *Ss*. A similar procedure was followed and 11 classes of tasks observed. When tokens were contingent upon the desired responses, the group spent an average of 45 hours on the tasks daily. When tokens were not contingent on responses, almost no time was spent on the tasks. The implications seem rather clear. When desired behavior is rewarded, it will be emitted, when it is not rewarded, it will not be emitted.

A great deal of related work has been reported. Allyon (1966) and Wolf, Risley, and Mees (1966) have shown how a reinforcement procedure can be effective in controlling the behavior of a psychotic patient and of an autistic child respectively. These are but a few of the many studies in a growing body of evidence.

More important for present purposes are the application of this approach in more complex social situations. The work of Hamblin *et al.* (1967) shows some of the interesting possibilities of the conditioning approach for school classes and aggressive children. A token system was used to shape desired behavior. Through the application of the conditioning approach to the school system, gains may be made in educating children from deprived backgrounds. Two examples will illustrate these possibilities.

The first example comes from a recent newspaper story. A record shop owner in a Negro area of Chicago reported seeing the report card of a Negro boy. The owner thought the boy was bright, but the report card showed mostly unsatisfactory performance. He told the boy he would give him $5 worth of free records if he got all "excellents" on the next report card. Ten weeks later the boy returned with such a card to collect his reward. The owner reported that similar offers to other children had a remarkable effect in getting them to study and do their homework. The anecdote demonstrates what everyone knows anyway: people will work for rewards. It also suggests the converse: people will not work if rewards do not exist. The problems of education in the ghetto and motivation to work in general, may be overcome by appropriate reinforcement. Further support for this statement comes from the work of Montrose Wolf.

Wolf (1966) ran a school for children, most of whom were sixth graders, in a lower class Negro area of Kansas City. The children attended this school for several hours after school each day and on Saturday. Rewards were given in the form of tickets which could be saved and turned in for different kinds of things like toys, food, movies, shopping trips, and other activities. Tickets were made contingent on academic performance within the remedial school itself, and on performance in the regular school system. The results were remarkable. The average regular school grade of the students was raised to C from D. The results on standard achievement tests showed the remedial group progressed over twice as much in one year as they had done the previous year. They showed twice as much progress as a control group. Other gains were also noted. Wolf reported that a severe punishment was not to let the children attend school. They expressed strong discontent when school was not held because of a holiday. He further noted that when reading was no longer rewarded with tickets, the students still continued to read more than before the training. Arithmetic and English did not maintain these increments. Thus, to some extent, reading appeared to be intrinsically rewarding.

A final point concerns the transferability of skills learned in such a school to society at large. Will the tasks that are not rewarding in themselves be continued? The answer is probably not, unless other rewards are provided. The task then becomes to develop skills and behavior which society itself will reward. If this method is applied to develop behavior which is rewarded by society, the behavior is apt to be maintained. The same argument holds for organizational behavior. It will be fruitless to develop behavior which is not rewarded in the organization.

In summary, evidence has been presented to show the relevance of the Skinnerian approach to complex social systems. Certainly the evidence is only suggestive of future possibilities. The rest of this paper attempts to suggest some of these implications for organizational management.

MANAGEMENT THROUGH POSITIVE REINFORCEMENT

The implications of the systematic use of positive reinforcement for management range over many traditional areas. Some of the more important areas include training and personnel development, compensation and alternative rewards, supervision and leadership, job design, organizational design, and organizational change.

Training and Personnel Development

The area of training has been the first to benefit from the application of conditioning principles with the use of programmed learning and the teaching machine. An example of future potential comes from the Northern Systems Company Training Method for assembly line work. In this system, the program objectives are broken down into subobjectives. The training employs a lattice which provides objective relationships between functions and objectives, indicates critical evaluation points, and presents a visual display of go-no-go functions. Progress through various steps is reinforced by rewards. To quote from a statement of the training method ". . . the trainee gains satisfaction only by demonstrated performance at the tool stations. Second, he quickly perceives that correct behaviors obtain for him the satisfaction of his needs, and that incorrect behaviors do not (p. 20)." Correct performance includes not only job skills, but also the performance of social interaction which is necessary in a factory setting. The skills taught are designed to allow for high mobility in the industrial world. The Northern System's method develops behavior which the economic and social system will normally reinforce and has been successful in training people in a wide variety of skills. Its potential in training such groups as the "hard-core" unemployed seems to be limited only by the resources and creativity of program designers.

The Skinnerian approach seems to have potential for all areas of personnel development, not only for highly programmed tasks. Reinforcement theory may be useful in the development of such behaviors as creativity. The work of Maltzman, Simon, Roskin, and Licht (1960) demonstrated this possibility. After a series of experiments employing a standard experimental training procedure with free association materials, these investigators concluded that a highly reliable increase in uncommon responses could be produced through the use of reinforcement. The similarity of their results to those of operant experiments with respect to the persistance of the responses and the effect of repetitions, led them to conclude that originality is a form of operant behavior. Positive reinforcement increased the rate at which original responses were emitted.

Support is also available for the efficacy of operant conditioning to more conventional personnel and leadership development. Three such contributions are discussed below. The first concerns the organizational environment as a shaper of behavior of which Fleishman's (1967) study is a case in point. He found that human relations training programs were only effective in producing on-the-job changes if the organizational climate was supportive of the content of the program. More generally it would appear that industrial behavior is a function of its consequences. Those responses which are rewarded will persist: those responses which are not rewarded or are punished will decrease in frequency. If the organizational environment does not reward responses developed in a training program, the program will be, at best, a total waste of time and money. As Sykes (1962) has shown, at worst, such a program may be highly disruptive. A second implication of operant conditioning concerns the content of personnel development programs in the area of human relations. If, as Homans (1961) and others have suggested, social interaction is also influenced by the same operant principles, then people in interaction are constantly "shaping" or conditioning each other. The behavior of a subordinate is to some degree developed by his boss and vice-versa. What more sensible, practical point could be taught to organizational members than that they are teaching their fellow participants to behave in a certain manner? What more practical, sensible set of principles could be taught than that, due to latent dysfunctions generated, punishment and extinction procedures are less efficient ways to influence behavior than positive reinforcement? Clearly, the behavioral scientists who have contributed so greatly to organizational practice and personnel development have not put enough emphasis on these simple principles. The third implication for personnel development is added recognition that annual merit interviews and salary increments are very inefficient development techniques. The rewards or punishments are so delayed that they can be expected to have little feedback value for the employees involved. More frequent appraisals and distribution of rewards are apt to be far more effective, especially to the degree that they are related to specific tasks or units of work.

Job Design

Recently, behavioral scientists have emphasized

the social psychological factors which need to be attended to in job design. McGregor and others have suggested job enlargement. Herzberg (1968) has argued that job enlargement just allows an individual to do a greater variety of boring jobs and suggests that "job enrichment" is needed. For present purposes, job enlargement and job enrichment will be lumped together. Both of these approaches are consistent with the conditioning view if two differences can be resolved. First, the definitions of motivation must be translated into common terms. Second, reinforcers operating in the newly designed jobs must be delineated and tested to see if the reinforcers postulated in the newly designed jobs are really responsible for behavioral changes or if there are other reinforcers operating.

With respect to the definitions of motivation, the two approaches are really similar in viewing the rate of behavior as the crucial factor. The major differences exist on the conceptual level. Both job enlargement and job enrichment are attempts to increase motivation. Conceptually, McGregor and Herzberg tend to view motivation as some internal state. The conditioning approach does not postulate internal states but rather deals with the manipulation of environmental factors which influence the rate of behavior. Actually, some combination of the two approaches may be most useful theoretically as Vinacke (1962) has suggested. However, if both approaches are viewed only at the operational level, it is quite probable that rates of behavior could be agreed on as an acceptable criterion. Certainly from the practitioners viewpoint, behavior is the crucial variable. When a manager talks about a motivated worker, he often means one who frequently makes desired responses at a high rate without external prompting from the boss. The traditional view of motivation as an inner-drive is of limited practical and theoretical value.

If both approaches could agree on the behavioral criterion, at least on an operational level, the operant approach could be employed to help resolve some practical and theoretical problems suggested by the work of McGregor and Herzberg. Since, generally speaking, the external conditions are most easily manipulated in an organization, attention can be focused on designing an environment which increases the frequency of the wanted responses. As a result, practitioners and students of organization could deal with motivation without searching for man's essence. We can avoid the metaphysical assumptions of Maslow and McGregor until they are better documented. The issue of a two-factor theory of motivation proposed by Herzberg which recently has been severely challenged by Lindsay, Marks, and Gorlow (1967) and Hulin and Smith (1967) among others can also be avoided. Attention can be confined to developing systems which produce high rates of desired behavior. Thus the conceptual differences about motivation do not cause unresolvable conflict at the present time.

The second area of difference between McGregor-Herzberg and the operant explanation of the effects of job enrichment stems from the failure of Herzberg and McGregor to recognize the great variety of possible rewards available in job design. The Skinnerian approach leads to the development of a more comprehensive discussion of the rewards from enriched or enlarged jobs. In terms of the operant approach, both job enrichment and job enlargement are apt to lead to what would generally be called greater motivation or what we will call higher rates of desired behavior. McGregor and Herzberg suggest feelings of achievement and responsibility explain these results. The reinforcement approach leads to a search for specific rewards in these newly designed jobs.

Job enlargement can be viewed simply as increasing the variety of tasks a person does. Recent research on self-stimulation and sensory deprivation has suggested that stimulation itself is reinforcing, especially when one has been deprived of it. The increased variety of tasks due to job enlargement may thus be intrinsically rewarding due to a host of reinforcers in the work itself rather than to any greater feeling of responsibility or achievement. These feelings may be a cause of greater productivity or merely correlates of the receipt of these intrinsic rewards from stimulation. The evidence is not clear, but the effects of job enlargement can at least be partially explained in operant terms.

Some additional support from this idea comes from Schultz's (1964) work on spontaneous alternation of behavior. Schultz suggested that spontaneous alternation of human behavior is facilitated (1) when responses are not reinforced and/or are not subjected to knowledge of correctness, (2) by the amount of prior exercise of one response alternative, and (3) by a short intertrial interval. Low feedback and reinforcement, short intervals between responses, and the frequent repetition of one response are all characteristic of many jobs which need enlargement. Merely making different responses may be rewarding to a worker, thereby explaining some of the benefits noted from job enlargement. It has also been noted that people create variation for themselves in performing monotonous tasks. For example, ritualized social interaction in the form of social "games" is a form of such alternation workers developed noted by Roy (1964).

By way of summary, much of the current work on job enlargement and enrichment has attributed the effects to feelings of achievement or responsibility, without taking into account numerous other possible reinforcers which may be more basic. Further research to determine the efficacy of these various possibilities is needed before definite conclusions can be drawn. Do the feelings of achievement or responsibility operate as reinforcers in an operant manner? Do these feelings come from other more basic rewards as task variety? Present data does not permit answers to these questions.

With respect to the benefits noted from job enrichment, an operant model may provide further insights. Herzberg (1968) maintained that some jobs can not be "enriched" or made more motivating in themselves. It is the contention of this paper that it is not the tasks which are the problem, but it is the reinforcement schedules. For example, what could be more boring, have less potential for achievement and realization of Herzberg's satisfiers, than the game of bingo. Yet people will sit for hours at bingo, often under punishing conditions (since the house takes in more than it pays out) and place tokens on numbers. Similar behavior is exhibited at slot-machines and other gambling devices. Most operational definitions of motivation would agree that these players are highly motivated. The reason is clear from the operant viewpoint. The reinforcement schedule employed in games of chance, the variable ratio schedule, is a very powerful device for maintaining a rapid rate of response. With respect to job design, the important requirement is that rewards follow performance on an effective schedule.

The type of rewards Herzberg (1968) called satisfiers may be important motivators because they are distributed on a variable ratio schedule. Herzberg's data does not rule out this explanation. Take achievement, for example. If a person is doing a job from which it is possible to get a feeling of achievement, there must be a reasonably large probability that a person will not succeed on the task. Often times, this condition means that some noncontinuous schedule of reinforcement is operating. An individual will succeed only on some variable ratio schedule. In addition, successful completion of the task is often the most important reward. The reward is, of course, immediate. A similar statement could be made about tasks which are said to yield intrinsic satisfaction, such as crossword puzzles or enriched jobs. Thus the factors Herzberg called motivators may derive their potency from the manner in which the rewards are administered. The task is immediately and positively reinforced by the environment on a variable ratio schedule. Often the schedule is one which rewards a very small fraction of a large number of responses. Since behavior is a function of its consequences, if jobs can be designed to reinforce desired behavior in the appropriate manner, "motivated" workers are apt to result. Some of Herzberg's results may be explained without resort to a two-factor theory more parsimoniously in terms of schedules of reinforcement. Herzberg's (1966) finding that recognition is only a motivator if it is contingent on performance further documents the operant argument.

Another suggestion for job design from the operant tradition was suggested by Homans. He explored the relationship of the frequency of an activity and satisfaction to the amount of a reward. He concluded that satisfaction is generally positively related to the amount of reward whereas frequency of an activity is negatively related to the amount of reward the individual has received in the recent past. In order to have both high satisfaction and high activity, Homans (1961) suggested that tasks need to be designed in a manner such that repeated activities lead up to the accomplishment of some final result and get rewarded at a very low frequency until just before the final result is achieved. Then the reinforcement comes often. For example, consider the job of producing bottled soda. An optimal design would have the reward immediate on the completion of putting the caps on the bottles, but the task would be designed such that all the operations prior to capping were completed before any capping was done. Near the end of a work day, all the capping could be done. High output and satisfaction might then exist simultaneously. In general then, the operant approach suggests some interesting possibilities for designing jobs in ways which would maximize the power of reinforcers in the job itself.

A similar argument can be applied to some problems faced in administration and management. For example, it is commonly recognized that programmed tasks tend to be attended to before unprogrammed ones. It is quite obvious that programmed functions produce a product which is often tangible. The product itself is a reinforcer. An unprogrammed task often requires behavior which has not been reinforced in the past and will not produce a reward in the near future. It may be beneficial to provide rewards relatively early for behavior on unprogrammed tasks. This suggestion will be difficult to put into practice because of the very nature of unprogrammed tasks. Perhaps the best that can be done is to reward the working on such tasks.

Compensation and Alternative Rewards

Although whether money is a true "generalized reinforcer" as Skinner suggests, has not been demonstrated conclusively, for years operant principles have been applied in the form of monetary incentive systems. Opsahl and Dunnette (1966) concluded that such programs generally do increase output. However, the restriction of output and other unanticipated consequences are associated with these programs. Many writers have attributed these consequences to social forces, such as the desire for approval from one's peers. Gewirtz and Baer (1958), for example, have shown that social approval has the same effects as other reinforcers in an operant situation. Dalton's (1948) famous study on rate-busters may be interpreted to show that people who are more "group-oriented" may place a higher value on social approval and hence are more apt to abide by group production norms than are less "group-oriented" people. Thus, it is not that money in piece-rate systems is not a potential reinforcer, but rather other reinforcers are more effective, at least after a certain level of monetary reward.

The successful use of the Scanlon Plan demonstrates the value of combining both economic and social rewards. This plan rewards improved work with several types of reinforcers, and often more immediately and directly than many incentive systems. The Scanlon Plan combines economic rewards, often given monthly, with social rewards. The latter are given soon after an employee's idea has been submitted or used.

Related arguments can be made for other group incentive programs. Often jobs are interdependent. The appropriate reinforcement for such tasks should be contingent upon interdependent responses, not individual ones. Even if the jobs are independent, the workers are social-psychologically interdependent. Social rewards are often obtainable by restricting output. It is hardly surprising that individual incentive programs have produced the unanticipated consequences so often noted. Further, since rewards and punishments from the informal group are apt to be administered immediately and frequently they are apt to be very powerful in controlling behavior.

In general then, money and other rewards must be made contingent on the desired responses. Further, the importance of alternative rewards to money must be recognized and incorporated into the design of the work environment. The widely known path-goal to productivity model expresses a similar point.

Another problem of compensation in organizations is also apparent in an operant context. Often, means of compensation, especially fringe benefits, have the unanticipated consequence of reinforcing the wrong responses. Current programs of sick pay, recreation programs, employee lounges, work breaks, and numerous other personnel programs all have one point in common. They all reward the employee for not working or for staying away from the job. These programs are not "bad," since often they may act to reduce problems such as turnover. However, an employer who relies on them should realize what behavior he is developing by establishing these costly programs. Alternative expenditures must be considered. If some of the money that was allocated for these programs was used to redesign jobs so as to be more reinforcing in themselves, more productive effort could be obtained. This idea is certainly not new. A host of behavioral scientists have suggested that resources devoted to making performance of the job itself more attractive will pay social and/or economic dividends.

Another interesting application of conditioning principles has to do with the schedule on which pay is distributed. The conventional pay schedule is a fixed interval one. Further, pay often is not really contingent on one's performance. The response needed to be rewarded is often attending work on pay day. Not only is pay often not contingent upon performance, but the fixed interval schedule is not given to generating a high response rate. In a creative article, Aldis (1966) suggested an interesting compensation program employing a variable ratio schedule. Instead of an annual Christmas bonus or other types of such expected salary supplements, he suggested a lottery system. If an employee produced above an agreed upon standard, his name would be placed in a hat. A drawing would be held. The name(s) drawn would receive an amount of money proportionate to the number of units produced during that period of time. This system would approximate the desired variable ratio schedule.

In addition to the prosperity of the owners of gambling establishments, there is some direct evidence that variable ratio schedules will be of use to those charged with predicting and controlling human behavior. A leading St. Louis hardware company[1] although apparently unaware of the work of the operant conditioners, has applied an approximate variable ratio schedule of reinforcement to reduce absenteeism and tardiness. Although the complete data is not available, the personnel department has reported surprising success. A brief description of the system will be presented below and a more detailed study will be written in the near future.

Under the lottery system, if a person is on time (that is, not so much as ½ minute late) for work at the start of his day and after his breaks, he is eligible for a drawing at the end of the month. Prizes worth approximately $20 to $25 are awarded to the winners. One prize is available for each 25 eligible employees. At the end of six months, people who have had perfect attendance for the entire period are eligible for a drawing for a color television set. The

[1] The author wishes to thank Mr. C. for making this information available and one of his students, Richard Weis, for informing him about this program.

names of all the winners and of those eligible are also printed in the company paper, such that social reinforcement may also be a factor. The plan was introduced because tardiness and absenteeism had become a very serious problem. In the words of the personnel manager, absenteeism and tardiness ". . . were lousy before." Since the program was begun 16 months ago, conditions have improved greatly. Sick leave costs have been reduced about 62%. After the first month, 151 of approximately 530 employees were eligible for the drawing. This number has grown larger, although not at a steady rate to 219 for the most recent month. Although the comparable figures for the period before the program were unfortunately not available, management has noted great improvements. It would appear that desired behavior by organization participants in terms of tardiness and absenteeism can be readily and inexpensively developed by a variable ratio schedule of positive reinforcement. The possibilities for other areas are limited largely by the creativity of management.

The operant approach also has some additional implications for the use of money as a reward. First, many recent studies have shown money is not as important as other job factors in worker satisfaction. Herzberg, (1968) among others, has said explicitly that money will not promote worker satisfaction. Undoubtedly, in many situations, Herzberg is correct. However, crucial factors of reward contingencies and schedules have not been controlled in these studies. Again, it appears that the important distinction that can be made between Herzberg's motivators and hygiene factors is that the former set of rewards are contingent on an individual's responses and the latter are not. If a work situation were designed so that money was directly contingent on performance, the results might be different. A second point has to do with the perception of money as a reward. Opsahl and Dunnette (1966) have recently questioned pay secrecy policies. They maintained that pay secrecy leads to misperception of the amount of money that a promotion might mean. The value of the reinforcers are underestimated by the participants suggesting that they are less effective than they might otherwise be. Certainly, alternative rewards are likely to be "over chosen." By following policies of pay secrecy, organizations seem to be failing to utilize fully their available monetary rewards.

In addition to under utilization of money rewards, organizations seem to be almost totally unaware of alternative reinforcers, and in fact see punishment as the only viable method of control when existing reinforcers fail. What are some alternatives to a punishment centered bureaucracy? Some, such as job design, improved scheduling of reinforcement, and a search for new reinforcers have already been suggested. There are other possible reinforcers, a few of which are discussed below.

The important thing about reinforcers is that they be made immediately contingent on desired performance to the greatest degree possible. The potential reinforcers discussed here also require such a contingent relationship, although developing such relationships may be a severe test of an administrator's creativity. One of the more promising reinforcers is leisure. It would seem possible in many jobs to establish an agreed upon standard output for a day's work. This level could be higher than the current average. Once this amount is reached, the group or individual could be allowed the alternative of going home. The result of experiments in this direction would be interesting to all concerned. Quite possibly, this method might lead to a fuller utilization of our labor force. The individual may be able to hold two four-hour jobs, doubling his current contribution. Such a tremendous increase in output is quite possible as Stagner and Rosen (1966) have noted, when the situation possesses appropriate contingencies. Certainly, the problems of industrial discipline, absenteeism, and grievances which result in lower productivity might be ameliorated. Another possible reinforcer is information. Guetzkow (1965) noted that people have a strong desire to receive communication. Rewarding desired performance with communication or feedback may be a relatively inexpensive reinforcer. Graphs, charts, or even tokens which show immediate and cumulative results may serve this function. Some of the widely accepted benefits from participative management may be due to the reinforcing effect of communication. Certainly the "Hawthorne effect" can be described in these terms. In addition, social approval and status may be powerful reinforcers. Blau's classic study described by Homans (1961) on the exchange of approval and status for help is but one example. People will work for approval and status. If these are made contingent on a desired set of responses, the response rate can be increased. At present, often social approval is given by one's peers, but is contingent on behavior which is in conflict with organizational goals.

In addition to these reinforcers, there are certain social exchange concepts such as justice, equity, reciprocity, and indebtedness which deserve attention. Recent research has demonstrated that an unbalanced social exchange, such as one which is inequitable or leaves one person indebted to someone else, may be tension producing in such a way that individuals work to avoid them. In other words, unbalanced exchanges are a source of punishment.

Relationships, such as those involving dependency, which result in such social imbalance can be expected to have the same latent consequences as punishment. Techniques which employ social imbalance to predict and control behavior can be expected to be less efficient in most respects than ones based on positive reinforcement.

The crucial variable in distributing any reward is contingency. Managers have been quick to point out that the problem with a "welfare-state" is that rewards do not depend on desired behavior. This point is well taken. It is surprising that the same point has not been recognized in current management practices.

Organizational Climate and Design

Important aspects of human behavior can be attributed to the immediate environment in which people function. The potential then exists to structure and restructure formal organizations in a manner to promote the desired behavior. Once this point is recognized and accepted by managers, progress can begin. The reaction of managers to this approach is often, "You mean my organization should reward people for what they ought to do anyway?" The answer is that people's behavior is largely determined by its outcomes. It is an empirical fact rather than a moral question. If you want a certain response and it does not occur, you had better change the reinforcement contingencies to increase its probable occurrence.

The first step in the direction of designing organizations on this basis involves defining explicitly the desired behaviors and the available reinforcers. The next step is to then make these rewards dependent on the emission of the desired responses. What are some of the implications of such reasoning for organizational design?

Already the importance of organizational climate has been discussed in connection with human development. Some additional implications merit brief consideration. A major one concerns conformity. Often today the degree to which people conform to a wide variety of norms is lamentably acknowledged and the question is asked, "Why do people do it?" The reasons in the operant view are quite clear: conformity is rewarded, deviance is punished. People conform in organizations because conformity is profitable in terms of the outcomes the individual achieves. In fact, Nord (in press) and Walker and Heyns (1962) presented considerable evidence that conformity has the same properties as other operant responses. If managers are really worried about the costs of conformity in terms of creativity and innovation, they must look for ways to reward deviance, to avoid punishing nonconformity, and to avoid rewarding conformity. Furthermore, the way in which rewards are administered is important. Generally, if rewards are given by a person or group of people, a dependency relationship is created, with hostility, fear, anxiety, and other emotional outcomes being probable. Dependence itself may be a discomforting condition. It is therefore desirable to make the rewards come from the environment. Rewards which have previously been established for reaching certain agreed upon goals are one such means. Meaningful jobs, in which achievement in itself is rewarding are another way. In general, to the degree that competition is with the environment or forces outside the organization, and rewards come from achievement itself, the more effective the reinforcers are apt to be in achieving desired responses.

A final point concerns the actual operation of organizations. Increasingly it is recognized that a formal organization, which aims at the coordination of the efforts of its participants, is dependent on informal relationships for its operation. As Gross (1968) noted,

> In administration, also, "the play's the thing" and not the script. Many aspects of even the simplest operation can never be expressed in writing. They must be sensed and felt . . . Daily action is the key channel of operational definition. In supplying cues and suggestions, in voicing praise and blame, in issuing verbal instructions, administrators define or clarify operational goals in real life (p. 406).

More generally, what makes an organization"tick" is the exchange of reinforcers within it and between it and its environment. The nature of these exchanges involves both economic and social reinforcers. Many of these are given and received without explicit recognition or even awareness on the part of the participants. The operant approach, focuses attention on these exchange processes. As a result, it may prove to be an invaluable asset to both administrators and students of administration and organization.

A final advantage of the operant approach for current organizational theory and analysis may be the attention it focuses on planned and rational administration. Gouldner (1966) noted "Modern organizational analysis by sociologists is overpreoccupied with the spontaneous and unplanned responses which organizations make to stress, and too little concerned with patterns of planned and rational administration (p. 397)." The Skinnerian approach leads to rational planning in order to control outcomes previously viewed as spontaneous consequences. This approach could expand the area of planning and rational action in administration.

REFERENCES

Aldis, O. Of pigeons and men. In R. Ulrich, T. Stachnik and J. Mabry (eds), *Control of human behavior.* Glenview, Ill.: Scott, Foresman, 1966, pp. 218–21.

Ayllon, T. Intensive treatment of psychotic behavior by stimulus satiation and food reinforcement. In R. Ulrich, T. Stachnik and T. Mabry (eds.), *Control of human behavior.* Glenview, Ill.: Scott, Foresman, 1966. 170–76.

Ayllon, T. and Azrin, N. H. The measurement and reinforcement of behavior of psychotics. *Journal of the Experimental Analysis of Behavior,* 1965, 8, 357–83.

Bijou, S. W. and Baer, D. M. *Child development.* Vol. 1. New York: Appleton-Century-Crofts, 1961.

Dalton, M. The industrial "rate-buster": A characterization. *Applied Anthropology,* 1948, 7, 5–18.

Fleishman, E. A. Leadership climate, human relations training, and supervisory behavior. In E. A. Fleishman, (ed.), *Studies in personnel and industrial psychology.* Homewood, Ill.: Dorsey, 1967. 250–63.

Free records given for E's, pupils report cards improve. *St. Louis Post Dispatch,* December 3, 1967.

Gewirtz, J. L. and Baer, D. M. Deprivation and satiation of social reinforcers as drive conditions. *Journal of Abnormal and Social Psychology,* 1958, 57, 165–72.

Gouldner, A. W. Organizational analysis. In Bennis, W. G., Benne, K. D. and Chin, R. (eds.), *The planning of change.* New York: Holt, Rinehart, and Winston, 1966, pp. 393–99.

Gross, B. M. *Organizations and their managing.* New York: Free Press, 1968.

Guetzkow, H. Communications in Organizations. In J. G. March, (Ed.), *Handbook of organizations.* Chicago: Rand McNally, 1965, 534–73.

Hamblin, R. L., Bushell, O. B., Buckholdt, D., Ellis, D., Ferritor, D., Merritt, G., Pfeiffer, C., Shea, D., and Stoddard, D. Learning, problem children and a social exchange system. Annual Report of the Social Exchange Laboratories, Washington University, and Student Behavior Laboratory, Webster College, St. Louis, Mo. August, 1967.

Herzberg, F. One more time: How do you motivate employees? *Harvard Business Review,* January–February 1968, pp. 53–62.

Herzberg, F. *Work and the nature of man.* Cleveland: World, 1966.

Homans, G. C. *Social behavior: Its elementary forms.* New York: Harcourt, Brace & World, 1961.

Hulin, C. L. and Smith, P. A. An empirical investigation of two implications of the two-factor theory of job satisfaction. *Journal of Applied Psychology,* 1967, 51, 396–402.

Lindsay, C. A., Marks, E., and Gorlow, L. The Herzberg theory: A critique and reformulation. *Journal of Applied Psychology,* 1967, 51, 330–39.

Maltzman, I., Simon, S., Roskin, D., and Licht, L. Experimental studies in the training of originality. *Psychological Monographs: General and Applied,* 1960, 74 (6, Whole No. 493).

Maslow, A. *Eupsychian management.* Homewood, Ill.: Dorsey, 1965.

McGregor, D. *The human side of enterprise.* New York: McGraw-Hill, 1960.

McGregor, D. *Leadership and motivation.* Cambridge, Mass.: M. I. T. Press, 1966.

Nord, W. R. Social exchange theory: An integrative approach to social conformity. *Psychological Bulletin,* (in press).

Northern Systems Company, A proposal to the department of labor for development of a prototype project for the new industries program. Part one.

Opsahl, R. L. and Dunnette, M. D. The role of financial compensation in industrial motivation. *Psychological Bulletin,* 1966, **66**, 94–118.

Reese, E. P. *The analysis of human operant behavior.* Dubuque, Ia.: William C. Brown, 1966.

Roy, D. F. "Banana time" Job satisfaction and informal interaction. In Bennis, W. G., Schein, E. H., Berlew, D. E., and Steele, F. I. (eds.), *Interpersonal dynamics.* Homewood, Ill.: Dorsey, 1964. 583–600.

Schultz, D. P. Spontaneous alteration behavior in humans, implications for psychological research. *Psychological Bulletin,* 1964, **62**, 394–400.

Skinner, B. F. *Science and human behavior,* New York: Macmillan, 1953.

Skinner, B. F. The science of learning and the art of teaching. *Harvard Educational Review,* 1954, **24**, 86–97.

Skinner, B. F. *Walden two.* New York: Macmillen, 1948.

Stagner, R. and Rosen, H. *Psychology of union-management relations.* Belmont, Cal.: Wadsworth, 1966.

Sykes, A. J. M. The effect of a supervisory training course in changing supervisors' perceptions and expectations of the role of management. *Human Relations,* 1962, **15**, 227–43.

Vinacke, E. W. Motivation as a complex problem. *Nebraska symposium on motivation,* 1962, **10**, 1–45.

Walker, E. L., and Heyns, R. W. *An anatomy of conformity.* Englewood Cliffs, N.J.: Prentice-Hall, 1962.

Wolf, M. M. Paper read at Sociology Colloquium, Washington University, December 5, 1966.

Wolf, M. M., Risley, T., and Mees, H. Application of operant conditioning procedures to the behavior problems of an autistic child. In R. Ulrich, T. Stachnik and T. Mabry (eds.), *Control of human behavior.* Glenview, Ill.: Scott, Foresman, 1966, pp. 187–93.

4. DESCRIPTIVE BEHAVIORISM VERSUS COGNITIVE THEORY IN VERBAL OPERANT CONDITIONING*

***Charles D. Spielberger and L. Douglas DeNike*†**

Operant behavior generally refers to responses which an organism in a given environment displays spontaneously without special training. Operant conditioning usually implies a variety of experimental techniques wherein a subject is rewarded after engaging in operant behavior of a selected kind. The successful conditioning of an operant response is inferred from an increase in its rate of occurrence as a function of reward (reinforcement) administered by the experimenter. Through the efforts of those who have used operant conditioning procedures, significant advances in our knowledge of animal learning have been made possible, and widespread interest has been generated in the use of such procedures for investigating human learning. The purpose of the present paper is to examine theoretical and methodological issues which have arisen in recent applications of operant conditioning techniques to verbal learning.

In verbal operant conditioning, hereafter termed verbal conditioning, the subject is typically instructed to speak in accordance with a particular task. He is not told that this task involves reinforcement or learning. The experimenter attempts to change the rate of emission of certain responses by the systematic application of a reinforcing stimulus, usually some form of social reward, such as the experimenter saying "Mmm-hmm" or "Good." Studies of verbal conditioning originated in close connection with the concepts and procedures developed by Skinner (1938) with infrahuman species. Greenspoon, a pioneer in verbal conditioning research, maintains that

> . . . it should be possible to work with verbal behavior in much the same way that experimenters have worked with the behavior of rats, pigeons, etc. It should also be possible to investigate the same kinds of variables that have been investigated with the non-verbal behavior of humans and infrahumans [1962, p. 511].

Thus, the Skinnerian (1957, 1963a, 1963b) approach has been clearly apparent both in the methods employed and the variables investigated in most verbal conditioning experiments.

In keeping with Skinner's emphasis on the "experimental analysis of behavior," many verbal conditioners have largely ignored the possibility that subjects' awareness of response-reinforcement contingencies might influence their conditioning performance. Investigators who have examined subjects' verbal reports in relation to their conditioning performance have discovered considerable evidence suggesting that cognitive processes mediate performance gains in verbal conditioning. But descriptive behaviorists have been quick to rejoin that the relationships between awareness and performance observed by cognitively oriented researchers have arisen from artifacts associated with the verbal report procedures from which awareness was inferred. Thus, in verbal conditioning, broadly opposed theoretical systems lock horns: Descriptive behaviorists argue for learning without awareness, those of cognitive persuasion argue against it, and proponents of each point of view generate methodological criticisms of the experimental work carried on in the opposing camp.[1]

It would appear that radically different epistemologies underlie the theoretical differences between Skinnerian and cognitive researchers. The epistemological issues, which revolve around the admissibility of conscious awareness as a desideratum for psychological science, have been discussed in detail elsewhere (Spielberger, 1965). Therefore, rather than restating these issues here, a simple analogy may better serve to illustrate how varying pretheoretical assumptions about the general nature and scope of science can lead to highly disparate approaches to a concrete scientific problem.

---

* *Psychological Review,* Vol. 73, No. 4 (1966), 306–25.

Work on this paper was supported in part by grants to the first author from the National Institutes of Mental Health (MH 7446) and Child Health and Human Development (HD 947), United States Public Health Service. We are indebted to Norman Cliff, Jum C. Nunnally, Henry Slucki and Donald L. Thistlethwaite for their critical comments on the manuscript.

† Florida State University and University of Southern California, respectively.

[1] It should be noted that S-R behavior theorists in the Hull-Spence tradition are not a party to this controversy. The model developed by these theorists was designed to account for the behavior phenomena exhibited by nonarticulate organisms or by humans in simple learning situations in which the operation of higher mental processes was minimal, for example, in eyelid conditioning and rote learning. A major difference between the views of descriptive behaviorists and those of Hull and Spence is that the latter never claimed that their theoretical concepts would hold for complex verbal processes. In his discussion of the postulates and methods of behaviorism nearly two decades ago, Spence (1948 p. 76) noted that:

> . . . in dealing with the more complex types of animal and human behavior, implicit emotional responses, covert verbal responses and not easily observable receptor-exposure and postural adjustments will have to be postulated . . .

and that:

> It is in this realm of theorizing that the verbal reports of human subjects are likely to be of most use to the behavior theorist, for presumably these reports can be made the basis on which to postulate the occurrence of these inferred activities.

It seems reasonable to conjecture that biologists of an earlier generation who did not believe in protozoa probably contended at times that objects too small to be observed by the naked eye were *irrelevant to scientific analysis* (of disease, for instance). Attempts to explore the domain of the microscopic world might have been disdained by such observers as revealing only illusory effects traceable to light diffusion in the microscope, and so on. Similarly, we might expect that present-day psychologists who consider thoughts and hypotheses to be beyond the limits of "scientific" inquiry would not vigorously search for them in experimental subjects. Furthermore, we should not be surprised to find that such psychologists were uninterested and unskilled in evaluating cognitive phenomena which for them do not exist. On the other hand, early biologists who believed in protozoa might occasionally have "seen" them when they were not there. Similarly, we might expect, as has been suggested by Farber (1963), that cognitively oriented verbal conditioning researchers, in their eagerness to attribute behavior to mediating conscious processes, would sometimes inadvertently suggest (or erroneously infer) awareness in questioning subjects who show performance gains.

One obvious implication of the above analogy is that competing scientific theories lead to different experimental procedures and often to observational errors which support the theoretical predilections of the investigator (Rosenthal, 1963). In most cases, however, such methodological differences and observational errors are eventually resolved since competing theories generally lead to more sensitive experiments. Furthermore, good experiments contribute to the accumulation of a composite set of facts which facilitate the convergence of theoretical schools and the establishment of an organized body of scientific knowledge (Campbell, 1963). But, if the epistemological assumptions which underlie competing scientific theories differ, the methodological consequences of such differences may lead to the collection of noncomparable data about which pointless theoretical controversy is generated. Unfortunately, this seems to be the case in verbal conditioning.

In this paper, we propose to examine the relative merits of cognitive and Skinnerian interpretations of verbal conditioning and the methodological assumptions on which these interpretations are based. The organization of the paper is as follows: In Section I the use of verbal report measures as indexes of awareness (mediating cognitive processes) will be discussed, and the various objections which investigators of a Skinnerian bent have raised concerning these measures will be enumerated and analyzed. In Section II methodological problems associated with the assessment of awareness from postconditioning interviews will be considered, and procedures for assessing awareness during conditioning will be described along with the results of two experiments in which such procedures were utilized. A theoretical analysis of verbal conditioning in terms of cognitive concepts will be presented in Section III. In Section IV the significance of the verbal conditioning paradigm for the more general question of learning without awareness will be taken up.

I. CAN VERBAL REPORTS BE INTERPRETED AS INDEXES OF MEDIATING COGNITIVE PROCESSES?

Methodological criticism has been associated with attempts to condition verbal behavior since Thorndike's early experiments in this area. In these Thorndike was interested in determining whether the law of effect operated when the subject was unaware of the contingency of reinforcement. Utilizing a word-association task, Thorndike and Rock (1934) reinforced sequential as opposed to denotative associations (*over*-the hill, as opposed to *over*-above). They reasoned that if subjects gained sudden insight (awareness) into the response-reinforcement contingency, the number of sequential responses which they gave would rise sharply. Hence, they regarded the gradual increase in sequential responses, which they in fact obtained, as providing evidence for learning without awareness. This interpretation, however, was immediately challenged by the demonstration that similar gradual performance gains ensued even when subjects were informed of the basis of reinforcement (Irwin, Kauffman, Prior, & Weaver, 1934). It is perhaps an unfortunate commentary on the narrow, behavioristic zeitgeist then prevailing that the simple procedure of questioning subjects was not utilized in either of these studies. Irwin et al. (1934), while they did not fill the need for measures of insight or awareness that are operationally independent of performance, helped at least to make the need evident. More recently, the quest for such measures has generally led to the use of systematically obtained verbal reports.

Now Skinnerian verbal conditioners do not hold that subjects should never be asked questions, nor do they assert that reliable relationships between verbal reports and performance measures cannot be found. They do argue that such relationships when found do not constitute adequate evidence that awareness plays a *causal* intervening role. However, descriptive behaviorists have not attempted to investigate the adequacy of verbal report procedures. Thus, their criticisms of them appear to stem chiefly from the implicit assumption that consciousness is in principle unknowable and/or that it is unnecessary to consider it. These epistemological biases are not often made explicit, but under their influence criticisms of cognitive interpretations of verbal conditioning phenomena are made on methodological and theoretical grounds. It is to such criticisms[2] that we now turn.

1. The first group of objections advanced by descriptive behaviorists to the interpretation of verbal reports in cognitive terms is concerned with the possibility that awareness is *suggested* by the procedures which are employed to assess it. Questioning techniques used to evaluate awareness may, it is argued, differentially suggest the contingency of reinforcement to subjects who condition as compared to those who do not. When both the conditioning task and the awareness interview are conducted by the same experimenter, it is certainly plausible that the experimenter might inadvertently ask questions and/or record answers in such a way as to suggest and/or impute awareness to those subjects who showed performance gains. A related way in which the interviewer might artifactually bring about a relationship between performance and awareness is through cues provided by the wording of interview questions. Questioning subjects about their experiences during an experiment obviously leads them to reflect on their performance and possibly also to develop hypotheses about the response-reinforcement contingency.

2. A second general class of criticism contends that subjects condition without awareness, notice their increasing outputs of the critical response class, and then *label* the response-reinforcement contingency. In other words, it is argued that the subjects' knowledge of the contingency emerges as a result of an automatic conditioning process, and those subjects who indicate in a postconditioning interview that their performance was mediated by their hypotheses are merely rationalizing their performance gains. This line of criticism calls into question correspondences between performance and awareness based on measures taken after performance gains have ensued and points up the theoretical significance of the temporal sequence of events in verbal conditioning, that is, whether in fact performance gains precede awareness or occur subsequent to the subjects' development of awareness.

3. A more complicated variant of the point of view indicated in 2 above, has been suggested by Postman and Sassenrath (1961)[3] who state that "awareness as reflected in verbalization may represent an advanced stage in the development of a habit under conditions of reinforcement [p. 124]." They go on to suggest that the verbalization of a response-reinforcement contingency "*may be considered at the same time a result of past improvement and a condition for further improvement* [p. 124]." The tenability of this formulation, which ascribes a secondary mediational role to awareness, rests upon the demonstration of significant amounts of learning prior to the subjects' verbalization of a correct or partially correct contingency.

4. Another line of criticism contends that awareness is merely a covert response which is conditioned over trials, in an automatic fashion, at the same time as the reinforced response class is strengthened. Postman and Sassenrath (1961), in discussing symbolic mediators, have posited this sort of mechanism to explain the acquisition of hypotheses in instrumental learning. They state: "The differential reinforcements administered for the overt instrumental responses will at the same time selectively strengthen the correct mediating responses [p. 132]." In this view, awareness is assigned the properties of an operant response, and it is hypothesized that covert verbalizations of the reinforcement principle (awareness) are directly and automatically strengthened by the same reinforcement process through which other instrumental responses are conditioned.[4]

The formulations described above are presented as schematic diagrams in Figure 1. These diagrams are not intended to represent particular viewpoints in detail, but are offered only tentatively as an aid in expressing interpretations of verbal conditioning which consider verbal reports primarily as responses rather than as indexes of mediating states. In each schematic, the temporal sequence of events is from left to right. Events which are merely temporally contiguous are indicated by dotted lines; presumed causal relationships between events are represented by solid arrows.

Schematic 1 illustrates the two possibilities whereby awareness might be suggested by ques-

[2] These criticisms have not been listed and treated in detail in any single article. What follows is an attempted coverage of relevant objections to interpretations of verbal reports in verbal conditioning in terms of mediating states. These have been adapted from friendly and unfriendly sources, including Dulany (1961, 1962), Eriksen (1958, 1960, 1962), Greenspoon (1962, 1963), Kanfer and his colleagues (Kanfer & Marston, 1961, 1962; Kanfer & McBrearty, 1961), Krasner (1962), Krasner and Ullmann (1963), Postman and Sassenrath (1961), Salzinger (1959), Spielberger (1962, 1965), and especially Dulany (1963).

[3] It should be noted that although Postman and Sassenrath cite findings of verbal conditioning investigations as relevant to this interpretation, their conclusions are based primarily upon Thorndikian experiments in which gradual increments in performance typically precede the point of verbalization.

[4] A similar interpretation is suggested by Kanfer and McBrearty (1961) who contend that:

> . . . verbalization of the response-reinforcement contingency may be independently affected by *different* antecedent conditions than the acquisition rate of the (reinforced verbal) response class, even though experimental conditions may sometimes facilitate an interaction between these two events [p. 116].

FIGURE 1 SCHEMATIC DIAGRAMS DEPICTING NON-COGNITIVE INTERPRETATIONS OF VERBAL REPORTS OF AWARENESS IN VERBAL CONDITIONING.

1. SUGGESTION

$R --- S_R \rightarrow R\uparrow$ — S_I, S_Q → Awareness

2. LABELING

$R --- S_R \rightarrow R\uparrow \rightarrow S_{R\uparrow} \rightarrow$ Awareness

3. SECONDARY MEDIATION

4. JOINT CONDITIONING EFFECTS

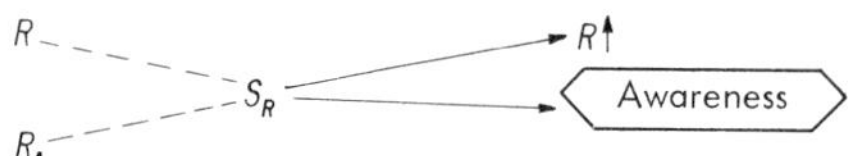

tioning procedures to subjects who showed performance gains. The symbol R stands for the subject's verbalization of responses belonging to the reinforced response class. S_R refers to the reinforcing stimulus administered by the experimenter for each R. $R\uparrow$ indicates performance gains. S_I represents biasing stimuli that might be transmitted unwittingly to the subject by an interviewer who had knowledge of the subject's conditioning performance. S_Q stands for possible cues conveyed by the wording of questions which might lead subjects who showed performance gains to construct correct hypotheses after the fact by reflecting on their performance.

Schematic 2 diagrams the hypothetical automatic strengthening-labeling sequence in which subjects are said to condition without awareness and then to become aware of the response-reinforcement contingency after noticing their increasing output of reinforced responses, $S_R\uparrow$.

Schematic 3 depicts the hypotential operation of mediating processes subsequent to automatic conditioning. As described in Schematic 2, the subject becomes aware as a result of increments in performance brought about by the automatic effects of reinforcement and utilizes this awareness further to enhance performance gains. In this diagram, $R\uparrow$ symbolizes augmented performance consequent upon the subject becoming aware of the correct contingency.

Schematic 4 illustrates the view that reinforcement acts simultaneously to condition both the reinforced response class and verbalization of the reinforcement principal. Presumably, reinforcement would operate in this paradigm to strengthen covert verbalizations of the correct response-reinforcement contingency, R_A.

Underlying all of the above formulations is the epistemological viewpoint mentioned earlier. It would appear that what descriptive behaviorists object to basically is the use of verbal reports as a Trojan horse for the reintroduction of private experiences into psychology. Since private experience does not meet positivistic canons of interobserver reliability, they argue largely on epistomological grounds that interest in it remains but a vestige of discredited introspectionism. However, the heuristic value of operationally defined awareness variables in verbal conditioning has been demonstrated empirically, and the numerous instances in which such measures have been found to relate consistently and meaningfully to other variables provides strong justification for their use, irrespective of how they are interpreted. Over and above this pragmatic value, the utilization of awareness as a systematic concept has led to experimental findings which the Skinnerian approach would not have predicted and can explain only with piecemeal augmenting assumptions (Dulany, 1962; Spielberger, 1962).

In this paper we will contend that the descriptive behaviorists' rejection on epistemological grounds, of verbal reports as indexes of mediating states has retarded the convergence of empirical findings and the development of adequate theory in verbal conditioning. We will argue moreover that this general approach has contributed little to the understanding of verbal behavior because, as Guttman (1963, p. 119) has recently suggested with respect to perception:

> . . . the effort to speak the language of behavior *only* is just inefficient, and to do so leads to bad experiments . . . , to a truncated set of laws of behavior, and to wide misinterpretation as to what our current knowledge of behavioral laws portends, theoretically and practically.

Having stated these goals and claims, we may now proceed to a discussion of procedures used for assessing awareness in verbal conditioning.

II. THE USE OF VERBAL REPORTS IN VERBAL CONDITIONING

The questioning techniques employed to assess awareness in verbal conditioning studies have included both oral interviews and written-response questionnaires. These have been utilized both during and after conditioning trials. In this section, we will first consider methodological factors associated with the assessment of awareness from postconditioning interviews. We will then describe procedures developed for assessing awareness during conditioning and the findings of two experiments in which such procedures were employed. Finally, the noncognitive formulations developed in Section I will be reviewed in the light of these studies.

The Assessment of Awareness after Conditioning

The assessment of awareness from postconditioning interviews is influenced by the style of questioning, the wording of questions and the number of questions asked, the interpolation of extinction trials, and the experimenter's concern with correlated hypotheses. Each of these factors will be discussed below in terms of its potential effect on reports of awareness obtained in postconditioning interviews.

Oral Interview versus Written Questionnaire Procedures. Both oral interviews and written-response questionnaires have been utilized for assessing awareness after the completion of conditioning trials. Either style of questioning would appear to have certain characteristic advantages and disadvantages. Written-response questionnaires eliminate the potential biasing influence of the experimenter who conducts an oral interview. However, the responses elicited by this procedure may not be as complete as those obtained from questions asked and answered orally, and clarification of unclear replies through additional inquiry is not generally feasible. Furthermore, some subjects may be inclined to avoid being incorrect by not responding when they are unsure of their hypotheses.

Number and Wording of Questions. In early verbal conditioning studies awareness interviews were very brief, and the questions were vaguely worded. For example, in one study (Sidowski, 1954) the postconditioning interview consisted of only two questions: *(a)* "Were you aware of the purpose of the experiment?" and *(b)* "Were you aware of the purpose of the light?" (the contingent reinforcing stimulus). In response to these questions, a subject who might have been perfectly aware of the response-reinforcement contingency might not have had any idea of the "scientific purpose" of the experiment nor of the reinforcing stimulus. Furthermore, questions asked in this form make it easier to say "No" than "Yes" since the latter response will obviously require elaboration. A series of questions in which subjects were asked to state their thoughts about when and why the light was blinking would have been more satisfactory.

Given minimal questioning, subjects tend to respond according to their own preconceptions about what is important and refer to the reinforcing stimulus only when asked about it. For example, after the conclusion of a pseudo-ESP verbal conditioning experiment, Krieckhaus and Eriksen (1960) held informal conversations with subjects who showed performance gains, but failed to verbalize a correct response-reinforcement contingency in a structured interview. They reported:

> Two (subjects) verbalized very clearly their awareness of the effects of reinforcement upon their behavior. When asked why they had not stated this in response to the postconditioning interview questions, both of them commented that they hadn't understood that this was what *E* was asking. They both stated that they thought *E* was concerned with whether or not they were getting ESP messages, rather than trying to find out whether the reinforcement of "good" had affected their choice of responses [p. 515].

Thus, the requirement of asking for information with clear and adequately worded questions is coordinate with the necessity of asking a sufficient number of questions.

Although more detailed questioning might be thought to increase the likelihood of suggesting awareness indiscriminately (Farber, 1963), a series of questions of gradually increasing specificity enables the interviewer to assess awareness and motivation while providing minimal *surplus* information. Furthermore, in studies in which such interviews were employed (see Spielberger, 1962), it has been demonstrated that: *(a)* Substantial numbers of subjects were identified as aware of correct response-reinforcement contingencies who were not so classified on the basis of brief interviews; and *(b)* performance gains were limited essentially to aware subjects and specific to those responses for which the individual subject was aware of a correct contingency.

Extinction Trials. In verbal conditioning, the practice of interpolating extinction trials (e.g., Cohen, Kalish, Thurston, & Cohen, 1954; Greenspoon, 1955) or other tasks (Gergen, 1965; Sassenrath, 1959) between acquisition trials and the interview in which awareness is assessed probably reduces the likelihood that awareness will be detected. Subjects who are aware of a correct contingency during conditioning may either forget their hypotheses, interpret the withdrawal of the reinforcing stimulus during extinction as a sign that they were wrong, or both. We have observed that, even during acquisition trials, instances of *accidental* nonreinforcement due to experimenter error sometimes suffice to disconfirm subjects' hypotheses (Spielberger & DeNike, 1963).

Correlated Hypotheses. The problem of assessing correlated hypotheses in learning experiments was first raised by Postman and Jarrett (1952). In verbal conditioning, a subject is considered to have a correlated hypothesis if he verbalizes a contingency which is different from, but correlated with, the reinforcement principle employed by the experimenter (Dulany, 1961). Thus, a subject need not be aware of the *experimenter's* definition of the contingency in order to show performance gains through conscious pursuit of his *own* hypotheses. For example, suppose one spring a whimsical millionaire were to emplace a few gold nuggets on some fertile ground on his estate and announce magnanimously to the townsfolk that all were welcome to come there and shovel around on the surface. Anyone inquiring among these townsfolk as they labored would find them highly aware that they were "digging for gold" and highly unaware that they were "spading a garden."

In the traditional verbal conditioning task in which plural nouns are reinforced (Greenspoon, 1955), a subject would receive 100% reinforcement if he said serially, "apples, oranges, peaches," etc. When interviewed, he might report as his hypothesis that reinforcement is contingent upon his naming "fruits." While the response class "fruits" is formally different from "plural nouns," the subject who named fruits would be reinforced for acting on this hypothesis and would be likely to develop the conviction that he was being encouraged to say words of similar meaning, as Dulany (1961) has convincingly shown. That subjects sometimes develop and pursue correlated ideas in response to less than 100% reinforcement points up the importance of *random* reinforcement rather than *no* reinforcement for control groups in verbal conditioning experiments (DeNike & Spielberger, 1963; Spielberger, DeNike, & Stein, 1965). And as Adams (1957) has pointed out, correlated hypotheses are typically *not* evaluated in investigations which have reported evidence for learning without awareness.

Thus far, we have discussed methodological factors which influence reports of awareness obtained from interviews or questionnaires conducted after the completion of the conditioning task. As previously noted, in recent verbal conditioning experiments in which such factors were taken into account, performance gains were limited essentially to subjects who verbalized a correct or correlated contingency. However, in these experiments, awareness was inferred from responses to interview questions asked *after* performance measures had been taken. Therefore, it could be argued that the performance gains of aware subjects were automatically produced by reinforcement and that the awareness-performance relationship could be accounted for by any of the noncognitive explanations described in Section I. The assessment of awareness during conditioning would provide a firmer basis for evaluating the temporal relationship between performance and awareness in verbal conditioning. Such procedures will now be considered.

The Assessment of Awareness during Conditioning

Most noncognitive explanations of verbal conditioning implicitly assume that increments in performance initially result from the direct and automatic effects of reinforcement and that performance gains occur prior to the time that the subject becomes aware of a correct response-reinforcement contingency. On the other hand, it is argued in cognitive explanations of verbal conditioning that awareness precedes performance increments. Thus, reinforcement theory and cognitive theory lead to differential predictions with regard to the temporal relationship between the development of awareness and the inception of performance gains. But in order to evaluate temporal factors in verbal conditioning, a procedure is required which will permit determination of whether or not subjects become aware of a correct contingency *during conditioning,* and if so, when. The results of two studies in which awareness was assessed during conditioning are discussed below.

Experiment I. DeNike (1964) reinforced female college students for giving *human-noun* responses in a word-naming task (Matarazzo, Saslow, & Pareis, 1960). His subjects were required to write down their "thoughts about the experiment" after each block of 25 response words. As a signal for the subject to record her thoughts, a light was turned on which remained lit until the subject indicated she was ready to resume saying words. No reinforcement was given during the first two word blocks, which provided a measure of operant rate. Beginning with the third word block, subjects in the Experimental Group were reinforced with "Mmm-hmm" for each human-noun response; those in the Control Group were reinforced with "Mmm-hmm" for 10% of their response words, according to a predetermined random schedule.

Awareness of the contingency between human-noun responses and the experimenter's "Mmm-hmm" was inferred from the thoughts (notes) which each subject recorded during conditioning. On the basis of these notes, subjects were independently rated by four judges as either *aware* or *unaware* of a correct contingency. Agreement between pairs of judges ranged from 90–95%, and there was unanimity or a 3–1 consensus among the judges with respect to the classification of 59 of the 61 subjects in the Experimental Group. For each aware subject, the judges also indicated the word block on which a correct contingency was first recorded.

If performance gains in verbal conditioning are automatically produced by reinforcement, it would be expected that gradual increments in performance would occur for all subjects, and that performance gains for aware subjects would occur prior to the word block on which they recorded a correct contingency in their notes. However, if acquisition of the reinforced response class in verbal conditioning is mediated by awareness, performance gains would be expected only for aware subjects, and these should occur on or subsequent to the word block on which such subjects recorded a correct contingency. The performance curves of DeNike's Aware, Unaware, and Control Groups are presented in Figure 2A. It may be noted that the output of human nouns for the Aware Group increased markedly over the reinforced word blocks and that the Unaware and Control Groups failed to show any performance gains. However, although only subjects who recorded correct contingencies in their notes gave more human nouns, it cannot be determined from the data as arrayed in Figure 2A whether or not aware subjects showed increments in performance prior to the word block on which they recorded a correct contingency.

In order to evaluate the temporal relationship between performance gains and awareness, the conditioning data for the aware subjects were examined as a function of the word block on which each first recorded a correct contingency in her notes. This word block was designated the "0" block. Word blocks prior to and subsequent to Block 0 were designated the preverbalization and postverbalization blocks and were labeled respectively with negative and positive integers, after the practice of Philbrick and Postman (1955). The 0 blocks of the aware subjects were then aligned, and the data for the preverbalization and postverbalization blocks were separately Vincentized (Munn, 1950). The Vincentized conditioning curve for the Aware Group is given in Figure 2B in which it may be noted that performance on the conditioning task: *(a)* remained at essentially the same level in the preverbalization blocks as in the operant blocks, *(b)* increased markedly on the 0 block, and *(c)* was maintained at a relatively high level during the postverbalization blocks. The finding that the performance increments of aware subjects first occurred during the word block on which they first recorded a correct contingency in their notes would appear to indicate that their increased output of human-noun responses was cognitively mediated. The absence of preverbalization performance gains would appear particularly difficult to explain by the use of learning theories which ascribe automatic trans-situational reinforcing effect to verbal stimuli.

Although it was possible, according to a cognitive theoretical interpretation of verbal conditioning, for aware subjects in DeNike's study to give essentially 100% human-noun responses on each postawareness word block, it may be noted in Figure 2 that the mean number of such responses given by these subjects never exceeded 35%. Interview data obtained by DeNike after the conclusion of the conditioning task revealed some aware subjects for whom the reinforcing stimulus had no incentive value, and these

FIGURE 2 CONDITIONING CURVES

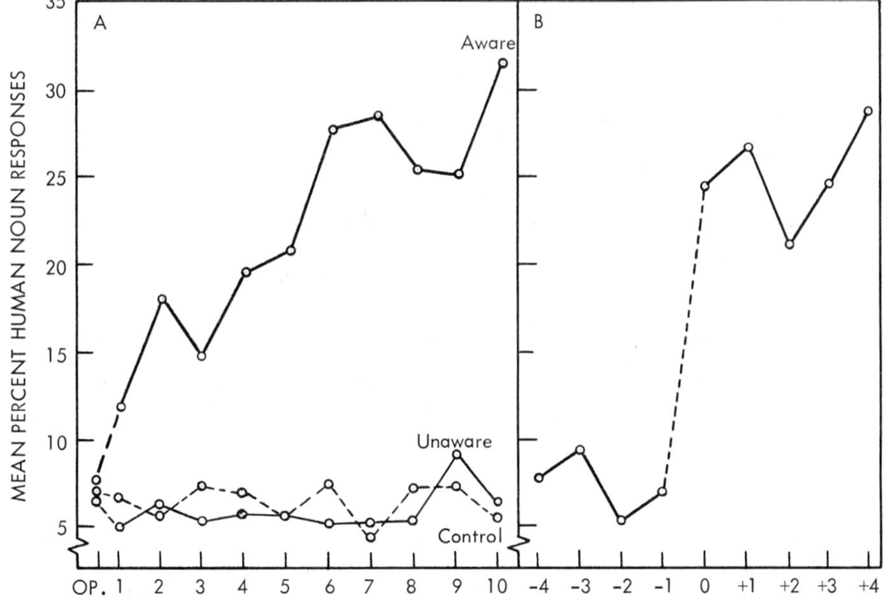

(A: Mean percentage of human-noun responses given by the Aware, Unaware, and Control Groups on the conditioning task. B: Conditioning curve for the Aware Group in which the data for preverbalization and postverbalization word blocks have been separately Vincentized. Adapted from DeNike, 1964.)

FIGURE 3 CONDITIONING CURVES

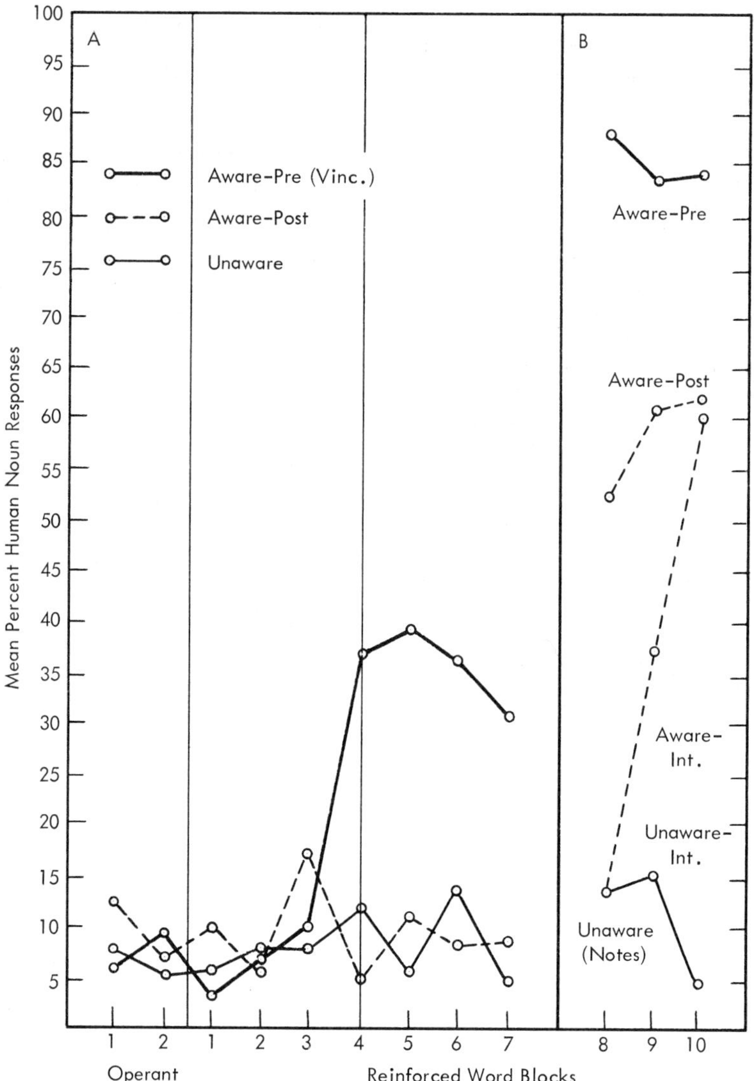

(A: Mean percentage of human-noun responses given by the Aware-Pre, Aware-Post, and Unaware Groups on the operant word blocks and the reinforced word blocks prior to the incentive-inducing instruction. B: Mean percentage of human-noun responses given by the Aware-Pre, Aware-Post, Aware-Int., and Unaware-Int. Groups on the word blocks subsequent to the incentive-inducing instruction. Adapted from Spielberger et al., 1966.)

subjects failed to show performance gains (DeNike, 1965). In contrast, aware subjects who reported that they wanted to receive reinforcement showed a marked increase in their output of human nouns on postawareness word blocks. In the next study to be reported, a uniformly high level of motivation to receive reinforcement was induced during conditioning in all subjects.

Experiment II. Using similar conditioning procedures to those described for Experiment I, female college students were reinforced with "Mmm-hmm" for giving human-noun responses (Spielberger, Bernstein, & Ratliff, 1966). Also, as in Experiment I, awareness of a correct response-reinforcement contingency was evaluated from the thoughts about the experiment (notes) which subjects recorded after each word block. However, the procedures differed from those of the previous experiment in that, between the seventh and eighth reinforced word blocks of the conditioning task each subject was told: "As you may have noted, there is a rule under which I say 'Mmm-hmm.' Try to act on that rule so as to make me say 'Mmm-hmm' as often as you can." The purpose of this instruction was to increase the incentive value of the reinforcing stimulus. Immediately after conditioning a different experimenter conducted an interview which checked on the incentive manipulation and provided additional data on subjects' awareness.

The notes which subjects recorded during conditioning were rated by two judges who had neither contact with the subjects nor knowledge of their performance on the conditioning task. The judges agreed perfectly in classifying each subject as either aware or unaware of a correct contingency. For the subjects rated aware, the judges also indicated the word block on which a correct contingency was first reported. Those subjects who recorded a correct contingency prior to the incentive-inducing instruction were designated the Aware-Pre Group; those who did so subsequent to this instruction were designated the Aware-Post Group; subjects who failed to record a correct contingency during conditioning were called the Unaware Group. The mean percentage of human-noun responses given by the three groups in the operant blocks and the reinforced blocks prior to the incentive-inducing instruction are given in Figure 3A in which the Aware-Pre Group's conditioning data have been Vincentized. Statistical analyses of these data indicated that: *(a)* The three groups did not differ during the operant blocks; *(b)* the performance gains of the Aware-Pre Group first occurred on the word block on which these subjects first recorded a correct contingency; and *(c)* the Aware-Post and Unaware Groups failed to show performance gains. Thus, prior to the incentive-inducing instruction, aware and unaware subjects performed much as did their counterparts in DeNike's study (see Figure 2).

Data obtained in the postconditioning interview indicated that the instruction to try to make the experimenter say "Mmm-hmm" had the desired effect on the subjects' motivation to receive reinforcement. Almost all the subjects indicated that, as a consequence of the instruction, they wanted more for the experimenter to say "Mmm-hmm," and they tried harder to make him say it. The performances of the Aware-Pre, the Aware-Post, and Unaware Groups in the word blocks subsequent to the instruction are indicated in Figure 3B. The immediate marked increase in the number of human nouns given by the Aware-Pre Group on Block 8 suggested that the incentive manipulation increased the motivation of these subjects to receive reinforcement and that their prior awareness of a correct contingency permitted them at once to give more human-noun responses. The somewhat less marked increase in human nouns for the Aware-Post Group subsequent to the instruction may be interpreted as indicating that these subjects, most of whom recorded a correct contingency in their notes on Block 8, had to become aware before heightened motivation induced by the instruction could influence their performance. Consistent with this interpretation, examination of the conditioning data for individual subjects in the Aware-Post Group revealed that initial performance increments tended to occur on the word block on which a correct contingency was first recorded.

The mean percentage of human-noun responses given by the Unaware Group increased gradually in the post-instruction word blocks, from 15% on Block 8 to 30% on Block 10 (not shown in Figure 3B), suggesting that these subjects conditioned without awareness. In order to evaluate this possibility further, the postconditioning interview protocols of all subjects who failed to record a correct contingency in their notes were examined by two judges who had neither contact with the subjects nor knowledge of their performance on the conditioning task. The judges agreed perfectly in rating approximately half of these subjects as aware of a correct contingency solely on the basis of their verbal reports in the interview.

The performance of subjects rated aware on the basis of their interview responses, but unaware on the basis of their notes (Aware-Int. Group), is compared, in Figure 3B, with the performance of subjects rated unaware on the basis of *both* their interview responses and their notes (Unaware-Int. Group). For the latter group, the output of human-noun responses subsequent to the instruction did not increase. Indeed, by the final word block, the number of human nouns given by the Unaware-Int. Group was below what it had been prior to the instruction. In contrast, the conditioning curve for the Aware-Int. Group showed a significant rise subsequent to the instruction, and performance increments for individual subjects tended to correspond with the word block on which they claimed they became aware. Furthermore, several of these subjects spontaneously reported that they had not recorded a correct response-reinforcement contingency in their notes because they did not become aware of it until the final word block and did not have sufficient confidence in their hypothesis to report it.

In sum, the findings in Experiments I and II are consistent with the hypothesis that "what is learned" in verbal conditioning is awareness of a correct response-reinforcement contingency. These findings would also appear to indicate that the reinforcing stimulus in verbal conditioning has both information and incentive value (Dulany, 1962), and that the latter influences the degree to which subjects who are aware of a correct contingency act on their awareness. The adequacy with which noncognitive explanations of verbal conditioning can account for the results in these experiments is considered below.

Noncognitive Interpretations of the Findings in Experiments I and II

The findings in Experiments I and II would appear difficult to account for in terms of a theory which does not include a concept of awareness as a mediating cognitive state or process. In these investigations, only subjects who were judged to be aware of a correct response-reinforcement contingency showed performance gains, and these tended to correspond with the word block on which each aware subject first recorded a correct contingency. However, the question remains whether the obtained relationships between performance gains and operational indexes of awareness can be explained without recourse to cognitive variables. The possibility that these relationships arose artifactually will now be examined in terms of each of the noncognitive formulations described in Section I (see Figure 1).

Suggestion. The possibility that awareness might

have been suggested to subjects who showed conditioning through cues provided by a biased experimenter was practically eliminated in Experiments I and II. In these studies, awareness was inferred primarily from notes recorded during conditioning, and these notes were *not* written in response to potentially biasing questions. The signal for the subject to record her thoughts, a light presented at uniform intervals, was a completely impersonal nonverbal stimulus which was in no way contingent upon the subject's conditioning performance. For those subjects in Experiment II whose awareness was inferred from their responses to the postconditioning interview, the experimenter who conducted this interview had neither prior contact with the subjects nor knowledge of their performance on the conditioning task.

Labeling. The findings in Experiments I and II do not support the interpretation that reinforcement automatically produced increments in performance and that the subjects' knowledge of a correct response-reinforcement contingency subsequently resulted from their noticing and labeling the relationship between the critical response class and the reinforcing stimulus. As may be noted in Figure 2B and 3A the performance gains of aware subjects first occurred on the word block on which these subjects recorded a correct contingency in their notes. Thus, the reinforcing stimulus had no apparent influence on performance prior to the subjects becoming aware of a correct contingency. And while it still might be argued that automatic reinforcement effects produced performance gains during the 0 word block, the absence of performance gains on the preceding word blocks would remain unaccounted for. Only the performance of the small group of subjects ($N = 4$) in the Aware-Int. Group of Experiment II might be interpreted as consistent with the labeling hypothesis. But even these subjects, who failed to record a correct contingency in their notes but reported it in the postconditioning interview, tended spontaneously to explain this discrepancy in terms of insufficient opportunity to test their hypotheses.

Secondary Mediation. The secondary-mediation hypothesis assumes that automatic performance increments precede the development of awareness of a correct contingency, and that awareness then facilitates further performance gains. This view is contradicted by the same findings in Experiments I and II which led us to challenge the labeling interpretation. The demonstration of automatic reinforcement effects prior to the verbalization of awareness would appear crucial in order to support the hypothesis of secondary mediation. No such evidence was found, except possibly for the subjects in the Aware-Int. Group in Experiment II. Thus, at the very least, the secondary-mediation hypothesis would require extensive modification if it is to account for *all* of the findings in Experiments I and II.

Joint Conditioning Effects. According to the joint conditioning hypothesis, gradual gains in performance on the conditioning task would be expected along with the simultaneous strengthening of the covert "awareness response." The absence of performance increments in Experiments I and II prior to the word block on which aware subjects recorded a correct contingency, and the striking temporal correspondence of the inception of performance gains with the verbalization of awareness would seem to dictate the additional assumption of a "threshold" concept in order to support the view that the reinforced response class and a covert awareness response were simultaneously and automatically strengthened. Moreover, it would also appear necessary to assume that the threshold at which awareness was verbalized corresponds to the threshold at which the cumulative effects of reinforcement influence performance on the conditioning task, and that performance and covert awareness responses were practically identically susceptible to influence by reinforcement in *each individual subject.* While such assumptions might provide tenuous post-hoc explanations for the findings obtained in Experiments I and II, the conclusion appears inescapable that a theory of automatic strengthening of verbal response by reinforcement requires extensive modification and radical augmentation before it can account for such findings. In the next section, a theoretical analysis of verbal conditioning in terms of the concepts of cognitive learning theory will be proposed.

III. AN ANALYSIS OF VERBAL CONDITIONING IN TERMS OF COGNITIVE CONCEPTS

The schematic diagram presented in Figure 4 reflects a general formulation of the sequence of hypothetical events which we believe mediate performance gains in verbal conditioning for subjects who show "conditioning" effects. The diagram is not intended to represent any particular cognitive theory in detail. Rather, it is offered to account for the findings of recent investigations of verbal conditioning, such as those described in Section II, at the same level of specificity as the noncognitive formulations presented in Figure 1. A similar more detailed and sophisticated theoretical analysis of verbal conditioning has been recently advanced by Dulany (1962).

The temporal sequence of events in Figure 4 is from left to right. Those events which are merely temporally contiguous are indicated by dotted lines;

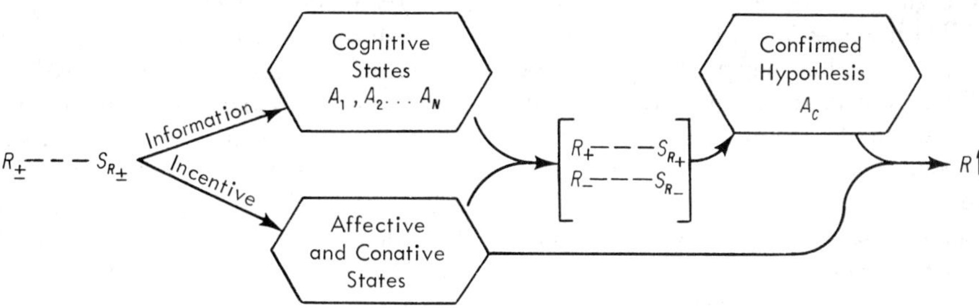

FIGURE 4 SCHEMATIC DIAGRAM INDICATING THE HYPOTHETICAL PROCESSES WHICH ARE ASSUMED TO MEDIATE PERFORMANCE GAINS IN VERBAL CONDITIONING FOR SUBJECTS WHO SHOW "CONDITIONING" EFFECTS

presumed causal relationships between events are represented by solid arrows. The symbol $R_\pm$ indicates that in verbal conditioning the subject initially emits a variety of responses, some of which belong to the reinforced class, R_+, and some of which do not, R_-. These are followed respectively by reinforcement, S_{R+}, and nonreinforcement, S_{R-}, which convey differential information and provide differential incentive to the subject.

The information provided by the reinforcing stimulus gives rise to one or more cognitive states, represented as $A_1, A_2, \ldots A_N$. For example, the sequence of cognitive states developed by a subject in a word-naming verbal conditioning task might be: "The experimenter sometimes says 'good' after some of my words" (A_1); "Perhaps his saying 'good' depends on what words I say" (A_2); "Perhaps he wants me to figure out what words he is saying 'good' to, and give more of those" (A_3), etc. Depending upon the pattern and amount of reinforcement which they receive and recall, some subjects may be able to skip some of these early logical steps and go directly to a tentative formulation of the correct hypothesis, A_N: "Perhaps he is saying 'good' when I say words denoting people." We have observed that subjects who verbalize a correct hypothesis approach the experiment essentially as a problem-solving task. Furthermore, in verbal conditioning experiments in which subjects are given explicitly a problem-solving set, they proceed more directly to test out their hypotheses, and a larger proportion verbalize a correct contingency (DeNike & Spielberger, 1963; Spielberger & Levin, 1962).

Concurrent with the concept-formation activity involved in arriving at a correct hypothesis, subjects also develop affective and conative states based on the *incentive* provided by the reinforcing stimulus. For example, if the reinforcing stimulus has positive incentive value for a particular subject, he will *want* to receive reinforcement, and generally will *try* to elicit it from the experimenter. On the other hand, if the reinforcing stimulus has neutral or negative incentive value for the subject, he may be indifferent to it or attempt to avoid it (Mandler & Kaplan, 1956). Thus, the subject's affective and conative states in conjunction with his cognitive states (hypotheses) lead him to give responses, R_+, which he believes are in the reinforced response R_-, which are not expected to elicit reinforcement. Following these responses, the selective administration of the reinforcing stimulus, S_{R+}, or the absence of the reinforcing stimulus, S_{R-}, either confirms the subject's hypothesis, A_C, or leads him to modify it. The confirmed hypothesis, if accompanied by appropriate affective and conative states, results in increased output of the reinforced response class, $R\uparrow$.

It should be noted that the schematic diagram in Figure 4 massively oversimplifies our view of verbal conditioning. In it, we have treated affective and conative states as essentially constant and independent of cognitive states; there is much reason to suspect that these fluctuate and interact with the subjects' hypotheses. We have diagramed the process for the successful subject and ignored the numerous blind alleys explored by both successful and unsuccessful subjects; such processes should receive consideration in any theory which claims completeness. The nature of the conditioning task, the status of the experimenter, the instructions given to the subject, the characteristics of the subject population —all of these have demonstrable influence on mediating states and performance in verbal conditioning. In the final section of this paper, the significance of the verbal conditioning paradigm for the more general question of human learning without awareness will be considered.

IV. VERBAL CONDITIONING AND THE QUESTION OF LEARNING WITHOUT AWARENESS

Few persons doubt that behavior occurs without awareness, as in, for example, shifting gears, fingernail biting, facial tics, etc. (Eriksen, 1960). Of theoretical interest, however, is the extent to which such behaviors are initially *learned* without the mediation of cognitive processes. Kimble (1962) has suggested that the question of whether learning without awareness is possible may not have the same answer for all forms of learning. In classical eyelid conditioning, according to Kimble, it would appear that the subject need only be aware of the unconditioned stimulus for learning to take place.

In verbal conditioning, the evidence for learning without awareness reported in early experiments (e.g., Cohen et al., 1954; Greenspoon, 1955; Taffel, 1955) now appears suspect because of short-comings in the evaluation of awareness in these studies. In recent experiments in which awareness was more carefully and thoroughly assessed (e.g., DeNike, 1964; Dulany, 1961, 1962; Spielberger, 1962), the absence of learning-without-awareness effects all but compels the conclusion that performance gains in verbal conditioning are consciously mediated.[5] However, for the reasons indicated below, the verbal conditioning paradigm may not provide an appropriate framework for clarifying the more general question of whether human operant learning can occur without awareness.

Subject Vigilance

Most subjects in psychological experiments, as Orne (1962) has pointed out, tend to be alert to manipulations that the experimenter may impose upon them and vigilant vis-à-vis their own behavior. In almost all verbal conditioning research, the subject is aware that he is participating in a psychological experiment. Thus, subjects in verbal conditioning experiments ordinarily notice the reinforcing stimulus and attempt to ascribe some meaning to it, making learning without awareness unlikely.

Response Monitoring

Despite reinforcement and no admonition to the contrary, reinforced words are rarely repeated in word-naming verbal conditioning tasks. This almost universal tendency not to repeat words would be difficult to explain by automatic reinforcement theories. When asked why they did not repeat reinforced words, subjects usually indicate that they believed they were supposed to give a variety of words. It would appear that the subject keeps both his past responses and their consequences in mind and monitors new responses according to his hypotheses about the experiment. Thus, on the assumption that selective responding is guided by response monitoring in accordance with the subjects' hypotheses, the tendency not to repeat reinforced words in verbal conditioning becomes understandable, and learning without awareness seems improbable.

Response Sets

Some subjects approach verbal conditioning with a problem-solving set, while others interpret the conditioning task as either a personality test or an attempt to make them "conform." When a problem-solving set is combined with response monitoring in a vigilant subject, the subject notices the reinforcing stimulus, proceeds to test out successive hypotheses about the experiment, and is likely to become aware of a correct or correlated response-reinforcement contingency. In contrast, subjects with a personality-test set may get so involved in their free associations (on a word-naming verbal conditioning task) that they are oblivious to the reinforcing stimulus or tend to regard it as annoying and disruptive. Other subjects with personality-test sets devote considerable effort to the selection of "innocuous" or "unrevealing" words or otherwise defensively edit their responses so that they will not reveal personal secrets or shortcomings. Subjects who believe the experimenter is attempting to manipulate their behavior often report that they deliberately ignored the reinforcing stimulus or tried to avoid it. Thus, while a "conformity" or "personality" interpretation of the verbal conditioning task tends to prevent learning without awareness by causing subjects to ignore or avoid the reinforcing stimulus and/or to perceive it as unpleasant, a problem-solving approach tends to preclude learning without awareness by making it easier for the subjects to become aware.

The foregoing analysis of the "demand characteristics" (Orne, 1962) of verbal operant conditioning suggests that it is unlikely that learning without awareness will be found in laboratory experiments which employ the methods traditionally associated with the verbal conditioning paradigm. Under such conditions, it might be expected on a priori grounds that subjects will be particularly vigilant about their own verbal responses which are likely to be more carefully monitored than most other behavior. Or, in Eriksen's (1960) words, ". . . any situation where the cues and the reinforcements are salient enough to

[5] It should be noted, however, that some subjects who are unaware of a correct contingency may nevertheless show slight gains in performance in verbal conditioning if they develop what may be termed a *correlated set.* For example, subjects (patients) who regard the Taffel (1955) sentence-construction task as a personality test sometimes assume they are supposed to make up sentences about themselves and their families. In response to either *random or systematic* reinforcement, subjects with such response dispositions may interpret the reinforcing stimulus as a sign of the experimenter's approval or encouragement and therefore give increasingly more sentences beginning with "I" or "We" (Spielberger, DeNike, & Stein, 1965).

produce learning, will not escape detection by awareness [p. 298]."

It would appear more plausible to seek evidence of learning without awareness in situations where subjects are not aware that they are participating in a psychological experiment and on tasks which do not induce intensive response monitoring or defensive response sets. A likely place to look for such evidence might be in settings where subjects are motivated not to be aware, as, for example, in experimental situations involving processes such as repression, dissonance reduction, conformity, and ingratiation. At present, only scattered attempts have been made to investigate human operant learning with research designs representative of some of the forenamed conditions (e.g., Centers, 1963; Gergen, 1965; Goldiamond, 1965; Hefferline, Keenan, & Harford, 1959; Kimmel & Baxter, 1964; Verplanck, 1956; Vogel-Sprott, 1964). In such studies, however, the role of awareness has ordinarily not been the focus of investigation, and, consequently, the methods employed to assess awareness are subject to the criticisms discussed earlier. Therefore, where learning-without-awareness effects have been found, little confidence may be placed in such results. This in no way implies that human operant learning cannot take place without awareness, but merely affirms Adams' (1957) observation that such learning has not been demonstrated convincingly in the laboratory.

Some Final Considerations

We have endeavored in this paper to compare the relative adequacy with which descriptive behaviorism and cognitive learning theory can account for the findings of verbal operant conditioning experiments. We have argued that the descriptive behaviorists' implicit rejection of awareness as a concept has had serious methodological consequences which have retarded the convergence of empirical findings and the development of adequate theory. We have also contended that the utilization of awareness as a systematic concept has led to experimental findings which the Skinnerian approach would not have predicted. Finally, we have presented evidence to support the view that the reinforcing stimulus in verbal conditioning has both information and incentive value and that "what is learned" in verbal conditioning is awareness of a correct (or correlated) response-reinforcement contingency.

With respect to whether human operant learning can occur without awareness, it should be noted that although this question would appear to have an empirical answer, in verbal conditioning the answer turns out to be inextricably tied to an investigator's theoretical orientation and, more fundamentally, to his epistemological assumptions concerning awareness as a concept (Spielberger, 1962, 1965). The issue is further complicated by the fact that different learning theories imply different operational definitions of the learned response (Campbell, 1954), leading in verbal conditioning to the collection of noncomparable data and to fruitless theoretical controversy. This controversy, which revolves about the role of awareness in verbal conditioning, is reminiscent of earlier disagreements among S–R and cognitive theorists concerning the role of reinforcement in learning. It has since been recognized that much of the controversy and confusion with respect to reinforcement stemmed from the failure of learning theorists to differentiate conceptually between the law of effect as an empirical statement and as a general theory of reinforcement (Spence, 1951).

On an empirical level, most would agree with the observation that performance in a variety of tasks is facilitated by reinforcement, but S–R and cognitive learning theories are still sharply divided on the question of whether reinforcement is required for learning to take place. Similarly, it is generally accepted that performance will be facilitated by the presence of appropriate cognitive states; that is, an "empirical law of cognition" is as supportable as the empirical law of effect,[6] but whether cognitive processes mediate any and all forms of learning is as dubious as a general theory of reinforcement. Thus, while a "theoretical law of cognition" might well serve to explain the findings in verbal conditioning experiments with human adults, it is quite another matter to demonstrate the role of cognitive processes in the learning of animals and preverbal children.

Nevertheless, the careful investigation of subjects' awareness in relation to other behavior is, we believe, requisite to the development of an adequate theory of human learning. Progress in this direction will depend upon the general acceptance of experimental procedures which permit sensitive evaluation of cognitive processes. These procedures must surely include subjects' verbal reports and must provide necessary safeguards against biasing or distorting such reports. Furthermore, it must be clearly recognized that the validity of verbal reports in any experimental context rests upon the willingness and linguistic competence of subjects to describe their mediating states when properly questioned (Dulany, 1961), and that verbal reports are but imperfectly related to the subjects' internal states (Eriksen, 1960). Paradoxically, perhaps the most significant contribution of verbal conditioning research has been

[6] We are grateful to Donald L. Thistlethwaite for suggesting the analogy between an empirical law of cognition in verbal conditioning and the empirical law of effect in traditional discussions of learning theory.

the stimulation of interest in verbal report procedures and in concepts such as awareness among psychologists who are inclined to insist that thoughts and ideas are beyond the limits of scientific inquiry.

REFERENCES

Adams, J. K. Laboratory studies of behavior without awareness. *Psychological Bulletin,* 1957, **54**, 383–405.

Campbell, D. T. Operational delineation of "what is learned" via the transposition experiment. *Psychological Review,* 1954, 61, 167–74.

Campbell, D. T. Social attitudes and other acquired behavioral dispositions. In S. Koch (ed.), *Psychology: A study of a science.* Vol. 6. New York: McGraw-Hill, 1963. Pp. 94–172.

Centers, R. A. Laboratory adaptation of the conversational procedure for the conditioning of verbal operants. *Journal of Abnormal and Social Psychology,* 1963, **67**, 334–39.

Cohen, B. D., Kalish, H. I., Thurston, J. R., and Cohen, E. Experimental manipulation of verbal behavior. *Journal of Experimental Psychology,* 1954, **47**, 106–10.

DeNike, L. D. The temporal relationship between awareness and performance in verbal conditioning. *Journal of Experimental Psychology,* 1964, **68**, 521–29.

DeNike, L. D. Recall of reinforcement and conative activity in verbal conditioning. *Psychological Reports,* 1965, **16**, 345–46.

DeNike, L. D. and Spielberger, C. D. Induced mediating states in verbal conditioning. *Journal of Verbal Learning and Verbal Behavior,* 1963, **1**, 339–45.

Dulany, D. E. Hypotheses and habits in verbal "operant conditioning." *Journal of Abnormal and Social Psychology,* 1961, **63**, 251–63.

Dulany, D. E. The place of hypotheses and intentions: An analysis of verbal control in verbal conditioning. In C. W. Eriksen (ed.), *Behavior and awareness.* Durham: Duke University Press, 1962. Pp. 102–29.

Dulany, D. E. How can we speak of awareness and volition as instrumental? In H. D. Kimmel (Chm.), Awareness as a factor in verbal operant conditioning. Symposium presented at Southeastern Psychological Association, Miami Beach, April 1963.

Eriksen, C. W. Unconscious processes. In M. R. Jones (ed.), *Nebraska symposium on motivation: 1958.* Lincoln: University of Nebraska Press, 1958. Pp. 169–228.

Eriksen, C. W. Discrimination and learning without awareness: A methodological survey and evaluation. *Psychological Review,* 1960, **67**, 279–300.

Eriksen, C. W. Figments, fantasies, and follies: A search for the subconscious mind. In C. W. Eriksen (ed.), *Behavior and awareness.* Durham: Duke University Press, 1962. Pp. 3–26.

Farber, I. E. The things people say to themselves. *American Psychologist,* 1963, **18**, 185–97.

Gergen, K. J. The effects of interaction goals and personalistic feedback on the presentation of self. *Journal of Personality and Social Psychology,* 1965, **1**, 413–24.

Goldiamond, I. Stuttering and fluency as manipulable operant response classes. In L. Krasner and L. P. Ullmann (eds.), *Research in behavior modification: New developments and their clinical implications.* New York: Holt, Rinehart, & Winston, 1965. Pp. 106–56.

Greenspoon, J. The reinforcing effect of two spoken sounds on the frequency of two responses. *American Journal of Psychology,* 1955, **68**, 409–16.

Greenspoon, J. Verbal conditioning and clinical psychology. In A. J. Bachrach (ed.), *Experimental foundations of clinical psychology.* New York: Basic Books, 1962, 510–53.

Greenspoon, J. Reply to Spielberger and DeNike: "Operant conditioning of plural nouns: A failure to replicate the Greenspoon effect." *Psychological Reports,* 1963, **12**, 29–30.

Guttman, N. Laws of behavior and facts of perception. In S. Koch (ed.), *Psychology: A study of a science.* Vol. 5. New York: McGraw-Hill, 1963, 114–78.

Hefferline, R. F., Keenan, B., and Harford, R. A. Escape and avoidance conditioning in human subjects without their observation of the response. *Science,* 1959, **130**, 1338–39.

Irwin, F. W., Kauffman, K., Prior, G., and Weaver, H. B. On "learning without awareness of what is being learned." *Journal of Experimental Psychology,* 1934, **17**, 823–27.

Kanfer, F. H. and Marston, A. R. Verbal conditioning, ambiguity and psychotherapy. *Psychological Reports,* 1961, **9**, 461–75.

Kanfer, F. H. and Marston, A. R. The effect of task-relevant information on verbal conditioning. *Journal of Psychology,* 1962, **53**, 29–36.

Kanfer, F. H. and McBrearty, J. F. Verbal conditioning: Discrimination and awareness. *Journal of Psychology,* 1961, **52**, 115–24.

Kimble, G. A. Classical conditioning and the problem of awareness. In C. W. Eriksen (ed.), *Behavior and awareness.* Durham: Duke University Press, 1962, 27–45.

Kimmel, H. D. and Baxter, R. Avoidance conditioning of the GSR. *Journal of Experimental Psychology,* 1964, **68**, 482–85.

Krasner, L. The therapist as a social reinforcement machine. In H. Strupp and L. Luborsky (eds.), *Research in psychotherapy.* Vol. 2. Washington, D.C.: American Psychological Association, 1962, 61–94.

Krasner, L. and Ullmann, L. P. Variables affecting report of awareness in verbal conditioning. *Journal of Psychology,* 1963, **56**, 193–202.

Krieckhaus, E. E. and Eriksen, C. W. A study of awareness and its effect on learning and generalization. *Journal of Personality,* 1960, **28**, 503–17.

Mandler, G. and Kaplan, W. K. Subjective evaluation and reinforcing effect of a verbal stimulus. *Science,* 1956, **124**, 582–83.

Matarazzo, J. D., Saslow, G., and Pareis, E. N. Verbal conditioning of two response classes: Some methodological considerations. *Journal of Abnormal and Social Psychology,* 1960, **61**, 190–206.

Munn, N. L. *Handbook of psychological research on the rat: An introduction to animal psychology.* Boston: Houghton Mifflin, 1950.

Orne, M. T. On the social psychology of the psychological experiment: With particular reference to demand characteristics and their implications. *American Psychologist,* 1962, **17**, 776–83.

Philbrick, E. B. and Postman, L. A further analysis of "learning without awareness." *American Journal of Psychology,* 1955, **68**, 417–24.

Postman, L. and Sassenrath, J. M. The mental analysis of learning without awareness. *American Journal of Psychology,* 1952, **65**, 244–55.

Postman, L. and Sassenrath, J. M. The automatic action of verbal rewards and punishments. *Journal of General Psychology,* 1961, **65**, 109–36.

Rosenthal, R. On the social psychology of the psychological experiment: The experimenter's hypothesis as unintended determinant of experimental results. *American Scientist,* 1963, **51**, 268–83.

Salzinger, K. Experimental manipulation of verbal behavior: A review. *Journal of General Psychology,* 1959, **61**, 65–94.

Sassenrath, J. M. Learning without awareness and transfer of learning sets. *Journal of Educational Psychology,* 1959, **50**, 205–12.

Sidowski, J. B. Influence of awareness of reinforcement on verbal conditioning. *Journal of Experimental Psychology,* 1954, **48**, 355–60.

Skinner, B. F. *The behavior of organisms: An experimental analysis.* New York: Appleton-Century-Crofts, 1938.

Skinner, B. F. *Verbal behavior.* New York: Appleton-Century-Crofts, 1957.

Skinner, B. F. Behaviorism at fifty. *Science,* 1963, **140**, 951–58.(a)

Skinner, B. F. Operant behavior. *American Psychologist,* 1963, **18**, 503–15.(b)

Spence, K. W. The postulates and methods of "behaviorism." *Psychological Review,* 1948, **55**, 67–78.

Spence, K. W. Theoretical interpretations of learning. In S. S. Stevens (ed.), *Handbook of experimental psychology.* New York: Wiley, 1951, 690–729.

Spielberger, C. D. The role of awareness in verbal conditioning. In C. W. Eriksen (ed.), *Behaviorism and awareness.* Durham: Duke University Press, 1962, 73–101.

Spielberger, C. D. Theoretical and epistemological issues in verbal conditioning. In S. Rosenberg (ed.), *Directions in psycholinguistics.* New York: Macmillan, 1965, 149–200.

Spielberger, C. D., Bernstein, I. H., and Ratliff, R. G. Information and incentive value of the reinforcing stimulus in verbal conditioning. *Journal of Experimental Psychology,* 1966, **71**, 26–31.

Spielberger, C. D. and DeNike, L. D. Implicit epistemological bias and the problem of awareness in verbal conditioning: A reply to Greenspoon. *Psychological Reports,* 1963, **12**, 103–06.

Spielberger, C. D., DeNike, L. D., and Stein, L. S. Anxiety and verbal conditioning. *Journal of Personality and Social Psychology,* 1965, **1**, 229–39.

Spielberger, C. D., and Levin, S. M. What is learned in verbal conditioning? *Journal of Verbal Learning and Verbal Behavior,* 1962, **1**, 125–32.

Taffel, C. Anxiety and the conditioning of verbal behavior. *Journal of Abnormal and Social Psychology,* 1955, **51**, 496–501.

Thorndike, E. L. and Rock, R. T. Learning without awareness of what is being learned or intent to learn it. *Journal of Experimental Psychology,* 1934, **17**, 1–19.

Verplanck, W. S. The operant conditioning of human motor behavior. *Psychological Bulletin,* 1956, **53**, 70–83.

Vogel-Sprott, M. E. Response generalization under verbal conditioning in alcoholics, delinquents, and students. *Behavior Research and Therapy,* 1964, **2**, 135–41.

5. EVALUATION OF RESEARCH ON EXPECTANCY THEORY PREDICTIONS OF EMPLOYEE PERFORMANCE*

Herbert G. Heneman III and Donald P. Schwab†

A central concern of industrial relations is the identification and measurement of factors associated with individual differences in employee job performance, since efficient utilization of manpower resources is dependent upon our ability to account for such differences. Recently, two statements of a theory of employee job performance, usually referred to as expectancy theory, have been advanced by Vroom (1964) and Porter and Lawler (1968). These formulations have stimulated considerable thought and research. Unfortunately, it appears that there is substantial confusion in interpretation of, and con-

* *Psychological Bulletin,* Vol. 78, No. 1 (July 1972), pp. 1–9.

† Graduate School of Business and Industrial Relations Research Institute, University of Wisconsin.

The authors thank R. J. Adams, L. L. Cummings, and W. E. Scott, Jr., for their critical comments on an earlier draft of this paper.

FIGURE 1 EXPECTANCY THEORY PREDICTIONS OF JOB PERFORMANCE, BASED UPON VROOM (1964) AND PORTER AND LAWLER (1968)

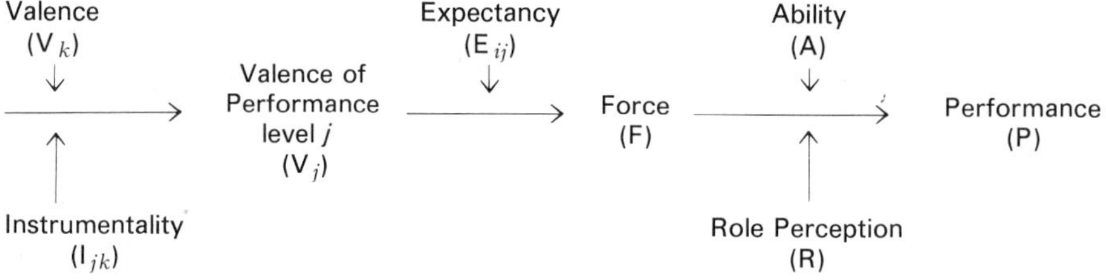

duct of research on, the theory. Our purposes are thus to attempt to resolve this state of confusion and make suggestions for improvement in future research on expectancy theory.

In subsequent sections, Vroom's (1964) and Porter and Lawler's (1968) descriptions of the theory are summarized and shown to be quite similar. Nine field studies that have tested hypotheses of expectancy theory are then summarized. Finally, these studies are critically evaluated and recommendations are made for needed additional research.

THE THEORY

Vroom (1964) hypothesized that employee job performance (P) is a function of the interaction between force to perform (F), or motivation, and ability (A).

$$P = f(F \times A). \qquad (1)$$

Porter and Lawler (1968), alternatively, hypothesized that performance is a function of the three-way interaction among exerted effort (E), or motivation, ability, and role perceptions (R).

$$P = f(E \times A \times R). \qquad (2)$$

Conceptualizations of motivation, ability, and role perceptions are described below. While terminological differences exist between the two theories, the only substantive difference between them is the inclusion of role perceptions as an additional performance determinant by Porter and Lawler. For this reason, and for purposes of clarification, the theories are combined into one comprehensive framework, shown in Figure 1.

Force or Effort

In Vroom's formulation, force to exert effort level i is a function of the sum of the interactions between *(a)* the valence of each performance level (V_j) and *(b)* the perceived probability that an ith amount of effort will result in the achievement of each performance level; this perception is termed expectancy (E_{ij}).

$$F_i = f[\sum_{j=1}^{n} (V_j \times E_{ij})]. \qquad (3)$$

It is hypothesized that the individual chooses the effort level exerting the strongest positive or weakest negative force.

A performance level (first-level outcome), in turn, acquires valence if it is perceived as leading to the attainment of valent second-level outcomes (V_k), such as pay and recognition. The perception that performance level j will result in the attainment of second-level outcome k is termed the instrumentality of the performance level (I_{jk}). The valence of performance level j is hypothesized to be a function of the sum of the interactions between *(a)* the valence of second-level outcomes and *(b)* the instrumentalities of the performance level.

$$V_j = f[\sum_{k=1}^{n} (V_k \times I_{jk})]. \qquad (4)$$

Porter and Lawler (1968) presented a theoretical treatment of motivation to perform, further refined by Lawler (1970), which is similar to Vroom's except for differences in terminology. Vroom's terminology, and the corresponding terminology by Porter and Lawler, is as follows: force (effort), valence of second-level outcomes (value of rewards), instrumentality (performance-reward probability), and expectancy (effort-performance probability). The latter two form what Porter and Lawler term the effort-reward probability.[1] For expository convenience the

[1] Another apparent discrepancy between Vroom (1964) and Porter and Lawler (1968) is that the latter first multiply the effort-performance and performance-reward probabilities, and then multiply this product and value of rewards to form their definition of effort. In the case of only one second-level outcome, this procedure results in a definition of effort identical to Vroom's (1964) definition of force. With more than one second-level outcome, however, this procedure leads to a definitional discrepancy between Vroom and Porter and Lawler. Consistency with Vroom requires that the value of reward and performance-reward probabilities be multiplied and summed across second-level outcomes, and that this total product be multiplied by the effort-performance probability. In his latest statement of expectancy theory, Lawler (1970) did combine the variables in this manner, and thus is consistent with Vroom.

terminology of Vroom is employed throughout the rest of this discussion.

Ability

Both Vroom (1964) and Porter and Lawler (1968) hypothesized that the individual's actual performance is additionally dependent upon his ability to perform. Vroom defined ability as characteristics of the individual that represent "a potential for performing some task which may or may not be utilized [p. 198]." Similarly, Porter and Lawler (1968) defined ability as "relatively stable, long-term individual characteristics (e.g., personality traits, intelligence, manual skills, etc.) that represent the individual's currently developed power to perform [p. 22]." In both models emphasis is placed on the individual's capacity, as opposed to his willingness, to perform at a task.

Role Perceptions

Porter and Lawler (1968) additionally included role perceptions as a determinant of performance. Role perceptions are defined as "the direction of effort—the kinds of activities and behaviors the individual believes he should engage in to perform his job successfully [p. 24]." Evaluation of these behaviors by his supervisor, however, is dependent upon the supervisor's role perceptions for the job. This suggests that accuracy of role perceptions may be a more important performance determinant than the individual's role perceptions per se.

THE EVIDENCE

Nine published field studies were found that investigated one or more hypotheses of expectancy theory using various measures of employee performance as the dependent variable. In reviewing these studies the terminology previously developed is employed. Reference to significant results indicates statistical significance at or beyond the .05 level. Critical evaluation of the studies is reserved for the following section since a number of the comments apply to more than one study.

Georgopolous, Mahoney, and Jones (1957) preceded Vroom's (1964) and Porter and Lawler's (1968) formulations by testing a portion of expectancy theory on 621 manufacturing operatives. Productivity was hypothesized to be a function of path-goal perceptions (i.e., instrumentality), level of need (i.e., valence), and freedom to alter one's performance behavior. Instrumentality and valence perceptions were obtained for three second-level outcomes. Freedom consisted of self-reported freedom, age, and length of service. Productivity was measured by subjects' reports of their productivity relative to established standards. A contingency problem format (Blalock, 1960) was employed to compute main and "interaction" effects of the three independent variables. Generally, significant differences and "interactions" were obtained for the outcome "making more money in the long run." For example, the percentage of high producers was significantly greater for the high money need–positive path-goal perception group than the high money need–negative path-goal perception group.

Lawler (1966) investigated the effects of instrumentality and ability on the performance of 211 state government managers. Subjects were asked to indicate the instrumentality[2] of three factors (quality, productivity, and effort) for the determination of their pay. Responses to these items were summed to form a composite instrumentality index. Ability was measured by supervisor rankings of managerial qualifications. Supervisor rankings and self-ratings of performance served as dependent variables. The independent variables were dichotomized and a two-way analysis of variance was performed for each dependent variable. The main instrumentality effect was significant for both dependent variables; ability and interaction effects were each significant for one dependent variable.

Galbraith and Cummings (1967) obtained ratings of the valence of seven second-level outcomes, and the instrumentality of performance for their attainment, from 32 operatives in a manufacturing organization. Ability was measured by length of time on the job, and performance was measured by daily output as a percentage of standard averaged over a 1-month interval. The independent variables were dichotomized, coded in dummy variable format (including interaction variables), and subjected to stepwise multiple regression analysis. No valence, instrumentality, or ability variables entered any of the regression equations significantly, and only 6 of 54 possible interaction variables entered the equations significantly.

Lawler and Porter (1967) examined the effects of valence, instrumentality, role perceptions, and their interactions on the performance of 154 managers. Subjects were asked to indicate how instrumental

[2] In this and several other studies (Gavin, 1970; Hackman & Porter, 1968; Lawler, 1968a; Lawler & Porter, 1967; Porter & Lawler, 1968), individuals were asked to indicate the relationship between "working hard" or "effort" and second-level outcomes. Their responses presumably represent the perceived effort-reward probability. As such, they confound the effort-performance (expectancy) and performance-reward (instrumentality) probabilities. For purposes of simplicity, however, such perceptions are referred to as instrumentality perceptions in this review.

three factors (effort, high productivity, and good job performance) were for the attainment of seven second-level outcomes and the valence of these outcomes. Responses to the instrumentality items were summed to form a composite instrumentality index. Role perceptions were obtained from 55 of the managers by having them rank 10 inner- and outer-directed traits (Riesman, 1950; Whyte, 1956) first on the basis of self-description and second on the basis of importance for success. Six criteria (three ratings of effort and three of performance) were obtained.

The median correlation between instrumentality and *(a)* performance was .11 and *(b)* effort was .18. Correlations between valence and the criteria were not reported. Out of 42 possible correlations between valence times instrumentality scores and the criteria, 29 were larger than the correlations between instrumentality and the criteria alone, 5 were the same, and 8 were smaller. Finally, high and low valence times instrumentality groups were formed, and correlations between role perceptions and performance were computed. Some of the correlations within groups were significant, but the correlations between groups were not significantly different. The results thus offer some support for the effects of role perceptions, but no support for the interaction of valence instrumentality and role perceptions.

Hackman and Porter (1968) obtained ratings of the instrumentality of working hard for the attainment of 18 second-level outcomes, and the valence of each outcome, from 82 female service representatives of a telephone company. Four summated scores were computed for each subject: valence, instrumentality, valence plus instrumentality, and valence times instrumentality. The scores were correlated with 10 subcriteria of job performance and a composite performance criterion. The median correlation between the 10 subcriteria and *(a)* valence was .16; *(b)* instrumentality was .11; *(c)* valence plus instrumentality was .17; *(d)* valence times instrumentality was .27. The correlation between valence times instrumentality and the composite criterion was a significant .40. Since the valence-instrumentality scores yielded greater correlations with performance than the other sets of scores, Hackman and Porter argued that the results tend to confirm the hypothesized valence-instrumentality interaction effect.

Lawler (1968a) used cross-lagged (Campbell & Stanley, 1963) and dynamic (Vroom, 1966) correlation analyses to test for causality between valence-instrumentality perceptions and performance. Data were collected from 55 public service managers twice, with a 1-year interval between collections. Subjects indicated how instrumental two factors (working hard and quality of job performance) were for attaining six second-level outcomes and the valence of each outcome. Six composite valence-instrumentality scores were computed for each subject. Three measures of job performance were obtained. The cross-lagged correlation analysis suggested that valence instrumentality was more likely the cause, rather than the result, of job performance. The dynamic correlation analysis, however, generally did not preclude the possibility that some third variable was responsible for the results obtained from the cross-lagged analysis.

Porter and Lawler (1968) investigated the effects of valence of pay, instrumentality, and role perceptions on the performance of 635 managers. These variables were measured as in the Lawler and Porter (1967) study. Dependent measures were self-ratings and supervisory rankings of effort and performance. Hypotheses were tested by the significance of difference between mean performance and effort of managers giving the highest and lowest third of responses to the independent variable(s) in question. In general, the results offered some support for the main effects of instrumentality and role perceptions. Less support was obtained for hypothesized interaction effects.

Gavin (1970) investigated the impact of valence, instrumentality, ability, and role perceptions on the performance of 192 male and 175 female managerial candidates of an insurance company. Each subject was asked to indicate the instrumentality of two factors (good job performance and working hard) for attaining 21 second-level outcomes, and the valence of each outcome. A total composite valence-instrumentality score was computed for each subject. Based upon the work of Barrett (1966), two measures of role perceptions were obtained by the correlations between *(a)* the subject's and his supervisor's rating of the importance of 22 work behaviors for the subject's performance and *(b)* the subject's importance and self-descriptiveness ratings of the same behaviors. Ability was measured by a general "in-house" mental aptitude test. Performance was measured by supervisory ratings. Of the independent variables, only ability did not correlate significantly with performance. Multiple regression procedures suggested by Cohen (1968) also were used. Additive regression models generally yielded significant multiple correlations on the order of .30. Interaction variables generally did not significantly "contribute to" these multiple correlations, thus indicating little support for hypothesized interaction effects.

Goodman, Rose, and Furcon (1970) interviewed 66 employees of a government research organization to obtain indications of the three most valent second-level outcomes, the instrumentality of seven factors for attaining these outcomes, and the amount of job control (in order to infer expectancy). A measure of force (see Formula 3) was derived for each of the seven factors. Actual measures of success on four of these seven factors were obtained and correlated with the appropriate force measure. Significant correlations were obtained in each instance.

Summary

Nine field studies that tested hypotheses derived from expectancy theory were reviewed. Generally, valence, instrumentality, and role perceptions were significantly related to performance, while ability was not. Little support was obtained for hypothesized interactions among these variables.

DISCUSSION OF THE EVIDENCE

The review suggests that limitations of existing research pertain primarily to the variables investigated and their measurement and to the analytical procedures employed. Measurement criticisms are aimed at each major independent[3] variable in the theory (force, ability, and role perceptions). In the analysis section, research objectives are specified, and the analyses performed in several of the studies are criticized in light of these objectives.

Force to Perform

Expectancy theory clearly places greatest emphasis on the role of motivation or force to perform as a determinant of job performance. It is disconcerting to observe, therefore, that force has consistently been measured incorrectly in the studies reviewed. Either instrumentality (performance-reward probability) and expectancy (effort-performance probability) has not been clearly delineated, or only instrumentality has been measured directly. For example, Hackman and Porter (1968) confounded instrumentality and expectancy perceptions by asking respondents to specify the probable linkage between effort and second-level outcomes. Gavin (1970), Lawler (1966, 1968a), Lawler and Porter (1967), and Porter and Lawler (1968) obtained overall perceived effort-reward and performance-reward probabilities. In each study the two probabilities were combined, again resulting in confounding. In the remaining three studies (Galbraith & Cummings, 1967; Georgopolous et al., 1957; Goodman et al., 1970) only instrumentality perceptions were measured directly. Attempts were made to infer expectancy by considering the nature of the job on such dimensions as autonomy and self-control, but subjects were never asked to indicate directly their expectancy perceptions.

Additionally, in five of the studies (Gavin, 1970; Lawler, 1966, 1968a; Lawler & Porter, 1967; Porter & Lawler, 1968) instrumentality alone has been confounded. According to the theory, the perceived instrumentality of each first-level outcome should be related separately to measured success on that outcome (e.g., as done by Goodman et al., 1970). For example, if "quality of job performance" is the first-level outcome, instrumentality perceptions of "quality of job performance" should be related empirically to actual "quality of job performance." Such a procedure was not followed in the five studies identified. Rather, managers rated the instrumentality of more than one first-level outcome, the ratings were combined to form a composite instrumentality index, and the composite index was related to actual success on various first-level outcomes.

Turning to valence, the number and type of second-level outcomes used in most of the studies may be questioned. Research on job satisfaction (e.g., Herzberg, Mausner, & Snyderman, 1959; Smith, Kendall, & Hulin, 1969; Vroom, 1964; Weiss, Dawis, England, & Lofquist, 1967) suggests that individuals experience a wide variety of satisfactions in work environments. These may be sorted (either conceptually or empirically) into a number of categories or factors, each of which may be viewed as a second-level outcome derived from participation in the organization and/or performance in a work role. A meaningful measure of force thus should tap valence and instrumentality perceptions for all relevant outcomes. The relevance of outcomes to the individuals under investigation, however, is difficult to determine a priori. This suggests that many outcomes should be included in the measure developed, or that preliminary investigation be conducted to determine the relevant second-level outcomes for the group studied. Unfortunately, the trend has been to include few second-level outcomes without preliminary investigation.

Finally, the problem of stability of responses appears to be serious, although only two studies have investigated this type of reliability. Galbraith and Cummings (1967) obtained a test-retest reliability of .80 for instrumentality, but only .50 for valence over a 1-month interval. Lawler (1968a) reported a test–retest reliability of .48 for valence-instrumentality responses over a 1-year interval.

[3] Discussion of the dependent measure, performance is omitted because the problem permeates a variety of research problems in organization settings and because excellent treatments are presented by Campbell, Dunnette, Lawler, and Weick (1970), Dunnette (1966), Guion (1965), Nagle (1953), and Ronan and Prien (1966).

Ability

In only three studies has ability even been considered as an explanatory variable. Lawler (1966) measured ability by having supervisors rank subordinates on overall qualifications. This ranking correlated significantly with the supervisor's ranking of his subordinates on overall job performance. Criterion contamination in some degree is likely, however, since both rankings were obtained from the same supervisor at the same time. Galbraith and Cummings (1967) defined ability as length of time on the job. The extent to which length of time on the job serves as a proxy for ability as defined, however, is at best unclear. Gavin (1970) used a psychometric ability measure. It did not correlate significantly with performance, nor did its interactions with force and role perceptions generally contribute significantly to the multiple correlations. In part, this was probably due to restriction of range since the measure was employed as a selection instrument by the organization. Gavin also argued that the measure may not tap the relevant intellectual capacities.

Future research requires experimentation with numerous psychometric ability measures. Use of these measures should be guided by the validity evidence of various aptitude and achievement tests used for predicting employee performance in a selection context (e.g., Ghiselli, 1966; Guion, 1965). In addition, given the broad definition of ability presented by Vroom (1964) and Porter and Lawler (1968), measures of interest, temperament, and personality also might be considered. Their use requires caution, however, for they generally have not correlated significantly with performance (Dunnette, 1966; Guion & Gottier, 1965; Nash, 1965), and they may tap motivational characteristics of individuals (Guion, 1965).

Role Perceptions

The effects of role perceptions have also been investigated in only three instances. Lawler and Porter (1967) and Porter and Lawler (1968) asked managers to rank a number of psychological traits in the order of perceived importance for determining success in their present position. By defining the traits with one word it is doubtful that even approximately equal meanings were triggered for all respondents (Stryker, 1958). Moreover, no attempt was made to tap role perception accuracy as defined by Porter and Lawler (1968).

Gavin's (1970) role perception measures appear to represent an improvement over Porter and Lawler's since Gavin employed more behaviorally descriptive items and included accuracy. Nevertheless, because the items that formed the basis of the measures were not developed with specific reference to the managerial positions investigated by Gavin, their relevance and completeness of description are open to question.

More attention should be devoted to accuracy of role perceptions in future research. Additionally, it seems that more meaningful measures would concentrate on the inclusion of the job duties and objectives derived from detailed analysis of the specific job under consideration. It is these duties and requirements that ultimately define the individual's job and form the basis of his performance evaluation.

Statistical Analysis

Expectancy theory hypothesizes that performance is a function of several independent variables operating in an interactive fashion. Thus, it is reasonable to assume that analytical procedures performed in tests of the theory would indicate *(a)* the amount of performance variance explained by additive and interactive variables and *(b)* the extent to which hypothesized interactions among variables made independent, significant contributions to explained performance variance beyond their additive (main) effects (i.e., the "usefulness" of interaction variables, Darlington, 1968).

The procedure employed by Gavin (1970) is the best to date in terms of these analytical objectives. He regressed performance on the additive variables, and then the additive and interactive variables, to obtain estimates of performance variance explained and the usefulness of the interactions investigated. This procedure thus has much to commend it in future research on expectancy theory.

Lawler (1966) also obtained interpretable indications of interaction effects by performing a two-way analysis of variance. Dichotomization of independent variables, however, may have led to an understatement of effects. Moreover, computation of omega squared (Hays, 1963) would have been desirable to indicate the strength of main and interaction effects.

Lawler and Porter (1967), and Hackman and Porter (1968), correlated valence, instrumentality, or both with performance. Valence and instrumentality scores were then multiplied, and the product score was correlated with performance. Generally, the latter correlations exceeded the former. The significance of the increase was not reported, however, and the usefulness of the valence-instrumentality interaction is thus indeterminant. Goodman et al. (1970) and Lawler (1968a) merely correlated valence-instrumentality scores with performance, and thus there is no indication of the usefulness of those interactions.

Galbraith and Cummings (1967) stepwise regressed performance against all independent variables, which were dichotomized. Two problems may be noted with this approach. First, the reduction of continuous variables to dichotomous ones may have lowered possible predictability. Second, such a procedure does not necessarily indicate the usefulness of interaction variables. If an interaction variable enters a stepwise regression before one or more of its component variables, it is impossible to demonstrate that the interaction variable made a unique contribution to the multiple correlation beyond the additive effects of its component variables.

In the remaining studies (Georgopolous et al., 1957; Porter & Lawler, 1968) significance of difference tests were performed on groups created by dichotomizing independent variable scores. Interactions, in turn, were assessed by performing significance of difference tests on the dependent variables between levels of one independent variable, within levels of one or more other independent variables. Such techniques are suboptimal for several reasons. First, dichotomization may result in an underestimate of possible effects. Second, no direct indications about the strengths of relationships are given. Third, it is difficult to precisely determine and convey interaction effects. Finally, a substantial number of significance tests are required, resulting in possible nonindependence of significance tests and an underestimate of the number of Type I errors.

CONCLUSIONS

Expectancy theory differs in several promising respects from much previous theorizing about the determinants of employee performance. Campbell et al. (1970), for example, pointed out that the concept of force to perform focuses on the major classes of variables (valence, instrumentality, and expectancy) that determine motivated behavior. This is in direct contrast to other industrial motivation theories (e.g., Herzberg et al., 1959; Maslow, 1965) that tend to emphasize only identification of second-level outcomes. Expectancy theory additionally includes ability and role perceptions as potential performance determinants. This multivariate approach seemingly has potential for increasing the proportion of explained variance in employee performance. Finally, interactions among independent variables are explicitly hypothesized, and presumably these interactions will account for significantly greater performance variance than additive formulations alone.

Unfortunately, these potential theoretical improvements have not been adequately reflected in the research. First, in only one study was a measure of force to perform developed according to its theoretical definition. Second, in only one study were measures of all three independent variables (force, ability, and role perceptions) included. The predictive power of the total theory is thus essentially unknown. Finally, while various interactions were supposedly computed in all of the studies, in only two was the contribution of the interactions to explained performance variance, beyond additive effects, appropriately computed. A minimum requirement for future research is thus that it avoid replication of these three general inadequacies in past research.

At the level of specific measurement issues, the review and discussion of the evidence warrants the following conclusions and suggestions for future research. First, in terms of force to perform, efforts should be made to incorporate an adequate number and type of second-level outcomes, and to develop measures of both instrumentality and expectancy that are more reflective of their corresponding constructs as defined by Vroom (1964) and Porter and Lawler (1968). Second, psychometrically sound ability measures should be employed. Finally, the development and use of behaviorally descriptive role-perception measures, and assessment of the impact of role perception accuracy, are required.

A noteworthy aspect of research on expectancy theory is the emphasis on investigating employees in their natural work environments, thus providing a high degree of external validity. In the case of motivation, this is in direct contrast to research on equity theory (Adams, 1965) and goal-setting theory (Locke, 1968), which has usually entailed student subjects working on laboratory tasks in experimental situations. The "cost" of external validity has been, of course, a general inability to make causal inferences. Lawler's (1968a) design exemplifies one potential compromise between the needs to study employees in their natural work environments and to obtain evidence that permits causal inferences. A variety of such designs are suggested by Campbell and Stanley (1963), and hopefully they will be used more fully in future research.

While there is an obvious need for substantial additional research on the validity of expectancy theory as formulated, work should also be performed on the determinants of valence, instrumentality, and expectancy perceptions. It has been hypothesized, for example, that the valence of second-level outcomes is a function of the satisfaction derived from their past attainment (Porter & Lawler, 1968) and their perceived equity (Lawler, 1968b). A number of specific variables have been hypothesized to influence instrumentality. In general, they all pertain to the nature of the actual relationships between performance and second-level outcomes, on the assumption that these "objective" relationships will influence instrumentality perceptions. This approach has been most noticeable in the discussions of compensation systems (Opsahl & Dunnette, 1966; Schneider & Olson, 1970). Recently it has been extended to considerations of job design as a means of more directly relating performance and intrinsic second-level outcomes (Lawler, 1969), and to considerations of the supervisor as a motivational agent to the extent that he can differentially reward the performance of his subordinates (Evans, 1970). In terms of expectancy determinants, Lawler (1970) hypothesized that past expectancy experiences and self-esteem influence expectancy. In addition, the nature of the task on such dimensions as difficulty, control over work pace, and length of job cycle may be important determinants. Considerably more theoretical and empirical work of this nature is necessary for the development of an expanded model of force to perform.

REFERENCES

Adams, J. S. Inequity in social exchange. In L. Berkowitz (ed.), *Advances in experimental social psychology.* Vol. 2. New York: Academic Press, 1965.

Barrett, R. S. The influence of supervisor's requirements on ratings. *Personnel Psychology,* 1966, **19**, 375–87.

Blalock, H. M. *Social statistics.* New York: McGraw-Hill, 1960.

Campbell, D. T. and Stanley, J. C. *Experimental and quasi-experimental designs for research.* Chicago: Rand-McNally, 1963.

Campbell, J. P., Dunnette, M. D., Lawler, E. E., and Weick, K. E. *Managerial behavior, performance, and effectiveness.* New York: McGraw-Hill, 1970.

Cohen, J. Multiple regression as a general data-analytic system. *Psychological Bulletin,* 1968, **70**, 426–43.

Darlington, R. B. Multiple regression in psychological research and practice. *Psychological Bulletin,* 1968, **69**, 161–82.

Dunnette, M. D. *Personnel selection and placement.* Belmont, Calif.: Wadsworth, 1966.

Evans, M. G. The effects of supervisory behavior on the path-goal relationship. *Organizational Behavior and Human Performance,* 1970, **5**, 277–98.

Galbraith, J. and Cummings, L. L. An empirical investigation of the motivational determinants of task performance: Interactive effects between valence-instrumentality and motivation-ability. *Organizational Behavior and Human Performance,* 1967, **2**, 237–57.

Gavin, J. F. Ability, effort, and role perception as antecedents of job performance. (Experimental publication system, manuscript number 190A) Washington, D.C.: APA, 1970.

Georgopolous, B. S., Mahoney, G. M., and Jones, N. W. A path-goal approach to productivity. *Journal of Applied Psychology,* 1957, **41**, 345–53.

Ghiselli, E. E. *The validity of occupational aptitude tests.* New York: Wiley, 1966.

Goodman, P. S., Rose, J. H., and Furcon, J. E. Comparison of motivational antecedents of the work performance of scientists and engineers. *Journal of Applied Psychology,* 1970, **54**, 491–95.

Guion, R. M. *Personnel testing.* New York: McGraw-Hill, 1965.

Guion, R. M. and Gottier, R. F. Validity of personality measures in personnel selection. *Personnel Psychology,* 1965, **18**, 135–64.

Hackman, J. R. and Porter, L. W. Expectancy theory predictions of work effectiveness. *Organizational Behavior and Human Performance,* 1968, **3**, 417–26.

Hays, W. L. *Statistics for psychologists.* New York: Holt, Rinehart & Winston, 1963.

Herzberg, F., Mausner, B., and Snyderman, B. *The motivation to work.* New York: Wiley, 1959.

Lawler, E. E. Ability as a moderator of the relationship between job attitudes and job performance. *Personnel Psychology,* 1966, **19**, 153–64.

Lawler, E. E. A correlational—causal analysis of the relationship between expectancy attitudes and job performance. *Journal of Applied Psychology,* 1968, **52**, 462–68. (a)

Lawler, E. E. Equity theory as a predictor of productivity and work quality. *Psychological Bulletin,* 1968, **70**, 596–610. (b)

Lawler, E. E. Job design and employee motivation. *Personnel Psychology,* 1969, **22**, 426–35.

Lawler, E. E. Job attitudes and employee motivation: Theory, research, and practice. *Personnel Psychology,* 1970, **23**, 223–38.

Lawler, E. E. and Porter, L. W. Antecedent attitudes of effective managerial job performance. *Organizational Behavior and Human Performance,* 1967, **2**, 122–42.

Locke, E. A. Toward a theory of task motivation and incentives. *Organizational Behavior and Human Performance,* 1968, **3**, 157–89.

Maslow, A. *Eupsychian management.* Homewood, Ill.: Irwin-Dorsey, 1965.

Nagle, B. F. Criterion development. *Personnel Psychology,* 1953, **6**, 271–89.

Nash, A. N. Vocational interests of effective managers: A review of the literature. *Personnel Psychology,* 1965, **18**, 21–37.

Opsahl, R. L. and Dunnette, M. D. The role of financial compensation in industrial motivation. *Psychological Bulletin,* 1966, **66**, 94–118.

Porter, L. W. and Lawler, E. E. *Managerial attitudes and performance.* Homewood, Ill.: Irwin-Dorsey, 1968.

Riesman, D. *The lonely crowd.* New Haven, Conn.: Yale University Press, 1950.

Ronan, W. W. and Prien, E. P. *Toward a criterion theory.* Greensboro, N.C.: Richardson Foundation, Creativity Research Institute, 1966.

Schneider, B. and Olson, L. K. Effort as a correlate of organizational reward system and individual values. *Personnel Psychology,* 1970, **23**, 313–26.

Smith, P. C., Kendall, L. M., and Hulin, C. L. *The measurement of satisfaction in work and retirement.* Chicago: Rand-McNally, 1969.

Stryker, P. On the meaning of executive qualities. *Fortune,* 1958, **57**, 116–19.

Vroom, V. H. *Work and motivation.* New York: Wiley, 1964.

Vroom, V. H. A comparison of static and dynamic correlation methods in the study of organizations. *Organizational Behavior and Human Performance,* 1966, **1**, 55–70.

Weiss, D. J., Dawis, R. V., England, G. W., and Lofquist, L. H. *Manual for the Minnesota Satisfaction Questionnaire.* Minneapolis: Industrial Relations Center, University of Minnesota, 1967.

Whyte, W. H. *The organization man.* New York: Simon and Schuster, 1956.

6. A DECADE OF MOTIVATION THEORY*

D. E. Berlyne†

A conspicuous part of contemporary psychology consists of what is coming to be known as "motivation theory." This term does not denote a coherent system of axioms and theorems, as "set theory" and "special relativity theory" do, or even to the extent that at least parts of "learning theory" do. Some psychologists regard motivation theory as indissociable from learning theory and place them both within "behavior theory." Others would be more inclined to annex motivation theory to "personality theory." Motivation theory consists of an area of inquiry, and, although it would be hard to obtain agreement on where precisely its boundaries lie, its territory is demarcated by questions rather than by answers.

For some time after the launching of psychology as a scientific discipline, experimental psychologists did their best to manage without motivational concepts and did not feel their lack. The earliest pioneers were interested largely in eliciting descriptions of the conscious experiences produced in human subjects whose sense organs were being exposed to particular kinds of stimuli or who were engaged in particular kinds of tasks. Motivational problems arise in these situations as elsewhere, but they were masked by the ease with which verbal instructions or requests can generate artificial motives in human subjects, especially when they are colleagues or graduate students of the experimenter, as was often the case in those days. A little later, men like Watson, Thorndike and Pavlov began to seek laws governing behavior, beginning with the simplest forms which could most conveniently be studied in animals. They likewise felt no need to consider the motivational condition of the organism, being content to analyze behavior in terms of "reflexes" or stimulus-response "connections," which meant relating muscular and glandular reactions to events in the external environment. Two of their contemporaries, Freud and McDougall, having become involved in abnormal psychology and in social psychology respectively, were brought face to face with some of the dramatic extremes reached by behavior outside the laboratory and felt compelled to denounce the vanity of attempting to explain animal or human actions without reference to "urges," "instincts," "purposes," "goals," etc.

Psychologists primarily interested in individual differences and personality were readily converted to this way of thinking. Experimental psychologists were more resistant, but, by the beginning of the 1930's, which is the time when the early behaviorism of Watson gave place to the various brands of neobehaviorism, they too had absorbed the lesson. The contentious concept of "instinct" had been replaced by the less provocative concept of "drive," a term apparently first taken over from mechanical engineering but later used in the plural under the influence of the German word "*Triebe*" (the word that Freud's translators rendered as "instincts"). Various techniques for measuring the strength of drive (or drives) experimentally had been introduced, and several experimenters had demonstrated that even the simplest forms of animal learning are profoundly affected by the motivational condition (drive level) of the subject. Theoreticians like Holt, Tolman, and Hull had devised ways in which the purposive, goal-striving nature of behavior could be acknowledged and yet treated in full conformity with the canons of scientific discourse. They studied the effects of motive and drive level as factors that fluctuate from moment to moment in the life-history of one individual. Personality theorists were more concerned with "motives" or "needs" as persistent factors varying from individual to individual.

To attack motivational problems means to seek

* *American Scientist,* Vol. 52 (1964), pp. 447–51.
† Department of Psychology, University of Toronto.

factors that govern the organism's degree of alertness and activation, that bias the organism towards certain forms of behavior, and that determine what events will provide reinforcement for learning processes and how effectively. This might seem to involve three distinct groups of problems rather than one psychological topic. Nevertheless, the three groups appear to be inter-related and are commonly treated together, because the best known drive states, e.g., hunger and fear, are apparently conditions that activate animals as well as conditions that bring certain forms of behavior to the fore (e.g., eating, being startled, moving in directions where food or safety has been found in the past) and "aversive" conditions whose termination is rewarding or reinforcing.

Since 1952, theoretical and experimental work on motivation has been carried on under watchful surveillance from Lincoln, Nebraska. The Nebraska Symposium on Motivation has annually summoned some five or six psychologists and near-psychologists to deliver themselves of their findings and ideas. This does not mean that the organizers of the Symposium have mustered 60 specialists in motivation. There are, actually, surprisingly few people who would accept that label. Many of the participants must have been quite surprised to find themselves associated with motivation, and a few were put to evident strain to find some connection between what they had been doing and motivational problems. Nevertheless, all psychological processes presumably have motivational aspects, and all the contributors had the experience, which must have been salutary for them and for their readers, of being forced to consider their areas of interest from this angle, which they might not have done otherwise.

The first decade of the Nebraska Symposium has been a singularly eventful one for motivation theory. First, there have been momentous neurophysiological advances whose psychological implications must take some time to work out and which show no prospects of slackening their pace. The discovery by Moruzzi and Magoun, reported in 1949, that the reticular formation of the brain stem governs the electroencephalographic patterns indicative of an alert brain gave rise, when put together with the proceeds of other lines of research, to the psychophysiological concept of "arousal level," a development whose potential consequences are far-reaching. The newer concept of "arousal" has obviously much in common with the older concept of "drive," especially in its activation aspect. We know of many conditions that will raise arousal in addition to the familiar conditions that have long been known to raise drive level, and we have at our disposal several convenient, relatively direct ways of measuring arousal to supplement the indirect, cumbersome techniques that have had to be used hitherto to measure drive.

Neurophysiological discoveries relating to response selection and reinforcement have also not been lacking. Stimulation and ablation experiments have identified numerous points in the lower parts of the brain—in the hypothalamus, thalamus, and limbic system—whose activity brings to the fore, or inhibits, behavior appropriate to specific motivational conditions, e.g., feeding, drinking, sleeping, sexual behavior, aggressive behavior, and flight. Since 1954, when Olds and Milner and Miller, Delgado, and Roberts reported finding structures in the lower cerebrum and brain-stem whose stimulation had effects resembling those of externally applied rewards and punishments, the study of the functioning and inter-relations of these structures has steadily intensified and proved extremely productive.

On a more purely psychological level, the last ten years has seen rapid growth of interest in exploratory behavior and related phenomena. It came to be realized that, in higher animals, a great deal of time is spent on the multifarious activities that are customarily placed under such headings as "curiosity" and "play" and bear no obvious and immediate relation to familiar, "organic" motives. Experimental work has revealed that the likelihood of these activities and the directions that they take depend largely on factors like novelty, surprisingness, and complexity of external stimulation. These factors (which are closely related to the concepts of information theory) seem, in their turn, to be capable of generating the kind of disturbance that motivates behavior and promotes acquisition of new learned responses, apparently because they involve the simultaneous initiation of discrepant or mutually interfering reactions.

This means that we must add disharmonious relations among neural processes to the visceral upheavals (e.g., hunger, fear) and the external irritations (e.g., pain, excessive cold) that have long been recognized as sources of drive. We must also add a large range of new rewarding conditions, working through relief of conflict, to the rewarding events that can reinforce learned responses. The new lines of thought that have thus been opened up by work on exploratory behavior are converging in significant ways with ideas that have emerged from recent work on attitude change, educational practice, child development, personality, aesthetics, and humor. Factors like novelty, complexity, and conflict now appear to play a prominent and previously overlooked role in all these areas.

Further impetus for rethinking has come from the ethological movement, which was launched by continental European zoologists interested in animal behavior, particularly in that of insects and lower vertebrates. Ethology was introduced to psychologists by the publication of Tinbergen's book, *The Study of Instinct,* in 1951. In consequence of the interchanges between ethologists and psychologists that resulted, some of the theoretical statements of the former have been criticized and refurbished. On the other hand, both animal and human psychology have appreciatively received a mass of new experimental problems, new experimental techniques, and new theoretical notions. The ethologists made clear the prevalence of patterns of "instinctive" or "species-specific" behavior in lower animals, stemming from inherited properties of the nervous system and yet much more complicated and flexible than the reflexes and chains of reflexes that were formerly thought to comprise inherited behavior patterns. Above all, these forms of behavior are profoundly affected by the animal's motivational condition. So, while the ethologists have raised the possibility that the kinds of instinctive behavior that they have brought to light may be present in higher animals, including human beings, their main contribution has perhaps been to indicate the close interpenetration of unlearned and learned elements in behavior and the susceptibility of both of them to common principles, especially common motivational principles.

Volume XI in the Nebraska series[1] shows a polarization reflecting the tension between old and new trends in current motivational theory. Rogers and Sears, in their articles on "actualizing tendency" and "dependency motivation," are concerned with motivational aspects of personality and extend inquiries that they have been pursuing for some years. The three remaining contributors, N. E. Miller, Pribram, and Magoun, discuss long-standing problems pertaining to reinforcement and to inhibition in the light of recent neurophysiological advances. Miller's paper is particularly interesting to anybody who likes to spot trends. Having been one of the most die-hard and ingenious defenders of the view that reinforcement depends on drive-reduction, Miller here outlines an alternative, and in some ways diametrically opposed, view that brain-stimulation experiments have forced him to consider. He now speculates that reinforcement depends on activation of a "go mechanism" which promotes learning by supplying a burst of extra excitation (arousal?). This new view has a great deal in common with the ways in which several other contemporary writers have begun to think, as well as with hypotheses suggested by some pioneers of learning theory quite a while ago and with current Russian conceptions of the physiological processes behind conditioning. Reinforcing agents commonly involve a rise in excitation or arousal, quickly followed by a fall. The rapid succession of the rise and the fall may account for our failure so far to disentangle the roles of these two phases.

What is going to happen in motivation theory over the next ten years? What solutions will impending psychological and physiological experimentation give to the still unsolved problem of the nature of reinforcement? Will the concepts of "drive" and "arousal" be swept aside, will they fragment into several distinct and more precisely defined concepts, or will they be firmly vindicated and more accurately pinpointed? Will motivation theory lose such autonomy as it now possesses or will its boundaries become clearer? The only prediction that it would be safe to venture is that anybody who continues to read the Nebraska Symposium for the next ten years will know the answers.

[1] M. R. Jones (ed.), *Nebraska Symposium on Motivation 1963* (Lincoln, Neb.: University of Nebraska Press, 1963).

Section B
ATTITUDES AND MOTIVES

Conditioning studies emphasize ongoing environmental variables as determinants of behavior. However, the study of human behavior is complicated by the fact that previous learning experiences modify the effects of stimuli or, at least interact with ongoing stimulation, to determine the behavioral outcome. Several investigators have recognized that we cannot explain the effects of reinforcement by examining *only* the current reinforcement schedule. We must also take into account the previous reinforcement history of the individual. Motives and attitudes, classed as intervening variables, have increasingly come to be considered as products of a previous reinforcement history and McClelland's theory of motive acquisition reflects this line of reasoning. He goes on to describe an interesting program designed to produce a motive change.

Peak's treatment of attitudes and attitude change recognizes, at least implicitly, that an attitude is reflective of a previous reinforcement history. She reminds us that we should not expect to find a direct relationship between attitudes and behavior and, in fact, a number of attempts to establish such a relationship have failed.

7. TOWARD A THEORY OF MOTIVE ACQUISITION*

***David C. McClelland*†**

Too little is known about the processes of personality change at relatively complex levels. The empirical study of the problem has been hampered by both practical and theoretical difficulties. On the practical side it is very expensive both in time and effort to set up systematically controlled educational programs designed to develop some complex personality characteristic like a motive, and to follow the effects of the education over a number of years. It also presents ethical problems since it is not always clear that it is as proper to teach a person a new motive as it is a new skill like learning to play the piano. For both reasons, most of what we know about personality change has come from studying psychotherapy where both ethical and practical difficulties are overcome by the pressing need to help someone in real trouble. Yet, this source of information leaves much to be desired: It has so far proven difficult to identify and systematically vary the "inputs" in psychotherapy and to measure their specific effects on subsequent behavior, except in very general ways (cf. Rogers & Dymond, 1954).

On the theoretical side, the dominant views of personality formation suggest anyway that acquisition or change of any complex characteristic like a motive in adulthood would be extremely difficult. Both behavior theory and psychoanalysis agree that stable personality characteristics like motives are laid down in childhood. Behavior theory arrives at this conclusion by arguing that social motives are learned by close association with reduction in certain basic biological drives like hunger, thirst, and physical discomfort which loom much larger in childhood than adulthood. Psychoanalysis, for its part, pictures adult motives as stable resolutions of basic conflicts occurring in early childhood. Neither theory would provide much support for the notion that motives could be developed in adulthood without somehow recreating the childhood conditions under which they were originally formed. Furthermore, psychologists have been hard put to it to find objective evidence that even prolonged, serious, and expensive attempts to introduce personality change through psychotherapy have really proven successful (Eysenck, 1952). What hope is there that a program to introduce personality change would end up producing a big enough effect to study?

Despite these difficulties a program of research has been under way for some time which is attempting to develop the achievement motive in adults. It

* *American Psychologist,* Vol. 20 (1965), pp. 321–33.

† Department of Social Relations, Harvard University.

"I am greatly indebted to the Carnegie Corporation of New York for its financial support of the research on which this paper is based, and to my collaborators who have helped plan and run the courses designed to develop the achievement motive—chiefly George Litwin, Elliott Danzig, David Kolb, Winthrop Adkins, David Winter, and John Andrews. The statements made and views expressed are solely the responsibility of the author."

was undertaken in an attempt to fill some of the gaps in our knowledge about personality change or the acquisition of complex human characteristics. Working with n Achievement has proved to have some important advantages for this type of research: The practical and ethical problems do not loom especially large because previous research (McClelland, 1961) has demonstrated the importance of high n Achievement for entrepreneurial behavior and it is easy to find businessmen, particularly in underdeveloped countries, who are interested in trying any means of improving their entrepreneurial performance. Furthermore, a great deal is known about the origins of n Achievement in childhood and its specific effects on behavior so that educational programs can be systematically planned and their effects evaluated in terms of this knowledge. Pilot attempts to develop n Achievement have gradually led to the formulation of some theoretical notions of what motive acquisition involves and how it can be effectively promoted in adults. These notions have been summarized in the form of 12 propositions which it is the ultimate purpose of the research program to test. The propositions are anchored so far as possible in experiences with pilot courses, in supporting research findings from other studies, and in theory.

Before the propositions are presented, it is necessary to explain more of the theoretical and practical background on which they are based. To begin with, some basis for believing that motives could be acquired in adulthood had to be found in view of the widespread pessimism on the subject among theoretically oriented psychologists. Oddly enough we were encouraged by the successful efforts of two quite different groups of "change agents"—operant conditioners and missionaries. Both groups have been "naive" in the sense of being unimpressed by or ignorant of the state of psychological knowledge in the field. The operant conditioners have not been encumbered by any elaborate theoretical apparatus; they do not believe motives exist anyway, and continue demonstrating vigorously that if you want a person to make a response, all you have to do is elicit it and reward it (cf. Bandura & Walters, 1963, pp. 238 ff.). They retain a simple faith in the infinite plasticity of human behavior in which one response is just like any other and any one can be "shaped up" (strengthened by reward)—presumably even an "achievement" response as produced by a subject in a fantasy test. In fact, it was the naive optimism of one such researcher (Burris, 1958) that had a lot to do with getting the present research under way. He undertook a counseling program in which an attempt to elicit and reinforce achievement-related fantasies proved to be successful in motivating college students to get better grades. Like operant conditioners, the missionaries have gone ahead changing people because they have believed it possible. While the evidence is not scientifically impeccable, common-sense observation yields dozens of cases of adults whose motivational structure has seemed to be quite radically and permanently altered by the educational efforts of Communist Party, Mormon, or other devout missionaries.

A man from Mars might be led to observe that personality change appears to be very difficult for those who think it is very difficult, if not impossible, and much easier for those who think it can be done. He would certainly be oversimplifying the picture, but at the very least his observation suggests that some theoretical revision is desirable in the prevailing views of social motives which link them so decisively to early childhood. Such a revision has been attempted in connection with the research on n Achievement (McClelland, Atkinson, Clark, & Lowell, 1953) and while it has not been widely accepted (cf. Berelson & Steiner, 1964), it needs to be briefly summarized here to provide a theoretical underpinning for the attempts at motive change to be described. It starts with the proposition that all motives are learned, that not even biological discomforts (as from hunger) or pleasures (as from sexual stimulation) are "urges" or "drives" until they are linked to cues that can signify their presence or absence. In time, clusters of expectancies or associations grow up around affective experiences, not all of which are connected by any means with biological needs (McClelland et al., 1953, ch. 2), which we label motives. More formally, motives are "affectively toned associative networks" arranged in a hierarchy of strength or importance within a given individual. Obviously, the definition fits closely the operations used to measure a motive: "an affectively toned associative cluster" is exactly what is coded in a subject's fantasies to obtain an n Achievement score. The strength of the motive (its position in the individual's hierarchy of motives) is measured essentially by counting the number of associations belonging to this cluster as compared to others that an individual produces in a given number of opportunities. If one thinks of a motive as an associative network, it is easier to imagine how one might go about changing it: The problem becomes one of moving its position up on the hierarchy by increasing its salience compared to other clusters. It should be possible to accomplish this end by such tactics as: *(a)* setting up the network—discovering what associations, for example, exist in the achievement area and then extending, strengthening, or otherwise "improving" the network they form; *(b)* conceptualizing the network—forming a clear and conscious construct that labels the network; *(c)* tying the network to as many cues as possible in everyday life, especially those preceding and following action, to insure that the network will be regularly rearoused once formed; and *(d)* working out the relation of the network to superordinate associative clusters, like the self-concept, so that these dominant schemata do not block the train of achievement thoughts—for example, through a chain of interfering associations (e.g., "I am not really the achieving type").

This very brief summary is not intended as a full exposition of the theoretical viewpoint underlying the research, but it should suffice to give a rough idea of how the motive was conceived that we set out to change. This concept helped define the goals of the techniques of change, such as reducing the effects of associative interference from superordinate associate clusters. But what about the techniques themselves? What could we do that would produce effective learning of this sort? Broadly speaking, there are four types of empirical information to draw on. From the animal learning experiments, we know that such factors as repetition, optimal time intervals between stimulus, response, and reward, and the schedule of rewards are very important for effective learning. From human learning experiments, we know that such factors as distribution of practice, repetitions, meaningfulness, and recitation are important. From experiences with psychotherapy (cf. Rogers, 1961), we learn that warmth, honesty, nondirectiveness, and the ability to recode associations in line with psychoanalytic or other personality theories are important. And, from the attitude-change research literature, we learn that such variables as presenting one side or two, using reason or prestige to support an argument, or affiliating with a new reference group are crucial for developing new attitudes (cf. Hovland, Janis, & Kelley, 1953). Despite the fact that many of these variables seem limited in application to the learning situation in which they were studied, we have tried to make use of information from all these sources in designing our "motive acquisition" program and in finding support for the general propositions that have emerged from our study so far. For our purpose has been above all to produce an effect large enough to be measured. Thus we have tried to profit by all that is known about how to facilitate learning or produce personality or attitude change. For, if we could not obtain a substantial effect with all factors working to produce it, there would be no point to studying the effects of each factor taken one at a time. Such a strategy also has the practical advantage that we are in the position of doing our best to "deliver the goods" to our course participants since they were giving us their time and attention to take part in a largely untried educational experience.[1]

Our overall research strategy, therefore is "subtractive" rather than "additive." After we have demonstrated a substantial effect with some 10–12 factors working to produce it, our plan is to subtract that part of the program that deals with each of the factors to discover if there is a significant decline in the effect. It should also be possible to omit several factors in various combinations to get at interactional effects. This will obviously require giving a fairly large number of courses in a standard institutional setting for the same kinds of businessmen with follow-up evaluation of their performance extending over a number of years. So obviously it will be some time before each of the factors incorporated into the propositions which follow can be properly evaluated so far as its effect on producing motive change is concerned.

The overall research strategy also determined the way the attempts to develop the achievement motive have been organized. That is to say, in order to process enough subjects to permit testing the effectiveness of various "inputs" in a reasonable number of years, the training had to be both of *short duration* (lasting one to three weeks) and *designed for groups* rather than for individuals as in person-to-person counseling. Fortunately these requirements coincide with normal practice in providing short courses for business executives. To conform further with that practice, the training has usually also been *residential* and *voluntary.* The design problems introduced by the last characteristic we have tried to handle in the usual ways by putting half the volunteers on a waiting list or giving them a different, technique-oriented course, etc. So far we have given the course to develop n Achievement in some form or another some eight times to over 140 managers or teachers of management in groups of 9–25 in the United States, Mexico, and India. For the most part the course has been offered by a group of two to four consultant psychologists either to executives in a single company as a company training program, or to executives from several different companies as a self-improvement program, or as part of the program of an institute or school devoted to training managers. The theoretical propositions which follow have evolved gradually from these pilot attempts to be effective in developing n Achievement among businessmen of various cultural backgrounds.

---

[1] Parenthetically, we have found several times that our stated desire to evaluate the effectiveness of our course created doubts in the minds of our sponsors that they did not feel about many popular courses for managers that no one has ever evaluated or plans to evaluate. An attitude of inquiry is not always an asset in education. It suggests one is not sure of his ground.

The first step in a motive development program is to create confidence that it will work. Our initial efforts in this area were dictated by the simple practical consideration that we had to "sell" our course or nobody would take it. We were not in the position of an animal psychologist who can order a dozen rats, or an academic psychologist who has captive subjects in his classes, or even a psychotherapist who has sick people knocking at his door every day. So we explained to all who would listen that we had every reason to believe from previous research that high n Achievement is related to effective entrepreneurship and that therefore business executives could expect to profit from taking a course designed to understand and develop this important human characteristic. What started as a necessity led to the first proposition dealing with how to bring about motive change.

Proposition 1. The more reasons an individual has in advance to believe that he can, will, or should develop a motive, the more educational attempts designed to develop that motive are likely to succeed. The empirical support for this proposition from other studies is quite impressive. It consists of *(a)* the prestige-suggestion studies showing that people will believe or do what prestigeful sources suggest (cf. Hovland et al., 1953); *(b)* the so-called "Hawthorne effect" showing that people who feel they are especially selected to show an effect will tend to show it (Roethlisberger & Dickson, 1947); *(c)* the "Hello-Goodbye" effect in psychotherapy showing that patients who merely have contact with a prestigeful medical authority improve significantly over waiting list controls and almost as much as those who get prolonged therapy (Frank, 1961); *(d)* the "experimenter bias" studies which show that subjects will often do what an experimenter wants them to do, even though neither he nor they know he is trying to influence them (Rosenthal, 1963); *(e)* the goalsetting studies which show that setting goals for a person particularly in the name of prestigeful authorities like "science" or "research" improves performance (Kausler, 1959; Mierke, 1955); *(f)* the parent-child interaction studies which show that parents who set higher standards of excellence for their sons are more likely to have sons with high n Achievement (Rosen & D'Andrade, 1959). The common factor in all these studies seems to be that goals are being set for the individual by sources he respects—goals which imply that his behavior should change for a variety of reasons and that it *can* change. In common-sense terms, belief in the possibility and desirability of change are tremendously influential in changing a person.

So we have used a variety of means to create this belief: the authority of research findings on the relationship of n Achievement to entrepreneurial success, the suggestive power of membership in an experimental group designed to show an effect, the prestige of a great university, our own genuine enthusiasm for the course and our conviction that it would work, as expressed privately and in public speeches. In short, we were trying to make every use possible of what is sometimes regarded as an "error" in such research—namely, the Hawthorne effect, experimenter bias, etc., because we believe it to be one of the most powerful sources of change.

Why? What is the effect on the person, theoretically speaking, of all this goal setting for him? Its primary function is probably to arouse what exists of an associative network in the achievement area for each person affected. That is, many studies have shown that talk of achievement or affiliation or power tends to increase the frequency with which individuals think about achievement or affiliation or power (cf. Atkinson, 1958). And the stronger the talk, the more the relevant associative networks are aroused (McClelland et al., 1953). Such an arousal has several possible effects which would facilitate learning: *(a)* It elicits what exists in the person of a "response" thus making it easier to strengthen that response in subsequent learning. *(b)* It creates a discrepancy between a goal (a "Soll-lage" in Heckhausen's—1963—theory of motivation) and a present state ("Ist-lage") which represents a cognitive dissonance the person tries to reduce (cf. Festinger, 1957); in common-sense terms he has an image clearly presented to him of something he is not but should be. *(c)* It tends to block out by simple interference other associations which would inhibit change—such as, "I'm too old to learn," "I never learned much from going to school anyway," "What do these academics know about everyday life?" or "I hope they don't get personal about all this."

After the course has been "sold" sufficiently to get a group together for training, the first step in the course itself is to present the research findings in some detail on exactly how n Achievement is related to certain types of successful entrepreneurial performance. That is, the argument of *The Achieving Society* (McClelland, 1961) is presented carefully with tables, charts and diagrams, usually in lecture form at the outset and with the help of an educational TV film entitled the *Need to Achieve.* This is followed by discussion to clear up any ambiguities that remain in their minds as far as the central argument is concerned. It is especially necessary to stress that not all high achievement is caused by high n Achievement—that we have no evidence that high n Achievement is an essential ingredient in success as a research scientist, professional, accountant, office or personnel manager, etc.; that, on the contrary, it seems rather narrowly related to entrepreneurial, sales, or promotional success, and therefore should be of particular interest to them because they hold jobs which either have or could have an entrepreneurial component. We rationalize this activity in terms of the following proposition.

Proposition 2. The more an individual perceives that developing a motive is consistent with the demands of reality (and reason), the more educational attempts designed to develop that motive are likely to succeed. In a century in which psychologists and social theorists have been impressed by the power of unreason, it is well to remember that research has shown that rational arguments do sway opinions, particularly among the doubtful or the uncommitted (cf. Hovland et al., 1953). Reality in the form of legal, military, or housing rules does modify white prejudice against Negroes (cf. Berelson & Steiner, 1964, p. 512). In being surprised at Asch's discovery that many people will go along with a group in calling a shorter line longer than it is, we sometimes forget that under most conditions their judgments conform with reality. The associative network which organizes "reality"—which places the person correctly in time, place, space, family, job, etc.—is one of the most dominant in the personality. It is the last to go in psychosis. It should be of great assistance to tie any proposed change in an associative network in with this dominant schema in such a way as to make the change consistent with reality demands or "*reasonable*" extensions of them. The word "reasonable" here simply means extensions arrived at by the thought processes of proof, logic, etc. which in adults have achieved a certain dominance of their own.

The next step in the course is to teach the participants the n Achievement coding system. By this time, they are a little confused anyway as to exactly what we mean by the term. So we tell them they can find out for themselves by learning to code stories written by others or by themselves. They take the test for n Achievement before this session and then find out what their own score is by scoring this record. However, we point out that if they think their score is too low, that can be easily remedied, since we teach them how to code and how to write stories saturated with n Achievement; in fact, that is one of the basic purposes of the course: to teach them to think constantly in n Achievement terms. Another aspect of the learning is discriminating achievement thinking from thinking in terms of power or affiliation. So usually the elements of these other two coding schemes are also taught.

Proposition 3. The more thoroughly an individual develops and clearly conceptualizes the associative network defining the motive, the more likely he is to develop the motive. The original empirical support for this proposition came from the radical behaviorist Skinnerian viewpoint: If the associative responses are the motive (by definition), to strengthen them one should elicit them and reinforce them, as one would shape up any response by reinforcement (cf. Skinner, 1953). But, support for this proposition also derives from other sources, particularly the "set" experiments. For decades laboratory psychologists have known that one of the easiest and most effective ways to change behavior is to change the subject's set. If he is responding to stimulus words with the names of animals, tell him to respond with the names of vegetables, or with words meaning the opposite, and he changes his behavior immediately and efficiently without a mistake. At a more complex level Orne (1962) had pointed out how powerful a set like "This is an experiment" can be. He points out that if you were to go up to a stranger and say something like "Lie down!" he would in all probability either laugh or escape as soon as possible. But, if you say "This is an experiment. Lie down!" more often than not, if there are other supporting cues, the person will do so. Orne has demonstrated how subjects will perform nonsensical and fatiguing tasks for very long periods of time under the set that "This is an experiment." At an even more complex level, sociologists have demonstrated often how quickly a person will change his behavior as he adopts a new role set (as a parent, a teacher, a public official, etc.). In all these cases an associative network exists usually with a label conveniently attached which we call set and which, when it is aroused or becomes salient, proceeds to control behavior very effectively. The purpose of this part of our course is to give the subjects a set or a carefully worked out associative network with appropriate words or labels to describe all its various aspects (the coding labels for parts of the n Achievement scoring system like Ga^+, I^+, etc; cf. Atkinson, 1958). The power of words on controlling behavior has also been well documented (cf. Brown, 1958).

It is important to stress that it is not just the label (n Achievement) which is taught. The person must be able to produce easily and often the new associative network itself. It is here that our research comes closest to traditional therapy which could be understood as the prolonged and laborious formation of new associative networks to replace anxiety-laden ones. That is, the person over time comes to form a new associative network covering his relations, for example, to his father and mother, which still later he may label an "unresolved Oedipus complex." When cues arise that formerly would have produced anxiety-laden associations, they now evoke this new complex instead, blocking out the "bad" associations by associative interference. But all therapists, whether Freudian or Rogerian, insist that the person must learn to produce these associations in their new form, that teaching the label is not enough. In fact, this is probably why so-called directive therapy is ineffective: It tries to substitute new constructs ("You should become an achiever") for old neurotic or ineffective ones ("rather than being such a slob") without changing the associative networks which underlie these surface labels. A change in set such as "Respond with names of vegetables" will not work unless the person has a whole associative network which defines the meaning of the set. The relation of this argument is obvious both to Kelley's (1955) insistence on the importance of personal constructs and to the general semanticists' complaints about the neurotic effects of mislabeling or overabstraction (Korzybski, 1941).

But, theoretically speaking, why should a change in set as an associative network be so influential in controlling thought and action? The explanation lies in part in its symbolic character. Learned acts have limited influence because they often depend on reality supports (as in typewriting), but learned thoughts (symbolic acts) can occur any time, any place, in any connection, and be applied to whatever the person is doing. They are more generalizable. Acts can also be inhibited more easily than thoughts. Isak Dinesen tells the story of the oracle who told the king he would get his wish so long as he never thought of the left eye of a camel. Needless to say, the king did not get his wish, but he could easily have obeyed her prohibition if it had been to avoid *looking* at the left eye of a camel. Thoughts once acquired gain more control over thoughts and actions than acquired acts do because they are harder to inhibit. But why do they gain control over actions? Are not thoughts substitutes for actions? Cannot a man learn to think achievement thoughts and still not act like an achiever in any way? The question is taken up again under the next proposition, but it is well to remember here that thoughts are symbolic acts and that practice of symbolic acts facilitates performing the real acts (cf. Hovland, 1951, p. 644).

The next step in the course is to tie thought to action. Research has shown that individuals high in n Achievement tend to act in certain ways. For example; they prefer work situations where there is a challenge (moderate risk), concrete feedback on how well they are doing, and opportunity to take personal responsibility for achieving the work goals. The participants in the course are therefore introduced to a "work" situation in the form of a business game in which they will have an opportunity to show these characteristics in action or more specifically to develop them through practice and through observing others play it. The game is designed to mimic real life: They must order parts to make certain objects (e.g., a Tinker Toy model bridge) after having estimated how many they think they can construct in the time allotted. They have a real chance to take over, plan the whole game, learn from how well they are doing (use of feedback), and show a paper profit or loss at the end. While they are surprised often that they should have to display their real action characteristics in this way in public, they usually get emotionally involved in observing how they behave under pressure of a more or less "real" work situation.

Proposition 4. The more an individual can link the newly developed network to related actions, the more the change in both thought and action is likely to occur and endure. The evidence for the importance of action for producing change consists of such diverse findings as *(a)* the importance of recitation for human learning, *(b)* the repeated finding that overt commitment and participation in action changes attitudes effectively (cf. Berelson & Steiner, 1964, p. 576), and *(c)* early studies by Carr (cf. McGeoch & Irion, 1952) showing that simply to expose an organism to what is to be learned (e.g., trundling a rat through a maze) is nowhere near as effective as letting him explore it for himself in action.

Theoretically, the action is represented in the associative network by what associations precede, accompany, and follow it. So including the acts in what is learned *enlarges* the associative network or the achievement construct to include action. Thus, the number of cues likely to trip off the n Achievement network is increased. In common-sense terms, whenever he works he now evaluates what he is doing in achievement terms, and whenever he thinks about achievement he tends to think of its action consequences.

So far the course instruction has remained fairly abstract and removed from the everyday experiences of businessmen. So, the next step is to apply what has been learned to everyday business activities through the medium of the well-known case-study method popularized by the Harvard Business School. Actual examples of the development of the careers or firms of business leaders or entrepreneurs are written up in disguised form and assigned for discussion to the participants. Ordinarily, the instructor is not interested in illustrating "good" or "bad" managerial behavior—that is left to participants to discuss—but in our use of the material, we do try to label the various types of behavior as illustrating either n Achievement and various aspects of the achievement sequence (instrumental activity, blocks, etc.), or n Power, n Affiliation, etc. The participants are also encouraged to bring in examples of managerial behavior from their own experience to evaluate in motivational terms.

Proposition 5. The more an individual can link the

newly conceptualized association-action complex (or motive) to events in his everyday life, the more likely the motive complex is to influence his thoughts and actions in situations outside the training experience. The transfer-of-training research literature is not very explicit on this point, though it seems self-evident. Certainly, this is the proposition that underlies the practice of most therapy when it involves working through or clarifying, usually in terms of a new, partially formed construct system, old memories, events from the last 24 hours, dreams, and hopes of the future. Again, theoretically, this should serve to enlarge and clarify the associative network and increase the number of cues in everyday life which will rearouse it. The principle of symbolic practice can also be invoked to support its effectiveness in promoting transfer outside the learning experience.

For some time most course participants have been wondering what all this has to do with them personally. That is to say, the material is introduced originally on a "take it or leave it" objective basis as something that ought to be of interest to them. But sooner or later, they must confront the issue as to what meaning n Achievement has in their own personal lives. We do not force this choice on them nor do we think we are brainwashing them to believe in n Achievement. We believe and we tell them we believe in the "obstinate audience" (cf. Bauer, 1964), in the ultimate capacity of people to resist persuasion or to do in the end what they really want to do. In fact, we had one case in an early session of a man who at this point decided he was not an achievement-minded person and did not want to become one. He subsequently retired and became a chicken farmer to the relief of the business in which he had been an ineffective manager. We respected that decision and mention it in the course as a good example of honest self-evaluation. Nevertheless, we do provide them with all kinds of information as to their own achievement-related behavior in the fantasy tests, in the business game, in occasional group dynamics sessions —and ample opportunity and encouragement to think through what this information implies so far as their self-concept is concerned and their responsibilities to their jobs. Various devices such as the "Who am I?" test, silent group meditation, or individual counseling have been introduced to facilitate this self-confrontation.

Proposition 6. The more an individual can perceive and experience the newly conceptualized motive as an improvement in the self-image, the more the motive is likely to influence his future thoughts and actions. Evidence on the importance of the ego or the self-image on controlling behavior has been summarized by Allport (1943). In recent years, Rogers and his group (Rogers, 1961; Rogers & Dymond, 1954) have measured improvement in psychotherapy largely in terms of improvement of the self-concept in relation to the ideal self. Indirect evidence of the importance of the self-schema comes from the discussion over whether a person can be made to do things under hypnosis that are inconsistent with his self-concept or values. All investigators agree that the hypnotist can be most successful in getting the subject to do what might normally be a disapproved action if he makes the subject perceive the action as consistent with his self-image or values (cf. Berelson & Steiner, 1964, p. 124).

The same logic supports this proposition. It seems unlikely that a newly formed associative network like n Achievement could persist and influence behavior much unless it had somehow "come to terms" with the pervasive superordinate network of associations defining the self. The logic is the same as for Proposition 2 dealing with the reality construct system. The n Achievement associations must come to be experienced as related to or consistent with the ideal self-image; otherwise associations from the self-system will constantly block thoughts of achievement. The person might be thinking, for example: "I am not that kind of person; achievement means judging people in terms of how well they perform and I don't like to hurt people's feelings."

Closely allied to the self-system is a whole series of networks only half conscious (i.e., correctly labeled) summarizing the values by which the person lives which derive from his culture and social milieu. These values can also interfere if they are inconsistent with n Achievement as a newly acquired way of thinking. Therefore, it has been customary at this point in the course to introduce a value analysis of the participants' culture based on an analysis of children's stories, myths, popular religion, comparative attitude surveys, customs, etc., more or less in line with traditional, cultural anthropological practice (cf. Benedict, 1946; McClelland, 1964). For example, in America we have to work through the problem of how being achievement oriented seems to interfere with being popular or liked by others which is highly valued by Americans. In Mexico a central issue is the highly valued "male dominance" pattern reflected in the patriarchal family and in the *macho* complex (being extremely masculine). Since data shows that dominant fathers have sons with low n Achievement and authoritarian bosses do not encourage n Achievement in their top executives (Andrews, 1965), there is obviously a problem here to be worked through if n Achievement is to survive among thoughts centered on dominance. The problem is not only rationally discussed. It is acted out in role-playing sessions where Mexicans try, and often to their own surprise fail, to act like the democratic father with high standards in the classic Rosen and D'Andrade (1959) study on parental behavior which develops high n Achievement. Any technique is used which will serve to draw attention to possible conflicts between n Achievement and popular or traditional cultural values. In the end it may come to discussing parts of the *Bhagavad Gita* in India, or the *Koran* in Arab countries, that seem to oppose achievement striving or entrepreneurial behavior.

Proposition 7. The more an individual can perceive and experience the newly conceptualized motive as an improvement on prevailing cultural values, the more the motive is likely to influence his future thoughts and actions. The cultural anthropologists for years have argued how important it is to understand one's own cultural values to overcome prejudices, adopt more flexible attitudes, etc., but there is little hard evidence that doing so changes a person's behavior. What exists comes indirectly from studies that show prejudice can be decreased a little by information about ethnic groups (Berelson & Steiner, 1964, p. 517), or that repeatedly show an unconscious link between attitudes and the reference group (or subculture to which one belongs—a link which presumably can be broken more easily by full information about it, especially when coupled with role-playing new attitudes (cf. Berelson & Steiner, 1964, pp. 566 ff.).

The theoretical explanation of this presumed effect is the same as for Propositions 2 and 6. The newly learned associative complex to influence thought and action effectively must somehow be adjusted to three superordinate networks that may set off regularly interfering associations—namely, the networks associated with reality, the self, and the social reference group or subculture.

The course normally ends with each participant preparing a written document outlining his goals and life plans for the next two years. These plans may or may not include references to the achievement motive; they can be very tentative, but they are supposed to be quite specific and realistic; that is to say, they should represent moderate levels of aspiration following the practice established in learning about n Achievement of choosing the moderately risky or challenging alternative. The purpose of this document is in part to formulate for oneself the practical implications of the course before leaving it, but even more to provide a basis for the evaluation of their progress in the months after the course. For it is explained to the participants that they are to regard themselves as "in training" for the next two years, that 10–14 days is obviously too short a time to do more than conceive a new way of life: it represents the residential portion of the training only. Our role over the next two years will be to remind them every six months of the tasks they have set themselves by sending them a questionnaire to fill out which will serve to rearouse many of the issues discussed in the course and to give them information on how far they have progressed towards achieving their goals.

Proposition 8. The more an individual commits himself to achieving concrete goals in life related to the newly formed motive, the more the motive is likely to influence his future thoughts and actions.

Proposition 9. The more an individual keeps a record of his progress toward achieving goals to which he is committed, the more the newly formed motive is likely to influence his future thoughts and actions. These propositions are both related to what was called "pacing" in early studies of the psychology of work. That is, committing oneself to a specific goal and then comparing one's performance to that goal has been found to facilitate learning (cf. Kausler, 1959), though most studies of levels of aspiration have dealt with goal setting as a result rather than as a "cause" of performance. At any rate, the beneficial effect of concrete feedback on learning has been amply demonstrated by psychologists from Thorndike to Skinner. Among humans the feedback on performance is especially effective if they have high n Achievement (French, 1958), a fact which makes the relevance of our request for feedback obvious to the course participants.

The theoretical justification for these propositions is that in this way we are managing to keep the newly acquired associative network salient over the next two years. We are providing cues that will regularly rearouse it since he knows he is still part of an experimental training group which is supposed to show a certain type of behavior (Proposition 1 again). If the complex is rearoused sufficiently often back in the real world, we believe it is more likely to influence thought and action than if it is not aroused.

As described so far the course appears to be devoted almost wholly to cognitive learning. Yet this is only part of the story. The "teachers" are all clinically oriented psychologists who also try to practice whatever has been learned about the type of human relationship that most facilitates emotional learning. Both for practical and theoretical reasons this relationship is structured as warm, honest, and nonevaluative, somewhat in the manner described by Rogers (1961) and recommended by distinguished therapists from St. Ignatius[2] to Freud. That is to say, we insist that the only kind of change that can last or mean anything is what the person decides on and works out

---

[2] In his famous spiritual exercises which have played a key role in producing and sustaining personality change in the Jesuit Order, St. Ignatius states: "The director of the Exercizes ought not to urge the exercitant more to poverty or any promise than to the contrary, not to one state of life or way of

by himself, that we are there not to criticize his past behavior or direct his future choices, but to provide him with all sorts of information and emotional support that will help him in his self-confrontation. Since we recognize that self-study may be quite difficult and unsettling, we try to create an optimistic relaxed atmosphere in which the person is warmly encouraged in his efforts and given the opportunity for personal counseling if he asks for it.

Proposition 10. Changes in motives are more likely to occur in an interpersonal atmosphere in which the individual feels warmly but honestly supported and respected by others as a person capable of guiding and directing his own future behavior. Despite the widespread belief in this proposition among therapists (except for operant conditioners), one of the few studies that directly supports it has been conducted by Ends and Page (1957) who found that an objective learning-theory approach was less successful in treating chronic alcoholics than a person-oriented, client-centered approach. Rogers (1961) also summarizes other evidence that therapists who are warmer, more emphatic, and genuine are more successful in their work. Hovland et al. (1953) report that the less manipulative the intent of a communicator, the greater the tendency to accept his conclusions. There is also the direct evidence that parents of boys with high n Achievement are warmer, more encouraging and less directive (fathers only) than parents of boys with low n Achievement (Rosen & D'Andrade, 1959). We tried to model ourselves after those parents on the theory that what is associated with high n Achievement in children might be most likely to encourage its development in adulthood. This does not mean permissiveness or promiscuous reinforcement of all kinds of behavior; it also means setting high standards as the parents of the boys with high n Achievement did but having the relaxed faith that the participants can achieve them.

The theoretical justification for this proposition can take two lines: Either one argues that this degree of challenge to the self-schema produces anxiety which needs to be reduced by warm support of the person for effective learning to take place, or one interprets the warmth as a form of direct reinforcement for change following the operant-conditioning model. Perhaps both factors are operating. Certainly there is ample evidence to support the view that anxiety interferes with learning (cf. Sarason, 1960) and that reward shapes behavior (cf. Bandura & Walters, 1963, pp. 283 ff.).

living more than another . . . [while it is proper to urge people outside the Exercizes] the director of the Exercizes . . . without leaning to one side or the other, should permit the Creator to deal directly with the creature, and the creature directly with his Creator and Lord."

One other characteristic of the course leads to two further propositions. Efforts are made so far as possible to define it as an "experience apart," "an opportunity for self-study," or even a "spiritual retreat" (though the term can be used more acceptably in India than in the United States). So far as possible it is held in an isolated resort hotel or a hostel where there will be few distractions from the outside world and few other guests. This permits an atmosphere of total concentration on the objectives of the course including much informal talk outside the sessions about Ga^+, Ga^-, I^+, and other categories in the coding definition. It still comes as a surprise to us to hear these terms suddenly in an informal group of participants talking away in Spanish or Telugu. The effect of this retreat from everyday life into a special and specially labeled experience appears to be twofold: It dramatizes or increases to salience of the new associative network, and it tends to create a new reference group.

Proposition 11. Changes in motives are more likely to occur the more the setting dramatizes the importance of self-study and lifts it out of the routine of everyday life. So far as we know there is no scientific evidence to support this proposition, though again if one regards Jesuits as successful examples of personality change, the Order has frequently followed the advice of St. Ignatius to the effect that "the progress made in the Exercizes will be greater, the more the exercitant withdraws from all friends and acquaintances, and from all worldly cares." Theory supports the proposition in two respects: Removing the person from everyday routine *(a)* should decrease interfering associations (to say nothing of interfering appointments and social obligations), and *(b)* should heighten the salience of the experience by contrast with everyday life and make it harder to handle with the usual defenses ("just one more course," etc.) That is to say, the network of achievement-related associations can be more strongly and distinctly aroused in contrast to everyday life, making cognitive dissonance greater and therefore more in need of reduction by new learning. By the same token we have found that the dramatic quality of the experience cannot be sustained very long in a 12–18 hour-a-day schedule without a new routine attitude developing. Thus, we have found that a period somewhere between 6 to 14 days is optimal for this kind of "spiritual retreat." St. Ignatius sets an outside limit of 30 days, but this is when the schedule is less intensive (as ours has sometimes been), consisting of only a few hours a day over a longer period.

Proposition 12. Changes in motives are more likely to occur and persist if the new motive is a sign of membership in a new reference group. No principle of change has stronger empirical or historical support than this one. Endless studies have shown that people's opinions, attitudes, and beliefs are a function of their reference group and that different attitudes are likely to arise and be sustained primarily when the person moves into or affiliates with a new reference group (cf. Berelson & Steiner, 1964, pp. 580 ff.). Many theorists argue that the success of groups like Alcoholics Anonymous depends on the effectiveness with which the group is organized so that each person demonstrates his membership in it by "saving" another alcoholic. Political experience has demonstrated that membership in small groups like Communist or Nazi Party Cells is one of the most effective ways to sustain changed attitudes and behavior.

Our course attempts to achieve this result *(a)* by the group experience in isolation—creating the feeling of alumni who all went through it together; *(b)* by certain signs of identification with the group, particularly the language of the coding system, but also including a certificate of membership; and *(c)* by arranging where possible to have participants come from the same community so that they can form a "cell" when they return that will serve as an immediate reference group to prevent gradual undermining of the new network by other pressures.

In theoretical terms a reference group should be effective because its members constantly provide cues to each other to rearouse the associative network, because they will also reward each other for achievement-related thoughts and acts, and because this constant mutual stimulation, and reinforcement, plus the labeling of the group, will prevent assimilation of the network to bigger, older, and stronger networks (such as those associated with traditional cultural values).

In summary, we have described an influence process which may be conceived in terms of "input," "intervening," and "output" variables as in Table 1. The propositions relate variables in Column A via their effect on the intervening variables in Column B to as yet loosely specified behavior in Column C, which may be taken as evidence that "development" of n Achievement has "really" taken place. The problems involved in evaluation of effects are as great and as complicated as those involved in designing the treatment, but they cannot be spelled out here, partly for lack of space, partly because we are in an even earlier stage of examining and classifying the effects of our training one and two years later preparatory to conceptualizing more clearly what happens. It will have to suffice to point out that we plan extensive comparisons over a two-year period of the behaviors of our trained subjects compared with matched controls along the lines suggested in Column C.

What the table does is to give a brief overall view of how we conceptualize the educational or treatment process. What is particularly important is that the propositions refer to *operationally defined* and *separable* treatment variables. Thus, after having demonstrated hopefully a large effect of the total program, we can subtract a variable and see how much that decreases the impact of the course. That is to say, the course is designed so that it could go ahead perfectly reasonably with very little advanced goal setting (P1), with an objective rather than a warm personal atmosphere (P11), without the business game tying thought to action (P9), without learning to code n Achievement and write achievement-related stories (P3), without cultural value analysis (P7), or an isolated residential setting (P1, P11, P12).

TABLE 1 VARIABLES CONCEIVED AS ENTERING INTO THE MOTIVE CHANGE PROCESS

A *Input or Independent Variables*	*B* *Intervening Variables*	*C* *Output or Dependent Variables*
1. Goal setting for the person (P1, P11)	Arousal of associative network (salience)	Duration and/or extensiveness of changes in:
2. Acquisition of n Achievement associative network (P2, P3, P4, P5)	Experiencing and labeling the associative network	1. n Achievement associative network
3. Relating new network to superordinate networks reality (P2) the self (P6) cultural values (P7)	Variety of cues to which network is linked Interfering associations assimilated or bypassed by reproductive interference	2. Related actions: use of feedback, moderate risk taking, etc. 3. Innovations (job improvements) 4. Use of time and money
4. Personal goal setting (P8) 5. Knowledge of progress (P3, P4, P9)		5. Entrepreneurial success as defined by nature of job held and its rewards
6. Personal warmth and support (P10)	Positive effect associated with network	
7. Support of reference group (P11, P12)		

Note. P1, P11, etc., refer to the numbered propositions in the text.

The study units are designed in a way that they can be omitted without destroying the viability of the treatment which has never been true of other studies of the psychotherapeutic process (cf. Rogers & Dymond, 1954).

But is there any basis for thinking the program works in practice? As yet, not enough time has elapsed to enable us to collect much data on long-term changes in personality and business activity. However, we do know that businessmen can learn to write stories scoring high in n Achievement, that they retain this skill over one year or two, and that they like the course—but the same kinds of things can be said about many unevaluated management training courses. In two instances we have more objective data. Three courses were given to some 34 men from the Bombay area in early 1963. It proved possible to develop a crude but objective and reliable coding system to record whether each one had shown *unusual* entrepreneurial activity in the two years prior to the course or in the two years after the course. "Unusual" here means essentially an unusual promotion or salary raise or starting a new business venture of some kind. Of the 30 on whom information was available in 1965, 27 percent had been unusually active before the course, 67 percent after the course ($x^2 = 11.2$, $p < 0.01$). In a control group chosen at random from those who applied for the course in 1963, out of 11 on whom information has so far been obtained, 18 percent were active before 1963, 27 percent since 1963.

In a second case, four courses were given throughout 1964 to a total of 52 small businessmen from the small city of Kakinada in Andhra Pradesh, India. Of these men, 25 percent had been unusually active in the two-year period before the course, and 65 percent were unusually active immediately afterwards ($x^2 = 17.1$, $p < 0.01$). More control data and more refined measures are needed, but it looks very much as if, in India at least, we will be dealing with a spontaneous "activation" rate of only 25 percent—35 percent among entrepreneurs. Thus we have a distinct advantage over psychotherapists who are trying to demonstrate an improvement over a two-thirds spontaneous recovery rate. Our own data suggest that we will be unlikely to get an improvement or "activation" rate much above the two-thirds level commonly reported in therapy studies. That is, about one-third of the people in our courses have remained relatively unaffected. Nevertheless the two-thirds activated after the course represent a doubling of the normal rate of unusual entrepreneurial activity—no mean achievement in the light of the current pessimism among psychologists as to their ability to induce lasting personality change among adults.

One case will illustrate how the course seems to affect people in practice. A short time after participating in one of our courses in India, a 47-year-old businessman rather suddenly and dramatically decided to quit his excellent job and go into the construction business on his own in a big way. A man with some means of his own, he had had a very successful career as employee-relations manager for a large oil firm. His job involved adjusting management-employee difficulties, negotiating union contracts, etc. He was well-to-do, well thought of in his company, and admired in the community, but he was restless because he found his job increasingly boring. At the time of the course his original n Achievement score was not very high and he was thinking of retiring and living in England where his son was studying. In an interview, eight months later, he said the course had served not so much to "motivate" him but to "crystallize" a lot of ideas he had vaguely or half consciously picked up about work and achievement all through his life. It provided him with a new language (he still talked in terms of standards of excellence, blocks, moderate risk, goal anticipation, etc.), a new construct which served to organize those ideas and explain to him why he was bored with his job, despite his obvious success. He decided he wanted to be an n-Achievement-oriented person, that he would be unhappy in retirement, and that he should take a risk, quit his job, and start in business on his own. He acted on his decision and in six months had drawn plans and raised over £1,000,000 to build the tallest building in his large city to be called the "Everest Apartments." He is extremely happy in his new activity because it means selling, promoting, trying to wangle scarce materials, etc. His first building is partway up and he is planning two more.

Even a case as dramatic as this one does not prove that the course produced the effect, despite his repeated use of the constructs he had learned, but what is especially interesting about it is that he described what had happened to him in exactly the terms the theory requires. He spoke not about a new motive force but about how existing ideas had been crystallized into a new associative network, and it is this new network which *is* the new "motivating" force according to the theory.

How generalizable are the propositions? They have purposely been stated generally so that some term like "attitude" or "personality characteristic" could be substituted for the term "motive" throughout, because we believe the propositions will hold for other personality variables. In fact, most of the supporting experimental evidence cited comes from attempts to change other characteristics. Nevertheless, the propositions should hold best more narrowly for motives and especially the achievement motive. One of the biggest difficulties in the way of testing them more generally is that not nearly as much is known about other human characteristics or their specific relevance for success in a certain type of work. For example, next to nothing is known about the need for power, its relation to success, let us say, in politics or bargaining situations, and its origins and course of development in the life history of individuals. It is precisely the knowledge we have about such matters for the achievement motive that puts us in a position to shape it for limited, socially and individually desirable ends. In the future, it seems to us, research in psychotherapy ought to follow a similar course. That is to say, rather than developing "all purpose" treatments, good for any person and any purpose, it should aim to develop specific treatments or educational programs built on laboriously accumulated detailed knowledge of the characteristic to be changed. It is in this spirit that the present research program in motive acquisition has been designed and is being tested out.

REFERENCES

Allport, G. W. The ego in contemporary psychology. *Psychological Review,* 1943, **50**, 451–78.

Andrews, J. D. W. The achievement motive in two types of organizations. *Journal of Personality and Social Psychology,* 1965, in press.

Atkinson, J. W. (ed.). *Motives in fantasy action and society.* Princeton, N.J.: Van Nostrand, 1958.

Bandura, A. and Walters, R. H. *Social learning and personality development.* New York: Holt, Rinehart & Winston, 1963.

Bauer, R. A. The obstinate audience: the influence process from the point of view of social communication. *American Psychologist,* 1964, **19**, 319–29.

Benedict, Ruth. *The chrysanthemum and the sword.* Boston: Houghton Mifflin, 1946.

Berelson, B. and Steiner, G. A. *Human behavior: An inventory of scientific findings.* New York: Harcourt, Brace, 1964.

Brown, R. W. *Words and things.* Glencoe, Ill.: Free Press, 1958.

Burris, R. W. The effect of counseling on achievement motivation. Unpublished doctoral dissertation, Indiana University, 1958.

Ends, E. J. and Page, C. W. A study of three types of group psychotherapy with hospitalized male inebriates. *Quarterly Journal on Alcohol,* 1957, **18**, 263–77.

Eynsenck, H. J. The effects of psychotherapy: An evaluation. *Journal of Consulting Psychology,* 1952, **16**, 319–24.

Festinger, L. *A theory of cognitive dissonance.* New York: Harper & Row, 1957.

Frank, J. *Persuasion and healing.* Baltimore: Johns Hopkins Press, 1961.

French, E. G. Effects of the interaction of motivation and feedback on task performance. In J. W. Atkinson (ed.), *Motives in fantasy, action and society.* Princeton, N.J.: Van Nostrand, 1958, pp. 400–408.

Heckhausen, H. Eine Rehmentheorie der Motivation in zehn Thesen. *Zeitschrift fur experimentelle und angewandte Psychologie,* 1963, X/4, 604–26.

Hovland, C. I. Human learning and retention. In S. S. Stevens (ed.), *Handbook of experimental psychology.* New York: Wiley, 1951.

Hovland, C. I., Janis, I. L., and Kelley, H. H. *Communication and persuasion: Psychological studies of opinion change.* New Haven: Yale Univer. Press, 1953.

Kausler, D. H. Aspiration level as a determinant of performance. *Journal of Personality,* 1959, **27**, 346–51.

Kelley, G. A. *The psychology of personal constructs.* New York: Norton, 1955.

Korzybski, A. *Science and sanity.* Lancaster Pa.: Science Press, 1941.

McClelland, D. C. *The achieving society.* Princeton, N.J.: Van Nostrand, 1961.

McClelland, D. C. *The roots of consciousness.* Princeton, N.J.: Van Nostrand, 1964.

McClelland, D. C., Atkinson, J. W., Clark, R. A. and Lowell, E. L. *The achievement motive.* New York: Appleton-Century, 1953.

McGeoch, J. A. and Irion, A. L. *The psychology of human learning.* (2d ed.). New York: Longmans, Green, 1952.

Mierke, K. *Wille und Leistung.* Göttingen: Verlag für Psychologie, 1955.

Orne, M. On the social psychology of the psychological experiment: With particular reference to demand characteristics and their implications. *American Psychologist,* 1962, **17**, 776–83.

Roethlisberger, F. J. and Dickson, W. J. *Management and the worker.* Cambridge: Harvard University Press, 1947.

Rogers, C. R. *On becoming a person.* Boston: Houghton Mifflin, 1961.

Rogers, C. R. and Dymond, R. F. (eds.). *Psychotherapy and personality change.* Chicago: University of Chicago Press, 1954.

Rosen, B. C. and D'Andrade, R. G. The psychosocial origins of achievement motivation. *Sociometry,* 1959, **22**, 185–218.

Rosenthal, R. On the social psychology of the psychological experiment: The experinmenter's hypothesis as unintended determinant of experimental results. *American Scientist,* 1963, **51**, 268–83.

Sarason, I. Empirical findings and theoretical problems in the use of anxiety scales. *Psychological Bulletin,* 1960, **57**, 403–15.

Skinner, B. F. *Science and human behavior.* New York: Macmillan, 1953.

8. ATTITUDE AND MOTIVATION*

Helen Peak†

Wherever one starts in a discussion of behavior the same general problems demand attention. Thus a treatise on learning will consider motivation and perception and attitudes and expectations. Or a book on perception finds it necessary to raise questions about predisposing background factors like attitudes, expectations, and motives, as well as problems of learning. The fact is that there is not a separate psychology for each of these areas, a point which has been vigorously maintained by Krech (28). Nevertheless, even in a dynamic system, there are eddies in the stream of events, to use William James' apt phrase, and one must analyze and make distinctions between events even at the risk of violating reality, for the only alternative is to lose oneself in the contemplation of the wholeness of the universe. However satisfying this may be, it is not the way of science. In this particular attempt at behavior theory we have chosen to break the circle of interrelated processes by focussing first on attitudes as they are abstracted from the matrix of psychological events.

The attitude concept has had a chequered career. At one time writers such as Allport (2) and W. I. Thomas (44) regarded it as the central feature of social psychology. More recently, Doob has suggested that it has no place as a systematic construct and that its functions should be taken over eventually by more fundamental variables like habit strength, drive and effective action potential (14). But through the years attitudes, or concepts like them, have played important roles in psychological systems of all kinds under the guise of many different names such as sentiments, complexes, sets, cathected objects, affective orientations. By this time it begins to look as though we cannot get along without a construct which testifies to the fact that our feelings are organized around the objects and the concepts of those objects that occupy our psychological world.

The task for today has two parts. First, we shall describe some of our research on attitude change with the purpose of demonstrating that attitudes towards any aspect of experience—the objects or people about us, our own acts, the issues of the day—depend in some measure on the utility of such events in helping us achieve our goals. In other words, attitudes are related to motive satisfaction. But they are not only dependent on motivation. They may also play a role in determining the motivation that leads to action; i.e., they may be independent variables. This suggests that our second task must be to state how attitudes are related to action.

I. ATTITUDE STRUCTURE AND ATTITUDE CHANGE

At the beginning of our research planning[1] it seemed to me that the barrenness of much of the work on attitudes arose from the lack of a guiding theory. There is no limit to the number and kinds of attitudes people can have, since any object, real or imaginary, any person, idea, act, or policy—indeed anything that one can react to—may be the object of an attitude. So all kinds of attitudes had been studied, but little in the way of a general theory was available. Nor is there any limit to the environmental variables that might be used to change attitudes. But questions about change had often been phrased with little reference to theory: should you use emotional or intellectual appeals, direct or indirect contact with the objects of attitude, group participation or lectures? It is difficult to know just what variables are to be tested in answering questions such as these, and this was another problem. Studies were beginning to appear that pointed to still another inadequacy in the thinking about attitudes; namely, their relation to other characteristics of the individual, such as his information, his motivations, and his other attitudes. The now famous California investigation of the authoritarian personality (1) was one of those which clearly implied that if you want to predict what will happen to attitudes and related behavior, you must know at the start what the attitude is like and this means you must know a great deal about the matrix of its relations with other psychological processes. The point is obvious enough to the chemist who would not think of using the same reagent in order to alter the structure of a molecule of sodium chloride as he would use to change a protein molecule. We too need to refine our reagents and select

* In M. R. Jones (ed.), *Nebraska symposium on motivation,* 1955 (Lincoln, Neb.: University of Nebraska Press, 1955), pp. 149–59 (abridged).

†Department of Psychology, University of Michigan

"Many colleagues and students at Michigan have helped me clarify the ideas presented in this paper, but special thanks are due to Professor J. W. Atkinson, Jr. for his stimulating suggestions and for the privilege of participating in his Seminar in Motivation."

[1] Some of the work which I shall report was part of a project carried out under Air Force Contract No. AF 33(038)–26646, with Dr. Daniel Katz as principal investigator (25). In Dr. Katz' absence (academic year 1951–52) the work was under my direction.

them in the light of the structure with which we are working. Knowing this structure, it then becomes relevant to ask how you can pin-point various parts of it in order to produce change. With specific targets to aim at, the change procedure may be selected intelligently and with more hope of predictable results.

A. Definition of Attitude

The meaning of attitude structure will become clear when we have set down the hypotheses that were the starting point of the experimental work to be described. But a working definition of attitude is called for before we go any further. We are using the term very broadly to refer to a hypothetical construct which involves organization around a conceptual or perceptual nucleus *and* which has affective properties. To put this in other words, attitudes have referents; i.e., they are always attitudes towards something (friends, tobacco, or bread), and they are affective reactions to that referent. By this I mean they involve preferences: liking and disliking, favoring or not favoring and so on.[2] Much more may be and usually is involved in the structure of the attitude, but these are the essentials as we define the term. You will notice that I have made no reference to certain properties that are often included in the definition of attitude, as, for example, the learned or unlearned character of the process, the degree of conscious awareness, whether or not there is a reality or a time dimension, the complexity of the attitude and its duration. The point is this: while attitudes all share the properties of affect and organization around an object or a concept, they differ from each other on other dimensions such as those listed.

The relation of attitude to action will be considered in some detail as we describe our theory of motivation. But I want to call your attention to one point at this time. It is often said that an attitude is a "readiness for action" which seems to imply that behavior is directly determined by attitudes. We regard this at best as a greatly oversimplified statement of the relationship between attitude and action. As we shall try to make plain, an attitude should not be expected to serve as an adequate basis for predicting all behavior, since it is rarely more than one of several components of motive structure. We have, therefore, omitted "readiness-for-action" from the definition of attitude.

[2]There are many closely related terms here. "Concept" is the broadest. It is process with a referent. It stands for, refers to something. "Attitudes" are a special class of concepts with affective properties. They may or may not involve a time referent. "Sentiments" and "complexes" are like attitudes in this respect. "Expectations," on the other hand, are a kind of conceptual organization involving a time referent but they may or may not carry affect.

B. Attitude Structure

With attitude defined as a process which involves affect organized around a conceptual or perceptual nucleus, we asked ourselves this question: if attitudes are reflected in performance on scales or in behavior as some degree of favorableness or preference for an object, what lies behind the affect which is thus manifested? More specifically, what in the individual's psychological structure do we need to take into account in order to predict his attitude toward psychology or toward his best girl?

We attempted to answer this question with the simplest, most plausible assumptions we could think of in an effort to formulate and study attitude structure. The first assumption was based on the idea that an attitude toward any object or situation is related to the ends which the object serves, i.e., to its consequences. This we have called the *instrumental relation.* Thus if Susie learns that screaming gets attention and she likes attention, screaming has an instrumental relation to a valued end and acquires positive affect thereby.

Another assumption about structure is the familiar principle of *generalization* as a function of *similarity:* if two situations are seen as similar, affect attached to one is some function of the affect attached to the other. This means that if Mary's boss and her father are regarded somehow as similar, changing her attitudes towards her father should be reflected in feelings about the boss. Our idea was that if we were able to predict attitude position from knowledge about the instrumental relations and similarity relations of the object of the attitude, then attitudes could be changed by altering these structural relations. We were not assuming, by the way, that these were necessarily the only structural features involved, but we thought they were doubtless among the most important. We are now about to begin work on other aspects of structure, but that is another story.

Let's look at the studies. The first was carried out by M. J. Rosenberg (39) and was completed in the spring of 1953. This investigation has no concern with changing attitudes but took as its central problem a test of the hypothesis that the position any person takes on an attitude scale is a function of the instrumental relations he attributes to the object of the attitude. More specifically, it was assumed that the affect attached to an attitude object would be some function of: (1) the judged probability that the object leads to good or bad consequences, and (2) the intensity of the affect expected from those consequences. Rosenberg collected data from 112 subjects in two attitude areas: attitudes toward free speech for Communists and attitudes toward removing

Negro housing segregation. He made these observations on his subjects: (1) Scales measuring attitudes toward segregation and free speech were given. (2) In a later session judgments were made of the amount of satisfaction or dissatisfaction to be gained from reaching each of 35 specific goals or values. A phrase designating each goal was written on a separate card and the cards were sorted into categories ranging from plus ten to minus ten. Goals such as gaining power over people, every one being assured a good standard of living, America having prestige in other countries, making one's own decisions, all people having equal rights, giving expression to feelings of anger or hostility, being good-looking, were included. (3) Judgements were also made of the probability that free speech for Communists (or segregation as a separate task) would lead to or block the attainment of each of the 35 goals. This time the subjects sorted each card into an instrumentality category, numbered from minus five (free speech will interfere) to plus five (will aid attainment of goal.)

Rosenberg was able to make highly significant predictions to attitude position from a number of different indices based on a combination of judgments of the satisfaction to be derived from reaching the various goals and the instrumental. relation of the attitude issue to these goals. Figure 1 provides a simplified example of one method of calculating an index from which these predictions were made.[3] The satisfaction judgment of each goal is multiplied by the corresponding instrumental judgment. Then these products are added algebraically to obtain an index of affective loading. Thus, assume that reduction in property values is seen as having a satisfaction score of minus six. The probability that removing segregation will reduce values is judged as 0.5. This relationship thus contributes minus 3.0 to the total affect load (-6×0.5).

C. Attitude Change

It follows from these findings that we should be able to alter attitude by way of the instrumentality structure in one of two ways: either by changing the perception of the probability that Negro segregation leads to goals with various satisfaction potentials, or by changing the satisfaction attached to any goal that is already seen as related to segregation. Earl R. Carlson (10) carried out a study in which he tested the prediction that attitude change would follow an alteration in instrumentality relations. He also predicted that this change would generalize to similar attitude objects. Again attitudes toward Negro housing segregation were studied. In an initial session Carlson made these observations: (1) He measured attitudes towards removing segregation for Negroes, for Jews, for Mexicans, and toward having Negroes as officers in charge of white enlisted men, Jews as officers, Mexicans as officers. These were given as separate scales. (2) Measures were made of the amount of satisfaction expected from the attainment of specified goals, which were sorted into categories in much the same fashion as in the Rosenberg experiment. (3) An instrumentality sort was made to determine the perceived probability that removing Negroes segregation would lead to each of these goals.

Ten days later another person administered the change procedure. The students were assigned, as part of their class work, participation in an experiment which was announced as an investigation of the relative objectivity of men and women. It was explained that objectivity would be reflected in their ability to argue on any side of a question regardless of their own points of view. The subjects were then given statements of four goals or values known to be regarded as important. These included such goals as maintaining property values and developing greater respect for this country on the part of other nations. The subjects were asked to write down reasons why abolishing Negro segregation would lead to each of these goals. Later a promised feedback of experimental results was given to them, along with a summary of reasons in favor of removing Negro segregation. After five weeks had elapsed attitude measures, measures of goal satisfaction, and of instrumentality were repeated. In general, attitudes changed significantly in the direction of the influence attempt and this change was correlated with alteration in the perception of instrumentality but not with change in judgments of goal satisfaction. Generalization of changed attitude was shown to occur in three related situations: Negroes serving as officers, Jews as officers, and abolishing Jewish segregation. There was no generalized change in attitudes towards Mexicans. We were not able in this experiment to demonstrate the relation of generalization to *degree* of similarity.

A third study represents the attempt to produce attitude change by attacking the intensity of the motivational state and thus the satisfaction to be gained from the attainment of related goals. The predictions were these. If an object or situation is seen as positively instrumental to a valued end, increasing the satisfaction of attaining that end by added motivation will increase the favorableness of

[3] Somewhat similar methods of combining indices of satisfaction and probability appear to have been employed more or less independently by a considerable number of people. Theorists concerned with economic utility (15), Coombs (11), W. Edwards (15), Escalona (16), Rotter (40), and Woodruff (47), as well as our own group are among those who have used similar operations.

FIGURE 1

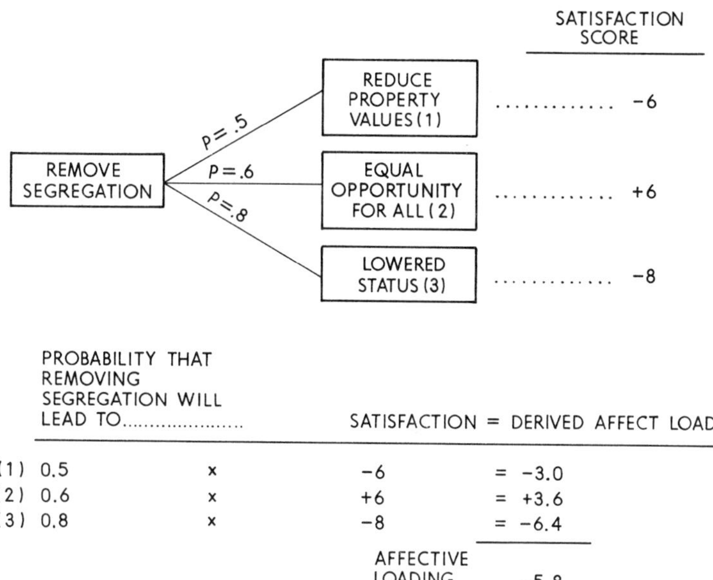

the attitude toward the instrumental object. If the object is seen as interfering with attaining the end, altering the value of the goal will make the attitude toward the instrumental object more negative. If the object is seen as having no relation to the goal, altering the value of the goal will not change the attitude. Fifteen different statements about procedures, techniques, and practices in the academic situation, such as taking books out of the library without signing up, having discussions, grading on the curve, having small classes, and so on, were used as attitude "objects." Attitudes toward these situations were measured once on a normal class day and at another time, immediately following a quiz. It was assumed on the basis of McClelland, Atkinson, Clark and Lowell's (33) results that need to achieve would be greater on the quiz day than on the normal class day. At the same time, measures were made of the subjects' perceptions of the probability that each of these 15 situations would lead to making good grades. That is, their instrumental value was measured.

In a preliminary analysis, predictions appear to be working out. Under increased arousal, people do more often increase their positive feelings about situations which are seen as leading to good grades. They become more negative about those which interfere with attaining this end. And they show no consistent direction of change where there is no instrumental relation.

It seems clear then that procedures which take as their target some specific aspect of structure can produce attitude change and that regularities can be more readily discovered when structural features of the attitude, such as its instrumental relations, are taken into account. Indeed, the effects on attitudes of aroused need to achieve good grades would have been unpredictable without information regarding the utility of each procedure in making grades.

In summary, the first point to be made about the connection of attitude and motivation is this: attitudes as dependent variables are a function of: (1) the instrumentality of their referent objects or situations for aiding or interfering with goal attainment, and (2) the satisfaction derived from reaching goals, and this in turn depends on the level of a motive state. It should be noted for later reference that such a statement about the source of attitude and attitude change is relevant to many important psychological problems. Attitude-like organizations may be built around all sorts of objects and situations, such as acts leading to goals, the people who reward and punish us, the self-concept, instrumental objects and policies of all kinds. These will suffer change in their affect loadings through their relation to valued goals and as a result of change in motive states. We shall have occasion to return to this point in the discussion of direction as a characteristic of motivated behavior.

But to say that attitudes are altered by motivational processes does not indicate anything about the way in which attitudes are related to action. We turn now to consider the problem from this angle. This will require spelling out in some detail a concept of the nature of motivation, where I hope that it will become clear that attitudes may be terms in a disparity relation which constitutes the fundamental structure of a motive. Motive structures do not always have attitude components but they often do.

REFERENCES

1. Adoring, T. W., Frenkel-Brunswick, E., Levinson, D. J., and Sanford, R. N. *The authoritarian personality.* New York: Harper Bros., 1950.
2. Allport, G. *Attitudes.* In *Handbook of social psychology.* C. Murchison (ed.), Worcester, Mass.: Clark University Press, 1936.
3. Asch, S. E. *Social psychology.* New York: Prentice-Hall, 1952.
4. Atkinson, J. W. Exploration using imaginative thought to assess the strength of human motives. In Marshall R. Jones (ed.). *Nebraska symposium on motivation, 1954,* Lincoln: University of Nebraska Press, 1954.
5. Bergmann, G. Theoretical psychology. In C. P. Stone (ed.), *Annual Review of Psychology,* 1953. Vol. 4. Stanford, 1953.
6. Bridgman, P. W. *The logic of modern physics.* New York: Macmillan Co., 1932.
7. Brown, J. S. and Farber, I. E. Emotions conceptualized as intervening variables—with suggestions toward a theory of frustration. *Psychological Bulletin,* 1951, **48**, 465–96.
8. Brownfain, J. J. Stability of the self concept as a dimension of personality, *Journal of Abnormal and Social Psychology,* 1952, **47**, 597–606.
9. Cannon, W. B. *The wisdom of the body.* New York: W. W. Norton & Co., 1932.
10. Carlson, E. R. Attitude change through modification of attitude structure. Unpublished Ph.D. dissertation, University of Michigan, 1953.
11. Coombs, C. H. and Beardslee, D.C. On decision making uncertainty. In R. M. Thrall, C. H. Coombs, and R. L. Davis (eds.), *Decision processes.* New York: John Wiley & Sons, 1954, pp. 255–86.
12. deCharms, R., Morrison, H. W., Reitman, W., and McClelland, D. C. Behavioral correlates of directly and indirectly measured achievement motivation. In D. C. McClelland (ed.), *Studies in motivation.* New York: Appleton-Century-Crofts, 1955.
13. Dollard, J. and Miller, N. E. *Personality and psychotherapy.* New York: McGraw-Hill, 1950.
14. Doob, L. W. The behavior of attitudes. *Psychological Review,* 1947, 54, 135–56.
15. Edwards, W. The theory of decision making. *Psychological Bulletin,* 1954, **51**, 380–417.
16. Escalona, S. K. The effect of success and failure on the level of aspiration and behavior in manic-depressive psychoses. *University of Iowa Studies in Child Welfare,* 1940, **16**, No. 3, 199–302.
17. Festinger, L., et al. *Theory and experiment in social communication.* Research Center for Group Dynamics, Institute for Social Research, University of Michigan, 1950.
18. Festinger, L. Motivation leading to social behavior. In *Nebraska symposium on motivation,* 1954, Marshall R. Jones (ed.). Lincoln: University of Nebraska Press, 1954.
19. French, J. R. P., Jr. Organized and unorganized groups under fear and frustration. Authority and Frustration: Studies in Topological and Vector Psychology, *University of Iowa Studies in Child Welfare,* 1944, **20**, 231–307.
20. Freud, S. *Beyond the pleasure principle,* London: Hogarth Press, 1922.
21. Harlow, H. F. Motivation as a factor in new responses. In *Current theory and research in motivation: A symposium.* Lincoln: University of Nebraska Press, 1953.
22. Hebb, D. O. *Organization of behavior.* New York: John Wiley & Sons, 1949.
23. Helson, H. Adaptation level as a basis for a quantitative theory of frames of reference. *Psychological Review,* 1948, **55**, 297–313.
24. Hull, C. L., Livingston, J. R., Rouse, R. O., and Barker, A. N. True, sham and esophageal feeding as reinforcements. *Journal of Comparative and Physiological Psychology,* 1951, **44**, 236–45.
25. Katz, Daniel. *Attitude change project.* Final Report of Research Conducted on AF Project 504–036–0010, Contract AF 33 (038)–26646, June 30, 1953.
26. Klein, G. S. Need and regulation. In Marshall R. Jones (ed.), *Nebraska symposium on motivation,* 1954. Lincoln: University of Nebraska Press, 1954.
27. Krech, D. and Crutchfield, R. S. *Theories and problems of social psychology.* New York: McGraw-Hill, 1946.
28. Krech, D. Notes toward a psychological theory. *Journal of Personality,* 1949, **18**, 66–87.
29. Lambert, W. W., Solomon, R. L., and Watson, P. D. Reinforcement and extinction as factors in size estimation. *Journal of Experimental Psychology,* 1949, **37**, 637–41.
30. Lewin, K. *Field theory in social science.* New York: Harper & Bros., 1951.
31. Maier, N. R. F. *Frustration.* New York: McGraw-Hill, 1949.
32. Matire, J. G. Relationships between the self concept and differences in the strength and generality of achievement motivation. Unpublished Ph.D. Dissertation, University of Michigan, 1953.
33. McClelland, D. C., Atkinson, J. W., Clark, R. A., and Lowell, E. L. *The achievement motive.* New York: Appleton-Century-Crofts, 1953.
34. Meehl, P. and McCorquodale, K. On a distinction between hypothetical constructs and intervening variables. *Psychological Review,* 1948, **55**, 95–107.
35. Murphy, G. *Personality.* New York: Harper & Bros., 1947.
36. Nissen, H. W. The nature of the drive as innate determinant of behavioral organization. In Marshall R.

Jones (ed.), *Nebraska symposium on motivation*, 1954. Lincoln: University of Nebraska Press, 1954.

37. Postman, L. Experimental analysis of the motivational factors in perception. In *Current theory and research in motivation: A symposium.* Lincoln: University of Nebraska Press, 1953.
38. Pratt, Cornelia. The effect of secondary reward value on perception. Honors Thesis, Connecticut College, 1949.
39. Rosenberg, M. J. A value theory of attitude. Unpublished Ph.D. Dissertation, University of Michigan, 1953.
40. Rotter, J. E. *Social learning and personality.* New York: Prentice-Hall, 1954.
41. Schrödinger, E. *What is life?* New York: Macmillan Co., 1946.
42. Shafer, R. and Murphy, G. The role of autism in a visual figure-ground relationship. *Journal of Experimental Psychology,* 1943, **32**, 335–43.
43. Sheffield, F. D. and Rody, T. B. Reward value of a non-nutritive sweet taste. *Journal of Comparative and Physiological Psychology,* 1950, **43**, 471–81.
44. Thomas, W. I. and Znaniecki, F. *The Polish peasant in Europe and America.* Vol. I. Chicago: University of Chicago Press, 1918.
45. Tolman, E. C., Hall, C. S., and Bretnall, L. P. A disproof of the law of effect and a substitution of the laws of emphasis, motivation and disruption. *Journal of Experimental Psychology,* 1932, **15**, 601–14.
46. Wiener, N. *Cybernetics.* New York: John Wiley & Sons, 1948.
47. Woodruff, A. D. The concept value theory of human behavior. *Journal of General Psychology,* 1949, **40**, 141–54.
48. Young, P. T. *Motivation of behavior.* New York: John Wiley & Sons, 1936.
49. Young, P. T. Food-seeking drive, affective process and learning. *Psychological Review,* 1949, **56**, 98–121.

Section C

COGNITIVE AND PERCEPTUAL PROCESSES

Attitude and motive constructs obviously refer to organismic or internal mediational processes as determinants of behavior. Cognitive and perceptual formulations are also quite frankly mediational. The underlying assumption is that overt behavior cannot be traced directly back to an environmental event. Rather, according to mediational models, the environmental event is somehow transformed into an implicit cue (a cognition, a belief, a perception) which controls behavior. Most cognitive theorists do not maintain that their hypothetical mediational processes are totally independent of environmental variables, but their formulations only rarely contain postulates which specify relationships between the hypothetical mediating process and the external environment.

We begin this section with a critical review of cognitive dissonance phenomena by Tedeschi, Schlenker, and Bonoma. Festinger's cognitive dissonance theory, one of a family of cognitive consistency theories, contains two basic postulates. The first is that two contradicting beliefs or cognitions will result in a state of dissonance. The second is that dissonance is a noxious or unpleasant state and, once aroused, will lead to behavior which is instrumental in reducing the dissonance. As Tedeschi et al. point out, cognitive dissonance theory has generated a great deal of research but it has also become the focal point of a great deal of skepticism. A basic criticism is that hypotheses presumably derived from the theory have not been consistently supported. Perhaps more fundamentally, the theory does not clearly specify the environmental circumstances under which dissonance phenomena are likely to be observed nor does it indicate how cognitions produce physiological tension (another internal mechanism). Nevertheless, dissonance phenomena can be reliably produced under certain circumstances, and Tedeschi et al. offer an impression-management hypothesis to account for it. They maintain that an individual must be perceived by others to be "truly" inconsistent in word and deeds before dissonance phenomena are manifested. An individual will be perceived by himself and others as truly inconsistent when the beliefs espoused by him are both contradictory and not under the obvious control of environmental variables. Under those circumstances, others are likely to punish him (by labeling him as psychologically unstable, unfit for leadership, stupid or simply inconsistent!), and he will, therefore, engage in instrumental, face-restoring behaviors.

In the next selection on perception, Zalkind and Costello discuss some of the implications of theory and research in interpersonal perception. Studies of illusions, hallucinations, and similar phenomena have indicated that the way in which we perceive environmental events is not solely dependent upon the characteristics of those events but upon mediating factors in the perceiver as well. Thus we say that the perceived world is not necessarily isomorphic with the real world, and this may be especially true when the stimulus events are other persons. Zalkind and Costello go on to describe some factors which influence one's perception of others and warn the administrator to avoid premature and categorical judgments in forming impressions of others.

9. PERSPECTIVE

(Writer Unknown)

"Dear Mother and Dad:

Since I left for college I have been remiss in writing and I am sorry for my thoughtlessness in not having written before. I will bring you up to date now, but before you read on, please sit down. You are not to read any further unless you are sitting down. Okay?

Well, then, I am getting along pretty well now. The skull fracture and the concussion I got when I jumped out of the window of my dormitory when it caught on fire shortly after my arrival here is pretty well healed now. I only spent two weeks in the hospital and now I can see almost normally and only get those sick headaches once a day. Fortunately, the fire in the dormitory, and my jump, was witnessed by an attendant at the gas station near the dorm, and he was the one who called the Fire Department and the ambulance. He also visited me in the hospital and since I had nowhere to live because of the burnt-out dormitory, he was kind enough to invite me to share his apartment with him. It's really a basement room, but it's kind of cute. He is a very fine boy and we have fallen deeply in love and are planning to get married. We haven't got the exact date yet, but it will be before my pregnancy begins to show.

Yes, Mother and Dad, I am pregnant. I know how much you are looking forward to being grandparents and I know you will welcome the baby and give it the same love and devotion and tender care you gave me when I was a child. The reason for the delay in our marriage is that my boy friend has a minor infection which prevents us from passing our premarital blood tests and I carelessly caught it from him.

I know that you will welcome him into our family with open arms. He is kind and, although not well educated, he is ambitious. Although he is of a different race and religion than ours, I know your often-expressed tolerence will not permit you to be bothered by that.

Now that I have brought you up to date, I want to tell you that there was no dormitory fire, I did not have a concussion or skull fracture, I was not in the hospital, I am not pregnant, I am not engaged, I am not infected, and there is no boy friend in my life. However, I am getting a D in History and F in Science and I want you to see those marks in their proper perspective.

Your loving daughter,
Susie."

10. COGNITIVE DISSONANCE: PRIVATE RATIOCINATION OR PUBLIC SPECTACLE?*

James T. Tedeschi, Barry R. Schlenker, and Thomas V. Bonoma†

In an 1877 volume of *Popular Science Monthly*, Charles Sanders Peirce wrote a powerful essay on "The Fixation of Belief," which was important not only as a milestone in the history of philosophy, and particularly the American school of pragmatism, but also in a clearly traceable way to the subsequent psychological thought of William James, John Dewey, Edward Tolman, and Leon Festinger. Peirce argued that men are motivated to attain states of belief and to avoid states of doubt. Doubt was considered to be an uncomfortable state, an irritant, from which men sought relief. When a man is in a state of belief, the cognitive basis for habit exists, since, given the proper circumstances, he will know how to act. But when a man is in a state of doubt, the basis for action does not exist. For Peirce, the sole object of individual inquiry was the settlement of doubtful opinions, to attain beliefs, and thus restore a comfortable state of mind. He stated: "as soon as a firm belief is reached we are entirely satisfied, whether the belief be true or false [reprinted in Fisch, 1951, p. 60]." This core idea has been represented in one form or another in the most important competing theories of contemporary social psychology.

It is not much of a step to extend Peirce's thesis to the conditions that cause doubt. For example, when a person is publicly caught in a contradiction of thought, doubt must be created in him about which element of the contradiction is true and which is false (or at least which is most useful). The person who is aware that he holds contradictory beliefs should experience an uncomfortable state and be motivated to resolve doubt and reestablish a noncontradictory belief system. This need for cognitive balance is at the base of the cognitive consistency theories in social psychology. Yet the evidence shows that sometimes a person demonstrates a need for cognitive consistency, but at other times obvious contradictions are not disconcerting at all. Social scientists have offered their theoretical insights to the problem, and many ingenious experiments have been carried out. No single theory proffered to date, however, seems capable of explaining all of the conditions under which cognitive or behavioral contradictions are "irritating" to a person. The present article offers a critical review of some of the major theoretical arguments and empirical results concerning the phenomenon of cognitive dissonance and then proffers a single integrating hypothesis that appears to enable a coherent reorganization of the existing data.

THEORETICAL BACKGROUND

Several varieties of cognitive consistency theory exist, including balance theory (Heider, 1946), congruity theory (Osgood & Tannenbaum, 1955), psycho-logic (Abelson & Rosenberg, 1958), and cognitive dissonance theory (Festinger, 1957). These theories have in common the treatment of the individual as an internally active processor of information who sorts through and modifies a multitude of cognitive elements in an attempt to achieve some type of cognitive coherence. Rather than attempt to deal with each type of consistency theory separately, or run the risk of inaccurate observations inherent in any blanket generalities, the present article focuses on the theoretical and assumptional ramifications of dissonance theory as opposed to other consistency formulations. Except in detail, however, the criticisms offered generate difficulties for most, if not all, of the consistency theories, regardless of their origin or specialized focus.

Festinger's (1957) theory of cognitive dissonance has probably generated more research than any other theory in social psychology and is to some extent representative of the flavor of the others. According to Festinger, any two cognitions (beliefs, opinions, attitudes, or ideas) are said to be dissonant if the "obverse" of one follows from the other. Once dissonance between cognitive elements has been uncovered or aroused, its presence is presumed to be noxious to the individual, and motivating tensions are created causing actions to be taken that reduce the dissonance.

Among the strongest claims for dissonance theory are: *(a)* it allows the prediction of nonobvious effects over a wide range of seemingly unrelated situations, and *(b)* similar results cannot be deduced from other theoretical schemes (Aronson, 1968; McGuire,

---

* *American Psychologist*, Vol. 26 (1971), pp. 685–95.

The present investigation was supported in part by Grant No. GS-27059 from the National Science Foundation to the senior author, by a National Science Foundation Predoctoral Fellowship to the second author, and by Grant No. ACDA-0331 from the United States Arms Control and Disarmament Agency (National Research Council) to the third author.

† State University of New York at Albany

1966). The prediction of intuitively nonobvious results is best illustrated by the now classic and often quoted experiment performed by Festinger and Carlsmith (1959). Subjects spent an hour participating in several very dull and boring tasks and then were offered either $1 or $20 to tell an alleged subject who apparently was waiting to participate in the experiment that the task was actually quite interesting. Later, when the subjects were asked their own "true" attitude about the experimental tasks, it was found that subjects who were paid the least said they found the experimental tasks more interesting. This finding had tremendous impact on social psychology because it contraverted predictions drawn from traditional learning theory. According to the law of effect, any response followed by reinforcement should be strengthened. Favorability ratings gathered from subjects at the experiment's conclusion should have been a direct and positive function of the magnitude of incentive offered for emitting the highly positive counterattitudinal statement regarding the task. Festinger and Carlsmith explained the obtained inverse relationship between incentive magnitude and favorability ratings by the theory of cognitive dissonance. The highest paid subjects had sufficient justification for lying about the task. "I didn't like the task" and "I was paid a lot of money for lying" are perfectly consonant cognitions and no dissonance should be generated. In the small-incentive conditions, however, insufficient justification was provided for lying. The cognitive elements "I disliked the task" and "I had little monetary reason to lie" are dissonant. To resolve the dissonance, subjects in the small-incentive conditions enhanced their post-experimental "true" opinion about the task and restored cognitive consistency: "I didn't really lie, because the task was actually enjoyable."

Behavior is relevant to dissonance only insofar as it puts the organism in relation to contradictory information or as it fosters readjustment of "out-of-tune" cognitions. Collins (1968) and Bem (1967) have been critical of dissonance theory on the grounds that it is only concerned with such cognitive relations. Collins has viewed dissonance not in terms of cognitive tensions that result from the simultaneous occurrence of contradictory attitudes or beliefs but in terms of attitudes that predispose the individual to make incompatible responses to particular stimulus situations. Collins claims that his behavioristic interpretation of dissonance as response conflict brings the phenomena back under the more inclusive theoretical rubric of traditional individual learning theory. The "connections" between cognitions and behaviors, however, are not specified by Collins, and little help can be gained from the empirical literature. For example, Wicker (1969), after reviewing over 50 studies, concluded that attitudes seldom are predictors of behavior.

A more radically behavioristic interpretation of the dissonance phenomena has been advanced by Bem (1967), who holds that what has been labeled dissonance is actually the consequence of the individual's own inferences about the causes of his own behavior. When the individual emits a behavior that appears to him to be caused by external pressures ("manded" behavior), both the individual and objective observers should attribute the behavior to the external pressures and not to any true beliefs or feelings of the actor. When the actor can find no obvious external cause for his behavior ("tacted" behavior), however, it must be attributed to internal causes in the form of true beliefs of the individual. A small reward may cause more liking for a boring task than a large reward because the individual infers that since he had little external reason for saying he liked the task, he must have intrinsic liking for the task. Though couched in the behavioristic language developed by Skinner (1957), the inference process postulated by Bem appears to be just as cognitive as dissonance theory. No mechanism is postulated by Bem to account for how the person decides whether a particular action is tacted or manded or what criteria are used to make that decision. For example, why would a $1 reward in the Festinger and Carlsmith (1959) study constitute an insufficient environmental "cause" of behavior, while $20 in reward allows the behavior to be attributed to external factors? Would $5 lead to attributions of tact or mand? This kind of questioning indicates that cognitive variables have been avoided only temporarily by Bem.

In contrast to the above alternatives to the dissonance explanation, a significant number of investigators have preferred to ascribe dissonance effects to various experimental artifacts and to maintain that when such artifactual variables are identified and controlled, attitude change is found to be a direct function of amount of reward as predicted by traditional reinforcement or incentive theory (cf. Elms, 1969). Thus, the offer of high versus low rewards for counterattitudinal behaviors has been criticized as differentially engendering guilt (Janis & Gilmore, 1965), suspicion and incredulity (Chapanis & Chapanis, 1964), or evaluation apprehension (Rosenberg, 1965, 1969) among the high-dissonance (low reward) subjects only. The net effect of any of these selective biases in experimental treatments would be less attitude change in the high-incentive than low-incentive groups.

For a number of reasons, dissonance theory has been the focus of skepticism and, in a few cases, outright attack (cf. Elms, 1969). The underlying motivation in cognitive dissonance theory is some type of physiological or psychological tension that is both unpleasant and ubiquitous. Once a particular threshold of tension is reached, the individual holding unbalanced or dissonant cognitions will carry out actions to reduce the inconsistency, thereby relieving the basis for the underlying unpleasant tension. Yet, most people seem to be able to tolerate a great deal of logical inconsistency among their behaviors and beliefs. Strong need for consistency would imply the development of coherent ideologies to integrate cognitive elements. But evidence indicates that only a few, if any, individuals reveal a high integration of their belief systems (cf. Campbell, Converse, Miller, & Stokes, 1960; Katz, 1968). Rosenberg and Abelson (1960) have obtained results which indicate that imbalanced relationships between cognitive elements are actually preferred to balanced relationships under conditions in which the latter precluded maximizing expected gains or minimizing expected losses (i.e., "minimaxing" outcomes); results supported balance theories only when minimaxing was compatible with choosing balanced structures.

If the tension aroused by dissonance is unpleasant, then individuals might be expected to selectively avoid tension-increasing information. Individuals should avoid information that would refute their beliefs and that would reflect unfavorably on prior decisions. A review of the evidence by Freedman and Sears (1965) indicates that people neither avoid information that is favorable to unchosen alternatives nor overexpose themselves to materials supporting prior decisions. Mills, Aronson, and Robinson (1959) have suggested that one reason that people frequently do not avoid dissonant information is that it often has value for them.

Regardless of the rather gelatinous and unparsimonious state of dissonance theory's assumptional base, and the stubborn refusal of the theoretical formulation to yield to the deductive generation of clear hypotheses, it is clear that, at least in the most simple cases, dissonance phenomena can be produced with some reliability. A problem faced by any would-be critic, however, is that cognitive dissonance theory does not state clearly the conditions under which the phenomena in question will be manifested; rather, it seems much more suitable for postdiction than prediction. Under the circumstances, it is common for post hoc explanations and theoretically ungrounded hypotheses to be offered for successful *or* unsuccessful demonstrations of the dissonance effect. One example of the upshot of such theoretical ambiguity is the inability of Collins and his associates (cf. Collins, Ashmore, Hornbeck, & Whitney, 1970) to replicate the classic Festinger and Carlsmith (1959) investigation prior to studying further conditions for the occurrence of the phenomenon. After numerous attempts in their Sisyphean effort, Collins et al. report, "Like the biologist unable to grow his culture in the laboratory, we could not continue our investigation(s) without an experimental paradigm that would reliably produce the dissonance-predicted negative relationship [p. 11]" (between incentive magnitude and attitude change). This somewhat unsightly state of affairs flows largely from the difficulty of determining precisely what "follows from" means in relation to two cognitions. Although there has been some attempt to delineate more precisely what the "core" of dissonance theory entails, the situation remains sufficiently ambiguous that Aronson (1968) suggests that predictions can be made, but "If you want to be sure, ask Leon [p. 8]."[1] Impatient of receiving theoretical clarification, the reaction has been the attempt to empirically determine the conditions under which dissonance effects occur.

CONDITIONS UNDER WHICH DISSONANCE PHENOMENA ARE DEMONSTRATED

Because only the behavioral manifestations of the underlying dissonance are directly observable, situations must be constructed in which the experimenter believes he can make a strong inference (Platt, 1964) that contradictory beliefs or attitudes have been induced in most of his subjects. After being asked to perform tasks that are obviously boring or noxious, subjects are subtly manipulated to make statements that the task was actually enjoyable, interesting, and important. An alternative paradigm is to pretest the subjects in order to ascertain their true or private attitudes and then induce subjects to engage in counterattitudinal behaviors. Posttests should reveal some change from the pretested true attitudes if dissonance was produced. Given these basic paradigms, certain conditions for the occurrence of dissonance have been isolated.

An important condition for producing dissonance effects is the degree of *volition* (Brehm & Cohen, 1962; Linder, Cooper, & Jones, 1967) or the degree of freedom (Bem, 1967; Steiner, 1970) the individual feels he has had in making the counterattitudinal statements. Studies have consistently found that only when volition or tacted behaviors are involved are dissonance predictions confirmed. Thus, if the counterattitudinal behavior is experienced as manded (i.e., the result of external pressures), no dissonance effects are found.

A condition closely related to volition is the con-

[1] The satirical comment was made to demonstrate the ambiguity of the theoretical formulation.

cept of commitment. Commitment has been considered to be operative when constraints exist that prevent an individual from changing particular behaviors (Kiesler, 1968) and, hence, demonstrate the degree of responsibility that he will take for these behaviors, or how persistently he expresses them, or how important they are to him. Commitment therefore consists of behaviors that enhance the individual's or other persons' attributions of self-volition for the counterattitudinal behaviors, consequently facilitating dissonance phenomena. Commitment to the counterattitudinal behaviors has been manipulated experimentally by asking subjects to make identifiable videotaped recordings rather than write anonymous essays (Carlsmith, Collins, & Helmreich, 1966), by not allowing subjects to elaborate to their audience the reasons for making counterattitudinal and generally unpopular statements (Helmreich & Collins, 1968), or by constraining subjects to continue for a long period of time in an undesirable group (Kiesler & Corbin, 1965). As with the effects of tacted behaviors, results confirmed dissonance theory, when commitment was strong, and incentive theory, when commitment was nonexistent or weak.

Jones and Davis (1965) and Kelley (1967) have developed attribution theories which state that behaviors that violate others' expectations allow observers to infer that the behaviors were tacted. In this context it is interesting that Aronson (1968) has stated that the most crucial factor in producing dissonance is the individual's firm expectation that a given behavior is inappropriate in a given situation. The more inappropriate a person perceives his own behavior, the more dissonance he should presumably experience. A person may engage in inappropriate behaviors despite the costs involved because of the importance of those behaviors to his self-concept (Aronson, 1968; Zimbardo & Ebbesen, 1969). The more relevant the actor's counterattitudinal behavior to his enduring self-concept, the more resistant to external constraints the actor should perceive himself to be. Hence, ego-relevant behaviors are more likely to be perceived as tacted. It is not clear, therefore, that inappropriateness of the counterattitudinal behaviors can be accepted as a clearly separate condition for the arousal of dissonance. The critical factor may be the person's perceived freedom to act.

There is evidence to suggest that some types of personalities display greater amounts of dissonance than do others. Persons who score high on Christie and Geis's (1970) measure of Machiavellianism display greater dissonance effects than persons who score low on the measure (Steiner & Spaulding, 1966). Chronic anxiety has also been related to "need for balance." Individuals who are classified as highly anxious demonstrate behavior in accord with dissonance predictions, while those who are classified as low in anxiety tend to behave according to incentive theory predictions (Steiner & Rogers, 1963). Similarly, Rosenberg (1969) has shown that persons who score high on a measure of social desirability display more dissonance than individuals who score low in need for social approval. Rosenberg interprets these latter findings in terms of his evaluation apprehension hypothesis.

The present authors believe that they observe some degree of commonality among the diverse conditions that have been proffered to limit and explicate dissonance theory. These common characteristics have been hinted at in the above discussion, but now will be made more explicit. The theory to follow will elaborate these commonalities and hopefully provide a basis to supplant dissonance theory. Volition, commitment, importance or relevance of the involved behaviors, and self-concept-related behaviors all affect the degree to which the individual can be held responsible by observers for his actions. Under all of these conditions, observers can and do gain information as to the enduring response predispositions of the actor since his actions can be attributed to internal causes rather than situational demands (cf. Jones & Davis, 1965; Kelley, 1967). These attributed dispositions then can be used by observers as a basis for their own behaviors in subsequent interactions with the actor. The personality variables of Machiavellianism and chronic anxiety, as well as situationally aroused evaluation apprehension, all relate to the degree to which the actor might be concerned about the observer's attributions. Before explicating the impression management theory, it is necessary to raise some further questions about dissonance theory.

SOME FURTHER QUESTIONS ABOUT DISSONANCE THEORY

In the last analysis, cognitive dissonance theory is and remains a theory of human motivation. However, the mechanism by which the organism is aroused to action in order to reduce dissonance remains unexplicated by either Festinger or his followers (cf. Abelson & Rosenberg, 1958; Aronson, 1968; Festinger, 1957), although the underlying motivating force apparently generates "tension." Given this rather vague assumptional statement, the origins of such tension are unclear, although two possible alternatives present themselves: *(a)* either dissonance theory must assume that a person is genetically endowed with some type of mysterious mechanism, like a gyroscope, that works in the fashion of a computing device automatically activated by any illogically formed cognition pair; or *(b)* the assumption must be made that there is a pervasive socially acquired drive, perhaps akin to Skinner's (1957) class of generalized secondary reinforcers, that functions to attach ubiquitous unpleasant consequences to psychologically inconsistent cognitions and pleasant consequences to psychologically consistent cognition pairs. In either case, there can be only certain conditions under which the genetically or socially governed mechanism can be activated, and sometimes it rather inexplicably exerts more energy in restoring the logical relations between cognitive elements than at other times. This type of implausible basis for dissonance effects is probably the weakest link in the theory. A more adequate theory would explain why inconsistency is motivationally activating.

Most of the discovered conditions for demonstrating dissonance effects have included the person's perception that his counterattitudinal behaviors are tacted or engaged in freely. But why should perceived freedom have this effect? Cognitive dissonance theory has not produced a satisfactory answer to this question. Perhaps it should be noted parenthetically that Brehm's (1966) concept of psychological reactance is related closely to dissonance theory and assumes that people resist manipulation by others by emitting boomerang-type behaviors, doing the opposite of that which the manipulator would prefer. The concept of reactance is based on the assumption of a need for freedom in the individual. This common assumption of dissonance and reactance theories suggests the possibility of including both phenomena within the same theory, a point we will come back to later.

There is a distinct tendency by dissonance theorists to take a limited and somewhat dehumanizing view of man. The subject in an experiment is viewed as a passive target of the clever manipulations performed by the experimenter. In a sense, given that his predictions are confirmed, the psychologist knows what the subject is going to do before the subject does because the experimental manipulations are carried out to achieve that very result. And, of course, the subject does not know what the experimenter knows. The experimenter, therefore, must feel superior to his subject, and in many ways these attitudes and postures by the experimenter get communicated and must help make the subject feel inferior (cf. Rosenberg, 1969). Once the manipulation "takes," and dissonance is aroused, the passive subject is presumed to cogitate actively in an effort to resolve his newly uncovered inconsistencies, sometimes modifying his behaviors or beliefs to restore balance and consistency. Allen (1968) has helped to partially rehumanize dissonance theory by pointing out that the individual in a dissonance experiment may be engaged in more than just cognitive reorganization. Following Goffman's (1959) analysis of social behavior, Allen suggests that social interactions always involve an intricate interplay between the individual's maintenance of his unique self-concept and the presentations he makes to others of his own social role position. Thus, the subject is sometimes more concerned with *appearing* to be consistently fulfilling others' expectations than he is with *actually* privately structuring his beliefs to *be* consistent. According to Allen, individuals are continually compromising the two objectives.

INTEGRATING THEORY: IMPRESSION-MANAGEMENT

A hypothesis that appears to coherently explain the dissonance phenomena is that the subjects in such experiments are engaged in managing the impressions that the experimenter forms about them, but not for the reasons that either Goffman (1959) or Allen (1968) suppose. Ralph Waldo Emerson in his famous "Essay on Man" pointed out that each man is concerned about being consistent in his beliefs because consistency over time is the orbit by which others judge him. And, if a person lacks consistency, he will be misunderstood. The present authors believe that Emerson's view that such consistency is foolish and the hobgoblin of little minds couldn't be more wrong. According to Dollard (1949), the consistency between words and deeds

> enables men to participate in organized social life with good confidence that others will do what they say they will do. . . . Every man is under compulsion to keep his promises, to make his acts correspond with his verbal expressions. He constantly watches others to see that they do likewise [p. 624].

Thus, consistency of words and deeds enhances the individual's own credibility and enables him to be more successful in influencing others.

An individual who states that he likes Person A or Object X one day and just as vehemently informs others that he hates both Person A and Object X the next day would hardly be viewed by others as a stable individual. Asch (1946) has shown that persons will attribute instability of mental health to a stimulus person described by contradictory adjectives. In any case, a person must keep his promises and back up his threats if he is to be effective in influencing others. Moreover, if one issues warnings of dire consequences if the target person persists in a particular behavioral direction, and the predicted outcome does not occur, there will be a loss of credibility for future warnings. In such a case, the source can be counted on to try and convince the target that conditions had changed or that the nonpredicted outcome was the outcome that really had been predicted all along.

According to attribution theory (Jones & Davis, 1965; Kelley, 1967), a perceiver will not be able to infer the true intentions of an actor as long as the latter's behavior is believed to be controlled by external, nonvolitional factors. Taking pairs of behaviors (rather than cognitions) as an actor's unit of analysis, either of his own behaviors may be perceived as tacted or manded, creating four possible patterns: mand-mand, mand-tact, tact-mand, and tact-tact. Unlike Bem (1967), who could accept the hypothesis that the individual must perceive his counterattitudinal behavior as tacted, we are postulating that it is not the actor's own perceptions that matter so much as the actor's beliefs about the impression that an observer gains. As long as one of the behaviors in any contradictory pair of behaviors is believed by the individual to be perceived by others as a mand, no contradiction will be apparent and no face-restoring behaviors will be required. Manded behaviors do not inform observers about the actor's true beliefs or intentions and therefore are irrelevant in developing a unified impression. Behaviors intended to restore impressions of consistency will be emitted only when the individual believes the *observer* has perceived two actions as tacted and, further, as contradictory in their attributional implications. When two behaviors are perceived by an observer to be manded, no attribution can be made about the actor other than that he has reacted to external pressures in the same way that most people would. When only one of the two behaviors are perceived as manded, incompatibility of the behaviors would not affect the attribution made by observers as to what the actor "is really like." That is, the tacted behavior will appear to represent the true attitudes of the actor while the manded behavior can be attributed to external pressures. Only when both behaviors appear as tacted and contradictory could an observer attribute inconsistency to the actor.

In contradistinction to dissonance theory, the impression maintenance theory suggests that there are conditions under which the actor will perceive two of his own actions as tacted and contradictory without experiencing any dissonance. For example, if the actor perceives both of his own contradictory behaviors as tacted but believes the observer perceives at least one of them as manded, no dissonance-like effects should be manifested; the impression that the observer has of the actor is already a consistent one. Again, if the actor should behave in a tacted manner to one person and in a contradictory but tacted manner to a second person, and the actor believes that the two persons will not compare their impressions, no dissonance should be manifested by the actor.

Collins (1969) has also observed that dissonance-like effects only occur when public behaviors are involved: "I suspect that an individual in our culture is not much concerned with the silly and foolish things he does while locked in a dark closet [p. 212]." Collins' statement, however, was predicated on the belief that inconsistent behaviors are a threat to self-esteem, whereas the present theory focuses on the individual's need to maintain credibility for purposes of social influence. The hypothesis that public behaviors must be involved for dissonancelike effects to occur has been indirectly supported by the studies investigating commitment and volition. When a subject is allowed to remain anonymous in expressing a counterattitudinal behavior or else is allowed to retract the behavior, results support incentive rather than consistency theory.

Impression management theory predicts that a person who believes he is perceived as engaging in contradictory tacted behaviors will weigh the costs and gains of leaving an inconsistent impression and will compare that alternative against the costs and gains of engaging in facework to mend his image. Often, the counterattitudinal behavior represents a "change of heart" and can be useful in gaining advantages from the observer, but not without a long-term loss in credibility. The gains are typically immediate, while the costs occur over the long run. Perhaps the nature of costs and gains explains why children and immature persons are more willing to appear inconsistent than are the more "socialized" members of society. Schelling (1960) has pointed out that it can sometimes be to the advantage of national decision makers to appear inconsistent and unpredictable in their behavior. Such a strategy fosters the impression of disregard for personal costs and, hence, has the effect of deterring would-be threateners. Similarly, Rapoport (1970) stresses that the mathematically "best" strategy in situations that do not admit of minimax solution consists of a random selection of alternatives so as to maximize expected gains and to yield the minimum amount of predictive information to the opponent.

It often has been remarked that laboratory situations are notorious for producing results in accord with cognitive dissonance interpretations of data, while such consistency is difficult to demonstrate in natural settings (cf. Freedman, 1968; McGuire, 1969). This observation is consonant with the impression management hypothesis. In the laboratory, subjects know they are participating in an experiment, and the experiment has been legitimized by the university, the department, and faculty scientists.

Subjects ordinarily take the experiment seriously and are inclined to believe it to be important. Additionally, the caricature of the scientist is that he is an objective observer, impressed above all by rationality, order, consistency, and coherence. Given such formidable cues for the appropriate presentation of self, it is little wonder that consistency results are obtained time and again. Then, too, the two tacted and contradictory behaviors occur close together in time and in front of the same observer (experimenter).[2] Such phenomena as evaluation apprehension, need for social approval, state anxiety, reactance, faking "good" and faking "bad" on personality tests, and dissonancelike behaviors may all be considered as demonstrating a concern by subjects for how the experimenter perceives them.

It would be much too glib to suggest that people need to be consistent only in front of psychologists. Most people do need to maintain consistent impressions, and much facework is devoted to shoring up the actor's credibility in the eyes of others. This need and the development of face-making behaviors, however, seem to be learned through the socialization process. Individuals learn that they must have reasons for their actions. Parents, teachers, friends, and acquaintances ask the child to justify his actions to them. If his actions are considered bad, and he has insufficient justification for them (they are perceived by others as tacted), he deserves to be punished. But if the person can justify his actions as actually desirable or at least necessary, then he may escape punishment. Obviously, good behaviors do not have to be justified in the same way as do bad behaviors. As a consequence, it could be suggested that if an actor performed two tacted and contradictory actions in relation to a particular observer, and the second tacted behavior was favorable to the observer, there may be no attempt to restore the impression of consistency. In fact, the contradiction may serve to indicate to the observer how committed to the second action the actor was. Commitment to the last in a series of inconsistent actions may help to explain Aronson and Linder's (1965) findings that an individual who switches from a negative to a positive evaluation of an observer is liked more by the observer than an individual who gives positive evaluations all along, while an individual who switches from a positive to a negative evaluation is disliked more than an individual who expresses dislike all along.

Perceived freedom also has import for the impression management theory due to the existence of vital social norms, particularly the norm of reciprocity (Gouldner, 1960) and the obverse norm of retaliation (cf. Helm, Bonoma, & Tedeschi, 1971). The positive norm of reciprocity specifies that a person should help those who help him and should not harm those who help him. The strength and universality of the reciprocity norm are seldom questioned. It is doubtful, however, that the norm applies when help is given inadvertently or under coercion. One does not feel gratitude if the neighbor boy's mother coerces him into sharing his jelly beans. When help has been received, the recipient must ascertain whether the beneficial behavior of the giver was tacted. If it was, favor for favor should result. If the helping behavior is perceived as manded, the norm of reciprocity should be inapplicable or at least less salient. Naturally, individuals who have helped others can be expected to manage the impression that the beneficial behaviors were tacted. If so, it can be predicted that when a counterattitudinal behavior is perceived as tacted and beneficial, the actor usually will not engage in facework to restore consistency. Inconsistency simply makes the beneficial behavior appear to be more tacted, while attempts to restore consistency would lower the commitment the recipient of help would attribute to the actor. If anything, the actor should attempt to enhance the inconsistency by insisting that he has had a change of heart or by attempting to show that the beneficial behavior was not just an accident but was actually intended. By emphasizing the inconsistency, the actor can increase the probability of reciprocation by maximizing the probability that the observer does not interpret the beneficial action as accidental.

The norm of retaliation stipulates that "an eye for an eye and a tooth for a tooth" should be applied only if a harm-doer's behavior is perceived as tacted. Under the law, excusing conditions *(mens rea)* for crimes do exist, including coercion, accident, and insanity. Each of these imply that the accused's behaviors were manded. Those who have perpetrated harm can be expected to engage in facework to create the impression that their harm-doing behavior was manded. The typical dissonance paradigm induces the experimental subject to engage in counternormative behaviors, such as lying to another person or misrepresenting his "true" opinions. Dissonance reduction in such situations serves two purposes: *(a)* restores credibility and *(b)* denies or rationalizes the counternormative behavior. Restoration of credibility is an investment in the future, while rationalization attempts to avoid the costs associated with the negative norm of reciprocity. Although few dissonance theorists would view a criminal's rationalizations for his crimes as manifestations of his need

[2] It is questionable that subjects in dissonance experiments ever perceive their counterattitudinal actions as tacted. It is more plausible to interpret such actions as manded from the subject's point of view, however subtle and clever the experimenter. But the rub is that the experimenter leads the subject to believe that the former perceives the latter's counterattitudinal behavior as tacted.

for cognitive consistency, it can be viewed as face-work to manage the impressions that others construct.

Brehm (1966) has hypothesized that psychological reactance is manifested when an individual's set of possible (free) behaviors have been threatened or actually have been constrained. The degree of reactance is hypothesized to depend on the number and importance of the behaviors threatened or eliminated and/or the magnitude of the threat. Reactance has as its goal the reestablishment by the individual of the threatened or eliminated behaviors. According to the present theory, reactance will be manifested only when it is important for the individual to demonstrate the tacted nature of his behavior to another. Presumably, then, reactance will occur only when commitment must be demonstrated to deter coercion from others, or when clear communication that a helping behavior was tacted appears necessary. In the first regard, it is commonly believed that to give in to the influence attempts of others simply encourages the influencer to attempt further influence. A person should endeavor to maintain the impression that he is acting freely whenever another attempts to influence him, even when behavioral compliance to coercion is consistent with gain maximization and the individual does comply. Hence, even when the actor might not have wanted to do what the influencer had demanded, the actor will attempt to make it clear that he is not complying because of the threat, but because he wanted to perform that behavior anyway. In so doing, he maintains his integrity and independence in the world of influence. Further, when compliance results in beneficial behaviors toward the source of influence or another individual, the target would want to show that the behavior was tacted so that the behavior could initiate a chain of positive reciprocity behaviors.

The impression management theory has several advantages when compared to cognitive consistency explanations for dissonance phenomena. Both dissonance and incentive effects are explained in terms of costs and gains, and the individual is considered to be motivated to minimax outcomes. In effect, each person must consider the impact of abrupt changes in self-presentation in terms of the gains that such strategy will mediate against the costs of the loss of credibility for future influence attempts. Unless a person is perpetrating harm in order to establish credibility for prior threats, he is likely to attempt to rationalize his harm-doing as manded in order to undermine the justification for retaliation from the victim. But when the harm-doing action is contradictory to a prior action, the actor has fewer means of rationalization at his disposal because he must restore his credibility at the same time that he justifies his harm-doing. Very often, an effective strategy is to attribute the wrongdoing to "uncontrollable" emotions and to make restitution to the victim or in some other way to demonstrate the actor's more permanent and enduring benevolent (contrite) character. In any case, the need for consistency is presumed to be rooted within the socialization process and is devoted to maintaining high perceived credibility for influence communications (i.e., threats, promises, warnings, and statements of fact).

Most of the current research on dissonance indicates that the subject must perceive his counterattitudinal behavior as tacted. The present theory suggests that the important factor is that the actor believes the observer perceives the counterattitudinal behavior as both tacted and counternormative. Perceived freedom or volition is a phenomenological reality to the actor and probably offers him cues as to how an observer perceives his actions. Nevertheless, the actor attempts to control the impressions that others have about his freedom to act. This line of reasoning is based on the universality and importance of reciprocity norms and the assumption that reciprocity norms are inappropriate when the beneficent or harm-doing behaviors are believed to be manded. The impression management explanation for dissonance phenomena makes no assumption that the individual has a need for freedom. Instead, it is postulated that the actor may wish to be perceived as acting under his own volition sometimes, but not at other times.

If McGuire (1966) could claim that accepting any other hypothesis "would require accepting a tremendous variety of alternative explanations, whereas dissonance theory alone explains a large subset of them [p. 493]," a stronger claim can be made that the impression management hypothesis is more coherent, leads to the development of further testable hypotheses, roots the mechanism of dissonance into the socialization process, and avoids assumptions about unpleasant tensions. Furthermore, the impression management hypothesis supplants Festinger's (1959) dissonance theory, Bem's (1967) tact-mand theory, Brehm's (1966) theory of psychological reactance, and Steiner's (1970) conceptualizations concerning perceived freedom. From the present view, these are not competing theories, and much discussion has been at cross-purposes. Instead, the effects and the conditions under which the various phenomena can be expected to occur can be predicted by a single coherent theory of social influence, a tactic within which are the actor's attempts to manage the impressions others have of him.

The conditions that have been isolated as those

producing dissonance effects lend coherence to the belief that dissonance phenomena can be most parsimoniously explained in terms of impression management. Commitment and importance of public counterattitudinal behaviors communicate the strength of the actor's inconsistent beliefs and/or intentions to an observer, and therefore require face-saving behavior to restore the others' impressions of consistency. Unless observers perceive the counterattitudinal behaviors as tacted, no inference can be drawn about the actor's *real* beliefs and intentions, and no face restoration is necessary. Role-inappropriate behaviors should elicit face-saving behaviors for two reasons: such behaviors are perceived as tacted, and they are ordinarily perceived as harmful to other members of the social group. Persons who are anxious or apprehensive about the manner in which others will evaluate them should demonstrate more behaviors relevant to impression management than individuals who have little concern for the impressions that others have of them. Similarly, the personality trait known as Machiavellianism is an indication of a person's concern about influencing or manipulating other people, and, therefore, those who score high on this measure should be particularly prone to demonstrate dissonance. It could be expected that other personality attributes related to involvement in influencing others, such as need for power or dominance, would be highly correlated with impression management behaviors.

The impression management theory does not view subjects in experiments as passive targets of the subtle or clever manipulations of the experimenter. Rather, subjects have been the originators of influence attempts directed at the experimenter. The effectiveness of subjects in manipulating the impressions that experimenters have of them has been made evident by the fact that social-psychological theory reflects the lack of awareness by experimenters about how they have been manipulated. Subjects have been quite successful in leaving the impression that they are rational and have a profound need to be consistent in their beliefs and behaviors.

In conclusion, impression management theory presents a plausible alternative to an entire family of cognitive consistency theories. The theory has strong integrative power for interpreting dissonance experiments and makes further predictions that are as yet untested. No assumptions are made concerning a person's need for freedom, intrapsychic tensions, or need for consistency. Undoubtedly, the latter assumptions will continue to be a matter of much debate. Finally, impression management theory roots dissonance phenomena into the social influence process and retains the view that the individual's behavior, even when managing the impression of consistency, is directed by the expectation of gains or the avoidance of costs.

REFERENCES

Abelson, R. P. and Rosenberg, M. J. Symbolic psychologic: A model of attitudinal cognition. *Behavioral Science,* 1958, **3**, 1–13.

Allen, V. L. Role theory and consistency theory. In R. P. Abelson, E. Aronson, W. J. McGuire, T. M. Newcomb, M. J. Rosenberg, and P. H. Tannenbaum (eds.), *Theories of cognitive consistency: A sourcebook.* Chicago: Rand McNally, 1968.

Aronson, E. Dissonance theory: Progress and problems. In R. P. Abelson et al. (eds.), *Theories of cognitive consistency: A sourcebook.* Chicago: Rand McNally, 1968.

Aronson, E. and Linder, D. Gain and loss of esteem as determinants of interpersonal attractiveness. *Journal of Experimental Social Psychology,* 1965, **1**, 156–72.

Asch, S. E. Forming impressions of personality. *Journal of Abnormal and Social Psychology,* 1946, **41**, 258–90.

Bem, D. J. Self-perception: An alternative interpretation of cognitive dissonance phenomena. *Psychological Review,* 1967, **74**, 183–200.

Brehm, J. W. *A theory of psychological reactance.* New York: Academic Press, 1966.

Brehm, J. W. and Cohen, A. R. *Explorations in cognitive dissonance.* New York: Wiley, 1962.

Campbell, A. A., Converse, P. E., Miller, W. E., and Stokes, D. E. *The American voter.* New York: Wiley, 1960.

Carlsmith, J. M., Collins, B. E., and Helmreich, R. L. Studies in forced compliance: I. The effect of pressure for compliance on attitude change produced by face-to-face role playing and anonymous essay writing. *Journal of Personality and Social Psychology,* 1966, **4**, 1–13.

Chapanis, N. P. and Chapanis, A. C. Cognitive dissonance: Five years later. *Psychological Bulletin,* 1964, **61**, 1–22.

Christie, R. and Geis, F. L. *Studies in Machiavellianism.* New York: Academic Press, 1970.

Collins, B. E. Behavior theory. In R. P. Abelson et al. (eds.), *Theories of cognitive consistency: A sourcebook.* Chicago: Rand McNally, 1968.

Collins, B. E. The effect of monetary inducements on the amount of attitude change produced by forced compliance. In A. C. Elms (ed.), *Role playing, reward, and attitude change.* New York: Van Nostrand, 1969.

Collins, B. E., Ashmore, R. D., Hornbeck, F. W., and Whitney, R. Studies in forced compliance: XIII and XV. In search of a dissonance-producing forced compliance paradigm. *Representative Research in Social Psychology,* 1970, **1**, 11–23.

Dollard, J. Under what conditions do opinions predict behavior? *Public Opinion Quarterly,* 1949, **12**, 623–32.

Elms, A. C. Role playing, incentive and dissonance. In A. C. Elms (ed.), *Role playing, reward, and attitude change.* New York: Van Nostrand, 1969.

Festinger, L. *A theory of cognitive dissonance.* Stanford: Stanford University Press, 1957.

Festinger, L. and Carlsmith, J. M. Cognitive consequences of forced compliance. *Journal of Abnormal and Social Psychology,* 1959, 58, 203–10.

Fisch, M. H. (ed.), *Classic American philosophers.* New York: Appleton-Century-Crofts, 1951.

Freedman, J. L. How important is cognitive consistency? In R. P. Abelson et al. (eds.), *Theories of cognitive consistency: A sourcebook.* Chicago: Rand McNally, 1968.

Freedman, J. L. and Sears, D. O. Selective exposure. In L. Berkowitz (ed.), *Advances in experimental social psychology.* Vol. 2. New York: Academic Press, 1965.

Goffman, E. *The presentation of self in everyday life.* New York: Doubleday, 1959.

Gouldner, A. W. The norm of reciprocity: A preliminary statement. *American Sociological Review,* 1960, **25**, 161–78.

Heider, F. Attitudes and cognitive organizations. *Journal of Psychology,* 1946, **21**, 107–12.

Helm, B., Bonoma, T. V., and Tedeschi, J. T. Reciprocity for harm done. *Journal of Social Psychology,* 1971, in press.

Helmreich, R. and Collins, B. E. Studies in forced compliance: Commitment and magnitude of inducement to comply as determinants of opinion change. *Journal of Personality and Social Psychology,* 1968, **10**, 75–81.

Janis, I. L. and Gilmore, J. B. The influence of incentive conditions on the success of role playing in modifying attitudes. *Journal of Personality and Social Psychology,* 1965, **1**, 17–27.

Jones, E. E. and Davis, K. E. From acts to dispositions: The attribution process in person perception. In L. Berkowitz (ed.), *Advances in experimental social psychology.* Vol. 2. New York: Academic Press, 1965.

Katz, D. Consistency for what? The functional approach. In R. P. Abelson et al. (eds.), *Theories of cognitive consistency: A sourcebook.* Chicago: Rand McNally, 1968.

Kelley, H. H. Attribution theory in social psychology. *Nebraska Symposium on Motivation,* 1967, **15**, 192–240.

Kiesler, C. A. Commitment. In R. P. Abelson et al. (eds.), *Theories of cognitive consistency: A sourcebook.* Chicago: Rand McNally, 1968.

Kiesler, C. A. and Corbin, L. H. Commitment, attraction, and conformity. *Journal of Personality and Social Psychology,* 1965, **2**, 890–95.

Linder, D. E., Cooper, J., and Jones, E. E. Decision freedom as a determinant of the role of incentive magnitude in attitude change. *Journal of Personality and Social Psychology,* 1967, **6**, 245–54.

McGuire, W. J. Attitudes and opinions. *Annual Review of Psychology,* 1966, **17**, 475–514.

McGuire, W. J. The nature of attitudes and attitude change. In G. Lindzey and E. Aronson (eds.), *The handbook of social psychology.* Vol. 3. Reading, Mass.: Addison-Wesley, 1969.

Mills, J., Aronson, E., and Robinson, H. Selectivity in exposure to information. *Journal of Abnormal and Social Psychology,* 1959, **59**, 250–53.

Osgood, C. E., and Tannenbaum, P. H. The principle of congruity in the prediction of attitude change. *Psychological Review,* 1955, **62**, 42–55.

Peirce, C. S. The fixation of belief. *Popular Science Monthly,* 1877. Reprinted in M. H. Fisch (ed.), *Classic American philosophers.* New York: Appleton-Century-Crofts, 1951.

Platt, J. R. Strong inference (certain systematic methods of scientific thinking may produce much more rapid progress than others). *Science,* 1964, **146**, 347–53.

Rapoport, A. Conflict resolution in the light of game theory and beyond. In P. Swingle (ed.), *The structure of conflict.* New York: Academic Press, 1970.

Rosenberg, M. J. When dissonance fails: On eliminating evaluation apprehension from attitude measurement. *Journal of Personality and Social Psychology,* 1965, **1**, 18–42.

Rosenberg, M. J. The conditions and consequences of evaluation apprehension. In R. Rosenthal & R. W. Rosnow (eds.), *Artifacts in behavioral research.* New York: Academic Press, 1969.

Rosenberg, M. J. and Abelson, R. P. An analysis of cognitive balancing. In M. J. Rosenberg, C. I. Hovland, W. J. McGuire, R. P. Abelson, and J. W. Brehm (eds.), *Attitude organization and change.* New Haven: Yale University Press, 1960.

Schelling, T. C. *The strategy of conflict.* New York: Oxford University Press, 1960.

Skinner, B. F. *Verbal behavior.* New York: Appleton-Century-Crofts, 1957.

Steiner, I. D. Perceived freedom. In L. Berkowitz (ed.), *Advances in experimental social psychology.* Vol. 5. New York: Academic Press, 1970.

Steiner, I. D. and Rogers, E. D. Alternative responses to dissonance. *Journal of Abnormal and Social Psychology,* 1963, **66**, 128–36.

Steiner, I. D. and Spaulding, J. *Preference for balanced situations.* (USPHS Tech. Rep. No. 1, Grant 4460) Urbana: University of Illinois Press, 1966.

Wicker, A. U. Attitudes versus actions: The relationship of verbal and overt behavioral responses to attitude objects. *Journal of Social Issues,* 1969, 25, 41–78.

Zimbardo, P. and Ebbesen, E. B. *Influencing attitudes and changing behavior.* Reading, Mass.: Addison-Wesley, 1969.

11. PERCEPTION: SOME RECENT RESEARCH AND IMPLICATIONS FOR ADMINISTRATION*

Sheldon S. Zalkind and *Timothy W. Costello*†

The administrator frequently bases decisions and actions on his perception of other people. Behavioral scientists have been systematically studying the process of perception, focusing in recent years on interpersonal perception. Although their work has been done largely in laboratory settings, their conclusions have relevance for the administrator. This paper examines some of the recent work on interpersonal perception and suggests some implications for administrative practice.[1] No easy means is proposed to make objective what is essentially a subjective process; nevertheless it is possible to indicate some guidelines and precautions to use in this complex aspect of interpersonal relations. Understanding the process of interpersonal perception is one means of trying to avoid gross errors in interpersonal judgments.

Management practice is being increasingly influenced by behavior science research in the areas of group dynamics, problem solving and decision making, and motivation. One aspect of behavior which has not been fully or consistently emphasized is the process of perception, particularly the recent work on person perception.

In this paper we shall summarize some of the findings on perception as developed through both laboratory and organizational research and point out some of the administrative and managerial implications. We discuss first some basic factors in the nature of the perceptual process including need and set; second, some research on forming impressions; third, the characteristics of the perceiver and the perceived; fourth, situational and organizational influences on perception; and finally, perceptual influences on interpersonal adjustment.

NATURE OF THE PERCEPTUAL PROCESS

What are some of the factors influencing perception? In answering the question it is well to begin by putting aside the attitude of naive realism, which suggests that our perceptions simply register accurately what is "out there." It is necessary rather to consider what influences distort one's perceptions and judgments of the outside world. Some of the considerations identified in the literature up to the time of Johnson's 1944 review of the research on object perception (where distortion may be even less extreme than in person perception) led him to suggest the following about the perceiver:[2]

1. He may be influenced by considerations that he may not be able to identify, responding to cues that are below the threshold of his awareness. For example, a judgment as to the size of an object may be influenced by its color even though the perceiver may not be attending to color.

2. When required to form difficult perceptual judgments, he may respond to irrelevant cues to arrive at a judgment. For example, in trying to assess honesty, it has been shown that the other person's smiling or not smiling is used as a cue to judge his honesty.

3. In making abstract or intellectual judgments, he may be influenced by emotional factors—what is liked is perceived as correct.

4. He will weigh perceptual evidence coming from respect (or favored) sources more heavily than that coming from other sources.

5. He may not be able to identify all the factors on which his judgments are based. Even if he is aware of these factors he is not likely to realize how much weight he gives to them.

These considerations do not imply that we respond only to the subtle or irrelevant cues or to emotional factors. We often perceive on the basis of the obvious, but we are quite likely to be responding as well to the less obvious or less objective.

In 1958, Bruner, citing a series of researches, described what he called the "New Look" in perception as one in which personal determinants of the perceptual process were being stressed.[3] Bruner summarized earlier work and showed the importance of such subjective influences as needs, values, cultural background, and interests on the perceptual process. In his concept of "perceptual readiness" he described the importance of the framework or category system that the perceiver himself brings to the perceiving process.

* *Administrative Science Quarterly,* Vol. 7 (1962), pp. 218–35.

† Baruch College, City College of New York and Adelphi University, respectively.

[1] Portions of this article were originally presented at the Eighth Annual International Meeting of The Institute of Management Sciences in Brussels, August, 1961.

[2] D. M. Johnson. A systematic treatment of judgment. *Psychological Bulletin,* Vol. 42 (1945), 193–224.

[3] J. S. Bruner. Social psychology and perception, in E. Maccoby, T. Newcomb, and E. Hartley (eds.). *Readings in social psychology* (3d ed.: New York, 1958), pp. 85–94.

Tapping a different vein of research, Cantril described perceiving as a "transaction" between the perceiver and the perceived, a process of negotiation in which the perceptual end product is a result both of influences within the perceiver and of characteristics of the perceived.[4]

One of the most important of the subjective factors that influence the way we perceive, identified by Bruner and others, is *set.* A study by Kelley illustrated the point.[5] He found that those who were previously led to expect to meet a "warm" person, not only made different judgments about him, but also behaved differently toward him, than those who were expecting a "cold" one. The fact was that they simultaneously were observing the same person in the same situation. Similarly, Strickland indicated the influence of set in determining how closely supervisors feel they must supervise their subordinates.[6] Because of prior expectation one person was trusted more than another and was thought to require less supervision than another, even though performance records were identical.

FORMING IMPRESSIONS OF OTHERS

The data on forming impressions is of particular importance in administration. An administrator is confronted many times with the task of forming an impression of another person—a new employee at his desk, a visiting member from the home office, a staff member he has not personally met before. His own values, needs, and expectations will play a part in the impression he forms. Are there other factors that typically operate in this area of administrative life? One of the more obvious influences is the physical appearance of the person being perceived. In a study of this point Mason was able to demonstrate that people agree on what a leader should look like and that there is no relationship between the facial characteristics agreed upon and those possessed by actual leaders.[7] In effect, we have ideas about what leaders look like and we can give examples, but we ignore the many exceptions that statistically cancel out the examples.

In the sometimes casual, always transitory situations in which one must form impressions of others it is a most natural tendency to jump to conclusions and form impressions without adequate evidence. Unfortunately, as Dailey showed, unless such impressions are based on important and relevant data, they are not likely to be accurate.[8] Too often in forming impressions the perceiver does not know what is relevant, important, or predictive of later behavior. Dailey's research furthermore supports the cliché that, accurate or not, first impressions are lasting.

Generalizing from other research in the field, Soskin described four limitations on the ability to form accurate impressions of others.[9] First, the impression is likely to be disproportionately affected by the type of situation or surroundings in which the impression is made and influenced too little by the person perceived. Thus the plush luncheon club in which one first meets a man will dominate the impression of the man himself. Secondly, although impressions are frequently based on a limited sample of the perceived person's behavior, the generalization that the perceiver makes will be sweeping. A third limitation is that the situation may not provide an opportunity for the person perceived to show behavior relevant to the traits about which impressions are formed. Casual conversation or questions, for example, provide few opportunities to demonstrate intelligence or work characteristics, yet the perceiver often draws conclusions about these from an interview. Finally, Soskin agrees with Bruner and Cantril that the impression of the person perceived may be distorted by some highly individualized reaction of the perceiver.

But the pitfalls are not yet all spelled out; it is possible to identify some other distorting influences on the process of forming impressions. Research has brought into sharp focus some typical errors, the more important being stereotyping, halo effect, projection, and perceptual defense.

Stereotyping

The word "stereotyping" was first used by Walter Lippmann in 1922 to describe bias in perceiving peoples. He wrote of "pictures in people's heads," called stereotypes, which guided (distorted) their perceptions of others. The term has long been used to describe judgments made about people on the basis of their ethnic group membership. For example, some say "Herman Schmidt [being German] is industrious." Stereotyping also predisposes judgments in many other areas of interpersonal relations.

[4] H. Cantril, Perception and interpersonal relations. *American Journal of Psychiatry,* Vol. 114 (1957), 119–26.

[5] H. H. Kelley. The warm-cold variable in first impressions of persons. *Journal of Personality,* Vol. 18 (1950), 431–39.

[6] L. H. Strickland, Surveillance and trust. *Journal of Personality,* Vol. 26 (1958), 200–215.

[7] D. J. Mason. Judgments of leadership based upon physiognomic cues. *Journal of Abnormal and Social Psychology,* Vol. 54 (1957), 273–74.

[8] C. A. Dailey. The effects of premature conclusion upon the acquisition of understanding of a person. *Journal of Psychology,* Vol. 33 (1952), 133–52.

[9] W. E. Soskin. Influence of information on bias in social perception. *Journal of Personality,* Vol. 22 (1953), 118–27.

Stereotypes have developed about many types of groups, and they help to prejudice many of our perceptions about their members. Examples of stereotypes of groups other than those based on ethnic identification are bankers, supervisors, union members, poor people, rich people, and administrators. Many unverified qualities are assigned to people principally because of such group memberships.

In a research demonstration of stereotyping, Haire found that labeling a photograph as that of a management representative caused an impression to be formed of the person, different from that formed when it was labeled as that of a union leader.[10] Management and labor formed different impressions, each seeing his opposite as less dependable than his own group. In addition each side saw his own group as being better able than the opposite group to understand a point of view different from its own. For example, managers felt that other managers were better able to appreciate labor's point of view, than labor was able to appreciate management's point of view. Each had similar stereotypes of his opposite and considered the thinking, emotional characteristics, and interpersonal relations of his opposite as inferior to his own. As Stagner points out, "It is plain that unionists perceiving company officials in a stereotyped way are less efficient than would be desirable.[11] Similarly, company executives who see all labor unions is identical are not showing good judgment or discrimination."

One of the troublesome aspects of sterotypes is that they are so widespread. Finding the same stereotypes to be widely held should not tempt one to accept their accuracy. It may only mean that many people are making the same mistake. Allport has demonstrated that there need not be a "kernel of truth" in a widely held stereotype.[12] He has shown that while a prevalent stereotype of Armenians labeled them as dishonest, a credit reporting association gave them credit ratings as good as those given other ethnic groups.

Bruner and Perlmutter found that there is an international stereotype for "businessmen" and "teachers."[13] They indicated that the more widespread one's experience with diverse members of a group, the less their group membership will affect the impression formed.

An additional illustration of stereotyping is provided by Luft.[14] His research suggests that perception of personality adjustment may be influenced by stereotypes, associating adjustment with high income and maladjustment with low income.

Halo Effect

The term halo effect was first used in 1920 to describe a process in which a general impression which is favorable or unfavorable is used by judges to evaluate several specific traits. The "halo" in such case serves as a screen keeping the perceiver from actually seeing the trait he is judging. It has received the most attention because of its effect on rating employee performance. In the rating situation, a supervisor may single out one trait, either good or bad, and use this as the basis for his judgment of all other traits. For example, an excellent attendance record causes judgments of productivity, high quality of work, and so forth. One study in the U.S. Army showed that officers who were liked were judged more intelligent than those who were disliked, even though they had the same scores on intelligence tests.

We examine halo effect here because of its general effect on forming impressions. Bruner and Taguiri suggest that it is likely to be most extreme when we are forming impressions of traits that provide minimal cues in the individual's behavior, when the traits have moral overtones, or when the perceiver must judge traits with which he has had little experience.[15] A rather disturbing conclusion is suggested by Symonds that halo effect is more marked the more we know the acquaintance.[16]

A somewhat different aspect of the halo effect is suggested by the research of Grove and Kerr.[17] They found that knowledge that the company was in receivership caused employees to devalue the higher pay and otherwise superior working conditions of their company as compared to those in a financially secure firm.

Psychologists have noted a tendency in perceivers to link certain traits. They assume, for example,

[10] M. Haire. Role perceptions in labor-management relations. An experimental approach. *Industrial and Labor Relations Review,* Vol. 8 (1955), 204–16.

[11] R. Stagner. *Psychology of industrial conflict* (New York, 1956), p. 35.

[12] G. Allport. *Nature of prejudice* (Cambridge, Mass., 1954).

[13] J. S. Bruner and H. V. Perlmutter. Compatriot and foreigner: A study of impression formation in three countries. *Journal of Abnormal and Social Psychology,* Vol. 55 (1957), 253–60.

[14] J. Luft. Monetary value and the perception of persons. *Journal of Social Psychology,* Vol. 46 (1957), 245–51.

[15] J. S. Bruner and A. Taguiri. The perception of people, ch. xvii in G. Lindzey (ed.), *Handbook of social psychology* (Cambridge, Mass., 1954).

[16] P. M. Symonds. Notes on rating. *Journal of Applied Psychology,* Vol. 7 (1925), 188–95.

[17] B. A. Grove and W. A. Kerr. Specific evidence on origin of halo effect in measurement of morale. *Journal of Social Psychology,* Vol. 34 (1951) 165–70.

that when a person is aggressive he will also have high energy or that when a person is "warm" he will also be generous and have a good sense of humor. The logical error, as it has been called, is a special form of the halo effect and is best illustrated in the research of Asch.[18] In his study the addition of one trait to a list of traits produced a major change in the impression formed. Knowing that a person was intelligent, skillful, industrious, determined, practical, cautious and warm led a group to judge him to be also wise, humorous, popular, and imaginative. When warm was replaced by cold, a radically different impression (beyond the difference between warm and cold) was formed. Kelley's research illustrated the same type of error.[19] This tendency is not indiscriminate; with the pair "polite—blunt," less change was found than with the more central traits of "warm—cold."

In evaluating the effect of halo on perceptual distortion, we may take comfort from the work of Wishner, which showed that those traits that correlate more highly with each other are more likely to lead to a halo effect than those that are unrelated.[20]

Projection

A defense mechanism available to everyone is projection, in which one relieves one's feelings of guilt or failure by projecting blame onto someone else. Over the years the projection mechanism has been assigned various meanings. The original use of the term was concerned with the mechanism to defend oneself from unacceptable feelings. There has since been a tendency for the term to be used more broadly, meaning to ascribe or attribute any of one's own characteristics to other people. The projection mechanism concerns us here because it influences the perceptual process. An early study by Murray illustrates its effect.[21] After playing a dramatic game, "Murder," his subjects attributed much more maliciousness to people whose photographs were judged than did a control group which had not played the game. The current emotional state of the perceiver tended to influence his perceptions of others; i.e., frightened perceivers judged people to be frightening. More recently, Feshback and Singer revealed further dynamics of the process.[22] In their study, subjects who had been made fearful judged a stimulus person (presented in a moving picture) as both more fearful and more aggressive than did nonfearful perceivers. These authors were able to demonstrate further that the projection mechanism at work here was reduced when their subjects were encouraged to admit and talk about their fears.

Sears provides an illustration of a somewhat different type of projection and its effect on perception.[23] In his study projection is seeing our own undesirable personality characteristics in other people. He demonstrated that people high in such traits as stinginess, obstinacy, and disorderliness, tended to rate others much higher on these traits than did those who were low in these undesirable characteristics. The tendency to project was particularly marked among subjects who had the least insight into their own personalities.

Research thus suggests that our perceptions may characteristically be distorted by emotions we are experiencing or traits that we possess. Placed in the administrative setting, the research would suggest, for example, that a manager frightened by rumored organizational changes might not only judge others to be more frightened than they were, but also assess various policy decisions as more frightening than they were. Or a general foreman lacking insight into his own incapacity to delegate might be oversensitive to this trait in his superiors.

Perceptual Defense

Another distorting influence, which has been called perceptual defense, has also been demonstrated by Haire and Grunes to be a source of error.[24] In their research they ask, in effect, "Do we put blinders on to defend ourselves from seeing those events which might disturb us?" The concept of perceptual defense offers an excellent description of perceptual distortion at work and demonstrates that when confronted with a fact inconsistent with a stereotype already held by a person, the perceiver is able to distort the data in such a way as to eliminate the inconsistency. Thus, by perceiving inaccurately, he defends himself from having to change his stereotypes.

[18] S. Asch. Forming impressions of persons. *Journal of Abnormal and Social Psychology,* Vol. 60 (1946), 258–90.

[19] Kelley, The warm-cold variable in first impressions of persons.

[20] J. Wishner. Reanalysis of "Impressions of personality," *Psychology Review,* Vol. 67 (1960), 96–112.

[21] H. A. Murray. The effect of fear upon estimates of the maliciousness of other personalities. *Journal of Social Psychology,* Vol. 4 (1933), 310–29.

[22] S. Feshback and R. D. Singer. The effects of fear arousal upon social perception. *Journal of Abnormal and Social Psychology,* Vol. 55 (1957), 283–88.

[23] R. R. Sears. Experimental studies of perception, 1. Attribution of traits. *Journal of Social Psychology,* Vol. 7 (1936), 151–63.

[24] M. Haire and W. F. Grunes. Perceptual defenses: Processes protecting an original perception of another personality. *Human Relations,* Vol. 3 (1958), 403–12.

CHARACTERISTICS OF PERCEIVER AND PERCEIVED

We have thus far been talking largely about influences on the perceptual process without specific regard to the perceiver and his characteristics. Much recent research has tried to identify some characteristics of the perceiver and their influence on the perception of other people.

The Perceiver

A thread that would seem to tie together many current findings is the tendency to use oneself as the norm or standard by which one perceives or judges others. If we examine current research, certain conclusions are suggested:

1. *Knowing oneself makes it easier to see others accurately.* Norman showed that when one is aware of what his own personal characteristics are he makes fewer errors in perceiving others.[25] Weingarten has shown that people with insight are less likely to view the world in black-and-white terms and to give extreme judgments about others.[26]

2. *One's own characteristics affect the characteristics he is likely to see in others.* Secure people (compared with insecure) tend to see others as warm rather than cold, as was shown by Bossom and Maslow.[27] The extent of one's own sociability influences the degree of importance one gives to the sociability of other people when one forms impressions of them.[28] The person with "authoritarian" tendencies is more likely to view others in terms of power and is less sensitive to the psychological or personality characteristics of other people than is a nonauthoritarian.[29] The relatively few categories one uses in describing other people tend to be those one uses in describing oneself.[30] Thus traits which are important to the perceiver will be used more when he forms impressions of others. He has certain constant tendencies, both with regard to using certain categories in judging others and to the amount of weight given to these categories.[31]

3. *The person who accepts himself is more likely to be able to see favorable aspects of other people.*[32] This relates in part to the accuracy of his perceptions. If the perceiver accepts himself as he is, he widens his range of vision in seeing others; he can look at them and be less likely to be very negative or critical. In those areas in which he is more insecure, he sees more problems in other people.[33] We are more likely to like others who have traits we accept in ourselves and reject those who have the traits which we do not like in ourselves.[34]

4. *Accuracy in perceiving others is not a single skill.* While there have been some variations in the findings, as Gage has shown, some consistent results do occur.[35] The perceiver tends to interpret the feelings others have about him in terms of his feelings towards them.[36] One's ability to perceive others accurately may depend on how sensitive one is to differences between people and also to the norms (outside of oneself) for judging them.[37] Thus, as Taft has shown, the ability to judge others does not seem to be a single skill.[38]

Possibly the results in these four aspects of person perception can be viewed most constructively in connection with earlier points on the process of perception. The administrator (or any other individual) who wishes to perceive someone else accurately must look at the other person, not at himself. The things that he looks at in someone else are influenced by his own traits. But if he knows his own traits, he can be aware that they provide a frame of reference for him. His own traits help to furnish the categories that he

---

[25] R. D. Norman. The interrelationships among acceptance-rejection, self-other identity, insight into self, and realistic perception of others. *Journal of Social Psychology,* Vol. 37 (1953), 205–35.

[26] E. Weingarten. A study of selective perception in clinical judgment. *Journal of Personality,* Vol. 17 (1949), 369–400.

[27] J. Bossom and A. H. Maslow. Security of judges as a factor in impressions of warmth in others. *Journal of Abnormal and Social Psychology,* Vol. 55 (1957), 147–48.

[28] D. T. Benedetti and J. G. Hill. A determiner of the centrality of a trait in impression formation. *Journal of Abnormal and Social Psychology,* Vol. 60 (1960), 278–79.

[29] E. E. Jones. Authoritarianism as a determinant of first-impressions formation. *Journal of Personality,* Vol. 23 (1954), 107–27.

[30] A. H. Hastorf, S. A. Richardson, and S. M. Dornbusch. The problem of relevance in the study of person perception, in R. Taguiri and L. Petrullo, *Person perception and interpersonal behavior* (Stanford, Calif., 1958).

[31] L. J. Cronbach. Processes affecting scores on "Understanding of others" and "Assumed similarity," *Psychological Bulletin,* Vol. 52 (1955), 177–93.

[32] K. T. Omwake. The relation between acceptance of self and acceptance of others shown by three personality inventories. *Journal of Consulting Psychology,* Vol. 18 (1954), 443–46.

[33] Weingarten, A study of selective perception in clinical judgment.

[34] R. M. Lundy, W. Katovsky, R. L. Cromwell, and D. J. Shoemaker. Self acceptability and descriptions of sociometric choices. *Journal of Abnormal and Social Psychology,* Vol. 51 (1955), 260–62.

[35] N. L. Gage. Accuracy of social perception and effectiveness in interpersonal relationships. *Journal of Personality,* Vol. 22 (1953), 128–41.

[36] R. Taguiri, J. S. Bruner, and R. Blake. On the relation between feelings and perceptions of feelings among members of small groups, in Maccoby *et al. Readings in social psychology.*

[37] U. Bronfenbrenner, J. Harding, and M. Gallway. The measurement of skill in social perception, in H. L. McClelland, D. C. Baldwin, U. Bronfenbrenner, and F. L. Strodtbeck (eds.). *Talent and society* (Princeton, N.J., 1958), pp. 29–111.

[38] R. Taft. The ability to judge people. *Psychological Bulletin,* Vol. 52 (1955), 1–21.

will use in perceiving others. His characteristics, needs, and values can partly limit his vision and his awareness of the differences between others. The question one could ask when viewing another is: "Am I looking at him, and forming my impression of his behavior in the situation, or am I just comparing him with myself?"

There is the added problem of being set to observe the personality traits in another which the perceiver does not accept in himself, e.g., being somewhat autocratic. At the same time he may make undue allowances in others for those of his own deficiencies which do not disturb him but might concern some people, e.g., not following prescribed procedures.

The Perceived

Lest we leave the impression that it is only the characteristics of the perceiver that stand between him and others in his efforts to know them, we turn now to some characteristics of the person being perceived which raise problems in perception. It is possible to demonstrate, for example, that the status of the person perceived is a variable influencing judgments about his behavior. Thibaut and Riecken have shown that even though two people behave in identical fashion, status differences between them cause a perceiver to assign different motivations for the behavior.[39] Concerning co-operativeness, they found that high status persons are judged as wanting to co-operate and low status persons as having to co-operate. In turn, more liking is shown for the person of high status than for the person of low status. Presumably, more credit is given when the boss says, "Good morning," to us than when a subordinate says the same thing.

Bruner indicated that we use categories to simplify our perceptual activities. In the administrative situation, status is one type of category, and role provides another. Thus the remarks of Mr. Jones in the sales department are perceived differently from those of Smith in the purchasing department, although both may say the same thing. Also, one who knows Jones's role in the organization will perceive his behavior differently from one who does not know Jones's role. The process of categorizing on the basis of roles is similar to, if not identical with, the stereotyping process described earlier.

Visibility of the traits judged is also an important variable influencing the accuracy of perception.[40] Visibility will depend, for example, on how free the other person feels to express the trait. It has been demonstrated that we are more accurate in judging people who like us than people who dislike us. The explanation suggested is that most people in our society feel constraint in showing their dislike, and therefore the cues are less visible.

Some traits are not visible simply because they provide few external cues for their presence. Loyalty, for example, as opposed to level of energy, provides few early signs for observation. Even honesty cannot be seen in the situations in which most impressions are formed. As obvious as these comments might be, in forming impressions many of us nevertheless continue to judge the presence of traits which are not really visible. Frequently the practical situation demands judgments, but we should recognize the frail reeds upon which we are leaning and be prepared to observe further and revise our judgments with time and closer acquaintance.

SITUATIONAL INFLUENCES ON PERCEPTION

Some recent research clearly points to the conclusion that the whole process of interpersonal perception is, at least in part, a function of the *group* (or interpersonal) context in which the perception occurs. Much of the research has important theoretical implications for a psychology of interpersonal relations. In addition, there are some suggestions of value for administrators. It is possible to identify several characteristics of the interpersonal climate which have direct effect on perceptual accuracy. As will be noted, these are characteristics which can be known, and in some cases controlled, in administrative settings.

Bieri provides data for the suggestion that when people are given an opportunity to interact in a friendly situation, they tend to see others as similar to themselves.[41] Applying his suggestion to the administrative situation, we can rationalize as follows: Some difficulties of administrative practice grow out of beliefs that different interest groups in the organization are made up of different types of people. Obviously once we believe that people in other groups are different, we will be predisposed to see the differences. We can thus find, from Bieri's and from Rosenbaum's work, an administrative approach for attacking the problem.[42] If we can produce an interacting situation which is cooperative rather than

[39] J. W. Thibaut and H. W. Riecken. Some determinants and consequences of the perception of social causality. *Journal of Personality,* Vol. 24 (1955), 113–133.

[40] Bruner and Taguiri, The perception of people.

[41] J. Bieri. Change in interpersonal perception following interaction. *Journal of Abnormal and Social Psychology,* Vol. 48 (1953), 61–66.

[42] M. E. Rosenbaum. Social perception and the motivational structure of interpersonal relations. *Journal of Abnormal and Social Psychology,* Vol. 59 (1959), 130–33.

competitive, the likelihood of seeing other people as similar to ourselves is increased.

Exline's study adds some other characteristics of the social context which may influence perception.[43] Paraphrasing his conclusions to adapt them to the administrative scene, we can suggest that when a committee group is made up of congenial members who are willing to continue work in the same group, their perceptions of the goal-directed behavior of fellow committee members will be more accurate, although observations of purely personal behavior (as distinguished from goal-directed behavior) may be less accurate.[44] The implications for setting up committees and presumably other interacting work groups seem clear: Do not place together those with a past history of major personal clashes. If they must be on the same committee, each must be helped to see that the other is working toward the same goal.

An interesting variation in this area of research is the suggestion from Ex's work that perceptions will be more influenced or swayed by relatively unfamiliar people in the group than by those who are intimates.[45] The concept needs further research, but it provides the interesting suggestion that we may give more credit to strangers for having knowledge, since we do not know, than we do to our intimates whose backgrounds and limitations we feel we do know.

The *organization*, and one's place in it, may also be viewed as the context in which perceptions take place. A study by Dearborn and Simon illustrates this point.[46] Their data support the hypothesis that the administrator's perceptions will often be limited to those aspects of a situation which relate specifically to his own department, despite an attempt to influence him away from such selectivity.

Perception of self among populations at different levels in the hierarchy also offers an opportunity to judge the influence of organizational context on perceptual activity. Porter's study of the self-descriptions of managers and line workers indicated that both groups saw themselves in different terms, which corresponded to their positions in the organization's hierarchy.[47] He stated that managers used leadership-type traits (e.g., inventive) to describe themselves, while line workers used follower-type terms (e.g., co-operative). The question of which comes first must be asked: Does the manager see himself this way because of his current position in the organization? Or is this self-picture an expression of a more enduring personal characteristic that helped bring the manager to his present position? This study does not answer that question, but it does suggest to an administrator the need to be aware of the possibly critical relationship between one's hierarchical role and self-perception.

PERCEPTUAL INFLUENCES ON INTERPERSONAL ADJUSTMENT

Throughout this paper, we have examined a variety of influences on the perceptual process. There has been at least the inference that the operations of such influences on perception would in turn affect behavior that would follow. Common-sense judgment suggests that being able to judge other people accurately facilitates smooth and effective interpersonal adjustments. Nevertheless, the relationship between perception and consequent behavior is itself in need of direct analysis. Two aspects may be identified: (1) the effect of accuracy of perception on subsequent behavior and (2) the effect of the duration of the relationship and the opportunity for experiencing additional cues.

First then, from the applied point of view, we can ask a crucial question: Is there a relationship between accuracy of social perception and adjustment to others? While the question might suggest a quick affirmative answer, research findings are inconsistent. Steiner attempted to resolve some of these inconsistencies by stating that accuracy may have an effect on interaction under the following conditions: when the interacting persons are co-operatively motivated, when the behavior which is accurately perceived is relevant to the activities of these persons, and when members are free to alter their behavior on the basis of their perceptions.[48]

Where the relationship provides opportunity only to form an impression, a large number of subjective factors, i.e., set, stereotypes, projections, etc., operate to create an early impression, which is frequently erroneous. In more enduring relationships a more balanced appraisal may result as increased interaction provides additional cues for judgment. In his study of the acquaintance process, Newcomb showed that while early perception of favorable traits caused attraction to the perceived person, over a four-month

[43] R. V. Exline. Interrelations among two dimensions of sociometric status, group congeniality and accuracy of social perception. *Sociometry*, Vol. 23 (1960), 85–101.

[44] R. V. Exline. Group climate as a factor in the relevance and accuracy of social perception. *Journal of Abnormal and Social Psychology*, Vol. 55 (1957), 382–88.

[45] J. Ex. The nature of the relation between two persons and the degree of their influence on each other. *Acta Psychologica*, Vol. 17 (1960), 39–54.

[46] D. C. Dearborn and H. A. Simon. Selective perception. A note on the departmental identifications of executives. *Sociometry*, Vol. 21 (1958), 140–44.

[47] L. W. Porter. Differential self-perceptions of management personnel and line workers. *Journal of Applied Psychology*, Vol. 42 (1958), 105–9.

[48] I. Steiner. Interpersonal behavior as influenced by accuracy of social perception. *Psychological Review*, Vol. 62 (1955), 268–75.

period the early cues for judging favorable traits became less influential.[49] With time, a much broader basis was used which included comparisons with others with whom one had established relationships. Such findings suggest that the warnings about perceptual inaccuracies implicit in the earlier sections of this paper apply with more force to the short-term process of impression forming than to relatively extended acquaintance-building relationships. One could thus hope that rating an employee after a year of service would be a more objective performance than appraising him in a selection interview—a hope that would be fulfilled only when the rater had provided himself with opportunities for broadening the cues heeded in forming his first impressions.

SUMMARY

Two principal suggestions which increase the probability of more effective administrative action emerge from the research data. One suggestion is that the administrator be continuously aware of the intricacies of the perceptual process and thus be warned to avoid arbitrary and categorical judgments and to seek reliable evidence before judgments are made. A second suggestion grows out of the first: increased accuracy in one's self-perception can make possible the flexibility to seek evidence and to shift position as time provides additional evidence.

Nevertheless, not every effort designed to improve perceptual accuracy will bring about such accuracy. The dangers of too complete reliance on formal training for perceptual accuracy are suggested in a study by Crow.[50] He found that a group of senior medical students were somewhat less accurate in their perceptions of others after a period of training in physician-patient relationships than were an untrained control group. The danger is that a little learning encourages the perceiver to respond with increased sensitivity to individual differences without making it possible for him to gauge the real meaning of the differences he has seen.

Without vigilance to perceive accurately and to minimize as far as possible the subjective approach in perceiving others, effective administration is handicapped. On the other hand, research would not support the conclusion that perceptual distortions will not occur simply because the administrator says he will try to be objective. The administrator or manager will have to work hard to avoid seeing only what he wants to see and to guard against fitting everything into what he is set to see.

We are not yet sure of the ways in which training for perceptual accuracy can best be accomplished, but such training cannot be ignored. In fact, one can say that one of the important tasks of administrative science is to design research to test various training procedures for increasing perceptual accuracy.

Section D

SOCIAL PSYCHOLOGICAL PROCESSES

The last set of readings in this chapter deals with social psychological processes. Organizations are comprised of groups of individuals. Consequently, it is imperative that we study the behavior of individuals as that behavior is influenced by the mere presence and the behavior of others.

Zajonc examines the literature on the behavioral effects of the presence of others and points out a rather consistent observation. The performance of well-learned responses is improved while the learning of new responses is hampered by the mere presence of passive spectators or co-actors. Zajonc advances the postulate that the presence of others raises the arousal level which, in turn, enhances dominant responses. Zajonc also notes that others may have more complex effects on the individual's behavior.

Hill's examination of evaluative reinforcers supports Zajonc's suggestion that the behavior of others can exert more complex effects. Hill reviews six explanations for the fact that facial expressions, tones of voice, and verbal expressions of praise and criticism are powerful reinforcers of behavior. He suggests that the reinforcing value of the evaluative acts of others is due to the fact that positive evaluations are frequently associated with a variety of rewarding events and negative evaluations are associated with the withdrawal of positive reinforcers and with stimulus events which are downright aversive.

There appears to be no substitute for the adminis-

[49] T. M. Newcomb. The perception of interpersonal attraction. *American Psychologist,* Vol. 11 (1956), 575–86, and *The acquaintance process* (New York, 1961).

[50] W. J. Crow. Effect of training on interpersonal perception. *Journal of Abnormal and Social Psychology,* Vol. 55 (1957), 355–59.

tration of reinforcement contingencies on an individual basis. This means, of course, that individuals in the work group should be differentially rewarded if there are differences in the behaviors which the leader wishes to strengthen. It also means that inequities may arise. Goodman and Friedman discuss inequity problems in a critical examination of Adams's theory of inequity and related empirical studies. Adams postulates that an individual is in a state of inequity when he perceives that the ratio of his own outcomes (rewards) to inputs (education, effort, cooperation, performance, etc.) is not equal to a comparison of others' ratio of outcomes to inputs. The state of inequity is presumed to result in tension which the individual attempts to reduce by restoring equity in some manner. There can be no doubt that inequities are serious problems, and Adams's theory has helped organizational leaders understand the problem and the conditions which give rise to it. However, it must be admitted that some refinements in the model are needed. For one thing, the induction operations (those instructions and procedures which are designed to lead the subject to believe that he is being under- or overpaid) are typically quite complex and variable. Consequently, as Goodman and Friedman point out, the behavioral outcomes are open to numerous alternative explanations. In addition, most of the studies designed to test hypotheses deduced from the theory constitute complex forms of propositional control as we have earlier discussed it rather than actual reinforcement control. That is, subjects are told that they will be paid more or less than is equitable, then consequent behavior is observed. This procedure is quite unlike the typical sequence in a formal organization where individuals first perform, then are rewarded and, after the fact, may come to perceive an inequity. Such a sequence may have a more profound and a more durable effect on behavior than the induction operations typically seen in equity research.

12. SOCIAL FACILITATION*

***Robert B. Zajonc*†**

Most textbook definitions of social psychology involve considerations about the influence of man upon man, or, more generally, of individual upon individual. And most of them, explicitly or implicitly commit the main efforts of social psychology to the problem of how and why the *behavior* of one individual affects the behavior of another. The influences of individuals on each other's behavior which are of interest to social psychologists today take on very complex forms. Often they involve vast networks of interindividual effects, such as one finds in studying the process of group decision-making, competition, or conformity to a group norm. But the fundamental forms of interindividual influence are represented by the oldest experimental paradigm of social psychology: social facilitation. This paradigm, dating back to Triplett's original experiments on pacing and competition, carried out in 1897 (1), examines the consequences upon behavior which derive from the sheer presence of other individuals.

Until the late 1930's, interest in social facilitation was quite active, but with the outbreak of World War II it suddenly died. And it is truly regrettable that it died, because the basic questions about social facilitation—its dynamics and its causes—which are in effect the basic questions of social psychology, were never solved. It is with these questions that this article is concerned. I first examine past results in this nearly completely abandoned area of research and then suggest a general hypothesis which might explain them.

Research in the area of social facilitation may be classified in terms of two experimental paradigms: audience effects and co-action effects. The first experimental paradigm involves the observation of behavior when it occurs in the presence of passive spectators. The second examines behavior when it occurs in the presence of other individuals also engaged in the same activity. We shall consider past literature in these two areas separately.

AUDIENCE EFFECTS

Simple motor responses are particularly sensitive to social facilitation effects. In 1925 Travis (2) obtained such effects in a study in which he used the pursuit-rotor task. In this task the subject is required to follow a small revolving target by means of a stylus which he holds in his hand. If the stylus is even momentarily off target during a revolution, the revolution counts as an error. First each subject was trained for several consecutive days until his performance reached a stable level. One day after the

---

* *Science*, Vol. 149 (1965), 269-74. The preparation of this article was supported in part by grants Nonr-1224(34) from the Office of Naval Research and GS-629 from the National Science Foundation.

† Department of Psychology, University of Michigan.

conclusion of the training the subject was called to the laboratory, given five trials alone, and then ten trials in the presence of from four to eight upperclassmen and graduate students. They had been asked by the experimenter to watch the subject quietly and attentively. Travis found a clear improvement in performance when his subjects were confronted with an audience. Their accuracy on the ten trials before an audience was greater than on any ten previous trials, including those on which they had scored highest.

A considerably greater improvement in performance was recently obtained in a somewhat different setting and on a different task (3). Each subject (all were National Guard trainees) was placed in a separate booth. He was seated in front of a panel outfitted with 20 red lamps in a circle. The lamps on this panel light in a clock-wise sequence at 12 revolutions per minute. At random intervals one or another light fails to go on in its proper sequence. On the average there are 24 such failures per hour. The subject's task is to signal whenever a light fails to go on. After 20 minutes of intensive training, followed by a short rest, the National Guard trainees monitored the light panels for 135 minutes. Subjects in one group performed their task alone. Subjects in another group were told that from time to time a lieutenant colonel or a master sergeant would visit them in the booth to observe their performance. These visits actually took place about four times during the experimental session. There was no doubt about the results. The accuracy of the supervised subjects was on the average 34 percent higher than the accuracy of the trainees working in isolation, and toward the end of the experimental session the accuracy of the supervised subjects was more than twice as high as that of the subjects working in isolation. Those expecting to be visited by a superior missed, during the last experimental period, 20 percent of the light failures, while those expecting no such visits missed 64 percent of the failures.

Dashiell, who, in the early 1930's, carried out an extensive program of research on social facilitation, also found considerable improvement in performance due to audience effects on such tasks as simple multiplication or word association (4). But, as is the case in many other areas, negative audience effects were also found. In 1933 Pessin asked college students to learn lists of nonsense syllables under two conditions, alone and in the presence of several spectators (5). When confronted with an audience, his subjects required an average of 11.27 trials to learn a seven-item list. When working alone they needed only 9.85 trials. The average number of errors made in the "audience" condition was considerably higher than the number in the "alone" condition. In 1931 Husband found that the presence of spectators interferes with the learning of a finger maze (6), and in 1933 Pessin and Husband (7) confirmed Husband's results. The number of trials which the isolated subjects required for learning the finger maze was 17.1. Subjects confronted with spectators, however, required 19.1 trials. The average number of errors for the isolated subjects was 33.7; the number for those working in the presence of an audience was 40.5.

The results thus far reviewed seem to contradict one another. On a pursuit-rotor task Travis found that the presence of an audience improves performance. The learning of nonsense syllables and maze learning, however, seem to be inhibited by the presence of an audience, as shown by Pessin's experiment. The picture is further complicated by the fact that when Pessin's subjects were asked, several days later, to recall the nonsense syllables they had learned, a reversal was found. The subjects who tried to recall the lists in the presence of spectators did considerably better than those who tried to recall them alone. Why are the learning of nonsense syllables and maze learning inhibited by the presence of spectators? And why, on the other hand, does performance on a pursuit-rotor, word-association, multiplication, or a vigilance task improve in the presence of others?

There is just one, rather subtle, consistency in the above results. It would appear that the emission of well-learned responses is facilitated by the presence of spectators, while the acquisition of new responses is impaired. To put the statement in conventional psychological language, performance is facilitated and learning is impaired by the presence of spectators.

This tentative generalization can be reformulated so that different features of the problem are placed into focus. During the early stages of learning, especially of the type involved in social facilitation studies, the subject's responses are mostly the wrong ones. A person learning a finger maze, or a person learning a list of nonsense syllables, emits more wrong responses than right ones in the early stages of training. Most learning experiments continue until he ceases to make mistakes—until his performance is perfect. It may be said, therefore, that during training it is primarily wrong responses which are dominant and strong: they are the ones which have the highest probability of occurrence. But after the individual has mastered the task, correct responses necessarily gain ascendency in his task-relevant behavioral repertoire. Now they are the ones which are more probable—in other words, dominant. Our tentative generalization may now be simplified: audience enhances the emission of dominant responses. If the dominant responses are the correct ones, as is the case upon achieving mastery, the presence of an audience will be of benefit to the individual. But if they are mostly wrong, as is the case in the early stages of learning, then these wrong responses will be enhanced in the presence of an audience, and the emission of correct responses will be postponed or prevented.

There is a class of psychological processes which are known to enhance the emission of dominant responses. They are subsumed under the concepts of drive, arousal, and activation (8). If we could show that the presence of an audience has arousal consequences for the subject, we would be a step further along in trying to arrange the results of social-facilitation experiments into a neater package. But let us first consider another set of experimental findings.

CO-ACTION EFFECTS

The experimental paradigm of co-action is somewhat more complex than the paradigm involved in the study of audience effects. Here we observe individuals all simultaneously engaged in the same activity and in full view of each other. One of the clearest effects of such simultaneous action, or co-action, is found in eating behavior. It is well known that animals simply eat more in the presence of others. For instance, Bayer had chickens eat from a pile of wheat to their full satisfaction (9). He waited some time to be absolutely sure that his subject would eat no more, and then brought in a companion chicken who had not eaten for 24 hours. Upon the introduction of the hungry co-actor, the apparently satisfied chicken ate two-thirds again as much grain as it had already eaten. Recent work by Tolman and Wilson fully substantiates these results (10). In an extensive study of social-facilitation effects among albino rats, Harlow found dramatic increases in eating (11). In one of his experiments, for instance, the rats, shortly after weaning, were matched in pairs for weight. They were then fed alone and in pairs on alternate days. Figure 1 shows his results. It is clear that considerably more food was consumed by the animals when they were in pairs than when they were fed alone. James (12), too, found very clear evidence of increased eating among puppies fed in groups.

FIGURE 1 DATA ON FEEDING OF ISOLATED PAIRED RATS [HARLOW (11)]

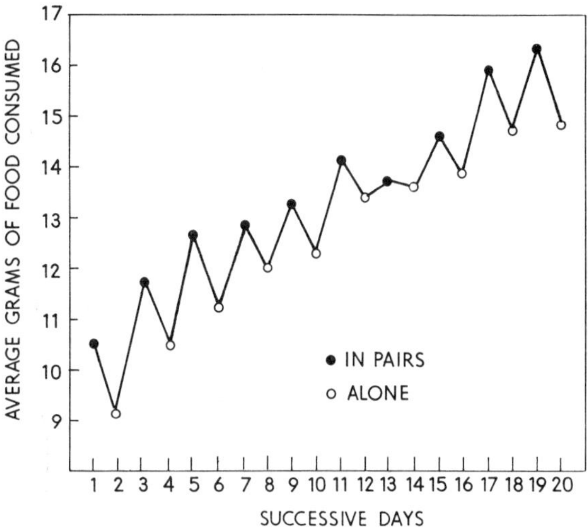

Perhaps the most dramatic effect of co-action is reported by Chen (13). Chen observed groups of ants working alone, in groups of two, and in groups of three. Each ant was observed under various conditions. In the first experimental session each ant was placed in a bottle half filled with sandy soil. The ant was observed for 6 hours. The time at which nest-building began was noted, and the earth excavated by the insect was carefully weighed. Two days afterward the same ants were placed in freshly filled bottles in pairs, and the same observations were made. A few days later the ants were placed in the bottles in groups of three, again for 6 hours. Finally, a few days after the test in groups of three, nest-building of the ants in isolation was observed. Figure 2 shows some of Chen's data.

There is absolutely no question that the amount of work an ant accomplishes increases markedly in the presence of another ant. In all pairs except one, the presence of a companion increased output by a factor of at least 2. The effect of co-action on the latency of the nest-building behavior was equally dramatic. The solitary ants of session 1 and the final session began working on the nest in 192 minutes, on the average. The latency period for ants in groups of two was only 28 minutes. The effects observed by Chen were limited to the immediate situation and seemed to have no lasting consequence for the ants. There were no differences in the results of session 1, during which the ants worked in isolation, and of the last experimental session, where they again worked in solitude.

If one assumes that under the conditions of Chen's experiment nest-building *is* the dominant response, then there is no reason why his findings could not be embraced by the generalization just proposed. Nest-building is a response which Chen's ants have fully mastered. Certainly, it is something that a mature ant need not learn. And this is simply an instance where the generalization that the presence of others enhances the emission of dominant and well-developed responses holds.

If the process involved in audience effects is also involved in co-action effects, then learning should be inhibited in the presence of other learners. Let us

FIGURE 2 DATA ON NEST-BUILDING BEHAVIOR OF ISOLATED AND PAIRED ANTS [CHEN (13)]

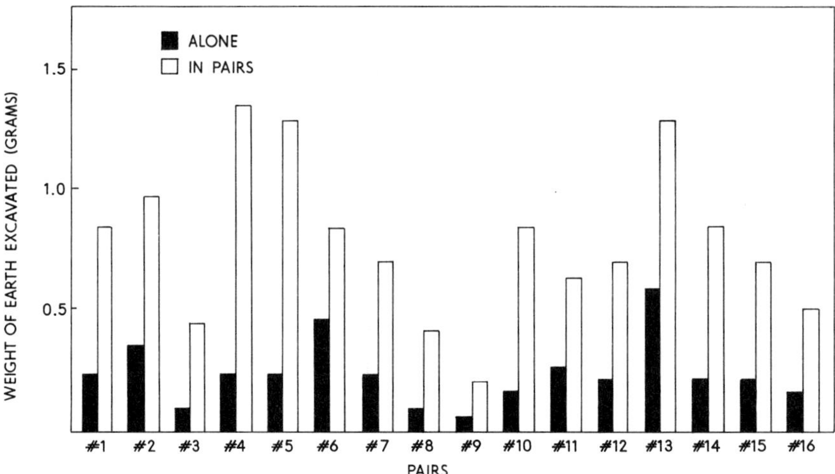

examine some literature in this field. Klopfer (14) observed greenfinches—in isolation and in heterosexual pairs—which were learning to discriminate between sources of palatable and unpalatable food. And, as one would by now expect, his birds learned this discrimination task considerably more efficiently when working alone. I hasten to add that the subject's sexual interests cannot be held responsible for the inhibition of learning in the paired birds. Allee and Masure, using Australian parakeets, obtained the same result from homosexual pairs as well (15). The speed of learning was considerably greater for the isolated birds than for the paired birds, regardless of whether the birds were of the same sex or of the opposite sex.

Similar results are found with cockroaches. Gates and Allee (16) compared data for cockroaches learning a maze in isolation, in groups of two, and in groups of three. They used an E-shaped maze. Its three runways, made of galvanized sheet metal, were suspended in a pan of water. At the end of the center runway was a dark bottle into which the photophobic cockroaches could escape from the noxious light. The results, in terms of time required to reach the bottle, are shown in Figure 3. It is clear from the data that the solitary cockroaches required considerably less time to learn the maze than the grouped animals. Gates and Allee believe that the group situation produced inhibition. They add, however (16, p. 357): "The nature of these inhibiting forces is speculative, but the fact of some sort of group interference is obvious. The presence of other roaches did not operate to change greatly the movement to different parts of the maze, but did result in increased time per trial. The roaches tended to go to the corner or end of the runway and remain there a longer time when another roach was present than when alone; the other roach was a distracting stimulus."

The experiments on social facilitation performed by Floyd Allport in 1920 and continued by Dashiell in 1930 (4, 17), both of whom used human subjects, are the ones best known. Allport's subjects worked either in separate cubicles or sitting around a common table. When working in isolation they did the various tasks at the same time and were monitored by common time signals. Allport did everything possible to reduce the tendency to compete. The subjects were told that the results of their tests would not be compared and would not be shown to other staff members, and that they themselves should refrain from making any such comparisons.

Among the tasks used were the following: chain word association, vowel cancellation, reversible perspective, multiplication, problem solving, and judgments of odors and weights. The results of Allport's experiments are well known: in all but the problem-solving and judgments test, performance was better in groups than in the "alone" condition. How do these results fit our generalization? Word association, multiplication, the cancellation of vowels, and the reversal of the perceived orientation of an ambiguous figure all involve responses which are well established. They are responses which are either very well learned or under a very strong influence of the stimulus, as in the word-association task or the reversible-perspective test. The problem-solving test consists of disproving arguments of ancient philosophers. In contrast to the other tests, it does not involve well-learned responses. On the contrary, the probability of wrong (that is, logically incorrect) responses on tasks of this sort is rather high; in other words, wrong responses are dominant. Of interest,

FIGURE 3 DATA ON MAZE LEARNING IN ISOLATED AND GROUPED COCKROACHES [GATES AND ALLEE (16)]

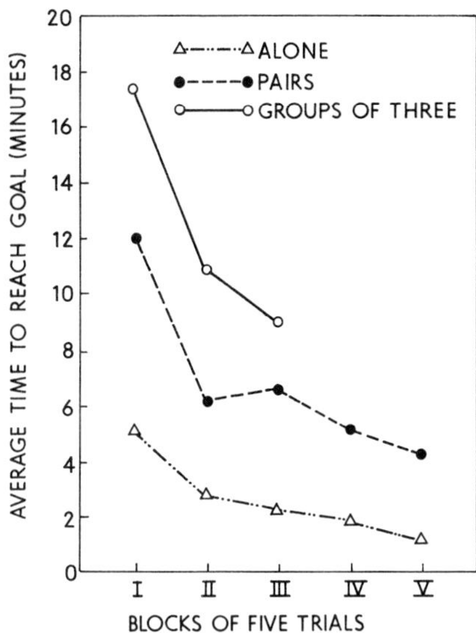

however, is the finding that while intellectual work suffered in the group situation, sheer output of words was increased. When working together, Allport's subjects tended consistently to write more. Therefore, the generalization proposed in the previous section can again be applied: if the presence of others raises the probability of dominant responses, and if strong (and many) incorrect response tendencies prevail, then the presence of others can only be detrimental to performance. The results of the judgment tests have little bearing on the present argument, since Allport gives no accuracy figures for evaluating performance. The data reported only show that the presence of others was associated with the avoidance of extreme judgments.

In 1928 Travis (18), whose work on the pursuit rotor I have already noted, repeated Allport's chain-word-association experiment. In contrast to Allport's results, Travis found that the presence of others decreased performance. The number of associations given by his subjects was greater when they worked in isolation. It is very significant, however, that Travis used stutterers as his subjects. In a way, stuttering is a manifestation of a struggle between conflicting response tendencies, all of which are strong and all of which compete for expression. The stutterer, momentarily hung up in the middle of a sentence, waits for the correct response to reach full ascendancy. He stammers because other competing tendencies are dominant at that moment. It is reasonable to assume that, to the extent that the verbal habits of a stutter are characterized by conflicting response tendencies, the presence of others, by enhancing each of these response tendencies, simply heightens his conflict. Performance is thus impaired.

AVOIDANCE LEARNING

In two experiments on the learning of avoidance responses the performances of solitary and grouped subjects were compared. In one, rats were used; in the other, humans.

Let us first consider the results of the rat experiment, by Rasmussen (19). A number of albino rats, all litter mates, were deprived of water for 48 hours. The apparatus consisted of a box containing a dish of drinking water. The floor of the box was made of a metal grille wired to one pole of an electric circuit. A wire inserted in the water in the dish was connected to the other pole of the circuit. Thirsty rats were placed in the box alone and in groups of three. They were allowed to drink for 5 seconds with the circuit open. Following this period the shock circuit remained closed, and each time the rat touched the water he received a painful shock. Observations were made on the number of times the rats approached the water dish. The results of this experiment showed that the solitary rats learned to avoid the dish considerably sooner than the grouped animals did. The rats that were in groups of three attempted to drink twice as often as the solitary rats did, and suffered considerably more shock than the solitary subjects.

Let us examine Rasmussen's results somewhat more closely. For purposes of analysis let us assume that there are just two critical responses involved: drinking, and avoidance of contact with the water. They are clearly incompatible. But drinking, we may further assume, is the domimant response, and, like eating or any other dominant response, it is enhanced by the presence of others. The animal is therefore prevented, by the facilitation of drinking which derives from the presence of others, from acquiring the appropriate avoidance response.

The second of the two studies is quite recent and was carried out by Ader and Tatum (20). They devised the following situation with which they confronted their subjects, all medical students. Each subject is told on arrival that he will be taken to another room and seated in a chair, and that electrodes will be attached to his leg. He is instructed not to get up from the chair and not to touch the electrodes. He is also told not to smoke or vocalize, and is told that the experimenter will be in the next room. That is all he is told. The subjects are observed either alone or in pairs. In the former case the subject is brought to the room and seated at a table equipped with a red button which is connected to an electric circuit. Electrodes, by means of which electric shock can be administered, are attached to the calf of one leg. After the electrodes are attached, the experimenter leaves the room. From now on the subject will receive ½ second of electric shock every 10 seconds unless he presses the red button. Each press of the button delays the shock by 10 seconds. Thus, if he is to avoid shock, he must press the button at least once every 10 seconds. It should be noted that no information was given him about the function of the button, or about the purpose of the experiment. No essential differences are introduced when subjects are brought to the room in pairs. Both are seated at the table and both become part of the shock circuit. The response of either subject delays the shock for both.

The avoidance response is considered to have been acquired when the subject (or pair of subjects) receives less than six shocks in a period of 5 minutes. Ader and Tatum report that the isolated students required, on the average, 11 minutes, 35 seconds to reach this criterion of learning. Of the 12 pairs which participated in the experiment, only two reached this criterion. One of them required 46 minutes, 40 seconds; the other, 68 minutes, 40 seconds! Ader and Tatum offer no explanation for their curious results. But there is no reason why we should not treat them in terms of the generalization proposed above. We are dealing here with a learning task, and the fact that the subjects are learning to avoid shock by pressing a red button does not introduce particular problems. They are confronted with an ambiguous task, and told nothing about the button. Pressing the button is simply not the dominant response in this situation. However, escaping is. Ader and Tatum report that eight of the 36 subjects walked out in the middle of the experiment.

One aspect of Ader and Tatum's results is especially worth noting. Once having learned the appropriate avoidance response the individual subjects responded at considerably lower rates than the paired subjects. When we consider only those subjects who achieved the learning criterion and only those responses which occurred *after* criterion had been reached, we find that the response rates of the individual subjects were in all but one case lower than the response rates of the grouped subjects. This result further confirms the generalization that, while learning is impaired by the presence of others, the performance of learned responses is enhanced.

There are experiments which show that learning is enhanced by the presence of other learners (21), but in all these experiments, as far as I can tell, it was possible for the subject to *observe* the critical responses of other subjects, and to determine when he was correct and when incorrect. In none, therefore, has the co-action paradigm been employed in its pure form. That paradigm involves the presence of others, and nothing else. It requires that these others not be able to provide the subject with cues or information as to appropriate behavior. If other learners can supply the critical individual with such cues we are dealing not with the problem of co-action but with the problem of imitation or vicarious learning.

THE PRESENCE OF OTHERS AS A SOURCE OF AROUSAL

The results I have discussed thus far lead to one generalization and to one hypothesis. The generalization which organizes these results is that the presence of others, as spectators or as co-actors, enhances the emission of dominant responses. We also know from extensive research literature that arousal, activation, or drive all have as a consequence the enhancement of dominant responses (22). We now need to examine the hypothesis that the presence of others increases the individual's general arousal or drive level.

The evidence which bears on the relationship between the presence of others and arousal is, unfortunately, only indirect. But there is some very suggestive evidence in one area of research. One of the more reliable indicators of arousal and drive is the activity of the endocrine systems in general, and of the adrenal cortex in particular. Adrenocortical functions are extremely sensitive to changes in emotional arousal, and it has been known for some time that organisms subjected to prolonged stress are likely to manifest substantial adrenocortical hypertrophy (23). Recent work (24) has shown that the main biochemical component of the adrenocortical output is hydrocortisone (17-hydroxycorticosterone). Psychiatric patients characterized by anxiety states, for instance, show elevated plasma levels of hydrocortisone (25). Mason, Brady, and Sidman (26) have recently trained monkeys to press a lever for food and have given these animals unavoidable electric shocks, all preceded by warning signals. This procedure led to elevated hydrocortisone levels; the levels returned to normal within one hour after the end of the experimental session. This "anxiety" reaction can apparently be attenuated if the animal is given repeated doses of reserpine one day before the experimental session (27). Sidman's conditioned avoidance schedule also results in raising the hydrocortisone levels by a factor of 2 to 4 (26). In this schedule the animal receives an electric shock every 20 seconds without warning, unless he presses a lever. Each press delays the shock for 20 seconds.

While there is a fair amount of evidence that adrenocortical activity is a reliable symptom of arousal, similar endocrine manifestations were found to be associated with increased population density

(28). Crowded mice, for instance, show increased amphetamine toxicity—that is, susceptibility to the excitatory effect of amphetamine—against which they can be protected by the administration of phenobarbital, chlorpromazine, or reserpine (29). Mason and Brady (30) have recently reported that monkeys caged together had considerably higher plasma levels of hydrocortisone than monkeys housed in individual cages. Thiessen (31) found increases in adrenal weights in mice housed in groups of 10 and 20 as compared with mice housed alone. The mere presence of other animals in the same room, but in separate cages, was also found to produce elevated levels of hydrocortisone. Table 1, taken from a report by Mason and Brady (30), shows plasma levels of hydrocortisone for three animals which lived at one time in cages that afforded them the possibility of visual and tactile contact and, at another time, in separate rooms.

Mason and Brady also report urinary levels of hydrocortisone, by days of the week, for five monkeys from their laboratory and for one human hospital patient. These very suggestive figures are reproduced in Table 2 (30). In the monkeys, the low weekend traffic and activity in the laboratory seem to be associated with a clear decrease in hydrocortisone.

TABLE 1

Subject	*Time*	*Conc. of 17-Hydroxycorticosterone in Caged Monkeys (μg per 100 ml of Plasma)*	
		In Separate Rooms	*In Same Room*
M-1	9 a.m.	23	34
M-1	3 p.m.	16	27
M-2	9 a.m.	28	34
M-2	3 p.m.	19	23
M-3	9 a.m.	32	38
M-3	3 p.m.	23	31
Mean	9 a.m.	28	35
Mean	3 p.m.	19	27

Basal plasma concentrations of 17-hydroxycorticosterone in monkeys housed alone (cages in separate rooms), then in a room with other monkeys (cages in same room). [Leiderman and Shapiro (35, p. 7)].

As for the hospital patient, Mason and Brady report (30, p. 8), "he was confined to a thoracic surgery ward that bustled with activity during the weekdays when surgery and admissions occurred. On the weekends the patient retired to the nearby Red Cross building, with its quieter and more pleasant environment."

Admittedly, the evidence that the mere presence of others raises the arousal level is indirect and scanty. And, as a matter of fact, some work seems to suggest that there are conditions, such as stress, under which the presence of others may lower the animal's arousal level. Boyard (32), for instance, hypothesized that the presence of another member of the same species may protect the individual under stress by inhibiting the activity of the posterior hypothalamic centers which trigger the pituitary adrenal cortical and sympatheticoadrenal medullary responses to stress. Evidence for Boyard's hypothesis, however, is as indirect as evidence for the one which predicts arousal as a consequence of the presence of others, and even more scanty.

SUMMARY AND CONCLUSION

If one were to draw one practical suggestion from the review of the social-facilitation effects which are summarized in this article he would advise the student to study all alone, preferably in an isolated cubicle, and to arrange to take his examinations in the company of many other students, on stage, and in the presence of a large audience. The results of his examination would be beyond his wildest expectations, provided of course, he had learned his material quite thoroughly.

I have tried in this article to pull together the early, almost forgotten work on social facilitation, and to explain the seemingly conflicting results. This explanation is, of course, tentative, and it has never been put to a direct experimental test. It is, moreover, not far removed from the one originally proposed by Allport. He theorized (33, p. 261) that "the sights and sounds of others doing the same thing" augment ongoing responses. Allport, however, proposed this effect only for *overt* motor responses, assuming (33, p. 274) that "*intellectual or implicit responses* of thought are hampered rather than

TABLE 2

Subjects	*Amounts Excreted (mg/24 hr)*								
	Mon.	*Tues.*	*Wed.*	*Thurs.*	*Fri.*	*Sat.*	*Sun.*	*Mon.*	*Tues.*
Monkeys	1.88	1.71	1.60	1.52	1.70	1.16	1.17	1.88	
Patient		5.9	6.5	4.5	5.7	3.3	3.9	6.0	5.2

Variations in urinary concentration of hydrocortisone over a 9-day period for five laboratory monkeys and one human hospital patient [Leiderman and Shapiro (35, p. 8)].

facilitated" by the presence of others. This latter conclusion was probably suggested to him by the negative results he observed in his research on the effects of co-action on problem solving.

Needless to say, the presence of others may have effects considerably more complex than that of increasing the individual's arousal level. The presence of others may provide cues as to appropriate or inappropriate responses, as in the case of imitation or vicarious learning. Or it may supply the individual with cues as to the measure of danger in an ambiguous or stressful situation. Davitz and Mason (34), for instance, have shown that the presence of an unafraid rat reduces the fear of another rat in stress. Boyard (32) believes that the calming of the rat in stress which is in the presence of an unafraid companion is mediated by inhibition of activity of the posterior hypothalamus. But in their experimental situations (that is, the open field test) the possibility that cues for appropriate escape or avoidance responses are provided by the co-actor is not ruled out. We might therefore be dealing not with the effects of the mere presence of others but with the considerably more complex case of imitation. The animal may not be calming *because* of his companion's presence. He may be calming *after* having copied his companion's attempted escape responses. The paradigm which I have examined in this article pertains only to the effects of the mere presence of others, and to the consequences for the arousal level. The exact parameters involved in social facilitation still must be specified.

REFERENCES

1. N. Triplett, *American Journal of Psychology*, 1897, **9**, 507.
2. L. E. Travis, *Journal of Abnormal and Social Psychology*, 1925, **20**, 142.
3. B. O. Bergum and D. J. Lehr, *Journal of Applied Psychology*, 1963, **47**, 75.
4. J. F. Dashiell, *Journal of Abnormal and Social Psychology*, 1930, **25**, 190.
5. J. Pessin, *American Journal of Psychology*, 1933, **45**, 263.
6. R. W. Husband, *Journal of Genetic Psychology*, 1931, **39**, 258. In this task the blindfolded subject traces a maze with his finger.
7. J. Pessin and R. W. Husband, *Journal of Abnormal and Social Psychology*, 1933, **28**, 148.
8. See, for instance, E. Dufy, *Activation and behavior* (New York: Wiley, 1962); K. W. Spence, *Behavior theory and conditioning* (New Haven: Yale University Press, 1956); R. B. Zajonc and B. Nieuwenhuyse, *Journal of Experimental Psychology*, 1964, **67**, 276.
9. E. Bayer, *Zoological Psychology*, 1929, **112**, 1.
10. C. W. Tolman and G. T. Wilson, *Animal Behavior*, 1965, **13**, 134.
11. H. F. Harlow, *Journal of Genetic Psychology*, 1932, **43**, 211.
12. W. T. James, *Journal of Comparative and Physiological Psychology*, 1953, **46**, 427; *Journal of Genetic Psychology*, 1960, **96**, 123; W. T. James and D. J. Cannon, *Journal of Genetic Psychology*, 1956, 87, 225.
13. S. C. Chen, *Physiological Zoology*, 1937, **10**, 420.
14. P. H. Klopfer, *Science*, 1958, **128**, 903.
15. W. C. Allee and R. H. Masure, *Physiological Zoology*, 1936, **22**, 131.
16. M. J. Gates and W. C. Allee, *Journal of Comparative Psychology*, 1933, **15**, 331.
17. F. H. Allport, *Journal of Experimental Psychology*, 1920, **3**, 154.
18. L. E. Travis, *Journal of Abnormal and Social Psychology*, 1928, **23**, 45.
19. E. Rasmussen, *Acta Psychology*, 1939, **4**, 275.
20. R. Ader and R. Tatum, *Journal of the Experimental Analysis of Behavior*, 1963, **6**, 357.
21. H. Gurnee, *Journal of Abnormal and Social Psychology*, 1939, **4**, 529; J. C. Welty, *Physiological Zoology*, 1934, **7**, 85.
22. See K. W. Spence, *Behavior Theory and Conditioning* (New Haven: Yale University Press), 1956.
23. H. Selye, *Journal of Clinical Endocrinology*, 1946, **6**, 117.
24. D. H. Nelson and L. T. Samuels, *Journal of Clinical Endocrinology*, 1952, **12**, 519.
25. E. L. Bliss, A. A. Sandberg, and D. H. Nelson, *Journal of Clinical Investigation*, 1953, **32**, 9; F. Board, H. Persky, and D. A. Hamburg, *Psychosomatic Medicine*, 1956, **18**, 324.
26. J. W. Mason, J. V. Brady, and M. Sidman. *Endocrinology* 1957, **60**, 741.
27. J. W. Mason and J. V. Brady, *Science*, 1956, **124**, 983.
28. D. D. Thiessen, *Texas Reports of Biology and Medicine*, 1964, **22**, 266.
29. L. Lasagna and W. P. McCann, *Science*, 1957, **125**, 1241.
30. J. W. Mason and J. V. Brady, in *Psychobiological Approaches to Social Behavior*. P. H. Leiderman and D. Shapiro, eds. (Stanford, Calif.: Stanford Univ. Press, 1964).
31. D. D. Thiessen, *Journal of Comparative and Physiological Psychology*, 1964, **57**, 412.
32. E. W. Boyard, *Psychological Review*, 1959, **66**, 267.
33. F. H. Allport, *Social Psychology* (Boston: Houghton-Mifflin, 1924).
34. J. R. Davitz and D. J. Mason, *Journal of Comparative and Physiological Psychology*, 1955, **48**, 149.
35. P. H. Leiderman and D. Shapiro, eds., *Psychobiological Approaches to Social Behavior* (Stanford, Calif.: Stanford University Press, 1964).

13. SOURCES OF EVALUATIVE REINFORCEMENT*

***Winfred F. Hill*†**

A large proportion of the reinforcers, positive and negative, that play a major part in human learning and motivation involve the evaluation of a person by others or by himself. They include the positive reinforcing value of being liked, praised, admired, accepted, superior, or successful, and the negative reinforcing value of being disliked, criticized, ridiculed, rejected, inferior, or a failure. Such reinforcers vary on a number of dimensions. Some are specifically social, others only indirectly social in that they refer to evaluative standards that are for the most part socially learned. Some refer directly to hierarchies of superiority, others do so only by vague implication. Some refer to single events, others to enduring conditions. What they all have in common is that they involve an evaluation of the subject, either by someone else or by himself, with positive evaluations functioning as positive reinforcers and negative ones as negative reinforcers. They may therefore be grouped under the term *evaluative reinforcers.*

REVIEW OF ATTEMPTED EXPLANATIONS

How do evaluative reinforcers acquire their positive or negative reinforcing properties? The whole question of how tastes and values are acquired is a difficult and controversial one in psychological theory, and the problem as applied to evaluative reinforcers is especially difficult. A number of suggestions are available in the literature about the sources of positive and negative reinforcers. The present paper reviews six such interpretations as they apply to evaluative reinforcers. These six interpretations represent not six different theories associated with different authors, but rather six hypothetical mechanisms which have been considered in various forms, singly or in combination, by a variety of theorists. With some adjustments in details, they represent a fairly thorough coverage of suggested sources of the reinforcing properties of stimuli.

Evaluative Reinforcers as Innate

The first interpretation, suggested by the strength and ubiquity of evaluative reinforcers, is that human beings inherit the tendency to be reinforced by certain behaviors which have evaluative significance. These evaluative reinforcers can therefore be treated as primary reinforcers, just as food reinforcement has traditionally been treated. (The simple statement that food is a primary reinforcer of course covers a multitude of complexities, but for the present purpose we can afford to overlook them.) For some evaluative reinforcers, this is a plausible interpretation. Caresses and other forms of body contact are very likely innately reinforcing to humans even when not specifically sexual (Harlow, 1958); smiles may well be innately positively reinforcing, and "harsh" tones of voice are quite possibly innately negatively reinforcing. Considerably more research, both developmental and cross-cultural, will be needed before we can say definitely which such behaviors, if any, have innate affective properties. Moreover, there may be a close relationship between such likely innate reinforcers as manipulation (Harlow, 1950) and effectance (White, 1959) and such partially evaluative reinforcers as power and achievement. In any case, however, those reinforcers for which such an interpretation is plausible constitute only a subset of evaluative reinforcers. Most evaluative reinforcers involve arbitrary, culturally patterned symbolism. The particular objects and acts which function as status symbols or as signs of friendship differ so much from one culture to another that to treat them as innate is hopeless. Even within a single culture, the evaluative significance of a given act, and hence its function as a positive or a negative reinforcer, may depend on very subtle supplementary cues. The same shove which in one context implies "We're buddies, and it's great fun to have you around," in another context implies "You're a contemptible nuisance, and all I want is to get you out of my way." This is not to deny that hereditary differences may be important in the case with which evaluative reinforcers are acquired. However, given the variation in the significance of symbols, both from culture to culture and from context to context within the same culture, it seems clear that some kind of learning must be involved in determining what symbols will have what affective significance.

Evaluative Reinforcers as Learned by Familiarity

The second interpretation is that evaluative rein-

* *Psychological Bulletin,* Vol. 69, No. 2 (1968), pp. 132–46.

† Northwestern University.

This article was prepared during the author's tenure as a Fellow at the Center for Advanced Study in the Behavioral Sciences, Stanford, California.

forcers acquire their effectiveness through sheer amount of experience. For many other kinds of reinforcers, this form of learning may be important. The work of Cairns (1966) with sheep and of Scott and Fuller (1965) with dogs, for example, suggests the importance of learning by familiarity for the formation of social attachments. Dember, Earl, and Paradise (1957) have provided some experimental support for the widely held view that experience alone is enough to change esthetic preferences from simpler to more complex stimuli. Such terms as canalization (Murphy, 1947) and sensitization imply that repeated experience itself enhances the affectivity of certain stimuli. (On the other hand, the terms satiation and habituation imply that repeated experience reduces affectivity.) It is possible that this process of affective learning by familiarity may play some small part in the acquisition of evaluative reinforcers. It is difficult to see, however, how it could be a major factor. A crucial characteristic of evaluative reinforcers is their polarity. Markedly similar communications can have opposite affective significance, depending on a small change in intonation or on the insertion of a "not." To say that the positive and the negative versions of the communication differ in their affective significance because of a difference in the sheer frequency with which they have been experienced would be a very difficult position to defend. In any case, it is highly unlikely that the frequency with which most people experience positive and negative evaluations differs in any systematic way which could explain either the typical preference for the positive evaluations or individual differences in the strength of this preference. It seems clear not only that the power of evaluative reinforcers must be learned, but that it must be learned by some process that goes beyond mere frequency of experience to make certain stimuli positively reinforcing and other, superficially similar stimuli negative reinforcing.

Evaluative Reinforcers as Learned Drives Based on Pain

The basic paradigm for the acquisition of a learned drive (or conditioned negative reinforcer) is that a previously neutral stimulus, as a result of pairing with an aversive stimulus, becomes aversive, and its reduction consequently reinforcing (Miller, 1951; Skinner, 1953). Ordinarily in experimentation, the primary aversive stimulus with which the neutral stimulus is paired is pain, in most cases electric shock. Other unconditioned stimuli have been used, such as cold (Howard, 1962), air blast (Ray, 1966), and momentary asphyxiation (Campbell, Sanderson, & Laverty, 1964), but without providing definite evidence that removal of the CS is sufficient to reinforce a new response. The theoretical suggestion then is that negative evaluative responses are paired with primary aversive stimuli and thus become conditioned aversive stimuli, stimuli for the arousal of secondary drive. By this interpretation, the aversiveness of negative evaluations is the more basic phenomenon, reflecting learned drive directly, whereas the positive reinforcing property of positive evaluations is a derived phenomenon, in that positive evaluations serve as a sort of insurance against or antidote to negative ones.

If the learned-drive paradigm is considered only in the narrow sense in which it has been clearly demonstrated—that is, with pain as the primary aversive stimulus—there are several reasons for doubting that it can explain the powerful role of evaluative reinforcers in human behavior. For one thing, what pain people suffer, at least in middle-class America, is largely the result of illness or accident rather than being inflicted in any systematic pairing with negative evaluations. The "penalty" for being disapproved by another, whether peer or superior, is much more likely to take the form of social isolation, loss of property or privileges, or some other such mistreatment which, while it may be highly unpleasant, can scarcely be construed as physically painful. (Admittedly, really systematic data are not available to support this dogmatic statement, though it receives some support from parents' reports of their disciplinary techniques—Sears, Maccoby, & Levin, 1957, p. 328.) These conditions for the occurrence of pain could much more readily result in evidences of carelessness becoming conditioned aversive stimuli than in evidences of negative evaluation becoming aversive. Moreover, what evidence we have suggests that there is a negative correlation between the use of pain as a disciplinary device and evidence of conscience in children (Sears et al., 1957, p. 386). Though there is something of a leap in going from "conscience" to "concern with evaluative reinforcers," such data nevertheless suggest that more frequent pairing of pain with negative evaluation does not necessarily make the child try harder to avoid negative evaluation. Finally, if pain is a crucial factor in the development of evaluative reinforcers, we would expect congenitally pain-free individuals to be profoundly different in personality from other people. Again, what limited evidence we have is to the contrary (Sternbach, 1963).

In principle, it is possible that other primary aversive stimulation, such as loud noise, loss of support, extreme temperature, or asphyxiation, might substitute for pain in this paradigm. Even though such aversive stimuli would circumvent some of the difficulties with pain, it would be even more difficult to make a case that they are systematically paired with negative evaluations in many people's lives. It therefore seems highly unlikely that they play any major part in the acquisition of evaluative reinforcers.

Brown (1961) has proposed a modification of the secondary drive hypothesis, in which certain words, tones of voice, and facial expressions become learned drive stimuli through pairing with pain on those occasions when the child is hurt and others about him display these various symptoms of distress. Then, through second-order conditioning, negative evaluations become paired with these signs of distress and thus also become learned drive stimuli. This two-stage interpretation solves some of the problems of the single-stage learned-drive interpretation. It also leads to at least one prediction which has some support: that the more closely the signs of negative evaluation resemble those of distress at injury, the more aversive negative evaluation should become for the child. This prediction is consistent with the finding (Sears et al., 1957) that disciplinary techniques which emphasize the parent's unhappiness at the child's misbehavior tend (with many qualifications) to be associated with higher development of conscience than techniques which emphasize the parent's "unhappiretribution." However, Brown's interpretation still has its difficulties. For one thing, it fails to deal with the problem of the congenitally pain-free person. For another, it implies a backward conditioning process for the first-order conditioning of secondary drive, in that the child first feels pain and then observes the signs of distress in others. The evidence from classical conditioning (see especially Barlow, 1956) suggests that such a backward paradigm would be quite a poor one for making signs of distress into conditioned aversive stimuli. Finally, Brown's model raises the question of why the aversiveness of distress signs does not extinguish when these signs occur so frequently in the absence of pain and so seldom in the presence of pain. Though there is ample evidence that conditioned aversiveness is highly resistant to extinction in an avoidance situation (e.g., Solomon & Wynne, 1954), there is no suggestion in Brown's theory that the child learns to avoid pain by making any particular response to signs of distress in other people. The classical aversive conditioning situation seems more relevant to Brown's hypothesis than does the avoidance situation, and there is no indication of such high resistance to extinction in classical aversive conditioning (e.g., Ayres, 1966; Strouthes & Hamilton, 1964). The suggested structure of second-order aversive conditioning thus appears to be built on a dangerously fragile base.

Evaluative Reinforcers as Learned Drives Based on Frustration

According to theory (e.g., Dollard & Miller, 1950), a neutral stimulus can become aversive not only through pairing with pain, but through pairing with any aversive stimulus. Under this broader interpretation, the frustration of any motive could serve as the primary aversive stimulus in the conditioning of secondary drive. Negative evaluations could thus become negative reinforcers through pairing with any of a great variety of frustrations. If disapproval from a parent or a peer means that a child is unable to eat the candy, play the game, get hold of the toy, or receive the caress that he wants, the resultant frustration should tend to make the signs of disapproval into negative reinforcers. This broader interpretation of secondary drive, not always clearly distinguished in the literature from that based on pain, eliminates all the objections to the interpretation which arises when only pain is considered as a primary aversive stimulus. However, the evidence that secondary drives can be learned on the basis of frustration is quite sparse. Several experiments (e.g., Ferster, 1958) have shown avoidance behavior in which the (presumably noxious) stimulus being avoided was a time-out from primary positive reinforcement. Such studies suggest that the time-out, which involves frustration of instrumental behavior, is aversive. However, a recent review of the topic (Leitenberg, 1965) raised the question of whether the avoidance behavior occurs because the time-out is aversive or because the avoidance behavior serves to maximize positive reinforcement. To separate the effects of these two factors, a situation is needed in which the avoidance behavior does not provide any differential positive reinforcement beyond that of a control group. Leitenberg's review cited two such studies. In one (Adelman & Maatsch, 1956), rats receiving extinction (and hence frustration) in a runway showed a marked tendency to jump out of the goal box when given the opportunity, much more so than rats that had never been rewarded in the goal box. However, interpretation is slightly confounded by the fact that during acquisition of the jump-out response the frustrated group ran to the goal box while the control group was placed there. In the other study (Wagner, 1963), rats jumped a hurdle to terminate a distinctive stimulus more readily if that stimulus had previously occurred on the nonreinforced trials of a partial reinforcement schedule in a runway than if it had occurred in another place, unassociated with reward. It is noteworthy, however, that neither of these studies separated the aversiveness of the frustrative stimulus from its activating properties (Amsel, 1962). Both activation and aversiveness are included in typical definitions of drive, but for purposes of explaining evaluative reinforcement it is the aversiveness which is crucial. Moreover, the difference in hurdle jumping between the experimental and control groups in the Wagner study was rather small compared to the difference in a similar study using electric shock to establish the aversiveness of a stimulus (Brown & Jacobs, 1949). Finally, Wong and Pavlik (1966) have shown a limitation on the aversiveness of stimuli associated with frustration, in that rats in a runway did not leave the start box any more rapidly when it was of a color previously associated with nonreward than when it was of a color associated with reward or of a neutral color.

Even if all these weaknesses in the evidence for the aversiveness of frustrative stimuli are ignored, there is an additional problem. In none of these apparent demonstrations of conditioned aversiveness based on frustration was the original training drive (generally hunger) satiated at the time of testing. Strictly speaking, therefore, all that can be predicted about evaluative reinforcers from this paradigm is that if a negative evaluation was paired with frustration of, for example, food-directed activity, negative evaluation would subsequently function as a negative reinforcer when the person was hungry. Yet it appears, anecdotally, that the aversiveness of disapproval or of conspicuous inferiority bears very little relation to the current primary drive state of the individual. Would the learned drive stimulus still be aversive if the training drive were satiated? There is little evidence on this point, but at least one study suggests that it would not. Myers and Miller (1954) trained hungry rats to run from a white box into a black one where they were fed. When satiated, these rats showed no more tendency to run from the white box into the black one, and to learn a new response which permitted them to do so, than did control rats without the prior training. Though the data do not rule out learned drive based on frustration as the basis for the aversiveness of negative evaluations, they certainly indicate that the experimental basis for this interpretation is very tenuous.

Still another interpretation of learned drive involves the conditioned consummatory response. In this paradigm, a stimulus associated with deprivation acquires the power to enhance subsequent consummatory behavior. For example, a rat eats more in a distinctive box when moderately food-deprived if his previous experience in that box was when highly deprived than if it was when satiated. Whether such conditioned consummatory behavior actually occurs with any consistency is highly controversial. (On the positive side: Calvin, Bicknell, & Sperling, 1953; Trost & Homzie, 1966; Wright, 1965. On the negative side: Brozovich, Malony, & Wright, 1963; Dyal, 1958; Novin & Miller, 1962; Siegel & MacDonnell, 1954.) Whether valid or not, this learning paradigm has little relevance to the problem of evaluative reinforcers since it deals with the eliciting function of the conditioned stimulus rather than with its positive or negative reinforcing function. We are concerned with, for example, whether the pairing of criticism with loss of candy makes criticism aversive, not with whether it makes criticism a stimulus for eating candy. (The latter may nonetheless be an important question, as in cases of bulimia.) Similarly, the literature on variables in hoarding (Morgan, 1947), though relevant in a general sense to the issue of learnable drives, is too closely tied to the original primary reinforcer (e.g., food pellets) to have much relevance for the question of evaluative reinforcers.

Evaluative Reinforcers as Secondary Reinforcers

The fifth interpretation, especially emphasized by Skinner (1953), is that positive evaluative reinforcers acquire their reinforcing properties through being paired with primary reinforcers, following the paradigm for secondary (conditioned) reinforcement. In contrast to the third interpretation, this one treats the reinforcing property of positive evaluation as the more basic phenomenon, with the aversiveness of negative evaluations as a derived phenomenon in which negative evaluations merely represent the most conspicuous failures to obtain positive ones.

Again, three difficulties appear. First, evalutive reinforcers appear to be highly resistant to extinction. The positive reinforcing value of liking and respect and the negative reinforcing value of inferiority, criticism, and rejection seem to persist little diminished through many experiences in which they occur without any tangible primary positive or negative reinforcer being paired with them. Secondary reinforcement in the laboratory, in contrast, does not ordinarily show any such high resistance to extinction. Such reviewers as Kelleher and Gollub (1962) and Razran (1955) commented on the weak resistance to extinction commonly found in laboratory studies of secondary reinforcement.

Second, evaluative reinforcers not infrequently appear to be more powerful than primary reinforcers assumed to have been involved in the acquisition of the evaluative (secondary) reinforcers. People will bear considerable degrees of physical discomfort and privation rather than incur the disapproval, from others or from themselves, that would result from sacrificing a goal, breaking an ethical rule, admitting weakness, or committing a breach of decorum. (As evidence for this point, our slavish adherence to the social niceties regarding proper clothing and proper times and places for excretion are fully as compelling as our occasional extreme sacrifices for God, Country, or the conquest of mountain peaks.) In contrast, Kelleher and Gollub (1962), in reviewing the topic of secondary reinforcement, concluded that in every study where appropriate comparisons were made, secondary reinforcers were less effective than the primary reinforcers from which they were learned. These authors suggested that superiority of a secondary to a primary reinforcer might be achieved by a multiple secondary reinforcer (i.e., one acquired through pairing with several different primary reinforcers). However, there is enough doubt as to whether multiple secondary reinforcers are really superior to single ones (Myers & Trapold, 1966; Wunderlich, 1961) so that their suggestion must be considered highly tentative.

Third, evaluative reinforcers appear to be independent of primary drives. The positive reinforcing effect of praise and the negative reinforcing effect of criticism do not seem to depend to any appreciable extent on whether the person is deprived or satiated with respect to food, water, exploration, activity, or much of anything else. The power of laboratory reinforcers, in contrast, depends heavily on the current state of drive. Miles (1956), using a secondary reinforcer learned through pairing with food, found responses for the secondary reinforcer to be a monotonic increasing function of food deprivation at the time of testing. Estes (1949a), using a secondary reinforcer learned through pairing with water, found no more responding by the secondarily reinforced group than by the control group when both were satiated for water. Similar results have been found when an inaccessible primary reinforcer was used as a special kind of secondary reinforcer. Although Brogden (1942), Wike and Casey (1954b), and MacCorquodale and Meehl (1949) found some evidence of the reinforcing value of food for satiated animals, these studies did not control for possible irrelevant primary reinforcing properties of food, properties which might perhaps have been found equally in wooden blocks. Seward and Levy (1953) demonstrated a preference for a secondarily reinforcing goal box by satiated rats in the absence of this confounding factor. However, the absence of a significant increase in preference over trials makes the results somewhat difficult to interpret. Subsequent studies (Platt & Wike, 1962; Schlosberg & Pratt, 1956) have shown that a preference for inaccessible food is found in hungry but not in satiated rats. Similarly, there is little evidence that token rewards are effective reinforcers for satiated primates, however effective they may be for hungry subjects (Howard & Young, 1962; Wolfe, 1936).

There is evidence to suggest that other drives can to some extent substitute for the training drive in maintaining the power of secondary reinforcers. This possibility is supported by Bower and Kaufman (1963), D'Amato (1955), Estes (1949a), and Wike and Casey (1954a). However, an attempt by Reid and Slivinske (1954) to replicate the Estes finding was unsuccessful. Moreover, since all of these experiments used hunger and thirst as the two drives to be manipulated, Verplanck and Hayes' (1953) emphasis on the nonindependence of hunger and thirst makes the generality of the suggestion suspect. Even if further research should clearly demonstrate a general tendency for irrelevant drives to activate secondary reinforcers, there is considerable doubt as to how helpful this law would be in supporting the conclusion that evaluative reinforcers are secondary reinforcers. It would not be enough that there was always some activated drive to explain why the evaluative (secondary) reinforcer is effective; there would also have to be evidence that the effectiveness of evaluative reinforcers is proportional to the total level of activation (drive) of the individual at the time. On the basis of casual observation, it seems unlikely that such evidence can be obtained.

Evaluative Reinforcers as Cognitively Mediated

The final interpretation is that evaluative reinforcement depends on a high level of cognitive mediation, involving rational considerations of the consequences of certain states of affairs. By this interpretation, a person wants positive evaluations because he can foresee that they are likely to be followed by positive primary reinforcers and dislikes negative evaluations because he expects them to be followed by pain or frustration. Though this interpretation is in some ways a combination of the three previous ones, it differs from all of them in postulating not simple learning processes akin to classical conditioning, but high levels of rational foresight. It assumes that the persistence and power of evaluative reinforcers depend on the person's constantly reminding himself of their importance to his ultimate goals. It is unconcerned with contrary data from animal experiments because it considers the processes in evaluative reinforcement to be uniquely human.

It is quite plausible to suppose that much evaluative reinforcement is of this sort. When a researcher earnestly desires positive evaluation of his grant proposal from one particular committee, we can safely assume that he is rationally evaluating means-end relationships in a manner beyond the reach of any nonhuman. However, as a general explanation for all evaluative reinforcement, this interpretation also has severe weaknesses. Introspectively, there is a difference between particular evaluative reinforcers based on such calculated means-end relationships and the broader range of evaluative reinforcers that maintain their effect in the absence of any perceivable gain with which they are associated. Ontogenetically, the latter kind of evaluative reinforcement appears remarkably early for a tendency dependent on complex mediational processes. Phylogenetically, the latter kind of evaluative reinforcement is alleged anecdotally to vary markedly among species other than man, for example, to be much more characteristic of dogs than of cats. Moreover, the high resistance to extinction of evaluative reinforcers is even more of a problem for this interpretation than for the secondary reinforcement interpretation, since by this interpretation evaluations should be positively or negatively reinforcing only as long as the person believes that they are instrumental to positive or negative primary reinforcers. These considerations suggest that those instances of evaluative reinforcement in humans which appear to be direct and nonrational are acquired by some process which does not require a high level of cognitive mediation and which is shared with at least some other species.

SOME INTEGRATIVE SUGGESTIONS

Consideration of these six attempted explanations of evaluative reinforcement suggests that all are quite weak. Are we forced to the conclusion that existing concepts of heredity and learning cannot deal with evaluative reinforcers, that their development is incapable of explanation within the framework of current knowledge and theory? If not, how can their development be explained? Psychologists interested in the relation between learning theory and personality development have been somewhat aware of this dilemma for a number of years, but no entirely adequate answer has yet appeared.

A Compromise Interpretation

In considering the six explanations of evaluative reinforcement discussed above, it is noteworthy that four of them are subject to a priori difficulties, to objections that do not involve experimental data. The other two, secondary drive based on frustration, and secondary reinforcement, appear quite plausible but are confronted by contradictory data. Is there a combination of these two processes that is adequate to deal with the contradictory data and to explain those cases of evaluative reinforcement that do not depend on rational foresight? The following is suggested as an interpretation consistent with a wide range of current thinking on the problem.

Assume that evaluative reinforcers tend to be correlated, particularly in childhood, with a variety of primary reinforcers, positive evaluations serving as cues to the relative availability of positive reinforcers and negative evaluations as cues to their relative unavailability (and also, but of much less importance, as cues to primary aversive stimulation). Although occasional exceptions suggest themselves, as in the extra demands or restrictions that sometimes accompany the positive evaluation of high status (noblesse oblige), on the whole this assumption seems quite plausible. Positive evaluations thus have the status S^D (positive discriminative stimulus) and negative evaluations the status of S^Δ (negative discriminative stimulus) with regard to primary reinforcers. Alternatively, evaluations may be regarded as forming a continuum from most positive to most negative, correlated with degree of availability of primary reinforcers. Through this correlation, positive evaluations become secondary reinforcers and negative evaluations become secondary aversive stimuli. The resistance to extinction of these secondary reinforcers is enhanced by two kinds of contingencies in the environment: *(a)* intermittency in the original pairing of positive and negative evaluations with positive and negative primary reinforcers, and *(b)* occasional repetitions of the appropriate pairing even during periods when most occurrences of positive and negative evaluations are not paired with appropriate primary reinforcement.

This interpretation, though cast in more traditional learning-theory terms, is quite consistent with the affective arousal theories of McClelland, Atkinson, Clark, and Lowell (1953) and of Young (1961). It is also consistent with the view that objective conditions of dependence on others are important in the development of evaluative reinforcement. Moreover, the interpretation can be extended to a variety of nonevaluative positive and negative reinforcers. Its application to the positive reinforcing value of money and of power is obvious and familiar. Its application to the negative reinforcing value of imprisonment, which constitutes an S^Δ for a great many primary reinforcers, is also straightforward. Even fear of the dark may be related to the greater difficulty which visual organisms have in obtaining reinforcers under conditions of darkness (Mowrer, 1960, pp. 180–81).

A Defense of the Interpretation

If this interpretation is correct, why has the experimental demonstration of the relevant learning processes proved so difficult, as noted earlier? Actually, when we consider the importance of the topic to personality theory, the variety of experiments is surprisingly limited. For one thing, although there is no evidence that cues associated with frustration remain aversive in the absence of the training drive, neither is there any very direct evidence that they do not. In fact, as already noted, the whole question of the aversiveness of conditioned frustration cues, though important in learning theory (e.g., Amsel, 1962), has received too little direct experimental exploration. In view of the large literature on secondary reinforcement, the sparsity of literature on such conditioned aversiveness (in contrast to aversiveness conditioned through the use of pain) is surprising.

In this connection, it is interesting to speculate on what Myers and Miller (1954) would have found if they had carried out their experiment on learned drive a little differently. As it was, they placed rats in one compartment while hungry and permitted them to run into the other compartment and eat. This training procedure did not endow the cues of the hunger compartment with secondary drive properties. Suppose, however, there had been two different sets of cues in the hunger compartment, one indicating that the rat would be forced to remain there hungry, the other indicating that it was now possible to enter the other compartment and eat. It is quite possible that subsequent tests could have demonstrated either drive properties of the "frustration" cue or reinforcing properties of the "reward" cue even for satiated animals. This change in procedure would have made their study much like Wagner's (1963), in which, however, the drive properties of the "frustration" stimulus were not tested under conditions of food satiation.

Second, although the total literature on secondary reinforcement is quite large, little effort has been made to test the limits of secondary reinforcement in the directions relevant to evaluative reinforcement. Several studies (Armus & Garlich, 1961; D'Amato, Lachman, & Kivy, 1958; others cited in Myers, 1958) suggest that a training procedure in which the secondary reinforcer is only intermittently paired with the primary reinforcer makes the secondary reinforcer more resistant to extinction. In addition, can repeated pairings of the secondary reinforcer with the primary reinforcer, interspersed among tests of the secondary reinforcer without the primary reinforcer, maintain the strength of the secondary reinforcer indefinitely, or will a discrimination be learned that will result in extinction of the secondary reinforcer when it occurs alone? Saltzman (1949) found greater resistance to extinction of secondary reinforcement in a T maze when such "retraining" trials were interspersed between test trials, but since he used only 15 test trials, the limits of this procedure were not tested. Likewise, Zimmerman and Hanford (1966) have shown that pecking by pigeons in a Skinner box can be sustained solely by secondary reinforcing cues whose reinforcing power is maintained through repeated pairings with primary reinforcement. However, Zimmerman and Hanford went to considerable trouble to prevent the formation of a discrimination, and when the conditions were changed, a discrimination did form.

Only recently has an attempt been made to test for secondary reinforcement in a satiated animal, making use of the possibilities of multiple reinforcement, multiple training techniques, and intermittent reinforcement to enhance the power of the secondary reinforcer. Nevin (1966) paired a buzzer sometimes with food and sometimes with water on an intermittent schedule for four rats. The pairing took several different forms. The buzzer served at various times for each rat as the magazine cue in a Skinner box on a DRL schedule, as the cue indicating which arm of a T maze was correct, and as the S^D on partial reinforcement in a runway. Finally, the efficacy of the buzzer as a secondary reinforcer for satiated animals was tested by giving each rat, when satiated for both food and water, a chance to press two levers, one of which produced the buzzer and the other did not. Although the overall rate of responding on the levers declined over time, following an initial burst when the buzzer contingency was first introduced, there was a persistent preference for the lever which produced the buzzer. Since this preference was not found in two control animals tested without the prior training, some secondary reinforcing effect was indicated. This conclusion was further supported by a subsequent phase of discrimination training in which the lever press produced the buzzer only when a light was on. Since a discrimination was formed, with more lever pressing in the light, the reinforcing effect of the buzzer is again indicated. However, since no control was run in this phase, it is harder to evaluate than the first test phase. Considering both the small number of animals and the fact that the major effect of secondary reinforcement was on preference between levers rather than on absolute level of responding, the results are quite weak relative to the demands of theory. Nevertheless, this study represents a promising attempt to make the complexity of the training more nearly match that which would be found in real-life situations.

Third, it is noteworthy that all studies so far reviewed have used adult, or at least adolescent, animal subjects. If there is a critical period for the most effective learning of evaluative reinforcers, as there apparently is for the learning of simple social attachments (Cairns, 1966; Hess, 1959; Scott & Fuller, 1965), the subjects in all of these experiments may have been too old to provide an adequate test of theory. Although secondary reinforcers can be acquired at any point in life, it is quite possible that only those acquired early in life have the exceptional power and persistence of many human evaluative reinforcers. It may be worthwhile to distinguish here, again, between those human evaluative reinforcers that are cognitively mediated and frankly instrumental and those that appear to be very direct and unrelated to anticipated consequences.

Fourth, the research both on secondary reinforcement and on the aversiveness of frustration cues has been almost completely restricted to food and water as the primary reinforcers. Since there is a clearer deprivation-satiation cycle for these two classes of primary reinforcers than for a number of others, these two may represent a quite unfortunate choice for demonstrating that reinforcers are not dependent on the training drive. Such other hypothetically primary reinforcers as novelty (Berlyne, 1960), activity (Hill, 1956), effectance (White, 1959), and contact comfort (Harlow, 1958) may be of considerably greater importance than hunger and thirst in the acquisition of evaluative reinforcers. The various distress inhibitors discussed by Kessen and Mandler (1961) may also be important as reinforcers which though not independent of drive, are effective under a variety of drive conditions. Even if the maximum power of such reinforcers as these is considerably less than the maximum power of food and water under appropriate deprivation, they may nevertheless be more effective as bases for establishing secondary reinforcers that will be relatively independent of drive conditions. These suggestions are highly speculative at present since very little is known about secondary reinforcement based on these classes of primary reinforcers. Whether or not such secondary reinforcers turn out to have the properties demanded by theories of evaluative reinforcement, research on these cases of secondary reinforcement would be worthwhile.

Finally, the phylogenetic range has not been adequately explored. The assumption that the relevant learning processes are not unique to man does not require that they be equivalent in all species of mammals and birds. Rats, on which a large part of the limited relevant research has been conducted, may be an especially poor species for demonstrating this kind of learning. The possibility that dogs might be a better species has already been suggested. If we assume that whatever is true of man is more true of primates than of most other orders, the results of token-reward studies on primates are somewhat discouraging to the hope that the proper selection of species will result in clearcut results (Cowles, 1937; Howard & Young, 1962; Wolfe, 1936). However, these data are not sufficiently definitive to rule out the possibility that the hypothesized learning process is shared by man with various other species much more than with the rat.

Experimental Predictions

At present we can only guess what experimental arrangements would be necessary in order to make a previously neutral stimulus into a reinforcer, positive or negative, with the strength, persistence, and independence of drive conditions that human evaluative reinforcers appear to have. However, on the basis of the considerations outlined above, the following speculation may be suggested. Two contrasting conditioned stimuli would be used. One would be an S^D for responses leading to a variety of reinforcers, including (for example) food, water, a varied sensory display, playthings, an activity wheel, a warm cuddly surface, and access to other animals of the same species, including appropriate sex objects. The subjects would be as young as the arrangements permitted (possibly too young for a sex partner to be an appropriate primary reinforcer). For very young animals, much of the above might be accomplished by making access to the mother the single, multifaceted primary reinforcer. (In fact, it is possible that access to the mother, whose importance has previously been established by contiguous conditioning, may be the most powerful "primary" reinforcer for the conditioning of evaluative reinforcers in young children.) The various reinforcers would be available on some intermittent schedule whenever S^D was present. The other stimulus would be an S^Δ, in the presence of which none of the reinforcers would ever be available. (Alternatively, probably making the analogy more precise, there might be a stimulus continuum correlated with frequency of reinforcement, instead of just two contrasting stimuli.) The training regime would be interspersed with appropriate tests for the positive reinforcing properties of the S^D and the negative reinforcing properties of the S^Δ, these tests to follow periods of free availability of all the relevant primary reinforcers. Such an arrangement should maximize the chance that the S^D and S^Δ could be shown to have acquired and to maintain the predicted reinforcing properties. If the results of such an experiment are positive, further research can then determine the relative contributions of the various primary reinforcers, of the schedule of reinforcement, of the age of the subjects, and of the procedure of interspersing retraining sessions among testing sessions. It would also be worthwhile to determine whether the effect is greater when control of S^D and S^Δ is entirely by the experimenter, as might be predicted from a paradigm of helplessness (Mowrer & Viek, 1948), or when the subject by his own efforts can exert some control over them, as might follow from a liberal interpretation of dissonance theory (Festinger, 1957).

Using some variant of this procedure (which is deliberately left somewhat open-ended), what sorts of phenomena should we be able to demonstrate if evaluative reinforcers are acquired on the basis of secondary reinforcement and of secondary drive resulting from frustration? To make predictions, we must consider further the characteristics of evaluative reinforcement as it appears to operate in humans.

As already noted, the same stimulus may have either positive or negative evaluative significance depending on the culture, the individual, and the context. When all of these variables are held constant, a person may still have difficulty deciding whether to interpret an evaluative stimulus as positive or negative, as in the familiar query, "What did he mean by that?" Even such standard positive reinforcers as smiles and compliments sometimes have negative significance, while insults and ridicule can sometimes be positive. Through learning, these significances can fairly readily be changed: One learns whose insults are really tokens of camaraderie and whose smiles denote sadistic glee. It follows that it should be fairly easy to produce a reversal shift in the significance of the cues, that is, to make the previous S^D aversive by changing it to an S^Δ and to make the previous S^Δ positively reinforcing by changing it to an S^D. Moreover, if a background stimulus is introduced to indicate when S^D and S^Δ have the original and when the reversed significance, their reinforcing values should become contingent on this background stimulus.

On the other hand, the great persistence of evaluative reinforcers under conditions where no differential primary reinforcement is present suggests that the S^D and S^Δ should maintain their original significance in the face of any equalization of their reinforcing significance. Neither extinction nor nondifferential reinforcement should eliminate the positive value of the S^D and the negative value of the S^Δ, at least not for a great many trials. This prediction is supported, though in a considerably different situation, by Ross's (1962) finding that the positive and negative cues in a discrimination situation remain differentiated even after long periods of nondifferential reinforcement, and by earlier evidence from repeated extra-dimensional shifts (Goodwin & Lawrence, 1955).

Finally, what would be expected if the discrimination became too difficult, either because the S^D and S^Δ were too similar or because their significance depended on a background stimulus in too complex a way? When a person finds the evaluative cues too difficult to interpret, either because of too great subtlety in social interaction or because of conflicting standards for his own self-evaluation, he does not simply shrug and ignore the whole matter of evaluation; he is more likely to try extra hard to interpret the subtle cues or to find some way of resolving the conflict. Failure in this effort is widely regarded as a source of neurotic behavior (e.g., Dollard & Miller, 1950). This conclusion is partially supported by observations on experimental neurosis in animals, in which a very difficult discrimination, rather than becoming simply a partial-reinforcement situation, becomes a highly stressful one, with attempts to escape and various abnormal symptoms. Though the evidence for experimental neurosis comes mainly from studies in which there was either painful stimulation or extreme confinement of the subjects (Liddell, 1944), the combination of human anecdotal evidence and animal experimental-neurosis data suggests the possibility that neurotic symptoms might result if the discrimination were made impossibly difficult.

Psychometric Predictions

It is common procedure in dealing with evaluative reinforcers (as with any other kind of reinforcers) to group them into a small number of categories corresponding to certain hypothetical motives. Categories of evaluative reinforcers are a major part of such lists as Murray's (1938) needs, Thomas's (see Volkart, 1951) four wishes (new experience, security, response, recognition), and Hsu's (1963) three "S's" (sociability, security, and status). There is considerable question as to whether even such broad categories as these can claim to be universal; at a minimum, they vary according to environmental contingencies and perhaps according to heredity as well. Certainly it is not always reinforcing to be liked (as by a tenacious bore), to be admired for one's superior ability (as a Victorian girl for her strength and athletic prowess), or to be recognized for the scrupulous propriety of one's behavior (as a young lower-class man for his sexual and aggressive restraint). It has even been suggested that whole cultures may be lacking in responsiveness to whole classes of evaluative reinforcers, as the Zuni to those involving admiration for one's superiority to others (Benedict, 1934). Even these very broad categories thus lack the universality that we ordinarily attribute to evaluative reinforcers.

What does seem to be universal is some concern with evaluation of oneself, whether by oneself or by others, according to whatever clear or unclear criteria. If the interpretation of evaluative reinforcement as secondary positive and negative reinforcement is correct, the universality of this very broad tendency is to be expected. Given the conditions of human life and the postulated resistance to extinction of evaluative reinforcement, we can expect to find every human susceptible to evaluative reinforcement, just as every animal given the training described above is predicted to be reinforcible by the S^D and S^Δ. On the other hand, individuals exposed to different contingencies should attach predictably different values to different reinforcers, just as an animal trained with a tone as S^D and silence as S^Δ would differ from one trained with light as S^D and darkness as S^Δ. Although this generalization would apply to all stimuli with evaluative significance, in the human case it would be of particular interest in connection with broad categories of evaluative reinforcers (such as those which enter into lists of human motives). The relative reinforcing value to an individual of being likable versus being superior, of being approved by others versus living up to his own standards, and of gaining positive evaluations versus avoiding negative ones should all be predictable from a knowledge of the conditions under which he has previously received reinforcement.

Consider, for example, two contrasting hypothetical situations in which a child might be reared. In the first, rules exist mainly for purposes of rhetoric rather than to be obeyed, and what a person does is mainly a question of what he can get away with. People express their feelings openly, without embarrassment or dissimulation. In the second, rules are taken seriously and exceptions rarely allowed. The people are cold, stoical, and unexpressive. What differences would we predict between children reared in these two situations as regards evaluative reinforcers? In the first environment, the cues as to whether a child would be able to get what he wanted (i.e., the S^D and S^Δ pairs) would be mainly cues from other people's reactions. He could not predict other people's reactions from abstract charateristics of his own behavior, since there would be few useful general rules. He could, however, judge other people's reactions readily from their expressive cues. He should therefore learn to be positively reinforced by signs of others' favor and negatively reinforced by signs of their disfavor, but develop little concern with evaluating his own behavior according to general principles. In other words, he should become other-directed. In the second environment, a child would find it harder to predict others' behavior toward himself from their expressive cues, since there would be few such cues, but easier to predict from his own adherence to general rules, since such rules would be strictly enforced. He would learn that signs of favor or disfavor which were not consistent with his own behavior (e.g., being condemned for obeying a rule) are of little importance because they would usually be soon reversed by the person giving the cues or overruled by others. He would thus learn to care more whether he was living up to fixed standards than whether he was momentarily receiving indications of others' approval or disapproval. In short, he would become inner-directed.

Similar predictions can be made about the environmental conditions favorable to learning preferences for one or another kind of evaluative reinforcement: popularity versus respect, obtaining positive evaluations versus avoiding negative ones, as well as any kind of socially structured evaluations versus concern with recognition of one's own objective competence in manipulating the nonhuman environment. Measurement, both of the environmental independent variables and of the dependent variables of evaluative reinforcement, offers many problems, but the approach also offers much promise for increasing our understanding of personality development.

CONCLUSION

The hypothesis that evaluative reinforcers represent secondary positive and negative reinforcers learned through their functions as S^D and S^Δ is certainly not well established, as the data cited here indicate. However, it is also far from refuted. Considering its a priori plausibility, its fruitfulness as a source of hypotheses, and its value in integrating learning theory with personality theory, further exploration of the hypothesis seems highly desirable. Some of the directions that such research might take have been indicated.

REFERENCES

Adelman, H. M. and Maatsch, J. L. Learning and extinction based upon frustration, food reward, and exploratory tendency. *Journal of Experimental Psychology,* 1956, 52, 311–15.

Amsel, A. Frustrative nonreward in partial reinforcement and discrimination learning: Some recent history and a theoretical extension. *Psychological Review,* 1962, **69,** 306–28.

Armus, H. L. and Garlich, M. M. Secondary reinforcement strength as a function of schedule of primary reinforcement. *Journal of Comparative and Physiological Psychology,* 1961, **54,** 56–58.

Ayres, J. J. B. Conditioned suppression and the information hypothesis. *Journal of Comparative and Physiological Psychology,* 1966, **62,** 21–25.

Barlow, J. A. Secondary motivation through classical conditioning: A reconsideration of the nature of backward conditioning. *Psychological Review,* 1956, **63,** 406–8.

Benedict, R. *Patterns of culture.* New York: Houghton Mifflin, 1934.

Berlyne, D. E. *Conflict, arousal, and curiosity.* New York: McGraw-Hill, 1960.

Bowen, G. and Kaufman, R. Transfer across drives of the

discriminative effect of a Pavlovian conditioned stimulus. *Journal of the Experimental Analysis of Behavior*, 1963, **6**, 445–48.

Brogden, W. J. Non-alimentary components in the food-reinforcement of conditioned forelimb-flexion in food-satiated dogs. *Journal of Experimental Psychology*, 1942, **30**, 326–35.

Brown, J. S. *The motivation of behavior.* New York: McGraw-Hill, 1961.

Brown, J. S. and Jacobs, A. The role of fear in the motivation and acquisition of responses. *Journal of Experimental Psychology*, 1949, **39**, 747–59.

Brozovich, R., Malony, N., and Wright, L. An attempt to establish a secondary drive based upon a primary appetitional drive. *Psychological Reports*, 1963, **13**, 283–88.

Cairns, R. B. Attachment behavior of mammals. *Psychological Review*, 1966, **73**, 490–26.

Calvin, J. S., Bicknell, E. A., and Sperling, D. S. Establishment of a conditioned drive based on the hunger drive. *Journal of Comparative and Physiological Psychology*, 1953, **46**, 173–75.

Campbell, D., Sanderson, R. E., and Laverty, S. G. Characteristics of a conditioned response in human subjects during extinction trials following a single traumatic conditioning trial. *Journal of Abnormal and Social Psychology*, 1964, **68**, 627–39.

Cowles, J. T. Food-tokens as incentives for learning by chimpanzees. *Comparative Psychology Monographs*, 1937, **14**(5, Serial No. 71).

D'Amato, M. R. Transfer of secondary reinforcement across the hunger and thirst drives. *Journal of Experimental Psychology*, 1955, **49**, 352–56.

D'Amato, M. R., Lachman, R., and Kivy, P. Secondary reinforcement as affected by reward schedule and the testing situation. *Journal of Comparative and Physiological Psychology*, 1958, **51**, 737–41.

Dember, W. N., Earl, R. W., and Paradise, N. Response by rats to differential stimulus complexity. *Journal of Comparative and Physiological Psychology*, 1957, **50**, 514–18.

Dollard, J. and Miller, N. E. *Personality and psychotherapy.* New York: McGraw-Hill, 1950.

Dyal, J. A. Secondary motivation based on appetites and aversions. *Psychological Reports*, 1958, **4**, 698.

Estes, W. K. Generalization of secondary reinforcement from the primary drive. *Journal of Comparative and Physiological Psychology*, 1949, **42**, 286–95. (a)

Estes, W. K. A study of motivating conditions necessary for secondary reinforcement. *Journal of Experimental Psychology*, 1949, *39*, 306–10. (b)

Ferster, C. B. Control of behavior in chimpanzees and pigeons by time-out from positive reinforcement. *Psychological Monographs*, 1958, **72** (8, Whole No. 461).

Festinger, L. *A theory of cognitive dissonance.* Evanston: Row, Peterson, 1957.

Goodwin, W. R. and Lawrence, D. H. The functional independence of two discrimination habits associated with a constant stimulus situation. *Journal of Comparative and Physiological Psychology*, 1955, **48**, 437–43.

Harlow, H. F. Learning and satiation of response in intrinsically motivated complex puzzle performance by monkeys. *Journal of Comparative and Physiological Psychology*, 1950, **43**, 289–94.

Harlow, H. F. The nature of love. *American Psychologist*, 1958, **13**, 673–685.

Hess, E. H. The relationship between imprinting and motivation. In M. R. Jones (ed.), *Nebraska symposium on motivation.* Lincoln: University of Nebraska Press, 1959, 44–77.

Hill, W. F. Activity as an autonomous drive. *Journal of Comparative and Physiological Psychology*, 1956, **49**, 15–19.

Howard, T. C. Conditioned temperature drive in rats. *Psychological Reports*, 1962, **10**, 371–73.

Howard, T. C. and Young, F. A. Conditioned hunger and secondary rewards in monkeys. *Journal of Comparative and Physiological Psychology*, 1962, **55**, 392–97.

Hsu, F. L. K. *Clan, caste, and club.* Princeton, N.J.: Van Nostrand, 1963.

Kelleher, R. T. and Gollub, L. R. A review of positive conditioned reinforcement. *Journal of the Experimental Analysis of Behavior*, 1962, **5**, 543–97.

Kessen, W. and Mandler, G. Anxiety, pain, and the inhibition of distress. *Psychological Review*, 1961, **68**, 396–404.

Leitenberg, H. Is time-out from positive reinforcement an aversive event? A review of the experimental evidence. *Psychological Bulletin*, 1965, **64**, 428–41.

Liddell, H. S. Conditioned reflex method and experimental neurosis. In J. McV. Hunt (ed.), *Personality and the behavior disorders.* New York: Ronald Press, 1944, 389–412.

MacCorquodale, K. and Meehl, P. E. "Cognitive" learning in the absence of competition of incentives. *Journal of Comparative and Physiological Psychology*, 1949, **42**, 383–90.

McClelland, D. C., Atkinson, J. W., Clark, R. A., and Lowell, E. L. *The achievement motive.* New York: Appleton-Century-Crofts, 1953.

Miller, N. E. Learnable drives and rewards. In S. S. Stevens (ed.), *Handbook of experimental psychology.* New York: Wiley, 1951, 435–72.

Miles, R. C. The relative effectiveness of secondary reinforcers throughout deprivation and habit-strength parameters. *Journal of Comparative and Physiological Psychology*, 1956, **49**, 126–30.

Morgan, C. T. The hoarding instinct. *Psychological Review*, 1947, **54**, 335–41.

Mowrer, O. H. *Learning theory and behavior.* New York: Wiley, 1960.

Mowrer, O. H. and Viek, P. An experimental analogue of fear from a sense of helplessness. *Journal of Abnormal and Social Psychology*, 1948, **83**, 193–200.

Murphy, G. *Personality: A biosocial approach to origins and structures.* New York: Harper, 1947.

Murray, H. A. *Explorations in personality.* New York: Oxford University Press, 1938.

Myers, A. K. and Miller, N. E. Failure to find a learned

drive based on hunger; evidence for learning motivated by "exploration." *Journal of Comparative and Physiological Psychology,* 1954, **47**, 428–36.

Myers, J. L. Secondary reinforcement: A review of recent experimentation. *Psychological Bulletin,* 1958, **55**, 284–301.

Myers, W. A. and Trapold, M. A. Two failures to demonstrate superiority of a generalized secondary reinforcer. *Psychonomic Science,* 1966, **5**, 321–22.

Nevin, J. A. Generalized conditioned reinforcement in satiated rats. *Psychonomic Science,* 1966, **5**, 191–92.

Novin, D. and Miller, N. E. Failure to condition thirst induced by feeding dry food to hungry rats. *Journal of Comparative and Physiological Psychology,* 1962, **55**, 373–74.

Platt, J. R. and Wike, E. L. Inaccessible food as a secondary reinforcer for deprived and satiated rats. *Psychological Reports,* 1962, **11**, 837–40.

Ray, A. J., Jr. Shuttle avoidance: Rapid acquisition by rats to a pressurized air unconditioned stimulus. *Psychonomic Science,* 1966, **5**, 29–30.

Razran, G. A note on second-order conditioning—And secondary reinforcement. *Psychological Review,* 1955, **62**, 327–32.

Reid, L. S. and Slivinske, A. J. A test for generalized secondary reinforcement during extinction under a different drive. *Journal of Comparative and Physiological Psychology,* 1954, **47**, 306–10.

Ross, L. E. The response to previous discriminanda during the learning of a new problem. *Journal of Comparative and Physiological Psychology,* 1962, **55**, 944–46.

Saltzman, I. J. Maze learning in the absence of primary reinforcement: A study of secondary reinforcement. *Journal of Comparative and Physiological Psychology,* 1949, **42**, 161–73.

Schlosberg, H. and Pratt, C. H. The secondary reward value of inaccessible food for hungry and satiated rats. *Journal of Comparative and Physiological Psychology,* 1956, **49**, 149–52.

Scott, J. P. and Fuller, J. L. *Genetics and the social behavior of the dog.* Chicago: University of Chicago Press, 1965.

Sears, R. R., Maccoby, E. E., and Levin, H. *Patterns of child rearing.* Evanston: Row, Peterson, 1957.

Seward, J. P. and Levy, N. Choice-point behavior as a function of secondary reinforcement with relevant drives satiated. *Journal of Comparative and Physiological Psychology,* 1953, **46**, 334–38.

Siegel, P. S. and MacDonnell, M. F. A repetition of the Calvin-Bicknell-Sperling study of conditioned drive. *Journal of Comparative and Physiological Psychology,* 1954, **47**, 250–52.

Skinner, B. F. *Science and human behavior.* New York: Macmillan, 1953.

Solomon, R. L. and Wynne, L. C. Traumatic avoidance learning: The principles of anxiety conservation and partial irreversibility. *Psychological Review,* 1954, **61**, 353–85.

Sternbach, R. A. Congenital insensitivity to pain: A critique. *Psychological Bulletin,* 1963, **60**, 252–64.

Stroutheis, A. and Hamilton, H. C. UCS intensity and number of CS-UCS pairings as determiners of conditioned fear R. *Psychological Reports,* 1964, **15**, 707–14.

Trost, R. C. and Homzie, M. J. A further investigation of conditioned hunger. *Psychonomic Science,* 1966, **5**, 355–56.

Verplanck, W. S. and Hayes, J. R. Eating and drnking as a function of maintenance schedules. *Journal of Comparative and Physiological Psychology,* 1953, **46**, 327–33.

Volkart, E. H. (ed.) *Social behavior and personality. Contributions of W. I. Thomas to theory and social research.* New York: Social Science Research Council, 1951.

Wagner, A. R. Conditioned frustration as a learned drive. *Journal of Experimental Psychology,* 1963, **66**, 142–48.

White, R. W. Motivation reconsidered: The concept of competence. *Psychological Review,* 1959, **66**, 297–333.

Wike, E. L. and Casey, A. The secondary reinforcing value of food for thirsty animals. *Journal of Comparative and Physiological Psychology,* 1954, **47**, 240–43. (a)

Wike, E. L. and Casey, A. The secondary reward value of food for satiated animals. *Journal of Comparative and Physiological Psychology,* 1954, **47**, 441–43. (b)

Wolfe, J. B. Effectiveness of token-rewards for chimpanzees. *Comparative Psychology Monographs,* 1936, **12**,(5, Serial No. 60).

Wong, R. and Pavlik, W. B. Cues associated with frustrative nonreward do not necessarily have aversive motivational properties. *Psychonomic Science,* 1966, **5**, 325–26.

Wright, J. H. Test for a learned drive based on the hunger drive. *Journal of Experimental Psychology,* 1965, **70**, 580–84.

Wunderlich, R. A. Strength of a generalized conditioned reinforcer as a function of variability of reward. *Journal of Experimental Psychology,* 1961, **62**, 409–15.

Young, P. T. *Motivation and emotion.* New York: Wiley, 1961.

Zimmerman, J. and Hanford, P. V. Sustaining behavior with conditioned reinforcement as the only response-produced consequence. *Psychological Reports,* 1966, **19**, 391–401.

14. AN EXAMINATION OF ADAMS' THEORY OF INEQUITY*

Paul S. Goodman and Abraham Friedman†

This paper examines the empirical evidence directly testing Adams' (1963a, 1965) theory of inequity.[1] Adams' theoretical statement and initial experimental design have stimulated considerable interest among researchers interested in motivation, organizational performance, and compensation systems. Although others (Homans, 1961; Jaques, 1961) have presented similar concepts of inequity, Adams' formulation has generated more systematic empirical evidence. Given this growing body of data, it is useful to assess critically the validity of the theory in order to determine possible directions for future research and possible implications of the theory for practice. This type of review is particularly important now because a number of researchers have recently questioned the utility of the theory (Lawler, 1968a; Pritchard, 1969; Wiener, 1970).

ADAMS' THEORY OF INEQUITY

Adams (1965: 280) defined inequity as follows: Inequity exists for Person whenever he perceives that the ratio of his outcomes to inputs and the ratio of Other's outcomes to Other's inputs are unequal. This may happen either *(a)* when Person and Other are in a direct exchange relationship or *(b)* when both are in an exchange relationship with a third party and Person compares himself to Other. Outcomes refer to rewards such as pay or job status which Person receives for performing his job. Inputs represent the contributions Person brings to the job, such as age, education, and physical effort. Outputs, a term not used in the definition, refer to products of Person's work, such as the number of interviews completed or pages proofed.

The basic assumptions, propositions, and derivations of the theory (Adams, 1965: 280–296) can be divided into two general classes: those dealing with the conditions of inequity and those dealing with the resolution of inequity. Propositions concerning conditions of inequity include: inequity is a source of tension; the greater the feeling of inequity, the greater drive to reduce this tension; inequity results from input-outcome discrepancies relative to Other versus absolute input-outcome discrepancies; the threshold for underpayment is lower than for overpayment; inputs and outcomes are additive. Sample propositions dealing with resolution of inequity include: Person will allocate rewards in a dyad proportionate to each member's contributions; Person will resist changing input-outcome cognitions about self more than about Other; Person who is overpaid in an hourly pay system will produce more than an equitably paid Other; Person who is overpaid in a piece-rate system will produce higher quality but fewer units than an equitably paid Other.

Listing these propositions serves two functions. (1) It indicates the range of the theory requiring empirical assessment. Previous reviewers (Lawler, 1968a; Pritchard, 1969) have considered propositions dealing mainly with the effect of inequity on performance. (2) It provides a logical basis for organizing the paper. The evidence relevant to propositions concerning resolution of inequity are analyzed first, because there are more studies in this area and because the evidence for these propositions bears on propositions concerning conditions of inequity. Empirical evidence about conditions of inequity are analyzed second.

RESOLUTION OF INEQUITY AND PERFORMANCE

Inequity-Performance

These studies examine how resolution of inequity affects job performance. The basic design is as follows: The experimenter, posing as an employer, advertises for individuals interested in part-time work—for example, interviewing for attitude survey. A contact is made, and the subject comes to the prospective employer. The experimenter creates the inequity induction by paying the subject more or less than the going rate, or by paying more or less than the going rate and also telling the subject that his qualifications for the job are lower than a comparison Other receiving the same pay. The pay is either on an hourly or piece-rate basis. After some initial job training, the subject performs the task over a stated period of time, returns to the employer, completes a postjob experimental questionnaire, and is paid. The number of units—for example, interviews—completed, quality of work, and attitudinal responses from the questionnaire represent the major dependent variables.

* *Administrative Science Quarterly,* vol. 16 (1971), pp. 271–88.

† Carnegie-Mellon University and Hebrew University.

[1] This paper was supported in part by Grant USPHS 5-ROI MH-18 512–02 to the senior author and Dr. L. Richard Hoffman.

There are four types of studies in this area: overpaid-hourly, overpaid-piece rate, underpaid-hourly, and underpaid-piece rate.

Overpaid-Hourly. The basic hypothesis is that overpaid subjects will raise their inputs by producing more as a means of reducing inequity. Four studies (Adams & Rosenbaum, 1962; Arrowood, 1961; Goodman & Friedman, 1969; Pritchard et al., 1970) have generally supported this hypothesis. Kalt (1969) provided nominal support for the hypothesis, but the induction in this study was not particularly effective. Studies by Valenzi and Andrews (1969), Evan and Simmons (1969), and Anderson and Shelly (1970) indicated no differences in productivity between over and equitably paid groups. Three studies (Friedman & Goodman, 1967; Lawler, 1968b; Wiener, 1970) have obtained findings which support and some which reject the hypothesis.

The studies which did not support the hypothesis had two distinguishing characteristics: their hourly rate of pay was lower and their induction of overpayment differed from the supporting studies. The lower rate of pay was a limitation because it undermined the notion of overpayment. The supporting studies, on the other hand, paid an hourly rate higher than the modal rate for most of the subjects and, therefore, produced a more powerful induction.

The second distinguishing characteristic of the nonsupporting studies was the use of an induction which overpays by circumstances. Subjects were told their pay exceeded the modal rate for the job because of a special circumstance—for example, a private foundation was subsidizing the work, or there was a mistake in the advertisement for the job. If subjects in these studies selected the most similar comparison Others—those working on the same job—their outcomes would be high relative to their inputs, but the same as their comparison Others and, therefore, although they may have reported their pay as high, they should not have experienced inequity. In Evan and Simmons' (1969: 234) study, using an overpaid-by-circumstance design, only 53 percent of their overpaid subjects reported they were overpaid. Also, in their second experiment they (1969: 234) concluded: "Although acknowledging the discrepancy between their authority and salary (it was higher) the overpaid subjects did not translate this awareness into a psychological feeling of being inequitably paid." Therefore, this evidence indicates that the overpaid-by-circumstance induction is not very successful in creating feelings of inequity, and studies using this induction, and the lower hourly rate are not suitable tests of the overpaid hypothesis (Adams, 1968). A similar induction is used in selected experimental groups in Lawler (1968b) and Pritchard et al. (1970); the results also do not support the hypothesis.

The main criticism against the supporting studies is that the results are attributed to devalued self-esteem rather than to feelings of inequity (Lawler, 1968a; Pritchard, 1969). The inductions in these studies (Adams & Rosenbaum, 1962; Arrowood, 1961) provided similar pay to equitably and overpaid subjects, but told the overpaid subject his qualifications were lower—devalued—and thus he was overpaid relative to the equitably paid Other. If the subject's increased productivity was an attempt to demonstrate valued abilities that had been devalued by the induction, then the results cannot be interpreted in equity terms even though the data appear in the predicted direction.

A number of studies (Friedman & Goodman, 1967; Andrews & Valenzi, 1970; Wiener, 1970) demonstrated that feelings of self-qualification can affect performance variation in equity experiments. However, it is difficult to extrapolate from these studies to those supporting the main hypothesis. For example, Wiener (1970) showed that overpaid subjects—those whose inputs were devalued—produced significantly more than equitably paid subjects in an ego-involved task, but not more in a less ego-involved task. Since these subjects only produced more in a condition where task abilities were central to one's self-concept, Wiener argued that their behavior represented a reaction to devalued self-esteem rather than to feelings of overpayment. Even if this interpretation is accepted, it is difficult to extrapolate from this study to those supporting the equity hourly hypothesis for two reasons. First, the induced ego orientation in this study far exceeded that in any other inequity study. Second, subjects in the overpaid-unqualified group did not report significantly greater feelings of overpayment than those in the equitably paid group; a relationship which does appear in the supporting studies. Empirically we know that reaction to devalued self-esteem can affect performance in inequity experiments. What has not been empirically demonstrated is that reaction to devalued self-esteem accounts for more production variance than feelings of inequity in studies supporting the hypothesis.

An analysis of supporting studies indicates that the inequity explanation is more tenable than the devalued self-esteem explanation. Some studies have minimized conditions likely to evoke feelings of devalued self-esteem by: (1) not hiring qualified subjects (Adams & Rosenbaum, 1962); (2) distinguishing in the analysis between qualified subjects and those who felt overpaid (Arrowood, 1961); (3) using a psuedotest to pretend to validate the subjects' lower qualifications (Goodman & Friedman, 1968); (4) not selecting an ego-involved task; and (5) using a reduced dissonance control group. In these studies inputs were devalued and pay was also reduced, commensurate with the lower qualifications. Since subjects in both the overpaid and reduced dissonance groups were devalued, then no differences should have appeared between these groups if reaction to devalued self-esteem was more salient than to wage inequity; however, the differences did appear (Goodman & Friedman, 1968).

A study by Pritchard et al. (1970) employed an induction which did not rely on devaluation of self or on overpaid-by-circumstance, and successfully supported the hourly hypothesis. In their induction the payment system was changed after several days' work so that subjects were getting more or less money for the same amount of work; that is, the relationship between past and present input and outcome ratios was modified to create feelings of inequity. Since their design used a relatively unambiguous method to create feelings of inequity, did not rely on devaluation of self nor on overpaid-by-circumstance (Wiener, 1970), and it embraced a longer experimental time period—greater than 30 hours—than in most experiments (for example, Valenzi & Andrews, 1969—2 hours), its supporting data provides one of the most powerful tests of the hourly hypothesis.

Another major criticism (Lawler, 1968a) of the supporting studies is that feelings of job insecurity evoked by the experimental induction reduce the efficacy of the equity explanation. That is, if the subject feels that subsequent employment is based on initial high job performance, and if this feeling is more salient in the overpaid-unqualified condition, then differential performance represents a way of buying job security rather than reducing inequity.

In a study on the possible effects of job insecurity, Arrowood (1961) found overpaid subjects produced more than control subjects in both high and low job-security conditions. Perhaps more important, however, is the likelihood of job-insecurity feelings being evoked by the inductions in the studies under consideration. Only the Adams and Rosenbaum (1962) study leaves the length of future employment ambiguous, and therefore, likely to evoke feelings of insecurity. The other studies seem quite clear in stating the employment period, and the employment period is relatively short—2 hours to part-time for 7 days. The authors' own experience indicates that presenting a clear, short work period with a statement that no future work is available substantially reduces the contamination from feelings of job insecurity.

Summary. There is some evidence to support the hypothesis that overpaid subjects increase their productivity as a way of bringing their inputs and outcomes in balance and thus of reducing feelings of inequity. Studies which used the overpay-by-circumstance induction and paid a lower rate were not considered adequate tests of the hypothesis. Although the effects of devalued self-esteem and job insecurity can affect performance variation in the equity studies, there is no compelling evidence that they represent the major source of production variance in the supporting studies. The Pritchard et al. (1970) study, which supports the hypothesis, offers a more useful way to test the hypothesis.

Overpaid-Piece Rate. The basic hypothesis is that overpaid subjects will produce higher quality and lower quantity than equitably paid subjects. The assumption for this hypothesis is: Overpaid subjects will increase their inputs as a means of achieving equity. These inputs can lead to greater quantity or quality. However, increases in quantity can only increase inequity because every unit is overpaid. Therefore, inputs are invested in increased quality and inputs and outcomes per unit achieve a balanced relationship.

The design for the piece-rate studies is the same as that described for the hourly system except that the job is advertised and paid by the piece.

The empirical support for this hypothesis seems relatively straightforward. Adams and Rosenbaum (1962), Adams (1963b), Adams and Jacobsen (1964), and Goodman and Friedman (1969) reported lower quantity and higher quality for the overpaid group. Lawler et al. (1968) supported this relationship for the initial work session but not over subsequent experimental sessions. Wood and Lawler (1970) reported lower quantity for the overpaid piece-rate subjects. Andrews (1967) reported lower quantity and higher quality for the overpaid subjects as compared to equitably paid subjects, but the differences were not statistically significant. Moore (1968) presented data contrary to the equity prediction; however, she used the overpaid-by-circumstance induction, which is not particularly effective. Moore (1968: 101) indicated that the connection between inputs and outcomes was not successfully created, hence the divergence between this and other piece-rate studies.

Although there seems to be support for the piece-rate hypothesis, alternative explanations should be considered. First, the piece-rate system probably does not initially evoke feelings of overpayment. Most of the subjects had never worked piece-rate and no referent in these studies was available to translate the piece-rate into some effective wage. Therefore, at the time of employment the subjects probably did not feel overpaid, which is in contrast to a basic assumption of the piece-rate hypothesis.

A second dimension of the induction is whether it evokes perception of pay on a global or a unit basis. The hypothesis assumes perception of pay on a unit basis; that is, to reduce inequity one cannot increase production since each unit is overpaid. Therefore, by increasing quality, balance per unit can be achieved. However, it is not clear that subjects perceived pay on a unit basis. Most of the subjects were unfamiliar with a piece-rate system. Their work time was limited and specified in hours. Also, the fact that overpaid subjects reduced the number of units produced, and thus their pay over time (Andrews, 1967), suggests that they evaluated in a global sense the amount earned, the amount they could earn in the next time period, and how much they thought they should earn as a function of the induction or past wages. This conclusion does not mean the subject did not feel overpaid. The process of overpayment could have worked as follows: The subject was hired and told his qualifications were low in comparison to some Other who received the same rate. At that time, feelings of inequity would not have been salient because the 30-cent rate was not translatable into a common referent. After a period of work, a global or dollar amount would have been calculated and compared to some minimal acceptable rate. If the amount earned seemed reasonable, the induction should have taken effect. That is, the subject knew he could earn an acceptable wage and he knew that his qualifications were less than those of Other receiving the same potential wage, therefore, it was congruent to reduce quantity and to invest more time in improving the quality of his inputs. Andrews (1967) reported overpaid piece-rate workers did produce fewer pieces in their second hour of production than in the first hour.

The implication of asserting that the individual adopts a global versus unit assessment is that this assertion rejects the assumption that differences in quality and quantity from the overpaid group are a function of intrinsic characteristics of the payment scheme, as Adams has hypothesized. The differential emphasis between quality and quantity can be traced to the nature of the induction and characteristics of the task. Most of the overpaid inductions (Adams & Jacobsen, 1964; Lawler, 1968b) emphasized the importance of quality, and thus focused on one salient way to achieve equity; that is, the induction provided the subjects with an instrumental way to reduce inequity. The task became an added dimension in this explanation for two reasons. First, in both proofreading and interviewing tasks quality is an important component; it is difficult for someone proofreading not to recognize quality as an intrinsic part of task performance. Second, in both tasks quality and quantity are inversely related; and if the induction and task focus on quality, it is not surprising that while quality increases as a means of dissonance reduction for the overpaid subjects, quantity decreases. Goodman and Friedman (1969) examined the effect of differential emphasis on quantity or quality in a piece-rate induction, indicating that the perceived instrumentality of quantity or quality in resolving overpayment led to the amount of quantity or quality produced. That is, overpaid subjects increased quality or quantity if it was perceived as instrumental to reducing inequity, not because of some characteristic of the payment scheme.

There are two other studies relevant to the quantity-quality issue. A study by Andrews (1967) used a task similar to most of the other studies but omitted statements emphasizing quality over quantity. Inequity was induced by varying the level of pay. The results seemed to suggest that overpaid piece-rate workers produce better quality and lower quantity. However, the quantity and quality differences between the experimental and control subjects were not statistically examined and were not very substantial. Therefore, this study does not provide strong support for Adams' basic hypothesis.

The second study, by Wood and Lawler (1970), also focused on whether subjects in an overpaid situation first reduce their outcomes to avoid inequity and as a consequence increase quality or first increase quality and as a consequence reduce quantity and their outcomes. A task was designed in which quantity was not dependent on quality. Wood and Lawler (1970) reported that overpaid subjects produced less than equitably paid subjects and that low productivity was not dependent on striving for increased quality. This study is not in conflict with the present paper's interpretation of the quality-quantity issue. It merely stated that given a task where quantity was not dependent on quality, and quantity was the focal output measure, then lower quantity in the overpaid situation was selected as a means of avoiding increased dissonance.

A third dimension of the induction which may reduce the internal validity of the piece-rate studies is the problem of devalued self-esteem. That is, as with the hourly studies, production differences may be a reaction to devalued self-esteem rather than to feelings of inequity. There are several studies which provide additional information on this problem. Lawler et al. (1968) used the unqualified induction in a piece-rate study but designed the study to cover several work periods rather than the single two-hour session found in most inequity experiments. He (1968) reported the modal finding—lower quantity-higher quality for overpaid subjects—in the initial session but no differences between overpay and controls in subsequent sessions, and also that feelings of self-qualification to perform the job increased over the three work sessions for the overpaid subjects. One interpretation of these findings is that subjects reduced productivity in the initial session as a reaction to devalued self-qualification, learned that they could perform the task, and then increased their feelings of confidence and produced more. Another interpretation, consistent with inequity theory, is that increasing quality and lowering the quantity in the initial work situation followed the hypothesized resolution strategy, but that the piece-rate system, which rewarded for increasing rather than reducing outputs, and the failure to repeat the inequity induction, caused the hypothesized differences not to reappear in the latter work sessions. The increase in feelings of self-qualification could reflect both a desire to increase inputs and a successful work experience. Therefore, either interpretation is tenable, and additional information is necessary to indicate a preferred choice.

On the self-qualification issue, Andrews (1967) used the same task and procedures as the other studies, but varied pay to induce inequity rather than to devaluate qualifications. His data supported Adams' hypothesis but the differences were not strong and did not provide definitive support to the inequity versus self-qualification argument. Because neither of these two studies demonstrated the importance of devalued self-esteem in explaining production variance in inequity studies, and because the supporting piece-rate studies tried to minimize the effect of reactions to devalued self-esteem, this alternative explanation of the piece-rate findings is not accepted.

Job security represents the last dimension which can affect internal validity of the piece-rate studies. The problem is exactly the same as in the hourly studies. The unqualified induction can increase feelings of job insecurity which can lead to higher quality productivity as a way of protecting the job. Adams and Jacobsen (1964) designed a study to deal with the job security issue by creating high and low job security conditions as well as the inequity experimental conditions. Because the high and low prospect condition did not contribute significantly to production variation, nor did it interact with the inequity conditions, job security was not considered a major confounding variable. Evans and Molinari (1970), employing a similar design, reported that for quality of work produced there was a weak inequity main effect ($p > .10$) and no significant inequity-security interaction effect; for quantity of work produced there was a significant inequity-security interaction. They (1970) suggested that in their secure condition the inequity effect paralleled Adams' hypothesis, but did not hold in the insecure condition. Although the present experiment indicated that feelings of insecurity could affect performance in inequity experiments, it did not indicate that this dimension is important in evaluating the internal validity of the supporting piece-rate studies. First, the insecurity induction was quite strong in the Evans and Molinari (1970) study and it had no parallel in the studies supporting the hypothesis. Second, the secure condition in their experiment paralleled the studies under consideration and provided data supporting the piece-rate hypothesis. Also, most researchers in the piece-rate studies had been quite clear in advertising that the job was for a limited time to minimize any insecurity effect.

Summary. The data from the overpaid piece-rate studies supported Adams' hypothesis more consistently than that from the hourly studies. However, it is less clear that the data supported some of the assumptions underlying the hypothesis. It is unlikely that piece-rate subjects initially felt overpaid or conceptualized overpayment on a unit basis—two assumptions necessary to explain the differential emphasis on quantity versus quality for overpaid subjects.

Although the data did not support some of the mechanisms underlying the piece-rate hypothesis, the findings could be interpreted in the inequity framework. That is, overpaid subjects did experience inequity after an initial performance period and differentially emphasized quantity or quality outputs—whichever seemed more successful in resolving inequity. The problem with most piece-rate studies is that the perceived instrumentality of quantity or quality outputs was a function of artifacts in the induction and task rather than intrinsic characteristics of the payment system as suggested by Adams.

Underpaid-Hourly. The basic hypothesis is that underpaid subjects decrease their inputs to achieve an input-outcome balance. Masters (1968) showed that increasing outcomes is also a relevant resolution strategy in the underpaid hourly condition. Since his population—young children—and design differ greatly from the studies under consideration, Masters' study is not included.

The change in inputs can affect the quantity or quality of outputs; Adams does not specify which output dimension would change. The emphasis on quality or quantity seems a function of the instrumental task characteristics and the relationship between quantity and quality. If quality is an instrumental task requirement, as in proofreading, then decreased inputs will lead to lower quality. If quality and quantity are inversely related, then quantity will increase as quality decreases. On the other hand, if quantity and quality are positively related, decreased inputs will decrease quantity.

Four underpaid-hourly studies, using the same general design of the other studies, tested Adams' hypothesis. An experiment by Evan and Simmons (1969) and one by Pritchard et al. (1970) supported the underpaid hourly hypothesis. Another experiment by Evan and Simmons (1969) and one by Valenzi and Andrews (1969) did not support the underpaid hypothesis.

In the Evan and Simmons (1969: 234) experiment which did not support the hypothesis, the induction probably did not create strong feelings of inequity. It was thus not an effective test of the hypothesis. The differences in results between the Valenzi and Andrews (1969) and the supporting studies are more difficult to reconcile because many factors—populations, rates of pay, tasks, length of employment—were different.

While it is difficult to delineate why there were no differences among underpaid and equitably paid groups in the Valenzi and Andrews (1969) study, the following factors seem relatively clear for the Evan and Simmons (1969) and Pritchard et al. (1970) studies. First, underpaid subjects did express feelings of underpayment. Second, the time periods for both studies were short and clearly stated, thus minimizing feelings of insecurity. In the Valenzi and Andrews (1969) study subjects were to work for at least six weeks, a more ambiguous recruitment procedure. Third, the Pritchard et al. (1970) study used an unambiguous referent for creating feelings of underpayment—past work and wages to present work and wages. Thus it created a powerful induction. From these three factors it seemed reasonable to conclude that the Evan and Simmons (1969) and Pritchard et al. (1970) studies did provide some positive evidence for the underpaid-hourly hypothesis.

Summary. There were not enough studies to adequately test the validity of the hourly underpaid hypothesis, but from the few existing studies there appears to be some preliminary support for the hypothesis.

Underpaid-Piece Rate. The basic hypothesis is that underpaid subjects will produce a large number of low quality outputs because the production of low quality outputs permits increasing outcomes without substantially increasing inputs.

Two studies (Andrews, 1967; Lawler & O'Gara, 1967) successfully tested this hypothesis. Both reported greater quantity and lower quality from the underpaid subjects. Lawler and O'Gara (1967) also reported that the underpaid subjects perceived the job as interesting—an outcome—and at the same time simpler and less challenging—inputs—than the equitably paid subjects. The attitudinal differences were congruent with Adams' hypothesis that inequity resolution would occur by increasing outcomes and decreasing inputs. Although Moore (1968) examined the underpaid condition, the induction in that study did not provide a satisfactory test of the hypothesis.

Many problems in interpreting the other inequity-performance studies have been avoided in this payment condition. In addition, by introducing new measures to capture additional forms of the resolution process these studies tested the hypothesis better. Because these studies specifically demonstrated that underpaid subjects cognitively devalued their inputs and raised their outcomes, one is more certain that the underpaid subjects were attempting to resolve inequity.

Summary. The data from these studies supported Adams' hypothesis. Although more studies are needed to provide full confirmation of the hypothesis, the two cited studies were probably freer of alternative explanations than the other inequity-performance studies.

Other Inequity Resolution Studies

The majority of studies testing Adams' theory focused on the effect of inequity on performance. Recently other studies have been designed to test resolution strategies unrelated to job performance. These studies were distinguished from the inequity-performance studies in one or more of the following ways: (1) The inequity resolution process between Person and Other was examined. Inequity-performance studies have focused on the employer-Person relationship, with Other's identity generally ambiguous. (2) The dependent variable in these studies concerned the allocation of rewards rather than changes in performance to achieve equity. (3) The studies occurred in either a laboratory setting or in an on-going organization. The inequity-performance studies were experiments in a simulated work situation in the field.

Leventhal and his associates (see Leventhal et al., 1969a) have conducted most of the laboratory experiments in this area. Typically, subjects participated in an experiment to fulfill a class requirement. The subject was led to believe he was performing with a partner on a task for monetary rewards. The experimenter varied the inputs contributed by each member, and Other initially allocated the rewards after the task performance on an overpaid, equitably paid or underpaid basis. The subject could then reallocate the rewards, thus providing a test of inequity theory.

Findings from these studies supported the general proposition from Adams' model that Person will allocate rewards earned by the dyad in accordance with each member's contributions. Each study by Leventhal attempted to test some theoretical elaboration of this general proposition: for example, Leventhal et al. (1969a) showed that when Person could not change his inputs he was likely to reduce inequity by reallocating available rewards. Overpaid subjects reduced their share of outcomes; underpaid subjects increased their share. Leventhal et al. (1969b) indicated that alternative theoretical explanations were not as useful as the inequity model in explaining this reallocation behavior. Leventhal and Bergman (1969) examined conditions in which the general proposition did not hold, and found that under extreme conditions of underpayment, Person would reduce rather than try to increase his outcomes. Leventhal and Lane (1970) and Leventhal and Anderson (1970), using a different strategy to refine the hypothesis, indicated that sex was a moderator of the inequity resolution process.

Lane and Messé (1969), using a similar design, reported some parallel findings. Given a task where inputs were equal, outcomes were most frequently allocated on an equal basis. Other variables which related to the selection of equal distribution of outcomes included: (1) the sex composition of the dyad—heterogeneity was associated with role symmetric choices, or, equal allocation of outcomes; (2) sex of chooser—females made more role symmetric choices; (3) whether choices were made publicly or privately—the former was more associated with role symmetric choices; and (4) personality—the greater the concern for others the more role symmetric choices. In a second experiment Lane and Messé (1969) varied the inputs of the chooser and receiver in the dyad and analyzed the allocation of rewards. The inputs of the receiver—high or low—seemed more important in affecting allocation of rewards than those of the chooser. That is, when the receiver's inputs were low the chooser allocated in his own favor, regardless of whether his own inputs were high or low. Also, there was some evidence that the chooser would distort the levels of his inputs as a way of alleviating feelings of dissonance. When choosers worked one-third as long as receivers, about 40 percent said they worked about the same as receivers and preferred a more equal distribution of outcomes.

These findings are directed to hypotheses not previously tested and deal with critical dimensions in the theory. For example, the definition of relevant inputs affects the resolution of inequity. Leventhal extended theoretically and empirically some aspects of this definition process, arguing that the locus of control for Other's behavior affects Person's assessment of Other's inputs. If Person believes Other operates under involuntary constraints, Person is more likely to attribute higher inputs to him. This hypothesis is based on the assumptions that Person's perception of inputs is affected by the difference between actual and expected performance and that Person expects lower performance when constraints on Other are high. Leventhal and Michaels (1970) varied the external constraints by telling Person that Other had useful or nonuseful training for a particular task. As predicted, with performance held constant, individuals with nonuseful training were considered more deserving of rewards than those with useful training.

These laboratory studies do represent a new direction in inequity research, but they have several limitations which should be noted. First, pay, the main outcome in the experiments, does not seem very relevant (Leventhal & Michaels, 1969). Subjects were recruited to participate in the study and course credits were the initial payments. At the conclusion of the experiment subjects returned the money they subsequently received. These conditions are not conducive to making pay a relevant outcome.

Second, the mechanisms for reallocating rewards, a critical dimension in testing for inequity resolution strategies, lack credibility. For example, in Leventhal et al. (1969b), subjects were told that the high-scoring member of their dyad would divide the money after the task was finished, but that the low-scoring member could modify the initial allocation. The subjects were then told that the two members of the dyad tied in their scores and a coin was flipped to determine who would allocate the money. The other member of the dyad, who really was nonexistent, won and then the subject was told that the winner had decided on the allocation himself or randomly selected the basis of allocation. Allocation occurred and then the subject reallocated. The low relevance of the pay, and the low credibility of this reallocation induction as further evidenced by the fact that some subjects recognized the deception (Leventhal & Michaels, 1969) increased the salience of experimental demand characteristics and thus chances for experimental error.

A third problem concerns how well the induction creates perceptions that one's inputs are related to outcomes. This relationship is basic to testing Adams' hypotheses. Because the subject had little time in these studies to test how his inputs were related to outcomes and because prior to task performance the subject knew that the other member of the dyad could determine his rewards, it was likely that his outcomes would not be perceived as directly dependent on his inputs (Leventhal et al., 1969b).

Weick and Nesset (1968) in using a different design to examine the inequity resolution process, developed a force choice format which contains 20 pairs of hypothetical work situations, the situations varying in degrees of inequity. Subjects have to select the preferred work situation and then to indicate preferred resolution strategies to make the least preferred choice in the pair more comfortable. Analysis of the resolution strategies indicated subjects were more likely to change individual circumstances by increasing effort than interpersonal circumstances by finding a new comparison Other. This was consistent with Adams' (1965: 294) hypothesis. Seeking higher wages was the most preferred strategy for underpaid subjects. It is interesting that this alternative had not been examined in the inequity resolution studies. Subjects did select quitting as an alternative, which seems contrary to Adams' hypothesis that leaving the field would occur only when other strategies were blocked. However, because the instrument permitted responding to more than one resolution strategy, it is not surprising to see that leaving the field was selected as an option, and therefore, Adams' hypothesis about withdrawal was not adequately tested.

Weick and Nesset's (1968) force choice instrument represents a new approach in testing inequity theory hypotheses. Refinements of this methodology would be important for assessing the validity of inequity theory because the use of different methods to test similar hypotheses is a very powerful validation strategy. Some of the limitations of this force choice instrument were discussed by Weick and Nesset (1968: 414). Other additions, such as assessing the instrument's reliability and using an independent criterion, would improve the instrument's validity.

In a correlational study in an organization, Penner (1967), directly testing dimensions of Adams' hypothesis, indicated that propensity to leave the company was twice as likely for those individuals who perceived their salary as inequitable. Although there has been other research on the satisfaction, absenteeism, and turnover relationships (Hulin, 1968), these studies were not direct tests of Adams' theory. Therefore more work is needed to test preferences for alternative resolution strategies in the field.

Summary. Studies in this section focused on inequity resolution between Person and Other, considered resolution strategies other than changing performance, and used designs different from the inequity-performance studies. The basic proposition tested is that Person allocates outcomes to himself and Other proportional to their respective inputs. The effects of the source of inequity, of how much control Other had over his inputs, and of Person's sex on the distribution of outcomes between Person and Other were investigated. Redefinition of Other's inputs and anticipation of future behavior from Other were other processes mediating the distribution of outcomes. These findings seemed congruent with Adams' theory, and in some cases (Weick & Nesset, 1968; Leventhal & Michaels, 1970) offered extensions to the theory. Additional studies are needed, however, to provide a more critical analysis.

CONDITIONS OF INEQUITY

Other studies which bear on Adams' theory concern determinants of feelings of inequity and the psychological state of inequity. The role of the comparison Other as a determinant of inequity has received surprisingly little attention. There have been field studies which indicated that an imbalance between Person and Other led to feelings of inequity (Penner, 1967; Lawler, 1965); these provided a confirmation of a basic assumption in the theory. An experiment by Wicker and Bushweiler (1970) indicated that the degree of liking between Person and Other could moderate perceptions of inequity during an exchange in this dyad. However, the complex processes leading to the selection of a comparison Other had not been pursued. Weick and Nesset (1968) made the most significant advance in this area, distinguishing between three comparison conditions of equity: own equity—Person had a balanced input-outcome ratio (L/L, low inputs-low outcomes) but it is unbalanced in regard to Other (H/L, high inputs-low outcomes); comparison equity—Person had an equal input-outcome ratio with Other but both were unbalanced (H/L, H/L); own comparison equity—Person had a balanced input-outcome ratio which equaled Other's (L/L, H/H). Weick and Nesset's (1968) findings indicated that subjects chose equitable conditions in terms of Other's input-outcome ratio (H/L, H/L) rather than in terms of their own input-outcome ratio. Subjects also chose situations where their own input-outcome ratio was in balance and equal to Other's ratio rather than a situation of own equity (L/L, H/L). Other analyses indicated that overpayment relative to one's own inputs (L/H, L/H) was preferred to overpayment in terms of Other's inputs (L/L, H/L). This study was especially important as the first that empirically examined some of the alternative comparison models, and focused on Person's input-outcome ratio as a source of inequity without reference to Other.

There are some very preliminary findings on the effect of past and future input-outcome ratios on the evaluation of present feelings of inequity, for example, Pritchard et al. (1970) indicated that past input-outcome ratio could induce present feelings of inequity. Although there is some data indicating that optimism about future outcomes is associated with present feelings of satisfaction (Goodman, 1966), the evidence supporting the effect of future input-outcome ratios on inducing present feelings of inequity is not yet clear (Lawler, 1970).

Other factors, such as characteristics of the individual and the organization providing the outcomes, can affect feelings of inequity. Penner (1967) indicated that high performers were more likely to feel dissatisfied with their pay; high inputs were more likely to lead to feelings of inequity. Klein and Maher (1966), using education as an input, indicated that college educated respondents were more likely to feel dissatisfied with their pay than noncollege respondents.

Organizational factors also seem to affect feelings of inequity. Penner (1967) reported that when pay and performance were not perceived as related, feelings of dissatisfaction with pay would more likely occur. In equity terms this reward system did not reward increased inputs for performance, and therefore, inequity resulted. A corollary finding was that when pay was determined by budgetary constraints rather than by inputs, dissatisfaction with pay resulted. Probably the most provocative finding from Penner's study was that increasing one organizational reward, like amount of freedom, could affect feelings of inequity about other rewards, like pay. Implicit in this finding was a hypothesis from Adams' theory which asserts that outcomes are additive. Although Penner's (1967) study represented an important test in the field of Adams' work, it lacked some important control procedures. For example, variables such as amount of pay, organizational level, and type of job should have been controlled in an analysis of the relationship between amount of freedom and feelings about pay. Since these controls were absent in Penner's (1967) analysis, the findings must be considered tentative.

The last set of studies to be reviewed concerns the psychological state of inequity. Adams argued that inequity is a source of tension which an individual is motivated to reduce. To some extent, all the studies confirming any inequity hypotheses are testing this assumption. Some studies, however, directly measured the affective state associated with inequity, and confirmed Adams' basic contention (Leventhal et al., 1969a; Pritchard et al., 1970). Pritchard et al.'s (1970) research went beyond confirming the inequity and dissatisfaction relationship to indicate that inequity with one input-outcome ratio may generalize to other outcomes. For example, their data indicated that subjects in a condition of pay inequity exhibited lower job satisfaction than equitably paid subjects.

Another hypothesis in inequity theory—that the threshold for underpayment is lower than for overpayment—received fairly consistent support from different investigators (Andrews, 1967; Weick & Nesset, 1968).

Summary. Studies in this section extended our understanding of inequity theory by examining how the comparison process affected feelings of inequity, individual and organizational factors which affected feelings of inequity, as well as some aspects of the state of inequity. Although none of the findings presented seriously challenged Adams' theory, more, better controlled studies are needed to adequately test the validity of the hypotheses discussed in this section.

METHODOLOGICAL ISSUES

Recruitment-Selection

There are a number of important moderators—ability (Bass, 1968; Moore, 1968); past work experience (Friedman & Goodman, 1967); past wages (Andrews, 1967); need preferences (Lawler & O'Gara, 1967)—which can affect interpretation of inequity studies. Some moderators, like need for money represent an alternative explanation for variation in the dependent variables, and therefore must be controlled to assess the role of the inequity explanation. For example individuals high in need for money may work hard in a piece-rate experiment not as a means of reducing inequity but to satisfy a need for more money. Although it can be argued that these moderators should be equally distributed across experimental conditions, given the relatively small sample size in most studies and the fact that despite random assignment the moderators often are not equally distributed (Goodman & Friedman, 1968), it seems desirable to measure and analyze the effects of the relevant moderators. The fact that few investigations (Lawler et al., 1968, is an exception) have done this casts doubt on the internal validity of the studies we have examined.

A recruitment-selection bias is also relevant for interpreting the external validity or generalizability of some inequity studies. For example, since the method of payment is often advertised during recruitment, there is probably a differential selection process for hourly and piece-rate studies, with the latter selecting out more subjects because of the ambiguity of how much they can make (Evans & Molinari, 1970). Although this differential selection does not limit the internal validity of a particular study, it does limit one's ability to compare hourly and piece-rate studies (Adams, 1963b). One solution to this problem would be to examine the differences between people who respond and do not respond to the simulated advertisements about either hourly or piece-rate jobs.

Induction

The induction is an important experimental event for explaining differences among studies. Inequity theory postulates an imbalance between Person's outcomes and inputs in comparison to Other as a condition of inequity. To successfully operationalize this concept, however, one must deal with the following cognitions (Vroom, 1964):

1. Person's evaluation of his inputs.
2. Person's perception of the relevance of his inputs for task performance.
3. Person's perception of E's perception of his inputs.
4. Person's perception of Other's outcome-input ratio.
5. Person's perception of future outcomes.
6. Person's perception of the outcomes relative to alternative outcomes—his past outcomes—the outcomes for this class of tasks, and so forth.
7. The relative importance Person attaches to using 4, 5, and 6 as comparison points.

These conditions are basic to assessing the internal validity of any inequity experiment. If, for example, the subject selects comparison Others different from those intended by the experimenter, then the substantive interpretation of an experiment is limited, and since the comparison Other in most experiments is ambiguously specified, this particular problem is likely to occur. Or subjects could define relevant outcomes differently from the experimenter. Because many of the studies are advertised as part of some research and because helping in research has been identified as an additional outcome which affects performance differences in inequity studies (Heslin & Blake, 1969), failure to control on definition of outcomes introduces a source of experimental error.

None of the studies reviewed recognized most of these conditions in specifying their experimental design; therefore, another source of error has not been controlled. These conditions could be controlled either by directly building them into the induction or measuring these cognitions and including them in the analysis.

Developing an adequate control group, a problem relevant to inequity resolution studies, is another aspect of the induction which deserves attention. The equitable condition, characterized by an absence of tension, has been the modal control group. At issue is the source and degree of motivation exhibited by subjects in this group. One equity study (Friedman & Goodman, 1967) showed that equitably paid control subjects, as a way of confirming their valued abilities, were actually highly motivated to produce. Although this problem has been identified by others (Weick, 1967b), it has not captured the attention of researchers concerned with inequity. The Pritchard et al. (1970) study illustrated how the subject's own performance could provide a baseline for assessing subsequent feelings of inequity. Also, by introducing various levels of inequity—high, medium, and low overpayment—more refined contrasts could be made and assumptions about the similarity between an overpaid and equitable induction could be avoided.

Task

The experimental task represents another source of error which should be controlled. The design of future studies, especially when performance is a major dependent variable, must reflect the following problems found in past inequity studies. First, if the hypothesis indicates a differential emphasis on quality or quantity, tasks in which these two are relatively independent should be developed. This issue is particularly important in studies where one wants to know if the subject is reducing quantity or increasing quality. Some recent studies (Wood & Lawler, 1970; Wiener, 1970) have reported tasks where quantity and quality are independent.

Second, if the subject modifies the task in a way unintended by the experimenter (Weick, 1967a), internal validity can be reduced. Although there are no data available to assess the effect of task modifiability in these studies, it does represent a problem in interpreting inequity studies. For example, it is possible for the subject to modify some of the scoring procedures in the questionnaire or proofreading tasks used in inequity-performance studies. The problem is how to evaluate the modification. On one hand, it might represent a new input and it should then be measured. However, it would be difficult to add this input to other measures of outputs such as the number of units produced and form some common index of contributions to the job. On the other hand, if this modification increases productivity, counting this additional productivity may not reflect an increase in inputs; the subject may merely have found a more efficient way to increase outputs without additional effort.

A third and related problem concerns the need for an independent assessment of the relationship between inputs and outputs for different tasks. Basic to the inequity-resolution studies in the strategy of modifying inputs to reduce inequity. Outputs are taken to be measures of inputs. The problem is to what extent do the number of outputs—questionnaires for example—reflect the amount of inputs—effort—expended. If the amount of effort per unit varies with the level of performance and type of task, then evaluation of inputs from outputs becomes a less desirable measure. Unfortunately, there is no evidence on this particular point, and therefore, the issue can only be raised for consideration in future studies.

The fourth task-related problem concerns the amount of time allocated for task performance. There has been considerable variation in the studies reviewed; some took less than 10 minutes (Leventhal et al., 1969b), others took more than 30 hours (Pritchard et al., 1970). Although there do not seem to be any clear differences between studies which support or do not support the inequity hypotheses on the time dimension, there is evidence that the time dimension is relevant in assessing the validity of inequity studies. For example, change over time in subject behavior within an experimental session (Andrews, 1967) was important in assessing whether subjects were overpaid in piece-rate studies. The fact that some studies (Lawler et al., 1968; Pritchard et al., 1970) have not supported the inequity hypotheses over several experimental sessions raises questions about the effectiveness of the theory or the induction over time. In any case, it would seem desirable to use multiple sessions over time in future studies—most studies have been single sessions—and to systematically assess behavior over time both within and between sessions and to identify factors like differential task success which affect performance over time.

Measurement and Data Analysis

There are a number of problems of measurement and analysis which confound the interpretation of the reviewed studies and should be eliminated in future studies. First, measures of the effectiveness of the induction must be introduced immediately after the induction. This would require one experimental group that would be tested after the induction but would not complete the experimental session. In many of the reviewed studies this measurement was taken after the experiment and thus was contaminated by the experimental experience. Second, and most important, inequity theory focuses on the complex interrelationship among multiple cognitions. Most of the research reviewed has dealt with only a few cognitions. One contribution to research would be to develop additional measures using different methods to capture the multiple cognitions used to define inequity (Zedeck & Smith, 1968) and to resolve it.

Problems in working with a small sample size, with subject mortality, and with weak statistical techniques which characterized some of the earlier studies (Arrowood, 1961; Goodman & Friedman, 1968), seem to have been avoided in the most recent studies (Pritchard et al., 1970; Wiener, 1970). Thus it seems that data analysis issues have been recognized and probably will receive continued attention in future studies.

THEORETICAL OVERVIEW

The purpose of this paper is to examine the empirical evidence testing Adams' theory of inequity. It is important in making this assessment to review all the varied propositions in the theory, not just inequity-performance; for this alone does not permit an adequate evaluation of the theory.

Three general conclusions about the relative validity can be offered. First, some assumptions and hypotheses derived from the theory have relatively clear empirical support; they are: inequity is a source of tension (Pritchard et al., 1970); the greater the inequity the greater the drive to reduce it—all supporting studies; input-outcome discrepancies relative to Other are a source of inequity (Weick & Nesset, 1968); the threshold for underpayment is lower than for overpayment (Leventhal et al., 1969b); Person maximizes positive outcomes in inequity resolution (Leventhal & Michaels, 1970); Person allocates rewards in a dyad in proportion to each member's contributions (Leventhal et al., 1969a); underpaid piece-rate subjects produce more than equitably paid subjects (Lawler & O'Gara, 1967).

Second, there are a set of assumptions and hypotheses which have tentative empirical support. The tentative label is applied to these hypotheses either because there have not been enough tests of the hypothesis or because the evidence is mixed. In this latter category, we have argued that the supporting evidence is greater than the nonsupporting evidence. Hypotheses in this second set include: Person will resist changing input-outcome cognitions central to his self-concept (Leventhal & Lane, 1970); Person will resist changing his comparison Other once Other has become a referent (Weick & Nesset, 1968); overpaid-hourly subjects produce more than equitably paid subjects (Pritchard et al., 1970); overpaid piece-rate subjects produce less quantity and higher quality than equitably paid subjects (Adams & Jacobsen, 1964); underpaid-hourly subjects will invest lower inputs than equitably paid subjects (Evan & Simmons, 1969).

Third, the following are a set of hypotheses which either have not been tested, or have been tested in a single study with poor controls: if input-outcome discrepancies are the same for Person and Other no inequity results; inequity is greater when both inputs and outcomes are discrepant for Other; inputs and outcomes are additive; within certain limits of inequity Person manipulates inputs and outcomes to reduce inequity; Person will resist changing cognitions about his own inputs and outcomes more than about Other's inputs and outcomes; Person will leave the field when inequity is high and other reduction strategies are unavailable.

The evidence seems to provide initial support for some of Adams' propositions, but the critical test of the theory will depend on: (1) empirical support for the propositions listed above that are not fully tested; (2) elaboration of conceptual areas not fully specified by Adams to generate new propositions for testing; and (3) contrasting of inequity theory with other theories to evaluate its comparative advantages in prediction.

Although the general concept of inequity has been well stated by Adams, the components of perceived inequity have not been theoretically specified in sufficient detail. One important problem concerns the process by which inputs and outcomes are defined as relevant. Advancing our knowledge in this area would permit identification of determinants of inequity and prediction of inequity. Weick (1966) and Leventhal and Michaels (1970) have provided some provocative thinking about the input-outcome specification problem which should stimulate further theorizing and research.

A related problem concerns how information is combined when Person evaluates his input-outcome ratio. Person must deal with information not only about his own multiple inputs and outcomes, but also about input-outcome ratios of Others. How is this information combined? Einhorn (1970a, 1970b) has developed a conceptual and operational procedure for testing whether people use linear or nonlinear models when combining information. This type of research could be applied to inequity studies to provide a better understanding of how different methods of combining information lead to feelings of inequity.

Another problem subsumed in the inequity concept is the selection and use of a referent in evaluating one's inputs and outcomes. The major theoretical focus has been derived from social comparison theory and Other has been critical in the determination of inequity. There are, however, other relevant referents in inequity evaluation such as Person's concept of his own self-worth, past input-outcome ratios, and future input-outcome ratios. The critical issue, then, is specifying a theoretical framework to permit the identification and weighting of multiple referents used in evaluating the input-outcome ratio.

The inequity resolution process requires further elaboration and testing before the utility of the theory can be assessed. The basic issues for both cognitive and behavioral resolution modes are how are salient resolution strategies defined and which strategies are most likely to be evoked. Expectancy theory (Lawler, 1970) might provide a general framework for predicting resolution processes. The expectancy and valence components could be defined for each resolution strategy and the expected force associated with each strategy assessed.

Testing competing hypotheses from inequity theory and other theoretical perspectives provides another way to assess its comparative validity. For example, expectancy theory (Porter & Lawler, 1968), which focuses primarily on the perceived relationship between behavior and valued rewards, would not predict increased performance for overpaid subjects in the hourly condition since performance is not related to pay; inequity theory does predict increased performance. Lawler (1968a) has argued that the reported performance differences in the hourly study are attributed to the characteristics of the induction, and that expectancy theory represents a preferred theoretical perspective. We would argue that there is an inequity effect in those studies, although expectancy theory probably is a more powerful long-run predictor. Pritchard et al.'s (1970) study suggests a future model for comparing both theories; it examines different levels of inequity in payment systems with different expectancies that pay and performance are related.

The concept of insufficient rewards (Weick, 1967b) represents another theoretical position which contrasts with inequity theory predictions. Inequity theory predicts no increase in effort from underpaid subjects in the hourly condition; the insufficient rewards concept predicts increased effort. A design incorporating different levels of underpayment would permit a test of these contrasting hypotheses. We would expect inequity theory predictions to be supported at moderate levels of underpayment, and insufficient reward predictions at greater levels.

Research on the norm of reciprocity (Pruit, 1968), the norm of social responsibility (Goranson & Berkowitz, 1966; Berscheid et al., 1968; Greenglass, 1969), or the belief in a just world (Simmons & Lerner, 1968) poses an interesting challenge to the development of inequity theory. To what extent, for example, is there a norm of equity? How would such a norm differ from the reciprocity or social responsibility norms? Levanthal et al. (1969b) have made some preliminary attempts to empirically separate these concepts; however, there seems to be little interchange in the development of these three perspectives. Messé et al. (1970) examined the effect of inequity in the resolution of interpersonal conflict;

another potentially useful area to expand inequity theory.

Until research in the above areas is well developed, it will be difficult to delimit with certainty the relevance of Adams' theory for organizational processes. However, there are some indications of directions in which the theory may contribute. First, and its most general contribution, inequity theory offers a relatively simple model to explain and to predict an individual's feelings about various organizational rewards. Although the experimental studies have focused primarily on feelings of inequity about pay, the model seems generalizable to other types of rewards such as promotion, supervisor support, status (Stephenson & White, 1968), and to other types of relationships such as that of buyer-seller (Leventhal et al., 1970). The primary contribution of the model will certainly not be in explaining performance. The data at the present time only indicate a very short term effect of inequity on performance. Also, it is important to remember that variations in performance represent only one inequity resolution mode. Neither the theory nor present research indicates it is the dominant resolution strategy. Unfortunately, the large number of studies in the inequity-performance area have led some people to think of Adams' theory as primarily a motivation-performance model.

Second, the delineation of the comparison model an individual uses in evaluating his input-outcome ratio should be relevant for organizational decision makers involved in determining appropriate levels of rewards. For example, identifying Others Person considers in evaluating his pay should indicate what groups of individuals should be included in a salary survey, one mechanism for setting levels of pay.

Another contribution of the inequity model to administration may be in the area of the interchangeability of rewards. A topic that needs further empirical analysis concerns how an individual combines his outcomes and inputs. This type of research should aid organizational decision makers by identifying what kind of rewards like freedom have an additive effect on other rewards like pay, and which rewards can be substituted for others (Penner, 1967).

Finally, research on allocation of rewards suggests that achieving balance between input and outcome is an important decision rule. However, there may be alternative forces or competing decision rules in organizations that conflict with an equitable allocation. For example, an experiment by Rothbart (1968) indicated supervisors consider competing models of inequity and of the relative effectiveness of different reward-punishment schedules in allocation of possible outcomes. Identifying individual or structural factors which evoke these competing decision rules and their consequences would represent another contribution of the theory.

REFERENCES

Adams, J. Stacy. Toward an understanding of inequity." *Journal of Abnormal and Social Psychology,* 1963, 67, 422–36. (a)

Adams, J. Stacy. Wage inequities, productivity and work quality. *Industrial Relations,* 1963, 3, 9–16. (b)

Adams, J. Stacy. Inequity in social exchange. In L. Berkowitz (ed.), *Advances in Experimental Social Psychology,* vol. 2. New York: Academic Press, 1965, 267–300.

Adams, J. Stacy. Effects of overpayment: Two comments on Lawler's paper. *Journal of Personality and Social Psychology,* 1968, 10, 315–16.

Adams, J. Stacy and Jacobsen, Patricia R. Effects of wage inequities on work quality. *Journal of Abnormal and Social Psychology,* 1964, 69, 19–25.

Adams, J. Stacy and Rosenbaum, William B. The relationship of worker productivity to cognitive dissonance about wage inequities. *Journal of Applied Psychology,* 1962, 46, 161–64.

Anderson, Bo and Shelly, Robert. A replication of Adams' experiment and a theoretical formulation. *Acta Sociologica,* 1970, 13, 1–10.

Andrews, I. R. Wage inequity and job performance: an experimental study. *Journal of Applied Psychology,* 1967, 51, 39–45.

Andrews, I. R. and Valenzi, E. Overpay inequity or self-image as a worker: A critical examination of an experimental induction procedure. *Organizational Behavior and Human Performance,* 1970, 53, 22–27.

Arrowood, Arthur J. Some effects on productivity of justified and unjustified levels of reward under public and private conditions. Doctoral dissertation, University of Minnesota, 1961.

Bass, Bernard M. Ability, values, and concepts of equitable salary increases in exercise compensation. *Journal of Applied Psychology,* 1968, 52, 299–303.

Berscheid, Ellen, Boye, David, and Walster, Elaine. Retaliation as a means of restoring equity. *Journal of Personality and Social Psychology,* 1968, 10, 370–76.

Einhorn, Hillel J. The use of nonlinear, noncompensatory models in decision making. *Psychological Bulletin,* 1970, 73, 221–30 (a)

Einhorn, Hillel J. Use of nonlinear, noncompensatory models as a function of task and amount of information. *Organizational Behavior and Human Performance,* 1970, 6, 1–27. (b)

Evan, William M. and Simmons, Roberta G. Organizational effects of inequitable rewards: Two experiments in status inconsistency. *Administrative Science Quarterly,* 1969, 14, 224–237.

Evans, Martin G., and Molinari, Larry. Equity, piece-rate overpayment, and job-security: Some effects on performance. *Journal of Applied Psychology,* 1970, 54, 105–14.

Friedman, Abraham, and Goodman, Paul S. Wage inequity, self-qualifications, and productivity. *Organizational Behavior and Human Performance,* 1967, 2, 406–17.

Goodman, Paul S. A study of time perspective: Measurement and correlates. Doctoral dissertation, Cornell University, 1966.

Goodman, Paul S., and Friedman, Abraham. An examination of the effect of wage inequity in the hourly condition. *Organizational Behavior and Human Performance,* 1968, 3, 340–52.

Goodman Paul S., and Friedman, Abraham. An examination of quantity and quality of performance under conditions of overpayment in piece rate. *Organizational Behavior and Human Performance,* 1969, 4, 365–74.

Goranson, Richard E., and Berkowitz, Leonard. Reciprocity and responsibility reactions to prior help. *Journal of Personality and Social Psychology,* 1966, 3, 227–32.

Greenglass, Esther R. Effects of prior help and hindrance on willingness to help another: Reciprocity or social responsibility. *Journal of Personality and Social Psychology,* 1969, 11, 224–31.

Heslin, Richard and Blake, Brian. Performance as a function of payment, commitment and task interest. *Psychonomic Science,* 1969, 15, 323–24.

Homans, George. *Social behavior.* New York: Harcourt, Brace & World, 1961.

Hulin, Charles L. Effects of changes in job-satisfaction levels on employee turnover. *Journal of Applied Psychology,* 1968, 52, 122–26.

Jaques, E. *Equitable payment.* New York: Wiley, 1961.

Kalt, Neil C. Temporal resolution of inequity: An exploratory investigation. Doctoral dissertation, University of Illinois, 1969.

Klein, S. M. and Maher, J. R. Education level and satisfaction with pay. *Personnel Psychology,* 1966, 19, 195–208.

Lane, Irving M. and Messé, Lawrence A. Equity and distribution of rewards. Working paper, Michigan State University, 1969.

Lawler, Edward E. Manager's perceptions of their subordinates' pay and their superiors' pay. *Personnel Psychology,* 1965, 18, 413–22.

Lawler, Edward E. Equity theory as a predictor of productivity and work quality. *Psychological Bulletin,* 1968, 70, 596–610. (a)

Lawler, Edward E. Effects of hourly overpayment on productivity and work quality. *Journal of Personality and Social Psychology,* 1968, 10, 306–13. (b)

Lawler, Edward E. *Pay and organizational effectiveness,* New York: McGraw-Hill, 1970.

Lawler, Edward E., and O'Gara, Paul W. Effects of inequity produced by underpayment on work output, work quality, and attitudes toward work. *Journal of Applied Psychology,* 1967, 51, 403–10.

Lawler, Edward E., Koplin, Cary A., Young, Terence F., and Fadem, Joel A. Inequity reduction over time in an induced overpayment situation. *Organizational Behavior and Human Performance,* 1968, 3, 253–68.

Leventhal, Gerald S., and Anderson, David. Self-interest and the maintenance of equity. *Journal of Personality and Social Psychology,* 1970, 15, 57–62.

Leventhal, Gerald S. and Bergman, James T. Self-depriving behavior as a response to unprofitable inequity. *Journal of Experimental and Social Psychology,* 1969, 5, 153–71.

Leventhal, Gerald S. and Lane, Douglas W. Sex, age, and equity behavior. *Journal of Personality and Social Psychology,* 1970, 15, 312–16.

Leventhal, Gerald S. and Michaels, James W. Extending the equity model: Perception of inputs and allocation of reward as a function of duration and quantity of performance. *Journal of Personality and Social Psychology,* 1969, 12, 303–09.

Leventhal, Gerald S., and Michaels, James W. Locus of cause and equity motivation as determinants of reward allocation. Working paper, North Carolina State University, 1970.

Leventhal, Gerald S., Allen, John, and Kemelgor, Bruce. Reducing inequity by reallocating rewards. *Psychonomic Science,* 1969, 14, 295–96. (a)

Leventhal, Gerald S., Weiss, Thomas, and Long, Gary. Equity, reciprocity, and reallocating rewards in the dyad. *Journal of Personality and Social Psychology,* 1969, 13: 300–05. (b)

Leventhal, Gerald S., Younts, Charles M., and Lund, Adrian K. Tolerance for inequity in buyer-seller relationships. Working paper, North Carolina State University, 1970.

Masters, John C. Effects of social comparison upon subsequent self-reinforcement behavior in children. *Journal of Personality and Social Psychology* 1968, 10, 391–401.

Messé, Lawrence, Dawson, Jack, and Lane, Irving. Equity as a mediator of the effect of reward level on behavior in the prisoner's dilemma game. Working paper, Michigan State University, 1970.

Moore, Loretta M. Effects of wage inequities on work attitudes and performance. Masters thesis, Wayne State University, 1968.

Penner, Donald. *A study of causes and consequences of salary satisfaction.* Crotonville, N. Y.: General Electric Behavioral Research Service, 1967.

Porter, Lyman and Lawler, Edward E. *Managerial attitudes and performance.* Homewood, Ill.: Irwin, 1968.

Pritchard, Robert D. Equity theory: A review and critique. *Organizational Behavior and Human Performance,* 1969, 4, 176–211.

Pritchard, Robert D., Jorgenson, Dale O., & Dunnette, Marvin D. The effects of perceptions of equity and inequity on worker performance and satisfaction. Working paper, Purdue University, 1970.

Pruit, Dean. Reciprocity and credit building in a laboratory dyad. *Journal of Personality and Social Psychology,* 1968, 8, 143–47.

Rothbart, Myron. Effects of motivation, equity and compliance on the use of reward and punishment. *Journal of Personality and Social Psychology,* 1968, 9, 353–62.

Simmons, Carolyn and Lerner, Melvin. Altruism as a search

for justice. *Journal of Personality and Social Psychology,* 1968, 9, 216–25.

Stephenson, G. M. and White, J. H. An experimental study of some effects of injustice on children's moral behavior. *Journal of Experimental Social Psychology,* 1968, 4, 367–83.

Valenzi, E. R. and Andrews, I. R. Effect of underpay and overpay inequity when tested with a new induction procedure. In *Proceedings,* 77th Annual Convention. Washington, D.C.: American Psychological Association, 1969, 593–94.

Vroom, Victor. *Work and motivation.* New York: Wiley, 1964.

Weick, Karl E. The concept of equity in the perception of pay. *Administrative Science Quarterly,* 1966, 11, 414–39.

Weick, Karl E. Organizations in the laboratory. In Victor Vroom (ed.), *Methods of organization research.* Pittsburgh: University of Pittsburgh, 1967. Pp. 1–56 (a).

Weick, Karl E. Dissonance and task enhancement: A problem for compensation theory, *Organizational Behavior and Human Performance,* 1967, 2, 189–207. (b)

Weick, Karl E. and Nesset, Bonna. Preferences among forms of equity. *Organizational Behavior and Human Performance,* 1968, 3, 400–16.

Wicker, Allan W. and Bushweiler, Gary. Perceived fairness and pleasantness of social exchange situations: Two factorial studies of inequity. *Journal of Personality and Social Psychology,* 1970, 15, 63–75.

Wiener, J. The effect of task and ego oriented performance on two kinds of overcompensation inequity. *Organizational Behavior and Human Performance,* 1970, 5, 191–208.

Wood, Ian and Lawler, Edward E. Effects of piece-rate overpayment on productivity. *Journal of Applied Psychology,* 1970, 54, 234–38.

Zedeck, Sheldon and Smith, Patricia Cain. A psychophysical determination of equitable payment: A methodological study. *Journal of Applied Psychology,* 1968, 52, 343–47.

FOCUS FOR CHAPTERS 2 THROUGH 5

In the first chapter, we presented a foundation of theory and principles believed to be relevant and perhaps crucial to our understanding of human behavior in organizations.

We are now going to shift our focus. The remainder of the book dwells upon several areas of knowledge and practical relevance in the administration of the human side of an organization. First, in Chapter 2, we examine several criteria by which the behavior of people in organizations can be and frequently is evaluated. We are concerned here with the measurement and interrelationships among these dependent variables. We then move to several important variables which can be significantly influenced by the administrator in directing human behavior toward organizational goals. Specifically, in Chapter 3 we examine the design of tasks, the role of organizational structure and size in influencing human performance and attitudes, and the impact of formal reward and penalty systems on behavior. In Chapter 4, our concern shifts to group processes and the role of leadership in organizational behavior. Finally, in Chapter 5, the emphasis is placed upon measuring, controlling, and changing behavior in organizations.

Two themes may be noted throughout these chapters. First, we are concerned with the practical relevance of knowledge about human behavior in organizations. Thus, we will be examining empirical evidence in search of trustworthy findings which suggest controllable variables in administration. Second, this search will lead us across three levels of analysis in organizational behavior, that is, individual, interpersonal, and organizational. We must, therefore, become involved with the concepts and findings drawn from the behavioral disciplines of psychology, social psychology, and sociology.

chapter 2

DEPENDENT VARIABLES IN ORGANIZATIONAL BEHAVIOR AND HUMAN PERFORMANCE

The dependent variable in organizational behavior is nearly always some aspect of behavior or the consequences of behavior. Both the administrator and the behavioral scientist are interested in the phenomena of productivity, absenteeism, and turnover. Both have shown a pervasive interest in what has been variously called "attitudes," "satisfaction," or "morale." The readings in this chapter are devoted to some important issues regarding the number of dependent variables, their interrelationships, and their relative significance.

In the first selection, Katz describes several dependent variables which he feels are related to organizational effectiveness. Since there is the possibility that the dependent variables may have different motivational bases, the relationships between them may be low, or at best, obscure. Katz also observes that certain kinds of behavior may not be specified as role requirements in spite of the fact that they may be essential to organizational success. The suggestion that our dependent variables may be unrelated should pique the curiosity of those who assume that satisfaction and performance, for example, are highly related.

In the next selection, Schwab and Cummings review a number of theoretical positions concerning the relationship between satisfaction and performance. For several years, the belief that satisfaction resulted in high levels of performance prevailed among laymen and organizational theorists alike. There were, however, a number of embarrassing exceptions to this hedonistic principle, and when concerted research efforts failed to provide evidence in support of a causal relationship, new conceptualizations began to emerge. They generally took the form of attempts to provide a theoretical rationale for the absence of a direct relationship including the postulation of a variety of moderator variables. In addition, the Porter-Lawler model reversed the previously assumed relationship and postulated that satisfaction, rather than causing performance was caused by it. A careful reading of the Porter-Lawler model reveals, however, that the assumed linkage between performance and satisfaction is somewhat complex with the implication that satisfaction is brought about not by performance but by rewards associated with performance. Schwab and Cummings frankly question the value of further satisfaction-performance theorizing. Like Katz, they suggest that a better approach might be to treat performance and satisfaction as unrelated dependent variables and to seek out the determinants of each.

Schwab and Cummings held up the work of Herzberg and his colleagues as an example of current theory reflecting the view that satisfaction leads to performance. We now turn to a comprehensive evaluation of the "two-factor theory" of job motivation by King. In 1959, Herzberg, Mausner, and Snyderman advanced the thesis that those factors which lead to satisfaction are different from those leading to dissatisfaction. A corollary is that the former (the motivators) are more important in determining high levels of performance and that as a consequence satisfaction with those factors should be related to productivity. As King points out, the theory has generated a great deal of research as well as a large measure of controversy in part because it has not been explicitly stated. King examines five distinct versions of the theory and concludes that all of them lack unequivocal empirical support. The two-factor theory is another example of an explanation of human behavior which, because it is based upon introspective reports, seems to have widespread intuitive appeal. However, we are of the opinion that it can only be viewed as another attempt to salvage a simplified hedonistic doctrine by the invention of new kinds of pleasures and pains. If the theory has any value at all, it is because it suggests that certain events are more reinforcing than others and that some reinforcers have more impact on behavior than others because they are more likely to be contingent upon performance. It is the nature of the relationship between behavior and its consequences rather than satisfaction as such which determines behavioral outcomes.

Cherrington, Reitz, and Scott contend that there is no inherent relationship between satisfaction and performance. Rather, they postulate a causal relationship between the occurrence of reinforcing stimuli and implicit affective and arousal responses assumed to underlie self-reports of satisfaction. One deduction from their reinforcement model is that one can produce a variety of relationships between satisfaction and performance merely by varying the contingencies between performance and reinforcing events. This deduction was generally supported by the study which they described. Subjects who were rewarded reported significantly higher levels of satisfaction than those who were not rewarded. Furthermore, there was a positive correlation between self-reports of satisfaction and performance for an appropriately reinforced group while a negative relationship was found for an inappropriately reinforced group.

We assume that human behavior is an important managerial concern because that behavior determines, to a significant degree, the effectiveness of the organization. But precisely what is meant by the term "organizational effectiveness"? Yuchtman and Seashore are critical of the assumption that organizations have immutable goals which can be identified either from the organization's charter or by deduction from a body of theory. Yuchtman and Seashore prefer to think of an organization as a functional entity in interaction with the broader environment in which it resides and to define organizational effectiveness in terms of its bargaining position or its ability to acquire scarce and valued resources. If this is the case, then many organizational goals in the usual sense are essentially courses of action presumably instrumental in procuring resources and should, therefore, vary as the contingencies change.

15. THE MOTIVATIONAL BASIS OF ORGANIZATIONAL BEHAVIOR*

***Daniel Katz*†**

How, and what extent, do people become involved in an organization and committed to its goals? If an organization is to survive and to function effectively, it must require not one, but several different types of behavior from most of its members, and the motivations for these different types of behavior may also differ. How does a business organization attract the kind of people it needs? How does it hold them? How does it induce both reliable performance and spontaneous innovation on the part of its members? This paper proposes an analytic framework for understanding the complexities of motivational problems in an organization.

The basic problem to which I shall address myself is how people are tied into social and organizational structures so that they become effective functioning units of social systems. What is the nature of their involvement in a system or their commitment to it?

The major input into social organizations consists of people. The economist or the culturologist may concentrate on inputs of resources, raw materials, technology. To the extent that human factors are recognized, they are assumed to be constants in the total equation and are neglected. At the practical level, however, as well as for a more precise theoretical accounting, we need to cope with such organizational realities as the attracting of people into organizations, holding them within the system, insuring reliable role performance, and in addition stimulating actions which are generally facilitative of organizational accomplishment. The material and psychic returns to organizational members thus constitute major determinants, not only of the level of effectiveness of organizational functioning, but of the very existence of the organization.

The complexities of motivational problems in organizations can be understood if we develop an

* *Behavioral Science,* 1964, pp. 131–33 (abridged).

† Department of Psychology, University of Michigan.

analytic framework which will be comprehensive enough to identify the major sources of variance and detailed enough to contain sufficient specification for predictive purposes. The framework we propose calls for three steps in an analysis process, namely, the formulation of answers to these types of questions: (1) What are the types of behavior required for effective organizational functioning? Any organization will require not one, but several patterns of behavior from most of its members. And the motivational bases of these various behavioral requirements may differ. (2) What are the motivational patterns which are used and which can be used in organizational settings? How do they differ in their logical and psycho-logic? What are the differential consequences of the various types of motivational patterns for the behavioral requirements essential for organizational functioning? One motivational pattern may be very effective in bringing about one type of necessary behavior and completely ineffective in leading to another. (3) What are the conditions for eliciting a given motivational pattern in an organizational setting? We may be able to identify the type of motivation we think most appropriate for producing a given behavioral outcome but we still need to know how this motive can be aroused or produced in the organization.

BEHAVIORAL REQUIREMENTS

Our major dependent variables are the behavioral requirements of the organization. Three basic types of behavior are essential for a functioning organization: (1) People must be induced to enter and remain within the system. (2) They must carry out their role assignments in a dependable fashion. (3) There must be innovative and spontaneous activity in achieving organizational objectives which go beyond the role specifications.

Attracting and Holding People in a System

First of all, sufficient personnel must be kept within the system to man its essential functions. People thus must be induced to enter the system at a sufficiently rapid rate to counteract the amount of defection. High turnover is costly. Moreover, there is some optimum period for their staying within the system. And while they are members of the system they must validate their membership by constant attendance. Turnover and absenteeism are both measures of organizational effectiveness and productivity, though they are partial measures. People may, of course, be within the system physically but may be psychological absentees. The child may be regular and punctual in his school attendance and yet day-dream in his classes. It is not enough then, to hold people within a system.

Dependable Role Performance

The great range of variable human behavior must be reduced to a limited number of predictable patterns. In other words, the assigned roles must be carried out and must meet some minimal level of quantity and quality of performance. A common measure of productivity is the amount of work turned out by the individual or by the group carrying out their assigned tasks. Quality of performance is not as easily measured and the problem is met by quality controls which set minimal standards for the pieces of work sampled. In general, the major role of the member is clearly set forth by organizational protocol and leadership. The man on the assembly line, the nurse in the hospital, the teacher in the elementary school all know what their major job is. To do a lot of it and to do it well are, then, the most conspicuous behavioral requirements of the organization. It may be, of course, that given role requirements are not functionally related to organizational accomplishment. This is a different type of problem and we are recognizing here only the fact that some major role requirements are necessary.

Innovative and Spontaneous Behavior

A neglected set of requirements consists of those actions not specified by role prescriptions which nevertheless facilitate the accomplishment of organizational goals. The great paradox of a social organization is that it must not only reduce human variability to insure reliable role performance but that it must also allow room for some variability and in fact encourage it.

There must always be a supportive number of actions of an innovative or relatively spontaneous sort. No organizational planning can foresee all contingencies within its operations, or can anticipate with perfect accuracy all environmental changes, or can control perfectly all human variability. The resources of people in innovation, in spontaneous co-operation, in protective and creative behavior are thus vital to organizational survival and effectiveness. An organization which depends solely upon its blueprints of prescribed behavior is a very fragile social system.

Co-operation

The patterned activity which makes up an organization is so intrinsically a cooperative set of interrelationships, that we are not aware of the co-operative nexus any more than we are of any habitual behavior like walking. Within every work group in a factory, within any division in a government bureau, or within any department of a university are countless acts of co-operation without which the system would break down. We take these everyday acts for granted, and few, if any, of them form the role prescriptions for any job. One man will call the attention of his companion on the next machine to some indication that his machine is getting jammed, or will pass along some tool that his companion needs, or will borrow some bit of material he is short of. Or men will come to the aid of a fellow who is behind on his quota. In a study of clerical workers in an insurance company one of the two factors differentiating high-producing from low-producing sections was the greater co-operative activity of the girls in the high-producing sections coming to one another's help in meeting production quotas. In most factories specialization develops around informal types of help. One man will be expert in first aid, another will be expert in machine diagnosis, etc. We recognize the need for cooperative relationships by raising this specific question when a man is considered for a job, How well does he relate to his fellows, is he a good team man, will he fit in?

Protection

Another subcategory of behavior facilitative of organizational functioning is the action which protects the organization against disaster. There is nothing in the role prescriptions of the worker which specifies that he be on the alert to save life and property in the organization. Yet the worker who goes out of his way to remove the boulder accidentally lodged in the path of a freight car on the railway spur, or to secure a rampant piece of machinery, or even to disobey orders when they obviously are wrong and dangerous, is an invaluable man for the organization.

Constructive Ideas

Another subcategory of acts beyond the line of duty consists of creative suggestions for the improvement of methods of production or of maintenance. Some organizations encourage their members to feed constructive suggestions into the system, but coming up with good ideas for the organization and formulating them to management is not the typical role of the worker. An organization that can stimulate its members to contribute ideas for organizational improvement is a more effective organization in that people who are close to operating problems can often furnish informative suggestions about such operations. The system which does not have this stream of contributions from its members is not utilizing its potential resources effectively.

Self-Training

Still another subcategory under the heading of behavior beyond the call of duty concerns the self-training of members for doing their own jobs better and self-education for assuming more responsible positions in the organization. There may be no requirement that men prepare themselves for better positions. But the organization which has men spending their own time to master knowledge and skills for more responsible jobs in the system has an additional resource for effective functioning.

Favorable Attitude

Finally, members of a group can contribute to its operations by helping to create a favorable climate for it in the community, or communities, which surround the organization. Employees may talk to friends, relatives, and acquaintances about the excellent or the poor qualities of the company for which they work. A favorable climate may help in problems of recruitment, and sometimes product disposal.

In short, for effective organizational functioning many members must be willing on occasion to do more than their job prescriptions specify. If the system were to follow the letter of the law according to job descriptions and protocol, it would soon grind to a halt. There have to be many actions of mutual co-operation and many anticipations of organizational objectives to make the system viable.

Now these three major types of behavior, and even the subcategories, though related, are not necessarily motivated by the same drives and needs. The motivational pattern that will attract and hold people to an organization is not necessarily the same as that which will lead to higher productivity. Nor are the motives which make for higher productivity invariably the same as those which sustain cooperative interrelationships in the interests of organizational accomplishment. Hence, when we speak about organizational practices and procedures which will further the attainment of its mission, we need to specify the type of behavioral requirement involved.

. . .

16. THEORIES OF PERFORMANCE AND SATISFACTION: A REVIEW*

***Donald P. Schwab and Larry L. Cummings*†**

. . . the animals worked like slaves. But they were happy in their work; they grudged no effort or sacrifice, well aware that everything that they did was for the benefit of themselves and those of their kind who would come after them. . . .[1]

A sizable portion of behavioral science research in organizations has focused on possible connections between job attitudes, particular job satisfaction, and various job behaviors.[2] Industrial psychologists and labor economists, for example, have explored the relationship between job satisfaction and job tenure.[3] Other scholars from various disciplines have examined the association between job satisfaction and such behavioral variables as absences, accidents, grievances, illnesses,[4] and even life expectancy.[5] More recently, a growing number of studies suggesting a controversy have emerged concerning the relationship between technology and task design and satisfaction with the job.[6]

Unquestionably, however, it is the hypothesized connection between employee satisfaction and job performance. The methodologies employed in these search and theoretical interest. In the last 40 years, investigators have examined these two variables in a wide variety of work situations: (1) among organization members ranging from the unskilled to managers and professionals, (2) in diverse administrative and technological environments, (3) using individuals or groups as the unit of analysis, and (4) employing various measures of both satisfaction and performance. The methodologies employed in these studies, and their findings have been reviewed by Brayfield and Crockett; Herzberg, Mausner, Peterson and Capwell; and Vroom.[7]

Whereas earlier reviews have focused on empirical research, this paper reviews and evaluates *theoretical* propositions concerning the relationship between satisfaction and performance. Three major points of view are considered: (1) the view that satisfaction leads to performance, a position generally associated with early human relations concepts, (2) the view that the satisfaction-performance relationship is moderated by a number of variables, a position which gained acceptance in the fifties and continues to be reflected in current research, and (3) the view that performance leads to satisfaction, a recently stated position. Conceptualizations of satisfaction-performance relations which represent each of these positions are reviewed, even though several do not represent theories in any rigorous sense.

---

* *Industrial Relations,* Vol. 9, No. 4 (October 1970), pp. 408–30.

† The authors are, respectively, Associate Professor of Personnel and Industrial Relations and Professor of Organizational Behavior, University of Wisconsin.

[1] George Orwell. *Animal farm* (New York: New American Library, Signet Classics, 1959), p. 63.

[2] The authors thank H. G. Heneman, Jr., H. G. Heneman, III, R. U. Miller, and W. E. Scott, Jr., for their critical comments on an earlier draft of this paper. Portions of this paper were presented at the American Psychological Association Convention, September 1970, Miami Beach.

[3] For a review of psychological research on this relationship, see Victor H. Vroom. *Work and motivation* (New York: Wiley, 1964), pp. 175–178. For more recent research investigating the relationship from a psychological point of view, see Charles L. Hulin. Effects of changes in job satisfaction levels on employee turnover. *Journal of Applied Psychology,* 52 (April 1968), 122–26; Charles L. Hulin. Job satisfaction and turnover in a female clerical population. *Journal of Applied Psychology,* 50 (August 1966), 280–85, and Patricia S. Mikes and Charles L. Hulin. Use of importance as a weighting component of job satisfaction. *Journal of Applied Psychology,* 52 (October 1968), 394–398. Labor economists have tended to be concerned with the relative impact of differing types of satisfaction on turnover. In particular, they have sought to determine the importance of satisfaction with money income in the decision to remain with or leave an organization. In this regard, see the studies by Lloyd G. Reynolds. *The structure of labor markets* (New York: Harper, 1951), pp. 79–101, and Charles A. Myers and George P. Shultz. *The dynamics of a labor market* (New York: Prentice-Hall, 1951), pp. 102–34. These and other economically oriented studies are reviewed in Herbert S. Parnes. *Research on labor mobility* (New York: Social Science Research Council, 1954), pp. 147–56. For a discussion which attempts to explain the labor market findings within the context of classical economic theory, see Simon Rottenberg. On choice in labor markets, *Industrial and Labor Relations Review,* 9 (January 1956), 183–99.

[4] Studies investigating these relationships are reviewed in Arthur H. Brayfield and Walter H. Crockett. Employee attitudes and employee performance, *Psychological Bulletin,* 52 (September 1955), 396–424; Frederick H. Herzberg, Bernard M. Mausner, Richard O. Peterson, and Dora F. Capwell. *Job attitudes: Review of research and opinion* (Pittsburgh: Psychological Service of Pittsburgh, 1957), pp. 107–11, and Vroom, *Work and motivation,* pp. 178–81.

[5] See, for example, Francis C. Madigan. "Role satisfactions and length of life in a closed population, *American Journal of Scoiology,* 67 (May 1962), 640–49.

[6] A recent study by Shepard concluded that job satisfaction and functional job specialization are inversely related. Jon M. Shepard. Functional specialization and work attitudes, *Industrial Relations,* 8 (February, 1969), 185–94. However, a recent thorough review of the literature challenges much of the research which purportedly shows a relationship between job satisfaction and task design. Charles L. Hulin and Milton R. Blood. Job enlargement, individual differences and worker responses, *Psychological Bulletin,* 69 (January 1968), 41–55.

[7] Brayfield and Crockett, employee attitudes and employee performance. Herzberg, *et al., job attitudes;* and Vroom, *Work and motivation.*

SATISFACTION → PERFORMANCE

. . . management has at long last discovered that there is greater production, and hence greater profit when workers are satisfied with their jobs. Improve the morale of a company and you improve production.[8]

Historical Perspective. Whatever their value as research, the Hawthorne studies had a significant impact on the thinking of a generation of behavioral scientists and business managers.[9] The quotation from Parker and Kleemeir was almost certainly inspired by the Hawthorne studies, although the original investigators probably never stated the relationship so unequivocally. Roethlisberger, for example, in discussing the implications of the study for managers, noted that ". . . the factors which make for efficiency in a business organization are not necessarily the same as those factors that make for happiness, collaboration, teamwork, morale, or any other word which may be used to refer to cooperative situations."[10]

Yet, despite Roethlisberger's caveat, the early human relationists have been interpreted as saying that satisfaction leads to performance. Vroom, for example, argues that ". . . human relations might be described as an attempt to increase productivity by satisfying the needs of employees."[11] Strauss states that ". . . early human relationists viewed the morale-productivity relationship quite simply: higher morale would lead to improved productivity."[12] In the final analysis the interpretation is perhaps more significant than the original views expressed.

A Current Satisfaction → Performance Interpretation. The work of Herzberg and his colleagues provides perhaps the best illustration of current theory and research formulated on the view that satisfaction leads to performance. These researchers separate job variables into two groups, hygiene factors and motivators.[13] Included in the hygiene group are such variables as supervision, physical working conditions, regular salary and benefits, company policies, etc. These are viewed as potential sources of dissatisfaction, but not as sources of positive work attitudes. Among the motivators, Herzberg lists factors closely associated with work itself and its accomplishment, i.e., challenging assignments, recognition, the opportunity for professional growth, etc. These factors presumably contribute to work satisfaction and are the key factors associated with performance. Thus, Herzberg feels that low performance-satisfaction correlations obtained in other research studies can thus be explained since ". . . the usual morale measures are confounded . . . they tap both kinds of attitudes . . ." (i.e., satisfiers and dissatisfiers).[14]

In fairness to the original authors of *The Motivation to Work*, it should be recognized that the conclusion relating performance to the satisfiers but not to the dissatisfiers has escalated somewhat with the passage of time. In the original study, care was taken to report the actual percentages obtained and to at least raise alternative explanations of the findings.[15] These qualifications are not present in subsequent restatements of the original findings by Herzberg[16] or by other advocates of the two-factor theory.[17] In short, it appears that the satisfaction-performance findings of *The Motivation to Work* are being overinterpreted in the same manner as were Roethlisberger and Dickson's findings in *Management and the Worker*.

Although there have been a number of partial replications of the two-factor theory,[18] they have not investigated the hypothesized performance consequences of job satisfaction and dissatisfaction.[19]

---

[8] Willard E. Parker and Robert W. Kleemeir. *Human relations in supervision: Leadership in management* (New York: McGraw-Hill, 1951), p. 10.

[9] Fritz J. Roethlisberger and William J. Dickson. *Management and the worker*, Science Editions (New York: Wiley, 1964). For two highly critical interpretations of the Hawthorne studies as research, see A. J. M. Sykes. Economic interests and the Hawthorne researchers: A comment, *Human Relations*, 18 (August 1965), 253-63, and Alex Carey, The Hawthorne studies: A radical criticism, *American Sociological Review*, 32 (June 1967), 403-16. For less critical but earlier re-examinations, see Michael Argyle. The relay assembly test room in retrospect, *Occupational Psychology*, 27 (April 1953), 98–103, and Henry A. Landsberger. *Hawthorne revisited* (Ithaca, N.Y.: Cornell University, 1958).

[10] Fritz J. Roethlisberger. *Management and morale* (Cambridge: Harvard University Press, 1941), p. 156.

[11] Vroom, *Work and motivation*, p. 181.

[12] George Strauss, Human relations—1968 style, *Industrial Relations*, 7 (May 1968), 264.

[13] Frederick Herzberg, Bernard Mauser, and Barbara Snyderman. *The motivation to work* (2d ed.; New York: Wiley, 1959), pp. 59–83.

[14] Ibid., p. 87.

[15] Ibid., pp. 86–87.

[16] Frederick Herzberg. *Work and the nature of man* (Cleveland: World Publishing, 1966), p. 74, and Frederick Herzberg, One more time, How do you motivate employees? *Harvard Business Review*, 66 (January–February 1968), 53–62.

[17] See, for example, David A. Whitsett and Erik K. Winslow. An analysis of studies critical of the motivator-hygiene theory, *Personnel Psychology*, 20 (Winter 1967), 391–415.

[18] Nine such replications are discussed in Herzberg, *Work and the nature of man*, pp. 96–129. See, however, a study by Schwab and Heneman which suggests that the analytical procedure employed in the original study and in the replications overstates the theory's predictability of individual responses to satisfying and dissatisfying experiences. Donald P. Schwab and Herbert G. Heneman, III. Aggregate and individual predictability of the two-factor theory of job satisfaction, *Personnel Psychology*, 23 (Spring 1970), 55–66.

[19] See, for example, Frederick Herzberg. The motivation to work among Finnish supervisors, *Personnel Psychology*, 18 (Winter 1965), 393–402; M. Scott Myers. Who are your motivated workers? *Harvard Business Review*, 62 (January–February 1964), 73–88; Shoukry D. Saleh. A study of attitude change in the pre-retirement period, *Journal of Applied Psychology*, 67 (October 1964), 310–12; and Milton M. Schwartz, Edmund Jenusaitis, and Harry Stark. Motivational factors

Thus, the empirical validity of the satisfaction-performance relationship specified in the two-factor theory rests entirely on the original study of 200 accountants and engineers.[20]

Moreover, the evidence employed to support the premise that satisfaction leads to performance has been nonexperimental in design. As such, the studies obviously do not show causality. In fact, neither human relationists in general, nor Herzberg in particular, have provided an adequate theoretical explanation for the causal relationship which they postulated.

In sum, it is our view that the popular interpretation of human relations research has probably been detrimental to the understanding of worker motivation. An essentially unsupported interpretation was so quickly and widely accepted that the underlying theory was neither questioned nor refined. By assuming, without adequate analysis, that observed satisfaction-performance linkages were casually and unidirectionally related, subsequent researchers may well have misinterpreted the meaning of their data.[21] Ultimately, however, it was probably the human relationist's failure to develop a sufficiently sophisticated theory, combined with ambiguous, often contradictory research evidence, which led to other formulations of the relationship between these two variables.

SATISFACTION—?—PERFORMANCE

> . . . high morale is no longer considered as a prerequisite of high productivity. But more than this, the nature of the relationship between morale and productivity is open to serious questioning. Is it direct? Is it inverse? Is it circular? Or, is there any relationship at all between the two; are they independent variables?[22]

The Development of Uncertainty. The statement by Scott (and others similar to it)[23] reflects perhaps more than anything else the pervasive influence of the previously mentioned review by Brayfield and Crockett, along with the conclusions reached in some of the early research conducted at the Institute for Social Research, University of Michigan.[24]

The Michigan findings are important for at least two reasons. First, they represent early empirical evidence offering little reason for optimism about the association between satisfaction and performance. In the insurance and railroad studies only one of the four attitude measures (pride in work group) was found to be positively associated with the productivity measures employed.[25] Second, unlike much previous research reported, the investigators carefully spelled out the limitations of their design for making causal inferences and specifically suggested alternative causal hypotheses which their data might support.[26]

A capstone to the development of uncertainty regarding the satisfaction-performance relationship was provided by Brayfield and Crockett in 1955.[27] Their review of over 50 studies represents, depending on one's point of view, either a council of despair or a challenge for theory development and extended research. As we will illustrate, the latter (at least the theoretical dimension) seems to have prevailed.

---

among supervisors in the utility industry, *Personnel Psychology,* 16 (Spring, 1963), 45–53.

[20] Moreover, a recent study examining the relationship between job attitudes and performance effects did not find support for Herzberg's hypothesis. Among a group of 80 managers, it was found that the dissatisfiers were as closely associated with variations in performance effects as were the satisfiers. Donald P. Schwab, William W. Devitt and Larry L. Cummings. A test of the adequacy of the two-factor theory as a predictor of self-report performance effects, *Personnel Psychology,* 24 (Summer 1971) 293–304.

[21] Several findings of the Herzberg, *et al.,* study suggest, for example, an alternative interpretation. They reported that 74 per cent of satisfying and 25 per cent of the dissatisfying sequences included feelings of achievement and/or recognition for successful or unsuccessful job performance. (Cf. Herzberg, *et al., The motivation to work,* pp. 72, 143.) In these instances, at least, it would seem plausible to argue that performance preceded, rather than followed, satisfaction. If one were to accept their conclusions about stated performance effects, it would seem appropriate to suggest a possible circular relationship between satisfaction and performance.

[22] William G. Scott. *Human relations in management: A behavioral science approach* (New York: McGraw-Hill, 1962), p. 93.

[23] See also, for example, March and Simon who stated that "Attempts to relate these variables (morale, satisfaction and cohesiveness) directly to productivity have failed to reveal any consistent simple relation." James G. March and Herbert A. Simon. *Organizations* (New York: Wiley, 1958), pp. 47–48. In the same vein, Carey, in commenting on the Hawthorne studies, noted ". . . the widespread failure of later (post-Hawthorne) studies to reveal any reliable relations between the social satisfaction of industrial workers and their work performance." Carey, The Hawthorne Studies, p. 403. Even Davis, an avowed human relationist, deferred to Brayfield and Crockett, conceding that one must ". . . recognize that high morale and high productivity are not absolutely related to each other." Keith Davis, *Human relations in business* (New York: McGraw-Hill, 1957), p. 182.

[24] Daniel Katz, Nathan Maccoby, and Nancy C. Morse. *Productivity, supervision and morale in an office situation* (Ann Arbor: University of Michigan, Survey Research Center, 1950), and Daniel Katz, Nathan Maccoby, Gerald Gurin, and Lucretia G. Floor. *Productivity, supervision and morale among railroad workers* (Ann Arbor: University of Michigan, Survey Research Center, 1951).

[25] Katz, *et al. Productivity . . . in an office situation,* p. 48 and Katz, *et al., Productivity . . . among railroad workers,* pp. 24–30. Factor items and analyses differed somewhat between the two studies and thus they are not strictly comparable. In summarizing this research, Kahn stated that "The persistence with which managers and managerial consultants place them (satisfaction and performance) in juxtaposition is much more revealing of their own value structure, I believe, than it is indicative of anything in the empirical research data on organizations." Robert L. Kahn. Productivity and job satisfaction, *Personnel Psychology,* 13 (Autumn 1960), 275.

[26] Katz, *et al Productivity . . . in an office situation,* pp. 14–15.

[27] Brayfield and Crockett, Employee attitudes and employee performance. p. 415.

Brayfield and Crockett hypothesized that employees govern their job seeking, job performing, and job terminating behavior by the law of effect, subsequently elaborated and relabeled by Vroom, and Porter and Lawler, as expectancy theory.[28] Regarding job terminating behavior, Brayfield and Crockett argued that: "One principal generalization suffices to set up an expectation that morale should be related to absenteeism and turnover, namely, that organisms tend to avoid those situations which are punishing and to seek out situations that are rewarding."[29]

Brayfield and Crockett encountered greater difficulty explaining satisfaction and job performance linkages through the simple application of the hedonistic principle. They suggested that satisfaction and job performance might be concomitantly rather than causally related. In addition, one ". . . might expect high satisfaction and high productivity to occur together when productivity is perceived as a path to certain important goals and when these goals are achieved. Under other conditions, satisfaction and productivity might be unrelated or even negatively related."[30]

Additional Models. Three lesser known theoretical expositions of the satisfaction-performance relation further illustrate the influence of the mixed and uncertain research findings in this area.[31] Each suggests that both satisfaction *and* performance can be viewed as criteria of organizational effectiveness. Moreover, each suggests that relationships between satisfaction and performance need be neither direct nor particularly strong.

A Theory of Work Adjustment. In the first of these, Dawis and his colleagues posit that work adjustment is a function of employee *satisfaction* and *satisfactoriness* (performance).[32] Satisfaction presumably results from the correspondence between the individual's need set and the organization's reinforcer system and has its major impact on individual decisions to remain with or withdraw from the organization. Satisfactoriness, alternatively, refers to the organization's evaluation (in terms of its goals) of the behavior of its members. It is assumed to be a function of the correspondence between the requirements imposed by the job and the abilities possessed by the employee and can result in one of several consequences, e.g., promotion, transfer, termination, or retention in present position. Incorporated in the Dawis *et al.* model is the possibility of a relation between satisfaction and satisfactoriness, although its form and strength are not developed. Moreover, their model allows one to explain variations in employee satisfaction without reference to performance (either as a cause or consequence).

Pressure for Production as an Intervening Variable. In a related statement, Triandis has proposed a theory which shares with Dawis *et al,* the notion that satisfaction and performance need not covary under all conditions.[33] Triandis hypothesized that organizational pressure for high production influences both satisfaction and performance, but not in the same fashion. As pressure increases, job satisfaction is hypothesized to decrease irrespective of the concomitant variation in performance. Employee performance, alternatively, is hypothesized to be curvilinearly related to production pressure. At several locations within the typical range of employee satisfaction increasing pressure is hypothesized to result in increased performance, while at other locations the relation between pressure and performance is assumed to be negative. Triandis also hypothesized that satisfaction and performance may be directly linked in certain circumstances. Finally, satisfaction may also lead to moderate performance under the utopian condition of no pressure to perform. This would be the case where a minimum level of performance is caused by intrinsic job satisfaction plus certain activity drives or needs for stimulus inputs and variation.[34]

Satisfaction and the Motivation to Produce. A model proposed by March and Simon perhaps best bridges the theoretical gap between the satisfaction → performance view of the human relationists and the performance → satisfaction view to be discussed in the following section.[35] The model suggests that both performance and satisfaction can serve as dependent variables.

Beginning with performance as the dependent variable, March and Simon hypothesized: "Motivation to produce stems from a present or anticipated

---

[28] Vroom, *Work and motivation,* and Lyman W. Porter and Edward E. Lawler, III, *Managerial attitudes and performance* (Homewood, Ill.: Irwin, 1968).

[29] Brayfield and Crockett, Employee attitudes and employee performance, p. 415.

[30] Ibid., p. 416. The tone of this quote anticipates a portion of the Porter-Lawler model to be discussed subsequently; namely that performance can lead to satisfaction when mediated by relevant goals (rewards in the terminology of the Porter-Lawler model).

[31] Rene V. Dawis, George E. England, and Lloyd H. Lofquist. *A theory of work adjustment: A revision* (Minneapolis: University of Minnesota, Industrial Relations Center, 1968), Bulletin 47; Harry C. Triandis. A critique and experimental design for the study of the relationship between productivity and job satisfaction, *Psychology Bulletin,* 56 (July 1959), 309-312, and March and Simon, *Organizations.*

[32] Dawis, *et al., A theory of work adjustment,* p. 8.

[33] Triandis, A critique and experimental design . . .

[34] For an elaborated treatment of the implications of activity drives or activation levels as correlates of task performance, see William E. Scott, Jr., Activation theory and task design, *Organizational Behavior and Human Performance,* 1 (September, 1966), 3-30.

[35] March and Simon, *Organizations.*

state of discontent and a perception of a direct connection between individual production and a new state of satisfaction."[36] The hypothesis states that performance is a function of two variables: (1) the degree of dissatisfaction experienced, and (2) the perceived instrumentality of performance for the attainment of valued rewards.

Thus, the model suggests that a state of dissatisfaction is a necessary, but not sufficient, condition for performance. It is necessary because dissatisfaction of some sort is assumed to be required to activate the organism toward search behavior. It lacks sufficiency, however, because a dissatisfied employee may not perceive performance as leading to satisfaction or may perceive nonperformance as leading to greater perceived satisfaction.

March and Simon also specify conditions where performance may lead to satisfaction although the linkage appears weaker (moderated by a greater number of variables) in their model than the satisfaction → performance linkage.[37] This is due to three factors. First, we have already noted that the hypothesized job satisfaction may result from the receipt of rewards which are not based on performance. Second, even if improved performance is the behavioral alternative chosen by the employee, satisfaction need not necessarily result since the actual rewards of performance may not correspond to the anticipated consequences. Third, in the process of searching for and evaluating the consequences of alternative behaviors, the worker's level of aspiration may be raised as much or more than the expected value of the rewards associated with the behavior. Thus, even if performance is chosen as the best alternative and its consequences are perfectly anticipated, the worker may find himself no more and perhaps less satisfied than before.

The Models Compared. The above three models can most easily be contrasted on the independent variables hypothesized to influence employee performance. The theory of work adjustment implies that the major determinant of performance is the structural fit between employee skills and abilities on the one hand and technical job requirements on the other. Thus, its implications for organizational practice are largely in the areas of employee selection, placement, and training. In contrast, March and Simon focus primarily on two motivational determinants of performance; namely, expected value of rewards and aspiration levels. Finally, Triandis emphasizes the importance of pressure for production, an organizational variable. As such, the Triandis model ignores the impact of either skill and ability or motivational differences between individuals.

It is also interesting to contrast Triandis, March, and Simon, and the Herzberg two-factor theory with regard to the circumstances leading to a causative linkage between performance and satisfaction. In the Triandis and March and Simon models, it is dissatisfaction which can have performance implications (negative in the former; positive in the latter). The two-factor theory alternatively suggests that it is predominately satisfaction which leads to high performance.

PERFORMANCE → SATISFACTION

> . . . good performance may lead to rewards, which in turn lead to satisfaction; this formulation then would say that satisfaction, rather than causing performance, as was previously assumed, is caused by it.[38]

The performance → satisfaction theory represents an important departure from earlier views about the relationship between these two variables. Human relationists, not without some qualification, postulated that high levels of satisfaction would result in high levels of performance. Subsequent models focused on the complexity of the relationship, incorporating various intervening variables in an attempt to account for frequently ambiguous findings of empirical studies. The performance → satisfaction theory, while it retains the idea of intervening variables, stresses the importance of variations in effort and performance as causes of variations in job satisfaction.

The Porter-Lawler Model.[39] Just as the Brayfield and Crockett review significantly influenced subsequent theoretical developments on the satisfaction → performance issue, a later review published by Vroom in 1964 has apparently had a similar impact on recent theorizing. While noting the generally low correspondence observed between measured satisfaction and performance, Vroom nevertheless found that in 20 of 23 cases the correlation was posi-

[36] Ibid., p. 51.

[37] Because March and Simon hypothesize that in certain circumstances performance leads to satisfaction, their theory could have been included in the following major section. We include it here because they hypothesize that performance is not necessary for satisfaction, while dissatisfaction is necessary for performance. Porter and Lawler's theory, discussed later, also hypothesizes a circular causal connection between satisfaction and performance. It reverses the emphasis of March and Simon, however, since it concentrates on the performance → satisfaction linkage.

[38] Edward E. Lawler, III, and Lyman W. Porter, The effect of performance on job satisfaction, *Industrial Relations,* 7 (October, 1967), p. 23.

[39] The performance → satisfaction theory is attributed to Porter and Lawler because they have developed it most fully. As we have already noted, March and Simon suggested conditions when performance could cause satisfaction. Vroom also suggests that performance as a cause of satisfaction is somewhat more tenable than the reverse (*Work and motivation,* p. 187).

FIGURE 1 PERFORMANCE → SATISFACTION

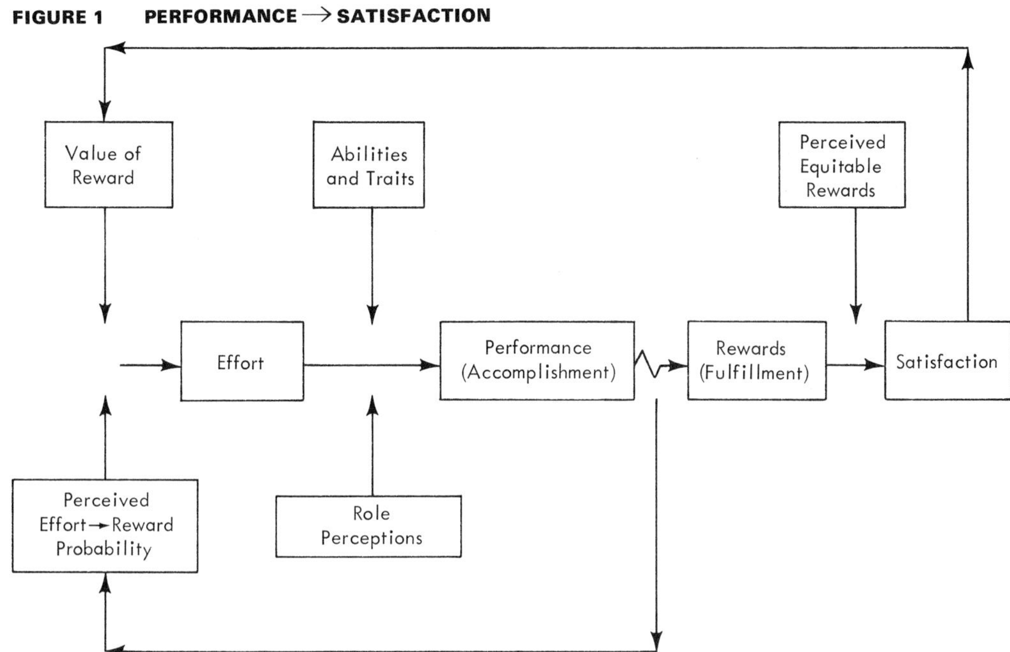

*Adapted from Porter and Lawler, *Managerial Attitudes and Performance,* p. 17.

tive and that the median correlation reported was +.14.[40] Porter and Lawler have cited this review and the generally positive nature of this association as a basis for suggesting that premature, pessimistic closure would be unwise and have expounded their model through a series of recent publications.[41]

Although the Porter-Lawler model posits circularity in the relationship between performance and satisfaction, Figure 1 shows that the most direct linkage has performance as the causal and satisfaction as the dependent variable. That relationship is mediated only by rewards (intrinsic and extrinsic) and the perceived equity of those rewards. When performance leads to rewards which are seen by the individual as equitable, it is hypothesized that high satisfaction will result.[42] The model suggests that the generally low performance-satisfaction relationships observed in previous empirical research may result from rewards, particularly extrinsic rewards, which are often not closely tied to performance.[43]

For satisfaction to exert an influence on performance in the Porter-Lawler model, it must affect the value of the rewards received, which in turn interacts with the perceived effort → reward linkage to determine the level of actual work effort. Finally, effort moderated by role perceptions and abilities and traits determines performance. Because of the number of intervening variables involved, it seems unlikely that satisfaction (or dissatisfaction) has as much impact on performance as performance has on satisfaction.

A Comparative Evaluation. The March and Simon model probably provides the most salient comparison with the Porter-Lawler model because both explicitly postulate a circular performance-satisfaction relation. The theories can be contrasted regarding the conditions necessary to avoid entropy or the "running down" of the level of employee motivation. In the March and Simon model, the function is performed primarily by aspiration level. It is hypothesized that as the expected value of reward increases,

[40] Ibid., p. 183.

[41] Edward E. Lawler, III, and Lyman W. Porter, Antecedent attitudes of effective managerial performance, *Organizational Behavior and Human Performance,* 2 (May 1967), 122–42; Edward E. Lawler, III, Attitude surveys and job performance, *Personnel Administration,* 30 (September–October 1967), 3-ff; Lawler and Porter, The effect of performance on job satisfaction; Lyman W. Porter and Edward E. Lawler, III. What job attitudes tell about motivation, *Harvard Business Review,* 46 (January–February 1968), 118–36, and Porter and Lawler. *Managerial attitudes and performance.*

[42] The concept of equity does not play the central role in the Porter-Lawler theory as it does say, in the works of Adams. See, for example, J. Stacy Adams. Toward an understanding of inequity, *Journal of Abnormal and Social Psychology,* 67 (November 1963), 422–36, and Wage inequities productivity and work quality, *Industrial Relations* 3 (October 1963), 9–16. In addition, at least one of the authors appears to have some serious reservations about the predictive utility of equity theory. See Edward E. Lawler, III. Equity theory as a predictor of productivity and work quality, *Psychological Bulletin,* 70 (December 1968), 596–610.

[43] Lawler and Porter, The effect of performance on job satisfaction, pp. 23–24.

level of aspiration increases, which in turn has a negative impact on satisfaction. Thus, the concept of aspiration level enables the model to be dynamic. That is, it is partially because of a rising aspiration level (resulting from the receipt of past rewards) that dissatisfaction is created, thereby leading to search behavior, one form of which can be performance.

Provision for the avoidance of entropy is more tenuous in the Porter-Lawler model. To sustain effort and performance over time, it is necessary to assume that satisfaction experienced from the receipt of intrinsic rewards leads to enhanced value being attached to such rewards. One must assume, for example, that feelings of worthwhile accomplishment increase the attractiveness or valence of such achievement.[44] As the authors note, however, the relation between satisfaction and value of reward can be interpreted in contrasting ways.[45] There exists some psysiological and psychological evidence to suggest that the greater the extrinsic reward satisfaction experienced, the less value attached to such rewards.[46] This would clearly lead to eventual entropy in the Porter-Lawler model. The point of contention between the two models on this issue centers on the causative factors in the continuity and preservation of behavior over time. Since both models are essentially based on need deprivation theories, some mechanism must be provided to prevent the system from attaining entropy.

Alternative Sources of Satisfaction. Porter and Lawler's model can be contrasted with both the March and Simon model and the theory of work adjustment on the question of the sufficiency of performance for satisfaction. The Porter-Lawler model shown in Figure 1 implies that satisfaction results from rewards associated with performance. It does not, therefore, appear to take into account all sources of employee satisfaction. Consider, for example, an organization which bases its rewards on seniority or organizational longevity. For persons with relatively strong security needs and low task involvement, seniority may represent the most rational means to the attainment of valued rewards and satisfaction. That is, the performance → reward linkage is not a necessary condition for attainment of meaningful satisfactions. Nor is it necessarily a condition for organizational survival. There are industrial jobs where minimally acceptable levels of performance are sufficient conditions for sustained participation. If system rewards are based on participation rather than individual performance and if they are perceived to be administered equitably, then, logically, satisfaction may be evident. This possibility is accounted for in the theory of work adjustment through the correspondence between employee needs and the reinforcer system of the job. It is accounted for in March and Simon's theory by their explicit hypothesis that satisfaction may result from rewards associated with various forms of nonperformance.

Implications for Administrative Practice. The Porter-Lawler model is quite rich in terms of its administrative implications. For example, it shares with the theory of work adjustment implications for high performance through the modification of abilities and traits via selection and training processes. In addition, their theory more than the others suggests a role for performance appraisal and salary administration in increasing employee performance levels. Both activities presumably have the potential of influencing the effort → reward and performance → reward probabilities. Furthermore, salary level, and particularly salary structure, would appear to be important determinants of perceived equity of rewards.

Alternatively, the Porter-Lawler model does not explicitly include supervisory and system pressure for high levels of effort and performance. These may be extremely important variables in some organizations. In this regard, Triandis' discussion is clearly more realistic. March and Simon's model also considers organizational pressure through its influence on the individual's evaluation of the perceived consequences of behavioral alternatives.

DISCUSSION

Two broad problems suggested by our review of the theoretical literature are discussed in the present section. First, although we have noted some obvious differences and points of contrast between various theoretical viewpoints, rigorous comparison and evaluation is made difficult by the fact that there are few commonly defined constructs across various theories. Second, it appears questionable whether present theorizing has adequately accounted for the variety of relevant variables that may moderate satisfaction-performance linkages in any specific work environment.

Conceptual Problems. In their review of empirical studies, Brayfield and Crockett observed: "Definitions are conspicuous by their absence in most current work in this area."[47] Much of the same conclusion can be stated after reviewing the theoretical

[44] On this point, satisfaction or dissatisfaction having performance consequences, Porter and Lawler are clearly closer to Herzberg and the early human relationists than to March and Simon or Triandis.

[45] Porter and Lawler, *Managerial attitudes and performance,* pp. 39–40.

[46] Charles N. Cofer and Mortimer H. Appley. *Motivation: Theory and research* (New York: Wiley, 1964), pp. 204–68.

[47] Brayfield and Crockett, "Employee attitudes and employee performance," p. 397.

literature, and the consequences are even more troublesome. In empirical research the measures employed ultimately define the variables. Thus, if operational procedures are adequately reported, one can identify the definitions and assess their appropriateness to the research question posed.[48] However, with regard to theory, it is impossible to ascertain the meaning of variables if the theoretician fails to define terms.

Satisfaction. The greatest ambiguity in theorizing about satisfaction-performance linkages has been in defining satisfaction. Three partially overlapping issues are raised by the literature reviewed here. First, it is often unclear whether satisfaction is being used in a "narrow," need deprivation sense, or in a "broad," attitudinal sense. Second, it is generally not clear which needs or which attitudinal referents are being considered. Third, there is a question whether feelings of job satisfaction are generated with or without reference to conditions on other jobs. These issues make comparisons among theoretical positions risky.

Beginning with the need deprivation versus attitude issue, satisfaction-dissatisfaction may be thought of in the context of "elementary" motivation theory.[49] Needs, demands, or drives generate tensions (feelings of dissatisfaction). The individual engages in behavior designed to obtain goals or incentives to reduce the tensions (satisfy the need).

Alternatively, satisfaction-dissatisfaction can be thought of as the evaluative component of an attitude. A person may respond affectively (feel satisfied or dissatisfied) about an object or referent in his work environment. Peak has argued that an attitude toward an object is a function of the object's perceived instrumentality for obtaining a valued end.[50] Thus, an object (e.g., economic rewards) could be positively valent (satisfying) in an attitudinal sense[51] while simultaneously deficient (dissatisfying) in a need sense. Illustrating these definitional differences, in the March and Simon model (dissatisfaction may lead to high performance), satisfaction appears to be defined in the need deprivation context.[52] Dissatisfaction (deprivation) in a sense, "pushes" the individual to behave. Satisfaction in the two-factor theory (satisfaction leads to performance), on the other hand, may refer to the affective feelings associated with certain job referents. A referent with positive valence may "pull" an individual to obtain it.[53]

Whether the theoretician chooses to work with needs or with attitudes, he must still identify the need types or attitude referents about which the individual feels satisfied or dissatisfied. There is evidence suggesting that global job satisfaction is made up of at least partially independent subcomponents.[54] Recent research at Cornell on the Job Description Index and other satisfaction measures, for example, has identified five subcomponents of overall satisfaction (work, pay, promotion, supervision, and co-workers) showing adequate convergent and discriminant validity.[55] The Minnesota Satisfaction Questionnaire has 20 factors which have shown only moderately high intercorrelations.[56]

[48] Evans recently identified five definitions of satisfaction generated by alternative measuring procedures. Martin G. Evans. Conceptual and operational problems in the measurement of various aspects of job satisfaction, *Journal of Applied Psychology,* 52 (April 1969), 93–101.

[49] See, for example, David Krech and Richard S. Crutchfield. *Theory and problems of social psychology* (New York: McGraw-Hill, 1948), pp. 40–43.

[50] Helen Peak, Attitude and motivation, in Marshall R. Jones (ed.). *Nebraska symposium on motivation* (Lincoln, Nebraska: University of Nebraska Press, 1955), pp. 149–59. Note the similarity between attitude as defined by Peak and valence as defined by Vroom. In Vroom's model, motivation (force) is a function of valence (attitude) times the expectation that a particular behavior will lead to the desired outcome (*Work and motivation,* pp. 15–19). Porter and Lawler use attitudes to refer to valence as well as other antecedents of job performance (*Managerial attitudes and performance* and Antecedent attitudes of effective managerial performance). For quite a different formulation of attitude, see Daryl J. Bem. Self-perception: The dependent variable of human performance, *Organizational Behavior and Human Performance,* 2 (May 1967), 105–21. He argued attitudes result from behavior. For evidence on a similar theme, see Aaron Lowin and James R. Craig. The influence of level of performance on managerial style: An experimental object-lesson in the ambiguity of correlation data, *Organizational Behavior and Human Performance,* 3 (November 1968), 440–58.

[51] And hence be a necessary, but not sufficient, condition for motivation given Vroom's model.

[52] Unfortunately, March and Simon do not define satisfaction in their discussion. In fact, they do not explicitly distinguish between satisfaction, morale, or cohesiveness (*Organizations,* pp. 47–48).

[53] While Herzberg *et al.* employ the term job attitude when referring to satisfaction, they do not define it (Herzberg, *et al., The motivation to work,* pp. 5–12). More importantly, they do not discuss the mechanism whereby performance is perceived as the path to the attainment of the satisfying referent. In this context, see Vroom's discussion of expectancy (*Work and motivation,* pp. 17–18).

[54] For a review, see Vroom, *Work and motivation,* pp. 101–5.

[55] Lorne M. Kendall, Patricia C. Smith, Charles L. Hulin, and Edwin A. Locke. Cornell studies of job satisfaction: IV The relative validity of the job description index and other methods of measurement of job satisfaction, unpublished paper, 1963. A recent thorough description of the development of the JDI can be found in Patricia C. Smith, Lorne M. Kendall, and Charles L. Hulin. *The measurement of satisfaction in work and retirement* (Chicago, Ill.: Rand McNally, 1969).

[56] David J. Weiss, Rene V. Dawis, George W. England, and Lloyd H. Lofquist, *Manual for the Minnesota Satisfaction Questionnaire* (Minneapolis: University of Minnesota, Industrial Relations Center, 1967), Bulletin 45, pp. 93–100. McCornack has shown how erroneous it may be to assume that because two variables correlate fairly highly with each other (e.g., two satisfaction measures) both will correlate about the same with some third variable (e.g., performance). Robert L. McCornack, A criticism of studies comparing item-weighting methods, *Journal of Applied Psychology,* 40 (October 1956), 343–44.

Hinrichs factored a 60-item satisfaction questionnaire and obtained nine fairly independent factors.[57]

Despite (or, perhaps because of) this type of research, little is known about the number of satisfaction objects, their interrelationship or their relationship to more global feelings of satisfaction.[58] With such basic questions about job satisfaction unanswered, it is imperative that theoreticians be specific about the satisfaction objects they have in mind. Performance implications may well differ depending upon the type of satisfaction under study.

One illustration is sufficient to show the ambiguity which results if the theorist fails to adequately confront this issue. As noted previously, Triandis hypothesized that pressure leads to dissatisfaction. In light of the previous discussion one might well ask, what type of dissatisfaction?[59] Suppose the pressure is induced by the supervisor.[60] An increase in dissatisfaction with supervision might be expected. There seems little reason to believe, however, that satisfaction with referents such as pay, promotion opportunities, working conditions, or co-workers will decrease.[61] One might even hypothesize that increases in supervisory pressure, in some circumstances, would increase informal group cohesiveness,[62] which in turn may increase satisfaction with co-workers. The impact of supervisory pressure on overall satisfaction, to say nothing of performance, is very much in doubt.

Comparison of one of the theories reviewed with recent empirical work suggests another issue that may bear on hypothesized satisfaction-behavior relations. Specifically, the definition and model in the theory of work adjustment clearly imply that satisfaction is perceived as an intra-job phenomenon, i.e., judgments of satisfaction or dissatisfaction are made without reference to the reinforcer system of other jobs in the same organization or jobs in other organizations.[63] Smith, on the other hand, suggests that job satisfaction may more appropriately be thought of in relative terms. She hypothesized that ". . . above a certain minimum, for example, a given annual income is a positive source of satisfaction, a source of dissatisfaction, or irrelevant to an individual, depending upon what other jobs might pay, upon what other people of comparable training, skills, and experience are obtaining (in the same labor market), upon what the same individual has earned in the past, and upon the financial obligations he has assumed and expenditures to which he has become accustomed."[64]

Without getting into the merits of the two approaches in an abstract sense, we simply wish to point out that expected relationships between satisfaction and other variables may differ depending upon the definition chosen. We would hypothesize, for example, that scores on an operational measure of Smith's definition would be more highly related to voluntary turnover than scores obtained from a measure conforming to the theory of work adjustment.[65] The former reflects labor market conditions, a variable which has been shown to influence voluntary turnover;[66] the latter does not.

The issues raised here do not exhaust those which might be considered when discussing conceptual problems associated with satisfaction. They do, however, serve to show that comparisons between different theories are difficult, if not impossible, without explicit definitions on the part of the theorist. They also suggest that one might expect quite dissimilar

---

See also Patricia C. Smith and Lorne M. Kendall. Cornell studies of job satisfaction: VI Implications for the future, unpublished paper, 1963.

[57] John R. Hinrichs. A replicated study of job satisfaction dimensions, *Personnel Psychology,* 21 (Winter 1968), 479–503.

[58] Weiss, *et al.,* found that the factor structure of measured satisfaction varied across occupational groups (*Manual for the Minnesota Satisfaction Questionnaire,* pp. 22–23). While the factor structure was relatively constant across five subsamples in Hinrichs' study, differences existed in terms of the degree to which various factors correlated with an overall measure of satisfaction (A replicated study of job satisfaction dimensions).

[59] In fairness to Triandis, it should be noted that the same criticism could be made of most of the other models. Only Herzberg *et al.* have specifically dealt with types of satisfaction.

[60] As noted above, Triandis did not specify the type of pressure induced either.

[61] All of these hypotheses are, of course, empirically researchable. We simply do not know whether increasing levels of supervisory pressure increase or decrease various types of dissatisfaction for all individuals and for all levels of pressure.

[62] If true, this would clearly complicate any pressure-satisfaction-performance linkage. Seashore, for example, concluded that identification with management goals moderated the relation between cohesiveness and performance. Stanley Seashore. *Group cohesiveness in the industrial work group* (Ann Arbor: University of Michigan, Survey Research Center, 1954).

[63] Dawis, *et al., A theory of work adjustment,* pp. 8, 13.

[64] Patricia C. Smith. Cornell studies of job satisfaction: I Strategy for the development of a general theory of job satisfaction, unpublished paper, 1963.

[65] It may be difficult to obtain an operational measure conforming to Dawis', *et al.,* definition. Results from a study conducted by Hulin suggest that individuals may respond from a relative frame of reference even when asked about satisfaction with a specific job. He found, for example, that satisfaction with pay was inversely related to such community factors as median income, percentage of residents earning over $10,000, percentage of acceptable housing units, and per capita retail sales. Since type of organization, job level, and sex of respondents was held relatively constant across communities, Hulin concluded variance in satisfaction was due to job opportunity differences in the communities sampled. Chalres L. Hulin. Effects of community characteristics on measure of job satisfaction, *Journal of Applied Psychology,* 59 (April 1966), 185–92.

[66] See, for example, Hilde Behrend. "Absence and labour turnover in a changing economic environment, *Occupational Psychology,* 27 (April 1953), 69–79; Gladys L. Palmer. *Labor mobility in six cities* (New York: Social Science Research Council, 1954), and Reynolds, *The structure of labor markets.*

relationships between satisfaction and other variables depending on one's definition of satisfaction.

Performance. In defining performance a fundamental issue pertains to the value of thinking in terms of some "ultimate" criterion as though it was a unidimensional construct.[67] This global approach is partially the result of efforts to arrive at operational measures of performance through overall ratings or rankings of the workers' effectiveness.[68] Recent theory and research severely questions the adequacy of this point of view.[69] Research has shown, for example, that alternative criterion measures are neither particularly stable over time[70] nor highly intercorrelated.[71] This suggests, of course, that relations between other variables and performance will vary depending upon the performance measure employed.

Despite this evidence, theorists interested in satisfaction-performance relations have generally treated performance as a homogeneous variable.[72] This position is particularly troublesome when one thinks of measuring performance across different kinds of tasks, organizations, and occupations.[73] For example, on some jobs performance would appear to be heavily influenced by rule compliance and programmatic behavior, while on others problem solving and creative behavior are probably much more important. One might well expect differences in relationships between some satisfaction measure and these two types of performance.

Potential Moderator Variables. Definitions aside, a commendable trend in recent theorizing and research is the inclusion of variables hypothesized to moderate the relationship between satisfaction and performance. In an experimental study, Korman found that subjects' self-esteem (a variable not explicitly accounted for in previous theorizing) moderated the relationship between task success (performance) and task liking (satisfaction).[74] Carlson recently reported that the measured correspondence between the individual's ability and the ability requirements of the job moderated the relationship between satisfaction and performance.[75] This evidence offers some support for the theory of work adjustment. Katzell *et al.* concluded that the positive satisfaction-performance relationship observed in their study probably resulted from variation in "urbanization" among the workers studied.[76] Finally, Harding and Bottenberg found that satisfaction did not contribute significantly to explained variance in performance above that accounted for by biographical data.[77]

A much larger body of evidence suggests that satisfaction and performance, when treated separately as dependent variables, are complexly related to a number of other variables. To the extent that these variables differentially affect satisfaction and performance, they become potential moderators of satisfaction-performance relationships. For example,

[67] For example, Bechtoldt defined the criterion as ". . . the performance of individuals on a success criterion." Harold P. Bechtoldt. Problems of establishing criterion measures, in Dewey B. Stuit (ed.). *Personnel research and test development in the Bureau of Naval Personnel* (Princeton: Princeton University, 1947), p. 357. At a somewhat more sophisticated level, Brogden and Taylor sought to quantify various performance dimensions on a single monetary continuum. H. E. Brogden and E. K. Taylor. The dollar criterion-applying the cost accounting concept to criterion construction, *Personnel Psychology,* 3 (Summer 1950), 133–54.

[68] Robert M. Guion. Personnel selection, *Annual Review of Psychology,* 18 (1967), 191–216.

[69] For a brief but excellent discussion, see Marvin D. Dunnette. A note on *The* Criterion, *Journal of Applied Psychology,* 47 (August 1963), 251–54.

[70] Edwin E. Ghiselli and Mason Haire. The validation of selection tests in the light of the dynamic character of criteria, *Personnel Psychology,* 13 (Autumn 1960), 225–31, and Edwin E. Ghiselli. Dimensional problems of criteria, *Journal of Applied Psychology,* 40 (February 1956), 1–4.

[71] See, for example, Charles L. Hulin. Relevance and equivalence in criterion measures of executive success, *Journal of Industrial Psychology,* 1 (September 1963), 67–78.

[72] Moreover, definitions differ among theories. Porter and Lawler identify but do not distinguish (in terms of relations with satisfaction) between three types of performance measures: objective, subjective-supervisor, and subjective-self (Porter and Lawler, *Managerial attitudes and performance,* pp. 26–28). Performance is measured by self-evaluations in the two-factor theory (Herzberg, *et al., The motivation to work,* pp. 51–52). In the theory of work adjustment, performance (satisfactoriness) is measured by the organization (Dawis, *et al., The theory of work adjustment,* p. 9). While Triandis does not explicitly define the term, he appears to be emphasizing quantity of performance (Triandis, A critique and experimental design . . . , see especially footnote 1, p. 309). March and Simon employ the term *motivation to produce* which appears to be more closely related to Porter and Lawler's effort than to any of the performance measures used (March and Simon, *Organization,* pp. 52–53). With such variability in definitions, it is not surprising that hypothesized relationships between satisfaction and performance vary.

[73] In this regard, see Alexander W. Astin. Criterion-centered research, *Educational and Psychological Measurement,* 24 (Winter 1964), 807–22. He argued for the need to think of criteria in terms of relationships between the individual worker and his environment.

[74] Abraham K. Korman. Task success, task popularity, and self-esteem as influences on task liking, *Journal of Applied Psychology,* 52 (December 1968), 484–90.

[75] Robert E. Carlson. Degree of job fit as a moderator of the relationship between job performance and job satisfaction, *Personnel Psychology,* 22 (Summer 1969), 159–70.

[76] Raymond A. Katzell, Richard S. Barrett, and Treadway C. Parker. Job satisfaction, job performance, and situational characteristics, *Journal of Applied Psychology,* 45 (April 1961), 65–72. Reanalysis of the data suggested that two factors, "urbanization" and "female employee syndrome" moderated the satisfaction-performance relation. Edward E. Cureton and Raymond A. Katzell. A further analysis of the relations among job performance and situational variables, *Journal of Applied Psychology,* 46 (June 1962), 230.

[77] Francis D. Harding and Robert A. Bottenberg, Effect of personal characteristics on relationships between attitudes and job performance, *Journal of Applied Psychology,* 45 (December 1961), 428–30.

measures of need satisfaction on the job have been found to be functionally related to occupational,[78] organizational,[79] individual,[80] and community[81] variables. Moreover, evidence suggests that at least in the case of organizational characteristics these variables tend to be related to satisfaction in a non-additive fashion.[82]

Knowledge of the determinants of performance has come primarily from researchers interested in employee selection and employee motivation. Both groups have concentrated on the impact of individual variables on performance.[83] Selection researchers have been concerned primarily with the impact on performance of such variables as abilities and aptitudes,[84] personality characteristics,[85] and interest.[86] Students of industrial motivation have also begun to look seriously at the determinants of performance. Recently research having performance as the dependent variable has been conducted within the framework of equity,[87] expectancy,[88] and goal-setting[89] theories.

While the selection and motivational approaches to predicting performance have had some success, a relatively small amount of performance variance is typically explained in any one study.[90] Part of the problem is perhaps attributable to measurement problems associated with both independent variables and performance. Part, however, is unquestionably due to the fact that insufficient attention has been paid to the variety of variables which may influence performance or to their probable interrelationships.[91]

---

[78] For a review of studies, see Harold L. Wilensky. Varieties of work experience, in Henry Borow (ed.). *Man in a world of work* (Boston: Houghton Mifflin, 1964), pp. 125–54. For a recent comprehensive study, see Gerald Gurin, Joseph Veroff, and Shelia Feld. *Americans view their mental health* (New York: Basic Books, 1960). See also George W. England and Carroll I. Stein. The occupational reference group—A neglected concept in employee attitude studies, *Personnel Psychology,* 14 (Autumn 1961), 299–304.

[79] Porter and Lawler have conducted a series of studies investigating the relationship between satisfaction and organizational variables such as job level, line/staff, company size and structure, and pay. These and other studies are reviewed in L. L. Cummings and A. M. El Salmi. Empirical research on the bases and correlates of managerial motivation: A review of the literature, *Psychological Bulletin,* 70 (August 1968), 127–44.

[80] For a review of studies, see Glenn P. Fournet, M. K. Distefano, Jr., and Margaret W. Pryer. Job satisfaction: Issues and problems, *Personnel Psychology,* 19 (Summer 1966), 165–83. See also studies by Charles L. Hulin and Patricia C. Smith. Sex differences in job satisfaction, *Journal of Applied Psychology,* 48 (April 1964), 88–92; Charles L. Hulin and Patricia C. Smith. A linear model of job satisfaction, *Journal of Applied Psychology,* 49 (June 1965), 209–16; and William H. Form and James A. Geschwender. Social reference basis of job satisfaction: The case of manual workers, *American Sociological Review,* 27 (April 1962), 228–37. In the latter study the subjects' job satisfaction was found to be associated with fathers' and brothers' job level.

[81] Hulin, Effects of community characteristics on job satisfaction. For a study which bears on this issue indirectly, see Arthur N. Turner and Paul R. Lawrence. *Industrial jobs and the worker: An investigation of response to task attributes* (Boston: Harvard Graduate School of Business Administration, 1965). See also Hulin and Blood. Job enlargement, individual differences, and worker responses.

[82] In one study, for example, it was found that several organizational variables were interactively related to satisfaction (A. M. El Salmi and L. L. Cummings. Managers' perceptions of needs and need satisfactions as a function of interactions among organizational variables, *Personnel Psychology,* 21 [Winter, 1968], 465–77). In another study individual values were found to moderate the relationship between organizational climate variables and satisfaction (Frank Friedlander and Newton Margulies. Multiple impacts of organizational climate and individual value systems upon job satisfaction, *Personnel Psychology,* 22 [Summer 1969], 171–83).

[83] Organizational variables have received less attention. Three exceptions are task complexity (see, again, Hulin and Blood. Job enlargement, individual differences, and worker responses), supervision (for reviews see Stephen M. Sales. Supervisory style and productivity: Review and theory, *Personnel Psychology,* 70 [Autumn 1966], 275–286; Abraham K. Korman. "Consideration," "initiating structure," and organizational criteria—A review, *Personnel Phychology,* 70 [Winter, 1966], 349–61), and wages (for a review see Robert L. Opsahl and Marvin D. Dunnette. The role of financial compensation in industrial motivation, *Psychological Bulletin,* 66 [August 1966], 94–118).

[84] Edwin E. Ghiselli. *The validity of occupational aptitude tests* (New York: Wiley, 1966).

[85] Robert M. Guion and Richard F. Gottier. Validity of personality measures in personnel selection, *Personnel Psychology,* 18 (Summer 1965), 135–64.

[86] Allan N. Nash. Vocational interests of effective managers: A review of the literature, *Personnel Psychology,* 18 (Spring, 1965), 21–37. For an excellent overview of the problems and accomplishments in predicting performance from a selection point of view, see Robert M. Guion. *Personnel testing* (New York: McGraw-Hill, 1965).

[87] For an early formulation of equity theory, see Adams. Toward an understanding of inequity. A large amount of research, sometimes nonsupportive, has been conducted on this theory. For a recent review, see Lawler. Equity theory as a predictor of productivity and work quality.

[88] See Basil S. Georgopoulos, Gerald M. Mahoney, and Nyle W. Jones. A path-goal approach to productivity, *Journal of Applied Psychology,* 41 (December, 1957), 345–53; Jay Galbraith and L. L. Cummings. An empirical investigation of the motivational determinants of task performance: Interactive effects between instrumentality-valence and motivation-ability, *Organizational Behavior and Human Performance,* (August 1967), 237–57; Edward E. Lawler, III, and Lyman W. Porter. Antecedent attitudes of effective managerial performance, *Organizational Behavior and Human Performance,* 2 (May 1967), 122–42; George Graen. Instrumentality theory of work motivation: Some experimental results and suggested modifications, *Journal of Applied Psychology monograph,* 53 (April 1969), 1–25; and J. Richard Hackman and Lyman W. Porter. Expectancy theory predictions of work effectiveness, *Organizational Behavior and Human Performance,* 3 (November 1968), 417–26.

[89] Locke and his colleagues have conducted a number of experimental studies on the impact of goal-setting on performance. These are reviewed in Edwin A. Locke. Toward a theory of task motivation and incentives, *Organizational Behavior and Human Performance,* 3 (May 1968), 157–89.

[90] In the selection context, see Edward A. Rundquist, The prediction ceiling, *Personnel Psychology,* 22 (Summer 1969), 109–16.

[91] As a case in point, equity and goal-setting theory have developed more or less independently of each other. Only one study (P. Goodman and A. Friedman. An examination of the effect of wage inequity in the hourly condition, *Organizational Behavior and Human Performance,* 3 [August 1968], 340–52)

While the discussion above does not exhaust the literature, one point is clear. Satisfaction and performance, studied alone or together, are associated with a large number of covariates. This suggests that even recent theoretical work has not accounted for a sufficient number of the variables which may influence the strength and perhaps even the direction of the relationship between satisfaction and performance. At the very least it suggests that if available theory were to be applied, these applications should be within the context of well-defined and specified individuals, organizations, occupations, and communities. However, the most pressing need would seem to be for additional research on the dimensionality of satisfaction and performance and on the specific conditions under which they are related.

CONCLUSIONS

We close with a few recommendations for investigators interested in job satisfaction and performance. Although pleas for the use of standardized research instruments generally fall on deaf ears, we are unlikely to sample the necessary variety of work environments in a meaningfully comparable fashion unless there is greater utilization of common measures. We additionally urge researchers to obtain as much information about potential moderating variables as their data sources and methodological skills permit. Experimental studies obviously permit control and observation of potential moderators and should be employed more frequently than in the past. But additional survey research is also needed. Adequate controls can be obtained through subject selection and by the greater utilization of multivariate analytical techniques.

We are frankly pessimistic about the value of additional satisfaction-performance theorizing at this time. The theoretically inclined might do better to work on a theory of satisfaction *or* a theory of performance. Such concepts are clearly complex enough to justify their own theories. Prematurely focusing on relationships between the two has probably helped obscure the fact that we know so little about the structure and determinants of each.

APPENDIX

Several articles have appeared recently which pertain directly to several of the issues raised in this paper. We were unable to discuss them in the appropriate sections of this article because of the lead-time required for publication. However, the interested reader may wish to see, W. W. Ronan, "Individual and Situational Variables Relating to Job Satisfaction," *Journal of Applied Psychology Monograph.* LIV (February 1970), 1–31; Edwin A. Locke, "What Is Job Satisfaction," *Organizational Behavior and Human Performance,* IV (November 1969), 309–336; Martin G. Wolf, "Need Gratification Theory: A Theoretical Reformulation of Job Satisfaction/Dissatisfaction and Job Motivation," *Journal of Applied Psychology,* LIV (February 1970), 87–94; Richard E. Doll and E. K. Eric Gunderson, "Occupational Group as a Moderator of the Job Satisfaction-Job Performance Relationship," *Journal of Applied Psychology,* LIII (October 1969), 359–361.

A partial test of the performance predictions of the Porter-Lawler model is presented in James F. Gavin, "Ability, Effort and Role Perceptions as Antecedents of Job Performance," *Experimental Publication System,* American Psychological Association, April 1970, Issue No. 5, Manuscript No. 190A. Recently data has appeared suggesting the JS-JP relation may be a function of organizational level and skill level within any given organizational level. See John W. Slocum, Richard B. Chase, and David Kuhn, "A Comparative Analysis of Job Satisfaction and Job Performance for High and Low Skilled Operatives," *Experimental Publication System,* American Psychological Association, April 1970, Issue No. 5, Manuscript No. 163A.

17. CLARIFICATION AND EVALUATION OF THE TWO-FACTOR THEORY OF JOB SATISFACTION*

***Nathan King*†**

According to the two-factor theory of job satisfaction, the primary determinants of job satisfaction are intrinsic aspects of the job, called motivators (e.g., achievement, recognition, the work itself, responsibility, and advancement), whereas the primary determinants of job dissatisfaction are extrinsic factors, called hygienes (e.g., company policy and administration, supervision, salary, interpersonal relations with co-workers and working conditions).

The two-factor theory originated from a study by Herzberg, Mausner, and Synderman (1959). These

has combined elements of the two theories. Interestingly, the goal-setting implications of their study are ignored by the authors.

* *Psychological Bulletin,* Vol. 74, No. 1 (1970), pp. 18–31.
The author is especially grateful to Charles L. Hulin and Milton R. Blood for reading earlier versions of this paper and providing helpful comments.

† Department of Psychology, University of Berkeley, California.

TABLE 1 PERCENTAGE OF GOOD AND BAD CRITICAL INCIDENTS IN WHICH EACH JOB FACTOR APPEARED (Herzberg et al., 1959)

Factor	Percentage* Good	Bad
Achievement (M)	41†	7
Recognition (M)	33†	18
Work itself (M)	26†	14
Responsibility (M)	23†	6
Advancement (M)	20†	11
Salary (H)	15	17
Possibility of growth (M)	6	8
Interpersonal relations—subordinate (H)	6	3
Status (H)	4	4
Interpersonal relations—superior (H)	4	15†
Interpersonal relations—peers (H)	3	8†
Supervision—technical (H)	3	20†
Company policy & administration (H)	3	31†
Working conditions (H)	1	11†
Personal life (H)	1	6†
Job security (H)	1	1
Percentage of total contributed by Ms	78	36
Percentage of total contributed by Hs	22	64

Note.—Abbreviations are: M = motivator; H = hygiene.

* The percentages total more than 100% since more than one job factor can be mentioned in a single critical incident.

† The difference between the percentage of good and bad critical incidents is significant at the .01 level.

investigators interviewed 203 accountants and engineers and asked them to describe specific instances when they felt exceptionally good or exceptionally bad about their jobs. Upon analyzing the content of these critical incidents, it was found that the good critical incidents were dominated by reference to intrinsic aspects of the job (motivators), while the bad critical incidents were dominated by reference to extrinsic factors (hygienes). As indicated in Table 1, this tendency was quite marked; in the reports of good critical incidents, motivators were alluded to almost four times as frequently as hygienes (78% vs. 22%), whereas in bad critical incidents, hygienes were mentioned about twice as frequently as motivators (64% vs. 36%).

Subsequent to the original study (Herzberg et al., 1959), a considerable number of empirical studies designed to test the validity of the two-factor theory were published, and a heated controversy has developed between supporters and critics of the theory.

It is the opinion of this writer that a major portion of the controversy stems from the lack of an explicit statement of the theory. At least five distinct versions of the two-factor theory have been stated or implied by various researchers. It is the purpose of this paper to explicate and to evaluate these various forms of the theory.

FIVE VERSIONS OF THE TWO-FACTOR THEORY

Table 2 lists five versions of the two-factor theory and an example of two types of data which might be used to support each of the different versions. The critical incident data (second column of Table 2) refer to data of the same type as is illustrated in Table 1; whereas correlational data (third column of Table 2) might be obtained, for example, by simultaneously measuring satisfaction with each of a group of job factors, overall job satisfaction, and overall job dissatisfaction. As almost all of the relevant empirical investigations have made use of the critical incident technique, the different versions of the two-factor theory are discussed in terms of critical incident data.

Theory I

Theory I states that all motivators combined contribute more to job satisfaction than to job dissatisfaction and that all hygienes combined contribute more to job dissatisfaction than to job satisfaction. Critical incident data support Theory I if *(a)* all motivators combined are mentioned proportionately more often in good critical incidents than in bad critical incidents, and *(b)* all hygienes combined are mentioned proportionately more often in bad than in good incidents. Clearly the data of Table I meet these two requirements; motivators composed 78% of the job factors mentioned in good critical incidents compared to only 36% mentioned in bad incidents, whereas the hygienes favored the bad incidents (64% compared to 22%).

Actually, Theory I requires that critical incident data meet only one condition, as conditions *a* and *b* (see the preceding paragraph) are redundant. That is, *a* implies *b*, and *b* implies *a*. This redundancy follows from the necessity that the proportion of motivators plus the proportion of hygienes mentioned in either type of critical incident must equal one.

Let M_g denote the proportion of factors mentioned in good critical incidents which are motivators, and let H_g be the proportion which are hygienes. Similarly, define M_b and H_b, where the subscript *b* denotes bad critical incidents. In this notation, *a* states that $M_g > H_b$, and *b* states that $H_b > H_g$.

$$\text{Since } M_g + H_g = 1, \text{ and } M_b + H_b = 1,$$

$$M_g > M_b \Rightarrow 1 - H_g > 1 - H_b \Rightarrow H_b > H_g.$$

That is, *a* implies *b*. The proof that *b* implies *a* is analogous.

Theory I appears to be the version of the two-factor theory adopted by Whitsett and Winslow

TABLE 2 FIVE VERSIONS OF THE TWO-FACTOR THEORY OF JOB SATISFACTION

Theory	Supporting Data: Critical Incident Data	Supporting Data: Correlation Data
I. All motivators (Ms) combined contribute more to job satisfaction (S) than to job dissatisfaction (D), and all hygienes (Hs) combined contribute more to D than to S.	All Ms combined are mentioned proportionately more often in good critical incidents (Gs) than in bad critical incidents (Bs), and all Hs combined are mentioned proportionately more often in Bs than in Gs.	The multiple correlation (R) between the Ms and S is greater than the R between the Ms and D, and the R between the Hs and D is greater than the R between the Hs and S.
II. All Ms combined contribute more to S than do all Hs combined, and all Hs combined contribute more to D than do all Ms combined.	All Ms combined are mentioned in Gs more frequently than are all Hs combined, and all Hs combined are mentioned in Bs more frequently than are all Ms combined.	The R between the Ms and S is greater than the R between the Hs and S, and the R between the Hs and D is greater than the R between the Ms and D.
III. Each M contributes more to S than to D, and each H contributes more to D than to S.	Each M is mentioned proportionately more often in Gs than in Bs, and each H is mentioned proportionately more often in Bs than in Gs.	Each M correlates more with S than with D, and each H correlates more with D than with S.
IV. Theory III holds, and in addition, each principal M contributes more to S than does any H, and each principal H contributes more to D than does any M.	The data support Theory III, and in addition, each principal M is mentioned in Gs more frequently than is any H, and each principal H is mentioned in Bs more frequently than is any M.	The data support Theory III, and in addition, each principal M correlates with S more than does any H, and each principal H correlates with D more than does any M.
V. Only Ms determine S, and only Hs determine D.	Only Ms are mentioned in Gs, and only Hs are mentioned in Bs.	Only Ms correlate with S, and only Hs correlate with D.

(1967) in their review of a study by Dunnette, Campbell, and Hakel (1967). In the Dunnette et al. study, subjects used a Q-sort technique in order to assign to each of 12 job factors, a score which represented the extent to which the factor determined a good and a bad critical incident. The mean scores of the motivator and hygiene factors in the good and bad critical incidents of workers in six different occupational groups are given in Table 3. As indicated in this table, the mean motivator score was greater in good than in bad critical incidents in all six occupational groups. Also, in each occupational group, the mean hygiene score was greater in bad than in good incidents. Although this critical incident data is not of the same type as that illustrated in Table 1, the results clearly support Theory I. In their review of the Dunnette et al. (1967) experiment, Whitsett and Winslow concluded:

> We feel that the direct data of this study are supportive of the M-H theory and what the author feels is nonsupportive is a misinterpretation of the underlying structure of the M-H theory [p. 404].

The M-H theory to which Whitsett and Winslow here referred appears to be Theory I, whereas Dunnette et al. must have been considering a "stronger" version of the two-factor theory.

Theory II

Theory II states that all motivators combined contribute more to job satisfaction than do all hygienes combined, and conversely, that the hygienes contribute more to job dissatisfaction than do the motivators. Critical incident data support Theory II if *(a)* all motivators combined are mentioned in good critical incidents more frequently than are all hygienes combined, and *(b)* all hygienes combined appear more frequently in bad incidents than do all motivators combined. The data of Table 1 exemplify these conditions; in good critical incidents, motivators were

TABLE 3 MEAN SCORES OF MOTIVATORS AND HYGIENES IN GOOD AND BAD CRITICAL INCIDENTS (Dunnette et al., 1967)

	Motivators		Hygienes	
Occupational Group	*Good*	*Bad*	*Good*	*Bad*
Store managers	4.59	4.22	3.43	3.84
Sales clerks	4.37	4.17	3.63	3.68
Secretaries	4.61	4.23	3.45	3.75
Engineers & scientists	4.71	4.22	3.34	3.74
Machine equipment salesmen	4.76	4.17	3.16	3.79
Army reservists & students	4.54	4.20	3.51	3.77

mentioned more frequently than hygienes (78% vs. 22%), whereas in bad incidents, hygienes appeared more frequently (64% vs. 36%).

Unlike the critical incident data used to support Theory I, conditions *a* and *b* are here *not* redundant. For example, it is possible for all motivators combined to be mentioned more frequently than all hygienes combined in both good *and* bad incidents.

Herzberg (1966) implied, in a review of a replication of the original study, that the "basic" two-factor theory is Theory II. In commenting on two arrows in a chart, which illustrated the relative frequencies of motivators and hygienes in the reports of good and bad critical incidents and which indicated that the data supported Theory II, Herzberg stated:

> Once again, the two arrows shown at the bottom of the chart, indicating the divergent trends for motivators and hygiene factors, serve to verify the basic theory as these factors are involved in positive and negative job-attitude sequences [p. 101].

Apparently the "basic theory" is here Theory II; however, it is puzzling to this writer why Herzberg (1966), in a review of nine replications of the original study, failed to mention the fact that Theory II was supported in every one of the 15 different occupational groups studied.

In terms of critical incident data, Theory II is a stronger theory than Theory I. That is, if specific critical incident data meet the requirements of Theory II, then the data also support Theory I; however, critical incident data which support Theory I do not necessarily meet the conditions of Theory II. The proof of the first statement follows from the necessity that the proportion of motivators plus the proportion of hygienes mentioned in either type of critical incident must equal one.

Using the notation of the proof given in the section on Theory I, the requirements of Theory II are denoted as $M_g > H_g$ and $H_b > M_b$, and Theory I is supported if $M_g > M_b$ and $H_b > H_g$.

Since $M_g + H_g = 1$, and $M_b + H_b = 1$,

$$M_g > H_g \text{ and } H_b > M_b$$
$$\Rightarrow M_g > .5, \quad H_g < .5, \quad H_b > .5, \quad \text{and} \quad M_b < .5$$
$$\Rightarrow M_g > M_b \text{ and } H_b > H_g.$$

The proof of the second statement is accomplished by producing a counterexample of its negation:

Let $M_g = .8$, $H_g = .2$, $M_b = .6$, and $H_b = .4$.

This example is admissible, for the conditions $M_g + H_g = 1$ and $M_b + H_b = 1$ are satisfied. Clearly Theory I is supported, as $M_g > M_b$ and $H_b > H_g$; however, Theory II is not supported because $M_b > H_b$.

Theory III

Theory III is essentially a strong version of Theory I. Instead of requiring that all motivators *combined* contribute more to job satisfaction than to job dissatisfaction, Theory III states that each motivator contributes more to satisfaction than to dissatisfaction (and conversely, that each hygiene contributes more to dissatisfaction than to satisfaction).

In the case of Theories I and II, where only one or two conditions are specified, it seems reasonable to conclude that a single critical incident study either supports or contradicts the particular theory depending upon whether or not the data meet the specifications indicated in Table 2. However, in the case of Theory III, where many more conditions are specified, sampling errors must be given more serious consideration. That is, one would not claim that a single critical incident study contradicted Theory III if it did not quite meet all the conditions specified in Table 2. For example, one would not claim that the data of Table 1 exemplify a contradiction of Theory III merely because the most infrequently mentioned motivator (possibility of growth) appeared in 8% of the bad incidents and in only 6% of the good incidents. It may thus be necessary to restrict a statement of the confirmation of Theory III to collections of similar studies rather than to individual studies. It should be noted, however, that a single study might be said to contradict Theory III if, for example, a frequently mentioned motivator appeared significantly more often in bad than in good critical incidents.

On at least one occasion Herzberg implied that the basic two-factor theory is Theory II; however, in summarizing the results of nine replications of the original study, Herzberg (1966) suggested that *the* theory is Theory III:

> The chart shows that of the 51 significant differences reported for the six motivator factors, *every one* was in the predicted direction. For the 57 significant hygiene factors, 54 were in the predicted direction. In sum, then, the predictions from the theory were wrong in less than 3 per cent of the cases [p. 125].

Evidently "the theory" is a theory which predicts that each motivator will appear proportionately more often in good than in bad critical incidents and that each hygiene will appear proportionately more often in bad than in good incidents—namely, Theory III.

Theory IV

Critical incident data support Theory IV if, in addition to supporting Theory III, each principal motivator is mentioned in good critical incidents more frequently than is any hygiene, and each principal hygiene is mentioned in bad critical incidents more frequently than is any motivator. The data illustrated in Table 1, for example, do not meet these conditions; recognition was mentioned in considerably more bad incidents than were working conditions and interpersonal relations with peers.

House and Wigdor (1967) apparently acknowledged that replications of the original experiment supported Theory III; however, in a secondary analysis of this data they criticized the two-factor theory for failing to meet the requirements of Theory IV. These investigators ranked 10 job factors according to the total number of individuals mentioning the factor in the bad critical incidents of six studies reported by Herzberg (1966). As indicated in Table 4, achievement and recognition were mentioned by more individuals than were three hygienes. House and Wigdor concluded:

> Our secondary analysis of the data presented by Herzberg (1966) in his most recent book yields conclusions contradictory to the proposition of the Two-Factor theory that satisfiers [factors appearing in good incidents] and dissatisfiers [factors appearing in bad incidents] are unidimensional and independent. Although many of the intrinsic aspects of jobs are shown to be more frequently identified by respondents as satisfiers, achievement and recognition are also shown to be very frequently identified as dissatisfiers. In fact, achievement and recognition are more frequently identified as dissatisfiers than working conditions and relations with the superior [p. 385].

Apparently "the Two-Factor theory" is here a theory which requires that each principal hygiene contributes more to job dissatisfaction than does any motivator, and conversely, that each principal motivator contributes more to job satisfaction than does any hygiene—namely, Theory IV.

Theory V

According to Theory V, only motivators determine job satisfaction, and only hygienes determine job dissatisfaction.

Herzberg (1964) suggested Theory V in a discussion of the events leading up to the original investigation:

> From a review and an analysis of previous publications in the general area of job attitudes, a two-factor hypothesis was formulated to guide the original investigation. This hypothesis suggested that the factors involved in producing job satisfaction were separate and distinct from the factors that led to job dissatisfaction [p. 3].

This "two-factor hypothesis," which states that the factors involved in producing job satisfaction are *separate* and *distinct* from the factors leading to job dissatisfaction, clearly appears to be Theory V.

However, it is questionable whether Herzberg intended to suggest Theory V; for in referring to the results of the original experiment, Herzberg (1964) stated, "The proposed hypothesis appears verified [p. 4]." Certainly these results (see Table 1) do not serve as verification of Theory V. The results of the original study might possibly be interpreted as supporting Theory V if evidence indicated that the measurement errors were considerably biased in opposition to Theory V; however, evidence presented in the evaluation section indicates that the Herzberg-type experiments were biased in *favor* of Theory V.

Regardless of Herzberg's intensions, other investigators have evidently interpreted the "two-factor hypothesis" as Theory V. For example, Lindsay, Marks, and Gorlow (1967) quoted Herzberg's statement of the hypothesis and then restated it in the following manner:

> Satisfaction(s) is a function of motivators (M) and other potential factors and/or error of measurement . . .; dissatisfaction (DS) is a function of hygienes (H) plus other potential factors and/or error of measurement [p. 331].

TABLE 4 NUMBER OF INDIVIDUALS MENTIONING EACH OF TEN JOB FACTORS IN THE BAD CRITICAL INCIDENTS OF SIX STUDIES REPORTED BY HERZBERG (1966) (House & Wigdor, 1967)

Factor	*Frequency*
Company policy & administration (H) . . .	337
Supervision (H)	182
Achievement (M)	122
Recognition (M)	110
Working conditions (H)	108
Work itself (M)	75
Relations with superior (H)	59
Relations with peers (H)	57
Advancement (M)	48
Responsibility (M)	35

Note.—Abbreviations are: M = motivator; H = hygiene

EVALUATION

Irrelevant Empirical Studies

Many of the empirical studies which have been considered relevant to the two-factor theory are not directly relevant to the validity of the theories of Table 2.

Extensions beyond the Domain of Job Satisfaction. The two-factor theories have been extended beyond the domain of job satisfaction. For example, Hamlin and Nemo (1962) attempted to explain differences between improved and unimproved schizophrenics in terms of a two-factor theory. Such an extension is beyond the scope of this paper.

Studies by Hinton (1968) and Levine and Weitz (1968) are ostensibly within the domain of job satisfaction. However, the job investigated in these studies was the "job" of student, which appears to this writer to be sufficiently unlike other jobs as to warrant exclusion from consideration in this paper.

Predictions on a Job Satisfaction-Dissatisfaction Continuum. Several investigators (Ewen, Smith, Hulin, & Locke, 1966; Graen, 1968; Hinrichs & Mischkind, 1967) adopted a version of the two-factor theory which makes statements about an overall job satisfaction-dissatisfaction (S-D) continuum. More specifically, these investigators adopted a two-factor theory which states that motivators account primarily for variance on the satisfaction portion of the S-D continuum and that hygienes account primarily for variance on the dissatisfaction end of the continuum. For example, Ewen et al. (1966) grouped subjects according to their degree of satisfaction with three job factors, and then assumed that the two-factor theory predicts differences between certain groups in terms of scores on an S-D continuum. This particular version of the two-factor theory, although possibly worthy of consideration in its own right, is considerably unlike the theories of Table 2; the theories of Table 2 make statements about a job satisfaction continuum and a job dissatisfaction continuum—*not* about an S-D continuum. These studies might be relevant to some of the theories of Table 2 if additional assumptions concerning the relationships among satisfaction, dissatisfaction, and S-D were made. However, the evaluation of such assumptions is beyond the scope of this paper.

Likewise, an experiment by Lindsay et al. (1967) is here irrelevant. Lindsay et al. created descriptions of hypothetical job situations and had subjects indicate the degree of S-D inherent in each situation, thus attempting to discover how motivators and hygienes interact in determining S-D.

Studies Concerning Aspects of the Job Other Than Satisfaction or Dissatisfaction. Several empirical studies investigated the extent to which individual job factors contributed to aspects of the job other than satisfaction or dissatisfaction. Friedlander and Walton (1964) had respondents indicate which factors operated to *keep* them with their present employer and which factors might cause them to *leave*. Similarly, Centers and Bugental (1966) had respondents indicate which three of six job factors were most important in *keeping* them on their present job. Friedlander (1966) measured the perceived importance of job factors to feelings of satisfaction *or* dissatisfaction—that is, contributions to job satisfaction and to job dissatisfaction were not measured separately; and similarly, Singh and Baumgartel (1966) had subjects rate job factors on a scale of importance *in general*—importance for job satisfaction and for job dissatisfaction were not measured separately. Although these four studies may be relevant to particular extensions of the two-factor theory, they are not directly relevant to the theories of Table 2.

Studies in Which Only Satisfaction with Individual Job Factors Were Measured. The theories of Table 2 are concerned with the relative contributions of individual job factors to overall job satisfaction and to overall job dissatisfaction. Any study which measures only satisfaction with individual job factors is not relevant, for without measures of overall job satisfaction and dissatisfaction, the relative contributions of individual factors to the overall measures cannot be determined. Such studies simply indicate what the most-liked characteristics of a specific job happen to be. Thus, studies by Friedlander (1965) and Wolf (1967) are irrelevant. Friedlander measured only the degree of satisfaction with individual job factors, and Wolf simply had respondents indicate which aspects of a job were the most liked and which were the least liked.

Factor Analytic and Scaling Studies. Although it may be desirable for the job factors to be factors in some factor analytic sense, the theories of Table 2 place no such restrictions on the motivators and hygienes. Thus, studies which merely consist of a factor analysis of characteristics of a job or of a job situation (Graen, 1966; Lodahl, 1964) are here considered irrelevant.

Likewise, a study by Burke (1966) is irrelevant. Burke used the unfolding technique in one dimension (Coombs, 1964) in order to determine whether or not subjects, along with Herzberg's principal job factors, could be placed on a latent unidimensional continuum so as to account for individual differences in relative preferences for job factors.

Studies Lacking Adequate Descriptions of Measures Used. Four studies (Friedlander, 1963; Halpern, 1966; Malinovsky & Barry, 1965; Weissenberg & Gruenfeld, 1968) in which overall job satisfaction was purportedly measured did not clarify whether the measure used was a measure of job satisfaction or overall satisfaction-dissatisfaction (S-D). In either case, however, little information is lost by the omission of these studies. If it was S-D that was measured, the study is not directly relevant to the theories of Table 2; and if it was job satisfaction that was measured, the study is irrelevant to Theories I and III and, at most, relevant to only parts of Theories II, IV, and V, as overall job dissatisfaction was measured in none of the four studies.

Relevant Empirical Studies

As there appear to be no relevant empirical

studies which support either Theory IV or Theory V, this evaluation is restricted to Theories I, II, and III.

Table 5 indicates whether or not each relevant empirical study supports Theories I, II, and III.

Replications of the Original Study. Herzberg (1966) reviewed nine studies (e.g., Herzberg, 1965; Myers, 1964; Saleh, 1964; Schwartz, Jenusaitis, & Stark, 1963) which, in toto, consist of replications of the original study in 15 different occupational groups. In two of the studies (Herzberg, 1965; Schwartz et al., 1963) an open-ended questionnaire patterned after the original interview, rather than an interview, was used. Theories I and II were supported in every one of the 15 occupational groups studied. That is (using the notation of the proof given in the section on Theory I), in each group studied, $M_g > M_b$, $H_{by} > H_g$, $M_g > H_g$, and $H_b > M_b$. These data, considered in toto, also support Theory III; in all replications combined, 42 hygienes and 36 motivators appeared significantly more ($p < .01$, according to Herzberg, 1966) in one type of critical incident than in the other, and of these, all the motivators and all but 3 hygienes were significant in the predicted direction.

Studies in Which Subjects Coded the Perceived Determinants of Their Critical Incidents. In the original study and in its replications, the experimenters coded the information given in the reports of critical incidents. Several critics (Ewen, 1964; Graen, 1966; House & Wigdor, 1967) pointed out that the coding system is not completely determined by the data and a preestablished rating system, but requires additional interpretation by the experimenter. Before one can rule out the possibility of experimenter coding biases, it is necessary to consider studies in which the subjects themselves coded the perceived determinants of their reported critical incidents (subject-coded studies). Four relevant studies (Dunnette et al., 1967; Friedlander, 1964; Lahiri & Srivastva, 1967; Wernimont, 1966) fall into this category.

Friedlander (1964) had respondents indicate, on a 4-point scale, the degree to which each of 18 job factors contributed toward producing the feeling of satisfaction inherent in a good critical incident and the feeling of dissatisfaction inherent in a bad critical incident. The mean scores of each job factor in good and bad incidents are given in the first two columns of Table 6. In analyzing the data Friedlander used these mean scores; however, an alternative analysis seems more appropriate. Since the satisfaction scores were scaled independently of the dissatisfaction scores (i.e., the satisfaction scores were first determined in response to a good critical incident, and then the dissatisfaction scores were determined in response to a bad incident), the two scales are not necessarily comparable. Assuming that the mean dissatisfaction scores represents scale values on a scale which is no stronger than an interval scale, it is admissible to transform these scores by any linear transformation. For purposes of comparison with the satisfaction scores, it thus seems most appropriate to transform the dissatisfaction scores by the unique linear transformation which yields mean

TABLE 5 EMPIRICAL STUDIES RELEVANT TO THE VALIDITY OF THEORIES I, II, OR III

Study	Theoretical Support: Theory I	Theory II	Theory III
Replications of the original study			
Saleh (1964)	yes	yes	yes* (considered collectively: Saleh through Herzberg 1965)
Myers (1964); 5 different occupational groups (Gps)	yes in all 5	yes in all 5	
Herzberg's (1966) review of 5 other studies; 7 Gps.	yes in all 7	yes in all 7	
Replications using a questionnaire			
Schwartz et al. (1963)	yes	yes	
Herzberg (1965)	yes	yes	
Subjects coded the perceived determinants of their critical incidents			
Friedlander (1964)	no	irrelevant	no* (considered collectively: Friedlander through Wernimont forced choice)
Lahiri and Srivastva (1967)			
Present job	yes	irrelevant	
Imaginary job	yes	irrelevant	
Dunnette et al. (1967); 6 Gps	yes in all 6	irrelevant	
Wernimont (1966); 2 Gps			
Forced choice	yes in both	irrelevant	
Free choice	yes in both	irrelevant	no data†
Correlational studies			
Hulin and Smith (1967); 2 Gps	irrelevant	irrelevant	

* Considered collectively.
† Relevant data were evidently collected but not published.

TABLE 6 A REANALYSIS OF FRIEDLANDER'S (1964) DATA

Job Factor	Mean scores: Satisfaction	Dissatisfaction	Rescaled dissatisfaction
Motivators			
Promotion	2.10	1.99	2.54
Challenging assignments	3.10	2.67	3.42
Recognition	3.23	2.61	3.35
Merit increases	1.80	1.60	2.03
Achievement	3.38	2.80	3.59
Responsibility	2.84	2.01	2.57
Growth	3.38	2.19	2.80
Work itself	3.46	2.39	3.06
Use of best abilities	2.99	2.89	3.71
Hygienes			
Relations with supervisor	3.06	2.09	2.67
Relations with co-workers	2.73	1.46	1.85
Technical supervision	2.56	1.75	2.23
Working conditions	2.31	1.60	2.03
Security	2.56	1.64	2.08
Employee benefits	1.46	1.30	1.64
Home life	1.63	1.61	2.04
Work group	2.19	1.77	2.25
Management policies	2.01	2.28	2.92
Mean score of motivators	2.92	2.35	3.01
Mean score of hygienes	2.28	1.72	2.19

scores having the same mean and variance as the satisfaction mean scores. The last column of Table 6 contains the mean dissatisfaction scores which result from applying this linear transformation to the original dissatisfaction scores, and the data are here analyzed by comparing the original satisfaction scores to the *rescaled* dissatisfaction scores.

As indicated in Table 6, the data do not support Theory I; the mean motivator score was greater in bad than in good incidents (3.01 vs. 2.92), and the mean hygiene score was greater in good than in bad incidents (2.28 vs. 2.19).

The data of Table 6 are irrelevant to Theory II. That is, it is inappropriate, for example, to claim that all motivators combined contributed more to good incidents than did all hygienes combined on the basis that the mean motivator score was greater than the mean hygiene score in good critical incidents (2.92 vs. 2.28), for the amount of overlap among the job factors was not taken into consideration. If the set of motivators represented broad overlapping categories relative to the set of hygienes, the contribution of all motivators combined would be over-represented by the mean motivator score. Comparing the mean motivator score to the mean hygiene score in either type of critical incident is, in terms of correlational data, analogous to comparing the means of sets of correlation coefficients rather than multiple correlation coefficients. Correlational data (third column of Table 2), however, *are* relevant to Theory II, because the multiple correlation coefficient takes into consideration the intercorrelations (or overlap) among the factors. And the Herzberg-type critical incident studies are also relevant to Theory II, for in these studies there is no overlap among the job factors (i.e., the factors represent mutually exclusive categories).

Lahiri and Srivastva (1967) had respondents indicate, on a 10-point scale, the degree to which each of 26 job factors contributed toward satisfaction and dissatisfaction in both actual and imaginary good and actual and imaginary bad critical incidents. (In the imaginary critical incidents, subjects were asked to think of a "best" and a "worst" job they could imagine themselves doing.) The general methodology of this study was the same as that of Friedlander's (1964) study; and thus, Lahiri and Srivastva's data were reanalyzed in the same way as Friedlander's data. Table 7 contains the mean satisfaction and rescaled dissatisfaction scores of each job factor in the two different situations.

As indicated in Table 7, the data supported Theory I in both the present and imaginary job situations. That is, for both situations, the mean motivator score was greater in good than in bad incidents, and the mean hygiene score was greater in bad than in good incidents.

The data of Lahiri and Srivastva (and also Dunnette et al., 1967; Wernimont, 1966) are irrelevant to Theory II on the same grounds that Friedlander's (1964) data are irrelevant to Theory II.

The experiment by Dunnette et al. (1967), which

is discussed in the section on Theory I, is also a subject-coded study. In describing both a good and a bad critical incident, the Q-sort items representing job factors were sorted into a 7-point quasi-normal distribution. Thus, the scores representing contributions of job factors to good incidents are comparable to the scores derived from the reports of bad incidents, and unlike the studies of Friedlander (1964) and Lahiri and Srivastva (1967), it is unnecessary to rescale the mean scores. As indicated in Table 3, Theory I was supported in all six occupational groups studied.

Wernimont (1966) constructed 50 pairs of positive items describing good critical incidents and 50 pairs of negative items describing bad incidents. One member of each pair represented a motivator, the other represented a hygiene, and the members of each pair were equated in terms of social desirability. The respondents were first required to indicate which member of each pair most closely described a good or a bad critical incident (forced choice situation), and they were then asked to go back over the items and indicate the 10 items which were the most descriptive of each type of critical incident (free choice situation). The data were analyzed separately for two different occupational groups—engineers and accountants. Theory I was supported in both occupational groups in both the forced choice and free choice situation. That is, in all four situations, motivator items were selected more often in good than in bad incidents, and hygiene items were selected more often in bad than in good incidents.

If Theory III is valid, one would not expect to find incorrect predictions made for the *same* job factors in all occupational groups. (Definition of an incorrect prediction for a job factor: if a motivator, the mean score in bad incidents is greater than the mean score in good incidents; and if a hygiene, the mean score in good incidents is greater than the mean score in bad incidents.) That is, if incorrect predictions are due entirely to sampling errors, one would expect the errors to be randomly distributed among the different job factors. However, as indicated in Table 8, recognition, advancement, and relations with peers were *consistently* linked to incorrect pre-

TABLE 7 A REANALYSIS OF LAHIRI AND SRIVASTVA'S (1967) DATA

	Mean Scores			
	Present Job		*Imaginary Job*	
Job Factor	*Satisfaction*	*Rescaled dissatisfaction*	*Satisfaction*	*Rescaled dissatisfaction*
Motivators				
Recognition	6.32	6.68	7.97	8.33
Challenging assignments	6.59	6.06	7.73	7.38
Growth	6.09	6.98	7.88	8.44
Achievement	7.03	6.47	8.68	7.74
Liking for the work	7.00	6.30	8.76	7.78
Accomplishment	7.65	6.02	8.21	7.96
Use of best abilities	7.18	5.96	8.53	8.11
Responsibility	8.00	5.79	8.68	7.45
Autonomy	6.35	6.10	7.29	8.68
Promotion	4.59	8.05	7.53	8.52
Prestige	6.91	6.82	8.18	8.64
Work itself	6.35	6.22	8.53	8.00
Status	6.73	6.88	8.26	8.15
Hygienes				
Relations with co-workers	6.82	5.30	8.09	7.20
Superior's help	6.12	7.36	7.41	7.96
Friendliness of superior	7.15	6.98	7.12	7.76
Technical competence of superior	5.44	6.82	7.47	7.65
Salary	4.94	7.91	7.38	8.56
Security	7.29	6.13	8.29	7.34
Working conditions	6.53	4.63	7.62	7.26
Benefits	6.47	5.69	7.53	7.57
Fairness of authority	6.12	6.33	7.91	8.58
Freedom of expression	5.79	6.47	7.76	8.42
Work group	5.12	5.96	7.03	7.36
Managerial policies	5.12	8.69	6.59	8.27
Home life	8.00	5.11	8.82	6.16
Mean score of motivators	6.68	6.49	8.17	8.09
Mean score of hygienes	6.22	6.41	7.62	7.70

dictions. Thus, the results of the subject-coded studies contradict Theory III, indicating that the support given Theory III by the Herzberg-type studies merely reflects experimenter coding biases.

Correlational Studies. In both the Herzberg-type studies and the subject-coded studies, the determinants of satisfaction and dissatisfaction were measured by direct self-report. While the very nature of satisfaction and dissatisfaction may require that these constructs be measured by a self-report technique, it is neither necessary nor desirable that the *determinants* of satisfaction and dissatisfaction be measured by direct self-report. As emphasized by several critics (Dunnette et al., 1967; House & Wigdor, 1967; Vroom, 1964), the use of these self-report measures permits an explanation of the results solely in terms of defensive biases inherent in such measures. For example, even though the subjects accurately report the determinants of critical incidents, the recall of the incidents may be selective so that those good incidents which happen to be recalled tend to be biased toward those incidents which were due to one's own efforts (motivators) as opposed to those incidents which were due to the efforts of others (hygienes).

In correlational studies, the extent to which job factors contribute toward satisfaction and dissatisfaction is not determined by self-report but is inferred from the correlations between measures of satisfaction with individual job factors and measures of overall satisfaction and dissatisfaction. Thus, in order to eliminate the possible defensive biases of the measures used in critical incident studies, correlational studies should be considered.[1] Although correlational data may not be sufficient to permit a determination of the causal relationships stated in the theories of Table 2, certainly correlational support is a necessary requirement.

One correlational study (Hulin & Smith, 1967) is relevant. Hulin and Smith measured satisfaction with each of the five job factors of the Job Description Index (JDI); (Smith, 1967). In addition, overall job satisfaction was measured on one-fourth of the subjects, overall job dissatisfaction was measured on another one-fourth of the subjects, and a measure of overall satisfaction-dissatisfaction (S-D) was obtained on the remaining half of the subjects, where the overall measures consisted of variations of the General Motors Faces Scale (Kunin, 1955).[2] Since the theories of Table 2 do not make statements about an S-D continuum, data from only half the respondents are directly relevant.

The correlations between satisfaction with each of the five job factors and the two relevant overall measures are given in Table 9. In the male group, the two hygienes, supervision and co-workers, correlated significantly more with overall satisfaction than with overall dissatisfaction. However, these differences may be partially explained by possible differences in the reliabilities of the satisfaction and dissatisfaction measures. That is, if the dissatisfaction measure is much less reliable than the satisfaction measure, the hygienes might be expected to correlate more with satisfaction than with dissatisfaction, even though Theory III is valid. Certainly this possibility should be considered, especially since Hulin and Smith mentioned that the variability of scores on the dissatisfaction measure was considerably less than the variability on the satisfaction measure. As the reliabilities of the overall satisfaction and dissatisfaction measures are not known, it is not possible to obtain a reasonable estimate of the "true" correlations. However, as shown in Table 10, if the largest conceivable discrepancy between the reliabilities of the overall measures was assumed, the two hygienes, supervision and co-workers, would still correlate considerably higher with satisfaction than with dissatisfaction. It is thus concluded that the results of this study contradict Theory III.

Since Hulin and Smith considered only five of Herzberg's principal job factors, this study is irrelevant to Theories I and II; Theories I and II contain statements about the effects of all motivators combined and all hygienes combined.

Conclusion

In considering all relevant empirical studies, the following conclusions seem justified:

1. Theory III, being supported by the Herzberg-type studies but not by the subject-coded studies, merely reflects experimenter coding biases.

2. Theory I, although being supported by both the Herzberg-type studies and the subject-coded studies, has not been adequately tested in studies where the determinants of satisfaction and dissatisfaction were measured by techniques other than direct self-report. It is thus possible that Theory I merely reflects defensive biases inherent in such self-report measures.

[1] It should be noted that in correlational studies, not only are defensive biases eliminated, but also, the assumption (implicit in the critical incident studies) that the determinants of critical incidents are identical to the determinants of less-than-critical incidents is not made. However, it is the opinion of the writer that this second distinction between correlational and critical incident studies is much less crucial than the defensive bias distinction.

[2] This description of the Hulin and Smith study is actually incomplete. However, the omitted portion of the study is not directly relevant, for it is essentially concerned with predictions on an S-D continuum.

TABLE 8 SUCCESS OF PREDICTIONS BASED ON THEORY III IN STUDIES WHERE SUBJECTS CODED THE PERCEIVED DETERMINANTS OF THEIR CRITICAL INCIDENTS

Job Factor	Friedlander (1964)	Lahiri and Srivastva (1967) Present	Lahiri and Srivastva (1967) Imaginary	Dunnette et al. (1967) (6 Groups)	Wernimont (1966), Forced Choice (2 Groups)	Total
Motivators						
Achievement	−	+	+	6+	2+	10+, 1−
Recognition	−	−	−	5−, 1+	2−	10−, 1+
Work itself	+	+	+	6+	2+	11+
Responsibility	+	+	+	6+	2+	11+
Advancement	−	−	−	6−	2−	11−
Hygienes						
Company policy & administration	+	+	+	5+, 1−	2+	10+, 1−
Supervision	−	+	+	5+, 1−	2+	9+, 2−
Working conditions	−	−	−	6+	2−	6+, 5−
Relations with superior	−	−	+	5+, 1−	no data*	6+, 3−
Relations with peers	−	−	−	6−	no data*	9−

Note.—A plus sign signifies a correct prediction, and a minus sign indicates an incorrect prediction.
* Relations with superior and relations with peers were grouped into a single category—interpersonal relations.

3. Theory II has not been adequately tested in studies other than the Herzberg-type critical incident studies. It is thus possible that Theory II merely reflects experimenter coding biases or defensive biases inherent in self-report measures.

TABLE 9 CORRELATIONS BETWEEN SATISFACTION WITH EACH OF FIVE JOB FACTORS AND MEASURES OF OVERALL JOB SATISFACTION AND OVERALL JOB DISSATISFACTION (Hulin & Smith, 1967)

Job Factor	Males Satisfaction	Males Dissatisfaction	Females Satisfaction	Females Dissatisfaction
Motivators				
Work itself	.68*	.44	.45	.43
Promotion	.40	.38	.46	.14
Hygienes				
Pay	.39	.24	.12	.18
Supervision	.53*	.25	.31	−.03
Co-workers	.48*	.13	.20	−.08

* The difference between the correlation with satisfaction and with dissatisfaction is significant at the .05 level.

TABLE 10 CORRELATIONS OF TABLE 9 "CORRECTED" FOR ATTENUATION SO AS TO SUPPORT THEORY III AS MUCH AS POSSIBLE

Job Factor	Males Satisfaction	Males Dissatisfaction
Motivators		
Work itself	.68	.66
Promotion	.40	.57
Hygienes		
Pay	.39	.36
Supervision	.53	.38
Co-workers	.48	.20

Note.—The correlations are "corrected" for the attenuation of one variable under the assumption that the reliability of the overall satisfaction measure was 1 and that the reliability of the overall dissatisfaction measure was .44—the highest observed correlation between overall dissatisfaction and any other variable (work itself).

The relationship between these conclusions and the principle of multiple operationalism (Garner, Hake, & Eriksen, 1956; Webb, Campbell, Schwartz, & Sechrest, 1966) should be noted. According to the principle of multiple operationalism, a hypothesis is validated only if it is supported by two or more different methods of testing, where each method contains specific idiosyncratic weaknesses, but where the entire collection of methods permits the elimination of all alternative hypotheses. The application of this principle to Theories I, II, and III indicates that none of these theories have been validated. In the case of Theory III, three distinct methods, each containing different weaknesses, were used: Herzberg-type studies, subject-coded studies, and a correlational study. And two alternative hypotheses were considered: *(a)* the support given Theory III by the Herzberg-type studies is due not to the validity of Theory III but to experimenter coding biases; and *(b)* this support is due to defensive biases inherent in the self-report measures used. Neither did all three types of studies support Theory III nor were the two alternative hypotheses eliminated. In the case of Theory I, only the Herzberg-type studies and the subject-coded studies were used. Although both types of studies supported Theory I and although the alternative hypothesis analogous to hypothesis *a* was eliminated, these studies did not eliminate the alternative hypothesis analogous to hypothesis *b*. Likewise, Theory II was not validated, for neither of the two alternative hypotheses were eliminated.[3]

[3]For a study examining the individual (versus aggregate) predictability of the two-factor theory against a satisfaction

SUGGESTIONS FOR FUTURE RESEARCH

The preceding section indicates a major gap in the relevant empirical studies—namely, studies which are relevant to Theories I and II and in which the determinants of satisfaction and dissatisfaction are measured by techniques other than direct self-report. It is thus suggested that correlational studies patterned after the study by Hulin and Smith (1967) be performed. However, three exceptions to the Hulin and Smith design should be made: *(a)* Satisfaction with each of Herzberg's principal motivators and hygienes, rather than with only the five JDI factors, are measured, *(b)* the use of a measure of overall dissatisfaction which is possibly more reliable than the measure used by Hulin and Smith, and *(c)* the calculation of the multiple correlation coefficients indicated in Table 2.

In both types of critical incident studies (Herzberg-type studies and subject-coded studies) there appeared to be no differences among different occupational groups in terms of the support given Theories I, II, and III; however, this similarity may merely reflect a similarity of defense mechanisms rather than a similarity of determinants of job satisfaction. It is thus desirable that subsequent correlational studies consider relatively homogeneous occupational groups separately, for it may be found that Theory I or II is valid for specific occupational groups.

REFERENCES

Burke, R. J. Are Herzberg's motivators and hygienes unidimensional? *Journal of Applied Psychology,* 1966, **50**, 317–21

Centers, R. and Bugental, D. E. Intrinsic and extrinsic job motivations among different segments of the working population. *Journal of Applied Psychology,* 1966, **50**, 193–97.

Coombs, C. H. *A theory of data.* New York: Wiley, 1964.

Dunnette, M. D., Campbell, J. P., and Hakel, M. D. Factors contributing to job satisfaction and job dissatisfaction in six occupational groups. *Organizational Behavior and Human Performance,* 1967, **2**, 143–74.

dependent variable, see D. P. Schwab and H. G. Herreman III, "Aggregate and Individual Predictability of the Two-Factor Theory of Job Satisfaction," *Personnel Psychology,* 1970, 23, 55–66.

For a study examining the motivational validity of the two-factor theory (i.e., against a performance criteria), see D. P. Schwab, H. W. DeVitt, and L. L. Cummings, "A Test of the Adequacy of the Two-Factor Theory as a Predictor of Self-Report Performance Effects," *Personnel Psychology,* 1971, 24, 293–303.

Neither study is supportive of the two-factor theory, either as a satisfaction or motivational model. For a more thorough review of the studies claiming relevance for the two-factor theory through 1967, see L. L. Cummings and A. M. El Salmi, "Empirical Research on the Bases and Correlation of Managerial Motivation: A Review of the Literature," *Psychological Bulletin,* 70, August 1968, 127–44.

Ewen, R. B. Some determinants of job satisfaction: A study of the generability of Herzberg's theory. *Journal of Applied Psychology,* 1964, **48**, 161–63.

Ewen, R. B., Smith, P. C., Hulin, C. L., and Locke, E. A. An empirical test of the Herzberg two-factor theory. *Journal of Applied Psychology,* 1966, **50**, 544–50.

Friedlander, F. Underlying sources of job satisfaction. *Journal of Applied Psychology,* 1963, **47**, 246–50.

Friedlander, F. Job characteristics as satisfiers and dissatisfiers. *Journal of Applied Psychology,* 1964, **48**, 388–92.

Friedlander, F. Relationships between the importance and the satisfaction of various environmental factors. *Journal of Applied Psychology,* 1965, **49**, 160–64.

Friedlander, F. Importance of work versus nonwork among socially and occupationally stratified groups. *Journal of Applied Psychology,* 1966, **50**, 437–41.

Friedlander, F. and Walton, E. Positive and negative motivations toward work. *Administrative Science Quarterly,* 1964, **9**, 194–207.

Garner, W. R., Hake, H. W., and Eriksen, C. W. Operationism and the concept of perception. *Psychological Review,* 1956, **63**, 149–59.

Graen, G. B. Motivator and hygiene dimensions for research and development engineers. *Journal of Applied Psychology,* 1966, **50**, 563–66.

Graen, G. B. Testing traditional and two-factor hypotheses concerning job satisfaction. *Journal of Applied Psychology,* 1968, **52**, 366–71.

Halpern, G. Relative contributions of motivator and hygiene factors to overall job satisfaction. *Journal of Applied Psychology,* 1966, **50**, 198–200.

Hamlin, R. M. and Nemo, R. S. Self-actualization in choice scores of improved schizophrenics. *Journal of Clinical Psychology,* 1962, **18**, 51–54.

Herzberg, F. The motivation-hygiene concept and problems of manpower. *Personnel Administration,* 1964, **27**(1), 3–7.

Herzberg, F. The motivation to work among Finnish supervisors. *Personal Psychology,* 1965, **18**, 393–402.

Herzberg, F. *Work and the nature of man.* Cleveland: World Publishing Company, 1966.

Herzberg, F., Mausner, B., and Snyderman, B. *The motivation to work.* (2d ed.) New York: Wiley, 1959

Hinrichs, J. R. and Mischkind, L. A. Empirical and theoretical limitations of the two-factor hypothesis of job satisfaction. *Journal of Applied Psychology,* 1967, **51**, 191–200.

Hinton, B. L. An empirical investigation of the Herzberg methodology and two-factor theory. *Organizational Behavior and Human Performance,* 1968, **3**, 217–38.

House, R. J. and Wagdor, L. A. Herzberg's dual-factor theory of job satisfaction and motivation: A review of the evidence and a criticism. *Personnel Psychology,* 1967, **20**, 369–89.

Hulin, C. L. and Smith, P. A. An empirical investigation of two implications of the two-factor theory of job satisfaction. *Journal of Applied Psychology,* 1967, **51**, 396–402.

Kunin, T. The construction of a new type of attitude measure. *Personnel Psychology,* 1955, 8, 65–77.

Lahiri, D. K. and Srivastva, S. Determinants of satisfaction in middle-management personnel. *Journal of Applied Psychology,* 1967, **51**, 254–65.

Levine, E. L. and Weitz, J. Job satisfaction among graduate students: Intrinsic versus extrinsic variables. *Journal of Applied Psychology,* 1968, **52**, 263–71.

Lindsay, C. A., Marks, E., and Gorlow, L. The Herzberg theory: A critique and reformulation. *Journal of Applied Psychology,* 1967, **51**, 330–39.

Lodahl, T. M. Patterns of job attitudes in two assembly technologies. *Administrative Science Quarterly,* 1964, 8, 482–519.

Malinovsky, M. R. and Barry, J. R. Determinants of work attitudes. *Journal of Applied Psychology,* 1965, **49**, 446–51.

Myers, M. S. Who are your motivated workers? *Harvard Business Review,* 1964, **42**(1), 73–88.

Saleh, S. D. A study of attitude change in the preretirement period. *Journal of Applied Psychology,* 1964, **48**, 310–12.

Schwartz, M. M., Jenusaitis, E., and Stark, H. Motivational factors among supervisors in the utility industry. *Personnel Psychology,* 1963, **16**, 45–53.

Singh, T. N. and Baumgartel, H. Background factors in airline mechanics' work motivations: A research note. *Journal of Applied Psychology,* 1966, **50**, 357–59.

Smith, P. C. The development of a method of measuring job satisfaction: The Cornell studies. In E. A. Fleishman (ed.), *Studies in personnel and industrial psychology.* Homewood, Ill.: Dorsey Press, 1967.

Vroom, V. H. *Work and motivation.* New York: Wiley, 1964.

Webb, E. J., Campbell, D. T., Schwartz, R. D., and Sechrest, L. *Unobtrusive measures: Nonreactive research in the social sciences.* Chicago: Rand McNally, 1966.

Weissenberg, P. and Gruenfeld, L. W. Relationship between job satisfaction and job involvement. *Journal of Applied Psychology,* 1968, **52**, 469–73.

Wernimont, P. F. Intrinsic and extrinsic factors in job satisfaction. *Journal of Applied Psychology,* 1966, **50**, 41–50.

Whitsett, D. A. and Winslow, E. K. An analysis of studies critical of the motivator-hygiene theory. *Personnel Psychology,* 1967, **20**, 391–415.

Wolf, M. G. The relationship of content and context factors to attitudes toward company and job. *Personnel Psychology,* 1967, **20**, 121–32.

18. EFFECTS OF REWARD AND CONTINGENT REINFORCEMENT ON SATISFACTION AND TASK PERFORMANCE*

***David L. Cherrington*†**
***H. Joseph Reitz* and *William E. Scott, Jr.*‡**

A persisting belief is that if an individual is satisfied or his "morale" is high, then his performance will be higher than that of an individual who is dissatisfied or whose "morale" is low. In other words, it appears intuitively obvious that satisfaction causes task performance. This cause and effect relationship is, of course, not obvious to those who have been studying it. Nevertheless, current speculations, reviewed by Schwab and Cummings (1970), still imply that satisfaction and task performance are related in a causal fashion although, in some cases, the cause has now become the effect with moderating variables tossed in for good measure.

In contrast our "theory" is that there is no inherent relationship between satisfaction and performance, and that, as a matter of fact, one can produce just about any sort of a relationship between self-reports of satisfaction and performance that one wishes. This position was derived from operational proposals by Skinner (1969) and Bandura (1969) and from speculations by a variety of reinforcement theorists (for example, Berlyne, 1967; Bindra, 1968; Rescorla & Solomon, 1967; Weiskrantz, 1968).

It is not necessarily contradictory to adopt a Skinnerian proposal while exhibiting an enduring interest in feelings or covert processes in general. Skinner (1969), for example, contends that autonomic reflex responses to stimuli are among the emotions that are felt and that what is felt is certainly relevant to a causal sequence. However, he insists that feelings are, at best, accompaniments rather than causes of behavior and that both are the products of common environmental variables. Bandura's (1969, p. 598) analysis of the empirical problem, while similar, may be more to the point. He suggests that we might better treat self-reports of satisfaction simply as another class of behavior rather than as indices of an under-

* An abbreviated version of this manuscript appeared in the *Journal of Applied Psychology,* Vol. 55 (1971), pp. 531–36.

† Graduate School of Business Adminstration, University of Illinois.

‡ Graduate School of Business, Indiana University.

lying state endowed with special causal powers. From this point of view, there exists no inherent relationship between self-reports of satisfaction and performance, and the empirical problem becomes that of examining the conditions under which the different response systems are correlated *or* independent.

While it is unlikely that Bandura's proposal will be greeted with wholesale enthusiasm, it may prove to be fruitful in at least two respects. First, we can proceed with our empirical investigations of environmental conditions leading to the presence or absence of covariation between self-reports of satisfaction and performance. Secondly, it does not preclude speculation about central neural processes which may underlie self-reports of satisfaction (Scott & Rowland, 1970), but it does serve to prevent the confusion of identity between hypothesized central states and the responses which are usually thought to index those states.

Very briefly, our position is that reinforcing events may be performance contingent, in which case their occurrence serves to influence performance. But whether performance-contingent or not, it is also true that the occurrence and withdrawal of reinforcers *produce* other responses, and these responses loom large in accounts of emotion (Weiskrantz, 1968, p. 50). In the theoretical arena, Berlyne (1969, pp. 205–211) has postulated that reinforcing stimuli produce changes in activation or arousal level. Since there are intimate relationships between the neural structures thought to subserve arousal and affective feelings, Berlyne has also postulated that positive reinforcers produce either a moderate increase or a decrease in arousal and are thus rewarding, while negative reinforcers result in a high arousal level and are thus aversive. At the empirical level, the occurrence of rewards is often reported by human beings as pleasant, satisfying, and relatively preferred while the occurrence of negative reinforcers are reported as unpleasant, dissatisfying or painful. Also at the empirical level, direct electrical stimulation of reward sites in the brain produces, in human subjects, reports of increased alertness, expressions of pleasant experiences and relief from intense pain while stimulation of the punishment areas induces expressions of pain (Heath, 1964).

Since we do not ordinarily apply punishing stimuli such as shock to a human being, the next question is whether a time-out or the withdrawal of a reward is aversive. At the theoretical level again, it has been postulated that the withdrawal or absence of a rewarding stimulus in situations in which the reward had previously occurred produces primary frustration which is thought to be aversive (Amsel, 1958). It does not represent a speculative leap to theorize that a time-out results in a large increase in arousal level and negative affect. At the empirical level, various kinds of "emotional" behavior are rather consistently observed when extinction procedures are introduced, and Wagner (1969) has concluded that frustrative non-reward qualifies as an aversive event in the sense that individuals will act to terminate or avoid a time-out from a positive reinforcer.

Following Skinner (1957) and Bem (1967), we assume that self-report measures of satisfaction and attitudes are "tacts" or descriptions of internal feeling states (I am satisfied-dissatisfied, emotional-unemotional, tense-relaxed, encouraged-discouraged, etc.), and of the reinforcing effects of stimulus objects or situations on the individual (my supervisor is fair-unfair, my job is interesting-boring, my pay is pleasing-annoying, etc.). These kinds of tacts are under the discriminative control of stimuli to which the individual, alone, may have access, and as such, they present certain problems for the culture in teaching an individual to describe his inner states. However, it has been contended that, under most conditions, the presence or absence of covert activities can be easily and reliably detected by the individual in whom they are occurring (Homme, 1965), although the number of independent discriminations among internal stimuli may be quite small (Osgood, Suci, & Tannenbaum, 1957).

We are led to postulate that there is no inherent relationship between satisfaction and performance, that variations in satisfaction and arousal are caused by the occurrence, non-occurrence, and other properties of reinforcing stimuli, and that one can produce varying degrees of covariation between satisfaction and performance by varying the contingencies between performance and reinforcing events.

In this study, it was hypothesized that those members of a work group who received a non-contingent monetary reinforcer would report greater satisfaction and more favorable attitudes towards components of the task setting than those members who were not rewarded. It was further hypothesized that when a reward is delivered randomly to half the members of a work group, the correlation between self-reports of satisfaction and subsequent task performance would not differ significantly from zero. However, by chance, some members would be appropriately reinforced (high performers—rewarded, low performers—not rewarded) and some members would be inappropriately reinforced (high performers—not rewarded, low performers—rewarded). Consequently, it was also hypothesized that for the appropriately reinforced group there would be a significant positive correlation between self-reports of satisfaction and subsequent task performance while for the inappropriately reinforced group there would be a significant negative correlation. Finally, it was

ME AT THIS TASK

	Extremely	Quite	Slightly	Neither One Nor the Other	Slightly	Quite	Extremely	
Appreciated	______	______	______	______	______	______	______	Unappreciated
Bored	______	______	______	______	______	______	______	Interested
Efficient	______	______	______	______	______	______	______	Inefficient

hypothesized that performance subsequent to appro priate reinforcement contingencies would be significantly higher than performance subsequent to inappropriate reinforcement contingencies.

METHODOLOGY

Subjects

Ss were 90 undergraduate students, both male and female, enrolled in a junior-level business course. To enlist Ss for the study, the students were told that volunteers were needed to score some psychological tests for which they would be paid at least $1.00 per hour.

Procedure and Task

Ss reported to the laboratory in groups which varied from seven to nine individuals and were met by E who introduced himself as a graduate student who would be their supervisor. While they were waiting for others to arrive, they were invited to look through a Closure Flexibility Test booklet to familiarize themselves with it before actually scoring the completed tests.

When all Ss had arrived and had sufficient time to look over the Closure Flexibility Test booklet each S was told that his task would be to score the tests at his work station. The Ss were also told that the tests had been completed by employees in a paper mill. However, all of the Closure Flexibility Test booklets had been marked according to 24 patterns of responses. Therefore, the difficulty of the task was controlled and the correct responses were known in advance.

All Ss were told that they would be paid a minimum of $1.00 per hour but that the best performers in terms of quality and quantity would receive an additional $1.00 bonus. All Ss were also led to believe that there was a 50-50 chance of receiving the bonus.

The Ss were then taken into the lab where the task of scoring the test booklets was explained to them. Diagrams on a blackboard showing an answer sheet that was partially marked were used to help the Ss understand the instructions.

After the Ss began the task, the experimenter returned every 10 minutes to bring additional booklets and collect the booklets and answer sheets which had been completed.

At the end of one hour, the experimenter stopped the Ss and asked them to indicate on four 7-point scales an estimate of their quantity, quality, and overall performance and probability of receiving a reward.[1] The experimental manipulations of financial reward were then performed, which consisted of the following statements and payments.

> I have collected the tests as you have scored them and selected a sample from each of you to check your work. I've used a rather complicated index which combines quantity and quality of performance into one index. Based upon this index four of you will received $2.00 for the last hour's work. The other four will get $1.00. The four winners are . . . and the four losers are . . .

In fact, the monetary bonus was randomly distributed to half of the Ss regardless of their performance.

The Ss were then asked to complete a self-report measure of satisfaction developed by Scott and his colleagues (Scott, 1967; Scott & Rowland, 1970). The format of the self-report measure was a semantic differential questionnaire as shown below. Bipolar adjective pairs were set against four concepts: Me At This Task, My Pay, My Fellow Workers, and The Task. The response to each scale was scored from one to seven with seven assigned to that response which appeared to indicate the most preferred condition. A factor score was computed for each S by averaging the S's responses to each of the scales previously found to comprise that factor.

Eight factor scores were computed for each S. A General Affective Tone score was obtained by averaging the Ss responses to the following bipolar scales set against the concept, Me At This Task: appreciated-unappreciated, rewarded-penalized, sat-

[1] There were no significant differences between the reward and non-reward group in either the subjective probability of being rewarded (5.42 vs. 5.22 respectively) or in estimated performance (5.37 vs. 5.32).

TABLE 1 COMPARISON OF MEAN PERFORMANCE AND SATISFACTION (Scores of rewarded versus non-rewarded subjects)

Item	*Mean Scores* Rewarded Ss	Non-Rewarded Ss	D_m
Performance:			
First Hour	285.6	286.6	−1.0
Second Hour	403.8	411.2	−7.4
Satisfaction Indices:			
General Affective Tone	5.16	3.83	+1.33‡
General Arousal	4.98	4.44	+0.54†
Personal Competence	5.82	5.01	+0.81‡
General Satisfaction with Pay	5.61	3.69	+1.92‡
Equity of Pay	5.24	3.74	+1.50‡
Adequacy of Pay	4.76	3.40	+1.36‡
Attractiveness of Fellow Workers	4.96	4.63	+0.33*
Attractiveness of Task	3.80	3.19	+0.61‡

*$p < .01$.
†$p < .005$.
‡$p < .001$.

isfied-dissatisfied, and encouraged-discouraged. The remaining self-report measures and the semantic scales defining each factor were as follows—General Arousal (Me At This Task): interested-bored, spirited-lifeless, and alert-listless; Personal Competence (Me At This Task): efficient-inefficient, productive-unproductive, reliable-unreliable, and effective-ineffective; General Satisfaction With Pay (My Pay): pleasing-annoying, reasonable-unreasonable, superior-inferior, and rewarding-penalizing; Equitableness of Pay (My Pay in Comparison with what Others in My Groups Received): fair-unfair, high-low, and reasonable-unreasonable; Adequacy of Pay (My Pay in Comparison with what Others Get for Similar Work on the Campus): superior-inferior, high-low, and reasonable-unreasonable; Interpersonal Attractiveness (My Fellow Workers): sociable-unsociable, helpful-obstructive, pleasant-unpleasant, unselfish-selfish, and cooperative-uncooperative; Task Attractiveness (The Task): attractive-repulsive, exciting-dull, good-bad, interesting-boring, superior-inferior, and wholesome-unwholesome.

The performance score for each S was the total number of rows of figures in the Closure Flexibility Test booklets which the S scored correctly. This was determined by subtracting the number of errors from the total number of rows scored. Thus performance scores were a measure of both quality and quantity.

After completing the semantic differential scales, the Ss were invited to take a five minute break. After this short break, the Ss were given more test booklets and asked to continue scoring them for another hour. The procedure at the end of the second

TABLE 2 COMPARISON OF MEAN PERFORMANCE AND SATISFACTION SCORES OF APPROPRIATELY VERSUS INAPPROPRIATELY REINFORCED SUBJECTS

Item	*Mean Scores* Appropriately Reinforced Ss	Inappropriately Reinforced Ss	D_m
Performance:			
First Hour	291.6	280.9	+10.7
Second Hour	428.4	385.9	+42.5†
Satisfaction Indices:			
General Affective Tone	4.26	4.11	+0.15
General Arousal	4.12	4.02	+0.10
Personal Competence	5.30	5.07	+0.23
General Satisfaction with Pay	4.56	4.11	+0.45
Equity of Pay	4.40	4.18	+0.22
Adequacy of Pay	4.18	3.64	+0.54*
Attractiveness of Fellow Workers	4.85	4.78	+0.07
Attractiveness of Task	3.31	3.27	+0.04

*$p < .05$.
†$p < .01$

hour was identical to that at the end of the first hour. First, the Ss were asked to estimate their perceived performance and probability of reward on the four scales. Then they were paid and asked to fill out the semantic differential questionnaire. The monetary bonus was distributed to the same Ss who received it at the end of the first hour.

After the questionnaires were filled out for the second time, the Ss were debriefed. They were told that all rewards were given at random and since it was only by chance someone received more than the others, the winners were asked to share their rewards with the losers, although the E did not insist that they do so.

RESULTS

We have hypothesized that there is no inherent relationship between satisfaction and performance but that there is a direct relationship between the occurrence of a reinforcer and self-reports of satisfaction. Whatever covariation one does observe between satisfaction and performance, then, may depend upon other environmental conditions, particularly the kind of performance-reinforcement contingency which has been arranged or has evolved.

To test this hypothesis, we first examined the effects of a noncontingent monetary reinforcer on both performance and self-reports of satisfaction, then the effects of variations in the performance-reinforcement contingency on performance and satisfaction and finally the correlations between performance and satisfaction under the different reinforcement contingencies.

Table 1 presents a test of the effects of a non-contingent monetary reinforcer on performance and satisfaction.[2] The nearly identical average performance scores of the rewarded and non-rewarded subjects during the first hour established that the reinforcer was administered randomly, without regard for performance. The average second-hour performance scores of rewarded Ss did not differ significantly from that of non-rewarded Ss. These results indicate that non-contingent reward had no effects on performance.

However, the results summarized in Table 1 clearly support the hypothesis that a non-contingent monetary reinforcer significantly affects self-reports of satisfaction. Mean satisfaction scores of rewarded subjects were significantly greater than mean scores of non-rewarded subjects on each of the eight satisfaction indices. This first set of results thus show that self-report measures of satisfaction can be highly dependent on the occurrence or non-occurrence of a monetary reinforcer, but if that reinforcer is delivered independent of performance, it fails to have incremental effects on subsequent performance.

To test the effects of variations in performance-reinforcement contingency, Ss were evaluated on the basis of first-hour performance. The 42 Ss whose performance scores were above the median are referred to as "high performers," and the 42 Ss below the median as "low performers." Since rewards at the end of the first hour were distributed randomly, half the Ss in each performance classification were rewarded, and half not rewarded. The appropriateness of each S's reinforcement was then defined by the performance-reward contingency which happened to occur for that S. The 21 rewarded high performers and the 21 non-rewarded low performers were classified as "appropriately reinforced." The 21 rewarded low-performers and the 21 non-rewarded high performers were classified as "inappropriately reinforced."

The results shown in Table 2 reveal first that the average second-hour (post-reinforcement) performance of appropriately reinforced subjects was significantly higher than that of inappropriately reinforced subjects, whereas the first-hour (pre-reinforcement) performance of the two classes did not differ. Although performance under both conditions increased from the first to the second hour, the mean increase of the appropriately reinforced subjects was significantly greater (136.8 vs. 105.0) than that of the inappropriately reinforced subjects ($F = 5.30$, $p < .025$).

However, comparisons between the two classes on self-reports of satisfaction revealed a significant difference on only one of the eight satisfaction indices: Adequacy of Pay. The tests summarized in Tables 1 and 2 thus establish that, as hypothesized, a monetary reinforcer is sufficient to increase self-reported satisfaction, but does not of itself bring about increments in performance. It is the contingency of that reinforcer on performance that enables it to bring about increments in performance. However, that contingency characteristic has little or no effect on satisfaction.

The next relationships examined were between satisfaction and performance.

Two different relationships between satisfaction and performance were investigated: (1) the relationship between self-reports of satisfaction and subsequent performance, and (2) the relationship between performance and subsequent self-reports of satisfaction.

Table 3 presents the results of correlational analyses performed between the eight satisfaction indices recorded at the end of the first hour and subsequent

[2] Raw scores are reported in the tables. However, normalized scores were utilized in all statistical analyses.

TABLE 3 CORRELATIONS BETWEEN SATISFACTION AT END OF FIRST HOUR AND SUBSEQUENT PERFORMANCE DURING SECOND HOUR

Satisfaction Indices	*All Subjects (n = 90)*	*Appropriately Reinforced Subjects (n = 42)*	*Inappropriately Reinforced Subjects (n = 42)*
General Affective Tone	.00	.56‡	—.32*
General Arousal	.10	.42†	—.15
Personal Competence	.21	.54‡	—.01
General Satisfaction with Pay	.04	.46†	—.29
Equity of Pay	—.17	.15	—.44†
Adequacy of Pay	.04	.39†	—.31*
Attractiveness of Fellow Workers	.22*	.33*	.13
Attractiveness of Task	.04	.21	—.08

* $p < .05$.
† $p < .01$.
‡ $p < .001$.

performance during the second hour. The data for all 90 subjects revealed only one significant correlation between satisfaction and subsequent performance.

However, when the data were separated according to the subjects' performance-reward contingencies, distinct differences in the satisfaction-performance relationships were observed. For the 42 *appropriately* reinforced subjects, significant *positive* correlations were found between six of the eight satisfaction indices and subsequent performance. But for the 42 inappropriately reinforced subjects, *negative* correlations were found between seven of the eight satisfaction indices and subsequent performance. Three of these latter correlations were statistically significant and one closely approached significance at the .05 level.

Table 4 presents the results of correlational analyses performed between performance during the second hour and the eight satisfaction indices subsequently recorded at the end of the second hour. The similarities between Tables 3 and 4 are striking. The data for all 90 subjects revealed no significant correlations between performance and subsequent satisfaction. However, when distinctions were made between appropriately and inappropriately reinforced subjects, where the performance classifications were based on the second-hour's productivity scores, widely disparate performance-satisfaction relationships were observed. For the appropriately reinforced subjects, significant positive correlations were obtained between performance and each of the eight satisfaction indices. For the inappropriately reinforced subjects, negative correlations were obtained between performance and seven of the eight satisfaction indices, with four of the correlations being highly significant.

DISCUSSION

The results of this study support the hypothesis that the manipulation of a monetary reinforcer will have significant effects on self-reports of satisfaction, and that the type and magnitude of the relationship between satisfaction and performance depends pri-

TABLE 4 CORRELATIONS BETWEEN PERFORMANCE DURING SECOND HOUR AND SATISFACTION AT END OF SECOND HOUR

Satisfaction Indices	*All Subjects (n = 90)*	*Appropriately Reinforced Subjects (n = 42)*	*Inappropriately Reinforced Subjects (n = 42)*
General Affective Tone	—.03	.55‡	—.51‡
General Arousal	.02	.42†	—.26
Personal Competence	.13	.48†	—.16
General Satisfaction with Pay	.03	.67‡	—.56‡
Equity of Pay	—.09	.45†	—.51‡
Adequacy of Pay	—.03	.59‡	—.57‡
Attractiveness of Fellow Workers	.20	.44†	.04
Attractiveness of Task	—.06	.32*	—.16

* $p < .05$.
† $p < .01$.
‡ $p < .001$.

TABLE 5 PRODUCTIVITY INCREASES AFTER REINFORCEMENT

Condition	*Mean Productivity Increase*
Low Performers, Not Rewarded	151.8
High Performers, Rewarded	121.8
Low Performers, Rewarded	111.9
High Performers, Not Rewarded	98.2

marily upon the performance-reinforcer contingencies that have been arranged. Such findings make very tenuous any theory which postulates a simplistic cause and effect relationship between satisfaction and performance in which either variable directly influences the other.

It was also found that performance improvements subsequent to the application of appropriate performance-reinforcer contingencies were significantly higher than performance improvements subsequent to the application of inappropriate performance-reinforcer contingencies. Somewhat unexpected was the finding that among the appropriately reinforced subjects, it was the non-rewarded, low performance group who showed the greatest increment in performance in the second hour (see Table 5). It might have been that it was physically impossible for the highest performing subjects to increase their productivity a great deal, while the lowest performing subjects had more room for improvement. On the other hand, merely to indicate to an individual that his performance was unsatisfactory (e.g., by withholding a reward) is usually not sufficient to effect improvements in his performance. Therefore, unless there are cues in the task setting which clearly suggest that one must expend greater effort or work faster, we would not expect the non-rewarded low performance group to show the greatest increment in productivity. In any event, this group did not show an increase in productivity *because* the members were satisfied for, if anything, they were dissatisfied.

Of course, it will be necessary to replicate this study utilizing different subjects and different tasks. Of even greater interest would be to investigate the effects of variations in the quality, scheduling, and other reinforcer parameters on performance, self-reports of overall satisfaction, and attitude toward the task, fellow workers, and the supervisor. Additional insight could be gained by systematically varying the performance-reinforcer contingencies while noting the effects on satisfaction and on the covariation between self-reports of satisfaction and performance measures.

In this study, it was difficult for subjects to differentiate their performance from that of others in the work group, and partly for that reason, the subjective probability of receiving the monetary bonus was nearly equal for all experimental groups. These conditions are not likely to hold within most work groups over a period of time. If there were variations in the subjective probability of receiving the bonus, then the effects of being rewarded or non-rewarded on self-reports of satisfaction might differ from those found here. However, despite variations in subjective probability of being rewarded, we would expect satisfaction-performance relationships for appropriately reinforced and for inappropriately reinforced groups to be similar to those found in this study.

REFERENCES

Amsel, A. The role of frustrative nonreward in noncontinuous reward situations. *Psychological Bulletin,* 1958, 55, 102–19.

Bandura, A. *Principles of behavior modification.* New York: Holt, Rinehart & Winston, 1969.

Bem, D. J. Self-perception: An alternative interpretation of cognitive dissonance phenomena. *Psychological Review,* 1967, 74, 183–200.

Berlyne, D. E. Arousal and reinforcement. In D. Levine (ed.), *Nebraska symposium on motivation: 1967.* Lincoln, Neb.: University of Nebraska Press, 1967.

Berlyne, D. E. The reward value of indifferent stimulation. In J. T. Tapp (ed.), *Reinforcement and behavior.* New York: Academic Press, 1969.

Bindra, D. Neuropsychological interpretation of the effects of drive and incentive-motivation on general activity and instrumental behavior. *Psychological Review,* 1968, 75, 1–22.

Heath, R. G. Pleasure response of human subjects to direct stimulation of brain: Physiologic and psychodynamic considerations. In R. G. Heath (ed.), *The role of pleasure in behavior.* New York: Harper and Row, 1964.

Homme, L. E. Perspectives in psychology: XXIV. Control of coverants, the operants of the mind. *Psychological Record,* 1965, 15, 501–11.

Osgood, C. E., Suci, G. J., and Tannenbaum, P. H. *The measurement of meaning.* Urbana, Ill.: University of Illinois Press, 1957.

Rescorla, R. A. and Solomon, R. L. Two-process learning theory: Relationships between Pavlovian conditioning and instrumental learning. *Psychological Review,* 1967, 74, 151–82.

Schwab, D. P. and Cummings, L. L. Employee performance and satisfaction with work roles: A review and interpretation of theory. *Industrial Relations,* 1970, in press.

Scott, W. E., Jr. The development of semantic differential scales as measures of "morale." *Personnel Psychology,* 1967, 20, 179–98.

Scott, W. E. and Rowland, K. M. The generality and significance of semantic differential scales as measures of "morale." *Organizational Behavior and Human Performance,* 1970, in press.

Skinner, B. F. *Verbal behavior.* New York: Appleton-Century-Crofts, 1957.

Skinner, B. F. *Contingencies of reinforcement: A theoretical analysis.* New York: Appleton-Century-Crofts, 1969.

Wagner, A. R. Frustrative nonreward: A variety of punishment. In B. A. Campbell and R. M. Church (eds.), *Punishment and aversive behavior.* New York: Appleton-Century-Crofts, 1969.

Weiskrantz, L. Emotion. In L. Weiskrantz (ed.), *Analysis of behavioral change.* New York: Harper & Row, 1968.

19. A SYSTEM RESOURCE APPROACH TO ORGANIZATIONAL EFFECTIVENESS*

Ephraim Yuchtman and Stanley E. Seashore†

We are badly in need of an improved conceptual framework for the description and assessment of organizational effectiveness. Nearly all studies of formal organizations make some reference to effectiveness; the growing field of comparative organizational study depends in part upon having some conceptual scheme that allows comparability among organizations with respect to effectiveness and that guides the empirical steps of operationalization and quantification.

Aside from these needs of social scientists, consideration should also be given to the esthetic and applied requirements of organization managers. They experience high emotional involvement, pleasurable or otherwise, in the assessment of the relative success of their organizations; they are, of course, intensively and professionally engaged, informally, in the formulation and testing of hypotheses concerning the nature of decisions and actions that alter organizational effectiveness. They need a workable conception of "effectiveness" to sustain their egos and their work.

The social scientist designing or interpreting an organizational study is presently in a quandary. Most of the research concerned with the problem has been devoted to the study of the *conditions* under which organizations are more or less effective. The classic paradigm consists of some measurement of effectiveness—productivity or profit, for example—as the dependent variable, and of various sociological and social-psychological measures as the independent variables. The independent variables are usually treated in a relatively sophisticated manner; little attention, however, has been given to the concept of effectiveness itself. The latter remains conceptually a vague construct; in consequence there is available a large amount of empirical data with little understanding of these data. As stated recently by Katz and Kahn:

> There is no lack of material on criteria of organizational success. The literature is studded with references to efficiency, productivity, absence, turnover, and profitability—all of these offered implicitly or explicitly, separately or in combination, as definitions of organizational effectiveness. Most of what has been written on the meaning of these criteria and on their interrelatedness, however, is judgmental and open to question. What is worse, it is filled with advice that seems sagacious but is tautological and contradictory.[1]

Similar conclusions, on the same or on different grounds, have been reached by other students of organizations.[2] While emphasizing different aspects of the problem, all agree that results from studies of organizational effectiveness show numerous inconsistencies, and are difficult to evaluate and interpret, let alone compare. The inconsistencies arise, often, from discrepant conceptions of "organizational effectiveness." In the present paper an attempt is made, first, to show some of the limitations inherent in traditional approaches to organizational effectiveness and, second, to provide an improved conceptual framework for dealing with that problem.

TRADITIONAL APPROACHES TO ORGANIZATIONAL EFFECTIVENESS

In spite of the variety of terms, concepts and operational definitions that have been employed with

* *American Sociological Review,* Vol. 32, No. 6 (December 1967), pp. 891–903.

The preparation of this paper was financially supported by the National Science Foundation under Grant GS-70. Since the preparation of this paper, the first author has taken up his new post at the University of Tel-Aviv.

† Survey Research Center, the University of Michigan.

[1] Daniel Katz and Robert L. Kahn. *The social psychology of organizations* (New York: Wiley, 1966), p. 149.

[2] Basil S. Georgopoulos and Arnold S. Tannenbaum, A study of organizational effectiveness, *American Sociological Review,* 22 (October 1957), pp. 534–540; Mason Haire, Biological models and empirical histories of the growth of organizations, in Mason Haire (ed.), *Modern organization theory* (New York: Wiley, 1959), pp. 272–306; Amitai W. Etzioni. Two approaches to organizational analysis: A critique and a suggestion, *Administrative Science Quarterly,* 5 (September 1960), pp. 257–78; Robert M. Guion. Criterion measurement and personnel judgments, *Personnel Psychology,* 14 (Summer 1961), pp. 141–49; Charles Perrow. Organizational goals, in *International encyclopedia of social sciences,* 1964 edition, pp. 854–66; Stanley E. Seashore. Criteria of organizational effectiveness, *Michigan Business Review,* 17 (July, 1965), pp. 26–30.

regard to organizational effectiveness, it is hardly difficult to arrive at the generalization that this concept has been traditionally defined in terms of goal attainment. More specifically, most investigators tend implicitly or explicitly to make the following two assumptions: (1) that complex organizations have an ultimate goal ("mission," "function") toward which they are striving and (2) that the ultimate goal can be identified empirically and progress toward it measured. In fact, the orientation to a specific goal is taken by many as the defining characteristic of complex organizations. A few organizational theorists[3] avoid making these assumptions, but they represent the exception rather than the rule.

Beyond these two common assumptions, however, one may discern different treatments of the matter, especially with regard to the rationale and operations for identifying the goals of organizations. It is useful to distinguish between two major doctrines in this respect. The first may be called the "prescribed goal approach." It is characterized by a focus on the formal charter of the organization, or on some category of its personnel (usually its top management) as the most valid source of information concerning organizational goals. The second may be referred to as the "derived goal approach." In it the investigator derives the ultimate goal of the organization from his (functional) theory, thus arriving at goals which may be independent of the intentions and awareness of the members. The prescribed and derived doctrines will be referred to as the *goal approach* and the *functional approach*, respectively.

THE GOAL APPROACH TO ORGANIZATIONAL EFFECTIVENESS

The goal approach, which itself has taken many forms, is the most widely used by students of organizations. Some have adopted it only as part of a broader perspective on organizations.[4] Others have employed it as a major tool in their study of organizations.[5] The goal approach has been attacked recently on various grounds. Katz and Kahn, while noting that ". . . the primary mission of an organization as perceived by its leaders furnishes a highly informative set of clues," go on to point out that:

> Nevertheless, the stated purpose of an organization as given by its by-laws or in the reports of its leaders can be misleading. Such statements of objectives may idealize, rationalize, distort, omit, or even conceal some essential aspects of the functioning of the organization.[6]

The goal approach is often adopted by researchers because it seems to safeguard them against their own subjective biases. But Etzioni attacks precisely this assumption:

> The (goal) model is considered an objective and reliable analytical tool because it omits the values of the explorer and applies the values of the subject under study as the criteria of judgment. We suggest, however, that this model has some methodological shortcomings, and it is not as objective as it seems to be.[7]

Furthermore, argues Etzioni, the assessment of organizational effectiveness in terms of goal attainment should be rejected on theoretical considerations as well:

> Goals, as norms, as sets of meanings depicting target states, are cultural entities. Organizations, as systems of coordinated activities of more than one actor, are social systems.[8]

We understand this statement as rejecting the application of the goal approach in the study of organizational effectiveness for two reasons: first, goals as ideal states do not offer the possibility of realistic assessment; second, goals as cultural entities arise outside of the organization as a social system and cannot arbitrarily be attributed as properties of the organization itself. A similar criticism is offered by Starbuck, who calls attention to a hazard in the inferring of organizational goals from the behavior of organizational members:

> To distinguish goal from effect is all but impossible. The relation between goals and results is polluted by environmental effects, and people learn to pursue realistic goals. If growth is difficult, the organization will tend to pursue goals which are not growth oriented; if growth is easy, the organization will learn to pursue goals which are growth oriented. What one observes are the learned goals. Do these goals produce growth, or does growth produce these goals?[9]

---

[3] James G. March and Herbert A. Simon. *Organizations* (New York: Wiley, 1958); Etzioni, Two approaches to organizational analysis"; Perrow, Organizational Goals; Seashore, Criteria of organizational effectiveness; Katz and Kahn, *The social psychology of organizations.*

[4] Chester I. Barnard. *The functions of the executive* (Cambridge: Harvard University Press, 1938); Peter F. Drucker. *The practice of management* (New York: Harper, 1954).

[5] Robert Michels. *Political parties* (Glencoe, Ill.: The Free Press, 1949); William J. Baumol. *Business behavior, value and growth* (New York: Macmillan, 1959); James K. Dent. Organizational correlates of the goals of business management, *Personnel Psychology,* 12 (Autumn 1959), pp. 365-93; Carl M. White. Multiple goals in the theory of the firm, in Kenneth E. Boulding and W. Allen Spivey (ed.), *Linear programming and the theory of the firm* (New York: Macmillan, 1960), pp. 181–201; Bertram M. Gross. What are your organization's objectives? A general-systems approach to planning, *Human Relations,* 18 (August, 1965), pp. 195–216.

[6] Katz and Kahn, *The social psychology of organizations,* p. 15.

[7] Etzioni, Two approaches to organizational analysis, p. 258.

[8] Etzioni, Two approaches to organizational analysis, p. 258.

[9] William H. Starbuck. Organizational growth and development, in James G. March (ed.), *Handbook of organizations* (Chicago: Rand McNally, 1965), p. 465.

It should be noted that the authors cited above tend to treat the problem as a methodological one even though, as we will show, theoretical differences and uncertainties are present as well. In order to escape some of these methodological shortcomings, several investigators have attempted to rely upon inferential or impressionistic methods of goal identification. Haberstroh, for example, makes the distinction between the formal objectives and the "common purpose" of the organization, the latter serving as the "unifying factor in human organizations."[10] But how, one may wonder, can that factor be empirically identified? Haberstroh maintains that it can be discovered through a systematic inquiry into the communication processes of the organization and by knowledge of the interests of its leadership, especially those in key positions. An empirical investigation conducted in accordance with that advice resulted in a list of operational (task) goals that, according to the investigator's own acknowledgment, do not adequately represent his notion of the "common purpose" of the organization. The latter remains therefore a rather vague concept and, it may be added, not surprisingly so. If one assumes that Haberstroh's "common purpose" stands for those objectives that are shared by the organization's members, he is reminded by several students of organizations[11] that such objectives are generally highly ambiguous, if not controversial, and therefore difficult to identify and measure.

The same kind of criticism can be applied to those who rely on the organization's charter, whether formal or informal, as containing the main identifying features of the organization, including its goals. Such an approach is represented by Bakke; he refers to the organization's charter, in the broad sense of the term, as expressing ". . . the image of the organization's unique wholeness." Such an image is created by ". . . selecting, highlighting, and combining those elements which represent the *unique* whole character of the organization and to which uniqueness and wholeness all features of the organization and its operations tend to be oriented."[12] The reader is left puzzled about how to discover the goals of the organization even after knowing that they are contained somewhere in the "image of the organization's unique wholeness."

The difficulty of identifying the ultimate goal of an organization is illustrated by some of the research on mental hospitals and other "total" institutions, as discussed by Vinter and Janowitz and, particularly, by Perrow and Etzioni.[13] Many of these institutions have been judged to be ineffective since they fail to achieve their presumed therapeutic goals. Vinter and Janowitz demonstrate, however, that the goal of therapy is held only by a limited segment of the public, and that the institutions themselves are oriented mainly to custody, not therapy.

Etzioni elaborates upon this issue as follows:

> When the relative power of the various elements in the environment are carefully examined, it becomes clear that, in general, the sub-publics (e.g., professionals, universities, well-educated people, some health institutions) which support therapeutic goals are less powerful than those which support the custodial or segregating activities of these organizations. Under such conditions, most mental hospitals and prisons must be more or less custodial.[14]

This observation, like Starbuck's argument quoted above, amounts to saying that organizational goals are essentially nothing more than courses of action imposed on the organization by various forces in its environment, rather than preferred end-states toward which the organization is "striving." Such a perspective on the nature of organizational goals seems to undermine the rationale behind the use of goals as a yardstick for assessing organizational effectiveness. How, we may ask, can a given social unit be regarded as "effective" if it cannot even determine its goals for itself, i.e., if the reference is wholly to the needs of entities other than itself? It would seem that the capacity of an organization to attain its own goals is a consideration of higher priority than that of success in attainment of imposed goals. An adequate conceptualization of organizational effectiveness cannot therefore be formulated unless factors of organization-environment relationships are incorporated into its framework.

Finally, it is not only in its external environment that the organization is faced with a variety of forces exerting influence on its behavior. The organization itself is composed of a large variety of individuals and groups, each having its own conceptions about any claims on the organization. The managers of an organization do not wholly agree among themselves

---

[10] Chadwick J. Haberstroh. Organization design and systems analysis, in James G. March (ed.), *Handbook of organizations* (Chicago: Rand McNally, 1965), pp. 1171–1211.

[11] Abraham D. H. Kaplan, Joel B. Dirlam, and Robert F. Lanzillotti. *Pricing in big business* (Washington: Brookings Institution, 1958); Richard M. Cyert and James G. March. A behavioral theory of organizational objectives, in Mason Haire (ed.), *Modern organization theory* (New York: Wiley, 1959), pp. 76–90.

[12] E. Wight Bakke. Concept of the social organization, in Mason Haire (ed.), *Modern organization theory* (New York: Wiley, 1959), pp. 16–75.

[13] Robert Vinter and Morris Janowitz. Effective institutions for juvenile delinquents: A research statement, *Social Service Review,* 33 (June 1959), pp. 118–30; Charles Perrow. The analysis of goals in complex organizations, *American Sociological Review,* 26 (December 1961), pp. 854–66.

[14] Etzioni, Two approaches to organizational analysis, p. 264.

about the organizational goals; in addition it is not certain that these goals, even if agreed upon, would prevail. This complicated reality is highlighted by the analysis of Cyert and March. They warn against the confusion in understanding organizational behavior whenever any one individual or group, such as the top management, is selected to represent the organization as a whole:

> The confusion arises because ultimately it makes only slightly more sense to say that the goal of the business organization is to maximize profit than it does to say that its goal is to maximize the salary of Sam Smith, Assistant to the Janitor.[15]

These considerations, taken together, seem to cast a serious doubt on the fruitfulness of the goal approach to organizational effectiveness. This is not to suggest that the concept of organizational goals should be rejected *in toto.* For certain analytical purposes it is useful to abstract some goal as an organizational property. In the study of persons in organizational settings, the concept of goal is useful and perhaps essential.[16] In the study of organizational effectiveness, however, the goal approach has appeared as a hindrance rather than as a help.

THE FUNCTIONAL APPROACH TO ORGANIZATIONAL EFFECTIVENESS

The functional approach to organizational effectiveness can be characterized as "normative" in the sense that the investigator reports what the goals of an organization are, or should be, as dictated by the logical consistency of his theory about the relationship among parts of larger social systems. From this point of view, the functional, or derived goal, approach has an important advantage over the prescribed goal doctrine since it appears to solve the problem of identifying the ultimate goals of complex organizations: Given the postulates and premises of the functional model about the nature of organizations and their interconnectedness with the total social structure one can derive from it the specific goals of an organization or of a class of organizations. This is evident mainly in the work of Parsons, one of the outspoken advocates of functional analysis, in his suggestions for a theory of organizations.[17] The Parsonian scheme also illustrates, however, a major weakness inherent in the functional approach. This weakness can be usefully discussed in terms of "frames of reference."

Organizations, or other social units, can be evaluated and compared from the perspectives of different groups or individuals. We may judge the effectiveness of an organization in relation to its own welfare, or we may assess how successful the organization is in contributing to the well-being of some other entities. While the selection of a given frame of reference is a question of one's values and interests, the distinction among them must be clearly made and consistently adhered to. Vital as this requirement appears to be, one encounters various treatments of effectiveness that implicitly or explicitly refer to different frames of reference interchangeably, as if effectiveness from the point of view of the organization itself is identical with, or corresponds to, effectiveness viewed from the vantage point of some other entity, such as a member, or owner, or the community, or the total society.

The point of departure for Parsons' analysis of complex organizations is the "cultural-institutional" level of analysis. Accordingly, "The main point of reference for analyzing the structure of any social system is its value pattern. This defines the basic orientation of the system (in the present case, the organization) to the situation in which it operates; hence, it guides the activities of participant individuals."[18] The impact of the value pattern, furthermore, is felt through institutional processes which ". . . spell out these values in the more concrete functional contexts of goal-attainment itself, adaptation to the situation, and integration of the system."[19] These functional prerequisites, including the value pattern, are universally present in every social system. Their specific manifestations and their relative importance, however, vary according to the defining characteristic of the system and its place in the superordinate system. In the case of complex organizations, their defining characteristic is the primacy of orientation to the attainment of a specific goal. This goal, like all other organizational phenomena, must be legitimated by the value pattern of the organization. The nature of this legitimation is a crucial element in Parsons' analysis; the following quotation shows its relevance for the present discussion as well:

> Since it has been assumed that an organization is defined by

---

[15] Cyert and March, A behavioral theory of organizational objectives, p. 80.

[16] Alvin F. Zander and Herman M. Medow. Individual and group levels of aspiration, *Human Relations,* 16 (Winter 1963), pp. 89–105; Alvin F. Zander and Herman M. Medow. Strength of group and desire for attainable group aspirations, *Journal of Personality,* 33 (January 1965), pp. 122–39.

[17] Talcott Parsons. Suggestions for a sociological approach to a theory of organizations—I, *Administrative Science Quarterly,* 1 (June 1956), pp. 63–85; Talcott Parsons. *Structure and processes in modern societies* (New York: The Free Press, 1960), pp. 16–96.

[18] Parsons, Suggestions for a sociological approach . . . , p. 67.

[19] Parsons, Suggestions for a sociological approach . . . , p. 67.

the primacy of a type of a goal, the focus of its value-system must be the legitimation of this goal in terms of the functional significance of its attainment for the superordinate system, and secondly, the legitimation of the primacy of this goal over other possible interests and values of the organization and its members.[20]

In terms of our analysis, this states explicitly that the focal frame of reference for the assessment of organizational effectiveness is not the organization itself but rather the superordinate system. Not only must the ultimate goal of the organization be functionally significant in general for that system but, in the case of a conflict of interests between it and the organization, the conflict is always resolved in favor of the superordinate system—since the value pattern of the organization legitimates only those goals that serve that system. In other words, the *raison d'être* of complex organizations according to this analysis, is mainly to benefit the society to which they belong, and that society is, therefore, the appropriate frame of reference for the evaluation of organizational effectiveness. In order to avoid misunderstanding in this respect the following illustration is provided by Parsons:

For the business firm, money return is a primary measure and symbol of success and is thus part of the goal structure of the organization. But it cannot be the primary organizational goal because profit-making is not by itself a function on behalf of the society as a system.[21]

Now there is no argument that the organization, as a system, must produce some important output for the total system in order to receive in return some vital input. However, taking the organization itself as the frame of reference, its contribution to the larger system must be regarded as an unavoidable and costly requirement rather than as a sign of success. While for Parsons the crucial question is "How well is the organization doing for the superordinate system?", from the organizational point of view the question must be "How well is the organization doing for itself?"

It was suggested earlier that a major weakness of the goal approach has been its failure to treat the issue of organizational autonomy in relation to organizational effectiveness. This seems to be the Achilles heel of the functional approach as well. In Parsons' conception of organizations, and of social systems in general, there exists the tendency to overemphasize the interdependence among the parts of a system and thus, as argued by Gouldner, fail ". . . to explore systematically the significance of variations in the degree of interdependence," ignoring the possibility that ". . . some parts may vary in their dependence upon one another, and that their interdependence is not necessarily symmetrical."[22]

Gouldner's proposition of "functional autonomy" may be examined on several different levels. For example, one may regard the organization itself as the total system, looking for variations in the degree of autonomy among its own parts; this has been the focus of Gouldner's analysis. But the same line of analysis can be attempted at a different level, where society is taken as the total system. Here the investigator may be exploring variations in the degree of autonomy of various parts and sub-systems, an instance of which are complex organizations. Such an analysis underlies the typology offered by Thompson and McEwen, in which the relations between organizations and their environments are conceived in terms of the relative autonomy, or dominance, of the organization vis-à-vis its environment.[23]

The proposition of functional autonomy implies that organizations are capable of gearing their activities into relatively independent courses of action, rather than orienting themselves necessarily toward the needs of society as the superordinate system. Under such assumptions it is difficult to accept as a working model of organizations the proposition that the ultimate goal of organizations must always be of functional significance for the larger system.

Comparing the goal and the functional approaches, it can be concluded that both contain serious methodological and theoretical shortcomings. The goal approach, while theoretically adhering to an organizational frame of reference, has failed to provide a rationale for the empirical identification of goals as an organizational property. The functional approach, on the other hand, has no difficulty in identifying the ultimate goal of the organization, since the latter is implied by the internal logic of the model, but the functional model does not take the organization as the frame of reference. Furthermore, neither of the two approaches gives adequate consideration to the conceptual problem of the relations between the organization and its environment.

A SYSTEM RESOURCE APPROACH TO ORGANIZATIONAL EFFECTIVENESS

The present need, to which we address our attention, is for a conception of organizational effectiveness that: (1) takes the organization itself as the focal

[20] Parsons, Suggestions for a sociological approach . . . , p. 68.

[21] Parsons, Suggestions for a sociological approach . . . , p. 68.

[22] Alvin W. Gouldner. Organizational dynamics, in Robert K. Merton *et al.* (eds.), *Sociology today* (New York: Basic Books, 1959), p. 419.

[23] James D. Thompson and William J. McEwen. Organizational goals and environment: Goal-setting as an interaction process, *American Sociological Review,* 23 (February 1958), pp. 23–31.

frame of reference, rather than some external entity or some particular set of people; (2) explicitly treats the relations between the organization and its environment as a central ingredient in the definition of effectiveness; (3) provides a theoretically general framework capable of encompassing different kinds of complex organizations; (4) provides some latitude for uniqueness, variability and change, with respect to the specific operations for assessing effectiveness applicable to any one organization, while at the same time maintaining the unity of the underlying framework for comparative evaluation; (5) provides some guide to the identification of performance and action variables relevant to organizational effectiveness and to the choice of variables for empirical use.

A promising theoretical solution to the foregoing problems can be derived from the open system model as it is applied to formal social organizations. This model emphasizes the distinctiveness of the organization as an identifiable social structure or entity, and it emphasizes the interdependency processes that relate the organization to its environment. The first theme supports the idea of treating formal organizations not as phenomena incidental to individual behavior or societal functioning but as entities appropriate for analysis at their own level. The second theme points to the nature of interrelatedness between the organization and its environment as the key source of information concerning organizational effectiveness. In fact, most existing definitions of organizational effectiveness have been formulated, implicitly or explicitly, in terms of a *relation* between the organization and its environment, since the attainment of a goal or the fulfullment of a social function imply always some change in the state of the organization vis-à-vis its environment. The crucial task, then, is the conceptualization of that relation. The system model, with its view of the nature of the interaction processes between the organization and its environment, provides a useful basis for such a conceptualization.

According to that model, especially as applied to the study of organization by Katz and Kahn,[24] the interdependence between the organization and its environment takes the form of input-output transactions of various kinds relating to various things; furthermore, much of the stuff that is the object of these transactions falls into the category of *scarce and valued resources*. We shall have more to say about "resources" below. For the moment it will suffice to indicate that the value of such resources is to be derived from their utility as (more or less) generalized means for organizational activity rather than from their attachment to some specific goal. This value may or may not correspond to the personal values of the members of the organization, including their conception of its goals. It should be noted also that scarce and valued resources are, for the most part, the focus of competition between organizations. This competition, which may occur under different social settings and which may take different forms, is a continuous process underlying the emergence of a universal hierarchical differentiation among social organizations. Such a hierarchy is an excellent yardstick against which to assess organizational effectiveness. It reflects what may be referred to as the "bargaining position" of the organization in relation to resources and in relation to competing social entities that share all or part of the organization's environment.[25]

We propose, accordingly, to define the effectiveness of an organization in terms of its bargaining position, as reflected in the ability of the organization, in either absolute or relative terms, to exploit its environment in the acquisition of scarce and valued resources.

The concept of "bargaining position" implies the exclusion of any specific goal (or function) as the ultimate criterion of organizational effectiveness. Instead it points to the more general capability of the organization as a resource-getting system. Specific "goals" however can be incorporated in this conceptualization in two ways: (1) as a specification of the means or strategies employed by members toward enhancing the bargaining position of the organization; and (2) as a specification of the personal goals of certain members or classes of members within the organizational system. The better the bargaining position of an organization, the more capable it is of

[24] Katz and Kahn, *The social psychology of organizations.*

[25] The differential amounts of success of organizations with regard to their bargaining positions implies the possibility of exploitation of one organization by another, a possibility which may endanger the stability of social order. This asymmetry in interorganizational transactions and its consequences for the problem of social order underlie the sociological interest in exchange processes and their normative regulation. As pointed out recently by Blau:

"Without social norms prohibiting force and fraud, the trust required for social exchange could not serve as a self-regulating mechanism within the limits of these norms. Moreover, superior power and resources, which often are the results of competitive advantages gained in exchange transactions, make it possible to exploit others." (*Exchange and power in social life* [New York: Wiley, 1964], p. 255)

Blau's discussion is concerned mainly with the more limited case of exchange between individuals as social actors. Nevertheless, it points to the potential asymmetry involved in exchange processes in general and the consequences of such asymmetry, namely, the emergence of a hierarchical differentiation among the interacting units with regard to their exploitative ability. For the purposes of the present discussion it is important to note that such an advantageous bargaining position, which may be dysfunctional for the system as a whole, is from the organization's point of view a sign of its success.

attaining its varied and often transient goals, and the more capable it is of allowing the attainment of the personal goals of members. Processes of "goal formation" and "goal displacement" in organizations are thus seen not as defining ultimate criteria of effectiveness, but as strategies adopted by members for enhancing the bargaining position of their organizations.

The emphasis upon the resource-getting capability of the organization is not intended to obscure other vital aspects of organizational performance. The input of resources is only one of three major cyclic phases in the system model of organizational behavior, the other two being the throughput and the output. From this viewpoint the mobilization of resources is a necessary but not a sufficient condition for organizational effectiveness. Our definition, however, points not to the availability of scarce and valued resources as such, but rather to the bargaining position with regard to the acquisition of such resources as the criterion of organizational effectiveness. Such a position at a given point of time is, so far as the organization's own behavior is concerned, a function of all the three phases of organizational behavior—the importation of resources, their use (including allocation and processing), and their exportation in some output form that aids further input.

By focusing on the ability of the organization to exploit its environment in the acquisition of resources we are directed by the basic yet often neglected fact that it is only in the arena of competition over scarce and valued resources that the performance of both like and unlike organizations can be assessed and evaluated comparatively. To put it somewhat differently, any change in the relation between the organization and its environment is affected by and results in a better or worse bargaining position vis-à-vis that environment or parts thereof.

It should be noticed that the proposed definition of effectiveness does not imply any specific goal toward which an organization is striving, nor does it impute some societal function as a property of the organization itself. Our definition focuses attention on *behavior,* conceived as continuous and never-ending processes of exchange and competition over scarce and valued resources.[26] We shall now discuss some of the concepts central to our definition of organizational effectiveness.

[26] One reader of an early draft of this paper, Dr. Martin Patchen, inquired about the sources of directive energy in goalless organizations. The answer is that persons who are members of the organization, and acting both within their role prescriptions and in indiosyncratic deviations from role prescriptions, import personal values and goals which may modify the system in a directed way.

COMPETITION AND EXCHANGE

Our emphasis upon the competitive aspects of interorganizational relations implies that an assessment of organizational effectiveness is possible only where some form of competition takes place. This raises the question of how general or limited is the scope of applicability of our definition, since interorganizational transactions take forms other than competition. An old and useful distinction in this respect has recently been formulated by Blau:

> A basic distinction can be made between two major types of processes that characterize the transactions of organized collectivities—as well as those of individuals, for that matter—competitive processes reflecting endeavors to maximize scarce resources and exchange processes reflecting some form of interdependence. Competition occurs only among like social units that have the same objectives and not among unlike units . . . Competition promotes hierarchical differentiation between more or less successful organizations and exchange promotes horizontal differentiation between specialized organizations of diverse sort.[27]

Blau's assessment that ". . . competition promotes hierarchical differentiation between more or less *successful* organizations" is, of course, in line with our definition of organizational effectiveness; furthermore, there is no question about the mainly competitive character of relations among "like" social units.

However, Blau's contention that competition occurs *only* among like organizations is an oversimplification. Indeed, it is difficult to point to any interrelated organizations that are not in competition with respect to some kinds of resources, and it is easy to point to organizations that are dominantly competitive, yet have some complementarity and interdependence in their relations. A university and a business firm, for example, may be involved in an exchange of knowhow and money, and still compete with respect to such resources as manpower and prestige. The type of pure complementarity of exchange is very limited indeed. We suggest, accordingly, that exchange and competition are the extremes of a continuum along which interorganizational transactions can be described. The proposed definition of effectiveness allows then for the comparative evaluation of any two or more organizations that have some elements of rivalry in their relations. Such a comparative evaluation becomes more meaningful—in the sense of encompassing the crucial dimensions of organizational behavior—as the variety and number of competitive elements in these relations increases. The clearest and most meaning-

[27] Peter Blau, *Exchange and power in social life* (New York: Wiley, 1964), p. 255.

ful comparison obtains when the evaluated organizations compete directly for the same resources. This condition implies that the compared organizations are engaged in like activities and share to a large degree the same temporal and physical life space. In such cases the comparison is facilitated by the fact that the competition refers to the same kinds of resources and that the assessment variables—both of input and output—are measured in like units. Comparisons are also possible, however, in the case of organizations that do not compete directly, but that compete in environments that are judged to be similar in some relevant respects.

As the characteristic transactions between organizations come closer to the exchange pole of the continuum the problem of comparison becomes more complex: first, the elements of competition may be very few in number and peripheral in importance, thus making the comparison trivial; second, the more unlike the organizations, the more difficult it is to measure their performance units on common scales. In any case, the identification of the competitive dimensions in interorganizational transactions is the key problem in the assessment of organizational effectiveness. Some clarification and possible ways of solution for this problem can be achieved through an examination of the concept of "resources."

RESOURCES

A key element in this definition is the term "resources." Broadly defined, "resources" are (more or less) generalized means, or facilities, that are potentially controllable by social organizations and that are potentially usable—however indirectly—in relationships between the organization and its environment. This definition, it should be noted, does not attribute directionality as an inherent quality of a resource, nor does it limit the concept of resources to physical or economic objects or states even though a physical base must lie behind any named resource. A similar approach to "resources" is taken, for example, by Gamson. He argues that the "reputation" of individuals or groups as "influentials" in their community political affairs is itself a resource rather than simply ". . . the manifestation of resources. . . ."[28]

One important kind of resource that is universally required by organizations, that is scarce and valued, and that is the focus for sharp competition, is energy in the form of human activity. The effectiveness of many organizations cannot be realistically assessed without some accounting for the organization's bargaining position with respect to the engagement of people in the service of the organization. One thinks, of course, of competition in the industrial or managerial labor market, but the idea is equally applicable to the competition, say, between the local church and the local political party, for the evening time of persons who are potentially active in both organizations.

Since human activity is such a crucial class of organizational resource, we elaborate on the meaning that is intended and one of the implications. We view members of an organization as an integral part of the organization with respect to their organizational role-defining and role-carrying activities, but as part of the environment of the organization with respect to their abilities, motives, other memberships, and other characteristics that are potentially useful but not utilized by the organization in role performance. An "effective" organization competes successfully for a relatively large share of the member's personality, engaging more of the personality in organizationally relevant ways, thus acquiring additional resources from its environment.

A number of other distinctions may usefully be made with respect to the resources that are involved in the effectiveness of organizations:

1. Liquidity. Some resources are relatively "liquid" in the traditional economic sense of that term and are readily exchangeable by an organization for resources of other kinds. Money and credit are highly liquid, being exchangeable for many other (but not all) kinds of resources. By contrast, the resource represented by high morale (among members) is relatively low in liquidity; under some conditions it is not directly exchangeable at full value in transactions with other organizations but must be internally transformed, e.g., into products or services, before exchange. Some organizations are characterized by having a large proportion of their resources in relatively non-liquid forms.

2. Stability. Some resources are transient in the sense that they must be acquired and utilized continuously by an organization, while other resources have the property of being stored or accumulated without significant depreciation. An organization that acquires a rapidly depreciating resource and fails to utilize this resource within an acceptable period will suffer loss of part of the value. The current high turnover among technical staff in some industrial firms is an example of loss of effectiveness through failure to utilize transient resources. By contrast, money is a highly stable resource that can be stored indefinitely at small loss and can be accumulated against future exchange requirements. Political influence is a resource of notorious instability.

[28] William A. Gamson. Reputation and resources in community politics, *American Journal of Sociology,* 72 (September 1966), pp. 121–31.

3. Relevance. In principle, all resources are relevant to all organizations to the extent that they are capable of transformation and exchange. The degree of relevance, however, is of considerable interest, since identification of resources of high relevance offers a guide to a useful classification of organizations and serves to direct priority in comparative analyses to those kinds of resources that most clearly reflect the relative bargaining power of organizations. Degree of relevance also has a bearing upon the analysis of symbiotic relationships among organizations (high rates of exchange with relatively little bargaining and high mutual benefit) and upon the analysis of monopolistic forces (dominance of a given resource "market" and consequent enhancement of bargaining power). The degree of relevance of a given resource can be estimated on an *a priori* basis from a knowledge of the typical outputs of an organization and a knowledge of its characteristic throughput activities. Critical resources might be discerned from an analysis of changes in the pattern of internal organizational activity, for such changes can be interpreted to be a response to an enhanced requirement or a threatened deficit with respect to a given type of resource. Organizations are frequently observed to mobilize activities in a way that enhances their power to acquire certain resources. A judgment of future organizational effectiveness might accordingly be improved by information concerning the organization's ease of adaptation to shifts among classes of resources in their degree of relevance.

4. Universality. Some resources are of universal relevance in the sense that all organizations must be capable of acquiring such resources. The universally required classes include: (1) personnel; (2) physical facilities for the organization's activities; (3) a technology for these activities; and (4) some relatively liquid resource, such as money, that can be exchanged for other resources. The amount required of each class may in some cases be very modest, but all organizations must have, and must be able to replenish, resources of these kinds. The non-universal resources are, in general, those for which competition is limited, either because of irrelevance to many organizations or because the particular resource is ordinarily obtained amply through symbiotic exchange.

5. Substitution. Organizations with similar typical outputs competing in a common environment do not necessarily share the same roster of relevant and critical resources. One reason for this is that the internal processes of organizational life may be adapted to exploit certain readily available resources rather than to acquire alternative scarce resources in hard competition. An example of this is seen in the case of a small, ill-equipped guerilla army facing a force of superior size and equipment. While exploiting rather different resources, they may compete equally for the acquisition of territorial and political control.

A crucial problem in this context is the determination of the relevant and critical resources to be used as a basis for absolute or comparative assessment of organizational effectiveness. In stable, freely competitive environments with respect to relatively liquid resources, this determination may be rather easy to make, but under other conditions the determination may be problematic indeed. The difficulties arise primarily in cases in which the competing organizations have differential access to relatively rich or relatively poor environments, where symbiotic exchange relationships may develop, where the resources are not universal, and where the possibilities of substitution are great. In such situations, the analytic approach must employ not a static conception of the relationships between an organization and its environment but rather, a conception that emphasizes adaptation and change in the organizational patterns of resource-getting.

OPTIMIZATION VS. MAXIMIZATION

In their recent analysis of complex organizations, Katz and Kahn proposed defining organizational effectiveness as "the maximization of return to the organization by all means."[29] This definition shares with the one we propose an emphasis on resource procurement as the sign of organizational success; it differs, however, in invoking the notion of maximization, a concept we have avoided. The position taken here is that maximization of return, even if possible, is destructive from the viewpoint of the organization. To understand this statement it should be remembered that the bargaining position of the organization is equated here with the ability to exploit the organization's environment—not with the maximum use of this ability. An organization that fully actualizes its exploitative potential may risk its own survival, since the exploited environment may become so depleted as to be unable to produce further resources. Furthermore, an organization that ruthlessly exploits its environment is more likely to incite a strong organized opposition that may weaken or even destroy the organization's bargaining position. Thus, the short-run gains associated with over-exploitation are likely to be outweighted by greater long-run losses. Also, the resource itself may lose value if over-exploited; for example, an effective voluntary community organization may enjoy extra-

[29] Katz and Kahn, *The social psychology of organizations,* p. 170.

ordinary bargaining power in the engagement of prestigeful people, but this power may not safely be used to the maximum, because excessive recruitment risks the diminishing of the value of membership when membership ceases to be exclusive.

These considerations lead to the proposition that the highest level of organizational effectiveness is reached when the organization maximizes its bargaining position and optimizes its resource procurement. "Optimum" is the point beyond which the organization endangers itself, because of a depletion of its resource-producing environment or the devaluation of the resource, or because of the stimulation of countervailing forces within that environment. As stated by Thompson and McEwen:

> It is possible to conceive of a continuum of organizational power in environmental relations, ranging from the organization that dominates its environmental relations to one completely dominated by its environment. Few organizations approach either extreme. Certain gigantic enterprises, such as the Zaibatsu in Japan or the old Standard Oil Trust in America, have approached the dominance-over-environment position at one time; most complex organizations, falling somewhere between the extremes of the power continuum, must adopt strategies for coming to terms with their environment.[30]

We may add, however, that the need "for coming to terms with their environments" applies to organizations that approximate the dominance-over-environment extreme as well. A powerful enterprise like General Motors must exercise its potential power with much restraint in order to avoid the crystalization of an opposition which may weaken its bargaining power considerably, through legislation or some other means.

It is of course very difficult, if possible at all, to determine in absolute terms the organization's maximum bargaining position and the optimal point of resource procurement that is associated with that position. Since most organizations, however, fall short of maximizing their bargaining position, the optimization problem, though theoretically important, is only of limited empirical relevance. In practice, organizational effectiveness must be assessed in relative terms, by comparing organizations with one another. The above discussion on the nature of "resources" provides at best a general outline for carrying out such a task. A more detailed discussion and a preliminary effort to apply empirically the conceptual scheme presented here is reported elsewhere.[31] Briefly, the following steps seem necessary for a meaningful comparative assessment of organizational effectiveness: (1) to provide an inclusive taxonomy of resources; (2) to identify the different types of resources that are mutually relevant for the organizations under study; and (3) to determine the relative positions of the compared organizations on the basis of information concerning the amount and kinds of resources that are available for the organization and its efficiency in using these resources to get further resources.

SOME IMPLICATIONS

We end this discussion with a few speculations about the impacts that might arise from a general acceptance and use of the conception of organizational effectiveness that we have proposed. These may affect theorists, empirical researchers and managers in various ways:

1. The rejection of the concept of an ultimate goal, and the replacement of this singular concept with one emphasizing an open-ended multidimensional set of criteria, will encourage a broadening of the scope of search for relevant criterion variables. Past studies have tended to focus too narrowly upon variables derived from traditional accounting practice or from functional social theory, or on narrowly partisan "goals" attributed to organizations. A conception of organizational effectiveness based upon organizational characteristics and upon resource-acquisition in the most general sense will encourage the treatment as criteria of many variables previously regarded as by-products or incidental phenomena in organizational functioning.

2. Past comparative studies of organizations have, in general, been of two kinds: (1) Comparison of organizations differing markedly in their characteristics, e.g. prisons and factories, so that issues of relative effectiveness were deemed irrelevant and uninteresting as well as impractical; and (2) comparisons among organizations of a similar type, so that they could be compared on like variables and measurement units. The conception we offer provides the possibility of making accessible for study the large middle range of comparisons involving organizations that have only limited similarities such that they compete with respect to some but not all of their relevant and crucial resources.

3. Case studies of single organizations will be aided by the provision of a conceptual basis for treating a more inclusive and more realistic range of vari-

[30] Thompson and McEwen, Organizational goals and environment, p. 25.

[31] Stanley E. Seashore and Ephraim Yuchtman. The elements of organizational performance. A paper prepared for a symposium on people, groups and organizations: An effective integration of knowledge, Rutgers University, November 1966. (This paper will appear in *Administrative Science Quarterly,* 1967.); Ephraim Yuchtman, A study of organizational effectiveness, unpublished Ph.D. dissertation, the University of Michigan, 1966.

ables that bear on the effectiveness of the organization.

4. The meaning of some familiar variables will need to be reassessed and in some cases changed. For example, distributed profit, a favorite variable for the comparative assessment of business organizations, will be more widely recognized as a cost of organizational activity and not as an unequivocal sign of success or goal achievement. Some managers have already adopted this view. Similarly, growth in size, usually interpreted as a sign of organizational achievement, can now be better seen as a variable whose meaning is tied closely to environmental factors and to the position of the organization with respect to certain other variables; the conception we have presented highlights the idea that growth in size is not in itself an unmitigated good, even though it may mean greater effectiveness under some conditions. In a similar fashion, it will be seen as necessary that the judgment of the meaning of each criterion variable rests not upon an absolute value judgment or a universal conceptual meaning, but rather upon the joint consideration of an extensive integrated set of organizational performance and activity variables.

chapter 3

STRUCTURAL AND ENVIRONMENTAL DETERMINANTS OF BEHAVIOR IN ORGANIZATIONS

In this chapter we will focus on the structural and other intraorganizational environmental determinants of participant behavior. We begin by examining several dimensions of the task structure of the work of an organization. Next we examine the effects on performance and attitudes of various organizational arrangements, designs and structures. Finally, having considered the task design and structural influences on behavior and attitudes we conclude Chapter 3 by examining the effects of the formal reward and penalty system of the organization on the employee behavior and goal accomplishment.

Much of the research and theory drawn upon in this chapter focuses on the individual level of analysis; therefore many of the contributors write from a psychological perspective. This is particularly the case in the first section. The importance of the contributions of the orthodox or classical management theorists, as well as several neoclassical and contemporary organization theorists, becomes apparent as we move to a consideration of organization structure. Our knowledge relevant to the design and administration of formal reward and penalty systems draws upon several levels of analysis and disciplines; e.g., industrial psychology and classical management theory with their emphasis upon the individual per se, organizational and social psychology with the associated emphasis upon individuals in interaction in relatively small groups, and contemporary organization theory and sociology with their emphasis upon the intergroup and organizational level of analysis.

We introduce this chapter with an important article by Forehand and Gilmer which overviews many of the intraorganizational influences on attitudes and behavior. The article strongly reflects one of the implicit values of Chapters 1 and 2; namely, the scientists' belief that behavior is determined. After restating the widely held premise that behavior is a function of the interaction between personal characteristics and environmental variables, they go on to define "climate" as a set of organizational properties which may influence the behavior of individuals in organizations. Forehand and Gilmer then introduce the various observational strategies which investigators have employed to determine the relationships between those properties and behavior. Finally, their discussion of some potentially significant organizational variables should be of some interest to the aspiring manager since all of these properties are amenable to change by organizational leaders.

20. ENVIRONMENTAL VARIATION IN STUDIES OF ORGANIZATIONAL BEHAVIOR*

Garlie A. Forehand and B. Von Haller Gilmer†

The desirability of incorporating environmental variation into research designs has often been pointed out, but few procedures for doing so have been developed. Attempts to operationalize the concept of "organizational climate" in studies of organizational behavior provide a number of methods for assessing environmental variation, and yield data relevant to hypotheses regarding the interaction of persons and environments. Methods for observing climate variation include field studies, assessments of participant's perceptions, observations of objective indices, and experimental control of organizational variables. Conditions may affect behavior by determining stimuli, by restraining freedom of response, and by rewarding and punishing behavior. Illustrative of the organizational properties meriting further study are size, structure, systems complexity, leadership pattern, and goal directions. Selected bibliography of 104 titles indicates how studies of organizations make possible the variation of both person and climate variables.

The concept of environment has been a difficult one for psychologists to deal with empirically. The postulate that behavior is a function of the interaction of organism and environment is widely accepted and both its theoretical and practical implications have been explored (Barton, 1961; Brunswik, 1956; Cronbach, 1957; Murray, 1938). Effort has been devoted to discovery of relevant dimensions of personal variables and to the precise definition of experimental treatments, but there have been few attempts to develop multivariate definitions of environment, and fewer still to study behavior as a function of the simultaneous variation of personal and situational factors. In the past few years several psychologists have noted the lack of such studies and have begun to develop models for systematically incorporating environmental variation in research design (e.g., Abelson, 1962; Sells, 1963a, 1963b). Models relevant to this problem of general psychology are emerging from the rapidly developing and multidisciplinary study of behavior of individuals in organizations.

The study of behavior of persons in organizations presents both a need and an opportunity for environmental analysis. Analyses of organizational behavior have multiple origins. An example of the diversity of approaches may be termed the institutional-individual continuum. Extremes on the continuum are represented by "classical" descriptions of organizations that derive their descriptive terms from formal, legalistic specifications (summarized by Strother, 1963) and by contemporary conceptions whose descriptive terms refer to the behavior of interacting individuals (Guetzkow & Bowes, 1957). Any segment of the continuum would, of course, have value in accounting for some observed events, and a given approach will handle some observations better than others. Not surprisingly, analyses focusing upon one end of the continuum are beset by devils whose home is at the other. Formal models of the organization and its parts provide neat symbolic devices, but members of the organization often do not behave as the model says they should (March & Simon, 1959). On the other hand, attempts to predict what an individual will do on the basis of his own personal characteristics often lead to the reluctant conclusion that behavior depends in part on the situation (Tagiuri, 1961).

Evidence that approaches to organizational behavior are coming together is summarized by Leavitt (1962a), who sees the emergence of "organizational psychology," a new multidisciplinary research field that "views organizations as curiosities deserving of research; and is therefore as much concerned with the nature of systems and the nature of human decision-making as with any applied problems [p. 27]." A consequence of such a perspective is intensified interest in human behavior as it is conditioned by organizational properties, and in organizations as they are influenced by the behavior of their members.

Organizational psychology offers unique opportunity for the study of environmental variation. Observers of—and participants in—organizations have noted differences in organizational personality or climate (Dill, Hilton, & Reitman, 1962; Gilmer, 1961), and some have written narrative descriptions reminiscent of early descriptions of personality types (e.g., Gellerman, 1960). The development of formal specification and measurement of such variation is a task of as much relevance to general psychology as to the specific study of organizations. An organiation has several properties that make it a particularly appropriate focus for studying environmental variation: (a) The organization represents a component of the environment of behavior known to be influential on certain subsets of behavior. (b) The organization is bounded, at least in a relative sense; a company or a department can be identified unam-

* *Psychological Bulletin,* Vol. 62, No. 6 (December, 1964), pp. 361–82.

† Both of Department of Psychology, Carnegie Institute of Technology.

biguously. And (c) there exist sources of information about an organization—in the form of records, statistical summaries, perceptions of participants, organiation charts and the like—that provide potential data for characterizing the personality of the organization.

What to call the desired conceptually integrated synthesis of organizational characteristics has been a problem for many researchers. The term organizational climate has been used by several of them, although the term means different things to different writers. We shall use the term in this paper to refer to the set of characteristics that describe an organization and that (a) distinguish the organization from other organizations, (b) are relatively enduring over time, and (c) influence the behavior of people in the organization. These defining properties were chosen in the effort to focus discussion upon features of organizational variation that are amenable to specification, measurement, and incorporation into empirical research.

Work on the problem of conceptualizing variation in climate has been done on many fronts. Relevant studies are found in the literature of psychology, sociology, administration, and education. This paper reviews a number of these efforts, but is in no sense a survey. The pertinent literature is too diffuse to make such an attempt profitable at present. Rather, we have searched for converging conclusions from samples of diverse approaches to the problem and have concentrated on studies in which variation in both climate and individual behavior was considered. Among the questions to be discussed are: How can organizational climate be measured? What dimensions of climate are meaningful? What kinds of relationship between climate and behavior may be expected? What do such relationships imply concerning the operation of organizations? What directions do these concepts suggest for future research?

MEASUREMENT OF ORGANIZATIONAL VARIATION

The measurement problem confronting the student of organizational climate is similar in some respects to that of the psychologist studying individual behavior. The problem may be conceived as one of constructing tests for organizations, and thus involves the systematic observation of the behavior of organizations. As in individual testing there are a variety of possible ways for making the required systematic observations. Approaches include: intensive observation in "field" situations, assessments of perceptions of organizations by organization members, observation of objective organization properties, and experimental variation of organizational properties and processes.

Field Studies

Intensive observations of the actual, ongoing activities of organizations may provide a researcher with a sensitive feel for the organization's climate, and, depending upon the skill of the observer, a communicable model of the organization's functioning. The sources of information available to the naturalistic observer are almost unlimited—observations of conferences, interviews with participants, diaries kept by participants, departmental memos, records and correspondence, and the history of the organization, to name only a few—and a wealth of descriptive material has been obtained in this way. Much of this material comes from case studies of single organizations. While hypotheses may sometimes be generated from such studies, an understanding of the effect of climate requires studies that systematically examine variations of climate as they influence the behavior of participants. Two approaches to the observation of climate variation have been (a) examining behavior in contrasting organizations (comparative studies) and (b) studying the effects of changing conditions in a single organization (longitudinal studies).

Designs for comparative studies have reflected varying perspectives of investigatiors. Two polar types of design will serve to illustrate the approach: the experimenter may begin with organizational systems that differ observably in properties hypothetically relevant to individual behavior, and look for differences in actual behavior; or he may focus upon groups whose behavior is observed to be contrasting and look for organizational correlates of that variation. The former design is illustrated by Barnes' (1960) study of two engineering work groups. The groups were approximately equal in size and had similar duties, but one was characterized by a "closed" authority system—tight control, low member autonomy, few opportunities for interaction of members, etc.—while the other presented a contrasting "open system." Other climate dimensions that have been chosen to define contrasts in field studies are informal social relations in small work groups (Blau, 1954), democratic versus authoritarian management policies (Stanton, 1960), and interdependence of employees in a work group (Vroom & Mann, 1960).

The second approach—investigation of organization correlates of observed differences in behavior—was taken by Dill (1958) in a study of two firms that differed markedly in the degree of personal autonomy of their members, as indicated by differences in perceived autonomy and in observed conference behaviors. The two firms were found to differ both with respect to task environment (inputs of information from external sources, e.g., stability and homogeneity of customers, suppliers, competitors, and regulatory groups) and with respect to internal restraints characteristic of the firms themselves (e.g., stress on formal rules and procedures, top management involvement in routine activities).

An example of a longitudinal study of a single organization is provided by Argyris (1958). From a model of the process by which the climate of an organization evolves from input variables (e.g., hiring process, formal policies, leadership style) Argyris generated and tested hypotheses about what would occur in a particular organization under particular conditions. The hypotheses concerned, for example, what would happen if an officer who is not the right type (i.e., the type congruent with the climate) is appointed, if employees are requested to communicate their true feelings, and if officers are asked to diagnose the organizations's human problems.

The richness of information available from field studies carries with it some serious disadvantages, notably the practical expense, demands upon the skill and sensitivity of the observer, the impracticality of obtaining a "sample size" of more than two or three organizations and, perhaps the most serious disadvantage, the inherent subjectivity of the classifications. Each of the remaining methods discussed here attempts to overcome one or more of these disadvantages, at the expense of detailed impressions.

Perceptions of Participants

Theoretical conceptions of the relationship of organizational properties to individual behavior often emphasize the role of perception of organizational properties as intervening variables. For example, Likert's interaction-influence model assigns central importance to organizational characteristics as they are perceived by the individual. The causal variables (structure, objectives, supervisory practices, etc.) interact with personality to produce perceptions, and it is only through perceptions that the relationship between causal and end-result variables may be understood (Likert, 1961, pp. 196 ff.). This point of view suggests the measurement of climate indirectly via the perception of the individuals whose behavior is being studied.

Another argument for assessing organizational climate by means of participant's perceptions is that such perceptions are based upon experience that is both more extensive and more involved than that of an outside observer. The developers of the College Characteristic Index (CCI) (Pace, 1961; Pace & Stern, 1958) make this rationale explicit:

> In answering the CCI, students act as observers, saying what they believe is generally true or not true of their college. The items refer to a wide range of topics—rules and regulations, facilities, student-faculty relationships, classroom methods, extra-curricular activities, etc. The argument is that all these characteristics and events and practices, added together, constitute an educational press on the awareness of students. The aggregate awareness of students about their college environments constitutes a press in the sense of exerting a directive influence [Pace, 1962, p. 47].

The CCI is one of a few inventories designed to assess a range of dimensions of climate. It contains 30 scales based upon Murray's concept of environmental press. The scales are named in terms of Murray's classification of needs, and include press toward humanism, impulsion deliberation, and reflectiveness. Thistlethwaite (1959, 1960) rescored the CCI to define scales reflecting faculty behavior as distinguished from student behavior. Hemphill (1956) has developed another set of scales for measuring dimensions of group performance. These 14 scales, based on factor-analytic studies, include measures of control, stability, and intimacy.

Other investigators have developed perceptually based measures of specific constructs, for purposes of testing specific hypotheses. For example, Forehand and Guetzkow (1962; Forehand, 1963) obtained a measure of executives' perceptions of the relative "rule centeredness" and "group centeredness" of their organizations by having subjects report the solutions to administrative problems that they thought would be most typically adopted in their organizations. Lodahl and Porter (1961) assessed necessity for work-group cooperation by means of judgments by supervisory personnel familiar with the work. Pelz (1951), in a study of employee behavior as a function of supervisor's influence, judged the degree of supervisor's "influence over the social environment in which his employees were functioning" from the supervisor's reports concerning his voice in decisions made by his own supervisor, lack of formal contact with his supervisor, and his salary.

Measures based on perception have advantages in research convenience, and may have theoretical meaning in their own right, but in such a measure characteristics of the individual and the organization are confounded. As Sells (1963a) has pointed out, analysis of the interaction between person and situation will require independent identification of the variation in each. For such analyses, it will be necessary to define organizational variation in terms of objectively observable measures, or to develop means of systematically manipulating organizational properties.

Objective Indices

There have been several attempts to examine objective properties of organizations, properties easily and reliably obtainable from records. Several studies, for example, have been concerned with organizational size as a variable (Baumgartel & Sobol, 1959; Talacchi, 1960; Thomas 1959). In a study of factors related to accidents, Sherman, Kerr, and Kosinar (1957) examined a long list of organizational variables, including union representation, extent of employee participation in incentive and profit-sharing plans, extent of seasonal layoffs, and the nature of the plant vicinity.

This method affords the possibility of studying a wide variety of organizations (e.g., the Sherman, Kerr, and Kosinar study included 147 plants), with consequent advantages for studying the generality of the conclusions. The principal difficulties of the procedure are the same as those confronted by the psychologist studying individual personality—the variables that may be examined are too numerous and too specific to be readily interpreted. Studies that examine in isolation specific objective properties of an organization leave unanswered the questions of how the properties are related to one another and how they are related to useful constructs of organizational functioning.

Evan (1963) has outlined an approach that has considerable promise for giving meaning to objective indices. Rather than taking administratively defined measures as given, he begins with an abstractly defined concept that has hypothetical relevance to behavior and suggests ways of constructing indices to reflect that concept. Specifically, Evan has worked with the concept of degree of hierarchical organization. He postulates that "different degrees of hierarchical organization have different consequences for total and partial social systems," and outlines several indices of the hierarchies of skills, rewards, and authority in organizations. Suggested indices of the authority hierarchy, for example, involve *(a)* ratio of higher level supervisors to foremen; *(b)* number of levels of authority from top management to workers; *(c)* ratio of administrative to production personnel; *(d)* the ratio of maximum to minimum time span of control—that is, the length of time an employee is authorized to make organization-committing decisions on his own initiative; *(e)* degree of decentralization of defined classes of decisions; and *(f)* the number of echelons for which "procedural due process of law" has been institutionalized. Such an approach to organization measurement has the valuable effect of rendering the criteria of construct validity, particularly the ideas of convergent and discriminant validity (Campbell & Fiske, 1959), applicable to organizational measurement. Another approach, taking cue from differential psychology, applies multi-variate statistical techniques to the analysis of organizational properties. In one such study, five situational characteristics of 72 wholesale warehousing divisions of a single firm were examined. The variables—size of work force, city size, wage rate, unionization and percentage of male employees—were found to be considerably intercorrelated and defined a single factor in a factor analysis. The factor was interpreted as:

> degree of urbanization of the setting in which the division is located, low urbanization being represented by relatively small community population, few employees in the division, lower wages, absence of a union, and lower proportion of male employees [Katzell, Barrett, & Parker, 1961, p.67].

Palmer (1961) analyzed measures of 21 organizational conditions (e.g., pension plan, recreation facilities, quality control methods) and nine personnel behaviors (e.g., productiveness, lateness, turnover) in 188 manufacturing firms. The variables could be accounted for by eight orthogonal factors, of which five—denoted retirement welfare, size of work force, thrift benefits, insurance benefits, and theft versus discounts—were defined by both organizational and behavioral measures.

Experimental Manipulation of Climate

Two characteristics of the organizational climate have been assumed in the foregoing discussion: that it is multidimensional in nature, and that it is characteristic of an existing organization, built upon factors beyond the investigator's control. We have thus talked of discovering rather than creating climate, although some investigators have envisioned the eventual possibility of selecting climates for maximum benefit. As a research device, the idea of identifying relevant dimensions of climate and varying them systematically has appeal. This would permit a clear-cut test of interaction hypotheses, among other advantages.

Such a strategy, applying to the concept of climate as we have defined it, is far from ready to be put to work, but there are several lines of effort that provide relevant models. The most detailed and voluminous work on the experimental control of social variables has involved small groups. Golembiewski (1962a, 1962b) and Leavitt and Bass (1964) have recently surveyed literature in this field with its relevance to organizations in mind; although, as the latter investigators point out, "extrapolations from small group data [to large organizations] have been free and easy." The group properties singled out by Leavitt and Bass as potentially relevant to organizations are group maturity, size, group composition (homogeneity, cohesion mutual esteem), and geographical distance. Golembiewski's longer reviews could be interpreted to suggest some 15-20 variables that might be defined experimentally, although they often are defined in other ways in small group studies. Examples are structural integration, status congruency, task, and threat.

Group experiments most clearly relevant to question about climate have come from two traditions. One is the study of communication networks (Glanzer & Glaser, 1961). These experiments permit variation of both the permitted pattern of communication and of individual position in the pattern. Highly "realistic" situations can be developed in this way; in a sense the experimenter actually "creates" an organization (Guetzkow & Bowes, 1957).

Perhaps the most extensive examinations of effects of organizational properties have developed from the "human relations" tradition in management. In attempts to demonstrate the relative superiority or inferiority of democratic, participative, employee-centered leadership practices, ingenious methods of varying organizational properties have been devised. Perhaps the most relevant studies here are those that build on the model of early research on leadership style (Lewin, Lippitt, & White, 1939) and whose experimental conditions are designed to reflect realistic characteristics of complex organizations.

Some of these experiments have approached the problem of realism by simulating organizational activities. For example, Kidd and Christy (1961) studied effects of several supervisory practices (laissez faire, direct participant, and active monitor) on productivity in a simulated air-traffic control center. In a well-controlled study, Day and Hamblin (1961) constructed a factorial design involving combination of close versus general supervision and punitive versus nonpunitive supervision in a simulated assembly-line situation. The independent variables were operationally defined by controlling the number of instructions given by supervisors and the number of sarcastic, negative, status-deflating remarks made by the supervisors, and by careful training of supervisors in the playing of their roles.

Several classic studies conducted by the Institute for Social Research have attempted experimental control of organizational variables in actual ongoing organizations. Coch and French (1948) varied the manner in which work groups were involved in a change in jobs. Experimental groups participated in decisions regarding the need and nature of job changes, with varying degrees of totality of participation in the planning, while a control group was instructed to carry out plans developed by the production department. In a further variation, participative treatment was introduced into the control group at a later time, and the production of this group before and after the change was contrasted. Morse and Reimer (1956) varied conditions of supervision in an organization by training supervisors in one group of offices to delegate and decentralize, and those in a similar group of offices to exercise closer supervision over employees.

An approach that has promise lies somewhere between the manipulation of existing organizations and the creation of laboratory group situations. It involves the simulation of complex organizational activity, varying factors that are more complex than those of the experimental situation and less complex than those of the real organization (Guetzkow 1962). Simulation has been used most often to date for purposes other than environmental variation: to provide a controlled context for training (Cohen & Rhenman, 1961), a constant background for the observation of behavioral processes (Chapman, Kennedy, Newell, & Biel, 1959), or constant conditions for the evaluation of individual performance (Hemphill, Griffiths, & Fredericksen, 1962). Simulation, however, offers a useful opportunity to vary some aspects of an organization while holding others constant, and for observing the effects of such variation on behavior. Bass (1963), for example, has developed simulated manufacturing organizations in which complexity of line-staff organization, among other properties, can be varied. Bass studied such variations with respect to both groups' productive efficiency (sales, costs, profits) and individual reactions (satisfaction, communication, style, and interpersonal relations).

EFFECTS OF CLIMATE

The literature would profit from surveys both of studies of dimensions of organizations (along the lines of the Golembiewski, 1962b, analysis of small group dimensions) and of studies of the effects of organizational variables (along the lines of the Thomas and Fink, 1963, review of the effects of group size). In this section and the next we have set for ourselves somewhat more modest objectives: an examination of some possible mechanisms by means of which climate might affect behavior, and of some classes of variables that will need to be considered in any attempt to define dimensions. This strategy stems in part from the difficulty of assembling—or even finding—the relevant literature. But it may also be argued that such an approach is a necessary component of any attempt to get order into this field. For example, one of the few general hypotheses concerning organizational variation that has been investigated with any degree of thoroughness might be stated as follows: An organization in which personnel policies are participative, democratic, unstructured, will differ from one whose practices are nonparticipative, authoritarian, or structured in that productivity, and employee satisfaction will be higher. There is evidence in support of this hypothesis, much of it summarized by Likert (1961). There is other evidence that the hypothesis may be true for satisfaction but not for productivity (Blau & Scott, 1962; Morse & Reimer, 1956), and that it may be true for some jobs or some parts of an organization, but not for others (Leavitt, 1962b). Uncertainty about whether the hypothesis is generally true, or if not, when it is true and when it is not, will have to prevail until certain questions are asked. First, what organizational properties differentiate a structured from a nonstructured environment? Barnes' (1960) open system, Morse and Reimer's (1956) decentralization of authority, and Day and Hamblin's (1961) general (as opposed to close) supervision are interpreted similarly but are defined by widely differing operational criteria. Can we assume that they have some organizational property in common to a degree sufficient to permit comparison of their effects? These questions concern dimensions of organizational variation and are considered further in the next section. The second question is: Why should we expect such an organizational property to have such an effect? With respect to the specific hypothesis stated above, answers to the question seem to rest more often on ideological than on theoretical grounds. The question of the way in which the environment impinges on the individual to affect behavior needs to be asked if the hypothesis is to have significance beyond its application in a specific context.

Two kinds of influence may be distinguished. A particular organizational property may influence the behavior of all or almost all members of the organization. This kind of relationship will be termed "direct influence": The general hypothesis of direct influence is that aggregate behavior under one organizational condition will differ from that under another. The second kind of influence, which will be termed "interactive influence," exists when an organizational condition has a certain effect upon the behavior of some independent identifiable persons, but another effect, or no effect, on that of others.

A number of studies have examined the influence of particular organizational variables, but few attempts have been made, either before or after the data are in, to posit a mechanism for such influence. Empirical results, therefore, give few clues as to the nature of such mechanisms. The following classification of ways in which climate may affect behavior is an attempt to formulate and clarify hypotheses concerning such effects with the realization that available results will not fall neatly into the categories. Organizational climate may affect behavior by: defining the stimuli which confront the individual, placing constraints upon the freedom of choice of behavior, and/or rewarding and punishing behavior.

Definition of Stimuli

If behavior of organization members is determined in part by their perceptions of the organizational environment, as several observers (e.g., Likert, 1961) have postulated, then behavior will be influenced by variations in the objects or events available to be perceived, that is, in stimuli. One difficulty in examining such effects is that of specifying the meaning of stimulus in a complex situation. Arnoult (1963) has described a social stimulus, in response to Gibson's (1960) questions, as follows:

> *(a)* it may have motivational properties; *(b)* it is the *occasion* rather than the *cause* of a response . . . ; *(c)* it must frequently be defined in terms of the response it elicits; *(d)* it exists in the environment and not just at the receptors; *(e)* it can be a pattern or sequence of events; *(f)* its structure must often be inferred from the structure of the response which it elicits; and *(g)* it carried information about its source in the environment [pp. 19–20].

Thus defined stimulus variation is essentially equivalent to environmental variation as we have discussed it here. Other investigators have also approached the entire problem in terms of stimulus properties of the situation (Helson, Blake, & Mouton, 1958; Rosenbaum, 1956; Sells, 1963c). The emphasis of this section is on Property b of Arnoult's classification and here we are concerned with ways in which organizational variation brings about variation in the occasion of a response.

The physical properties of organizational situations are recognized more or less explicitly in systems research. Chapman et al. (1959), for example, outlined procedures used in the experimental evaluation of an air control system for presenting stimuli, controlling extraneous stimuli, and directing the attention of subjects. Stimulus elements of machine design have been a classical focus for research on man-machine systems (Gregg, 1961).

A second, and more complex, set of occasions for response consists of the task-relevant information available to the individual. The likelihood that information is differentially distributed among members of an organization is suggested by Cyert and March's (1963, pp. 101 ff.) model of the organization as a communication system. One of the functions performed by operating procedures in such a system is the distribution and condensation of information that comes into the organization. The effect of social structure upon the transmission of this information is illustrated by Blau's (1954) study of interviewers in an employment agency. Competitiveness among work group members—which varied with "climate" conditions, such as security of employment, opportunity for development of a common professional orientation, and supervisory evaluation procedures—was manifested most clearly in the hoarding of information concerning job openings: members of the more competitive group resorted to various illicit means to withhold such information from their colleagues, in an effort to maximize their comparative record of job placements. Similar information-withholding practices have been observed by Argyris (1962). One source of behavioral effects of variations in information transmission is the likelihood that, regardless of the motivational and freedom-of-choice variables in a situation, some behaviors never occur because the stimuli that would elicit them are never presented. Another is suggested by evidence that one's expectations and evaluation of his own performance are influenced by information about the expectations and evaluation of co-workers (Neimark & Rosenberg, 1959; Rosenberg & Hall, 1958; Zander & Curtis, 1962).

A third subset of stimulus elements that depend upon climate variables includes the behavior of individuals and social interactions within the organization. Organizations may define certain patterns of behavior to be appropriate, as discussed below, and thus restrict the social stimuli available to organization members. Studies of interpersonal perception have indicated that social judgments are influenced by a number of properties of the perceived, including status, role, and visibility of the trait to be judged (Costello & Zalkind, 1963, pp. 46–47). All of these properties can be influenced by organizational climate; the visibility variable will serve as an illustration. Goffman (1959) suggests that the stimulus qualities of a person's behavior result from a more-or-less conscious role-taking strategy. An organizational rule of thumb that limits or defines appropriate role-taking behaviors (e.g., formality of relationships with subordinates) might, therefore, suppress or heighten the visibility of a particular behavioral cue.

There is, of course, much evidence that perceptions are influenced by abilities, values, and personality traits of the perceiver (Bruner, 1958; Costello & Zalkind, 1963, pp. 45–46; Taft, 1955) and by his organizational role (Dearborn & Simon, 1958). Individuals are thus expected to be differentially sensitive to organizational stimuli, and if variation in organizational and personal variables is observed simultaneously, we might expect to find interactions. For example, ability to perceive subtle variations in standard operating procedures, sources of influence, and status may be more relevant to success as an administrator when information about these organizational characteristics is made available informally, inaccurately, or not at all, than when it is disseminated systematically in bulletins or memos. One source of conflict in organizations stems from uncertainty about organizational goals (March & Simon, 1959). An information transition system that produces such uncertainty will increase the relevance of the personality characteristic that has been called uncertainty absorption—the capacity to set premise for the decision of subordinates and peers despite the ambiguity of the environment (Guetzkow & Forehand, 1961). There could be many more examples; these serve to illustrate the interaction hypotheses that might be investigated by varying stimulus characteristics of organizational climate.

Constraints upon Freedom

The stimulus conditions of the organizational environment place bounds upon the set of behaviors that might be selected. Within these bounds, there are additional restrictions imposed by the formal and informal characteristics of an organization, in the form of routine, institutionalized procedures, or of intended or unintended evaluation criteria that place a premium on particular kinds of solution to problems. Hauge (1964), for example, argues that specialization is a threat to diversity and freedom because it "spells a narrowing of the alternatives."

The constraining effects of environment have been emphasized by theorists concerned with creativity. Rogers (1954), for example, maintained that psychological freedom, psychological safety, and a nonevaluative atmosphere are essential conditions in the environment for creativity. Studies of organizational conditions under which scientists work indicate that the extent of constraint varies among organizations, and that it has an effect upon the satisfactions and productivity of the scientists (Vollmer, 1962, 1963).

The origins of such constraints often lie in rules and procedures designed to enable the efficient conduct of complex organizational activities (Cyert & March, 1963) and for keeping delegated decision on the track of organizational goals (Strauss, 1963). It is clear that such procedures are necessary but also that they can have unintended consequences of ruling out certain kinds of behavior (March & Simon, 1959). There is evidence of variations in the degree to which organizations rely upon rules and procedures (Dill, 1958; Forehand & Guetzkow, 1962), and of concomitant variation in degree of autonomy of individuals (Dill, 1958) and of satisfactions (Herzberg, Mausner, & Snyderman 1959), and for the general proposition that "programmed activity drives out unprogrammed acitivity" (March & Simon, 1959).

The most notable effect of such constraints, however, may be interactive in nature. There is evidence from differential studies (e.g., Crites, 1961) that individuals vary in their preference for constraining versus free environments. Thus the performance and satisfaction of individuals would depend upon the particular combination of person and environment. A number of studies provide evidence of interactions between environmental freedom and personal traits. Forehand and Guetzkow (1962) found different patterns of correlations between test-measured characteristics and ratings of innovative behaviors in different climates. With supervisors' ratings as a criterion, interpersonal variables such as dominance and need for aggression were most highly related in rule-centered organizations, while cognitive variables such as flexibility and sensitivity to problems were more highly related in group-centered organizations. Barnes (1960) found differential relations between satisfaction and productivity in a closed versus an open system of work-group interrelations. Lodahl and Porter (1961) found that in small (4–13 men) industrial work groups, homogeneity of members with respect to supervisory attitudes was related to productivity when necessity for work-group cooperation was high, but not when it was low or moderate. Thus, the importance of being like other people in the group depends upon an organizational characteristic.

Another source of constraining influence stems from outside the boundaries of the organization—from the cultural setting in which the organization functions. Haire, Ghiselli, and Porter (1963) found that managers' attitudes toward management in different countries followed a pattern more closely associated with cultural variation than with degree of industrialization, which has frequently been posited as a determinant of attitudes. Thus, managers from Spain and Italy tended to agree more in attitudes toward management—despite their dissimilarity in degree of industrialization—than did, for example, managers from Italy and Denmark whose degrees of industrialization are more similar. Dill (1958) has noted variations in the environment of organizations on a much smaller geographical scale, that is, within countries or even within cities.

The effects of restraint of freedom are not always negative. Blau and Scott (1962) conclude from a review of communication studies, that a hierarchical organization may be more effective than a nonhierarchical organization in facilitating the coordination of work because of the restriction in the flow of communication, while a nonhierarchical organization is more effective in producing new ideas. The establishment of functional roles in a group can also aid the attainment of group goals, while at the same time restricting the freedom of choice of individuals (Golembiewski, 1962b).

Reward and Punishment

Two kinds of effects of stimulus restriction and behavioral constraint have been assumed in the literature. In the first place, they have the result of selecting behaviors simply by permitting some possible responses and precluding others. It has also been assumed that these organizational properties have motivating effects. The human relations emphasis, for example, has assumed that freedom from constraint will generally result in greater satisfaction. Several bases for motivating effects are plausible. First, different organizational properties carry differential opportunity for satisfying the values that employees bring with them into the organization (Vroom, 1960). Secondly, there is growing support for the hypothesis that diversity of stimulation is intrinsically motivating (Fiske & Maddi, 1961). Finally, the mechanism that has received most attention in the literature is the capacity of groups and organizations to reward and punish behavior systematically.

The power of the work group to reward and punish is illustrated in many studies. Among the properties of work groups that may serve a motivating function are cohesiveness (Likert, 1961) and congruence of attitudes (Blau & Scott, 1962). Blau and Scott find evidence that behavior shifts from that which accords with the individual's own values to that which accords with the values of his work group, and interpret such shifts in terms of rewards and punishments provided by the work group.

Properties of larger organizational units also have motivational effects. The findings of Herzberg et al. (1959) suggest that such properties are more likely to have a punishing than a rewarding effect. The factors most often mentioned by the respondents as determinants of dissatisfaction centered about the context of the job—for example, supervision and working conditions—while the factors determining satisfaction were more often characteristics of the job itself—for example, the nature of the work, accomplishment, and responsibility. It should be pointed out that defense mechanisms affecting the perceptions of respondents might account for this finding (Vroom & Maier, 1961).

Among the hypothetically influential properties of organizational reward systems identified by March and Simon (1959, pp. 61 ff.) are: amount of reward, dependence of promotion and monetary reward on performance, the perceived operationality of criteria, and independence of individual rewards. These variables may have both direct and interactive effects.

For example, March and Simon proposed (p. 70) that competition among group members will be inversly related to independence of individual rewards; observations of behavior in zero-sum games support this hypothesis (Blake & Mouton, 1961, 1962). Conditions that lead to intragroup competition would be expected to differentially affect persons depending on their own typical level of competitiveness. Blau (1954) in fact, found that personal competitiveness was related to productivity in a competitive work group, but not in a noncompetitive work group.

DIMENSIONS OF ORGANIZATIONAL VARIATION

What we have called organizational climate has often been discussed in terms of analogy with individual personality. The validity and implications of the analogy are discussed below, but the analogy is particularly useful in discussing the problem of dimensions. Organizational behavior, like human behavior, is characterized by an overwhelming number of variations. Talking about them requires some way to select and classify them; hence, the search for dimensions—or traits—of organizations. The question of dimensions might be approached empirically in two different ways. First, dimensions might be defined in terms of covariation among many indices of organizational behavior, directly in the tradition of statistical definition of traits. Secondly, organizational variables might be organized according to the effects that they exert, or might be expected to exert, on individuals. These approaches are neither mutually dependent nor mutually exclusive; it is probable that both kinds of analyses will need to be undertaken. Several writers have proposed taxonomies of environmental situations, on the basis of both empirical (Hemphill, 1956; Palmer, 1961) and logical (Golembiewski, 1962b; Sells, 1963b) grounds, while others have reviewed the evidence of dependable effects of specific organizational properties (Thomas & Fink, 1963).

The variables discussed below have been established neither as factors accounting for covariation nor as dependable determinants of behavior; they may be considered as likely candidates for such status in future research. The five variables discussed here—size, organization structure, systems complexity, leadership pattern, and goal directions—were culled from a list of about 30 properties mentioned in studies and discussions of organizational variation.

Size

Thomas & Fink (1963) reviewed 31 studies of effects of group size—with size varying from two to twenty members—on group performance, distribution of participation, nature of interaction, group organization, individual performance, conformity, and consensus and member satisfaction. They point out that size may be considered "phenotypic and really but a correlate of the social and psychological condition capable of producing changes in member and group behavior," and suggest, as intervening variables, resource input (e.g., skills, knowledge), demand input (e.g. members' need for recognition, social interaction), and potential relational complexity.

As one moves from small groups to large organizations, size takes on a different significance. As the number of possible person-to person interactions increase, the capacity of individuals to form relationships becomes exhausted. A result is the development of small face-to-face subgroups within the large organization, and of pressures toward cohesiveness and adoption of subgroup norms, sometimes at the expense of larger organizational goals (Blau & Scott, 1962; Golembiewski, 1962b; Thomas & Fink, 1963).

The effects of group size upon an individual depend in large measure on the individual's position within the organization. The Thomas-Fink review, as well as studies in applied settings (e.g., Baumgartel & Sobol, 1959; Talacchi, 1960; Thomas, 1959), suggests that satisfaction of work-group members decreases as size of work group increases. Frequently mentioned as factors in this relationship are varying opportunities for participation and for satisfaction of achievement and affiliation needs. In the large organization, the existence of sub-groups has the effect of removing the individual from goals of the organization. If the individual is to be evaluated according to production criteria, his evaluated performance may be influenced by conflicts between organizational and subgroup goals (e.g., with regard to quotas). The accoutrements of procedures for efficiency—systems of authority, status, technology, and financial control—place even greater constraints on the individual's opportunity to satisfy personal needs.

For the manager, increasing organizational size may require different sets of skills (Ghiselli, 1963; Haire, 1959). The face-to-face techniques of management must give way to dealing with subgroups and coordinating their outputs. Thus, size may well be a factor influencing correlates of managerial success (Guetzkow & Forehand 1961).

Structure

Closely related to variables in size, and often varying with them, are variations in the structure of authority and relationships among persons and groups. Evan (1963) summarized evidence that organizations differ widely in the degree of hierarchical organizations of skills, rewards, and authority. There have been many assumptions about behavioral consequences of different kinds of structure, but relatively few empirical attempts to verify them.

Porter and Lawler (1963) examined the proposition most clearly put forward by Worthy (1950) that "flat" (i.e., decentralized) organizations are superior to "tall" (centralized) organizations with respect to satisfaction of employees' needs. They studied responses of over 1,900 managers, classified as belonging to tall, intermediate, and flat organizations, according to the ratio of levels of supervision relative to size. They found no evidence of superiority of flat organizations across all the organizations. There was evidence, however, of interaction between size and shape of the organization: in relatively small organizations (under 5,000 employees), the extent to which managers report their needs to be satisfied was higher for flat than for tall organizations, but in companies with more than 5,000 employees, reported need satisfaction was greater for tall organizations.

Experimental studies, especially those involving communication networks, indicate that satisfaction with job and results are greater in structures with a wider spread of participation. In more centralized structures, satisfaction is highest in the more central positions (Glanzer & Glaser, 1961; Golembiewski, 1962b). There is also evidence that centralized structures are more effective than noncentralized structures for coordinating results, the responsibility for which falls mainly to persons in central positions. These results help to explain why the managers studied by Porter and Lawler (1963) found the tall organization more satisfying in large organizations. Such a structure may give the manager more control over organizational activity and more opportunity for creative contribution than would a flat structure. Porter and Lawler suggest that the effect of structure on need satisfaction might depend upon the individuals position in the organization and that nonmanagers might respond differently.

Another structural variation has been noted by some observers, but has received little research attention; that is, the tendency of the model organizational pattern to shift from a "pyramidal" structure—with workers in the majority at the base—to a "hexagonal structure." The hexagonal structure has blue-collar workers at the base, about equal in number to the top management team, with the largest group, represented in the middle, being professional staff people and those who support them. An implication of the structure of difference of the performance of managers is the problem of the effective supervision of these highly individualistic staff professionals. For the "man in the middle" the difference might be associated with increased conflicts between organizational and professional objectives, decreased opportunity to select assignments and working patterns, and decreased apparent relevance of his work to the functioning of the organization as a whole.

Systems Complexity

The concept of system as a collection of elements functioning together has generated a wide variety of research relevant to organizational behavior. Since analysis of a system implies definition of its elements and quantitative study of their interactions (Peach, 1962), such research can result in unprecedentedly precise descriptions of organizational units (e.g., Chapman et al., 1959; Miller, 1962). While this approach has not yet reached the point of providing comparisons of complex organizational properties and their effects, it appears likely to contribute to that objective.

The systems concept provides several ways of describing environmental variation, and there is little basis for predicting which ones will be useful. One potentially definable variable will serve as an example. Organizations may vary in the complexity of the systems that they employ. Complexity can be defined in terms of the number of components and the number and nature of the interactions among them. It seems likely that variations in systems complexity will be associated with variation in both stimulus availability and behavioral constraint. The part that social elements play in the system offers other opportunities for defining variations in climate (Michael, 1959).

Leadership Style

The various approaches to defining leadership traits (Petrullo & Bass, 1961) also can be applied to the description of organizations, since significant organizational properties are controlled by persons in leadership positions. Thus a tentative measure of aspects of climate may be obtained by simply taking personality measurements of leaders. For example, Vroom and Mann (1960) and Haythorn, Couch, Haefner, Langham, and Carter (1956) studied follower behavior as a function of leaders' degree of authoritarianism.

The studies of participative management practices, summarized in preceding pages, also illustrate the feasibility of defining leadership style as a dimension of organizational climate. These studies, for the most part, created the contrast experimentally by training or instructing leaders. A further question would ask whether the influence of such variation extends past the individual—whether the variation is truly characteristic of organizations rather than simply of certain individuals. There is some evidence that organizations can be reliably described in terms of typical leadership practices (Baumgartel, 1957; Forehand & Guetzkow, 1962) and that such variation has systematic effects. There is, however, insufficient data as yet to make a conclusion about the generality of such findings.

Goal Directions

Variation in organizational goals is obvious to observers of organizations. Such variation has provided one basis for classifying organizations, for example, as business, government, or philanthropic organizations. Even among business organizations, of which the profit motive might be the most characteristic feature, there is variation with regard to the relative weight placed on subsidiary goals (e.g., dominance of market, avoidance of conflict with government). That such variation would affect behavior of organization members should be expected, in view of the role played by organizational goals in defining the aspects of behavior to be rewarded and punished.

The range of variation in factors affecting behavior may not be as great as that of overall organizational objectives. The sub-goals chosen to accomplish the overall objectives (e.g, efficiency, cooperation) may be quite similar despite wide differences in the ultimate goals, and hence the pressures on individuals may be similar. Evidence of relationships between organizational goals and participants' behavior is scarce, partially because of the difficulty of specifying such goals unambiguously and partially because the influence of goals cannot be separated from other organizational qualities (e.g., leadership style). Studies of college environments (Thistlethwaite, 1960) indicate that such effects may exist, however. It was possible to identify schools associated with students' motives to seek higher education in humanities and social sciences as contrasted with those associated with motivation to seek advanced degrees in the natural and biological sciences. The former are characterized by faculty affiliation, enthusiasm and emphasis on achievement, humanism and independence; the latter by a lack of emphasis on compliance. Goals of work groups defined on more specific and more structured situations have received more intensive research attention, and the mechanisms by which conformity pressures are exerted have been explored (Blau & Scott, 1962; Lawrence & Smith, 1955).

Organizational goals may also interact with personal characteristics, particularly the motives of individual organization members. Such interaction may be manifested in several ways: *(a)* The extent to which the individual perceives and understands the organization's goals may depend upon his own skills and attitudes (Vroom, 1960). *(b)* The individual who, for one reason or another, responds to his own goals, ignoring those of his organization, can succeed to the extent that his goals coincide with those of the organization. *(c)* The individual who responds both to his own and to his organization's goals faces the possibility of conflict, depending upon what his own goals are. The particular form of the conflict and the attempted resolution both depend in large part on personal factors.

DISCUSSION

This paper has focused mainly upon opportunities for the operational study of environmental variation afforded by organizational research. We have on several occasions drawn an analogy between the climate of an organization and the personality of an individual in order to bring attention to issues in the study of environment. There often appear in the literature, particularly the management literature, suggestions and assumptions that the analogy can be taken more literally, that climate may be treated as a construct, and the "personality of an organization" identified and dealt with.

It has sometimes been suggested that the matching of organizational and individual characteristics would maximize both organizational effectiveness and individual satisfaction. Such a conclusion is suggested by theories and evidence of interactive effects. If the suggestion is implemented mechanically, however, it does not allow room for change, either of the organization or the person. The matching strategy may hinder both the organization and the person from adapting readily to new situations—the former by the inbreeding of inflexibility, and the latter by the limitation placed on the individual's range of experience (McMurray, 1958).

A number of social scientists have suggested a different kind of application of the climate concept: the achievement of organizational change by means of changing the climate. Leavitt (1964) reviews a number of plans for organizational change that focus on "people variables" in the organizational system (in contrast with plans focusing on structure, technology, and task variables). The most influential of these Leavitt terms "power equalization" approaches. The power equalization approaches include client-centered therapy, "T-group" training, and economic distribution devices like the Scanlon Plan.

They share an emphasis upon pushing the power and responsibility for decision making as far down in the organizational hierarchy as possible, establishing relationships of mutual trust and authenticity, and keeping all channels of communication open. They also share assumptions that employees, in general, will be more satisfied and more productive when working under such conditions; individual differences in response to climate are not taken into account. Finally, the climate concept has been invoked to account for differences in results of management training programs (Fleishman, 1953; Guetzkow, Forehand & James, 1962).

These and similar suggestions are promising leads for research and strategy. They rest on the assumption that there is such a thing as a general atmosphere, personality, or climate within an organization. Several implications of this assumption will need to be investigated before the usefulness of climate as a construct is established.

1. Identification of Comparable Organizational Units. According to the personality analogy, organizational climate is a concept based upon covariation of individual differences among organizations. The identification of what organizational units are to serve the role of persons in this model is a complex problem. An individual is a member of many organizations—a face-to-face work group, department, divisions, etc.—which coexist and interact within a larger organizational unit. Environmental characteristics need not covary systematically between levels of a single organization: a department may be rule centered even if the company is not, and vice versa. When a group of organizations are chosen for study some effort to establish their comparability is needed, unless the study deliberately focuses on variation across levels of organization. One possible approach when individual subjects are involved is to focus on an individual's superior and all of the superior's subordinates or the superior's superior and all of his subordinates, etc. In this way, one can obtain comparable organizational units from widely ranging organizations (Forehand, 1963).

2. Homogeneity within the Organizational Unit. The description of a company personality implies a degree of homogeneity within the company that may be seldom found. The definition of a climate dimension requires evidence that: the objective determinants of the dimension are applicable to all subunits, and the dimension is perceived comparably by individuals in the subunits.

3. Relative Permanence. One of the major ambiguities in definitions of climate has resulted from failure to come to grips with the problem of permanence. The term has been used to refer to organizational properties defined by a given leader and thus sensitive to normal personnel change. On the other hand, it sometimes refers to properties that have become traditionalized through policy, procedures, or objective constraints. If climate is to have meaning as a construct, with meaning distinguished from that of leadership, a criterion of relative permanence would seem appropriate to its definition.

4. Mode of Combination of Organizational Properties. As the preceding discussion has stated, present evidence permits no definitive description of dimensions of organizational variation. The attempt to define the climate of an organization raises a different and more complex question about which there is available no evidence: the question of the way in which dimensions are best combined to describe a particular organization. A meaningful combination may be a linear one, but it seems more likely that it will be a pattern or configuration.

The usefulness of the procedures developed for studying climate need not depend upon the establishment of climate as a generally applicable theoretical construct, for the procedures are applicable to the much more general problem of specification of the environment. We have mentioned a number of hypotheses and research approaches toward this end in this paper, and they need not be repeated. They may be summarized in terms of two directions for research that seem especially salient to the problem of studying environmental variation.

1. Measurement. As we have seen, there is no lack of ingenious ideas for the measurement of organizational properties. It is seldom clear, however, that two investigators using the same names for their variables are talking about the same, or even correlated, dimensions. It is for this problem that borrowing from the techniques of differential psychology seems most appropriate. Two approaches can be suggested. The attempt to define dimensions of organizational variation via factor analyses (Hemphill, 1956; Katzell et al., 1961; Palmer, 1961) has yielded results encouraging extensions to a wider range of organizations and organizational properties. A second differential concept that needs emphasis is that of validity, particularly convergent and discriminant validity (Campbell & Fiske, 1959). The multitrait multimethod matrix recommended by Campbell and Fiske for validation of personality tests also provides a model for validating climate measures. Rule centeredness, for example, measured by participants' perceptions, ought to correlate more highly with the same variable measured by an objective count than with a different variable measured by perceptions. Otherwise the perceptual process, rather than the organization's properties, accounts for variance in the measure. Studies of this sort would not only validate the measures for use in future experiments, but would also contribute information about the nature of effective organizational variation.

2. Interaction Studies. Many approaches to the study of behavior assume that either the person or the environment varies, but not both at the same time. Both the theoretical disadvantage and the practical inutility of such an approach have been demonstrated (Cronbach, 1957; Helson, 1964). Studies of organizations make possible the variation of both sets of variables, and thus provide not only a greater understanding of the functions of organizations, but also a chance to test psychological hypotheses about the interaction of the individual and his environment.

REFERENCES

Abelson, R. P. Commentary: Situational variables in personality research. In S. Messick and J. Ross (eds.), *Measurement in personality and cognition.* New York: Wiley, 1962.

Argyris, C. Some problems in conceptualizing organizational climate: A case study of a bank. *Administrative Science Quarterly,* 1958, **2**, 501–20.

Argyris, C. *Interpersonal competence and organizational effectiveness.* Homewood, Ill.: Dorsey Press, 1962.

Arnoult, M. D. The specification of a "social" stimulus. In S. B. Sells (ed.), *Stimulus determinants of behavior.* New York: Ronald Press, 1963.

Barnes, L. B. *Organizational systems and engineering groups.* Boston: Harvard University, Graduate School of Business Administration, 1960.

Barton, A. H. *Organizational measurement and its bearing on college environments.* New York: College Entrance Examination Board, 1961.

Bass, B. M. Experimenting with simulated manufacturing organizations. In S. B. Sells (ed.), *Stimulus determinants of behavior.* New York: Ronald Press, 1963.

Baumgartel, H. Leadership style as a variable in research administration. *Administrative Science Quarterly,* 1957, **2**, 344–60.

Baumgartel, H. and Sobol, R. Background and organization factors in absenteeism. *Personnel Psychology,* 1959, **12**, 431–43.

Blake, R. R. and Mouton, Jane S. Loyalty of representatives to in-group positions during interpersonal competition. *Sociometry,* 1961, **24**, 177–83.

Blake, R. R. and Mouton, Jane S. Comprehension of points of communality in competing solutions. *Sociometry,* 1962, **25**, 56–63.

Blau, P. M. Co-operation and competition in a bureaucracy. *American Journal of Sociology,* 1954, **59**, 530–35.

Blau, P. M. and Scott, W. R. *Formal organizations.* San Francisco, Calif.: Chandler, 1962.

Bruner, J. Social psychology and perception. In Eleanor Maccoby, T. Newcomb, and E. Hartley (eds.), *Readings in social psychology.* (3d ed.) New York: Holt, Rinehart, & Winston, 1958.

Brunswik, E. *Perception and the representative design of psychological experiments.* Berkeley: University of California Press, 1956.

Campbell, D. T. and Fiske, D. W. Convergent and discriminant validation by the multitrait-multimethod matrix. *Psychological Bulletin,* 1959, **56**, 81–105.

Chapman, R. L., Kennedy, J. L., Newell, A., and Biel, W. C. The Systems Research Laboratory's air defense experiments. *Management Science,* 1959, **5**, 250–69.

Coch, L. and French, J. R. P. Overcoming resistance to change. *Human Relations,* 1948, **1**, 512–32.

Cohen, K. J. and Rhenman, E. The role of management games in education and research. *Management Science,* 1961, **7**, 131–66.

Costello, T. W. and Zalkind, S. S. *Psychology in administration: A research orientation.* Englewood Cliffs, N.J.: Prentice-Hall, 1963.

Crites, J. O. Factor analytic definitions of vocational adjustment. *Journal of Applied Psychology,* 1961, **45**, 330–37.

Cronbach, L. J. The two disciplines of scientific psychology. *American Psychologist,* 1957, **12**, 671–84.

Cyert, R. M. and March, J. G. *A behavioral theory of the firm.* Englewood Cliffs, N.J.: Prentice-Hall, 1963.

Day, R. C. and Hamblin, R. L. Some effects of close and punitive styles of supervision. Technical Report No. 8, 1961, Contract Nonr 816(11), Office of Naval Research.

Dearborn, D. C. and Simon, H. A. Selective perception: A note on the departmental identification of executives. *Sociometry,* 1958, **21**, 140–44.

Dill, W. R. Environment as an influence on managerial autonomy. *Administrative Science Quarterly,* 1958, **2**, 409–43.

Dill, W. R., Hilton, T. L., and Reitman, W. R. *The new managers.* Englewood Cliffs, N.J.: Prentice-Hall, 1962.

Evan, W. M. Indices of the hierarchical structure of industrial organizations. *Management Science,* 1963, **9**, 468–77.

Fiske, D. W. and Maddi, S. (eds.). *Functions of varied experience.* Homewood, Ill.: Dorsey Press, 1961.

Fleishman, E. A. Leadership climate, human relations training and supervision. *Personnel Psychology,* 1953, **6**, 205–22.

Fleishman, E. A. and Harris, E. F. Patterns of leadership behavior related to employee grievances and turnover. *Personnel Psychology,* 1962, **15**, 43–56.

Forehand, G. A. Assessments of innovative behavior: Partial criteria for the assessment of executive performance. *Journal of Applied Psychology,* 1963, **47**, 206–13.

Forehand, G. A. and Guetzkow, H. Characteristics related to innovative administrative behavior in varying organizational climates. In *Education for innovative behavior in executives.* (Final report, Cooperative Research Project No. 975) Washington, D.C.: United States Office of Education, 1962.

Gellerman, S. W. *People, problem and profits.* New York: McGraw-Hill, 1960.

Ghiselli, E. E. Managerial talent. *American Psychologist,* 1963, **18**, 631–42.

Gibson, J. J. The concept of the stimulus in psychology. *American Psychologist,* 1960, **15**, 694–703.

Gilmer, B. v. H. *Industrial psychology.* New York: McGraw-Hill, 1961.

Glanzer, H. and Glaser, R. Techniques for the study of group structure and behavior: II. Empirical studies of the effects of structure in small groups. *Psychological Bulletin,* 1961, **58**, 1–27.

Goffman, E. *The presentation of self in everyday life.* New York: Anchor Books, 1959.

Golembiewski, R. T. *Behavior and organization: O & M and the small group.* Chicago: Rand-McNally, 1962. (a)

Golembiewski, R. T. *The small group: An analysis of research concepts and operations.* Chicago: University of Chicago Press, 1962. (b)

Gregg, L. W. Engineering psychology. In B. v. H. Gilmer, *Industrial psychology.* New York: McGraw-Hill, 1961.

Guetzkow, H. (ed.). *Simulation in social science: Readings.* Englewood Cliffs, N.J.: Prentice-Hall, 1962.

Guetzkow, H. and Bowes, A. E. The development of organizations in the laboratory. *Management Science,* 1957, **3**, 380–402.

Guetzkow, H. and Forehand, G. A. A research strategy for partial knowledge useful in the selection of executives. In R. Tagiuri (ed.), *Research needs in executive selection.* Boston: Harvard University, Graduate School of Business Administration, 1961.

Guetzkow, H., Forehand, G. A., and James, B. J. An evaluation of educational influence on executive judgment. *Administrative Science Quarterly,* 1962, **6**, 483–500.

Haire, M. Biological models and empirical histories of the growth of organizations. In M. Haire (ed.), *Modern organization theory.* New York: Wiley, 1959.

Haire, M., Ghiselli, E. E., and Porter, L. W. Cultural patterns in the role of the manager. *Industrial Relations,* 1963, **2**, 95–117.

Hauge, G. *The individual in the modern economic world.* Pittsburgh, Pa.: Carnegie Press, 1964.

Haythorn, W., Couch, A., Haefner, D., Langham, P., and Carter, L. F. The behavior of authoritarian and equalitarian personalities in groups. *Human Relations,* 1956, **9**, 58–74.

Helson, H. Current trends and issues in adaptation-level theory. *American Psychologist,* 1964, **19**, 26–38.

Helson, H., Blake, R. R., and Mouton, Jane S. Petition-signing as adjustment to situational and personal factors. *Journal of Social Psychology,* 1958, **48**, 3–10.

Hemphill, J. K. *Group dimensions: A manual for their measurement.* Columbus, O.: Ohio State University, Bureau of Business Research, 1956.

Hemphill, J. K., Griffiths, D. E., and Fredericksen, N. *Administrative behavior: A study of the principal in a simulated elementary school.* New York: Columbia University, Teachers College, 1962.

Herzberg, F., Mausner, B., and Snyderman, Barbara B. *The motivation to work.* New York: Wiley, 1959.

Katzell, R. A., Barrett, R. S., and Parker, T. C. Job satisfaction, job performance, and situational characteristics. *Journal of Applied Psychology,* 1961, **45**, 65–72.

Kidd, J. S. and Christy, T. Supervisory procedures and work-team productivity. *Journal of Applied Psychology,* 1961, **45**, 388–92.

Lawrence, L. C. and Smith, P. C. Group decision and employee participation. *Journal of Applied Psychology,* 1955, **39**, 334–37.

Leavitt, H. J. Toward organizational psychology. In B. v. H. Gilmer (ed.), *Walter Van Dyke Bingham Memorial Program.* Pittsburgh, Pa.: Carnegie Institute of Technology, 1962. (a)

Leavitt, H. J. Unhuman organization. *Harvard Business Review,* 1962, **40**, 90–98. (b)

Leavitt, H. J. Applied organizational change in industry: Structural, technological and humanistic approaches. In J. G. March (ed.), *Handbook of organizations.* Chicago: Rand-McNally, 1964.

Leavitt, H. J. and Bass, B. M. Organizational psychology. *Annual Review of Psychology,* 1964, **15**, 371–98.

Lewin, K., Lippitt, R., and White, R. K. Patterns of aggressive behavior in experimentally created "social climates." *Journal of Social Psychology,* 1939, **10**, 271–99.

Likert, R. *New patterns of management.* New York: McGraw-Hill, 1961.

Lodahl, T. M. and Porter, L. W. Psychometric score patterns, social characteristics, and productivity of small industrial work groups. *Journal of Applied Psychology,* 1961, **45**, 73–79.

McMurry, R. N. Recruitment, dependence, and morale in the banking industry. *Administrative Science Quarterly,* 1958, **3**, 87–117.

March, J. G. and Simon, H. A. *Organizations.* New York: Wiley, 1959.

Michael, D. N. The social environment. *Operations Research* 1959, **7**, 506–23.

Miller, R. B. Task description and analysis. In R. M. Gagné (ed.), *Psychological principles in systems development.* New York: Holt, Rinehart, & Winston, 1962.

Morse, Nancy and Reimer, E. The experimental change of a major organization variable. *Journal of Abnormal and Social Psychology,* 1956, **52**, 120–29.

Murray, H. A. *Explorations in personality.* New York: Oxford University Press, 1938.

Neimark, Edith D. and Rosenberg, S. The effect of "social" discriminative cues. *Journal of Experimental Psychology,* 1959, **58**, 302-11.

Pace, C. R. Implications of differences in campus atmosphere for evaluation and planning of college programs. In R. L. Sutherland, W. H. Holtzman, E. A. Koile, and B. K. Smith (eds.), *Personality factors on the college campus.* Austin, Tex.: Hogg Foundation for Mental Health, 1962.

Pace, C. R. and Stern, G. C. An approach to the measurement of psychological characteristics of college environments. *Journal of Educational Psychology,* 1958, **49**, 269–77.

Palmer, G. J. Test of a theory of leadership and organization behavior with management gaming. Second annual report, 1961, Louisiana State University, Contract Nonr 1575 (05), Office of Naval Research, Group Psychology Branch.

Peach, P. What is system analysis? In H. W. Karn and B. v. H. Gilmer (eds.), *Readings in industrial and business psychology.* New York: McGraw-Hill, 1962.

Pelz, D. C. Leadership within a hierarchical organization. *Journal of Social Issues,* 1951, **7**, 47–63.

Petrullo, L. and Bass, B. M. (eds.). *Leadership and interpersonal behavior.* New York: Holt, Rinehart, and Winston, 1961.

Porter, L. W. and Lawler, E. E. The effects of "tall" vs. "flat" organizations on managerial satisfactions. Paper read at American Psychological Association, Philadelphia, September, 1963.

Rogers, C. R. Toward a theory of creativity. *Etc.,* 1954, **4**, 249–60.

Rosenbaum, M. The effect of stimulus and background factors in the volunteering response. *Journal of Abnormal and Social Psychology,* 1956, **53**, 118–121.

Rosenberg, S. and Hall, R. L. The effects of different social feedback conditions upon performance in dyadic teams. *Journal of Abnormal and Social Psychology,* 1958, **58**, 271–77.

Sells, S. B. Dimensions of stimulus situations which account for behavior variance. In S. B. Sells (ed.), *Stimulus determinants of behavior.* New York: Ronald Press, 1963. (a)

Sells, S. B. An interactionist looks at the environment. *American Psychologist,* 1963, **18**, 696–702. (b)

Sells, S. B. (ed.). *Stimulus determinants of behavior.* New York: Ronald Press, 1963. (c)

Sherman, P. A., Kerr, W., and Kosinar, W. A study of accidents in 147 factories. *Personnel Psychology,* 1957, **10**, 43–51.

Stanton, E. S. Company policies and supervisors' attitude toward supervision. *Journal of Applied Psychology,* 1960, **44**, 22–26.

Strauss, G. Some notes on power equalization. In H. J. Leavitt (ed.), *The social sciences of organization: Four perspectives.* Englewood Cliffs, N.J.: Prentice-Hall, 1963.

Strother, G. B. Problems in the development of a social science of organizations. In H. J. Leavitt (ed.), *The social science of organizations: Four perspectives.* Englewood Cliffs, N.J.: Prentice-Hall, 1963.

Taft, R. The ability to judge people. *Psychological Bulletin,* 1955, **52**, 1–21.

Tagiuri, R. (ed.). *Research needs in executive selection.* Boston: Harvard University, Graduate School of Business Administration, 1961.

Tagiuri, R. and Petrullo, L. (eds.). *Person perception and interpersonal behavior.* Stanford: Stanford University Press, 1958.

Talacchi, S. Organization size, individual attitudes and behavior: An empirical study. *Administrative Science Quarterly,* 1960, **5**, 398–420.

Thistlethwaite, D. L. College press and student achievement. *Journal of Educational Psychology,* 1959, **50**, 183–91.

Thistlethwaite, D. L. College press and changes in study plans of talented students. *Journal of Educational Psychology,* 1960, **51**, 222–34.

Thomas, E. J. Role conceptions and organizational size. *American Sociological Review,* 1959, **24**, 30–37.

Thomas, E. J. and Fink, C. F. Effects of group size. *Psychological Bulletin,* 1963, **60**, 371–84.

Vollmer, H. M. A preliminary investigation and analysis of the role of scientists in research organizations. I. *USAF OSR Technical Report,* 1962, Task No. 37707, Project No. 9778.

Vollmer, H. M. Adaptations of scientists in an independent research organization: A case study. IIa. *USAF ORD Technical Report,* 1963, Task No. 37707, Project No. 9778.

Vroom, V. H. The effects of attitudes on perception of organizational goals. *Human Relations,* 1960, **13**, 229–40.

Vroom, V. H. and Maier, N. R. F. Industrial social psychology. *Annual Review of Psychology,* 1961, **12**, 413–46.

Vroom, V. H. and Mann, F. C. Leader authoritarianism and employee attitudes. *Personnel Psychology,* 1960, **13**, 125–40.

Worthy, J. C. Factors influencing employee morale. *American Sociological Review,* 1950, **15**, 169–79.

Zander, A. and Curtis, T. Effects of social power on aspiration level and striving. *Journal of Abnormal and Social Psychology,* 1962, 64 63–74.

Section A
TASK DESIGN

Quite often the behavioral ramifications of task design are ignored either because the consequences are considered unimportant or because the nature of the task is assumed to be determined by the technology and therefore unalterable. However, it is obvious that the task can be modified in a variety of ways and behavioral scientists are accumulating evidence which suggests that significant behavioral consequences may be attributable to variations in task design.

We begin our treatment of task design with a poem by Pack pointing to some of the humorous, yet somewhat pathetic, reactions to repetitive clerical tasks. Pack's characterization is dramatic and extreme; yet it does serve to set the stage for a more systematic and analytical examination of the effects of task design on human performance and attitudes.

In the next selection Scott reviews a number of studies of task design and concludes that behavior in repetitive tasks can be accounted for by theory and research in the field of neuropsychology. Scott's paper is an example of attempts to build two-way bridges between psychological theory and research on the one hand, and practical, managerial problems on the other. Activation theory seems to explain some facets of human performance that have remained somewhat enigmatic. However, further developments are needed before we can consider it a prediction system which tells us precisely how to structure tasks for best results.

Hulin and Blood are critical of the more recent assumption that job enlargement is inevitably salutary. They advance the thesis that white-collar and rural blue-collar employees will benefit from job enlargement while urban blue-collar employees would reject, and be dissatisfied with, enlarged jobs. The evidence which they hold up in support of their thesis is not very convincing, as the authors admit. On the other hand, Hulin and Blood make two points which can hardly be overemphasized. First, significant individual differences in response to changes in task structure have been consistently observed even among white-collar and urban blue-collar workers. The authors' suggestion that the observed differences may be attributable to differences in reinforcement histories is an interesting one and should be pursued. Secondly, our theories and research concerned with the effects of task structure are still relatively crude. More rigorous experimental studies of the behavioral effects of variations in task design are needed.

Hackman and Lawler refer to a number of studies which have shown that when repetitive jobs are enlarged, increases in productivity and satisfaction are the consequence. But they also agree that job enlargement studies have typically involved a number of changes so that it is difficult to know which, if any, of those changes produced the outcomes. Drawing upon expectancy formulations and Maslow's need theory, Hackman and Lawler propose a conceptual framework which emphasizes both individual difference variables and certain job characteristics as determinants of performance and satisfaction. The job characteristics which they signify are the extent to which there is a perceived contingency between the individual's behavior and the observable outcomes, the value of those outcomes both to the performer and others, and the amount of feedback provided. Hackman and Lawler contend that it is not the objective job characteristics themselves but rather the individual's perceptions of those characteristics which determine his performance and attitudes. They hypothesize that only among employees desirous of higher order need satisfaction will there be a positive relation between perceived job characteristics and performance and attitudes. After describing an extensive correlational study (not included here) which supported their hypothesis,[1] the authors conclude that a better understanding of the impact of task designs will presumably consider the interaction between characteristics of the individuals and task variables. They warn the reader that their study does not establish a direct causal link between objective task parameters and either performance or attitudes. On the other hand, they believe that their own as well as other studies provide ample evidence that task structure has a substantial impact on employee behavior and that many organizations could benefit from job enrichment programs.

---

[1] For a discussion of the practical implications of this study, see E. E. Lawler, and J. R. Hackman, Corporate profits and employee satisfaction: Must they be in conflict, *California Management Review,* Vol. 14 (1971), pp. 46–55.

21. ROUTINE*

***Robert Pack*†**

Today was a hard one at the office.
The secretary, who always seems
so shy
And never starts a conversation,
wore
a skin-tight glass dress.
Nobody seemed to notice, so I asked.
"Yes, it's true," she said, "touch it
and see."
Forcing that serene objective smile
I use when addressing superiors,
I tapped her arm with my fingernail.
A silver crack appeared—
As in ice. "Don't worry," she said,
and returned to her typewriter.
By noon the crack had spread up her
shoulder
To her neck below the ear, and
down past her elbow
Where it branched out, like on a
map, in rivulets.
She strained hard not to turn her head.
Then, below her left breast, I noticed
A dark spot, like a beebee hole,
and I was anxious.
"Hadn't you better change?" I asked,
And she replied, "Proceed at your
own risk."—
Which was, I thought, a gauche
thing to say.
I began to chip and peel away the
glass,
Getting better at it as I went along,
becoming, I might say,
Really quite adept, though in some
places
Innate modesty impeded my work.
When I finished, I discovered she
was completely dressed—
In a ski outfit. "Why?" I asked.
"I'm planning a vacation," she said.
By then I was curious and had lost
much of my reserve,
So I carried her to the supply room
Where I stripped away a mink coat,
a raccoon coat,
Two cashmere sweaters, three dresses,
a blouse
With a round collar and a butterfly
pin on it, and a dickey,
But when at last I reached her
underclothes,
She sniffled and whimpered, "Haven't
you gone too far!"
Naturally, I felt ashamed, so I folded
her
Into a manila envelope, and mailed
her, with no return address,
To the office manager of a competing
firm.

22. ACTIVATION THEORY AND TASK DESIGN*

***William E. Scott, Jr.*†**

Performance decrements and dissatisfactions at the work place have long been observed but have not been adequately explained. Activation research and selected studies of work behavior are reviewed to show that decrements in performance may be better understood in the light of recent neuropsychological findings. This review indicates that activation theory and the research upon which it is based anticipates behavior related to variations in task design and suggests new avenues of investigation for those interested in the determinants of work behavior.

Industrial psychologists have been accused of being largely atheoretical, which is to say that in attempting to resolve the important problems of individuals at work, the first response is to develop measures of concepts derived more from vague intuition and the vernacular at hand than from psychological theory. If it could be said in reply that

---

* Reprinted from *The American Scholar*, Vol. 35, No. 2 (Spring 1966), pp. 275-76. Copyright © 1966 by the United Chapters of Phi Beta Kappa. By permission of the publishers.

† Robert Pack is currently teaching at Middlebury College, and completing work on a new collection of poems, *The Last Will and Testament of Art Evergreen*. His other recent books of poetry are *Guarded by Women* and *Selected Poems*.

* Reprinted from *Organizational Behavior and Human Performance*, Vol. 1, No. 1 (August 1966), pp. 3-30. Copyright © 1966 by Academic Press, Inc.

† Indiana University.

we are inductive animals who prefer to let theory emerge from data, the criticism could be taken as a plaudit. The fact is, however, that most of us remain disturbed. There are, to be sure, certain advantages to empirical heterogeneity, but those advantages do not accrue when we consistently fail to look beyond the immediate significance of our data or make few attempts to refine our constructs by seeking the relationships between the several measurements operations which have been devised.

If we would rather approach the investigation of work behavior with a theoretical orientation, and there are promising signs that we have reached this stage of maturity, the first problem is that of having to choose from the many theories available. For example, there has been a sustained interest in the problems of maintaining performance levels, in morale or satisfaction, and in behavior generally classified as dysfunctional where organizational goals are concerned. Such phenomena would seem to call for a theory of motivation as a basis for research and explanation. This being the case, one might choose any one of a number of theories ranging from psychoanalytic motivational theory to the motivational cores of perceptual and learning theory. The difficulties are compounded with the realization that most of these theories are poorly developed and largely inadequate for the task with which the industrial psychologist is confronted. Many applied psychologists find it impossible to employ the hypothetical constructs prevalent in psychoanalytic theory, and need or drive reduction models are found to be increasingly inadequate either as explanations for the behavior we observe at the work place or as a basis for developing and testing fruitful hypotheses.

Under these circumstances, the only recourse might be to continue gathering data by employing constructs from our "common-sense" observations. However, the writer contends that recent and profoundly significant discoveries in neuropsychological research and early formulations of activation theory, which remain closely tied to this research, provide a more desirable alternative for those who wish to extend our knowledge of work behavior. Psychologists in widely diverse fields have acknowledged the importance of activation and affective constructs originating in the investigations of the reticular formation and brain stimulation experiments. In the area of work behavior, activation theory offers an explanation for performance decrements and dissatisfactions frequently observed in repetitive industrial tasks. It also appears to account for the unequivocal effects of high-intensity, intermittent noise on performance, the equivocal effects of music, the "Hawthorne" effect, and at least some of the unexplained variance in accident behavior.

The purpose of this paper is to restate the first of these problems, that of "motivational drift" or performance decline, to describe activation research, and to point out that activation theory anticipates performance decrements as well as the results of our studies in task design.

THE BEHAVIORAL PROBLEM

A perennial problem in industry has been that of sustaining human productivity over extended periods of time. It has been most acute where the principles of specialization and work simplification have been carried to the extreme indicated in the following observation.

> In the days of craftsmanship when the worker was responsible for the making of the complete article, the cycle of repetition was often so long that it contained within itself the elements of the variety which is often assumed to be an important factor in eliminating boredom, "monotony," and want of interest in the work and which is ostensibly lacking in much of the highly specialized tasks of today when the cycle of repetition may consist of but a fraction of a second (Vernon, 1924).

The date of the article in which this statement was elaborated indicates that it is not a new problem. Nor is it one which we have been inclined to tackle head on. In a cultural setting which has supported and materially benefited from the principles of specialization, it has not often occurred to us that when we design a task we are specifying the behavior of those who are to perform it in the absence of a great deal of knowledge about the psychological demands we are placing on the individual. We have, of course, observed a number of behavioral patterns which are *not* prescribed. Vernon (1924), for example, observed employees in a number of jobs in which the cycle of repetition was less than a minute and found that workers frequently took short breaks beyond those authorized, changed posture, and reported feelings of monotony and boredom. More recently, a number of writers (e.g., Strauss & Sayles, 1960; Walker & Guest, 1952) have noted the difficulties of maintaining performance in assembly-line tasks and the widespread dissatisfaction of those engaged in mass production work.

Performance decrements have often been attributed to fatigue, but continued research has raised serious problems for this construct. While performance decrements, momentary lapses of attention, and irritability are often the consequence of prolonged mental and psychomotor activities, the above phenomena are not always accompanied by physicochemical changes in the muscles (Ghiselli & Brown, 1955, p. 259; Scott, 1957; Tiffin & McCormick, 1965, p. 469). Furthermore, Broadbent (1958, p.

138) has cited some studies in which the performance decrement was found to be a function of the number of times the stimulus situation had been presented rather than a function of the number of repeated responses, and performance has been sustained or restored in some cases by the introduction of factors irrelevant to muscular exhaustion (Broadbent, 1958, p. 111; Mackworth, 1950).

It is interesting to note that response decrements have also been consistently observed in learning experiments. Quite early, Pavlov (1927) noted that a continued presentation of a conditioned stimulus with or without the unconditioned stimulus led to a gradual weakening of the response. Following the lead of Pavlov, Hull (1943) developed the concept of reactive inhibition (Ir) to account for decrements in response with repeated elicitation of the response. He postulated that each occurrence of a response generated an increase in Ir which had the property of decreasing the tendency to repeat the response and which, because it dissipated over time, allowed for spontaneous recovery of the response.

Hull's Ir and conditioned inhibition (sIr) constructs were taken over by Ammons (1947) to explain performance decrements and related phenomena frequently observed in studies of motor skill acquisition. Ammons (1947) noted that in many reported curves of motor performance, performance after rest was characterized by an abrupt rise to a level much higher than that expected if there had been no rest, a gradual flattening followed by a decremental segment after the abrupt rise, a resumption of the prerest curve of gradual improvement, and a fairly definite permanent difference in performance levels between groups practicing under different conditions of distributed practice. Since Ir is assumed to be produced by every motor response and diminishes with time after response cessation, Ir is viewed as an explanation for performance superiority with distributed practice as opposed to massed practice. However, Ammons (1947) had to call on sIr, a nonresponding habit reinforced by the dissipation of Ir and presumed to be more permanent than Ir, to account for the seemingly permanent and lower performance levels achieved with massed practice.[1] Ammons (1947) did not feel that the post-rest phenomena of sharp initial rise, relative decrement, and resumption of rise were directly accounted for by the Ir and sIr constructs. It may be noted here that while Feldman (1963) still insists that a significant portion of the post-rest rise in performance is due to the extinction of sIr, the Ammons' and their associates (e.g., Ammons, Ammons, & Morgan, 1958) have reported data not wholly in accord with the extinction hypothesis.

Performance decrements have also been frequently observed in studies of human vigilance (Adams, 1956; Bakan, 1955; Jerison, 1958; Mackworth, 1950). However, certain experimental treatments have been found to eliminate or reduce the decrement. Mackworth (1950) found that a telephone message in the middle of the second hour of a clock-monitoring task resulted in a performance level usually obtained only by fresh subjects. Mackworth (1950) also found that when subjects were supplied complete accounts of their performance as the clock-monitoring task proceeded, their performance was sustained. Fraser (1953) found that the presence of the experimenter in the test room reduced the decrement in a prolonged visual task, and Sipowicz, Ware, and Baker (1962) found that an experimental treatment combining knowledge of results and a monetary reward individually administered and made contingent upon the maintenance of a high level of performance resulted in no decrement over a 3-hour period. Jerison and Wallis (1957) found a large decrement for a one-clock monitoring task but were hard pressed to locate a decrement when their subjects were required to monitor three clocks. Deese and Ormand (1953), Holland (1958), and Jenkins (1958) have reported studies in which performance decrements appeared to be reduced when subjects had to respond to multiple signal sources and more frequent signal rates. Frankman and Adams (1962) have noted in their review that decrements are more prominently associated with simple vigilance tasks and are absent or small in complex visual tasks with multiple stimulus sources. It is therefore tempting to conclude unequivocally, in view of the theory presented below, that increases in stimulus or response complexity or both, up to some point will reduce vigilance decrements. However, it must be admitted that negative results have also been reported (Adams & Boulter, 1962; Kidd & Micocci, 1964).

Inhibition constructs have been advanced to account for vigilance decrements (Mackworth, 1950) as well as the performance decrements observed in motor skill acquisition. However, the inadequacies of those constructs have been succinctly pointed out by Adams (1963), Broadbent (1958), Deese (1955), and Frankman and Adams (1962). It may be noted that the results of many of the vigilance studies cited above are not in agreement with inhibition postulates.

Other explanatory constructs (Dember & Earl, 1957; Glanzer, 1953; Scott, 1957; Walker, 1958) have been developed to account for performance decrements so widely observed not only at the work

[1] Adams (1963) cites evidence supporting the contention that lower performance levels achieved with massed practice are merely temporary.

site but also in the psychological laboratory. In designing industrial tasks, the attempts to explain this "fading" or "motivational drift" have been generally ignored either because they have appeared irrelevant to task design or because performance can be sustained, at least temporarily, by a variety of programs extrinsic to the task itself. The fact that such programs tend to lose their effectiveness or lead to dysfunctional behavior merely emphasizes the lack of knowledge about the factors inherent in task design which affect performance.

BRAIN STIMULATION RESEARCH LEADING TO ACTIVATION THEORY

Activation theory has developed from extensive investigations of the reticular formation, a neural structure extending from the lower part of the brain stem upwards through the pons and midbrain tegmentum to portions of the hypothalamus and thalamus.[2] This diffuse nonspecific projection system is to be distinguished from the classical sensory pathways which can be traced in a point-to-point fashion from the sensory receptors to thalamic relays and thence to primary sensory areas in the cortex. The reticular formation consists of a dense network of neurons with short fibers and multiple relays. Consequently, it does not preserve information about the location and quality of stimulation as does the specific projection system. However, this formation does receive collaterals from the classical sensory pathways as the latter rise toward the cortex, and receives projections from limited regions in the cortex.

Although it has been known for some time that distinctive electroencephalogram (EEG) patterns correspond to various arousal states, the role of the recticular formation in producing generalized arousal or activation was not known until the late 1940's. Moruzzi and Magoun (1949) were among the first to discover that electrical stimulation of the reticular formation changed the EEG pattern characteristic of sleep to one corresponding to activation or alert wakefulness. Then Lindsley, Bowden, and Magoun (1949) gradually transecting higher and higher portions of the brain stem, found that as the reticular formation was eliminated, the EEG recording changed to that of deep sleep or somnolence.

It is now believed that the reticular formation is comprised of two systems: the lower or brain stem reticular formation (BSRF) and the upper or thalamic reticular formation (TRF). The properties of the BSRF, which are somewhat different from those of the TRF, appear to be more germane to the behavioral phenomena with which this paper is concerned.

Studies by Lindsley et al. (1949) and French and Magoun (1952) have shown that lesions in the BSRF with the classical sensory pathways intact produce a chronically comatose animal which cannot be aroused. Under this condition, impulses from the various sensory modalities reach the cortex via the classical pathways, but EEG recordings indicate that this stimulation does not outlast the presentation of the stimulus. With the classical sensory pathways transacted and the BSRF intact, direct electrical stimulation of the BSRF or its excitation by the stimulation of any peripheral nerve (auditory, visual, proprioceptive, visceral, etc.) will produce behavior arousal which persists after stimulation has stopped (French, Amerongen, & Magoun, 1952; French and Magoun, 1952; Lindsley, Schreiner, Knowles, & Magoun, 1950).

With all systems intact, a sleeping animal may be aroused by electrical stimulation of the BSRF, and at somewhat higher voltages the animal will awake, vocalize, and show signs of negative affect. With further increases in voltage, the animal will show abrupt arousal, extreme agitation, escape responses, and behavioral disorganization (Worden & Livingston, 1961). Studies reviewed by Lindsley (1957) and Samuels (1959) have shown that collaterals from the classical sensory pathways converge on the BSRF and that stimulation of any receptor, interoceptive and exteroceptive, will initiate an increase in BSRF activity and, in turn, a diffuse activation pattern in the cortex. It has also been found that stimulation from the various sensory modalities has differential affects on the BSRF. Bernhaut, Gellhorn, and Rasmussen (1953) report that painful stimuli elicit the most widespread and intense cortical arousal patterns followed by proprioceptive, auditory, and visual stimuli in that order.

Stimulation of specific cortical areas also produces widespread activity in the BSRF (French, Hernandez-Peon, & Livingston, 1955; Hernandez-Peon & Hagbarth, 1955). Projections from the cortex into the reticular formation, therefore, provide a means for cortical influence on arousal (Lindsley, 1961).

A number of studies have indicated that the BSRF is critically involved in habituation or response decrement phenomena. Sharpless and Jasper (1956) found generalized cortical arousal to diminish rapidly with repeated presentations of auditory stimuli. After habituation has been established, increases in the arousal pattern could be obtained with changes in the frequency or pattern of the auditory stimulus, and arousal could be reinstated after a period of rest following discontinuation of the stimulus. Further studies reviewed by Worden and Livingston (1961, pp. 271–74) have indicated that

[2] For a more comprehensive review of the research which has illuminated the structure and functions of the reticular formation, see Samuels (1959).

electrophysiological activity and behavioral arousal decrements are primarily a function of the BSRF. Once habituation has been established, nembutal anesthesia (which acts upon the reticular formation) eliminates the habituation effect. Habituation is reinstated when the animal recovers from the anesthesia while lesions in the BSRF permanently eliminate habituation effects.

In summary, stimulation from exteroceptive, interoceptive, and cortical sources sets up recurrent discharges in the BSRF. This activity outlasts the presentation of the stimulus, diminishes rapidly with repeated presentation of the stimulus, and can be reinstated after periods of rest following the discontinuation of that stimulus. (Of course cortical rearousal can occur with the simultaneous presentation of other stimulation. For example, pairing the habituated stimulus with a primary reward or punishment.) Diffuse BSRF activity is projected widely into the cortex effecting a generalized cortical arousal upon which the perception and integration of messages (arriving more quickly and consistently by the classical sensory pathways) is dependent. As stimulus habituation occurs, activity in the cortex may still be observed but it becomes relatively restricted to the area serving the sensory modality through which the stimulus has been presented.

Latency studies cited by Samuels (1959) have indicated that stimulation arrives at the cortex more quickly through the classical sensory pathways and the TRF than through the BSRF. It has also been indicated that activity shows up more quickly in the BSRF after stimulation of the cortical areas than activity in the cortex after stimulation of the BSRF (French, Hernandez-Peon, & Livingston, 1955). Thus a stimulus which has taken on significance through learning has time to reach the cortex through the classical sensory pathways, cue off cortical associations, and then be relayed to the BSRF in time to effect increased or sustained cortical arousal.

Affective Processes. Discoveries by Olds and Milner (1954) have led to brain stimulation research which has been relatively more concerned with central neural mechanisms mediating affect than activation or arousal. Although hedonism has been a controversial issue for many years, the results of these studies support those who postulate a mediating affective component in behavior.

While experimenting with electrodes implanted in the brains of normal rats, Olds and Milner (1954) found that electrical stimulation in certain areas of the brain seemed to produce a behavioral effect similar to that of a primary reward.

Later studies by Olds (1956a, 1956b) have indicated that there is a concentration of "pleasure" and "punishment" centers as one proceeds from the cortex down to the brain stem, that they lie for the most part just above the BSRF, and that rats with electrodes in hypothalamic areas would run faster for electrical stimulation than for food when they were food-deprived.

A number of studies reviewed by McGeer (1962) have shown similar results for cats, monkeys, and dolphins. In human patients undergoing surgery for brain tumor and epilepsy, reward centers have been found which, when stimulated electrically, result in intense but nonspecific feelings of well-being, pleasant sensations ascribed to different parts of the body, and sexual arousal. Other "punishment" areas when stimulated resulted in terror, pain, and anger.

A great deal of research has followed the discovery by Olds and Milner; and while the findings are by no means conclusive, they indicate that there are neural structures which mediate reward and punishment and that they are distinct from those which mediate generalized arousal or activation but contiguous enough to permit interaction effects. Consequently, and in agreement with Young (1961), who supports the objective existence of an affective component in behavior, the writer postulates an affective dimension which is perceived as a bipolar continuum ranging from extreme negative affect (feelings characterized as unpleasant) through indifference to extreme positive affect (feelings characterized as pleasant). Like the activation dimension to be described below, this affective construct does not specify behavior direction, but also like activation, it is one of the determinants of overt response.

ACTIVATION THEORY

Following the lead of Duffy (1951), a number of writers (Berlyne, 1960; Bindra, 1959; Fiske & Maddi, 1961; Lindsley, 1951; Malmo, 1959) have presented cogent evidence to support their views that the *degree of activation* of an organism is a major variable in a wide range of behavior processes.

More recently, Duffy (1962) defined the level of activation "as the extent of release of the stored energy of the organism through metabolic activity in the tissues." She perceives the activation construct as a continuum ranging from somnolence through varying degrees of alertness to agitated states such as hypertension, hyperactivity, and loss of coordination. This writer agrees that it is a neuropsychological dimension and with Duffy's description of the outward manifestations of varying degrees of activation—that is, from coma through hyperactivity or extreme excitement. However, Duffy herself recognized that the organism is not equally activated in all its parts and suggested a definition which is more in accord with that given by Malmo (1959) and Fiske and Maddi (1961). At the present time it appears more fruitful to conceive of activation as the *degree of excitation of the brain stem reticular formation.* It is believed that subsequent investigations of the sources and properties of stimulation which result in varying degrees of activation as defined above, and consideration of the behavioral manifestations of variations in activation will prove to be enlightening in our search for the determinants of human work behavior.

Determinants of Activation. By virtue of the physiological properties of the reticular mechanism and its location in the central nervous system, it is to be expected that stimulation from exteroceptive, interoceptive, and cerebral sources will cause variations in the individual's level of activation. Evidence in support of this relationship is seen in numerous studies reviewed by Berlyne (1960), Fiske and Maddi (1961), and Duffy (1962).

A number of methodological difficulties confront those who attempt to isolate the properties of stimulation which result in changes in activation. However, different investigators have consistently agreed upon certain properties which either have some empirical support or are suggested by common experience. (Most of the empirical evidence is indirect in that no measures of activity in the BSRF were obtained while introducing changes into the external stimulus surround. Rather, changes in various arousal measures, GSR, EEG, muscle tension, etc., which are considered to be manifestations of activation, were obtained.)

Stimulus intensity appears to be one of the most straightforward variables affecting activation level. The greater the intensity of a stimulus, the greater the frequency of impulses reaching the BSRF; hence, the higher the activation level. Fiske and Maddi (1961) postulate *stimulus variation* as another property affecting activation level, but there are a number of ways in which stimulation can vary. There may be variation in the total number of different stimuli impinging upon the individual, periodic fluctuations in stimulus intensity, variation in the degree to which novel stimuli are introduced into the stimulus field and the relative degree of stimulus novelty for the individual, variation in the relative speed and unexpectedness with which the stimulus complex is introduced, and so on. Other properties which have been suggested are *stimulus complexity, uncertainty,* and *meaningfulness.* Obviously, the stimulus properties hypothesized by various authors overlap in meaning and are probably not independent in their effect on activation. It is also clear that, as one moves from the physical intensity of a stimulus to such properties as complexity and meaningfulness, individual perceptions and interpretations of the external stimulus configuration become increasingly significant as determinants of activation level.[3] This is simply another indication of the complex interaction between the properties of external stimulation and cortical processes, a conceptual and methodological problem which has plagued psychologists for years but which is not insurmountable.

Activation level is assumed to covary with the sum total of stimulation from all sources. Berlyne (1960) reports some studies which support this assumption in his discussion of "arousal potential." Fiske and Maddi (1961) also postulate a covariation between "total impact" and level of activation, where total impact is defined as "an additive function of the contextual and inherent properties of stimulation from all three sources at a point in time."

Activation and Performance. Duffy (1962) reviews a host of studies reporting changes in muscle tension, electrical resistance of the skin, EEG recordings, reaction time, and sensory sensitivity with changes in the stimulus configuration.[4] She then concludes, as have others, that the general quality of performance will vary with changes in activation.

The relationship between activation level and performance is generally described by an inverted *U.* At low activation levels, performance is handicapped by lack of alertness, a decrease in sensory sensitivity, and lack of muscular coordination (all of which are due to insufficient cortical stimulation from the BSRF). At intermediate levels of activation, performance is optimal, and at high levels performance is again handicapped by hypertensiveness, loss of muscular control, "impulsion to action," and in the extreme, total disorganization of responses. The direct evidence in support of this relationship is meager in that few if any investigations have obtained measures of activity in the brain stem and observed concomitant variations in performance. A number of investigations, however, have introduced variables assumed to effect the level of activation while noting changes in the quality of task performance. Although these studies were not designed to systematically vary activation from low to high levels but rather started at some presumably high or low level, nearly

[3] The neuropsychological explanation of central neural processes advanced by Hebb (1949) provides the rationale for the postulated relationship between the "meaningfulness" of a stimulus and activation level. In essence, an external stimulus which is more meaningful for the experiencing organism cues off a greater degree of cortical activity which, in turn, leads to an increase in activation level through the feedback systems from the cortex to the BSRF.

[4] It may be recalled that muscle tension, skin conductance, and other measures of physiological arousal are here considered as manifestations of activation level. Duffy prefers a definition of activation level in terms much closer to these measures rather than in terms of activity in the BSRF. The difficulty with Duffy's proposal, however, is that interindividual correlations between these measures is seldom high.

all suggest that task performance is at first enhanced and then diminishes in quality as the activation level varies from low to high.

Relationship between Affect and Activation. Many of the studies cited above, as well as common experience, suggest an interaction between affective states and activation level, and a number of writers have advanced the hypothesis that both low and high levels of activation result in negative affect. Fiske and Maddi (1961), drawing upon the work of Leuba (1955), Berlyne (1960), Stein and Ray (1959), and others, postulate a characteristic activation level which is an organismic norm independent of external demands and then advance the proposition that negative affect is experienced when activation differs markedly from the individual's characteristic level; positive affect is associated with shifts of activation toward the characteristic level.

While the above is a straightforward statement of the relationship between affect and activation, it must be admitted that the precise nature of the characteristic activation level as well as the interaction remains to be worked out. Fiske and Maddi relate the characteristics activation level to a sleep-wakefulness cycle (Fiske & Maddi, 1961, p. 39), noting that activation is often discussed in terms of drowsiness and alertness. However, recent evidence suggests that sleep is not a part of the activation continuum but rather a different phenomena attributable, perhaps, to other mechanisms. Nakajima (1964) points out that there has been no experimental evidence that drowsiness and sleep are intermediate states between wakefulness and coma. Injecting both neural excitants and neural depressants into the reticular formation, he observed that neural excitants produced alertness followed by escape responses, behavioral freezing and finally convulsions. On the other hand, small injections of neural depressants produced hyperactivity and a state which might be called delirium. Larger injections produced a comatose state which was not preceded by drowsiness or sleep. Brownfield (1964), in a review of sensory deprivation research, insists that it is impossible to completely deprive the intact organism of sensory stimulation. If it were possible, a kind of psychological suspended animation (coma?) would result. He feels that a condition of minimal, diffuse stimulation obtained in most sensory deprivation studies is a primary requisite for disorganizations of cognitive and perceptual function. The hallucinatory activity which accompanies this deafferentiation process (low activation level) may lead to negative affect and a greater effort on the part of the organism to increase stimulation. If this fails, coma may result.

These observations may overcome the objections to Fiske and Maddi's propositions that conditions leading to low activation levels produce negative affect (there seems to be little question that high activation levels produce negative affect) and attempts by the organism to increase impact and restore activation to its characteristic level. However, the construct of characteristic level of activation is left more vague.

Lindsley (1961) has noted that the reticular formation as well as the cortex and other systems may become conditioned to a characteristic pattern of regulation imposed by habitual excitation and adaptation. This could give rise to a characteristic activation level as indicated by fast or slow reactions, alertness or lack of alertness, interindividual variations in "emotionality," etc. Also the results of studies recently reviewed by Denenberg (1964) indicate that variations in amount and types of stimulation applied at certain critical times in infancy lead to later differences in chronic or general level of arousal.

All of the above observations lead this writer to suggest slight modifications in two of the constructs—the activation dimension and the characteristic activation level—proposed by Fiske and Maddi in their very excellent work.

The writer would exclude drowsiness and sleep from the activation dimension, and conceive of this continuum as ranging from coma to delirium states to alert attentiveness up to extreme agitation and convulsions. These behavioral manifestations are attributable to varying degrees of BSRF excitation from minimal to maximal.

The characteristic activation level is defined as the degree of sensitivity of the BSRF to stimulation from all sources. It is conceived as a generalized threshold, throughout the BSRF, which is primarily a function of its biochemical structure. The biochemical structure is, in part, genetically determined. But it is also subject to enduring and perhaps major modifications effected by variations in stimulus inputs during critical pre- and postnatal periods, and to enduring but small modifications after those periods. Of course, experimental or accidental lesions in the BSRF could permanently modify its sensitivity, and the application of drugs could be expected to produce gross but temporary modifications in BSRF sensitivity. The diurnal patterns of sleep and activity could also effect relatively small cyclical changes in the BSRF threshold; that is, continued activity may produce true neural fatigue and decreases in sensitivity whereas sleep would restore it to its original level.

ACTIVATION THEORY AND TASK BEHAVIOR

Activation theory anticipates a number of behavioral outcomes in tasks which require the constant repetition of a limited number of responses to stimulation which is configuratively simple and temporally unvarying.

As the individual becomes familiar with the surroundings and learns the responses required in the repetitive task, a decline in activation level is expected. With continued exposure at the task site, habituation in the BSRF may lead to a decrement in performance. If the activation level falls below the characteristic norm, the individual will experience negative affect and will attempt to increase impact. If he is prevented from engaging in impact-increasing behavior, the result is a continuous decline in performance. When confronted with these circumstances, the individual may temporarily or permanently leave the task situation if these alternatives are readily available. If the individual is successful in increasing stimulus impact, the result would be an increase in the activation level and positive affect which is postulated to occur with shifts in activation toward the characteristic level. The quality or quantity of performance, or both, may then be sustained or restored to its original level depending upon the nature of the impact-modifying behavior.

It may be noted that any of a wide range of behaviors may be utilized to increase activation level. Additional cortical stimulation resulting from thoughts of an anticipated hunting trip or the recall of a recent encounter with a sexual partner may offset a decline in activation level. The individual may increase proprioceptive stimulation and thus sustain activation level by stretching, alternating positions, or otherwise varying their position at the task site. Leaving to visit the water fountain, another department, or the rest room not only increases proprioceptive stimulation but results in greater stimulus variation. Social activity including conversation with fellow employees, the development of complex group relationships, gambling, and horseplay also introduces variation which may serve to increase activation level.

It is obvious that much of the impact-increasing behavior which is described above and which is generally available to the individual is extrinsic to the task and may be incompatible with task performance. If the impact-increasing behavior is incompatible with task performance, we have the possibility of sustained activation levels and "high morale" but low performance. If it does not interfere with task performance, we have the possibility of successful adaptation to a repetitive task.

The individual may also introduce variation into the task itself. In a wide variety of work activities, individuals, when confronted with a repetitive task of long duration, may be observed dividing the total task into discrete units and then responding until each unit is completed. The experience seems to be pleasant and associated with a feeling of reduced effort (Baldamus, 1951, p. 42). This type of variation is probably most effective where the individual can arbitrarily set intermediate goals, can obtain immediate feedback regarding progress as responding continues, and can be reasonably certain of a change in activity such as a rest period when the goal is reached. This is only one example of what must be a wide variety of ways of increasing functional variation by modifying the task itself. If the individual is successful, the effect may be to sustain activation level over a long period of time in which case there is the possibility of continued high performance and moderately high morale in what is otherwise a repetitive task.

Management may introduce variation extrinsic to the task. The anticipation of monetary rewards may effect some changes in activation level as may rest periods and music. As will be noted below, however, the effects of introducing variation extrinsic to the task may be to reduce the performance decrement only temporarily or not at all.

From activation theory it may be anticipated that as more variation is introduced into a repetitive task, the result would be a reduction in habituation and a sustained activation closer to that required for optimal behavioral efficiency. If the increase in variation results in an activation level near the individual's characteristic norm or perhaps just above that level so that responding in the task results in consistent shifts back to the norm, increases in performance and positive affect could be expected. Thus, "job enlargement" requiring the individual to attend to stimulation of greater variety or complexity or both should have more potential for effecting long-run productivity and satisfaction than variation extrinsic to the task.

Molar Studies of Task Behavior. Several studies of behavior in repetitive tasks have shown that forced repetition of a limited number of responses to unchanging stimuli results in a decrement of responsiveness, discomfort reactions, and a tendency to alternate responses. Wyatt and Ogden (1924) observed female operatives who selected and packed tablets in paper envelopes, a task which took about 12 seconds to complete and was repeated approximately 2,500 times a day. They found that the average time to complete the operation consistently increased and the standard deviation to increase out of proportion to the increase in the average as the day progressed. Furthermore, the workers often showed signs of discomfort and became increasingly restless as the task was continued. In a laboratory experiment in the same study Wyatt found a consistent decrease in output and an increase in errors when subjects were required to perform simple, repetitive tasks five hours per day. His subjects also reported feelings of boredom and monotony and overestimated time intervals. Bills (1931), in a series of studies of worker efficiency, found that individuals engaged in repetitive work show lapses of attention often after short periods of time at the task. These lapses, which Bills referred to as blocking, resulted in performance decrements, increases in errors, greater variability in performance, and an increase in the likelihood of accidents. Fiske (Fiske & Maddi, 1961, pp. 106–44), in a review of the research on the effects of monotonous and restricted stimulation, reports that performance decrements on continuous, repetitive tasks have consistently been observed often within minutes after performance was initiated. In addition to decreased output, boredom, irritability, daydreaming, and restlessness were reported in many of the studies.

In a series of studies deserving of far more attention than they have received, Wyatt, Fraser, and Stock (1928) observed the behavior of individuals in repetitive tasks and then introduced changes in task design while noting the effects on output, work stoppages, and affective tone. In one of their preliminary examinations, female employees first walked to stores for tablets of soap and wrapping materials. Returning to the work site, they sat down to perform two hand-wrapping operations and then labeled and packed the soap into cardboard boxes. They then stood up to wrap, seal, and place the cardboard boxes in wooden cases, processing 144 bars of soap in a like manner before returning to stores for more supplies. Subsequently, the task was made more repetitive by eliminating the necessity for procuring their own supplies. The results over a five-day period showed that the less varied procedure resulted in slight increases in productivity. It may be noted, however, that the increases were quite small (from 0.5 to 6.2 percent), much smaller than one might expect considering that the women could not wrap and pack while procuring supplies. Furthermore, performance was significantly more uniform throughout the day when the employees were required to get their own supplies. Observations of behavior over a longer period of time may have revealed an increase in alternation behavior in the more repetitive task further reducing or eliminating the slight gains in productivity that were noted.

In their next study, Wyatt et al. (1928) observed eight women who manually folded and smoothed handkerchiefs into two different shapes. The two shapes differed in appearance although the folding and smoothing responses were essentially the same for both. On some days, the same shape was folded and smoothed throughout the workday. On alternate days, the women worked on one shape for approximately one hour, after which the other shape was folded and smoothed for the same period of time. There were no significant differences in productivity. However, it was reported that the women were unanimous and emphatic in their preference for more varied procedure.

Performance decrements in vigilance tasks, which often present the individual with a limited number of unchanging stimuli over time, have been discussed above. More comprehensive reviews of vigilance studies by Broadbent (1958), Frankman and Adams (1962), Mackworth (1950), and Scott (1957) indicate with striking regularity that performance decrements are more likely to occur when the vigilance task is repetitive. Mackworth's (1950) clock test, which is representative of the more simple vigilance tasks, requires the subject to sit in a small room and attend to a black pointer which moves clockwise on a plain white vertical surface. The subject is alone and noise, except for a constant drone from the apparatus, is excluded. The subject is instructed to look for double-jumps in the pointer and to press a morse key when one is observed. This task is continued for varying time periods, and under the usual experimental conditions, significant increases in the number of double-jumps missed are observed after one-half hour.

Several studies have shown that when extrinsic factors such as rest pauses, music, and knowledge of results are introduced into the repetitive task situation, performance improves at least temporarily. Vernon and Bedford (1924) found that the introduction of a 10-minute rest period increased hourly production by 20 percent in a repetitive labeling task. Similarly, McGehee and Owen (1940) found a significant increase in productivity with the introduction of two rest pauses in a routine clerical task. Mackworth (1950) found that alternating half-hour periods in the clock test with half-hour rest periods reduced the number of signals missed, and Bergum and Lehr (1962) found that the introduction of 10-minute rest pauses at the end of each 30 minutes of a vigilance task overcame the decrement observed when the task was continued for 90 minutes without rest. Uhrbrock (1961) reviewed the research on the effects of music and found that where significant increases in productivity were observed with the introduction of music, the tasks were usually of a simple, repetitive nature. Mackworth (1950) found that a telephone message in the second half-hour of the clock test reduced the number of signals missed. He estimated that the effects of the telephone message lasted for 25 minutes and then disappeared. Mackworth (1950) also found that knowledge of results (KR) provided by the experimenter sustained performance in the clock test over the two-hour period. Gibbs and Brown (1955) found that output in a repetitive task of copying pages from scientific reports and historical reviews with a copying machine was significantly higher when KR was provided by a counter which tallied each page as it was copied. The subjects in this experiment were not instructed to meet daily quotas and were paid uniformly. Chapanis (1964), however, found no significant differences in output in a repetitive task between a control group and experimental groups who were provided KR by a counter. Again, KR was provided casually, the subjects were paid uniformly, and there was no emphasis on individual performance. Sipowicz, Ware and Baker (1962) investigated the effects of KR, a monetary reward (R), and a combination of the two on performance in a simple vigilance task and found that KR and R administered singly and in combination resulted in improved performance over a control group who were provided neither one. The combined treatment of KR and R resulted in better performance than KR and R administered singly. They found also that the performance curve of the control group revealed the typical vigilance decrement but that the decrement was not shown by any of the experimental groups. A cursory inspection of their data, however, reveals what appears to be a small decrement in the KR group.

Studies involving modifications in task design also lend support to the prediction that when the repetitive task is enlarged, habituation effects may be reduced leading to gains in productivity and increases in positive affect. In three studies by Wyatt et al. (1928), substantial increases in productivity were found when greater variation was introduced into a repetitive task. In a cigarette-making task, for example, each worker was provided with a supply of tobacco from which a small quantity was taken and rolled by hand before being inserted into the cylindrical cigarette paper. The protruding tobacco ends were then cut off with a pair of scissors. The investigators modified the task as shown below and observed the hourly output under the different task designs.

Series one: Making and cutting alternately according to the worker's inclination. (The time required for making was approximately three times that for the cutting operation.)
Series two: Making for one hour, then cutting.
Series three: Making for one and a half hours, then cutting.
Series four: Making for three hours, then cutting.
Series five: Making all day.

Twenty subjects were observed, ten in the sequence indicated above and ten in the reverse sequence. The results showed that the highest output was obtained under Series two and three. An average decrease of 5.7 percent in output was observed when the duration of the making period was extended to three hours, and a reduction of 11.2 percent occurred when making was required all day. Decrements in behavioral efficiency were also seen in the tendency to cut away cigarette paper along with the loose tobacco when the workers were required to cut for long periods of time (Series four). Eighteen out of the 20 workers stated that the more repetitive task was unpleasant and boring. The investigators reported that such expressions as "The day seems doubly long" and "Making all day almost puts me out" were fairly typical.

Davis (1957) reviews three more recent studies of task design, and while they were obviously not "pioneering" or "one of the first controlled experiments on job design," the results are in accord with predictions from activation theory. In one study, a hospital appliance was being assembled on a line which was manned by 29 female employees. Nine different operations, each performed at stations along the conveyor belt, were required to assemble the product. Each task consisted of performing only one of the nine assembly operations, but the employees rotated between difficult and easy stations every two hours so each employee had learned to perform all nine assembly tasks. Material handlers brought supplies to the line and inspection personnel inspected the completed product. The investigator introduced two modifications in task design while recording output in terms of average daily productivity and percentages of kinked assemblies in consecutive lots. In the original assembly line task, the average daily productivity index for a period of 26 days was 100. In the first design modification which consisted merely of eliminating the conveyor belt, the index for 14 days dropped to 89. In the second modification, each employee performed all nine operations necessary for complete assembly of the product, procured his own supplies, and performed a final inspection. The productivity index resulting from the latter task design was 95.3 for a 27-day period, but the author notes that during this trial period, average output was consistently upward and that on the sixth day the group achieved an average productivity index above that achieved under the other two task designs. There was also a significant reduction in the percentage of *kinked* assemblies under the more varied procedure. There were large interindividual differences in both quantity and quality of performance when the workers were not paced alike by the conveyor belt. That a reduction in intraindividual variations in performance over the work period may have resulted could not be determined from the data given by Davis.

The results of the vigilance studies (Deese & Ormond, 1953; Holland, 1958; Jenkins, 1958; Jerison & Wallis, 1957), in which the introduction of multiple signal sources or more frequent signal rates reduced the performance decrement, are also believed to be in accord with predictions from activation theory. More relevant, perhaps, are vigilance studies in which the primary objective was to test the "activation hypothesis" that increased task complexity would reduce the vigilance decrement. Studies by Adams and his colleagues (Adams & Boulter, 1960; Adams, Stenson, & Humes, 1961) have shown that increasing the number of identical stimulus sources did not have a significant effect on vigilance decrement, but a more complex decision response of four choices associated with each signal detection reduced the decrement. In a subsequent study (Adams & Boulter, 1962), however, neither a more complex response pattern nor what appeared to be a more complex presentation of the stimulus signals produced a significant increase in performance. Measures of activation were not utilized in any of the above studies so it is impossible to directly assess the effects of the experimental treatments in activation terms, but the studies point to the problems of empirical verification of activation postulates. They also represent a step in the direction of operational clarification of the constructs found in activation theory.

EXPLANATORY VALUE OF ACTIVATION THEORY COMPARED WITH INHIBITION POSTULATES

The results of those studies in which the task required the repetition of a limited number of responses to a nonvarying stimulus configuration appear to be explained equally well by either activation or simple inhibition postulates with possibly two exceptions. If reactive inhibition is response-produced and grows as a function of the number of responses, one would expect a steady decline in performance with continued responding. However, Broadbent (1958, p. 118) has pointed out that performance in vigilance tasks does not merely decline but improves or oscillates. This tendency was also observed in the studies by Wyatt and Ogden (1924), Wyatt *et al.* (1928), and Mackworth (1950). From activation theory, one might expect to see evidence of impact-increasing behavior such as growing restlessness and stretching which, if not incompatible with continued responding, would provide momentary increases in activation level and thereby partial recovery in performance. Secondly, if reactive inhibition is a negative drive state much like pain or tissue injury,[5] then one would not have expected the preference shown by the women for the more varied handkerchief folding task since the responses were essentially the same in both tasks.

The effects of rest pauses on repetitive task performance are also anticipated by simple inhibition theory and the fatigue postulate as well as by activation theory, but the differences in explanation are worth noting. Since both Ir and fatigue are assumed to be response-induced and to dissipate with nonresponding, a reduction in performance decrement with rest is expected. On the other hand, Scott (1957) has suggested that the rest pause is effective not so much because it allows fatigue or Ir to dissipate but because it results in additional stimulus variation. A study in which an experimental group continued responding in a different stimulus configuration while the control group rested before both groups returned to the original task should provide an indirect test of the differential predictions. Another study in which the experimental group was forced to remain immobile and alone but not responding at the task site while the control group was permitted to leave the site to rest in a different stimulus surround should provide a similar test. In the first case, activation theory would anticipate near comparable performance from both groups after the experimental treatment whereas simple inhibition theory would expect lower performance from the experimental group. In the second case, activation theory would anticipate lower performance from the experimental group after the treatment, but no differences are expected from inhibition theory.

It is difficult if not impossible to anticipate the consequences of introducing other extrinsic factors such as noise, music, and knowledge of results from simple inhibition theory. Mackworth (1950), however, made an attempt. He attributed the performance decline in the usual clock test to partial experimental extinction (which he regarded as one form of internal inhibition) of a conditioned response. The response was originally conditioned through the use of derived reinforcement, namely knowledge of results provided by the experimenter during the instruction trial and withheld during most of the tests proper. Mackworth also concluded that while his subjects usually obtained some information about their performance from the task itself, when KR was specifically provided during the KR clock test, the reduction in performance decrement was due to increased reinforcement inherent in KR. However, he had to call on yet another Pavlovian construct,

[5] Cofer and Appley (1964, p. 155) have pointed out the vagueness of reactive inhibition as a negative drive state. However, it is commonly interpreted as such.

disinhibition, to account for the effects of the telephone message. Still other constructs of expectancy, set, and attitude had to be called upon to explain the significant fluctuations in the extinction curves obtained by Mackworth.

It is difficult to separate, experimentally, the corrective effects from the rewarding and activation effects of KR. The two studies (Chapanis, 1964; Gibbs & Brown, 1955) which attempted to determine the more purely arousal effects of KR resulted in contradictory findings. It may therefore prove instructive to note the differences in those experiments from the viewpoint of activation theory. Scott (1957) suggested that the beneficial effects of KR are at least partly due to the fact that in providing KR, new stimuli are introduced into the task. As with any other novel stimuli, an increase in activation level is expected and performance may be sustained or improved depending upon the level of activation prior to the introduction of KR. Should KR be continued as an integral part of the task or artificially provided at regular intervals, then its effects may habituate leading once again to a possible decline in performance. In Chapanis' study, the subjects were assigned to one experimental treatment throughout the test period (one hour per day for 24 days). The control subjects never received KR but the experimental subjects always received KR from a counter that was set at zero at the beginning of each test period. There were no significant differences in performance between the control and experimental groups, but after five days all groups showed a significant performance decrement after the first 15 minutes of task onset. In the Gibbs and Brown study, half of the subjects worked with KR and the other half with the counter concealed, and then the two groups were reversed. Output was significantly higher when the subjects were provided KR than when KR was withheld.

Significant increases for the group going from no KR to the KR condition might be accounted for by the fact that KR was a novel stimulus introduced into an otherwise repetitive task situation. It is more difficult to account for the decrement for the group going from KR to no KR from activation postulates.

There are other indications that the effects of introducing KR, or any other novel stimulus extrinsic to the task, may be temporary. Freedman, Hafer, and Daniel (1966) found that the EEG pattern first showed signs of arousal (low incidence of alpha waves) which then declined during a paired-associate learning task with meaningful KR provided. The decline in the arousal pattern appeared to precede evidence of learning; this fact led the investigators to suggest that decreased arousal may have been due to KR effects. Thompson and Spencer (1966) have hypothesized that the presentation of another stimulus results in recovery of the habituated response, but that the repeated application of the dishabituatory stimulus will cause that stimulus to lose its dishabituation effects. Their studies support the above hypotheses.

Studies of noise by Broadbent (cited by Scott, 1957) indicate that the effects of introducing extraneous noise into a vigilance task are a slight initial performance decrement, followed by an actual advantage which decreases gradually with repeated presentations of the noise.

Inhibition theory, with the emphasis on the learned response-evoking properties of stimuli and the drive reduction hypothesis, does not enable one to anticipate the positive effects of the task enlargement studies. If the net effort of task enlargement is to increase the number of different responses that are required or to increase the variety of stimuli to which the individual must attend or both, then as Berlyne (1960, p. 11) has pointed out, mutual conditioned inhibition may occur. Thus, unless added reinforcement accompanies each of the responses, a gradual accumulation of sIr is anticipated that will lead to a performance decrement. One possible exception may be that when added stimulation does not require additional responses, in which case the added stimulation may serve to disinhibit the inhibited response. However, the added stimulation may also serve as distraction, evoking responses incompatible with task performance.

While inhibition theory generally anticipates negative results from task enlargement, activation theory accounts for the positive results that have often been observed by the increases in activation resulting from the more variable task requirements. As noted below, however, it is not yet possible to state precisely how to enlarge the task nor the conditions under which task enlargement might have beneficial effects.

CONCLUSIONS

Activation theory, in its present stage of development, provides a conceptual framework which not only integrates an impressive number of empirical observations of task behavior but also anticipates them in a general way. On the other hand, Fiske and Maddi (1961, p. 446) have warned that relatively precise predictions can only be made when the constructs have been operationally defined. Such a program, while not easy, is far from impossible. On the environment side, Berlyne (1960, p. 18) has noted that such stimulus properties as uncertainty, novelty, complexity, variation, and intensity are eminently quantitative properties. Since these properties are obviously interdependent, it may prove fruitful to attempt operational definitions of each in order that their interrelationships as well as their relative significance for task behavior may be investigated.

Studies previously cited (Adams & Boulter, 1960; 1962; Adams et al., 1961) suggest that simply increasing the *number* of stimuli to which the individual must attend, holding overt task responses constant, may not have an appreciable effect on activation level. This writer would further speculate that increasing the *variety* of responses, holding the stimulus configuration constant, would not influence activation level as much as increasing the number of distinguishable stimuli with overt task responses held constant. Increasing the variety of responses would perhaps have the greatest effects when some of those responses either led to modifications of the stimulus configuration or consisted of movement to a different stimulus configuration. Thus it may be that our attention should be directed toward the clarification and operational definitions of *stimulus variation.* The definition may be comprised of an intricate measure which takes into account the number of distinguishable stimuli to which the individual must attend, the length of time each stimulus configuration must be responded to before a shift to another stimulus configuration is required, and/or the time elasped before returning to each stimulus configuration. A more immediate alternative, of course, is to develop global rating scales of sustained stimulus variation. The latter should also consider stimuli extrinsic to the task (those which do not require overt responses as an inherent part of the task), but extrinsic stimulus variation should ultimately be treated as a separate problem experimentally.

The direct measurement of activation level will be difficult since students and employees alike will not be eager to have electrodes implanted in their brain stems. However, Fiske and Maddi (1961, p. 53) have reported that measures of physiological arousal, including changes in pupillary size, have been tried with some success. Equipment is now available which will allow the investigator to obtain several arousal measures simultaneously from subjects unencumbered by wires.

Applied psychologists seeking to test the implications of activation theory in an ongoing organization may have to develop psychometric techniques based upon the subject's judgment. While undoubtedly less satisfactory, such techniques should be investigated. The writer factor-analyzed the responses to a number of semantic differential scales set against the concept *Me At Work* and found "activation" and "affective" dimensions to emerge as dominant factors (Scott, 1965). Locke (1965), in working with the Cornell Job Description Index, observed a number of analytically distinguishable subdimensions among those being an "evaluative" dimension, a "monotony" dimension, and an "arousal" dimension. These measures and similar ones could be developed and utilized to test the postulated relationships between variations in task, affective tone, activation level, and performance. Incidentally, here is a case where activation theory may aid in the clarification and understanding of morale. Gordon (1955) has observed that morale measures have typically emphasized affective orientations toward things, whereas there are definitions of morale which emphasize an intraorganismic condition in the absence of specified external referrents. Child (1941), who noted the intraorganismic emphasis, also pointed out the "energetic" and "enthusiastic" dimensions of that condition. Activation theory seems to confirm these ideas and, moreover, suggests the significance of the task itself in morale development.

Other implications of activation theory could be cited but enough has been given to indicate its potential. The writer believes that activation theory provides for those interested in the determinants of task behavior an opportunity to develop more fruitful research programs while contributing to psychological theory. It is not necessary to point out the advantages of developing concepts which are sufficiently abstract to enable us to see the conceptual "sameness" of tasks across phenomenal differences. The clarification and operational specifications of such constructs as stimulus variation and complexity may provide that advantage.

Activation theory is not proposed as a complete behavior theory capable of explaining all the variance in task behavior. In fact, one of the criticisms has been that it has not gone far beyond the empirical data upon which it is based. However, a functional theory which avoids the dangers of premature closure and rank speculation while suggesting new parameters to be investigated is more to be applauded than criticized.

REFERENCES

Adams, J. A. Vigilance in the detection of low-intensity visual stimuli. *Journal of Applied Psychology,* 1956, **52**, 204–08.

Adams, J. A. Comment on Feldman's Reconsideration of the extinction hypothesis of warm up in motor behavior. *Psychological Bulletin* 1963, **60**, 460–63.

Adams, J. A. and Boulter, L. R. Monitoring of complex visual displays: I. Effects of response complexity and intersignal interval on vigilant behavior when visual load is moderate. *United States Air Force CCDD Technical Note,* 1960, No. 60–63.

Adams, J. A. and Boulter, L. R. An evaluation of the activationist hypothesis of human vigilance. *Journal of Experimental Psychology,* 1962, **64**, 495–504.

Adams, J. A., Stenson, H. H., and Humes, J. M. Monitoring of complex visual displays: II. Effects of visual load and response complexity on human vigilance. *Human Factors,* 1961, **3**, 213–21.

Ammons, R. B. Acquisition of motor skill: I. Quantitative analysis and theoretical formulation. *Psychological Reviews,* 1947, **54**, 263–81.

Ammons, R. B., Ammons, C. H., and Morgan, R. L. Subskills in rotary pursuit as affected by rate and accuracy requirements and by distribution of practice. *Journal of General Psychology,* 1958, **58**, 259–79.

Bakan, P. Discrimination decrement as a function of time in a prolonged vigil. *Journal of Experimental Psychology,* 1955, **50**, 387–90.

Baldamus, W. Incentives and work analysis. *University of Birmingham Studies in Economics and Sociology,* 1951, Monograph **A1**, 1–78.

Bergum, B. O. and Lehr, D. J. Vigilance performance as a function of interpolated rest. *Journal of Applied Psychology,* 1962, **46**, 425–27.

Berlyne, D. E. *Conflict, arousal and curiosity.* New York: McGraw-Hill, 1960.

Bernhaut, M., Gellhorn, E., and Rasmussen, A. T. Experimental contributions to the problem of consciousness. *Journal of Neurophysiology,* 1953, **16**, 21–35.

Bills, A. G. Blocking: A new principle of mental fatigue. *American Journal of Psychology,* 1931, **43**, 230–45.

Bindra, D. *Motivation: A systematic reinterpretation.* New York: Ronald Press, 1959.

Broadbent, D. E. *Perception and communication.* New York: Pergamon Press, 1958.

Brownfield, C. A. Deterioration and facilitation hypotheses in sensory deprivation research. *Psychological Bulletin,* 1964, **61**, 304–13.

Chapanis, A. Knowledge of performance as an incentive in repetitive monotonous tasks. *Journal of Applied Psychology,* 1964, **48**, 263–67.

Child, I. L. Morale: A bibliographic review. *Psychological Bulletin,* 1941, **38**, 393–420.

Cofer, C. N. and Appley, M. H. *Motivation: Theory and research.* New York: Wiley, 1964.

Davis, L. E. Job design and productivity: A new approach. *Personnel,* 1957, **33**, 418–30.

Deese, J. Some problems in the theory of vigilance. *Psychological Review,* 1955, **62**, 359–68.

Deese, J. and Ormond, E. Studies of detectability during continuous visual search. *United States Air Force Wright Air Development Center Technical Report,* 1953, No. 53-8.

Dember, W. N. and Earl, R. W. Analysis of exploratory, manipulatory, and curiosity behaviors. *Psychological Review,* 1957, **64**, 91–96.

Denenberg, V. H. Critical periods, stimulus input, and emotional reactivity: A theory of infantile stimulation. *Psychological Review,* 1964, **71**, 335–51.

Duffy, Elizabeth. The concept of energy mobilization. *Psychological Review,* 1951, 58, 30–40.

Duffy, Elizabeth. *Activation and behavior.* New York: Wiley, 1962.

Feldman, M. P. A reconsideration of the extinction hypothesis of warm-up in motor behavior. *Psychological Bulletin,* 1963, **60**, 452–59.

Fiske, D. W. and Maddi, S. R. (eds.) *Functions of varied experience.* Homewood, Ill.: Dorsey Press, 1961.

Frankman, Judith P. and Adams, J. A. Theories of vigilance. *Psychological Bulletin,* 1962, **59**, 257–72.

Fraser, D. C. The relation of an environmental variable to performance in a prolonged visual task. *Quarterly Journal of Experimental Psychology,* 1953, **5**, 31–32.

Freedman, N. L., Hafer, Brenna M., and Daniel, R. S. EEG arousal decrement during paired-associate learning. *Journal of Comparative and Physiological Psychology,* 1966, **61**, 15–19.

French, J. D., Amerongen, F. K., and Magoun, H. W. An activating system in the brainstem of monkeys. *Archives of Neurological Psychiatry (Chicago),* 1952, **68**, 577–90.

French, J. D., Hernandez-Peon, R., and Livingston, R. B. Projections from cortex to cephalic brain stem in monkeys. *Journal of Neurophysiology,* 1955, **18**, 74–95.

French, J. D. and Magoun, H. W. Effects of chronic lesions in central cephalic brain stem of monkeys. *Archives of Neurological Psychiatry (Chicago)* 1952, **68**, 591–604.

Ghiselli, E. E. and Brown, C. W. *Personnel and industrial psychology.* New York: McGraw-Hill, 1955.

Gibbs, C. B. and Brown, I. D. Increased production from the information incentive in a repetitive task. *Medical Research Council, Applied Psychological Research Unit, Great Britain,* 1955, No. 230.

Glanzer, M. Stimulus satiation: An explanation and related phenomenon. *Psychological Review,* 1953, **8**, 257–68.

Gordon, O. J. A factor analysis of human needs and industrial morale. *Personnel Psychology,* 1955, **8**, 1–18.

Hebb, D. O. *The organization of behavior.* New York: Wiley, 1949.

Hernandez-Peon, R. and Hagbarth, K. E. Interaction between afferent and cortically induced reticular responses. *Journal of Neurophysiology,* 1955, **18**, 44–55.

Holland, J. G. Human vigilance. *Science,* 1958, **128**, 61–67.

Hull, C. L. *Principles of behavior.* New York: Appleton-Century-Crofts, 1943.

Jenkins, H. M. The effect of signal rate on performance in visual monitoring. *American Journal of Psychology,* 1958, **71**, 647–61.

Jerison, H. J. Experiments on vigilance: Duration of the vigil and the decrement function. *United States Air Force Wright Air Development Center Technical Report,* 1958, No. 58-369.

Jerison, H. J. and Wallis, R. M. Experiments on vigilance: One-clock and three-clock monitoring. *United States Air Force Wright Air Development Center Technical Report,* 1957, No. 57-206.

Kidd, J. S. and Micocci, A. Maintenance of vigilance in an auditory monitoring task. *Journal of Applied Psychology,* 1964, **48**, 13–15.

Leuba, C. Toward some integration of learning theories: The concept of optimal stimulation. *Psychological Reports,* 1955, **1**, 27–33.

Lindsley, D. B. Emotion. In S. S. Stevens (ed.), *Handbook of experimental psychology.* New York: Wiley, 1951, pp. 473–516.

Lindsley, D. B. Psychophysiology and motivation. In M. R. Jones (ed.), *Nebraska symposium on motivation, 1957.* Lincoln: University of Nebraska Press, 1957, pp. 44–105.

Lindsley, D. B. The reticular activating system. In D. E. Sheer (ed.), *Electrical stimulation of the brain.* Austin: University of Texas Press, 1961, pp. 331–49.

Lindsley, D. B., Bowden, J., and Magoun, H. W. Effect upon the EEG of acute injury to the brain stem activating system. *Electroencephalography and Clinical Neurophysiology,* 1949, **1**, 475–86.

Lindsley, D. B., Schreiner, L. H., Knowles, W. B., and Magoun, H. W. Behavior and EEG changes following chronic brain stem lesions in the cat. *Electroencephalography and Clinical Neurophysiology,* 1950, **2**, 483–98.

Locke, E. A. The relationship of task success to task liking and satisfaction. *Journal of Applied Psychology,* 1965, **49**, 379–85.

McGeer, P. L. Mind, drugs and behavior. *American Scientist,* 1962, **50**, 322–38.

McGehee, W. and Owen, E. B. Authorized and unauthorized rest pauses in clerical work. *Journal of Applied Psychology,* 1940, **24**, 605–14.

Mackworth, N. H. Researches in the measurement of human performance. *Medical Research Council Special Report Series,* 1950, No. 268, London.

Malmo, R. B. Activation: A neuropsychological dimension. *Psychological Review,* 1959, **66**, 367–86.

Moruzzi, G. and Magoun, H. W. Brain stem reticular formation and the activation of the EEG. *Electroencephalography and Clinical Neurophysiology,* 1949, **1**, 455–73.

Nakajima, A. Effects of chemical injection into the reticular formation of rats. *Journal of Comparative and Physiological Psychology,* 1964, **58**, 10–15.

Olds, J. A preliminary mapping of electrical and reinforcing effects in the rat brain. *Journal of Comparative and Physiological Psychology,* 1956, **49**, 281–85. (a)

Olds, J. Runway and maze behavior controlled by basomedial forebrain stimulation in the rat. *Journal of Comparative and Physiological Psychology,* 1956, **49**, 407–512. (b)

Olds, J. and Milner, P. Positive reinforcement produced by electrical stimulation of septal area and other regions of the rat's brain. *Journal of Comparative and Physiological Psychology,* 1954, **47**, 419–27.

Pavlov, I. P. *Conditioned reflexes.* Oxford: Clarendon Press, 1927.

Samuels, Ina. Reticular mechanisms and behavior. *Psychological Bulletin,* 1959, **56**, 1–25.

Scott, T. H. Literature review of the intellectual effects of perceptual isolation. *Defence Research Board,* 1957, Rep. No. HR **66**, Department of National Defence, Ottawa.

Scott, W. E. Some motivational determinants of work behavior. *Indiana Business Information Bulletin No. 54,* 1965, 116–31. Bureau of Business Research, Bloomington, Indiana.

Sharpless, S. and Jasper, H. H. Habituation of the arousal reaction. *Brain,* 1956, **79**, 655–80.

Sipowicz, R. R., Ware, J. R., & Baker, R. A. The effects of reward and knowledge of results on the performance of a simple vigilance task. *Journal of Experimental Psychology,* 1962, **64**, 58–61.

Stein, L. and Ray, O. S. Self-regulation of brain-stimulating current intensity in the rat. *Science,* 1959, **130**, 570–71.

Strauss, G. and Sayles, L. R. *Personnel: The human problems of management.* Englewood Cliffs, N.J.: Prentice-Hall, 1960.

Thompson, R. F. and Spencer, W. A. Habituation: A model phenomenon for the study of neuronal substrates of behavior. *Psychological Review,* 1966, **73**, 16–43.

Tiffin, J., and McCormick, E. J. *Industrial psychology.* (5th ed.) Englewood Cliffs, N.J.: Prentice-Hall, 1965.

Uhrbrock, R. S. Music on the job: Its influence on worker morale and production. *Personnel Psychology,* 1961, **14**, 9–38.

Vernon, H. M. On the extent and effects of variety in repetitive work. *Industrial Fatigue Research Board* Report No. 26. London: H. M. Stationery Office, 1924.

Vernon, H. M. and Bedford, T. The influence of rest pauses on light industrial work. *Industrial Fatigue Research Board* Report No. 25. London: H.M. Stationery Office, 1924.

Walker, C. R. and Guest, R. H. *The man on the assembly line.* Cambridge: Harvard University Press, 1952.

Walker, E. L. Action decrement and its relation to learning. *Psychological Review,* 1958, **55**, 129–42.

Worden, F. G., and Livingston, R. B. Brain-stem reticular formation. In D. E. Sheer (ed.), *Electrical stimulation of the brain.* Austin: University of Texas Press, 1961, pp. 263–76.

Wyatt, S., Fraser, J. A., and Stock, F. G. L. The comparative effects of variety and uniformity in work. *Industrial Fatigue Research Board* Report No. 52. London: H.M. Stationery Office, 1928.

Wyatt, S. and Ogden, A. D. On the extent and effects of variety in repetitive work. *Industrial Fatigue Research Board* Report No. 26. London: H.M. Stationery Office, 1924.

Young, P. T. *Motivation and emotion.* New York: Wiley, 1961.

23. JOB ENLARGEMENT, INDIVIDUAL DIFFERENCES, AND WORKER RESPONSES*

***Charles L. Hulin and Milton R. Blood*†**

The literature bearing on the job-enlargement thesis and the literature relating job size to job satisfaction and behavior are reviewed. The conclusion is reached that the positive relationship between job size and job satisfaction cannot be assumed to be general but rather is dependent to a great extent on the backgrounds of the workers in the sample. Evidence is also reviewed which indicates that the hypothesized relationships between repetition and monotony, monotony and satisfaction, and satisfaction and behavior must be questioned. Finally, a model which relates job size to satisfaction depending on a third variable (alienation of the workers from middle-class work-related values and norms) is presented. This model adequately accounts for most of the problems and contradictions which exist in the literature.

One of the most pervasive and dominant themes which exists in the attempts of industrial psychologists to provide guidelines and frameworks for the motivation of industrial workers is the notion of job enlargement. Job enlargement is a concerted attempt to stem and even reverse the current trends among industrial engineering programs toward job simplification and specialization. The attack on job specialization and job simplification has a long and impressive history going back nearly 200 years to the writings of Adam Smith. In 1776, Smith (reported in Lewis, 1963) stated that

> It [division of labor] corrupts even the activity of his body, and renders him incapable of exerting his strength with vigour and perseverance, in any other employment than that to which he has been bred. His dexterity at his own particular trade seems, in this manner, to be acquired at the expense of his intellectual, social, and martial virtues [p. 237].

Further early support for this position has been found in the writings of Durkheim (1933). However, the support from Durkheim is more in the eye of the reader than in the writings since Durkheim did not attack the division of labor *per se,* only the anomic division of labor. He stated that normally the division of labor produces social solidarity and that there is nothing noble about a man doing a large job in a mediocre fashion nor nothing debasing about a man doing a small job well. Unfortunately, most of the references to Durkheim are to his discussion of the anomic division of labor, which he considered a pathological state of society. The problem in the discussion presented by Durkheim is to define that point at which the division of labor ceases to be beneficial and becomes pathological and produces anomie. We raise the question of whether such a point exists and is indeed definable. If it does exist, can it be considered a constant or does it vary from worker to worker with some workers regarding extremely specialized short-time-cycle, simple jobs as good jobs?

Most modern writers (Argyris, 1957; Kornhauser, 1965; Likert, 1961; MacGregor, 1957; Whyte, 1955) regard nearly all division of labor, with the resulting job simplification and specialization, as leading almost inevitably to monotony, boredom, job dissatisfaction, and inappropriate (from the point of view of management) behavior patterns. The evidence on this point will be reviewed in this paper, along with an analysis of the effects of the individual differences of workers on their responses to job enlargement and job simplification. An attempt will also be made to specify a model based on the cultural differences of workers which can be used to resolve the contradictions in the literature and to predict responses to larger (or enlarged) jobs.

DEFINITION

For the purposes of this review, job enlargement has been considered as the process of allowing individual workers to determine their own working pace (within limits), to serve as their own inspectors by giving them responsibility for quality control, to repair their own mistakes, to be responsible for their own machine setup and repair, and to attain choice of method. In this sense, job enlargement is qualitatively different from job extension, which consists of merely adding similar elements to the job without altering job content (e.g., soldering the red wires as well as the black wires). However, changing from a line-paced job to a self-paced job would be regarded as job enlargement. It can also be seen that the process of job enlargement produces jobs at a higher level of skill, with varied work content and relative autonomy for the worker. On the other hand, the process of job simplification results in jobs requiring less skill which are more repetitive and have less autonomy. The process of job simplification has progressed much further with some jobs than with others. Thus, jobs at different points in the process of simplification exist contemporaneously. While we do not normally think of differences

* *Psychological Bulletin,* Vol. 69, No. 1 (1968), pp. 41–55.

† Departments of Psychology, University of Illinois, and University of California (Berkeley), respectively.

between jobs in such terms, it seems to be a veridical way of organizing thinking about job levels. Also, such categorizations of jobs enable us to consider both experimental and correlational methods of analyzing differences or changes in worker responses. That is, changes in workers' responses which correlate with the degree of job simplification should also be observed if changes in job specialization are made experimentally.

TRADITIONAL MODEL

According to the theorists, as jobs become increasingly specialized the monotony (perception of the *sameness* of the job from minute-to-minute, perception of the unchanging characteristic of the job) increases. That is, short-time-cycle, simplified jobs lead to monotony. Monotony is supposedly associated with feelings of boredom and job dissatisfaction. Boredom and job dissatisfaction lead to undesirable (from management's point of view) behavior. This reasoning could be diagrammed as follows:

Stimulus Condition		*Perception*		*Affective Response*		*Behavioral Response*
Simplified, low skill level, short-cycle jobs	→	Monotony	→	Boredom, job dissatisfaction	→	Absenteeism, turnover, restriction of output

Several assumptions in this line of reasoning deserve discussion. Consider the assumption that repetitiveness leads to monotony and, conversely, that uniqueness and change lead to a lack of monotony. Smith (1955) has demonstrated that there are important individual differences in susceptibility to monotony among workers on the same job. Apparently, some workers do not report monotony even in the face of a job with an extremely short work cycle. Baldamus (1961) has pointed out that repetitive work can often have positively motivating characteristics (traction) which tend to "pull the worker along" and are pleasant. This notion has been experimentally verified by Smith and Lem (1955) using a sample of industrial workers. Thus the assumption of repetitiveness leading to monotony could be questioned on two grounds—effects of individual differences and positive motivational characteristics of repetition.

The second assumption is that monotony leads to boredom and job dissatisfaction. Even granting that the physical reality of short time cycles or repetition leads to monotony, can we assume that workers respond with negative affect to this perception? This assumption can be questioned on much the same grounds as the first. At the very least, we should allow the possibility that some workers prefer the safety of not being required to make decisions. Vroom (1960) has demonstrated that not all workers are satisfied when they are allowed to take part in the decision-making process about their jobs, and there are significant individual differences (F scale scores) between workers who respond positively to the opportunity to make decisions and those who do not. While not exactly to the point, these data at least indicate that some workers prefer routine, repetition, and specified work methods to change, variety, and decision making.

The final assumption is that boredom and job dissatisfaction are associated with undesirable behavior patterns. This assumption is probably the least crucial to the argument since trite as it may seem, a high level of job satisfaction among industrial workers may be an appropriate goal in itself. If job enlargement had no other result than decreased boredom and increased job satisfaction, it would be appropriate. Also, there is evidence (Hulin, 1966; Weitz & Nuckols, 1953) that in certain circumstances, job satisfaction is significantly related to individual decisions to quit. The relationship between satisfaction and productivity and other on-the-job behaviors is somewhat more elusive. The fact that this relationship has been so difficult to obtain indicates the weakness of the final assumption of the traditional model.

EVIDENCE

Empirical studies linking job satisfaction to job size have a long history but have generally been poorly controlled, and most of the authors have attempted to generalize from severely limited data. In an early study, Wyatt, Fraser, and Stock (1929a) reported that workers on a soap-wrapping job gave higher outputs when working conditions were uniform than when conditions were varied. Outputs were not different in the two conditions when the jobs were folding handkerchiefs and making bicycle chains. From this they concluded that varied conditions were better and they began studying optimum spacing of task changes! There are obvious problems with this study. The *N*s were small and results did not reach statistical significance, most of the results do not support their conclusions, and they did not control for variations in output which may have been caused by the change *per se* as opposed to the particular variations of their hypotheses. Their writings also fail to distinguish among the effects of fatigue, inhibition, boredom, and monotony. In later studies, Wyatt, Fraser, and Stock (1929b) and Wyatt, Langdon, and Stock (1937) investigated the effects of jobs having short time cycles. Smith (1953) has pointed out "certain deviations from normally acceptable methods of scientific investigation . . . [p. 69]." Part of their measure of boredom consisted of questions about slowing of output during the middle of the day. Those who reported such slowing were regarded as bored. Also, those who reported such slowing did indeed slow down at these times. Therefore, Wyatt *et al.* were able to obtain good matches between their measure of boredom and "typical" boredom output curves. The circularity is evident. The results relating boredom, IQ, and production cause concern. High-IQ workers were more bored and boredom reduced the rate of working, but high-IQ workers were more productive. Boredom was less likely to occur on fully automated work, and the experience of boredom was largely dependent on individual characteristics. The workers in all these studies were female which serves as an additional restriction on generalization. All in all, both the measures and the conclusions of these studies are extremely suspect. Roethlisberger and Dickson (1941) and Smith (1953) were unable to replicate the original results of Wyatt *et al.* Generalizations from these data must, indeed, be cautious.

Walker (1950) presented a report of the benefits of a job-enlargement program which was undertaken at IBM. Though some might consider this article a heuristic success, it presented little in the way of data. There was no control for a Hawthorne effect, and no data were presented which concerned satisfaction, turnover, costs, etc.

Walker and Marriott (1951) provided data indicating that more than a third of the employees of mass production factories complained of boredom, but in rolling mills the proportion was only 8 percent. Boredom was more widespread among conveyor workers, and workers were less satisfied on such jobs if they had previously held a skilled job. Data came from interviews with 976 men from three large factories. This seems to be evidence supporting the traditional model which relates uniformity and repetition in work to dissatisfaction. While we have no disagreement with the results as presented, there are some problems associated with the generality of the conclusions. Individual differences in worker responses were considerable, and, in fact, "Many liked their work because it was simple, straightforward, and carried no responsibility." Differences between factories were attributed to differences in production techniques rather than to differences between the persons making up the work forces of the factories. A subsequent interview study (Walker & Guest, 1952) related increased dissatisfaction, increased absences, and increased turnover to assembly line work. The basic conclusion was that very little could be said in favor of assembly line work.

While Walker and Guest were careful not to generalize beyond their sample, their conclusions and recommendations were stated in very general terms, and sound as if they are cures for ills everywhere. In light of the sample described by Walker and Guest and the findings of Blood and Hulin (1967) and Turner and Lawrence (1965), there is little doubt that Walker and Guest's results would be anticipated by the model to be presented in this paper. Typical descriptive statements given by Walker and Guest (1952) are: "The area from which [the workers] were recruited has few mass production factors [p. 4]." "Only two in our sample had ever worked in an automobile plant before [p. 19]" and ". . . 34.5 percent of all those [in the sample] with manual work experience were skilled persons. Considering the relatively unskilled nature of automobile assembly work, this high proportion of skilled workmen . . . is of interest [p. 31]." While our model would predict negative responses to simplified, line-paced jobs from workers such as those described by Walker and Guest, we would not expect such negative responses to be a general characteristic of the United States work force. In subsequent papers (Guest, 1955, 1957; Walker, 1954), these investigators have extolled the virtues of job flexibility, job rotation, and job enlargement without contributing any additional data. Their claims are unjustifiable because of the peculiarities of their sample and their lack of acceptable experimental controls.

The Detroit Edison Electric Utility Company carried out a program of job enlargement among first-line supervisors and clerical workers (Elliott, 1953). Though there were no controls and no statistical information was provided, Elliott claimed that job enlargement reduced costs and increased production. He then assumed a positive relationship between productivity and morale. On the basis of this assumed relationship, he argued that satisfaction had increased! Cost reduction and production increase are more easily explained in this case as a result of the elimination of duplications in the work process. The report did include the recognition that some workers prefer repetitive jobs.

Marks (1954) reported a study of 29 female employees in the manufacturing department of a company on the West Coast. A similar department was monitored as a control. Production was poorer with enlarged jobs, but quality improved.[1] After experience with the enlarged job, some workers disliked the lack of personal responsibility of an assembly line design. The conclusion, however, which is normally drawn

[1] Quality improvement would be expected in nearly all programs of job enlargement since the worker serves as his own inspector. If he makes a mistake and discovers it he can repair it on the spot. Such repairs on assembly line work are, of course, impossible since the worker cannot stop to make the repairs. This improvement in quality, however, should be regarded as a direct result of the technical changes in the jobs

from this study is that enlarged jobs are better.

When assembly operations were enlarged in the Maytag Company plant in Newton, Iowa, there were quantity and quality improvements in production (Biganne & Stewart, 1963). These workers would be expected by the model to be presented in this paper to be more satisfied with enlarged jobs. No statistical evidence was presented, but it was reported that most of the workers came to like their new jobs and they seemed to become involved.

In a study of the attitudes of skilled and semiskilled workers to job enlargement, Davis and Werling (1960) surveyed a West Coast plant employing 400 operating and 250 clerical and administrative personnel. The interests of skilled workers, similar to those of management, included company success, improvement of self, and improvement of operations. Semiskilled workers, on the other hand, lacked concern for company goals and they attached little importance to job content. From this, Davis and Werling concluded that semiskilled jobs are insufficiently enlarged. Such a conclusion requires evidence that the size of the job determines attitude. Of course there is no evidence of this sort, and, indeed, attitudes toward company goals and job content may be as influenced by many subcultural and personal background factors as by one aspect of the task. Further, the inference that the workers *should* think job content important is an evaluative assumption not necessary for empirical analysis of the data.

Argyris (1959) provided information from content analysis of interviews with 34 employees from a department with high skill demands and 90 unskilled and semiskilled employees from another department. As compared with the skilled employees, those of lower skill expressed *(a)* less aspiration for high-quality work, *(b)* less need to learn more about their work, *(c)* more emphasis on money, *(d)* lower estimates of personal abilities, *(e)* less desire for variety and independence, *(f)* high work spoilage (subjectively judged since the tasks were different), *(g)* fewer lasting friendships formed on the job, and *(h)* less creative use of leisure time. Also, the lower skilled employees expressed needs "to be left alone," "to be passive," and "to experience routine or sameness." According to the theories of Argyris, these differences are caused by the organization's stifling the maturity of individuals on the job. However, just as in the Davis and Werling study, there is no reason to believe that these differences were caused by the job rather than brought to the work situation.

In a study auspiciously titled "Job Enlargement: Antidote to Apathy," Reif and Schoderbek (1966) reported the results of a survey of companies regarding their use of job enlargement. Questionnaires were mailed to 276 companies. Replies were received from 210, and of these, 41 said they had used job enlargement. The most popular reasons for undertaking job enlargement were cost reduction and profit increase. Twenty-three respondents checked "increase in job satisfaction" as an advantage of job enlargement. It is significant that only 23 of the 41 companies which used job enlargement noted an increase in job satisfaction in spite of *(a)* the popularity of the traditional notion that workers want larger jobs, and *(b)* the opportunity for bias in this sample. Reif and Schoderbek seemed unaware that their data may have been atypical even though the sample represented less than 15 percent of their initial population. Returns perhaps should not be expected from companies who have tried job enlargement unsuccessfully, and if an executive from such a company did reply he would probably be hesitant to admit that an executive policy of his firm had failed. Reif and Schoderbek's conclusions in favor of job enlargement and the proposal of job enlargement as an "antidote for apathy" are unjustified.

In a study of the effects of repetitive work on the mental health of industrial workers, Kornhauser (1965) found that many production workers from an urban area gave interview responses which he considered indicative of poor mental health. He showed that, in general, such indications of poor mental health increased as job level decreased (from skilled workers to semiskilled workers with repetitive tasks). He has gleaned a large amount of information from interviews with 655 men, and his data and his conclusions merit discussion. He convincingly showed that there are systematic differences in the interview responses of workers at different job levels. From the nature of the response differences he concluded that the persons in the lower skilled jobs were in poorer mental health and, furthermore, that their occupational situation caused this condition. He argued that job simplification is a cause of poor mental health. Before accepting these conclusions, some of the methods of his study must be examined.

First, all data were obtained from interview responses. Therefore, they are open to such biasing factors as social acceptability, interviewer bias, and bias of the coder who arranged the interview transcripts into quantitative material. Social acceptability bias would enter the situation and distort responses in the obtained direction if the interviewee shaped his answers to his expectations of the responses desired by his middle-class-oriented interviewer. That is, persons in repetitive jobs may feel hesitant to ad-

and not of changes in worker motivation or satisfaction. Kilbridge (1960b) has also pointed out that many of the positive results obtained in studies of job enlargement could be attributed to reductions in balance-delay time and nonproduction time and not to changes in worker motivations or satisfaction.

mit that they are not dissatisfied with their work if they feel that such admission will lead to an unfavorable judgment from the interviewer. If the interviewer or coder was familiar with the hypothesis of the study (either explicitly or implicitly), there is the additional possibility that responses were systematically interpreted in the manner most favorable to the hypothesis. Since no information was presented which would either confirm or disconfirm the existence of these biases, we must approach the results with proper caution and the realization that such distortions *might* have taken place.

Second, Kornhauser attempted to generalize from an urban blue-collar sample to all production workers. Recent studies by Turner and Lawrence (1965) and Blood and Hulin (1967) have demonstrated that we cannot generalize from urban blue-collar workers to all blue-collar workers.

Further, Kornhauser chose to ignore differences in workers' personal backgrounds. Perhaps this is justified since he explained that these differences were not the point of his discussion. However, we should not overlook his data which show the relationship between personal background variables and the Mental Health Index score to be at least as strong as that between job level and the Mental Health Index score. He pointed to the relative independence of these influences, but his analytic techniques were such that they would not have been sensitive to interaction effects so this conclusion must be attributed to his personal judgment.

Finally, it is inevitable that the Mental Health Index depends on value judgments as to what constitutes good or poor health. In this case, good mental health seems to depend more on striving for personal betterment than on a realistic evaluation of the situation. For example, the interview response "There's such a thing as beating your brains against the wall. Some things you just can't change; might as well accept them and adjust yourself to them" was said by Kornhauser to "call attention to the very limited self-expectations, the degree of passivity, fatalism, and resignation that characterize many of the workers [p. 241]." Thus, Kornhauser shows that he himself subscribes to what he considers to be a middle-class concept—that every person is responsible for his own situation rather than being influenced by forces beyond his control. He saw as evidence of poor mental health that members of a lower-class subculture do not hold middle-class ideals. What these data show most convincingly is that there are differences by job level among urban workers in the extent to which workers adhere to a middle-class value system. Another problem with the Mental Health Index results is that we are not able to compare them with any kind of base line. Some comparison data were provided from a small sample of low-ranking white collar workers and a small sample of production workers from outside Detroit. Because of the sample sizes, these comparison data are less trustworthy than the experimental data. Statistical probabilities of the differences between these comparison samples and the larger, Detroit blue-collar sample were not provided and in many cases the results look similar.

In several ways Kornhauser's study demonstrates the dangers of trying to index a culture-bound concept such as mental health when using a research sample which may contain subcultural differences and may be culturally different from the investigators and persons who are judging the validity of the research instrument. Nonetheless, the study confirms that there are response differences between different job levels. This is not a new concept, but whereas blue-collar and white-collar differences have been discussed in the past, Kornhauser showed that within the gross blue-collar category finer discriminations will provide additional information. Porter (1961) has shown that such differentiation is profitable in the white-collar realm. Certainly job level is an influential dimension in the determination of workers' responses and the extent to which class ideals prevail. If we can find other useful dimensions, we will increase our ability to understand, and hence predict, workers' reactions to job enlargement and other aspects of their work situation.

Scott (1966) has generalized the activation theory of vigilance behavior to the area of task and job design. The activation theory of vigilance behavior is a physiological explanation of behavior in situations characterized by low levels of stimulation and has been found to summarize much of the literature on vigilance decrement (Frankmann & Adams, 1962). Briefly, this theory holds that stimuli impinging on the human receptor serve two purposes. One is a cue or information function which is accomplished when the stimulation travels directly to the appropriate cortical projection area. The other is an arousal or activation function and is accomplished when the neural stimulation also travels through the ascending reticular formation and is diffused over a wide area of the cortex. This pathway serves no cue or information function but does serve to maintain the organism at a high state of arousal or activation. Generalizing from the activation theory and the results of vigilance studies, Scott argued that amount and variety of stimulation serve to motivate the worker and enable him to maintain a high level of performance. In short, nonroutine, nonrepetitive jobs are likely to serve as positive motivators of behavior. Basing a theory of industrial motivation in physiology would, of course, tend to give it the appearance of being more basic, general, and valid.

While we have no disagreement with the efficacy of the activation theory when applied to vigilance data, we do feel there are a number of problems involved with generalizing the theory to the area of industrial task design. First, the similarity between the experimental settings *where vigilance decrements are reliably obtained* and even the most routine and repetitive of industrial jobs is slight. The presence of other people, random intermittent noise, illumination changes, multiple tasks, the opportunity to move about, stretch, talk to other workers, etc., all summate to produce a situation far removed from the usual vigilance situations. Considering the fact that vigilance decrements can be eliminated by the introduction of multiple tasks, other people in the room, etc., industrial tasks are so different from vigilance tasks that any generalizations are exceedingly dangerous. Second, whenever tasks are enlarged, several derived social motivation variables are changed along with the desired changes in amount and variety of the physical stimulation. When more elements are added to a task, a greater variety of skills is required and, at the extreme, greater involvement in the job is required. Whether all or even most workers are willing to make this investment in their jobs is a matter for investigation, not assumption. Finally, while not an inherent problem of the activation theory, there is the matter of individual differences in the optimal levels of stimulation. While parameters for individual differences could be built into the theory, there are at present no such parameters nor are there any indications in the activation theory as to the source of information for predicting such individual differences parameters. Considering the variance controlled by these ubiquitous individual differences in the behavior and motivation of industrial workers, such an omission amounts to a very serious gap in the theory.

In addition to the references cited above, Worthy (1950), Argyris (1957, 1964), Davis (1957a, 1957b), and Davis and Canter (1955) presented the traditional viewpoint that larger jobs are "better" jobs. Though the human relations approach has gained widespread popular support, the data are unconvincing. These supportive data present us with severe restrictions either because of methodological problems or because of the nature of the samples. Warren (1958) reviewed the traditional literature and the research data and called for the research-team approach to the evaluation of job enlargement. He concurred in some of the human relations concepts, but he made clear the difference between monotony and boredom. An approach to the problem of dissatisfaction with repetitive work which is notable for its novelty was presented by Behling (1964). He began with the human relations assumption that repetitive work leads to dissatisfaction. He then invoked the Maslow hierarchy of needs to explain this dissatisfaction, saying it results from the fact that our present civilization is able to satisfy our lower level needs thus making our higher level needs more potent. Of course while the lower level needs of workers are unsatisfied, these higher level needs are not motivators of behavior. He concluded that many of the needs of workers would be more properly fulfilled outside of the work organization. MacKinney, Wernimont, and Galitz (1962) reviewed the studies relating job specialization and job satisfaction, and they concluded that the issue was not settled by the data at that time. We obviously feel that the issue is still not structured, and also agree with MacKinney *et al.*'s (1962) statement:

> The most compelling argument against specialization as a major cause of job dissatisfaction lies in the fact of individual differences. This is the central fact of life in the behavioral sciences, and yet the would-be reformers apparently believe that all people must react in exactly the same way to the same job. The observer says to himself, "That job would drive me nuts in half an hour." From this he somehow concludes that it must drive everyone else nuts as well. This simply is not so! (For that matter, it's highly probable that many of the workers interviewed by sympathetic social scientists privately regard their questioners' activities as a pretty terrible way to earn a living, too) [p. 17].

More recent data presented by Whyte (1955), Kennedy and O'Neill (1958), Kilbridge (1960a), Katzell, Barrett, and Parker (1961), Kendall (1963), Conant and Kilbridge (1965), Kornhauser (1965), and Blood and Hulin (1967) indicate that the general conclusion regarding the effects of job enlargement on job satisfaction and/or motivation is overstated and may be applicable to only certain segments of the working population. Further, it seems that each of the assumptions in the job-enlargement model can be seriously questioned by numerous other studies.

Perhaps the most dramatic of these studies was done by Turner and Lawrence (1965). Turner and Lawrence attempted a comprehensive study of the attitudinal and behavioral responses of workers to different aspects of their jobs. The original hypotheses were that workers respond favorably (high satisfaction and low absence rates) to jobs which are more complex, have more responsibility, more authority, more variety, etc. In short, "good" responses would accompany high-level jobs. The hypothesis concerning attendance was confirmed for a sample of 470 workers from 11 industries working on 47 different jobs. The hypothesized positive relationship between job level and satisfaction was *not* supported. This finding plus the presence of a number of curvilinear relationships led Turner and Lawrence to the conclusion that the workers in the sample had been drawn from two separate and distinct populations whose members responded in different ways to similar job characteristics. The investigators, by splitting their group of workers on a succession of variables and analyzing the relationship between task attributes and job satisfaction, were able to determine that workers from factories located in small towns responded dramatically differently from workers who came from more urban settings. The workers from small-town settings tended to respond to task attributes in the manner predicted by Turner and Lawrence. Workers from cities indicated no relationship between task attributes and attendance and responded with *low* job satisfaction to supposedly desirable job attributes and with high satisfaction to such "undesirable" attributes as repetitiveness. Turner and Lawrence posited an explanation based on a notion of alienation *qua anomie*. They argued that workers in large cities with their extremely heterogeneous social cultures would be more likely to be normless (anomic). They would fail to develop strong group or subcultural norms and values due to the extreme size and heterogeneity of the city population and would fail to respond positively to the white-collar-oriented values attached to larger, more autonomous, more skilled jobs. Rather than ignoring the effects of individual differences or attributing them to chance, Turner and Lawrence were able to determine that the unexpected results could not be attributed to chance or poor mental health but could be attributed to differences in cultural backgrounds.

Blood and Hulin (1967) argued that workers from large cities could not be considered as being anomic on the basis of the evidence but could be considered to be alienated from the "work" norms of the middle class (positive affect for occupational achievement, a belief in the intrinsic value of hard work, a striving for the attainment of responsible positions, and a belief in the work-related aspects of Calvinism and the Protestant ethic) and integrated with the norms of their own particular subculture. Simply because blue-collar workers do not share the work norms and values of the middle classes does not mean they have no norms. In the case of the industrial workers sampled by Turner and Lawrence, there is no compelling reason to suspect that workers in large industrialized cities would adhere to the dominant work value systems of the white middle-class groups. In fact, it would be somewhat surprising if these workers whose grandfathers and fathers had (likely) worked as unskilled or semiskilled laborers and had failed to rise above their initial job or, even worse, had been replaced by a machine or a younger worker at age 50 would behave in the way demanded by the Protestant ethic. (Work hard and you will get ahead. You are responsible for your own destiny. Acceptance into the Kingdom of Heaven is dependent on hard work on this mortal earth.) Starting from this position, Blood and Hulin reanalyzed some data gathered by Patricia C. Smith. These data had been gathered from some 1,300 blue-collar workers employed in 21 plants located throughout the eastern half of the United States. Using results of Kendall's (1963) principal component analysis based on variables available in the census tracts, Blood and Hulin ordered the 21 plants along a number of dimensions which they felt would reflect the degree to which the blue-collar workers in the communities would feel alienated from middle-class work norms. Kendall (1963) labeled the principal components which were chosen for this analysis as extent of slums, urbanization, population density, standard of living, etc. (see Kendall, 1963, or Blood and Hulin, 1967, for a description of how these variates were constructed). These community variates were then used to predict a number of variables obtained from each of the 21 plants. These dependent variables included extent of preparation for retirement, correlation between pay satisfaction and overall job satisfaction, etc. The predictions made were that blue-collar workers in communities where one could expect integration with an acceptance of middle-class work norms (small community, low standard of living, few slums, etc.) would respond as the human relations theory or the striving type of motivation theory (Maslow, 1943) would expect. However, workers in communities where we would expect alienation from middle-class work norms (large, industrialized communities with large slum areas, etc.) would not respond as expected and, in some cases, would respond in an opposite manner from the counterparts in the "integrated" communities. These predictions were confirmed beyond the chance level. Of particular interest to the present review are their findings regarding job level and work satisfaction. In the most "alienated" community the correlation between job level and work satisfaction was approximately -0.50, while among the workers drawn from the plant located in the most "integrated" community the correlation between these two variables was approximately 0.40. These results raise questions for the generality of the job-enlargement model.

Similar evidence regarding the importance of plant location has been presented by Kendall (1963). While his analysis was not designed to answer the questions crucial to this review, he did present canonical regression variates indicating the role played by community characteristics in predicting different combinations of specific job satisfaction and general job satisfaction.

Katzell et al. (1961) determined that among a sample of warehouse workers drawn from a number of locations there existed strong relationships between both satisfaction and productivity on the response side and community characteristics on the input side. They demonstrated that the location of the plant and hence the backgrounds of the workers, since these would seem to be correlated variables, play important roles in shaping the attitudes of the workers and influencing their behavior.

Whyte's (1955) descriptions of rate busters and quote restricters also indicate the importance of the worker's cultural backgrounds. In his analysis, based on a group of workers working under a piece-rate bonus system, he found that workers who were likely to be "rate busters" (produce above the group standards) were those workers with rural or small-town backgrounds, whose fathers had been entrepreneurs or farmers, who were Protestants, who were Republicans, and who had tended to look "upward" toward their parents for authority sanctions rather than toward their peer group. Quota restricters were more likely to have been reared in large cities, have come from working-class families who were Catholic, have belonged to a boy's gang as a youth, and to be Democrats. It could be argued that the rate busters *rejected* the norms of their peer group and *accepted* the norms of management (middle-class norms). If this is true, then we can predict on the basis of background those workers who will be alienated from middle-class work norms and those who will be integrated with these norms.

Kilbridge (1960a) attacked the question of the preference of workers for larger versus smaller jobs and the issue of mechanical pacing versus self-pacing. Of a sample of 202 (141 females, 61 males) assembly line workers employed by a radio and television set factory in Chicago, 51 percent stated they would prefer a smaller job, 37 percent were indifferent, and only 12 percent preferred a larger job. Further, 84 percent stated they preferred mechanical pacing, 6 percent were indifferent, and only 10 percent preferred a self-paced job. Considering the location of this factory and the results of Turner and Lawrence (1965), Blood and Hulin (1967), and Whyte (1955), these results are not surprising.

Kennedy and O'Neill (1958) surveyed workers in four automotive production departments. They determined that assembly operators performing highly routine and repetitive tasks held opinions toward their supervisors or work situations no more negative than those held by utility men who were performing a much more varied set of tasks.

Finally, Turner and Miclette (1962) interviewed 115 female assembly workers from an electronics plant. Even though the work was extremely repetitive and routine, most of the workers expressed satisfaction with the work itself. The main sources of dissatisfaction came from the sense of being caught in a quantity-quality squeeze and the interruptions from staff and supervisory personnel. Object, batch, line, and process traction were discussed as sources of satisfaction (cf. Baldamus, 1961; Smith & Lem, 1955). Thus, repetition (job size) alone is a poor indicator of worker response and the various sources of positive motivations of repetitive work must be considered.

DISCUSSION

The studies reviewed appear to be of two types. Those which have used acceptable methodology, control groups, appropriate analysis, and multivariate designs have generally not yielded evidence which could be considered as supporting the job-enlargement thesis. Those studies which do appear to support such a thesis frequently contain a number of deviations from normally acceptable research practice. Unfortunately, the former studies are in the minority and the latter studies have generated the greatest fervor and have been accepted as gospel by a large number of psychologists and human relations theorists.

The case for job enlargement has been drastically overstated and overgeneralized. Further, the evidence of the simultaneous effects of plant location and job size (or job level) provides a means of summarizing the literature and resolving the contradictions. Specifically, the argument for larger jobs as a means of motivating workers, decreasing boredom and dissatisfaction, and increasing attendance and

Figure 1

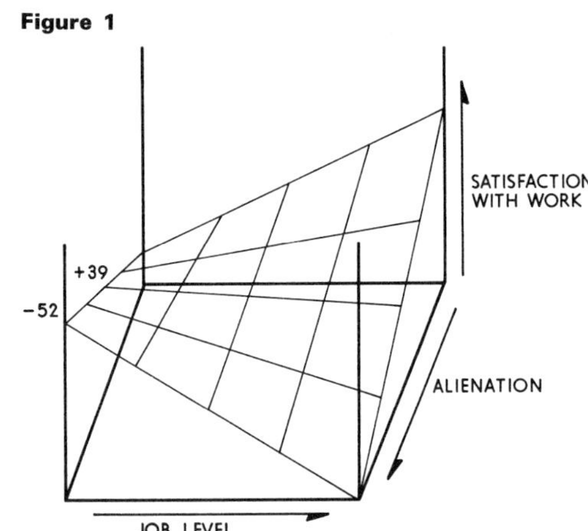

Response surface depicting the interrelationship between job level, satisfaction with work, and alienation of blue-collar workers from middle-class work norms. (Based on data from Blood and Hulin, 1967.)

productivity is valid only when applied to certain segments of the work force—white-collar and supervisory workers and nonalienated blue-collar workers. That is, if we choose the urban-rural dimension of the location of the plant as a crude but useful index of the expected alienation of the blue-collar workers in the community we could construct Table 1.

TABLE 1 PLANT-LOCATION INDEX OF EXPECTED WORKER ALIENATION FROM MIDDLE-CLASS WORK NORMS

Type of Worker	*Urban Location*	*Rural Location*
Blue-collar	Alienated	Nonalienated
White-collar	Nonalienated	Nonalienated

We would expect the job-enlargement hypothesis to predict the behavior of the white-collar workers and the rural or small-town blue-collar workers. Such a hypothesis would not predict responses and behavior of the urban blue-collar workers. This interaction between job size, job satisfaction, and plant location could be further amplified by the following representation of a three-dimensional plot.

Figure 1 is based on data taken from Blood and Hulin (1967). The communities in which the 21 plants in their sample were located were ordered on one of the alienation indexes (or, more properly, dimensions of communities which may be used to index the extent of predicted alienation among the blue-collar workers), and the extremes of the alienation index were used to obtain the slopes of the front and back edge of the surface. In this instance, the back edge of the surface, which represents a community which should foster integration with middle-class work norms, has been drawn to indicate a correlation of 0.39 between job level and work satisfaction. The front edge of the surface, which represents a community which should develop feelings of alienation from middle-class norms among the blue-collar workers, has been drawn to indicate a correlation of −0.52 between job level and work satisfaction.[2]

This response surface indicates that as we move from nonalienated to alienated communities, we should expect the relationship of job level to work satisfaction to change linearly from positive through zero to negative. It further indicates that if we hold job level constant at high-skill-level jobs, we would expect greater job satisfaction among nonalienated workers. However, if we look only at low levels of blue-collar jobs, we would expect greater work satisfaction among the alienated workers.

This response surface summarizes a great deal of the literature on job enlargement, job level, and job satisfaction. It seems evident, for example, that the rural workers sampled by Turner and Lawrence would have been drawn from the nonalienated end of the continuum while the urban workers would have come from plants located at the alienated end of the continuum. Likewise, those workers Katzell *et al.* found to be the most satisfied and the most productive should have been drawn from the nonalienated end of the continuum since they were located in small towns with nonunionized work forces. The workers interviewed by Walker and Guest (1952) seem to have been drawn from a plant located in a community which would be described as having workers who were nonalienated since "The area from which [the workers] were recruited has few mass production factories [p. 4]," "Only two in our sample had ever worked in an automobile plant before [p. 8]," etc. Thus, the workers' negative responses to assembly line work would be predicted by the model. The workers in the Maytag study (Biganne & Stewart, 1963), being drawn from a small community, should have also responded positively to job enlargement. On the other hand, the workers studied by Kilbridge should have responded negatively to job enlargement since they were drawn from the Chicago metropolitan area (only 10 percent preferred a self-paced job and only 12 percent preferred a "larger" job). Whyte's (1955) descriptions of rate busters and quota restricters could also be explained by such a response surface. His rate busters appear to have been reared in an environment which would cause them to internalize the norms and value systems of the middle class. This was not true for the quota restricters. Also, this model would be expected to summarize the results of Blood and Hulin (1967) since these were the data used to verify the tenability of the response surface.

Finally, support for the part played by individual differences can be found even in these studies which make the strongest arguments for job enlargement. For example, Walker and Marriott reported that "many liked their [assembly line] work because it was simple, straightforward, and carried no responsibility." Argyris (1959) found lower skilled employees tending to express a desire "to experience routine or sameness." While these last two studies provide no direct support for such a model, they do indicate that the search for individual differences will be fruitful.

It would also seem that this response surface is reasonable from a theoretical point of view since it is consistent with most of the literature on anomie

[2] A very convenient property of a response surface of this type is that any slice taken parallel to either of the stimulus planes results in a linear function relating the other stimulus variable to job satisfaction. This of course means we need not be concerned with any other than first degree functions with this particular model.

and alienation. Blue-collar workers living in small towns or rural areas would not be members of a work group large enough to develop and sustain its own work norms and values and would be more likely to be in closer contact with the dominant middle class. On the other hand, blue-collar workers living and working in large metropolitan areas would likely be members of a working-class population large enough to develop a set of norms particular to that culture. There is no compelling reason to believe that the norms developed by an urban working-class subculture would be the same or similar to those of the middle class.

If these arguments are correct, then we could expect that workers living in small towns would be more likely to be integrated with middle-class norms and workers in large cities would be more likely to feel alienated from the middle class and its norms and values. Turner and Lawrence (1965), provided discussion of the effects of heterogeneity and homogeneity of population on values and norms. However, it is not necessary to apply an argument based directly on number of blue-collar workers and social heterogeneity. One could argue that the dominant norms and values that all children learn in school and at home are those brought by the Anglo-Saxon Protestants from Europe in the 17th and 18th centuries. These norms and values have become the standard in American middle-class society. Children are taught these values in school by their middle-class teachers and attempt to reach goals defined in terms of these values by means of behavior consistent with these values. However, children raised in slums, where the cost of living is high, or where there is a great deal of migration are more likely to be frustrated in these attempts. Also, the lower-class American city dweller is less likely to be Anglo-Saxon Protestant (Turner & Lawrence, 1965) and less sympathetic to American middle-class values. Therefore, the acquisition by the lower-class city dweller of goals consistent with the Anglo-Saxon Protestant value system is likely to be met with criticism from his peer group (Whyte, 1955). Such frustration or negative reinforcement should extinguish behavior and beliefs consistent with American middle-class ideals.[3]

While we have cast our explanation of these results into a static model which implies fixed values of alienation from middle-class work norms, this is not a necessary aspect of the response surface. It would be possible to postulate a second moderating variable related to length of time since the job was enlarged or changed. This second moderator effect would be expected to indicate initial strong rejection of the enlarged job and initial dissatisfaction. As time on the enlarged job increases, however, we would expect less rejection and less dissatisfaction. The extent of the moderating effect of this latter variable is open to empirical study, but it does indicate the possibility of this model fitting into the current emphasis on dynamic as opposed to static models of work behavior (Vroom, 1966).

Even though such a model appears to summarize a great deal of the published evidence on job size and job satisfaction and is consistent with much of the theorizing regarding alienation and anomie, there are a number of unanswered problems. Nearly all of the data which have been published regarding the joint effects of job size and cultural variables on job satisfaction have used the environmental characteristics of the plant as one of the stimulus conditions. The assumption is that the environmental setting of the plant serves to index certain psychological variables of the individual workers. We have no disagreement with the use of index variables *per se*. However, the environmental setting of the plant or office is thoroughly confounded with the cultural backgrounds of the workers. Plants located in rural areas are more likely to have a work force with rural backgrounds who are Protestants, third or fourth generation Americans, etc. On the basis of the data, we have no way of disentangling the effects of plant location from the effects of the backgrounds of the workers. To attribute the changes in the relationship between job size and satisfaction to differences in the norms and value systems of the workers, as we have done, may not be warranted. On the other hand, the description of rate busters and quota restricters provided by Whyte does indicate that cultural and background differences are important. It would be incredible if the location of the plant had such an effect without operating through an intervening psychological variable. There is also evidence (Bronfenbrenner, 1958) that with socioeconomic status held constant, rural mothers adhere to more rigid patterns of socialization in their child-rearing practices. The probable effect of such practices (as opposed to permissiveness) is to result in children who are more likely to adopt the values of those who are in positions of authority (the middle-class oriented foremen and plant managers).

Finally, the writings of Durkheim, Weber, and Marx on the values and behavior of the industrial proletariat all point in the direction we have taken in the explanation of these findings.

There are also a number of problems raised by the studies relating job level to job satisfaction. For example, Ash (1954), Hoppock (1935), Hulin and Smith (1965), Inlow (1951), Katz (1949), Mann

[3]The authors would like to thank Harry C. Triandis for pointing out this line of argument. We are, of course, fully responsible for its exposition.

(1953), Miller (1940), and Morse (1953) have all presented data which indicate that higher satisfaction levels are associated with higher job levels. However, most of these studies contained problems mitigating against their being regarded as evidence negative to the model presented in Figure 1. Many of these studies used white-collar as well as blue-collar workers as subjects. Others did not specify the location of the plant from which the workers were drawn. Thus, there is no way of knowing whether the findings are consistent with the model. Further, Blood and Hulin (1967) reanalyzed the data originally presented by Hulin and Smith (1965) and concluded that Hulin and Smith's conclusions had to be modified to take plant location into account. Finally, many of these studies did not separate the effects of job size from the effects of salary or wages.

In addition to the problems already mentioned, we are making the assumption that well-designed correlational studies can provide evidence on effects of basically manipulative programs. That is, the job-enlargement thesis states that if jobs are reengineered to make them larger, then certain desirable consequences will take place—notably decreases in monotony, increases in satisfaction, and decreases in turnover and restriction in output. We have made several inferences regarding this thesis and have based these inferences to a great extent on information contained in studies which have *correlated* job level or job size with satisfaction. Being *placed* on a high-skill-level job may be qualitatively different than having a present job *enlarged.* However, predictions based on a model (Figure 1) which has been generated by such correlations appear to be valid for several of the job-enlargement studies. Second, we would expect differences between skilled and unskilled blue-collar workers to operate against the hypotheses. Highly skilled workers who have gone through an extensive training period should be more likely to adopt the norms and values of the middle class. Yet, we find that the highly skilled blue-collar workers do not necessarily report the higher satisfaction levels expected of them.

In summary, studies bearing on the job-enlargement thesis have been reviewed and analyzed. These studies do not support the hypothesis that job size or job level is positively correlated *in general* with job satisfaction. Such hypotheses must be modified to take into account the location of the plant and the cultural backgrounds of the workers.

REFERENCES

Argyris, C. *Personality and organization.* New York: Harper, 1957.

Argyris, C. The individual and organization: An empirical test. *Administrative Science Quarterly,* 1959, **4**(2), 145–67.

Argyris, C. *Integrating the individual and the organization.* New York: Wiley, 1964.

Ash, P. The SRA employee inventory—A statistical analysis. *Personnel Psychology,* 1954, **7**, 337–60.

Baldamus, W. *Efficiency and effort.* London: Tavistock, 1961.

Behling, O. C. The meaning of dissatisfaction with factory work. *Management of Personnel Quarterly,* 1964, **3**(2), 11–16.

Biganne, J. F. and Stewart, P. A. Job enlargement: A case study. Research Series No. 25, 1963, State University of Iowa, Bureau of Labor and Management.

Blood, M. R. and Hulin, C. L. Alienation, environmental characteristics, and worker responses. *Journal of Applied Psychology,* 1967, **51**, 284–90.

Bronfenbrenner, U. Socialization and social class through space and time. In E. E. Maccoby, T. M. Newcomb, & E. L. Hartley (eds.), *Readings in social psychology.* New York: Holt, 1958, pp. 400–25.

Conant, E. H. and Kilbridge, M. D. An interdisciplinary analysis of job enlargement: Technology, costs, and behavioral implications. *Industrial and Labor Relations Review,* 1965, **18**(3), 377–95.

Davis, L. E. Job design and productivity: A new approach. *Personnel,* 1957, **33**, 418–30. (a)

Davis, L. E. Toward a theory of job design. *Journal of Industrial Engineering,* 1957, **8**, 305–9. (b)

Davis, L. E. and Canter, R. R. Job design. *Journal of Industrial Engineering,* 1955, **6**(1), 3–6, 20.

Davis, L. and Werling, R. Job design factors. *Occupational Psychology,* 1960, **34**, 109–32.

Durkheim, E. *The division of labor.* Glencoe, Illinois: Free Press, 1933.

Elliott, J. D. Increasing office productivity through job enlargement. In, *The human side of the office manager's job.* (No. 134, Office Management Series) New York: American Management Association, 1953, pp. 3–15.

Frankmann, J. P. and Adams, J. A. Theories of vigilance. *Psychological Bulletin,* 1962, **59**, 257–72.

Guest, R. H. Men and machines: An assembly-line worker looks at his job. *Personnel,* 1955, **31**, 496–503.

Guest, R. H. Job enlargement—A revolution in job design. *Personnel Administration,* 1957, **20**(2), 9–16.

Hoppock, R. *Job satisfaction.* New York: Harper, 1935.

Hulin, C. L. Job satisfaction and turnovers in a female clerical population. *Journal of Applied Psychology,* 1966, **50**, 280–85.

Hulin, C. L. and Smith, P. C. A linear model of job satisfaction. *Journal of Applied Psychology,* 1965, **49**, 209–16.

Inlow, G. M. Job satisfaction of liberal arts graduates. *Journal of Applied Psychology,* 1951, **35**, 175–81.

Katz, D. Morale and motivation in industry. In W. Dennis (ed.), *Current trends in industrial psychology.* Pittsburgh: University of Pittsburgh Press, 1949, pp. 145–71.

Katzell, R. A., Barrett, R. S., and Parker, T. C. Job satisfaction, job performance, and situational characteristics. *Journal of Applied Psychology,* 1961, **45**, 65–72.

Kendall, L. M. Canonical analysis of job satisfaction and behavioral, personal background, and situational data. Unpublished doctoral dissertation, Cornell University, 1963.

Kennedy, J. E. and O'Neill, H. E. Job content and worker's opinions. *Journal of Applied Psychology,* 1958, **42**, 372–75.

Kilbridge, M. D. Do workers prefer larger jobs? *Personnel,* 1960, **37**, 45–48. (a)

Kilbridge, M. D. Reduced costs through job enlargement. *Journal of Business,* 1960, **33**(10), 357–62. (b)

Kornhauser, A. W. *Mental health of the industrial worker: A Detroit study.* New York: Wiley, 1965.

Likert, R. *New patterns of management.* New York: McGraw-Hill, 1961.

MacGregor, D. M. Adventure in thought and action. In, *Proceedings of the fifth anniversary convocation of the school of industrial management.* Cambridge, Mass.: MIT Press, 1957.

MacKinney, A. C., Wernimont, P. F., and Galitz, W. O. Has specialization reduced job satisfaction? *Personnel,* 1962, **39**(1), 8–17.

Mann, F. C. A study of work satisfaction as a function of the discrepancy between inferred aspirations and achievement. Unpublished doctoral dissertation, University of Michigan, 1953.

Marks, A. R. N. An investigation of modifications of job design in an industrial situation and their effects on some measures of economic productivity. Unpublished doctoral dissertation, University of California, 1954. (Summarized in L. E. Davis and R. R. Canter, Job design research. *Journal of Industrial Engineering,* 1956, **7**(6), 275–82.)

Maslow, A. H. A theory of human motivation. *Psychological Review,* 1943, **50**, 370–96.

Miller, D. C. Morale of college-trained adults. *American Sociological Review,* 1940, **5**, 880–89.

Morse, N. C. *Satisfactions in the white-collar job.* Ann Arbor: University of Michigan, Institute for Social Research, Survey Research Center, 1953.

Porter, L. A study of perceived need satisfactions in bottom and middle management jobs. *Journal of Applied Psychology,* 1961, **45**, 232–36.

Reif, W. E. and Schoderbek, P. P. Job enlargement: Antidote to apathy. *Management of Personnel Quarterly,* 1966, **5**(1), 16–23.

Roethlisberger, F. J. and Dickson, W. J. *Management and the worker.* Cambridge: Harvard University Press, 1941.

Scott, W. E., Jr. Activation theory and task design. *Organizational Behavior and Human Performance,* 1966, **1**, 3–30.

Smith, A. The education of the worker. (Orig. publ. 1776). Reported in A. O. Lewis (ed.), *Of men and machines.* New York: Dutton, 1963, pp. 236–39.

Smith, P. C. The curve of output as a criterion of boredom. *Journal of Applied Psychology,* 1953, **37**, 69–74.

Smith, P. C. Individual differences in susceptibility to industrial monotony. *Journal of Applied Psychology,* 1955, **39**, 322–29.

Smith, P. C. and Lem, C. Positive aspects of motivation in repetitive work: Effects of lot size upon spacing of voluntary rest periods. *Journal of Applied Psychology,* 1955, **39**, 330–33.

Turner, A. N. and Lawrence, P. R. *Industrial jobs and the worker: An investigation of response to task attributes.* Boston: Harvard University, Graduate School of Business Administration, 1965.

Turner, A. N. and Miclette, A. L. Sources of satisfaction in repetitive work. *Occupational Psychology,* 1962, **36**, 215–31.

Vroom, V. H. *Some personality determinants of the effects of participation.* Englewood Cliffs, N.J.: Prentice-Hall, 1960.

Vroom, V. H. A comparison of static and dynamic correlational methods in the study of organizations. *Organizational Behavior and Human Performance,* 1966, **1**, 55–70.

Walker, C. R. The problem of the repetitive job. *Harvard Business Review,* 1950, **28**(3), 54–58.

Walker, C. R. Work methods, working conditions, and morale. In A. Kornhauser, R. Dubin, and A. M. Ross (eds.), *Industrial conflict.* New York: McGraw, 1954, pp. 345–58.

Walker, C. R. and Guest, R. H. *The man on the assembly line.* Cambridge: Harvard University Press, 1952.

Walker, C. R. and Marriott, R. A study of attitudes to factory work. *Occupational Psychology,* 1951, **25**, 181–91.

Warren, N. D. Job simplification versus job enlargement. *Journal of Industrial Engineering,* 1958, **9**(5), 435–39.

Weitz, J. and Nuckols, R. C. The validity of direct and indirect questions in measuring job satisfaction. *Personnel Psychology,* 1953, **6**, 487–94.

Whyte, W. F. *Money and motivation: An analysis of incentives in industry.* New Yorker: Harper, 1955.

Worthy, J. C. Organizational structure and employee morale. *American Sociological Review,* 1950, **15**, 169–79.

Wyatt, S., Fraser, J. A., and Stock, F. G. L. The comparative effects of variety and uniformity in work. Report No. 52, 1929, Industrial Fatigue Research Board. (a)

Wyatt, S., Fraser, J. A., and Stock, F. G. L. The effects of monotony in work. Report No. 56, 1929, Industrial Fatigue Research Board. (b)

Wyatt, S., Langdon, J. N., and Stock, F. G. L. Fatigue and boredom in repetitive work. Report No. 77, 1937, Industrial Fatigue Research Board.

24. EMPLOYEE REACTIONS TO JOB CHARACTERISTICS*

J. Richard Hackman and Edward E. Lawler III†

Researchers and managers alike are increasingly attending to the way jobs are designed as an important factor in determining the motivation, satisfaction, and performance of employees at work. This is not to say that jobs previously have been seen as irrelevant to organizational administration. On the contrary, earlier in this century when scientific management was in its prime, considerable research effort was expended to find ways that jobs could be simplified, specialized, standardized, and routinized. At the same time, industrial psychologists were developing rather complex and sophisticated procedures for describing and analyzing jobs in terms of their simplest components, as a means of evaluating the skill levels required for different jobs. The results of job analyses have been used to establish fair rates of pay, for training purposes, and in personnel selection (see, e.g., Ghiselli & Brown, 1955; Lytle, 1946; Stigers & Reed, 1944). The general expectation of the scientific management approach was that by simplifying jobs, work could be carried out more efficiently; less-skilled employees would be required; the control of management over production would be increased; and, ultimately, organizational profits would be enhanced.

In recent years, numerous scholars have documented a number of unintended and unfortunate consequences of the trend toward work simplification (e.g., Argyris, 1964; Blauner, 1964; Davis, 1957; Friedmann, 1961; Guest, 1955; Herzberg, Mausner, & Snyderman, 1959; Walker, 1950; Walker & Guest, 1952). In brief, it has been shown that simple, routine nonchallenging jobs often lead to high employee dissatisfaction, to increased absenteeism and turnover, and to substantial difficulties in effectively managing employees who work on simplified jobs.[1] The expected increases in profitability from work simplification have not materialized as had been hoped, and the reasons apparently have very much to do with the human problems encountered when jobs are standardized and simplified.

Partially in response to the above findings, a number of researchers began experimentally enlarging various jobs to determine whether or not worker productivity and satisfaction would increase if jobs were designed so as to be more generally meaningful and challenging to employees. By and large, those job enlargement experiments which have been reported in the literature have been considered successful (see, e.g., Biganne & Stewart, 1963; Conant & Kilbridge, 1965; Davis & Valfer, 1965; Ford, 1969; Kilbridge, 1960; Pelissier, 1965). With few exceptions, however, job enlargement experiments have been case studies and often have lacked appropriate experimental controls. Hulin and Blood (1968) review the research literature on job enlargement in some detail and are especially attentive to possible difficulties in procedure and methodology which may cast doubt on the generality or the validity of the findings reported.

Perhaps equally as disturbing as the uneven level of methodological rigor which has characterized job enlargement studies is the almost total absence of any systematic conceptual or theoretical basis for the studies which have been done. As a result, after dozens of experiments, little cumulative knowledge has been gained regarding the effects and effectiveness of job redesign. Job enlargement experiments, for example, typically have involved a number of simultaneous changes—such as in the amount of variety in the work, the amount of responsibility required, the degree to which working with others is an important part of the enlarged job, etc. Very little is known about which of these (or of other) aspects of the redesigned job are in fact responsible for observed behavioral and attitudinal changes. Further, the generality of job enlargement effects is largely unknown (e.g., whether they are effective only for certain types of workers or whether they are relevant only to certain kinds of jobs). More case studies are not likely to contribute very much to the development of answers to crucial questions such as these. Instead, what appears to be needed are conceptual frameworks which generate testable propositions about how job characteristics affect employees under various circumstances, and empirical research which is designed explicitly to test these propositions. This article proposes one way of conceptualizing the

---

* *Journal of Applied Psychology Monograph,* Vol. 55, No. 3 (June 1971), pp. 259-86.

This research was supported in part by United States Air Force Office of Scientific Research Grant AF-AFOSR-68-1600, Effects of Task Characteristics on Performance (J. Richard Hackman, principal investigator). The cooperation and assistance of employees and managers in the company where the research was done is gratefully acknowledged, as is the assistance of Ann Garvin and Lloyd Suttle in collecting and analyzing the data. Clayton Alderfer and Chris Argyris provided helpful comments on an earlier draft of this article.

† Yale University and University of Michigan, respectively.

[1] These observations have not, however, gone unchallenged. See, for example, Kilbridge (1961) and MacKinney, Wernimont, and Galitz (1962).

impact of job characteristics on individual work behavior and attitudes. It then reports data which were collected to provide a preliminary test of that conceptualization.

Previous Theory and Research

Some progress toward the development of theory relevant to job design has been made in recent years. The well-known two-factor theory of Herzberg (Herzberg, Mausner, & Snyderman, 1959; Herzberg, 1966), for example, can be used to derive general propositions regarding conditions on the job which will be motivating and satisfying to employees. In particular, the theory suggests that a job should enhance employee motivation to the extent that it provides opportunities for *(a)* achievement, *(b)* recognition, *(c)* responsibility, *(d)* advancement, and *(e)* growth in competence. These principles have given rise to a series of generally successful job enlargement experiments in the American Telephone and Telegraph Company (summarized by Ford, 1969).

Unfortunately, a number of researchers have been unable to provide empirical support for some of the major tenets of the theory from which the principles used in the AT&T studies are derived (e.g., Dunnette, Campbell, & Hakel, 1967; Hinton, 1968; King, 1970), and the general conceptual status of the theory must presently be considered uncertain. Further, the theory has not yet been elaborated to specify how characteristics of workers interact with the presence or absence of the five motivating conditions in determining worker performance and satisfaction. Finally, the theory in its present form does not specify how the presence or absence of the motivating conditions can be measured for existing jobs. This makes it very difficult to test the theory and to generate unambiguous predictions from it about the effects of specific changes which may be contemplated for existing jobs.

The problem of measuring job characteristics has been explicitly and carefully dealt with by Turner and Lawrence (1965). These authors developed operational measures of six "requisite task attributes" which, on the basis of a review of existing literature and an a priori conceptual framework, were predicted to be positively related to worker satisfaction and attendance. The six attributes are: *(a)* variety, *(b)* autonomy, *(c)* required interaction, *(d)* optional interaction, *(e)* knowledge and skill required, and *(f)* responsibility. Scores on each attribute for each of 47 different jobs were obtained from field observations and interviews by the researchers, and precise specification of how scores on each of the attributes is determined is provided. Examination of the relationships among the six requisite task attributes for the 47 jobs revealed that the attributes were very closely related to one another. Therefore, Turner and Lawrence developed a summary measure called the Requisite Task Attribute Index (RTA Index) by formulating a linear combination of the six separately measured attributes. This summary index was then used in ascertaining the relationships between the attributes of the jobs and worker job satisfaction and attendance.

The authors' expectation that employees working on jobs which were high on the RTA Index would have higher job satisfaction and lower absenteeism was not fully supported. Instead, it appeared that the predicted relationship between the RTA Index and employee reactions held only for workers from factories located in small towns. Workers in urban settings reported less satisfaction with their jobs when the jobs were high on the RTA Index, and the RTA Index was unrelated to absenteeism for urban workers. Turner and Lawrence (1965) argued that the obtained differences in reactions to good (i.e., high RTA Index) jobs were substantially moderated by differences in the cultural backgrounds of employees.

Blood and Hulin (1967) and Hulin and Blood (1968) provide additional data on the importance of subcultural factors in determining worker responses to the makeup of their jobs. These authors hypothesize that an important moderating factor is alienation from the traditional work norms which characterize the middle class. When employees hold traditional values regarding the value of work and achievement in work settings (as would be expected of the employees in small town factories in the Turner and Lawrence study), more complex jobs should be responded to positively. When employees are alienated from these norms (as might be expected of urban workers), more complex jobs should be responded to negatively. Blood and Hulin (1967) provide data supporting this general proposition and propose a three-dimensional response surface (Hulin & Blood, 1968) which specifies the expected interrelationships among worker alienation, job level, and satisfaction with work.

The data of Turner and Lawrence (1965) and of Blood and Hulin (1967) are sufficiently compelling that the generality of the strong proposition that enlarged jobs (in the sense of being high, e.g., on the dimensions which make up the RTA Index) lead to improved satisfaction, attendance, and/or performance on the job must be called into question. Instead, it appears that certain characteristics of the employees themselves must be taken into account simultaneously with the characteristics of their jobs in order to generate valid predictions about the behavioral and affective responses of employees at work.

If the above conclusion is accepted, thorny questions then arise about how the relevant differences among employees are to be conceptualized and measured. Both Turner and Lawrence (1965) and Hulin and Blood (1968) choose to deal with individual differences on a subcultural or sociological level (i.e., in terms of differences between town and city workers or in terms of the alienation of city workers from middle-class work norms).

An alternative strategy would be to attempt to conceptualize and measure the relevant individual differences directly at the individual level of analysis. The town-city conceptualization assumes a substantial homogeneity of worker characteristics and response tendencies for employees within the two cultural settings. To the extent that there are substantial individual differences among town workers and among city workers, an attempt to measure relevant individual differences directly at the individual level would seem to have considerable merit. The difficulty in implementing this alternative approach, of course, is that it requires prior specification on a conceptual level of what specific differences among people are responsible for the results reported by Turner and Lawrence (1965) and Blood and Hulin (1967) (i.e., what it is about people that moderates the way they react to their jobs). In the following paragraphs, we will propose such a conceptualization, and derive from it a number of predictions about the effects of job characteristics on employee satisfaction and motivation.

Jobs and Individuals: A Conceptual Framework

The present conceptualization of the interaction between job characteristics and individual differences is based primarily on the expectancy theory of motivation, as formulated by Lewin (1938) and Tolman (1959), and as applied to work settings by Vroom (1964), Porter and Lawler (1968), and others. In particular, five propositions based on expectancy theory are suggested below, which address the specific problem of how employee motivation can be enhanced through the design of jobs.

1. To the extent that an individual believes that he can obtain an outcome he values by engaging in some particular behavior or class of behaviors, the likelihood that he will actually engage in that behavior is enhanced. Relevant valued outcomes can be both intrinsic (e.g., feelings of accomplishment or of personal worth) and extrinsic (e.g., material goods); the only requirement is that the outcomes be valued by the individual. When an individual anticipates obtaining some valued outcome as a result of a contemplated action or course of action, that outcome may be termed an incentive for engaging in the action.

2. Outcomes are valued by individuals to the extent that they satisfy the physiological or psychological needs of the individual, or to the extent that they lead to other outcomes which satisfy such needs or are expected by the individual to do so. Such need satisfaction need not, of course, be in the objective best interest of the individual. People frequently strive for satisfying states of affairs which are quite inconsistent with their long-term well-being (Locke, 1969). Nevertheless, if an outcome is not somehow linked to satisfaction, it will not continue to be valued and therefore cannot continue to serve as an incentive.

3. Thus, to the extent that conditions at work can be arranged so that employees can satisfy their own needs best by working effectively toward organizational goals, employees will in fact tend to work hard toward the achievement of these goals (McGregor, 1960).

4. Most lower level needs (e.g., physical well-being, security) can be (and often are) reasonably well satisfied for individuals in contemporary society on a continuing basis and, therefore, will not serve as motivational incentives except under unusual circumstances. This is not the case, however, for certain higher order needs (e.g., needs for personal growth and development or for feelings of worthwhile accomplishment). A person may experience higher order need satisfaction on a continuing basis without the strength of desire for additional satisfaction of these needs diminishing. Indeed, it may be that additional satisfaction of higher order needs actually increases their strength (Alderfer, 1969). This is an important possibility since it suggests that the opportunity for the development of continuing (and possibly even increasing) motivation is much more a reality when higher order needs are engaged than is the case for more easily satisfied lower order needs. There is, of course, a major cost associated with any motivational approach in which higher order needs are central: Not all employees can or will respond to opportunities for the satisfaction of higher order needs, and thus motivational approaches based on these needs cannot be applied indiscriminantly. Maslow (1943, 1954) and Alderfer (1969, 1971) discuss in much more complete detail the nature of higher order needs and their motivational implications.

5. Individuals who are capable of higher order need satisfaction will in fact experience such satis-

faction when they learn that they have, as a result of their own efforts, accomplished something that they personally believe is worthwhile or meaningful (see Argyris, 1964; Lewin, Dembo, Festinger, & Sears, 1944). Specifically, individuals who desire higher order need satisfactions should be most likely to obtain them when they work effectively on meaningful jobs which provide feedback on the adequacy of their personal work activities. To establish conditions for internal work motivation, then, it appears that a job must: *(a)* allow workers to feel personally responsible for an identifiable and meaningful portion of the work, *(b)* provide work outcomes which are intrinsically meaningful or otherwise experienced as worthwhile, and *(c)* provide feedback about performance effectiveness. The harder and better an individual works on such a job, the more opportunities he will have to experience higher order need satisfactions and the more incentive there can be for continued effective performance. Higher order need satisfactions, therefore, are seen both as *(a)* a result of (rather than a determinant of) effective performance (Lawler & Porter, 1967), and *(b)* an incentive for continued efforts to perform effectively.[2]

The five propositions outlined above lead to the conclusion that it may be possible under specifiable conditions simultaneously to achieve high employee satisfaction and high employee effort toward organizational goals. Specifically, the long term congruence of high satisfaction and high effort is seen as depending upon *(a)* the existence of employee desires for higher order need satisfaction and *(b)* conditions on the job such that working hard and effectively toward organizational goals will bring about satisfaction of these needs.

Characteristics of Motivating Jobs

The three general job characteristics identified above as central in developing a congruence between individual need satisfaction and organizational goal achievement must be describable in more measurable terms if the validity of the conceptualization proposed here is to be tested. In the following paragraphs, therefore, each of the three general characteristics are examined in somewhat more detail. In addition, it will be proposed that four of the requisite task attributes proposed by Turner and Lawrence (1965) are likely to be useful as measures of the three general job characteristics.

[2] It should be noted that only higher order satisfactions are predicted to be increased by effective work on a job with the characteristics outlined above; other satisfactions (e.g., pay satisfaction, satisfaction with supervision) may not be affected.

1. The job must allow a worker to feel personally responsible for a meaningful portion of his work. What is accomplished must be through the individual's own efforts. He must realize that the work he does is his own. And he must believe that he personally is responsible for whatever successes and failures occur as a result of his work. Only if what is accomplished is seen as one's own can an individual experience a feeling of personal success and a gain in self-esteem. This does not mean, of course, that feelings of personal responsibility for work outcomes cannot occur in team projects; all that is required is for team members to feel that their own efforts are important in accomplishing the task at hand.

The autonomy dimension, as specified by Turner and Lawrence (1965), would seem to tap the degree to which workers feel personal responsibility for their work. In jobs high on measured autonomy, workers will tend to feel that they own the outcomes of their work; in jobs low on autonomy, a worker may more often feel that successes and failures on the job are more often due to the good work (or to the incompetence) of other workers or of his supervisor.[3]

2. The job must provide outcomes which are intrinsically meaningful or otherwise experienced as worthwhile to the individual. If a worker feels that the results of his efforts are not very important, it is unlikely that he will feel especially good if he works effectively. Instead, he must achieve something that he personally feels is worthwhile and important if he is to be able to experience positive feelings about himself as a result of his efforts. It clearly is not possible to indicate for people in general what kinds of job characteristics will be likely to provide outcomes seen as meaningful and worthwhile; people differ too much in the kinds of things they value for any statement of such generality to be made. It is possible, however, to provide some such specifications for indiviuals who have high desires for higher order need satisfaction and, of course, these are the individuals to whom the present conceptualization is intended to apply.

There are at least two ways that work can come to be experienced as meaningful for employees with relatively high desires for higher order need satisfaction. The first is for the job to be a sufficiently whole piece of work that the worker can perceive

[3] Having high autonomy on the job does not, of course, necessarily imply that one will have major control over the work outcomes achieved. There may be a number of factors in the work environment which affect the nature of work outcomes, over which the worker has little meaningful control. For example, a football quarterback has high autonomy in selecting plays but only a moderate level of personal control over the outcomes obtained from execution of the plays. Thus, work autonomy is probably best viewed as a necessary but not sufficient condition for feeling personal responsibility for work outcomes.

that he has produced or accomplished something of consequence. In terms of a Turner and Lawrence task attribute, this would be expected to be the case when a job is high on task identity. According to Turner and Lawrence (1965, p. 157), jobs high on task identity are characterized by *(a)* a very clear cycle of perceived closure—the job provides a distinct sense of the beginning and ending of a transformation process, *(b)* high visibility of the transformation to the worker, *(c)* high visibility of the transformation in the finished product, and *(d)* a transformation of considerable magnitude. For a worker who has high needs for developing and using his competence, a job with such characteristics generally would be expected to be experienced as highly meaningful and worthwhile.

In addition, the experienced meaningfulness of work may be enhanced when a job provides a worker with the opportunity to accomplish something by using skills and abilities which he personally values. For example, a strongly motivated duffer feels good when he hits a solid tee shot, even though the broader significance of this event is doubtful. His golfing skills are on the line when he steps to the tee; those skills are important to him; he performs well—and that, in itself, is enough.

Jobs high on the Turner and Lawrence (1965) dimension of variety would be expected to provide opportunities for workers to experience this kind of meaningfulness on the job, since high variety jobs typically tap a number of different skills which may be important to the employee. Thus, working on high variety jobs may become personally meaningful to some employees through a process very analogous to that which makes golf meaningful to the duffer. It should be noted, however, that only variety which does in fact challenge the worker will be expected to be experienced as meaningful to workers with desires for higher order need satisfaction; screwing many different sizes of nuts on many different colors of bolts, if this could be considered variety, would not be expected to be experienced as meaningful.[4]

To summarize, it may be that jobs can come to be experienced as meaningful to employees to the extent that they involve doing a whole piece of work of some significance (i.e., have high task identity) and, at the same time, to the extent that they give employees the chance to use their valued skills and abilities (i.e., to be challenged) in doing the work. In many cases the latter condition may be met on jobs which have high variety.

3. The job must provide feedback about what is accomplished. Even if the two general conditions discussed above are met, an employee cannot experience higher order need satisfaction when he performs effectively unless he obtains some kind of feedback about how he is doing. Such feedback may come from doing the task itself (e.g., when a telephone operator successfully completes a long distance person-to-person call), but performance feedback also may come from some other person—an esteemed co-worker, a supervisor, etc. The crucial condition is that feedback be present in a form that is believable to the worker, so that a realistic basis exists for the satisfaction (or frustration) of higher order needs.

It should be emphasized that, for all of the job characteristics discussed above, it is not their objective state which affects employee attitudes and behavior, but rather how they are experienced by the employees. Regardless of the amount of feedback (or variety, or autonomy, or task identity) a worker really has in his work, it is how much *he perceives that he has* which will affect his reactions to the job. Objective job characteristics are important because they do affect the perceptions and experiences of employees. But there are often substantial differences between objective job characteristics and how they are perceived by employees, and it is dangerous to assume that simply because the objective characteristics of a job have been measured (or changed) that the way that job is experienced by employees has been dealt with as well.

In summary, then, it has been argued that the characteristics of jobs can establish conditions which will enhance the intrinsic motivation of workers who desire higher order need satisfaction. In particular, it has been suggested, in terms of a subset of the Turner and Lawrence (1965) dimensions, that such individuals will be able to obtain meaningful personal satisfaction when they perform well on jobs which they experience as high on variety, autonomy, task identity, and feedback. Further, the harder and better an individual performs on a job which is perceived as high on these dimensions (hereafter will be called the four core dimensions), the more satisfaction he is likely to feel.

Strategy of the Present Research

The conceptualization presented above provides the basis for the present empirical research on the relationships among job characteristics; individual differences in need strength; and employee motiva-

[4] It is also possible, of course, for a job to have too much variety. Activation theory (e.g., Scott, 1966) suggests that when variety is too high, employees may experience a general state of muscular and mental hypertension which can greatly handicap performance effectiveness. In addition, Hall and Lawler (1970) found that among research scientists, high job variety can be associated with low job satisfaction, apparently because jobs with high variety also tended to be low in task identity and feedback.

tion, satisfaction, performance, and absenteeism on the job. In particular, the research to be reported here follows the strategy steps listed below:

1. Measures of the following six job dimensions were developed: *(a)* variety, the degree to which a job requires employees to perform a wide range of operations in their work and/or the degree to which employees must use a variety of equipment and procedures in their work; *(b)* autonomy, the extent to which employees have a major say in scheduling their work, selecting the equipment they will use, and deciding on procedures to be followed; *(c)* task identity, the extent to which employees do an entire or whole piece of work and can clearly identify the result of their efforts; *(d)* feedback, the degree to which employees receive information as they are working which reveals how well they are performing on the job; *(e)* dealing with others, the degree to which a job requires employees to deal with other people (either customers, other company employees, or both) to complete the work; *(f)* friendship opportunities, the degree to which a job allows employees to talk with one another on the job and to establish informal relationships with other employees at work.

The latter two dimensions were included to permit exploration of the impact of the interpersonal characteristics of job design. These dimensions were adapted with very minor revision from the task attributes "required interaction" and "optional interaction" proposed by Turner and Lawrence (1965). They are not, however, directly relevant to the conceptualization about job-based work motivation proposed above, and no specific predictions regarding them were made. Thirteen different jobs were described on these six dimensions by the researchers, by employees who worked on the jobs, and by members of the management of the telephone company in which the research was carried out.

2. A measure was developed which was expected, on an a priori basis, to reflect the level of employee desire for the satisfaction of higher order needs.

3. Based on the mean scores of the employees on the measure of need strength, predictions were made regarding the expected relationships between the job characteristics as measured by the four core dimensions and the dependent variables: satisfaction, performance, and absenteeism. Relevant data were collected from 208 employees, and correlations between each of the four core dimensions and each of the dependent measures were computed.

4. The theory outlined above indicates that how a job is experienced or perceived by an individual employee should determine his reactions to it, rather than the objective characteristics of the job. This possibility can be examined by analyzing the relationship between the characteristics of a single job (as they are perceived by employees) and the behavioral and attitudinal reactions of individuals who hold that job. By restricting the scope of the analysis to individuals working on the same job, it is possible to rule out objective differences in jobs as an explanation for obtained empirical relationships—and, thereby, to address the possibility that the perceived characteristics of jobs affect employees in the same general fashion as do objectively measured characteristics. Therefore, relationships between perceived job characteristics and the dependent variables of interest were computed separately for employees who worked on each of the 13 objectively different jobs included in the study, and these relationships were compared to those obtained in the overall analyses involving all *S*s and all 13 jobs.

5. The theory implies that satisfaction, performance, and attendance should be highest when all four of the core dimensions are present. That is, being high on, say, variety and task identity but low on autonomy and feedback should not provide the conditions that are necessary for positive behavioral and affective responses. Under such circumstances, a worker would be expected to have neither a sense of personal ownership of his work activities and outcomes (low autonomy) nor a trustworthy gauge of the adequacy of his performance (low feedback). The conditions for the development of internal work motivation specified earlier would therefore not be met. The importance of having all four core dimensions present was tested by comparing the dependent variable scores of employees who saw their jobs as moderately high on all four core dimensions both with the scores of employees who saw their jobs as high on some dimensions and low on others, and with the scores of employees who saw their jobs as moderately low on all four dimensions.

6. The theory states that individual differences in desire for higher order need satisfactions should moderate the relationships between job characteristics and dependent variables. In order to test this possibility, relationships were computed separately and compared for the third of the employees highest on desire for higher order need satisfaction and for those employees lowest on desire for higher order need satisfaction.

7. Finally, exploratory analyses were made of the relationships between the two interpersonal job dimensions (dealing with others, and friendship opportunities) and the dependent variables.

METHOD

Research Setting and Subjects

The research was carried out in an eastern telephone company, and focused on employees who worked on 13 different jobs in the plant and traffic departments of the company. The jobs were selected so as to include *(a)* several varieties of operators, installers, central office repairmen, and cable splicers; *(b)* to range widely in complexity and in the level of employee skill required; and *(c)* to be located in both rural and urban settings.

Data were collected from 208 employees and 62 supervisors. Employees in the traffic department (about one-third of the sample) were female; all plant department employees were male.

Procedure

All data were collected on site at each of the 13 job locations. One to three days were spent at each location, and all data were collected from each location before moving on to another location. Data were collected over a period of about 9 mo. At each location, the following five procedural steps were followed (although the order of the steps sometimes varied because of local circumstances).

1. Local second- or third-level management was visited to obtain permission to collect data from employees working on a particular job. When permission was secured (it was never denied), the managers were interviewed about the general nature of the job as they perceived it.

2. First-level supervisors on the local job were interviewed about the nature of the job and employees' reactions to it and were given a questionnaire which tapped the supervisors' perceptions of the employee job in a format similar to that used for obtaining the employees' own job perceptions.

3. Employees working on the job were observed and interviewed informally. These observations and interviews were conducted by two researchers and continued until the researchers felt that they were no longer obtaining substantial new information about the job. Observation typically lasted approximately one working day. Ratings of the job characteristics by the researchers were made on the basis of these observations and interviews.

4. A questionnaire was administered to a sample of 15–20 employees on the job. The questionnaire took between ½–1 hr. to complete and usually was administered to employees in groups of three or four. The general nature of the research was explained to each group of employees before they began work on the questionnaire, although the hypotheses of the study and the dependent variables to be analyzed were not mentioned. It was emphasized to each individual that participation was voluntary, and a few individuals did decline to participate. In addition, employees were told that putting their names on the questionnaires, while desirable for research purposes, also was voluntary. About 10% of the employees who participated declined to give their names.

5. Ratings of the performance of those employees who had taken the questionnaire and provided their names were made by first-line supervisors. Absence data were collected later from company records.

Instruments and Measures

Job Descriptions. Each of the 13 jobs examined in the research was described in terms of the six general dimensions described earlier (variety, autonomy, task identity, feedback, dealing with others, and friendship opportunities). The jobs were described on all six dimensions using four different methods: *(a)* a sample of employees on the job completed several questionnaire scales relevant to the six dimensions; *(b)* first- and second-level management on the job completed identical questionnaire scales; *(c)* the researchers, after observing the job and interviewing employees and supervisors, completed similar scales; and *(d)* the researchers utilized a set of objective coding procedures adapted from Turner and Lawrence (1965) to obtain a set of nonsubjective assessments of each job.

The job descriptions completed by employees and supervisors involved three separate questionnaire items for five of the six dimensions; two items were used for the dimension "dealing with others." One section of the questionnaire involved making direct ratings of the job on six 7-point scales. The scales used in this section of the employee questionnaire, together with the labels attached to each of the scale end points and the midpoint, are listed below.

a. How much *variety* is there in your job?
   Very little; I do pretty much the same things over and over and use the same pieces of equipment and procedures almost all the time. (Scored 1)
   Moderate variety (Scored 4)
   Very much; I do many different things and use a wide variety of equipment and procedures. (Scored 7)
b. How much *autonomy* do you have on your job; how much are you left on your own to do your own work?
   Very little; I have almost no "say" about scheduling my work; the work and the procedures are all laid out for me in detail.
   Moderate autonomy; I make some of the decisions about my work, but many of them are made for me.
   Very much; I have almost all of the "say" about

the scheduling of my own work; I alone decide what procedures will be used.

c. To what extent do you *do a "whole" piece of work* (as opposed to doing part of a job which is finished by some other employee)?
I do one small part of a job; there are many others who do other parts of the job; I may not see the final result.
I do a moderate size "chunk" of the work; there are others involved too, but my contribution is clear.
I do an entire piece of work; I do the job from start to finish, and what is done is clearly "mine."

d. To what extent do you *find out how well you are doing* on the job as you are working?
Very little; I often work for long stretches without finding out how I am doing.
Moderately; sometimes I know how I am doing and other times I do not.
Very much; I get almost constant "feedback" on my performance as I work.

e. To what extent do you have the *opportunity to talk informally* with other employees while at work. (That is, is your job arranged so that you can chat with other workers while on the job—even though the job does not require you to talk to these people?)
Very little; there is almost no chance to talk to other employees except about "business."
Moderately; there is some chance to talk, but you may have to arrange it ahead of time.
Very much; there is almost always an opportunity to talk with other employees about non-business topics.

f. To what extent is *dealing with other people* a part of your job?
Very little; working with other people is *not* a very important part of my job.
Moderately; I have to deal with some other people, but this is not a major part of my job.
Very much; probably the single most important part of my job is working with other people.

A second section of the questionnaire asked employees on 7-point scales how much of the various job attributes was actually present on their jobs. These scales ranged from "none or a minimum amount" (scored 1) through "a moderate amount" (scored 4) to "a maximum amount" (scored 7). Scales which were used in this section of the questionnaire include:

(a) For variety: The amount of variety in my job.
The opportunity to do a number of different things.

(b) For autonomy: The opportunity for independent thought and action.
The freedom to do pretty much what I want on my job.

(c) For task identity: The opportunity to do a job from the beginning to end (i.e., the chance to do a whole job).
The opportunity to complete work I start.

(d) For feedback: The opportunity to find out how well I am doing in my job.
The feeling that I know whether I am performing my job well or poorly.

(e) For dealing with others: The opportunity, in my job, to give help to other people.

(f) For friendship opportunities: The opportunity in my job to get to know other people.
The opportunity to develop close friendships in my job.

The items described above were randomly spread throughout a 23-item section of the questionnaire which asked about the presence or absence of a number of heterogeneous aspects of the work setting.

Scores on all items describing each of the six job dimensions were averaged to arrive at a set of six summary scores from the employee ratings described above. The questionnaire items given to supervisors were identical in every respect, except that supervisors were asked to describe "the job you supervise" rather than "your job" as was the case for the employees.

Internal consistency reliabilities for the items making up each of the six job dimension scores are presented separately for employees and supervisors in Table 1. Also included are interjudge reliabilities for the researchers' assessments of the jobs. With the exception of supervisors' data on the dimension "dealing with others," the reliabilities are adequate.

Comparison of the scores obtained for each job by the four rating procedures reveals high agreement

TABLE 1 ESTIMATED RELIABILITIES OF THE SIX DESCRIPTIVE DIMENSIONS

	Source of Ratings		
Dimension	*Employees*	*Supervisors*	*Turner-Lawrence*
Variety	.90	.91	.86
Autonomy	.77	.68	.89
Task identity	.77	.86	.95
Feedback	.75	.75	.97
Dealing with others	.47	.17	.88
Friendship opportunities	.43	.42	.92

Note.—Reported reliabilities for employee and supervisor ratings are estimated internal consistencies. Each dimension score for these ratings consists of the average of three questionnaire items, except for "dealing with others" which is the average of two items. The reliability reported for the Turner-Lawrence procedure is the estimated reliability of the average of two judges, adjusted by Spearman-Brown procedures. Ratings by the researchers (the fourth procedure used) were made collaboratively and reliability data are not available.

TABLE 2 CORRELATIONS AMONG THE FOUR RATING PROCEDURES

Correlation Between	Job Dimensions					
	Variety	*Autonomy*	*Task Identity*	*Feedback*	*Dealing with Others*	*Friendship Opportunities*
Employees & supervisors	.87*	.85*	.65*	.09	.31	.49*
Employees & researchers	.94*	.94*	.79*	−.22	.91*	.73*
Employees & Turner-Lawrence	.89*	.72*	.63*	−.66	.95*	.52*
Supervisors & researchers	.94*	.79*	.63*	−.15	.37	.38
Supervisors & Turner-Lawrence	.84*	.49*	.62*	.23	.26	.35
Researchers & Turner-Lawrence	.90*	.80*	.69*	.16	.93*	.67*

Note.—$N = 13$ jobs.
* $p < .05$ (one-tailed test).

on all but one of the dimensions. These correlations are presented in Table 2. There is no agreement about which jobs are high and which jobs are low on the feedback dimension. One possible source of confusion regarding this dimension is that some feedback is provided directly by the job as an employee works (e.g., an installer successfuly installing and testing a telephone), while additional feedback may be provided by supervision (e.g., a foreman telling an installer that he has taken too long to do a particular job). It may be that employees, supervisors, and researchers were not attending to the same aspect of the feedback process in making their judgments, thereby lowering the level of agreement.

In addition to the problem with the feedback dimension, there is a tendency for correlations involving supervisors to be lower than others. This is especially true for the two dimensions involving interpersonal relationships: dealing with others, and friendship opportunities. Examination of the mean scores of employees and supervisors on these two jobs reveals no consistent differences. Supervisors did not see the jobs as having either consistently more or consistently less of an interpersonal component than employees—they simply did not agree well with the employees (or with the researchers) about the extent of interpersonal activities relevant to the job. Part of the reason for this lack of agreement may be the low internal consistency reliability of supervisors on the dimension "dealing with others." In addition, on-site observations indicated that, by and large, supervisors were considerably more attentive to and concerned with the technical and production aspects of the jobs they supervised than with interpersonal issues. This tendency may partially account for both the unreliability of the supervisors on the "dealing with others" dimension and the low level of agreement between supervisors and the other raters on the two interpersonal dimensions.

Table 2 shows that employees themselves provide judgments of the characteristics of their jobs which, in general, agree quite well with those made by outsiders and (with the exceptions noted above) by their supervisors. It is not, of course, possible to demonstrate conclusively that the employee judgments are objectively accurate, because no unambiguous standard of accuracy is available. Nevertheless, the strong convergence of the employee judgments with the assessments obtained from the researchers, from supervisors, and from the Turner-Lawrence procedures does suggest that the employees were able to provide generally nondistorted descriptions of the characteristics of their jobs. In most of the analyses reported in this article, employee judgments are used as the primary measures of job characteristics. This is appropriate and necessary, given that it was argued earlier that employees' perceptions of their jobs (rather than objective characteristics) are causal in affecting the reactions of employees to their work. Fortunately, the data in Table 2 establish that employee perceptions have convergent validity as descriptors of jobs—and, therefore, that they are probably reasonably well-grounded in reality.

The relationships among the six job dimensions themselves are presented in Table 3. Although there is some tendency for the six dimensions to be positively related to one another, only two of the correlations are of substantial magnitude: jobs seen as having high variety also are seen as being high in autonomy and in friendship opportunities. The level of interrelationship among the six dimensions as measured in the present research is lower than that reported by Turner and Lawrence (1965), and does not mitigate against use of the six dimensions separately as descriptors of job characteristics.

Table 4 presents a listing of the 13 jobs studied, the number of employees on each job who participated in the research, and the mean employee ratings of the characteristics of each job.[5]

[5] Descriptions of the 13 jobs on Turner-Lawrence dimensions are not included in Table 4 for two reasons. First, the Turner-Lawrence procedures were modified somewhat for use in the present study, and therefore the scores obtained are not directly comparable to those reported by Turner and Lawrence (1965) for their sample of 47 jobs. Second, the

TABLE 3 CORRELATIONS AMONG THE SIX DESCRIPTIVE DIMENSIONS: EMPLOYEE RATINGS

Dimensions	*Variety*	*Autonomy*	*Task Identity*	*Feedback*	*Dealing with Others*	*Friendship Opportunities*
Variety	—					
Autonomy	.67*	—				
Task identity	.17	.24*	—			
Feedback	.11	.06	.12	—		
Dealing with others	.05	—.05	.19*	.26*	—	
Friendship opportunities	.41*	.21*	.07	.32*	.13	—

Note.—$N = 208$ employees.
*$p < .01$ (two-tailed test).

TABLE 4 SUMMARY OF THE CHARACTERISTICS OF THE JOBS STUDIED

			X Employee Ratings of Job Characteristics					
Job Description	*Sex*	*N*	*Variety*	*Autonomy*	*Task Identity*	*Feedback*	*Dealing with Others*	*Friendship Opportunities*
Director assistance (DA) operators	F	16	3.08	3.64	5.66	4.88	6.06	4.13
Toll operators	F	18	2.87	3.06	5.15	4.80	6.03	3.69
Combined DA & toll operators	F	17	3.97	3.29	5.87	5.59	6.32	5.02
Traffic service position (TSP) operators	F	18	2.78	2.91	5.06	5.09	6.14	4.23
TSP operators with "enriched" jobs	F	19	2.94	2.96	5.26	5.08	5.90	4.05
Tip & ring (residence) installers	M	18	4.78	5.23	6.38	4.41	5.23	4.14
Key (commercial) installers	M	19	5.72	5.06	6.26	4.87	5.60	4.85
Private branch exchange installers	M	15	6.31	5.61	5.25	4.11	5.07	4.87
Cable splicers	M	16	5.14	4.67	5.04	5.12	4.59	4.67
Combined tip & ring & key installers	M	17	4.94	5.09	6.11	4.23	4.85	4.45
Central office framemen	M	8	4.50	3.89	4.42	5.43	5.12	5.44
Central office repairmen: Step equipment	M	11	5.30	4.84	5.32	4.30	4.77	4.70
Central office repairmen: Crossbar equipment	M	16	5.91	4.92	5.03	5.15	5.47	5.19

Individual Need Strength. To obtain a measure of the degree to which *Ss* were desirous of obtaining higher order need satisfactions from their work, a questionnaire was administered which asked how much of various opportunities and attributes the employees "would like" to have on their job. In a space beside each item, employees entered a number ranging from 1 (would like to have none or a minimum amount) to 7 (would like to have a maximum amount). Content of the questionnaire ranged widely, and included items relevant to pay, promotion, security, working conditions, peer relationships, and supervisory relationships. Twelve of the items were judged on a priori basis to measure desire for higher order need satisfactions. These items are:

(*a*) The opportunity for personal growth and development on my job.
(*b*) The opportunity for independent thought and action on my job.
(*c*) The opportunity to find out how I am doing.
(*d*) The opportunity to complete work I start.
(*e*) The opportunity to do challenging work.
(*f*) The feeling that I know whether I am performing my job well or poorly.
(*g*) The opportunity to do a number of different things.
(*h*) The opportunity to do a job from the beginning to the end (that is, the chance to do a whole job).
(*i*) The freedom to do pretty much what I want on my job.
(*j*) The amount of variety in my job.
(*k*) The feeling of worthwhile accomplishment in my job.
(*l*) The opportunity, in my job, for participation in the determination of methods, procedures, and goals.

Scores of each employee on the 12 items were summed to obtain an overall measure of the level of higher order need strength. Internal consistency reliability of the 12-item scale was .89.

Employee Reactions to Their Jobs. Four types of employee reactions to their jobs were obtained

primary use of the Turner-Lawrence scores in the present research was to demonstrate the convergence of employee assessments of their jobs with more objectively based job descriptions (see Table 2). Substantive analyses using the modified Turner-Lawrence scores are not reported, since the scores of specific jobs on the six dimensions are confounded both with traffic versus plant functions in the telephone company and with employee sex (see Table 4). It was concluded on these grounds that the sample of 13 jobs was not adequate for analysis of relations between objective job descriptions and mean dependent variable scores using jobs as observations.

TABLE 5 INTERCORRELATIONS AMONG DEPENDENT VARIABLES

			Correlations																					
Variable	*X*	*SD*	*1*	*2*	*3*	*4*	*5*	*6*	*7*	*8*	*9*	*10*	*11*	*12*	*13*	*14*	*15*	*16*	*17*	*18*	*19*	*20*	*21*	*22*
1. Level of intrinsic motivation	5.96	.87	—																					
Focus of motivation																								
2. Taking personal responsibility	6.39	.99	.30*	—																				
3. Doing large quantities of work	5.21	1.53	.01	.17*	—																			
4. Doing high quality work	5.22	1.09	.25*	.44*	.08	—																		
Rated performance																								
5. Quantity	5.24	1.45	.04	−.09	.09	−.05	—																	
6. Quality	5.24	1.27	.13	.05	.08	−.04	.63	—																
7. Overall effectiveness	5.53	1.11	.18*	.02	.10	.06	.79*	.85*	—															
8. General job satisfaction	4.97	1.26	.39*	.18*	.01	.23*	.07	.08	.16*	—														
9. Job involvement	3.00	1.37	.39*	.20*	.04	.16*	.07	.07	.11	.44*	—													
10. Absenteeism (no. of times absent)	2.69	2.16	−.23*	−.14*	−.10	−.06	°−.12	−.26*	−.33*	−.10	−.15*	—												
Specific satisfaction items																								
11. Self-esteem obtained from job	4.34	1.44	.23*	.04	−.01	.06	−.07	−.02	−.04	.49*	.34*	−.06	—											
12. Personal growth and development	4.33	1.48	.26*	.18*	.04	.11	.07	.03	.07	.58*	.38*	−.02	.66*	—										
13. Prestige of job inside company	3.95	1.44	.16*	−.01	.10	.04	−.09	.03	−.03	.44*	.29*	−.09	.63*	.50*	—									
14. Amount of close supervision received	4.46	1.45	.25*	.14*	−.01	.13	.04	.06	.10	.28*	.25*	−.07	.31*	.45*	.30*	—								
15. Independent thought and action	4.62	1.58	.21*	.13	−.11	.10	.11	.12	.17*	.36*	.34*	−.09	.39*	.50*	.32*	.62*	—							
16. Security	5.32	1.47	.15*	.13	.02	.16*	−.01	.06	.09	.47*	.23*	−.08	.43*	.46*	.39*	.40*	.40*	—						
17. Pay	3.68	1.74	.07	.04	−.02	.10	−.06	−.13	−.11	.44*	.16*	.02	.41*	.43*	.39*	.21*	.15*	.45*	—					
18. Feeling of worthwhile accomplishment	4.82	1.61	.45*	.22*	.01	.19*	.09	.14*	.11	.58*	.39*	−.02	.58*	.58*	.41*	.32*	.49*	.53*	.42*	—				
19. Participation in job-related decisions	3.86	1.50	.23*	.08	.05	.13	.04	.04	.07	.31*	.28*	−.04	.38*	.52*	.39*	.37*	.46*	.30*	.31*	.50*	—			
20. Development of close friendships	4.78	1.28	.06	.06	−.11	−.02	−.09	−.04	−.14*	.19*	.05	.15*	.24*	.34*	.21*	.25*	.31*	.28*	.22*	.33*	.33*	—		
21. Promotion	3.98	1.64	.16*	.16*	.08	.15*	.07	−.04	.03	.39*	.34*	.09	.43*	.60*	.42*	.38*	.29*	.44*	.48*	.43*	.51*	.22*	—	
22. Respect and fair treatment from boss	5.34	1.47	.23*	.08	−.06	.14*	.10	.06	.15*	.33*	.10	−.07	.42*	.40*	.35*	.43*	.41*	.57*	.34*	.45*	.35*	.25*	.42*	—

Note.—$N = 208$.

* $p < .05$ (two-tailed test).

from the questionnaires employees completed, for use as dependent variable measures. The four types of reactions are described separately below.

1. Experienced work motivation: measures were derived from the questionnaire to reflect both the amount of intrinsic motivation employees experienced on the job and the focus of their motivation. The amount of intrinsic motivation was assessed by three questionnaire items: *(a)* I feel a great sense of personal satisfaction when I do my job well. *(b)* Doing my job well increases my feeling of self-esteem. *(c)* I feel bad when I do my job poorly. The items were placed on 7-point scales ranging from "strongly disagree" (scored 1 to "strongly agree" (scored 7). Scores on the three items were averaged to yield a score indicative of the degree to which an employee experiences positive affective outcomes when he performs well, and negative affective outcomes when he performs poorly (Lawler & Hall, 1970). Internal consistency reliability of this scale was .72.

The focus of employee motivation was tapped by three questionnaire items which addressed the kinds of internal pressures for performance which were experienced on the job. Three items were used, which dealt with three different (but not mutually exclusive) foci of work motivation: *(a)* Being personally responsible for what you do, checking your own work. *(b)* Producing a large quantity of work. *(c)* Doing high quality work. Each item was on a separate 7-point scale, which ranged from high experienced pressure (e.g., "It is *extremely* important for a worker on this job to do high quality work") to low experienced pressure (e.g., "It is not especially important for a worker on this job to do high quality work").

2. Job involvement: three questionnaire items, in the same format as the intrinsic motivation items, were averaged to yield a score indicative of the degree employees felt personally involved in their work. The items were selected from those used by Lodahl and Kejner (1965). Internal consistency reliability of the scale was .81. The three items are: *(a)* The most important things that happen to me involve my work. *(b)* I live, eat, and breathe my job. *(c)* I am very much personally involved in my work.

3. General job satisfaction: employees completed three questionnaire items designed to tap overall job satisfaction. The three items also were in the same format as the intrinsic motivation items and were averaged to provide an index of general satisfaction. Internal consistency reliability of the 3-item scale was .76. The items are: *(a)* Generally speaking, I am very satisfied with my job. *(b)* I frequently think of quitting my job (reversed scoring). *(c)* Generally speaking, I am very satisfied with the kind of work I have to do on my job.

The nine items used in the general satisfaction, job involvement, and intrinsic motivation scales were randomly spread throughout a 23-item section of the employee questionnaire which addressed various types of reactions to work. Lawler and Hall (1970) have argued that it is useful, on a conceptual level, to treat satisfaction, involvement, and intrinsic motivation separately. In addition, they demonstrated that the three variables do have discriminant validity in predicting other employee attitudes and behaviors —even though the variables are moderately positively intercorrelated. The correlations obtained in the present research among intrinsic motivation, general satisfaction, and the three items reflecting the specific focus of employee motivation are included in Table 5.

4. Specific satisfaction items: Employees indicated on 12 questionnaire items the degree to which they were satisfied with particular aspects of their job. The items ranged from "extremely dissatisfied" (scored 1) to "extremely satisfied" (scored 7). The 12 items were not summed but were retained as separate indicators of specific satisfactions of the job. Median intercorrelation among the 12 items was .40. The items queried how satisfied employees were with:

(a) The feeling of self-esteem or self-respect a person gets from being in my job.
(b) The opportunity for personal growth and development in my job.
(c) The prestige of my job inside the company (that is, the regard received from others in the company).
(d) The amount of close supervision I receive.
(e) The opportunity for independent thought and action in my job.
(f) The feeling of security in my job.
(g) The pay for my job.
(h) The feeling of worthwhile accomplishment in my job.
(i) The opportunity, in my job, for participation in the determination of methods, procedures, and goals.
(j) The opportunity to develop close friendships in my job.
(k) The opportunity for promotion.
(l) The amount of respect and fair treatment I receive from my boss.

Performance Measures. Supervisors rated the performance of each employee on several dimensions, three of which are used in this report: *(a)* quantity of work produced, *(b)* quality of work produced, and *(c)* overall performance effectiveness.

The quantity and quality scores for each employee were obtained by averaging the ratings he received on 7-point rating scales from his supervisors (when more than one supervisory rating was available). The overall performance measure was obtained by summing average supervisory ratings across seven separate performance scales, including quantity and quality. Interjudge reliabilities of the quantity and quality scales were .71 and .79, respectively, and the internal consistency reliability of the overall performance effectiveness scale was .92. The correlation between the quantity and the quality scales was .63.

Anchors for the performance ratings were phrased in absolute terms, and supervisors were encouraged to assess each employee against the highest conceivable level of performance possible for the job in making his assessments. Nevertheless, the degree to which ratings made by different supervisors on different jobs are directly comparable is open to question, and results involving the performance ratings must be interpreted with caution.

Absenteeism Measure. The number of occasions an employee was absent during the 12-mo. period during which the study took place was derived from company payroll records. Occasions absent rather than days absent were used to discount the effects of single long periods of absence. For example, if an employee were ill for a 2-wk. period, the data would show the event as one occasion of absence, rather than as 10 working days of absence.

Summary of Measures. The various measures used in the research are summarized below. The means, standard deviations, and intercorrelations of all dependent variable measures are presented in Table 5. The measures include: *(a)* Job descriptions: variety, autonomy, task identity, feedback, dealing with others, and friendship opportunities. Descriptions were made by employees, by supervisors, by the researchers using the Turner-Lawrence procedures, and by the researchers subjectively after job observations and interviews. Because there was generally high convergent validity among the four sets of job descriptions, and because the conceptual basis of the study suggests that jobs as experienced by employees should be most directly causal of employee reactions to their jobs, the employee job descriptions are used in the analyses to be reported in subsequent sections. *(b)* Level of higher order need strength of employees: a summary score of employee reactions to 12 need strength items. *(c)* Employee reactions to their jobs and work. Questionnaire-derived measures of: the amount of intrinsic motivation experienced by employees, and the focus of their motivation; general job satisfaction; personal job involvement; and 12 specific satisfactions or dissatisfactions with the job or the work situation. *(d)* Rated performance effectiveness of employees, in terms of quantity of work produced, work quality, and overall performance effectiveness. *(e)* Absenteeism, measured by the number of occasions an employee was absent during a 12-mo. period.

RESULTS[6]

Core Dimensions: Toward Internal Motivation

Results showed that the higher jobs are on the four core dimensions, the more employees feel internal pressures to take personal responsibility for their work and to do high quality work. Supervisory ratings and company records confirmed that employees who experience their jobs as high on the core dimensions are in fact among the most effective performers on the job. Further, the data support the interpretation of these relationships which was proposed earlier in this paper: when jobs are high on the core dimensions, employees indicate that good performance results in *positive internal feelings*—and that when they do poorly, they feel bad. Apparently the core dimensions are centrally important in creating conditions whereby it is possible for employees to obtain personally rewarding experiences by doing well on the job.

Also as expected, results showed that the core dimensions were strongly and positively related to overall job satisfaction, to the degree employees feel personally involved in their work, and to low absenteeism. Finally, there were substantial relationships between the core dimensions and several specific types of job satisfaction. The core dimensions most *strongly* related to satisfaction with *(a)* the opportunity for independent thought and action on the job, *(b)* the feeling of worthwhile accomplishment derived from working on the job, *(c)* the opportunity for personal growth and development provided by the job, and *(d)* the self-esteem and self-respect a person can get from working on the job. The core dimensions were only *negligibly* related to satisfaction with *(a)* pay, *(b)* the opportunity to develop close friendships on the job, *(c)* promotion opportunities, and *(d)* the amount of respect and fair treatment received from the supervisor. These results confirm that the four core dimensions are most strongly related to the satisfaction of higher order needs; those

[6] This section is a radical condensation of the text and tabular material presented in pages 271–80 of the *Journal of Applied Psychology Monograph* from which this article was abridged.

satisfactions which are *not* substantially affected by the job characteristics, on the other hand, have mainly to do with needs classified as "lower-order" (for example, security, interpersonal, pay) in the hierarchies of Maslow (1943) and Alderfer (1969).

It should be noted that the results summarized above were based on all 208 employees in the sample, who were distributed across 13 different jobs. The initial analyses did not address the question of whether the relationships between the core dimensions and the dependent measures are primarily a result of *objective* differences among the 13 jobs studied—or whether they are more a consequence of *perceptual* differences among employees. Internal analyses designed to examine this question revealed that employees' perceptions of their jobs are, in fact, of central importance in affecting job attitudes and behaviors—but that the major determinant of such perceptions is the objective make-up of the job itself.

Exploration of Conditions for Enhancing Motivation and Satisfaction

The theory on which the research was based specifies that when jobs are high on the four core dimensions, employees have the opportunity to find out *(feedback)* that they personally *(autonomy)* have accomplished something meaningful and worthwhile (*variety* and *task identity*) when they perform well. The implication of this assertion is that, for maximum motivation and satisfaction, jobs should be high simultaneously on all four of the core dimensions. Analyses designed to test this proposition revealed that while motivation, satisfaction and performance are enhanced when jobs are high simultaneously on all four core dimensions, the theory-specified disjunctive model for combining the core dimensions is not necessarily the optimal one.

Finally, the theory specifies that jobs which are high on the core dimensions should be motivating *only* to individuals who are desirous of the kinds of intrinsic rewards that such jobs can provide—namely, higher-order need satisfactions. Employees in the present sample all were moderately high on the measure of higher-order need strength (the mean score on the 12-item need strength scale was 6.01 out of a possible 7.0). Therefore, generally positive relationships between the core dimensions and the dependent variables were expected (and found) for the sample as a whole. Despite the high overall mean of employees on the need strength measure, analyses were performed to test the possibility that employees who differ in measured need strength would, in fact, show differential responsiveness to jobs high on the core dimensions. Correlations between the core dimensions and the dependent variables were computed separately for those employees whose higher-order need strength scores were in the top one-third of the distribution of scores for all employees, and for those employees whose scores were in the bottom one-third of the same distribution. Even though most of the obtained correlations were positive (because of the relatively high mean need strength score even for the "low" one-third of the employees), substantial differences in the magnitude of the correlations were obtained for the two groups of employees. For example, correlation between a summary index (reflecting the degree to which the job was high on all four core dimensions) and employee satisfaction with the opportunity for independent thought and action was .70 for the "high" need strength employees—and only .45 for the "low" need strength employees. Similar differences were obtained for many other dependent variables. All in all, the results make a strong case for the moderating effect of individual higher-order need strength in determining the effects of job characteristics on employee behavior and attitudes at work.

DISCUSSION AND IMPLICATIONS

Job Design and Individual Differences

The results of this study suggest that there are important interdependencies among the characteristics of individuals and the characteristics of jobs which must be taken account of in the development of any full understanding of the impact of various kinds of job designs. Both the advocates of a "scientific management" approach to job design (make the work routine, simple, and standardized) and the more recent supporters of "job enlargement" (make the work complex, challenging, and demanding of individual responsibility and decision making) appear to have attached insufficient importance to individual-job interactions in determining affective and behavioral reactions to jobs. Those of the scientific management persuasion, for example, have tended to assume that the typical employee will be content, if paid judiciously for his cooperation, to work on jobs which provide little or no opportunity for personal feelings of accomplishment or achievement. Those of the job enlargement school, on the other hand, have tended to assume that most employees are desirous of such opportunities and will work hard and effectively when they have a job which provides them. The present research suggests that, depending on the characteristics of the workers involved, both points of view would lead to job design practices which are appropriate some of the time and inappropriate other times.

The present findings and conclusions fit well with the previous research of Turner and Lawrence (1965) and Hulin and Blood (1968). In both of these studies a sociological-level variable (urban vs. rural background) was shown to moderate the relationship between job characteristics and employee satisfaction. The relationship between job level (i.e., jobs which would be high on the four core dimensions) and satisfaction was found to be high for rural workers and low for urban workers. The present study demonstrates that individual higher-order need strength also moderates the relationship between job level and satisfaction (as well as the relationship between job level and other dependent variables). In particular, individuals with strong desires for higher-order need satisfaction respond much more positively to high level jobs than do individuals who have weaker higher order needs.

It may be that urban workers desire higher-order need satisfaction less than do rural workers—in which case the findings of the earlier studies and the present study would be highly congruent. This possibility was tested with the present data and a small difference in the expected direction was in fact found: workers with rural backgrounds were higher on higher-order need strength than were workers with urban backgrounds ($t = 1.47$, $p < .10$). Thus, the present research has taken the previous finding regarding urban-rural differences from the sociological level to the psychological level, refined it, and successfully replicated it. The present results also substantially extend the previous results in that the moderating effect of individual differences has been shown to apply to a number of dependent variables in addition to job satisfaction (i.e., job involvement, work motivation, quality of performance). Presumably it now should be possible to make considerably more specific predictions about how different individuals will respond to jobs with various characteristics.

It has been assumed throughout the above discussion that job characteristics actually cause the differences in employee satisfaction, motivation, performance, and absenteeism which were observed. Although the predictions which were made (and confirmed by the data) were based on a conceptual

TABLE 6 GENERAL RELATIONSHIPS BETWEEN JOB CHARACTERISTICS AND EMPLOYEE REACTIONS

	Core Dimension				*Interpersonal Dimension*	
Dependent variable	*Variety*	*Autonomy*	*Task Identity*	*Feedback*	*Dealing with Others*	*Friendship Opportunities*
Level of intrinsic motivation	.32*	.30*	.16*	.18*	.07	.09
Focus of motivation						
Taking personal responsibility	.14*	.12*	.19*	.06	.08	.05
Doing large quantities of work	−.10	−.12	.01	.02	.06	−.17
Doing high quality work	.16*	.12*	.13*	.10	.04	.12*
Rated performance						
Quantity	−.03	.12*	.05	.00	−.02	−.18
Quality	.17*	.16*	.07	.02	−.11	−.02
Overall effectiveness	.20*	.26*	.11*	−.03	−.07	−.09
General job satisfaction	.38*	.39*	.20*	.28*	.17*	.21*
Job involvement	.24*	.22*	.12*	.24*	.03	.16*
Absenteeism (no. of times absent)	.02	−.14*	−.22*	−.10	.01	−.05
Specific satisfaction items						
Self-esteem obtained from job	.32*	.32*	.15*	.35*	.15*	.27*
Personal growth and development	.36*	.34*	.14*	.31*	.11*	.29*
Prestige of job inside company	.30*	.25*	.15*	.35*	.14*	.28*
Amount of close supervision received	.31*	.35*	.13*	.30*	.07	.16*
Independent thought and action	.53*	.62*	.25*	.15*	.00	.25*
Security	.22*	.27*	.19*	.39*	.15*	.28*
Pay	.04	.05	.04	.34*	.25*	.24*
Feeling of worthwhile accomplishment	.29*	.32*	.28*	.42*	.23*	.31*
Participation in job-related decisions	.28*	.27*	.20*	.34*	.12*	.25*
Development of close friendships	.25*	.12*	.09	.29*	.09	.47*
Promotion	.17*	.20*	.15*	.34*	.21*	.19*
Respect and fair treatment from boss	.19*	.26*	.22*	.35*	.14*	.24*

Note.—$N = 208$.
* $p < .05$ (one-tailed test).

framework which includes causal propositions, the study design was correlational and at no point were the causal links in the theory directly tested. There is, however, reason to believe that the causal directions specified in the theory may be correct. While the simple correlations between job characteristics and the dependent variables (see Table 6) are open to alternative causal interpretations, this appears to be much less the case for those data which support other, more specific, predictions of the theory. In particular, it is difficult even after the fact to imagine an alternative causal model which would predict simultaneously that *(a)* all four of the core dimensions need to be present to realize the most positive affective and behavioral reactions on the part of employees, and that *(b)* the strength of desire for higher-order need satisfaction will substantially moderate the relationships between the core dimensions and the dependent variables. It appears, therefore, that a cautious interpretation of the results in terms of the causal impact of job characteristics may be reasonable. This does not deny the fact that any theory can best be tested by experimental alternation of the independent variables, and manipulation of the core dimensions in an experimental setting would seem to be a clear next step in research on job effects.

Use of Perceived Job Characteristics

One of the major conceptual and methodological problems which pervades studies of task and job effects on behavior has to do with the differences between task materials as they exist in objective reality and as they are perceived by individual performers. Tasks and jobs are invariably redefined by the individuals who perform them, sometimes deliberately and sometimes without full awareness by the performers of the changes or re-emphases that are being made. Further, it is the redefined task rather than the objective task which the individual tries to perform, and thus only those aspects of tasks or jobs which are actually perceived or experienced by a performer can have an impact on his performance and attitudes. This would seem to argue for the use of task and job characteristics as described by the performers themselves in research aimed at ascertaining the effects of these characteristics on performance. Yet when such subjective assessments are used, many of the important conceptual and methodological advantages associated with the use of independently and objectively described independent variables are lost.[7]

[7] The conceptual and methodological implications of the task redefinition phenomenon are discussed in more detail elsewhere (Hackman, 1969b; Weick, 1965).

There are at least two strategies for dealing with this problem in research on task and job effects on behavior. One, which was used in the present research, is to employ subjective assessments of the tasks or jobs by the performers themselves, but simultaneously to develop means of determining the relationship between these assessments and others, including objective measures when possible. Thus, in addition to employee descriptions of the characteristics of their jobs in the present study, jobs were rated by three other methods: by company managers, by the researchers, and by an adaptation of the Turner and Lawrence (1965) procedures for describing jobs in operational terms. As was shown in Table 2, there was high convergence among the four methods for all job dimensions except feedback. Thus, while the job descriptions used in the analyses are those actually experienced by the employees (and thus presumably are more directly causal of their behavior than would be the case for objectively described characteristics), they also have been shown to have substantial convergent validity and to be based upon the objective job characteristics.

A second strategy for dealing with the redefinition problem has been proposed by Hackman (1970) and, while methodologically more difficult to implement, probably has more potential for the development of a general understanding of the effects of tasks and jobs. In essence, this strategy suggests that the redefinition process should be viewed as the first stage of the performance process itself, and the redefined task should be conceived of as a potentially measurable intervening variable in the causal chain between the objective task input and the dependent variables of interest (e.g., performance, satisfaction). Just as individual differences in need strength have been shown in this research to moderate the effects of job characteristics on employee behavior and attitudes, so would individual needs, values, and goals be expected to interact with the objective task or job in influencing task redefinition. It might be, for example, that individuals with a particular pattern of needs tend to redefine the tasks they perform to be more consistent with those needs than is actually the case. These individuals might then develop hypotheses about appropriate on-the-job behavior which they expect to lead to need-satisfying outcomes, but which, because of the lack of congruence between the objective and the redefined task, might in fact serve only to set the stage for disillusionment and frustration. In any case, it appears that research on the ways different individuals redefine tasks and jobs may have considerable potential for furthering general understanding of the effects of tasks and jobs on the behavior and attitudes of performers.

Nature of the Four Core Dimensions

The results of the present research show that, in general, employees with moderately high desires for higher-order need satisfaction tend to work harder and be more satisfied when they perceive their jobs as being relatively high on the four core dimensions. In addition, it was shown that for the most favorable outcomes, jobs need to be at least moderately high on all four of the dimensions.

Further refinement of the core dimensions and exploration of their impact on individuals clearly is called for by the research. For example, the relationship between variety and task identity needs further examination. In one sense, since both of these dimensions are viewed as enhancing the meaningfulness of the work (although by different means), it might be argued that it is not necessary for both to be present (i.e., that one can effectively substitute for the other). The finding of Hall and Lawler (1970), that jobs which were very high on variety and low in task identity are not associated with high quality performance among researchers, would tend to argue against this possibility, however. An alternative possibility which would not be contrary to the Hall and Lawler findings is that some moderate level of variety is essential simply to keep the employee from being bored with his work (Scott, 1966), and that once this is achieved, experienced meaningfulness of the work will vary directly with the amount of task identity present. Finally, it may be that increases in variety can serve two different functions, depending on the amount initially present on a given job. For low initial levels of variety an increase may serve mainly to decrease the monotony of the work and make it possible for perceived meaningfulness to vary as a function of the amount of task identity present, as suggested above. At some point, however, variety may assume a different function, namely, introducing challenge into the work which, when successfully dealt with, can be satisfying to many individuals. Clearly, additional research on the psychological impact of these dimensions is called for.

Additional work also needs to be done on the operationalization of the feedback dimension, since no convergence was obtained among the several methods for measuring this dimension. The fact that the dimension operated as predicted in the data analyses indicates that the employee judgments of the dimension have some validity, but because the various groups who rated the jobs did not agree on the amount of feedback present, the exact meaning of the dimension remains highly uncertain.

Finally, the generality of the moderately high correlation ($r = .67$) between variety and autonomy should be tested. The descriptions of the scales used to measure these two dimensions were quite dissimilar, and it may be that the high correlation was obtained simply because jobs which had high variety in the particular organization where the study took place also tended to be jobs which provided considerable autonomy. The fact that most telephone traffic jobs (i.e., various kinds of operators) were low on both variety and autonomy would certainly facilitate obtaining a positive correlation between the dimensions, and might suggest that the high correlation is to some extent organization specific. There is reason, however, to believe that the positive relationship between variety and autonomy is at least moderately general. Turner and Lawrence (1965) found an analogously high relationship between these two dimensions across 47 different jobs, and Alderfer (1967) obtained a very high correlation between variety and "decision time" (which has some conceptual similarity to autonomy) across a sample of 30 jobs which included management jobs. It appears well worth examining the possibility that the psychological meaning of the two dimensions is similar in ways that have not been attended to in the present conceptualization.

Interpersonal Components of Jobs

The two job dimensions reflective of the interpersonal components of jobs (dealing with others, and friendship opportunities) did not relate to employee work motivation or performance. The dimensions did relate positively to certain kinds of satisfaction, but the relationships were not as substantial as those involving the four core dimensions.

According to the conceptualization on which the present study is based, the degree to which jobs require interpersonal activities should relate to work motivation only when *(a)* workers have high desires for the satisfaction of social needs, and *(b)* working hard on the job can lead to the satisfaction of these needs. Even those jobs which scored relatively high on the two interpersonal dimensions (e.g., some operators' jobs) fail to meet the latter criterion. Operators reported in fact that they could obtain social satisfactions best when they were not "working hard" by company standards (i.e., completing a large number of calls), since when the load of calls was heavy they had little time for meaningful interpersonal activities with either customers or fellow employees.

Even if jobs were designed so that relating meaningfully to others was an integral part of doing the job well, there is reason to doubt whether such jobs would have long-term motivational payoffs. The reason for skepticism is the arguments of Maslow (1943) and of Alderfer (1971) (presented earlier in this article) that when individuals have had ample opportunities to satisfy their social needs, the level of desire for additional social satisfaction will decrease and the level of desire for higher order need satisfaction will increase. When this occurs, of course, then jobs should be high on the four core dimensions (rather than high on an interpersonal dimension) to provide conditions for internal work motivation.

All of the above is not to suggest that the interpersonal aspects of work are unimportant. They do affect satisfaction and it is also possible that they affect other variables which were not considered in this study (e.g., problem-solving effectiveness, turnover). It should also be noted that all of the jobs in the present study were at least moderately high on the interpersonal dimensions; it is very likely that important negative reactions might be obtained from employees on jobs which were very low or totally lacking in interpersonal aspects. Further, the present data address only the degree to which the existing structure of jobs requires or provides opportunities for interpersonal activities. Alderfer (1967) has shown that when jobs are changed, interpersonal relationships (especially between the worker and his supervisor) are markedly affected, and that "relationship problems" clearly have the potential of negating or reversing increases in motivation and satisfaction which are anticipated as a result of job enlargement.

Nature of the Impact of Jobs on Behavior

Until relatively recently, research attention given to jobs has focused mainly on the ways jobs can be designed for most efficient production, or on the analysis of jobs into component parts to facilitate employee selection, placement, and compensation. Since the mid-1950s, however, research attention gradually has shifted toward examination of the effects jobs can have on the people who do them, and how jobs can be designed so that these effects are desirable for both employees and organizations.

Many studies, including this one, have shown that jobs can and often do have a substantial impact on employee behavior and attitudes; this finding is by now rather well documented. It appears that additional understanding of the nature and implications of job effects will require more direct investigation of the process by which these effects take place.

The present study represents some progress in this direction by providing data which show that certain job characteristics and certain individual differences interact in determining behavior and satisfaction. Apparently, individuals who are desirous of higher order need satisfactions will, when working on a job high on the core dimensions, gradually develop and/or verify the hypothesis that personally valued rewards can be obtained by working hard and effectively on the job. When this occurs, the job can be said to have influenced the behavior of these employees by affecting their personal hypotheses about what kinds of behaviors will lead to favorable outcomes. Thus, one general way that jobs can influence behavior is by creating conditions whereby employees are likely to develop and validate specific behavioral hypotheses about what they can do on the job to obtain work outcomes favorable to themselves (or to avoid unfavorable outcomes).

The general process outlined briefly above represents only one of several possible ways that jobs can influence behavior and attitudes on the job. For example, jobs also can affect behavior by influencing the level of activation of employees at work (Scott, 1966), or by arousing (or depressing) particular employee need states themselves. The general question of how jobs and tasks influence behavior is discussed in some detail by Hackman (1969a; 1970). The point of emphasis here is that job effects can and do come about via a number of different (albeit interrelated) psychological processes, only one of which was given focal attention in the present research. It is likely that sometimes these processes will operate simultaneously and will be mutually reinforcing; other times they may work at cross purposes. Further work toward a more general understanding of the several processes by which jobs affect behavior and how they interact with individual differences would seem to be warranted.

Implications for Organizational Practice

Standard organizational selection and placement procedures attempt to match the skills and abilities of a prospective employee with the skill requirements of the job for which he is being considered. The results of the present research suggest that it may be equally critical for long-term organizational effectiveness to achieve a match between the psychological makeup of the prospective employee and the psychological demands and opportunities of the job. In particular, the present results suggest that individuals who desire higher-order need satisfaction will be likely to contribute most effectively to organizational goals (and simultaneously to satisfy their own needs) if they are placed on jobs which are high on the four core dimensions. Other employees, of course, who may be neither desirous of higher-order need satisfactions nor capable of dealing with complex jobs requiring considerable autonomy, would be ineffective on such jobs and dissatisfied with them.

It appears from research cited earlier in this article that many organizations err rather consistently by designing jobs which are too low on the core dimensions. The present study supports this conclusion. It suggests that there are many workers who want to obtain more higher-order need satisfactions from their work, but few who are overwhelmed by the psychological demands of their jobs. The implication of this argument, of course, is that organizations might be well advised to consider redesigning many of their jobs.

When job enlargement is carried out, the question often arises whether the changes should be toward horizontal enlargement (i.e., increasing the number of different things an employee does) or toward vertical enlargement (i.e., increasing the degree to which an employee is responsible for making most major decisions about his work) or both. Lawler (1969) has reviewed the literature regarding the effects of vertical and horizontal job enlargement and concludes that simultaneous enlargement in both directions may be optimal in most cases. The results of the present study provide some support for this contention. Only if a job is enlarged vertically is an employee likely to feel personally responsible for his work outcomes; and only if a job has some amount of horizontal enlargement is he likely to experience his work as meaningful—although it should be kept in mind that too much horizontal enlargement apparently can cause problems. Simultaneous vertical and horizontal enlargement should increase the likelihood that a redesigned job will be high on all four of the core dimensions.

It should be re-emphasized in conclusion, however, that while jobs appear to be highly potent in determining employee motivation and satisfaction, there is no single best way to design a job. Instead, the results of the present research suggest that the substantial motivational potential of jobs can be realized only when the psychological demands and opportunities of jobs mesh well with the personal needs and goals of employees who work on them. This kind of matching can be developed through selection and placement of employees, through job redesign, or (perhaps optimally) by attempting to fit people to jobs and jobs to people simultaneously and continuously as both the organization and the characteristics of its employees change over time.

REFERENCES

Alderfer, C. P. An organizational syndrome. *Administrative Science Quarterly,* 1967, **12**, 440–60.

Alderfer, C. P. An empirical test of a new theory of human needs. *Organizational Behavior and Human Performance,* 1969, **4**, 142–75.

Alderfer, C. P. *Human needs in organizational settings.* New York: The Free Press of Glencoe, 1971.

Argyris, C. *Integrating the individual and the organization.* New York: Wiley, 1964.

Biganne, J. F. and Stewart, P. A. *Job enlargement: A case study.* (Research Series No. 25) State University of Iowa, Bureau of Labor and Management, 1963.

Blauner, R. *Alienation and freedom.* Chicago: University of Chicago Press, 1964.

Blood, M. R. and Hulin, C. L. Alienation, environmental characteristics, and worker responses. *Journal of Applied Psychology,* 1967, **51**, 284–90.

Conant, E. H. and Kilbridge, M. D. An interdisciplinary analysis of job enlargement: Technology, costs, and behavioral implications. *Industrial and Labor Relations Review,* 1965, **3**, 377–95.

Davis, L. E. Job design and productivity: A new approach. *Personnel,* 1957, **33**, 418–29.

Davis, L. E. and Valfer, E. S. Intervening responses to changes in supervisor job designs. *Occupational Psychology,* 1965, **39**, 171–89.

Dunnette, M. D., Campbell, J. P., and Hakel, M. D. Factors contributing to job satisfaction and job dissatisfaction in six occupational groups. *Organizational Behavior and Human Performance,* 1967, **2**, 143–74.

Ford, R. N. *Motivation through the work itself.* New York: American Management Association, 1969.

Friedmann, G. *The anatomy of work.* New York: The Free Press of Glencoe, 1961.

Ghiselli, E. E. and Brown, C. W. *Personnel and industrial psychology.* New York: McGraw-Hill, 1955.

Guest, R. H. Men and machines: An assembly-line worker looks at his job. *Personnel,* 1955, **31**, 3–10.

Hackman, J. R. Nature of the task as a determiner of job behavior. *Personnel Psychology,* 1969, **22**, 435–44. (a)

Hackman, J. R. Toward understanding the role of tasks in behavioral research. *Acta Psychologica,* 1969, **31**, 97–128. (b)

Hackman, J. R. Tasks and task performance in research on stress. In J. E. McGrath (ed.), *Social and psychological factors in stress.* New York: Holt, Rinehart & Winston, 1970.

Hall, D. T. and Lawler, E. E., III. Job design and job pressures as facilitators of professional-organization integration. *Administrative Science Quarterly,* 1970, **15**, 271–81.

Herzberg, F. *Work and the nature of man.* Cleveland: World, 1966.

Herzberg, F., Mausner, B., and Snyderman, B. *The motivation to work.* New York: Wiley, 1959.

Hinton, B. L. An empirical investigation of the Herzberg methodology and two-factor theory. *Organizational Behavior and Human Performance,* 1968, **3**, 286–309.

Hulin, C. L. and Blood, M. R. Job enlargement, individual differences, and worker responses. *Psychological Bulletin,* 1968, **69**, 41–55.

Kilbridge, M. D. Reduced costs through job enlargement: A case. *Journal of Business of the University of Chicago,* 1960, **33**, 357–62.

Kilbridge, M. D. Turnover, absence, and transfer rates as indicators of employee dissatisfaction with repetitive work. *Industrial and Labor Relations Review,* 1961, **15**, 21–32.

King, N. A clarification and evaluation of the two-factor theory of job satisfaction. *Psychological Bulletin,* 1970, **74**, 18–31.

Lawler, E. E., III. Job design and employee motivation. *Personnel Psychology,* 1969, **22**, 426–35.

Lawler, E. E., III and Hall, D. T. The relationship of job characteristics to job involvement, satisfaction and intrinsic motivation. *Journal of Applied Psychology,* 1970, **54**, 305–12.

Lawler, E. E., III and Porter, L. W. Antecedent attitudes of effective managerial performance. *Organizational Behavior and Human Performance,* 1967, **2**, 122–42.

Lewin, K. *The conceptual representation of the measurement of psychological forces.* Durham, N.C.: Duke University Press, 1938.

Lewin, K., Dembo, T., Festinger, L., and Sears, P. Level of aspiration. In J. McV. Hunt (ed.), *Personality and the behavior disorders.* New York: Ronald Press, 1944.

Locke, E. A. What is job satisfaction? *Organizational Behavior and Human Performance,* 1969, **4**, 309–36.

Lodahl, T. M. and Kejner, M. The definition and measurement of job involvement. *Journal of Applied Psychology,* 1965, **49**, 24–33.

Lytle, C. W. *Job evaluation methods.* New York: Ronald Press, 1946.

McGregor, D. *The human side of enterprise.* New York: McGraw-Hill, 1960.

MacKinney, A. C., Wernimont, P. F., and Galitz, W. O. Has specialization reduced job satisfaction? *Personnel,* 1962, **39**, 8–17.

Maslow, A. H. A theory of human motivation. *Psychological Review,* 1943, **50**, 370–96.

Maslow, A. H. *Motivation and personality.* New York: Harper, 1954.

Pelissier, R. F. Successful experience with job design. *Personnel Administration,* 1965, **28**, 12–16.

Porter, L. W. and Lawler, E. E., III. *Managerial attitudes and performance.* Homewood, Ill.: Irwin, 1968.

Scott, W. E. Activation theory and task design. *Organizational Behavior and Human Performance,* 1966, **1**, 3–30.

Stigers, M. F. and Reed, E. G. *The theory and practice of job rating.* New York: McGraw-Hill, 1944.

Tolman, E. C. Principles of purposive behavior. In S. Koch (ed.), *Psychology: A study of a science.* Vol. 2. New York: McGraw-Hill, 1959.

Turner, A. N. and Lawrence, P. R. *Industrial jobs and the worker.* Boston: Harvard University Graduate School of Business Administration, 1965.

Vroom, V. H. *Work and motivation.* New York: Wiley, 1964.

Walker, C. R. The problem of the repetitive job. *Harvard Business Review,* 1950, **28**, 54–58.

Walker, C. R. and Guest, R. H. *The man on the assembly line.* Cambridge: Harvard University Press, 1952.

Weick, K. E. Laboratory experimentation with organizations. In J. G. March (ed.), *Handbook of organizations.* Chicago: Rand-McNally, 1965.

Section B

ORGANIZATIONAL STRUCTURE

Having examined several factors influencing the optimum design of tasks (as well as several consequences associated with different task designs), we now turn our attention to the structuring of the relationships among tasks. Here we will be concerned with both the antecedents and consequences of differing organizational structures. The readings we have selected focus on four themes: (1) on theoretical development of models which attempt to describe the dimensions of organizational structure, (2) the indentification of environmental and technological determinants of structural variations, (3) the effects of structural differences on employee feelings, behavior, and performance, and (4) projections concerning likely organizational structures of the future.

We begin with a comic relief depicting how some view the personal implications of the bureaucratic structure. Several of the subsequent selections illustrate the oversimplification of the implied strategy for getting ahead.

Lichtman and Hunt provide a linkage between the individual level of analysis, upon which we have been focusing, and the organizational level. They point to the varying themes which attempt to provide a synthesis of personality (or person) and the structure of organizations. They make a strong argument for a situationally based or contingency model of the interaction between organizations and their participants. This theme will be extended later in this section by Pugh and his colleagues as well as by Fiedler and

House in our analysis of leadership later in the book.

The characterization of the bureaucratic organization in terms of several dimensions and an emphasis on *size* as a key variable in determining bureaucratization are foundations upon which Blau bases his formal theory of differentiation. In Blau's framework, size leads to differentiation which generates increasing problems of coordination which, in turn, cause the enlargement of the administrative component.

Perrow conceptualizes organizations in terms of their technologies. Technology is seen as composed of two dimensions: (1) the number of exceptions that must be handled and (2) the degree to which search or problem solving is an analyzable, routine procedure. Four types are described: (1) nonroutine, (2) routine, (3) craft, and (4) engineering. Organizational and social structure within the organization, as well as organizational goals, are seen as partially determined by the technology employed.

The themes of dimensional analysis and determinants of structure are carried forward by Pugh, Hickson, Hinings, and Turner. These authors focus on three major dependent variables which define intraorganizational structure in their analysis: (1) the structuring of activities, (2) the concentration of authority and (3) the locus of control over the flow of work. They then look to the historical as well as contemporary *context* or *environment* of organizations in an attempt to explain differences in internal structure. Two important characteristics of the Pugh *et al.* study should be noted: (1) the explicit attempt to link several dimensions of structure to their context, and (2) the actual measurement of these constructs and their interrelationships.

In the next selection, Porter and Lawler review a series of research studies investigating the effects of organizational structure and size on employee performance and attitudes. In most of these studies one or more organizational variables are treated as independent or causal factors generating certain specified behavioral or attitudinal consequences on the part of the participants in the organization. Many of the organizational factors reviewed by Porter and Lawler are to some degree variable or controllable from the viewpoint of the executive and therefore provide possibilities for changing and enhancing member attitudes and, in some cases, behaviors.

Several of the research studies reviewed by Porter and Lawler suggest that the traditional, pyramidal, bureaucratic organization may not be the most functional design for some purposes. This theme is carried forward by Bennis. He reviews the work of several contributors to the organizational literature and classifies their efforts within a useful typology. Bennis suggests that emerging developments in education, aspirations, and informational technology will necessitate a move toward more adaptive and flexible organizational forms.[1]

There are at least three major contributions to the literature on organizational theory which relate to the theme of this section. Even though they are outside the explicit focus of this book, the reader should be aware of their existence and importance. These are *Industrial Organization: Theory and Practice* (1965) by Joan Woodward, *Organizations in Action* (1967) by James Thompson and *Organization and Environment* (1967) by Paul Lawrence and Jay Lorsch. Each is rich in ideas, and none can be done complete justice here. Woodward was one of the first to both conceptually and empirically examine the link between technology (unit, mass, and process) and organizational structure. You will note that her work is frequently referenced in the selections in this section, and her ideas have provided a theme upon which many contemporary organizational theorists and researchers have built. Related to our purposes in this section, Thompson's major focus is on structural differentiation as a function of technology and environmental uncertainty. Lawrence and Lorsch share this emphasis on environmental uncertainty which, in their framework, results in varying degrees of differentiation (both structural and psychological) within the organization. Integrative mechanisms then must be established to coordinate the differentiated structure. Thompson's work is purely conceptual while Lawrence and Lorsch combine analysis and empirical data.[2]

---

[1] One reflection of these developments has been the emergence of "matrix models" of organizational design; see F. A. Shull, A. L. Delbecq and L. L. Cummings, *Organizational Decision Making* (New York: McGraw-Hill Book Co., 1970), chap. 6. For suggestions regarding the implementation of the matrix design, see Jay Galbraith, "Matrix organization designs: How to combine functional and project forms," *Business Horizons,* February 1971, pp. 29–40.

[2] For elaboration of the differentiation-integration theme, see P. Lawrence and J. Lorsch, "Differentiation and Integration in Complex Organizations," *Administrative Science Quarterly,* Vol. 12, No. 1 (June 1967), and J. Morse and J. Lorsch, "Beyond Theory Y," *Harvard Business Review,* June 1970.

25. ORGANIZATIONAL CHART

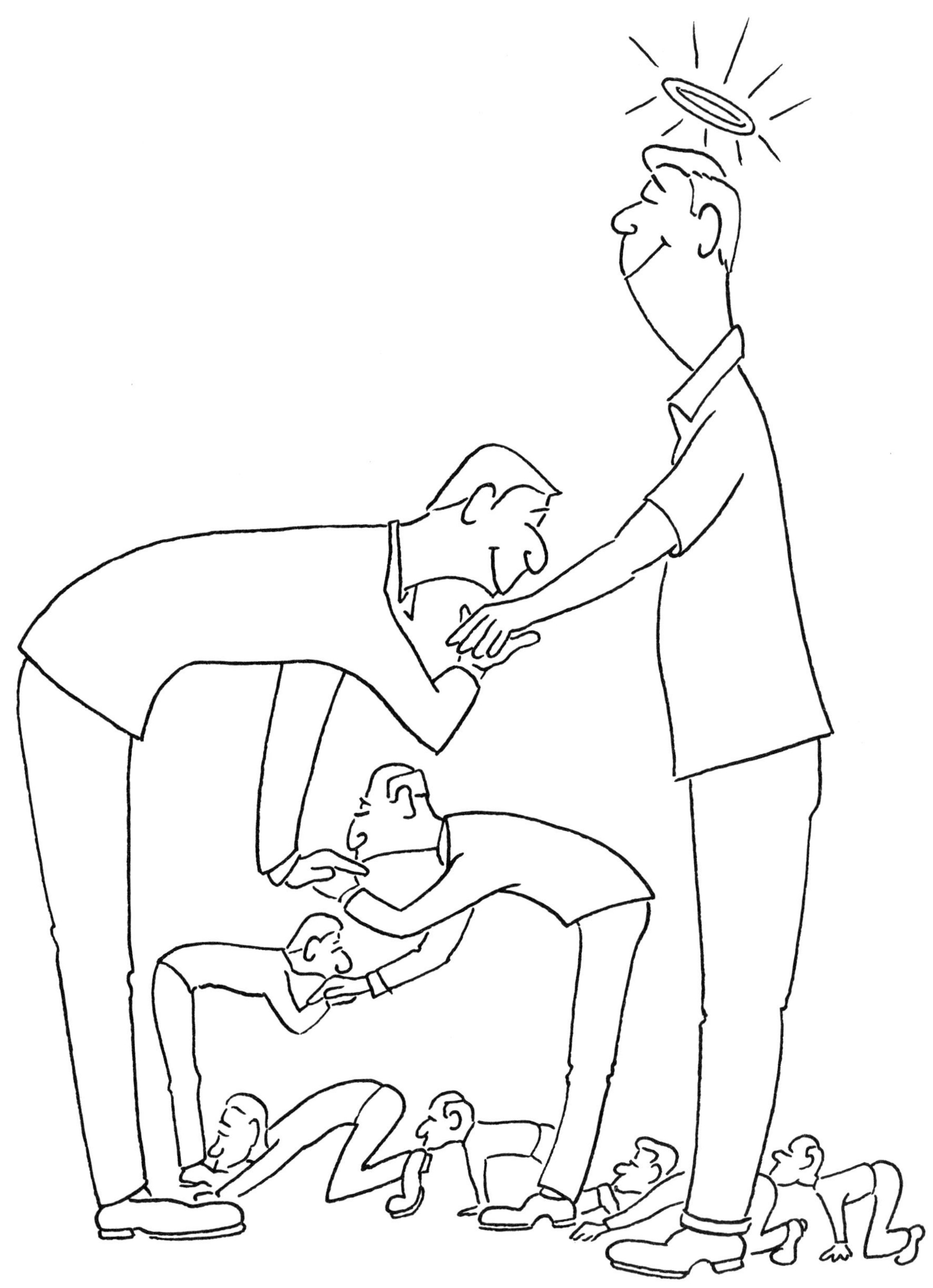

26. PERSONALITY AND ORGANIZATION THEORY: A REVIEW OF SOME CONCEPTUAL LITERATURE*

Cary M. Lichtman and Raymond G. Hunt†

Since a theory of organization can be no better than the assumption it makes about the human personality, this paper reviews and comments on the ways different theories have dealt with, or contributed to, the "structuralistic" versus "personalistic" dilemma. The several views are classed under four conceptual rubrics: *(a)* tradition structural approaches (e.g., Marx and Weber), *(b)* modern structural approaches (e.g., Argyris and McGregor), *(c)* personalistic views (e.g., perceptual theories), and *(d)* integrating approaches (e.g., system and role models). It is concluded that the extreme variability found within and among organizations renders the one-sided normative theories less useful in understanding organizational behavior than models that recognize situational contingencies.

When viewing the phenomena of human behavior, it has been a custom among social scientists to debate the relative importance to it of individual characteristics and properties of the social situation. Sometimes they hide from the problem, and, of course, accommodations have been sought, but the question still divides "personalists" and "situationalists" despite the efforts of a growing school of "interactionist" peacemakers (cf. Hollander & Hunt, 1967, especially Sections I and III for fuller discussion of these issues).

Theories of organization, dealing as they do with human collective undertakings, could hardly expect to escape the conceptual fallout from this "debate." Nor have they. And because we believe a theory of organization can be no better than the assumptions it makes about the human personality, we propose to review and comment on the ways different theories have chosen to resolve (or evade) the issue of relating persons and organizations.

In this discussion we construe organizations, after W. R. Scott (1964), as "collectivities . . . established for the pursuit of relatively specific objectives on a more or less continuous basis [p. 488]." Although organizational policies and structures may be elaborated separately from their memberships, people populate and work them, and the interplay of people and structures defines the phenomena of organization (cf. Hollander & Hunt, 1967, pp. 352–353).

Early theories of social organization emphasized the more general sociological conviction that the social structure was the primary determinant of differential human characteristics. Classical organization theorists, therefore, proposed that these structural determinants be utilized in the design of organizations to maximize human potential and organizational efficiency. Some two decades later, however, the so-called neoclassical organization theorists offered models based on the personalistic views of psychology. Reacting to early sociological notions, this school of thought rejected the formal organizational structure as of small importance and placed the locus of the organization within the phenomenal fields of its individual incumbents. Then, reacting in turn to the one-sidedness of these two earlier approaches, many modern organization theorists acknowledged the value of each and attempted to integrate them into a unitary systemic conceptual scheme. Thus, modern organization theory (cf. Scott, 1961) proposes that human behavior in organizational settings can be understood in terms of three elements: *(a)* the stated design of functions, that is, the requirements of the organization; *(b)* the characteristics of people who populate the organization, that is, the attributes they bring with them into the organization, including those derived from other social affiliations; *(c)* the relations between the organization's defined properties and the characteristics of people who populate it. The last element is a system concept that provides for prospects of organization-level emergents and is a hallmark of "modern" organization theory.

In their entirety, particular theories of organization do not always fit neatly into any one of these categories. The limited conceptual scope of some theories obviously places them with either the structural or personalistic camps; others seem to be a combination of both, without necessarily being full-fledged systemic theories. Grouping conceptual formulations into categories may not always do maximum justice to many of their nuances, but it does help to integrate the diverse ideas contained in the organizational literature. And the task of grouping theories becomes somewhat simpler if the classification is done, as we have tried to do here, according to the actual content of particular theoretical statements rather than what their authors claim to be the domain of their conceptualizations.

VARIETIES OF THEORY

For classificatory purposes we elected to employ

* *Psychological Bulletin,* Vol. 76, No. 4 (1971), pp. 271–94.

† Wayne State University and State University of New York at Buffalo, respectively.

four categories instead of the traditional three. The first two sections of this discussion deal in sequence with *traditional structural approaches* and *modern structural approaches* to organizational behavior. What the old and new structural theories have in common is the use of a global theory of personality as a premise upon which an organizational structure is designed. "All men are thus," they say, "and organizational theory and practice had best take account of such truths [Quinn & Kahn, 1967, p. 451]." In the case of traditional structuralists (classical organization theorists) the grounding assumption is that man is lazy, untrustworthy, and works only for money. The resulting organizational design suggested by this assumption, of course, has been of the bureaucratic variety, and the motivational presuppositions of traditional structuralism still underly much modern "incentive" theory and associated modes of compensating performance (cf. Opsahl & Dunnette, 1966).

Modern structural theorists follow quite the same logic, although basing it on a different initial premise. They argue that all men are interested in self-actualizing or realizing their full potential, and to allow for this they recommend a looser, more decentralized structure than did the bureaucrats. Both views are logically committed to the position that since people share certain important characteristics, differences in people or performance can best be explained in terms of differential positional occupancy in the organizational structure. The implication of this typology is that theorists such as Argyris and McGregor (and some others as well), who have usually been considered personalistic theorists, emerge as structural theorists in the present context.

The third section of the discussion deals with those theories that emphasize the *personalistic approach* to the understanding of organizational behavior. In this category are viewpoints that stress individual cognitive attributes, human experience, and individual differences as behavioral determinants. Some of these assume that employees act as individuals, while others assume that individual behavior is mediated by informal groups. In either case, however, the bias is in the direction of personalism or "psychologism" rather than "sociologism" or structuralism.

The fourth section deals with *integrative approaches* to organizations, which attempt to synthesize the various one-sided views into a single framework represented to be a more accurate model of organizational functioning.

Traditional Structural Approaches

Probably the most ambitious attempt to deal with the social-psychological aspects of the social structure was that of Marx (cf. 1887; or more particularly the collection of writings, 1964). Marx was concerned with properties of the social environment as they influence the characteristics of people who populated that environment. In this view, social stratification is seen collectively in the form of ideology; the stratification system is a way of organizing the social order. Ideology, then, is an expression of the stratification system and develops after the stratification system is established.

Thus, for Marx, the individual is influenced entirely by the social order and has no important characteristics aside from the system of which he is a part. The only way to change people is to change the society.

Following Marx's lead, Durkheim (1902) maintained that once a society establishes a division of labor, the properties of that society can be defined independently of people. The characteristics of people can be examined as a function of the categories to which they belong. In other words, people can be characterized as a function of the structural properties of society.

Ironically, then, the earlier sociological writings of theorists such as Marx and Durkheim can be seen to provide a broad theoretical base for classical organization theorists who founded such schools of organizational thought as scientific management, administrative management, and bureaucracy. By implication the Marxes and Durkheims introduced questions of distinctions between organization theory and personality theory, whose solutions still tend to elude us (cf. Hunt, 1969b).

Scientific Management

In his scientific management, Taylor (1911) set out to study organizations with "scientific precepts." He was interested primarily in work performance, and his goal was to integrate properties of the man with properties of the job. To this end, Taylor worked out procedures, by means of time and method studies, that would utilize less energy and yield more work. This view (and its complements, e.g., Gilbreth, 1911) shows little concern with the worker as a person; rather, the worker was seen as an extension of the job. So far as the model was concerned, the worker simply had no life outside his job or separate from his tasks. The implications of this "ascribed status" have been illuminated by Daniel Bell (1956). And it is interesting to note in passing that many Tayloristic polemics are today reechoed in passionate debates about "computerism." What was written before about Taylor and scientific management is being written again about the inhumanity of the computer (cf., e.g., Simon, 1965).

In the Tayloristic model, work gets done by providing employees with work routines (or programs). There is no point, thought Taylor, in having men work at less than capacity because the work is poorly organized (the man-machine concept). The assembly line, therefore, can be run as fast as people can work, and time-method studies can be used to discover how fast people can work. In other words, experiments could be performed to discover the *one best method* or *best conditions* for doing the job.

Apart from a kind of Calvinist work-ethic and a trust in monetary inducements, Taylor had no motivational terms in his models. Motivation was largely assumed as an intrinsic moral matter. Furthermore, the "essential ability to work" was simply taken as given (cf. Neff, 1968, pp. 5–11, for a pointed discussion of this idea). But, if motivation and ability tended to be treated as intrinsic, organizational operation was viewed as dependent on extrinsic control.

For Taylor, the organization was an authority structure to be described in terms of *span of control.* This was the key to organizational design and created a system based on a centralized pyramidal authority structure. Taylor's plan was to devise a rational structure based on an authority hierarchy, with varying support functions (clerical, research, and development, etc.) where and when necessary—the line-staff notion. Thus, for Taylor, the guiding principle of organization was the span of control (or the authority structure), with components laid out in terms of vertical line and lateral staff.

According to Taylor, the organization could then be specified in terms of organizational charts (authority and line-staff) and job specifications. This was the organization, the *formal system.* Nothing else mattered. The organization was thus defined in terms of scientific principles used to describe the formal system.

Confined almost exclusively to the vantage point of top management, Taylor's view of the organization suffers from a severe lack of conceptual richness. Furthermore,

> Scientific management achieves conceptual closure of the organization by assuming that goals are known, tasks are repetitive, output from production processes somehow disappears, and resources in uniform qualities are available [Thompson, 1967, p. 5].

Administrative Management

The administrative management views fostered by Gulick and Urwick (1937) stressed the structural relationships among production, personnel, supply, and other service units of the organization. Here again the emphasis is on efficiency, and many Tayloristic principles are invoked. Efficiency is maximized by task specialization and the grouping of similar tasks into departments. Responsibility is fixed according to such principles as span of control or delegation and by insuring adequate control over employees so that action conforms to plans. The assumption in this view is that a master plan is known so that specialization, departmentalization, and control can be determined rationally. (Simon, 1957, for one, has criticized this view by enumerating the difficulties in attaining agreement with and constancy in master plans.)

Like its relative, scientific management, administrative management commonly ignores the organization's environment and boundary functions necessary to transact matters of organizational survival with that environment.

We might interject at this point the observation that reviews of scientific management concepts frequently convey a not altogether accurate sense of ancient history. To be sure, there have been sequences of appearance and development, but the scientific management movement is hardly dead, even if it appears more often now in the form of computer-oriented management science exercises in model building, operations research, cost-benefit analysis, etc. Moreover, it often disguises itself today in a more dynamic "systems" terminology and posture, sometimes leaving behind many of its earlier oversimplifications (cf. Haberstroh, 1965; Koontz, 1962). In anticipation, the same cautionary comment might be made about the human relations tradition (discussed below), which sometimes is painted as if it were solely a manifestation of the 1930s and 1940s. However, unlike Australopithicus (or Che), it lives (cf., e.g., Whyte, 1969—note especially p. 708).

Bureaucracy

Similar in many ways to the above views, bureaucracy (cf. Mouzelis, 1967; Weber, 1947) focuses on staffing and structure as a means of dealing with clients and disposing of cases—and the achievement of efficiency. In this view, efficiency is maximized by organizing offices according to jurisdiction and hierarchical position, appointing experts to offices, utilizing procedural devices for work situations, the promulgation of rules governing behavior of positional incumbents, providing differential rewards by office to provide incentive and patterns for career advancement (Quinn & Kahn, 1967; Thompson, 1967). As with other structural theories of organization, Weber felt that the proper use of rules, rewards, and punishments could render the human component negligible by divorcing the individual's private life from his role as an officeholder. Once more the significance of individual identity was uncomprehended: Indeed, the belief was widely implicit that "workers," unlike managers and other "good" people, had none.

The static nature of the organization as described by Weber inspired numerous eloquent attacks on bureaucratic theory. Notable among these were the criticisms suggested by Merton (1957) and Gouldner (1954), dealing with the unintended consequences of bureaucratic rule enforcement. Merton argued that reliance on depersonalized relations and strict enforcement of rules and jurisdictions in order to reduce human variability lead to rigid behavior on the part of position incumbents. This rigidity, based on the need to defend individual actions, leads to reliance on organizational precedent and use of the most easily invoked rule in dealings with clients. Often, however, the rule most easily invoked is least appropriate to the client's case. The client's challenge of the bureaucrat's judgment serves only to increase his drive to defend his actions and thence to increasingly rigid and inappropriate behavior.

In a somewhat similar vein, Gouldner (1954) pointed out an additional self-defeating consequence of reliance, stemming from demands for control, on the use of general and impersonal rules. He argued that the use of such rules offers little incentive for employees to do any more than the minimum amount of work that will avoid punishment. When management discovers that productivity has fallen behind goals, pressure is placed on supervisors to supervise more closely. This serves to increase the visibility of power relations within the work group and leads to even more dogged determination on the part of the workers to do as little as possible.

Thompson (1961) added that bureaucracies tend to attract monocratic types to supervisory positions who tend to enhance feelings of helplessness and insecurity in subordinates. Jasinski (1956) has found even more problems with the overreliance on efficiency controls. He specified seven: wasted time, higher maintenance costs, figure "fudging," low morale, impaired labor recruitment, higher unit costs, and lowered product quality. Schlesinger has provided an especially amusing account of bureaucratic blundering and job protectiveness in the United States Department of State in his book *A Thousand Days* (1965), and Bell (1956) has penned a scathing indictment of the Tayloristic-bureaucratic "cult of efficiency."

Other writers (e.g., Argyris, 1964; Bennis, 1969; Haire, 1963) have objected to bureaucratic theory because it is based on the assumption that man is lazy and not to be trusted. They further object to the accompanying moral notion of the intrinsic goodness of work and the punishment orientation implicit in classical theory. These critics agree that classical models of organization serve to stifle workers in their quest for "psychological success."

Argyris (1964), for example, has argued that to the degree that the dictates of classical theory are followed in an organization, the lower level employee will suffer because

> few of his abilities will be used . . . [he] will tend to experience a sense of dependence and submissiveness toward his superior because decisions of whether or not he works, how much he shall be paid, and so on, will be largely under his superior's control . . . [and] the worker will tend to experience a decreasing sense of self-responsibility and self-control [pp. 38-39].

Although most of the critics of classical organization theory view bureaucracy as either an ideal type or an undifferentiated lump, Hall (1963) has shown that the major discussants of bureaucracy cannot themselves completely agree on a list of definitive characteristics. Furthermore, in an empirical study, Hall demonstrated that organizations that are highly bureaucratized on one dimension may not be so on another. The dimensions studied by Hall were hierarchy of authority, division of labor, system of rules, system of procedures, impersonality, and emphasis on technical competence; other variables have been dealt with by Woodward (1965), Perrow (1967), and Harvey (1968) with comparable results. Clearly, then, bureaucracy exists in degrees, and there are very few so-called bureaucracies conforming in all ways to an ideal type. Nevertheless, most of the critical writing in this area tends to view it as an all-or-none phenomenon. The conclusion to be drawn is that classical organization theory is often used as a straw man or figurative foil for both critical virtuosos and theorists advancing alternative models.

Modern Structural Views

Sharing the same general rationale of organizational design as the traditional structural theorists—that the organization must be designed to fit the nature of people—the modern structural theorists, by altering their assumptions concerning people, have proposed alternative designs to bureaucracy. Instead of assuming as did classical theorists, that all workers are motivated by rational economic factors, modern structuralists undertake to view the worker as a total human being striving for self-improvement, self-expression, autonomy, recognition, or whatnot. It is further assumed that these strivings exist in equal amounts in all people but that their expression depends on the degree to which the social structure is able to accommodate such strivings.

The model used by this approach is nicely exemplified in Merton's (1957) reformulation of the concept of *anomie.* The problem for Merton was to explain why the frequency of deviant behavior varies in different social structures. He viewed the task as one of locating groups which typically engage in deviant behavior (or maladjustive behavior from the societal viewpoint) as *normal* responses to the social situation in which they find themselves.

Specifically, Merton argued that certain cultural axioms prescribing the means and ends of success have been well internalized by virtually all members of American society. He defined success as the attainment of wealth and stature, and the means to this end are hard, honest work and no horseplay. The culture, however, while vigorously stressing the ends, provides a social structure that severely limits access to the means. Anomie arises from the conflict between the goals that culture sets up and the ineffectiveness of the prescribed means for attaining these goals. The incidence of this conflict is differentially observable in various strata of society, being more pronounced where an individual's position is weakened by the structure of society. Thus, people occupying positions in the lower social strata are more likely to be anomic as evidenced by criminal or ritualistic life styles employed as a means of coping with or defending against structural restrictions. The solution to problems of deviance then, of course, is to work at modifying the societal structure to allow for more freedom of legitimate goal attainment for incumbents of lower social strata (Gordon, 1964).

Several organization theorists have applied similar logic to social organizations. They maintain that all people have certain important common needs and that the structure of the organization interferes with the expression of these needs, especially for incumbents of positions low in the organization's hierarchy. This restrictiveness results in coping and adaptive responses such as minimal productivity, sabotage, low morale, and job satisfaction. Most of these theorists acknowledge the existence of individual differences, but they proceed to build their models as if these differences are of no account.

The immediate influences on these views rest with the Hawthorne studies (discussed later) and Maslow's (1954) theoretical formulations emphasizing man's inherent need to use his capacities and skills in a mature and productive way. Maslow specified a need hierarchy common to all normal people and consisting, in ascending order, of safety and survival needs, social needs, ego needs, autonomy needs, and self-actualization needs. A higher-level need cannot be satisfied until the needs below it in the hierarchy have been served. Maslow argued that it is universally true that all manner of human activity is an attempt to work upward in the hierarchy. Using this basic notion, modern structural theorists feel that since membership in a work organization is a central fact in men's lives, it is to the best interest of the organization and the people in it to alter the organization's structure to allow for the human quest for self-actualization.

Among the major advocates of this view is Argyris (1957, 1964), whose chief premise was that there is a lack of fit between requirements of bureaucratic organizations (the formal structure) and the needs of individual members to achieve "psychological success." Argyris wrote:

> our selection of the individual who aspires toward psychological success is not an arbitrary one . . . [T]here is an increasing number of psychologists who believe that self-esteem, self-acceptance, and psychological success are some of the most central factors that constitute individual mental health in our culture. If we are able to understand better how one may enhance the opportunity for individual psychological success, we believe that this will contribute toward individual mental health [1964, pp. 36–37].

As evidence for his premise, Argyris cited a number of empirical studies showing that workers at the lower end of the organizational hierarchy, as opposed to those at higher levels, suffer from poorer mental health, lower job satisfaction, lower levels of self-esteem, feelings of insecurity, and other related variables. The resulting feelings of dependence, subordination, and passivity on the part of the workers can only result in "frustration, failure, short-term perspective, and conflict [1964, p. 40]."

Further, Argyris took the position that an organization operated on classical premises suffers inefficiency to the extent that employees waste energy by engaging in activities of a compulsive, defensive nature. Thus, there is less human energy available for genuine productivity. As an outline for a solution, Argyris proposed a "mix model" in which "changes in the organization toward increasing opportunity for psychological success and self-esteem be made as long as we are able to show that they are decreasing the unproductive compulsive activities [1964, p. 147]." Argyris is quick to point out that this does not necessarily imply a people-centered organization because self-esteem is strongly coupled with responsibility to others. Furthermore, organizational changes designed to accommodate psychological success should continue only so long as the organization can more efficiently achieve its objectives, maintain its internal system, and adapt to its environment.

Argyris' view, then, contains a powerful belief in the reality of the forces exerted on individuals by an organizational structure. Since personality is considered a constant, individual differences can only be explained in terms of differential positional incumbency, and, indeed, the lower organizational levels are seen as the most restricting with respect to human need satisfaction.

McGregor (1960) embraced a similar view when he proposed "Theory Y" as a general solution to the problem of organizational improvement. Theory Y represents a set of assumptions about human motivation, based on Maslow's need hierarchy, which he felt should serve as a basis for organizational design. McGregor argued:

> Above all, the assumptions of Theory Y point up the fact that the limits of human collaboration in the organizational setting are not limits of human nature but of management's ingenuity in discovering how to realize the potential represented by its human resources. Theory X offers management an easy rationalization for ineffective organizational performance: It is due to the nature of human resources with which we must work. Theory Y, on the other hand, places problems squarely in the lap of management. If employees are lazy, indifferent, unwilling to take responsibility, intransigent, uncreative, uncooperative, Theory Y implies that the causes lie in management's methods of organization and control [p. 48].

In other words, the structure of the organization is responsible for difficult employees, and an alteration in this structure is called for.

Other theorists have, in whole or in part, fostered a similar point of view. Likert (1961, 1967) did so by arguing that "System 4" (trust and participation) is the only leadership style which can yield maximum effectiveness. Gellerman (1963) posited competence and power as general motives and suggested that the structure take these into account. And Blake and his co-workers (cf. Blake & Mouton, 1968) also proposed a "one best" route to managerial effectiveness—the 9–9 theory.

The solutions proposed by the several writers holding to modern structural viewpoints suggest reordering organization away from bureaucratic designs so that they will allow for participative decision making, face-to-face work groups, mutual confidence between superior and subordinate, job enlargement, increased responsibility at lower positions, and so on.

The modern structural theorists have met with criticism on two main grounds: Their global personality assumptions and their propensity to blame the structure of the organization for all of its ills. Examples of the first type of criticism have emanated from the pen of Strauss (1963, 1968). Strauss felt that the notions of such people as Argyris (1959), Herzberg, Mausner, and Snyderman (1959), Maier (1955), Maslow (1954), and McGregor (1960) are laden with an inner-directed academic bias in which righteous professors impose their own values on members of population segments who may have quite a different idea of self-development. J. K. Galbraith (1967), however, felt that modern structural theorists seem to feel that if workers gain most of their satisfactions away from their jobs, then the organization has somehow failed in both efficiency and elementary humanism and must, of necessity, be restructured. Strauss (1963) continued by asserting that the injudicious use of power-equalization practices may actually adversely affect the security needs of those workers who are not prepared for the added responsibilities that accompany an expanded role. Indeed, a closely related phenomenon figured prominently as a source of disturbance in Levinson, Price, Munden, Mandel, and Solley's Midland Utilities study (1962). Further, power-equalization techniques may be more expensive to employ than they are worth in highly programmed situations where simply adequate performance or keeping up with the assembly line is all that is required (cf. Perrow, 1967, for a discussion of this and related matters in a wider context of reviewing relations between technology and organization). Moreover, like their traditional counterparts, the modern structuralists are susceptible to criticism for their advocacy of "one best way" notions, albeit this time applied mostly to managerial methods (cf. Fiedler, 1965).

Sayles and Strauss (1966) maintained that the personality versus organization model is most applicable to employees who do highly skilled or creative work in large companies (e.g., research and development scientists, industrial designers—people similar to the model builders). For the workers who must perform jobs that are more difficult to make intrinsically interesting, Sayles and Strauss (1966) predicted a reemergence of the kind of leisure-based culture characteristic of ancient Greece and Rome. It is too late, they feel, for our society to revert to a production system based on individual craftsmanship. Katz and Kahn (1966) have pointed out, for instance, that a good many mass-produced automobiles can be bought for the price of one Rolls Royce. As noted above, Galbraith (1967), too, has voiced similar sentiments, although Bell (1956), while acknowledging the trend, has expressed skepticism as to whether there can be adequate substitutes for loss of satisfaction from work.

At any rate, a challenge to the structural suppositions of the human relations theorists has come from an extensive review of the empirical literature by Porter and Lawler (1965). These authors studied the literature pertaining to seven aspects of organizational structure: Organizational levels, line and staff hierarchies, span of control, subunit size, total organization size, hierarchical steepness, and degree of centralization or decentralization; they concluded:

Five of the seven properties of organization structure (span of control and centralization/decentralization being the two possible exceptions) have been shown to have some kind of significant relationship to either job attitudes or job behavior, or to both of these types of variables. However, . . . experimental "proof" of cause-effect relationships between structure and employee attitudes and behavior is elusive and almost nonexistent [p. 47]

[T]here are already enough indications in the literature to support a greater research effort to investigate the interactions among structural properties of organizations in their relationship to employees' job behavior and attitudes. Too much previous theorizing in the area of organizations has neglected such interaction possibilities and hence, there has been an unfortunate tendency to oversimplify vastly the effects of particular variables. Organizations appear to be much too complex for a given variable to have a consistent unidirectional effect across a wide variety of types of conditions [p. 48].

Similar sentiments relative to the contingent nature of organizational processes have become commonplace in the literature. And their pertinence is underscored by recent work on determinants of formal organization structure and the impact of formal structures on member characteristics (cf., e.g., Hickson, Pugh, & Pheysey, 1969; Whyte, 1969, especially Chapter 3). Structural properties of organizations surely "seep into" their members, as Udy (1965) stated, but the reverse is also true, and, in any case, the relations usually are not simple.

Other criticisms have also been leveled against the human relations structuralists. Pugh (1966) has noted that the theorists reacting against the classical school seem to have an implicit bias against formal organization. Leavitt (1962) felt that much organizational restructuring based on human relations philosophies has been done on the principle of defeating Taylorism and has too often thrown out the baby with the bath water. Leavitt felt, in particular, that the overreaction against classical theories has served to impede the salutary introduction of principles from communication and information theory into organizational design. Hunt and Lichtman[1] have cautioned managers against giving their employees the impression that productivity is somehow not important; in the first place, it is not true; second, it only serves to confuse employees and may create stress in those places where a human relations orientation is supposed to relieve it. And Katzell (1962) has cited evidence of conventional organizations that seemed to be functioning perfectly well and of human relations programs that were rejected by workers.

[1] R. G. Hunt and C. M. Lichtman. Concepts and strategies for training work supervisors as employee counselors. Buffalo, N.Y.: State University of New York, 1969. (Ditto)

It would seem, then, that current structural theories with emphases on human relations have made many of the same errors of theoretical presumption as did the classical theorists against whom they were ostensibly reacting. Notably, their assumptions of global personality characteristics give their theories the same one-side, closed system, quality of the classical theories. They have a way of proposing the one *best* solution to the efficiency of all organizations and the *one best way* to motivate all members. Their view then is not only simplistically one-sided, but unidirectional: Effects flow almost entirely from the organization's properties to the individual. As compared with modern varieties, traditional structuralism might, however, be said to hold a somewhat friendlier attitude toward organizations and a somewhat less humanistic one toward its members. Traditional structuralists tend to see organizations as societal benefactors needful only of augmented efficiency, whereas the modernists look upon the organization as a more oppressive agency suitable for reform. In either case, however, the belief prevails that apt structuring of the features of the organization will allow the individual's natural inclinations to issue forth as more effective performance. (And Taylor was as convinced as anybody that this would be accompanied by happier workers.)

In his discussion of "work as a psychological problem," Neff (1968), however, argued that it is evident that people exist who cannot (or will not) work effectively under even the best of conditions. The question he raised under the rubric of the "work personality" is, in essence, What psychological characteristics are requisite to entry and performance in "work roles"? (cf. also Dawis, Lofquist, & Weiss, 1968).

Personalistic Views

Although global theories of personality have been of benefit to organization and management theory—especially their implications for organizational design—they are often difficult to study in a precise empirical manner, and they do not provide sufficient differential predictive power to be useful by themselves for an understanding of organizational behavior. As a result, many students of organizations have chosen to concentrate their theoretical and empirical efforts on the discovery of the influence of more particularized measures of personality. Schein (1965) commented:

Man is not only complex, but also highly variable; he has many motives which are arranged in some sort of hierarchy of importance to him, but this hierarchy is subject to change from time to time and situation to situation; furthermore, motives interact and combine complex motive patterns (for example, since money can facilitate self-actualization, for some people economic strivings are equivalent to self-actualization). Man is capable of learning new motives through his organizational experiences . . . and . . . is the result of a complex interaction between initial needs and organizational experiences. Man's motives in different organizations or different subparts of the same organization may be different. . . . Man can become productively involved with organizations on the basis of many different kinds of motives . . . [p. 60] .

Many of the same points have been made by Hunt (1969a) in discussion of the role of profit in business affairs. In any event, the general assumption of the personalistic view is that people react to their organization on the basis of their perceptions of it. These perceptions are based on people's needs, motives, and values. Therefore, to understand human behavior in organizations, one must understand how individuals differ with respect to personalistic variables; to change organizations, one must alter the perceptions of people. The impetus to this view rests largely with the writings of Kurt Lewin and the Hawthorne group.

Lewin's field theory and his group dynamics work (cf. Lewin, 1951) prefigured more than one important contemporary pattern of organizational analysis. The group dynamics research, of course, was one of the roots of T-grouping, while field theory per se constituted one of the early gestures in psychology toward a systemlike interpretation of individual and group behavior. Among other things, for instance, Lewin argued that action was no simple outcome from mechanical stimulus-response linkages, but was a complex resultant of coacting mutually influential elements coalescing as dynamically shifting momentary fields of force in a psychological environment, the life space.

Broadly phenomenological in orientation, Lewin held the characteristics of the life space to be indefinable apart from the cognitions of the person-actor; overt behavior was construed as essentially derivative from fields of force consequent upon modes of organization of that cognitive space. Through his cognitive contributions, the actor is thus viewed as active in the behavioral process and not as just a passive recipient of discret stimuli. Indeed, in the Lewinian scheme, although constrained ecologically, the frame of behavior was phenomenal; the life space was a perceptual or experiential creation. Furthermore, little room was left for examining the accuracy of perception. The field of behavior was, so to say, principally "intrapsychic."

Now, if an organization has no properties aside from people's perceptions of it based on their needs, values, and attitudes, it can have no real structure because it cannot exist independently of its particular time-relative membership (cf. Hunt, 1968). The process of organizational analysis must then consist largely of personnel assessments and identification of ad hoc liaisons; organizational change must consist solely in the changing of people. Such a premise is fundamental (if implicit) to what may be termed "clinical" approaches to organization development (e.g., those associated with T-group perspectives; cf. Schein & Bennis, 1965).

About the same time as Lewin was writing, the Hawthorne or Western Electric studies (Mayo, 1933; Roethlisberger & Dickson, 1939) were being conducted. Although originally conceived as a test of Taylorism—a search for the one best level of illumination, among other things—the findings indicated that there was no one best level. Rather, workers stepped up production at all levels. The Hawthorne studies became important principally because the investigators went on to ask *why* there was no relation between illumination and output, and the studies conducted to discover the answer led to neoclassical organization theory.

From their studies the investigators concluded that friendship patterns were the heart of organization. They subsequently advocated human relations as a set of techniques by which people could be motivated. By maintaining that the organization is what is perceived by the employees to be the case, the proponents of neoclassical organization theory abandoned the formal structural notions of the classical theorists. The important system was no longer the formal organizational structure, but the informal relations at all organizational levels. What had traditionally been called the formal structure, then, was nothing but the manifestation of the workings of the informal system (or else somebody's idealization of it).

As the Hawthorne researchers saw it, however, the implications for management did not lie in any gross restructuring of the organization, but rather in a program of individual counseling designed to change the perceptions of individual workers toward the organization. The classic studies of Coch and French (1948) and Lewin (1958) were direct offshoots of this line of thinking. In both of these studies the persuasive potential of informal group membership was used as a vehicle for changing people's perceptions of the structure *as it is;* there was no intention of changing the basic structure of the system, there was only the attempt to get people to accept it. Although this new approach came to be called participative management, the fact was that management had no intention of altering the organization—only of changing people's attitudes toward work. Among others, Bell (1956) has been vocal about the "manipulative" qualities of human relations operations, and recently even Bennis (1970) has commented on this tendency.

Individuals and Informal Groups

The Hawthorne researchers have been subject to sweeping critique. Carey (1967) has argued that their conclusions neither followed from nor were they supportable from their data; if anything, they demonstrated exactly what they maintained had been disproven. Yet, be that as it may, few more influential works could be found—they ushered in an era. But as Katz (1965) has pointed out, the Hawthorne studies led to the demise of the notion of economic man without, however, actually making social organization the focus of analysis. The Hawthorne studies argued that man is motivated by a good deal more than monetary self-interest; indeed, that the worker's peer group could actually guide a man away from his own self-interest by establishing a norm of restricted output. Although the group factor in work situations was emphasized, and the concept of social system introduced, an individual focus was retained. The function of the group, in this view, was to relieve the boredom of the individual.

Roy (1960), however, has argued that the function of the group is a good deal more than that. The work-group culture reaches outside the organization by defining the social reality not only of the work situation but also of the worker's place in the larger society. The work group as an informal structure, argued Roy, provides a continuity between life outside and inside the organization. This general position has received wide support in the literature (e.g., Bennis & Shepard, 1965; Festinger, 1950; Walker, 1958).

Likert (1961, 1967) typifies the group dynamics approach in his advocacy of group decision processes at all levels. He proposed a type of organizational structure consisting of many overlapping groups that extend across adjacent management levels. Each foreman, for example, would be a member not only of the work group but also a full-fledged member of the next higher supervisory level. Thus, the supervisor in one group is a subordinate in the next, and so on, at successive levels. Horizontal as well as vertical linkages are built into this system. The emphasis is clearly on groups rather than on individuals. "An organization will function best when its personnel function not as individuals but as members of highly effective work groups with high performance goals [Likert, 1961, p. 105]." Likert felt that employee participation in decision making, when accomplished according to his "linking pin" notion, will not reduce supervisory influence (a view shared by Tannenbaum, 1966), but rather will serve to change the attitudes of work-group members to better conform to organizational goals. Moreover, like others of its genre, Likert's solutions to organizational problems rarely carry important implications of a basic structural order; indeed, by and large they presume a generally bureaucratic system and speak mainly to operations within it (cf. Bennis, 1970).

Despite contemporary recognition of the influence of informal groups on the formal organization, many modern theorists have preferred to limit the domain of their analysis to individual experience. Vroom (1964), for instance, has recently applied Lewin's general theory of personality to the study of organizational behavior, hypothesizing performance to be a function of the worker's perception of the abilities required by the job, the degree to which the person perceives himself as having these abilities, and the degree to which he values the possession of such abilities. Vroom, thus, stressed the affective consequences of the degree of consistency between a person's performance and his self-concept. In this view a person is motivated to perform effectively when effective performance is consisent with his conception of his abilities and with the value he places on them. Porter and Lawler (1968) have similarly hypothesized that managerial performance is a function of the perceived value of the reward, the probability that effort will bring the reward, and the accuracy of role perceptions. Smith and Cranny (1968) have presented a similar formulation, and March and Simon (1958) and Cyert and March (1963) have also stressed personalistic variables in their individual decision-making models of organizations. They have used such expressions as "the perceived consequence of evoked alternatives," "the expected value of reward," placing the locus of the organization within the individuals who populate it.

Katz (1964) has posited that the motivation to produce and motivation to belong are orthogonal dimensions, and this independence helps to explain the corresponding lack of relationship between job satisfaction and productivity. Bass (1965) argued that it is not necessary to study workers with reference to any basic needs or tensions; rather, there is just as much predictive power to be had by restricting research to "organizationally relevant" motivational dispositions. Task orientation, self-orientation, and interpersonal orientation are the three proposed by Bass. These and some related ideas have been well-summarized by Quinn and Kahn (1967).

In his book *Eupsychian Management,* Maslow (1965) took a more radical view by arguing that work in itself has a kind of symbiotic quality. Satisfaction can indeed be gotten out of good work, but this is not a social or socially derived (ego) need. Rather, work is a primitive need independent of social need satisfaction and can be intrinsically interesting. In principle, Maslow's view is not altogether unlike that of Bell (1956), which we have cited, or of Herzberg et al. (1959), who have claimed that the only true job satisfaction can come out of work itself. Good working conditions and satisfactory social relationships around the job can only serve to make the job tolerable.

A review of the literature concerned with studies of individual worker differences was written by Smith and Cranny (1968) and provides further evidence for the value of such research. In sum, recognizing the inadequacies of classical organization theory, many writers have turned the coin and concentrated their theoretical efforts toward evaluating the role of the individual and the work group as a determinant. They have also encouraged an individual differences approach to the study of organizational behavior, by proposing intrapersonal dimensions along which people may vary. An especially clear illustration of this can be found in Hackman's recent (1969) reworking of the Herzberg two-factor notions about work motivation.

But this view is no less one-sided than the structural approaches because it has little to say about the formal organization. Any comprehensive theory of organizational behavior, of necessity, has to integrate the formal structure, the processes occurring within individuals, and the function of informal groups (cf. Hunt, 1968; Perrow, 1967).

The solution, according to Scott (1961), lies in the remembrance that the main problem with the structural and personalistic views was not one of inaccurracy but rather incompleteness and shortsightedness. In neither approach is there adequate integration among the numerous facets of human behavior studied by it. The task of the modern organization theorist, therefore, is to combine the several views into a more accurate model of organizational functioning.

Mechanic (1963) has championed the use of the multivariable or "eclectic" approach to organizational studies, as opposed to "one sided" approaches committed to a single view of human nature. He maintained that one-sided approaches tend to encourage strong partisanship to a particular view and thus engender misunderstandings, communication difficulties, unjustified attacks, while they also discourage interdisciplinary cooperation.

> However, if "one-sided" analysis is defined openly as a strategy of approach rather than a dogmatic assertion of priority, the dialogue between theories may be improved and communication and cross-fertilization may be preserved at the same time . . . [W]hile it may be valuable to urge antieclecticism in theory building, it is essential to urge eclecticism in the use of research approaches and methodologies. Perhaps the most significant recent trend in organization studies is the utilization of various modes of data collection in the same study [Mechanic, 1963, pp. 172–173].

The virtues of the one-sided versus the eclectic approach depend, in part, on the purposes of the theorist. If his purpose is to convince bureaucratic managers of the advantages of human relations practices, there is probably no harm in taking a more extreme personalistic view of human behavior in organizations; presumably, the target is already familiar with the operations of formal rules. If, however, the theorist's intent is to build an accurate and workable general model of organizational functioning, then it is clear that none of the one-sided views proposed to date can do that job. The next section deals with some approaches to the discovery of a general solution to the organizational dilemma.

Integrating Approaches

Increasing disenchantment with the myriad of one-sided and normative approaches to organization theory has led many writers to favor the use of alternative models. Such models typically represent attempts to integrate existing approaches and/or reflect the influence of situational factors on organizational functioning. Katzell, for example, wrote:

> by concerning themselves with certain preselected dependent variables . . . and not with others that are relevant to the system, by relying heavily on unproven assumptions, and by their tendency to generalize rather than paying due attention to surrounding circumstances, such theories typically take the form of a blueprint or master plan which is prescribed as the one best way to organize and manage all work [1962, p. 104].

Katzell felt that many factors must be taken into account before it can be decided what organizational policies and practices are likely to work best. As a starting point, he suggested five such parameters:

1. The first parameter mentioned by Katzell is size, or the number of interdependent organizational members. Hickson et al. (1969) have also given prominence to size factors in their analyses of determinants of structure. Indik (1963) reviewed the literature relating organizational size to member participation in terms of absence and turnover (a finding which calls to mind Barker's ecological studies of schools, cf., e.g., 1963). In another paper, Indik (1965) interpreted these findings by positing that larger organizations contain more potential and necessary communication linkages among members, rendering adequate communication more difficult to achieve. The result of inadequate communication

among members serves to decrease interpersonal attractiveness and, in turn, member participation rates. Porter and Lawler (1965) also reviewed the literature on organizational size and concluded that although job satisfaction and morale tend to be lower in large organizations, the general findings relevant to this area are neither reliable nor clear. These authors felt that perhaps subunit size is a more crucial determinant of employee reactions than is total organization size. Woodward (1965), too, has pressed for a more differentiated concept of size, stressing the importance of indexing size by reference to the size of managerial subsystems. There is clearly a need for more research in this area.[2]

2. The degree of interaction and interdependence is another parameter suggested as important by Katzell. Katz and Kahn (1966) have theorized that the degree of task interdependence is an important consideration in choosing the appropriate authority structure for an organization. They argued that where such interdependence is high, where creative requirements are minimal, and where identification with organizational goals is not required, a hierarchical authority structure, with its implication of close supervision, is indicated. Where the opposite circumstances obtain, a more democratic alternative should be used for maximum efficiency. Vroom and Mann (1960) have proposed that differences in work-group task interdependence account for the choice of autocratic supervisors by some groups and democratic supervisors by others.

More generally, Hackman[3] has shown the importance of task structure to patterns of group interaction; Sommer (1967, 1968) has demonstrated the pervasive influence of broader ecological factors in group (and, by inference, organization) processes, and W. F. Whyte (1969) may be consulted for a wide-ranging discussion of various aspects and implications of "the structuring of the work environment" (cf. especially Chapter 3) Hunt (1970) has discussed at length the organizational significance of task uncertainty and has identified distinctive modes of structural adaptation to it. Relatedly, Haberstroh (1965) provided a review of the role of information systems in task modeling and organizational design. He noted, for instance, that "the coherence and unity of an organization is intimately related to its information system [p. 1192]." Therefore, he maintained, variations in such systems will precipitate "major [organizational] repercussions." Haberstroh promoted the idea of close and explicit integration of information systems and task models (cf. also Cleland & King, 1968; Glans, Grad, Holstein, Meyers, & Schmidt, 1968).

3. Another variable to be considered is the personalities of organization members. Their motivations, expectations, abilities, and other personal qualities seem to be of paramount importance in determining policies and practices of organizations. Employee satisfactions and attitudes have been linked to subcultural differences (Katzell, Barrett, & Parker, 1961) and cross-cultural differences (French, Israel, & Aas, 1960), as well as to individual difference measures (Smith & Cranny, 1968) and patterns of immediate supervision (Ronan, 1970).

4. The degree of congruence or disparity between organizational goals and the needs and goals of the members is a fourth factor to be considered as a determinant of organizational design. Katz and Kahn (1966) distinguished between two types of goal internalization that might be aroused in an employee. The first of these occurs when the employee identifies with the job itself and is, therefore, conducive to high quantity and high quality role performance. Job identification is exemplified by the craftsman or scientist who delights in the work he does and is rewarded by the opportunity to express his abilities and to make his own decisions. Although morale and satisfaction are well-linked to the variety and challenge of the job and the gratifications that accrue to workers, such individual craftsmanship is infeasible and expensive to apply to many positions in a company concerned with the mass production of consumer goods and also in some service operations. One solution is to eliminate dull assembly-line jobs through automation (cf. Bell, 1956, for a useful general discussion of this issue). Mann and Hoffman (1960) and Blauner (1964) have argued that after automation has occurred, the remaining jobs provide more freedom, responsibility, and dignity. The result is a decrease rather than an increase in worker alienation.

The second type of identification proposed by Katz and Kahn occurs through internalization of organizational goals rather than through the job itself. This type of motivation is associated with value expression and self-identification. In industrial organizations this type of internalization is usually found among management personnel, although in voluntary organizations it may extend to the rank and file. Katz and Kahn argued, however, that complete internalization of organizational goals is less common than two types of partial internalization. The first

[2] Recently Blau (1970) (see article 27) has published a systematic theory relating organization size and structural differentiation that could prove a productive guide for such research. He touches on various nuances of both dimensions, but his "basic generalizations are *(a)* increasing organizational size generates differentiation along various lines at decelerating rates; and *(b)* differentiation enlarges the administrative component in organizations to effect coordination [Abstract, p. 201]."

[3] J. R. Hackman. Functions of group interaction. Paper presented at Colloquium of the State University of New York, Buffalo, October 1969.

of these concerns general organizational purposes that are not unique to a particular organization. A scientist, for example, may internalize the research values of his profession and, to the extent that the organization that employs him shares similar goals, coincidence in worker and organizational goals will occur. However, the scientist could work in many other organizations just as easily. The same, of course, could be said of teachers and other professionals whose attachments to particular organizations are derivative and chiefly as a simple locus of occupational activity.

The other subtype proposed by Katz and Kahn is the internalization of subsystem goals and values. Since one's own organizational unit is often more visible to him and is frequently his immediate source of reward, it is often easier to internalize the smaller unit goal than that of the entire organization. This often leads to the aggrandizement effect (Caplow & McGee, 1958; Morane, 1967), that is, tendencies to rate one's subsystem higher than outsiders do. This may lead in turn to empire building, parochialism, petty jealousies, and factionalism within the organization. Thus, depending on which tendencies are involved, a high degree of goal internalization on the part of employees may not always be a bed of roses for the organization; but, in general, it is clear that the degree and variety of employee identification can have a profound influence on organizational policy and practice.

5. Katzell's final parameter has to do with who in the organization has the necessary ability and motivation to take action that will further its objectives. Rubin and Hunt (1969) have discussed this matter with special reference to what they called "mission identification." After reviewing some of the literature on supervision, Katzell observed that

> the best way to organize and manage work is heavily conditioned by those in the organization who have the knowledge and motivation to get the job done. More specifically, it would seem necessary to mold the organizational system so that it maximizes freedom of action and initiative for those who can and will take effective action, while eliciting compliance, support, or noninterference from others. Depending on the organizational loci of expertise and dedication, the appropriate work system may vary widely from situation to situation [1962, p. 107].

Katzell concluded that "the sheer number of variables that can be used to describe organizations is staggering [1962, p. 105]" and that ways must be found to work with them meaningfully (and we have hardly even mentioned technological variables; cf. Hunt, 1970). One way to do this, he proposed (not surprisingly), is to discover the genotypic dimensions that underlie phenotypic complexities.

It is the recognition of the vast number and complexity of organizational variables that has been responsible for a decided shift in emphasis on the part of many organization theorists over the past decade or so. Perhaps it is more accurate to say that recognition of the complexity of the facts of social structure and social organization was responsible for the belated development of the psychological approach to the study of organizations. Until perhaps two decades ago the social sciences lacked the conceptual tools for dealing with many important facets of social life (Katz & Kahn, 1966). With the introduction of the biological notion of an open system (von Bertalanffy, 1950) into the social sciences (Miller, 1968; Morane, 1967) came a practicable possibility for integrating the plethora of one-sided views of social organizations.

Social Systems

Among the earliest and most generally useful systemic theories of organizational behavior was the theory put forth by Homans (1950). Homans commenced by positing that any social system exists in a three-part environment: a *physical* environment (geography, climate, etc.), a *cultural* environment (the norms and values and goals of the society at large), and a *technological* environment (the state of knowledge and instrumentation available to the system). At the next level the social system itself has certain requirements and goals that are translated into specified activities and interactions for members of the system. The behavior required by the system or determined by its environment is called the *external* system by Homans. For example, in a work organization, management constitutes a large element of the external system by making decisions that bring certain people together in particular ways, for instance, through job specifications, work methods, prescribed layouts, and selection of personnel.

Although the people brought together by the management may be strangers at first, they eventually come to know one another, develop cliques and friendships, socialize on and off the job, help one another in their work, agree to restrict production, and so on. They now have another basis on which to associate, one that modifies and influences their behavior over and above (and perhaps instead of) the effects of the external system. The new form of behavior comes about as a reaction to the demands of the external system. Homans called this phenomenon the *internal system.*

Homans further specified that the elements of a social system can be sorted into three categories which contain aspects of both the internal and external systems: *Activities* (the things people do, the acts they perform), *interactions* (activities that link people together so that the activity of one person has an effect on the activity of another), and *sentiments* (internal psychological states, e.g., emotions, feelings, beliefs, values). Homans postulated that activities, interactions, and sentiments are mutually dependent on one another so that a change in any one will produce a change in the others. For example, positive sentiments between two people lead to increased interaction, or vice versa. Homans further argued that the internal and external systems are mutually dependent; for instance, technology influences interaction, which affects informal relationships. Conversely, the Hawthorne studies demonstrated how the informal system influenced "formal" production quotas.

Lastly, the two systems and the environment are mutually dependent. The environment may change the formal organizations (e.g., through federal and state legislation, union activities), which, in turn, will serve to alter informal organizational relations. Contained in Homans' formulations is the explicit recognition that a social organization, at any point in time, is the outcome of a pattern of interactions between the organization's stated requirements, its environment, and the characteristics of the people who populate it. It ties the emergent system of people's actual everyday behavior to organizations and the external system of formal plans, culture, and other groups that mold emergent behavior.

A more recent comprehensive discussion of organizations as open social systems is *The Social Psychology of Organizations* in which Katz and Kahn (1966) give precision to many concepts of organization by including them as part of a formal model within which a concept is defined partly in terms of its relations to other concepts.

At the outset of their book, Katz and Kahn discuss nine common characteristics of open systems:

1. Open systems, like biological organisms, must import some form of energy from the environment in order to survive.

2. Open systems contain a through-put process by which the imported energy is transformed; the through-put of an organization may be the creation of a new product, the providing of a service, the modification or treatment of human beings, etc.

3. "Open systems export some product into the environment, whether it be the invention of an inquiring mind or a bridge constructed by an engineering firm [p. 20]."

4. An open system consists of cycles of events. The product exported to the environment furnishes sources of energy renewal for the input so that the cycle may be repeated. It is important to note in this context that the structure of a social system

> is to be found in an interrelated set of events which return upon themselves to complete and renew a cycle of activities. It is events rather than things which are structured, so that social structure is a dynamic rather than a static concept [p. 21].

5. Open systems are further characterized by negative entropy. An open system imports more energy from its environment than it expends; it can thus store energy to counter entropic forces.

6. Energic inputs, which become transformed or altered by the through-put, are not the only form of system inputs. Information inputs, negative feedback, and the coding process are inputs of an informative character and serve to provide the system with information concerning its own functioning in relation to its environment.

7. An open system is characterized by a steady state and dynamic homeostasis. This does not imply a motionless or true equilibrium, but rather a force that seeks to preserve a constant ratio between the parts of the system. Thus, when one element in the system changes, forces are exerted to preserve the character of the system by the proportional alteration of all other elements. Thus, as with living organisms, organizational evolution is a symmetrical process.

8. Open systems become more differentiated and elaborated over time. Diffuse global patterns give way to more specialized functions.

9. Finally, open systems are characterized by the principle of equifinality. There is no *one best way* for a system to reach a given final state from a particular initial state. Contrariwise, given similar initial states, open systems may reach quite different final states. In short, there are a variety of paths between any two given points in a system's existence.

The underlying notion of open-system theory is that everything that does or can happen is dependent on everything else that does or can happen; that is, all events are correlated. Thus, the concept of cause and effect is discarded. While a closed system uses up all its energy in the through-put process and becomes simpler over time as a result of entropic processes, an open system has a permeable boundary that allows it to draw sustenance from its environment. Newcomb (1959) has written:

> I have chosen to emphasize "system properties" rather than single variables which contribute to them, and consequently none of the variables has an enduring status either as independent or as dependent . . . a change in one system variable is likely (under certain conditions) to be followed by a specified change in another system variable, but ac-

cording to others a change in the second is a precondition for a change in the first [p. 388].

All elements of the system change when the value of any one is changed. That is, there is a redistribution of energy through some form of equilibration process. An open system is, therefore, dynamic; it is expending energy, and, as a result, it is in process and ongoing. (Doubtless the most wide-ranging treatment of system concepts and applications will be found in Buckley's 1968 compendium.)

The open-system model has also been vigorously advanced by the Tavistock group (e.g., Rice, 1963; Trist, Higgin, Murray, & Pollack, 1963) who have combined it with the less general concept of the sociotechnical system. The purpose of the sociotechnical concept is to bring into the same framework both the ideal efficiency of the system and the practicability of attaining the ideal with human beings and realistic conditions of work. Any productive organization, in this view, is the result of the interaction between technology and the system of relationships between those who perform the jobs (the social system). Each system influences the other (cf. Hunt, 1970, for a detailed discussion of these relations). This notion, of course, is not unlike Homans'.

However, the Tavistock group, by adding the notion of a sociotechnical system to the open-system model, served thereby to add recognition of the importance of the channels of interaction between the organization and its environment. Thus, the organization suffers constraints from two sources. On the one hand, the environment controls raw material, labor, money, and so on, all at the input side, while the output of the organization depends on such variables as consumer preferences, the state of the economy, and government regulation. And if that is not enough, additional constraints are imposed on the organization by the expectations, values, and norms of its human incumbents.

Of utmost importance in this model, however, is the notion that human capacities, preferences, and expectations are not necessarily personalistic elements, but may be influenced by experiences within the organization. Thus, the functions of personnel selection and organizational design are of *equal* importance—human behavior in organizations is the result of the interaction between formal role requirements and the nature of people (cf. Hunt, 1967).

In a more recent volume from the Tavistock Institute, Miller and Rice (1967) have employed a boundary model as a framework for examining problems of organizational control (see also Tannenbaum, 1968). The focus of this model is to make a distinction between the boundaries of the activity system ("the complex of activities which is required to complete the process of transforming an intake into an output [p. 6]"), task group (comprising those individuals employed in an activity system), and sentient group ("being the group to which individuals are prepared to commit themselves and on which they depend for emotional support [p. 253]"). Miller and Rice presented various organizational models that represent different degrees of coincidence between task, sentient, and administrative boundaries and evaluate each in terms of their ability to control task performance, to ensure the commitment of members to the organizational objectives, and to regulate relations between task and sentient systems.

One of the major hypotheses posited by Miller and Rice is that in organizations in which task and sentient groups coincide on a more or less permanent basis, only short-term effectiveness can be achieved. "In the longer term such groups can inhibit change and hence can lead eventually to deterioration of performance and, in consequence, to social and psychological deprivation rather than to satisfaction [p. 253]." As an alternative, Miller and Rice promoted temporary project systems as a general solution. These authors felt that such temporary work groups (such as an airline flight crew) will discourage the formation of group standards detrimental to organization efficiency, while providing sufficient social relationships to satisfy relevant employee needs. Bennis and Slater (1968), of course, have made of such ideas as these a basis for general societal design.

In a related vein, Crozier (1964) has argued that for a given organization there is no such thing as *a* structure; rather, each organization may best be characterized as an aggregate of structures, for instance, a power structure, a communication structure, or a friendship structure. Thus, an organizational member may be seen as occupying a variety of positions with respect to the various structures in which he is included. In Crozier's view, such dimensions as work flow and dependence as well as those mentioned above, may reveal numerous relationships not accounted for by the formal structure.

The recognition by the open-system model of the legion of variables and relationships affecting the behavior of social systems need not, however, imply that such phenomena are randomly distributed throughout an organization; they tend to be specialized by location. For example, Parsons (1960) has proposed that organizations exhibit three distinct levels of responsibility and control—technical, managerial, and institutional.

In his view, an organization contains substructures that exert forces to maintain a specific category of functions necessary to organizational survival. The technical or production structures are primarily concerned with the through-put of the organization—the processing or conversion of the input—and strive to achieve technical proficiency. The managerial structure services the technical subsystem by procuring necessary resources for the input and by mediating between the technical structure and the environmental elements to which the product will be exported. The managerial level controls or administers the technical substructure (not necessarily unilaterally or even unidirectionally, it should be noted) by deciding such matters as what the business of the organization shall be, the scale of its operations, and employment and purchasing policy.

Finally, the organization itself is part of a wider social system, which is the source of higher level support for the organization's goals. Although an organization may be relatively independent with regard to its formal controls, it must depend on its environment for meaning, legitimation, and resources. The overall responsibility for maintaining a favorable environment for the organization lies at the institutional level.

Parsons further argued that at each of the two points of articulation between the three levels there is a qualitative break in the simple continuity of line authority because the functions at each level are qualitatively different. The difference is one of kind, not degree. Organizational survival consists of the adequate functioning of these three levels as well as adequate interaction. If any level withholds its contribution, the system is dissipate.

Katz and Kahn (1966) have expanded Parsons' notion by offering a somewhat finer articulation of basic organizational substructures. Production structures are concerned with the work that gets done; supportive structures procure the input, dispose of the output, and deal with institutional relations; maintenance structures promote adequate role performances; adaptive subsystems serve to change the organization in line with a changing environment; and managerial subsystems direct, adjudicate, and control the several subsystems and activities of the organization.

The upshot of this line of thinking is that since these basic substructures are interdependent, a change in any one will bear implications of change for the others: For instance, differences in technology will make for differences at the managerial, supportive and other levels; differences in environment will, in turn, place different demands on the productive, managerial, supportive, and other levels (cf. Hunt, 1970; Udy, 1965).

Thus a strong case has been made by several recent theories of organization for the recognition of the nature of the interaction between a social system and its environment, on the one hand, and its people on the other. By the use of the open-system model as a framework and conceptual language for describing organizations there is the possibility for a more thorough (but also more complex) understanding of organizational behavior:

> It is too soon to predict whether this approach will become a dominant guide to empirical work or whether "system" will become merely the latest "in" word among organizational psychologists [Quinn & Kahn, 1967, p. 461].

Contribution of Role Theory

In years past, the mind-body problem was a leading topic for philosophical discussion. For many, the tenability of the mind-body model depended on discovering the precise locus of the meeting of the two. The contemporary person-environment dilemma has prompted a similar search for a conceptual meeting point for social structural forces and individual personalistic forces. Programmatically, at least, probably the most satisfactory solution came about when Linton (1936) gave the notion of *role* a central place in the social sciences. Introduced to social psychology by Newcomb (1950), this concept has been explicated and advanced by such writers as Merton (1957), Shibutani (1961), Banton (1965), and Sarbin and Allen (1968). Until rather recently, however, the concept of role occupied only a secondary position among social science concepts, partly because earlier sociological and anthropological role notions tended to focus solely upon structural influences on personality. The advent of systems approaches to the study of large groups, however, gave the concept of role a new lease on life by balancing it with the personalistic forces that have traditionally been the concern of psychology.

Somewhere within the action system that is the functioning organization, structural and personal forces jointly draw a bead, as it were, on the individual, controlling his performances. And we have now reached the point of development in role concepts where, in their exemplary analysis of organizations, Katz and Kahn (1966) proposed role concepts as:

> the major means for linking the individual and organizational levels of research and theory; it is at once the building block of social systems and the summation of the requirements with which such systems confront their members as individuals [p. 197].

Highlighting distinctions between structure and person while concerned with their integration, Hunt (1967) pointed out that a social system may be viewed conceptually as an interlocking complex of positions (the structural aspect), or functional divisions of labor, which are to be populated by people who are expected to fulfill certain behavior requirements and possess certain personal attributes associated with each position. Since a social system is a system of interdependent activities, positions within a social structure exist in relationships with certain other positions. Thus, the "rights and duties" of a particular *focal position* exist with respect to a *counterposition.*

> This complementary contrast is, of course, a function basically of the complex patterns of behavior organized around these positions and embodying the relevant mutual expectations (the rights and duties) *vis à vis* one another held by occupants of positions. It is possible, therefore, to regard social process as an interaction of positions patterned in terms of these complementary expectations which are themselves called *roles* [p. 259].

Thus, role and its personalistic correlate, identity, represent the implications of social position incumbency and can be comprehensively described only with reference to other roles, which bear a complementary relation to the focal role.

We cannot explicate the ideas here, but we can say simply that since persons occupy multiple positions in life and are only partly involved in any single position they occupy, they have multiple identities that combine in various ways to affect their views and the enactments of their singular roles. And, whatever else may be involved, the modes of a man's participation in structured social intercourse will be reflected in his concept of himself and in the fabric of his personality.

The essential point, then, is not simply that role serves a linking function; more than that. In its modern forms, it exemplifies and operationalizes the merging of social and individual phenomena heretofore treated separatistically. Roles are undoubtedly social phenomena. However, they are not only external "demands," they are dynamic interactional processes carried out by individuals who color their performances personal. By way of reciprocity, however, through their identity implications roles become operationally integral to individual personality. Thus, roles more than link the individual and the social (or structural)—they unite them.

Role Conflict

Cyert and MacCrimmon (1968) made some of these same points, in their discussion of organizational processes, and accorded a prominent place to role concepts. In particular, they identified organizational roles as points of linkage and also as principal sources of conflict between individuals and organizations. In the study cited earlier, Hunt (1967) explicated five role varieties that are helpful in conceptualizing role differentiation. These focus attention on the interplay of patterns of expectation and performance within the role system. The importance of the distinctions he draws between aspects of role taking is that a lack of fit between any of them will result in some degree of role conflict, the effects of which have been the topic of two relatively recent major organizational studies and resulting theories.

Gross, Mason, and McEachern (1958) studied the perception and resolution of role conflict among school superintendents. They focused on both interrole conflicts (resulting from the occupancy of multiple positions) and intrarole conflicts (resulting from the perception of conflicting sent-roles[4] vis à vis a single focal position). On the basis of their data, they concluded that there were three major cognitive styles employed by superintendents in the resolution of perceived role conflict.

The first style they call the *moral* orientation. Individuals in this category give most weight to evaluating the legitimacy of the conflicting expectations or the *right* of others to hold such expectations. With minimal attention to the likelihood of sanctions for nonconformity, this style emphasizes conformity to the demand seen as most legitimate. The second type of orientation is called *expedient.* Priority here is given to a consideration of the sanctions others will bring to bear if the individual does not conform to their expectations. The resolution style in this case is to minimize negative sanctions involved in the role-conflict situation. The nature of the right of others to hold particular expectations is not nearly so important in this case as the perceived severity of the probable sanctions. This superintendent, therefore, will choose to conform to the expectations of those whose sanctions he fears most. *Moral expedient* is the third orientation toward role conflict resolution. Here no primacy is given to the dimensions of legitimacy or sanctions; rather, both are considered equally in choosing a course of resolution.

Among the numerous empirical findings of these authors was the high job satisfaction reported among superintendents who perceived agreement between the sent-role from the school board and their own role stereotypes. What is probably conceptually more important was the consistent finding of Gross et al. (1958) that the effects of role conflict on job satisfaction and expressions of worry among the superintendents were mediated by the characteristic anxiety level of the individual. Implicit in this finding is the notion that personality may be the result of an interaction of social structural conditions and personalistic dispositions. The difficulty in this particular study is that Gross and his colleagues dealt only with perceptions of role conflict and did not attempt to deal with the accuracy of perception. So the social structure is not truly represented in their research.

Clearly the most ambitious attempt to employ the

[4] Communications by persons intended to influence the role behavior of others (cf. Kahn, Wolfe, Quinn, Snoek, & Rosenthal, 1964).

role concept in organizational studies is that of Kahn et al. (1964). Borrowing Merton's (1957) formulation of a role set, these authors built a model that is specifically designed to integrate properties of a social structure with characteristics of people who populate it. They called their model a role episode and posited that it consists of a series of events. Specifically, role pressures emanate from members of the role set—the discrepancy between their own expectations and their evaluations of how well the focal person's behavior measures up. Members of the role set attempt to reduce this discrepancy by exerting pressures on the focal person to adjust his behavior to conform with their expectations. These pressures induce perceptual and cognitive experiences in the focal person that can lead to certain adjustive or maladjustive responses. The role-senders monitor any subsequent behavior of the focal person and reward him if they are satisfied with his adjustment or exert further pressures if they are not. This is a cyclic, ongoing process.

Role conflict and ambiguity may thus occur in two ways. In the first case it may occur as a property of the social structure where, in fact, the sent-roles from role-set members exert pressures for various mutually exclusive behaviors on the part of the focal person (cf. also Hunt, 1967). Role ambiguity exists where the sent-role expectations lack sufficient clarity to be translated into behavior by the focal person. The second variety of role conflict occurs at the perceptual level and may or may not correspond with an actual state of affairs. Thus the focal person may not perceive conflict where it actually exists, or he may perceive it where it does not exist, or he may perceive it where it does indeed exist.

Furthermore, Kahn and his associates hypothesized that the degree of structural and perceived role conflict varies as a function of several enduring organizational and personal characteristics. For example, organizational positions vary in their vulnerability to conflicting expectations. Typically, the less structured and explicit the job requirement, the closer the position is to the boundary of the organization, and the larger the number of bosses, subordinates, and equals associated with a given position, the greater is the likelihood that role conflict (and the tensions and frustrations, which may occur as a result of its experience) will vary with such personalistic dispositions as needs for cognition, tolerance of ambiguity, neurotic anxiety, or need achievement.

Thus, these authors posited that the degree of role conflict and its relation to individual experience and reactions is highly conditional and depends on numerous organizational and personal attributes. Furthermore, variables such as job satisfaction and general mental health are anchored, via the role-set concept, to both the social structure and individual dispositions. These authors have further contributed to knowledge by operationalizing and testing their hypotheses—successfully.

The theories and data of the Kahn et al. (1964) study and the Gross et al. (1958) study have seriously challenged many old and static notions of organizational behavior. They have demonstrated crucial functions of personalistic dispositions as mediators between formal system requirements and individual outcomes. In other words, neither can stand alone as a comprehensive explanation of human behavior in organizations. Furthermore, they have provided evidence of the inadequacy of the personality versus organization hypothesis. While Gross et al. have shown that simply holding a high-ranking position does not render a man free from emotional problems, Kahn et al. have provided data comparing six hierarchical organizational levels and showing that tension induced by role strain increases with increasing rank. Since role conflict is linked with emotional reactions and mental health in general, it is apparently true that if the right measures are chosen, management positions may not be as rosy as the personality-organization theorists hold. Kahn et al. have clearly shown that the organizational locus of emotional maladjustment can occur anywhere in an organization and is not necessarily restricted to unskilled or low level workers. Employee reactions apparently depend on the nature of the organization, the nature of the job, and the nature of the person. It seems plain that Katzell's (1962) thesis warrants being taken seriously (and Quinn & Kahn's, 1967, as well). It is neither meaningful nor useful to promote normative, one-sided theories intended to account for all organizational situations. There is good evidence that organizational behavior is the outcome of a variety of highly conditional and highly contingent relationships and situations. Future theory will need to build on the foundations of those premises.

REFERENCES

Argyris, C. *Personality and organization.* New York: Harper, 1957.

Argyris, C. Understanding human behavior in organizations: One viewpoint. In M. Haire (ed.), *Modern organization theory.* New York: Wiley, 1959.

Argyris, C. *Integrating the individual and the organization.* New York: Wiley, 1964.

Banton, M. *Roles.* New York: Basic Books, 1965.

Barker, R. G. On the nature of the environment. *Journal of Social Issues,* 1963, **19**, 17–38.

Bass, B. M. *Organizational psychology.* Boston: Allyn & Bacon, 1965.

Bell, D. *Work and its discontents.* Boston: Beacon Press, 1965.

Bennis, W. G. Organizational developments and the fate of bureaucracy. In L. L. Cummings and W. E. Scott (eds.), *Organizational behavior and human performance.* Homewood, Ill.: Irwin-Dorsey, 1969.

Bennis, W. G. Organic populism. *Psychology today,* 1970, **3**, 48–71.

Bennis, W. G. and Shepard, H. A theory of group development. *Human Relations,* 1965, **9**, 415–57.

Bennis, W. G. and Slater, P. E. *The temporary society.* New York: Harper & Row, 1968.

Blake, R. R. and Mouton, J. *Corporate excellence through grid organizational development.* Houston, Tex.: Gulf Corporation, 1968.

Blau, P. A formal theory of differentiation in organizations. *American Sociological Review,* 1970, **35**, 201–219.

Blauner, R. *Alienation and freedom: The factory worker and his industry.* Chicago: University of Chicago Press, 1964.

Buckley, W. (ed.) *Modern systems research for the behavioral scientist.* Chicago: Aldine, 1968.

Caplow, T. and McGee, R. *The academic marketplace.* New York: Basic Books, 1958.

Carey, A. The Hawthorne studies: A radical criticism. *American Sociological Review,* 1967, **32**, 403–17.

Cleland, D. I. and King, W. R. *Systems analysis and project management.* New York: McGraw-Hill, 1968.

Coch, L. and French, J. R. P. Overcoming resistance to change. *Human Relations,* 1958, **1**, 512–33.

Crozier, M. *The bureaucratic phenomenon.* Chicago: University of Chicago Press, 1964.

Cyert, R. M. and MacCrimmon, K. R. Organizations. In G. Lindzey and E. Aronson (eds.), *Handbook of social psychology.* Vol. I. (2d ed.) Boston: Addison-Wesley, 1968.

Cyert, R. M. and March, J. G. *A behavioral theory of the firm.* Englewood Cliffs, N.J.: Prentice-Hall, 1963.

Dawis, R. V., Lofquist, L. H., and Weiss, D. J. A theory of work adjustment. *Minnesota Studies in Vocational Rehabilitation,* 1968, **23**, Bulletin 47.

Durkileim, E. *De la division du travail social.* [Division of labor in society] (Translation, G. Simpson, New York: Macmillan, 1933, 1947) Paris: F. Alcan, 1902.

Festinger, L. Informal social communication. *Psychological Review,* 1950, **57**, 271–82.

Fiedler, F. E. Engineer the job to fit the manager. *Harvard Business Review,* 1965, **43**, 115–22.

French, J. R. P., Israel, J., and Aas, D. An experiment on participation in a Norwegian factory. *Human Relations,* 1960, **13**, 3–19.

Galbraith, J. K. *The new industrial state.* Boston: Houghton Mifflin, 1967.

Gellerman, S. W. *Motivation and productivity.* New York: American Management Association, 1963.

Gilbreth, F. B. *Motion study.* New York: Van Nostrand, 1911.

Glans, T. B., Grad, B., Holstein, D., Meyers, W. E., and Schmidt, R. N. *Management systems.* New York: Holt, Rinehart & Winston, 1968.

Gordon, M. M. *Assimilation in American life: The role of race, religion, and national origins.* New York: Oxford, 1964.

Gouldner, A. W. *Patterns of industrial bureaucracy.* New York: Free Press, 1954.

Gross, N., Mason, W. S., and McEachern, A. W. *Explorations in role analysis.* New York: Wiley, 1958.

Gulick, L. and Urwick, L. (eds.) *Papers on the science of administration.* New York: Institute of Public Administration, 1937.

Haberstroh, C. J. Organization design and systems analysis. In J. March (ed.), *Handbook of organizations.* Chicago: Rand McNally, 1965.

Hackman, R. *The motivated working adult.* New York: American Management Association, 1969.

Haire, M. Philosophy of organizations. In D. M. Bowerman and F. M. Fillerup (eds.), *Management: Organization and planning.* New York: McGraw-Hill, 1963.

Hall, R. The concept of bureaucracy: An empirical assessment. *American Journal of Sociology,* 1963, **69**, 32–40.

Harvey, E. Technology and the structure of organizations. *American Sociological Review,* 1968, **33**, 247–59.

Herzberg, F., Mausner, B., and Snyderman, B. *The motivation to work.* (2d ed.) New York: Wiley, 1959.

Hickson, D. J., Pugh, D. S., and Pheysey, D. C. Operations technology and organization structure. *Administrative Science Quarterly,* 1969, **17**, 378-97.

Hollander, E. P. and Hunt, R. G. (eds.) *Current perspectives in social psychology.* New York: Oxford, 1967.

Homans, G. C. *The human group.* New York: Harcourt, Brace & World, 1950.

Hunt, R. G. Role and role conflict. In E. P. Hollander and R. G. Hunt (eds.), *Current perspectives in social psychology.* (2d ed.) New York: Oxford, 1967.

Hunt, R. G. Review of E. J. Miller and A. K. Rice, *Systems of organization. Administrative Science Quarterly,* 1968, **13**, 360–62.

Hunt, R. G. An essay on the profit motive. *Defense Management Journal,* 1969, **5**, 6–11. (a)

Hunt, R. G. Review of R. C. Hackman, *The Motivated Working Adult. Administrative Science Quarterly,* 1969, **14**, 614–15. (b)

Hunt, R. G. Technology and organization. *Academy of Management Journal,* 1970, **13**, 235–53.

Indik, B. P. Some effects of organization size on member attitudes and behavior. *Human Relations,* 1963, **16**, 369–84.

Indik, B. P. Organization size and member participation: Some empirical tests of alternative explanations. *Human Relations,* 1965, **18**, 339–50.

Jasinski, F. J. Use and misuses of efficiency controls. *Harvard Business Review,* 1956, **34**, 105-12.

Kahn, R. L., Wolfe, D. M., Quinn, R. P., Snoek, J. D., and Rosenthal, R. A. *Organizational stress: Studies in role conflict and ambiguity.* New York: Wiley, 1964.

Katz, D. The motivational basis of organizational behavior. *Behavioral Science,* 1964, **9**, 131–46.

Katz, D. and Kahn, R. L. *The social psychology of organizations.* New York: Wiley, 1966.

Katz, F. E. Explaining informal work groups in complex organizations: The case for autonomy in structure. *Administrative Science Quarterly,* 1965, **10**, 204–21.

Katzell, R. A. Contrasting systems of work organization. *American Psychologist,* 1962, **17**, 102–8.

Katzell, R. A., Barrett, R. S., and Parker, T. C. Job satisfaction, job performance, and situational characteristics. *Journal of Applied Psychology,* 1961, **45**, 65–72.

Koontz, H. Making sense of management theory. *Harvard Business Review,* 1962, **40**, 25.

Leavitt, H. J. Unhuman organizations. *Harvard Business Review,* 1962, **40**, 90–98.

Levinson, H., Price, C. R., Munden, K. J., Mandel, H. J., and Solley, C. M. *Men, management and mental health.* Cambridge: Harvard University Press, 1962.

Lewin, K. *Field theory in social science.* New York: Harper, 1951.

Lewin, K. Group decision and social change. In E. Maccoby, T. Newcomb, and E. Hartley (eds.), *Readings in social psychology.* (3d ed.) New York: Holt, Rinehart & Winston, 1958.

Likert, R. *New patterns of management.* New York: McGraw-Hill, 1961.

Likert, R. *The human organization.* New York: McGraw-Hill, 1967.

Linton, R. *The study of man.* New York: Appleton-Century, 1936.

Maier, N. *Psychology in industry.* Boston: Houghton Mifflin, 1955.

Mann, F. C. and Hoffman, L. R. *Automation and the worker. A study of social change in power plants.* New York: Holt, 1960.

March, J. G. and Simon, H. A. *Organizations.* New York: Wiley, 1958.

Marx, K. *Capital.* London: Allen & Unwin, 1887. (Translation reproduced and supplemented, 1943.)

Marx, K. *Selected writings in sociology and social philosophy.* (ed. and trans. by T. B. Bottomore and M. Rubel) New York: McGraw-Hill, 1964.

Maslow, A. H. *Motivation and personality.* New York: Harper, 1954.

Maslow, A. H. *Eupsychian management.* Homewood, Ill.: Irwin-Dorsey, 1965.

Mayo, E. *The human problems of industrial civilization.* New York: Macmillan, 1933.

McGregor, D. *The human side of enterprise.* New York: McGraw-Hill, 1960.

Mechanic, D. Some considerations in the methodology of organizational studies. In H. Leavitt (ed.), *The social science of organizations.* Englewood Cliffs, N.J.: Prentice-Hall, 1963.

Merton, R. K. *Social theory and social structure.* (Rev. ed.) New York: Free Press, 1957.

Miller, E. J. and Rice, A. K. *Systems of organization: The control of task and sentient boundaries.* London: Tavistock, 1967.

Miller, J. G. *Living systems.* New York: Wiley, 1968.

Morane, J. H. *A sociology of human systems.* New York: Appleton-Century-Crofts, 1967.

Mouzelis, N. P. *Organization and bureaucracy.* Chicago: Aldine, 1967.

Neff, W. S. *Work and human behavior.* New York: Atherton, 1968.

Newcomb, T. M. *Social psychology.* New York: Dryden, 1950.

Newcomb, T. M. Individual systems of orientation. In S. Koch (ed.), *Psychology: A study of a science.* Vol. 3. New York: McGraw-Hill, 1959.

Opsahl, R. L. and Dunnette, M. D. The role of financial compensation in industrial motivation. *Psychological Bulletin,* 1966, **66**, 94–118.

Parsons, T. *Structure and process in modern societies.* New York: Free Press, 1960.

Perrow, C. A framework for the comparative analysis of organizations. *American Sociological Review,* 1967, **32**, 194–209.

Porter, L. W. and Lawler, E. E. Properties of organization structure in relation to job attitudes and job behavior. *Psychological Bulletin,* 1965, **64**, 23–51.

Porter, L. W. and Lawler, E. E. *Managerial attitudes and performance.* Homewood, Ill.: Irwin-Dorsey, 1968.

Pugh, D. S. Modern organization theory: A psychological and sociological study. *Psychological Bulletin,* 1966, **66**, 235–51.

Quinn, A. P. and Kahn, R. L. Organizational psychology. *Annual Review of Psychology,* 1967, **18**, 437–66.

Rice, A. K. *The enterprise and its environment.* London: Tavistock, 1963.

Roethlisberger, F. J. and Dickinson, W. J. *Management and the worker.* Cambridge, Mass.: Harvard University Press, 1939.

Ronan, W. W. Individual and situational variables relating to job satisfaction. *Journal of Applied Psychology Monograph,* 1970, **54**, No. 1, Part 2.

Roy, D. F. Banana time: Job satisfaction and informal interaction, *Human Organization,* 1960, **18**, 158–68.

Rubin, I. and Hunt, R. G. *Some aspects of managerial control in interpenetrating systems: The case of government-industry relations.* (Tech. Rep. No. 7) State University of New York at Buffalo: Grant NGR 33-015-061, National Aeronautics and Space Administration, July 1969.

Sarbin, T. R. and Allen, V. L. Role theory. In G. Lindzey and E. Aronson (eds.), *Handbook of social psychology.* Vol. 1, (2d ed.) Boston: Addison-Wesley, 1968.

Sayles, L. and Strauss, G. *Human behavior in organizations.* Englewood Cliffs, N.J.: Prentice-Hall, 1966.

Schein, E. H. *Organizational psychology.* Englewood Cliffs, N.J.: Prentice-Hall, 1965.

Schein, E. H. and Bennis, W. G. *Personal and organizational change through group methods: The laboratory approach.* New York: Wiley, 1965.

Schlesinger, A. *A thousand days.* Boston: Houghton Mifflin, 1965.

Scott, W. G. Organization theory: An overview and an appraisal. *Academy of Management Journal,* 1961, **4**, 7–27.

Scott, W. R. Theory of organizations. In R. E. L. Farris (ed.), *Handbook of modern sociology.* Chicago: Rand McNally, 1964.

Shibutani, T. *Society and personality.* Englewood Cliffs, N.J.: Prentice-Hall, 1961.

Simon, H. *Administrative behavior.* (2d ed.) New York: Macmillan, 1957.

Simon, H. *The shape of automation for men and management.* New York: Harper & Row, 1965.

Smith, P. C. and Cranny, C. J. Psychology of men at work. *Annual Review of Psychology,* 1968, **19**, 467–96.

Sommer, R. Small group ecology. *Psychological Bulletin,* 1967, **67**, 145–52.

Sommer, R. *Personal space.* Englewood Cliffs, N.J.: Prentice-Hall, 1968.

Strauss, G. Some notes on power equalization. In H. Leavitt (ed.), *The social science of organizations.* Englewood Cliffs, N.J.: Prentice-Hall, 1963.

Strauss, G. Human relations—1968 style. *Industrial Relations,* 1968, **7**, 262–72.

Tannenbaum, A. S. *Social psychology of the work organization.* Belmont, Calif.: Wadsworth, 1966.

Tannenbaum, A. S. *Control in organizations.* New York: McGraw-Hill, 1968.

Taylor, F. W. *Scientific management.* New York: Harper & Row, 1911.

Thompson, J. D. *Organization in action.* New York: McGraw-Hill, 1967.

Thompson, V. *Modern organization.* New York: Knopf, 1961.

Trist, E. L., Higgin, G. W., Murray, H., and Pollack, A. B. *Organizational choice.* London: Tavistock, 1963.

Udy, S. H. The comparative analysis of organizations. In J. March (ed.), *Handbook of organizations.* Chicago: Rand McNally, 1965.

von Bertalanffy, L. The theory of open systems in physics and biology. *Science,* 1950, **111**, 23–38.

Vroom, V. H. *Work and motivation.* New York: Wiley, 1964.

Vroom, V. H. and Mann, F. Leader authoritarianism and employee attitudes. *Personnel Psychology,* 1960, **13**, 125–40.

Walker, C. R. Life in the automatic factory. *Harvard Business Review,* 1958, **36**, 111–19.

Weber, M. *Theory of social and economic organization.* (Trans. by A. M. Henderson & T. Parsons of Pt. I, *Wirtschaft and Gesellschaft*) New York: Oxford, 1947. (2d ed., Free Press, 1964.)

Whyte W. F. *Organization behavior: Theory and application.* Homewood, Ill.: Irwin-Dorsey, 1969.

Woodward, J. *Industrial organization: Theory and practice.* London: Oxford University Press, 1965.

27. A FORMAL THEORY OF DIFFERENTIATION IN ORGANIZATIONS*

***Peter M. Blau*†**

The objective of this paper is to develop a deductive theory of the formal structure of work organizations, that is, organizations deliberately established for explicit purposes and composed of employees. The differentiation of a formal organization into components in terms of several dimensions—spatial, occupational, hierarchical, functional—is considered to constitute the core of its structure. The theory is limited to major antecedents and consequences of structural differentiation. It has been derived from the empirical results of a quantitative study of government bureaus. The extensive analysis of these empirical data on the interrelations between organizational characteristics, too lengthy for presentation in an article, is reported elsewhere (Blau & Schoenherr, in press).[1] The topic of this paper is not the analysis of the research findings but the deductive theory that can be inferred from them and that therefore explains them and the parallel empirical regularities that the theory predicts to exist in other work organizations. Although the findings are not fully presented, the relevant empirical relationships observed are cited, since they are the basis of the theoretical generalizations advanced, and since they must logically follow from these generalizations to satisfy the requirements of deductive theory.

* Reprinted from *American Sociological Review,* Vol. 35, No. 2 (April 1970), pp. 201–18.

† Columbia University.

[1] The assistance of Sheila R. Klatzky with this research is gratefully acknowledged, and so is grant GS—553 of the National Science Foundation, the source of support of the Comparative Organization Research Program at the University of Chicago, of which this is report No. 11.

DEDUCTIVE THEORY

The conception of systematic theory adopted is explicated by Braithwaite (1953; see also Hempel & Oppenheim, 1948; Popper, 1959). An empirical proposition concerning the relationship between two or more variables is explained by subsuming it under a more general proposition from which it can be logically derived. A systematic theory is a set of such logically interrelated propositions, all of which pertain to connections between at least two variables, and the least general of which, but only those, must be empirically demonstrable. "A scientific theory is a deductive system in which observable consequences logically follow from the conjunction of observed facts with the set of fundamental hypotheses in the system" (Braithwaite, 1953:22). The theoretical generalizations that explain the empirical findings are in turn explained by subsuming them under still more general hypotheses, so that the theoretical system may have propositions on several levels of abstraction. These principles apply not only to universal hypotheses—if A, then B—but also to the statistical ones characteristic of the social sciences—the more A, the more likely is B.

The explanatory thrust of a formal theory of this kind resides completely in the generality of the theoretical propositions and in the fact that the empirical findings can be deduced from them in strict logic. Theorizing in the social sciences usually assumes not this form of a deductive model but what Kaplan calls the pattern model, according to which "something is explained when it is so related to a set of other elements that together they constitute a unified system" (1964:333). The psychological experience of gaining understanding by the sudden insight the theory brings of how parts fit neatly into a whole is largely missing in deductive theorizing. Instead, the theorist's aim is to discover a few theoretical generalizations from which many different empirical propositions can be derived. Strange as it may seem, the higher-level hypotheses that explain the lower-level propositions are accepted as valid purely on the basis that they do explain them, in the specific sense that they logically imply them, and without independent empirical evidence; whereas acceptance of the lower-level propositions that need to be explained is contingent on empirical evidence (see Braithwaite, 1953:303). Indeed, the reason for developing a deductive system is to empower empirical findings, confirming low-level hypotheses indirectly to establish an abstract body of explanatory theory, and empirical evidence for any lower-level proposition strengthens confidence in all propositions.

In Braithwaite's words:

> One of the main purposes in organizing scientific hypotheses into a deductive system is in order that the direct evidence for each lower-level hypothesis may become indirect evidence for all the other lowest-level hypotheses; although no amount of empirical evidence suffices to prove any of the hypotheses in the system, yet any piece of evidence for any part of the system helps toward establishing the whole of the system (1953:17–18).

In an attempt to start building a deductive theory of the formal structure of organizations, theoretical generalizations about differentiation in the structure are inferred from a large number of empirical findings of a study of government bureaus. Several middle-level propositions are deduced from two basic generalizations, and empirical findings supporting the derived generalizations are cited. Inasmuch as the generalizations subsume many empirically demonstrated propositions, that is, logically imply them, they explain these empirical regularities. There are several crosswise connections which strengthen the interdependence in the theoretical system.

The aim, in short, is to develop a small number of interrelated general propositions that account for a considerable variety of empirical regularities about differentiation in organizations. The contribution the paper seeks to make rests not on the originality of the particular propositions, several of which have been noted in the literature, but on the attempt to derive lower-level propositions systematically from higher-level ones and thus to construct a limited body of coherent theory that is supported by numerous empirical findings. The theory is explicitly confined to inferences from the most trustworthy and pronounced empirical relationships between organizational characteristics observed in 1,500 component organizations and the 53 larger government agencies to which they belong, in the hope that these strong associations observable under a variety of conditions reflect underlying forces that would also be manifest in other types of organizations than the ones studied. A test of most propositions has been conducted in another study of 416 government bureaus of a different kind, but only future research can tell whether and to which extent the generalizations advanced are also applicable to still other types of organizations. Since the theory is restricted to the interdependence among relatively few factors, it ignores other conditions on which these factors undoubtedly are dependent as well. Thus, the theory pays no attention to the influences of the technology employed, nor to those of the organization's environment. The assumption here is that such other influences may complement but do not suppress those of the factors incorporated in the theory, because these factors are of great general importance, and the empirical data available support this assumption.[2]

FORMAL STRUCTURE

The formal structure of organizations is conceptualized here more narrowly than is usually the case. The term "social structure" is often used broadly, and sometimes loosely, to refer to the common value orientations of people, the traditional institutions in a society, cultural norms and role expectations, and nearly everything that pertains to life in groups. But it has a more specific meaning. The gist of a social structure is that people differ in status and social affiliation, that they occupy different positions and ranks, and that they belong to different groups and subunits of various sorts. The fact that the members of a collectivity are differentiated on the basis of several independent dimensions is the foundation of the collectivity's social structure. This differentiation into components along various lines in organizations is the object of the present analysis. The theory centers attention on the social forces that govern the interrelations among differentiated elements in a formal structure and ignores the psychological forces that govern individual behavior. Formal structures exhibit regularities that can be studied in their own right without investigating the motives of the individuals in organizations.

Formal organizations cope with the difficult problems large-scale operations create by subdividing responsibilities in numerous ways and thereby facilitating the work of any operating employee, manager, and subunit in the organization. The division of labor typifies the improvement in performance attainable through subdivision. The more completely simple tasks are separated from various kinds of complex ones, the easier it is for unskilled employees to perform the routine duties and for skilled employees to acquire the specialized training and experience to perform the different complex ones. Further subdivision of responsibilities occurs among functional divisions, enabling each one to concentrate on certain kinds of work. Local branches may be established in different places to facilitate serving clients in various areas, and these branches may become functionally specialized. The management of such a differentiated structure requires that managerial responsibilities too become subdivided among managers and supervisors on different hierarchical levels.

Weber recognized the vital importance the subdivision of responsibilities has for administrative organizations and placed it first in his famous enumeration of the characteristics of modern bureaucracy.[3] His focus on a structure of differentiated responsibilities is also evident in his emphasis on the division of labor, specialized competence, and particularly the hierarchy of authority (see Weber, 1946:196–197; 1947:330–331). An apparent implication of this stress on structural differences is that the analysis of differentiation in the formal structure constitutes the core of the systematic study of formal organizations, but Weber himself does not pursue this line of inquiry. It is the primary concern here.

The central concept of differentiation in organizations must be clearly defined in terms that permit translation into operational measures. A dimension of differentiation is any criterion on the basis of which the members of an organization are formally divided into positions, as illustrated by the division of labor; or into ranks, notably managerial levels; or into subunits, such as local branches, headquarters divisions, or sections within branches or divisions. A structural component is either a distinct official status (for example, employment interviewer or first-line supervisor), or a subunit in the organization (for example, one branch or one division). The term differentiation refers specifically to the number of structural components that are formally distinguished in terms of any *one* criterion. The empirical measures used are number of branches, number of occupational positions (division of labor), number of hierarchical levels, number of divisions, and number of sections within branches or divisions.

The research from which the theory of structural differentiation has been derived is a study of the 53 employment security agencies in the United States, which are responsible for administering unemployment insurance and providing public employment services in the 50 states, the District of Columbia, Puerto Rico, and the Virgin Islands.[4] These are autonomous state agencies, although they operate under federal laws and are subject to some federal supervision. The empirical data were collected by a team of three research assistants who visited every agency in the country to interview key informants and obtain data from records. Most of the informa-

---

[2] The research of Blau and Schoenherr (in press) presents data that show that the empirical relationships implied by the theory persist when important differences in technology and numerous variations in environmental conditions are controlled.

[3] "I. There is the principle of fixed and official jurisdictional areas . . . 1. The regular activities required for the purposes of the bureaucratically governed structure are distributed in a fixed way as official duties" (Weber, 1946:196).

[4] The only agency excluded is the smallest one, on Guam, which has less than a dozen employees, compared to 1,200 for the mean of the other agencies. In the four jurisdictions in which unemployment insurance and employment services are carried out by separate bureaus, they were combined for the purpose of the analysis, since it became evident that these two functions are hardly more separate there than in some other jurisdictions where they are legally in the same bureau.

tion about the formal structure comes from personnel lists and from elaborate organizational charts specially prepared for the research, all of which were much more detailed than the charts kept by the agencies. In addition to analyzing the formal structure of the 53 total agencies or their entire headquarters, the structure of the 1201 local branches and that of the 354 headquarters divisions were also analyzed; these include all local branches and headquarters divisions in the country meeting minimum criteria of size (five employees) and structure (three hierarchical levels). Headquarters divisions were, moreover, divided on the basis of their function into six types, making it possible to analyze structure while controlling function. (The six types are the two basic line functions —employment services and unemployment insurance—and four staff functions—administrative services, personnel and technical, data processing, and legal services.)

FIRST GENERALIZATION

Increasing size generates structural differentiation in organizations along various dimensions at decelerating rates (1). This is the first fundamental generalization inferred from the empirical findings. From it can be deduced several middle-range propositions, which subsume additional empirical findings. One can consider this theoretical generalization about the structure of organizations to comprise three parts, in which case the middle-level and lower-level propositions are derived from the conjunction of the three highest-level ones. In this alternative formulation, the three highest-level propositions composing the first basic generalization about the formal structure of organizations are: (1A) large size promotes structural differentiation; (1B) large size promotes differentiation along several different lines; and (1C) the rate of differentiation declines with expanding size. The assumption is that these generalizations apply to the subunits within organizations as well as to total organizations, which can be made explicit in a fourth proposition: (1D) the subunits into which an organization is differentiated become internally differentiated in parallel manner.

A considerable number of empirical findings on employment security agencies can be accounted for by the generalization that differentiation in organizations increases at decreasing rates with increasing size, and none of the relevant evidence conflicts with this generalization. The operational definition of size is number of employees. When total state agencies

FIGURE 1 SIZE OF AGENCY AND NUMBER OF HIERARCHICAL LEVELS AT HEADQUARTERS

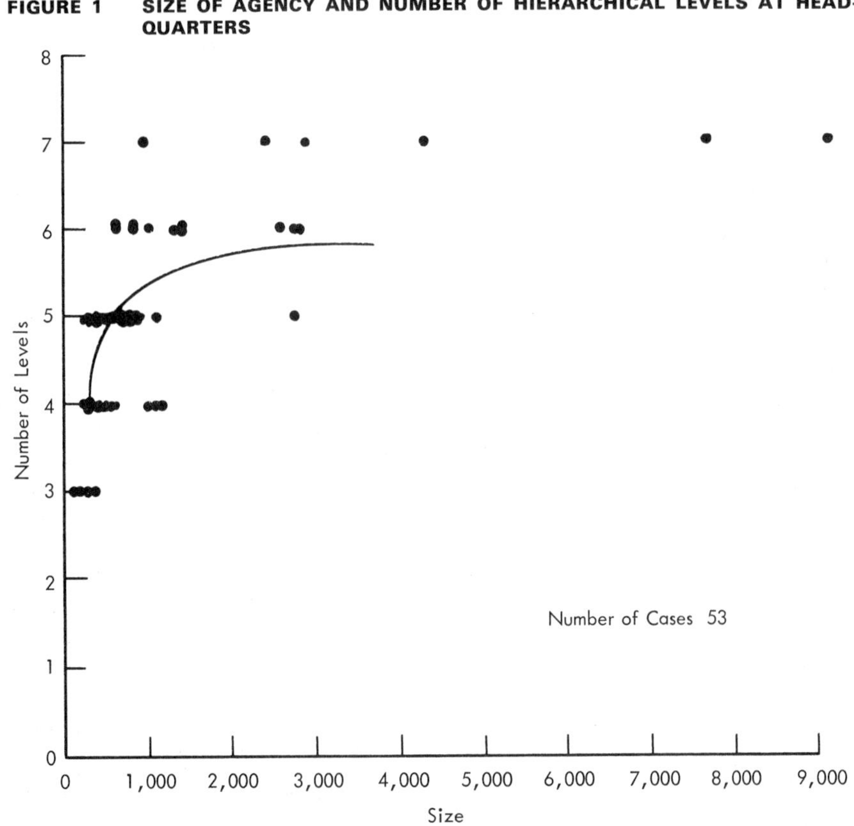

FIGURE 2 SIZE OF LOCAL OFFICE AND DIVISION OF LABOR

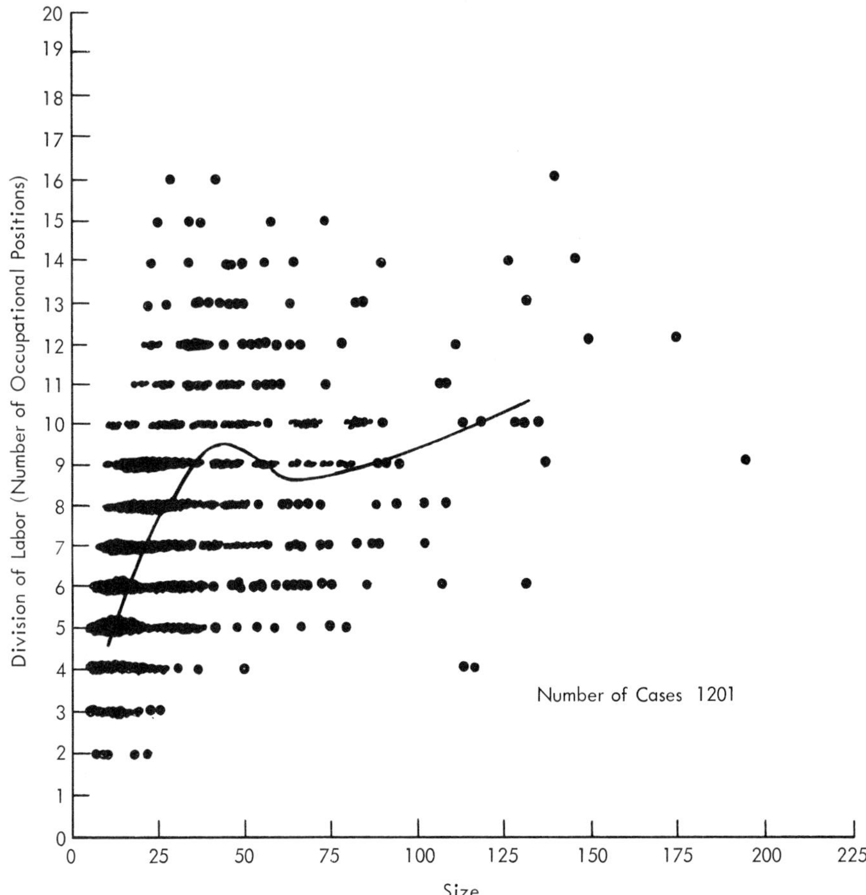

are compared, increases in size are accompanied by initially rapid and subsequently more gradual increases in the number of local branches into which the agency is spatially differentiated; the number of official occupational positions expressing the division of labor; the number of levels in the hierarchy; the number of functional divisions at the headquarters; and the number of sections per division. The profound impact that agency size has upon differentiation is indicated by its correlations of .94 with number of local offices; .78 with occupational positions; .60 with hierarchical levels; and .38 with functional divisions. Logarithmic transformation of size further raises these correlations (except the one with local offices); for example, that with number of divisions becomes .54; and that with sections per division, which was before an insignificant .16, is after transformation .43. The improvements in the correlations logarithmic transformation of size achieves reflect the logarithmic shape of the regression lines of the numbers of structural components on size, and thus the declining rate of differentiation with expanding size. For an illustration of this pattern, the scatter diagram for agency size and number of hierarchical levels is presented in Figure 1.

The internal differentiation within the subunits that have become differentiated in the agencies assumes the same form. The larger a local branch, the greater the differentiation into occupational positions ($r = .51$), hierarchical levels (.68), and functional sections (.61). This differentiation occurs at declining rates with increasing size (and the correlations are somewhat raised when size is logarithmically transformed). The scatter diagram of office size and division of labor (occupational positions) in Figure 2 illustrates the logarithmic curve expressing this pattern.[5] Similar logarithmic curves characterize the differentiation within the functional divisions at

[5] The curves shown are rough estimates. They were drawn by dividing size into three categories for Figure 1 and seven categories for Figure 2; determining the means for both size and the y-variable (ordinate) in each category; and making a smooth curve between those points. The same procedure is used for the other figures below.

the agency headquarters. The larger a division, the larger is the number of its occupational positions, hierarchical levels, and functional sections; and differences between very small and medium-sized divisions have again more impact on variations in these three aspects of differentiation than differences between medium-sized and very large divisions. Moreover, this tendency for differentiation at decelerating rates to occur with increasing size is observable in six separate types of divisions with basically different functions, which suggests that it is independent of function and thus provides some support for the claim that the same tendency will be found in other organizations which have different functions from those of employment security agencies.[6]

PROPOSITION 1.1

The first proposition that can be derived from the first fundamental generalization is the following: as the size of organizations increases, its marginal influence on differentiation decreases (1.1). As a matter of fact, this is hardly a derived proposition, since it is merely a restatement of one part of the original proposition (1C). But by translating the initial proposition into different concepts, the new proposition directs attention to a distinctive implication and an important parallel with the economic principle of diminishing returns or, in technical terms, of the eventually diminishing marginal physical productivity. In the words of Boulding: "As we increase the quantity of any one input which is combined with a fixed quantity of the other inputs, the marginal physical productivity of the variable input must eventually decline" (1955:589).

In a factory, production output can be raised by adding workers, but the marginal increment in output resulting from adding more and more workers without changing plant size and equipment eventually declines. In parallel fashion, a larger complement of employees in an organization makes its structure more differentiated, but as the number of employees and the differentiation of the structure increase, the marginal influence of a given increase in personnel on further differentiation declines. It seems that the differentiation produced by the expanding size of organizations stems the power of additional expansions in size to make the structure still more differentiated.

But why does the marginal influence of size on differentiation in organizations decline? If the analogy with the economic principle of diminishing returns is appropriate, it should provide some clues for answering this question. The reason for the eventually declining marginal productivity of increments in only one type of economic input is that such increments create an imbalance of inputs and the growing need for other inputs depresses productivity. For example, additional workers cannot be efficiently utilized in production without parallel increases in equipment and space. We may speculate that the influence of increasing organizational size on differentiation produces a growing need which in turn diminishes the influences of further increases in size.

The existence of differentiation in a formal organization implies a need for coordination. There are at least two inputs, using the terminology of economics, on which the development of structural differentiation in organization depends. The first is a sufficient number of employees (the measure of size) to fill the different positions and man the various subunits, and the second is an adequate administrative machinery to meet problems of coordination. The advancing differentiation to which an increasing number of employees gives rise intensifies the need for coordination in the organization, and this need restrains the further development of differentiation, which is reflected in the declining marginal influence of increasing size on differentiation. The implication of these considerations extrapolated from economic theory is that differentiation in organizations creates pressures to find ways to meet the need for coordination. We shall later return to the analysis of this problem, after discussing five other propositions that can be derived from the first basic generalization.

PROPOSITION 1.2

The second derived proposition is that the larger an organization is, the larger the average size of its structural components of all kinds (1.2). This proposition logically follows from the principle of the decelerating rate of differentiation with increasing organizational size (1C), which is graphically expressed by the decline in the slopes (the logarithmic curves) of the regression lines of the number of structural components of various kinds on size. In a diagram with total size or number of employees on the horizontal and number of structural components on the vertical axis, the average size of the structural components of an agency represented by a point is indicated by the ratio of the horizontal to the vertical coordinate of this point. As the positive slope of the regression line declines, this ratio is larger

[6] This pattern is reflected in the finding that the logarithmic transformation of size improves its zero-order correlations, for all types of divisions combined, with division of labor (from .64 to .76), hierarchical levels (from .71 to .85), and functional sections (from .38 to .68). If the six functional types are analyzed separately, logarithmic transformation of size raises the corresponding correlations in 15 of 18 cases.

for most large agencies than for most small agencies.[7] If the structural components increase more slowly than organizational size, the average size of these components necessarily becomes larger. Even in those cases in which the decline in the slope of the regression line is not pronounced, the average size of the structural components is strongly associated with the size of the organization. Two examples are the mean size of local branches, which variable has a zero-order correlation with agency size of .65, and the number of incumbents of the average occupational position, which variable is correlated .94 with agency size.

Thus, the large size of an organization raises the average size as well as the number of its structural components. Large agencies have more and larger local offices than small agencies, more and larger headquarters divisions, and the same holds true for every one of their structural components. The large size of the local offices within an agency and of its headquarters divisions, whatever their function, in turn tends to increase both the number and the average size of sections, and both the number of occupational positions and of managerial ranks and the mean number of employees occupying each position and each rank.

This double effect of organizational size has the paradoxical result that large offices and headquarters divisions constitute at the same time a more homogeneous and a more heterogeneous occupational environment for most employees than small ones. For larger offices or divisions contain comparatively many employees in nearly every occupational specialty, providing a congenial ingroup of colleagues for most employees—often not available in small organizational units—and they simultaneously contain a relatively great variety of different specialties, enhancing opportunities for stimulating contacts with people whose training and experience are unlike their own. However, the greater opportunity for social interaction with a colleague ingroup in large offices may prove so attractive that social contacts with persons from different specialties are rarer there than in small ones, despite the fact that opportunities for outgroup contacts are better in large offices too.

PROPOSITION 1.3

A third derived proposition is that the proportionate size of the average structural component, as distinguished from its absolute size, decreases with increases in organizational size (1.3). This follows directly from (1A): if the number of structural components, the criterion of differentiation, increases as organizational size does, the proportion of all employees who are in the average component must decrease. Hence, most groups or categories of employees in big organizations are larger in absolute numbers but constitute a smaller proportion of the total personnel than in small organizations. A consequence is that the average *(mean)* relative size of employee complements on a given dimension decreases with increasing organizational size, though not necessarily the proportion of any particular complement.

But we may reformulate this proposition (1.3) into a probability statement about groupings of employees: *ceteris paribus,* chance expectations are that the proportionate size of any personnel complement decreases with increasing organizational size. The empirical data show that this proposition applies to various kinds of administrative overhead or supportive services for the majority work force. The size of an agency is inversely related to the proportionate size of its administrative staff ($r = -.60$) and of its complement of managerial personnel (−.45). (The terms "manager" and "supervisor," unless qualified, are used interchangeably to refer to all levels.) The proportion of managers is also inversely related to size in local offices (−.64) and in headquarters divisions regardless of function.[8]

When a certain personnel complement is singled out for attention—the staff or the managerial component—and exhibits the expected decrease in proportionate size with increasing organizational size, the remainder of the total personnel—the line or the nonsupervisory employees—must naturally reveal a complementary increase in proportionate size. This is mathematically inevitable, and it indicates that the reformulated proposition (1.3) cannot possibly apply to both parts of a dichotomy. The plausible assumption is that the residual majority actually consists of numerous personnel categories while the specialized personnel complement focused upon can be treated as a single one, which implies that the proportion of the minority complement is the one that should decrease with increasing organizational size. The data support this assumption. If employees in various organizational units are divided into cleri-

[7] This can be readily seen by looking at the regression lines in Figures 1 and 2. For a point moving along either line from left to right, the horizontal coordinate increases more rapidly than the vertical one, indicating that the ratio of the first to the second coordinate increases.

[8] The zero-order correlations for the six types of divisions are: −.49 (employment services); −.51 (unemployment insurance); −.30 (adminstrative services); −.12 (personnel and technical); −.18 (data processing); and −.36 (legal services). Size in all cases (agencies and local offices as well as divisions) has been logarithmically transformed.

cal and professional personnel, the proportion of whichever of the two is in the minority tends to decrease as unit size does. The conclusion that may be drawn, which extends beyond what can be derived in strict logic from the premise, is that the proportionate size of any supportive service provided by a distinctive minority to the majority work force is likely to decline with increasing organizational size.

PROPOSITION 1.4

Another proposition can be derived either from the last one (1.3) or from the one preceding (1.2): the larger the organization is, the wider the supervisory span of control (1.4). If chances are that the proportionate size of any organizational component declines with increasing size (1.3), and if this applies to the proportion of managers, it follows that the number of subordinates per manager, or the span of control, must expand with increasing size (1.4). Besides, if chance expectations are that the absolute average size of any structural component or grouping of employees increases with increasing size (1.2), and if this applies to the various work groups assigned to supervisors, it follows that the size of the group under each supervisor, or his span of control, tends to expand with increasing size (1.4). Here again the logical implications specifying the *mean* absolute and proportionate size for *all* components have been translated into *probabilities* or statistical expectations referring to *any* component. Whether these derived propositions apply to a *particular* personnel component, like the managerial staff, must be empirically ascertained. If the evidence is negative, it would not falsify the theory, though it would weaken it. If the evidence is positive, it strengthens the theory, and makes it possible to extend it beyond the limits of its purely logical implications by taking into account the empirical data confirming this particular application of the merely statistical deduction from the theory.[9]

The empirical data on employment security agencies confirm the proposition that the span of control of supervisors expands with increasing organizational size. This is the case for all levels of managers and supervisors examined in these agencies and their subunits. The larger an agency, the wider is the span of control of its director and the average span of control of its division heads. The larger a headquarters division, whatever its function, the wider is the span of control of its division heads, the average span of control of its middle managers, and the average span of control of its first-line supervisors. The larger a local office is, the wider the span of control of the office manager and that of the average first-line supervisor.[10] Moreover, the size of the total organization has an independent effect widening the supervisory span of control when the size of local offices is controlled.[11] Big organizations and their larger headquarters divisions and local branches tend to have more employees in any given position with similar duties than small organizations with their smaller subunits, as we have seen, thus making it possible to use superviors more efficiently in large units by assigning more subordinates with similar duties to each supervisor.

The additional influence of the size of the total organization, independent of that of the size of the office, on the number of subordinates per supervisor, may reveal a structural effect (see Blau, 1960). The prevalence of a wide span of supervisory control in large organizations, owing to the large size of most of their branch offices, creates a normative standard that exerts an influence in its own right, increasing the number of subordinates assigned to supervisors; and the same is the case, *mutatis mutandis,* for the prevalence of a narrow supervisory span of control in small organizations with their smaller branches. To direct attention to the substantial influence of organizational size on the supervisory span of control is, of course, not to deny that this span is also influenced by other conditions, such as the nature of the duties.

PROPOSITIONS 1.5 AND 1.6

Organizations exhibit an economy of scale in management. This proposition (1.5) is implicit in the

[9] Two kinds of statistical or probability statements must be distinguished, empirical and theoretical ones. On the one hand, it is only probable that any given large agency has a lower ratio of supervisors than any given small agency, since the correlation is less than 1.00; this empirical probability is *not* what is referred to in the text. On the other hand, and this is what is discussed above, it is only probable that the ratio of supervisory personnel is inversely related to agency size, since the theory only predicts that the proportionate size of most components of the agency is inversely related to its own size and that it is probable that such an inverse relationship will be observed with respect to any particular component, such as the supervisory ratio.

[10] The zero-order correlations of size (log) of the respective organizational units and mean span of control of various managers are: agency director, .39; head of division, from .22 to .44 for the six functional types; middle managers in divisions, with one exception (.05) from .17 to .78; first-line supervisors in divisions, from .39 to .69 in the six types; managers of local offices, .40; and first-line supervisors in local offices, .66.

[11] In the multiple regression problem with the average span of control of the first-line supervisors in each of the 1201 local offices as dependent variable, and with office size and a number of other conditions controlled, the standardized regression coefficient of the size of the agency to which the local office belongs is .27.

two foregoing ones. For if the proportion of managerial personnel declines with size (1.3) and their span of control expands with size (1.4), this means that large-scale operations reduce the proportionate size of the administrative overhead, specifically, of the complement of managers and supervisors. In fact, the relative size of administrative overhead of other kinds, such as staff and supportive personnel, also declines with increasing size, as has been noted. The question arises whether this economy of scale in administrative overhead produces overall personnel economies with an increasing scale of operations. The data on employment security agencies are equivocal on this point. The only index of personnel economy available, the ratio of all employees engaged in unemployment benefit operations to the number of clients served by them, is inversely correlated with size, but with a case base of only 53 agencies the correlation is too small (—.14) to place any confidence in it. Logarithmic transformation of size raises the correlation to —.24, which suggests that large size might reduce the man-hour costs of benefit operations slightly.

Whereas this finding is inconclusive, not inconclusive are the numerous findings that indicate that the relative size of administrative overhead declines with increasing organizational size. Large-scale operations make it possible to realize economies in managerial manpower. This can be explained in terms of the generalization that the number of structural components increases at a declining rate with increasing size (1), which implies that the *size* of work groups under a supervisor, just as that of most personnel components, increases with increasing size, and that the *proportion* of supervisors, just as that of most personnel components, decreases with increasing size, and these relationships account for the economy of scale in management.

A final derived proposition in this set is that the economy of scale in administrative overhead itself declines with increasing organizational size (1.6). This proposition follows from two parts of the basic generalization (1A and 1C) in conjunction with one derived proposition (1.3). If the number of structural components increases with increasing organizational size (1A), the statistical expectation is that the proportionate size of any particular personnel component decreases with size (1.3). The empirical data showed that the proportion of managerial personnel and that of staff personnel do in fact decrease as size increases, in accordance with these expectations. But since the increase in the number of components with expanding size occurs at a declining rate (1C), the decrease in the proportionate size of the average component, implicit in this increase in number, must also occur at a declining rate with expanding organizational size. Reformulation in terms of statistical probability yields the proposition that chance expectations are that the proportionate size of any particular personnel complement decreases at a decelerating rate as organizations become larger.

Whether this statistical proposition about most personnel components holds true for the managerial and the staff component is an empirical question, and the answer is that it does. The proportion of staff personnel decreases at a declining rate as organizational size increases (see Figure 3), and so does the proportion of managerial personnel at the agency headquarters as well as in local offices (see Figure 4). The marginal power of organizational size to produce economies in administrative overhead diminishes with growing size, just as its marginal power to generate structural differentiation does. Both of these patterns are implied by the generalization that the number of structural components in an organization increases at a declining rate with expanding size.

TRANSITION

The structure of formal organizations seems to undergo repeated social fission with growth. In a large organization, its broad responsibilities tend to be subdivided to facilitate their performance, and it thereby becomes differentiated into a number of structural components of diverse sorts. The larger an organization, however, the larger is typically not only the number but also the average size of the components into which it is differentiated. These larger segments of larger organizations, in turn, tend to become internally differentiated along various lines. Thus, the process of social fission recurs within the differentiated units which that process produced. Differentiation lessens the difficulties the performance of duties entails by reducing the scope of the responsibilities assigned to any individual or unit, but it simultaneously enhances the complexity of the structure. Social fission makes duties less complex at the expense of greater structural complexity.

When responsibilities become extensively subdivided, many employees will have the same duties and entire units will have similar ones, and savings in supervisory manpower may occur. At the same time, however, the greater structural complexity implicit in the pronounced subdivision of large organizations intensifies problems of communication and coordination, which make new demands on the time of managers and supervisors at all levels. In short, the very differentiation of responsibilities through which large organizations facilitate the performance of duties and reduce the need for supervision creates fresh administrative problems for supervisory person-

FIGURE 3 SIZE OF AGENCY AND PERCENT STAFF PERSONNEL

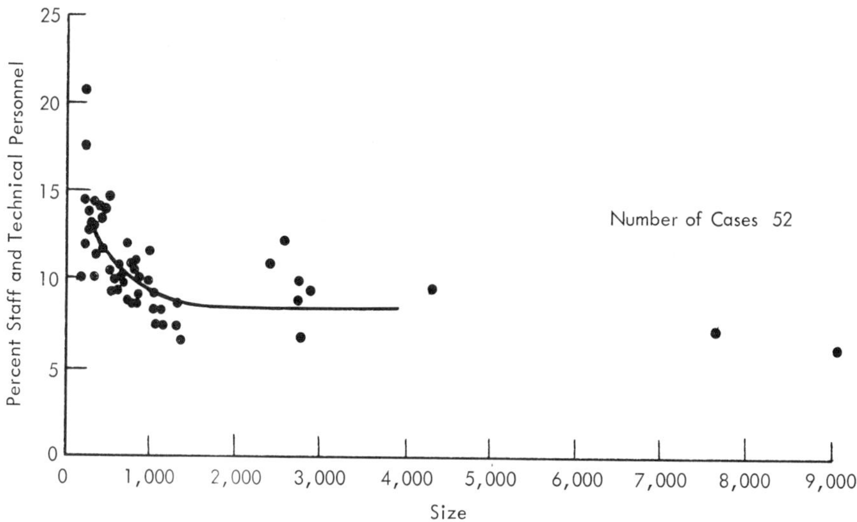

nel. The theory presented so far accounts for the effect of size on savings in supervisory manpower (1.4, 1.5) as well as for its effect on differentiation (1A), but it does not yet include an explicit proposition concerning the effect of differentiation on supervision and administration.

To be sure, the analysis of the proposition that the marginal influence of an organization's size on differentiation declines with increasing size (1.1) has already led to the inference that differentiation intensifies administrative problems. The assumption is that the problems of coordination and communication in differentiated structures have feedback effects that create resistance to further differentiation, which is the reason why the marginal influence of size on differentiation declines with increasing size. The expanding size of an organization is a social force that produces differentiation. The more differentiated an organization is, according to this interpretation, the more resistance a force must overcome to produce still more differentiation, and the more of an expansion in size it therefore takes to effect a given increment in differentiation.

This interpretation seeks to explain the decel-

FIGURE 4 SIZE OF LOCAL OFFICE AND PERCENT SUPERVISORY PERSONNEL

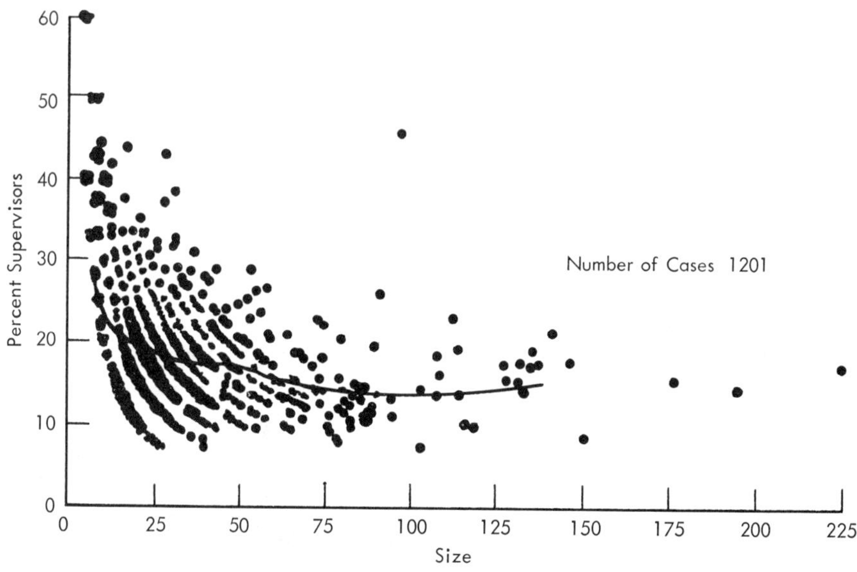

erating rate at which increasing size generates differentiation in organizations, but it cannot be logically deduced from the propositions referring to this decelerating rate. It is important in this connection to keep in mind the distinction between inferring a higher-order generalization from a lower-order proposition, in an inductive argument, and logically deriving a lower-order from a higher-order proposition, in deductive reasoning. What is logically implied by the generalization that the rate of differentiation declines with expanding size (1C), as well as by the derived proposition that the marginal influence of increasing size on differentiation diminishes (1.1), is that differentiation gives rise to *some* problems and needs that stifle the further development of differentiation, as indicated by the decreasing power of size to effect differentiation. It does not follow, though it is a plausible inference, that these are problems of coordination and communication calling for administrative solutions. Hence, another basic generalization is postulated incorporating these ideas, which explains some of the propositions in the first set, and which in conjunction with earlier propositions yields three more derived propositions.

SECOND GENERALIZATION

Structural differentiation in organizations enlarges the administrative component (2), because the intensified problems of coordination and communication in differentiated structures demand administrative attention. In this second fundamental generalization of the deductive theory, the first part subsumes many empirical findings, whereas the second part introduces theoretical terms not independently measured in the research but inferred. The assumptions are that differentiation makes an organization more complex; that a complex structure engenders problems of communication and coordination; that these problems create resistance to further differentiation; that managers, the staff, and even first-line supervisors spend time dealing with these problems; and that consequently more supervisory and administrative manpower is needed in highly differentiated structures than in less differentiated structures. Although these assumptions of the intervening connections are not empirically tested, the implications of the conclusion are. If, in accordance with the inferred assumptions, much of the time of supervisors on all levels in the most differentiated structures is occupied with problems of communication and coordination, it follows that these supervisors have less time left for guiding and reviewing the work of subordinates.

Hence, the more differentiated the formal structure, the more administrative personnel of all kinds should be found in an organization of a given size, and the narrower the span of control of first-line supervisors as well as higher managers. This is precisely the pattern the empirical findings reveal. Vertical differentiation into levels and horizontal differentiation into divisions or sections are both positively related to the proportion of supervisors among the total personnel, controlling size, in the whole organization, in local branches, and in the six functional types of headquarters divisions. They are also positively related to the proportionate size of the staff in agencies of a given size.

Moreover, both vertical and horizontal differentiation, with size held constant, are negatively related to the span of control of managers and supervisors on different levels in local offices and in headquarters divisions, regardless of function.[12] The finding that the second generalization and its derivations discussed below are supported when the span of control of supervisors on a given level is substituted for the ratio of all supervisors is of special importance. The more levels organizations of a given size have, the larger is necessarily the proportion of their supervisors, that is, of their personnel above the lowest level. The positive relationship of number of levels with proportion of supervisors does not merely reflect this mathematical nexus, which would make it trivial, as demonstrated by its positive relationship with supervisory span of control, which is not affected by this nexus. Hence, the empirical data support the principle that hierarchical as well as horizontal differentiation, presumably by engendering problems of coordination, enlarges requirements for managerial manpower.

PROPOSITIONS 2.1 AND 2.2

One derived proposition is that the large size of an organization indirectly raises the ratio of administrative personnel through the structural differentiation it generates (2.1). If increasing organizational size generates differentiation (1A), and if differentiation increases the administrative component (2), it follows that the indirect effect of size must be to increase the administrative component. Decomposi-

[12] This statement and those in the preceding paragraph are based on a multiple regression analyses with size (log) and a number of other conditions controlled; two or three measures of differentiation as the independent variables (levels, divisions, and sections per division in agencies; levels and sections in local offices and in divisions); and the following dependent variables: for agencies, managerial ratio and staff ratio; for local offices, managerial ratio, span of control of office manager, and mean span of control of first-line supervisors; for the six types of divisions, managerial ratio, span of control of division head, mean span of control of middle managers, and mean span of control of firstline supervisors.

tion of the zero-order correlations of size with various ratios of managerial and staff personnel in multiple regression analysis makes it possible to isolate the indirect effects of size mediated by differentiation from its direct effects. In every problem analyzed, the empirical findings confirm the prediction that the indirect effects of size mediated by both vertical differentiation into levels and horizontal differentiation into divisions or sections raise the ratio of administrative to total personnel. This is the case whether the dependent variable under consideration is the staff ratio or the managerial ratio at the agency headquarters; the ratio of supervisors on all levels; or the span of control of first-line supervisors in any of the six types of functional divisions or in local branches. In all these instances, the indirect effects of size mediated by the differentiation it generates and its direct effects are in opposite directions. The savings in administrative overhead large-scale operations make possible are counteracted by the expansion in administrative overhead the structural complexity of large organizations necessitates.

Another derived proposition is that the direct effects of large organizational size lowering the administrative ratio exceed its indirect effects raising it owing to the structural differentiation it generates (2.2). This is a logical consequence of propositions (1.5) and (2.1). If the overall effect of large size reduces management overhead (1.5), and if large size, by fostering differentiation, indirectly increases management overhead (2.1), it follows that its effect of reducing overhead must outweigh this indirect effect. All the decompositions of the zero-order correlations of size with various measures of management reflect this, as they inevitably must. For example, the direct effect of agency size on the managerial ratio at the agency headquarters, which is represented by the standardized regression coefficient when three measures of differentiation are controlled, is −1.13, whereas its overall effect, indicated by the zero-order correlation, is −.45, the difference being due to the strong counteracting effect mediated by differentiation.[13] For the staff ratio at the agency, with the same conditions controlled, the direct effect of size is −1.04, and its overall effect is −.60, revealing again a substantial indirect counteracting effect due to structural differentiation. The direct and indirect effect of the size of a division on its managerial ratio and of the size of a local office on its managerial ratio reveal parallel differences.[14]

Ceteris paribus, a large scale of operations would effect tremendous savings in administrative overhead, but these savings are much reduced by the structural differentiation of large organizations. Consistently, however, the economies of scale exceed the costs of differentiation, so that large organizations, despite their greater structural complexity, require proportionately less administrative manpower than small ones.

PROPOSITION 2.3

The last proposition to be derived is that the differentiation of large organizations into subunits stems the decline in the economy of scale in management with increasing size, that is, the decline in the decrease in the proportion of managerial personnel with increasing size (2.3). The derivation of this proposition is rather complicated and must be approached in several steps. The new proposition is not as well knit into the system as the others and should be regarded as a mere conjecture.

The concept of economy of scale in administration refers to the fact that the proportion of various kinds of administrative personnel decreases with the increasing size of the organization or its subunits. The operational indication is a negative correlation between any of these proportions and size, which is represented on a graph by a negative slope of the regression line of the proportion on size. These negative correlations and slopes are evident in all empirical data on employment security agencies: size of local branch and either proportion of all managerial personnel or ratio of first-line supervisors to operating employees (the reverse of span of control); size of functional division and either ratio of all managerial personnel or ratio of supervisors to subordinates on three levels; size of total agency and either proportion of staff personnel, or proportion of managerial personnel at the headquarters, or proportion of managerial personnel in the total organization.

A decline in this economy of scale means that the *rate of decrease* in the ratio of managerial personnel itself *decreases* with increasing size. This is reflected

[13] The three aspects of differentiation controlled in this problem, as well as in the one mentioned in the next sentence, are number of *(a)* levels, *(b)* divisions, and *(c)* sections per division.

[14] In the multiple regression analysis for all divisions combined (with sections, levels, clerical ratio, division of labor, agency size, and agency managerial ratio controlled), the standardized regression coefficient indicating the direct effect of a division's size (log) on its managerial ratio is −1.32, and the zero-order correlation indicative of the overall effect is only −.23, with differentiation into levels (.65) and sections (.35) being responsible for most of the difference. The separate regression analyses for the six types yield parallel results. In the analysis of local offices (with levels, sections, specialization, manager's span of control, and division of labor controlled), the standardized regression coefficient of office size (log) on the managerial ratio is −1.43, but this incredibly strong direct effect is reduced to a still substantial overall effect, represented by the zero-order correlation, of −.64, most of the reduction being due to differentiation into levels (.41) and sections (.40).

FIGURE 5 SIZE OF AGENCY AND PERCENT SUPERVISORY PERSONNEL IN TOTAL AGENCY

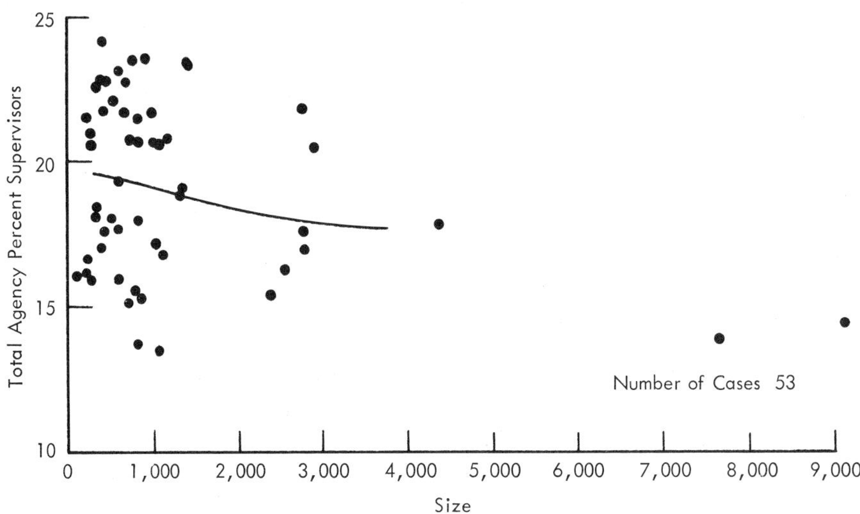

on a graph by a curve in the negative slope of the regression line of the ratio on size that shows that the ratio of overhead personnel drops first sharply and then more gradually with increasing size. The percent of supervisors in local offices illustrates a decrease at such a decreasing rate (Figure 4), and so does the ratio of staff personnel in the agency (Figure 3) and that of the supervisors at the agency headquarters (not shown), and the same pattern is observable in most other relationships mentioned in the above paragraph. The major exception is that the proportion of managerial personnel in the total agency does not reveal such a declining rate of decrease but a fairly linear decrease with increasing agency size, as Figure 5 shows. Although this appears to be a deviant case, the principle it expresses can be deduced from the propositions in the theory.

In local offices, the smallest organizational unit examined, the proportion of all supervisory personnel drops rapidly as size increases from ten, or fewer, to about fifty employees, but it drops much more slowly with further increases to one and two hundred employees (see Figure 4). From a projection of this trend, one would expect that further increases in size to several thousand employees are hardly accompanied by any decline in the proportion of supervisory personnel. As the size of the entire organization increases from about one hundred to several thousand employees, however, the total proportion of supervisory personnel decreases on the average at a constant rather than declining rate, as Figure 5 reveals, though there is much scatter. Although this decline is not pronounced, it is by no means inconsequential; the zero-order correlation is —.34, which compares with a correlation of —.46 between size of office and its proportion of supervisors. (However, the latter correlation is raised to —.64 if size is logarithmically transformed: In contrast, the former correlation is reduced to —.23 by such a transformation, which is another indication that the regression line does not exhibit a logarithmic curve.) Why does the decrease in the proportion of managerial personnel with increasing size, which is already very small as office size expands beyond fifty employees, not become virtually zero but is again considerable as agency size expands from several hundred to several thousand? The answer suggested by the theory is that the differentiation of large organizations into many branch offices (and divisions), while raising the proportion of managers needed, simultaneously restores the economy of scale in the managerial component, that is, it recreates the decline in the proportion of managerial personnel with increasing size observed among very small organizational units.

The growing need for managerial manpower resulting from the structural differentiation engendered by expanding size (2.1) increasingly impinges upon the savings in managerial manpower that a large scale of operations realizes (1.5), which helps to explain why the economy of scale in management declines as size and differentiation increase (1.6).[15] In other words, the *rate* of savings in management overhead with increasing size is higher among comparatively small than among comparatively large organizational units, although, or perhaps because, the management overhead is bigger in small than in large organizational units. Differentiation in a large organization (1A) means that it consists of relatively many smaller rather than relatively few larger organizational subunits, such as local offices. Inasmuch as the *rate* of savings in management overhead is higher in smaller than in larger organizational units, the reduction in the size of units created by differentiation raises this rate of savings and stems the decline in the economy of scale with respect to management overhead that would be otherwise expected once organizations have grown beyond a certain size (2.3).

CONCLUSIONS

A formal theory of the formal structure of formal organizations has been presented. Its subject is formally established organizations with paid employees, not emergent social systems or voluntary associations of people. It is confined to the analysis of the formal structure—specifically, its differentiation—of organizations, ignoring the informal relations and behavior of individuals within these organizations. And the endeavor has been to develop a formal theory by inferring from many empirical findings a minimum number of generalizations that can logically account for these findings. These findings come from a quantitative study of all employment security agencies and their subunits in the United States. The two basic generalizations, from which nine other propositions were deduced, are: (1) the increasing size of organizations generates structural differentiation along various dimensions at decelerating rates; and (2) structural differentiation enlarges the administrative component in organizations.

The concluding review of the theory rearranges the order of presentation of propositions to call attention to alternative connections between them and to some of the unmeasured terms assumed to underlie these connections. Organizing the work of men means subdividing it into component elements. In a formal organization, explicit procedures exist for systematically subdividing the work necessary to achieve its objectives. Different tasks are assigned to different positions; specialized functions are allocated to various divisions and sections; branches may be created in dispersed locations; administrative responsibilities are subdivided among staff personnel and managers on various hierarchical levels. The larger an organization and the scope of its responsibilities, the more pronounced is its differentiation along these lines (1A, 1B), and the same is the case for its subunits (1D). But large-scale operations, despite the greater subdivision of tasks than in small scale operations—involve a larger volume of most organizational tasks. Hence, large organizations tend to have larger as well as more structural components of various sorts than small organizations (1.2).

The pronounced differentiation of responsibilities in large organizations enhances simultaneously intra-unit homogeneity and inter-unit heterogeneity. Inasmuch as duties are more differentiated and the amount of work required in most specialties is greater in large organizations than in small ones, there are comparatively many employees performing homogeneous tasks in large organizations. The large homogeneous personnel components in large organizations simplify supervision and administration, which is reflected in a wider span of control of supervisors (1.4) and a lower administrative ratio (1.3) in large than in small organizations. Consequently, organizations exhibit an economy of scale in administrative manpower (1.5). At the same time, however, the heterogeneity among organizational components produced by differentiation creates problems of coordination and pressures to expand the administrative personnel to meet these problems (2). In this formulation, the unmeasured concepts of intra-unit homogeneity and inter-unit heterogeneity have been introduced to explain why large size has two opposite effects on administrative overhead, reducing it owing to the enlarged scale of similar tasks, and raising it owing to the differentiation among parts.

By generating differentiation, then, large size indirectly raises administrative overhead (2.1), and if its influence on differentiation were unrestrained, large organizations might well have disproportionately large administrative machineries, in accordance with the bureaucratic stereotype. However, the administrative ratio decreases with expanding organizational size, notwithstanding the increased administrative ratio resulting from the differentiation in large organizations (2.2). Two feedback effects of the administrative costs of differentiation may be inferred, which counteract the influences of size on administration and differentiation, respectively. The first of these apparently reduces the savings in administrative manpower resulting from a large scale of operations, as implied by the decline in the rate of decrease of administrative overhead with increasing organizational size (1.6). (Although differentiation into local branches may keep the rate of overhead savings with increasing size constant (2.3), it also raises the amount of overhead.) The second feedback process, probably attributable to the administrative problems engendered by differentiation, creates resistance to further differentiation, which is reflected in the diminishing marginal influence of expanding size on differentiation (1.1) and the declining rate at which size promotes differentiation (1C).

In short, feedback processes seem to keep the amount of differentiation produced by increasing

---

[15] This alternative derivation of proposition (1.6) illustrates the type of crosswise connections that creates a more closely knit theoretical system. Other alternative connections are presented in the conclusions.

FIGURE 6 CHART OF CONNECTIONS

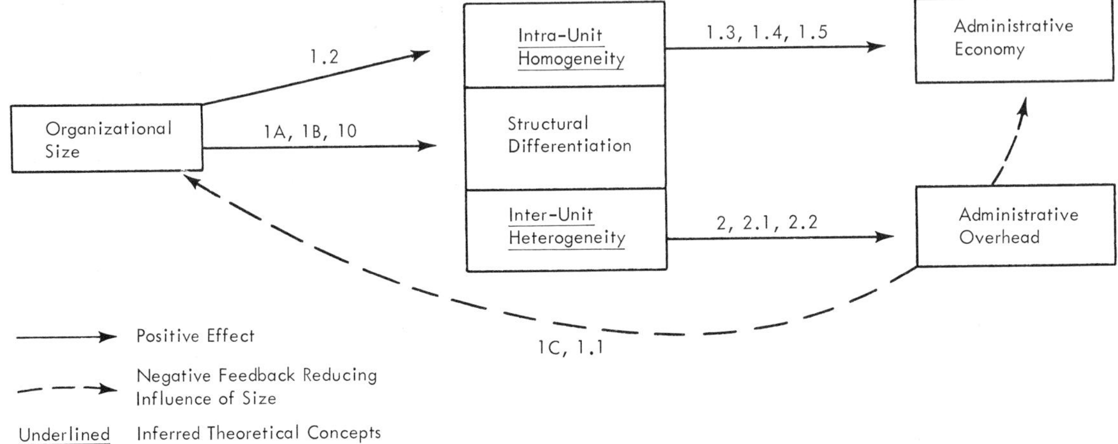

organizational size below the level at which the additional administrative costs of coordination would equal the administrative savings realized by the larger scale of operations. Hence, organizations exhibit an economy of scale in administration, despite the extra administrative overhead required by the pronounced differentiation in large organizations, but this economy of scale declines with increasing size, on account of this extra overhead due to differentiation. The feedback effects inferred, though not directly observable, can explain why the influence of size on differentiation, as well as its influence on administrative economy, declines with increasing size. Figure 6 presents these connections graphically.

A final question to be raised is how widely applicable the theory is to organizations of different types. Since the theory was constructed by trying to formulate generalizations from which the empirical findings on employment security agencies can be derived, the fact that these data conform to the propositions advanced does not constitute a test of the theory. But it should be noted that several of the specific propositions included in the theory are supported by findings from previous empirical studies of other kinds of organizations, for example, that administrative overhead in organizations decreases with size and increases with complexity or differentiation (see Anderson & Warkov, 1961; Pondy, 1969, and references therein), and that its decrease with size occurs at a declining rate (Indik, 1964). Moreover, an empirical test of the entire body of theory has been conducted in a study of another type of government bureau, the 416 major finance departments of American states, large cities, and large counties. This independent test confirms the propositions implied by the theory.[16] Whether the theoretical generalizations are also valid for private and other public organizations, and how they must be modified or refined to make them widely applicable, only further research can tell.

REFERENCES

Anderson, Theodore R. and Warkov Seymour. Organizational size and functional complexity. *American Sociological Review*, 26, 23–28.

Blau, Peter M. Structural effects. *American Sociological Review*, 1960, 25, 178–93.

Blau, Peter M. and Schoenherr, Richard A. *The structure of organizations.* New York: Basic Books, in press.

Boulding, Kenneth E. *Economic analysis.* (3d ed.). New York: Harper, 1955.

Braithwaite, Richard B. *Scientific explanation.* Cambridge (England): University Press, 1953.

Hempel, Carl G. and Oppenheim, Paul. The logic of explanation. *Philosophy of Science*, 1948, 15, 135–75.

Indik, Bernard P. The relationship between organization

[16] The number of occupational positions, that of hierarchical levels, and that of functional divisions in these finance departments increases at decelerating rates with increasing size, as indicated by regression lines with positive slopes and logarithmic curves (1, 1.1, 1.2, 1.3). The span of control of first-line supervisors is positively correlated with size (1.4), which implies that the supervisory ratio decreases with size (1.5), and this relationship reveals a logarithmic curve, indicating that the economy of scale in supervisory manpower declines with size (1.6). The numbers of levels and that of divisions both raise the ratio of supervisors to nonsupervisory personnel (2), and large size indirectly does so through its influences on levels and divisions (2.1), but these indirect effects of size are exceeded by its direct effect reducing the ratio of supervisors by widening their span of control (2.2). The absence of local branches in finance departments makes it impossible to test proposition (2.3).

size and supervision ratio. *Administrative Science Quarterly,* 1964, 9, 301–12.

Kaplan, Abraham. *The conduct of inquiry.* San Francisco: Chandler, 1964.

Pondy, Louis R. Effects of size, complexity, and ownership on administrative intensity. *Administrative Science Quarterly,* 1969, 14, 47–60.

Popper, Karl R. *The logic of scientific discovery.* New York: Basic Books, 1959.

Weber, Max. *Essays in sociology.* New York: Oxford University Press, 1946.

Weber, Max. *The theory of social and economic organization.* New York: Oxford University Press, 1947.

28. A FRAMEWORK FOR THE COMPARATIVE ANALYSIS OF ORGANIZATIONS*

Charles Perrow†

This paper presents a perspective on organizations that hopefully will provide a basis for comparative organizational analysis, and also allow one to utilize selectively the existing theories of organizational behavior. There are four characteristics of this perspective.

First, technology, or the work done in organizations, is considered the defining characteristic of organizations. That is, organizations are seen primarily as systems for getting work done, for applying techniques to the problem of altering raw materials —whether the materials be people, symbols or things. This is in contrast to other perspectives which see organizations as, for example, cooperative systems, institutions, or decision-making systems.

Second, this perspective treats technology as an independent variable, and structure—the arrangements among people for getting work done—as a dependent variable. Goals are conceived of as being in part a dependent variable. What is held to be an independent and dependent variable when one abstracts general variables from a highly interdependent and complex social system is less of an assertion about reality than a strategy of analysis. Thus, no claim is made that for all purposes technology need be an independent variable.

Third, this perspective attempts to conceptualize the organization as a whole, rather than to deal only with specific processes or subparts. Thus, while the importance of technology has often been demonstrated within work groups or for particular organizational processes, here it will be used as a basis for dealing with the organization as an organization.

Finally, and in the long run perhaps most importantly, the perspective holds that technology is a better basis for comparing organizations than the several schemes which now exist.[1]

None of these points in itself is new, and the last section of this article discusses the uses to which the concept of technology has been put by others. However, the attempt to deal with all four points simultaneously, or, to put it differently, to pay systematic attention to the role of technology in analyzing and comparing organizations as a whole, is believed to be distinctive.

Technology and Raw Materials

By technology is meant the actions that an individual performs upon an object, with or without the aid of tools or mechanical devices, in order to make some change in that object. The object, or "raw material," may be a living being, human or otherwise, a symbol or an inanimate object. People are raw materials in people-changing or people-processing organizations; symbols are materials in banks, advertising agencies and some research organizations; the interactions of people are raw materials to be manipulated by administrators in organizations; boards of directors, committees and councils are usually

* Reprinted from *American Sociological Review,* Vol. 32, No. 2 (April 1967), pp. 194–208.

Revision of a paper read at the 1966 Annual Meeting of the American Sociological Association. This paper was prepared during the course of research on industrial corporations supported by Grant No. GS-742, National Science Foundation. Numerous colleagues criticized an earlier version unstintingly, but I would like to single out Ernest Vargas, Geoffrey Guest and Anthony Kovner, who transcended their graduate student roles at the University of Pittsburgh during the formulation of these ideas in sticky field situations.

† State University of New York at Stony Brook and London Graduate School of Business Studies, London, England.

[1] E.g., social function (schools, business firms, hospitals, etc.), as used by Talcott Parsons in *Structure and process in modern society* (Glencoe, Ill.: The Free Press, 1960), pp. 44–47; who benefits, proposed by Peter M. Blau and William R. Scott in *Formal organizations* (San Francisco: Chandler, 1962), pp. 42–45; or compliance structure, as used by Amitai Etzioni. *A comparative analysis of complex organizations* (New York: The Free Press, 1961).

FIGURE 1 TECHNOLOGY VARIABLE (industrial example)

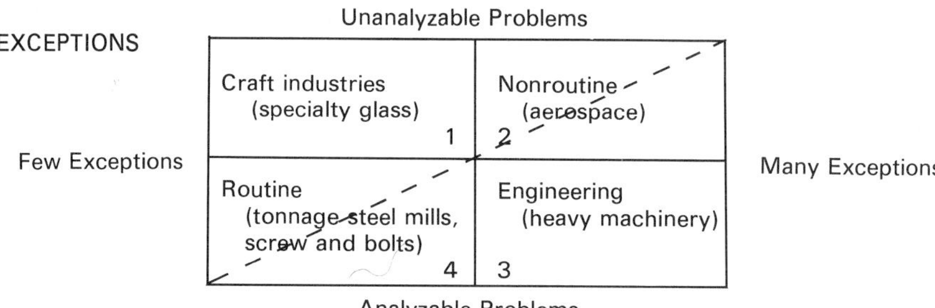

involved with the changing or processing of symbols and human interactions, and so on.

In the course of changing this material in an organizational setting, the individual must interact with others. The form that this interaction takes we will call the structure of the organization. It involves the arrangements or relationships that permit the coordination and control of work. Some work is actually concerned with changing or maintaining the structure of an organization. Most administrators have this as a key role, and there is a variety of technologies for it. The distinction between technology and structure has its gray areas, but basically it is the difference between an individual acting directly upon a material that is to be changed and an individual interacting with other individuals in the course of trying to change that material. In some cases the material to be changed and the "other individuals" he interacts with are the same objects, but the relationships are different in each case.

There are a number of aspects of technology which are no doubt important to consider in some contexts, such as the environment of the work (noise, dirt, etc.) or the possibilities of seductive or exploitative relationships with clients, patients or customers. For our purposes, however, we are concerned with two aspects of technology that seem to be directly relevant to organizational structure. The first is the number of exceptional cases encountered in the work,[2] that is, the degree to which stimuli are perceived as familiar or unfamiliar. This varies on a scale from low to high.

The second is the nature of the search process that is undertaken by the individual when exceptions occur. We distinguish two types of search process. The first type involves a search which can be conducted on a logical, analytical basis. Search processes are always exceptional actions undertaken by the individual. They are nonroutine. No programs exist for them. If a program exists, only a very trivial search is involved in switching from one program to another program when the stimuli change.[3] But though nonroutine, one type of search may be logical, systematic and analytical. This is exemplified by the mechanical engineering unit of a firm building large machinery, or by programmers writing individual programs for slow readers in a special school. The second type of search process occurs when the problem is so vague and poorly conceptualized as to make it virtually unanalyzable. In this case, no "formal" search is undertaken, but instead one draws upon the residue of unanalyzed experience or intuition, or relies upon chance and guesswork. Examples would be work with exotic metals or nuclear fuels, psychiatric casework, and some kinds of advertising. We can conceive of a scale from analyzable to unanalyzable problems.

If we dichotomize these two continua into the presence or absence of exceptional cases and into the presence or absence of analyzable problems, we have a four-fold table as in Figure 1. The upper right-hand quadrant, cell 2, where there are many exceptional cases and a few analytic techniques for analyzing them, is one extreme to which we will refer as nonroutine. In the lower lefthand quadrant, cell 4, we have the routine extreme, where there are few exceptions and there are analytic techniques for handling those that occur. A one-dimensional scheme would follow the dotted line from routine to nonroutine. But note that the other two quadrants may represent viable cases in themselves and they have been labeled with some industrial examples. Few cases would probably fall in the upper left-hand corner of cell 1, or lower right-hand corner of cell 3, but otherwise many organizations are expected to appear in these two cells.

Techniques are performed upon raw materials.

[2] Cf. James March and Herbert Simon, *Organizations* (New York: Wiley, 1958), pp. 141–42, where a related distinction is made on the basis of search behavior. In our view the occurrence of an exceptional case is prior to search behavior, and various types of search behavior can be distinguished.

[3] Ibid., p. 142.

The state of the art of analyzing the characteristics of the raw materials is likely to determine what kind of technology will be used. (Tools are also necessary, of course, but by and large, the construction of tools is a simpler problem than the analysis of the nature of the material and generally follows the analysis.) To understand the nature of the material means to be able to control it better and achieve more predictability and efficiency in transformation. We are not referring here to the "essence" of the material, only to the way the organization itself perceives it.

The other relevant characteristic of the raw material, besides the understandability of its nature, is its stability and variability; that is, whether the material can be treated in a standardized fashion or whether continual adjustment to it is necessary. Organizations uniformly seek to standardize their raw material in order to minimize exceptional situations. This is the point of de-individualizing processes found in military academies, monasteries and prisons, or the superiority of the synthetic shoe material Corfam over leather.

These two characteristics interact, of course. On the one hand, increased knowledge of the nature of the material may lead to the perception of more varieties of possible outcomes or products, which in turn increases the need for more intimate knowledge of the nature of the material. Or the organization, with increased knowledge of one type of material, may begin to work with a variety of related materials about which more needs to be known, as when a social service agency or employment agency relaxes its admission criteria as it gains confidence, but in the process sets off more search behavior, or when a manufacturing organization starts producing new but related products. On the other hand, if increased knowledge of the material is gained but no expansion of the variety of output occurs, this permits easier analysis of the sources of problems that may arise in the transformation process. It may also allow one to prevent the rise of such problems by the design of the production process.

A recent analysis of a public defender system by Sudnow highlights the twin characteristics of the material variable.[4] On the one hand, offenders are distributed into uniform categories by means of the conception of the "normal crime," and on the other hand, control over the individual offender is insured because the public defender well understands the offender's "nature"—that is, his low status, limited understanding and intellectual resources, and his impecunious condition. The technology, then, can be routine because there are few exceptions (and these are handled by a different set of personnel) and no search behavior on the public defender's part is required. The lawyer in private practice, of course, is a contrasting case.[5]

It will readily be seen that these two characteristics of the raw material are paralleled in the fourfold table of technology (Figure 2). If the technology of an organization is going to move from cell 2 to any of the other cells, it can only do so either by reducing the variability of the material and thus the number of exceptional cases that occur, or by increasing the knowledge of the material and thus allowing more analytic techniques to be used, or both. One may move from cell 2 to cell 1 with increasing production runs, clients served, accounts handled, research projects underway, agency programs administered and so forth, since this allows more experience to be gained and thus reduces the number of stimuli seen as exceptions. If technical knowledge increases, increasing the reliability of search procedures, one

[4] David Sudnow. Normal crimes: Sociological features of the penal code in a public defender office, *Social Problems,* 12 (Winter 1965), pp. 255–276.

[5] For a more extensive treatment of raw material somewhat along these lines, see David Street, Robert Vinter and Charles Perrow. *Organization for treatment, A comparative study of institutions for delinquents* (New York: The Free Press, 1966), Chap. 1.

FIGURE 2 RAW MATERIAL VARIABLES (people-changing examples)

PERCEIVED NATURE OF RAW MATERIAL

VARIABILITY OF MATERIAL

	Not Well Understood		
Perceived as Uniform and Stable	Socializing Institutions (e.g. some schools) 1	Elite psychiatric agency 2	Perceived as Non-uniform and Stable
	Custodial Institutions vocational training 4	Programmed learning school 3	
	Well Understood		

may move from cell 2 to cell 3. If both things happen —and this is the aim of most organizations—one may move from cell 2 to cell 4.[6]

TASK AND SOCIAL STRUCTURE

For our purpose, the task structure of an organization is conceived of as consisting of two dimensions, control and coordination. Control itself can be broken up into two components. They are the degree of discretion an individual or group possesses in carrying out its tasks, and the power of an individual or group to mobilize scarce resources and to control definitions of various situations, such as the definition of the nature of the raw material. Discretion here does not mean freedom from supervision or freedom simply to vary task sequences or pace of work. Both of these are compatible with routine activities, and some nonroutine tasks must be closely supervised or have precise sequences of tasks, once a program is selected, because of their critical nature. Nor does the length of time between performance reviews[7] necessarily indicate discretion. Rather, discretion involves judgments about whether close supervision is required on one task or another, about changing programs, and about the interdependence of one's task with other tasks.[8] Discretion and power may often be correlated,[9] but there is an important distinction. Power affects outcomes directly because it involves choices regarding basic goals and strategies. Discretion relates to choices among means and judgments of the critical and interdependent nature of tasks. The consequences of decisions in the case of discretion have no direct influence on goals and strategies; these decisions are formed within the framework of accepted goals and strategies.

Coordination, on the other hand, can be achieved through planning or feedback, to use the terms proposed by March and Simon.[10] Coordination by planning refers to the programmed interaction of tasks, which interaction is clearly defined by rules or by the very tools and machinery or the logic of the transformation process. Coordination by feedback, on the other hand, refers to negotiated alterations in the nature or sequence of tasks performed by two different units.

It is now necessary to distinguish three functional or task areas within management in organizations. Area One, the design and planning function, entails such major decisions as what goods or services are to be produced, who the customers will be, the technology employed, and the source of legitimacy and capital. Area Two, the technical control and support of production and marketing, includes such functions (to use industrial terms) as accounting, product and process research, quality control, scheduling, engineering, plant management, purchasing, customer service, advertising, market research, and general sales management. (Not all are important, or even existent, of course, in all industrial organizations.) This is distinguished as a function, though not necessarily in terms of actual persons or positions, from Area Three, the supervision of production and marketing. This area involves the direct supervision of those dealing with the basic raw materials and those doing direct selling.[11] In the subsequent discussion we shall ignore marketing, and, for a time, Area One.

Figure 3 shows crudely the kinds of values that might be expected to appear in the task structure, considering only Areas Two and Three—technical control and support of production, and the supervision of production. Some global organizational characterizations of structure are given at the bottom of each cell. Those familiar with Burns and Stalker's work will recognize cell 2 as closest to the organic structure and cell 4 as closest to the mechanistic structure.[12]

In cell 2, we have nonuniform raw materials in both areas which are not well understood, and thus

---

[6] Some organizations, such as mental hospitals, perceive that their technology is inadequate to their goals, and try to move from cell 4 to cell 2 in the search for a new technology.

[7] Eliot Jaques. *The measurement of responsibility* (Cambridge, Mass.: Harvard University Press, 1959).

[8] This raises serious operationalization problems. In my own work, first-line supervisors were said to have considerable independence in some routine production situations, and to have little in some nonroutine situations, according to a questionnaire, though it was observed that the former had little discretion and the latter a good deal. Kovner found the same kind of responses with a similar question regarding control of job and pace of work among nurses in routine and nonroutine nursing units. See Anthony Kovner. The nursing unit: A technological perspective, unpublished Ph.D. dissertation, University of Pittsburgh, 1966. See also the discrepancy between scores on a similar matter resulting from different interpretations of discretion in two studies: Rose L. Coser. Authority and decisionmaking in a hospital, *American Sociological Review,* 23 (February 1958), pp. 56–64, and James L. Hawkins and Eugene Selmanoff. Authority structure, ambiguity of the medical task, absence of doctor from the ward, and the behavior of nurses, Indiana University, mimeo.

[9] See, for example, a developmental scheme which holds that critical tasks requiring considerable discretion are the basis for group domination in hospitals and other organizations, in Charles Perrow. Analysis of goals in complex organizations, *American Sociological Review,* 26 (April 1961), pp. 335–41. See also the compelling illustration presented in the discussion of maintenance personnel in a thoroughly routinized cigarette factory by Michel Crozier. *The bureaucratic phenomenon* (Chicago: University of Chicago Press, 1964), chap. 4.

[10] March and Simon, *Organizations,* p. 160.

[11] The distinction between Areas Two and Three is based upon a more limited distinction used by Joan Woodward in her brilliant study, *Industrial organization* (London: Oxford University Press, 1965).

[12] Tom Burns and G. M. Stalker. *The management of innovation* (London: Tavistock Publications, 1961).

FIGURE 3 TASK STRUCTURE (task-related interactions)

	Discretion	*Power*	*Coordination within Groups*	*Interdependence of Groups*	*Discretion*	*Power*	*Coordination within Groups*	*Interdependence of Groups*
Technical	Low	Low	Plan	Low	High	High	Feed	High
Supervision	High	High	Feed		High	High	Feed	
		Decentralized		1	2	Flexible, Polycentralized		
				4	3			
Technical	Low	High	Plan	Low	High	High	Feed	Low
Supervision	Low	Low	Plan		Low	Low	Plan	
		Formal, Centralized				Flexible, Centralized		

present many occasions for exceptional handling. However, the search required cannot be logically conducted, but must involve a high degree of experimentation and "feel." In such a technological situation, the discretion of both those who supervise the transformation of the basic raw material, and those who provide technical help for this process, must be high. The supervisors will request help from technical personnel rather than receive orders from them, or there may not even be a clear line of distinction between the two in terms of persons. That is, the clinical psychologist or the quality control engineer will find himself "on the line" so to speak, dealing directly with patients or exotic metals and working side by side with the supervisors who are nominally of lower status. The power of both groups will be high, and not at the expense of each other. The coordination will be through feedback—that is, considerable mutual adjustment must be made. The interdependence of the two groups will be high. The development of product groups and product managers in industry provides an example, as does the somewhat premature attempt of one correctional institution to utilize a cottage system bringing both clinical and line personnel together with joint responsibility for running autonomous cottages.[13]

In the case of cell 4, uniform stable materials whose relevant nature is perceived as well understood can be handled with few exceptions occurring, and those that do occur can be taken care of with analytical search processes. In such a situation the discretion of both groups is likely to be low. This is a well-programmed production process and there is no need to allow much discretion. Indeed, there is danger in doing so. However, the power of the technical group over the supervisory group is high, for they direct the activities of the supervisors of production on the basis of routine reports generated by the supervisors. Those in Area Three are likely to see those in Area Two as hindrances to their work rather than aides. Coordination can be through planning in both groups, and the interdependence of the two groups is low; it is a directive rather than an interdependent relationship.

Cell 3 represents a variation from either of these extremes, for here, in contrast to cell 2, the existence of many exceptions which require search procedures increases both the power and the discretion of the technical group, which handles these exceptions, at the expense of the supervisory group. The supervisors of production respond to the results of these search processes rather than undertake search themselves. In the case of cell 1, the situation is reversed. Because search cannot be logical and analytical, when the infrequent exceptions occur they are handled by those in closest contact with the production process such as teachers and skilled craftsmen, and there is minimal development of administrative services. Of course, in schools that attempt to do little

[13] Street, *et al., Organization for treatment,* chaps. 5, 6. The organization is called Milton.

FIGURE 4 SOCIAL STRUCTURE (the bases of non-task-related interaction)

Social identity (communal) 1	2 Goal identification (mission, "character" of organization, distinctive competence, etc.)
4 Instrumental identity (job security, pay, protection from arbitrary power)	3 Work or task identification (technical satisfactions)

socialization but simply offer instruction and provide custody, technical (administrative) services grow and we move to cell 2.

Having thus related technology to task structure, let us turn to another aspect of structure—the non-task-related but organizationally relevant interactions of people. We call this the social structure.

Figure 4 follows our previous four-fold classification and indicates the variety of bases for non-task-related interactions. All are present in all organizations, but the saliency varies. In cell 2, these interactions are likely to revolve more around the mission, long-range goals, and direction of development of the organizations than around the other three bases. This is because of the task structure characteristic of a flexible, polycentric organization, or at least is related to it. The category "social identity" in cell 1 is meant to convey that the non-task-related interactions of personnel that are organizationally relevant revolve around communal or personal satisfactions born of long tenure and close working relationships. This is true especially at the supervisory level, which is a large management group in this type of structure. However, it is very possible, as Blauner and others have shown, for communal relations to develop in cell 4 types of organizations if the organization is located in a rural area where kinship and rural ties are strong.[14] The basis of interaction in cell 3 is instrumental identity and in cell 4, work or task identification. These would also be predicted upon the basis of the technology.

So far we have ignored Area One—design and planning. This area receives more inputs from the environment than the other areas, and thus its tasks and technologies are derived from both internal and external stimuli. If the product environment of the organization—a term meant to cover competitors, customers, suppliers, unions and regulatory agencies—were the same in all four cells of Figure 3, we would expect the design and planning areas in cell 4 to have routine tasks and techniques, and nonroutine ones in cell 2. This is because the occasions for design and long-range planning would be few in the one and many in the other. For example, at least until very recently, the decisions that executives in the primary metals industries, railroads and surface mining had to make were probably rather routine, while those of executives in new industries such as electronics and aerospace were probably nonroutine.[15] One would expect that cell 1 would also be routine, and cell 3 somewhat nonroutine. But the product environment can alter all this. Organizations in cell 4 can be in a rapidly changing market situation even though the technical control and the supervision of production are fairly routine. Consumer goods industries probably deal with many decisions where the search behavior confronts unanalyzable problems such as the hemline of women's clothes, fads in the toy industry, or the length of time that tail fins or the boxy look in autos will last. Generally speaking, however, though the intrinsic characteristics of the product remain the same, rapid changes in the extrinsic characteristics will introduce nonroutine tasks in the design and planning area, even though it hardly alters the routine character of the technical control and the supervision of production.[16]

These are industrial examples, but it also seems likely that the tasks of Area One in custodial mental hospitals are quite different from those in treatment-oriented hospitals. Relations with the regulatory agencies, supplying agencies, the consumers such as courts and families, and the other agencies that compete for funds or clients, will be rather routine in the first, while they will be quite nonroutine and sensitive in the second. This would not be true, of course, if the latter have the means of isolating themselves from their environment.[17] Similarly, the market situation of vocational training institutions may change rather quickly as industrial technologies change, requiring changes in the design and planning of the institution, while the market of a public school that attempts to socialize youths will not change as often.

GOALS

Finally, let us turn to the last major variable, goals. Three categories of goals can be distinguished for present purposes.[18] These are system goals,

[14] Robert Blauner. *Alienation and freedom: The factory worker and his industry* (Chicago: University of Chicago Press, 1964), chap. 4. Blauner's theory, incidentally, is entirely consistent with the perspective proposed here, even though we do not concern ourselves explicitly in this article with the morale of hourly employees.

[15] On the former see Alfred D. Chandler, Jr. *Strategy and structure* (Cambridge, Mass.: MIT Press, 1962), pp. 329–330, and chap. 7 in general. The discussion of social structure and time periods by Stinchcombe can be interpreted in this manner also. Those exceptions that occur in his data appear to be examples of nonroutine technologies established in periods of predominantly routine technologies, or *vice versa.* See Arthur Stinchcombe. Social structure and organizations in James March (ed.), *Handbook of organizations* (Chicago: Rand McNally, 1965), pp. 142–69, esp. p. 158.

[16] On the distinction between intrinsic and extrinsic prestige, see Charles Perrow. Organizational prestige, some functions and dysfunctions, *American Journal of Sociology,* 66 (January 1961), pp. 335–41.

[17] Cf. Street, et al., *Organization for treatment,* chap. 4.

[18] For a full discussion of these and three others see Charles Perrow. Organizational goals, *International Encyclopedia of the Social Sciences,* (rev. ed.), forthcoming. (Draft copies, mimeo. 18 pp., can be obtained from the author.)

FIGURE 5 GOALS

System	Product	Derived	System	Product	Derived
Stability Few risks Moderate to low profit emphasis	Quality No innovations	Conservative 1	2 High growth High risks Low emphasis on profit	High quality Innovative	Liberal
Stability Few risks High profit emphasis	Quantity No innovations	4 Conservative	3 Moderate growth Some risks Moderate profit emphasis	Reliability Moderate innovations	Liberal

which relate to the characteristics of the system as a whole, independent of its products; product characteristic goals, which relate to the characteristics of the products the organization decides to emphasize; and derived goals, which refer to the uses to which power generated by organizational activities can be put, independent of system or product goals.

We would expect completely routinized organizations to stress those "system" goals of organizational stability, low risk, and perhaps high profits or economical operations rather than growth. (See Figure 5.) In terms of "product characteristic" goals, they would be more likely to emphasize quantity than quality, stable lines over unstable or diversified lines, superficial transformations (e.g., instilling discipline in deviant clients) over basic transformation (such as character restructuring), and so forth. Their "derived" goals are likely to emphasize conservative attitudes towards the government, conservative political philosophies, conservative forms of corporate giving. Also, they are perhaps more likely to have individuals who exploit, for their own benefit, relations with suppliers, and who have collusive arrangements with competitors and devious and excessive forms of management compensation. Obviously, these comments upon possible goals are open to serious question. For one thing, we lack such data on goals for a large number of organizations. Furthermore, personalities and the environment may shape goals more than the other variables of technology and structure. Finally, the link between structure and goals is an intuitive one, based upon unproven assumptions regarding attitudes generated by task relations. But the comments are meant to suggest how goals may be shaped or constrained, though hardly specified, through the influence of technology and structure.

SOME CAUTIONS

This truncated perspective ignores the role of the cultural and social environment in making available definitions of raw material, providing technologies, and restricting the range of feasible structures and goals.[19] It also ignores, for the most part, the role of the product environment—customers, competitors, suppliers, unions and regulatory agencies—and the material and human resources. These will have their independent effect upon the major variables.

In addition, it is not proposed here that there are four types of organizations. The two-dimensional scheme is conceived of as consisting of two continua. Nor are the dimensions and the specifications of the variables necessarily the best. It is argued, however, that the main variables—raw materials, technology, task and social structure, goals, and some differentiation of task areas within organizations, are critical ones. As to the assignment of independent and dependent variables, occasions can be readily cited where changes in goals, for example those brought about by changes in the market place or the personalities of top executives, have brought about changes in the technology utilized. The argument is somewhat more subtle than one of temporal priorities. Rather, it says that structure and goals must adjust to technology or the organization will be subject to strong strains. For a radical change in goals to be a successful one, it may require a change in technology, and thus in structure, or else there will be a large price paid for the lack of fit between these variables.[20] Furthermore, as one proceeds, analytically, from technology through the two kinds of structure to goals, increasingly the prior variable only sets limits upon the range of possible variations in the next variable. Thus, technology

[19] The role of the cultural and social environment is developed in somewhat more detail in a review of studies of general and mental hospitals in Charles Perrow. Hospitals: Technology, structure and goals, in James March, *Organizations,* chap. 22.

[20] This is argued in detail in Perrow, Hospitals, pp. 926–946. Kovner finds those nursing units with the greatest divergence between technology and structure to have the lowest scores on a dimension of goal realization. The nursing unit, pp. 96–97.

may predict task structure quite well in a large number of organizations,[21] but these two predict social structure less well, and these three only set broad limits upon the range of possible goals.

COMPARATIVE ANALYSES

If all this is at all persuasive, it means that we have a powerful tool for comparing organizations. The first implication of this for comparative studies is that we cannot expect a particular relationship found in one organization to be found in another unless we know these organizations are in fact similar with respect to their technology. Thus, the fact that the cosmopolitan-local relationship that worked so well in Antioch College was not found in the outpatient department of a hospital should not surprise us; the work performed by the professionals in each case was markedly different.[22] That morale was associated with bureaucracy in fairly routine public schools, but not in research organizations, is understandable.[23] Less obvious, however, is the point that types of organization—in terms of their function in society—will vary as much within each type as between types. Thus, some schools, hospitals, banks and steel companies may have more in common, because of their routine character, than routine and nonroutine schools, routine and nonroutine hospitals, and so forth. To assume that you are holding constant the major variable by comparing several schools or several steel mills is unwarranted until one looks at the technologies employed by various schools or steel mills. In fact, the variations within one type of organization may be such that some schools are like prisons, some prisons like churches, some churches like factories, some factories like universities, and so on.[24] Once this is recognized, of course, analysis of the differences between churches or whatever can be a powerful tool, as witness the familiar contrast of custodial and treatment-oriented people-changing institutions.

Another implication is that there is little point in testing the effect of a parameter variable, such as size, age, auspices, geographical dispersion, or even national culture, unless we control for technology. For example, in the case of size, to compare the structure of a small R and D lab where the tasks of all three areas are likely to be quite nonroutine with the structure of a large bank where they are likely to be quite routine is fruitless. The nature of their tasks is so different that the structures must vary independently of their different sizes.[25] A meaningful study of the effect of size on structure can be made only if we control for technology, and compare, say, large and small banks all of which have similar services, or large and small R and D labs. Similarly, though the brilliant work of Crozier on French culture is very suggestive, many of his conclusions may stem from the fact that only very routine organizations were studied, and even those lacked many critical elements of the bureaucratic model.[26] Equally routine organizations in a protected product environment in the U.S. might have displayed the same characteristics.

Finally, to call for decentralization, representative bureaucracy, collegial authority, or employee-centered, innovative or organic organizations—to mention only a few of the highly normative prescriptions that are being offered by social scientists today—is to call for a type of structure that can be realized only with a certain type of technology, unless we are willing to pay a high cost in terms of output. Given a routine technology, the much maligned Weberian bureaucracy probably constitutes the socially optimum form of organizational structure.

If all this is plausible, then existing varieties of organizational theory must be selectively applied. It is increasingly recognized that there is no "one

---

[21] Unfortunately, verification of the predicted relationships would require a large sample of organizations since there are bound to be many examples of incompatibility between the variables. However, even in a small sample, those whose structure was appropriate to their technology should have fewer "strains" than those whose structure was inappropriate. Joan Woodward, using a similar approach with 100 industrial firms found strong relationships between production systems and certain aspects of structure, though the rudimentary information and analysis on the 100 firms leaves one in doubt as to how strong. See Joan Woodward, *Industrial organization.*

[22] Cf. Alvin Goudner. Cosmopolitans and locals: Toward an analysis of latent social roles, *Administrative Science Quarterly,* 2 (December 1957, March 1958), pp. 281–306, 444–80, and Warren G. Bennis, N. Berkowitz, M. Affinito, and M. Malone. Reference groups and loyalties in the out-patient department, *Administrative Science Quarterly,* 2 (March 1958), pp. 481–500.

[23] Gerald H. Moeller and W. W. Charters. Relation of bureaucratization to sense of power among teachers, *Administrative Science Quarterly,* 10 (December 1966), pp. 444–65. In addition, for this reason one becomes wary of propositional inventories that fail to make sufficient distinctions among organizations, but attempt to support the propositions by illustrations that are likely to restrict the scope of the proposition to the particular type of organization used in the illustration. For the most recent example, see William A. Rushing. Organizational rules and surveillance: Propositions in comparative organizational analysis, *Administrative Science Quarterly,* 10 (December 1966), pp. 423–43.

[24] Many of the frameworks for comparative analysis, such as those cited in footnote 1, break down because of their broad categories. The failure of some of these schemes to meaningfully order the data from a large sample of a great variety of organizations is discussed in J. Eugene Haas, Richard H. Hall and Norman J. Johnson. Toward an empirically derived taxonomy of organizations, in Raymond V. Bowers (ed.), *Studies on behavior in organizations* (Atlanta: University of Georgia Press, 1966), pp. 157–80.

[25] This may be a basic error in the ambitious survey conducted by Haas and his associates, ibid.

[26] Crozier, *The bureaucratic pheonomenon.*

best" theory (any more than there is "one best" organizational structure, form of leadership, or whatever) unless it be so general as to be of little utility in understanding the variety of organizations. The perspective proposed here may allow us to utilize existing theories selectively.

For example, a characteristic of thoroughly routinized organizations is the programmatic character of decisions, and perhaps the infrequency with which important decisions have to be made. A decision-making framework that attempts to simulate executive behavior would be fruitful in such cases, for decisions are programmed and routinized. There are fairly clear guidelines for decisions, and clear routing maps, flow charts, and so forth. (See the examples in the second half of the Cyert and March volume, *The Behavioral Theory of the Firm.*[27]) However, a decision-making perspective which emphasizes uncertainty, such as Herbert Simon's, or that illustrated in the first part of the Cyert and March volume, would not be fruitful here.[28] It would be fruitful where nonroutine tasks are involved.

The study of organizations with a moderate or high component of nonroutine activities, especially at the design and planning level, would benefit from the institutional analysis proposed by Selznick, whereas more routine organizations would not. Selznick, himself, would see them as technical tools. The Communist Party is engaged in nonroutine activities and Selznick chose to analyze the nonroutine rather than the routine aspects of the multiorganization, the Tennessee Valley Authority.[29] Except for its Bell Laboratories, the American Telephone and Telegraph Corporation is probably a rather routine organization in a stable product environment and Barnard's equilibrium analysis works well.[30] Equilibrium analysis also works well for the routine operatives at the production level in economic organizations that constitute most of the subjects for the discussion by March and Simon of the contribution-inducement model.[31] Where nonroutine activities are involved, however, the measurement of both inducements and contributions tends to be difficult, and little is gained by this model except the unenlightening assertion that if the person stays in the organization and produces, there must be some kind of an inducement at least to match his contribution.[32]

There are, of course, many aspects of the general perspectives or theories of organizations that apply to all organizations, and many more will be forthcoming. What is asserted here is that we know enough about organizations in general, at this point, to suggest that more of our effort should be directed toward "middle range" theories which attempt to increase their predictive power by specifying the types of organizations to which they apply. To do this we need far better classification systems than we now have. A better classification system will be based upon a basic aspect of all organizations. In this paper we have suggested that a better system would be one which conceptualizes organizations in terms of the work that they do rather than their structure or their goals.

OTHER STUDIES UTILIZING TECHNOLOGY

If there is anything novel in the present essay it is the setting forth of an integrated and somewhat comprehensive viewpoint on technology and complex organizations. Numerous studies have dealt with specific aspects of this viewpoint and some are discussed here.

There have been a few general theoretical statements regarding technology and structure. The one closest to the perspective presented here is a seminal essay by Litwak[33] which distinguishes uniform and nonuniform tasks. His framework received some empirical support in an interesting essay by Hall.[34]

---

[27] Richard M. Cyert and James G. March. *The Behavioral theory of the firm* (Englewood Cliffs, N.J.: Prentice-Hall, 1963), chaps. 7–11.

[28] Ibid., chaps. 1–4, 6.

[29] Philip Selznick. *The organizational weapon* (New York: McGraw-Hill, 1952), and *TVA and the grass roots* (Berkeley: University of California Press, 1949). See also *Leadership in administration* (Evanston, Ill.: Row, Peterson, 1957), chap. 1.

[30] Chester Barnard. *The functions of the executive* (Cambridge, Mass.: Harvard University Press, 1938).

[31] March and Simon, *Organizations,* chap. 4.

[32] Woodward's remarkable book offers several implicit examples of selective utility. It seems clear, for example, that firms in her middle category (large batch, assembly and mass production) exhibit the characteristics of political science models such as Melville Dalton (*Men who manage* [New York: Wiley, 1959]) and the first part of Cyert and March *(The behavioral theory of the firm).* But this view would not illuminate the other two categories in her scheme; application must be selective.

[33] Eugene Litwak. Models of organization which permit conflict, *American Journal of Sociology,* 67 (September 1961), pp. 177–84.

[34] Richard H. Hall. Intraorganizational structural variation: Application of the bureaucratic model, *Administrative Science Quarterly,* 7 (December 1962), pp. 295–308. However, the normative anti-bureaucratic tone of many of Hall's questionnaire items precludes an adequate test. An affirmative response to an item such as "I have to ask my boss before I do almost anything" probably indicates a very poor boss, rather than a situation where a bureaucratic structure is viable. A factor analysis of Hall's items was utilized to construct several discrete dimensions of some aspects of bureaucracy in connection with research reported by Aiken and Hage. It appears that the groupings are not on the basis of content, but on the evaluative wording of the items. Those stated negatively, as in the above example, group together, and those implying "good" leadership techniques (rather than bureaucratic or

One of the first attempts to specify some structural and goal concomitants of technology in general terms was by Thompson and Bates.[35] March and Simon,[36] and Simon alone,[37] proposed and discussed a distinction between programmed and nonprogrammed decisions in general terms. Bennis[38] verges upon a technological conceptualization in parts of his excellent review of leadership theory and adminstrative behavior.

There have been numerous studies of the role of technology in work groups and small groups. One of the most widely cited is that of the long-wall coaling method by Trist and Bamforth.[39] In our terms this represents a premature attempt at rationalizing nonroutine activities. An assembly-line work layout was imposed on a craft and job-shop operation which was essentially nonroutine, and the results were predictably unfortunate, as were similar attempts to impose a bureaucratic structure on the nonroutine underground mining operations described by Gouldner.[40] Those interested in human relations in organizations have increasingly toyed with technology as an independent variable, but with mixed feelings and reluctance, since it appears to jeopardize some implicit values of this school of thought. See, for example, the curious chapter in Likert[41] where many of the central hypotheses of previous and subsequent chapters are undermined by observing that the consequences of leadership style varied with the routine and nonroutine nature of the work. More sophisticated statements of the impact of technology upon work groups can be found in Dubin[42] and in the comparative study of Turner and Lawrence.[43] The most sophisticated statement of the impact upon workers is presented by Blauner,[44] who uses a comparative framework to great effect; he also summarizes the vast literature on this topic which need not be cited here. Studies of experimental groups have provided evidence of the effect of technology upon small group structure. See the work of Bavelas,[45] Guetzkow and Simon,[46] and Leavitt.[47]

The impact of routine technologies upon both managerial and nonmanagerial personnel is apparent, though not explicit, in Argyris' study of a bank,[48] in Sudnow's study of a court system,[49] and in two studies of French organizations by Crozier.[50]

Technology plays an explicit and important role in a number of studies of single types of organizations, such as Janowitz's outstanding study of the military,[51] and Rose Coser's contrast of two units in a long-term hospital.[52] It is implicit in her contrast of a medical and a surgical ward.[53] It is also implicit in Rosengren's analysis of milieu therapy.[54] It plays the key role in the author's analysis of the literature on general and mental hospitals,[55] and in his longi-

---

nonbureaucratic techniques) group together. It is doubtful that anything but good or bad leadership in a gross sense is being tested here. A valid item for degree of bureaucratization would permit respondents to approve of the necessity for close supervision, for example, as well as to indicate it is not appropriate. See Michael Aiken and Jerald Hage. Organizational alienation: A comparative analysis, *American Sociological Review,* 31 (August 1966), pp. 497-507

[35] James D. Thompson and Frederick L. Bates. Technology, organization, and administration, *Administrative Science Quarterly,* 2 (March 1957), pp. 325-43.

[36] March and Simon, *Organizations.*

[37] Herbert Simon. *The new science of management decisions* (New York: Harper, 1960).

[38] Warren G. Bennis. Leadership theory and administrative behavior: The problem of authority, *Administrative Science Quarterly,* 4 (April 1959), pp. 259-301.

[39] Eric L. Trist and E. K. Bamforth. Some social and psychological consequences of the long-wall method of coal-getting, *Human Relations,* 4 (1951), pp. 3-38.

[40] Alvin W. Gouldner. *Patterns of industrial bureaucracy* (Glencoe, Ill.: The Free Press, 1954).

[41] Rensis Likert. *New patterns of management* (New York: McGraw-Hill, 1961), chap. 7.

[42] Robert Dubin. Supervision and productivity: Empirical findings and theoretical considerations, in Robert Dubin, George C. Homans, Floyd C. Mann and Delbert C. Miller. *Leadership and productivity* (San Francisco: Chandler, 1965), pp. 1-50.

[43] Arthur N. Turner and Paul R. Lawrence. *Industrial jobs and the worker* (Cambridge, Mass.: Harvard University Press, 1965).

[44] Robert Blauner. *Alienation and freedom: The factory worker and his industry* (Chicago: University of Chicago Press, 1964).

[45] Alex Bavelas. Communication patterns in task-oriented groups, *Journal of the Statistical Society of America, 22* (1950), pp. 725-30.

[46] Harold Guetzkow and Herbert Simon. "The impact of certain communication nets upon organization and performance in task-oriented groups," in Albert H. Rubenstein and Chadwick J. Haverstroh (eds.), *Some theories of organization* (Homewood, Ill.: The Dorsey Press, 1960), pp. 259-77.

[47] Harold J. Leavitt. Some effects of certain communication patterns on group performance, Eleanor Maccoby *et al.* (eds.), *Readings in Social Psychology,* (New York: Holt, Rinehart & Winston Inc. 1958), pp. 546-563.

[48] Chris Argyris. *Organization of a bank* (New Haven, Conn.: Yale University Press, 1954).

[49] David Sudnow. Normal crimes: Sociological features of the penal code in a public defender office, *Social Problems,* 12 (Winter 1965), pp. 255-76.

[50] Michel Crozier. *The bureaucratic phenomenon* (Chicago: University of Chicago Press, 1964).

[51] Morris Janowitz. *The professional soldier* (Glencoe, Ill.: The Free Press, 1960).

[52] Rose L. Coser. Alienation and the social structure: A case analysis of a hospital, in Eliot Freidson (ed.), *The hospital in modern society* (New York: The Free Press, 1963), pp. 231-65.

[53] Rose L. Coser. Authority and decision-making in a hospital, *American Sociological Review,* 23, (February 1958), pp. 56-64.

[54] William R. Rosengren. Communication, organization and conduct, *Administrative Science Quarterly,* 9 (June 1964), pp. 70-90.

[55] Charles Perrow. Hospitals: Technology, structure and goals, in James March (ed.), *Handbook of organizations* (Chicago: Rand McNally, 1965), chap. 22.

tudinal study of a maximum security institution for juveniles.[56] It plays an ambiguous role in the Street *et al.*, study of six correctional institutions where its impact is obscured by a competing emphasis upon executive goals and behavior, and an inappropriate reliance upon a simple custodial-treatment continuum which leads to many ambiguities about the middle organizations where components of treatment vary independently.[57]

Explicit contrasts of organizations have utilized technological variables. The most ambitious, of course, is Udy's analysis of simple organizations in nonindustrial societies where the emphasis upon technology is explicit.[58] Unfortunately, it is difficult to import his techniques of operationalization and his theory into the world of complex organizations in industrialized societies. As is noted in the preceding essay, technology is a relevant variable, and is sometimes made explicit, in Stinchcombe's discussion of structure and time periods.[59] It also plays a role, though not the key one, in his discussion of craft and bureaucratic organization.[60] The key role is reserved for market factors, and this is true of two other comparative studies—the study of two business concerns by Dill[61] and an ambitious study of two industrial firms by Lorsch.[62] In both these cases it would appear that technology is an important variable but is absorbed in the broader variable, environment. A study of several British firms by Burns and Stalker[63] uses technology as an important variable, though in a quite nonrigorous fashion; their one explicit comparison of a routine and a nonroutine firm is excellent.[64]

The most ambitious and stimulating comparative study using technology as an independent variable is Joan Woodward's survey of 100 industrial organizations.[65] Her independent variable is not, strictly speaking, technology, but is a mixture of type of production, size of production run, layout of work and type of customer order. These distinctions overlap and it is difficult to decide how a particular kind of organization might be classified in her scheme, or how she made her final classification. An examination of the actual types of organizations (bakery, electronic firm, etc.) utilized in her study, kindly provided by Miss Woodward, suggests that most of those in the general category "small batch and unit" are probably involved in nonroutine production; those in the "large batch and unit" are probably involved in routine production; those in the "large batch and mass production" category have a mixture of routine and nonroutine technologies, but are predominantly routine. If so, her findings would be consistent with our perspective. However, her analysis of continuous process firms unfortunately cannot easily be incorporated in the scheme advanced here. Efforts to do so after her book appeared floundered because of lack of crucial data.

Considering the strong empirical tradition of sociology, it is surprising that so few studies actually give details regarding the kind of work performed in organizations that permit technological generalizations. Two of the best are Gouldner's contrast of mining and manufacturing within a gypsum plant,[66] and Blau's implicit contrast of a routine employment agency and a nonroutine regulatory agency.[67] The works of Argyris,[68] Crozier,[69] Sudnow,[70] and Trist and Bamford[71] also are exceptions.

Finally, we should mention the problem of operationalizing the various concepts of technology—programmed and nonprogrammed decisions, uniform and nonuniform events, routine and nonroutine techniques, simple and complex technologies, and so forth. This has rarely been systematically handled. Udy's procedures do not seem to be applicable to complex organizations.[72] Neither Lorsch[73] nor Hall[74] indicate in detail how they make their distinctions. March and Simon provide some general guidelines,[75] but Litwak[76] provides none. It is impossible to deter-

[56] Charles Perrow. Reality adjustment: A young organization settles for humane care, *Social Problems,* 14 (Summer 1966), pp. 69–79.

[57] David Street, Robert Vinter and Charles Perrow. *Organization for treatment: A comparative study of institutions for delinquents* (New York: The Free Press, 1966).

[58] Stanley Udy. *Organization of work* (New Haven: Human Relations Area Files Press, 1959).

[59] Arthur L. Stinchcombe. Social structure and organization, in James March (ed.), *Handbook of organizations* (Chicago: Rand McNally, 1965), chap. 4.

[60] Arthur L. Stinchcombe. Bureaucratic and craft administration of production: A comparative study, *Administrative Science Quarterly,* 4 (September 1959) pp. 168–87.

[61] William Dill. Environment as an influence on managerial autonomy, *Administrative Science Quarterly,* 2 (March 1958), pp. 409–43.

[62] Jay W. Lorsch. *Product innovation and organization* (New York: Macmillan, 1965).

[63] Tom Burns and G. M. Stalker. *The management of innovation* (London: Tavistock Publications, 1961).

[64] Ibid., chap. 5.

[65] Joan Woodward. *Industrial organization: Theory and practice* (London: Oxford University Press, 1965).

[66] Gouldner, *Patterns of industrial bureaucracy.*

[67] Peter Blau, *Dynamics of bureaucracy* (Chicago: University of Chicago Press, 1955).

[68] Argyris, *Organization of a bank.*

[69] Crozier. *The bureaucratic phenomenon.*

[70] Sudnow, Normal crimes.

[71] Trist and Bamford, *Some social and psychological consequences. . . .*

[72] Udy, *Organization of work.*

[73] Lorsch, *Product innovation and organization.*

[74] Hall, Intraorganizational structural variation.

[75] March and Simon, *Organizations.*

[76] Litwak, Models of organization which permit conflict.

mine how Woodward[77] or Burns and Stalker[78] arrived at their classifications of companies. Street *et al.*,[79] provide indications of operationalization, but these are not particularly applicable to other types of organizations nor are the authors particularly sensitive to the problem. Only Turner and Lawrence[80] have approached the problem systematically and fully described in an appendix the measurement of their variables. The level of conceptualization is not general enough to apply to other types of organizations than industrial firms, and the material is limited to blue-collar workers, but it is at least encouraging that in our own study of industrial firms we arrived independently at some roughly similar measures.

Udy, in a discussion of this paper, aptly noted the difficulty of reconciling the respondent's perception of the nature of his work with the observer's perception, which is based upon a comparative view. Few organizations will characterize themselves as routine, and most employees emphasize the variability of their jobs and the discretion required. Nevertheless, contrasts between extreme examples of a single type of organization appear to present no problem. It seems clear that the technology of custodial and therapeutic mental hospitals, or of firms producing ingot molds and those producing titanium-based metals, differ greatly. On the other hand, to say precisely wherein these differences occur, and how one might compare the two routine examples, is far more difficult. Such operationalization, however, depends first upon adequate conceptualization. That proposed in this essay—the two continua of exceptions and search procedures—hopefully can be operationalized for a variety of settings. (An attempt is made, with fair success, by Kovner in his study of nursing units.[81]) But much more research and theory will be required to determine if these concepts are relevant and adequate. Meanwhile, we are aware of a number of other studies of technology and organization currently under way or even in press; other concepts will no doubt be formulated and perhaps will be given systematic operational definition.

29. THE CONTEXT OF ORGANIZATION STRUCTURES*

D. S. Pugh, D. J. Hickson, C. R. Hinings, and C. Turner†

The structure of an organization is closely related to the context within which it functions, and much of the variation in organization structures might be explained by contextual factors. Many such factors, including size, technology, organizational charter or social function, and interdependence with other organizations, have been suggested as being of primary importance in influencing the structure and functioning of an organization.

There have been few attempts, however, to relate these factors in a comparative systematic way to the characteristic aspects of structure, for such studies would require a multivariate factorial approach in both context and structure. The limitations of a unitary approach to organizational structure have been elaborated elsewhere (Hinings *et al.*, 1967), but its deficiencies in the study of contextual factors are no less clear. Theorists in this area seem to have proceeded on the assumption that one particular contextual feature is the major determinant of structure, with the implication that they considered the others less important. Many writers from Weber onwards have mentioned size as being one of the most important causes of differences between structures, and large size has even been considered as characteristic of bureaucratic structure (Presthus, 1958). Others argue for the pre-emptive importance of the technology of production or service in determining structure and functioning (Dubin, 1958; Perrow, 1967; Woodward, 1965; Trist *et al.*, 1963). Parsons (1956) and Selznick (1949) have attempted to show in some detail that the structure and functioning of the organization follow from its social function, goals, or "charter." Eisenstadt (1959) emphasized the importance of the dependence of the organization on its

[77] Woodward, *Industrial organization.*

[78] Burns and Stalker, *The management of innovation.*

[79] Street et al., *Organization for treatment.*

[80] Turner and Lawrence, *Industrial jobs and the worker.*

* From: *Administrative Science Quarterly*, Vol. 14 (1969), pp. 91–114.

† D. S. Pugh, director of research and reader in organizational behavior at the London Business School, England. D. J. Hickson, C. R. Hinings, and C. Turner, members of the Industrial Administration Research Unit, The University of Aston in Birmingham, England.

[81] Anthony Kovner, "The Nursing Unit: A Technological Perspective," unpublished Ph.D. dissertation, University of Pittsburgh, 1966.

TABLE 1 CONCEPTUAL SCHEME FOR EMPIRICAL STUDY OF WORK ORGANIZATIONS

Contextual variables	*Structural variables*†
Origin and history	*Structuring of activities*
Ownership and control	Functional specialization
Size	Role specialization
Charter	Standardization (overall)
Technology	Formalization (overall)
Location	*Concentration of authority*
Resources	Centralization of decision making
Dependence	Autonomy of the organization
*Activity variables**	Standardization of procedures for selection and advancement
Identification (charter, image)	*Line control of workflow*
Perpetuation (thoughtways, finance, personnel services)	Subordinate ratio
Workflow (production, distribution)	Formalization of role performance recording
Control (direction, motivation, evaluation, communication)	Percentage of workflow superordinates
Homeostasis (fusion, leadership, problem solving, legitimization)	*Relative size of supportive component*
	Percentage of clerks
	Percentage of nonworkflow personnel
	Vertical span (height)
	Performance variables
	Efficiency (profitability, productivity, market standing)
	Adaptability
	Morale

* Bakke (1959). †Pugh et al. (1968).

TABLE 2 ELEMENTS OF ORGANIZATION CONTEXT

Elements of Context	*Product-Moment Correlation with Structural Factors*		
	Structuring of Activities	*Concentration of Authority*	*Line Control of Workflow*
*Origin and history (3)**			
Impersonality of origin	—0.04	0.64	0.36
Age	0.09	—0.38	—0.02
Historical changes	0.17	—0.45	—0.03
Ownership and control (7)			
Public accountability	—0.10	0.64	0.47
Concentration of ownership with control	—0.15	—0.29	—0.21
Size (3)			
Size of organization†	0.69	—0.10	—0.15
Size of parent organization†	0.39	0.39	—0.07
Charter (7)			
Operating variability	0.15	—0.22	—0.57
Operating diversity	0.26	—0.30	—0.04
Technology (6)			
Workflow integration	0.34	—0.30	—0.46
Labor costs	—0.25	0.43	0.32
Location (1)			
Number of operating sites	—0.26	0.39	0.39
Dependence (10)			
Dependence	—0.05	0.66	0.13
Recognition of trade unions	0.51	0.08	—0.35

* Numbers in parentheses indicate number of primary scales. †Logarithm of number of employees.

TABLE 3 INTERCORRELATIONS OF CONTEXTUAL VARIABLES (product-moment coefficients, $N = 46$)

Scale Title	Impersonality of Origin	Age	Historical Changes	Public Accountability	Concentration of Ownership with Control*
Impersonality of origin	—				
Age	—0.20	—			
Historical changes	—0.34	0.50	—		
Public accountability	0.66	0.00	—0.25	—	
Concentration of ownership with control*	—0.40	—0.03	0.02	—0.50	—
Size of organization†	0.07	0.16	0.29	0.00	—0.21
Size of parent organization†	0.45	—0.12	—0.10	0.51	—0.55
Operating variability	—0.26	—0.24	—0.16	—0.34	0.29
Operating diversity	—0.23	0.00	0.13	—0.14	0.00
Workflow integration	—0.24	0.07	0.05	—0.35	0.10
Labor Costs	0.41	—0.24	—0.31	0.34	—0.09
No. of operating sites	0.14	—0.07	—0.08	0.34	—0.20
Dependence	0.53	—0.32	—0.38	0.53	—0.50
Recognition of trade unions	0.04	—0.04	—0.11	0.17	—0.21

* $N =$ for all correlations with this variable.
† Logarithm of number of employees.

social setting, particularly its dependence on external resources and power, in influencing structural characteristics and activities. Clearly all of these contextual factors, as well as others, are relevant; but without a multivariate approach, it is not possible to assess their relative importance.

A previous paper described the conceptual framework upon which the present multivariate analysis is based (Pugh *et al.*, 1963), and a subsequent paper its empirical development (Pugh *et al.*, 1968). It is not a model of organization in an environment, but a separation of variables of structure and of organizational performance from other variables commonly hypothesized to be related to them, which are called "contextual" in the sense that they can be regarded as a setting within which structure is developed. Table 1 summarizes the framework and also includes a classification of activities useful in the analysis of organization functioning (Bakke, 1959).

The design of the study reported in the present paper treats the contextual variables as independent and the structural variables as dependent. The structural variables are (i) *structuring of activities;* that is, the degree to which the intended behavior of employees is overtly defined by task specialization, standard routines, and formal paper work; (ii) *concentration of authority;* that is, the degree to which authority for decisions rests in controlling units outside the organization and is centralized at the higher hierarchical levels within it; and (iii) *line control of workflow;* that is, the degree to which control is exercised by line personnel instead of through impersonal procedures. The eight contextual variables were translated into operational definitions and scales were constructed for each of them. These were then used in a multivariate regression analysis to predict the structural dimensions found.

This factorial study using cross-sectional data does not in itself test hypotheses about *processes* (e.g. how changes in size interact with variations in structuring of activities), but it affords a basis for generating such hypotheses.

SAMPLE AND METHODS

Data were collected on fifty-two work organizations, forty-six of which were a random sample stratified by size and product or purpose. The sample and methods have been described in detail in a previous paper, (Pugh *et al.*, 1968). For scaling purposes, data on the whole group were used, but for correlational analyses relating scales to each other, and for prediction analyses relating contextual variables to structural ones, only data on the sample of forty-six organizations were used. None of the data was attitudinal.

The data were analyzed under the heading of the conceptual scheme. To define the variables operationally, scales were constructed that measured the degree of a particular characteristic. The scales varied widely. Inkson *et al.* (1967) discussed the variety of scaling procedures used. Some were simple dichotomies (such as impersonality of origin) or counts (such as number of operating sites); some were ordered category scales, locating an organization at one point along a postulated dimension (such as closeness of link with customers of clients). Some were stable, ordered scales established by linking together a large number of items exhibiting the characteristic on the basis of cumulative scaling procedures, such as workflow rigidity, an aspect of technology. Some were summary scales extracted by principal-components analysis to summarize a whole dimension, such as operating variability, an aspect

Size of Organization†	Size of parent Organization†	Operating Variability	Operating Diversity	Workflow Integration	Labor Costs	No. of Operating Sites	Dependence	Trade Unions
—								
0.43	—							
−0.24	−0.19	—						
0.26	−0.10	0.02	—					
0.07	−0.09	0.57	0.33	—				
−0.28	0.08	−0.27	0.01	−0.50	—			
0.14	0.16	−0.56	−0.05	−0.58	0.16	—		
−0.17	0.63	0.05	−0.19	−0.05	0.26	0.05	—	
0.36	0.37	0.19	0.01	0.20	−0.15	−0.12	0.22	—

of charter. In this way, forty primary scales of context were constructed and then reduced to fourteen empirically distinct elements, which are listed in Table 2 together with their correlations with the main structural variables as defined in Table 1. Table 3 gives their intercorrelations. The methodological implications of this analysis are discussed in Levy and Pugh (1969).

The study of contextual aspects of organizations will inevitably produce a much more heterogeneous set of scales than the comparable study of the structural aspects; for the scales are selected, not from a common conceptual base, but for their postulated links with structure. One of the objectives of using the multivariate approach described here would be to test the relationship between disparate aspects of context, and to attempt a conceptual clarification of those aspects demonstrated to be salient in relation to organizational structure.

It was not possible to investigate the variable "resources" adequately. For human and ideational resources, the wide-ranging interviews within a comparatively short time span made it impossible to obtain adequate data. Material and capital resources were found to reduce to aspects of size, and the relative disposition of these resources (e.g. capital versus labor) was found to be better regarded as an aspect of technology.

CONTEXTUAL VARIABLES

Origin and History

An organization may have grown from a one-man business over a long period of time, or it may have been set up as a branch of an already existing organization and so developed rapidly. During its development it may have undergone many or few radical changes in purpose, ownership, and other contextual aspects. An adequate study of the impact of these factors on organizational structure must be conducted on a comparative longitudinal basis (Chandler, 1962); but even in a cross-sectional study such as this, it is possible to define and make operational three aspects of this concept.

Impersonality of Origin. This variable distinguishes between entrepreneurial organizations, personally founded, and bureaucratic ones founded by an existing organization. Impersonally founded organizations might be expected to have a higher level of structuring of activities, whereas personally founded organizations would have a higher degree of concentration of authority. The data on the present sample, however, show no relationship between impersonality of origin and structuring of activities ($r = -0.04$), but a strong relationship between impersonality of origin and concentration of authority ($r = 0.64$). (With $N = 46$, all correlations 0.29 and above are at or beyond the ninety-five percent level of confidence.) To a considerable extent this relationship is due to the fact that government-owned, and therefore impersonally founded, organizations tend to be highly centralized. Such organizations tend to be line controlled in their workflow, thus contributing to the relationship ($r = 0.36$) between impersonality of origin and line control of workflow. The lack of relationship with structuring of activities, which is common to all three scales of this dimension, underlines the need to examine present contextual aspects in relation to this factor rather than historical ones.

Age. The age of the organization was taken from the time at which the field work was carried out. The range in the sample varied from an established metal goods manufacturing organization, founded over 170 years previously, in 1794, to a government inspection department, which began activities in the area as a separate operating unit 29 years previously. No clear relationship was found between age and impersonality of origin ($r = -0.20$). Stinchcombe (1965) has argued that no relationship should be expected between the age of an organization and its structure but rather between the structure of an organization and the date that its industry was founded. The present data support this conclusion in that no relationship is found between age and structuring of activities ($r = 0.09$) or line control of workflow ($r = 0.02$). Age was related to concentration of authority ($r = -0.38$), older organizations having a tendency to be more decentralized and to have more autonomy.

Historical Changes. The organizations in this sample did not have adequate historical information on the extent of contextual changes for use in a cross-sectional investigation; but it was possible to obtain limited information as to whether particular changes had occurred, and thus to develop a scale for the *types* of contextual changes that had occurred, namely whether at least one change had occurred *(i)* in the location of the organization, *(ii)* in the product or service range offered, and *(iii)* in the pattern of ownership. Item analysis carried out using the Brogden-Clemens coefficient (Brogden, 1949) gave a mean item-analysis value of 0.85, suggesting that it was possible to produce a scale of historical changes by summing the items. The organizations were distributed along the scale from no changes to all three types of changes. As expected, there was a strong correlation of this scale with age ($r = 0.51$), older organizations tending to have experienced more types of change. There was also a strong relationship, perhaps mediated by age, between historical changes and concentration of authority ($r = -0.45$), such changes being associated with dispersion of authority.

Ownership and Control

The differences in structure between a department of the government and a private business will be due to some extent to the different ownership and control patterns. Two aspects of this concept, public accountability and the relationship of the ownership to the management of the organization were investigated. For wholly owned subsidiary companies, branch factories, local government departments, etc. this form of analysis had to be applied to the parent institution exercising owning rights, in some cases through more than one intermediate institution (e.g. committees of the corporation, area boards, parent operating companies, which were themselves owned by holding companies, etc.). The ultimate owning unit is referred to as the "parent organization."

Public Accountability. This was a three-point category scale concerned with the degree to which the parent organization, (which could, of course, be the organizational unit itself, as it was in eight cases) was subject to public scrutiny in the conduct of its affairs. Least publicly accountable would be a company not quoted on the stock exchange; next, organizations that raised money publicly by having equity capital quoted on the stock exchange, also public cooperative societies; and most publicly accountable were the departments of the local and central government. On the basis of the classical literature on bureaucracy as a societal phenomenon, it might be hypothesized that organizations with the greatest exposure to public accountability would have a higher degree of structuring of activities, and a greater concentration of authority. The data on the

TABLE 4 OWNERSHIP AND CONTROL ($N = 42$)

	Scale Number and Title	*Range %*	*Mean*	*S.D.*
12.01	Concentration of voteholdings. (Percentage of equity owned by top twenty shareholders.)	0–100	38.47	32.37
12.03	Voteholdings of individuals. (Percentage of individuals among top twenty shareholders.)	0–100	17.19	26.89
12.04	Directors among top twenty voteholders. (Percentage of directors among top twenty shareholders.)	0–100	20.69	29.39
12.05	Directors' voteholdings. (Percentage of equity owned by all directors combined.)	0– 99.9	9.40	19.61
12.06	Percentage of directors who are executives.	0–100	46.11	32.73
12.09	Interlocking directorships. (Percentage of directors with other directorships beyond owning organization.)	0–100	45.22	33.73

TABLE 5 OWNERSHIP AND CONTROL: INTERCORRELATION MATRIX (product-moment coefficients, $N = 42$)

	Concentration of Voteholdings	Voteholdings of Individuals	Directors among Top Twenty Voteholders	Directors' Voteholdings	Percentage of Directors Who Are Executives	Interlocking Directorships
Concentration of voteholdings	—					
Voteholdings of individuals	0.62	—				
Directors among top twenty voteholders	0.54	0.87	—			
Directors' voteholdings	0.55	0.90	0.78	—		
Percentage of directors who are executives	0.26	0.30	0.37	0.20	—	
Interlocking directorships	0.32	0.03	0.04	0.09	0.33	—

present sample show relationships more complicated than this, however.

First, it must be emphasized that although this sample included eight government departments, all the organizations had a nonadministrative purpose, which could be identified as a workflow, Pugh, *et al.* (1968) Table 1. This is not surprising in this provincial sample, since purely administrative units of the requisite size (i.e., employing more than 250 people) are few outside the capital. The relationships between public accountability and structure must be interpreted in the light of this particular sample.

No relationship was found between public accountability and structuring of activities ($r = -0.10$). This structuring factor applies to the workflow as well as administrative activities of the organization, and it appears that government organizations with a workflow are not differentiated from nongovernment organizations on this basis. On the other hand there was a positive relationship between public accountability and concentration of authority ($r = 0.63$) standardization of procedures for selection and advancement ($r = 0.56$) and line control of workflow ($r = 0.47$). These all point to centralized but line-controlled government workflow organizations (Pugh *et al.*, 1969). The scale of standardization was a bipolar one, and a high score meant that the organization standardized its procedures for personnel selection and advancement, and also that it did *not* standardize its procedures for workflow. The relationship between public accountability and this standardization scale suggests that the government workflow organizations standardize their personnel procedures, but rely on professional line superordinates for workflow control.

Relationship of Ownership to Management. The concepts of Sargent Florence (1961) were found most fruitful in studying this aspect of ownership and control, but the method used was the selection of variables for a correlational approach, rather than classification on the basis of percentages. Florence studied the relationships of shareholders, directors, and executives. Where these groups were completely separate there was full separation of ownership, control, and management; where they were the same, then ownership, control and management coalesced. Between these two extremes, the scales were designed in the present study to measure the degree of separation. Company records and public records were examined and five scales developed for the patterns of shareholding and the relationships between the ownership and the management of the organization. For the four foreign-owned organizations in the sample, this information was not available in England; the analysis was therefore based on $n = 42$ (Table 4). A sixth scale was developed for interlocking directorships; that is, the percentage of directors who held other directorships outside the owning group. The intercorrelation matrix of these six variables suggested that factor analysis would be helpful in summarizing an extensive analysis of ownership (Table 5). A principal-components analysis was thus applied to the matrix, and a large first factor accounting for 56 percent of the variance was extracted, which was heavily loaded on all variables except interlocking directorships and was therefore termed "concentration of ownership with control."

As would be expected, there was a negative relationship between public accountability and concentration of ownership with control ($r = -0.51$); the more publicly accountable the ownership, the less concentrated it was, with central and local government ownership epitomizing diffuse ownership by the voting public.

The discussion about the effects of differing patterns of personal ownership on organizations and society originated with Marx, and has since polarized into what Dahrendorf (1959) has called the "radical" and "conservative" positions. It is generally agreed that there has been a progressive dispersion of share ownership following the rise of the corporation, but there is little agreement, or systematic evidence, on the effects of this. The radicals (Burnham, 1962; Berle & Means, 1937) argue that present ownership patterns have produced a shift in control away from the entrepreneur to managers, who become important because of their control over the means of production and the organization of men, materials, and equipment. The result then of dispersion of ownership is likely to be dispersion of authority. However, the conservatives (Mills, 1956; Aaronovitch, 1961) argue that the dispersion of capital ownership makes possible the concentration of economic power in fewer hands, because of the inability of the mass of shareholders to act, resulting in a concentration of authority.

The results obtained with this sample support neither of these positions. The correlation given in Table 2 of concentration of ownership with control with concentration of authority ($r = -0.29$) might suggest that concentration of ownership is associated with dispersion of authority; but it must be remembered that this correlation is obtained for the whole sample, which includes government-owned organizations, whereas the discussion of the effects of ownership patterns has been concerned entirely with private ownership. When the government organizations were extracted from the sample, the correlation disappeared ($r = -0.08$ for $N = 34$). No relationships were found between the structure of an organization and the ownership pattern of its parent organization. This lack of relationship is quite striking, particularly in view of the extent of the correlation found with other contextual variables. Since ownership and control seemed to have its impact through the degree of public accountability, and the other variables did not have an additional effect, there seemed to be grounds for not proceeding with them in a multivariate analysis.

Size

There has been much work relating size to group and individual variables, such as morale and job satisfaction, with not very consistent results (Porter & Lawler, 1965). With few exceptions, empirical studies relating size to variables of organization structure have confined themselves to those broad aspects of the role structure which are here termed "configuration" (Starbuck, 1965). Hall and Tittle, (1966), using a Guttman scale of the overall degree of perceived bureaucratization obtained by combining scores on six dimensions of Weberian characteristics of bureaucracy in a study of twenty-five different work organizations, found a small relation between their measurement of perceived bureaucratization and organization size ($\tau = 0.252$ at the 6 percent level of confidence).

In this study the aspects of size studied were number of employees, net assets utilized, and number of employees in the parent organizations.

Number of Employees and Net Assets. It was intended that the sample be taken from the population of work organizations in the region employing more than 250 people, but the sample ranges from an insurance company employing 241 people to a vehicle manufacturing company employing 25,052 (mean 3,370; standard deviation 5,313). In view of this distribution, it was felt that a better estimate of the correlation between size and other variables would be obtained by taking the logarithm of the number of employees (mean 3.12; standard deviation 0.57).

"Net assets employed by the organization" was also used, because financial size might expose some interesting relationships with organization structure that would not appear when only personnel size was considered. The sample ranged from under £ 100,000 — an estimate for the government inspection agency whose equipment was provided by its clients — to a confectionery manufacturing firm with £ 38 million. The attempt to differentiate between these two aspects of size proved unsuccessful, however, as the high correlation between them ($r = 0.78$) shows. Taking the logarithm of the two variables raised the correlation ($r = 0.81$). For this sample, therefore, a large organization was big both in number of employees and in financial assets. The logarithm of the number of employees was therefore taken to represent both these aspects of size.

The correlation between the logarithm of size and structuring of activities ($r = 0.69$) lends strong support to descriptive studies of the effects of size on bureaucratization. (This correlation may be compared with that between actual size and structuring of activities, $r = 0.56$, to demonstrate the effects of the logarithmic transformation.) Larger organizations tend to have more specialization, more standardization and more formalization than smaller organizations. The *lack* of relationship between size and the remaining structural dimensions, i.e., concentration of authority ($r = -0.10$) and line control of workflow ($r = -0.15$) was equally striking. This clear differential relationship of organization size to the various structural dimensions underlines the necessity of a multivariate approach to context and structure if oversimplifications are to be avoided.

Indeed, closer examination of the relationship of size to the main structural variables underlying the dimension of concentration of authority (Pugh *et al.*, 1968: Table 4) points up a limitation in the present approach, which seeks to establish basic dimensions by means of factor analysis. As was explained in that paper, the structural factors represent an attempt to summarize a large amount of data on a large number of variables to make possible empirically based comparisons. But the cost is that the factor may obscure particular relationships with the source variables which it summarizes. For some purposes therefore, it may be interesting to examine particular relationships. The lack of relationship between size and concentration of authority, for example, summarizes (and therefore conceals) two small but distinct relationships with two of the component variables. There is no relationship between size and autonomy ($r = 0.09$), but there is a negative relationship between size and centralization ($r = -0.39$), and a positive one between size and standardization of procedures for selection and advancement ($r = 0.31$). The relationship with centralization has clear implications for the concept of bureaucracy. Centralization correlates *negatively* with all scales of structuring of activities except one: the more specialized, standardized, and formalized the organization, the *less* it is centralized. Therefore on the basis of these scales, there can be no unitary bureaucracy, for an organization that develops specialist offices and associated routines is decentralized. Perhaps when the responsibilities of specialized roles are narrowly defined, and activities are regulated by standardized procedures and are formalized in records, then authority can safely be decentralized. Pugh *et al.* (1969) discuss the interrelationship of the structural variables in particular types of organization.

Size of Parent Organization. This is the number of employees of any larger organization to which the unit belongs. The literature on bureaucracy often implies that it is the size of the larger parent organization that influences the structure of the sub-unit. The important factor about a small government agency may not be its own size, but that of the large ministry of state of which it is a part. Similarly, the structure of a subsidiary company may be more related to the size of its holding company. The number of employees in the parent organizations ranged from 460 to 358,000 employees. The size of the parent organization correlated positively (after logarithmic transformation) with structuring ($r = 0.39$) and concentration of authority ($r = 0.39$) but not with line control of workflow ($r = -0.07$). The classical concept of bureaucracy would lead to the hypothesis that the size of the parent organization would be highly correlated with structuring of activities and concentration of authority, therefore the support from this sample was relatively modest. The correlation with structuring ($r = 0.39$) is much lower than the correlation of *organization* size and structuring ($r = 0.69$). The impact of the size of an organization is thus considerably greater than the size of the parent organization on specialization, standardization, formalization, etc. But a relationship with concentration of authority is not found with organization size ($r = -0.10$). Thus large groups have a small but definite tendency to have more centralized subunits with less autonomy. This relationship would be partly due to the government-owned organizations, inevitably part of large groups, which were at the concentrated end of this factor.

Charter

Scales. Institutional analysts have demonstrated the importance of the charter of an organization; that is, its social function, goals, ideology, and value systems, in influencing structure and functioning (Parsons, 1956, Selznick, 1949). To transform concepts which had been treated only descriptively into a quantitative form that would make them comparable to other contextual aspects, seven ordered category scales were devised. Four of them characterized the purpose or goal of the organization in terms of its "output," the term being taken as equally applicable to products or services: *(i)* multiplicity of outputs—ranging from a single standard output to two or more outputs; *(ii)* type of output—a manufacturing-service dichotomy, *(iii)* consumer or producer outputs or a mixture of both, and *(iv)* customer orientation of outputs—ranging from completely standard outputs to outputs designed entirely to customer or client specification. Three scales were devised for ideological aspects of charter: *(v)* self-image—whether the ideology of the organization as indicated by slogans used and image sought emphasized the qualities of its outputs; *(vi)* policy on multiple outputs—whether the policy was to expand, maintain, or contract its range of outputs; and *(vii)* client selection—whether any, some, or no selectivity was shown in the range of customers or clients served by the organization. Table 6 gives the details of the seven scales and Table 7 the intercorrelation matrix between them. This suggested that factor analysis would be helpful in summarizing the data, and a principal components analysis applied to the matrix gave the results shown in Table 8.

Operating Variability. This factor, accounting for 30 percent of the variance was highly loaded on the variables, consumer or producer outputs, customer orientation of outputs, and type of output. It was therefore conceptualized as being concerned with manufacturing nonstandard producer goods

TABLE 6 CHARTER

Distribution N = 46	Score	Scale Number and Title
		Scale No. 14.02
		Multiplicity of outputs
19	1	Single output with standard variations
8	2	Single output with variations to customer specification
19	3	Two or more outputs
		Scale No. 14.03
		Type of output
14	1	Service (nonmanufacturing)
32	2	Manufacturing (new physical outputs in solid, liquid or gaseous form)
		Scale No. 14.04
		Type of output
16	1	Consumer (outputs disposed of to the general public or individuals)
7	2	Consumer and producer
23	3	Producer (outputs disposed of to other organizations which use them for, or as part of, other outputs)
		Scale No. 14.06
		Customer orientation
11	1	Standard output(s)
7	2	Standard output(s) with standard modifications
6	3	Standard output(s) with modification to customer specification
22	4	Output to customer specification
		Scale No. 14.07
		Self-image
24	1	Image emphasizes qualities of the *organization itself*
6	2	Image emphasizes both the organization and the output
16	3	Image emphasizes qualities of the *output* of the organization
		Scale No. 14.08
		Policy on outputs multiplicity
5	1	Contracting the range of outputs
26	2	Maintaining the range
15	3	Expanding the range
		Scale No. 14.09
		Ideology: client selection
28	1	No selection, any clients supplied
14	2	Some selection of clients
4	3	Clients specified by parent organization

TABLE 7 INTERCORRELATION MATRIX (product-moment coefficients, N = 46)

	Multiplicity of Outputs	*Service-Manufacturing*	*Consumer-Producer*	*Customer Orientation*	*Self-Image*	*Client Selection*	*Expansion-contraction of Range*
Multiplicity of outputs	—						
Service-manufacturing	0.15	—					
Consumer-producer	0.05	0.37	—				
Customer orientation	0.38	0.18	0.59	—			
Self-image	−0.05	−0.17	−0.33	−0.13	—		
Client selection	−0.14	−0.02	0.28	−0.04	−0.18	—	
Expansion-Contraction of range	0.07	−0.14	−0.09	0.07	0.10	−0.09	—

TABLE 8 CHARTER: PRINCIPAL-COMPONENTS ANALYSIS

Scales	Factor Loadings: *Operating Variability**	*Operating Diversity†*
Consumer-producer output .	0.85	0.16
Customer orientation of outputs.	0.74	—0.41
Type of output (service-manufacturing)	0.57	0.00
Self-image	—0.52	—0.34
Multiplicity of outputs	0.37	—0.66
Client selection	0.23	0.66
Expansion-contraction of range	—0.15	—0.48

* Percentage of variance = 30%
† Percentage of variance = 20%

as against providing standard consumer service. The manufacturing producer end of the scale was linked with an organizational emphasis on self-image, whereas the consumer service end emphasized outputs. The scale was therefore constructed by a weighted summing of the scores on all these variables (the weighting being necessary to equate the standard deviations) and then standardizing the sums to a mean of 50 and a standard deviation of 15. This produced the range of scores on the scale given in Table 9. The lower scores distinguished organizations giving only a standard service (e.g., teaching, transport, retailing), from organizations (with high scores) producing nonstandard producer outputs to customer specification (metal goods firm, engineering repair unit, packaging manufacturer, etc.), with those organizations having a standard output range in the middle.

Operating Diversity. This factor of charter, accounting for 20 percent of the variance, emphasized multiplicity of outputs, policy on whether to expand the range of kinds of outputs, client selection, and self-image. The more diversely operating organizations were a glass manufacturer, a metal manufacturer, and a brewery; the more restricted were a motor component manufacturer, a domestic appliance manufacturer, and a scientific inspection agency.

Eisenstadt (1959), Parsons (1956), Selznick (1949, 1957), Wilson (1962), and Clarke (1956) have discussed the effects of the goals of an organization on its structure, but there has been almost no detailed empirical work on the actual relationship between goals and structure. Selznick (1949) showed how the goal of democracy led to decentralization in the TVA, and also suggested that the role structure of an organization is the institutional embodiment of its purpose. Wilson (1962) suggested a relationship between goals and methods of recruitment and means of selection. Clarke (1956) as well as Thompson and Bates (1957) emphasized both the marginality and the degree of concreteness of the goal as a determinant of the direction of organizational adaptation. Blau and Scott (1962) made one of the few attempts to classify organizations by their goals, suggesting that internal democracy goes with mutual benefit goals, efficiency with business goals, a professional structure with service goals and bureaucratic structure with commonweal goals.

Scales of organizational charter were related to structure, and operating variability was shown to be strongly associated with line control of workflow ($r = -0.57$). Thus the more an organization is concerned with manufacturing nonstandard producer goods, the more it relies upon impersonal control of workflow; the more it is providing a standard consumer service, the more it uses line control of its workflow through the supervisory hierarchy. Organizations showing operating diversity, however, tended to be more structured in activities ($r = 0.26$) and more dispersed in authority ($r = -0.30$).

Technology

Scales. Technology has come to be considered increasingly important as a determinant of organizational structure and functioning, although comparative empirical studies of its effects on structure are few, mainly case studies on the effects on the operator's job and attitudes (Walker, 1962). Thompson and Bates (1957), however, compared a hospital, a university, a manufacturing organization, and a mine for the effects of their technologies on the setting of objectives, the management of resources, and the execution of policy. The main work on the classification of technology in relation to organization structure has been that of Woodward (1965). She related mainly "configuration" aspects of the structure of manufacturing organization (e.g., number of levels of authority, width of spans of control) to a classification of their production systems according to the "controlability and predictability" of the process.

In the present study the need to develop suitable measurements of overall organizational technology made the level of generality achieved by the Woodward classification desirable; but the need to develop concepts of technology that applied to all the organizations in the sample precluded the direct adoption of that scale. A full account of the development of scales of technology and their relationship to organization structure is given in Hickson *et al.* (1969). Only the scales included in the present analysis are described here.

Technology is here defined as the sequence of physical techniques used upon the workflow of the

TABLE 9 OPERATING VARIABILITY

Number of Organizations N = 46	Score	Type of Organization
1	48	Component manufacturer
6	45	Two metal goods manufacturers Component manufacturer Abrasives manufacturer Packaging manufacturer Glass manufacturer
2	43	Printer Repairs for government department
4	42	Two component manufacturers Motor component manufacturer Metal motor component manufacturer
2	41	Vehicle manufacturer Engineering tool manufacturer
1	40	Component manufacturer
3	37	Civil engineering firm Carriage manufacturer Metal goods manufacturer
3	36	Vehicle manufacturer Confectionery manufacturer Local authority water department
2	35	Motor-tire manufacturer Commercial vehicle manufacturer
4	34	Motor component manufacturer Non-ferrous metal manufacturer Research division Food manufacturer
3	33	Engineering component manufacturer Domestic appliances manufacturer Local authority civil engineering department
1	32	Component manufacturer
2	31	Government inspection department Toy manufacturer
3	30	Brewery Insurance company Food manufacturer
1	27	Local authority transport department
6	25	Local authority baths department Co-operative chain of retail stores Chain of retail stores Savings bank Chain of shoe repair stores Department store
1	23	Omnibus company
1	21	Local authority education department

organization, even if the physical techniques involve only pen, ink, and paper. The concept covers both the pattern of operations and the equipment used, and all the scales developed are applicable to service as well as to manufacturing organizations. Five scales of related aspects of technology were developed.

Thompson and Bates (1957) defined the "adaptability" of the technology as "the extent to which the appropriate mechanics, knowledge, skills and raw materials can be used for other products" and, it may be added, services. An attempt to operationalize some aspects of this definition is given in Table 10, which shows a scale of *workflow rigidity*. This consists of eight biserial items concerned with the adaptability in the patterns of operations; for example, whether the equipment was predominantly multipurpose or single-purpose, whether rerouting of work was possible, etc. Since this was a scale of composite items, item analysis was used to test the scaleability. The mean item-analysis value of 0.84 indi-

TABLE 10 SCALE OF WORKFLOW RIGIDITY

Item	Number of Organizations (N = 52)†	Item Analysis Value*
No waiting time possible (versus waiting time)	8	0.82
Single-purpose equipment (versus multi-purpose)	13	0.78
Production or service line (versus no set line)	42	1.00
No buffer stocks and no delays possible (versus buffer stocks and delays)	8	0.71
Single-source input (versus multisource input)	12	0.67
No rerouting of work possible (versus rerouting possible)	15	0.80
Breakdown stops all workflow immediately (versus not all workflow stops)	6	0.97
Breakdown stops some or all workflow immediately (versus no workflow stops)	35	0.95

* Mean item analysis value = 0.84.

† Since this is a test of internal consistency and scaleability, the whole group of 52 organizations was used. (D. S. Pugh *et al.*, 1968.)

cates that it is legitimate to add the scores on these items to form a workflow rigidity score for an organization.

Two other scales of technology utilized the concepts outlined by Amber and Amber (1962). They postulated that "the more human attributes performed by a machine, the higher its automaticity" and compiled a scale of automaticity together with clear operational definitions, which could be applied to any piece of equipment from a pencil to a computer, and which categorized each into one of six classes. The two scales based on these concepts were: the *automaticity mode,* i.e., the level of automaticity of the bulk of the equipment of the organization; and the *automaticity range;* i.e., the highest-scoring piece of equipment an organization used, since every organization also scored the lowest possible by using hand tools and manual machines.

The fourth scale, *interdependence of workflow segments,* was a scale of the degree of linkage between the segments of an organization; a segment being defined as those parts into which the workflow hierarchy was divided at the first point of division beneath the chief executive. The three points on the scale were: *(i)* segments duplicated in different locations, all having the same final outputs; *(ii)* segments having different final outputs, which are not inputs of other segments; *(iii)* segments having outputs which become inputs of other segments. The final scale, *specificity of criteria of quality evaluation,* was a first attempt to classify the precision with which the output was compared to an acceptable standard. The three points on the scale were: *(i)* personal evaluation only; *(ii)* partial measurements, of some aspect(s) of the output(s); *(iii)* measurements used over virtually the whole output, to compare against precise specification (the "blueprint" concept).

Correlations. As expected, these measures tend to be highly intercorrelated. A principal components analysis extracted a large first factor accounting for 58 percent of the variance, with loadings of over 0.6 on all scales, and of over 0.8 on three of them. A scale of *workflow integration* was therefore constructed by summing the scores on the component scales. Among organizations scoring high, with very integrated, automated, and rather rigid technologies, were an automobile factory, a food manufacturer, and a swimming baths department. Among those scoring low, with diverse, nonautomated, flexible technologies, were retail stores, an education department, and a building firm.

There were no clear relationships between workflow integration and the variables of size, origin and history, or concentration of ownership with control and negative relationship with public accountability ($r = -0.35$), largely because the government-owned organizations in the sample were predominantly service and therefore at the diverse end of the workflow integration scale. The correlations between workflow integration and operating variability ($r = 0.57$) and diversity ($r = 0.33$) reflect the close relationship between the ends of the organization and the means it employs to attain them.

Workflow integration showed modest but distinct correlations with all the three structural factors, the only contextual variable to do so, as can be seen from Table 2. The relationships of technology are therefore much more general than is the case with size, for example, which has a greater but more specific effect. The positive correlation between workflow integration and structuring of activities ($r = 0.34$) would be expected since highly integrated and therefore more rigid technologies would be associated with a greater structuring of activities and procedures. Similarly, the correlation with concentration of authority ($r = -0.30$) suggests that because of the increasing control resulting directly from the workflow itself in an integrated technology, decisions tend to become more routine and can be decentralized. But the fact that the correlations are not higher than this emphasizes that structuring may be related to other contextual factors, such as size. The relationship of technology to line control of workflow, however, was very clear ($r = 0.46$); the more integrated the technology, the more the reliance on impersonal control. It must be emphasized, however, that these relationships were found on the whole sample of manufacturing and service organizations. When manufacturing organizations only were considered, some of the relationships showed considerable change (Hickson *et al.*, 1969).

Labor Costs. This is a second related, but conceptually distinct, aspect of the technology of the workflow and is expressed as a percentage of total costs. The range in the sample was from 5 to 70 percent, with engineering organizations scoring low and public services high. The scale correlated with workflow integration ($r = -0.50$), high integration being associated with reduced labor costs. Its correlations with the structural factors are comparable with those for technology (after adjusting the signs).

Location

The geographical, cultural, and community setting can influence the organization markedly (Blau & Scott, 1962). This study controls for some of these effects in a gross way, for all organizations of the sample were located in the same large industrial conurbation, and the community and its influence on the organizations located there were taken as given (Duncan *et al.*, 1963). Compared with the national distribution, the sample was overrepresented in the engineering and metal industries, and unrepresented in mining, shipbuilding, oil refining and other industries. Because of the location, however, regional cultural differences of the sort found by Thomas (1959) as to role conceptions, were avoided.

One aspect of location which discriminated between organizations in the sample, was *number of operating sites.* The range formed a Poisson distribution, with 47 percent of the sample having one site; but six organizations had over a hundred sites, and two over a thousand. This distribution did not appear to be a function of size ($r = 0.14$) but of the operating variability aspect of charter ($r = -0.56$). Manufacturing organizations were concentrated in a small number of sites (the largest number being nine), whereas services ranged across the scale. The number of operating sites was therefore correlated with the workflow integration scale of technology ($r = -0.58$), and with public accountability ($r = 0.34$), this last correlation reflecting the predominantly service function of the group of government-owned organizations.

This pattern of inter-relationships among the contextual variables led to the expectation of relationships between number of operating sites and the structual dimensions which would be congruent with those of operating variability and workflow integration. The correlations of number of operating sites with structuring of activities ($r = -0.26$), concentration of authority ($r = 0.39$) and line control of workflow ($r = 0.39$) confirm the relationships with charter and technology, and suggest a *charter-technology-location* nexus of interrelated contextual variables having a combined effect on structure.

Dependence

The dependence of an organization reflects its relationships with other organizations in its social environment, such as suppliers, customers, competitors, labor unions, management organizations, and political and social organizations.

Dependence on Parent Organization. The most important relationship would be the dependence of the organization on its parent organization. The *relative size* of the organization in relation to the parent organization was calculated as a percentage of the number of employees. This ranged from under one percent in two cases—a branch factory of the central government, and a small subsidiary company of one of the largest British private corporations in the country—to 100 percent in eight independent organizations. The distribution was Poisson in form with a mean and standard deviation of 37 percent. The next scale was a four-point category scale concerned with the *status* of the organization in relation to the parent organization: *(i)* principal units (8 organizations) where the organization was independent of any larger group although it might itself have had subsidiaries or branches; *(ii)* subsidiary units (18 organizations) which, although part of a larger group, had their own legal identity with, for example, their own boards of directors; *(iii)* head branch units (4 organizations) which did not have separate legal identity although they were the major operating components of the parent organization and the head office of the parent organization was on the same site; *(iv)* branch units (16 organizations) operating parts of a parent organization which did not satisfy the preceding criteria.

The third aspect of the relation between the organization and the parent organization was given by the degree of *organizational representation on policy-making bodies.* This three-point scale ranged from the organization being represented on the policy-making body of the parent organization (e.g. board of directors, city council), through the organization being represented on an intermediate policy-making body (e.g. board of directors of an operating company but not of the ultimate owning holding company, committee of the city council), to the organization having no representative on any policy-making body of the parent organization. As would be expected, these three variables were highly correlated (Tables 11, 12).

A related variable was the number of *specializations contracted out* by the organization. In many cases these would be available as services of the parent organization to the organization, although account was also taken of the various specialist services (e.g., consultants) used outside the parent organization. The specializations were as defined in the structural scale of functional specialization (Pugh *et al.*, 1968: Appendix A), and ranged from one specialization contracted out (two engineering works, a printer, and a builder) to no less than fifteen of the sixteen specializations contracted out (an abrasives manufacturer and a packaging manufacturer) with a mean 7.2 and standard deviation 4.0.

Dependence on Other Organizations. The suppliers and customers or clients of the organization must also be considered. The operating function of the organization can be regarded as being the processing of inputs and outputs between supplier and client, and the degree to which the organization is integrated into the processual chain by links at either end can be measured. Five category scales were developed to elucidate this concept (with details given in Table 11). They were concerned with the integration with suppliers and clients, and response in the output volume to client influence, etc. To establish a single dimension measuring the degree to which the organization was integrated into this system, the five scales were transformed into biserial form. Item analysis was carried out on the 18-item scale generated and yielded a mean item analysis value of 0.70 which seemed to justify the addition of the items into a total scale, *vertical integration.* At one extreme was a confectionery manufacturer and an engineering components firm supplying goods from stock with a large number of customers after obtaining their supplies from a large variety of sources; at the other extreme were organizations (vehicle components, civil engineering, scientific research) obtaining their resources from a small number of suppliers and supplying their product or service to a small number of clients (often the owning group only) who had a marked effect upon their workflow scheduling.

For *trade unions,* a scale of five ordered categories was developed of the extent to which unions were accepted as relevant to the activities of the organization. The scale was *(i)* no recognition given; *(ii)* only partial recognition given (i.e., discussions for certain purposes, but not negotiations); *(iii)* full recognition given to negotiate on wages and conditions of service on behalf of their members; *(iv)* full recognition given plus facilities for union meetings to be held regularly on the time and premises of the organization; *(v)* as in the preceding plus the recognition of a works convenor to act on behalf of all unions with members in the organization. Organizations in the sample were located in all the categories, with the modal position being full recognition; but five organizations did not recognize unions, and eleven gave the maximum recognition including a works convenor.

Examination of the intercorrelations between these six variables of dependence (Table 12) and of their correlations with other important aspects of context (Table 13) shows considerably higher correlations with size of parent organization than with size of organization, and considerably higher correlations with concentration of ownership with control (a variable applied to the parent organization) than with operating variability or workflow integration (variables applied to the operations of the individual organizations themselves). This pattern lends support to the view that these measures are tapping aspects of the dependence of the organization, particularly its dependence on external resources and power as in Eisenstadt's (1959) formulation. The one exception was the variable of recognition of trade unions, which had its largest contextual correlation with organization size, and is therefore concerned with a different aspect of interdependence. Impersonality of origin (from origin and history) and public accountability (from ownership and control) show the same pattern of higher correlation with the parent organization than with the unit, indicating that impersonally founded organizations are likely to be more dependent on their founding organizations; and that more publicly accountable organizations are more likely to be dependent on outside power with government-owned organizations being the extreme case.

These relationships suggested the application of factor analysis to a correlation matrix containing the seven variables. A principal-components analysis applied to the matrix produced a large first factor *dependence*[1] accounting for 55 percent of the variance, which was heavily loaded on all seven scales (on six of the seven, the loadings were above 0.7; the remaining loading on vertical integration was

[1]We are grateful to our colleague Diana C. Pheysey for suggesting this formulation and for much valuable critical comment on an earlier draft of this paper.

TABLE 11 DEPENDENCE

Distribution N = 46	Score	Scale Number and Title
		Scale No. 18.07
		*Relative Size**
		Range = 0–100 Mean = 37.4 S.D. = 37.3
		Scale No. 12.10
		Status of Organization Unit
16	1	Branch
4	2	Head branch (headquarters on same location)
18	3	Subsidiary (legal identity)
8	4	Principal unit
		Scale No. 12.11
		Organizational representation on policy-making bodies†
19	1	Organization not represented on top policy-making body
4	2	Organization represented on local policy-making body but not on top policy-making body
23	3	Organization represented on policy-making body
		Scale No. 18.06
		Number of specializations contracted out‡
		Range = 1–16 Mean = 7.2 S.D. = 4.0
		Scale No. 18.17
		Vertical integrations§
		Range = 1–16 Mean = 7.7 S.D. = 3.5
		Scale No. 18.03
		Integration with suppliers
4	1	No ownership ties and single orders
7	2	No ownership and single contracts or tenders
8	3	No ownership and short-term contracts, schedule and call-off
6	4	No ownership and yearly contracts, standing orders
7	5	Ownership and contractual ties
14	6	Ownership and tied supply
		Scale No. 18.05
		Response in outputs volume to customer influence
12	1	Outputs for stock
5	2	Outputs for stock and to customer order
21	3	Outputs to customer order
2	4	Outputs to customer order and to schedule and call-off
6	5	Outputs to schedule and call-off
		Scale No. 18.08
		Integration with customers: type of link with customers
24	1	Single orders
9	2	Regular contracts
10	3	Long-term contracts (over two years)
3	4	Ownership
		Scale No. 18.09
		Integration with customers: dependence of organization on its largest customer
30	1	Minor outlet (less than 10% of output)
10	2	Medium outlet (over 10% of output)
3	3	Major outlet (over 50% of output)
3	4	Sole outlet
		Scale No. 18.10
		Integration with customers: dependence of largest customer on organization
11	1	Minor supplier (less than 10% of particular item)
5	2	Medium supplier (over 10% of particular item)
21	3	Major supplier (over 50% of particular item)
9	4	Sole supplier with exclusive franchise

* Size of unit as a percentage of size of parent organization.

† Internal and parent organizations.

‡ The specializations are those of functional specialization (D. S. Pugh et al., 1968: Appendix A). Scores are out of a possible 16

§ This scale is formed by the total of the scores on the 18 items representing the following five scales: 18.03, 18.05, 18.08, 18.09, 18.10.

TABLE 12 DEPENDENCE INTERCORRELATION MATRIX (product-moment coefficient $N = 46$)

	Relative size	*Status of Organization Unit*	*Organizational Representation on Policy-making Body*	*Specializations Contracted out*	*Vertical Integration*	*Trade Unions*
Relative size	—					
Status of organization unit	0.68	—				
Organizational representation on policy-making body	0.50	0.65	—			
Specializations contracted out	−0.60	−0.51	−0.52	—		
Vertical integration	−0.40	−0.34	−0.36	0.45	—	
Trade unions	−0.09	−0.16	−0.25	0.19	0.28	—

0.58). The scores for dependence were obtained by an algebraic weighted sum of the scores on the four most highly loaded component scales, the weightings being obtained by a multiple regression analysis of the component scales on the factor. A high score characterized organizations with a high degree of dependence, which tended to be impersonally founded, publicly accountable, vertically integrated, with a large number of specializations contracted out, small in size relative to their parent organization, low in status, and not represented at the policymaking level in the parent organization (e.g., branch units in packaging, civil engineering, and food manufacture, a central government repair department, and a local government baths department). Organizations with low dependence were independent organizations characterized by personal foundation, low public accountability, little vertical integration, few specializations contracted out, and where the parent organization was the organization itself (e.g., a printing firm, the very old metal goods firm, a chain of shoe repair stores, and an engineering component manufacturer).

The correlation of dependence with the structural factors was focused largely on concentration of authority ($r = 0.66$), in every case, for dependence and its component scales the correlation being much greater than with the other factors, as Table 13 shows. Indeed, apart from the correlations with impersonality of origin and public accountability, none of the other correlations reached the 5 percent level of confidence. Dependent organizations have a more centralized authority structure and less autonomy in decision making; independent organizations have

TABLE 13 DEPENDENCE

	Concentration of Ownership with Control	*Size*	*Size of parent Organization*	*Operating Variability*	*Workflow Integration*	*Size of Organization*	*Structuring of Activities*	*Concentration of Authority*	*Line Control of Workflow*
Status of organization unit	−0.45	0.11	−0.27	0.01	0.05	0.17	0.13	−0.63	−0.07
Organizational representation on policy-making bodies	0.41	0.15	−0.19	−0.01	0.19	0.20	0.14	−0.63	−0.18
Number of specializations contracted out	−0.32	0.14	0.40	0.11	0.09	0.01	0.18	0.53	0.00
Relative size	0.47	0.06	−0.38	−0.08	−0.03	0.16	0.03	−0.40	−0.13
Vertical integration	−0.15	−0.01	0.39	0.21	−0.12	−0.06	0.06	0.29	−0.04
Trade unions*	−0.21	0.26	0.25	0.19	0.21	0.36	0.51	0.08	−0.35
Impersonality of of origin	−0.40	0.13	0.36	−0.27	−0.25	0.07	−0.04	0.64	0.36
Public accountability of parent organization	−0.51	0.04	0.45	−0.35	−0.35	0.01	−0.10	0.64	0.47
Dependence	−0.49	−0.06	0.37	0.05	−0.05	−0.17	−0.05	0.66	0.13

* This variable was not included in the scale of dependence.

more autonomy and decentralize decisions down the hierarchy.

The relationships between dependence and the component scales of concentration of authority vary. Centralization, as defined and measured in this study, is concerned only with the level in the organization which has the necessary authority to take particular decisions, (Pugh *et al.*, 1968: 76); the higher the necessary level, the greater the centralization. No account was taken of the degree of participation or consultation in decision-making as in Hage and Aiken's (1967) formulation of the concept. These were regarded as aspects for study at the group level of analysis. Neither is it possible for such a statement as the following to hold: "The decisions were centralized on the foreman since neither the superintendent nor the departmental manager had the necessary experience." In the present formulation this would be regarded as relative decentralization. Autonomy was measured by the proportion of decisions that could be taken within the organization as distinct from those which had to be taken at the level above it. Thus independent organizations of necessity had more autonomy, since there was no level above the chief executive, and the correlation between dependence and this component of concentration of authority was $r = -0.72$. The relation of centralization (which is concerned with the whole range of levels in the hierarchy) with dependence is less, but still high ($r = 0.57$). Dependent organizations also have a distinct tendency to standardize the procedures for selection and advancement ($r = 0.40$), a major component of concentration of authority. So dependent units have the apparatus of recruitment routines, selection panels, formal establishment figures, etc. of their parent organizations.

Relation between Structure and Context

In this investigation of the relationship of organization structure to aspects of the context in which the organization functions, the use of scaling and factor analytic techniques has made possible the condensation of data and reorganization of concepts and has established eight distinctive scales of elements of context. These scales, shown in Table 14 together with their correlations with the structural dimensions, denote the variables that are salient among those which have been thought to affect structure. Relationships between structure and age, size, charter (operating variability, operating diversity), technology (workflow integration) location (number of operating sites) and dependence on other organizations are exposed by the correlations. At the same time the correlations raise questions about the relationship between ownership pattern and administrative structure.

THE MULTIVARIATE PREDICTION OF STRUCTURE FROM CONTEXT

From inspection of Table 14 and of the intercorrelation matrix in Table 3, certain elements of context can now be identified. The variables in Table 14 are now used as independent variables in a prediction analysis of the structural dimensions. The pattern of these correlations, that is, that where they are high they are specific, and where they are low, they are diffused, indicates that the predictions should be attempted on a multivariate basis. In this case consideration had to be given to choosing not only predictors with high correlations with the criterion, but also having low intercorrelations among themselves. If high intercorrelations among the predictors were allowed, then, since the high correlations with the criterion would be aspects of the same relationship, the multiple correlation would not be increased to any extent. If the intercorrelations between the predictors were low, then each would make its distinct contribution to the multiple correlation.

These problems can be illustrated from the attempt to obtain a multiple prediction of structuring of activities from the three contextual variables correlated with it (Table 14). Size is clearly the first

TABLE 14 SALIENT ELEMENTS OF CONTEXT (product-moment correlations with structural factors)*

Elements of Context	*Structuring of Activities*	*Concentration of Authority*	*Line Control of Workflow*
Age	—	−0.38	—
Size of organization†	0.69	—	—
Size of parent organization†	0.39	0.39	—
Operating variability	—	—	−0.57
Operating diversity	—	−0.30	—
Workflow integration	0.34	−0.30	−0.46
Number of operating sites	—	0.39	0.39
Dependence	—	0.66	—

* With $N = 46$, correlations of 0.29 are at the 5% level of confidence, and correlations of 0.38 are at the 1% level of confidence.

† Logarithm of number of employees.

TABLE 15 MULTIPLE PREDICTION ANALYSIS OF STRUCTURAL FACTORS

Contextual Predictors of Structural Factors	*Single Correlation*	*Multiple Correlation*	*F Ratio*	*Degrees of Freedom*	*Level of Confidence*
Structuring of activities					
Size.	0.69	0.69	39.6	1:44	>99%
Workflow integration	0.34	0.75	8.2	1.43	>99%
Size of parent organization	0.39	0.76	1.9	1:42	NS
Concentration of authority					
Dependence.	0.66	0.66	34.2	1:44	>99%
Location (number of operating sites).	0.39	0.75	12.5	1:43	>99%
Age of organization	−0.38	0.77	2.5	1:42	NS
Operating diversity.	−0.30	0.78	3.0	1:41	NS
Workflow integration	−0.30	0.78	0.0	1:40	NS
Size of parent organization	0.39	0.79	0.4	1:39	NS
Line control of workflow					
Operating variability	−0.57	0.57	20.7	1:44	>99%
Workflow integration	−0.46	0.59	1.7	1:43	NS
Number of sites	0.39	0.59	0.1	1:42	NS

predictor, with a correlation of $r = 0.69$, and the question is whether taking account of size of parent organization and workflow integration will increase predictive accuracy. In spite of its greater correlation with the criterion, the size of the parent organization would be expected to make a smaller contribution to the prediction than workflow integration, since it has a strong correlation with the first predictor ($r = 0.43$); whereas the technology measure is not correlated with organization size ($r = 0.08$). This is in fact the case as shown in the first section of Table 15, which gives the multiple prediction analyses for the three structural factors.

Table 15 shows for each predictor variable, the single correlation with the criterion, the multiple correlation obtained by adding this predictor to the preceding ones, the F ratio corresponding to the increase obtained on the addition of this predictor, the degrees of freedom corresponding to the F ratio when $N = 46$, and the level of confidence at which the increase due to this predictor can be quoted. It will be seen from the first section of Table 15 that the correlation 0.69, between size and structuring of activities, is increased to a multiple correlation of 0.75 when workflow integration is added as a predictor. But the multiple correlation shows no noticeable increase when size of parent organization is added as a third predictor; that is, its predictive power has already been tapped by the two previous variables.

It must be emphasized that this procedure assesses only the predictive power of the contextual variables, not their relative importance in any more general sense. It cannot be concluded that the relationship of size of parent organization to structuring of activities is less important than that of workflow integration, because it adds less to the multiple correlation. Indeed the original higher correlation shows that this is not the case. Because of the interaction of the variables, the effects of organizational size and size of parent organization are confounded, in this study, as the correlation between them shows. A full examination of their relative effects would require a sample in which they were not correlated, as is the case with the technology measure.

The same argument applies to the multiple prediction of concentration of authority (Table 15). Here again there is a clear first predictor, dependence, with a correlation of 0.66 but then a choice of intercorrelated variables. The selection was made in order to get as high a multiple correlation as possible with as few predictors as possible, but the fact that the later predictors add nothing to the multiple correlation does not mean that they have no impact, only that predictive power has been exhausted by previous related variables. The existence of the charter-technology-location nexus referred to above is supported by the fact that when any one of these variables is used as a predictor, the remaining two do not add to the multiple correlation. Table 15 shows the multiple correlation of 0.75 obtained by using the location measure together with dependence as predictors. When the technology scale of workflow integration is substituted as the second predictor, the multiple correlation is 0.71; when the operating diversity scale of charter is used, the multiple correlation is 0.70.

The prediction of line control of workflow shows this same phenomenon, where the addition of predictors, because of their interrelationships, does not improve on the original single correlation of operating variability with the criterion.

The size of the multiple correlations obtained with the first two factors, each 0.75 with two predictors, together with the small number of predictors needed, strongly supports the view that in relation to organization structure as defined and measured in this study, salient elements of context have been identified. Thus a knowledge of the score of an organization on a small number of contextual variables makes it possible to predict within relatively close limits, its structural profile. Given information about how many employees an organization has, and an outline of its technology in terms of how integrated and automated the work process is, its structuring of activities can be estimated within fairly close limits. Since in turn the score of the organization on structuring of activities summarizes an extensive description of broad aspects of bureaucratization, the organization is thereby concisely portrayed in terms of this and similar concepts. Likewise, knowing the dependence of an organization on other organizations and its geographical dispersion over sites tells a great deal about the likely concentration of authority in its structure. *Size, technology, dependence and location* (number of sites) are critical in the prediction of the two major dimensions (structuring of activities, concentration of authority) of the structures of work organizations.

Multiple predictions of the order of magnitude obtained are as high as can be expected with this level of analysis. Higher values would imply that there were no important deviant cases, and that differences as to policies and procedures among the members of an organization have no effect on its structure. And this is obviously not so. The multiple predictions discussed here are applicable only to this sample. When the regression equations obtained are applied to another similar sample for prediction purposes, there is likely to be a reduction in the multiple correlations. The extent of this reduction can be strictly gauged only by investigating another similar sample of organizations. This cross-validation study is at present being undertaken, but a first attempt to estimate the likely amount of reduction was made by splitting the sample into two subsamples of 23 organizations, each stratified in the same way as the whole sample. Table 16 gives the multiple regressions on structuring of activities and concentration of authority for the whole sample and for the two subsamples separately. The multiple correlations and the weightings are of the same order of magnitude. A "robust" prediction on the basis of simple weightings was also calculated. These correlations should be less subject to shrinkage. The stability of the correlation of 0.57 between operating variability and line control of workflow is indicated by correlations on the two subsamples of 0.50 and 0.65.

SUMMARY AND DISCUSSION

This study has demonstrated the possibilities of a multivariate approach to the analysis of the relationships between the structure of an organization and the context in which it functions. Starting from a framework as outlined in the conceptual scheme summarized in Table 1, aspects of the context and structure of the organization were sampled in order to establish scales which discriminated among organizations in a large number of aspects. From this sampling 103 primary scales of structure and context were developed as a basis for the analysis of the interrelationships among them.

By scaling and factor analytic techniques, these were then summarized to form three basic dimensions of structure and eight salient elements of context (Table 14). The analogy with the psychological test constructor who samples behavior in order to establish dimensions of personality is clear, and the same limitations apply. Thus while a claim can be made for the internal consistency and scaleability of these measures, no claim can be made as to the com-

TABLE 16 MULTIPLE REGRESSION ON STRUCTURAL FACTORS

Structural Factors	Whole Sample	Subsamples 1	Subsamples 2	"Robust" Weightings
Structuring of activities				
Weightings of predictors				
Size	0.67	0.72	0.60	2
Workflow Integration	0.29	0.14	0.43	1
Multiple correlation	0.75	0.73	0.79	0.74
Concentration of authority				
Weightings of predictors				
Dependence	0.64	0.50	0.77	2
Location	0.36	0.40	0.33	1
Multiple correlation	0.75	0.66	0.84	0.75

prehensiveness with which they cover the field. This is particularly clear in the attempt to elucidate aspects of context, a concept which, although in some respects narrower than that of environment, is still very wide. Emphasis was therefore placed on those aspects of context that had been held to be relevant to structure on the basis of previous writings. The size of the multiple correlations obtained indicates that at least some of the salient aspects of context were tapped.

The predicability of the structural dimensions from contextual elements serves as external validating evidence for the structural concepts themselves. It has now been shown that besides being internally consistent and scaleable, as previously demonstrated, they can also be related in a meaningful way to external referents. Indeed the size of the correlations inevitably raises the question of causal implications. It is tempting to argue that these clear relationships are causal—in particular, that *size, dependence, and the charter-technology-location nexus largely determine structure.*

It can be hypothesized that size causes structuring through its effect on intervening variables such as the frequency of decisions and social control. An increased scale of operation increases the frequency of recurrent events and the repetition of decisions, which are then standardized and formalized (Haas & Collen, 1963). Once the number of positions and people grows beyond control by personal interaction, the organization must be more explicitly structured. In so far as structuring includes the concept of bureaucracy, Weber's observation that "the increasing bureaucratic organization of all genuine mass parties offers the most striking example of the role of sheer quantity as a leverage for the bureaucratization of a social structure" is pertinent (Gerth & Mills, 1948).

Dependence causes concentration of authority at the apex of publicly owned organizations because pressure for public accountability requires the approval of central committees for many decisions. The similar position of small units in large privately owned groups is demonstrated by the effect that a merger may have upon authority. After a merger, a manager of the smaller unit "may no longer be able to make a certain decision and act upon it independently. He may have to refer matters to people who were complete strangers to him a few months earlier" (Stewart *et al.,* 1963).

Integrated technology may be hypothesized to cause an organization to move towards the impersonal control end of the line-control dimension. Line control is adequate in shops or in municipal schools or building maintenance gangs, where the technology of the tasks is not mechanized and each line supervisor and primary work group is independent of all the others. But as workflow integration reaches the production line or automated stages, where large numbers of tasks are interdependent, more control is needed than can be exercised by the line of command alone. Udy (1965) summarizes this in his proposition, "The more complex the technology . . . , the greater the emphasis on administration."

The causal argument need not run only one way. It can be suggested that a policy of specializing roles and standardizing procedures, that is, of structuring, would require more people, that is, growth in size. Concentration of decisions in the hands of an owning group is likely to result in more economic integration among the subsidiaries concerned, that is, more dependence; while the production control, inspection, and work-study procedures of staff control might raise the level of workflow integration in the technology.

But a cross-sectional study such as this can only establish relationships. Causes should be inferred from a theory that generates a dynamic model about changes over time. The contribution of the present study is to establish a framework of operationally defined and empirically validated concepts, which will enable processual and dynamic studies to be carried out on a much more rigorous and comparative basis than has been done previously. The framework is also seen as a means of controlling for organizational factors when individual and group level variables are being studied. Such studies must now be conducted with reference not only to differences in size, but also in dependence, operating function, workflow integration, etc., and with reference to the demonstrated relationship between these aspects of context and organization structure.

REFERENCES

Aaronovitch, S. *The ruling class.* London: Lawrence and Wishart, 1961.

Amber, G. H., and Amber, P. S. *Anatomy of automation.* Englewood Cliffs, N.J.: Prentice-Hall, 1962.

Bakke, E. W. Concepts of the social organization. In M. Haire (ed.), *Modern organization theory.* New York: Wiley, 1959.

Berle, A. A. and Means, G. *The modern corporation and private property.* New York: Macmillan, 1937.

Blau, P. and Scott, W. R. *Formal organizations.* San Francisco: Chandler, 1962.

Brogden, H. E. A new coefficient: Application to biserial correlation and to estimation of selective efficiency. *Psychometrika,* 1949, **14**, 169–82.

Burnham, J. *The managerial revolution.* London: Penguin, 1962.

Chandler, A. D. *Strategy and structure.* Cambridge, Mass.: M.I.T. Press, 1962.

Clarke, B. R. Organizational adaptation and precarious values. *American Sociological Review,* 1956, **21**, 327-336.

Dahrendorf, R. *Class and conflict in industrial society.* Stanford, Calif.: Stanford University Press, 1959.

Dubin, R. *The world of work.* Englewood Cliffs, N.J.: Prentice-Hall, 1958.

Duncan, O. D., Scott, W. R., Liberson, S., Duncan B., and Winsborough, H. *Metropolis and region.* Baltimore, Md.: Johns Hopkins University Press, 1963.

Eisenstadt, S. N. Bureaucracy, bureaucratization and debureaucratization. *Administrative Science Quarterly,* 1959, **4**, 302-20.

Florence, P. S. *Ownership, control and success of large companies.* London: Sweet and Maxwell, 1961.

Gerth, H. H. and Wright Mills, C. (eds.). *From Max Weber: Essays in sociology.* London: Routledge and Kegan Paul, 1948.

Haas, E. and Collen, L. Administrative practices in university departments. *Administrative Science Quarterly,* 1963, **8**, 44-60.

Hage, J. and Aiken, M. Relationship of centralization to other structural properties. *Administrative Science Quarterly,* June 1967, **12**, 72-92.

Hall, R. H. and Tittle, C. R. A note on bureaucracy and its correlates. *American Journal of Sociology,* 1966, **72**, 267-72.

Hickson, D. J., Pugh, D. S., and Pheysey, D. C. Operations technology and formal organization: An empirical reappraisal. *Administrative Science Quarterly,* 1969 (to appear).

Hinings, C. R., Pugh, D. S., Hickson, D. J., and Turner, C. An approach to the study of bureaucracy. *Sociology,* January 1967, **1**, 62-72.

Inkson, J. H. K., Payne, R. L., and Pugh, D. S. Extending the occupational environment: The measurement of organizations. *Occupational Psychology,* 1967, **41**, 33-47.

Levy, P. and Pugh, D. S. Scaling and multivariate analyses in the study of organizational variables. *Sociology,* 1969, **3**.

Mills, C. Wright. *The power elite.* London: Oxford University Press, 1956.

Parsons, T. Suggestions for a sociological approach to the theory of organizations, I and II. *Administrative Science Quarterly,* June and September 1956, **1**, 63-85, 225-39.

Perrow, C. A framework for the comparative analysis of organizations. *American Sociological Review,* April 1967, **32**, 194-208.

Porter, L. W. and Lawler, E. E. III. Properties of organization structure in relation to job attitudes and job behavior. *Psychological Bulletin,* 1965, **64**, 25-51.

Presthus, R. V. Towards a theory of organizational behavior. *Administrative Science Quarterly,* 1958, **3**, 48-72.

Pugh, D. S., Hickson, D. J., and Hinings, C. R. An empirical taxonomy of work organization structures. *Administrative Science Quarterly,* 1969, 115-26.

Pugh, D. S., Hickson, D. J., Hinings, C. R., Macdonald, K. M., Turner, C., and Lupton, T. A conceptual scheme for organizational analysis. *Administrative Science Quarterly,* 1963, **8**, 289-315.

Pugh, D. S., Hickson, D. J., Hinings, C. R., and Turner, C. Dimensions of organization structure. *Administrative Science Quarterly,* 1968, **13**, 65-105.

Selznick, P. *T.V.A. and the grass roots.* Berkeley, Calif.: University of California Press, 1949.

Selznick, P. *Leadership in administration.* Evanston, Ill.: Row and Peterson, 1957.

Starbuck, W. H. Organizational growth and development. In J. G. March (ed.), *Handbook of organizations.* Chicago: Rand McNally, 1965.

Stewart, R., Wingate, P., and Smith, R. *Mergers: The impact on managers.* London: Acton Society Trust, 1963.

Stinchcombe, A. L. Social structure and organization. In J. G. March (ed.), *Handbook of organizations.* Chicago: Rand McNally, 1965.

Thomas, E. J. Role conceptions and organizational size. *American Sociological Review,* 1959, **24**, 30-37.

Thompson, J. D. and Bates, F. E. Technology, organization and administration. *Administrative Science Quarterly,* 1957, **2**, 323-43.

Trist, E. L., Higgin, G. W., Murray, H. and Pollock, A. B. *Organizational choice.* London: Tavistock, 1963.

Udy, S. H. The comparative analysis of organizations. In J. G. March (ed.), *Handbook of organizations.* Chicago: Rand McNally, 1965.

Walker, C. R. *Modern technology and civilization.* New York: McGraw-Hill, 1962.

Wilson, B. R. Analytical studies of social institutions. In A. T. Welford *et al., Society: Problems and methods of study.* London: Routledge and Kegan Paul, 1962.

Woodward, J. *Industrial organization, theory and practice.* London: Oxford University Press, 1965.

30. PROPERTIES OF ORGANIZATION STRUCTURE IN RELATION TO JOB ATTITUDES AND JOB BEHAVIOR*

***Lyman W. Porter and Edward E. Lawler, III*†**

This article reviews the results of empirical field studies that have investigated the relationships between properties of organization structure and job attitudes and job behavior in business and industrial organizations. The following seven structural properties were examined: organizational levels, line/staff hierarchies, span of control, subunit size, total-organization size, tall/flat shape, and centralized/decentralized shape. At least five of these seven variables (with the possible exceptions being span of control and centralized/decentralized shape) were found to be significantly related to one or more attitude or behavioral variables. Implications of these findings for organization theory and future research are discussed.[1]

All organizations are structured, in the sense of having positions and parts which are systematically related to other positions and parts. Since organizations vary in their structure, it is appropriate to examine the question of whether differences in the structure of organizations are related to differences in the attitudes and behavior of their members. The purpose of this article is to review the results of published research (prior to 1964) relevant to such relationships existing in business and industrial organizations.

Although organizations have been the focus of research and interest in sociology since the time of Weber's first writings on bureaucracy in the 1920s, and in industrial psychology since the time of the Hawthorne studies in the early 1930s, it has been only in the past decade or so that intensive and concentrated attention has been given to organizations in the behavioral sciences. The major development in this area in psychology over the past 10 years has been the advent of so-called "modern organization theory." Such theory, as developed by Likert, Haire, McGregor, Argyris, and others, has been advocated as a contrast with, and improvement on, so-called "classical organization theory" as developed by Fayol, Urwick, Taylor, and others. Whereas the classical theorists, with their discussions of chain of command, specialization of function, span of control and so forth, placed heavy emphasis on factors related to organization structure, the modern psychological theorists, such as those mentioned previously, have paid relatively little attention to the structural aspects of organizations. Bennis (1959) aptly summed up this point several years ago when he pointed out that classical theorists talked about "organizations without people," while modern theorists often seem to talk about "people without organizations." Instead of emphasizing the structure of organizations, latter-day theorists have advocated supervisory human relations training, *T* groups, attention to the nonfinancial needs of the employees and the like, as methods for improving organizational administration and leadership. The efficacy of such methods, however, may well be reduced by failure to take into account the structural characteristics of organizations.

Not only have organization theorists tended to ignore structural variables, but also so have many of the researchers in this area. Despite the apparent lack of concentrated empirical efforts to understand the effects of structural variables (other than the variable of work-group size), there are, nevertheless, a number of studies in the psychological, sociological, and management-science literature that are pertinent to a consideration of structure. Although many of these studies were not conceived by their authors as investigations pertaining to structure as such, they do provide relevant and important evidence and thus will be included in this review.

For the purposes of this paper, structure has been defined to mean the positions and parts of organizations and their systematic and relatively enduring relationships to each other. Thus, we are referring to the formal structure of organizations as might be indicated, in a superficial way at least, in the formal "organization chart." Within the boundaries of this broad definition of structure, we have identified the following seven structural properties or variables:

Suborganization properties
1. Organizational levels
2. Line and staff hierarchies
3. Span of control
4. Size: subunits

Total-organization properties
5. Size: total organizations
6. Shape: tall or flat
7. Shape: centralized or decentralized

* *Psychological Bulletin*, Vol. 64, No. 1 (1965), pp. 23–51.

† Graduate School of Administration, University of California, Irvine, and Institute of Social Research, University of Michigan, respectively.

[1] The authors are indebted to the following individuals for their comments and suggestions regarding earlier versions of this paper: Chris Argyris, Peter M. Blau, Edwin E. Ghiselli, Thomas M. Lodahl, George Strauss, and Victor H. Vroom. We should also like to acknowledge the financial support of the Institute of Industrial Relations, University of California, Berkeley.

The first four variables above can be considered as suborganization properties of structure inasmuch as they permit comparisons of positions or parts contained within organizations with other positions or parts, either contained within the same organizations or within other organizations. The last three variables can be considered total-organization properties of structure because they require comparisons among organizations as complete entities. This sort of distinction between suborganization and total-organization types of properties will be shown to be especially crucial in the discussion of the effects of "size." It is also important to stress that these seven properties or dimensions of structure should not be considered mutually exclusive. For example, "span of control" has an obvious connection to the variable of "tall/flat" shape of total organizations. Although such variables are not clearly distinct from each other, we have discussed them separately since they are typically considered separately in both the research and textbook literature on organizations.

In essence, for this review these seven properties of organization structure will be regarded as the "independent" variables. Since almost none of the studies reviewed were experimental studies in the strict use of the term "experiment," any relationships found between structural variables and job attitudes or job behavior cannot be considered "cause-effect" relationships. Thus, neither the studies nor our conclusions from them can prove that the variations in structure cause the particular attitudes or behavior. However, the structural properties are referred to as the independent variables in the sense that if there are any cause-effect relationships present they probably are due either to the variation in structure causing the variation in attitudes or behavior, or else to some third variable determining both the structure and the attitudes and behavior. Although it is conceivable that the kinds of attitudes or behavior usually investigated in these studies could determine the structure of organizations, this seems unlikely (at least in a direct fashion) in most cases.

Turning now to our "dependent" variables, job attitudes and job behavior, we have used the term "attitude" in its broadest and loosest sense of "opinion concerning some object," in this case jobs or aspects of jobs. Included under job-attitude studies would be the typical morale study, where the specific attitude questions are concerned with opinions about the organization, the supervisors, the working conditions and other factors directly connected with the job situation in which the employee operates. Excluded from the review are studies focusing on attitudes toward the self, such as self-description and vocational-interest studies, on the assumption that they are more likely to describe what groups or types of people are like rather than what positions or parts of organizations are like.

Considered under the heading of job behavior are studies that were (with a few exceptions) concerned with the following types of information: performance and output rates or ratings, turnover rates, absenteeism rates, accident rates, and employee-grievance rates. In this review the problem of the relationship between job attitudes and these various indices of behavior have not been dealt with; these have merely been considered to be two categories of dependent variables that are of interest to social scientists studying organizations.

Finally, the three major criteria for the inclusion of studies reviewed can be listed:

1. Studies of Industrial and Business Organizations. The review is purposely restricted to studies dealing with these types of organizations—rather than also including other kinds of organizations such as governmental agencies, military units, schools, churches, and the like—in order to keep the discussion reasonably focused and delineated.

2. Comparative Studies. Only those studies which have dealt with at least two (preferably, three or more) positions or degrees of structure along a given property or dimension are included. Thus, for example, a study of only foremen's attitudes would not be included in the section on organizational levels since such a study did not compare foremen's attitudes with those of employees at some other organizational level. Likewise, a study of only small companies would not be included in the section on studies of total size, since no comparisons within that study are possible between small organizations and other-sized organizations. Under this criterion, case studies of single organizations were also excluded.

3. Empirical Studies. With very few exceptions, only those studies providing empirical data are included. Articles based wholly or mostly on the opinions of the author unsupported by actual data have been excluded. In addition, articles based on casual observations where it seemed unlikely that the procedures could be easily repeated by other researchers have also been excluded.

The sections of the review to follow are arranged in the same order as the previously-listed set of seven properties of organization structure. Thus, we first take up properties permitting suborganization comparisons, followed by properties concerned with total-organization comparisons.

ORGANIZATIONAL LEVELS

For many years social scientists interested in industrial organizations have tended either to ignore the effect of organizational levels or else to concentrate on the simple dichotomy between managers and workers. In the 1940's most textbook writers in the area of human relations, following the lead of the Hawthorne investigations, spotlighted the plight of workers vis-à-vis managers in terms of the types of physical, social, and psychological conditions they had to endure. The emphasis was almost completely on the worker-management comparison. This tradition carried over into the 1950's when the "modern" management theorists, such as Argyris (1957), Haire (1956), Leavitt (1958), Likert (1961), and McGregor (1960), continued to focus, for the most part, on the relationship of managers to nonmanagement subordinates.

This relative lack of attention to the effects of differentiation among levels within management is somewhat surprising when one considers the amount of interest that industrial psychologists and sociologists have shown in the effects of division of labor. Almost always, however, division of labor has been studied as it occurs along a horizontal dimension at the rank-and-file worker level. The fact that there is not only a division of labor horizontally but also vertically within industrial organizations has frequently been neglected. The importance of paying closer attention to this vertical dimension of structure has been well stated by Pfiffner and Sherwood (1960) when they point out that:

> [The] differentiation of task between echelons is of more significance to the selection and training of leaders at the several levels than may be indicated by the attention accorded it in the past. The psychological adjustment necessary when one goes from one level to another is often difficult because of the tendency to continue former behavior patterns. . . . At first glance this might appear to be a problem of human relations rather than of formal organization, but such a conclusion would be only partially true. Good job descriptions should reflect task differentiation at the various echelons. It is a matter of tasks combined with behavior. . . . [p. 139].

In surveying the literature pertinent to organizational levels and their impact on, or relationship to, job attitudes and behavior, we encounter several difficult boundary or definitional problems. The first such problem concerns the question of whether studies of *occupational* levels should be included in the review. For our purposes, since the focus is on *organizational* structural variables, such occupational level studies will be generally omitted on the basis that they ordinarily investigate levels in a societal or cultural setting rather than levels within an organizational setting. A second problem in defining studies of organizational levels is posed by the investigation directed toward superior-subordinate relationships. Although in one sense these are studies that compare two different organizational levels, they in fact seldom provide data that contribute to our knowledge of the effects of the vertical dimension of structure. This is because such studies are usually concerned with implications for superior-subordinate authority relationships and not with implications for attitudes or behavior that may be differentially required or exhibited at various *job levels* within organizations. Most such studies, therefore, will not be covered in this review.

Within these broad limits, this section of the review will analyze the results of studies containing two or more organizational levels as the independent type of variable and one or more categories of directly job-related attitudes or behavior as the dependent type of variable.

Attitudes

Job Satisfaction and Morale. The first studies to be considered will be those that compare management with nonmanagement employees; after that, studies dealing with comparisons among levels within management will be reviewed.

Herzberg, Mausner, Peterson, and Capwell (1957) have summarized the literature through 1954 relevant to job satisfaction attitudes associated with organizational levels. They conclude that "one unequivocal fact emerges from the studies of job satisfaction; the higher the level of occupation, the higher the morale [p. 20]." It is clear from this statement that their review included studies of occupational level. The problem of drawing conclusions from these studies is that frequently the occupational level categories include people who do not work in industrial or business organizations (e.g., professional people included in a category of "executive and professional"). Nevertheless, the Herzberg review does cite five studies "in which the morale of workers was compared to that of their supervisors (Ash, 1954; Browne & Neitzel, 1952; Campbell, 1948; Hull & Kolstad, 1942; Kolstad, 1944)." The study by Browne and Neitzel was actually based on different supervisory levels and will thus be reviewed below. The other four studies, however, did show greater job satisfaction among supervisory personnel when compared to workers.

In a study not included in the Herzberg review, Morse (1953) reported on the satisfactions of 61 supervisory personnel compared with 600 workers in a single company. She found that:

> The supervisors are considerably more satisfied with their jobs and with the company as a place to work. They are somewhat less satisfied than the employees with their salaries and are about equal in satisfaction with the employees

regarding the advancement they have received in the company [p. 98].

Thus, Morse's conclusions are in general agreement with the other studies cited above, although, as she points out, first-level supervisors may not be as satisfied as the rank and file with the specific aspect of wages.

Since the publication of the Herzberg review, only one study (Handyside, 1961) has appeared that has focused on management versus nonmanagement differences in job satisfaction. This study involved 30 managers and supervisory personnel and 467 production workers and found that "median satisfaction" (toward jobs) was higher for managerial personnel.

In recent years the content of job satisfaction studies of different organizational levels seems to have shifted from an exclusive focus on comparisons of supervisory personnel versus rank-and-file workers to comparisons among different levels of management within organizations.

A major point at issue in these studies of levels within management seems to be whether satisfaction increases with each higher level of management, or whether middle levels may have poorer morale than either lower or upper managerial levels. In their review of the literature through 1954, Herzberg *et al.* (1957) state that: "In large concerns, middle levels of management often have very poor morale [p. 23]." Their review refers to two articles relevant to this point (Benge, 1944; *Fortune,* 1950), but neither article presents enough data on either the samples of respondents or the results to draw any meaningful conclusions. Thus, there seems to be no substantial basis in the literature prior to 1954 to support this conclusion.

Recent studies, plus one appearing prior to the Herzberg review, seem to be nearly unanimous in concluding that job satisfaction or morale does increase monotonically with increasing levels of management, and that therefore middle managers are more satisfied than those below them in the organization but less satisfied than those above. The first such study, by Browne and Neitzel (1952), found that morale scores for three levels of supervision were "positively related to the echelon level of the supervisors [p. 90]." In 1961 two articles reporting on different levels of management appeared (Porter, 1961; Rosen, 1961a). Rosen's study, which was concerned with satisfaction with conditions of work, presented findings for three levels of management within a single plant. He found that the top managers in the plant and the middle managers did not differ significantly from each other in satisfaction, but both groups of managers were significantly more satisfied than first-level supervisors. Rosen also noted, however, that there was a similarity of profiles of satisfaction among the three levels of management, such that there were high rank-order correlations (ranging from 0.67 to 0.93) between each pair of levels in terms of the degree of satisfaction with the 24 items.

In Porter's study (1961), two levels of management, first-line supervisors and lower-middle management, were surveyed in three different types of companies with a questionnaire designed to tap satisfaction of different types of needs relevant to a Maslow hierarchical classification of needs. The results showed that the higher of the two management levels generally reported greater satisfaction and, as was the case in Rosen's investigation, the pattern of need satisfactions tended to be similar between the two levels.

Subsequent to these 1961 studies by Porter and Rosen, Porter has completed a large scale investigation of managerial need satisfactions across all levels of management, from first-level supervisors to company presidents. This study (Porter, 1962, 1964) sampled more than a thousand managers from a wide variety of different types and sizes of companies located throughout the country. The results were in general agreement with those from the previous Porter and Rosen studies. Satisfaction increased with each higher level of management for three of five needs (esteem, autonomy, and self-actualization needs), and profiles of satisfaction were generally similar across levels. (For security and social needs, satisfaction was roughly equal across all levels of management.) It should be emphasized that satisfaction in this study was measured by the difference between obtained and expected fulfillment. This is important because it means that for at least three types of needs lower-level managers were not just getting less fulfillment, as might be obvious, but there was a larger difference between their expectations and their fulfillment than was found at upper levels of management.

Much of the same sort of results were reported in a study published by the Opinion Research Corporation (1962). Attitude data were collected from 1,200 managers showing that the percentage of unfulfilled needs decreased from lower to middle to top management. For almost all of the specific questions asked of the respondents there were no reversals wherein a higher level of management expressed greater dissatisfaction than a lower level.

Finally, in a study as yet unpublished in detail, Haire, Ghiselli, and Porter (1963) found that in a cross-cultural investigation of managerial attitudes in 14 countries, higher levels of management on the whole reported greater degrees of need satisfaction in their jobs than did lower-level managers. It thus appears that the phenomenon of increased job satisfaction with increasing level of management is not confined to the situation existing in American companies but tends to be a worldwide fact of industrial organizations.

To summarize briefly at this point, it can be stated with some degree of assurance that the available literature on job satisfaction across different levels of organizations shows increasing job satisfaction at each higher level. This is true both for nonmanagement versus management comparisons and also for comparisons within the management parts of hierarchies. In addition, one other finding appears with some consistency: Patterns of satisfaction are roughly similar across different organizational levels, at least within management.

Other Attitudes. A number of studies have been concerned with the relationship of organizational levels to attitudes other than degree of satisfaction. However, such studies are somewhat difficult to classify and summarize since they cover a great diversity of types of attitudes.

There are, nevertheless, several groupings that are reasonably discernible. The first of these comprises studies of the relative importance of different types of needs and motives at different organizational levels. Two studies (*Fortune,* 1947; Kahn, 1958) have made direct comparisons between nonmanagement and management levels with regard to the importance of different motivating factors. The two studies seem to present somewhat conflicting results for these comparisons. Kahn's findings indicated that both workers and their supervisors attached high importance to security, but that supervisors attached less importance to high wages than did the workers. The *Fortune* study, on the other hand, indicated that when security was pitted against high wages in an "either-or" choice situation, high-level executives chose the high wage situation. It is obviously difficult to compare the two sets of findings since both the samples and the procedures differed. What is clear is that we need considerably more evidence from a wide variety of types of organizations before we can make any broad generalizations concerning manager-worker differences in the importance attached to different motivating factors.

Several studies in the past five years have made comparisons of the importance attached to different needs and conditions of work among different levels within management. The first of these studies was by Rosen and Weaver (1960) who studied the degree of importance attached to 24 conditions of work by three levels of management within one plant. They found high rank-order correlations (ranging from 0.76 to 0.90) between each pair of levels with regard to the degree of importance attached to each of the 24 items. In terms of overall importance, the first-level supervisors attached generally more importance to most of the items. Subsequent to the Rosen and Weaver study, Porter published two articles dealing with the importance attached to different psychological needs by different managerial levels (Porter, 1961; 1963a). Both studies confirm one aspect of the findings of Rosen and Weaver; namely, different managerial levels tend to be similar with regard to what they consider most important. However, the later and more comprehensive of the Porter studies differed in one respect from both the earlier Porter study and the Rosen and Weaver study. It showed that higher-level managers tended to attach somewhat more rather than less importance to various needs, whereas the earlier studies indicated that higher managerial levels regarded most needs or conditions as less important compared to lower levels. The difference in these findings may lie in the fact that in the later Porter study the degree of formal education of the respondents was about equivalent across management levels, while in the earlier studies the degree of education was either not controlled or else the lower-level respondents had less education. It is conceivable that employees with less education may be more prone to consider everything as important, whereas those with greater formal schooling may be somewhat more discriminating in attaching importance to different needs and conditions. Therefore, it may be necessary to control for differences in formal education when comparing different management levels with regard to the importance attached to different psychological needs or conditions of work.

Finally, the cross-cultural study by Haire, Ghiselli, and Porter (1963) showed that for almost all of the countries in their sample there was again a strong similarity between upper-level and lower-level managers in the relative importance attached to different needs.

Turning to a different area of job attitudes, we find a small group of studies that can be put under the general heading of role perception studies (Coates & Pellegrin, 1957; Porter & Henry, 1964a; Rosen, 1961b; Triandis, 1959b). Although each of these studies was in some way concerned with role perceptions, it should be noted that they were addressed to rather different aspects of role perceptions, they utilized different types of samples, and, particularly, they employed quite different methods to obtain their data. For instance, Triandis (1959b) utilized the semantic differential technique to study the "differential perception of certain jobs and people" by upper-level managers, lower-level managers, and clerks and workers from one company. He concluded that "the most significant variable in the perception of jobs is the *level* of the job [being perceived; p. 224]." In addition, he also found that managers made finer discriminations among their job perceptions than did workers. Rosen (1961b) investigated how three levels of management in a particular company ranked 16 "role prescriptions." His findings showed that managers at the two lower levels tended to be similar in how they evaluated their role as supervisors, but each level differed somewhat from the highest of the three levels. Porter and Henry (1964a) studied the perceptions of managers in terms of the type of behavior each level believed was most important for jobs at their particular level, and found that at each higher level of management increasing emphasis was put on "inner-directed" (as opposed to "other-directed") personality traits. Coates and Pellegrin (1957), in a study directed primarily toward self-perceptions, found that both supervisors and subordinates tended to "be aware of the rewards, penalties, and sacrifices associated with high-level roles. Such an awareness differentially influences achievement desires on the two levels [p. 220]."

An overall look at these diverse studies of role perception among different organizational levels reveals that again the variable of level seems to have a strong relationship to these types of perceptions, just as it did to perceptions of need and job satisfaction.

Two investigations have compared the factorial structures of attitudes of lower-level personnel versus those at higher levels. Baehr (1954), factoring the Science Research Associates (SRA) Employee Inventory for a "high-status" group of managers and white collar personnel and a "low-status" group of factory workers and routine clerical personnel, found considerable, but not complete, similarity in the factors emerging from the two groups. What differences there were indicated that the factors of the high-status group tended to be more concerned with the overall functioning of the organization while those of the low-status group were more relevant to specific aspects of the immediate work situation. Triandis (1960) factored the semantic job structures of managers and supervisors in a manufacturing plant and compared these with the factored job structures of workers in the same plant. He found even greater factorial similarity between the two groups than did Baehr and concluded that: "Management and workers, one might expect, will differ in their factorial structures when the domain of jobs is considered. The answer is that this is not true. The factor structures are surprisingly similar [p. 300]." It appears therefore, from these two studies, that organizational level does not have a strong relationship to the structure of job attitudes.

The salience of different features of jobs and jobholders appears to be related to the level at which a person is working in an organization. Two studies which demonstrate this are another article by Triandis and one by Pellegrin and Coates. Triandis (1959a) found that upper-level managers focused on such "expensive" categories of description as "graciousness" and "polish," while lower-level managers and workers emphasized "instrumental" categories such as "intelligence," "skill," and "dependability," in describing different groups of employees. Likewise, he also found differences associated with the three levels of respondents when they were describing different jobs. The two managerial groups tended to use the criterion of the "nature of the work" to distinguish among different jobs, whereas the workers made their distinction among jobs primarily on the basis of job requirements, particularly intelligence. Pellegrin and Coates (1957), in interviews with a sample of 50 "top-level" executives and 50 "first-level" supervisors, found that the former emphasized the intrinsic features of their jobs whereas the latter viewed their jobs more as means to off-job rewards. This may indicate, in the terms of Herzberg, Mausner, and Synderman (1959), that managers in higher-level positions focus more on "motivating" aspects of their positions while supervisors in lower-level jobs are oriented more toward concern with the "hygienic" conditions of their positions.

One other area of job attitudes in relation to organizational levels has received some attention, namely, types of leadership attitudes at different levels. The Ohio State studies (e.g., Fleishman, 1953; Fleishman, Harris, & Burtt, 1955) have demonstrated that attitudes about how supervisors should behave in relation to their workers vary depending on the organizational level of the respondent. For example, Fleishman's (1953) article showed that the higher the level of a manager, the less likely he was to believe that a supervisor should show "Consideration" attitudes toward his subordinates and the more likely he was to think a supervisor should put emphasis on "Initiating Structure" in dealing with subordinates.

Behavior

Studies of the relationships between organizational levels and individuals' behavior are relatively infrequent. The nature of five such studies that were located in the literature, including the sizes of their samples, is indicated in Table 1. This table shows that the sampling, in terms of both individual subjects

TABLE 1 STUDIES OF RELATIONSHIPS OF ORGANIZATIONAL LEVELS TO JOB BEHAVIOR

Investigators	*Type of Behavior*	*N of Individuals*	*N of Levels*	*N of Companies*
Burns (1954)	Interactions and activities	4	3	1
Davis (1953)	Communications (grapevine)	65	6	1
Dubin and Spray (1964)	Interactions and activities	8	2	3
Martin (1959)	Decision making	?	4	1
Shartle (1956)	Activities	14	2	7

and organizations, is extremely limited. Any conclusions emerging from these studies, therefore, must be regarded with great caution. One other point should be noted in Table 1. These five studies dealing with behavior in relation to organizational level are not concerned with rates of production, absenteeism, safety, turnover, and the like. Instead, they concentrate on interpersonal interaction patterns, types of decisions, and types of functional activities performed by the individual in his job. The reason these studies do not focus on the types of behavior usually studied in the typical field investigation is that they are all concerned with differences in behavior between or among levels of management. Thus, output or production in the usual sense is not easily measured. Also, it is probably assumed that turnover, absenteeism, and accident rates are so negligible at managerial levels that there would be little or no variation in these indices from level to level.

Keeping in mind the severely restricted nature of the samples in these five studies, there are several conclusions that seem to be supported by the data so far obtained:

*1. **Informal Communication (Informational) Patterns.*** Davis' (1953) study of the grapevine operating in the management sector of a particular company indicated that higher-level managers are much better informed on informal communication (as well as, presumably, on formal communication) items than lower-level managers and supervisors. Davis stressed the fact that, in this company at least, first-level supervisors were the most isolated from news traveling through the informal communication channels.

*2. **Interpersonal Interaction Patterns.*** Four major types of interaction variables have been examined in several studies: *(a)* The ratio of upward (or superior) contacts to downward (or subordinate) contacts—the three studies (Burns, 1954; Dubin & Spray, 1964; Martin 1959) that deal with this variable present contradictory findings. Burns' data (as pointed out by Dubin, 1962) show that the ratio of superior to subordinate contacts decreases the higher the level of management; Dubin and Spray's data seem to indicate the opposite; Martin's results show no changes in the ratio in relation to level. *(b)* Percentage of peer contacts—both Burns' and Martin's findings indicate that the relative number of contacts with peers decreases the higher the level of management. Dubin and Spray's data are inconclusive on this point. *(c)* Percentage of contacts with individuals outside the organizational unit (e.g., factory, office, or company)—the data of both the Martin and the Dubin and Spray studies show a definite trend for such outside contacts to increase the higher the level of management, as one might expect. Burns' study indirectly supports this point, as does one by Shartle (1956), who found that the heads of seven organizations spent a greater proportion of their time on public relations acitivities than did their immediate assistants. *(d)* Percentage of direct (face-to-face) contacts—Martin found the proportion of face-to-face contacts decreasing at higher management levels.

*3. **Types of Decisions.*** Martin's study is the only one of the five studies to focus on the differences in the types of decisions made at different levels of management. In his investigation of four levels (from works manager down to shift foreman) within a single plant, he found that the higher the managerial level, *(a)* the greater the "duration" of the decision (i.e., increase in time between the inception of the decision process and the actual implementation of this decision and the verification of its correctness or incorrectness), and hence the greater the increase in the "riskiness" of the decision, and *(b)* the more abstract the decision (i.e., an increasing lack of "structure" of the data relevant to the decision).

*4. **Types of Activities*** (e.g., planning, coordinating, production, etc.). Data concerning differences in patterns of activities at different levels of management are so meager that generalizations cannot be made in this area, even though several studies (Burns, 1954; Dubin & Spray, 1964; Shartle, 1956) have attempted to collect such information.

Summary

A review of the relevant literature demonstrates that organizational levels are strongly related to both attitudes and behavior. The evidence shows that perceived job and need satisfactions increase not only from rank-and-file positions to managerial positions, but also from lower management positions to middle- and upper-level positions. Thus, level seems clearly to be related to what individuals think they are receiving from their jobs. Level also seems to show a relationship to what employees think they must put into their jobs, in terms of the behavior they perceive to be required by their jobs. On the other hand, it should also be stressed that level does not necessarily affect all types of job attitudes. For example, it seemed to have only a slight relationship to the relative importance attached to different kinds of needs.

In terms of behavior that is actually exhibited by employees, especially within managerial ranks, level seems to affect the amount of information a person receives in his job, the types of interpersonal relationships he has on his job, and the types and nature of the decisions he must make in his position. However, the evidence concerning these behavioral variables in relation to level is limited, and hence conclusions concerning them must be regarded as tentative at the present time.

The major research trend in this area in recent years, both in studies of attitudes and of behavior, seems to be a shift toward an increasing focus on the differentiation of organizational levels within management in contrast with the former (almost complete) concentration on management versus nonmanagement differences. Eventually, it may be possible to describe organizational differences in major aspects of attitudes and behavior for at least four discrete points along the hierarchical or level dimension of structure: rank-and-file positions, first-line supervision, middle management, and top management. To date, however, we have no major sets of attitudinal or behavioral data from a specific study that adequately sample these four levels across different kinds of industrial or business organizations.

Future research on organizational levels will need to focus on the question of what it is about different levels that seems to create different job attitudes and job behavior. In other words, "organizational level" is merely a convenient label for other, more fundamental, variables that must be operating in the situation. An understanding of the nature of these other variables and how they are distributed along the vertical dimension of structure is a research task for the future in this area.

Future research will also need to focus on the necessity of disentangling the effects of individual-difference variables from the effects of organizational-level variables. Practically all of the studies so far carried out in this area have failed to consider the fact that individuals at different organizational levels may vary systematically in intelligence and/or personality traits. To what extent the obtained differences in attitudes and behavior are a function of these types of differences relative to differences due to job level is an open question. It is a question that will require sophisticated research for an answer.

LINE AND STAFF HIERARCHIES

The distinction between line and staff hierarchies is an old one in the study of formal organizations. Traditionally, positions concerned with the main operations of the organization and within the direct chain of command have been considered part of the line hierarchy, while positions concerned with auxiliary services and outside the direct chain of command have been considered part of the staff hierarchy. The staff's function is to provide specialized aid to the line, which is composed of "generalists." Recently, this traditional distinction has received attention from two sources. One group of writers (Brown, 1954; Fisch, 1961; Leavitt & Whisler, 1958; McGregor, 1960) has contended that the distinction between these two parallel hierarchies is disappearing under the impact of modern technology. A second group of writers has dealt with the type of relationships that exist between line and staff managers. Both Dalton (1959) and Whyte (1961) have illustrated the types of conflicts that can develop between managers in these two hierarchies existing within organizations.

Attitudes

The evidence available concerning the amount of satisfaction provided by line and staff positions is consistent in showing line managers to be more satisfied than staff managers. Three studies by the Opinion Research Corporation (1959) reported that engineers and scientists in staff positions were less satisfied with their jobs than engineers and scientists in line positions. In more recent studies using broader samples of managers, Rosen (1961a) and Porter (1963b) found that line managers reported a greater incidence of desirable conditions of work and perceived greater need satisfactions, especially in esteem and self-actualization need areas.

Three studies compared line and staff managers on the amount of importance they attached to job-related factors and needs, and all three found essentially no differences between the two groups of managers. Rosen and Weaver (1960) found that managers in line and staff positions did not differ substantially in their ratings of the importance of 24 desirable conditions of work. Porter (1963b) found that there were no line-staff differences in the importance attached to four of five need areas; only on the need for autonomy did the two groups differ, with staff managers feeling this need was more important. Lawler and Porter (1963) found no differences between the two types of managers in the importance attached to pay.

In a study involving a somewhat different type of attitude, Porter and Henry (1964b) asked line and staff managers to rank five other-directed and five inner-directed personality traits on the basis of how important they are for success in their management positions. The results showed that staff managers, as Whyte (1956) and others might have predicted, felt they have to show more other-directed behavior to succeed in their jobs than line managers.

Behavior

Only three studies were located that permitted comparisons of line and staff personnel on behavioral indices. A frequently cited study by Dalton (1950) found that staff managers in three plants had a turnover rate between two and four times that of line managers. Davis (1953), in a study of one company, reported that staff managers were better informed than line managers. He attributed this superior knowledge on the part of staff managers to their greater mobility.

> Staff executives in such areas as personnel and control found that their duties both required and allowed them to get out of their offices, made it easy for them to walk through other departments without someone wondering whether they were "not working," to get away for coffee, and so on—all of which meant they heard more news from the other executives they talked with [p. 47].

Burns' study (1954) also appears to support the notion of greater communication flexibility for managers in staff positions.

Summary

Since the studies that have compared the attitudes and behavior of employees in line and staff positions are all relatively recent, it is impossible to determine if the amount of difference between the two types of hierarchies has been decreasing over the long term, as some writers have suggested. The validity of this contention probably will not be established until we have strictly comparative data on line-staff differences from different time periods. In the meantime, however, the available evidence indicates that differences in conditions between the two types of positions are still large enough to produce significant differences in both attitudes and behavior. Staff managers derive less satisfaction from their jobs, feel they have to be more other-directed, and exhibit different patterns of behavior. The only area that failed to produce consistent differences was the degree of importance attached to various job-related factors and needs. Apparently this type of attitude was little affected by organizational conditions surrounding line and staff jobs.

The evidence on the attitude and behavior differences between managers in line and staff positions presents a picture of several factors that may be responsible for line and staff conflicts. The staff manager's position, for instance, requires him to be knowledgeable about his specialty and spend considerable time with a variety of types of executives; yet it provides him with little opportunity to use his knowledge for decision making unless he usurps the authority of the line. The line manager's position, on the other hand, places him in a situation in which he is expected to take advice, on decisions for which he has responsibility, from a man who frequently is younger and has been with the company a shorter period of time and who is not supposed to know the whole picture as he is. This is not a situation that lends itself to harmonious line-staff relations. The fact that managers in line and staff hierarchies see different traits being required for success and report different levels of satisfaction suggests that one way of easing some of the potential line-staff conflicts may be to take into account the psychological demands of the two different types of jobs in the selection and placement of managers.

SPAN OF CONTROL

Span of control is defined as the number of subordinates a manager is responsible for supervising. Since the early days of classical organization theory (Urwick, 1935), writers have prescribed what they felt to be an optimum span of control. In most instances, the classical theorists have assumed that a small span of control (few subordinates) is a "good thing" for any organization. Typical prescriptions have recommended spans of control between three and six (Dale, 1952). However, classical organization theorists generally have failed to consider what factors might call for a change in the size of the span of control. Recognizing this, Fisch (1963) has recently argued that such factors as level of management, company product diversification, and the personalities of the managers should be considered in determining the optimum span of control.

A vigorous dissent from the classical approach to the span of control was made by Worthy (1950). His radical suggestion was that a large span of control is good since it provides better communication and greater opportunities for individual growth and initiative. With this statement by Worthy, the battle line between the two approaches to organization theory was clearly drawn. However researchers have not been quick to join in the fray, and as late as 1960 Pfiffner and Sherwood stated: "There has been relatively little, if any, empirical study of span of control [p. 156]." The majority of the research that has been done on the topic has been concerned with discovering variables that are related to the size of the span of control found in existing organizations. Entwisle and Walton (1961), for example, found that the size of the organization and the function of the organization were both related to existing spans of control. This type of research undoubtedly represents a necessary first step in determining which conditions favor a large span of control and which favor a small span of control, but it does not provide data on relationships to job attitudes or performance. In fact, only one such study was located in the literature.

Attitudes

No empirical studies were found that attempted to determine the relationship between span of control and employee job attitudes. Worthy (1950) did report that in one company a large span of control had been found to be positively related to high morale; however, he presented no published data to support this point, and thus it is difficult to evaluate his claims.

Behavior

A study by Woodward (1958) found a relationship between the size of the span of control at the first level of supervision and company performance when several English companies were viewed. The companies were divided into three groups based upon the methods of production used—unit (e.g., production of unique units to customer's orders), mass (e.g., production of large numbers of identical units by assembly-line techniques), and process (e.g., production of chemicals, etc., by continuous processing). For each of the three types of production, the most successful companies were those that were near the median span of control for that production type. These median spans of control (23 for mass, 49 for process, and 13 for unit) for the successful companies were substantially larger than those suggested as optimum by the classical theorists. Woodward's study thus gives at least tentative support to Worthy's point that a large span of control can produce high performance. However, it is important to remember that Woodward's study was concerned with the span of control of first-line supervisors, and although a relatively large span of control may have proved to be optimum at this level, there is no reason to believe the same necessarily will be true of the upper levels of management. Perhaps the most significant point about the Woodward study is that the method of production was found to be an important variable in determining which span of control at the first level of supervision was optimum for producing high performance.

Summary

The lack of research makes it impossible to state that any particular span of control is best for producing high performance or positive job attitudes. What data there are suggest that it is not reasonable to expect any one span of control to be ideal for all organizational situations. Level of management and type of production appear to be two variables that influence the optimum span of control for a given situation, and undoubtedly further research will uncover other variables that are important.

SIZE: SUBUNITS

For the purposes of this review, any grouping of the members of a business organization that systematically excludes part of the membership of that organization is considered an organization subunit. Primary work groups, departments, and factories (in multifactory companies) have been frequently studied organization subunits. Previous summaries of the research evidence on the relationship between organization subunit size and job attitudes and performance typically have concluded that small organization subunits are superior on all counts (e.g., Strauss & Sayles, 1960; Viteles, 1953). Morale, absence rates, turnover rates, accident rates, and productivity are all considered to be better in small than in large organization subunits. An example of the broad statements supporting small organization subunits is Viteles' conclusion that "The size of the work group affects output and attitudes, which both tend to be better in smaller sized groups [p. 146]."

Recently several articles (Herbst, 1957; Indik & Seashore, 1961) have contained theories attempting to explain the beneficial effects of small organization subunits. Undoubtedly the appearance of these theories is due to the aforementioned widespread acceptance of the belief that the experimental evidence conclusively supports the proposition that smaller organization subunits are always beneficial. Virtually ignored in the rush to accept this simple picture of the effects of subunit size and completely ignored in theoretical attempts to explain this picture has been the effect of two other variables: job level within the organization subunit, and type of organization subunit (e.g., work group, department, factory). These variables may well function to limit the degree to which it is possible to generalize about the beneficial effects of small organization subunits. For example, increasing the size of a department may raise the absence rate among the department's production workers, but it is doubtful that it will also increase the absence rate of the department's management force. Likewise, increasing the size of a primary work group may cause lower morale in that work group, but increasing the size of a factory by adding more small work groups may very well not decrease the morale of the total plant. Thus, before we accept the conclusion that all types of large subunits, regardless of job level being considered, are always inferior to small ones, it may be well to see if the evidence justifies such a conclusion.

Since there are a relatively large number of studies that have investigated the relationship of subunit size to both attitudes and behavior, Table 2 was constructed to summarize most (but not all) of these studies. This table will serve as the basis for most of the subsequent discussion in this section on subunit size.

Attitudes

Job Satisfaction and Morale. As Table 2 indicates, there is little doubt that subunit size is significantly related to differences in job attitudes. The evidence is strong that workers in small departments and work groups are better satisfied than workers in large departments or groups, as six of the seven studies reviewed show results in this direction. However, the evidence does not yet support the sweeping conclusion that all types of employees in smaller organization subunits are more satisfied than those in larger subunits, since no studies were located, for example, that compared managerial job attitudes in different size organization subunits. Thus, it is impossible to reach any conclusion about the relationship between subunit size and the job satisfaction of managers.

Talacchi (1960) studied the level of job satisfaction among employees in 41 plants that were subunits of five larger organizations. His results showed a strong trend (r's ranging from -0.42 to -0.81) for job satisfaction to decrease as plant size increased. Kerr, Koppelmeier, and Sullivan (1951) found that for 894 workers in 29 departments in two electronics plants job satisfaction was correlated -0.46 with size of department. Indik and Seashore (1961) measured the amount of intrinsic job satisfaction expressed by workers in 32 package delivery departments, varying in size from 15 to 61, and found that increased size led to lower satisfaction. Likewise, Katzell, Barrett, and Parker (1961) found a significant trend for workers in large warehouses to express lower job satisfaction than workers in small warehouses (with 23 out of 23 correlations being in this direction). Campbell (1952), in studying workers' satisfaction with incentive pay plans as a function of the size (from under 20 to over 100) of the work group to which they belonged, found that workers in the smaller groups felt they had better knowledge of how their pay plan operated and were more satisfied with their pay. Finally, Worthy (1950) reported: "Our researches demonstrate that mere size is unquestionably one of the most important factors in determining the quality of employee relationships: the smaller the unit the higher the morale, and vice versa [pp. 172–73]." Regrettably, Worthy failed to document this strong statement with any published data on the size of the units studied, the type of employees studied, or the measure of morale used.

The only study that failed to show a negative relationship between subunit size and job satisfaction was one reported in the previously mentioned publication by Indik and Seashore (1961) which concerned employee job satisfaction in automobile dealerships. Since these dealerships were relatively autonomous, and perhaps not completely accurately classified as subunits, the failure to find a strong negative relationship in this particular instance is probably not too significant.

Other Attitudes. Three studies (not shown in Table 2) investigated the relationship between organization subunit size and job attitudes other than those concerned with satisfaction. Hemphill (1950) found that as group size increased, members expressed attitudes of greater tolerance for leader-centered direction of group activities. In addition, Hemphill (1956) found that small groups were better characterized by attitudes of high intimacy, high hedonic tone, and low control than were large groups. It should be noted that both studies by Hemphill employed subjects from very diverse types of groups (ranging from industrial work groups to members of a sorority), and thus it is difficult to assess their relevance for industrial organizations.

Seashore (1954) studied the relationship between group cohesiveness and size of work group for more than 200 groups in a large industrial organization. The results showed a general trend for feelings of cohesiveness to decrease with increasing subunit size. However, there was also a tendency for the

TABLE 2 STUDIES OF RELATIONSHIPS BETWEEN ORGANIZATION SUBUNIT SIZE AND JOB ATTITUDES AND JOB BEHAVIOR

Attitude or Behavior Studied	*Investigators*	*Type of Subunit Considered*	*Relationship Found**
Job satisfaction	Talacchi (1960)	Factories	Negative
	Kerr, Koppelmeier, & Sullivan (1951	Departments	Negative
	Indik & Seashore (1961)	Departments	Negative
	Katzell, Barrett, & Parker (1961)	Departments	
	Campbell (1952)	Work groups	Negative
	Worthy (1950)	?	Negative
	Indik & Seashore (1961)	Automobile dealerships	Zero
Absenteeism	Revans (1958)	Gas works	Positive
	Revans (1958)	Factories	Positive
	Revans (1958)	Factories	Positive
	Acton Society Trust (1953)	Factory	Positive
	Baumgartel & Sobol (1959)	"Plants" (airline locations)	Positive
	Research Council for Economic Security (Baumgartel & Sobol, 1959)	Plants	Positive (?)
	Hewitt & Parfitt (1953)	Departments	Positive
	Indik & Seashore (1961)	Departments	Positive
	Kerr, Koppelmeier, & Sullivan (1951)	Departments	Positive
	Metzner & Mann (1953)	Work groups (blue-collar)	Positive
	Argyle, Gardner, & Cioffi (1958)	Work groups	Curvilinear
	Metzner & Mann (1953)	Work groups (white-collar)	Zero
Turnover	Indik & Seashore (1961)	Automobile dealerships	Positive
	Kerr, Koppelmeier, & Sullivan (1951)	Departments	Positive
	Mandell (1956)	Departments	Positive
	Argyle, Gardner, & Cioffi (1958)	Work groups	Zero
Accidents	Revans (1958)	Mines (Britain)	Positive
	Revans (1958)	Factories (Britain)	Positive
	Revans (1958)	Departments (Asia)	Positive
	Revans (1958)	Mines (U.S.A.)	Curvilinear
	U.S. Department of Labor (Revans, 1958)	Factories (U.S.A.)	Curvilinear
	National Safety Council (Revans, 1958)	Factories (U.S.A.)	Negative
Labor disputes	Cleland (1955)	Factories	Positive
	Revans (1958)	Mines	Positive
Productivity	Katzell, Barrett, & Parker (1961)	Company divisions	Negative
	Indik & Seashore (1961)	Departments	Negative
	Marriott (1949)	Work groups	Negative
	Revans (1958)	Mines	Curvilinear
	Revans (1958)	Retail stores	Curvilinear
	Herbst (1957)	Retail stores	Curvilinear
	Indik & Seashore (1961)	Automobile dealerships	Zero
	Argyle, Gardner, & Cioffi (1958)	Work groups	Positive

* A positive relationship indicates a trend for the attitude or behavior to become more frequent as size increases. A negative relationship indicates a trend for the attitude or behavior to become less frequent as size increases. A curvilinear relationship indicates a trend for the middle-sized subunit to exhibit the greatest or the lowest frequency of the attitude or behavior.

smallest size groups to fall at the two extremes of cohesiveness; that is, they were either extremely high or extremely low in cohesiveness. Nevertheless, Seashore's general conclusion was that group size is negatively related to group cohesiveness attitudes.

Behavior

Absenteeism. The greatest amount of evidence demonstrating a relationship between organization subunit size and job behavior appears on the topic of absence rates. As shown in Table 2, 10 of the 12 studies reviewed found positive linear relationships between absence rates and the size of subunits. This finding appeared for factories, departments, and primary work groups. Again, however, the finding is limited to absence rates among employees at the blue-collar level, since the only study that separately looked at white-collar workers' absences found no relationship between subunit size and absence rates.

Revans (1958) has provided an excellent review of much of the data on the topic of subunit size in relation to absenteeism. He reported that in five randomly chosen gas works,[2] ranging in size from 67 to 3,430 employees, the duration of absence due to accidents and the log of the size of the works were correlated +0.91. In addition, size of works was correlated +0.62 with absence rates due to sickness and other factors. Revans also reported two further studies dealing with size of factory in multifactory organizations. Each study found significant positive correlations between log size of factory and absence rates. A study by the Acton Society Trust (1953) reported a correlation of +0.44 between size of factory (ranging from under 100 employees to more than 1,000) and absence rates. Baumgartel and Sobol (1959) did a well-controlled study on the relationships between the size of work locations or "plants" of an airline and absenteeism and found a strong tendency for absenteeism to increase with size of the work location. These investigators also cited the report on Prolonged Illness Absenteeism rates. And Metzner and Mann for Economic Security, which showed that smaller-sized plants had lower prolonged illness rates than medium-sized plants. However, the same report indicated that there was not a consistent linear relationship between plant size and illness. Several other studies, Hewitt and Parfitt (1953), Indik and Seashore (1961), and Kerr, Koppelmeier, and Sullivan (1951), have all found that larger departments of a company have higher absenteeism rates. And Metzner and Mann (1953) found that among blue-collar workers small work groups (seven and under) had fewer absences than did large work groups (over seven).

Only two of the 12 studies dealing with subunit size and absenteeism failed to show positive relationships between these two variables. Argyle, Gardner, and Cioffi (1958) reported that they found a curvilinear relationship between absence rates and workgroup size (ranging from 1 to 20+), with the lowest absence rates occurring in the middle-sized groups. Metzner and Mann, in their above-cited study (1953), found an insignificant relationship, although in the expected direction, between absence rates and workgroup size for white-collar workers. (It should also be noted that in the previously cited Baumgartel and Sobol study of airline locations, the effects of location size were less for white-collar workers than for blue-collar workers.)

Turnover. Table 2 shows that three of four studies found that turnover is greater in large units compared to small units. However, none of the studies compared the turnover rates of different-sized factories, and none of the studies considered turnover rates among managerial personnel. Indik and Seashore (1961) found that more employees were terminated in large than in small automobile dealerships. Kerr, Koppelmeier, and Sullivan (1951) found a significant relationship between turnover and department size ($r = +0.49$). Likewise, Mandell (1956), in a study of 320 companies, found that large offices tended to have higher turnover rates than did small offices. On the other hand, Argyle, Gardner, and Cioffi (1958) did not find any relationship between subunit size and turnover.

Accident Rates. Revans (1958) has thoroughly reviewed the literature on the relationship between accident rates and organization subunit size. As the six sets of data covered in his review indicate, there is not a consistent pattern of relationship between these two variables. In fact, three different patterns were found: positive, curvilinear, and negative relationships. A review of the evidence cited by Revans leads to the conclusion that accident rates may be dependent upon the type of industry considered and upon the technological development of the country in which a study is carried out. At the present time it seems wise to speak only of the type of relationship that exists for a given industry in a given country, and not for industry in general. For example, as shown in Table 2, the evidence is fairly convincing that for United States industry large size is not associated with high accident rates, while for

[2] Much of the literature on the relationship between behavior and size fails to point out whether the units studied (e.g., gas works, factories, or mines) are parts of larger organizations or are separate corporations. For the purposes of this review, it was decided that unless the author specified he was dealing with separate companies or firms, all data on factories, gas works, and mines would be dealt with as data on organization subunits.

British industry large size does appear to be associated with increased accident rates.

Revans' analysis of the accident rate for British coal miners and quarriers in 1950 showed a strong positive relationship between mine size and number of accidents. Likewise, the Annual Report of the Chief Inspector of Factories for 1956 (cited by Revans) showed that the compensable accident rate rises steadily with the average size of factory for British industrial firms. Also reported by Revans was a strong positive correlation (+0.47) between accident rates and department size for steel companies operating in Asia.

Turning to the data for American industry, Revans cited three studies that indicated either a curvilinear or negative relationship between subunit size and accident rates. The data for American mines, in contrast to similar data for mines in Britain, showed the highest accident rates occurring in middle-sized mines employing 100 to 300 workers. Data for United States factories were provided in two studies which showed somewhat different results from each other. Bulletin 1164 of the United States Department of Labor (cited by Revans) on "Work Injuries in the United States during 1952" points to a curvilinear relationship in the following quotation:

> The larger establishments, which can afford trained safety engineers and which conduct intensive safety programs, generally have the lowest rates. Usually the medium-size plants have the highest rates, and the smallest establishments show rates somewhat below the medium-size plants but above the average for the industry [quoted by Revans, 1958, p. 209].

In a report from the National Safety Council on 3,500 United States manufacturing plants, Revans cited data showing a strongly declining accident rate with increasing plant size.

Labor Disputes. Data contained in two sources (Cleland, 1955; Revans, 1958) show a positive relationship between subunit size and labor disputes. Cleland's data demonstrated that as plant size increases, the probability of an industrial strike rises significantly. Similarly, Revans noted that British coal miners in larger mines were more sensitive to nonmonetary issues (although not to monetary issues) than were miners in smaller locations. On the basis of these two reports it is tempting to conclude that small subunits are more likely to have fewer labor problems than larger subunits. However, one must be cautious in making this interpretation, since it is not size of operation, as such, that affects the number of labor disputes, but rather the type of technology that is associated with size (see Summary at the end of this section).

Productivity. As Table 2 shows, the studies on the relationship between performance and organization subunit size do not present a clear-cut picture. Thus, the available evidence does not support the widely believed assumption that small subunits are superior to large ones in terms of job performance.

Three studies found better performance in smaller subunits than in larger units. For example, Katzell, Barrett, and Parker (1961) found that product value, productivity, and profitability were all lower in the large divisions of the company they studied. Indik and Seashore (1961) found a negative correlation between the size of delivery organizations and rated overall performance of these units. Marriott (1949), in a widely cited study of the relationship between work-group size and production in two automobile factories, concluded from his data that: "Low, but significant correlations were obtained which demonstrate an inverse relationship between output and size, the smaller sized groups showing consistently larger output in each factory [p. 56]."

In contrast to the results from the above three studies, were the findings from five other studies and reports; three of them found curvilinear relationships between subunit size and production, one found essentially no relationship, and one a positive relationship. Revans (1958) reported that data gathered by the National Coal Board in Britain for Years 1948–53 showed a curvilinear relationship between mine size and output per miner, with the highest output being obtained in middle-sized mines where 1,500 to 2,000 men were employed. Revans (1958) and Herbst (1957) both present data on sales of retail sales units, and both report curvilinear relationships to size, with the middle-sized units again performing best. Indik and Seashore (1961), on the other hand, reported a lack of significant relationship between size of automobile dealerships and job performance, and Argyle, Gardner, and Cioffi (1958) found a slight tendency for larger work groups to achieve higher productivity than smaller groups.

Summary

The literature on subunit size shows that when blue-collar workers are considered, small size subunits are characterized by higher job satisfaction, lower absence rates, lower turnover rates, and fewer labor disputes. The evidence does not show, however, a consistent relationship for blue-collar workers between accident rates and subunit size, or between productivity and subunit size. Furthermore, none of the studies reviewed investigated the relationship between managers' job attitudes and job behavior and organization subunit size.

Future research might well consider the problem

FIGURE 1 HYPOTHESIZED EFFECTS OF SUBUNIT SIZE

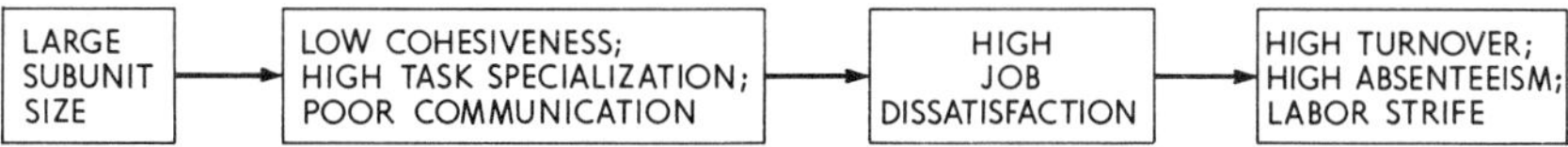

of assessing the relative impact on attitudes and behavior of the size of the different organization subunits of which an individual is a member. A typical worker is a member of at least three organization subunits: a primary work group, a department, and a factory or office. Although the evidence indicates that large-sized subunits are associated, for example, with high absenteeism, it is impossible to know on the basis of past studies if it is large size in the primary work group, department, or factory that is crucial in this relationship. Previous investigators have failed to control for variation in the size of the other types of subunits of which an individual is a member while they are studying the effects of size of one type of unit. For example, no study has compared absenteeism among work groups that are part of the same size departments and factories. Similarly, we do not know if factory size is related to absenteeism when all factories considered have the same size departments and work groups. It may well be that absenteeism is determined by work-group size but because large work groups are found in large factories and departments a spurious relationship exists between absenteeism and department size and between absenteeism and factory size.

At the present time, the weight of the evidence clearly suggests that small-sized subunits are desirable for a number of reasons. Although small-sized units may not improve job performance directly, the fact that they are associated with low turnover and low absenteeism argues strongly for their value. The question then arises as to why small subunits seem to have certain advantages over large units in affecting attitudes and behavior. Figure 1 presents a diagram that offers a possible explanatory model for the effects of organization subunit size on satisfaction, turnover, absenteeism, and labor strife. As subunits increase in size, it is probably increasingly difficult to maintain high cohesiveness and good communications. Further, task specialization may be more prevalent. The factors of low cohesiveness, high task specialization, and increased communication difficulties might tend in turn to lead to high job dissatisfaction. As Brayfield and Crockett (1955), among others, have pointed out, there is good reason to believe that dissatisfaction leads to higher turnover and absenteeism rates. Also, labor strife logically would seem to be affected by increases in job dissatisfaction.

On the basis of the diagram presented in Figure 1, there is no necessary reason for large units to lead directly to decreases in productivity. Although the model does predict that large units will be characterized by, among other things, higher job dissatisfaction, reviews of the literature have not found that job dissatisfaction is associated with low productivity. Nor is there evidence that task specialization, low cohesiveness, and communications problems must necessarily lead to lower productivity. It is not surprising, therefore, that the evidence on the relationship between productivity and subunit size is inconsistent.

SIZE: TOTAL ORGANIZATIONS

All of the studies discussed in the previous section were concerned with the relationships between size of some type of organizational subunit and attitude and behavioral indices. In the present section we will review only those studies that have dealt specifically with the total organization as the unit of size. It will become evident that the number of such studies on total organization size is much lower than the number of studies on subunit size.[3]

The distinction between subunit size and total-organization size has seldom been made clear either in previous empirical studies dealing with size or in various interpretations of these studies presented in textbooks concerned with organizational behavior. It is conceivable, for example, that although working in a large subunit has disadvantages (as demonstrated by the evidence in the preceding section), working in a large total organization might have advantages as long as the subunits within the organization are relatively small. Therefore, it seems necessary to keep the subunit/total-organization distinction clearly in focus because the effects of one type of size (e.g., total organizational size) may be confounded by the effects of the other type of size (i.e., size of subunits within total organizations).

[3] By the term "total organization" we mean a total operating company headed by an executive with the title "President." It is admittedly difficult at times to determine whether a "company," in the loose sense of the word, should be considered a separate total organization, in our terms, or merely a subunit of an even larger "corporation." In general, if a company has a chief executive with the title of president and if that company can sell stock independently of other "companies" all under the same corporate holding entity, we would consider it a total organization.

The absence, in most previous studies of size, of a distinction between subunits and total organizations has been compounded by the failure to take into account the job level of the employees. As was pointed out in the previous section, organizational level may interact with size such that conclusions pertaining to lower-level employees may not hold up when applied to higher-level personnel. This possible interaction effect of level could presumably influence results both for studies of subunit size and for studies of total-organization size. With the foregoing considerations in mind, we now turn to a review of the few studies that have been concerned with total-organization size.

Attitudes

At the rank-and-file worker level, two articles have appeared in the literature that *seem* to be concerned with the relationship of total-organization size (rather than subunit size) to job attitudes. The first of these two articles was by Benge (1944). Apparently sampling from a number of different companies and using the "composite attitude of employees in each company toward the boss" as an index of morale, he found that "morale of employees of small companies is appreciably better than that in larger companies [p. 104]." These results are extremely difficult to evaluate, however, since neither the number or type of respondents nor the number of companies on which the results were based was specified in the article.

The second study that seems to be concerned with the relationship of total-organization size to job attitudes of rank-and-file workers is one reported by Talacchi (1960). The study is described as an investigation involving 93 "organizations"; however, as one of the tables (Table 2 in the article, p. 411) indicates, at least 45 of the 93 organizations are in reality "plants" that comprise parts of only five companies. Thus, most of the findings reported in this article are difficult to interpret if one is interested in the effects of total-organization size, since the distinction between subunits and total organizations has been completely blurred. Nevertheless, it appears that the article does present some evidence bearing on the effects of size of the total organization on employee job satisfaction. The key result reported in Talacchi's article was a correlation of −0.67 between organization size and the overall index of employee satisfaction as measured by the SRA Employee Inventory. Employee dissatisfaction was, therefore, apparently greater within large organizations (which ranged up to a maximum size of 1,800 employees). Aside from the limitations in the study that have already been pointed out, this finding must be interpreted cautiously because it is possible that the larger organizations contained larger subunit work groups. In other words, it is possible that what seemed to be an effect of organization or, at least, plant size may have been due to work-group size.

At the management level of organizations, several recent articles by Porter (1963c, 1963d, 1964) examined the relationship between three types of job attitudes and the size of company for which each manager worked.[4] In this questionnaire study of more than 1,500 managers, respondents were placed into one of three size-of-company categories: small (companies of under 500 employees), medium (500–4,900 employees), and large (more than 5,000 employees). One part of the data dealt with need satisfactions and indicated that the effects of size were modified by the level of management being considered. At the lower and lower-middle management levels, managers from smaller companies were more satisfied than those from larger companies. At the upper-middle and vice-president levels, the reverse was true, with the managers from the larger companies indicating greater satisfaction. With respect to a different area of perceptions, when respondents were asked to rank 10 personality traits in terms of their importance for job success, it was found that managers from larger companies placed more emphasis than did managers from smaller companies on inner directed or nonorganization-man traits compared to other directed or organization-man traits. When respondents (across the intermediate three levels of management) were asked to use semantic differential scales to describe their jobs, managers from larger companies were slightly more likely to apply the terms "challenging," "interesting," and "competitive" to their jobs than were small company managers. (For both the personality trait and job-description results, management level did not seem to affect the findings. In other words, the effects of size were fairly consistent from one management level to the next.) These latter findings were interpreted as indicating that large companies place no more emphasis, perhaps even less, on conforming, organization-man type of behavior than do smaller companies.

[4] It should be pointed out that Porter also did not control for size of work groups or subunits in which an individual manager worked within his company. However, it is assumed that the concept of work group—number of individual reportings to a single supervisor—is a less meaningful and important variable at managerial levels because of the nature of the work situation. Hence, it is probably not as necessary to control its effects in assessing the effects of total size when the employees being considered are managers. Nevertheless, it is possible that this variable did have some undetermined effect on Porter's findings.

Behavior

With the exception of one quite limited area of investigation, there are almost no studies that specifically compare large total organizations or companies to small total organizations on behavioral measures other than attitude data.[5] Undoubtedly the major reason for this lies in the difficulty of obtaining a sample of organizations (as compared to a sample of individuals or a sample of subunits within organizations) in sufficient quantity and with sufficient variation in total size.

The one type of behavior that has been investigated in relation to total-organization size concerns the rate of managerial succession into top-level jobs. The first such study, by Grusky (1961), utilized *Fortune's* annual list of the 500 largest United States companies to select two groups of organizations differing on total size. His results indicated that the frequency or rate of succession was positively related to size such that there was more rapid turnover in the uppermost management positions within larger-sized companies. A study by Kriesberg (1962) seemed to confirm Grusky's findings. However, a later study by Gordon and Becker (1964), which involved a reanalysis of the data used by Grusky, showed very little relationship between size and rate of managerial succession. Thus, the possible effects of size on this particular variable of organizational behavior remain obscure at this point.

Summary

A review of relevant journals shows that very few studies have been carried out on the relationship of size of total organization to either job attitudes or job behavior. Two studies of worker attitudes that seem to fit in this category of investigations indicated that job satisfaction and morale were lower in larger organizations. However, both studies were reported in such a way that it is difficult to draw accurate or meaningful conclusions concerning the effects of organization size. At the managerial level, Porter (1963c, 1963d, 1964) found no overall advantage for either large or small organizations in relation to need satisfactions; he did find, however, that managerial jobs in larger companies were seen as requiring a somewhat greater emphasis on inner-directed behavior and as having a slightly greater amount of challenge and interest when compared to similar managerial jobs in smaller companies.

Overall, the findings relating total-organization size to job attitudes do not present as clear a picture as is the case for findings dealing with subunit size. It is entirely possible that the negative effects of large subunit size on job attitudes may not extend to large total-organization size. As has been suggested,

> An increase in the total size of an organization—with the consequent technological advantages of large-scale operation—will not necessarily reduce the morale and job satisfaction of employees as long as intra-organization work units are kept small [Porter, 1963d, p. 61].

This is a hypothesis that could be fairly easily confirmed or disconfirmed by future studies. Further research on total-organization size should also take into account the possibility that size of the total units may have one kind of effect on attitudes at the rank-and-file level, but a reversed effect at managerial levels, especially the higher levels. Again, this possibility would not be too difficult to test with additional research.

In the area of behavior, there is almost a complete lack of information on the effects of total-organization size. It would seem that future studies on size could, among other things, attempt to obtain measures of absenteeism, turnover, and similar rates in relation to total-unit size just as past studies have obtained this kind of data in relation to subunit size. At the moment, at least in the psychological literature, we do not even know whether the United States Steels, the Standard Oils, the General Motors, etc., have higher or lower turnover or absenteeism rates throughout their total organizations than do the local Acme or Ace manufacturing companies. (Again, it must be emphasized that if such comparisons of total organizations are to be meaningful, the effects of differences in the sizes of various subunits among the organizations must be partialed out and job level controlled.) Perhaps total-organization size will turn out to be an irrelevant variable in affecting such behavioral indices. At any rate, it would seem worthwhile to know whether this is the case or not.

SHAPE: TALL OR FLAT

Tall and flat organization structures are generally distinguished on the basis of the number of levels in the organization relative to the total size of the organization. A flat organization structure is one where

[5] The previously discussed article by Talacchi (1960) has sometimes been cited as an article that presents data on the relationship of "organization" size to job behavior, such as turnover rates and absenteeism rates, but no such data are given in the article. Instead, the findings are presented in terms of the relationship of size to satisfaction (as already noted above) and the relationship of satisfaction to turnover and absenteeism. Not only are there no data presented on the direct relationship of size to turnover and absenteeism, but also the data that are presented concerning these latter two variables involve intraorganization rather than interorganization comparisons. Thus, this article does not provide behavioral data in relation to size of total organization.

there are few levels relative to the total size of the organization and a tall organization structure is one where there are many levels relative to the total size of the organization. Another way of stating this is to say that the degree to which a structure is tall or flat is determined by the average span of control within the organization.

Attention has been focused on the relative merits of these two types of structures since 1950, when Worthy published his widely cited article on "Organizational Structure and Employee Morale" (see Gardner & Moore, 1955; Viteles, 1953; Whyte, 1961). Worthy's (1950) basic conclusion was that: "Flatter, less complex structures, with a maximum of administrative decentralization tend to create a potential for improved attitudes, more effective supervision, and greater individual responsibility and initiative among employees [p. 179]." Although Worthy published no empirical evidence to support his statements, and although his observations were based upon his experiences in a single company, his opinions are frequently cited by other authors to support their contention that flat organization structures produce better performance and better job attitudes than do tall ones. Worthy's opinions represent direct contradiction to those put forth by the classical organization theorists (e.g., Graicunas, 1937) who contend that a tall organization structure improves performance by allowing for close supervision and therefore complete understanding by the supervisor of the subordinate's activities.

Despite the fact that this significant disagreement about the relative advantages of tall and flat organization structures has provoked considerable comment in the literature, the topic did not generate any empirical research until 1962.

Attitudes

Three studies have compared the job satisfactions of employees in tall organizations with those in flat organizations. Meltzer and Salter (1962) published a study that reported on the job satisfactions of 704 physiologists (in nonuniversity organizations). They classified their questionnaire respondents by size of company (fewer than 20 professional employees, 21–50, and 51 or more), and by number of levels of administration within the organization (1–3 levels, 4–5, and 6 or more), and found generally insignificant relationships between tallness or flatness and job satisfaction. Their results, therefore, did not confirm Worthy's theory about flat structure producing better job attitudes. However, it should be noted that Meltzer and Salter studied research organizations of extremely small size, and hence their results may have limited generality.

A study by Porter and Lawler (1964) investigated the relationship between the need satisfaction of over 1,500 managers and the type of organization structure in which they worked. As in the Meltzer and Salter study, managers were classified as working in either a tall or flat organization structure based upon the number of levels in the organization relative to its total size. The results showed no clear overall superiority of flat over tall organizations in producing greater need satisfaction among managers. However, two qualifications to this general finding were noted: First, organization size seemed to have some effect on the relationship between type of structure and the degree of need satisfaction. In companies employing fewer than 5,000 people, managerial satisfaction was greater in flat rather than in tall organizations. For companies with 5,000 employees and over, the picture was reversed with a tall type of structure producing perceptions of greater need satisfaction. The second qualification was that the effects of organization structure on need satisfaction appeared to vary with the type of psychological need being considered. A tall type of structure was associated with greater satisfactions in the security and social need areas, whereas a flat structure was associated with greater satisfaction in the self-actualization need area.

Porter and Siegel (1964) have replicated the Porter and Lawler study with one essential difference—the sample. The Porter and Siegel sample of close to 3,000 managers was an international sample representing middle and upper levels of management in a wide variety of sizes and types of companies in 13 countries. The results of the newer study generally agreed with those found by Porter and Lawler. Porter and Siegel found that for companies of less than 5,000 employees, flat structures produced greater managerial need satisfaction, whereas for companies of 5,000 and over, there was no difference between tall and flat structures in producing managerial need satisfactions.

Behavior

Meltzer and Salter's (1962) study was the only empirical investigation that compared the job performances of individuals working in organizations with tall and flat structures. They found generally insignificant relationships between tallness and flatness and job performance (as measured by the publication of research articles). Only in large-size organizations did they find a significant trend and there it was in the direction of greater productivity in tall than in flat organizations.

Summary

The evidence does not support Worthy's (1950) sweeping generalization that a flat organization structure produces greater job satisfaction and improved job performance. The evidence points to organization size as one of the factors affecting the relative advantages of tall and flat organization structures. Two of the studies reviewed found that in relatively small organizations a flat organization did appear to be advantageous in terms of producing managerial job satisfactions. However, for relatively large organizations one study found that tall organization structures produced greater job satisfaction, and one study found that tall organization structures fostered greater productivity. Thus, it appears that the advantages of a flat structure not only decrease with increasing organization size, but that in relatively large organizations a flat structure may sometimes even be a liability.

One explanation for the tendency for the advantages of a flat organization structure to decrease with increasing organization size can be found in the characteristics generally attributed to tall and flat organization structures. Advocates of flat organization structures claim that because of the large average span of control subordinates will have greater freedom and autonomy to make decisions. As a result of this relatively greater freedom and autonomy, individuals are supposed to contribute more to the organization and receive greater satisfaction from their jobs. On the other hand, a tall structure increases supervisory controls and allows superiors to better coordinate the activities of their subordinates. In a small organization problems of coordination and communication do not tend to be severe, simply because the organization is small. Thus, in a small organization there would be little advantage in a tall structure and, in fact, since it tends to amplify the disadvantages associated with tight managerial control, a tall structure probably is a liability in a typical small organization. In large organizations, on the other hand, problems of coordination and communication are complex. Thus, for large organizations a taller type of structure may be needed to overcome these problems and allow managers to supervise their subordinates more effectively.

Future research will undoubtedly show that other variables such as type of company—for example, retail trade versus manufacturing firms—will have an important bearing on which type of structure is more advantageous in terms of job attitudes and job performance. Worthy (1959) himself has pointed out that different degrees of flatness may be desirable depending upon the type of organization considered.

SHAPE: CENTRALIZED OR DECENTRALIZED

> The contemporary trend in large-scale organization is toward decentralization, but we must realize that decentralization is several things to different people. There are those who view it entirely in terms of decision-making; others see it from the standpoint of geographical dispersion of plants and installations; and still others approach it as a philosophy of corporate life, a set of organization values with sociological, psychological, and spiritual facets [Pfiffner & Sherwood, 1960, p. 190].

There is no reason to believe that these different types of decentralization produce similar effects on job attitudes and performance. Thus, the first point that should be considered about any study concerned with the effects of decentralization is the measure of decentralization that is used.

According to Chandler (1956), the movement to decentralization can be dated to the 1920s and the management policies of Alfred P. Sloan, Jr., at General Motors. That the topic of decentralization is currently in the air is clearly demonstrated by the great number of recent articles that have dogmatically set forth plans for a decentralized corporate way of life (see Cordiner, 1956; Ginzberg & Reilley, 1957; Lawrence, 1958; Smith, 1958). Most writers have claimed that by offering increased autonomy for the individual regardless of his level within the company, decentralization improves both job attitudes and performance. Since the topic of decentralization has received considerable attention for the last forty years, it is not surprising that there has been a certain amount of research on the topic. However, most of the research on the effects of decentralization has been of the case study variety (e.g., Drucker, 1946; Given, 1949; Selznick, 1949), and therefore not within the scope of this review. In fact, only four studies were found that compared the job attitudes and behavior of employees in centralized and decentralized companies.

Attitudes

A study by Baker and France (1954) compared the attitudes of managers in centralized and decentralized industrial relations departments. Their classification of centralized or decentralized departments was based upon the level at which decisions relative to industrial relations were made. When they asked managers which type of structure produced the best intramanagement relations, managers who worked in companies with centralization favored centralization, and managers who worked in companies with decentralization favored decentralization. Baker and France further found the companies with decentralized industrial relations departments revealed no greater satisfaction among their plant managers than did those companies with centralized industrial relations departments. Although this latter finding does not support the claims of those who favor decentralization, it is important to remember that the study was concerned with decentralization in only one type of department, and the attitudes of only one level of management. Thus, it is impossible to know if the findings of Baker and France are applicable to the effects of decentralization on a company-wide basis.

Litzinger (1963) has compared the attitudes of bank managers who were under centralized management with those who were under decentralized management. His results indicated no clear attitude differences between the centralized and the decentralized groups of managers. However, the results are difficult to interpret because it is not clear from the article what measure of decentralization was used.

Behavior

Two studies were found that compared the behavior of employees in centralized companies with the behavior of employees in decentralized companies. Carlson (1951) found that executives in decentralized companies spent only 6.3 percent of their time "taking decisions," while executives in centralized companies spent 14.6 percent of their time "taking decisions." He further found that executives in decentralized companies spent less time giving orders (6.8 percent versus 13.8 percent) than did executives in centralized companies. Carlson's finding that executives in decentralized companies gave fewer orders and made fewer decisions supports the claim that decentralization can lead to greater autonomy at the lower levels of the organization. However, there is a problem with this study that makes the results difficult to interpret. It is not clear what Carlson used as his criteria for classifying organizations as centralized or decentralized. Thus, it is impossible to know which particular type of decentralization Carlson's findings support. His findings are further limited by the fact that he had only nine managers as subjects in the study.

Weiss (1957) studied the relationship between centralized and decentralized organization structures and several measures of behavior. He classified 34 companies as either centralized or decentralized based upon their answers to a 22-item questionnaire about the level at which decisions were made in the company. Weiss found no significant differences between centralized and decentralized companies on any of the following variables: turnover rate, number of grievances, number of white-collar workers, absenteeism, accident frequency, accident severity, and age of managers. It should be pointed out that although Weiss found no statistically significant differences, the trend on each of the factors considered was favorable to decentralized organizations.

Summary

The studies reviewed offer no clear support for the proposition that decentralization can produce either improved job attitudes or performance. Thus, Pfiffner and Sherwood's (1960) conclusion that decentralization must be accepted partially on faith seems completely justified. The fact that two of the studies reviewed obtained a few significant results and that another showed interesting trends suggest that the topic is a meaningful one for research. Perhaps the chief obstacle to research in this area, though, is the lack of an adequate method for measuring the degree of decentralization that exists in an organization. Until such a measure is developed the research evidence gathered will undoubtedly remain difficult to interpret.

It is doubtful that future research will ever prove that any of the three types of decentralization mentioned earlier are superior to centralization in all situations. Marschak (1959) has presented a model graphically illustrating that the efficiency of decentralization of decision making varies greatly depending upon the type of business in which the company is engaged. Sloan (1963) has made a similar point by stating that different degrees of decentralization appeared to be optimum for DuPont and General Motors because of their different product lines. Thus, for companies in a business where there is a high degree of complementarity among the members' actions (e.g., airlines or railroads), such that one member's action depends directly upon what his fellow employees are doing, a high degree of centralization is crucial. However, for companies in a business where there is a great deal of independence among the action of the members (e.g., chains of retail stores), such that one member's action does not depend on what his fellow employees are doing, increased decentralization may be desirable.

CONCLUSIONS

In this final section, two broad questions will be considered: First, what is the status of our current knowledge concerning the possible effects of structure? Second, where should future research efforts in this area be directed?

With respect to the first question, a review of the literature demonstrates the following:

1. Five of the seven properties of organization structure (span of control and centralization/decentralization being the two possible exceptions) have been shown to have some kind of significant relationship to either job attitudes or job behavior, or to both of these types of variables. However, as we stressed in the introduction, experimental "proof" of cause-effect relationships between structure and employee attitudes and behavior is elusive and almost nonexistent.

2. Certain structural variables seem to have stronger relationships to attitudes and behavior than other structural variables. On the basis of the evidence to date, the two properties of structure that have the strongest relationships with, or effects on, the two types of "dependent" variables are two suborganization properties: organizational levels and subunit size. Level was shown to have a definite connection with several types of attitudes, and subunit size was found to be associated strongly with both job satisfaction attitudes and several types of behavior. Three other properties—line/staff type of position, total-organization size, and tall/flat shape—accounted for some significant relationships to several of the dependent variables, but the strength and clarity of their relationships were not as great as was the case with organizational levels and subunit size. Each of these three former variables has not been researched as extensively as have the latter two variables, and hence it is possible that future results will show them to have somewhat stronger relationships than appears to be the case at the moment. The other two variables, span of control and centralization/decentralization, have so far not been found to be significantly related to attitudes or behavior. Again, however, relatively little research has been carried out on these two structural variables and they may yet be found to have more important influences on employees than seems apparent at the moment.

3. Certain dependent variables are more highly related to properties of structure than are other kinds of dependent variables. For example, indices of need satisfaction seem to be much more strongly correlated with structural properties than are indices of need importance. This makes good sense logically and psychologically, in that satisfactions presumably should be determined more by environmental factors (e.g., the degree of job responsibilities, supervisory behavior toward subordinates, size of work group, etc.) than by personal factors (e.g., degree of extroversion), whereas employee wants and desires are likely to come about more from personal factors than from aspects of the work environment. On the behavioral side, absenteeism and turnover seem somewhat more clearly related to structural factors than does employee output *per se.* The reasons why this should be so probably revolve around the fact that output or performance rates seem to be much more complexly determined phenomena than are absenteeism and turnover rates. That is, the latter types of behavior are within the employee's repertory of potential actions; however, all levels of output are not within his repertory of actions both because of personal limitations and because of possible environmental factors such as work-group pressure and equipment limitations. Therefore, if structure affects various aspects of behavior largely through its influence on employees' motivations, absenteeism and turnover rates will be more directly affected than will output levels.

In general, the impact of structural variables appears to be clearer on attitudes than on behavioral variables. However, this conclusion should be interpreted with caution because a search of the literature reveals that for most of the structural properties somewhat more research has been carried out on their relationships to attitudes than to types of behavior.

4. The direction of relationships of certain structural variables to certain dependent variables seems clear. The following directional relationships seem to be well supported by the research evidence to date: *(a)* organizational levels—positive relationship between height of level and degree of job and need satisfaction, positive relationship between height of level and perceived necessity for inner directed type of job behavior; *(b)* line/staff hierarchies—positive relationship between line type of position and degree of need satisfaction; *(c)* subunit size—negative relationship between size and degree of job satisfaction, positive relationship between size and absenteeism rates, positive relationship between size and turnover rates.

For certain other structural variables, the direction of their impact on certain dependent variables is not clear, even though particular studies found statistically significant relationships. Thus, it is not at all certain whether a flatter type of organization structure is always associated with greater employee satisfaction compared to a taller structure, or that a smaller total organization results in greater employee satisfaction than does a larger total organization. As will be pointed out below, the direction of relationship in each case seems to be affected by the interaction of some second structural variable. Also, the evidence on the relationship between subunit size and output shows a wide scattering of types of relationships, going all the way from negative through curvilinear to positive relationships. Thus, it may be that subunit size is an important determinant of employee productive behavior, but that the direction of its effects depends on relatively local and particularized conditions.

We now turn to our second question: Where should research efforts be directed in the future?

First, we would suggest that future research investigations in this area must be addressed to more complex questions. It seems evident that a great deal more attention has to be given to the possible interrelationships between and among different organization structural variables than has been the case so far. There is already some indication in the literature that such interactions among two or more properties or dimensions of structure are likely. For example, the available evidence indicates that in order to determine the effects of either subunit size or total-organization size, one must specify or take into account the organizational level or levels being considered. It seems probable that certain effects of size, either subunit or total, that are present when rank-and-file workers are the objects of investigation may be greatly reduced or possibly even reversed at management levels, especially middle and upper executive levels. With respect to a different structural variable, tall/flat organization shape, the available data indicate that its relationship to job satisfaction is modified considerably by the total size of the organizations being studied. In other cases there are, as yet, few data to support (or deny) a notion of interaction effects, yet logic would lead one to predict the likelihood of this kind of situation. As just one example, it appears probable that success, or lack of it, in cases of deliberate organizational decentralization may well depend upon which organizational levels are to be involved in the decentralization and upon such other intraorganizational structural variables as the spans of control and sizes of subunits created by the change.

To sum up this point, there are already enough indications in the literature to support a greater research effort to investigate the interactions among structural properties of organizations in their relationship to employees' job behavior and attitudes. Too much previous theorizing in the area of organizations has neglected such interaction possibilities, and hence there has been an unfortunate tendency to oversimplify vastly the effects of particular variables. Organizations appear to be much too complex for a given variable to have a consistent unidirectional effect across a wide variety of types of conditions.

Second, there is an obvious need for field experimental studies, as well as the more typical field comparative studies. We need, in other words, investigations where one or more structural variables are systematically manipulated in field, not laboratory, conditions. There are admittedly great practical difficulties in carrying out such investigations, yet with the study of organizations occupying such an important place in the behavioral sciences today, it is time that researchers in this area faced up to the necessities for this kind of undertaking. Perhaps this will require projects of greater scope and support than in the past, and most certainly it is likely to require a cross-discipline approach. But such projects are definitely not out of the realm of the possible. As examples, one can conceive without too much difficulty of the possibilities of manipulating such variables as span of control or size of subunit. The results of such studies would provide firm support for some aspects of organization theories, where such support is largely lacking at the present time.

Third, longitudinal studies are probably necessary to draw valid conclusions concerning certain structural variables. Results from studies so far carried out on the relationships of organizational level or line/staff hierarchies to job attitudes are subject to the limitation that any obtained relationships might in part be due to differences among types of people rather than to differences among types of positions within organizations. One profitable method of sorting out the relative effects of these two types of variables, that is, individual and organizational, would be to conduct longitudinal studies where the same individuals are followed in their careers from one kind of organizational position to another. Such longitudinal studies are conspicuous by their rarity in the literature on organization structure.

In conclusion, we feel that the importance attached to the study of organization structure is not misplaced. Increased attention in the future to research on structural properties of organizations should improve our understanding of the way people think and behave when they function in their jobs within organizations.

REFERENCES

Acton Society Trust. *Size and morale.* London: AST, 1953.

Argyle, M., Gardner, G., and Cioffi, I. Supervisory methods related to productivity, absenteeism, and labor turnover. *Human Relations,* 1958, **11**, 23–40.

Argyris, C. *Personality and organization.* New York: Harper, 1957.

Ash, P. The SRA Employee Inventory: A statistical analysis. *Personnel Psychology,* 1954, 7, 337–64.

Baehr, Melany E. A factorial study of the SRA Employee Inventory. *Personnel Psychology,* 1954, 7, 319–36.

Baker, Helen and France, R. R. *Centralization and decentralization in industrial relations.* Princeton: Industrial Relations Section, 1954.

Baumgartel, H. and Sobol, R. Background and organizational factors in absenteeism. *Personnel Psychology,* 1959, **12**, 431–43.

Benge, E. J. How to learn what workers think of job and boss. *Factory Management and Maintenance,* 1944 (May), **102** (5), 101–4.

Bennis, W. G. Leadership theory and administrative behavior: The problem of authority. *Administrative Science Quarterly,* 1959, **4**, 259–301.

Brayfield, A. H. and Crockett, W. H. Employee attitudes and employee performance. *Psychological Bulletin,* 1955, **52**, 396–424.

Brown, A. Some reflections on organization: Truths, half-truths, and delusions. *Personnel,* 1954, **31** (1) 31–42.

Browne, C. G. and Neitzel, Betty J. Communication, supervision, and morale. *Journal of Applied Psychology,* 1952, **36**, 86–91.

Burns, T. The direction of activity and communication in a departmental executive group: A quantitative study in a British engineering factory with a self-recording technique. *Human Relations,* 1954, **7**, 73–97.

Campbell, H. Group incentive payment schemes: The effects of lack of understanding and of group size. *Occupational Psychology,* 1952, **26**, 15–21.

Campbell, J. W. An attitude survey in a typical manufacturing firm. *Personnel Psychology,* 1948, **1**, 31–39.

Carlson, S. *Executive behavior, a study of the work load and the working methods of managing directors.* Stockholm: Stromberg, 1951.

Centers, R. Motivational aspects of occupational stratification. *Journal of Social Psychology,* 1948, **28**, 187–217.

Chandler, A. D. Management decentralization: An historical analysis. *Business History Review,* 1956, **30**, 111–74.

Cleland, S. *Influence of plant size on industrial relations.* Princeton: Princeton Univer. Press, 1955.

Coates, C. H. and Pellegrin, R. J. Executives and supervisors: Contrasting self-conceptions and conceptions of each other. *American Sociological Review,* 1957, **22**, 217–20.

Cordiner, R. J. *New frontiers for professional managers.* New York: McGraw-Hill, 1956.

Dale, E. *Planning and developing the company organization structure.* New York: American Management Association, 1952.

Dalton, M. Conflicts between staff and line managerial officers. *American Sociological Review,* 1950, **15**, 342–51.

Dalton, M. *Men who manage.* New York: Wiley, 1959.

Davis, K. Management communication and the grapevine. *Harvard Business Review,* 1953, **31** (5), 43–49.

Drucker, P. *Concept of the corporation.* New York: Day, 1946.

Dubin, R. Business behavior *behaviorally* viewed. In G. B. Strother (ed.), *Social science approaches to business behavior.* Homewood, Ill.: Dorsey Press, 1962.

Dubin, R. and Spray, S. L. Executive behavior and interaction. *Industrial Relations,* 1964, **3**, 99–108.

Entwisle, Doris, & Walton, J. Observations on the span of control. *Administrative Science Quarterly,* 1961, **5**, 522–33.

Fisch, G. G. Line-staff is obsolete. *Harvard Business Review,* 1961, **39** (5), 67–79.

Fisch, G. G. Stretching the span of management. *Harvard Business Review,* 1963, **41** (5), 74–85.

Fleishman, E. A. The measurement of leadership attitudes in industry. *Journal of Applied Psychology,* 1953, **37**, 153–58.

Fleishman, E. A., Harris, E. F., and Burtt, H. E. Leadership and supervision in industry: An evaluation of a supervisory training program. *Ohio State University, Bureau of Educational Research Monograph,* 1955, No. 33.

Fortune. The Fortune survey: A self-portrait of the American people—1947. *Fortune,* 1947, **35** (1), 5–16.

Fortune. Effective morale. *Fortune,* 1950, **42** (2), 46–50.

Gardner, B. B. and Moore, D. G. *Human relations in industry.* (3rd ed.) Homewood, Ill.: Dorsey Press, 1955.

Ginzberg, E., & Reilley, E. W. *Effecting change in large organizations.* New York: Columbia Univer. Press, 1957.

Given, W. B. *Bottom-up management; people working together.* New York: Harper, 1949.

Gordon, G. and Becker, S. Organizational size and managerial succession: A reexamination. *American Journal of Sociology,* 1964, **70**, 215–23.

Graicunas, V. A. Relationship and organization. In L. Gulick and L. Urwick (eds.), *Papers on the science of administration.* New York: Institute of Public Administration, 1937.

Grusky, O. Corporate size, bureaucratization, and managerial succession. *American Journal of Sociology,* 1961, **67**, 261–69.

Haire, M. *Psychology in management.* New York: McGraw-Hill, 1956.

Haire, M., Ghiselli, E. E., and Porter, L. W. Cultural patterns in the role of the manager. *Industrial Relations,* 1963, **2**, 95–117.

Handyside, J. D. Satisfactions and aspirations. *Occupational Psychology,* 1961, **35**, 213–44.

Hemphill, J. K. Relations between the size of the group and the behavior of "superior" leaders. *Journal of Social Psychology,* 1950, **32**, 11–22.

Hemphill, J. K. Group dimensions: A manual for their measurement. *Ohio State University, Bureau of Business Research Monograph,* 1956, No. 87.

Herbst, P. G. Measurement of behavior structure by means of input-output data. *Human Relations,* 1957, **10**, 335–46.

Herzberg, F., Mausner, B., Peterson, R. O., and Capwell, Dora F. *Job attitudes: Review of research and opinion.* Pittsburgh: Psychological Service of Pittsburgh, 1957.

Herzberg, F., Mausner, B., and Snyderman, Barbara B. *The motivation to work.* (2nd ed.) New York: Wiley, 1959.

Hewitt, D. and Parfitt, Jessie. A note on working morale and size of group. *Occupational Psychology,* 1953, **27,** 38–42.

Hull, R. L. and Kolstad, A. Morale on the job. In G. B. Watson (ed.), *Civilian morale.* New York: Houghton Mifflin, 1942.

Indik, B. P. and Seashore, S. E. *Effects of organization size on member attitudes and behavior.* Ann Arbor: University of Michigan, Survey Research Center of the Institute of Social Research, 1961.

Kahn, R. L. Human relations on the shop floor. In E. M. Hugh-Jones (ed.), *Human relations and modern management.* Amsterdam: North-Holland Publishing, 1958, pp. 43–74.

Katzell, R. A., Barrett, R. S., and Parker, T. C. Job satisfaction, job performance, and situational characteristics. *Journal of Applied Psychology,* 1961, **45,** 65–72.

Kerr, W. A., Koppelmeier, G. J., and Sullivan, J. J. Absenteeism, turnover and morale in a metals fabrication factory. *Occupational Psychology,* 1951, **25,** 50–55.

Kolstad, A. Attitudes of employees and their supervisors. *Personnel,* 1944, **20,** 241–50.

Kreisberg, L. Careers, organization size, and succession. *American Journal of Sociology,* 1962, **68,** 355–59.

Lawler, E. E. and Porter, L. W. Perceptions regarding management compensation. *Industrial Relations,* 1963, **3,** 41–49.

Lawrence, P. R. *The changing of organizational behavior patterns: A case study of decentralization.* Boston: Harvard University, Graduate School of Business Administration, Division of Research, 1958.

Leavitt, H. J. *Managerial psychology.* Chicago: Univer. Chicago Press, 1958.

Leavitt, H. J. and Whisler, T. L. Management in the 1980's. *Harvard Business Review,* 1958, **36**(6), 41–48.

Likert, R. *New patterns of management.* New York: McGraw-Hill, 1961.

Litzinger, W. D. Entrepreneurial prototype in bank management. *Academy of Management Journal,* 1963, **6**(1), 36–45.

McGregor, D. *The human side of enterprise.* New York: McGraw-Hill, 1960.

Mandell, M. M. *Recruiting and selecting office employees.* New York: American Management Association, 1956.

Marriott, R. Size of working group and output, *Occupational Psychology,* 1949, **23,** 47–57.

Marschak, J. Efficient and viable organizational forms. In M. Haire (ed.), *Modern organization theory.* New York: Wiley, 1959, pp. 307–20.

Martin, N. H. The levels of management and their mental demands. In W. L. Warner and N. H. Martin (eds.), *Industrial man.* New York: Harper, 1959, pp. 276–94.

Meltzer, L. and Salter, J. Organizational structure and the performance and job satisfaction of physiologists. *American Sociological Review,* 1962, **27,** 351–62.

Metzner, Helen and Mann, F. Employee attitudes and absences. *Personnel Psychology,* 1953, **6,** 467–85.

Morse, Nancy C. *Satisfactions in the white-collar job.* Ann Arbor: University of Michigan, 1953.

Opinion Research Corporation. *The conflict between the scientific and the management mind.* Princeton: ORC, 1959.

Opinion Research Corporation. *Motivating managers.* Princeton: ORC, 1962.

Pellegrin, R. J. and Coates, C. H. Executives and supervisors: Contrasting definitions of career success. *Administrative Science Quarterly,* 1957, **1,** 506–17.

Pfiffner, J. M. and Sherwood, F. P. *Administrative organization.* Englewood Cliffs, N.J.: Prentice-Hall, 1960.

Porter, L. W. A study of perceived job satisfactions in bottom and middle management jobs. *Journal of Applied Psychology,* 1961, **45,** 1–10.

Porter, L. W. Job attitudes in management: I. Perceived deficiencies in need fulfillment as a function of job level. *Journal of Applied Psychology,* 1962, **46,** 375–84.

Porter, L. W. Job attitudes in management: II. Perceived importance of needs as a function of job level. *Journal of Applied Psychology,* 1963, **47,** 141–48. (a)

Porter, L. W. Job attitudes in management: III. Perceived deficiencies in need fulfillment as a function of line vs. staff type of job. *Journal of Applied Psychology,* 1963, **47,** 267–275.(b)

Porter, L. W. Job attitudes in management: IV. Perceived deficiencies in need fulfillment as a function of size of company. *Journal of Applied Psychology,* 1963, **47,** 386–97.(c)

Porter, L. W. Where is the organization man? *Harvard Business Review,* 1963, **41**(6), 53–61.(d)

Porter, L. W. *Organizational patterns of managerial job attitudes.* New York: American Foundation for Management Research, 1964.

Porter, L. W. and Henry, Mildred M. Job attitudes in management: V. Perceptions of the importance of certain personality traits as a function of job level. *Journal of Applied Psychology,* 1964, **48,** 31–36.(a)

Porter, L. W. and Henry, Mildred M. Job attitudes in management: VI. Perceptions of the importance of certain personality traits as a function of line vs. staff type of job. *Journal of Applied Psychology,* 1964, **48,** 305–9.(b)

Porter, L. W. and Lawler, E. E. The effects of tall vs. flat organization structures on managerial job satisfaction. *Personnel Psychology,* 1964, **17,** 135–48.

Porter, L. W. and Siegel, J. The effects of tall vs. flat organization structures on managerial satisfactions in foreign countries. Unpublished manuscript, University of California, Berkeley, 1964.

Revans, R. W. Human relations, management and size. In E. M. Hugh-Jones (ed.), *Human relations and modern management.* Amsterdam: North-Holland Publishing, 1958, pp. 177–220.

Rosen, H. Desirable attributes of work: Four levels of management describe their job environments. *Journal of Applied Psychology,* 1961, **45,** 156–60.(a)

Rosen, H. Managerial role interaction: A study of three

managerial levels. *Journal of Applied Psychology,* 1961, **45**, 30–34.(b)

Rosen, H. and Weaver, C. G. Motivation in management: A study of four managerial levels. *Journal of Applied Psychology,* 1960, **44**, 386–92.

Seashore, S. E. *Group Cohesiveness in the industrial work group.* Ann Arbor: University of Michigan, Institute for Social Research, 1954.

Selznick, P. *T.V.A. and the grass-roots: A study in the sociology of formal organization.* Berkeley: Univer. California Press, 1949.

Shartle, C. L. *Executive performance and leadership.* Englewood Cliffs, N.J.: Prentice-Hall, 1956.

Sloan, A. P. My years with General Motors—Part II. *Fortune,* 1963, **68**(4), 145–48.

Smith, G. A., Jr. *Managing geographically decentralized companies.* Boston: Harvard University, Graduate School of Business Administration, Division of Research, 1958.

Strauss, G. and Sayles, L. R. *Personnel: The human problems of management.* Englewood Cliffs, N.J.: Prentice-Hall, 1960.

Talacchi, S. Organization size, individual attitudes and behavior: An empirical study. *Administrative Science Quarterly,* 1960, **5**, 398–420.

Triandis, H. C. Categories of thought of managers, clerks, and workers about jobs and people in an industry. *Journal of Applied Psychology,* 1959, **43**, 338–44.(a)

Triandis, H. C. Differential perception of certain jobs and people by managers, clerks, and workers in industry. *Journal of Applied Psychology,* 1959, **43**, 221-25.(b)

Triandis, H. C. A comparative factorial analysis of job semantic structures of managers and workers. *Journal of Applied Psychology,* 1960, **44**, 297–302.

Urwick, L. F. Executive decentralization with functional coordination. *Management Review,* 1935, **24**, 355–68.

Viteles, M. S. *Motivation and morale in industry.* New York: Norton, 1953.

Weiss, E. C. Relation of personnel statistics to organization structure. *Personnel Psychology,* 1957, **10**, 27–42.

Whyte, W. F. *Men at work.* Homewood, Ill.: Dorsey Press, 1961.

Whyte, W. H., Jr. *The organization man.* New York: Simon and Schuster, 1956.

Woodward, Joan. *Management and technology.* London: Her Majesty's Stationery Office, 1958.

Worthy, J. C. Organizational structure and employee morale. *American Sociological Review,* 1950, **15**, 169–79.

Worthy, J. C. *Big business and free men.* New York: Harper, 1959.

31. ORGANIZATIONAL DEVELOPMENTS AND THE FATE OF BUREAUCRACY*

***Warren G. Bennis*†**

Organizations are complex, goal-seeking social units. In addition to the penultimate task of realizing goals, they must undertake two related tasks if they are to survive: (1) they must maintain the internal system and coordinate the "human side," and (2) they must adapt to and shape the external environment.

The means employed for the first task is a complicated system of social processes which somehow or other gets organizations and their participants to accommodate to their respective goals. This process of mutual compliance, where the two parties conform to and accommodate one another is called *reciprocity.* The means for the second task has to do with the way the organization transacts and exchanges with its environment; this is called *adaptability.*

This social arrangement developed to accomplish the tasks of reciprocity and adaptability in contemporary society is called bureaucracy. I use that term descriptively, not as an epithet or as a metaphor *a la Kafka's Castle* which conjures up an image of red tape, faceless masses standing in endless lines, and despair. Bureaucracy, as I use it, is a social invention, perfected during the Industrial Revolution to organize and direct the activities of the firm and later (at the turn of the century) conceptualized by the great German sociologist, Max Weber.

Ironically, though Weber worked heroically to create a value-free science, the term bureaucracy has taken on such negative connotations that even dictionaries use the term in the vernacular. For example, the *Oxford Dictionary* quotes Carlyle as saying: "The Continental nuisance called 'Bureaucracy.'" It also defines a bureaucrat as "one who endeavors to concentrate power in his bureau." However empirically valid these descriptions may be, bureaucracy in a more technical sense, revered in theory by sociologists and in practice by most businessmen,

* Invited address delivered before the Division of Industrial and Business Psychology, American Psychological Association on September 5, 1964. Parts of this article have been published in *Trans-Action,* July-August, 1965. Permission of the publisher has been granted.

† President, University of Cincinnati.

has become the most successful and popular device for achieving the major tasks of organization. To paraphrase Churchill's ironic remark about democracy, we can say of bureaucracy that it is the worst possible theory of organization, apart from all others that have so far been tried.

Now is the time to challenge the conceptual and empirical foundations of bureaucracy. To jump to my conclusion first, I will argue that bureaucracy which has served us so well in the past, both as an "ideal type" and a practical form of organization, will not survive as the *dominant* form of human organization in the future. Social organizations behave like other organisms: they transform themselves through selective adaptation, and new shapes, patterns, models—currently recessive—are emerging which promise basic changes. This argument is based on the assertion that the methods and social processes employed by bureaucracy to cope with its internal environment (reciprocity) and its external (adaptability) are hopelessly out of joint with contemporary realities. So within the next 25 to 50 years we will all witness and participate in the end of bureaucracy.[1]

The remainder of this paper elaborates this viewpoint. First, I shall take up the problem of linkage one: how organizations get men to comply, the problem of reciprocity. In this section I shall discuss how contemporary psychologists and students of organizational behavior attempt to resolve this issue. Then I shall discuss the second crucial linkage: adaptability, and then present current thinking about this. Finally, I shall sketch the conditions and structure for organizations of the future.

1. LINKAGE ONE: THE PROBLEM OF RECIPROCITY

The problem of reciprocity, like most human problems, has a long and venerable past. The modern version of this one goes back at least 160 years and was precipitated by an historical paradox: the twin births of modern individualism and modern industrialism. The one brought about a deep concern for the constitutional guarantees of personal rights and a passionate interest in individual emotions and growth. The other brought about increased rationalization and mechanization of organized activity. By coinciding, the growth of technology and enterprise tended to subvert the newly won individual freedoms and to subordinate them to the impersonal dictates of the workplace. De Tocqueville, writing in 1835 about his American experience, managed to sum up an epoch and its controversies in a paragraph:

> When a workman is unceasingly and exclusively engaged in the fabrication of one thing, he ultimately does his work with singular dexterity; but at the same time he loses the general faculty of applying his mind to the direction of the work. He every day becomes more adroit and less industrious: so that it may be said of him that in proportion as the workman improves, the man is degraded. . . . Thus at the very time at which the science of manufacture lowers the class of workmen, it raises the class of masters. . . . The object (of managerial elite) is not to govern that population (of workers), but to use it . . . it first impoverishes and debases the men who serve it and then abandons them to be supported by the charity of the public.[2]

So as technology and rationalization increase, man's passions and liberties are suppressed: as organization becomes more efficient, man's work becomes more demeaning and depersonalized. Thus, De Tocqueville wrote an indictment of industrialization which has not only stuck to the present times but which provided Marx and other nineteenth century radicals with their main themes. It is also an issue which has captivated the imagination of many scholars and researchers currently interested in the human organization.

In its crudest form, the controversy is a conflict over priorities of criteria: the individual's needs, motives, goals, and growth *versus* the organization's goals and rights. And no matter how often the *Panglosses* of the right and left attempt to minimize this conflict—the former with a "What's good for General Motors is good for the workers" and the latter with "Satisfied workers are effective workers" —I am convinced that is a truly consequential dilemma.

Enter Bureaucracy

Bureaucracy is a unique solution in that it links man's needs to organizational goals. It achieves this linkage through an influence structure based on *legal-rational* grounds instead of on the vagaries of personal power. The governed agree to obey through the rights of office and the power of reason: superiors rule because of their role incumbency and their technical (rational) competence. In short, bureaucracy is a machine of social influence which relies exclusively on reason and law. Weber once likened the bureaucratic mechanism to a judge *qua* computer:

> Bureaucracy is like a modern judge who is a vending machine into which the pleadings are inserted together with

[1] The number of years necessary for this transition, of course, is an estimate based on forecasts for the prospects of industrialization. Sociological evolutionists are substantially agreed that within a 25 to 75 year period, most of the people in the world will be living in industrialized societies. But generally speaking, I am talking about the so-called advanced, not the under, semi, or partially advanced countries.

[2] [6], chapters XVII-XVIII.

the fee and which then disgorges the judgement together with its reasons mechanically derived from the code.[3]

The bureaucratic machine model was developed as a reaction against the personal subjugation, nepotism, cruelty, emotional vicissitudes and subjective judgments which passed for managerial practices in the early days of the Industrial Revolution. For Weber, the true hope for man lay in his ability to rationalize, calculate, to use his head, as well as his hands and heart. Roles, institutionalized and reinforced by legal tradition, rather than personalities; rationality and predictability, rather than irrationality and unanticipated consequences; impersonality, rather than close personal relations; technical competence rather than arbitrary rule or iron whims—these are the main characteristics of bureaucracy.[4]

This is bureaucracy: the pyramidal organization which dominates so much of our thinking and planning related to organizational behavior, and which mediates the organization-individual dilemma through a rational system of role constraints.

Critiquing Bureaucracy

It does not take a great critical imagination to detect the flaws and problems in the bureaucratic model. We have all *experienced* them: bosses with less technical competence than their underlings; arbitrary and zany rules; an informal organization which subverts or replaces the formal apparatus; confusion and conflict among roles; and cruel treatment of subordinates based not on rational grounds but on quasi-legal, or worse, inhumane grounds. Unanticipated consequences abound and provide a mine of material for those comics, like Chaplin or Tati, who can capture with a smile or a shrug the absurdity of authority systems based on pseudologic and inappropriate rules.

Almost everybody else—certainly many students of organizational behavior—approaches bureaucracy with a chip on his shoulder. It has been attacked for many different reasons: for theoretical confusion and contradictions, for moral and ethical reasons, on practical grounds or for inefficiency, for methodological weaknesses, for containing too many implicit values and for containing too few. I have recently cataloged the criticisms of bureaucracy (omitting those related to its boundary maintenance, which will be taken up in the next section), and they outnumber and probably outdo the 95 theses tacked on the church door at Wittenberg in attacking another bureaucracy.[5] The criticisms can be categorized as the following:

a) Bureaucracy does not adequately allow for the personal growth and the development of mature personalities.
b) It develops conformity and "group-think."
c) It does not take into account the "informal organization" and the emergent and unanticipated problems.
d) Its systems of control and authority are hopelessly outdated.
e) It has no adequate juridical process.
f) It does not possess adequate means for resolving differences and conflicts between ranks, and most particularly, between functional groups.
g) Communication (and innovative ideas) are thwarted or distorted due to hierarchical divisions.
h) The full human resources of bureaucracy are not utilized due to mistrust, fear of reprisals, etc.
i) It cannot assimilate the influx of new technology or scientists entering the organization.
j) It modifies the personality structure such that man becomes and reflects the dull, gray, conditioned "organization man."

Weber himself came around to condemn the apparatus he helped immortalize. While he felt that bureaucracy was inescapable, he also thought it might strangle the spirit of capitalism or the entrepreneurial attitude, a theme which Schumpeter later developed. And in a debate on bureaucracy Weber once said, more in sorrow than in anger:

> It is horrible to think that the world could one day be filled with nothing but those little cogs, little men clinging to little jobs and striving towards bigger ones—a state of affairs which is to be seen once more, as in the Egyptian records, playing an ever increasing part in the spirit of our present administrative system, and especially of its offspring, the students. This passion for bureaucracy . . . is enough to drive one to despair. It is as if in politics . . .

---

[3] [5], p. 421.

[4] For the sake of brevity, I simplify Weber's thinking more than I should. Within the year, a commemorative Weberian conference was held at his former university, Heidelberg. According to most reports, the conference ended in a mood of controversy and chaos caused by a disagreement in interpreting Weber's thoughts. Certainly many students of bureaucracy (Blau, Gouldner, Etzioni and Bendix—see References) have been attempting to clarify, order, and reconceptualize Weber's ideas. Weber, for example, never distinguished between the two types of authority he implied, the authority of office and the authority of reason. He was also easy to misinterpret. For example, his theory of bureaucracy could be viewed in a variety of ways: as an ethical system, as a series of hypotheses, as a conceptual framework, and as an anti-utopian model: various scholars have seen his theory in at least those ways. Most contemporary students of organizations would argue that bureaucracy must be viewed as a condition which can be dimensionalized and which can be found to vary empirically from firm to firm. The six dimensions most frequently cited are:
a) A division of labor based on functional specialization.
b) A well-defined hierarchy of authority.
c) A system of rules covering the rights and duties of the incumbents.
d) Impersonality of interpersonal relations.
e) A system of procedures for dealing with work situations.
f) Promotion and selection based on technical competence (Hall, 1963).

[5] See [7].

we were deliberately to become men who need "order" and nothing but order, who become nervous and cowardly if for one moment this order wavers, and helpless if they are torn away from their total incorporation in it. That the world should know no men but these: it is such an evolution that we are already caught up in, and the great question is therefore not how we can promote and hasten it, but what can we oppose to this machinery in order to keep a portion of mankind free from this parcelling-out of the soul, from this supreme mastery of the bureaucratic way of life.[6]

I think it would be fair to say that a good deal of the work on organizational behavior over the past two decades has been a footnote to the bureaucratic "back-lash" which aroused Weber's passion: saving mankind's soul "from the supreme master of bureaucracy." Very few of us have been indifferent to the fact that the bureaucratic mechanism is a social instrument in the service of repression, that it treats man's ego and social needs as a constant, or as nonexistent or as inert, that these confined and constricted needs insinuate themselves into the social processes of organizations in strange, unintended ways, that those very matters which Weber claimed escaped calculation—love, power, hate—are not only calculable and powerful in their effects, but must be reckoned with.

Resolutions of Linkage One: The Reciprocity Dilemma

Of the three resolutions to the discrepancy between individual and organizational needs, only the last truly holds our interest now. The first resolution minimizes or denies the problem; it asserts that there is no basic conflict. The second is more interesting than this. It allows for conflict, but resolves it through an absolute capitulation on the side of the organization *or* the individual; one or the other, total victory or unconditional surrender. Essentially it is a way *out* of the conflict: for it seems to exclude ambiguity or conflict or the mutual adaption that provides chronic tension.

It might be useful to say more about the second resolution, for it is far from unpopular. Too often, it is chosen by those who view organization solely as a system of impersonal forces *or* solely as a function of individual personalities. Daniel Levinson[7] calls this split vision the "mirage and sponge" theories of organization. The former view, implied in most psychoanalytic literature and held by most romantics, asserts that all role behaviors are functions of personality or mere byproducts of unconscious motivations and fantasy. The "sponge" theorists, seen most commonly in sociological circles, hold that man is infinitely plastic and will yield to or be shaped by role demands. If, for example, you view Eichmann solely as an unwitting instrument of the system, of the German bureaucracy, and see the "*banality* of evil," then the sponge theory seems to dominate. If, on the other hand, you tend to focus exclusively on Eichmann himself as evil, and as the victim of aggressive instincts, then the mirage theory seems to hold.

There are many interesting derivatives of the sponge theory. For example, Coser[8] has recently uncovered evidence which shows that "eunuchism" was characteristic of many upwardly mobile people in the early Chinese and Middle Eastern bureaucracies. Emperors could trust them and depend on their loyalty more than on the average citizen. (Originally eunuchs were trusted servants in the large harems of the rulers, but later they were retained because of their lack of social and family ties.) And Khrushchev, when asked if he was worried about the possibility of a Goldwater victory, replied that he wasn't particularly concerned: "High office," he said, "tends to moderate extreme positions." And, of course, the so-called "cult of personality" is an attack by Marxist theory on the mirage point of view.

Mirage theories are equally popular and undoubtedly less dull, partly because they oversimplify and partly because they tend to glamorize events through personalization. It is gossip-column analysis: Cuba went Communist because Fidel's brother Raoul was jilted by a capitalistic girl. It is the Homeric prose of *Time* magazine and it tends to reinforce our narcissism more than the eunuchism of the sponge theories.

Resolutions one and two interest us only a little because they tend to conceal the predicament: the first, by pretending it doesn't exist and the second, by camouflaging it through imputing false victories. But the problem cannot be disguised or suppressed, and the "giveaway," it seems to me, is the proliferation of paired-opposite terms mutually antagonistic in nature, which flaunt the basic nature of this duality. I refer to the following: individual-organization, personality-pyramid, democratic-autocratic, participative-hierarchical, rational-natural, formal-informal, mechanic-organic, task-maintenance, rational-illogical, human relations-scientific management, external-internal, hard-soft, achievement-socialization, theory X-theory Y, concern for people-concern for production, etc.

These paired dualities—ancient relics, as it were, from a distant, Manichaean world—reflect the two distinct traditions in the study of organizational behavior: the orderly, rational, predictable, Apolonian world of human strivings. Over the past several decades, a number of students of organiza-

[6] [5], pp. 455–56.

[7] [23].

[8] [11].

tions, mindful of this dilemma, have been proposing a number of interesting, theoretical, and practical resolutions which go a long way in revising, if not transforming, the very nature of the bureaucratic mechanism. Let us now sample some of those resolutions.

TEN APPROACHES TO THE PROBLEM

By way of introduction, I should say a few words about the ten approaches I will present and how I came to choose them. First of all, they are a diverse lot, with only one trait in common: an explicit recognition of the inescapable tension between individual and organizational goals. Aside from that, they approach the problem in a variety of ways using different value systems, theoretical and research traditions, and assigning divergent priorities to the centrality of the problem. Second of all, I have not—nor could I—include all the possible solutions or suggestions that are available. I have ignored, as well, those ubiquitous and important mechanisms of socialization which operate spontaneously and naturally in human organizations such as reward systems, identification, etc. Nor have I cited the work of personnel psychology or human engineering, both of which are concerned with reducing the discrepancy between individual and organizational goals. Strictly speaking, I have selected for inclusion a number of recent, moderately well-known ideas, associated with a particular author.

The ten approaches can be grouped under five categories:

Exchange theories

1. Barnard-Simon: inducement-contribution exchange
2. H. Levinson: psychological contract

Group theories

3. Mayo: the managerial elite
4. Likert: the key role of the primary group and "linking pins" between groups

Value theories

5. Argyris: interpersonal competence
6. Blake and Mouton: the managerial grid

Structural theory

7. Shepard: organic systems

Situational theories

8. McGregor: management by objective
9. Leavitt: management by task
10. Thompson and Tuden: management by decision

Exchange Theories

1. The Barnard-Simon theory of exchange is an equilibrium model, very similar to an economic transaction, which specifies the conditions under which an organization can induce participation. On the one hand, there are inducements offered to the participants by the organization. These usually are wages, income, services. For each inducement there is a corresponding utility value. On the other hand, there are contribution utilities: these are the payments the participant makes to the organization, usually specified as work.

From this abstract generalization, predictions can be made concerning the participants' services by estimating the inducement-contributions balance. The greater the difference between inducement and contributions, the more satisfied—and the more compliant—the participant. In addition, a zero point on the utility scale can be derived which shows the point at which the individual is indifferent to leaving the organization as well as a point at which the participants' dissatisfactions cause search behavior and withdrawal from the organization.

2. The Levinson[9] model of reciprocity is also an equilibrium model, but the terms of the inducement-contribution ratio are converted into motivational units, usually of an unconscious kind. These units of exchange represent the psychological contract. According to Levinson, reciprocity is established by the participants and the organization through fulfilling the terms of the contract. The employees' contributions to the organization are energy, work, and commitment. The organization, for its part, provides a psychological anchor in times of rapid social change and a hedge against personal losses. In addition, the organization, through transference phenomena, provides the employees with defense mechanisms through social structure, an opportunity for growth and mastery, and a focal point for cathexis.

Group Theories

3. Elton Mayo challenged the fundamental basis of a society which was organized around archaic, economic hypotheses which grew out of an eighteenth century, purely competitive model of society. Mayo referred to these as the Rabble Hypothesis: society consists of unorganized individuals, every individual acts in a manner calculated to secure his own self-interest, and man is logical. Mayo believed that management was blinded by the economic facts of life to the importance of association and human affiliation as a motivating force. Mayo and his associates were really among the first to view industrial organization as a social system as well as an economic-technical system.

With this profound (now seemingly mundane) insight, Mayo saw the possibilities in using *coopera-*

9 [24].

tion as an instrument to mediate the reciprocity dilemma. But in order to realize the norm of cooperation, a managerial elite, trained in the facts of social life, must take the responsibility, He wrote:

> The administrator of the future must be able to understand the human-social facts for what they are, unfettered by his own emotions or prejudice. He cannot achieve this ability except by careful training—a training that must include knowledge of relevant technical skills, of the systematic order of operations, and of the organization of cooperation.[10]

Thus, success of the organization was based on the manager's ability to develop the effective organization of sustained cooperation.

4. The Likert[11] theory of management also depends heavily on the importance of the cohesive, primary work group as a motivator: to this extent it resembles the Mayo orientation. Yet, there are important differences at the *strategic* level. For Mayo, a managerial elite was a necessity, while for Likert, cooperation between groups could be maintained through points of articulation which Likert refers to as "linking pins." Furthermore, in Likert's theory, decisions should be made at that point of the organizational social space where they are most relevant and where the data are available. Thus, the Likert solution entails a key role performing the linking pin solution—rather than a managerial elite—and the use of the group to mediate the reciprocity dilemma.

Value Theories

5. Argyris starts from the position that the value system of bureaucracy itself has to be modified before individual growth and productivity can be attained.[12] He argues that bureaucratic values, which dominate organizational life, are basically impersonal values. These bureaucratic values lead to poor, shallow, and mistrustful relationships between members of the organization, or what Argyris calls, "nonauthentic" relationships. These, in turn, reduce interpersonal competence, which leads to mistrust, intergroup conflict, rigidity, lowered problem-solving capacity, and eventually to a decrease in whatever criteria the organization uses to measure over-all effectiveness. Managers brought up under this system of values are badly cast to play the intricate human roles now required of them. Their ineptitude and anxieties lead to systems of discord and defense which interfere with the effectiveness of the system.

Argyris' solution is to develop the interpersonal competence of the management group such that they can accept and install new values, values which permit and reinforce the expression of feeling, of experimentalism and the norms of individuality, trust, and concern.

6. Blake and Mouton[13] have developed a solution for the reciprocity dilemma which is referred to as the managerial grid. They conceptualize the organization-individual dilemma by dimensionalizing the problem along two axes. On the basis of this twofold analytic framework, it is possible to locate eight types of managerial styles. One dimension is "concern for people" and the other dimension is "concern for production." Management, according to Blake and Mouton, has to maximize both of these concerns, rather than one or the other. They call this desired state "team management." To arrive at this state, an elaborate system of *organizational training* and *development* is developed which encompasses both the linking pin function and development of interpersonal competence.

Structural Theory

7. Shepard,[14] Burns and Stalker,[15] and others have attempted to replace the mechanical structure of bureaucracy with what they call an "organic" structure. Their structural approach presents a strong reaction against the idea of organizations as *mechanisms* which, they claim, has given rise to false conceptions (such as static equilibria, frictional concepts like "resistance to change," etc.) and worse, false notions of social engineering and change such as "pushing social buttons," thinking of the organization *à la* Weber as a machine, etc. Organic systems are proposed as the natural alternative to mechanical systems. They emerge and adapt spontaneously to the needs of the internal and external systems rather than operate through programmed codes of behavior which are contained in formal role specifications of the mechanical structure. As in the Likert group theory, decisions are made at the point of greatest relevance, and roles and jobs devolve to the "natural" incumbent. Shepherd claims that the bureaucratic (or mechanical) systems differ from the organic systems in the ways shown at the top of the next page.

Situational Theories

A number of resolutions have been worked out which stress situational demands as a mediating factor. Three of the most significant of these are:

[10] [28], p. 122.
[11] [25].
[12] [1], [2], [3].
[13] [8].
[14] [33].
[15] [10].
[16] [30].

Mechanical Systems	*Organic Systems*
Individual skills	Relationships between and within groups
Authority-obedience relationships	Mutual confidence and trust
Delegated and divided responsibility rigidly adhered to	Interdependence and shared responsibility
Strict division of labor and hierarchical supervision	Multigroup membership and responsibility
Centralized decision making	Wide sharing of control and responsibility
Conflict resolution through suppression, arbitration or warfare	Conflict resolution through bargaining or problem solving

8. Management by Objective, first noted by Drucker and further developed by McGregor,[16] attempts to link organizational goals to individual needs through the principle of "integration." It is a complicated process which entails a "working through" of the conflicts between individual objectives and organizational goals (almost in the psychotherapeutic sense) by the manager and his subordinates. The working through depends, to some extent, on the self-control and maturity of the individuals concerned and on a norm of collaboration between superiors and subordinates. Thus integration can be realized only if attention is kept on the objectives of management and on the human processes which develop collaborative relationships between ranks.

9. Leavitt[17] stresses the task constraints of the organization and the development of managerial practices which are appropriate to the task. Thus he views the organization as a differentiated set of subsystems, rather than as a unified whole, which leads to the recognition that the organization must fit the task, rather than the other way around. In this way, he seriously challenges some of the other theories proposed above by asserting that in some parts of the system, highly authoritative (sponge theory) systems of management will have to be employed which under-stress participative norms and which resolve the organization-individual tension in favor of the system. At the same time, other parts of the system will apparently operate with close to minimum discrepancy between organizational goals and individual needs.

In a provocative article with Whisler,[18] Leavitt suggests, keeping an eye on the computerized organizations of the future, that organizations will resemble not the pyramid, but a football (top management) which represents a ruling group very like Coleridge's idea of clerisy, a scholarly elite (trained in the arts of computers, mathematics, and statistics) balanced on the point of a churchbell. "Within the football," they write, "problems of coordination, individual autonomy, and group decision making, and so should arise more intensely than ever. We expect they will be dealt with quite independently of the bell portion of the company, with distinctly different methods of remuneration, control, and communication."

Thus, management-according-to-task will lead to a number of divergent forms of organization within the over-all system. In the football and the churchbell resolution, for example, we can envision an organic head and a mechanical bottom.

10. Thompson and Tuden[19] have developed a typology of organizational processes based on the types of decision issues called for. They derive four types of organizational structures which appear appropriate to a particular decision issue. Along one dimension are beliefs about causation of decision and agreement *versus* non-agreement. The diagram following shows the relationships among the fourfold classification:

Beliefs about Causation	*Preference about Possible Outcomes*: *Agreement*	*Non-agreement*
Agreement	Computation in *bureaucratic* structure	Bargaining in *representative* structure
Non-agreement	Majority judgement in *collegial* structure	Inspiration in *"anomic"* structure

From this analytic classification, Thompson and Tuden derive four *strategies:* computation, compromise, judgment, and inspiration: and four organizational *structures* appropriate to the particular strategy. Where decisions are clearcut, beliefs about causation and agreement about consequences are present, the bureaucratic structure is appropriate for the strategy of computation. Where there is agreement about outcomes but disagreement about causality, then majority judgment is required. Thompson and Tuden argue that a collegial structure, typical

[17] [21].

[18] [22].

[19] [35].

Author	Resolution	Strategy
1. Barnard-Simon	Inducement-contribution	Economic incentives
2. Levinson	Psychological contract	Psychological reciprocity
3. Elton Mayo.	Organization of cooperation	Managerial elite
4. Likert.	Group involvement	Linking pin and group development
5. Argyris.	Value change	Interpersonal competence
6. Blake	Team management	Group and organization development
7. Shepard	Organic structures	Group and organization development
8. McGregor	Management by objective	Integration through collaboration and self-control
9. Leavitt	Management by task	Task determines organizational arrangements
10. Thompson and Tuden . . .	Organization by decision	Decision determines organizational arrangements

of the university and some voluntary organization, would be appropriate. Where there is agreement about causation but disagreement about outcomes of decision, then compromise through representative government—typical of government operations—would be appropriate.[20]

Summary

The table on this page summarizes the major resolutions presented and the strategies implied to resolve the reciprocity issue.

These ten resolutions provide a perspective on revisions to the theory of bureaucracy. Some, like the Barnard-Simon model, are conservative, basically neo-Weberian in tone. Others, like the proposals of Argyris and Shepard, call for radical alterations in the value system or structure of bureaucracy. Still others, more moderate in tone, suggest a flexible arrangement based on situational demands. In all cases, they raise serious questions about the viability and nature of the bureaucratic mechanism.

I would like to make one additional remark about these revisions before going on to the next section. In a way, all of them reflect reactions for or against certain humanistic and democratic values and the authors' desires to optimize—certainly assert—these values. The argument is based on the idea that the effectiveness of bureaucracy should be evaluated on human and economic criteria. To this extent, they represent normative resolutions in that they aim to supplement a restrictive view of organizational effectiveness criteria by including not only some variant of efficiency (productivity, profit, etc.), but also human gains, such as satisfaction or personal growth. Furthermore, their revisions tend to be "inner-directed," if I can use that term in this context. That is, they tend to concentrate on the internal system and its human components rather than the external relations and problems of the environmental transactions.

The emphasis on the normative side and the accompanying inner-directedness has been off target, I believe, and ironically so. For though it appears on the surface that the case against bureaucracy has to do with its ethical-moral posture and its social fabric, the real *coup de grace* to bureaucracy has come from a totally unexpected direction, from the environment. While various proponents of "good human relations" have been fighting bureaucracy on humanistic grounds and for Christian values, bureaucracy seems most likely to founder on its inability to adapt to rapid changes in the environment.

2. LINKAGE TWO: THE PROBLEM OF ADAPTABILITY

The capability of bureaucracy to succeed in its transactions and exchanges with its external environments has, until recently, gone unchallenged. For good reason: it was an ideal weapon to harness and routinize the human and mechanical energy which fueled the Industrial Revolution. It could also function in a highly competitive, fairly undifferentiated and stable environment. The pyramidal structure of bureaucracy, where power was concentrated at the top—perhaps by one person or a group that had the knowledge and resources to control the entire enterprise—seemed perfect to "run a railroad." And undoubtedly for tasks like building railroads, for the routinized tasks of the nineteenth and early twentieth centuries, bureaucracy was and is an eminently suitable social arrangement.

Now three new elements, already visible, promise to give new shape to American society and its organizational environments. They are: (1) the exponential growth of science, (2) the growth of intellectual technology, and (3) the growth of research and development activities.[21] As Barbara Ward has said recently:

[20] For analytic and empirical reasons, namely, its non-existence in organized activities, the "anomic" structure will not be discussed here.

[21] [4], p. 44.

Modern industrial civilization, with its technical evolution and intellectual drive, is, as we know, the most aggressive form of civilization that mankind has ever known. Its twin impact of science and industry is one that involves a total transformation of all aspects of life—not only of organization and technique but of fundamental habits of thought and social behavior. . . .[22]

Science and technology have profoundly changed the shape and texture of the organizational environment in the following ways:

The Rate of Change Is Accelerating at an Increasing Rate. As Ellis Johnson said:

> . . . in those large and complex organizations the once-reliable constants have now become "galloping variables." Because of the impact of increasing complexity, trial and error must give way to an organized search for opportunities to make major shifts in the means of achieving organizational objectives.[23]

The Boundary Position of the Firm Is Changing. As A. T. M. Wilson[24] has pointed out, the number and pattern of relations between the manager and eight areas of relevant social activity have become more active and complicated. The eight areas are: government, distributors and consumers, shareholders, competitors, raw material and power suppliers, source of employees (particularly managers), trade unions, and groups within the firms. Over the last twenty-five years, the rate of transactions with these eight social institutions has increased and their importance in conducting the enterprise has grown.

The Causal Texture of the Environment Has Become Turbulent. Emery and Trist,[25] in an important paper, have conceptualized the field of forces surrounding the firm as a turbulent environment which contains the following characteristics:

a) The environment is a field of forces which contains *causal* mechanisms and pose important choices for the firm.

b) The field is dynamic with increasing interdependencies among and between the eight social institutions specified above.

c) There is, among the institutions relating to the firm, a deepening interdependence between the economic and other facets of society. This means that economic organizations are increasingly enmeshed in legislation and public regulation.

d) There is increasing reliance on research and development to achieve competitive advantage and a concomitant change gradient which is continuously felt in the environmental field.

e) Finally, maximizing cooperation rather than competition between firms appears desirable because their fates may become basically positively correlated.

The upshot of all this is that the environmental texture of the firm, shaped by the growth of science and technology, has changed in just those ways which make the bureaucratic mechanism most problematical. Bureaucracy thrives under conditions of competition and certainty, where the environment is stable and above all, predictable. The texture of the environment now holds in its turbulent and emergent field of forces causal mechanisms so rapidly changing and unpredictable that it poses insuperable problems for—and implies the end of—bureaucracy.

My argument so far can be summarized quickly. The first assault on bureaucracy arose from its incapacity to resolve the tension between individual and organizational goals. A number of resolutions emerged to mediate this conflict by supplementing the ethic of productivity with the ethic of personal growth and/or satisfaction. The second and more major shock to bureaucracy is caused by the scientific and technological revolution. It is the requirement of adaptability to the environment which leads to the predicted demise of bureaucracy as we know it.

Now, some students of organization have attempted to resolve this current dilemma, though not nearly in the same number or with the same vigor as they have the reciprocity issue. It is noteworthy that those who have made the attempt, like Burns, Stalker, Shepard, Leavitt, Argyris, and Simon, have been particularly attentive to—and have derived many of their ideas from—research and development organizations or professional associations, such as hospitals, universities, and the like. For the organizations of the future will undoubtedly resemble these, and will inherit their problems and attributes.

A FORECAST FOR ORGANIZATIONS OF THE FUTURE

A forecast falls somewhere between a prediction and a prophecy. It lacks the divine guidance of the latter and the empirical foundation of the former. But somewhere between inspiration and scientific certainty is a vision of the future of organizational life, which can be pieced together by detecting certain trends of the past and certain changes in the present that are on top of us. On this thin empirical ice, I want to set forth some of the conditions of organizational life in the next 25 to 50 years.

The Environment. As I mentioned before, the environment will be shifting and hold relative uncertainty due to the increase of research and development activities. The external environment will become increasingly differentiated, interdependent,

[22] [20], p. 266.
[23] [17].
[24] [36].
[25] [12].

and more salient to the firm. There will be greater interpenetration of the legal policy and economic factors, leading more and more to imperfect competition and other features of an oligopolistic and government-business controlled economy. (Telstar and similar operations, partnerships between industry and government, will become typical.) And because of the immensity and expense of the projects, there will be fewer identical units competing for the same buyers or sellers. In short, three main features of the environment will be: interdependence rather than competition, turbulent rather than steady competition, and large rather than small enterprises.

Aggregate Population Characteristics. We are living in what Peter Drucker calls the "educated society," and I think this feature is the most distinctive characteristic of our times. Within fifteen years, two-thirds of our population (living in metropolitan areas) will attend college. Adult education programs, not the least of which are the management development courses of such universities as M.I.T., Harvard, and Stanford, are expanding and adding intellectual breadth. All this, of course, is not just "nice" but necessary. For Secretary of Labor Wirtz recently pointed out that computers can do the work of most high school graduates—more cheaply and effectively. Fifty years ago education used to be called nonwork and intellectuals on the payroll (and many staff) were considered "overhead." Today, the survival of the firm depends, more than ever before, on the proper exploitation of brain power.

One other characteristic of the population which will aid our understanding of organizations of the future is increasing job mobility. The lowered expense and ease of transportation, coupled with the very real needs of a dynamic environment, will change drastically the idea of "owning" a job—or "roots," for that matter. Participants will be shifted and will change from job to job and employer to employer with much less fuss than we are accustomed to.

Work-Relevant Values. The increased level of education and rate of mobility will bring about certain changes in the values the population will hold regarding work. People will tend to: (1) be more rational, be intellectually committed, and rely more heavily on forms of social influence which correspond to their value system; (2) be more "other-directed," and will rely on their temporary neighbors and workmates for companionships; and (3) require more involvement, participation and autonomy in their pattern of work.

The first value stems from the effects of education and professionalization. The second is the best empirical guess I can make based on Riesman's ideas[26] and McClelland's data[27] that as industrialization increases, other-directedness increases. My own experience also leads me to think that "having relatives" and "having relationships" are negatively correlated. So we will tend to rely more heavily than we do now on temporary social arrangements, on our immediate and constantly changing colleagues. The third prediction is based on the idea that jobs of the future will require more responsibility and discretion, and that education and need-for-autonomy are positively correlated.

Tasks and Goals of the Firm. The tasks of the firm will be more technical, complicated, and unprogrammed. They will rely far more on intellectual power and the higher cognitive processes than on muscle power. They will be far too complicated for one man to comprehend, not to say control; they will call for the collaboration of professionals in a project organization.

Similarly, goals will become more differentiated and complicated, and oversimplified clichés, like "increasing profits," and "raising productivity" will be heard less than goals having to do with adaptive-innovative-creative capabilities. For one thing (as is true in universities and laboratories today), productivity cannot easily be quantified with the number of budgets produced, articles published, or number of patents. And hospitals have long ago given up the idea of using the number of patients discharged as an index of efficiency. For another thing, meta-goals will have to be articulated and developed: that is, supra-goals which shape and provide the foundation for the goal structure. For example, one meta-goal might be the system for detecting new and changing goals of the firm, or methods for deciding priorities among goals.

Finally, there will be an increase in goal conflict, more and more divergency and contradictoriness between and among effectiveness criteria. Just as in hospitals or universities today, there is conflict between the goal of teaching and the goal of research, so there will be increased conflict among goals in organizations of the future. Part of the reason for this is implied in the fact that there will be more professionals in the organization. Professionals tend to identify as much with their professional organizations as with their employers. In fact, if universities can be used as a case in point, more and more of their income stems from outside professional sources, such as private or public foundations. Professionals tend not to make good "company men" and are divided in

---

[26] [32].

[27] [29].

their loyalty between professional values and organizational demands.[28] This role conflict and ambiguity are both cause and consequence of the goal conflict.

Organizational Structure. Given the task structure, population characteristics, and features of environmental turbulence, the social structure in organizations of the future will take on some unique characteristics. First of all, the key word will be temporary: Organizations will become adaptive, rapidly changing *temporary systems.*[29] Second, they will be organized around *problems-to-be-solved.* Third, these problems will be solved by relative groups of *strangers* who represent a diverse set of professional skills. Fourth, given the requirements of coordinating the various projects, *articulating points* or "linking pin" personnel will be necessary who can speak the diverse languages of research and who can relay and mediate between various project groups. Fifth, the groups will be conducted on *organic* rather than on mechanical lines; they will emerge and adapt to the problems, and leadership and influence will fall to those who seem most able to solve the problems rather than to programmed role expectations. People will be differentiated, not according to rank or roles, but according to skills and training.

Adaptive, temporary systems of diverse specialists solving problems, coordinated organically *via* articulating points will gradually replace the theory and practice of bureaucracy. Though no catchy phrase comes to mind, it might be called an *organic-adaptive* structure.

(As an aside: what will happen to the rest of society, to the manual laborers, to the poorly educated, to those who desire to work in conditions of dependency, and so forth? Many such jobs will disappear; automatic jobs will be automated. However, there will be a corresponding growth in the service-type of occupation, such as organizations like the Peace Corps and AID. There will also be jobs, now being seeded, to aid in the enormous challenge of coordinating activities between groups and organizations. For certainly, consortia of various kinds are growing in number and scope and they will require careful attention. In times of change, where there is a wide discrepancy between cultures and generations, an increase in industrialization, and especially urbanization, society becomes the client for skills in human resources. Let us hypothesize that approximately 40 percent of the population would be involved in jobs of this nature, 40 percent in technological jobs, making an organic-adaptive majority with, say, a 20 percent bureaucratic minority.)

[28] See [13].

[29] See [31].

Motivation in Organic-Adaptive Structures. The way organizations tie people into their systems so that they become effective units is the motivational basis of organizational behavior and its most pressing problem.[30] In fact, the first part of this paper on reciprocity explains how the theory and practice of bureaucracy fail to solve this problem. In the organic-adaptive structure, the reciprocity problem will be eased somewhat because individual and organizational goals should coincide more. This is made possible because organizations will provide more meaningful and satisfactory tasks. In short, the motivational problem will rely heavily on the satisfaction intrinsic to the task and to the participant's identification with his profession.

Of course, professional identification and high task-involvement bring in a cargo of problems just as they ameliorate the reciprocity issue. Professionals are notoriously "disloyal" and tend to split their loyalty between professional values and organizational demands. For example, during the Oppenheimer hearings, Boris Pash of the F.B.I. reported:

> . . . It is believed that the only undivided loyalty that he (Oppenheimer) can give is to science and it is strongly felt that if in his position the Soviet government could offer more for the advancement of scientific cause he would select that government as the one to which he would express his loyalty.[31]

There is another consequence which I find inescapable but which many will deplore. There will be a reduced commitment to work groups. These groups, as I have already mentioned, will be transient and changing. While skills in human interaction will become more important due to the necessity of collaboration in complex tasks, there will be a concomitant reduction in group cohesiveness. I would predict that in the organic-adaptive system people will have to learn to develop quick and intense relationships on the job, and learn how to endure their loss.

In general, I do not agree with the Kerr *et al.*[32] emphasis on the "New Bohemianism" whereby leisure—not work—becomes the emotional-creative sphere of life, or with Leavitt and Whisler[33] who hold similar views. They assume a technological slowdown and leveling off, and a stabilizing of social mobility. This may be the society of the future, but long before then we will have the challenge of creating that push button society and a corresponding

[30] [19].

[31] [18], p. 147.

[32] [20].

[33] [22].

need for service-type organizations of the organic-adaptive structure.

Jobs in the next century should become *more*, rather than less, involving; man is a problem-solving animal and the tasks of the future guarantee a full agenda of problems. In addition, the adaptive process itself may become captivating to many.

At the same time, I think the future I describe is far from a Utopian or necessarily a "happy" one. Coping with rapid change, living in temporary systems, setting up (in quick-step time) meaningful relations—then breaking them all augur strains and tensions. Learning how to live with ambiguity and to be self-directing will be the task of education and the goal of maturity.

Structures of Freedom

I should mention now one last consequence of the new adaptive-organic structure which has a profound interaction with the reciprocity issue which concerned us earlier. In these new organizations, participants will be called on to utilize their minds and imagination more than any society previously has allowed. New standards will be sought for the development of creative and imaginative cognitive processes. In other words, fantasy and imagination will be legitimized in ways that today seem strange. And if we think of our social structures as instruments of repression with the necessity of repression and suffering derived from it, as Marcurse[34] says varying with the maturity of the civilization, then perhaps we are approaching an age where organizations can sanction the play and freedom which imagination and thought involve. The need for instinctual renunciation decreases as man achieves rational mastery over nature. In short, organizations of the future will require fewer restrictions and repressive techniques because of the legitimization of play and fantasy, accelerated through the rise of science and intellectual achievements.

Not only will the problem of adaptability be overcome through the organic-adaptive structure, but the problem we started with, reciprocity, will be resolved. Bureaucracy, with its "surplus repression," was a monumental discovery for harnessing muscle power *via* guilt and instinctual renunciation. In today's world, it is a prosthetic device, no longer useful. For we now require organic-adaptive systems as structures of freedom to permit the expression of play and imagination and to exploit the new pleasure of work.

---

[34] [27].

REFERENCES

1. Argyris, C. *Integrating the individual and the organization.* New York: John Wiley, 1964.
2. Argyris, C. *Interpersonal competence and organizational effectiveness,* Homeward, Ill.: Irwin-Dorsey Press, 1962.
3. Argyris, C. *Personality and organization.* New York: Harper, 1957.
4. Bell, D. The post-industrial society, *Technology and social change,* E. Ginzberg (ed.). New York: Columbia University Press, 1964.
5. Bendix, R. *Max Weber: An intellectual portrait.* New York: Doubleday, 1960.
6. Bendix, R. *Work and authority in industry.* New York: John Wiley, 1956.
7. Bennis, W. G. Theory and method in applying behavioral science to planned organizational change. Paper presented at the International Operations Research Conference. Cambridge University, England, September 14, 1964.
8. Blake, R. R. and Mouton, J. S. *The managerial grid.* Houston, Tex.: Gulf Publishing, 1964.
9. Blau, P. M. Critical remarks on Weber's theory of authority. *The American Political Science Review,* 1963, **47**, 305–16.
10. Burns, T. and Stalker, G. M. *The management of innovation.* Chicago: Quadrangle, 1961.
11. Coser, L. The political functions of eunuchism. Waltham, Mass.: Brandeis University, 1964.
12. Emery, F. E. and Trist, E. L. The causal texture of organizational environments. Paper read at the International Congress of Psychology, Washington, D.C., September, 1963.

12a. Etzioni, A. *A Comparative analysis of complex organizations,* Glencoe, Ill.: Free Press, 1961.

13. Gouldner, A. W. Cosmopolitans and locals: Toward an analysis of latent social roles, I. *Administrative Science Quarterly,* 1957, **2**, 281–306.
14. Gouldner, A. W. Organizational analysis, *Sociology today,* R. K. Merton, Leonard Broom, and Leonard S. Cottrell, Jr. (eds.). New York: Basic Books, 1959, pp. 400–428.
15. Gouldner, A. W. *Patterns of industrial bureaucracy.* Glencoe, Ill.: Free Press, 1954.
16. Hall, R. H. The concept of bureaucracy: an empirical assessment. *American Journal of Sociology,* 1963, **49**, 33.
17. Johnson, E. A. Introduction. *Operations research for management,* McClosky and Trefethen (eds.), p. xii. Baltimore: Johns Hopkins Press, 1954.
18. Jungk, R. *Brighter than a thousand suns.* New York: Grove Press, 1958, p. 147.
19. Katz, D. The motivational basis of organizational behavior. *Behavioral Science,* 1964, **9**, 131–46.

20. Kerr, C., Dunlop, J. T., Harbison, F., and Myers, C. *Industrialism and industrial man.* Cambridge, Mass.: Harvard U. Press, 1960.

21. Leavitt, H. J. Unhuman organizations. *Readings in managerial psychology,* H. J. Leavitt and L. Pondy (eds.). Chicago: University of Chicago Press, 1964.

22. Leavitt, H. J. & Whisler, T. L., Management in the 1980's in (21).

23. Levinson, D. Role, personality, and social structure in the organizational setting. *Journal of Abnormal and Social Psychology* 1959, **48**, 170–80.

24. Levinson, H. Reciprocation: The relationship between man and organization. Invited address at the Division of Industrial and Business Psychology, American Psychological Association, September 3, 1963.

25. Likert, R. *New Patterns of management.* New York: McGraw-Hill, 1961.

26. March, J. G. and Simon, H. A. *Organizations.* New York: John Wiley, 1958.

27. Marcurse, H. *Eros and civilization.* Boston: Beacon Press, 1955.

28. Mayo, E. *The social problems of an industrial civilization,* Cambridge, Mass.: Harvard U. Press, 1945.

29. McClelland, D. *The achieving society.* Princeton, N.J.: Van Nostrand, 1961.

30. McGregor, D. *The human side of enterprise.* New York: McGraw-Hill, 1960.

31. Miles, M. B. On temporary systems. *Innovation in education,* M. B. Miles (ed.). New York: Bureau of Publications, Teachers College, Columbia U., 1964, 437–90.

32. Riesman, D., with Glazer, N. and Denny, R. *The lonely crowd.* New Haven, Conn.: Yale U. Press, 1950.

33. Shepard, H. A. Changing interpersonal and intergroup relationships in organizations. *Handbook of organization.* J. March (ed.), New York: Rand McNally (in press).

34. Simon, H. A. The corporation: Will it be managed by machines? in [21].

35. Thompson, J. D. and Tuden, A. Strategies and processes of organizational decision. *Comparative studies in administration,* J. D. Thompson, P. B. Hammond, R. W. Hawkes, B. H. Junker, and A. Tuden (eds.). Pittsburgh: U. Of Pittsburgh Press, 1959, 195–216.

36. Wilson, A. T. M. The manager and his world. *Industrial Management Review,* 1961, fall.

Section C

DESIGN AND ADMINISTRATION OF FORMAL REWARD AND PENALTY SYSTEMS

The development of optimal organizational designs for varied purposes was the theme of the previous group of readings. From the viewpoint of the manager, however, this constitutes only a segment of the task of the effective management of manpower. We now turn our attention to an examination of one of the most powerful, and frequently most controllable, components of the organizational environment; namely, the design and administration of the organization's formal reward and penalty systems.

Katz leads off our treatment of reward and penalty systems by outlining six motivational patterns which may be thought of as providing the basis of organizational behavior. As defined by Katz these are (1) conformity to legal norms (rule compliance), (2) instrumental, systemwide rewards, (3) instrumental individual rewards, (4) intrinsic satisfaction derivable from the content of the job, (5) internalization of organizational goals, and (6) primary-group involvement. Katz examines the consequences of the motivational patterns for organizational performance as well as the specific conditions which the manager must establish for the emergence of these consequences. In a sense, the remaining selections in this section amplify and elaborate the broad themes initiated by Katz.

Opsahl and Dunnette summarize a good deal of knowledge regarding the motivational effects of financial rewards by reviewing an extensive history of research on compensation. They emphasize what they perceive to be the major conclusions to be derived from this research and point to the areas of research expected to yield the most fruitful results.

Lawler puts pay (as a reward) and its administration into an explicit organizational context. Lawler's reasoning is that the type of pay system which will generate effective performance and positive attitudes is dependent on the psychological climate, the technology, the size and the structure of the organization. We are also reminded that the pay plan of an organization and the manner in which it is administered can represent an important instrument of change in moving an organization toward new ways of functioning. It is important to note that the ideas explored by Lawler in relation to pay can also be related to other components of formal reward and penalty systems of an organization. (e.g., promotion, formal status differentiation, demotion, and disciplinary procedures).

Effective management involves more than merely using or not using various rewards and penalties. Schmitt points out that *scheduling* of these reinforcers has a major impact on employee performance. Schmitt reports laboratory data which indicate that both the magnitude and scheduling of a penalty exert a significant impact on the direction in which an individual focuses his behavior. Even though Schmitt did not explicitly study the intensity of behavior, there would be no reason to expect significantly different results with that dependent variable.[1]

Huberman describes the disciplinary procedures of a company which has attempted to incorporate constructive self-correction as a method of discipline into its disciplinary program. By contrast, the program described by Huberman points to several assumptions underlying traditional approaches to discipline which may be psychologically inappropriate.

32. MOTIVATIONAL BASIS OF ORGANIZATIONAL BEHAVIOR*

Daniel Katz†

TYPES OF MOTIVATIONAL PATTERNS

It is profitable to consider the possible motivational patterns in organizations under six major headings. Before considering their specific modes of operation and their effects, let me briefly describe the six motivational patterns which seem most relevant. These patterns are: (1) conformity to legal norms or rule compliance; (2) instrumental system rewards; (3) instrumental individual rewards; (4) intrinsic satisfaction from role performance; (5) internalization of organizational goals and values; and (6) involvement in primary-group relationships.

Rule Compliance or Conformity to System Norms. Conformity constitutes a significant motivational basis for certain types of organizational behavior. Though people may conform for different reasons I am concerned here with one common type of reason, namely, a generalized acceptance of the rules of the game. Once people enter a system they accept the fact that membership in the system means complying with its legitimate rules. In our culture we build up during the course of the socialization process a generalized expectation of conforming to the recognized rules of the game if we want to remain in the game. We develop a role readiness, i.e. a readiness to play almost any given role according to the established norms in those systems in which we become involved.

Instrumental System Rewards. These are the benefits which accrue to individuals by virtue of their membership in the system. They are the across-the-board rewards which apply to all people in a given classification in an organization. Examples would be the fringe benefits, the recreational facilities, and the working conditions which are available to all members of the system or subsystem. These rewards are instrumental in that they provide incentives for entering and remaining in the system and thus are instrumental for the need satisfaction of people.

Instrumental Reward Geared to Individual Effort or Performance. System rewards apply in blanket fashion to all members of a subsystem. Individual rewards of an instrumental character are attained by differential performance. For example, the piece rate in industry or the singling out of individuals for honors for their specific contributions would fall into this category of instrumental individual rewards.

Intrinsic Satisfactions Accruing from Specific Role Performance. Here the gratification comes not because the activity leads to or is instrumental to other satisfactions such as earning more money but because the activity is gratifying in itself. The individual may find his work so interesting or so much the type of thing he really wants to do that it would take a heavy financial inducement to shift to a job less congenial to his interests. It is difficult to get professors in many universities to take administrative posts such as departmental chairmanships or deanships because so many of them prefer teaching and re-

* *Behavioral Science,* 1964, pp. 134–46.

† Department of Psychology, University of Michigan.

[1] Schmitt has extended his work to examine the effects of reinforcing consequences on the choice made between two tasks. He found these reinforcing consequences to be highly similar in their effects to the punitive consequences reported in this article. The impact of rewards, however, was greater when administered according to a variable interval rather than a fixed interval schedule (see David R. Schmitt, "Effects of Intermittent Reinforcing Consequences on Task Choice," *Psychological Reports,* 1971, 78, pp. 771–76).

search. This motivational pattern has to do with the opportunities which the organizational role provides for the expressions of the skills and talents of the individual.

Internalized Values of the Individual which Embrace the Goals of the Organization. Here the individual again finds his organizational behavior rewarding in itself, not so much because his job gives him a chance to express his skill, but because he has taken over the goals of the organization as his own. The person who derives his gratifications from being a good teacher could be equally happy in teaching in many institutions but unhappy as an administrator in any one. The person who has identified himself with the goals of his own particular university and its specific problems, potentialities, and progress wants to stay on at his university and, moreover, is willing to accept other assignments than a teaching assignment.

Social Satisfactions Derived from Primary-Group Relationships. This is an important source of gratification for organizational members. One of the things people miss most when they have to withdraw from organizations is the sharing of experiences with likeminded colleagues, the belonging to a group with which they have become identified. Whether or not these social satisfactions become channelled for organizational objectives leads us to a consideration of the two basic questions with which we started: (1) What are the consequences of these motivational patterns for the various organizational requirements of holding people in the system, maximizing their role performances, and stimulating innovative behavior? and (2) What are the conditions under which these patterns will lead to a given organizational outcome?

MOTIVATIONAL PATTERNS: CONSEQUENCES AND CONDITIONS

Compliance with Legitimized Rules

In discussing bureaucratic functioning Max Weber pointed out that the acceptance of legal rules was the basis for much of organizational behavior (Weber, 1917). Compliance is to some extent a function of sanctions but to a greater extent a function of generalized habits and attitudes toward symbols of authority. In other words, for the citizen of modern society the observance of legitimized rules has become a generalized value. A great deal of behavior can be predicted once we know what the rules of the game are. It is not necessary to take representative samplings of the behavior of many people to know how people will conduct themselves in structural situations. All we need is a single informant who can tell us the legitimate norms and appropriate symbols of authority for given types of behavioral settings. Individuals often assume that they can control their participation with respect to organizational requirements when they enter an organization. Before they are aware of it, however, they are acting like other organizational members and complying with the rules and the authorized decisions.

The major impact of compliance with the legitimate rules of the organization primarily concerns only one type of organizational requirement, namely reliable role performance. The way in which any given role occupant is to perform in carrying out his job can be determined by the rules of the organization. But individuals cannot be held in the system by rule enforcement save for exceptions like the armed services. Nor can innovative behavior and actions beyond the call of duty by prescribed.

Though compliance with legitimate rules is effective for insuring reliable role performance it operates to insure minimal observance of role requirements. In other words, the minimal standards for quantity and quality of work soon become the maximum standards. The logic of meeting legal norms is to avoid infractions of the rules and not to go beyond their requirements, for as Allport has pointed out (1934), it is difficult, if not impossible, to be more proper than proper. Why, however, cannot the legal norms be set to require high standards with respect to both quantity and quality of production? Why cannot higher production be legislated? It can, but there is an important force working against such raising of standards by changing rules. The rule which sets a performance standard in a large organization is also setting a uniform standard for large number of people. Hence it must be geared to what the great majority are prepared to do. If not, there will be so many defections that the rule itself will break down. Timing of jobs in industry illustrates this principle. Management does not want a loose standard, but if the standards are set so that many workers can meet them only with difficulty, management is in for trouble.

In the third area of behavior necessary for effective organizational functioning, namely innovative and spontaneous acts which go beyond the call of duty, rule compliance is useless by definition. There can be exceptions, in that rules can be devised to reward unusual behavior under specified conditions. The army, for example, will move the man who has pulled off a brilliant military exploit from a court martial to a court of honors. Though such exceptions may occur, organizations cannot stimulate innovative actions by decreeing them. In general the greater the emphasis upon compliance with rules the less the motivation will be for individuals to do more than is specified by their role prescriptions. The great weakness of a system run according to rules is the lack of the corrective factor of human enterprise and spontaneity when something goes wrong. Two years ago in a hospital in New York State several infants died because salt rather than sugar was put into the formula. The large container for sugar had been erroneously filled with salt. The tragic fact was that day after day for about a week the nurses fed the babies milk saturated with salt in spite of the fact that the infants reacted violently to the food, crying and vomiting after each feeding session. But the hospital continued poisoning the children until many of them died. Not a single nurse, attendant, supervisor, or person connected with the nursery tasted the milk to see what was wrong. The error was discovered only when a hospital employee broke a rule and used some of the substance in the sugar container in her own coffee.

Conditions Conducive to the Activation of Rule Acceptance

Though compliance with rules can bring about reliable role performance, the use of rules must take account of the following three conditions for maximum effectiveness: (1) the appropriateness of the symbols of authority and the relevance of rules to the social system involved; (2) the clarity of the legal norms and rule structure; and (3) the reinforcing character of sanctions.

Appropriateness and Relevance. The acceptance of communications and directives on the basis of legitimacy requires the use of symbols and procedures recognized as the proper and appropriate sources of authority in the system under consideration. The worker may grumble at the foreman's order but he recognizes the right of the foreman to give such an order. The particular directives which are accepted as legitimate will depend upon their matching the type of authority structure of the system. The civilian in the army with officer status, uniform, and unassimilated rank is not accepted by the enlisted man as the proper giver of orders. In a representative democracy a policy decision of an administrator may be rejected since it lacks the legal stamp of the accepted procedures of the system. An industrial company may have a contract with a union that changes in the speed of the assembly line have to be agreed to by both organizations. The workers accordingly will accept a speedup in the line if it is sanctioned by the union-management agreement, but not if it is the work of a foreman attempting to impress his superiors.

The acceptance of legal rules is also restricted to the relevant sphere of activity. Union policy as formulated in its authority structure is binding upon its members only as it relates to relations with the company. The edicts of union officials on matters of desegregation or of support of political parties are not necessarily seen as legal compulsions by union members. In similar fashion, employees do not regard the jurisdiction of the company as applying to their private lives outside the plant. And areas of private behavior and personal taste are regarded in our democratic society as outside the realm of coercive laws. The most spectacular instance of the violation of a national law occurred in the case of the Volstead Act. While people were willing to accept laws about the social consequences resulting from drinking, such as reckless driving, many of them were not willing to accept the notion that their private lives were subject to federal regulation.

Another prerequisite to the use of rules as the appropriate norms of the systems is their impersonal character. They are the rules of the systems and are not the arbitrary, capricious decisions of a superior aimed at particular individuals. The equivalents of bills of attainder in an organization undermine rule compliance. We speak of the officiousness of given individuals in positions of authority when they use their rank in an arbitrary and personal fashion.

Clarity. A related condition for the acceptance of legal norms is the clarity of authority symbols, of proper procedures, and the content of the legitimized decisions. Lack of clarity can be due to the vagueness of the stimulus situation or to the conflict between opposed stimulus cues. In some organizations, symbols of authority are sharply enough defined, but the relationship between competing symbols may lack such clarity of definition. One difficulty of using group decision in limited areas in an otherwise authoritarian structure is that group members may not perceive the democratic procedure as legitimized by the structure. They will question the compelling effect of any decisions they reach. And often they may be right. Moreover, the procedure for the exercise of power may not be consistent with the type of authority structure. The classic case is that *of ordering* a people to be democratic.

Specific laws can be ambiguous in their substance. They can be so complex, so technical, or so obscure that people will not know what the law is. The multiplication of technical rulings and the patchwork of legislation with respect to tax structure means that while people may feel some internal compulsion to pay taxes, they also feel they should pay as little as they can without risking legal prosecution. A counter dynamic will arise to the tendency to comply with legal requirements, namely, the use of legal loopholes to defy the spirit of the law. Any complex maze of rules in an organization will be utilized by the guardhouse lawyers in the system to their own advantage.

Though our argument has been that legal compliance makes for role performance rather than for holding people in a system, the clarity of a situation with well-defined rules is often urged as a condition making for system attractiveness. People know what is expected of them and what they should expect in turn from others, and they much prefer this clarity to a state of uncertainty and ambiguity. There is merit in this contention, but it does not take into account all the relevant variables. The armed services were not able to hold personnel after World War II, and recruitment into systems characterized by rules and regulations is traditionally difficult in the United States. The mere multiplication of rules does not produce clarity. Even when certainty and clarity prevail they are not relished if it means that individuals are certain only of nonadvancement and restrictions on their behavior.

In brief, the essence of legal compliance rests upon the psychological belief that there are specific imperatives or laws which all good citizens obey. If there is doubt about what the imperative is, if there are many varying interpretations, then the law is not seen as having a character of its own but as the means for obtaining individual advantage. To this extent, the legitimacy basis of compliance is undermined.

Reinforcement. To maintain the internalized acceptance of legitimate authority there has to be some reinforcement in the form of penalties for violation of the rules. If there is no policing of laws governing speeding, speed limits will lose their force over time for many people. Sometimes the penalties can come from the social disapproval of the group as well as from legal penalties. But the very concept of law as an imperative binding upon everyone in the system requires penalties for violation either from above or below. Where there is no enforcement by authorities and no sanctions for infractions from the group itself, the rule in question becomes a dead letter.

Instrumental System Rewards

It is important to distinguish between rewards which are administered in relation to individual effort and performance and the system rewards which accrue to people by virtue of their membership in the system. In the former category would belong piece-rate incentives, promotion for outstanding performance, or any special recognition bestowed in acknowledgement of differential contributions to organizational functioning. In the category of system rewards would go fringe benefits, recreational facilities, cost of living raises, across-the-board upgrading, job security save for those guilty of moral turpitude, pleasant working conditions. System rewards differ, then, from individual rewards in that they are not allocated on the basis of differential effort and performance but on the basis of membership in the system. The major differentiation for system rewards is seniority in the system—a higher pension for thirty years of service than for twenty years of service. Management will often overlook the distinction between individual and system rewards and will operate as if rewards administered across the board were the same in their effects as individual rewards.

System rewards are more effective for holding members within the organization than for maximizing other organizational behaviors. Since the rewards are distributed on the basis of length of tenure in the system, people will want to stay with an attractive setup which becomes increasingly attractive over time. Again the limiting factor is the competition with the relative attraction of other systems. As the system increases its attractions, other things being equal, it should reduce its problems of turnover. In fact, it may sometimes have the problem of too low turnover with too many poorly motivated people staying on until retirement.

Systems rewards will not, however, lead to higher quality of work or greater quantity than the minimum required to stay in the organization. Since rewards are given across-the-board to all members or differentially to them in terms of their seniority, they are not motivated to do more than meet the standards for remaining in the system. It is sometimes assumed that the liking for the organization created by system rewards will generalize to greater productive effort within the system. Such generalization of motivation may occur to a very limited extent, but it is not a reliable basis for the expectation of higher productivity. Management may expect gratitude from workers because it has added some special fringe benefit or some new recreational facility. The more likely outcome is that employees will feel more desirous of staying in an enterprise with such advantages than of working harder for the company for the next twelve months.

System rewards will do little, moreover, to motivate performance beyond the line of duty, with two possible exceptions. Since people may develop a liking for the attractions of the organization they may be in a more favorable mood to reciprocate in cooperative relations with their fellows toward organizational goals, provided that the initiation of task-oriented cooperation comes from some other source. Otherwise, they may just be cooperative with respect to taking advantage of the system's attractions, such as the new bowling alley. Another possible consequence of system rewards for activity supportive of organizational goals is the favorable climate of opinion for the system in the external environment to which the members contribute. It may be easier for a company to recruit personnel in a community in which their employees have talked about what a good place it is to work.

Though the effects of systems rewards are to maintain the level of productivity not much above the minimum required to stay in the system, there still may be large differences between systems with respect to the quantity and quality of production as a function of system rewards. An organization with substantially better wage rates and fringe benefits than its competitors may be able to set a higher level of performance as a minimal requirement for its workers than the other firms and still hold its employees. In other words, system rewards can be related to the differential productivity of organizations as a whole, though they are not effective in maximizing the potential contributions of the majority of individuals within the organization. They may account for differences in motivation between systems rather than for differences in motivation between individuals in the same system. They operate through their effects upon the minimal standards for all people in the system. They act indirectly in that their effect is to make people want to stay in the organization; to do so people must be willing to accept the legitimately derived standards of role performance in that system. Hence, the direct mechanism for insuring performance is compliance with legitimacy, but the legal requirements of the organization will not hold members if their demands are too great with respect to the demands of other organizations. The mediating variable in accounting for organizational differences based upon system rewards is the relative attractiveness of the system for the individual compared to other available systems in relation to the effort requirements of the system. If the individual has the choice of a job with another company in the same community which requires a little more effort but offers much greater system rewards in the way of wages and other benefits, he will in all probability take it. If, however, the higher requirements of the competing system are accompanied by very modest increases in system rewards, he will probably stay where he is.

Conditions Conducive to Effective System Rewards

We have just described one of the essential conditions for making system rewards effective in calling attention to the need to make the system as attractive as competing systems which are realistic alternatives for the individual. In this context seniority becomes an important organizational principle in that the member can acquire more of the rewards of the system the longer he stays in it. The present trends to permit the transfer of fringe benefits of all types across systems undercuts the advantages to any one system of length of membership in it, though of course there are other advantages to permitting people to retain their investment in seniority when they move across systems.

Another condition which is important for the effective use of system rewards is their uniform application for all members of the system or for major groupings within the system. People will perceive as inequitable, distinctions in amounts of rewards which go to members by virtue of their membership in the system where such differences favor some groups over other groups. Management is frequently surprised by resentment of differential system rewards when there has been no corresponding resentment of differential individual rewards. One public utility, for example, inaugurated an attractive retirement system for its employees before fringe benefits were the acceptable pattern. Its employees were objectively much better off because of the new benefits and yet the most hated feature about the whole company was the retirement system. Employee complaints centered on two issues: years of employment in the company before the age of thirty did not count toward retirement pensions, and company officials could retire on livable incomes because of their higher salaries. The employees felt intensely that if they were being rewarded for service to the company it was unfair to rule out years of service before age thirty. This provision gave no recognition for the man who started for the company at age twenty compared to the one who started at age thirty. Moreover, the workers felt a lifetime of service to the company should enable them to retire on a livable income just as it made this possible for company officials. The company house organ directed considerable space over a few years to showing how much the worker actually benefited from the plan, as in fact was the case. On the occasion of a company-wide survey, this campaign was found to have had little effect. The most common complaint still focused about the patent unfairness of the retirement system.

The critical point, then, is that system rewards have a logic of their own. Since they accrue to people by virtue of their membership or length of service in an organization, they will be perceived as inequitable if they are not uniformly administered. The perception of the organization member is that all members are equal in their access to organizational benefits. Office employees will not be upset by differences in individual reward for differences in responsibility. If, however, their organization gives them free meals in a cafeteria and sets aside a special dining room for their bosses, many of them will be upset. In our culture we accept individual differences in income but we do not accept differences in classes of citizenship. To be a member of an organization is to be a citizen in that community, and all citizens are equal in their membership rights. A university which does not extend the same tenure rights and the same fringe benefits accorded its teaching staff to its research workers may have a morale problem on its hands.

Instrumental Individual Rewards

The traditional philosophy of the free-enterprise system gives priority to an individual reward system based upon the quality and quantity of the individual effort and contribution. This type of motivation may operate effectively for the entrepreneur or even for the small organization with considerable independence of its supporting environment. It encounters great difficulties, however, in its application to large organizations which are in nature highly interdependent cooperative structures. We shall examine these difficulties in analyzing the conditions under which individual rewards of an instrumental character are effective.

Basically the monetary and recognition rewards to the individual for his organizational performance are directed at a high level of quality and quantity of work. In other words, they can be applied most readily to obtain optimal role performance rather than to innovative and nonspecific organizational needs. They may also help to hold the individual in the organization, if he feels that his differential efforts are properly recognized. Nonetheless there is less generalization, or rubbing off, of an instrumental individual reward to love for the organization than might be anticipated. If another organization offers higher individual rewards to a person, his own institution may have to match the offer to hold him.

Individual rewards are difficult to apply to contributions to organizational functioning which are not part of the role requirements. Spectacular instances of innovative behavior can be singled out for recognition and awards. In the armed services, heroism beyond the call of duty is the basis for medals and decorations, but the everyday cooperative activities which keep an organization from falling apart are more difficult to recognize and reward. Creative suggestions for organizational improvement are sometimes encouraged through substantial financial rewards for employees' suggestions. The experience with suggestion systems of this sort has not been uniformly positive though under special conditions they have proved of value.

Conditions Conducive to Effective Individual Instrumental Rewards

If rewards such as pay incentives are to work as they are intended they must meet three primary conditions. (1) They must be clearly perceived as large enough in amount to justify the additional effort required to obtain them. (2) They must be perceived as directly related to the required performance and follow directly on its accomplishment. (3) They must be perceived as equitable by the majority of system members many of whom will not receive them. These conditions suggest some of the reasons why individual rewards can work so well in some situations and yet be so difficult of application in large organizations. The facts are that most enterprises have not been able to use incentive pay, or piece rates, as reliable methods for raising the quality and quantity of production (McGregor, 1960).

In terms of the first criterion many companies have attempted incentive pay without making the differential between increased effort and increased reward proportional from the point of view of the worker. If he can double his pay by working at a considerably increased tempo, that is one thing. But if such increased expenditure means a possible 10 percent increase, that is another. Moreover, there is the tradition among workers, and it is not without some factual basis, that management cannot be relied upon to maintain a high rate of pay for those making considerably more than the standard and that their increased efforts will only result in their "being sweated." There is, then, the temporal dimension of whether the piece rates which seem attractive today will be maintained tomorrow.

More significant, however, is the fact that a large-scale organization consists of many people engaging in similar and interdependent tasks. The work of any one man is highly dependent upon what his colleagues are doing. Hence individual piece rates are difficult to apply on any equitable basis. Group incentives are more logical, but as the size of the interdependent group grows, we move toward system rather than toward individual rewards. Moreover, in large-scale production enterprises the role performance is controlled by the tempo of the machines and their coordination. The speed of the worker on the assembly line is not determined by his decision but by the speed of the assembly line. An individual piece-rate just does not accord with the systemic nature of the coordinated collectivity. Motivational factors about the amount of effort to be expended on the job enter the picture not on the floor of the factory but during the negotiations of the union and management about the manning of a particular assembly line. Heads of corporations may believe in the philosophy of individual enterprise, but when they deal with reward systems in their own organizations they become realists and accept the pragmatic notion of collective rewards.

Since there is such a high degree of collective interdependence among rank-and-file workers the attempts to use individual rewards are often perceived as inequitable. Informal norms develop to protect the group against efforts which are seen as divisive or exploitive. Differential rates for subsystems within the organization will be accepted much more than invidious distinctions within the same subgrouping. Hence promotion or upgrading may be the most potent type of individual reward. The employee is rewarded by being moved to a different category of workers on a better pay schedule. Some of the same problems apply, of course, to this type of reward. Since differential performance is difficult to assess in assembly-type operations, promotion is often based upon such criteria as conformity to company requirements with respect to attendance and absenteeism, observance of rules, and seniority. None of these criteria are related to individual performance on the job. Moreover, promotion is greatly limited by the technical and professional education of the worker.

It is true, of course, that many organizations are not assembly-line operations, and even for those which are, the conditions described here do not apply to the upper echelons. Thus General Motors can follow a policy of high individual rewards to division managers based upon the profits achieved by a given division. A university can increase the amount of research productivity of its staff by making publication the essential criterion for promotion. In general, where assessment of individual performance is feasible and where the basis of the reward system is clear, instrumental individual rewards can play an important part in raising productivity.

Intrinsic Job Satisfaction

The motivational pathway to high productivity and to high-quality production can be reached through the development of intrinsic job satisfaction. The man who finds the type of work he delights in doing is the man who will not worry about the fact that the role requires a given amount of production of a certain quality. His gratifications accrue from accomplishment, from the expression of his own abilities, from the exercise of his own decisions. Craftsmanship was the old term to refer to the skilled performer who was high in intrinsic job satisfaction. This type of performer is not the clock watcher, nor the shoddy performer. On the other hand, such a person is not necessarily tied to a given organization. As a good carpenter or a good mechanic, it may matter little to him where he does work, provided that he is given ample opportunity to do the kind of job he is interested in doing. He may, moreover, contribute little to organizational goals beyond his specific role.

Conditions Conducive to Arousal of Intrinsic Job Satisfaction

If intrinsic job satisfaction or identification with the work is to be aroused and maximized, then the job itself must provide sufficient variety, sufficient complexity, sufficient challenge, and sufficient skill to engage the abilities of the worker. If there is one confirmed finding in all the studies of worker morale and satisfaction, it is the correlation between the variety and challenge of the job and the gratifications which accrue to workers (Morse, 1953). There are, of course, people who do not want more responsibility and people who become demoralized by being placed in jobs which are too difficult for them. (These are, however, the exceptions.) By and large people seek more responsibility, more skill-demanding jobs than they hold and as they are able to attain these more demanding jobs, they become happier and better adjusted. Obviously, the condition for securing higher motivation to produce, and to produce quality work, necessitates changes in organizational structure—specifically job enlargement rather than job fractionation. And yet the tendency in large-scale organizations is toward increasing specialization and routinization of jobs. Workers would be better motivated toward higher individual production and toward better quality work if we discarded the assembly line and moved toward the craftsmanlike operations of the old Rolls Royce type of production. Industry has demonstrated, however, that it is more efficient to produce via assembly-line methods with lowered motivation and job satisfaction than with highly motivated craftsmen with a large area of responsibility in turning out their part of the total product. The preferred path to the attainment of production goals in turning out cars or other mass physical products is, then, the path of organizational controls and not the path of internalized motivation. The quality of production may suffer somewhat, but it is still cheaper to buy several mass-produced cars, allowing for programming for obsolescence, than it is to buy a single quality product like the Rolls Royce.

In the production of physical objects intended for mass consumption, the assembly line may furnish the best model. This may also apply to service operations in which the process can be sufficiently simplified to provide service to masses of consumers. When, however, we move to organizations which have the modifications of human beings as their product, as in educational institutions, or when we deal with treating basic problems of human beings, as in hospitals, clinics, and remedial institutions, we do not want to rely solely upon an organizational control to guarantee minimum effort of employees. We want employees with high motivation and high identification with their jobs. Jobs cannot profitably be fractionated very far and standardized and coordinated to a rigorous time schedule in a research laboratory, in a medical clinic, in an educational institution, or in a hospital.

In addition to the recognition of the inapplicability of organizational devices of the factory and the army to all organizations, it is also true that not all factory operations can be left to institutional controls without regard to the motivations of employees. It frequently happens that job fractionation can be pushed to the point of diminishing returns even in industry. The success of the Tavistock workers in raising productivity in the British coal mines through job enlargement was due to the fact that the specialization of American long-wall methods of coal mining did not yield adequate returns when applied to the difficult and variable conditions under which British miners had to operate (Trist & Bamforth, 1951). The question of whether to move toward greater specialization and standardization in an industrial operation or whether to move in the opposite direction is generally an empirical one to be answered by research. One rule of thumb can be applied, however. If the job can be so simplified and standardized that it is readily convertible to automated machines, then the direction to take is that of further institutionalization until automation is possible. If however, the over-all performance requires complex judgment, the differential weighing of factors which are not markedly identifiable, or creativity, then the human mind is a far superior instrument to the computer.

The paradox is that where automation is feasible, it can actually increase the motivational potential among the employees who are left on the job after the changeover. Mann and Hoffman (1960) conclude from their study of automation in an electric power plant that the remaining jobs for workers can be more interesting, that there can be freer association among colleagues, and that the elimination of supervisory levels brings the top and bottom of the organization closer together.

Internalization of Organizational Goals and Values

The pattern of motivation associated with value expression and self-identification has great potentialities for the internalization of the goals of subsystems and of the total system, and thus for the activation of behavior not prescribed by specific roles. Where this pattern prevails individuals take over organizational objectives as part of their own personal goals. They identify not with the organization as a safe and secure haven but with its major purposes. The internalization of organizational objectives is generally confined to the upper echelons or to the officer personnel. In voluntary organizations it extends into some of the rank-and-file, and in fact most voluntary organizations need a core of dedicated people—who are generally referred to as the dedicated damn fools.

Now the internalization of organizational goals is not as common as two types of more partial internalization. The first has to do with some general organizational purposes which are not unique to the organization. A scientist may have internalized some of the research values of his profession but not necessarily of the specific institution to which he is attached. As long as he stays in that institution, he may be a well-motivated worker. But he may find it just as easy to work for the things he believes in in another institution. There is not the same set of alternative organizations open to liberals who are political activists and who are part of the core of dedicated damn fools in the Democratic party. They have no other place to go, so they find some way of rationalizing the party's deviation from their liberal ideals.

A second type of partial internalization concerns the values and goals of a subsystem of the organization. It is often easier for the person to take over the values of his own unit. We may be attached to our own department in a university more than to the goals of the university as a whole.

Conditions Conducive to Internalization of System Goals

Internalization of organization objectives can come about through the utilization of the socialization process in childhood or through the adult socialization which takes place in the organization itself. In the first instance, the selective process, either by the person or the organization, matches the personality with the system. A youngster growing up in the tradition of one of the military services may have always thought of himself as an Air Force officer. Similarly, the crusader for civil liberties and the American Civil Liberties Union find one another.

The adult socialization process in the organization can build upon the personal values of its members and integrate them about an attractive model of its ideals. People can thus identify with the organizational mission. If the task of an organization has emotional significance, the organization enjoys an advantage in the creation of an attractive image. If the task is attended by hazard, as in the tracking down of criminals by the FBI, or of high adventure, as in the early days of flying, or of high service to humanity, as in a cancer research unit, it is not difficult to develop a convincing model of the organization's mission.

The imaginative leader can also help in the development of an attractive picture of the organization by some new conceptualization of its mission. The police force entrusted with the routine and dirty business of law enforcement carried out by dumb cops and "flatfeet" can be energized by seeing themselves as a corps of professional officers devoted to the highest form of public service. Reality factors limit the innovative use of symbols for the glorification of organizations. Occupational groups, however, constantly strive to achieve a more attractive picture of themselves, as in the instances of press agents who have become public relations specialists or undertakers who have become morticians.

Internalization of subgroup norms can come about through identification with fellow group members who share the same common fate. People take over the values of their group because they identify with their own kind and see themselves as good group members, and as good group members they model their actions and aspirations in terms of group norms. This subgroup identification can work for organizational objectives only if there is agreement between the group norms and the organizational objectives. Often in industry the norms of the work group are much closer to union objectives than to company objectives.

This suggests three additional factors which contribute to internalization of group objectives: (1) participating in important decisions about group objectives; (2) contributing to group performance in a significant way; and (3) sharing in the rewards of group accomplishment. When these three conditions are met, the individual can regard the group as his, for he in fact has helped to make it.

Social Satisfactions from Primary-Group Relationships

Human beings are social animals and cannot exist in physical or psychological isolation. The stimulation, the approval, and the support they derive from interacting with one another comprise one of the most potent forms of motivation. Strictly speaking, such affiliative motivation is another form of instrumental-reward-seeking, but some of its qualitative aspects are sufficiently different from the instrumental system and individual rewards previously described to warrant separate discussion.

The desire to be part of a group in itself will do no more than hold people in the system. The studies of Elton Mayo and his colleagues during World War II showed that work groups which provided their members social satisfactions had less absenteeism than less coheisve work groups (Mayo & Lombard, 1944). Mann and Baumgartel (1953) corroborated these findings in a study of the Detroit Edison Company. With respect to role performance, moveover, Seashore (1954) has demonstrated that identification with one's work group can make for either above-average or below-average productivity depending upon the norms of the particular group. In the Seashore study the highly-cohesive groups, compared to the low-cohesive groups, moved to either extreme in being above or below the production standards for the company.

Other studies have demonstrated that though the group can provide important socioemotional satisfactions for the members it can also detract from task orientation (Bass, 1960). Members can have such a pleasant time interacting with one another that they neglect their work. Again the critical mediating variable is the character of the values and norms of the group. The affiliative motive can lead to innovative and cooperative behavior, but often this assumes the form of protecting the group rather than maximizing organizational objectives. So the major question in dealing with the affiliative motive is how this motive can be harnessed to organizational goals.

The Likert Theory

What are the conditions under which the cohesive group with all the motivational force of primary-group relationships can gear into organizational goals? There is the possibility that our fifth factor of internalization of organizational objectives can be mediated through identification with subgroups whose informal norms reflect these purposes. Likert (1961) has devoted his book *New Patterns of Management* to this problem. The Likert thesis is that the factors making for internalization of organizational objectives can be realized by involving all the subgroups of the organization in group decision-making of a task-oriented character. The task orientation is provided by an over-lapping set of organizational families and by giving each such family some responsibility in decision-making.

Specifically the Likert theory is based upon four

essential concepts: (1) the efficacy of group process in maximizing motivation of organization members; (2) the channeling of this motivation toward group goals by the use of overlapping organizational families; (3) the key role of a member of two families in his linking-pin function; and (4) the development of short feedback cycles through the use of research on the functioning of both the social and the technical system. This theory thus takes account of the hierarchical authority structure of organizations, but also ties in every individual in the organization through his attachment to his own group, and presumably integrates the needs of all subgroups. For example, the president of an organization can meet with his vice-presidents as the top organizational family, and as a group they can work through problems ordinarily handled by the president alone or by the president meeting individually with his vice-presidents. In turn each vice-president meets with his department heads and again the problems at this level are met through group process, with the vice-president forming the link to top management and interpreting company policy. Department heads meet with their division heads, and so on down the line. When a department head meets with his fellow department heads and their superior, the vice-president, he functions not only as a member of that group but as a representative of his own group of division heads. These meetings take on a task-oriented character, in good part through the continuing use of research and measurement of the group's own activities.

Decisions are made at the level of the structure which is the relevant focus for the amount of organizational space involved. If a decision affects only the people within a subunit, then it should be made in that subunit. Thus top management is relieved of many small decisions which can well be made down the line. Every member of the organization, save at the very top and bottom levels, thus serves as a linking-pin in functioning as a member of two organizational families. The bond between organizational levels is always personally mediated. Every group in the organizational structure has a voice in decision-making. It decides how its task should be implemented. Though its task is set primarily by the level above it, it has some participation at this higher level through its representative.

Problems

There are, however, difficulties with the Likert theory, not because of the nature of the approach but because the approach is not pushed far enough in dealing with the walls of the maze. Specifically, the following problems still remain.

1. The voice of the rank-and-file member of the organization is greatly attenuated in its representation up the line. By the time the ordinary member's voice is reinterpreted through several levels of the organizational structure it may be so faint as to be ghost-like.

2. A related weakness is that the Likert model is primarily directed at the technical and task problems of the organization. The interest-group conflicts in organizations over the distribution of rewards, privileges, and perquisites between hierarchical levels are difficult to meet in this system of organizational families. In contrast the worker's union, which cuts across all organizational families at the rank-and-file level, is still the worker's best chance of gaining representation of his interests. Legitimate differences in interests between groups may in fact be obscured by an application of the Likert model.

3. Not all motivational problems of the large-scale organization are solved by decisions made in overlapping family groups. The loss of a feeling of worth in an organization when an individual performs a routinized role which can be performed by ten million others or by a machine is still a basic issue. The internalization of organizational goals is not insured by involvement in very limited decisions. In other words, the specialization of labor, the job fractionation, and the alienation of the worker from any meaningful work process are matters of organizational structure which may still prove to be overriding factors in sociotechnical systems.

4. Finally, there is the limitation upon group process when it has to be carefully kept to a limited set of decisions, especially when these limits are imposed upon the group as fixed policies and boundaries. Workers may prefer their own unions, where their elected officers make some of their decisions for them, to their work group where they do not elect their leader and have no voice in larger issues. Group process generates its own dynamic and people involved in it want to go beyond their limited directives. Students who are given disciplinary policies by the university administration and given the task of their implementation soon raise questions about the policies themselves. Representative democracy may be a more powerful organizational form than group process hamstrung by being restricted to means rather than to goals.

REFERENCES

Allport, F. H. The J-curve hypothesis of conforming behavior. *Journal of Social Psychology*, 1934, 5, 141–83.

Bass, B. M. *Leadership, psychology, and organizational behavior.* New York: Harper, 1960.

Katz, D. Human interrelationships and organizational

behavior. In S. Mailick and E. H. Van Ness (eds.), *Concepts and issues in administrative behavior.* New York: Prentice-Hall, 1962, pp. 166–86.

Katz, D., Maccoby, N., and Morse, Nancy. *Productivity, supervision and morale in an office situation.* Ann Arbor, Mich.: Institute for Social Research, Univ. of Michigan, 1950.

Likert, R. *New patterns of management.* New York: McGraw-Hill, 1961.

Mann, F. C. and Baumgartel, H. J. *Absences and employee attitudes in an electric power company.* Ann Arbor, Mich.: Institute for Social Research, Univ. of Michigan, 1953.

Mann, F. C. and Hoffman, R. L. *Automation and the worker.* New York: Holt, Rinehart and Winston, 1960.

Mayo E. and Lombard, G. *Teamwork and labor turnover in the aircraft industry of Southern California. Business Research Studies No. 32.* Cambridge, Mass.: Harvard Univ., 1944.

McGregor, D. *The human side of enterprise.* New York: McGraw-Hill, 1960.

Morse, Nancy. *Satisfactions in the white collar job.* Ann Arbor, Mich.: Institute for Social Research, Univ. of Michigan, 1953.

Seashore, S. *Group cohesiveness in the industrial work group.* Ann Arbor, Mich.: Institute for Social Research, Univ. of Michigan, 1954.

Trist, E. and Bamforth, K. W. Some social and psychological consequences of the long wall method of coal-getting. *Human Relations,* 1951, **4**, 3–38.

Weber, M. *The theory of social and economic organization.* Glencoe, Illinois: Free Press, 1947.

33. THE ROLE OF FINANCIAL COMPENSATION IN INDUSTRIAL MOTIVATION*

Robert L. Opsahl **and** ***Marvin D. Dunnette***†

Theories and research studies related to the effects of financial compensation on employee motivation are reviewed and critically evaluated. Such theories are based primarily on limited studies conducted on subhuman species; no deductions from these theories have been adequately tested in industry. Most compensation practices in industry are based on impressionistic evidence characterized by anecdotal accounts and data gathered by means of self-report questionnaires. Studies of the effects of money on employee behavior need to be conducted in laboratory or in tightly controlled field settings. A commendable start in this direction has been made by a few investigators, but more empirical tests of the bases of current compensation practices are needed. Such research should lead eventually to a sound theory of money and employee motivation from which more effective and more behaviorally relevant compensation practices may be derived.[1]

Widespread interest in money as a motivational tool for spurring production was first stimulated in this country by Frederick Taylor. Some years before the turn of the century, Taylor observed an energetic steelworker, who, after putting in a 12-hour day of lifting pigs of iron, would run 12 miles up a mountainside to work on his cabin. If this excess energy could be used to produce more on the job, thought Taylor, higher profits from lower fixed costs could be used to pay the worker significantly more for his increased efforts. Such was the beginning of *scientific management,* which is based essentially on the assumption that workers will put forth extra effort on the job to maximize their economic gains. This became a guiding principle in pay practices until the late 1920s when the *human relations movement* in industrial psychology was ushered in with the Western Electric studies directed by Elton Mayo. As a result of these studies, recognition of man's ego and social needs became widespread, and job factors other than pay came to be emphasized as the major reasons why men work. To a large extent, these later ideas are still with us. Yet, few would disagree that money has been and continues to be the primary means of rewarding and modifying human behavior in industry.

Strangely, in spite of the large amounts of money spent and the obvious relevance of behavioral theory for industrial compensation practices, there is probably less solid research in this area than in any other field related to worker performance. We know amazingly little about how money either interacts with other factors or how it acts individually to affect job behavior. Although the relevant literature is voluminous, much more has been written about the subject than is actually known. Speculation, accompanied by compensation fads and fashions, abounds; research studies designed to answer fundamental

* *Psychological Bulletin,* Vol. 66, No. 2 (1966), pp. 94–118.

† Both of Department of Psychology, University of Minnesota.

[1] This investigation was supported in part by a Public Health Service Fellowship (5-F1-MH-21,814-03 PS) from the National Institute of Mental Health, United States Public Health Service, and in part by a behavioral science research grant to Marvin D. Dunnette from the General Electric Foundation.

questions about the role of money in human motivation are all too rare.

In this review, we have attempted to identify and summarize research studies designed to show how opportunities to get money affect the way people actually do their work. It was decided to focus attention on the role of money in motivating behavior *on the job*. The large body of literature on manpower economics relevant to relationships between wage and salary practices and manpower mobility has been largely ignored. Thus, we review here those theories and studies designed to illuminate possible effects of financial compensation for inducing greater effort in the job setting, and we ignore those theories and studies related to money's effects in inducing employees to take jobs, persist in them, or to leave them. First, several theories offered to explain how money affects behavior and research studies relevant to these theories are considered. Second, the behavioral consequences of compensation are examined by stressing and analyzing the variables relevant to the money-motivation relationship. Throughout, our purpose is to pinpoint the role of financial compensation in industrial job motivation. We seek to summarize and to evaluate critically what is already known and to suggest directions for future research.

THEORIES OF THE ROLE OF MONEY

Does money serve to stimulate job effort? If so, why does it do so? How does it take on value in our industrial society? There are at least five theories or interpretations of the role of money in affecting the job behavior of employees.

Money as a Generalized Conditioned Reinforcer

One widely held hypothesis is that money acts as a generalized conditioned reinforcer because of its repeated pairings with primary reinforcers (Holland & Skinner, 1961; Kelleher & Gollub, 1962; Skinner, 1953). Skinner (1953) has stated that such a generalized reinforcer should be extremely effective because some deprivation will usually exist for which the conditioned reinforcer is appropriate. Unfortunately, solid evidence of the behavioral effectiveness of such reinforcers is lacking, and what evidence there is has been based almost entirely on animal studies.

In a series of experiments conducted by Wike and Barrientos (1958) a goal box (containing wet mash) paired with both food and water deprivation proved to be a more effective reinforcer for rats than different goal boxes paired with food or water deprivation alone. The implications of these results are that money ought to be more potent when its attainment is paired with many, rather than only single, needs. Unfortunately, the magnitude of the difference in preferences in the above study, though statistically significant, was extremely small. In 15 test trials in a T-maze, rats turned to the goal box previously paired with both deprivations an average of only 0.62 trials more often than to the goal box paired only with food deprivation.

Moreover, this and most other studies on generalized conditioned reinforcers can be criticized because of the nonindependence of food and water as primary reinforcers (Grice & Davis, 1957; Verplanck & Hayes, 1953). A water-deprived rat eats less than his normal intake of food. What is needed are studies with human subjects in which a stimulus has been paired with many independent reinforcers. In one such study (Ferster & DeMeyer, 1962), coins paired with games and candy were used successfully with autistic children to develop and maintain complex operant behaviors. Although the effectiveness of the coins was well-demonstrated by the increased frequences of responding contingent on their presentation, their effectiveness under different conditions of deprivation was not studied, nor was their relative effectiveness compared with that of coins operating as simple conditional reinforcers.

Some theorists (e.g., Brown, 1961; Dollard & Miller, 1950) have referred to the token-reward studies of Wolfe (1936) and Cowles (1937) as examples of how money acquires value. In these studies, initially neutral poker chips apparently acquired reinforcement value because they could be exchanged for various foods. The analogy between the poker chips and the industrial use of money as wages is incomplete, however, because the reinforcement value of the poker chips came about because of their association with removing deprivation in a single primary area, whereas the theory of money's generalized reinforcing role would hypothesize that it is valued quite aside from and independent of any particular state of deprivation. It should be apparent that evidence in support of money as a generalized conditioned reinforcer is, at best, limited and inconclusive.

Money as a Conditioned Incentive

According to this hypothesis, repeated pairings of money with primary incentives[2] establish a new learned drive for money (Dollard & Miller, 1950). For example, in Wolfe's (1936) study, the sight of

[2] Incentive: "an object or external condition, perceived as capable of satisfying an aroused motive, that tends to elicit action to obtain the object or condition [English & English, 1958]."

a poker chip out of reach served as an incentive to motivate the chimpanzee to pull it in. The fact that chimpanzees refused to work if given a free supply of poker chips suggests that the act of obtaining the chips served a drive-reducing function (Dollard & Miller, 1950). Presumably, money could become a generalized conditioned incentive in the same manner that it is presumed by some to become a generalized conditioned reinforcer—that is, by many pairings with many different types of incentives. Perhaps the main difference between the conditioned reinforcer and conditioned incentive interpretations is the introduction of drive reduction in the incentive hypothesis. In contrast, no such drive need be hypothesized under empirical reinforcement principles.

Money as an Anxiety Reducer

Brown (1953, 1961) also utilized the concept of drive in an effort to explain how money affects behavior. He suggested that one learns to become anxious in the presence of a variety of cues signifying the absence of money. Presumably, anxiety related to the absence of money is acquired in childhood through a process of higher-order conditioning. The first stage consists of pairings of pain with cues of warning or alarm provided by adults. For example, before a child actually touches a hot stove, a nearby adult may provide facial gestures of alarm and warnings such as "Look out, you'll get hurt!" These cues eventually elicit anxiety without the unconditioned stimulus. In the second stage, anxiety-arousing warnings are conditioned to a wide variety of cues, indicating lack of money. After such learning, the child becomes anxious upon hearing phrases such as "That costs too much money," or "We can't afford to buy you that." The actual presence of money produces cues for the cessation of anxiety. This concept of anxiety as a learned motivating agent for money-seeking responses in no way contradicts the possible action of money according to the two previous hypotheses; money as an anxiety-reducer could operate jointly with them as an additional explanatory device.

Harlow (1953), however, has taken issue with Brown's thesis, stating: "It is hard to believe that parental expression at the time a child suffers injury is identical with or highly similar to a parent's expression when he says 'we have no money' [p. 22]." Harlow pointed out further that an infant's ability to recognize emotional expression when suffering pain has not been reliably demonstrated. Unfortunately, Brown presented no experimental evidence bearing on his theory.

Money as a "Hygiene Factor"

Herzberg, Mausner, and Snyderman (1959) postulated that money is a so-called "hygiene factor" serving as a potential dissatisfier if it is not present in appropriate amounts, but not as a potential satisfier or positive motivator. According to them, improvements in salary may only remove impediments to job satisfaction but do not actually generate job satisfaction. The main value of money, according to them, is that it leads to both the avoidance of economic deprivation and the avoidance of feelings of being treated unfairly. Thus, its hygienic role is one of avoiding pain and dissatisfaction ("disease") but not one of promoting heightened motivation ("health"). These notions were originally derived from content analyses of anecdotal accounts of unusually satisfying and unusually dissatisfying job events elicited from 200 engineers and accountants. Fifteen percent of their descriptions of satisfying events involved the mention of salary and 17 percent of their descriptions of dissatisfying events involved salary. Moreover, Herzberg *et al.* suggested that salary may be viewed as a "dissatisfier" because its impact on favorable job feelings was largely short-term while its impact on unfavorable feelings was long-term—extending over periods of several months. Herzberg *et al.*'s use of this finding to argue that money acts only as a potential dissatisfier is mystifying. It becomes even more so when their data are examined more carefully. In all of the descriptions of unusually good job feelings, salary was mentioned as a major reason for the feelings 19 percent of the time. Of the unusually good job feelings that lasted several months, salary was reported as a causal factor 22 percent of the time; of the short-term feelings, it was a factor 5 percent of the time. In contrast, salary was named as a major cause of unusually bad job feelings only 13 percent of the time. Of the unusually bad job feelings lasting several months, it was mentioned only 18 percent of the time (in contrast with the 22 percent of long-term good feelings, mentioned above).

These data seem inconsistent with the interpretations and lend no substantial support to hypotheses of a so-called differential role for money in leading to job satisfaction or job dissatisfaction.

Money as an Instrument for Gaining Desired Outcomes

Vroom's (1964) cognitive model of motivation has implications for understanding how money functions in affecting behavior. According to Vroom's interpretation, money acquires valence as a result of its perceived instrumentality for obtaining other desired outcomes. The concept of valence refers simply to affective orientations toward particular outcomes and has no direct implications for behavioral consequencces. However, the "force" impelling a person toward action was postulated to be the product of the valence of an outcome and the person's expectancy that a certain action will lead to attainment of the outcome. Thus, for example, if money is perceived by a given person as instrumental to obtaining security, and if security is desired, money itself acquires positive valence. The probability, then, of his making money-seeking responses depends on the degree of his desire for security *multiplied* by his expectancy that certain designated job behaviors lead to attaining money. Although Vroom summarized studies giving general support to his theory, the specific role of money in his theory was not dealt with in any detail.

Gellerman's (1963) statement of how money functions in industry also stressed its instrumental role. According to him money in itself has no intrinsic meaning and acquires significant motivating power only when it comes to symbolize intangible goals. Money acts as a symbol in different ways for different persons, and for the same person at different times. Gellerman presented the interesting notion that money can be interpreted as a projective device—a man's reaction to money "summarizes his biography to date: his early economic environment, his competence training, the various nonfinancial motives he has acquired, and his current financial status [p. 166]." Gellerman's evidence was largely anecdotal, but nonetheless rather convincing.

Summary of Theoretical Speculations

Much remains to be learned before we will understand very well what meaning money has for different persons, how it affects their job behaviors, which motives it serves, and how its effectiveness may come about. It is probably doubtful that there will ever be a "theory of money" in the sense that money will be given a unique or special status as a psychological variable. It is true that money functions in many ways, depending upon the setting, the antecedent conditions, and the particular person involved. According to Brown, money must be present to avoid anxiety. For Herzberg *et al.*, it serves to avoid feelings of being unfairly treated or economically deprived. Reinforcement theories, on the other hand, seem to treat money either as a generalized entity, functioning independently of specific deprivations, or as a general incentive that has been coupled with variously valued goals during a person's total learning history. Obviously, the answers are not yet available, and it is probably best to view money symbolically, as Vroom and Gellerman do, and to begin to learn and measure the personal, situational, and job parameters that may define more fully what it is the symbol of and what its attainment is instrumental to. Only by mapping the domain in this way will we come to know the relevant factors associated with money as a "motivator" of behavior in industry.

BEHAVIORAL CONSEQUENCES OF COMPENSATION

The major research problem in industrial compensation is to determine exactly what effects monetary rewards have for motivating various behaviors. More specifically, we need to understand more precisely how money can be used to induce employees to perform at high levels. Relevant research centers around two major groupings: studies related to the job or the job content and studies related to personal characteristics—preferences, perceptions, opinions, and other responses—made by the job incumbent. The first of these, the job or task variables, include primarily the policies and practices constituting the "compensation package" for any given job or setting. The personal or subject variables influence not only the way a job holder responds to the specific policies and practices in any given situation, but they also vary as a function of these task or job variables. Thus, it is necessary to give careful attention to the interaction between job and personal variables which is frequently overlooked in research designs and has an important bearing on the interpretations to be attached to the results of such research studies.

JOB AND TASK VARIABLES

Compensation Policies

Our assumption is that the manner in which financial compensation is administered may account for a large amount of the variation in job behavior. The particular schedule of payment, the degree of secrecy surrounding the amount of pay one receives, how the level of salary or pay is determined, and the individual's long-term or career pay history all have important potential effects on how the employee responds to any specific amount of money.

Schedules of Pay. In this review we shall be concerned solely with "incentive" payment systems[3] which are based on behavioral criteria (usually amount of output) rather than biographical factors

[3] We will not attempt to evaluate all the evidence on incentive plans. For an excellent review and evaluation of these, see Marriott (1957).

such as education, seniority, and experience. Incentive pay schemes of various sorts are believed to function primarily to "increase or maintain some already initiated activity or . . . to encourage some new form of activity . . . [Marriott, 1957, p. 12]."

There is considerable evidence that installation of such plans usually results in greater output per man hour, lower unit costs, and higher wages in comparison with outcomes associated with straight payment systems (e.g., Dale, 1959; Rath, 1960; Viteles, 1953). However, the installation of an incentive plan is not and can never be an isolated event. Frequently, changes in work methods, management policies, and organization accompany the changeover, and it is difficult to determine the amount of behavioral variance that each of these other events may contribute. This would seem to constitute a persuasive argument for placing workers in a controlled laboratory situation and analyzing the effectiveness of different methods of payment, isolated from the usual changes accompanying their installation. Unfortunately, there have been few studies of this nature.[4]

Incentive plans can be used on either the worker's own output or on the total output of his working group. The relative efficiency of the two methods are dependent upon such factors as the nature of the task performed (Babchuk & Goode, 1951; Marriott, 1957), the size of the working group (Campbell, 1952; Marriott, 1949, 1951; Marriott & Denerley, 1955; Shimmin, Williams, & Buck, 1956), the social environment (Selekman, 1941), and the particular group or individual plan employed. The chief disadvantage with group incentives is the likelihood of a low correlation between a worker's own individual performance and his pay in larger groups. There is also evidence (Campbell, 1952) that individual output decreases as the size of the work group increases, and this is apparently due to workers' perceiving a decreased probability that their efforts will yield increased outcomes (i.e., the workers have less knowledge of the relationships between effort and earnings). Both of these effects run counter to the main principle of incentive plans—immediate reward for desired job behaviors.

Not only do financial incentives operate with different efficacy in different situations, but often they do not even lead to increased production. Group standards and social pressures frequently induce workers to perform considerably below their potential. Most of the data on such rate restriction are either observational (e.g., Dalton, 1948; Dalton, Collins, & Roy, 1946; Dyson, 1956; Mathewson, 1951; Myers, 1920; Roethlisberger & Dickson, 1939; Roy, 1952; Whyte, 1955) or in the form of verbal responses to surveys (Opinion Research Corporation, 1949; Viteles, 1953). The results of these studies suggest that changes in the monetary consequences of performance are usually accompanied by changes in other expected consequences of performance. Thus, instituting an incentive plan may alter not only the expected consequences in terms of amount of money received, but also expected consequences related to possible loss of esteem in the eyes of one's co-workers or the presumed bad connotations of "selling out" or accepting the goals of management.

Hickson (1961) has divided the causes of rate restriction into five categories. Three of the causes are essentially negative or avoidance reasons: uncertainty about the continuance of the existing "effort-bargain" between the workers and management, uncertainty about the continuance of employment, and uncertainty about the continuance of existing social relationships. The other two causes are positive or approach-type factors: the desire to continue social satisfactions derived from the practice of restriction, and a desire for at least a minimal area of external control over one's own behavior. Hickson stated that we haven't studied sufficiently the positive reasons or advantages of rate restriction. We shall go a step further and state that the main method of studying rate restriction—on the job observation—is essentially a loose and ineffective way of determining any causative linkages. Just as schedules of pay can best be assessed by experimental manipulations under controlled conditions, so should rate restriction be studied by laboratory investigations characterized by controlled and objective observations.

The most intensive analysis of rate restriction was undertaken by Whyte (1952, 1955). It was the thesis of Whyte and his co-workers that many piece-rate incentive situations actually resemble the conditions of experimentally induced neurosis. He reasoned that most incentive "packages" do not provide the employee with sufficient cues to allow him to discriminate effectively between stimuli signaling the onset of punishment circumstances (loss of co-worker respect, etc.) and stimuli signaling the onset of rewarding circumstances (more pay, higher job success, etc.) (Whyte, 1955). Thus, money itself is only *one* of many possible rewards and punishments that invariably accompany any incentive situation.

Whyte's effort to show similarity between piece-rate incentive systems and the conditions accompanying experimental neurosis is misleading. The discriminative stimuli for the rewards and punishments administered by the work group and by management seem to be clearly differentiable. A double approach-

[4] Marriott (1957) mentioned only three experimental studies, all in an industrial setting and all conducted at least 30 years ago: Burnett (1925); Roethlisberger and Dickson (1939), and Wyatt (1934).

avoidance conflict between the rewards and punishments of management and the work group is more descriptive of the situation. If this is the case, the conditions necessary for maintaining the group as an effective reinforcing agent even in the face of an incentive piece-rate plan should be studied more thoroughly. Variables for study would include group cohesiveness; interaction patterns within the group; amount of intergroup competition; identification of individuals within the group; uniformity of group opinion; group control over the environment; and the extent to which group pressures support rather than subvert organizational goals and demands (March & Simon, 1958, pp. 59–61).

Thus, although "everyone knows" that incentive pay schemes work very effectively some of the time, it is painfully apparent that they are far from uniformly effective. The emphasis in research should now turn to more controlled observations of the effects of money in the context of the many other sources of reward and punishment in the work setting. So far, we have only a wealth of field observations. It is necessary now to learn more exactly just what employees will or will not give up for money or, more importantly, to learn how incentive payments may be made without engendering the painful and onerous circumstances which so often seem to accompany such payments.

Secret Pay Policies. In addition to the particular kind of pay plan, the secrecy surrounding the amount of money given an employee may have motivational implications. Lawler's (1965) recent study indicates that secret pay policies may contribute to dissatisfaction with pay and to the possibility of lowered job performance. He found that managers overestimated the pay of subordinates and peers, and underestimated their superior's pay; they saw their own pay as being too low by comparison with all three groups. Moreover, they also underestimated the financial rewards associated with promotion. Lawler argued that these two results of pay secrecy probably reduce the motivation of managers both to perform well on their present jobs and to seek higher level jobs. Another disadvantage of secrecy is that it lowers money's effectiveness as a knowledge-of-results device to let the manager know how well he is doing in comparison to others. Lawler advocates the abandonment of secrecy policies—"there is no reason why organizations cannot make salaries public information [p. 8]."

Lawler's assertion seems to have a good deal of merit; his results are impressive and his arguments sound. It would be very useful, at this stage, to conduct "before-after" studies of the effects of instituting policies of openness concerning wage and salary payments on employees' perceptions of relationships between pay and job performance. At the very least, Lawler's data suggest that useful effects would be produced by informing employees (particularly managers) about how their salaries are derived; the next logical step would be to provide normative data (e.g., percentile distributions of employee pay levels); and, finally, salary administrators might even publicize actual salary levels of persons in the firm.

This is not to say, of course, that there might not be negative outcomes from the sudden implementation of such policies. For example, one obvious possibility is that such action might crystallize present hierarchical "pecking orders"; group cohesiveness could be disrupted by the sudden awareness of substantial intra-work-group differences. Most such fears stem from the prevalence of actual pay inequities related to inadequate job-performance appraisal systems and current weaknesses in administering salary payments in such a way as to reflect valid relationships with job performance. We believe, with Lawler, that present policies of secrecy are undoubtedly due, in part, to fear on the part of salary administrators that they would have a difficult time mustering convincing arguments in favor of many of their present practices. Thus, it is true that until salaries are determined more rationally and until money becomes more firmly accepted as a way of rewarding outstanding job behavior, public disclosure of salary arrangements may probably not have the desirable consequences suggested by Lawler. Perhaps his results are merely symptomatic of present unsuccessful efforts to use pay effectively for motivating employees. If this is true, it seems all the more important and timely to undertake thorough studies of the effects of relaxing present policies of pay secrecy.

Pay Curves. An employee's periodic pay increases, as he progresses in his career with a company, constitutes another job or task variable with the potential for differentially motivating effects. Wittingly or not, every company "assigns" each employee a "pay curve" which is the result of successive alterations in compensation and compensation policies through the years. One way of doing this (the usual way) is with little or no advanced planning: increments are given haphazardly on a year to year basis and the resulting career pay curve simply "grows" somewhat akin to Topsy. Another alternative is to plan the future compensation program shortly after the individual enters the organization and then to modify it subsequently on the basis of his job behavior as his career unfolds. No matter which pay policy is adopted, the results will most likely affect the employee's job behavior, his aspirations and anticipations of future earnings, and his feelings of fairness with respect to his career-pay "program."

Most companies administer pay increments on a periodic (e.g., year-to-year) basis.[5] The rationale for this is quite simple, the usual idea being that differential pay increments may be given for differential results produced by employees on their jobs. Over a span of many years, then, we might expect a consistent pattern of positive correlations for the salary increments received by the individuals comprising any particular group of employees. This expectation would be based on two rather reasonable and closely related assumptions—first, that the acquisition of job skills is a predictable process; and, second, that the effectiveness of a person's job performance in any given period is predictable from his own past patterns of job performance.

In fact, however, career pay histories for employee groups do *not* usually show such patterns of consistently positive relationships between year-to-year salary gains. Haire (1965) mapped the correlations between salary levels at the end of each year and raises over 5- and 10-year periods in two large national companies. In one company, the correlations decreased over the 5-year span from 0.38 to −0.06 for one executive group (median salary $41,600), and from 0.36 to −0.25 for a second group (median salary $18,000). In the second firm, the correlations between salaries and raises for adjacent years over the 10-year period varied between −0.33 and 0.83 with no consistent pattern discernible. Haire believed that his results constituted damning evidence that these two companies had no consistent policies with respect to the incentive use of salarly increases; he suggested that the trend in the first company reflected a shift from a policy of distributing raises under the assumption that good performance is related to past excellence to the assumption that it is either not related at all or that it is negatively related. He also asserted that a pattern showing extremely low correlations between present salary levels and salary increments indicates that wage increases might just as well be distributed by lottery—that the incentive character of a raise is thereby nullified and that consistent striving for job excellence would seem futile under such circumstances. Haire's assertions are provocative and they may indeed follow from his results, but we believe that other explanations may be equally compatible with his findings. For example, low correlations could just as reasonably be viewed as reflecting a successfully administered wage policy allowing for greater rather than less flexibility in using money to reward top job performance. Such a policy might suggest, in effect, that an employee who has done well in the past cannot rest on his laurels in expectation of future "rewards" and that a lower salaried employee (with presumably a history of less effective performance) still has rich opportunities to be recognized and appropriately rewarded for improved job performance in the future. It is true that a finding of consistently low correlations would tend to refute our earlier stated assumptions about the acquisition of job skills and the consistency of job performance over time.

Be that as it may, future analyses of historical pay patterns such as these provided by Haire will probably yield more explicit insights about company wage policies if they focus more closely on individual employee pay and job performance histories rather than rely solely on coarse within-group comparisons and correlations such as those reported by Haire. The idea of inspecting historical patterns in the relationships between job performance, salaries, and raises is a good one and should be utilized more broadly.

The idea of specifying individual career pay curves has received extensive attention by Jaques (1961), through his "standard payment and progression method." By analyzing the pay histories of 250 male workers, he derived a family of negatively accelerated pay curves extending from ages 20 to 65. It should be noted, however, that his curves were plotted with a log scale for the ordinate (salary). If actual dollar values were plotted, the data would very likely yield positively rather than negatively accelerated curves. However, as plotted by Jaques, the curves rise rapidly in the younger age groups, slow down at older ages, and show a greater rate of progression at the higher earning levels. According to Jaques, these smoothed curves (called standard earning progressions), follow "the sigmoidal progression characteristic of biological growth [1961, p. 185]," and are the basis for his payment theory. Jaques believed that the standard earning progression curves represent a close approximation to the lines of growth of "time-span of discretion" in individuals. This time-span of discretion is the maximum period of time during which the work assigned by a manager requires his subordinate to exercise discretion, judgment, or initiative in his job without that discretion being subject to review by the manager. This objective yardstick can supposedly be used for direct comparison of work levels between any two jobs, regardless of content. The major significance of the time-span, according to Jaques, is that workers in jobs having different contents but the same time-span of discretion privately perceive the same wage or salary bracket to be equitable for the work they are doing.

Assuming that individuals seek an equitable level of payment for the level of work consistent with their

[5] Since there are innumerable ways to administer pay on a periodic basis, and since these methods are largely administrative and have little interest of a psychological nature, we will not attempt to review them.

capacity, an employee's future pay curve can be determined by: *(a)* determining the employee's present time-span of discretion along with the equitable payment for that time-span; *(b)* plotting the employee's achieved earning progression to date; *(c)* allowing the manager once-removed to determine the employee's potential progress assessment (i.e., the manager's assessment of the level of work a person is likely to achieve—this can be expressed in terms of the earning progression that the employee would likely achieve given that he receives equitable payment for his work); *(d)* letting the immediate manager assess the employee's performance, and altering the employee's wage or salary according to this assessment; *(e)* having the once-removed manager revise the potential progress assessment if performance continues above or below the original potential progress assessment.

The above is only a brief sketch of Jaques' theory of payment. It is a highly interesting one, but until further data concerning its motivational consequences are compiled, it must be regarded as highly tentative.

The "sigmoidal biological growth" pay curves that Jaques described are not the only possible ones; Ghiselli (1965) has pointed out other possibilities and has attempted to provide the rationale behind them. For instance, one suggested possibility was having average increments in pay increase from year to year. The result would be a positively accelerated pay curve consonant with the philosophy of paying an employee a substantial amount only after he becomes highly effective in the organization instead of when he is in the early stages of his career and easily tempted to move to another organization. If the organization wished to budget a fixed amount for pay increases each year, linear pay curves would result. If, on the other hand, it is assumed that an employee is unlikely to leave a firm after he has been with it a long time and has a huge personal investment in it (such as retirement benefits, stock options, etc.), it might be advantageous to reward him generously when he first starts his job to help insure that he will not go to another firm (i.e., assign him a negatively accelerated curve). To our knowledge, no empirical studies on the relative effectiveness of different possible pay curves have been undertaken.

Although it would appear that pay curves have a significant influence on job behavior, parametric experiments in this area are practically nonexistent. Several aspects of pay curves need to be studied before these curves can be constructed or used with even a moderate degree of effectiveness.

First and most important, it must be determined how a given pay curve differentially affects employees' motivation and job behaviors. It is not plausible to assume that one best curve can be found for *all* employees, or even for a subgroup of employees at a given job level or with common job duties. Some evidence of this was revealed by Festinger (1965) who found that promotions (with related pay increases, presumably) *increased* the aspired-to job level and perceived importance of pay for about 30 percent of a sample of employees within one company but *decreased* the job level-of-aspiration and perceived importance of pay in another 30 percent of the cases. It is not known why these groups reacted so differently to promotions. The overall level-of-aspiration of the employees certainly would be a prime variable; need Achievement might be another. Little is known about the stability of these two variables; therefore, assessment of them early in an employee's career may not be a valid index of later expectations or the effectiveness of career pay-curve policies. It is necessary to conduct longitudinal studies over extended periods of time—studies which are all too infrequent in the area of compensation. Some of the data necessary for this type of study are already on file in computer memory banks in the larger companies and need only to be retrieved and analyzed.

Since pay curves do not operate within a vacuum, the effect of one employee's pay curve on another employee must not be overlooked. Ghiselli's (1965) rationale for positively and negatively accelerated curves, for instance, may not prove effective in the context of the total industrial situation. Since pay is on a competitive basis across companies, a negatively accelerated curve in one company might lead to feelings of inequality and possible job termination for a young employee if other companies offered linear or positively accelerated pay increments in a similar situation. It is not implied that the effectiveness of the different curves should not be studied. However, the concept of equity applies to pay-curve comparisons as well as to wage comparisons, and this is an important potential area for investigation.

Several methods of deriving pay curves deserve further investigation. One option would be to inform the employee of the tentative curve agreed upon for him. This could be done piecemeal, by setting monetary goals for him to shoot at within a specific time period. An interesting variation of this procedure that, to our knowledge, has not been studied, would be to include pay goals in the goal-setting interviews given high level managers in some companies. The behavioral goals set in these interviews could have monetary rewards attached to them, thereby providing further incentive for their attainment. Informing an employee of his progress along his proposed pay curve might also serve a valuable feedback function, helping him evaluate his progress to date.

Other relevant research problems are numerous. Important ones include determining how to alter an employee's subsequent curve on the basis of under- or overachievement, discovering valid criteria for constructing a tentative curve, and determining which variables influence the perception of pay increments and *how* they influence it. With expanded knowledge in these areas, pay curves and their determination may come to play a central role in industrial compensation practices of the future.

Industrial psychologists have too often turned prematurely to the study of employee characteristics without giving sufficient attention to the job context. The significant research reviewed here and the questions suggested testify to the potential importance of task and job content variables. Certainly the complexities of the interaction between task and job variables and subject (employee) variables, discussed in the following section, demand research evidence bearing on both. The failure to place research emphasis in either area will very likely impede progress and understanding in the other.

SUBJECT VARIABLES

Perceived Relations between Performance and Pay

According to Vroom's (1964) theory of work motivation, the valence of effective performance increases as the instrumentality of effective performance for the attainment of money increases, assuming that the valence of money is positive. Vroom cited supporting evidence from experiments by Atkinson and Reitman (1956), Atkinson (1958), and Kaufman (1962) showing a higher level of performance by subjects who were told that their earnings were contingent on the effectiveness of their performance. Georgopoulos, Mahoney, and Jones' (1957) Path-Goal Approach theory similarly states that if a worker has a desire for a given goal and perceives a given path leading to that goal, he will utilize that path if he has freedom to do so. Georgopoulos *et al.* found that workers who perceived higher personal productivity as a means to increased earnings performed more effectively than workers who did not perceive this relationship.

The effectiveness of incentive plans in general depends upon the worker's knowledge of the relation between performance and earnings. The lack of this knowledge is one cause of failure in incentive schemes. As already mentioned, Campbell's (1952) study showed that one of the major reasons for lower productivity in large groups under group incentive plans is that the workers often do not perceive the relation between pay and productivity as well as they do in smaller groups. In the Georgopoulos *et al.* (1957) study, only 38 percent of the workers perceived increased performance as leading to increased earnings. More amazingly, 35 percent perceived *low* productivity as an aid to higher earnings in the long run. Lawler (1964) recently found that 600 managers perceived their training and experience to be the most important factors in determining their pay—not how well or how poorly they performed their jobs. Since Lawler found that the relation between their pay and their rated job performance also was low, their perceptions were probably quite accurate. A separate analysis of the most highly motivated managers, however, indicated that they attached greater importance to pay and felt that good job performance would lead to higher pay.

These studies confirm the importance of knowing how job performance and pay are related. The relation between performing certain desired behaviors and attainment of the pay-incentive must be explicitly specified. The foregoing statement seems so obvious as hardly to warrant mentioning. Unfortunately, as we have seen, the number of times in industry that the above *rule* is ignored is surprising. Future research must determine how goals or incentives may best be presented in association with desired behaviors. Practically nothing has been done in this area—especially for managers. In fact, programs for the recognition of individual merit are notoriously poor. Methods for tying financial compensation in with management-by-results (Schleh, 1961) or with systematic efforts to set job goals and methods of unambiguously outlining what the end result of various job behaviors will be should be developed and studied.

Personality-Task Interactions

Under some conditions, it appears that even specifying the relation between performance and pay is not sufficient. Early studies (Wyatt & Fraser, 1929; Wyatt, Fraser, & Stock, 1929; Wyatt & Langdon, 1937) conducted on British factory workers showed that feelings of boredom are associated with reduced output even under a carefully developed program of incentive pay. More recent studies have failed to reproduce the daily output curve found by the British investigators, and, moreover, indicate that boredom is not *necessarily* accompanied by reduced output (Cain, 1942; Smith, 1953; Ryan & Smith, 1954). Thus, boredom *may* lead to a decrease in performance; but, as in most other areas of investigation, a ceteris paribus clause must be included. Little is known of the factors which may outweigh the effects of boredom in a particular situation.

It is obvious that repetitiveness and uniformity

in job tasks are likely to contribute to feelings of boredom, but personality variables are also important determinants. Smith (1955) found that susceptibility to boredom is associated with such factors as youth, restlessness in daily habits and leisure-time activities, and dissatisfaction with personal, home, and plant situations not directly concerned with uniformity or repetitiveness. The commonly held assumption that workers of higher intelligence are more easily bored with repetitive work, however, is based on meager and conflicting data (Ryan & Smith, 1954).

One possible method of alleviating feelings of boredom is suggested by Wyatt and Fraser's (1929) finding that piece-rate systems lead to fewer symptoms of boredom than does straight hourly pay. This is in keeping with Whyte's (1955) contention that, in addition to money, there are three other sources of reward in a piece-rate situation: escape from fatigue, because the worker has a meaningful goal to shoot at; escape from management pressure and gain of control over one's own time; and "playing the game" of trying to attain quota.

Even if piece-rate systems relieve boredom, output under such plans may still suffer if the task is disliked. This was Wyatt's (1934) finding when he compared the levels of performance of 10 female workers in a British candy factory under hourly, bonus, and piece-rate payment methods. He observed a strong positive relation between an incentive plan's effectiveness (defined as increased productivity) and liking for the job. The best liked job was wrapping the candy and employees increased their output on it 200 percent when payment was changed from straight pay to a group bonus and finally to piece-rate payment. In contrast, unwrapping damaged packages was viewed as most onerous —"an aimless and destructive process"—and output on this task showed no changed under different conditions of pay.

The net conclusion from these studies is that repetitive tasks, destructive tasks, boring tasks, and disliked tasks are apparently much less susceptible to monetary incentives. Little has been done, however, to explore other possible interactions in this area. What little data we do have suggest that nonmonetary incentives are more effective for subjects who have high ability on the task being measured. Thus, Fleishman (1958) found that subjects high in ability on a complex coordination task increased their performance under incentive conditions significantly more than did low ability subjects. However, we do not know if such findings would generalize to situations in which monetary incentives are used or how the effectiveness of incentives varies as a function of other important variables such as the type of task, the amount of physical effort demanded, or the degree of interpersonal interaction involved, to mention but a few examples. Without knowledge of the range of behaviors susceptible to incentives or the degree to which they are susceptible, we cannot make optimal use of them in any specific situation. Should we use incentives for maintaining or improving leadership behavior? And how about jobs which are highly challenging and intrinsically rewarding? Are incentives in this situation a cause of mercenary feelings which detract from the main source of reinforcement—the job itself—and ultimately lower job effectiveness? Or do they spur the employees on to yet greater heights? Of course, we do not know; and, even more unfortunately, little research seems to be under way to test assumptions implicitly made by many firms' present compensation policies.

Perceived Importance of Pay

It seems obvious that employees must regard money as a highly desirable commodity before increased amounts of it motivate increased behavfor. Results of studies in this area are extremely confusing because of the almost exclusive dependence on self-reports to estimate the relative importance of pay. For example, when Wilkins (1949, 1950) asked 18- and 19-year-old males at the British Army Reception Center to rank various job incentives on importance, "pay" was placed second only to "friendly workmates." Only 8 percent ranked pay as most important. "Friendly workmates," "security," and "future prospects" all received more first-place rankings than pay. Factor analysis of the responses revealed two broad factors: One was of long-term appeal and included "security," "future prospects," "variety," and "efficient organization." The other factor included "pay," "workmates," "working hours," and "leave." The second factor was interpreted as consisting of items incidental to the job and mainly of short-term appeal. When Wilkins divided the group into high and low intelligence, he found that both "pay" and "workmates" were relatively more important for the low intelligence group —41 percent of the youth in this group gave "workmates" top ranking. He concluded that "a large proportion of such workers would be prepared to accept lower wages if they could be with workmates they liked [1950, p. 562]."

In a study by Watson (1939), employees ranked pay third in importance on a list of eight "morale" factors. However, when their employers were asked to rank the eight factors according to how they thought the employees would respond, pay was selected as the most important factor. This differential perception of the importance of money by employees and higher management has been confirmed in a survey conducted by the National Industrial Conference Board (1947), showing that executives ranking 71 morale factors in terms of overall importance gave top rank to compensation, while fewer than 30 percent of the rank-and-file employees included this among the five most important factors.

Worthy's (1950) analysis of surveys conducted by Sears, Roebuck, and Company over a 12-year period showed that pay ranked eighth among factors related to high morale, whereas rates of pay ranked fourteenth. Over a span of nearly 20 years, Jurgensen[6] has asked applicants for employment with the Minneapolis Gas Company to rank 10 job factors in order of their importance. Now with a total accumulation of over 42,000 cases, he finds that pay has consistently ended up in sixth place. On the other hand, when Ganuli (1954) asked employees in a Calcutta, India, engineering factory to rank eight items relating to working conditions in order of importance, he found that "adequate earnings" was ranked first, above such factors as "job security," "opportunity for promotion," and "personal benefits." Graham and Sluckin (1954) also found pay the most important job factor in a survey of skilled and semiskilled workers in England.

The discrepancies in the above-mentioned studies can be partially explained by the different samples of employees used. One would not expect executives to have the same values and goals as blue-collar workers (nor, for that matter, should it be assumed that executives or blue-collar workers are homogeneous groups in themselves). Another cause of the discrepant findings is the variety in the dimensions of job incentives used. Seldom are the same variables ranked in any two studies. Also, it is probable that many of the factors are not independent. Bendig and Stillman (1958) have criticized the bulk of studies for these last two reasons. They further contended that the factors used were not selected within any theoretical framework of hypothesized dimensions of job incentives. In an attempt to isolate the fundamental dimensions of job incentives, Bendig and Stillman (1958) factor-analyzed eight incentive statements given to college students. They found three orthogonal bipolar factors that they tentatively named "need achievement vs. fear of failure," "interest in the job vs. the job as an opportunity of acquiring status," and "job autonomy of supervision vs. supervisor dependency." Salary loaded highest on "the job as an opportunity for acquiring status," and had small loadings on "fear of failure" and "job autonomy." Still another possible reason for discrepancies in the above studies is that they have failed to assess the degree to which various respondents' job circumstances are or are not providing sufficient rewards in each job area. For example, a respondent who perceives his present pay as adequate may rate pay as relatively less important than he would if he perceived his present pay level to be low. It is probably impossible for respondents to detach themselves sufficiently from their present circumstances to be able to give completely accurate self-report estimates of the relative importance of different job aspects.

While most self-report surveys place salary in a position of only moderate importance, it is easy to find people in industry who *behave* as if they value money highly. Executives strive mightily to advance to high-paying jobs; entertainers work toward more and more lucrative arrangements; bankers embezzle; robbers rob; university professors publish to win increased salary and to enjoy royalty checks. Why is it then that money or pay seldom is ranked commensurate with these behaviors? The answer is not simple, but it may include at least the following possibilities: *(a)* There is probably a social desirability response set pervading the self-reports. The Protestant Ethic is still with us; one may not readily admit that he is running after the almighty dollar without feeling some twinge of conscience which can be dissipated by relegating pay to a relatively low position on the value hierarchy and giving lip service to other more acceptable factors such as "job autonomy" or "intrinsic job satisfaction." *(b)* The reinforcement contingencies present in filling out a self-report questionnaire are quite different from those in the real life situation. It is apparent that an individual is reinforced generously for actually obtaining money, but it is much less evident what the reinforcement contingencies are when he simply *admits* in a self-report checklist that attaining money may be a prime goal. Certainly one is reinforced for engaging in a bit of rationalization while filling out such self-reports. *(c)* Finally, as implied above, people are poor judges (and therefore poor reporters) of what they really want in a job. They do not know with certainty which job factors really attract and hold them; hence they cannot validly describe or rank these job factors.

Thus, research on the valence of money must move beyond the dependency of self-report measures and strive to establish the actual linkages between money and behavior by more sophisticated observational techniques. It is not implied that bankers embezzle *only* for money or that university professors publish *only* for money or that executives strive *only* for money. Money plays a role in all these—a role probably far greater than that suggested by the

[6] Personal communication, 1965.

self-report studies. The self-report studies are based on oversimplified notions tending to ignore the complexities and multidetermined aspects of human behavior. Further accumulation of such rankings or ratings will add little to our understanding of the behavioral effects of compensation. Laboratory studies and experimental observations of the behavioral effects of money are needed here just as in the many other areas we have discussed.

These may, in part, be supplemented with more sophisticated techniques of scaling. Some modification of the paired-comparison technique used by Jones and Jeffrey (1964) in which a more inclusive domain of job incentive aspects are compared against some monetary standard would be a promising start. We should also heed Bendig and Stillman's (1958) plea for the isolation of basic independent job incentive dimensions in future research in order to unify research and allow for cross-study comparisons. In sum, the question, "How do people value money?" will not be answered accurately simply by asking them.

Pay Preferences

Although money *per se* is usually accorded a middle position in any ranking of job factors, different ways of making salary payments are differently preferred. Mahoney (1964) found that managers prefer straight salary over various types of management incentive payments (such as stock options, deferred compensation, etc.). This is in keeping with the results of other surveys. Jaques, Rice, and Hill (1951), for example, reported that the majority of both workers and management in an English factory were in favor of a change from individual piece-rates to hourly wages. Likewise, Davis (1948) found that 60 percent of a sample of building operatives were opposed to incentive schemes, with only 21 percent expressing definite or conditional approval. The main arguments against incentive systems, as reported by Davis, include the fear that the incentive would inhibit other strong and pleasurable motives for working, such as the pleasure of work for its own sake and the solidarity and good fellowship of the working group.

A study conducted by the Michigan Survey Research Center (Larke, 1953) revealed that group incentive payments were favored by fewer than 50 percent of the employees who already were under such plans. Similarly, Mahoney (1964) found that his sample of managers also preferred individual to group pay plans. On the other hand, Wyatt and Marriott (1956) found more approval than disapproval of group incentives by 62 percent of the workers sampled in three factories. With respect to particular types of incentives, Spriegel and Dale (1953) found individual piecework much more popular than group piecework.

Using paired-comparison techniques, Nealey (1963) found that a large sample ($N = 1{,}133$) of electrical workers accorded direct pay increases a lower position than such fringe benefits as sick leave, extra vacation time, or hospital insurance. He also discovered that such preferences do not follow a simple dollar value. For example, dental insurance cost the company less than life insurance but was preferred by more workers. Jones and Jeffrey (1964) asked employees in two electrical equipment plants to make paired comparisons among 16 alternative compensation plans, each characterized by a combination of four features and having identical overall costs to the company. The unique aspect of this study is the possibility of directly comparing the average value of each compensation characteristic with that of a pay raise and, thus, attaching a monetary equivalent to each preferred characteristic. Results showed that the average value of a change from hourly wage to weekly salary is judged to be equivalent to a pay increase of between 1 and 2 cents an hour. A piece-rate incentive plan was perceived as equivalent to a 5- to 10-cent hourly pay increase and was preferred mainly by the skilled workers who already had experience with such a plan. At the nonunion plant, a supervisory merit-rating incentive was considered equal to a 4-cent pay raise. At the union plant, however, the scheme was so disliked that the absence of the plan was considered worth more than a 6-cent hourly raise.

Jones and Jeffrey believed that their approach may have direct bearing upon administrative decisions concerning changes in compensation plans. If the monetary value equivalent of the change, perceived by the worker, substantially exceeds the actual cost to the company of a change in benefits, then it may be considered—if it does not hinder other compensation goals. Basing company compensation policies directly on the measured perceptions of employees regarding the policies also has the additional advantage of designating the pay schemes directly to fit the motive (or preference) systems of the employees being compensated under the plans. The Nealey study and the Jones and Jeffrey study provide rare examples of the analysis of employees' preferences by sophisticated scaling techniques. They well deserve to be emulated by other researchers in this area.

Mahoney (1964, p. 144) concluded that preference for alternative forms of compensation are relatively uniform and that "fine distinctions among alternative forms of compensation probably are considerably less important in managerial motivation than is often suggested." Such preferences should not be the sole criterion for assessing the effects of compensation on motivation if we are mainly interested in actual job behavior, not satisfaction,[7] since the relation between the two is complex and, in many instances, unknown. From stated preferences one cannot easily infer that the compensation program is optimally motivating.

Although there has been a fair amount of research done in determining the pay preferences of managers and other employees, no work has been done on the relation between preference for a particular plan and the actual incentive value of that plan. The implicit, but unwarranted, assumption in all the above-mentioned studies is that if a person has a pay plan he likes, this plan will motivate behavior more than one that he does not like. Although this is an appealing assumption, future studies, in addition to determining employees' pay-plan preferences, should seek to map the relation between such preferences and the incentive value of different plans. The motivation of behavior, *not* the preference for compensation policies, is the prime goal of company pay plans, and research strategies should be directed toward this end.

Concept of Equitable Payment

Several theories have been independently advanced proposing that employees seek a just or equitable return for what they have contributed to the job (Adams, 1963a, 1965; Homans, 1961; Jaques, 1961; Patchen, 1961; Sayles, 1958; Zaleznik, Christenson, & Roethlisberger, 1958). A common feature of these theories is the assumption that compensation either above or below that which is perceived by the employee to be "equitable" results in tension and dissatisfaction due to dissonant cognitions. The tension, in turn, causes the employee to attempt to restore consonance by a variety of behavioral or cognitive methods.

One of the earlier theorists in this area was Homans, who suggested the concept of distributive justice—that is, justice in the way the rewards and costs of activities are distributed among men. He postulated that:

> A man in an exchange relation with another will expect that the rewards of each man be proportional to his costs—the greater the rewards, the greater the costs—and that the net rewards, or profits, of each man be proportional to his investments—the greater the investments, the greater the profits [Homans, 1961, p. 232].

Schematically, then, there is distributive justice when

$$\frac{\text{Person A's rewards minus his costs}}{\text{A's investments}} = \frac{\text{Person B's rewards minus his costs}}{\text{B's investments}}$$

(after Adams, 1965). If the two ratios are unequal, the members of the exchange experience feelings of injustice, one or the other perceiving that he is on the short end in terms of profits. Either member sensing injustice will attempt to bring his profits and investments into line through various behaviors or, perhaps, by changing his perception of the situation.

Homans briefly treated the relation between distributive justice and satisfaction. He proposed that if there is a state of injustice, the person at a disadvantage will "display the emotional behavior we call anger [1961, p. 75]." If, on the other hand, the injustice is in his favor, the person will feel guilty. He implied that the threshold for guilt is higher than that for anger.

Zaleznik et al. (1958) applied Homans' theory to compensation and tested the postulates on 50 production workers. They constructed a reward-investment index to determine whether a worker was receiving an equitable return for his services. When the index was related to worker satisfaction, however, a completely random distribution of high- and low-satisfied workers was found, no matter how favorable the reward-investment index. Since the index was crude and nonempirical, the lack of any relation between satisfaction and distributive justice is not particularly surprising.

Jaques' (1961) theory of equitable payment differs from Homans' mainly in its psychoanalytic orientation. His theory is based on the assumptions that *(a)* there exists "an unrecognized system of norms of fair payment for any given level of work, unconscious knowledge of these norms being shared among the population engaged in employment work [1961, p. 124]"; and that *(b)* an individual is "unconsciously aware" of his own potential capacity for work, as well as the equitable pay level for that work. Jaques claimed that this optimal level of payment is that which allows an optimal consumption of

[7] There is correlational evidence that amount of pay is positively associated with satisfaction with pay (Andrews & Henry, 1963; Lawler & Porter, 1963), job satisfaction (Barnett, Handelsman, Stewart, & Super, 1952; Centers & Cantril, 1946; Marriott & Denerley, 1955; Miller, 1951; Smith & Kendall, 1963; Thompson, 1939; all as reported in Vroom, 1964), and with need satisfaction (Lawler & Porter, 1963; Porter, 1962). However, it is not known to what degree the satisfaction is a result of the level of pay or the changes in job status, duties, and privileges that so often accompany higher pay.

goods and services consistent with "dynamic psychological equilibrium." He stated that equitable payments are accompanied by feelings of satisfaction, but that deviations in payment below or above the equitable level are usually accompanied by feelings of dissatisfaction or uneasiness.

As Vroom (1964) has pointed out, however, Jaques did a rather poor job of scientific reporting. He failed to specify the methods employed in measuring dissatisfaction, the means and variances in his dependent variable, and, frequently, the number of workers on whom various observations were made. Until these and other aspects of Jaques' research are adequately reported, his conclusions, as Vroom indicated, must be regarded with caution.

A third formulation of a theory of equity is found in the work of Patchen (1961). He postulated that equitable payment is achieved when the following two ratios are congruent:

$$\frac{\text{My pay}}{\text{His (their) pay}} \text{ compared to } \frac{\text{My position on dimensions related to pay}}{\text{His (their) position on dimensions related to pay}}$$

A unique aspect of this theory is the concept of potential, or future, perceived equitable payment. This results from the congruence of these ratios:

$$\frac{\text{My pay now}}{\text{His (their) pay now}} \text{ compared to } \frac{\text{My future position on dimensions related to pay}}{\text{His (their) present position on dimensions related to pay}}$$

Thus, although a person perceives a wage comparison as presently equitable, he may still perceive future inequity. This would occur, for example, if the comparison person(s) is someone more skilled, but the person feels he should receive gradual pay increases as his own skill improves—that is, as he becomes more like his comparison person(s) on dimensions related to pay. Such dissonant comparisons may provide a basis for mobility (promotional) aspirations for the person; he may feel that a higher status would be more appropriate for him. Under these circumstances, it is quite possible that dissatisfaction from future perceived inequity may be tolerated.

Substantiation of Patchen's theory comes from interviews with 489 employees in a Canadian oil refinery (Patchen, 1961). The employees were asked to name two persons whose yearly earnings were different from theirs. Those who chose objectively dissonant comparisons (e.g., comparison persons who were of similar status but whose earnings were greater) judged the comparison unsatisfactory. They explained their feelings in terms of dissonance between the wage difference and other related differences. For examples, 75 percent of the employees justified their feelings by pointing out their own equality or superiority with respect to the comparison person on factors directly relevant to pay—such as education, seniority, and skill. Those employees who were satisfied with their comparisons based their feelings of satisfaction on a perceived consonance between the wage difference and other related differences between the workers. Other interesting findings were that men relatively low in pay were less satisfied than others in the comparisons they chose; and, as a worker's mobility chances improved, these men would more frequently choose potentially dissonant comparisons and be more dissatisfied with the idea of remaining below their comparison persons in wages. However, workers who had the best mobility chances *within* the company chose fewer *presently* dissonant comparisons than workers who had the best mobility chances *outside* the company. Since those with good mobility chances within the company were virtually assured of rapid advancement in rank and wages, Patchen believed that the difference between the two groups depended largely upon whether advancement had to be fought for or was largely assured. If it was assured, as typified by the high within-company mobility group, presently dissonant comparisons need not have been chosen as justification for advancement or as a protest against one's present status. These reasons, however, become highly salient when advancement must be earned the hard way.

Further effects of within and outside company wage comparisons are found in Andrews and Henry's (1963) study of 228 managers in five companies. They found that, at a given level of management, overall satisfaction with pay was more highly related to the similarity between the pay of managers in one company and the average pay of managers in the other four companies than to the similarity between their pay and the average pay of other managers in their own company. Together, these two studies suggest that both mobility aspirations and wage comparisons, particularly comparisons outside of one's own company, are important determinants of wage satisfaction. Further studies along these lines should increase our meager knowledge concerning the factors influencing wage comparisons.

The most rigorous and best researched theory of equity is that of Adams (1963a, 1965). His theory is derived mostly from the postulates of Festinger's cognitive dissonance theory (1957) but was influenced also by Stouffer *et al.*'s (1949) earlier work on relative deprivation and by Homans' (1961) research on distributive justice. Adams' most recent definition of inequity stated that

> inequity exists for Person[8] whenever he perceives that the ratio of his outcomes to inputs and the ratio of Other's outcomes to Other's inputs are unequal, either *(a)* when he and Other are in a direct exchange or *(b)* when both are in an exchange relationship with a third party and Person compares himself to Other [1965, p. 22].

This implies, as do all the above-mentioned theories, that an inequitable relation occurs not only when the exchange is not in Person's favor, but when it is to his advantage as well. Adams, like Homans, hypothesized that the thresholds for underreward and overreward differ. Thus, a certain amount of overreward may be written off as "good luck," whereas similar deviations in the direction of underrewards will not be so easily tolerated.

Inputs mentioned in the definition are anything a worker perceives as constituting his contribution to the job—age, skill, education, experience, and amount of effort expended on the job. Outcomes, or rewards from the job, are also dependent upon the worker's perception and would normally include pay, status symbols, intrinsic job satisfaction, and fringe benefits, to mention a few examples.

The existence of equity or inequity is not an all-or-none phenomenon. Many degrees of inequity can be distinguished, and the magnitude of the inequity is assumed to be some increasing monotonic function of the size of the difference between the ratios of outcomes to inputs. Thus, it is not the absolute magnitudes of perceived inputs and outcomes that are important, but rather the discrepancy between the two ratios. Inequity may exist for both Person and Other, so long as each perceives discrepant ratios. The greatest inequity exists when both inputs and outcomes are discrepant.

The presence of inequity creates tension within a person in an amount proportional to the magnitude of the inequity. This tension creates a drive to reduce the inequity feelings, the strength of the drive being proportional to the tension created. Adams (1963a, 1965) suggested several possible avenues of achieving an equitable state. A person may increase or decrease his inputs (e.g., by increasing or decreasing either the quality or quantity of his work); he may increase or decrease his outcomes (by asking for a raise, or by giving part of his pay to charity, for example); he may change his comparison group or cognitively alter its inputs or outcomes, or force it out of the field; he may leave the field himself (by quitting, transferring, or being absent); or he may cognitively distort his own inputs and outcomes. It is not yet clear what principles govern the choice of method for inequity reduction, although Lawler and O'Gara (in press) have recently obtained evidence that the choice is related to such personality "traits" as self-esteem and responsibility.

A series of experiements to test this theory have been undertaken (Adams, 1963a 1963b, 1965; Adams & Jacobsen, 1964; Adams & Rosenbaum, 1962; Arrowood, 1961). These studies have all been directed toward the effects of overcompensation on behavior. In the first of these (Adams & Rosenbaum, 1962), the hypothesis that workers who felt they were overpaid would reduce their feelings of inequity by increasing the amount of work performed was tested. Twenty-two college students were hired to conduct interviews at $3.50 per hour; half of them were made to feel qualified and equitably paid, and the other half were made to feel unqualified and thus overpaid. As predicted, the overpaid group conducted significantly more interviews within the allotted time than did the control group.

It could reasonably be hypothesized that the group made to feel overpaid for the job worked harder because they felt insecure and were afraid of being fired. Another experiment was performed by Arrowood (1961,) reported in Adams, 1963a, 1965) with the same design—but with the addition of a "private" group that was under the impression that their employer would never see their work. Within this private group, the students who felt overcompensated also conducted significantly more interviews than the students who felt equitably compensated, thus showing the predicted effect is still obtained when pains are taken to remove the insecurity motive.

Although it is predicted from the theory that workers overpaid on an hourly basis will increase the quantity of their work, workers overpaid on a piecework basis would actually increase feelings of inequity if they produced more since they would be increasing the amount of their overpayment. Therefore, it was hypothesized that these workers would reduce inequity by reducing the quantity of their output—a procedure which increases inputs and decreases outcomes. Adams and Jacobsen (1964) tested this hypothesis on students hired for a proofreading task. Persons in the overpaid, experimental group were told they were not qualified but would be paid the usual rate of 30 cents per page anyway. Persons in one equitably paid control group were made to feel qualified and were also paid 30 cents

[8] Person is anyone for whom equity or inequity exists. Other is any individual or group used by Person as a referent in social comparisons of what he contributes to and what he receives from an exchange.

per page. Persons in a second equitably paid control group were made to feel unqualified but were paid the more equitable rate of only 20 cents per page. Adams also sought to assess any possible effects due to differing feelings of job security by manipulating the perceived possibility of future employment. This was done because it was reasoned that subjects made to feel overpaid and unqualified might perceive an implication that their tenure was in jeopardy unless they showed they were good workers. Thus, for half the subjects in each group, Adams created a condition in which they perceived that there was something to lose (i.e., insecurity) and for the other half a condition in which they perceived that there was nothing to lose (i.e., relative security). Adams reasoned that if job security were important, the overpaid secure subjects would work fast but carelessly whereas the overpaid insecure subjects ought to work with much greater care.

The index of quantity was the number of pages proofread, and the index of quality was the number of implanted errors detected (each page, averaging 450 words, had an average of 12 errors implanted in the text, such as misspellings or grammatical, punctuational, and typographical errors).

At first glance, the results substantiate the hypothesis. They show that the overpaid, experimental group proofed significantly more implanted errors per page than the two equitably paid groups. The job security manipulation had no significant effect, which was in keeping with the hypothesis that quality and productivity should vary with feelings of equity and not as a function of perceived job security.

It should be noted, however, that quality was not entirely adequately measured in the experiment. Detecting implanted errors is only one possible evidence of quality in proofreading. Another aspect of quality not included in Adams' quality score is the number of words detected as errors, but which were actually correctly spelled or punctuated. If a proofreader detected all of the real errors in a text, but also claimed several words or punctuation marks to be in error when they actually were correct, his stay on the job probably would be short-lived. Yet, in the experiment just described, he would get a perfect quality score because the specification of detecting nonerrors as errors was ignored. Significantly more of these nonerrors were falsely called errors by the overpaid group. If these "errors" had been taken into account, their quality scores would have been considerably lower. It can be argued, of course, that such nonerror detection simply illustrates the increased effort and consciousness that these subjects were devoting to the task, and this would then be further evidence in favor of the theory and of the effectiveness of the experimental manipulation. Even so, the net effect of "correcting" nonerrors is to reduce the job effectiveness of a proofreader; and it is not entirely clear whether this aspect of ineffectiveness was due to the equity manipulation, the different emphasis on detecting errors in two sets of directions,[9] or some interaction of the two.

Recent research (e.g., Freedman, 1963; Leventhal, 1964; Weick & Penner, 1965—all mentioned in Weick, 1965; Linder, 1965) indicates that predictions derived from equity theory in cases of underreward may require modification. All of the above studies showed that underpaid persons work harder, and also like the task more than persons who are overpaid or equitably paid.

Weick (1965) hypothesized that high effort for insufficient pay represents an attempt to raise outcomes, and suggested that proponents of equity theory give greater consideration to the proposition that persons may control their outcomes to reduce inequity. Thus, in the above-mentioned studies, increased satisfaction gained from performing the task may heighten outcomes and bring them more in line with the person's inputs. So far, with the exception of the recent paper by Lawler and O'Gara (in

[9] The two sets of instructions used in the experiment are as follows: First, the overpaid group and the "reduced rate" equitable group were told about their qualifications in the following manner:

"Well, you don't have nearly enough experience of the type we're looking for. We were hoping to find someone who had previously had actual job experience correcting publisher's proofs of a manuscript. It's really important that this be done by someone who is experienced in this sort of work. It takes special training to have the skill necessary to catch all the sorts of errors that can creep into the proofs. They will have to be returned to the publishers soon, and we can't afford to have any mistakes slip by. (Pause) Your score on this proofreading test isn't really satisfactory either. Would you wait here just a moment?" (Brief exit).

After a brief exit by the experimenter, the persons in the overpaid group were told they would be paid the usual rate anyway, whereas the persons in the "reduced rate" equitable group were informed that they would be paid at a lower, more equitable rate. The other group, the qualified equitable group, was instructed as follows:

"This is fine; you're just what we were looking for. You meet all the qualifications that were required, and your score on this proofreaders' test looks very good. So far as pay is concerned, you are probably aware that we pay 30 cents per page This rate is standard for work of this kind done by qualified people." [Adams & Jacobsen, 1964, p. 21.]

The different emphases on quality in the two sets of instructions are obvious; thus, it appears that the first two groups were given very different sets concerning the expectations of the employer about the quality demands of the work to be done. It can still be argued, of course, that the reduced-rate group should then have shown an increase in quality of about the same magnitude as that shown by the overpaid group. We do not believe this would necessarily obtain. It is likely, for example, that the pay reduction would be sufficient to suggest to an "unqualified" subject that his expected poor performance was already being taken into account, and he might then work in accordance with his employer's implied expectation. The confounding of the differing emphases on quality with the equity manipulation in this study seems to us to confuse seriously the interpretation of the results obtained by Adams and Jacobsen.

press), research directed toward testing equity theory has dealt with overpayment, but the effects of insufficient reward are equally important in industry. We hope that more attention is devoted to this area in future research on equity theory.

Several additions to the theory may help to increase its efficiency of prediction. First and most important, there is need for specifying the conditions governing the choice of one mode of resolution over another. The theory itself does not specify any priority of different methods, and, since there are so many potential methods of reducing inequity, the mere prediction that some one of them will occur is not a very useful or meaningful one. Several propositions about the choice of a method have been advanced tentatively by Adams (1965). These include the following hypotheses:

1. Person will maximize positively valent outcomes and the valence of outcomes.
2. He will minimize increasing inputs that are effortful and costly to change.
3. He will resist real and cognitive changes in inputs that are central to his self-concept and to his self-esteem.
4. He will be more resistant to changing cognitions about his own outcomes and inputs than to changing his cognitions about Other's outcomes and inputs.
5. Leaving the field will be resorted to only when the magnitude of inequality is high and other means of reducing it are unavailable [p. 46].

However, the above hypotheses have not yet been tightly incorporated into equity theory. Since so many modes for resolving inequity are possible, the difficulty of specifying exactly when any specific mode may or may not be used renders the theory more "hazy" and less directly testable than we would like to see it. For example, if an overcompensated group failed to show increased input (in the form of higher quantity or quality), might this be regarded as disconfirmation of the theory or merely an instance of the subject's choosing another mode (e.g., altering their perceptions of their own or others' inputs or of the nature of the job being performed) for reducing feelings of inequity? Because the principles specifying the choice of mode have not yet been specified, tightly reasoned deductions cannot yet be derived from the theory.

As implied above, it is quite likely that people differ substantially from one another in the mode they might choose for resolving feelings of inequity; moreover, these differences are undoubtedly a function of individual motive configurations and ability, interest, and personality variables. Lawler and O'Gara (in press) have shown, for example, that persons scoring higher on the Responsibility scale of the California Psychological Inventory (CPI) were less likely to sacrifice quality of work for quantity, when underpaid, than were persons scoring low on the scale. In similar fashion, underpaid persons scoring high on CPI scales of Dominance and Self Assurance were less likely to react with high productivity than those scoring low. Apparently, there are distinct differences in the way different kinds of people respond to feelings of inequity. The incorporation of such variables into the theory may increase its explanatory power. As it stands, the theory ignores individual differences.

Not only may motivational variables determine methods of resolution, but it has been hypothesized that the number and kinds of similarities on which Person compares himself to Other may also affect his choice of how he resolves inequity (Weick, 1965): For example, if a person compares himself with someone who is similar only with respect to education, perhaps education inputs will be the only salient means for resolving inequity when it occurs. Similarly, as Weick pointed out, as comparability increases and Person compares himself to Other with respect to many variables, it is plausible to expect that the intensity of discomfort associated with inequity will change. These two hypotheses, unfortunately, have not yet been investigated.

As it stands, the theory fails to specify methods of resolution relating to various kinds of perceptual alteration. Weick (1965) has pointed out that the theory overlooks such possibilities as denial, differentiation, toleration of the discrepancy, alteration of the object of judgment, bolstering, and task enhancement. This last method seems particularly important. If a person had proportionately low outcomes, task enhancement would be a relatively easy way to increase his outcomes without alienating his coworkers in the process.

One of the major problems with which equity theory must cope, therefore, is the obvious fact of the large number of variables, the complexities of their interaction, and the inadequacy of the operational definitions. Vroom (1964) pointed out that, according to the theory, a worker's satisfaction with his pay is a function of:

1. His beliefs concerning the degree to which he possesses various characteristics;
2. His convictions concerning the degree to which these characteristics should result in the attainment of rewarding outcomes from his job, i.e., their value as inputs;
3. His beliefs concerning the degree to which he receives these rewarding outcomes from his job;
4. His beliefs concerning the degree to which others possess these characteristics;

5. His beliefs concerning the degree to which others receive rewarding outcomes from their jobs; and
6. The extent to which he compares himself with these others [p. 171].

We agree with Vroom's conclusion that the complexity of equity theory makes conclusive tests difficult, and that "a great deal of theoretical and methodological refinement remains to be carried out before this approach can be properly evaluated [1964, p. 172]."

Nonetheless, Adams is to be commended for beginning the difficult task of trying to work through some of the complexities related to an understanding of how pay and employees' perceptions of pay affect the way they work on the job. These early studies on equity, though subject to some criticism, certainly bear the stamp of careful thought and careful experimentation, and we hope that Adams and others will continue in their efforts to explicate more fully some of the questions which have been raised here.

FUTURE RESEARCH

Although it is generally agreed that money is the major mechanism for rewarding and modifying behavior in industry, we have seen that very little is known about how it works. Haire remarked at a recent symposium on managerial compensation that, in spite of the tremendous amount of money spent and the obvious relevance of behavioral theory for compensation practices, there is less research and theory in this area than in almost any other field related to management (Haire, 1965). Similarly, Dunnette and Bass (1963), in a critique of current personnel management practices, pointed out that personnel men have relied on faddish and assumptive practices in administering pay which lack empirical support. One reason for this is the dearth of sound research upon which to base practices. The following are some suggested directions for research which may help to remedy these current deficiencies.

The principal research problem is to discover in what way money motivates employees and how this, in turn, affects their behavior. For this, we must know more about the motives of employees—which motives are dominant, and how employees differ from one another in the configuration of their motives. We must also determine which of these motives can be linked to money as an incentive. Can money be linked with insatiable needs so goal attainment does not cause cessation of behavior? Can money act as an incentive for the "higher order" needs? The two main hypotheses here—that money can serve only "lower order" needs, and that it can serve essentially all needs—have very different implications for compensation practices. Investigation of this question requires not only the discovery of the motives for which money has instrumental value but also the extent to which money can serve to fulfill or satisfy these needs. Quite obviously, money serves to satisfy needs for food, clothing, and shelter, but it is much less obvious how money may be related to such other areas as need Achievement or need Power. It seems obvious that money serves these needs too, but solid evidence of a relationship is lacking. To what extent may money be a primary way of dispensing feelings of achievement, competence, power and the like? In other words, what needs are currently served by money, and what needs, not now perceived as associated with money, may it be called upon to serve? Moreover, we believe that future studies of the effects of money on behavior will prove more fruitful if they are conducted in laboratory or in tightly controlled field settings rather than continuing to depend on survey and self-report instruments as is characteristic of so much of the research now available.

As this review shows, very little is known about the behavioral laws regulating the effectiveness of incentives. We continue to dole out large sums of money under the guise of "incentive pay" without really knowing much about its incentive character. We do not know, for instance, the nature of the effect of a pay raise or the length of time before that effect occurs; or, for that matter, how long the raise may be effective. Nor do we know the optimal reinforcement schedule to be used in giving salary increases for obtaining desired changes in job behavior. A simple monitoring of work outputs on jobs where amount of production is under the direct control of the employee and where it is easily assessed, may provide valuable information here. Such knowledge would have important implications for how often and in what amounts incentive raises should be built into the compensation package.

We also need to investigate the relation between amount of money and the amount of behavior money motivates. Is there some point beyond which increases in compensation are no longer related to increases in relevant behavior? That is, do humans show the same negatively accelerated relation between amount of reward and number of responses that lower organisms display? Or do increases in money "whet the appetite" and lead to behavior that follows some exponential or positively accelerated function?

If we are to effectively manipulate incentives, more information is needed about how they function. Money's incentive character, to be fully understood, must also take account of the perceptions of money by the recipient. For example, if it is assumed that the amount of extra pay needed in a raise before it assumes incentive character is partly determined by the value of a jnd of money, recent evidence (Haire, 1965) shows that not only the amount of money but also how a person perceives his work role are vital factors. Presidents apparently need a larger percentage increase than vice-presidents before they see it as constituting an incentive raise. Is this difference a function of the work role alone? Or do anticipations of future earnings, differences in abilities and dominant motives, and past earning history account for a good share of the variance? So far, these research questions are virtually untapped.

We have seen from Wyatt (1934) that money can be cheapened or lowered in value by the behavior demanded to attain it. To understand more about this relationship, it would be helpful to scale money values against behaviors demanded for money's attainment. This could best be done in a laboratory setting and by using actual workers. Such controlled laboratory experiments have been utilized *almost not at all* with actual employees as subjects. So far, we have depended heavily on rats and psychology sophomores to build a psychology of motivation. We sorely need studies in which real workers are brought into the laboratory and the effects of incentives under different conditions studied.

A very important variable influencing money's effectiveness is the schedule by which it is administered. Of the simple reinforcement schedules, the fixed interval—reinforcement following a fixed period of time after the last reinforced response—leads to notoriously poor performance in lower organisms (Ferster & Skinner, 1957). Yet this is the present pay schedule of most industrial employees. Lower organisms on this schedule tend not to respond very rapidly until just before their "payday." The notable exception to this type of pay schedule in industry occurs for commission salesmen (e.g., life insurance selling) and for entrepreneurs. It is probably worth noting that these two groups contain "workers" who must certainly be viewed as being among the most highly motivated persons in our industrial society.

Although more is known about the simple schedules of reinforcement, the complex schedules—composed of both interval and ratio elements—may be applicable in an industrial setting. In particular, the effects of alternative, conjunctive, and interlocking schedules are worth investigating. With these schedules, it would be possible to follow the suggestion of Haire, Ghiselli, and Porter (1963); that is, divide the paycheck into several parts: so much for tenure, so much for minimum services rendered, so much for excellent performance, etc. For example, about 70 percent of the total available might be given on a fixed interval for minimum services. The rest of the potential pay could be divided and incorporated into different variable ratio schedules, made contingent on outstanding performance.

Finally, evidence seems to indicate that, at various times, employees seek to maximize the amount of their reward, the fairness of their reward, and their acceptance by the group in which they work. The research question is: in which situations, and in what ways is behavior directed toward maximizing one or more of these goals? Which goals are maximized at the expense of others? What are the relative saliences of each goal in differing situations? What are the functional relationships between goals? Which goals account for most of the variance in productivity, and under what conditions? These are vital questions that must be answered before we can effectively utilize incentives.

As research on the role of financial compensation in industrial motivation becomes more and more prevalent, answers to many of the questions posed above should be forthcoming. Increased knowledge should be accompanied by more effective use of money in industry. It is hoped that the firm of the future will be able to establish compensation policies and practices based on empirical evidence about the behavioral effects of money as an incentive rather than on the nontested assumptions, hunches, and time worn "rules-of-thumb" so common in industry today.

REFERENCES

Adams, J. S. Toward an understanding of inequity. *Journal of Abnormal and Social Psychology,* 1963, **67**, 422–36. (a).

Adams, J. S. Wage inequities, productivity, and work quality. *Industrial Relations,* 1963, **3**, 9–16. (b)

Adams, J. S. Injustice in social change. In L. Berkowitz (ed.), *Advances in experimental social psychology.* Vol. 2. New York: Academic Press, 1965, pp. 267–99.

Adams, J. S. and Jacobsen, P. Effects of wage inequities on work quality. *Journal of Abnormal and Social Psychology,* 1964, **69**, 19–25.

Adams, J. S. and Rosenbaum, W. B. The relationship of worker productivity to cognitive dissonance about wage inequities. *Journal of Applied Psychology,* 1962, **46**, 161–64.

Andrews, I. R. and Henry, M. M. Management attitudes toward pay. *Industrial Relations,* 1963, **3**, 29–38.

Arrowood, A. J. Some effects on productivity of justified and unjustified levels of reward under public and private conditions. Unpublished doctoral dissertation, University of Minnesota, 1961.

Atkinson, J. W. (ed.). *Motives in fantasy, action, and society.* Princeton: Van Nostrand, 1958.

Atkinson, J. W. and Reitman, W. R. Performance as a function of motive strength and expectancy of goal attainment. *Journal of Abnormal and Social Psychology*, 1956, **53**, 361–66.

Babchuk, N. and Goode, W. J. Work incentives in a self-determined group. *American Social Review*, 1951, **16**, 679–87.

Barnett, G. J., Handelsman, I., Stewart, L. H., and Super, D. E. The Occupational Level scale as a measure of drive. *Psychological Monographs*, 1952, **66**, (10, Whole No. 342).

Bendig, A. W. and Stillman, E. L. Dimensions of job incentives among college students. *Journal of Applied Psychology*, 1958, **42**, 367–71.

Brown, J. S. Problems presented by the concept of acquired drives. In, *Current theory and research in motivation: A symposium*. Lincoln: University of Nebraska Press, 1953, pp. 1–21.

Brown, J. S. *The motivation of behavior*. New York: McGraw-Hill, 1961.

Burnett, F. *An experimental investigation into repetitive work*. (Industrial Fatigue Research Board Report No. 30) London: His Majesty's Stationery Office, 1925.

Cain, P. A. Individual differences in susceptibility to monotony. Unpublished doctoral dissertation, Cornell University, 1942.

Campbell, H. Group incentive payment schemes: The effects of lack of understanding and group size. *Occupational Psychology*, 1952, **26**, 15–21.

Centers, R. and Cantril, H. Income satisfaction and income aspiration. *Journal of Abnormal and Social Psychology*, 1946, **41**, 64–69.

Cowles, J. T. Food-tokens as incentives for learning by chimpanzees. *Comparative Psychology Monographs*, 1937, **14**, 1–96.

Dale, J. Increase productivity 50 percent in one year with sound wage incentives. *Management Methods*, 1959, **16**, 38–42.

Dalton, M. The industrial "rate-buster": A characterization. *Applied Anthropology*, 1948, **7**, 5–18.

Dalton, M., Collins, O., and Roy, D. Restriction of output and social cleavage in industry. *Applied Anthropology*, 1946, **5** (3), 1–14.

Davis, N. M. Attitudes to work among building operatives. *Occupational Psychology*, 1948, **22**, 56–62.

Dollard, J. and Miller, N. E. *Personality and psychotherapy*. New York: McGraw-Hill, 1950.

Dunnette, M. D. and Bass, B. M. Behavioral scientists and personnel management. *Industrial Relations*, 1963, **2**, 115–30.

Dyson, B. H. Whether direct individual incentive systems based on time-study, however accurately computed, tend over a period to limitation of output. Paper read at Spring Conference, British Institute of Management, London, 1956.

English, H. B. and English, C. A. *A comprehensive dictionary of psychological and psychoanalytical terms*. New York: McKay, 1958.

Ferster, C. B. and DeMeyer, M. K. A method for the experimental analysis of the behavior of autistic children. *American Journal of Orthopsychiatry*, 1962, **32**, 89–98.

Ferster, C. B. and Skinner, B. F. *Schedules of reinforcement*. New York: Appleton-Century-Crofts, 1957.

Festinger, L. *A theory of cognitive dissonance*. Evanston, Ill.: Row, Peterson, 1957.

Festinger, L. How attitudes toward compensation change with promotion. In R. Andrews (ed.), *Managerial compensation*. Ann Arbor: Foundation for Research on Human Behavior, 1965, pp. 19–20.

Fleishman, E. A. A relationship between incentive motivation and ability level in psychomotor performance. *Journal of Experimental Psychology*, 1958, **56**, 78–81.

Freedman, J. L. Attitudinal effects of inadequate justification. *Journal of Personality*, 1963, **31**, 371–85.

Ganuli, H. C. An inquiry into incentives for workers in an engineering factory. *Indian Journal of Social Work*, 1954, **15**, 30–40.

Gellerman, S. W. *Motivation and productivity*. New York: American Management Association, 1963.

Georgopoulos, B. S., Mahoney, G. M., and Jones, N. W. A path-goal approach to productivity. *Journal of Applied Psychology*, 1957, **41**, 345–53.

Ghiselli, E. E. The effects on career pay of policies with respect to increases in pay. In R. Andrews (ed.), *Managerial compensation*. Ann Arbor: Foundation for Research on Human Behavior, 1965, pp. 21–34.

Graham, D. and Sluckin, W. Different kinds of reward as industrial incentives. *Research Review, Durham*, 1954, **5**, 54–6.

Grice, G. R. and Davis, J. D. Effect of irrelevant thirst motivation on a response learned with food reward. *Journal of Experimental Psychology*, 1957, **53**, 347–52.

Haire, M. The incentive character of pay. In R. Andrews (ed.), *Managerial compensation*. Ann Arbor: Foundation for Research on Human Behavior, 1965, pp. 13–17.

Haire, M., Ghiselli, E. E., and Porter, L. W. Psychological research on pay: An overview. *Industrial Relations*, 1963, **3**, 3–8.

Harlow, H. F. Comments on Professor Brown's paper. In, *Current theory and research in motivation*. Lincoln: University of Nebraska Press, 1953, pp. 22–23.

Herzburg, F., Mausner, B., and Snyderman, B. *The motivation to work*. (2nd ed.) New York: Wiley, 1959.

Hickson, D. J. Motives of work people who restrict their output. *Occupational Psychology*, 1961, **35**, 110–21.

Holland, J. G. and Skinner, B. F. *The analysis of behavior*. New York: McGraw-Hill, 1961.

Homans, G. C. *Social behavior: Its elementary forms*. New York: Harcourt, Brace & World, 1961.

Jaques, E. *Equitable payment*. New York: Wiley, 1961.

Jaques, E., Rice, A. K., and Hill, J. M. The social and psychological impact of a change in method of wage payment. *Human Relations*, 1951, **4**, 315–40.

Jones, L. V. and Jeffrey, T. E. A quantitative analysis of expressed preferences for compensation plans. *Journal of Applied Psychology,* 1964, **49**, 201–10.

Kaufman, H. Task performance, expected performance, and responses to failure as functions of imbalance in the self-concept. Unpublished doctoral dissertation, University of Pennsylvania, 1962.

Kelleher, R. T. and Gollub, L. R. A review of positive conditioned reinforcement. *Journal of the Experimental Analysis of Behavior,* 1962, **5**, 543–97.

Larke, A. G. Workers' attitudes on incentives. *Dun's Review and Modern Industry,* Dec. 1953, 61–63.

Lawler, E. E., III. Managers' job performance and their attitudes toward their pay. Unpublished doctoral dissertation, University of California, Berkeley, 1964.

Lawler, E. E., III. Managerial perceptions of compensation. Paper read at Midwestern Psychological Association convention, Chicago, April 1965.

Lawler, E. E., III and O'Gara, P. W. The effects of inequity produced by underpayment on work output, work quality, and attitudes toward the work. *Journal of Personality and Social Psychology,* in press.

Lawler, E. E., III and Porter, L. W. Perceptions regarding management compensation. *Industrial Relations,* 1963, **3**, 41–49.

Leventhal, G. S. Reward magnitude and liking for instrumental activity: Further test of a two-process model. Unpublished manuscript, Yale University, 1964.

Linder, D. E. Some psychological processes which mediate task liking. Unpublished doctoral dissertation, University of Minnesota, 1965.

Mahoney, T. Compensation preferences of managers. *Industrial Relations,* 1964, **3**, 135–44.

March, J. G. and Simon, H. A. *Organizations.* New York: Wiley, 1958.

Marriott, R. Size of working group and output. *Occupational Psychology,* 1949, **23**, 47–57.

Marriott, R. Socio-psychological factors in productivity. *Occupational Psychology,* 1951, **25**, 15–24.

Marriott, R. *Incentive payment systems: A review of research and opinion.* London: Staples Press, 1957.

Marriott, R. and Denerley, R. A. A method of interviewing used in studies of workers' attitudes: II. Validity of the method and discussion of the results. *Occupational Psychology,* 1955, **29**, 69–81.

Mathewson, S. B. *Restriction of output among unorganized workers,* New York: Viking Press, 1951.

Miller, D. C. and Form, W. H. *Industrial sociology.* New York: Harper, 1951.

Myers, C. S. *Mind and work.* London: University of London Press, 1920.

National Industrial Conference Board. Factors affecting employee morale. (Studies in Personnel Policy No. 85) New York: Author, 1947.

Nealey, S. Pay and benefit preferences. *Industrial Relations,* 1963, **1**, 17–28.

Opinion Research Corporation. *Productivity from the worker's standpoint.* Princeton: Author, 1949.

Patchen, M. *The choice of wage comparisons.* Englewood Cliffs, N.J.: Prentice-Hall, 1961.

Porter, L. W. Job attitudes in management: I. Perceived deficiencies in need fulfilment as a function of job level. *Journal of Applied Psychology,* 1962, **46**, 375–84.

Rath, A. A. The case for individual incentives. *Personnel Journal,* 1960, **39**, 172–75.

Roethlisberger, F. J. and Dickson, W. J. *Management and the worker.* Cambridge: Harvard University Press, 1939.

Roy, D. Quota restriction and gold bricking in a machine shop. *American Journal of Sociology,* 1952, **57**, 427–42.

Ryan, R. A. and Smith, P. C. *Principles of industrial psychology.* New York: Ronald Press, 1954.

Sayles, L. R. *Behavior of industrial work groups: Prediction and control.* New York: Wiley, 1958.

Schleh, E. C. *Management by results: The dynamics of profitable management.* New York: McGraw-Hill, 1961.

Selekman, B. M. Living with collective bargaining. *Harvard Business Review,* 1941, **22**, 21–23.

Shimmin, S., Williams, J., and Buck, L. Studies of some factors in incentive payment systems. Report to the Medical Research Council. London: Industrial Psychology Research Group, 1956. (Mimeo).

Skinner, B. F. *Science and human behavior.* New York: Macmillan, 1953.

Smith, P. C. The curve of output as a criterion of boredom. *Journal of Applied Psychology,* 1953, **37**, 69–47.

Smith, P. C. The prediction of individual differences in susceptibility to industrial monotony. *Journal of Applied Psychology,* 1955, **39**, 322–29.

Smith, P. C. and Kendall, L. M. Cornell Studies of job satisfaction: VI: Implications for the future. Unpublished manuscript, Cornell University, 1963.

Spriegel, W. R. and Dale, A. G. Trends in personnel selection and induction. *Personnel,* 1953, **30**, 169–75.

Stouffer, S. A., Suchman, E. A., DeVinney, L. C., Star, S. A., and Williams, R. M. *The American Soldier: Adjustment during army life.* Vol. 1. Princeton, N.J.: Princeton University Press, 1949.

Thompson, W. A. Eleven years after graduation. *Occupations,* 1939, **17**, 709–14.

Verplanck, W. S. and Hayes, J. R. Eating and drinking as a function of maintenance schedule. *Journal of Comparative and Physiological Psychology,* 1953, **46**, 327–33.

Viteles, M. S. *Motivation and morale in industry.* New York: Norton, 1953.

Vroom, V. H. *Work and motivation.* New York: Wiley, 1964.

Watson, G. Work satisfaction. In G. W. Hartmann and T. Newcomb (eds.), *Industrial conflict.* New York: Cordon Co., 1939, pp. 114–24.

Weick, K. E. The concept of equity in the perception of pay.

Paper read at Midwestern Psychological Association, April, 1965.

Weick, K. E. and Penner, D. D. Comparison of two sources of inadequate and excessive justification. Unpublished manuscript, Purdue University, 1965.

Whyte, W. F. Economic incentives and human relations. *Harvard Business Review,* 1952, **30**, 73–80.

Whyte, W. F. *Money and motivation: An analysis of incentives in industry.* New York: Harper, 1955.

Wike, E. L. and Barrientos, G. Secondary reinforcement and multiple drive reduction. *Journal of Comparative and Physiological Psychology,* 1958, **51**, 640–43.

Wilkins, L. T. Incentives and the young worker. *Occupational Psychology,* 1949, **23**, 235–47.

Wilkins, L. T. Incentives and the young male worker in England. *International Journal of Opinion and Attitude Research,* 1950, **4**, 541–62.

Wolfe, J. B. Effectiveness of token-rewards for chimpanzees. *Comparative Psychology Monographs,* 1936, **12**, No. 60, 1–72.

Worthy, J. C. Factors influencing employee morale. *Harvard Business Review,* 1950, **28**, 61–73.

Wyatt, S. *Incentives in repetitive work: A practical experiment in a factory.* (Industrial Health Research Board Report No. 69) London: His Majesty's Stationery Office, 1934.

Wyatt, S. and Fraser, J. S. *The comparative effects of variety and uniformity in work.* (Industrial Fatigue Research Board Report No. 52) London: His Majesty's Stationery Office, 1929.

Wyatt, S., Fraser, J. A., and Stock, F. G. L. *The effects of monotony in work.* (Industrial Fatigue Research Board Report No. 56) London: His Majesty's Stationery Office, 1929.

Wyatt, S. and Langdon, J. N. *Fatigue and boredom in repetitive work.* (Industrial Health Research Board Report No. 77) London: His Majesty's Stationery Office, 1937.

Wyatt, S. and Marriott, R. *A study of attitudes to factory work.* Her Majesty's Stationery Office, 1956.

Zaleznik, A., Christenson, C. R., and Roethlisberger, F. J. *The motivation, productivity, and satisfaction of workers: A prediction study.* Boston: Harvard University, Graduate School of Business Administration, 1958.

34. THE ROLE OF PAY IN ORGANIZATIONS*

Edward E. Lawler, III†

In the last fifty years, scholars have advanced a number of rather completely developed yet different approaches to organization management (see, e.g., Miles, 1965; Scott, 1961). All of these approaches deal to some extent with pay administration. Not surprisingly, they tend to assign pay relatively different roles. The scientific management approach, for example, assigns it the primary role in motivating employees to follow the orders of their superiors, while modern management theory tends to ignore pay almost entirely or to see it as only one of a large number of possible influences on motivation (see e.g., Likert, 1961). Probably the one issue which should be considered by all organization theories is the relationship between pay and performance. Time and time again the issue has come up as a crucial issue in our discussion of pay and organizational effectiveness. No theory of organization can be said to be complete unless it deals with this issue. If the decision is made to try to relate pay to performance, then the issue of how this can be accomplished must also be dealt with. It is a difficult problem and one that is not adequately dealt with by most theorists.

Given our discussion of pay, it is difficult to argue with the view that relating pay to performance can contribute to organizational effectiveness. But it is also clear that under some conditions (e.g., subjective criteria, low trust) it cannot be done effectively. When pay is tied to performance, it can motivate performance. In addition, satisfaction will be related to performance, and as a result, turnover and absenteeism will be lower among high performers. Further, tying pay to performance leads to high pay satisfaction. Finally, it can increase the importance of pay. Figure 1 shows that tying pay to performance influences all the major psychological issues that have been discussed in this book. It also shows that an organization can realize a number of tangible benefits from relating the two closely.

THEORIES OF ORGANIZATION AND PAY

Not all theories of organization argue that pay should be tied to performance. Those that do differ widely on how they say this should be done and on how important they feel it is that it be done. Figure 2 shows one way of classifying the different approaches to administering pay in an organization.

* From: Edward E. Lawler, III, *Pay and Organizational Effectiveness: A Psychological View,* McGraw-Hill Book Co., 1971. Copyright held by and permission to reprint granted by McGraw-Hill, Inc.

† University of Michigan.

FIGURE 1 EFFECTS OF RELATING AND NOT RELATING PAY TO PERFORMANCE

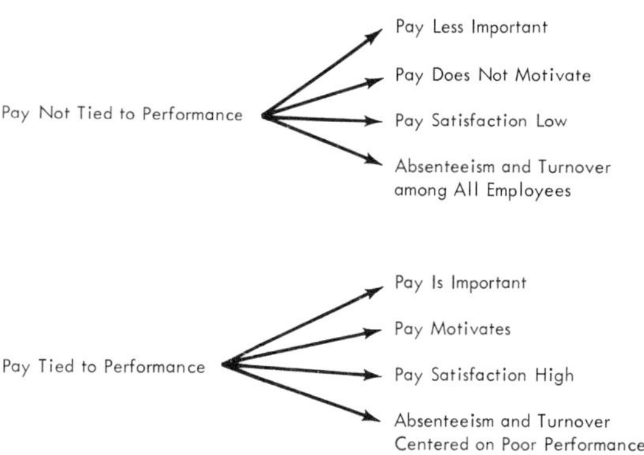

It presents a four-cell table that divides approaches according to whether they tie pay to performance and according to whether pay is administered on a democratic or an authoritarian basis.

In Figure 2 the names of different approaches to management and organizations are placed in three of the four cells. Paternalistic management is placed

FIGURE 2 MANAGEMENT STYLE AND THE RELATIONSHIP BETWEEN PAY AND PERFORMANCE

	Approach to administering rewards	
	Authoritarian	Democratic
Pay not related to performance	Paternalism	Human relations Socialism
Pay related to performance	Scientific management	

in the cell where authoritarian control is practiced and pay is not related to performance. This approach is called paternalistic because of the dependency relationship this type of pay administration creates between employer and employee and because, like the parent, the employer gives rewards for things other than performance. Scientific management falls under the approach of autocratically tying pay to performance: Taylor's work emphasizes the primary role of management in setting piece rates and tying pay to performance. There clearly is no room in Taylor's system for employee participation in discussions about how pay should be administered. Using democratic or participative management but not tying pay to performance is called the "human relations" or "socialist management" approach. In one sense, neither of these labels perfectly fits this approach to administering pay. There is a strong current of this kind of thinking in the writing of most writers who are identified with the human relations movement (e.g., Mayo, Roethlisberger), and certainly there is an element of this kind of thinking in the socialist management approach. The socialist approach stresses involving the workers in administrative decisions and relating their pay more to their needs than to their performance.

The name of no management style appears in the cell in which pay is democratically tied to performance. The reason for this is simple: none of the currently identifiable approaches to management have articulated this point of view adequately. The spirit of this approach is partially contained in the writings of many of the modern organization theorists. They are, however, far from unanimous in expressing this orientation toward pay administration. Many of them are more interested in the motivating power of higher-order needs, the importance of self-control, and the inappropriateness of the pyramidal structure.

Writers like Argyris (1964), Haire (1956), and McGregor (1960, 1967) are the exceptions here. They emphasize the importance of tying pay to performance, and they also express a preference for participative management. But even these writers put forward only tentative views of how pay and performance are to be related. Typically, they single out the Scanlon Plan for praise and cite it as an example of what can be done. The Scanlon Plan is an interesting effort in this direction. Clearly, however, there are problems associated with it, and it is not universally applicable.

Most modern organization theorists concentrate their fire on building an organization in which people will be motivated by intrinsic rewards such as a desire for growth and competence. Indeed, as Schein (1965) has stated, they are concerned with motivating "self-actualizing man." There is, of course, some validity to this view, just as there is validity to the view of scientific management. Schein has said that organization theorists should think in terms of what he calls "complex" man. Such a view of man is necessary, particularly if we wish to see the role of pay in its proper perspective—somewhere between the high place given it by scientific management and the low place given it by many of the human relations movement writes. The research evidence reviewed in this book shows that pay is important and that, if related to performance, it can contribute to organizational effectiveness. Still some organizations probably should not try to relate pay to performance, and among those that should, widely different approaches are needed. As we shall see, such things as the climate, technology and structure of an organization strongly influence whether and how pay should be related to performance.

ORGANIZATION CLIMATE AND PAY

The pay system in an organization must, above all, fit the human relations climate of that organization. Although it makes some sense to talk about general principles of pay administration, specific procedures must fit the conditions that exist in a particular organization. Consider for a moment the suggestion that salaries be made public. In the kind of organization that generally adopts a democratic or participative approach to management, this practice should develop naturally. As employees begin to participate more in evaluating themselves and others, they will gradually come to know other people's salaries, as well as the general pay structure of the organization. On the other hand, in an autocratically run organization the policy of openness just will not fit. Salary openness demands trust, open discussion of performance, and justification of salaries. None of these are likely to occur in an authoritarian organization. They are, however, an integral part of a democratic approach to management. Participative performance appraisal is another practice that is necessary if salary is to be clearly tied to performance. It too is likely to fit well in a participative, but not in an authoritarian, style of management. Similarly, widespread employee participation in a job evaluation program should present no problem in an organization that practices participative management day in and day out; but in one that does not, it may be quite impossible.

Piece rate plans with rates set by industrial engineers and other "semiautomated" payment plans were developed within the context of scientific management. Traditionally, such plans have been established as a management control device. Only with the advent of unions were workers given some say in how they were set up and administered. The fact that piece rate plans have typically been run in an authoritarian manner does not, of course, mean that they have to be. They could fit into a democratic approach to management if they were participatively developed and if greater self-control were built into the system. These plans are so strongly identified with more traditional styles of management, however, that it is difficult to convince people that they can be democratically administered. In fact, the traditional association of incentive pay and authoritarian management may account for the slight attention that many modern organization theorists have given to incentive plans.

What kind of pay incentive plan will work in an organization run on traditional lines? The evidence reviewed in this book suggests that the more "objectively" based the plan, the more likely it is to be successful. Plans that tie pay to "hard" criteria, such as quantity of output, profits, or sales, and thus require a minimum level of trust, stand a much better chance of succeeding in the traditional organization than approaches which depend on joint goal setting and soft criteria. Piece rate plans that are administered in a consistent and fair manner and have rates that are set fairly do work sometimes. So do sales bonuses for salesmen and profitsharing plans in small organizations. But where trust is low, these plans seldom reach their full potential.

The problem for traditional organizations occurs in jobs where there are no hard criteria for measuring performance and where trust and participation are needed if pay is to act as an incentive. Here, the traditionally managed organization has difficulty in getting pay to work as a motivator because the conditions are not right for participative performance appraisal and joint goal setting. In this kind of job situation, a Theory Y organization is in a better position to use pay to motivate performance than is the traditional scientific management approach. In such job situations, this approach, which is built upon the idea of using pay as an incentive, cannot be used because it does not believe in employee participation or the other power-equalization approaches to management. On the other hand, many of the newer approaches to organization theory—approaches which were not designed to rely on pay to motivate—can use it. Many modern organization theorists do not capitalize on this advantage of their approach by actually saying how pay can be used to motivate performance within their system.

In summary, it has been argued that one of the factors which influences the type of pay plan an organization can use is the human relations climate or management style that exists in the organization. For illustrative purposes, organizations characterized by an authoritarian style of management were contrasted with those characterized by a more participative approach. It was stressed that the potential for using pay to motivate performance is greater in the latter than in the former, despite the fact that the authoritarian approach has given greater emphasis to the use of pay to motivate performance.

TECHNOLOGY AND PAY

The human relations climate that exists in an organization is only one of the factors that determine how appropriate different pay plans will be. Certainly, the kind of product that is being produced must be considered, since it influences how an organization is technically organized, and this in turn influences the appropriateness of different pay plans.

Woodward (1965) distinguishes among industrial

organizations that engage in mass production, unit production, and process production. Piece rate incentives probably can be used in unit and mass production plants, but they hardly make sense in a process production firm. Plantwide bonuses would seem to be well suited to many process production plants but not to most unit and mass production plants. This difference arises because of the difficulty of identifying individual contributions in process production. If we expand our discussion to include nonindustrial professionally staffed service organizations, such as hospitals and schools, this point becomes even more obvious. Neither of these types of organizations could use piece rate plans or organizationwide bonuses. They could, perhaps, use a system based upon participative performance appraisals and joint goal setting if the climate were right.

In short, the type of product an organization produces influences the technology and production method of the organization. Production methods in turn differ in the degree to which individual performance is identifiable and measurable, as well as in the degree to which cooperation among the members of the organization is necessary. Because of this, organizations that differ in the kinds of products they produce need different pay systems, even though they may be similar in other ways. For example, it has been stressed that group plans lead to cooperation. In process production plants where cooperation is important and individual performance is difficult to measure, a group plan makes sense. In a consulting firm, however, where cooperation probably is not so important and individual performance is measurable, a more individualized plan makes sense, but not a piece rate plan, since individual performance in this situation probably does not lend itself to piece measurement.

ORGANIZATION STRUCTURE AND PAY

In addition to the human relations climate and technological factors, other characteristics affect the kind of pay system that will be appropriate for an organization. Size is a crucial variable. Another is the degree of centralization. Small organizations can do things that large organizations cannot. They can, for example, use incentive and bonus pay plans that are based upon organizationwide performance. In a small organization, most employees will feel that their behavior affects the performance of the total organization. In a large organization this is not likely to be so (except at the very top), and as a result an organizationwide plan is not likely to motivate performance. Pressures toward uniform policy statements and systematic pay and appraisal practices are also more prevalent in large organizations. Thus, it is more difficult to tailor an individual's pay package to his own situation. This is unfortunate, because much can be gained by individualizing fringe benefit packages and setting up individual pay incentive plans. People differ in how frequently they should be evaluated, in how they should be evaluated, and in the kind of pay system (i.e., bonus increase, stock options) that is most likely to motivate them. Using individualized pay programs to capitalize on these differences is difficult in large organizations because they entail tremendous increases in administrative overhead. They can be installed, however, in small organizations. In short, small organizations have a potential advantage over large organizations because they have more options open to them.

The degree of centralization-decentralization is relevant to pay administration because it affects the kind of performance criteria data that are available. In a centralized organization, for example, the performance of a subpart, or a particular plant, is often difficult to measure unless a decentralized responsibility-based accounting system is used. Even if it is possible to measure an individual plant's performance, this is often not a good criterion upon which to base pay, because the plant employees often are not in control of the plant. As a result they do not feel responsible for the plant's performance. If substantial decision-making power is vested in the central office, local plant management can hardly be evaluated on the basis of how the plant performs. In fact, the management may resent being evaluated on this basis. This is not true when decision making is decentralized and accounting data are gathered on subparts of the organization. This point is particularly important in a large organization. It means that pay plans that use large group, plantwide, or divisionwide performance as a criterion are practical only if the organization is to some extent decentralized. It is only within the context of a decentralized organization that this type of criterion can be meaningful.

Compared with firms with centralized authority, decentralized organizations have more pay administration options. As has already been mentioned, they can more easily use plantwide and subunitwide plans. In addition, they can more easily tolerate different pay practices in different parts of the organization. In fact, decentralization would seem to encourage different parts of an organization to establish different pay practices, while centralization would seem to discourage such tailoring. To the extent that it makes sense to tailor pay plans to fit the organization—which is the thesis on which this chapter is based—decentralization should have the advantage over centralization.

Table 1 attempts to summarize the points made so

TABLE 1 RELEVANCE OF FOUR ORGANIZATIONAL FACTORS TO PAY PLANS

Human relations climate	Authoritarian	Need objective hard criteria; pay clearly tied to performance
	Democratic	Can use participative goal setting and softer criteria
Production type	Mass and unit	Can usually develop hard criteria; rewards on individual or small group basis
	Process	Need to encourage cooperation; individual performance not highly visible or measurable
	Professional organizations (i.e., hospital, school, consulting firms)	Individually based plans; soft criteria; high individual involvement in own evaluation
Size	Large	Organizationwide bonuses poor for all but a few top-level managers
	Small	Organizationwide bonuses possible in some situations
Degree of centralization	Centralized	Hard to base performance on subunit (i.e., plant) performance
	Decentralized	Pay can be based on profit center or subunit performance for members of management

far on the relevance of organization factors to pay plans. The human relations climate of an organization, the type of production it engages in, its size, and its degree of centralization—all affect the kind of pay system that is appropriate for an organization. Each of these factors limits the possible types of merit pay plan that can be successfully used. Only certain kinds of plans are appropriate for large organizations, for example, and only certain kinds are appropriate for mass production organizations. In order to state what kind of plan can be used in a specific organization, one must classify the organization according to each of the four variables listed in Table 1. An organization might, for example, practice authoritarian management, engage in mass production, and be large and centralized. The pay plan that is appropriate for this organization is determined by all these factors. In other words, the plan that is chosen for this firm must be one that cannot be ruled out on the basis of any of these four characteristics.

Since each of the factors (being of a certain size, having a highly centralized administration, etc.) serves to rule out some kinds of pay plans, it is possible that for some organizations there is no pay plan that can be labeled appropriate. Table 2 shows this by listing all the types of organizations that can be identified, using the crude classification system developed here. As indicated, in some (e.g., authoritarian, centralized, large, and professionally staffed service organizations), there is simply no type of merit or performance-based pay system that is appropriate. In these organizations, it is advisable not to try to base pay on performance, and to pay on the basis of attendance and membership. In fact, in many types of organizations there is no really satisfactory merit pay system, but it is possible to design merit pay systems that will be adequate (e.g., most authoritarian organizations).

The most important point that Table 2 illustrates is that pay systems exist in the context of organizations and that the characteristics of the organizations must be taken into account when pay systems are developed. No one pay system will fit all organizations; there are too many situational factors that must be considered. Our discussion has emphasized only a few of the most salient. There are others which, if considered, would fruther complicate the thinking shown in Table 2 (e.g., age of company, hiring policies, characteristics of workers). One of the problems with the research on pay is that little of it has tried to identify the relevant situational factors and to elaborate on their treatment. There is a good deal of research showing what basic conditions must exist if pay is to motivate (e.g., it must be important, and it must be related to performance) and what must happen if people are to be satisfied with their pay (e.g., inputs must match outcomes). Missing, however, is "developmental" research (Haire, 1964)—that is, research concerned with (1) how these broad principles can be applied to the situations existing in particular organizations and (2) what the specific situational factors are that determine how the principles can be converted into practice. However, investigators are showing a growing tendency to do re-

TABLE 2 APPROPRIATE MERIT PAY PLANS FOR VARIOUS TYPES OF ORGANIZATIONS

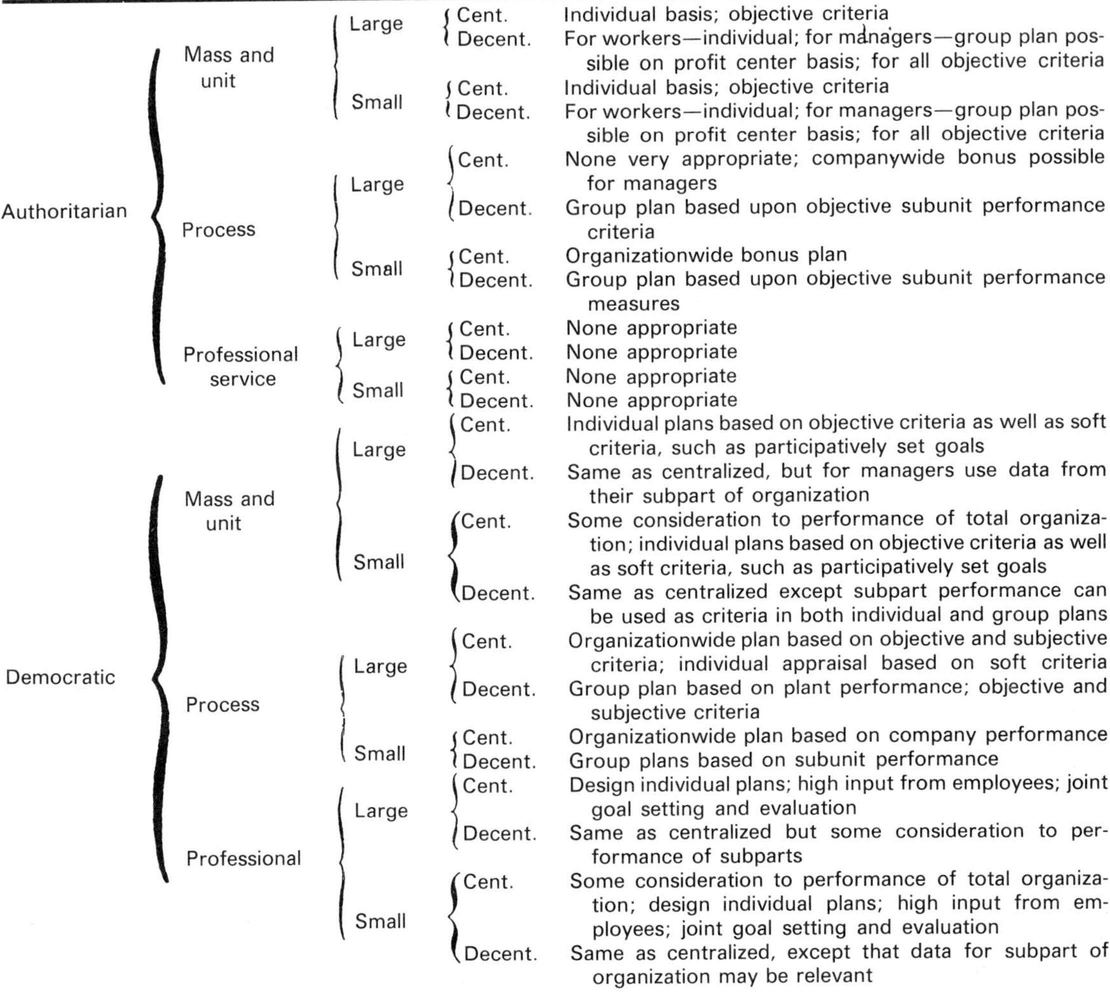

Climate	Technology	Size	Structure	Appropriate merit pay plan
Authoritarian	Mass and unit	Large	Cent.	Individual basis; objective criteria
			Decent.	For workers—individual; for managers—group plan possible on profit center basis; for all objective criteria
		Small	Cent.	Individual basis; objective criteria
			Decent.	For workers—individual; for managers—group plan possible on profit center basis; for all objective criteria
	Process	Large	Cent.	None very appropriate; companywide bonus possible for managers
			Decent.	Group plan based upon objective subunit performance criteria
		Small	Cent.	Organizationwide bonus plan
			Decent.	Group plan based upon objective subunit performance measures
	Professional service	Large	Cent.	None appropriate
			Decent.	None appropriate
		Small	Cent.	None appropriate
			Decent.	None appropriate
Democratic	Mass and unit	Large	Cent.	Individual plans based on objective criteria as well as soft criteria, such as participatively set goals
			Decent.	Same as centralized, but for managers use data from their subpart of organization
		Small	Cent.	Some consideration to performance of total organization; individual plans based on objective criteria as well as soft criteria, such as participatively set goals
			Decent.	Same as centralized except subpart performance can be used as criteria in both individual and group plans
	Process	Large	Cent.	Organizationwide plan based on objective and subjective criteria; individual appraisal based on soft criteria
			Decent.	Group plan based on plant performance; objective and subjective criteria
		Small	Cent.	Organizationwide plan based on company performance
			Decent.	Group plans based on subunit performance
	Professional	Large	Cent.	Design individual plans; high input from employees; joint goal setting and evaluation
			Decent.	Same as centralized but some consideration to performance of subparts
		Small	Cent.	Some consideration to performance of total organization; design individual plans; high input from employees; joint goal setting and evaluation
			Decent.	Same as centralized, except that data for subpart of organization may be relevant

search on the psychology of pay. It is hoped that the trend will continue and that this kind of research problem will be attacked.

PAY AS A CHANGE AGENT

The discussion so far has emphasized the important relationship between organization climate and pay administration. We have said that the kind of climate that exists very much limits the kind of pay practices that an organization can use. Further, we have assumed that pay practices must be adjusted to fit the climate. This assumption is open to question. Is it not possible that the pay system can change the climate? There is some evidence that this has happened in companies that have tried the Scanlon Plan and the Lincoln Electric Plan. The installation of these plans seemed to help the organizations move toward a more democratic style of management. In effect, the pay plans seemed to be agents of change.

It is not difficult to see how pay administration policies can affect organization climate. Pay is important to people, and decisions about pay are carefully watched by everyone in an organization. Pay is a common language shared by all, and because of this it is a medium through which an organization can communicate with all its employees. Thus, pay practices can influence the whole climate of the organization. Pay administration is one place where management philosophy can be clearly and immediately converted into action. It is a concrete manifestation of leadership and management style. Because of this, changes in pay policy can be a direct indication to employees of a change in management thinking or management style. Actually delivering on promised pay raises or merit increases, for example, can be concrete evidence that management means what it says. Such acts can increase the credibility of management and potentially lead to greater trust between management and workers. Actually involving workers in pay decisions is a clear way to indicate that management is moving toward a more democratic climate. Similarly, giving employees a share of company profits is a clear way to indicate that the organization wants to establish a climate in which employee-employer relations are characterized by trust, cooperation, and, indeed, respect.

Little research has been done on the use of pay as a change agent in organizations. With the exception of the Scanlon Plan and a few others, pay plans simply have not been thought of as a way of changing organizations. This is unfortunate because potentially pay administration represents a powerful tool for effecting change. Interest in organization change at this time emphasizes interpersonal issues rather than structural changes. The typical change program seems to begin with management training, using T-groups, grid sessions, role playing, etc. This may be the best approach in many organizations, but in others, changes in organization policy or procedures may be better. At present, we know very little about which approach is more effective. In particular, we know little about when to choose a specific approach.

Even when an organization decides that the pay system is not a good place to start a change effort, it is important that the pay system not be forgotten or overlooked. In the long run, an anachronistic or inappropriate pay system can be a powerful retarding force. For example, where an attempt is being made to change toward a more participative style of management, keeping the traditional pay plan can slow progress considerably. Unfortunately, many attempts at organizational change have concentrated only on revising leadership styles or increasing interpersonal competence. For maximum effectiveness these changes should be accompanied by changes in the pay system; changes in the pay system can reinforce the other changes and make it clear that they are not just another management gimmick. Money speaks, and administered in a traditional way, it can say that an avowed move toward participative management is not sincere; administered in new ways, it can say that a real change is taking place. It is hoped that, as more is learned about the psychological aspects of pay administration, more people interested in organizational change will see pay system changes as an important element in any change effort.

SUMMARY

The major theme of this chapter has been that a pay plan must fit the characteristics of an organization if it is to be effective; it must be individualized in terms of organization size, management style, etc. There are two ways organizations and pay systems can be matched. First, the task can be viewed as a problem of choosing the correct pay plan for an organization, taking into account the characteristics of the organization as it is presently administered. But as the last part of the chapter emphasized, there is a second way. Instead of fitting the plan to the organization, management can change the organization to fit the plan. The pay plan can be viewed as a stimulant or lever to effect change in the organization. A pay plan can be used to initiate movement toward a more participative management style. This can be done but we are just beginning to understand the process. The key would seem to be in choosing a pay plan that will start the organization moving and reinforce any movement that is made.

REFERENCES

Argyris, C. *Intergrating the individual and the organization.* New York: Wiley, 1964.

Haire, M. *Psychology in management.* New York: McGraw-Hill, 1956.

Haire, M. The social sciences and management practices. *California Management Review,* 1964, 6(4), 3–10.

Likert, R. *New patterns of management.* New York McGraw-Hill, 1961.

McGregor, D. *The human side of enterprise.* New York: McGraw-Hill, 1960.

McGregor, D. *The professional manager.* New York: McGraw-Hill, 1967.

Miles, R. E. Human relations or human resources. *Harvard Business Review,* 1965, 43(4), 148–63.

Scott, W. G. Organization theory: An overview and an appraisal. *Journal of the Academy of Management,* 1961, 4(1), 7–26.

Woodward, J. *Industrial organization: Theory and practice.* London: Oxford University Press, 1965.

35. PUNITIVE SUPERVISION AND PRODUCTIVITY: AN EXPERIMENTAL ANALOG*

David R. Schmitt†

As generally understood, supervision involves various activities which bear directly or indirectly on the job performance of the supervised individual: job planning, delegation of duties, communication of orders, and enforcement of work rules. The focus of a number of studies involving a variety of types of work groups has been the effects of the presence or absence of such activities or their combinations on worker productivity (Argyle, Gardner, & Coifi, 1957; Coch & French, 1948; Day & Hamblin, 1964; Gouldner, 1954; Katz, Maccoby, Gurin, & Floor, 1951; Katz, Maccoby, & Morse, 1950; Likert, 1961).

Supervision, however, is characterized by more than simply the presence or absence of various activities. The supervisor's choice of activities constitutes only one of the dimensions of what may be defined as his style of supervision. Of additional importance, although largely unexplored, may be the manner in which these activities are scheduled. Two characteristics define the schedule of an activity—its *frequency* and its *regularity*. Thus any supervisory activity can occur at various frequencies and at intervals which may be either regular or irregular.

The potential effects of schedules would appear to be greater for some supervisory activities than for others. For activities such as job planning which usually occur infrequently and involve little interpersonal contact, the effects may be slight. However, for those which occur often and involve interaction between the supervisor and worker, the effects may be substantial. For example, a common function of supervision is to control the amount of work activity on an assigned job. In many settings supervisors "check up" on a subordinate to ensure that he is following his assignment. The importance of the frequency of such checkups has been suggested in research by Katz and his associates (Katz, Maccoby, Gurin, & Floor, 1951; Katz, Maccoby, & Morse, 1950) comparing the effects of close and general styles of supervision. In these studies supervisors of the less productive workers were found to be more likely to use close supervision involving frequent checkups and task instructions. In explanation, Kahn and Katz (1960) suggest that most workers desire maximum autonomy and that supervision in a manner that does not permit it leads to lower morale and motivation. Other research, however, suggests that these effects may be limited to certain types of settings and production technologies (Argyle et al., 1957; Dubin, 1965).

Although unexplored, the regularity of the supervisory activities might have other important effects on work patterns. For example, in the use of supervisory checkups to ensure job performance, it might be predicted that regular checks will be less effective than irregular ones. With regular checkups the worker may learn when he needs to be present to coincide with the appearance of the supervisor, and thus may spend little additional time on the job. With irregular checkups, however, he may find such anticipation difficult or impossible, and thus must remain on the job for longer periods. Examples such as these suggest the potentially important effects of the schedule of an activity in supervisory situations and recommend its more systematic investigation in evaluating the effectiveness of various supervisory practices.

The general lack of research on schedule as an element of supervision style may have been dictated in part by the field research techniques that have typically been used in previous research on supervision. In general, field methods do not permit the measurement and control necessary to determine the effects which this aspect of supervision many have on productivity even though under some conditions it may determine the effectiveness of the supervisory activity.

The effects of the schedules of various consequences have been studied, however, in the experimental laboratory where sufficient measurement and control may be obtained. It may prove desirable, then, first to describe the effects of this variable experimentally, and then to determine the extent to which the results may be generalized to nonexperimental supervisory situations.

In the experimental study of task choice, a minimal task situation has been developed which permits the introduction of several conditions which appear to be functionally analogous to those in a nonexperimental situation involving the supervisor's use of

**Journal of Applied Psychology*, Vol. 53, No. 2 (1969), pp. 118–23.

This study was supported by the Cooperative Research Program of the Office of Education (Project No. S-319) and by the Graduate Research Committee of the University of Wisconsin. The author wishes to thank Lois Loddeke for her assistance in the research and L. Keith Miller and Robert Shotola for their suggestions and criticisms.

† Department of Sociology, University of Washington.

checkups and sanctions to maximize the amount of time spent in work. The *S* in the experimental setting is confronted by two concurrent operants—spacially distinct tasks or responses simultaneously available to *S* (Catania, 1966; Ferster & Skinner, 1957). As with single operants, these tasks are simple, readily repeatable, and easily measured, for example, pressing a lever or button, pulling a knob. Different schedules of reinforcement or punishment are generally programmed for each of the operants. In such a multitask situation, various consequences may be manipulated to attempt to eliminate an individual's behavior on one of these operants while increasing it on a second. Such a condition appears to be functionally equivalent to the supervisor's use of various means to attempt to maximize the amount of time a worker spends in task activity while minimizing various unauthorized behaviors. While previous research in experimental psychology has explored some of the variables controlling concurrent behavior, unfortunately the combinations of conditions which might be generalized to a supervisory setting have not been studied.

This study attempts to demonstrate the manner in which the effects of one type of consequence, punishment, can be explored under conditions relevant to the study of the effectiveness of supervision. Punishment of various magnitudes was administered on two basic schedules for behavior on one of the two tasks. The study is the first in a series of laboratory experiments using variables analogous to various supervisory and task work conditions.

In its broadest sense punitive control includes a variety of punishing behaviors ranging from fines, threats, or physical abuse to more subtle acts such as criticism, ridicule, slights, snubs, or avoidance, and thus is manifest, at least to some degree, in almost all supervisory situations. This study focused on two variables relevant to the use of punishment in affecting the choice of activities: the magnitude of the punitive consequences and the schedule with which they are administered. Two types of schedules, fixed and variable interval, were explored. Studies of two task settings have not investigated the effect of interval punishment on task choice. Rather, in previous research involving concurrent operants (Reynolds, 1963) or two choice risk-taking situations (Kogan & Wallach, 1967), punishment of one of the choices either has been continuous or has occurred for a particular proportion of the task responses. In general such studies suggest a tendency toward the elimination of the punished behavior as the negative consequences become high, The effects of fixed and variable interval schedules of punishment have been compared using a single operant (Azrin, 1956). These results indicate that variable interval schedules tend to produce more response suppression.

METHOD

Setting

The experimental setting in this study involved a choice of two activities each of which was reinforced. Both activities were button-pressing tasks located at opposite ends of a small work room. For each task, *S* was reinforced for pressing a large button mounted on an instrument panel. The reinforcer was money. A counter mounted on the panel indicated how much money *S* had earned. The tasks differed in the amount of money that could be earned on them. The number of presses required before a reinforcement count was registered was greater for one of the tasks. To standardize the rate at which different *S*s could work on either task, a 3-sec. time-out occurred after each response. The number of responses for each cent earned on the higher paying task (Task B) was half that on the other (Task A). With four responses for each cent required on Task B, *S*s could earn approximately $2.80/hr; with eight responses required for each cent on Task A, *S*s could earn $1.40. Thus, of the two, Task B was the more attractive.

The effectiveness of the punitive consequences in changing task behavior was studied under conditions in which its interpretation would be relatively unambiguous. The consequences were evaluated regarding the degree to which they produced behavior on Task A, the less attractive task. Thus work on Task B, the more attractive task, was punished. In most nonexperimental settings the unauthorized activities which the supervisor punishes are probably not consistently more attractive than any other activity including the work itself, as in this study. Thus, if the consequences are effective in eliminating an activity which is considerably more attractive than any other situational alternative, they are likely to be at least as effective in other situations where the alternatives are of more equal attractiveness.

Work on Task B, the higher paying alternative, was periodically penalized by a loss of money. Only one of the two tasks was operable at a time. An *S*-controlled switch on Task A determined which task could be used. The time at which work on Task B would be penalized was indicated by the sounding of a buzzer, regardless of which task *S* was operating. A penalty was administered only if *S* had Task *B* switched on when the buzzer sounded. A penalty count was added on a separate counter in the workroom; the amount of the penalty for that session was posted next to the counter. No consequences accompanied the buzzer if Task A was being operated. Since the changeover from work on Task B to Task A resulted in a several second delay while *S* crossed the room and turned on Task A, frequent switching to avoid penalties resulted in reduced reinforcement on either task. A clock on the wall was visible at all times. All events and measures were programmed and recorded by automated equipment in an adjacent room.

Procedure

The *S*s were told only how to operate the tasks and that the sound of the buzzer would be followed by a loss of money if they were working on Task B. The *S*s were college students who were told before volunteering that they would have an opportunity to make money on a laboratory task.

The effects of penalty magnitudes were explored under both fixed interval (FI) and variable interval (VI) schedules of supervision. Different *S*s were used for each of the schedules. Within a schedule, however, *S*s were exposed to several different penalty magnitudes. Changes in penalty were made only after *S*s evidenced stability in task work under a given condition. Since this investigation focused on the extensive study of several *S*s in each variation, a statistical analysis of the performance was judged not to be appropriate. Rather, similar patterns of response were sought in response to changes in the experimental conditions. The *S*s worked in sessions of 1–4 hr. in length several times a week. Payment was made at the conclusion of the total hours of work.

RESULTS

Fixed Interval Supervision Schedules

Seven *S*s worked over periods ranging from 4 to 14 hr. on several FI schedules in which the buzzer sounded after time periods of equal length throughout a work session. The different schedules included time intervals of 1, 3, 5, or 10 min. Penalties from \$.02 to \$2.00 were used. The *S*s worked at least 1 hr. under each of the penalties.

FIGURE 1 PERCENT OF TIME SPENT ON TASK A UNDER VARIOUS PENALTY CONDITIONS USING A FIXED INTERVAL SCHEDULE (FI 3 MIN.)

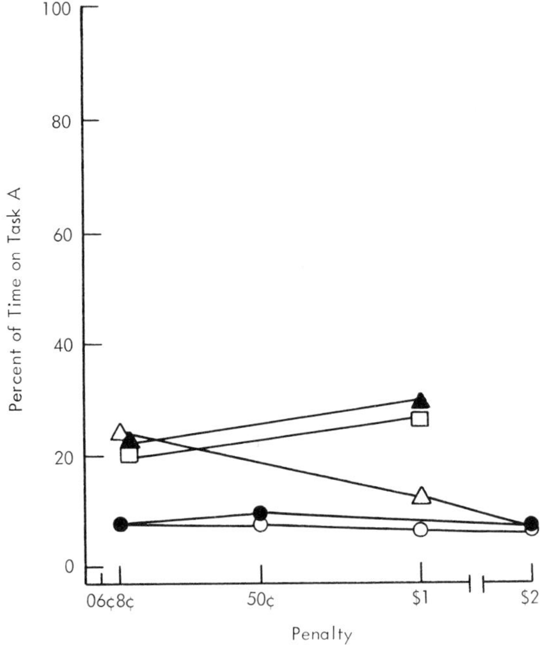

The results indicated that none of the FI punishment schedules was effective in producing a substantial amount of activity on Task A. Figure 1 shows the percentage of time spent by five *S*s on Task A working on one of the schedules (FI 3 min.) under various penalty conditions. After less than 1 hr. of work under any of the schedules and penalty magnitudes, none of the *S*s spent more than 30% of his time on Task A. With experience on a schedule, *S*s avoided virtually all penalties by switching from Task A immediately after the buzzer and switching back again a few seconds before the next buzzer.

Variable Interval Schedule

Four *S*s worked over periods ranging from 24 to 37 hr. on VI schedules in which the buzzer sounded after time periods of varying lengths. One schedule was used with an average of 4 min. for each interval. The intervals varied between 10 sec. and 8 min. Penalties from \$.01 to \$1.00 were used.

During the *S*s' first 2 hr. of work on this schedule, no penalties were administered although the buzzer continued to sound at the various intervals. In the remaining hours for each *S*, one of two progressions of penalties was used. Two *S*s were begun on high penalties which were progressively decreased when intersession stability was achieved. The other two *S*s were begun on low penalties which were progressively increased. Several penalty magnitudes were repeated following intervening periods of work under other penalties to determine the replicability of their effects. The *S*s worked at least 2 hr. under each penalty condition.

Figure 2 shows the proportion of time *S*s spent on Task A under the various penalty magnitudes. The results indicate that VI punishment was effective in producing activity on Task A. For all *S*s the proportion of time spent on Task A increased with increasing penalty size. Small penalties of less than \$.03 had a small effect on task behavior while moderate penalties from \$.05 to \$.15 considerably increased the time spent on Task A. High penalties of \$.25 or more generally resulted in time spent only on Task A after several hours of work. No pronounced effects appear to be caused by penalty sequence. Task performance under the various penalty conditions showed considerable stability and replicability particularly under the penalty extremes. For example, hourly differences in proportion of time on Task A under a given penalty averaged 9%.

DISCUSSION

The data clearly indicate the importance of different schedules in determining the effects of pun-

FIGURE 2 PERCENT OF TIME SPENT ON TASK A UNDER VARIOUS PENALTY CONDITIONS USING A VARIABLE INTERVAL SCHEDULE (VI 4 MIN.). (THE Ss JR AND CM WORKED UNDER PROGRESSIVELY INCREASING PENALTIES WHILE AR AND PW WORKED UNDER PROGRESSIVELY DECREASING ONES.)

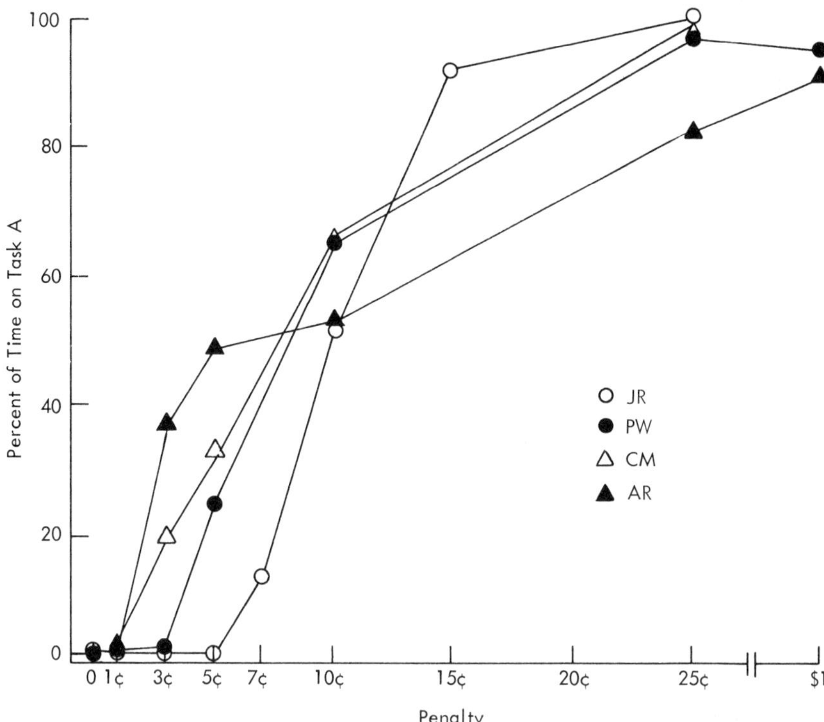

ishment on task choice. When penalties for work on one of the tasks were scheduled at equal intervals throughout a work period, *Ss* learned quickly to avoid them. Thus regardless of their magnitude the penalties proved relatively ineffective in increasing activity on the unpunished task. In contrast, when the penalties were scheduled at unequal intervals, no *S* spent a large amount of time on the punished task without receiving a number of penalties. Under this condition, the larger the penalties the greater the time spent on the unpunished task.

Importantly, however, the effectiveness of VI penalties was not predictable as a direct function of their effect on total earnings. Low and moderate penalties produced more than the predicted amount of work on the unpunished task. The *Ss* tended to avoid losses often to the detriment of their total earnings. For example, *Ss* working on Task A earned approximately $1.40/hr., on Task B $2.80/hr. Thus with an average of 14–15 penalties randomly distributed per hour, *Ss* could maximize their earnings by working only on Task A with penalties greater than $.10 and only on Task B with penalties less than $.10. With $.10 penalties, remaining on either task would result in approximately the same earnings. The results, however, indicate that with $.03 penalties, only two *Ss* spent no time on Task A during these periods. The other *Ss* spent 20 and 38% of their time, respectively, on the lower paying task. With $.05 penalties only one *S* spent no time on Task A with the other *Ss* spending 26, 32, and 49% of their time, respectively, on that task. For each of these penalty magnitudes the rank orders of the average amount earned by each *S* and the proportion of time spent on the higher paying task correspond exactly. With .$10 penalties, the point at which either task could be selected with little difference in earnings, all *Ss* spent more than half of their time on Task A.

In conclusion, the inference drawn from these findings appears to be an important one for an analysis of the effectiveness of supervision. The results strongly recommend the consideration of not only the type of supervisory activity but also the schedules with which it is performed. As the case of punitive control illustrates, schedule type in conjunction with the magnitude of the punishment may determine in large part the effectiveness of that activity.

A generalization of these results to nonexperimental settings, however, should take note of the various limiting characteristics of this research. For example, punishment in the experimental setting was impersonal, specific to a given activity, and involved loss of money as the only aversive consequence. Much supervision in nonexperimental settings, however, is personal, associated with a number of poorly specified activities, and may involve a number of different consequences. In the experimental situation only two activities were available and money was used as the reinforcer for both, while in other settings workers often have many alternatives available which are reinforced in a variety of ways. In addition, workers on the job are often participants in formal or informal groups in which additional standards, pressures, or sanctions are imposed. To what extent such conditions alter the relationships found in this research in a "minimal" task situation will need to be determined.

REFERENCES

Argyle, M., Gardner, G., and Coifi, F. The measurement of supervisory methods. *Human Relations,* 1957, **10**, 295–313.

Argyle, M., Garnder, G., and Coifi, F. Supervisory methods related to productivity, absenteeism and labor turnover. *Human Relations,* 1958, **11**, 23–40.

Azrin, N. H. Effects of two intermittent schedules of immediate and nonimmediate punishment. *Journal of Psychology,* 1956, **42**, 3–21.

Catania, A. C. Concurrent operants. In W. K. Honig (ed.), *Operant behavior: Areas of research and application.* New York: Appleton-Century-Crofts, 1966.

Coch, L. and French, J. R. P. Overcoming resistance to change. *Human Relations,* 1948, **1**, 512–32.

Day, R. C. and Hamblin, R. L. Some effects of close and punitive styles of supervision. *American Journal of Sociology,* 1964, **69**, 499–510.

Dubin, R. *Leadership and productivity.* San Francisco: Chandler, 1965. Professors Mann, Miller, and Homans are coauthors of this book.

Ferster, C. B. and Skinner, B. L. *Schedules of reinforcement.* New York: Appleton-Century-Crofts, 1957.

Gouldner, A. W. *Patterns of industrial bureaucracy.* Glencoe, Ill.: Free Press, 1954.

Kahn, R. L. and Katz, D. Leadership practices in relation to productivity and morale. In D. Cartwright & A. Zander (eds.), *Group dynamics.* (2d ed.) Evanston, Ill.: Row, Peterson, 1960.

Katz, D., Maccoby, N., Gurin, G., and Floor, L. G. *Productivity, supervision and morale among railroad workers.* Ann Arbor: Survey Research Center, University of Michigan, 1951.

Katz, D., Maccoby, N. and Morse, N. C. *Productivity, supervision and morale in an office situation,* Part 1. Ann Arbor: Survey Research Center, University of Michigan, 1950.

Kogan, N. and Wallach, M. A. Risk taking as a function of the situation, the person, and the group. In *New directions in psychology. III.* New York: Holt, Rinehart & Winston, 1967.

Likert, R. *New patterns of management.* New York: McGraw-Hill, 1961.

Reynolds, G. S. Potency of conditioned reinforcers based on food and on food and punishment. *Science,* 1963, **139**, 833–39.

36. DISCIPLINE WITHOUT PUNISHMENT*

***John Huberman*†**

Discipline on the production floor is necessary, as is the maintenance of good workmanship and acceptable levels of output. An entirely different question, however, is whether demotion, temporary suspension, or similar forms of punishment are necessary, desirable, or effective methods for dealing with lapses from discipline or satisfactory workmanship. I don't believe they are.

This conviction results from a searching inquiry conducted in a large Douglas-fir plywood mill. The study resulted in the adoption of a new philosophy, policy, and set of procedures which exclude punishment (in the usual sense of the word) as a means of dealing with sub-standard performance and with such breaches of discipline as late arrival for work, unnecessary absenteeism, overstaying of rest periods, and disregard of a foreman's instructions.

While the new methods were developed to handle more effectively a specific situation which had arisen in one plant (the largest one in the company), they may well be considered for general application in industry, because they appear to be based on a realistic appraisal of well-known principles governing human behavior. In retrospect, they may even consti-

*For a report of the result of the plan's second year of operation, plus some additional notes of the author about its probable general applicability, see the *From the Thoughtful Businessman* column of *Harvard Business Review,* Vol. 43, No. 5 (October 1965), pp. 182–86.

Harvard Business Review, Vol. 42 (1965), pp. 62–68.

†Private Consultant, Vancouver, British Columbia and special lecturer, Department of Psychology, University of British Columbia.

tute a small step in the direction of applying "Theory Y" advocated by Douglas McGregor.[1]

To introduce and discuss the subject of this article, and give the reader a better "feel" of the practicality of our solutions, I shall use a case-history approach. As many businessmen will recognize, the problems we faced are common ones in industry today. Indeed, to a greater or lesser extent they should be familiar to almost all managers of organizations.

THE SETTING

Our mill is a typical Douglas-fir plywood mill. At the time our story begins it had a work force of about 300 hourly paid (and unionized) employees, which rose to about 550 just at the time the "new look" plan became operational.

The company has been in operation for 20 years. The founders started the business with a benevolent-paternalistic philosophy. Turkeys were handed out at Christmas and bonuses at Christmas and Easter; interestfree (and unsecured) loans were available to employees, along with certain other unusual benefits. During an industry-wide strike, the canteen was kept open solely for use of the pickets, and employees could obtain payroll advances to tide them over. A real "family atmosphere" prevailed.

As the corporation grew, its philosophy gradually took a more businesslike direction. Dealings with employees became more impersonal. As competition stiffened, wages rose, and a few lean years followed; the special benefits mentioned earlier were gradually withdrawn. There were also repeated changes in mill managers, whose approach ranged from the highly permissive to the strongly authoritarian.

At the same time, a strong personality arose among the union members. This man skillfully rallied around himself those who resented the gradual dwindling away of what they had considered their "privileges"; soon a tightly knit union organization grew up, spurred by dissatisfaction over the withdrawn benefits. Whenever a union brother got into trouble, the union stood behind him to the last man, regardless, in most instances, of the merits of the particular case.

THE PROBLEM

When shifts in top management's philosophy are sudden, there is likely to be an explicit statement of the new thinking. But when, as so frequently happens, the changes are slow and almost unconscious, no announcement at all may be forthcoming. Lower levels of management then have to interpret the change from occasional acts of top management which do not seem to fit into the previous pattern. Such gradual changes are likely to create uncertainties in many management areas, and insofar as they include a shift in attitude regarding employee relations, they are likely to create an ambiguous situation for the foreman and superintendent who are in daily contact with the workers.

The problem of how unsatisfactory work performance and disciplinary matters should be handled can become particularly vexing. Should one deal with them in a casual manner as in the "good old days," or begin to take a stern, businesslike attitude? Should one try to reason with the individual, or tell him "either you do things right or you will be sent home?"

Deterioration and Unhappiness

Such uncertainties did arise, of course, and where there was uncertainty there was also a tendency to delay action. The relatively frequent change of plant managers who had widely differing beliefs about how best to deal with problem cases did not help matters. Gradually, the following pattern developed:

> Foremen would let minor infringements of the rules go by. A few individuals who noticed this would then start to test just how far they could go. After several annoying incidents, a foreman would get sufficiently angry to decide on immediate discharge.
>
> At this point, the union would step in. Since no record of previous misdemeanors of the individuals would be on file (because no action had been taken), the union usually experienced little difficulty in convincing management, including the angry foreman, that no arbitrator would sustain the discharge. Under the collective agreement, any grievance could be brought to arbitration (which was binding). Agreement was then usually reached on commuting the discharge to a temporary suspension without pay.
>
> At other times, the discharge might be changed to demotion to a lesser paid job.
>
> At still other times, management's original decision may have been a temporary suspension without pay. In these cases the union would institute negotiation directed toward reducing the period of the suspension. In at least one case it became known that the union had actually paid the penalized worker his full wages during the suspension, thereby enabling him to enjoy his penalty in the form of a paid vacation.

Management, and the foremen in particular, were showing signs of increasing unhappiness over the

[1] *The human side of enterprise* (New York, McGraw-Hill Book Company, 1960); for a brief description of "Theory Y," see Alva F. Kindall and James Gatza, Positive program for performance appraisal, *Harvard Business Review,* November–December 1963, at top of page 165.

union's success in protecting individuals who had repeatedly demonstrated a lack of discipline or interest in good workmanship. Not that the company was in any way "anti-union" in its attitude. On the contrary, management prided itself on the many constructive solutions it had worked out to presumably "insoluble" problems in full cooperation with the union; some of these solutions gradually filtered through to the rest of the industry. The company also realized that there was an obligation on the part of the union to act as lawyer and defender for its members. This knowledge, however, did little toward dissipating the irritation of the foremen who felt that whatever action they took to enforce discipline or sustain good workmanship was effectively counteracted by the union.

Other Annoyances

Other, almost equally annoying, features resulted from management's efforts to use the standard disciplinary tools:

In case of demotion, a new man had to be trained to replace the one who was demoted. Also, vigilant supervision was required to make sure that the latter individual would not act out his annoyance over the punishment by lowering production or quality.

Suspension brought with it the nuisance of multiple temporary job movements: the next senior man would be entitled to the job temporarily vacated, his job would be taken by the next senior man, and so on down.

Upon return from suspension, the man obviously had to save face. The method usually chosen for this purpose was for him to inform everyone how pleasantly and usefully he spent the "time off." Occasionally a few unprintable remarks would be dropped about management in general and about the foreman in particular, followed by the recommendation that others follow his example. The motto became: "As long as you don't burn down the plant, or punch a foreman in the nose, nothing will happen to you—the union will protect you!"

Lastly, the whole procedure was very costly in terms of the time of the foremen, personnel manager, superintendent, and occasionally the general manager himself. It took time to deliberate the initial action to be taken; also, more time was spent in the grievance meetings which followed the action. The grievance meetings regularly involved not only the supervisory staff but also the full plant committee; members of the committe who were on shift had to be replaced on the mill floor and also received full wages for the time spent in the meetings.

This then, was the situation which seemed to call for some remedy, especially as the plant was in the last phases of preparation for the doubling of its capacity. If experienced foremen were uncertain how to deal with unsatisfactory work performance and annoyed about the results of the system then in effect, the problem would take on unmanageable proportions with the influx of about 200 new workers and several new, partly inexperienced foremen.

It was therefore decided to analyze the philosophy and results of our past methods of dealing with unsatisfactory workmanship and problems of discipline, with a view to developing something better.

CHANGE IN THINKING

The first thoughts which occurred to management ran something like this: Shoddy workmanship or flagrant violations of discipline did not normally occur without some warning signs. The man would usually drift into such behavior gradually. If the foreman paid attention to such signs and, when observed, sent the man to the Personnel Office for a counseling interview, many outbreaks requiring disciplinary action might perhaps be forestalled.

This thought was put into action and had remarkably good results. It did not, however, prevent all trouble. At times foremen may have lacked the perspicacity to observe the gradual deterioration of behavior; at other times they may have been too busy solving problems brought about by expansion of the plant (e.g., introduction of new machinery and methods).

The second thought was to retread the well-worn path of enforcement. Management would establish a system of written warning slips to be handed out on the plant floor when an infraction occurred. A "criminal code" would also be developed which would list the appropriate penalty for the more usual infractions if the first or second warning slip failed to produce the desired behavioral change. This system would give the foreman a well-defined method to deal with such matters and would also make the workers aware of the type of penalty they could look forward to if they didn't toe the line.

To arrive at such a code, it seemed logical first to analyze all events which had led to some type of disciplinary action over the previous three years. Concurrently, the results which these penalties appeared to have had on the individuals involved would be assessed.

The outcome of the analysis was the sad picture of the undesirable results mentioned in the preceding section. This was not entirely unexpected; what surprised the team working on this project was that *not a single desirable result* could be detected.

The people who had been disciplined were generally still among the poorest workers; their attitude was sulky, if not openly hostile, and they seemed to be spreading this feeling among the rest of the crew. Some were known to play little games to frustrate the foremen, but were taking increased care not to get caught.

Pitfalls of Punishment

Could it be that "punishment does not pay"? We thought of a statistic which is well known but is seldom considered thoughtfully enough: 85 percent of all those who entered the local prison returned there within three years of their release, not counting those who found their way to other penal institutions.

This experience was not then—and is not in many prisons today—unusual. Experience indicates that even severe punishment achieves nothing to redirect behavior into more desirable channels, at least in the large majority of cases. The "penal ritual" we are engaging in seems entirely futile. Are we making the same mistake when we demote or suspend people in the mill?

It might be argued that an analysis of the effect of punishment on criminals cannot throw light on the efficacy of punishment in the "normal" industrial situation. Theoretically, this is a valid argument. In practice, however, the troubles experienced in our mill seem more consistent with the hypothesis that, in adults, punishment generally produces many undesirable—and few, if any, desirable—results.

These thoughts directed the team's attention to consideration of the possibility that it might be useful to eliminate all forms of punishment as unsuitable instruments for maintaining good workmanship and discipline.

At first the idea seemed preposterous. However, the more management thought about it, the more logical it appeared. Finally, after many discussions, a philosophy, a policy, and a system of procedures were evolved which promised to deal more effectively with the difficulties we had experienced and which were free of "punishment" or the threat of "punishment."

NEW PHILOSOPHY

Having told the story of our change in thinking about discipline and punishment, I wish now to describe the principles and policies we try to follow. We believe that:

The presence or absence of certain personality variables and environmental conditions exercises a decisive influence on a person's general adherence to, or disregard of, high standards of workmanship and disciplined behavior. The variables and conditions which we consider most important in this respect are set out in Exhibit 1.

It takes time and money to train individuals. We also acknowledge that industry has certain responsibilities to act in a humane manner. Both considerations require that we give each individual every possible and reasonable chance to play a positive and satisfactory role in the company's operations. We believe, however, that it is only possible to play such a role if the individual has adequate self-respect. By this we do not mean that an individual will never lapse from excellent workmanship or strict discipline. We believe, rather, that in a person with adequate self-

EXHIBIT 1 MOTIVATIONAL FACTORS IN EMPLOYEE PERFORMANCE

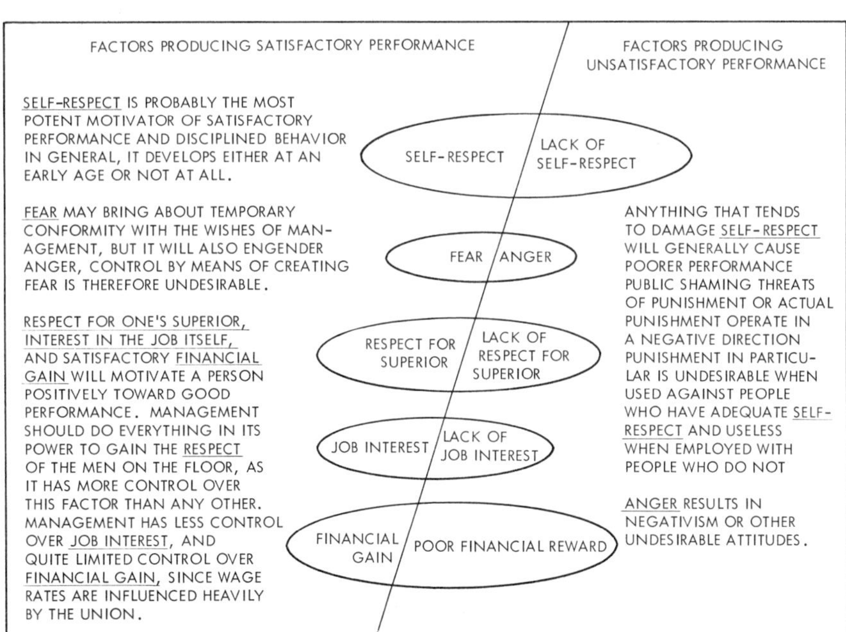

respect such lapses will happen rarely and will stop promptly if brought to his attention in a friendly manner.

Repeated demonstrations, within a relatively short interval, that such friendly methods do not produce the desired results are taken as indications of lack of adequate self-respect. When such a regrettable conclusion has been reached about an individual, we do not wish to keep him in our employment. We shall use orderly methods to terminate his services.

Policies and Procedures

How is such a philosophy implemented? Six policies and procedures seem of especial importance to us and have been adopted:

1. *No disciplinary demotions, suspensions, or other forms of punishment will henceforth be applied.*

2. *In case of unsatisfactory work performance (e.g., carelessness in handling materials, inattention to duty) or breach of discipline (e.g., overstaying rest or lunch periods, unnecessary absenteeism, disregard of safety, failure to carry out the foreman's instructions), the following steps will be followed:*

Step One. The foreman will offer the worker a casual and friendly reminder on the job.

Step Two. Should another incident arise within four to six weeks of Step One, the foreman will again correct it casually on the job but will later call the individual to his office for a serious but friendly chat. He will explain the need for and purpose of the rule(s); make sure the person understands the explanation; and express his confidence that the person will henceforth decide to abide by them. He will also listen to any reasonable excuse the employee may bring up. If he decides that the transgression was unintentional or based on a misunderstanding, he of course informs the employee that the matter is closed.

Step Three. In case of further incidents within about six weeks, Step Two is repeated with some variation. First, the shift foreman is also present at the discussion; secondly, the employee's attention is directed to the possibility that he may dislike the work we have to offer, or he may find the relatively strict industrial discipline distasteful. In such case, would it be better to look for some other job or line of work? (Vocational counseling is available through the Personnel Office.) The foreman then expresses his hope that the employee will, in fact decide that he likes the work and the company and will adapt himself to the requirements. This conversation is confirmed in a letter to the employee's home.

Step Four. The employee who perpetrates another incident of poor workmanship or breach of discipline within six to eight weeks of Step Three is called off the floor into the foreman's office, again in the presence of the shift foreman. There his is directed to go home for the rest of the shift and consider seriously whether he does or does not wish to abide by company standards. He is informed that he will get full pay for the time, as a last expression of the company's hope that he will wish to stay and abide by the rules. He is also told that another occurrence of trouble within reasonable time will lead—regretfully—to termination.

3. *If another incident should occur within reasonable time, the employee's services are terminated.*

4. *In case several incidents happen at unusually close intervals, Step Two or Step Three may be skipped.*

5. *If no further incident occurs within six to eight weeks of any one step (except Step four), such step is cleared from the employee's record. Should another incident happen at a later time, the last step will be repeated. Considerable time—in the range of a year—would have to elapse without incident before Step Four is cleared from the records.*

6. *In case of discovery of criminal behavior or in-plant fighting, termination results without preliminary steps. Such behavior is taken as conclusive evidence of lack of adequate self-respect and discipline even if it happens only once.*

Is Discharge Punitive?

A question invariably asked by those who hear about our plan is: "How can you pretend that your method eliminates punishment? Are you not eliminating minor forms of punishment (e.g., demotion and suspension) while retaining the most severe of all, namely, discharge?" What the questioners imply here is that termination, by the very fact that it inflicts severe unpleasantness on the recipient, must logically be regarded as a form of punishment.

We believe that this is not necessarily so: termination may, or may not, belong logically to the general class of "punishment," depending on the presence or absence of extraneous factors. The most important of these is the desire for retribution. If we fire someone "to pay him back" for what he has done to us, our act would take on the nature of punishment. But if we take the same action for any number of other reasons (e.g., to avoid expected future trouble) *and exclude retribution* as a motive, then we are not dealing out "punishment."

The distinction we are trying to make here may appear subtle, but it is not a semantic sleight of hand. What we say, in effect, is that if we terminate a person's employment, we do not do it *even partially* as retribution for whatever undesirable action he was involved in. We do it only because his act or acts lead us to believe that he lacks self-respect and, therefore, that his future behavior is going to be troublesome and contrary to the legitimate aims of the company. We agree with psychologists who state that the best predictor of a person's future behavior is his past behavior under similar circumstances, and that when the same behavior is elicited by dissimilar circumstances, it is likely to be of a general character and hence repeated in the future.

Accordingly, during Steps One to Four we attempt to establish the individual's tendency toward disruptive behavior. It is future trouble we wish to avoid. Thus, our system is future-oriented. In contrast, the punitive approach is past-oriented; it seeks to apportion the "proper punishment" for a given "crime."

This difference can be made even clearer by examining the typical arguments which someone might present under each system concerning the appropriateness of a decision to terminate an employee's services:

> In the punishment-oriented system, a man sympathetic with the "offender" would probably plead that "the punishment doesn't fit the crime," that the sentence is too harsh, that the individual doesn't quite deserve it, and that it should be commuted to a lesser one.
>
> In the system used in our company, such a sympathizer would have to argue that the observations of the person's behavior are inaccurate or insufficient in number for reliable prediction, or that the theory behind the prediction is not sufficiently reliable or is outright wrong.

The difference between the punishment-oriented and the predictive systems is a reflection of the different views taken of deviant behavior in criminal law and the behavioral sciences.[2]

If termination were considered the ultimate punishment, the rest of our system would have little chance of functioning. The system as described here places on the employee the onus of deciding whether he wishes (or is able) to conform to the requirements of a particular work situation. During Steps One to Four he is reminded of the requirements without any implication that if he does not conform, he commits something morally wrong for which he deserves condemnation and punishment. The supervisory staff is trained to avoid giving any such impression. We feel that if we condemn an individual, we give up all hope of changing him.

It is very questionable whether any supervisory staff could be trained to take a friendly, blame-free approach in its dealings with employees if it considered termination the ultimate punishment. If superiors took this attitude, they might regard Steps One to Four as a nuisance, to be gotten over as quickly as possible on the way to the "big stick." Such an attitude would also manifest itself in their discussions with employees under Steps One to Four and would create the same psychological effect as if overt punishment had been administered.

[2] See E. J. Sachar, Behavioral Science and Criminal Law, *Scientific American,* November 1963, pp. 39–45.

Rationale for Payment

People who hear about our new approach also often ask: "Why does a man receive pay for the rest of the shift if he is sent home?"

First, let me explain why the employee is sent home. We feel that after a supervisor has had several discussions with him which prove fruitless, a dramatic gesture may be the only means to induce him to consider the situation seriously. Being sent home from work would appear to fulfill this requirement. The payment—perhaps the most novel part of the plan—makes sense for several reasons:

1. Sending a person home *without* pay would undoubtedly be interpreted as punishment and would, therefore, be contrary to the avowed policy and philosophy.
2. The foreman is instructed to tell the person that paying him is a demonstration of the company's interest in keeping him—in seeing him decide that he will conform to acceptable standards in the future. This is a basically supportive statement, and we hope that it will be difficult for the foreman to make it without being supportive himself.
3. Since there is no loss of income, there are no grounds for grievance. (In the past, a grievance always resulted when a person was sent home without pay.) The expense of grievance meetings is much greater than the cost of paying an employee to take an afternoon off.
4. Should a perons's employment have to be terminated at a later date, the company's good faith, manifested by its paying him to think over whether he wished to abide by company standards, would certainly minimize any chance of an arbitrator's reversing the dismissal decision.

Theoretically, at least, the procedures outlined would appear to solve all the problems which we set out to tackle. They make it mandatory for the supervisory personnel to deal with problem cases in a constructive, nonpunitive manner. They eliminate all forms of "punishment," along with all undesirable and time-consuming side effects that we experienced in the past. And, should termination become necessary, they minimize the danger of reversal by arbitration. Lastly, the procedure seems, at least to us, fair.

So much for theory. What are the practical results? This brings us back to the story of what actually happened.

THE RESULTS

The policy was put into effect in the summer of 1963. It had the full backing of the superintendent, the personnel manager, and the shift foremen, who had participated in its formulation. The junior foremen were called in for meetings and were given instructions regarding the background, philosophy, and techniques involved in the plan.

As the next step, we were going to advise the

union of the new policy. Before this could be arranged, an in-plant fight occurred as a consequence of horseplay. Both individuals involved (one of them a young shop steward) were discharged. The shop steward initiated the expected grievance procedure; the union agreed that in-plant fights were dangerous and could not be tolerated, but pleaded for commutation of the termination to suspension.

We refused this request and proceeded to give the union the whole background for our decision to eliminate all forms of "punishment," much in the same manner as described in this article. We also expressed our hope that it would support us in our efforts to deal with grown-up union members as men and not as a collection of schoolboys.

The union did not seem too pleased with this unexpected turn of events but found it difficult to argue the point. The terminations stood.

Since then, three individuals have been processed to Step Four: i.e., sent home for the rest of the shift with pay. Two of them returned to work for a period of a few weeks and then quit. The third person, a young man, returned at the end of the shift to see his foreman. He was ostensibly moved.

> "I would never have thought the company would be that fair, and take so much interest in me," he said. "When I got home, I started to think about the way I used to act for the first time. I now realize that I have been taking a very childish attitude all along. I came to thank you for what you have done for me and I assure you there will be no more trouble."

At the time of this writing, seven months have elapsed and the boy's work, as well as his attitude, have so far left nothing to be desired.

There has been no occasion for terminating anyone's employment. Several employees were dealt with up to Steps Two and Three. In each case there was adequate improvement or the individual left quietly and voluntarily. Some even stated that they were quitting "in fairness to the company." There were no grievances.

The morale of the foremen and the superintendents has shown marked improvement. They seem to feel that for the first time they have a strong, reliable, and fair tool to deal with unsatisfactory work performance and breaches of discipline.

chapter 4

INTERPERSONAL PROCESSES AS DETERMINANTS OF BEHAVIOR IN ORGANIZATIONS

We have examined several of the dimensions of the intraorganizational environment, the structural features of organization design, and formal reward and penalty systems as factors in influencing behavior within the organization. We now turn our attention to the interpersonal and social processes within this organizational context. We will again be concerned with the nature of these processes and their effects on the various dependent variables of organizational behavior.

As we focus our attention on a more aggregate level of analysis, it should be kept in mind that the individual variables examined in Chapters 1 and 3 are basic inputs for our analysis of interpersonal, group and leadership processes. Furthermore, since behavior in organizations is realistically conceived as determined by an interacting system of causal factors, interpersonal processes will also influence the nature of individual motivation, perception, and learning as well as responses to environmental and structural determinants. We treat these various subsystems of causal factors separately solely for purposes of analysis and communication.

We shall segment our treatment of interpersonal processes into a discussion of *(a)* group structure and processes, and *(b)* leadership. In terms of the reality of organizational behavior this division is admittedly artificial. Such an analysis will allow us, however, to draw more easily on group processes on the one hand and leader behavior on the other and allows the detailed examination of these variables. Such intensive analysis facilitates the development of insights regarding the application of specific research findings. Processes that appear overwhelmingly complex and quite theoretical when viewed in their entirety can become more operational when examined with empirical detail.

Section A

GROUP STRUCTURE AND PROCESSES

The power of groups in influencing employee performance and attitudes is well known. The much publicized (and criticized) Hawthorne Studies conducted by Elton Mayo and his colleagues at the Western Electric Company contributed to our awareness of the significance of group processes. The work of Coch and French on "overcoming resistance to change" in the Harwood Manufacturing Company contributed to our understanding of the impact of group participation on individual motivation to change one's behavior in an organizationally desirable manner. These two studies have had wide exposure. Their implications for practice as well as their weaknesses as behavioral science studies have been discussed frequently in the literature. We will not continue this dialogue here.

Rather, in this section we will focus on several group dimensions or characteristics and their relationships to several of the important dependent variables of organizational behavior; namely individual behavior and satisfaction, group performance on computational tasks as well as on problem-solving or decision-making tasks, group cohesion, and group risk taking. We examine several characteristics of groups as they influence the above dependent variables. Imbedded in several of the selections is a consideration of the role of informal groups in encouraging and resisting organizational purposes.

We have attempted to impose two criteria in selecting the readings for this section: (1) each of the selections discusses variables of practical significance to the manager of human effort and (2) the articles reviewed present data and theory based on sound scientific methodology. The imposition of these two criteria reflects, once again, our general position that "good practice" and "good science" can be mutually supportive.

The ecology within a group can exert a major impact on both member feelings and group performance. Sommer reviews several studies on the effects of different spatial arrangements on intragroup processes and performances. From the viewpoint of the executive, these studies serve to emphasize several "controllables" or "tools" available to the manager through which he can develop, focus, and constrain group activity.

One of the most visible, and yet powerful (in terms of its impact on group processes) characteristics of a group is its size. Thomas and Fink review the research on the effects of group size. The size of a group, measured in terms of the number of its members, influences the group's structure, cohesion, and several dimensions of its performance. Group size also directly conditions the behaviors and attitudes of the group's members as individuals. The studies reviewed by Thomas and Fink suggest practical insights for managers making decisions regarding organization structures and work group assignments. The size of formal operative and managerial groups (both line and staff) is frequently controllable through managerial decisions.

One of the most interesting findings of the last decade is the fact that apparently it is possible to create conditions under which individuals will take (and recommend that others take) greater risks when making decisions in groups than when making the same decisions as individuals. This finding has become known as the risky-shift phenomenon. Clark discusses the conditions under which it has been found and reviews the evidence for and against four contending explanations for this shift toward riskier decisions in groups. This phenomenon and the associated explanations are of obvious relevance to the manager faced with the decision whether to assign problems to individuals per se or to groups of individuals for discussion and decision.[1]

As noted, one of the frequent uses of groups in organizations relates to the formulation and solving of problems. There exists a healthy stream of literature discussing the relative advantages and disadvantages of group processes for solving various types of problems. Maier reviews several studies relevant to this important practical question and integrates the major conclusions to be derived from such a review into a coherent theoretical system.

[1] For a special issue of the *Journal of Personality and Social Psychology* devoted to the choice shifts exhibited by groups including reviews of findings and theories, see Vol. 20, No. 3 (December 1971), pp. 339–510.

37. SMALL GROUP ECOLOGY*

***Robert Sommer*†**

The systematic study of the arrangement of individuals in small groups began in 1950 using post hoc analysis of data collected for other purposes. Only recently have investigators begun to design experiments with group ecology as the major independent variable. Results have shown that spatial arrangement is a function of group task, the degree of relationship of individuals, personalities of the individuals, and the amount and kind of available space. The resulting arrangement in turn affects communication, friendship, and status differentiation between individuals. Knowledge of small group ecology can help in developing a theory of social relationships that includes the environ-

* *Psychological Bulletin,* Vol. 67, No. 2 (1967), pp. 145–52.

† Department of Psychology, University of California, Davis.

ment in which interaction takes place as well as principles for designing functional environments from the standpoint of human relationships.

Systematic study of spatial arrangements in face-to-face groups, or small group ecology as the field has been termed, is a comparatively recent development. Typically, the arrangement of people has been an incidental or background variable in psychological experimentation. The use of spatial arrangements as an independent variable in small group research can be traced to Steinzor (1950), who noted some unusual spatial effects of interaction. This pattern persists to the present, since at least half the published studies of small group arrangements involve the reanalysis of data collected for other purposes. Despite consistent and clear data, psychologists seem reluctant to make the arrangement of people a major independent variable. As Hall (1959) put it, "We treat space somewhat as we treat sex, it is there but we don't talk about it." Yet, enough studies, experimental as well as ex post facto, have accumulated to warrant some attempt to integrate the findings and indicate what directions further studies may profitably take.

This review focuses upon the arrangement of individuals in face-to-face groups. Studies of residential living units such as dormitories, housing developments, and communities are omitted. These phenomena require a different level of analysis (community or societal) than the relationship between individuals in face-to-face groups. The study of larger stable human aggregations has fallen to the fields of demography, human ecology, and geography. Because of space limitations, studies of crowding and density are excluded from consideration since these important topics deserve treatment in their own right. This study concentrates instead on two aspects of small group ecology—the way groups arrange themselves under various conditions, and the ways in which the resulting arrangements affect communication, productivity, and social relationships.

LEADERSHIP AND SPATIAL ARRANGEMENTS

Many concepts used in discussion of leadership, such as central figure, dominant position, upper echelon, and high status are based on spatial analogies. Studies of group dynamics and leadership have shown that concepts such as social distance, inner circle, and isolate have some geographic reference but there is no simple isomorphism between psychological and geographic concepts. While investigating discussion groups, Steinzor noticed a participant changing his seat in order to sit opposite another person with whom he had recently had a verbal altercation. In an ex post facto design using data already collected, Steinzor found that when one person stopped speaking, someone opposite rather than alongside was next to speak, an effect he attributed to the greater physical and expressive value a person has for those opposite him in a circle. Following this, Bass and Klubeck (1952) reanalyzed their discussion group data to determine if leadership ratings varied as a function of location in an inverted V or a parallel row arrangement. Although they found that persons occupying end positions attained higher status than people in middle seats, there were so many confounding factors, including a nonrandom selection of seats by people of different status levels, that their results were equivocal. Hearn (1957) reanalyzed small group data collected for other purposes and found that leadership style had a significant influence on what was termed the "Steinzor effect." With minimal leadership, members of a discussion group would direct more comments to people sitting opposite than people adjacent; when a strong leader was present, people directed more comments to adjacent seats than to people opposite; and when direction of the group was shared equally among the members, no spatial effect appeared. These results may be explained in terms of eye contact. Since it is impermissible to look directly at a dominant individual at close quarters, the individual restricts his gaze to his immediate neighbors when a strong leader is close by. Steinzor's expressive contact hypothesis has been further refined by Argyle and Dean (1965) who studied the connection between eye contact, distance, and affiliation. A one-way mirror was used to chart interaction between a näive subject and a confederate who gazed continually at the subject. There was less eye contact and glances were shorter when the people were close together, and this effect was most pronounced for mixed-sex pairs. The authors believed that eye contact is a component of intimacy, which is governed by both approach and avoidance forces kept in a state of equilibrium during any given encounter. When this equilibrium is disturbed by increasing physical proximity or decreasing eye contact, there are compensatory changes along the other dimensions.

Communication flow as a function of spatial relationship was emphasized by Leavitt (1951), who continued the work of Bavelas (1950). Leavitt used groups of five subjects each who were seated at a table but separated from one another by vertical partitions. Channels of communication could be changed by manipulating slots in the partitions. Group leadership was closely correlated with a member's position in the communication net. Centrally located individuals enjoyed the task most and those in the peripheral positions enjoyed it least. Howells and Becker (1962) hypothesized that people who received greater numbers of messages would be more likely to be designated leaders than people who received fewer messages. They arranged groups of five subjects around small rectangular tables with three people on one side, two on the other. The results confirmed their predictions that more leaders than would be expected by chance would emerge from the two-man side of the table.

The studies described thus far have involved *relational* space, or the way people orient themselves towards one another. A second line of research has emphasized the cultural import of various fixed locations. In studies of leadership, the head chair at the table has a special significance. Sommer (1959) found that leaders in small discussion groups gravitated to the head position at rectangular tables. Strodtbeck and Hook (1961) reanalyzed data from experimental jury deliberations and found that people at end positions participated more and were rated as having greater influence on the decision process than people at the sides. It was also found that jurors from the managerial and professional classes selected the head chair more than did individuals of lower status. Hare and Bales (1963) did not work with leadership per se, but rather with dominance as measured by a paper-and-pencil personality test. Reanalyzing the data collected by Bales and his associates from five-man discussion groups, they found that subjects high on dominance tended to choose the central seats and do the most talking. Felipe (1966) used the semantic differential to assess dyadic seating arrangements along these dimensions: intimate-unacquainted, hostile-friendly, talkative-untalkative, and unequal-equal. The cultural influence of the head position was evident on the equality dimension—if one member of a pair was at the head of the table, this pair was rated significantly less equal than if members were both at ends of the table or only at the sides.

A weakness of all these studies is the limited range of cultures and populations sampled, almost all taking place in the United States. This would not be a serious limitation except that Hall indicated that leaders in other parts of the world use space differently. An equally serious problem concerns the confounding of location, status, and personality. All studies agreed that choice of seats is nonrandom with respect to status and personality. High status, dominant individuals in American culture gravitate to the head position, and people who occupy the head position participate more than people at the side positions (Strodtbeck & Hook, 1961), but there is no way to disentangle status from location in these studies. It is possible that occupancy of certain locations automatically raises an individual's status and/or dominance. On the other hand, it may be that dominant individuals choose these locations for reasons of tradition and would participate more wherever they sat, and thus their location has no essential connection with their participation. It may be that high status people tend to participate more *and* certain locations also increase participation, but the combination of the two results in greater participation than either by itself. The only way to disentangle these variables is to conduct experiments in which people are assigned randomly to various locations and their relative contributions noted. It must be recognized that these conditions are highly artificial in a society that typically allocates space according to status considerations. From the standpoint of designing experiments in natural settings, the policies of random assignments of location are not always adhered to in practice. In the prison camp studied by Grusky (1959), inmate leaders received the most desirable job assignments as well as the bottom bunks (which were status symbols in the dormitories) despite the official policy of random bed assignment. It is likely that the same pressures responsible for the connection between status and location operate against any assignment scheme in conflict with accepted spatial norms.

TASK AND LOCATION

The quest for effective spatial arrangements in working units such as relay assembly teams, seminars, and buzz groups has been a subject of considerable concern to applied psychologists. Textbooks of group dynamics recommend horseshoe or semicircular rather than straight-row arrangements for discussion groups and classrooms, rectangular tables have been criticized for fostering authoritarian leadership, and the improper location of individuals has been blamed for the failure of the working teams. Intuitively it would seem that the proper arrangement of people would increase production, smooth the flow of communication, and reduce the "friction of space," but the data are largely of the anecdotal variety. Perhaps more convincing data lie buried somewhere in applied psychology or human engineering journals and, if so, a valuable service could be rendered by bringing them to light.

Several recent studies have explored the connection between spatial arrangement and group task. Sommer (1965) and Norum (1966) studied the arrangement of conversing, competing, coacting, and cooperating individuals. At a rectangular table, cooperating pairs sat side-by-side, conversing pairs sat corner-to-corner, and competing pairs sat across from one another, while coacting individuals sat in distant arrangements. In a separate study of cooperative and competitive working conditions using a like-sex decoy, the subjects sat opposite the decoy in the competitive condition and on the same side of the table in the cooperative condition.

The extent to which similar attitudes produce greater physical proximity remains in some dispute. Little, Ulehla, and Henderson (1965), using silhouette figures, found that pairs reputed to be Goldwater supporters were placed closer together than Goldwater-Johnson pairs, but the effect did not occur with Johnson-Johnson pairs. However, Elkin (1964), using actual discussion groups involving pro-pro, pro-anti, and anti-anti Medicare pairs of college students, found no differences in seating between concordant and discordant pairs. It is possible that the intensity of the discussion and the interest shown by each of the participants influences proximity more than attitude concordance or discordance.

Several psychiatrists and clinical psychologists have written speculative articles on the significance of various spatial arrangements in psychotherapy. Goodman (1959) made an intriguing comparison between the Freudian use of the couch, Sullivan's cross-the-table therapy, and the spatial freedom of the Gestalt therapists. Wilmer (1958), Winnick and Holt (1961), and Horowitz (1965) all discussed seating position from the standpoint of nonverbal communication in group psychotherapy.

INDIVIDUAL DISTANCE

The term individual distance was first used by Burckhardt (1944) to refer to the spacing that animals maintain between themselves and others of the same species. Several studies have been directed toward the question of how close people come to one another and to physical objects. Hall (1959) developed a detailed schema for conversational distance under various conditions of social and psychological closeness which ranged from 3–6 inches for soft intimate whispers to 8–20 feet for talking across the room in a loud voice. It is also likely that noise, bustle, or threat brings people together. To measure conversational distance, Sommer (1961) sent pairs into a large lounge where they could sit either side-by-side or across from one another to discuss designated topics. On the basis of previous work, it was assumed that people would sit across from one another rather than side-by-side unless the distance across was too great. It was found that the upper limit for comfortable conversation *under these specified conditions* was approximately 5.5 feet between individuals. A subsequent study used four chairs instead of couches so that the distance side-by-side as well as the distance across could be varied. Again the 5.5-foot conversational distance prevailed. However, a cursory examination of conversational distance in private homes revealed a much greater conversational range than this, something like 8–10 feet between chairs.

Other investigators have used paper-and-pencil or projective tests to study individual distance. Keuthe (1962, 1964) instructed students to pin yellow felt figures (a woman, man, child, dog, rectangles of various sizes) on a blue felt background in various combinations. Kuethe found that the woman and the child were placed closer together than the man and the child, while the dog was typically placed closer to the man than the woman. In all conditions, the people were placed closer together than the rectangles. Little (1965) used line drawings of males and females to examine concepts of individual distance. It was found that the degree of prior acquaintance attributed to cardboard figures influenced the distance they were placed apart. A replication using silhouettes and another using live actresses who were posed by the subject in scenes involving different activities also showed that the distance apart which the figures were placed was a function of the closeness of the relationship between them.

Horowitz, Duff, and Stratton (1964) investigated individual distance among schizophrenic and nonschizophrenic mental patients. Each subject was instructed to walk over to either another person or a hatrack, and the distance between his goal and his stopping place was measured. It was found that both groups approached the hatrack closer than they approached a person. Each subject tended to have a characteristic individual distance which was shorter for inanimate objects than for people. McBride, King, and James (1965) did a similar study testing GSR to varying amounts of closeness between subject and male or female experimenters. It was considered that GSR effects would provide an indication of the level of arousal associated with the proximity of neighbors. The authors found that GSR was greatest (skin resistance was least) when the subject was approached frontally, while a side approach yielded a greater response than a rear approach. The response to experimenters of the same sex was less than to experimenters of the opposite sex. Being touched by an object produced less of a GSR than being touched by a person. Argyle and Dean (1965) invited the subjects to participate in a perceptual experiment in which they were to "stand as close as comfortable to see well" to a book, a plaster head, and a cutout life-sized photograph of the senior author with his eyes closed and another with his eyes open. Among other results, the subjects placed themselves closer to the eyes-closed photograph than the eyes-open photograph.

Systematic violation of individual distance was undertaken by Garfinkel (1964) and Felipe and

Sommer (1966). Garfinkel reported that the violation of individual distance produced avoidance, bewilderment, and embarrassment, and that these effects were most pronounced among males. Felipe and Sommer systematically staged invasion sequences under natural conditions (people seated on benches and at library tables) and demonstrated observable flight reactions. Two recent studies have dealt with the relationship between individual distance and personality variables. Williams (1963) showed that introverts placed themselves further from other people than did extroverts. The same conclusion was reached by Leipold (1963), who noted the chair a person occupied vis-à-vis a seated decoy under anxiety and praise conditions. There was greater closeness under the praise than the anxiety conditions, and extroverts placed themselves closer to the decoy than introverts.

Sex differences in spacing have been found on a number of occasions, but the number of cultures sampled is limited. Several investigators (Elkin, 1964; Norum, 1966; Sommer, 1959) have found that females make more use of the side-by-side arrangements than do males. Side-by-side seating, which is generally considered to be the most intimate of all seating arrangements for people already acquainted, is comparatively rare among males if they are given the opportunity to sit across from one another. The idea that females can tolerate closer physical presence than males is underscored by observations of women holding hands or kissing one another, practices which are uncommon between males in this culture.

Campbell, Kruskal, and Wallace (1966) used seating arrangements of Negroes and whites as an index of attitude in three Chicago colleges. Clustering of Negroes and whites was found to be associated with differences in ethnic attitudes in the three schools. These authors and Strodtbeck and Hook (1961) attempted to develop appropriate statistical techniques for analyzing aggregation data. Tabulating the results of a single observation involving a large number of individuals whose behavior at times relates to one another and at times to aspects of the physical environment is no small achievement, but when one assembles the records of repeated observations of individuals, some observed many times and some just one, the difficulties multiply. It is fortunate than animal ecologists and zoologists have encountered these problems over the years and have developed useful methods for measuring aggregation, dispersion, home range, and social distance. McBride (1964) has developed computer programs to assess the degree of non-randomness within an aggregation. Esser (1965), working on a closed research ward of a mental hospital with the available area divided into squares so that the location of each patient can be charted during the entire working day, has obtained detailed records of individual behavior similar to those of the better tracking studies by animal biologists, but he has not yet reached the same level of precision in relating the individual patients' locations one to another. The problems in analyzing the interdependency between a large number of individuals with $n(n-1)$ dyadic relationships has led some investigators to use physical aspects of the environment such as walls, partitions, and chairs as coordinates for locating individuals. A new approach (Bechtel & Srivastava, 1966) is the development of the Hodometer, an electronic recording device placed on the floor of a building to measure use of given areas as well as pathways. A much cruder index of area usage was suggested by Webb, Campbell, Schwartz, and Sechrest (1966), who examined the wear on floortiles in front of different museum exhibits.

DISCUSSION

Knowledge of how groups arrange themselves can assist in fostering or discouraging group relationships. A library which is intended to be *sociofugal space* (Osmond, 1957), aimed at discouraging interaction, requires knowledge of how to arrange people to minimize unwanted contact. It may be possible to use the rank order of preferred arrangements by interacting groups as arrangements *to be avoided* in sociofugal space. On this basis, corner-to-corner seating would be less satisfactory than opposite or distant seating in a sociofugal setting. An Emily Post or Amy Vanderbilt may know these principles intuitively, and diplomatic protocol may codify them, but there is value in making them explicit and subjecting them to empirical test. To an increasingly greater extent we find ourselves being arranged by impersonal environments in lecture halls, airports, waiting rooms, and lobbies. Many aspects of the proximate environment, including furniture and room dividers have been placed for ease of maintenance and efficient cleaning with little cognizance to their social functions. These principles will be of most help in institutional settings such as schools, hospitals, public buildings, and old folk's homes where the occupants have little control over their surroundings. The straight-row arrangement of most classrooms has been taken for granted for too long. The typical long narrow shape of a classroom resulted from a desire to get light across the room. The front of each room was determined by window location, since pupils had to be seated so that window light came over the left shoulder. However, new developments in lighting, acoustics, ventilation, and fireproofing have rendered invalid many of the arguments for the boxlike room with straight rows. In mental hospitals, the isolation of schizophrenic individuals can be furthered by sociofugal settings which minimize social contact, or reduced through sociopetal buildings aimed at reinforcing social behavior. The former approach is valid if one wants to provide an optimal environment in terms of the individual's present needs, the latter if society desires to shape the patient's social behavior to facilitate his return to society. It is mindless to design mental hospitals without taking cognizance of the connection between physical environment and social behavior. The study of small group ecology is important not only from the standpoint of developing an adequate theory of relationships that takes into account the context of social relationships, but also from the practical standpoint of designing and maintaining functional contexts in which human relationships can develop.

Several problems of method must be resolved before a relevant theory of group ecology can be developed. Having reviewed the studies themselves, problems in recording and some special characteristics of the settings in which the studies have taken place should be mentioned. The studies described have generally tabulated gross categories of behavior without any real specificity or precision. A person's location has been plotted as if this described his orientation, head angle, arm position, etc. Stated another way, the investigators whose work has been described here have relied almost exclusively on the eyeball technique of recording. Some, such as Esser and McBride, are moving into the electronic processing of observational data, but the improved precision is in data analysis rather than the integration of various facets of spatial behavior. Very little use has been made of photographic recordings. One would hardly undertake the study of comparative linguistics without a tape recorder, but only a handful of investigators whose work we have discussed have used still photographs, much less moving pictures. Twenty-five years ago, Efron (1941) hired a professional artist to sketch conversing groups. A few anthropologists, such as Birdwistell and Hall, are currently accumulating film libraries of interaction data. McBride found it necessary to photograph aggregations of fowl from small towers above the coops. It is difficult to get good photographs of the spatial arrangements of people from the horizontal plane, particularly if there are more than two individuals involved. Yet, it seems likely that the real breakthroughs in this field will occur when methods for monitoring angle of orientation, eye contact, and various other nonverbal cues are developed for use in standard interaction situations. The argument for and against laboratory studies of group behavior which involve one-way mirrors, microphones, and hidden photographic equipment compared to field studies in playgrounds, schools, and city streets will not be reviewed here. However, a promising solution is the field-laboratory method used by Sherif (1954) in his camp studies where he employed a standard controlled situation, in the sense that relevant variables were specified in advance and introduced in specified ways by the experimenter but always under conditions that appeared natural and appropriate to the subjects. Another limiting element in the work to date is that almost all the studies have involved discussion groups around tables and chairs. We know little about the ecology of working groups (apart from sociometric data) or coacting individuals, particularly if they are standing or moving. Again, the technical problems of recording interaction patterns of moving individuals are much greater than if the individuals are seated in a classroom or around a conference table.

Along with this is a disproportionate number of environmental studies that have taken place under conditions of confinement, particularly in mental hospitals. At this time there are at least seven studies underway on the use of space by mental patients. As far as the writer knows, this exceeds the number of current studies of spatial behavior on nonhospitalized individuals. Mental hospital studies allow greater control and environmental manipulation than can be achieved outside a total institution, but they also confound the effects of schizophrenia and institutionalization as a social process over time with the effects of captivity and locked doors as spatial variables.

REFERENCES

Argyle, M. and Dean, J. Eye contact, distance, and affiliation. *Sociometry,* 1965, **28**, 289–304.

Bass, B. M. and Klubeck, S. Effects of seating arrangements on leaderless group discussions. *Journal of Abnormal and Social Psychology,* 1952, **47**, 724–27.

Bavelas, A. Communication processes in task-oriented groups. *Journal of the Acoustical Society of America,* 1950, **22**, 725–30.

Bechtel, R. B. and Srivastava, R. Human movement and architectural environment. *Milieu,* 1966, **2**, 7–8.

Burckhardt, D. Mowenbeobachtungen in Basel. *Ornithologische Beobachter,* 1944, **5**, 49–76.

Campbell, D. T., Kruskal, W. H., and Wallace, W. P. Seating aggregation as an index of attitude. *Sociometry,* 1966, **29**, 1–15.

Efron, D. *Gesture and environment.* New York: Kings Crown Press, 1941.

Elkin, L. The behavioral use of space. Unpublished master's thesis, University of Saskatchewan, 1964.

Esser, A., *et al.* Territoriality of patients on a research ward. In, *Recent advances in biological psychiatry.* Vol. 7. New York: Plenum Press, 1965.

Felipe, N. Interpersonal distance and small group interaction. *Cornell Journal of Social Relations,* 1966, **1**, 59–64.

Felipe, N. and Sommer, R. Invasions of personal space. *Social Problems,* 1966, 13, 25–45.

Garfinkel, H. Studies of the routine grounds of everyday activities. *Social Problems,* 1964, **11**, 225–50.

Goodman, P. Meaning of functionalism. *Journal of Architectural Education,* 1959, **14**, 32–38.

Grusky, O. Organization goals and the behavior of informal leaders. *American Journal of Sociology,* 1959, **65**, 59–67.

Hall, E. T. *The silent language.* Garden City, N.Y.: Doubleday, 1959.

Hare, A. P. and Bales, R. F. Seating position and small group interaction. *Sociometry,* 1963, **26**, 480–86.

Hearn, G. Leadership and the spatial factor in small groups. *Journal of Abnormal and Social Psychology,* 1957, **54**, 269–72.

Horowitz, M. J. Human spatial behavior. *American Journal of Psychotherapy,* 1965, **19**, 20–28.

Horowitz, M. J., Duff, D. F., and Stratton, L. O. Body-buffer zone. *Archives of General Psychiatry,* 1964, **11**, 651–56.

Howells, L. T. and Becker, S. W. Seating arrangement and leadership emergence. *Journal of Abnormal and Social Psychology,* 1962, **64**, 148–50.

Kuethe, J. L. Social schemas. *Journal of Abnormal and Social Psychology,* 1962, **64**, 31–38.

Kuethe, J. L. Pervasive influence of social schemata. *Journal of Abnormal and Social Psychology,* 1964, **68**, 248–54.

Leavitt, H. J. Some effects of certain communication patterns in group performance. *Journal of Abnormal and Social Psychology,* 1951, **46**, 38–50.

Leipold, W. D. Psychological distance in a dyadic interview. Unpublished doctoral dissertation, University of North Dakota, 1963.

Little, K. B. Personal space. *Journal of Experimental Social Psychology,* 1965, 1, 237–47.

Little, K. B., Ulehla, J., and Henderson, C. Value homophily and interaction distance. Unpublished manuscript, University of Denver, 1965.

McBride, G. *A general theory of social organization and behavior.* St. Lucia: University of Queensland Press, 1964.

McBride, G., King, M. G., and James, J. W. Social proximity effects on GSR in adult humans. *Journal of Psychology,* 1965, **61**, 153–57.

Norum, G. A. Perceived interpersonal relationships and spatial arrangements. Unpublished master's thesis, University of California, Davis, 1966.

Osmond, H. Function as a basis of psychiatric ward design. *Mental Hospitals,* 1957, **8**, 23–29.

Sherif, M. Integrating field work and laboratory in small group research. *American Sociological Review,* 1954, **19**, 759–71.

Sommer, R. Studies in personal space. *Sociometry,* 1959, **22**, 247–60.

Sommer, R. Leadership and group geography. *Sociometry,* 1961, **24**, 99–110.

Sommer, R. Further studies in small group ecology. *Sociometry,* 1965, **28**, 337–48.

Steinzor, B. The spatial factor in face to face discussion groups. *Journal of Abnormal and Social Psychology,* 1950, **45**, 552–55.

Strodtbeck, F. L. and Hook, L. H. The social dimensions of a twelve man jury table. *Sociometry,* 1961, **24**, 397–415.

Webb, E. J., Campbell, D. T., Schwartz, R. D., and Sechrest, L. *Unobtrusive measures: Non-reactive research in the social sciences.* Chicago: Rand McNally, 1966.

Williams, J. L. Personal space and its relation to extroversion-introversion. Unpublished master's thesis, University of Alberta, 1963.

Wilmer, H. A. Graphic ways of representing some aspects of a therapeutic community. In, *Symposium of preventive and social psychiatry.* Washington, D.C.: United States Government Printing Office, 1958.

Winnick, C. and Holt, H. Seating position as non-verbal communication in group analysis. *Psychiatry,* 1961, **24**, 171–82.

38. EFFECTS OF GROUP SIZE*

***Edwin J. Thomas and Clinton F. Fink*†**

This paper reviews 31 empirical studies of small groups in which the major independent variable, group size, was related to several classes of dependent variables: group performance, distribution of participation, the nature of interaction, group organization, member performance, conformity and consensus, and member satisfaction. Many of these variables were found to be significantly affected by group size, but methodological shortcomings characterizing this group of studies preclude the assertion of broad generalizations. Several dependable and nondependable intervening variables are suggested which may help to account for many of the observed effects. Conclusions are: group size is an important variable which should be taken into account in any theory of group behavior, and future research on group size should proceed more systematically than in the past.[1]

This report is an effort to formulate generalizations about the effects of group size from a critical review of past research and an analysis of methods and problems relating to this subject. It is focused mainly on studies of face-to-face groups ranging in size from 2–20 members, in which behavior was studied directly by observations, questionnaires, or interviews. Because of their relevance a few studies are included that depart in some respect from these criteria. While making no claim to comprehensiveness, we have included all studies that we could locate through 1960 meeting the above standards. In earlier reviews of research relating to small groups there were sections on group size (Kelley & Thibaut, 1954; Lorge, Fox, Davitz, & Brenner, 1958), but no thorough review has been written. Studies of the size of families, organizations, cities, and societies are only generally relevant in this context and therefore have been excluded (see Caplow, 1957, for a review of studies relating to organizational size).

The studies discussed here do not represent an integrated attack upon a single problem or set of problems. Instead, they deal with a wide range of dependent variables and are concerned with establishing empirical relationships rather than with testing the implications of some general theory. To order the findings meaningfully, we have found it convenient to discuss them as specific topics under one of two major categories: *(a)* effects on the group as a whole, which include group performance, the distribution of participation, the nature of interaction, and group organization; and *(b)* effects on member behavior, including individual performance, conformity and consensus, and member satisfaction.

EFFECTS FOR THE GROUP AS A WHOLE

Group Performance

Ten experimental studies dealt with the effects of group size on group performance in problem solving or judgmental tasks. These findings are summarized according to four main classes of dependent variables: quality of performance, speed, efficiency, and productivity.

The quality of group solving was examined in four studies with mixed results. Taylor and Faust (1952) found that in playing the game Twenty Questions, four-man groups correctly solved more problems than did two-man groups. Similarly, Fox, Lorge, Weltz, and Herrold (1953) found that the quality of solutions to complex human-relations problems was significantly greater for groups of 12 and 13 than for groups of 6, 7, and 8. In contrast, Lorge and Solomon (1959, 1960) discovered no relation between group size (2–5 members in the first study and 3, 4, 6, and 7 members in the second) and the proportion of groups which arrived at the correct solution to the Tartaglia problem.

The quality of group judgments based on collective decisions also showed mixed relationships to group size. South (1927) found no difference between three-person and six-person groups in their ability to judge emotional expressions from photographs, but he did find that the six-person groups were better (i.e., agreed more with expert opinion) at judging the quality of English compositions. Ziller (1957) presented groups of two to six Air Force officers with two types of task: he found a positive relationship between group size and the quality of the group's judgment concerning the importance of certain facts for making military decisions; however, there was a curvilinear relationship between size and the accuracy of the group's judgment of the number of dots on a card with four- and five-man groups doing less well than two-, three-, and six-man groups. Perlmutter's study (1953) involved group memory rather than judgment: he found that three-person groups had somewhat better immediate

* *Psychological Bulletin,* Vol. 60, No. 4 (1963), pp. 371–84.

† School of Social Work, University of Michigan and Mental Health Research Institute, University of Michigan, respectively.

[1] This article reports portions of a research project financed by a grant from the Horace H. Rackham School of Graduate Studies of the University of Michigan.

recall for a story (The War of the Ghosts) than did two-person groups, but the difference was not statistically significant.

Speed of group performance was observed in three of the above studies (Perlmutter, 1953; South, 1927; Taylor & Faust, 1952) as well as in the study by Kidd (1958). In each case, speed was measured in terms of the amount of time required for the group to complete the task. Group size did not influence speed in the case of four problem solving tasks or the memory task. However, in the two judgmental tasks used by South, three-person groups were faster than six-person groups. South suggested that the judgmental tasks required the group to reach a compromise; to the extent that more discussion is needed in order to reconcile a wider variety of initial opinions, this would account for the fact that the larger groups took longer to reach a decision.

The efficiency with which the group solves a problem was considered in connection with two tasks we have designated as "concept attainment" tasks. According to Taylor and Faust, two-person groups were more efficient than four-person groups since they expended fewer man minutes of "labor." However, this is not really a new finding, since it is mathematically implied by the fact that there was no difference in speed as a function of size. Another meaning of problem solving efficiency involves the amount of intellectual effort expended, which in this case is measured by the number of questions asked by the group before they reached a solution. This measure of efficiency failed to differentiate between two- and four-person groups in the Taylor and Faust study, but South found that six-person groups were more efficient than three-person groups.

Group productivity, defined as the number of correct units produced in a given time period, was examined in three experiments. Comparing groups of Sizes 3–10 Watson (1928) found a correlation of 0.65 between size and the number of different correct words created in an anagrams task. With a similar task, unscrambling sentences, Kidd found no differences in productivity between groups of two, four, and six. Gibb (1951) briefly reported a comparison between individuals and groups of Sizes 2, 3, 6, 12, 24, 48, and 96 and reported that the number of suggested solutions to a complex problem increased as a negatively accelerated function of group size.

Considering the group performance findings as a whole, it appears that both quality of performance and group productivity were positively correlated with group size under some conditions, and under no conditions were smaller groups superior. In contrast, measures of speed showed no difference or else favored the smaller groups. The heterogeneity of tasks and of measurement procedures prevent more precise generalizations.

Distribution of Participation

Four studies were focused on the relative degree of participation of each member. In one of the earliest investigations in this area Dawe (1934) kept a record of the number of remarks made by each child in kindergarten classes ranging in size from 14 to 46. The total number of remarks decreased with increasing size, but not to a statistically significant degree. While an increase in the size of the group was accompanied by an increase in the total number of children who spoke ($r = 0.82$), there was a decrease in the proportion of the group who spoke ($r = 0.58$). Dawe reported also that the members who were seated toward the front of the room tended to speak more often than those seated further back, indicating that a spatial factor may be one determinant of the relationship between size and participation.

Using Bales' categories, Bales, Strodtbeck, Mills, and Roseborough (1951) observed interaction in leaderless discussion groups ranging in size from three to eight members. As size increased there was an increase in the relative discrepancy between the percentage of participation for the person ranked first and that for the person ranked second and a reduction in the difference between the percentage of participation for the person ranked second and for all those with less participation. The authors attempted to fit a harmonic function to these curves, but with no success. Later Stephan (1952) was able to fit an exponential curve more successfully to the same data.

Stephan and Mishler (1952) conducted an experiment to assess the generality of their exponential model beyond the type of group and method of gathering data used in the study by Bales *et al.* (1951). The unit of participation was all the verbal behavior exhibited by an individual between the time the previous speaker finished and the next began—a much larger unit than was used in the earlier study. In groups ranging in size from 4 to 12 members, they obtained results essentially the same as those of Bales *et al.*

The relationship between group size and the distribution of acts was analyzed by Miller (1951) for groups of Sizes 3–10, 12, 14, 16, 18, and 20. Although Miller used the same unit of participation as Stephan and Mishler, the task was different: the game Twenty Questions. As in Dawe's study, it was found that the average number of participations per member decreased as size increased ($r = -0.80$).

This of course is what would be expected when the length of the discussion period and the rate of participation are both held constant: as the group increases in size there is less opportunity for any individual to speak. However, this reduction in opportunity to speak did not seem to be accompanied by decreasing participation of the members not ranked highest, for there was found a small, nonsignificant negative correlation between group size and the number of persons who deviated from their expected percentage of participation based on equal distribution. Thus Miller's study casts doubt on the generality of the findings of Bales *et al.* and Stephan and Mishler and of the models developed to depict the results.

Nature of Interaction

Four additional studies provided information about the qualitative characteristics of group interaction. To study the "interaction profile" of the acts in the 12 categories of Bales' scheme, Bales and Borgatta (1955) observed discussion groups ranging in size from two to seven. The raw number of acts in each category was made a percentage of the total number of acts in the 12 categories and then converted by an arc-sine transformation. Analysis indicated that as size increased, there was an increase in the categories of showing tension release and giving suggestions; and a decrease in categories of showing tension, showing agreement, and asking for opinion. In addition, two-person groups appeared to have certain unique properties, namely, a high rate in the category of showing tension coupled with low rates in the categories of showing disagreement and showing antagonism. An odd-even effect was also apparent: groups of four and six showed higher rates than did groups of three, five, and seven in the categories of showing disagreement and showing antagonism, but lower rates in the category of asking for suggestions. These findings must be interpreted as representing *relative* increases or decreases in an interaction category. Bales and Borgatta offer intriguing speculations to interpret the trends, but it is difficult to draw conclusions about what the *critical changes* may be as size increases from two to seven because a relative increase in one category may come about due to either an absolute increase for the category may come about due to either an absolute increase for the category or an absolute decrease for all other categories, or both.

Bales and Borgatta also analyzed variability over four sessions for individuals and groups. They found increased variability for each individual's performance as size increased. The authors claimed that scores may have been less reliable in the larger groups because of partitioning scores among a greater number of persons. Another interpretation given by these researchers is that there may have been more shifting of roles in larger groups because there were more persons to perform role functions. Trends of variability among individuals, of given groups over successive sessions and among groups, revealed no clear-cut size effects.

Slater (1958) used Bales' categories with groups ranging from two to seven and concluded that there were inhibiting forces in the smallest groups which prevented the expression of dissatisfaction and disagreement. Scores on an Inhibition Index (the ratio of the number of acts in four agreement categories to the number of acts in five disagreement categories) were significantly higher in groups of two, three, and four than in groups of five, six, and seven. Slater's explanation was that the consequences of alienating a single member may have been more severe in the smaller than in the larger groups.

A study by Berkowitz (1958) of groups of 3, 4, 6, 7, 9, and 10 members revealed that there was more disagreement in solving logical problems in the larger groups than in the smaller groups—a finding consistent with those of Slater and Bales and Borgatta.

Bass and Norton (1951) observed leaderless discussion groups of 2, 4, 6, 8, and 12 members in which each member was rated on nine aspects of leadership behavior. As group size increased, the average leadership rating assigned to group members decreased significantly—group size accounting for 83 percent of the variance. There was also a nonsignificant tendency for the within-group variance of ratings to increase with size. The authors concluded that opportunity to adopt leadership functions decreased directly with an increase in group size.

Tentatively it would appear that smaller groups inhibit expression of disagreements and dissatisfactions more than larger groups and give each individual more opportunity to interact and to exhibit leadership behavior. The possibility that there are unique, odd-even and near-linear size effects on the nature of interaction, as Bales and Borgatta suggest, should be pursued further, possibly using different methods from the ones employed by these researchers.

Group Organization

The last set of studies related to effects on the group as a whole concerns group organization. In Berkowitz's study of the social organization of problem solving groups, 20 variables were found to be significantly affected by group size and most of these were reduced by a cluster analysis to two relatively independent sets of variables. The first cluster was called group cohesion, consisting mainly of sociometric variables such as the number of friendship choices. The components of this cluster were negatively related to size. The second cluster consisted of variables reflecting organization and division of labor. The variables in this cluster and their relationship to size follow: as size increased, there was decreasing contribution of the least active member, higher member variation of interaction, higher variation in the number of rules for solving the problem suggested by members and subsequently adopted by the group, increasing number of leaders, higher variation of rules suggested by each man, increasing number of votes required to reach decisions, increasing suggestions conveyed by those who did not originally make the suggestion, and higher specialization in the use of rules to solve the problems.

In a study of factors affecting consensus in decision making groups, Hare (1952) found a greater tendency for groups of 12 than for groups of five to break into factions or cliques. This trend was not significant, however, and was based on the reports of group members. Probably more reliable are the findings of Miller who observed directly the frequency with which two or more members of a group talked or whispered among themselves rather than to the group as a whole. A significant correlation of 0.77 was found between the number of members (3–10, 12, 14, 16, 18, and 20) and the number of cliques. Also, Miller found that this increase in cliques was associated with a decrease in group cohesiveness: a Cohesiveness Index correlated −0.52 with group size and −0.60 with the number of cliques.

After familiarizing subjects with the concept of the primary group, Fisher (1953) asked them to describe the primary groups to which they belonged and rank them for intimacy. Within the size range of 2–12 members, smaller groups were ranked as significantly more intimate.

Taken together, these studies indicate that as size increases there will be decreasing group cohesiveness and increasing organization and division of labor in the group, along with the development of cliques and possibly of factions.

EFFECTS ON MEMBER BEHAVIOR

Individual Performance

The effect of group size on individual performance has been considered primarily in connection with practical problems. In education, for example, there is a long history of concern with class size as a possible influence on classroom learning. We will not attempt to review this literature here, since it has been covered by Hudelson (1928), Von Borgersrode (1941), Goodlad (1960), and McKeachie (1963). Hudelson reported on 59 controlled experiments of the effects of class size, 46 of which favored large over small classes. In Von Borgersrode's review 73 studies were appraised, 19 of which were classified as semicontrolled and 24 as controlled; his conclusion was that "On the whole the statistical findings definitely favor the large classes at every level of instruction except kindergarten" (p. 199). In his review of the effects of lecture size at the college level, McKeachie noted that more recent studies have not been as complimentary to large lectures as were the earlier studies done during the 1920s. Nevertheless, he concluded that large lectures were not generally inferior. Lorge *et al.* (1958) made reference in their review of together-alone studies to some of the literature on classroom learning and concluded that there was probably an interaction between class size, teaching methods, and study methods as determinants of educational effectiveness. But even so, the consensus of the reviewers was that large classes are either superior to small classes or at least not inferior.

A second area of practical concern is the productivity of individual workers as a function of the size of work groups. Marriot (1949) found that the amount produced by male workers in a British factory, as measured by average piecework earnings per man, declined significantly as the size of the work group increased from 10 to 50 members. In contrast, Gekoski (1952) found a non-significant positive relation between individual productivity and size of work group (4–19 members) among female clerical workers in an American insurance company. Because these studies differed simultaneously along several dimensions, we have no basis for speculation as to the specific conditions which determine whether group size will be positively or negatively correlated with individual productivity.

Two experiments dealt with the individual's improvement in problem solving as a result of his interacting in groups of varying size. Taylor and Faust (1952) found that practice in playing Twenty Questions enhanced the individual's ability to solve such problems, but it did not matter whether the practice was obtained alone, as a member of a two-person group or as a member of a four-person group. By contrast, positive results were reported by Utterback and Fotheringham (1958) in regard to the quality of solutions to human relations problems. Individual answers were recorded both before and after a discussion in groups of 3, 6, 9, or 12 members. Improvement in quality of the individual's solutions was significantly greater for the larger groups.

However, there was also a significant interaction between group size and the manner in which the discussion was led: when the moderator intervened a great deal ("full moderation"), individual improvement was greatest for 12-person groups; but when the moderator intervened very little ("partial moderation"), individual improvement was greatest for three-person groups. Thus group size sometimes is related to individual problem solving, but the direction of the relationship is highly dependent on group conditions other than size.

Conformity and Consensus

In his famous experiment on yielding to a group of peers who, unknown to the naïve subject, had been instructed to report unanimous but incorrect judgments of the length of visually presented lines, Asch (1953) manipulated the size of the unanimous opposition. He found that as the number of confederates increased from 1 to 3, the amount of yielding to their unanimous judgment increased significantly; but there was no further increase in conformity as the confederates increased in number to 4, 8, or 16. In two related studies, Goldberg (1954) and Kidd (1958) failed to find any effect of group size even though their manipulations of group pressure did succeed in producing a significant amount of conformity. Goldberg's subjects, in groups of 2 or 4, made individual judgments of the intelligence of persons from their photographs; while Kidd's subjects, in groups of 2, 4, or 6 made individual judgments of flicker frequency. In both experiments, each individual made a second judgment after being exposed to false feedback concerning the group's average first judgment. Conformity, as measured by shifting toward the bogus group average, occurred in all groups, but the amount of yielding was not related to group size in either experiment. In contrast, Kishida (1956) found a significant size effect using groups of 5, 10, and 30 Japanese university students. Subjects responded individually to an opinion questionnaire, then received true feedback as to the majority opinion, and finally responded a second time to the questionnaire. Although there was a shift toward conformity in all groups, magnitude of opinion change showed a curvilinear relationship to group size, being greatest in 10-person groups and least in five-person groups. The results of these four studies indicate that the magnitude of the group's influence on the individual is a function of group size under some conditions, but differences in task and procedure again preclude specification of the relevant conditions.

A second set of findings involved measurement of the individual's opinion both before and after group discussion of a problem. Half of Kishida's (1956) groups discussed the opinion items and arrived at a group decision. Analysis of the individual postdiscussion responses indicated that shift toward the group opinion bore the same curvilinear relationship to group size under discussion conditions as in the condition involving feedback of the majority opinion. A negative effect of group size was found by Hare (1952) with groups of 5 and 12 Boy Scouts, with two measures showing that consensus increased more in the smaller groups. Finally, Utterback and Fotheringham (1958) reported a significant interaction between group size and the amount of intervention by the discussion moderator. Increase in consensus was greatest in 12-person groups under full moderation, but greatest in 3-person groups under partial moderation. However, there was no main effect of group size in this study. These findings lend further weight to the conclusion that group size is an important factor in determining the amount of yielding to conformity pressures.

Member Satisfaction

Questionnaire measures of members' subjective reactions to the group were included in four of the studies cited above. Both Hare (1952) and Slater (1958) found that members of larger groups were significantly less satisfied with the amount of time available for discussion, with their opportunity to participate, and with the group meeting or its decision. In addition, Slater found that his subjects considered five members to be optimum (i.e., neither too large nor too small) for the task of discussing a human relations problem. In contrast to the others, Ziller (1957) found no clear relationship between group size and members' satisfaction with their own part in the discussion, and Miller (1951) found no relationship between group size and three measures of satisfaction. With this exception, the general trend of the findings indicates that the smaller the group, the more likely it is that the individual will be satisfied with the discussion and with his own part in it. McKeachie's (1963) review of studies on discussion groups at the college level also indicated that larger groups were less satisfying to both students and instructors. It must be remembered, however, that the studies referred to here all dealt with discussion groups attempting to solve particular problems, and that the generalization may not apply to other types of groups.

EVALUATION

More converging findings emerged from this review than one might have expected considering that only 31 empirical investigations of group size were found to be relevant. But many more studies will have to be conducted and appraised before general conclusions can be drawn with confidence about the numerous effects of group size. Aside from their relatively small number, this set of studies, when considered collectively, has other limitations as a basis for generalized inferences. These shortcomings and problems are discussed below.

Methodological Difficulties

The arbitrary and unsystematic selection of sizes for comparison is perhaps one of the most serious methodological shortcomings of this group of studies. The pertinent range of sizes in order to generalize safely about small groups would seem to be two through at least 20. Two biases in drawing samples from this range are common. One is to sample a truncated series of the range, such as Sizes 2–4, and the other is to draw samples omitting various adjacent sizes so that there is an overrepresentation of odd or even sizes. Such biases may obscure the true functional relationship between size and the dependent variable. There is no reason to expect only a single type of function, such as a linear relationship, to hold between size and any dependent variable: in the studies reviewed here it was not uncommon to find a curvilinear relationship (cf. Asch, 1953; Gibb, 1951; Kishida, 1956; Ziller, 1957). From information about a limited portion of the size range, it is of course impossible to extrapolate with confidence to the type of functional relationship characterizing the entire range. As Borgatta and Cottrell (1957) have noted, the effects of size may be quantitative or discrete. The apparent linear effects, the odd-even differences, and the uniqueness of Size 2 would not have been noted by Bales and Borgatta had they sampled a more limited series of sizes.

A second limitation of this group of studies is that many independent variables other than group size were involved. The most conspicuous of these were the population characteristics of the subjects. In many cases, the observed groups were composed of either all male or all female members; in other cases, the groups were mixed; and a few investigators failed to report the sex of their subjects. The age and education of subjects were other population characteristics with respect to which the studies differed. The tasks employed were similarly heterogeneous, and like the population characteristics, could have interacted with group size to produce the obtained results. In general, these studies provide very little information concerning the conditions under which group size is related in some specific way to some particular variable.

Another shortcoming of this group of studies is the failure of the majority of the investigators to seek to determine *why* changes in group size had the observed effects. Rather than focusing on causal analysis, most of the researchers have used what might be called a "correlational" approach, which generally begins and ends with an empirical concern with the relationship between group size and a given dependent variable. It is as if many of the studies proceeded on the assumption that size should somehow have an immediate effect upon some aspect of behavior, and, as a consequence, relevant intervening variables were almost never measured or varied experimentally.

A basically different approach to the study of group size follows from the view that the size variable will have no behavioral effects when stripped of various social and psychological accompaniments. It is apparent, for example, that if there is no interdependence or communication between members, the size of the group is irrelevant to the prediction of behavioral changes for the members. An analysis and design oriented toward isolating the critical intervening variables in the relationship between size and the dependent variables should be the objective of studies which aspire to understand why size has effects.

Indik's (1961) study of the relationship between the size of voluntary organizations and the tendency of members to participate, clearly illustrates the importance of establishing a procedure to search for, and examine, the effects of possible intervening variables. Although voluntary organizations ranging in membership from 15 to 2,983 were studied, the method illustrated is fully applicable to the small group. It was hypothesized that the negative relationship between size of organization and tendency of members to participate (as indicated by absenteeism in a service company and attendance in a women's association) is mediated by organizational variables (e.g, amount of communication, job and task specialization, higher level interpersonal control and coordination) and psychological variables (e.g., attraction of members to the organization, satisfaction with one's activities performed in the organization, and perceived bureaucratic inflexibility). Four explanatory schemas were proposed in each of which size was linked to an organizational and a psychological intervening variable. The schema which found the strongest support was the one which hypothesized that the size of the organization would be negatively related to the amount of communication among members, that the amount of communication of each member would be positively associated with the attraction of members to the organization, and that the attraction of the members to the organization would be positively associated with tendency to participate. Analyses were also made of the other schemas and from these it was concluded that various intervening variables mediated the relationship between size and participation. This approach to the problem is distinctly more sophisticated than that of relating size to a given dependent variable without considering possible intervening conditions. However, Indik did not let the problem rest with the results reported above, for he ran higher order partial correlations, holding constant pairs of intervening variables, to see what effects this would have on the magnitude of the original correlation of −0.53 between size and tendency to participate. When the combined effects of the specialization-satisfaction linkage were removed the correlation between size of organization and tendency to participate dropped from −0.53 to −0.26; when the effects of lack of coordination and perceived bureaucratic inflexibility were removed, the correlation dropped further to −0.17; and finally, when the communication-attraction linkage was removed, the partial correlation was left at −0.08.

Dependable Intervening Variables

If group size is phenotypic and really but a correlate of the social and psychological conditions capable of producing changes in member and group behavior, it would be fruitful to stipulate what these intervening variables are. Can we say that some intervening variables will always or most always be influenced by variations in group size? If there are such variables and if these variables also produce relevant outcomes, then hypotheses predicating such outcomes as a function of size should be more or less axiomatically correct. Various classes of such variables are discussed below, along with examples and probable effects.

Input Quantity. Two types of input may be assumed to increase with group size. The first is *resource input,* such as interaction skills, knowledge, capacities, and physical strength. If we designate the amount of any given resource brought to the group by an individual as r, and the total amount of the resources of all group members made use of in the group as R, then $R = f(r, n)$ where n equals group size. For some resources each individual will contribute approximately equal amounts in which case $R = r \times n$; for other resources the amounts will vary widely among individuals and the functional relationship between r and n will be more complex. Whether R is greater than, less than, or equal to the sum of the individual resources $\left(\sum_{i=1}^{n} r_i\right)$ depends upon facilitating and hindering group conditions. But in general, R increases with increasing group size, whether or not the relationship is linear.

The relevance of viewing resource input as a dependable intervening variable is clear in the case of group problem solving. If knowledge is needed to solve a problem and each individual brings particular knowledge that others do not have, with increasing size there will be greater likelihood that the total amount of knowledge pertinent for solving the problem will be available in the group. If intelligence is the resource required for solving the problem, then the addition of each individual increases the likelihood that someone will have the capacity to solve the problem. Assuming that problem difficulty is known, the application of elementary probability theory to this problem readily makes possible the writing of formulas to express the likelihood of intellectual capacities being brought to the group with the addition of each individual. Thus one may state the likelihood that there will be at least one member in the group with the correct answer, that there will be more than half with the correct answer, that everyone will be correct, that everyone will be incorrect, or that there will be mixed correct and incorrect answers. If p equals the probability of the success of the individual working alone on the problem, n is the number of individuals in the group and q equals $1 - p$, then the probability that there will be at least one person in the group arriving at the right answer equals $1 - (1 - p)^n$. Taylor (1954), Ekman (1955), and Lorge and Solomon (1955) have all applied this basic idea to group problem solving where it is useful to compare results against theoretical probabilities based on the assumption that if one member gets the correct answer the group will accept it.

The formula given above applies to problems having one stage in their solution, but may be extended to multistage problems, as Lorge and Solomon have done. Their formula for the probability of a group solving a multistage problem is the product of the probabilities that the group can solve the problem for each stage. Steiner and Rajaratnam (1961) have further extended the basic idea by developing formulas, applicable to interval data, which make it possible to test the null hypothesis that groups function at the level of the most competent member, of the least competent member, or at any level of competence. In considering group solutions that can be represented as distributions of individual answers, Thomas and Fink (1961) have elaborated three models (independence, rational, and consensus) which state varying antecedent group conditions and the associated theoretical probabilities of having everyone correct, some correct and incorrect, and everyone incorrect for problems involving two- alternative and multialternative solutions.

A second type of input that increases with size is *demand input.* The demands each individual brings to the group include the need for recognition, affection, a minimum amount of social interaction, and so on. As size increases the sum of these individual demands increases. One of the main implications of an increase in demand input with increasing size is that larger groups will need more resources than smaller groups in order to meet the demand. Furthermore, we may assume that to the extent that larger groups are unable to satisfy demands of the members there will be decreased attractiveness, lack of reward, resulting in dissatisfaction, lowered morale, and a tendency to leave the group. If we assume that each person has some desire to communicate in group discussions, then restricting the amount of time to discuss a problem, as Hare (1952) did, will result in greater demand on time in the larger groups. Hare's finding that there was decreased satisfaction with the discussion in the larger groups as compared with the smaller groups is understandable in terms of the above comments.

Increasing Sample Size. As the size of the group increases, there is obviously an increase in the size of the sample of individuals. One consequence of increasing sample size is that there is more accurate estimation of parameters of the parent population when the sample is taken from a nonhomogeneous universe and the individuals are not added to the group by a biased method. Parameter estimation is illustrated by the results of a study by Eysenck (1939) in which the rankings of a sample of 200 subjects concerning their preferences for 12 black and white pictures were compared with the criterion of the average rankings by 700 subjects. It was found that as the number of unbiased judges increased, the correlation of their pooled rankings with a criterion increased. Sampling and test theory abound with other illustrations. In Ziller's study, judgments of the number of dots on a card should have been more accurate with increasing group size in the same way that he found increasing correspondence between the judgment of military experts on human relations problems with the judgments of the group members as size increased. One can only conclude that the errors in judgment were not random in the problem of judging dot numerosity, or that biased samples of judges were drawn, or both.

A second consequence of increasing sample size is that the heterogeneity of the variates sampled increases due to the inclusion of more variates from the extremes of the distribution. Applied to social groups, it follows that with an increase in size there will be more varied talents, more individuals with requisite skills and knowledge for performing specialized tasks, and more individuals who are likely to be liabilities. The foregoing review revealed that as size increased there was increasing variability of individual performance and increasing organization and division of labor in the group; both effects are probably due in part to an increase in the heterogeneity of the sample.

Potential Relational Complexity. Various writers, among them Bossard (1944) and Kephart (1950), have pointed out that as group size increases arithmetically there is a geometric increase in the number of relational possibilities among the members. For example, the number of possible diadic relations in any group increases according to the familiar formula: $(n^2 - n)/2$. Potential complexity becomes important in groups because most individuals have a limited capacity to establish relationships with others. For example, Jennings (1960) has indicated that the average repertoire of choices for associating closely with others (working, etc.) is about eight and that this number is increased to about 12 when leisure time activities are included. Individual relational capacities limit the varieties of informal and formal organization and the degree of role differentiation that may develop. Thus an upper bound is automatically set on the actual relational complexity of a group by the limited capacity of individuals to establish particular relationships and by the potential relational possibilities.

Several studies reviewed here indicate that as group size increases there is a decrease in cohesiveness, along with the development of cliques and possibly of factions. These findings are understandable generally when the limited choice capacities of individuals are placed against the potential relations that multiply with group size. First consider cohesiveness, for which we may assume that positive attraction among all members at some degree of intensity is generally required. If we acknowledge that individuals have a limited capacity to like others (as the findings of Jennings, 1960, suggest), and that the sociometric structure of a group must be filled up with a certain relatively high number of liking linkages in order for cohesiveness to exist, then as group size increases the potential relations will exceed the capacity of individuals to fill them, the average member attraction in the group will decrease, and consequently so will group cohesiveness. The development of cliques and factions should eventually occur, for as size increases a smaller proportion of the possible linkages will be made.

Differences between diads and triads can be understood partially in terms of relational possibilities. As Bales and Borgatta (1955) have noted, in a two-person group there can be no majority other than by unanimity, whereas in a three-person group there can be a majority of two against a minority of one. In a three-person group there are eight possible coalition possibilities (Caplow, 1959) whereas in a diad the power relations are much simpler: one member may have power over the other or they may be equal.

Nondependent Intervening Variables

Nondependent intervening variables are those which are affected by changes in group size only under certain conditions. Almost any social or psychological condition influencing group process or outcome may be a nondependable intervening variable. There are numerous examples: the time allowed for group discussion may be held constant while group size is increased, thereby reducing the opportunity to participate; a group payoff may be held constant in cooperative groups of different sizes, thus varying the amount of reward that each member may possibly get when the payoff is divided among them; expectancy of reward may decrease with increasing size of a competitive group; the relative contribution of each member in cooperative groups may decrease with size, thereby decreasing the individual's sense of importance and worth in the group: the interdependence of the members may be high, thus increasing the likelihood that with increasing size there will be at least one individual who will perform poorly and hinder the group's progress; the cost in time and money represented by each additional group member may eventually exceed the possible gain to be derived from having more individuals work on the problem; and the complexity of the cognitive field may become great with increasing size to the extent that members try to attend to impinging social stimuli.

Most of the observed effects of size reviewed here appear to be contingent upon the operation of one or more of these nondependable intervening variables. Where such mediating variables are affecting an outcome, the proper focus for explanation should be on the theoretical framework of which the intervening variable is a part and only secondarily on size.

CONCLUSIONS

On the basis of this review it is apparent that group size has significant effects on aspects of individual and group performance, on the nature of interaction and distribution of participation of group members, on group organization, on conformity and consensus, and on member satisfaction. This appraisal suggests that the variable of group size should be included in theories of group behavior, distinguishing where possible between the effects that result from the interaction of group size with other independent variables and the effects arising from intervening variables that are dependently and nondependently associated with size.

It is concluded furthermore that future research on group size should proceed systematically, making every effort *(a)* to vary size in complete sequence over a suitably large range; *(b)* to conceptualize, identify, and measure relevant intervening variables; *(c)* to determine in advance whether these variables should be expected axiomatically to be correlated with size or would be only contingent variables; and *(d)* to use multivariate designs, where appropriate, in which group size and significant intervening variables are both manipulated experimentally.

REFERENCES

Asch, S. E. Effects of group pressure upon the modification and distortion of judgments. In D. Cartwright and A. Zander (eds.), *Group dynamics.* Evanston, Ill.: Row, Peterson, 1953, pp. 151–63.

Bales, R. F. and Borgatta, E. F. Size of group as a factor in the interaction profile. In A. D. Hare, E. F. Borgatta, and R. F. Bales (eds.), *Small groups.* New York: Knopf, 1955, pp. 396–413.

Bales, R. F., Strodtbeck, F., Mills, T., and Roseborough, Mary E. Channels of communication in small groups. *American Sociological Review,* 1951, **16**, 461–68.

Bass, B. M. and Norton, F. T. Group size and leaderless discussions. *Journal of Applied Psychology,* 1951, **35**, 397–400.

Berkowitz, M. I. An experimental study of the relation between group size and social organization. Unpublished doctoral dissertation, Yale University, 1958.

Borgatta, E. F. and Cottrell, L. S., Jr. Directions for research in group behavior. *American Journal of Sociology,* 1957, **63**, 42–48.

Bossard, J. H. S. The law of family interaction. *American Journal of Sociology,* 1944, **50**, 289–93.

Caplow, T. Organizational size. *Administrative Science Quarterly,* 1957, **1**, 484–506.

Caplow, T. Further developments of a theory of coalitions in the triad. *American Journal of Sociology,* 1959, **64**, 488–93.

Dawe, Helen C. The influence of size of kindergarten group upon performance. *Child Development,* 1934, **5**, 295–303.

Ekman, G. The four effects of cooperation. *Journal of Social Psychology,* 1955, **41**, 149–53.

Eysenck, H. J. The validity of judgments as a function of the number of judges. *Journal of Experimental Psychology,* 1939, **25**, 650–54.

Fisher, P. H. An analysis of the primary group. *Sociometry,* 1953, **16**, 272–76.

Fox, D., Lorge, I., Weltz, P., and Herrold, K. Comparison of decisions written by large and small groups. *American Psychologist,* 1953, **8**, 351. (Abstract.)

Gekoski, N. The relationship of group characteristics to productivity. Unpublished doctoral dissertation, Ohio State University, 1952.

Gibb, J. R. Effects of group size and threat reduction on creativity in a problem-solving situation. *American Psychologist,* 1951, **6**, 324. (Abstract.)

Goldberg, S. C. Three situational determinants of conformity to social norms. *Journal of Abnormal and Social Psychology,* 1954, **49**, 325–29.

Goodlad, I. I. Classroom organization. In C. W. Harris (ed)., *Encyclopedia of educational research.* New York: Macmillan, 1960, pp. 221–25.

Hare, A. P. Interaction and consensus in different sized groups. *American Sociological Review,* 1952, **17**, 261–67.

Hudelson, E. *Class size at the college level.* Minneapolis: University of Minnesota Press, 1928.

Indik, B. P. Organization size and member participation. Unpublished doctoral dissertation, University of Michigan, 1961.

Jennings, Helen, H. Sociometric choice process in personality and group formation. In J. L. Moreno (ed.), *The sociometry reader.* Glencoe, Ill.: Free Press. 1960, pp. 87–113.

Kelley, H. H. and Thibaut, J. W. Experimental studies of group problem solving and process. In G. Lindzey (ed.), *Handbook of social psychology.* Cambridge, Mass.: Addison-Wesley, 1954, pp. 735–85.

Kephart, W. M. A quantitative analysis of intragroup relationships. *American Journal of Sociology,* 1950, **60**, 544–49.

Kidd, J. S. Social influence phenomena in a task-oriented group situation. *Journal of Abnormal and Social Psychology,* 1958, **56**, 13–17.

Kishida, M. A study of the effects of group norm upon the change of opinions. *Japanese Journal of Psychology,* 1956, **27**, 172–73. (Abstract.)

Lorge, I., Fox, D., Davitz, J., and Brenner, M. A survey of studies contrasting the quality of group performance and individual performance. *Psychological Bulletin,* 1958, **55**, 337–70.

Lorge, I. and Solomon, H. Two models of group behavior in the solution of Eureka-type problems. *Psychometrika,* 1955, **20**, 139–49.

Lorge, I. and Solomon, H. Individual performance and group performance in problem solving related to group size and previous exposure to the problem. *Journal of Psychology,* 1959, **48**, 107–14.

Lorge, I. and Solomon, H. Group and individual performance in problem solving related to previous exposure to problem, level of aspiration, and group size. *Behavioral Science,* 1960, **5**, 28–39.

McKeachie, W. J. Research on teaching at the college and university level. In N. Gage (ed.), *Handbook of research on teaching.* Chicago, Ill.: Rand McNally, 1963, pp. 1118–72.

Marriot, R. Size of working group and output. *Occupational Psychology,* 1949, **26**, 47–57.

Miller, N. E., Jr. The effect of group size on decision-making discussions. Unpublished doctoral dissertation, University of Michigan, 1951.

Perlmutter, H. V. Group memory of meaningful material. *Journal of Psychology,* 1953, **35**, 361–70.

Slater, P. E. Contrasting correlates of group size. *Sociometry,* 1958, **21**, 129–39.

South, E. B. Some psychological aspects of committee work. *Journal of Applied Psychology,* 1927, **11**, 348–68.

Steiner, J. D. and Rajaratnam, N. A model for the comparison of individual and group performance scores. *Behavioral Science,* 1961, **6**, 142–48.

Stephan, F. F. The relative rate of communication between members of small groups. *American Sociological Review,* 1952, **17**, 482–86.

Stephan, F. F. and Mishler, R. G. The distribution of participation in small groups: An exponential approximation. *American Sociological Review,* 1952, **17**, 598–608.

Taylor, D. W. Problem solving by groups. In *Proceedings of the XIV International Congress of Psychology: 1954.* Amsterdam: North Holland Publishing, 1954.

Taylor, D. W. and Faust, W. L. Twenty questions: Efficiency in problem-solving as a function of size of group. *Journal of Experimental Psychology,* 1952, **44**, 360–68.

Thomas, E. J. and Fink, C. F. Models of group problem solving. *Journal of Abnormal and Social Psychology,* 1961, **63**, 53–63.

Utterback, W. E. and Fotheringham, W. C. Experimental studies of motivated group discussion. *Speech Monographs,* 1958, **25**, 268–77.

Von Borgersrode, F. Class size. In W. S. Monroe (ed.), *Encyclopedia of educational research.* New York: Macmillan, 1941, pp. 197–200.

Watson, G. B. Do groups think more efficiently than individuals? *Journal of Abnormal and Social Psychology,* 1928, **23**, 328–36.

Ziller, R. C. Group size: A determinant of the quality and stability of group decision. *Sociometry,* 1957, **20**, 165–73.

39. GROUP-INDUCED SHIFT TOWARD RISK: A CRITICAL APPRAISAL*

***Russell D. Clark, III*†**

It is often assumed that group arrangements for solving problems and making decisions suppress or dampen individual tendencies toward boldness, innovation, and daring. One set of circumstances for which this assumption no longer appears to hold is in decisions or choices that embody a clear dimension of risk. By now, a host of studies, initiated by Stoner[1] in 1961 and given great impetus by Wallach and Kogan, has demonstrated that, on the average, individuals advocate greater degrees of risk taking following participation in a group than they had previously advocated in private (Bem, Wallach, & Kogan, 1965; Blank, 1968; Kogan & Wallach, 1967a; Pruitt & Teger, 1969; Stoner, 1968; see Footnote 1; Teger & Pruitt, 1967; Wallach & Kogan, 1965; Wallach, Kogan, & Bem, 1962, 1964). The phenomenon occurs when subjects in experiments are asked to serve as advisers to hypothetical persons who are described on paper as being confronted by a choice dilemma (Kogan & Wallach, 1964; Stoner, see Footnote 1); the hypothetical persons must choose between an alternative that is less attractive but safe and a situation that is more attractive but less likely to succeed. An example is an electrical engineer who may remain at his current job at a modest but adequate salary or take a new job that offers a much higher potential income but no assurance of long-range security. Subjects in the typical experiment make their recommendations regarding the engineer's accepting the new job, on a scale of odds varying from 1 in 10 through 10 in 10 that the new job will succeed. They choose their recommendation in terms of the minimum odds of success they would find acceptable before recommending that the engineer take the new job. After making their recommendations for a whole set of such items, subjects meet in groups and discuss each item in open-ended discussion. After the discussion they make new individual recommendations for each item. The typical finding is that on the average, subjects shift toward greater risk; that is, they recommend accepting alternatives at lower odds of success after the group discussion than they did before. This is the prototype of the group-induced shift toward risk or, simply, the risky shift.

This group-induced shift toward risk has been obtained with a wide range of decision content, including hypothetical decisions (Teger & Pruitt, 1967; Wallach & Kogan, 1965; Wallach et al., 1962) and situations where positive and negative consequences to subjects may actually result from their decisions (Bem et al., 1965; Blank, 1968; Pruitt & Teger, 1969; Wallach et al., 1964). The phenomenon has been found with graduate business students (Stoner, see Footnote 1), English students (Bateson, 1966), Israeli students (Rim, 1964a), and American students (Kogan & Wallach, 1967a), senior executives (Marquis, 1962), and males and females (Wallach et al., 1962). It occurs in groups who engage in direct, face-to-face interactions (Kogan & Wallach, 1967a), groups who simply exchange information (Clark & Willems, 1969a; Teger & Pruitt, 1967), groups who communicate over an intercom system (Kogan & Wallach, 1967b), and groups who merely observe other groups interacting (Lamm, 1967).

Two important things stand out regarding the risky-shift phenomenon: the recency of its discovery and the fact that none of the most common social psychological theories explains it adequately. Social psychologists have long been interested in the differences between decisions arrived at through some group process and those that are the product of individuals' efforts (Jones & Gerard, 1967; Kelley & Thibaut, 1969). However, the prevailing views are either that group decisions will be more conservative than individual decisions or that group decisions will represent an averaging, or simple convergence, of individual decisions. Many experimental results can be cited to support each view.

An experiment by Schachter (1951), as well as others cited in Cartwright and Zander (1960, pp. 165–341), found that group members tend to exert the most influence attempts toward those group members who deviate at the extremes; as the opinion of a deviant member is perceived to move toward

* *Psychological Bulletin,* Vol. 76, No. 4 (1971), pp. 251–70.

This review was supported in part by Training Grant BTTBT 217 from the National Institute of Mental Health to the Graduate Training Program in Social Psychology, University of Kansas; and in part by Grant MH17605-01 from the National Institute of Mental Health to Edwin P. Willems. The author is indebted to Walter H. Crockett, Anthony J. Smith, and Edwin P. Willems for making numberous suggestions on previous drafts of this manuscript.

† Florida State University.

[1] J. A. F. Stoner, A comparison of individual and group decisions involving risk. Unpublished master's thesis, School of Industrial Management, Massachusetts Institute of Technology, 1961.

the group's central tendency, the amount of communication directed toward him decreases.

In support of the view that groups exert conservative influences on the individual, Barnlund (1959), comparing groups with individuals on drawing logical conclusions from prepared arguments, found that group members were more cautious and deliberate. He concluded: "the necessity of explaining a conclusion forced many students to be more self-critical [p. 58]"; and, "group discussion was found to stimulate more careful thinking, to lead to a consideration of a wider range of ideas, and to provoke more objective and critical testing of conclusions [pp. 59–60]." Schein (1965), in reviewing studies on group discussion, made a similar point. The group is more likely than the individual to identify errors of judgment before action is taken. Greater care and deliberation as a function of group influence is also reflected in the finding by Zander and Medow (1963) that subjects working in groups more often lowered their aspirations following an unexpectedly poor performance than did those working alone. Evidence from Allport (1924) and Farnsworth and Behner (1931) suggests that subjects tend to give more moderate judgments of weights and odors when in a group situation than when alone.

While a variety of studies indicate that groups make more conservative judgments than individuals, it should be emphasized that none of the above studies offers a systematic basis for distinguishing between group and individual risk taking. Few, if any, of the studies have been directly concerned with the dimension of risk.

Finally, the findings from studies of conformity can account for the reduction in groups of the initial variation among the responses of group members (Asch, 1958; Festinger, 1954; Krech, Crutchfield, & Ballachry, 1962; Sherif, 1935, 1936). However, as Brown (1965) pointed out, conformity cannot account for the most important feature of the risky-shift phenomenon: the systematic shift toward risk. While variability in decisions is reduced after discussion, individuals are more willing to accept risky decisions after participating in interacting groups than they had been initially.

Perhaps in the recognition that other hypotheses than conformity would have to be formulated to account for the risky shift, a variety of explanations have been proposed in recent years to explain the phenomenon. The four that have generated the greatest amounts of empirical research may be called the familiarization hypothesis, the leadership hypothesis, the diffusion-of-responsibility hypothesis, and the risk-as-value hypothesis. The evidence for each of these hypotheses is discussed in turn.

THE FAMILIARIZATION HYPOTHESIS

It might be argued that the risky shift is not a true group effect, but a pseudogroup effect as defined by Secord and Backman (1964). Pseudogroup effects occur in groups, but do not actually result from group processes. They can be reproduced in individuals operating independently under appropriate circumstances. Two studies, one by Bateson (1966) and the other by Flanders and Thistlethwaite (1967), indicate that the risky-shift phenomenon might be attributed to a pseudogroup phenomenon.

Bateson argued that group discussion allows persons to become more familiar with the situations being discussed, and contended that this increased familiarity with the situations is responsible for the observed shift toward risk. According to this hypothesis, any procedure that will increase familiarity with an issue involving risk will cause persons to become more risky on that issue. Informal observation and anecdotal evidence provide some support for this hypothesis. For many animals in unfamiliar situations or humans in strange circumstances (e.g., boys at a strange swimming hole) initial periods of caution, exploration, and "feeling out" are usually followed by behaviors that are much more bold and daring. To test this general hypothesis, Bateson compared the riskiness of groups who discussed five of the choice dilemmas with that of individuals who merely wrote briefs on these items indicating the points in favor of and against the various alternatives. Results were consistent with his hypothesis. Both procedures resulted in risky shift that differed from zero, but the two procedures did not differ significantly in the amount of shifts toward risk. Since the group discussion appeared to be irrelevant, Bateson concluded that the risky shift may be a simple matter of familiarization with the choice dilemmas. However, Pruitt and Teger[2] conducted two similar studies and were unable to replicate Bateson's results. They found no evidence that familiarity with the items, by itself, produced a risky shift.

On the other hand, Flanders and Thistlethwaite (1967) did obtain results similar to Bateson's. After preliminary measurement on the hypothetical dilemmas, each subject was assigned at random to one of four conditions. Subjects in the first condition worked individually, familiarizing themselves with the items on the assumption that they were going to discuss them later with other subjects; they were asked to concentrate on the important issues, making

[2] D. G. Pruitt and A. I. Teger, Is there a shift toward risk in group discussion? If so, is it a group phenomenon? If so, what causes it? Paper presented at the annual meeting of the American Psychological Association, Washington, D. C., September 1967.

lists of "pros" and "cons." In the second condition, groups of three subjects discussed the items, according to the typical group discussion procedure. To determine whether discussion would add effects not already induced by familiarization, subjects in a third condition both familiarized themselves with the items and participated in three-man discussions of them. Finally, in a control condition, subjects merely filled out the questionnaire twice. There was a significant shift toward risk in all conditions except the control condition, and the familiarization procedure alone produced as much risky shift as the discussion condition or the discussion-plus-familiarization condition. The authors concluded that group discussion adds nothing to the effects of familiarization with the items; that is, discussion is the occasion for familiarization, but it is not a necessary condition of the risky shift. In other words, by this account, the risky-shift phenomenon is a pseudogroup effect.

Kogan and Wallach (1967c), however, have questioned the results of the familiarization studies. They compared groups who discussed the items with groups who merely listened to tape recordings of the group discussions, a condition that may be regarded as familiarization procedure. Risky shifts were found in both conditions, but the shifts under the discussion condition were significantly larger than under the listening condition. They argued that similar information was available to subjects in both conditions, so that if familiarization was sufficient to account for the risky shift, there should be no difference between the conditions. Since a difference was found, the authors felt that an explanation involving the vicarious experiencing of the group interaction is needed to account for the risky-shift phenomenon.

The difference in results between these two experiments may be due to subtle differences in procedure. In their familiarization instructions, Flanders and Thistlethwaite created the expectation in their subjects that they were to engage in a group discussion later on. Part of their instructions read, "We want each of you to be prepared to discuss the choices to be made so that you will not have to spend group discussion time restudying the problem [p. 93]." In contrast, Kogan and Wallach did not lead their subjects to expect that a group discussion would follow the familiarization procedure. To test the effects of differences in instructions, Teeger, Pruitt, St. Jean, and Haaland (1970) compared two familiarization conditions. In one condition, subjects wrote out the pros and cons of the various dilemmas items under the impression that they were subsequently to make new choices that would be revealed in a group discussion. In the other condition, subjects also wrote out the pros and cons of the various items, but they were under the impression that their subsequent choices would remain private. Neither familiarization condition produced significant shifts toward risk, but the traditional group discussion conditions did. Teger et al. have conducted additional tests of the familiarization hypothesis with nonsupporting results.

In the light of this evidence, it seems fair to conclude that the familiarization hypothesis cannot account for the risky-shift phenomenon. Blank's findings (1968) add further weight to this conclusion. In this experiment, subjects placed bets for upcoming throws of dice over many trials. Bets were selected from a table of odds on which outcomes with high probabilities had low winnings attached, and outcomes with low probabilities had high winnings attached. Subjects either played the betting game alone or in the simple, noninteractive presence of others. Since all subjects were exposed to the same materials and similar choices, there should have been no differences in degree of familiarization. And yet, over trials, subjects who played in the presence of others came to place more low-probability bets than subjects who played alone.

THE LEADERSHIP HYPOTHESIS

According to the second hypothesis, risk takers are perceived as group leaders.[3] Those who are initially more inclined to take risks also tend to be more dominant and influential in the group discussion; hence, the risky shift can be accounted for in terms of the influence of risky leaders. Marquis (1962) and Collins and Guetzkow (1964) have argued that this is the most likely explanation of the phenomenon.

In one test of this hypothesis, Wallach et al. (1962) asked group members to rank each other for degree of influence exerted in the group discussion. There was general agreement as to who had been most influential. In support of the hypothesis, group members with high initial levels of risk taking were perceived as more influential in the discussion. However, this study is not an adequate test of the hypothesis, since the outcome may simply reflect the fact that the group ends up at a riskier position, prompting group members to attribute greater influence to those who initially favored higher risk taking, regardless of whether they were actually more influential.

It is not necessary that the group reach a consensus in order for the relationship between initial level of risk and persuasiveness to hold. Wallach, Kogan, and Burt (1965) showed that even when the risky shift was produced by discussion without con-

[3] Roger Brown (1965) has completed a thorough discussion of the leadership hypothesis, with particular emphasis on general social-psychological issues.

sensus, group members judged the higher risk takers to be more forceful in the group discussion. Once again, however, group members may have reasoned that those who initially favored a risky position must have been more influential.

A more adequate test of the leadership hypothesis was undertaken by Wallach, Kogan, and Burt (1968) who reasoned that if risk takers are generally persuasive, they should be more persuasive than most group members even when discussing issues that have nothing to do with risk taking. Groups, whose members varied widely with respect to their initial level of risk taking, were formed for discussion of issues, some of which contained alternatives that were balanced for riskiness. After the discussions, group members were asked to rank one another for *(a)* degree of influence in the group discussion, *(b)* contribution of the best ideas, and *(c)* greatest provision of effective guidance to the discussions. Among men, high risk takers were not considered more persuasive by any of these criteria, although the relationship was obtained among women.

Evidence from other studies reveals that the leadership hypothesis can hardly qualify as a major explanation of the group-induced shift toward greater risk taking, let alone its sole cause. Wallach, Kogan, and Burt (1967) had groups, homogeneous as to the field dependence or field independence of their members, meet for discussion to consensus of the choice-dilemmas items. The two kinds of groups did not differ with respect to initial risk-taking levels, both field-independent and field-dependent groups shifted toward greater risk taking following discussion to consensus, and the risky shifts were of about the same magnitudes. In addition, high initial risk takers were perceived as more forceful by field-independent subjects but not by field-dependent subjects. The important point for present purposes is that a significant risky shift was found for the latter group, but there was no relationship between initial risk taking level and perceived influence. This result could not be accounted for by the possibility that field-dependent subjects are unable to detect differences in the exertion of influence, for members of field-dependent groups showed significant within-group agreement in their rankings of group members for relative forcefulness in the discussion.

In a related study, Kogan and Wallach (1967d) varied groups in terms of members' test anxiety and defensiveness levels. Despite the fact that the groups shifted toward risk, there was no significant relationship between level of initial risk taking and degree of perceived influence in the discussion. For groups composed of high-defensive, low-anxiety members the reverse was even true: low risk takers were slightly more influential than high risk takers. Once again, the result could not be attributed to differential ability of group members to detect degrees of influence.

Brown (1965) reported a study by Nordhøy, who constructed situations on which groups shifted in the opposite direction, that is, toward caution. When the group members were asked to indicate the more persuasive members on these items, they named those who had been more conservative, not more risky, in their initial positions. Rabow, Fowler, Bradford, Hofeller, and Shibuya (1966) found similar results. These findings suggest not that risk takers are more persuasive but that group members attribute greater persuasiveness to those individuals whose initial views were closer to the final position of the group.

A study by Edwards and Willems (personal communication, July 1970) questions the leadership hypothesis. If the risk-prone person is naturally influential in group discussion, his influence should be exerted whether he argues for a risky position or a conservative position.[4] Edwards and Willems asked persons who initially had risky positions to put aside their real views and argue instead for the conservative positions, while persons who were initially conservative were requested to argue for the risky positions. Group members were much more likely to shift toward risk, the position held by initially conservative members who were arguing for the risky positions, than toward caution, the position defended by initially risky members who were arguing for the cautious alternative.

A final study by Vidmar (1970) casts serious doubts on the leadership hypothesis. Experimental groups were formed that were homogeneous as to their initial level of risk taking; that is, all members of a group showed either high, medium, or low risk on the first administration of the questionnaires. If the leadership hypothesis were correct, no shift should have occurred in groups composed of low risk takers because influential high risk persons were absent from the groups. However, a significant shift toward risk was found. In addition, whereas Wallach et al. (1968) found a relation between rated persuasiveness and high risk taking in their female groups, in Vidmar's study female as well as male group members shifted toward risk even when high risk takers were absent.

We can only conclude that the leadership hypothesis is not a major contender among explanations

[4] Rim (1963, 1964a, 1964b, 1966a, 1966b) suggested that high risk takers are characterized by a pattern of personality traits that predispose them to leadership and influence. Some of the traits of high risk takers are high in extraversion, Machiavellianism, need for achievement, tolerance of ambiguity, radicalism, and interpersonal values of leadership and recognition.

of the risky-shift phenomenon. The finding that high risk takers are perceived to be more persuasive and influential is consistent with the hypothesis. However, as we noted before, caution must be used in attributing causal status to the persuasiveness of high risk takers. The findings *(a)* that group members shift toward greater risk even when high risk takers do not exert greater persuasiveness than low risk takers, *(b)* that it is easier for group members to shift toward risk than toward caution, and *(c)* that risky shifts have been obtained in groups without high risk takers where the leadership hypothesis would predict no shift suggest that other processes than leadership are responsible for the risky-shift phenomenon.

THE DIFFUSION-OF-RESPONSIBILITY HYPOTHESIS

In its present form, the diffusion-of-responsibility hypothesis emphasizes that discussion *(a)* produces emotional bonds between members and *(b)* frees the individual from full responsibility for his later decision because he perceives that his decision has been partially shaped by the group.

The concept of diffusion of responsibility is appealing because of its usefulness in other contexts. It has been used to explain the risky actions of mobs and crowds. The individual's temporary impression of universality among the members of a crowd or mob and his perception of a guaranteed anonymity is used to explain why individuals perform inhuman acts in a group setting where such acts would only bring disgust outside the setting.

Kogan, Wallach, and their collaborators have carried out a number of studies that they feel strongly support the diffusion-of-responsibility hypothesis. In one of these (Wallach et al., 1964), stakes, the probability of achieving these stakes, and group responsibility were varied to reach a clearer understanding of the factors involved in the risky shift. Subjects, who meet in groups of three, were told that their main task would be to answer 10 multiple-choice questions taken from old college board examinations and that they would be paid for correct answers but not for incorrect ones. Furthermore, each subject had to determine beforehand the difficulty level for each of the 10 questions he would answer. The more difficult the question, the more money he would receive for a correct answer.

After the subjects had chosen the level of difficulty for Problems 1–5, the following experimental interventions were introduced for the remaining five questions. In a control condition, subjects merely continued to work individually. In the group-decision condition, subjects were to discuss difficulty levels for the first five problems until they had reached a unanimous group consensus, but each individual would eventually have to solve each problem by himself. In the responsibility-for-group condition, subjects were told that the last five questions would actually be attempted by a randomly determined member of the group, but the winnings of the other two would be entirely dependent upon the outcome of his performance; each subject had to decide on a difficulty level of the five problems before the solver for each was randomly designated, and the solver would receive the problem at the level he had selected. In a group-responsibility—group-decision condition, subjects were to discuss and reach a unanimous decision concerning difficulty levels of the problems to be randomly assigned later. This condition differed from the previous one only in that there was a group discussion. Finally, in a group-designation condition, the group not only determined the difficulty level for each problem but also was to designate a representative who would attempt to solve each problem.

The results showed that the control group differed significantly from each of the other experimental conditions. A significant risky shift occurred in the decision conditions where subjects had to reach a unanimous group decision that would be binding on each member. The designation of an individual to solve a problem had a different effect when it occurred in connection with a group consensus about the problem than when there was no such consensus. In the latter condition, subjects actually became more conservative. Apparently, in the absence of the discussion to consensus, the individual had no way of knowing at what level of difficulty the other individuals would prefer to work; the burden of failure rested squarely on the shoulders of the individual decision maker. Hence, greater conservatism occurred when responsibility for others was created without opportunity for additional communication. However, when the group decided on a particular level of difficulty and then a member was chosen, randomly or by the group, to solve a given problem, there was a maximal diffusion of responsibility. In this case the individual was neither personally responsible for choosing the difficulty level nor responsible for deciding whether to work on a problem. If he was chosen to work on a problem and failed, there would be the consoling fact that the decision had not been his alone.

In a second study, Bem et al. (1965) asked subjects to participate in a study of physiological effects on problem solving. Six experiments were described to three subjects at a time, the subjects' being separated from each other by partitions. The six experiments, involving olfactory stimulation, chromatic stimulation, movement, taste, audition, and sensitivity to odorless gases, were concerned with the effects of various physiological stimulations on the ability to solve simple verbal and mathematical problems. It was explained that subjects would be randomly selected to appear in one of these experiments during their second session. If a subject was selected to participate in one of these six experiments, he could specify the extent to which he was willing to undergo painful temporary side effects so as to obtain more money. The more probable a side effect, the more money he would receive, except that he would be excluded from the study if he actually suffered the side effects. The payments ranged from $2.80 if the subject chose the alternative that had a 10% probability of producing side effects to $25 if he chose the alternative with a 90% probability. Subjects choosing the latter probabilities obviously had made risky decisions.

After the subjects filled out the risk-taking questionnaire, the partitions between subjects were removed, and they were requested to discuss each of the six experiments and reach a unanimous decision about the type of stimulation they would endure if the group were chosen to participate in a subsequent experiment as a group. Group decisions were significantly more risky than the mean of the decisions made by the group members as individuals. Furthermore, the private decisions of these same subjects, obtained after completion of a group discussion, had also shifted significantly in a risky direction. Responses in other conditions in the experiment showed that the mere anticipated public disclosure of personal decisions did not lead to a risky shift and that subjects became more conservative when they anticipated undergoing the consequences of the decisions in the company of others or when they anticipated discussion to consensus. The authors concluded that the latter findings clearly support the diffusion-of-responsibility hypothesis at the expense of alternative explanations.

Wallach et al. (1967) systematically composed groups of male adults in terms of field dependence-independence of their members. Although both field-dependent and field-independent groups shifted toward greater risk taking after discussion, longer discussion among field-dependent subjects enhanced the risky shift, while longer discussion among field-independent subjects reduced or even reversed the risky shift. The authors accounted for this result by arguing that field-dependent subjects are more gregarious and affectionate than field-independent subjects. Longer discussion in the former group would emphasize the affective linkage among group members and, hence, the diffusion of responsibility. On the other hand, long discussions by field-independent subjects would emphasize the cognitive analysis of issues, which, according to the authors, would not be conducive to the formation of the emotional ties necessary for diffusion of responsibility to take place. In addition, the authors found a significant positive correlation between the amount of risky shift exhibited by a field-dependent member and the degree of risky shift he attributed to the group of which he was a member. The authors viewed this projection of one's own behavior onto the group as a means of minimizing personal responsibility for one's actions. No such relationship was found for the field-dependent subjects, who presumably are not prone to minimize a sense of personal responsibility for their actions.

Kogan and Wallach (1967d) conducted another personality-oriented study testing the diffusion-of-responsibility hypothesis. They divided female undergraduates into four homogeneous groups: low anxious–low defensive; low anxious--high defensive; high anxious–low defensive; high anxious–high defensive. Significant risky shifts were found for all four groups, but the magnitude of shift varied, with anxious subjects shifting the most and defensive subjects, the least. The authors' interpretation is that homogeneous groups of anxious individuals are uniformly fearful of failure: Discussion of the choice dilemmas makes these individuals more willing to diffuse responsibility in an effort to relieve the burden of possible personal failure. In contrast, homogeneous groups of defensive individuals are quite guarded and careful in their approach to others for fear of exposing personal weaknesses: This orientation interferes with affective interchange among group members and hence tends to inhibit diffusion of responsibility.

The diffusion-of-responsibility hypothesis is strongly supported in these studies by the introduction of personality variables, which presumably reflect the individual's own concern about personal responsibility. In every case, subjects who were expected to shift toward risk when responsibility was diffused did show greater shifts than subjects at the other pole of the relevant personality continuum. Nevertheless, diffusion of responsibility cannot account for all of the variance in the risky-shift studies, for otherwise defensive subjects, field-independent subjects, and subjects with low anxiety would not have shown the significant risky shifts that did occur. In short, the work on personality variables that is supposed to stem directly from the diffusion-of-responsibility hypothesis does not unequivocally support that hypothesis as the exclusive determinant of the risky shift. There is additional evidence that points out weaknesses in the hypothesis and some that contradicts it.

Improving on Wallach and Kogan's (1965) design,

Teger and Pruitt (1967) compared information exchange with discussion conditions. In the former condition, subjects gave each other information about their preferred risk levels on various issues without discussing the issues; in the latter, the issues were discussed at some length. The authors found significant risky shifts for both conditions, though the shift was considerably greater in the discussion-to-consensus condition. Kogan and Wallach (1967c) contended that providing subjects with complete information about the views of others is not sufficient to account for the greater risky shifts found in the group discussion condition. However, the results of Teger and Pruitt's study show that discussion is not necessary for a significant shift toward risk to occur. The results of Teger and Pruitt's information-exchange condition have been replicated by Clark and Willems (1969a) and by Willems and Clark (1969, 1971).

Furthermore, the diffusion-of-responsibility hypothesis fails to predict the high correlation that Pruitt and Teger (see Footnote 2) found between the initial riskiness of items and risky shift. Items that initially receive the riskiest judgment produce the most shift. The diffusion-of-responsibility hypothesis would have to predict the opposite, since the low-initial-risk items are mostly those in which the risky alternative has important negative consequences (Clark & Willems, 1969b); thus, initial responsibility should be very strongly felt on these items, and there should be greater effects of diffusion of responsibility.

In addition, Kogan and Wallach have not made explicit the relationship between the development of emotional bonds, formed during discussion, and the negative consequences of the group decision. They stated that discussion allows each member to feel less than proportionately to blame in the event of failure, because he sees others as contributing to the decision with him. How this makes the subject more willing to risk the negative consequences of the decision remains unclear. Does the discussion allow subjects to avoid or repress the negative consequences? Does it somehow lessen the subjective probability of a negative outcome? Or, do the negative consequences actually come to be viewed more positively? Kogan feels that a discussion of the situations lessens the perceived severity of the negative consequences (N. Kogan, personal communication, April 1969). However, empirical research is needed to establish that such is the case.

Willems and Clark (1971) and Pruitt and Teger (1969) have found disconfirming evidence for the relationship between the establishment of emotional bonds among subjects and risky shift. Willems and Clark varied relevancy of the content of discussion orthogonally across conditions of information exchange and discussion. The obtained shifts for subjects who either exchanged risk-relevant information or who discussed risk-relevant content differed significantly from zero; such subjects shifted more toward risk than those who either exchanged irrelevant information or discussed the irrelevant propositions. Since discussion of irrelevant propositions should produce emotional bonds among group members, and since this did not result in a significant shift, Willems and Clark feel that this aspect of the diffusion-of-responsibility hypothesis was refuted.

One could argue that these experimental arrangements did not really test the second part of the diffusion-of-responsibility hypothesis: the implication of others in the final decision. However, a betting experiment conducted by Pruitt and Teger (1969) found no risky shift in a group decision where the members of the group had engaged in past discussions about other issues but were not permitted to discuss or exchange information about the current issue. In this experiment, satisfactory conditions were set for the creation of emotional bonds among group members, and responsibility of the group for the decision was achieved by informing each member that group decisions would be the average of the individuals' decisions. Each individual would have to face the positive or negative outcomes of this averaged decision. No shift was found even when there were emotional bonds among group members and when others were implicated in the group decision. Also, Dion, Miller, and Magnan[5] found in disagreement with the diffusion-of-responsibility hypothesis, that low cohesive groups exhibited greater risky shift than high cohesive groups. At the least, this finding indicates that the creation of emotional bonds is not necessary for the risky shift to occur. The authors, however, do see the finding as consistent with a diffusion-of-responsibility explanation. They suggested that as group members become more attracted to each other, they also become less willing to diffuse personal responsibility onto other group members for the negative consequences of a risky action.

Although the diffusion-of-responsibility hypothesis seems to have been refuted in experiments involving the choice dilemmas or betting, it should be pointed out that it may have explanatory value in other contexts, for instance, the behavior of bystanders in emergencies. Darley and Latané (1968) caused subjects to overhear another subject appear to suffer an epileptic seizure. More subjects from two-person groups responded with help than from three-person

[5] K. L. Dion, N. Miller, and M. A. Magnan. Group cohesiveness and social responsibility as determinants of the risky shift. Unpublished manuscript, University of Minnesota, Minneapolis, Minnesota, 1969.

groups, and more from three-person than from six-person groups. Darley and Latané argued persuasively that the diffusion-of-responsibility hypothesis more appropriately accounts for bystander inaction than the often acclaimed explanations of apathy, alienation, and anomie.[6] When there are several observers present, responsibility for helping is shared among all observers and does not fall to any one person. Also, when others are known to be present, it is convenient to believe that somebody has either already helped the victim or is about to do so. In either case, the result is that no one helps.

Latané and Darley (1968) conducted another experiment on bystander intervention in which the diffusion-of-responsibility bypothesis was less clearly confirmed. Male undergraduates found themselves in a smoke-filled room either alone, with two non-reacting confederates, or in groups of three naive subjects. They found, as predicted, that subjects were less likely to report the smoke when in the presence of passive others or in groups of three than when alone. On the basis of these results and from the postexperimental questionnaire, the authors inferred that the presence of unresponsive bystanders leads the individual to assume that the emergency is not serious and causes him not to react. The authors contend that diffusion of responsibility does not explain these results because they do not see how the "individual's responsibility for saving himself is diffused by the presence of other people [p. 221]." A major difference between this experiment and the previous one was that in the latter case an individual finds himself in danger; in the former, other people seriously need his help. The different results in the two types of situations are intriguing and should be systematically studied.[7]

Notwithstanding the apparent intuitive appeal of the diffusion-of-responsibility hypothesis and its usefulness in accounting for research on bystander intervention, it shows serious shortcomings when applied to the risky shift because: *(a)* Contrary to the hypothesis, discussion is not necessary for the risky shift to occur; *(b)* the hypothesis cannot account for cautious shifts; *(c)* the hypothesis cannot account for the finding that initially risky items are those for which the greatest shift occurs; *(d)* the hypothesis is inconsistent with the finding that the most shift occurs with those items that are perceived to have the least serious consequences; *(e)* the hypothesis does not specify how the creation of emotional bonds among subjects makes them less concerned about the negative consequences of risky decisions; *(f)* finally, most damaging of all, it appears to be the exchange of relevant information, not the development of emotional bonds, that is necessary for the risky shift to occur. In short, it seems rather clear that some other factor in the communication among group members is responsible for producing the shift toward risk.

THE RISK-AS-VALUE HYPOTHESIS

The most persistent and popular interpretation of the risky shift (Brown, 1965; Levinger & Schneider, 1969; Teger & Pruitt, 1967; Wallach & Wing, 1968; Willems, 1969) makes the key assumption that moderate risk is a stronger cultural value than caution and that individuals come to view themselves as being *at least as willing* as their peers to take risks. When a group of such persons meets and discusses matters of risk taking, those whose initial private positions were less risky than the group average will recognize their relative cautiousness and will subsequently recommend greater risk than before in order to restore their perceptions of themselves as relatively risky. On this view, the principal function of the group discussion is to allow group members to compare their positions on the issue to those of other people.

There is considerable evidence that persons perceive themselves to be at least as willing as their peers to take risks. Hinds[8] asked male graduate students in industrial management to try to guess for two choice dilemmas what alternatives would be chosen by other people like themselves. He found that subjects very consistently guessed that others would choose more cautiously than had the subjects themselves. Brown (1965) asked one undergraduate class of 30 students and one graduate seminar of 16 to answer one choice-dilemmas problem for themselves and then to guess how other people like themselves would respond. Not one subject guessed that others would answer more riskily than himself. Brown interpreted this finding as indicating that each individual conceives himself to be at least as risky as the average of his peers.

The generality of this finding is affirmed in the following studies. Wallach and Wing (1968), using six of the choice dilemmas, found that both males and females perceived themselves to be more risky than their peers. Levinger and Schneider (1969) found the same results for 9 of the 12 items. Willems (1969) made the same inquiry in the case of a

[6] Darley and Latané do not assume a linkage between emotional bonds and diffusion of responsibility; furthermore, the creation of emotional bonds is conceptually unnecessary to account for the behavior of individuals in emergencies.

[7] An excellent summary of the author's work on bystander intervention in emergencies is provided by Latané and Darley (1969).

[8] W. C. Hinds, Jr. Individual and group decisions in gambling situations. Unpublished master's thesis, Sloan School of Management, Massachusetts Institute of Technology, Cambridge, 1962.

single risk-taking item and found that 81% of his subjects perceived themselves to be at least as willing as their peers to take risks. Willems found the same results in a replication of this experiment. Thus, the data unequivocally reveal a strong and pervasive tendency by persons of both sexes to view themselves as being at least as risky as their peers.

From the risk-as-value hypothesis, however, it would follow that those subjects who perceive themselves as more *cautious* than their peers should not change toward risk following group discussions. Clark, Crockett, and Archer (1971) tested this proposition by comparing discussion groups whose members perceived themselves as being at least as risky as their peers with groups of subjects who perceived themselves to be more cautious than their peers. The results showed that only the former group shifted significantly from zero; the magnitude of shift in the latter group did not differ from that in a control group. Thus, Brown's second assumption was confirmed, for instance, persons who actually shifted toward risk were the ones who perceived themselves to be at least as willing as their peers to take risks.

According to the risk-as-value hypothesis, the main function of the group discussion is informative; it makes clear the level of risk that others will assume in a given situation. Bem et al.'s (1965) experiment on aversive consequences was designed to test this hypothesis. Instead of responding to the choice dilemmas, subjects in a psychophysiological experiment were asked to select the experimental treatment they would endure from a set of treatments that varied in their likelihood to involve disagreeable physical side-effects. The investigators reasoned that in this situation, risk taking would connote the valued properties of courage and boldness and that a risky shift should result when the subjects anticipated that their decisions would be revealed to others. In one condition, subjects were told that each person's decisions would subsequently be made public in the others' presence; in a second condition, subjects were told their decisions would be available to each other so that they could discuss them and make a unanimous selection on just what stimulation they wanted to be employed. The investigators felt that the social desirability of risk taking should be particularly enhanced under these circumstances because the subjects thought they would have to defend their positions in a subsequent discussion. However, no evidence of shift toward risk was found in the first condition, and a conservative rather than a risky shift in the second one. The authors concluded that the shift to risk in group decisions cannot be attributed to a social value on greater risk taking. However, the relevance of this study to the risk-as-value hypothesis must be called into question. As Brown (1965) pointed out, the subjects in both conditions who thought their decisions would be made public were not actually informed of one another's decisions, and since each subject may have already thought himself bold and venturesome, there was no need for him to become more risky.

A more adequate test of the role of information was provided by Teger and Pruitt (1967), who compared groups that discussed the choice dilemmas with groups that merely exchanged information with one another about their initial choices. By the risk-as-value hypothesis, the exchange of information should be enough to show many subjects that they are not as risky as most others in the group; those subjects should then shift toward greater risk. This, in fact, was what Teger and Pruitt found. Similarly, Kogan and Wallach (1967c) found that listening to a tape recording of an actual group discussion led to increased risk taking. In this study, as in the former study, information was made available that permitted the subject, in the absence of discussion, to compare his own risk-taking position with the positions advanced by others. Nevertheless, in both of the studies just cited, simple exchange of information was not as effective in promoting the risky shift as was the group discussion; this suggests that the risk-as-value hypothesis by itself does not account for the phenomenon. However, if one assumes that the discussion condition provides experiences that enhance the value of risk taking, then the centrality of this hypothesis can be defended. The discussion condition not only provides information concerning each individual's position on the issues but it also presents each individual's arguments in defense of his position, making the objectively less risky person more aware of the value he and others place on risk (Teger & Pruitt, 1967).

In support of this interpretation, Lamm (1967) found that subjects who observed a group discussion through a one-way mirror shifted toward greater risk in an amount that did not differ significantly from the shift observed among subjects who actually participated in a group discussion.

Kogan and Wallach's (1967c) listening condition and Lamm's (1967) observation condition might also be interpreted as supporting the diffusion-of-responsibility hypothesis since the groups did, after all, engage in discussion. It is possible to untangle this theoretical issue by initiating experiments in which one of the hypotheses makes a prediction that the other one does not. Vidmar (1970) has done such a study. Three relatively homogeneous sets of groups, consisting of high, medium, and low risk takers, were compared with mixed groups composed of two high, one medium, and two low risk takers. All four types of groups showed the risky shift, but the mixed, or heterogeneous groups showed significantly greater shifts than the more homogeneous groups; the three homogeneous groups did not differ significantly from one another in magnitude of risky shift. Vidmar also found that the magnitude of individual risky shift was inversely related to the member's initial risk position in the group. That is, the objectively conservative members in a group shifted more than did the risky members, exactly as the risk-as-value hypothesis predicts. It should be pointed out that the familiarization hypothesis and the diffusion-of-responsibility hypothesis cannot account for the twin facts that the heterogeneous groups shifted more toward risk than the homogeneous groups and that the objectively conservative subjects shifted more than the objectively risky members.

Willems and Clark (1971) varied homogeneous and heterogenous groups of females orthogonally across conditions of information exchange and discussion, using the six choice-dilemmas items that had produced the most risky shift in previous studies. The criteria for group compositions were as follows: On three critical items (4, 6, and 7 by Kogan and Wallach's numbering) each person in the homogeneous groups did not differ by more than two scale points. For heterogeneous groups, at least two persons differed by at least four scale points on each of the three items. Under both information-exchange and discussion conditions, only the heterogeneous groups gave shifts significantly greater than zero. These findings were interpreted as reflecting the fact that in heterogeneous groups the probability was increased that some subjects would discover that their choices were not as risky as their peers, producing motivation to shift. In the homogeneous groups, in which subjects differed by no more than two scale points, there was no real need for persons to shift toward risk because nobody was less risky than his peers; all subjects were already actualizing the value of risk.

The results of the study by Willems and Clark differ in one important way from those reported by Vidmar. While both found significant shifts in heterogeneous groups, Willems and Clark did not find a significant shift toward risk in the homogeneous groups, as Vidmar did. The difference may be due to a subtle difference in procedure. Vidmar formed his groups of high, medium, and low risk takers by summing each subject's scores over 10 choice dilemmas. Summing scores over items, however, can conceal diversity of responses on certain key items, like Items 4 and 7 of the Wallach and Kogan questionnaire. Since these items seem to be responsible for most of the shift found in a variety of studies, Willems and Clark argued that persons in homogeneous groups must respond similarly on those key items. Otherwise, apparently homogeneous groups may, in fact, be heterogeneous.

There is empirical evidence that supports this contention. Using the same criteria as Vidmar (1970), Hoyt and Stoner (1968) found significant shifts toward risk in their homogeneous groups, while the magnitude of shift in these groups did not differ significantly from that in previous studies in which groups were randomly composed and, therefore, assumed to be heterogeneous. At the same time, Hoyt and Stoner found a significant positive relation between dispersion of individual preferences on an item and the magnitude of group shift. They remarked:

> Thus it appears that homogeneous grouping reduced the ranges of total individual risk scores within each group very substantially (by almost three-fourths) but did not reduce individual item ranges very appreciably (by about one-seventh) [Hoyt & Stoner, 1968, p. 281].

Pruitt and Teger (see Footnote 2) cited other evidence supporting the risk-as-value hypothesis. They compared initial risk level with amount of risky shift across the items in a number of studies and found a very high correlation between the initial position on an item and the risky shift for that item. That is, judgments on items that elicit a risky response initially become even more risky after discussion; items that elicit a cautious response initially become even more cautious after discussion. Pruitt and Teger argued that this finding favors the risk-as-value hypothesis, on the proposition that the average initial position on an item indicates whether the value of risk or the value of caution is appropriate to that issue. Clark and Willems (1969b) also found a very high correlation between the mean initial responses to the 12 items of the Kogan and Wallach questionnaire and the national norms of risky shift for these items.

Further compelling evidence for the risk-as-value hypothesis comes from a betting experiment by Blank (1968). Subjects chose bets in either a group or an individual situation. Under individual conditions, subjects chose a significantly greater number of high-probability bets than did subjects in the group condition. More importantly, subjects who transferred from the individual condition to the group condition did not differ significantly in the riskiness of their bets from subjects who continued in the individual condition; however, subjects who transferred from the individual condition to the group condition showed a significant shift to greater risk. This study clearly indicated that the risky shift occurs in games of chance, that it may occur even when there has been no group discussion, and that it does not endure when subjects are switched to an individual condition.[9] Since no discussion was allowed in the groups, Blank asserted that the diffusion-of-responsibility hypothesis could not easily explain this finding.

The most attractive feature of the risk-as-value hypothesis is that it can be easily extended to account for items on which judgments consistently shift toward either risk or caution and for items on which no consistent shift in judgments is evident. If an issue invokes values favoring the risky alternative, then the hypothesis would predict that most individuals would consider themselves to be at least as willing as their peers to take risks, so that the effect of group discussion would be to produce a shift toward risk. For those items that elicit cautious values, the hypothesis predicts that individuals will perceive themselves to be at least as cautious as their peers, and we would expect a shift toward caution as a result of the group discussion. Stoner (1968) has performed a study that confirms these predictions. He presented his subjects with a 12-item questionnaire in which 6 items were assumed to elicit risky values and 6 to elicit cautious values. Subjects also completed a value-rating instrument that required them to rank in order of importance 18 phrases that reflected values that were implicit in the outcomes of the 12 dilemmas items. On the basis of the subjects' rankings, the 12 dilemmas items were divided into two groups: those for which the risky alternatives implied values that were ranked higher in importance than the cautious alternatives and those for which the opposite was true.[10] Subsequently, subjects discussed items in groups and arrived at a group decision. Results generally supported the risk-as-value predictions. Subjects were more risky initially on risk-oriented items and more cautious initially on cautious-oriented items. Significant differences between individuals' perceptions of their own and others' riskiness were also found. On risk-oriented items, subjects judged themselves to be relatively risky and, after unanimous group decisions, gave responses that were more risky than the average of the initial individual decisions. On caution-oriented items, however, the results were less clear-cut. Subjects perceived themselves to be more cautious than most people on only three of six cautious-oriented items; of the remaining items, two showed nonsignificant judgments in the direction of caution, while the third showed nonsignificant judgments in the direction of risk. In addition, only two of the six cautious-oriented items resulted in cautious shifts, the other four showing nonsignificant changes. Whether these results reflect the nature of the specific items that were employed or the fact that risk is a stronger value than caution in our culture is a matter for future research.

Stoner's assessment of the importance of values related to the risky and cautious items was an attempt to solve one of the major problems with the risk-as-value hypothesis, that of distinguishing in advance those issues on which a shift to risk will occur from those associated with a shift to caution. An additional distinction can be made between risk-oriented and caution-oriented items. Clark and Willems (1969b) have suggested that the perceived consequences of failure in each situation play a crucial role in determining the level of risk subjects will take in that situation. They asked subjects to assume that the hypothetical person in each situation chose the attractive alternative and that it failed. Subjects were asked to indicate how serious the consequences would be. The mean ratings of the consequences of failures were then correlated with Pruitt and Teger's national norms for the likelihood of risky shifts; the two sets of ratings correlated very highly ($r = -.70$, $p < .01$); that is, the greatest risky shifts occur for items with the least serious perceived consequences. In addition, the mean riskiness of subjects' initial positions on the items was correlated with the perceived consequences: those items that initially elicit risk are perceived to have relatively trivial consequences, those that initially elicit caution are perceived to have severe consequences. At the least, these data suggest that subjects' perceived consequences of failure play a part in their proneness toward risk and caution.

Taken together, the evidence available converges to suggest that *(a)* treatment of risk-relevant content, *(b)* in situations for which the consequences of failure are not severe, *(c)* in groups whose members vary in their initial riskiness, and *(d)* for individuals who perceive themselves to be at least as willing as their peers to take risks *jointly* represent the necessary and sufficient conditions for the risky shift. This is so because when all four of these conditions are not met, the shift occurs (sufficient conditions) and when *any* of the four conditions is not met, the shift does not occur (necessary conditions). Since three of the conditions (except Condition *b*) are direct derivatives

---

[9] Kogan and Wallach (1967a) reported several studies using the choice dilemmas where the shift did endure after discussion.

[10] If risk-taking items do involve values and if the importance of risky and cautious alternatives can be determined, then perhaps we may have a way of distinguishing between those items that produce cautious shifts and those items that produce risky shifts—hence, the risk-as-value hypothesis would not be an ex post facto explanation since subjects' perception of their own relative riskiness would tend to be consistent with and a good predictor of the subsequent group shift toward either caution or risk.

of the risk-as-value hypothesis, the evidence is strong support for that view.[11]

CURRENT STATUS OF THE RISKY-SHIFT PHENOMENON

The empirical shift toward risk using the choice dilemmas as a measure can be shown to have at least four main characteristics: *(a)* Regular and systematic average shift toward risk; *(b)* the convergence of risk preferences; *(c)* the ceiling effect, that is, that no individual's risk preference exceeds the preference of the riskiest individual before the group process occurs;[12] and *(d)* the preponderance of comments in the discussion favors risk (Brown, 1965).

On a post hoc basis, the familiarization hypothesis would seem to account for the systematic shift but none of the other three aspects. Not only does the familiarization hypothesis fail to account for the convergence of views, the ceiling effect, and the preponderance of comments favoring risk but, given the hypothesis, one cannot derive predictions concerning these key characteristics of the risky shift. This is because these characteristics refer to group processes, and the familiarization hypothesis regards the risky-shift phenomenon as a pseudogroup phenomenon. In addition, recent studies show that the original familiarization findings cannot be replicated.

On a post hoc basis, the leadership hypothesis, with its emphasis on the leader's persuasibility, would appear to account for the systematic shift, the ceiling effect, the convergence around the opinion of the leader, and the preponderance of comments favoring risk. However, on an empirical basis, the review of studies has shown that derivations from the leadership hypothesis do not predict and account for the phenomenon.

On a post hoc basis, the diffusion-of-responsibility hypothesis would seem to account for the systematic shift and perhaps the preponderance of comments in the discussion favoring risk, but not the convergence of views or the ceiling effect. The former two characteristics can be derived from the hypothesis but not the latter two, since it is possible for each person in a group to become more risky without changes in variability occurring as a result. Since the hypothesis emphasized generalized group processes, a prediction concerning the ceiling effect cannot be made. In fact, one might wonder why, as a result of diffusion of responsibility, the final decisions are not riskier than the riskiest individual. Although the hypothesis does predict the systematic shift toward risk and the preponderance of comments favoring risk, experimental studies reported above, especially the ones involving relevance of content, perception of self as relatively risky, and diversity of opinion, suggest that diffusion of responsibility as a postulated process is not necessary or sufficient to produce the shift.

In contrast to the other three hypotheses, on a post hoc basis, the risk-as-value hypothesis would account for all four aspects of the risky shift. The hypothesis predicts: *(a)* The systematic shift toward risk occurs when persons are not, in fact, expressing positions at least as risky as the norm; *(b)* the convergence of risk preferences around a central value is the result of value attainment; *(c)* the reason for the ceiling effect is that persons want to be at least as risky as their peers, and the fact that most individuals move toward the riskiest individual achieves this; and *(d)* the preponderance of discussion favors risk because the discussion of risk-relevant material allows the individual to compare his level of risk taking with that of others. Furthermore, the experimental studies reported above, particularly the ones in relevance of content, heterogeneity of initial opinions, and perception of riskiness, demonstrate that risky shifts occur under the conditions specifically predicted by the hypothesis. Finally, this hypothesis has the potential advantage of being able to account for cautious as well as for risky shifts.

However, one troublesome problem is the dependence of the risky shift on instructions. The stability and replicability of the risky-shift phenomenon have been firmly established. In fact, most investigators begin by assuming its stability and have been searching for explanations of the shift. The two most popular interpretations, the diffusion-of-responsibility and risk-as-value hypotheses, both point to group processes as producing the risky shift. That is, as they now stand, both interpretations are stated in terms that are independent of the specific experimental instructions used to elicit risk preferences. However, there is evidence from recent experiments by Clark and Willems (1969a) and Willems and Clark (1969) that the risky shift is a function of the instructions that are normally used in experiments on this topic.

Risk taking was measured by the Kogan and Wallach choice-dilemmas instrument, the format most widely used in the research on the risky shift. On this questionnaire, the experimental subject's task is to serve as a hypothetical adviser to the focal person by choosing the *lowest probability* of success that he would consider acceptable for the hypothetical per-

[11] Jellison and Riskind (1970) have recently completed studies that relate risk-as-value theory to Festinger's theory of social comparison.

[12] In the author's research, among 1,320 events (220 Subjects × 6 Choice-Dilemmas Items) only 57 outcomes involved final decisions that were more risky than the initial positions of the riskiest members of the groups. In other words, only 4% of the possible outcomes violated this assertion of a ceiling effect.

son to select the more attractive risky alternative. Clark and Willems reasoned that the phrase *lowest probability* in the instructions may orient either the individual in his responding or the group in its discussion toward riskiness and that more neutral instructions might reduce the risk-shift effect. Half of the subjects were given neutral instructions that requested them simply to choose, for each item, the probability of success they would consider acceptable to recommend the more attractive alternative; the other half of the subjects received the standard instructions. These two sets of instructions, risk-oriented and neutral, were varied orthogonally across information-exchange, discussion, listening, and control conditions. The results showed a significant risky shift only for the groups that received the standard risky instructions. Since no significant shifts occurred in any of the groups that received the neutral instructions, the authors concluded that the risk-oriented instructions provide directional expectations for risk preferences.[13] One might still argue, however, that since risky shifts have occurred in varying magnitudes from different manipulations, other concepts have to be formulated for a complete understanding of the risky-shift phenomenon.

Furthermore, the findings on instruction dependence do nothing to distinguish between the two major hypotheses now used to account for the risky shift. Diffusion-of-responsibility proponents might suggest that the lowest probability instruction becomes salient in the discussion and enhances the feeling of less potential blame. The risk-as-value proponents would probably suggest that the instructions operate to persuade subjects to move in a direction of the more risky alternatives. However, the findings do suggest that some conceptual and methodological restrictions must be placed on the range of generalizations we can make about the phenomenon. Specifically, the findings suggest that care must be exercised in interpreting the Kogan and Wallach questionnaire as a measure of risk taking. Until further research is conducted on instruction dependence and risk choices involving other experimental formats—for example, betting with payoffs—we cannot generalize instruction dependence to them. The importance of such research should be clear.

These data suggest, then, that instruction dependence must be added to relevance of context, in situations for which the consequences of failure are not severe, heterogeneity of opinions and distribution of perception of peers as a condition of the risky shift. When those conditions *and* risky-oriented instructions occur together, the risky shift will be obtained; when any of the four conditions is not met, it seems, the shift will not occur. Until recently, this seemed to be the case. But, as noted below, new research has raised some new and troublesome issues.

One difficulty, as discussed earlier, with the risk-as-value hypothesis as it was originally formulated by Brown is that it cannot account for the discrepancies found between information-exchange, listening, and discussion conditions. Teger and Pruitt (1967), however, argued for a modification of Brown's hypothesis, pointing out that in the discussion condition there is greater opportunity for group members to acquaint themselves with the arguments in favor of the value of risk.

Clark et al. (1971) performed an experiment relevant to this issue. They had subjects either *(a)* exchange information about their choices on the risk dilemmas; *(b)* discuss the dilemmas and indicate their choices on each item and their arguments for those choices; or *(c)* discuss the choice dilemmas, but only give their arguments in favor of the various alternatives without specifying which alternatives they had chosen. In both discussion conditions, judgments shifted significantly toward risk, in amounts significantly greater than in the information-exchange condition, which did not differ significantly from zero. This result appears to be inconsistent with the risk-as-value hypothesis, for since risk is a value, and we perceive ourselves to be at least as willing as our peers to take risks, we should need to reevaluate our own positions only when we actually discover that others choose riskier alternatives than we do; however, a significant shift occurred in the discussion condition when numerical preferences for specific alternatives were not exchanged. The hypothesis can be rescued only by assuming that listening to and participating in a discussion of arguments in favor of risk, even without clear commitment from each subject to an alternative, permit the discussant to learn that his peers are riskier than he had thought. There is evidence from this previous study, however, that suggests that subjects did change their perceptions of others' responses to specific alternatives. Subjects indicated before and after discussion of the choice dilemmas what they thought the majority of people like themselves would mark for each item. Subjects in both discussion groups—with and without exchange of the alternatives chosen—came to change their judgments to represent other people as riskier than initially; the two conditions

[13] The finding that risk-oriented instructions generate conservative rather than risky shifts, or do not cause shifts, for materials of certain kinds, is not a serious contradiction to an instructional demand characteristic interpretation of the risky shift, but it does suggest that instructions are not the only factor that generate shifts. Wallach and Mabli's (1970) view that Clark and Willems' neutral instructions encourage a wider range of choices and induce a force toward compromise and concession ignores the finding that there were no differences between the risk-oriented and neutral-oriented instructions in initial responses or variability.

did not differ significantly. Thus, the data do suggest that the mediation of the cultural value of risk through the specification of probabilities is still tenable.[14] However, a more adequate test is needed to substantiate this view.

Nevertheless, the idea that information exchange leads to social comparison processes is still a troublesome possibility. According to the risk-as-value hypothesis, the risky shift occurs because the individual discovers that he is not as risky as his peers; in order to maintain the implicit norm of riskiness, he becomes more risky. Recent evidence, however, suggests that risky and cautious shifts do not occur when social comparison processes and elicitation of arguments in favor of risky or cautious items, respectively, are not biased toward the implicit values of the decision items. In a pilot investigation, Steiner (cited in Dion, Baron, & Miller, 1970), using both risk-oriented and cautious-oriented items, presented false feedback that disconfirmed the subjects initial expectation concerning the responses of others. The manipulated norms produced marked shifts of own riskiness in the direction of the position advocated in the false feedback.

Baron, Dion, and Baron[15] conducted a similar study. Subjects discussed either risk-oriented or caution-oriented items. Using confederates, the investigators created a majority consensus that was either two scale positions riskier or more conservative than the naive subject's initial decision. Subjects exhibited marked conformity to the artificially established group consensus, regardless of whether the group norm coincided or conflicted with the underlying value elicited by the type of item. Furthermore, these shifts remained intact in private, posttest measures of risk taking.

Clark and Crockett (1971) had low, medium, or high risk takers listen to contrived tape recordings of discussion groups composed of low, medium, or high risk takers on six risky items. The results were striking. Subjects always conformed to the position advocated by the taped discussion groups, regardless of whether the positions advocated coincided with the underlying value of risk.

These results do not argue well for an interpretation that assumes that social comparison pressures operate in conjunction with elicited values. If risk and caution are strong cultural values, individuals should selectively adjust their levels of risk and caution to coincide with the dominant values underlying risk-oriented and caution-oriented items. Yet, the previous studies showed that subjects conform dramatically to the majority consensus provided them. Thus, it appears that the social comparison mechanism of value theory fares poorly.

Evidence from a recent experiment makes this conclusion premature. Wallach and Mabli (1970), testing the social comparison mechanism process of value theory against conformity, composed three-person groups that contained either a conservative minority and risky majority or a conservative majority and risky minority. As predicted by value theory, in contrast to the conformity interpretation, whether they constituted a minority or a majority of the group membership, conservatives showed strong and similar shifts toward greater risk as a result of discussion of the choice dilemmas. In contrast, whether they constituted a minority or a majority of the group membership, risk takers showed essentially no shift as a result of discussion. For the results of Steiner, of Baron, Dion, and Baron and of Clark and Crockett to hold up, one would have expected conservatives not to shift toward risk when they were in a majority, and risky persons to shift toward caution when they were in the minority. Procedural differences in how the groups were constituted may account for the discrepancies in results. Wallach and Mabli did not directly manipulate scale position in their groups, particularly on an item-by-item basis as did the other investigators. In addition, Wallach and Mabli's risky subjects had the opportunity to persuade the more cautious subjects.

We can only conclude that individuals are culturally disposed to generate and favor risky arguments when considering risky items and cautious arguments when considering cautious items (Brown, 1965; Madaras & Bem, 1968), but when forced to consider cautious arguments and judgments on risky items and risky arguments and judgments on cautious items, individuals do change their judgments in the direction advocated by the arguments to minimize the discrepancy themselves and others. Whether these results hold up when an individual is exposed to more heterogeneous judgments and arguments (persons in the above experiments heard only judgments and arguments that were homogeneously discrepant from their own), selected so that the individual is exposed to views that are the same or slightly different from his own as well as those that are very different, will have to wait for further experimental analysis. Such further work is important because, as they stand, these results raise questions about the risk-as-value hypothesis and risky-shift phenomenon itself.

Future research is needed to determine whether modifications of the above five necessary conditions

[14] Madaras and Bem (1968) presented evidence that they interpreted as indicating that cultural value of risk is mediated by the knowledge of others' arguments, for instance, information about risk alternatives.

[15] R. S. Baron, K. L. Dion, and P. Baron, Group norms, elicited values, and risk-taking. Unpublished manuscript, University of Minnesota, Minneapolis, Minnesota, 1968.

are needed or if additional conditions have to be found to account for situations where social comparison pressures and elicitation of arguments that are not biased toward the implicit values of the risk-taking dilemmas. At present, it is particularly unclear just what distribution of arguments (percentage of risky and cautious arguments) must occur for risky or cautious shifts to result.

REFERENCES

Allport, F. H. *Social psychology.* Boston: Houghton, Mifflin, 1924.

Asch, S. E. Forming impressions of personality, *Journal of Abnormal and Social Psychology,* 1946, **41**, 258–90.

Asch, S. E. Effects of group pressure upon the modification and distortion of judgments. In E. E. Maccoby, R. M. Newcomb, and E. L. Hartley (eds.), *Readings in social psychology.* New York: Holt, Rinehart & Winston, 1958.

Barnlund, D. C. A comparative study of individual, majority, and group judgment. *Journal of Abnormal and Social Psychology,* 1959, **58**, 55–60.

Bateson, N. Familiarization, group discussion, and risk taking. *Journal of Experimental Social Psychology,* 1966, **2**, 119–29.

Bem, D. J., Wallach, M. A., and Kogan, N. Group decision making under risk of aversive consequences. *Journal of Personality and Social Psychology,* 1965, **1**, 453–60.

Blank, A. D. Effects of group and individual conditions on choice behavior. *Journal of Personality and Social Psychology,* 1968, **8**, 294–98.

Brown, R. *Social psychology.* New York: The Free Press, 1965.

Cartwright, D. and Zander, A. (eds.) *Group dynamics.* New York: Harper and Row, 1960.

Clark, R. D. and Crockett, W. H. Subjects initial positions, exposure to varying opinions, and the risky shift. *Psychonomic Science,* 1971, **23**, 277–79.

Clark, R. D., III, Crockett, W. H., and Archer, R. L. The relationship between perception of self, others, and the risky shift. *Journal of Personality and Social Psychology,* 1971, in press.

Clark, R. D., III and Willems, E. P. Where is the risky shift? Dependence on instructions. *Journal of Personality and Social Psychology,* 1969, **13**, 215–21. (a)

Clark, R. E., III and Willems, E. P. Risk preferences as related to judged consequences of failure. *Psychological Reports,* 1969, **25**, 827–30. (b)

Collins, B. E. and Guetzkow, H. A. *A social psychology of group processes for decision making.* New York: Wiley, 1964.

Darley, J. M. and Latané, B. Bystander intervention in emergencies: Diffusion of responsibility. *Journal of Personality and Social Psychology,* 1968, **8**, 377–83.

Dion, D. L., Baron, R. S., and Miller, N. Why do groups make riskier decisions than individuals? In L. Berkowitz (ed.), *Advances in experimental social psychology.* Vol. 5. New York: Academic Press, 1970.

Farnsworth, P. R. and Behner, A. A note on the attitude of social conformity. *Journal of Social Psychology,* 1931, **2**, 126–28.

Festinger, L. A theory of social comparison processes. *Human Relations,* 1954, **7**, 117–40.

Flanders, J. P. and Thistlethwaite, D. L. Effects of familiarization and group discussion upon risk taking. *Journal of Personality and Social Psychology,* 1967, **5**, 91–97.

Hoyt, G. C. and Stoner, J. A. F. Leadership and group decisions involving risk. *Journal of Experimental Social Psychology,* 1968, **4**, 275–84.

Jellison, J. M. and Riskind, J. A social comparison of abilities interpretation of risk-taking behavior. *Journal of Personality and Social Psychology,* 1970, **15**, 375–90.

Jones, E. E. and Gerard, H. B. *Foundations of social psychology.* New York: Wiley, 1967.

Kelley, H. H. and Thibaut, J. W. Group problem solving. In G. Lindzey & E. Aronson (eds.), *Handbook of social psychology.* Vol. IV. Reading, Mass.: Addison-Wesley, 1969.

Kogan, N. and Wallach, M. A. *Risk taking: A study in cognition and personality.* New York: Holt, Rinehart & Winston, 1964.

Kogan, N. and Wallach, M. A. Risk taking as a function of the situation, the person, and the group. In, *New directions in psychology.* Vol. III. New York: Holt, Rinehart & Winston, 1967. (a)

Kogan, N. and Wallach, M. A. Effects of physical separation of group members upon group risk taking. *Human Relations,* 1967, **20**, 41–48. (b)

Kogan, N. and Wallach, M. A. The risky-shift phenomenon in small decision-making groups: A test of the information-exchange hypothesis. *Journal of Experimental Social Psychology,* 1967, **3**, 75–84. (c)

Kogan, N. and Wallach, M. A. Group risk taking as a function of members' anxiety and defensive levels. *Journal of Personality,* 1967, **35**, 50–63. (d)

Krech, D., Crutchfield, R. S., and Ballachry, E. L. *Individual in society: A textbook of social psychology.* New York; McGraw-Hill, 1962.

Lamm, H. Will an observer advise higher risk taking after hearing a discussion of the decision problem? *Journal of Personality and Social Psychology,* 1967, **6**, 467–71.

Latané, B. and Darley, J. M. Group inhibition of bystander intervention in emergencies. *Journal of Personality and Social Psychology,* 1968, **10**, 215–21.

Latané, B. and Darley, J. M. Bystander apathy. *American Scientist,* 1969, **2**, 244–68.

Levinger, G. and Schneider, D. J. A test of the risk is a value hypothesis. *Journal of Personality and Social Psychology,* 1969, **11**, 165–69.

Madaras, G. R. and Bem, D. J. Risk and conservatism in group decision-making. *Journal of Experimental Social Psychology,* 1968, **4**, 350–65.

Marquis, D. G. Individual responsibility and group decisions involving risk. *Industrial Management Review,* 1962, **3**, 8–23.

Pruitt, D. G. and Teger, A. I. The risky shift in group betting. *Journal of Experimental Social Psychology,* 1969, **5**, 115–26.

Rabow, J., Fowler, F. J., Bradford, D. L., Hofeller, M. A., and Shibuya, Y. The role of social norms and leadership in risk taking. *Sociometry,* 1966, **29**, 16–27.

Rim, Y. Risk taking and need for achievement. *Acta Psychologica,* 1963, **21**, 108–15.

Rim, Y. Personality and group decision involving risk. *Psychological Record,* 1964, **14**, 37–45. (a)

Rim, Y. Social attitudes and risk taking. *Human Relations,* 1964, **17**, 259–65. (b)

Rim, Y. Who are the risk-takers in decision making? *Personnel Administration,* 1966, **29**, 26–30. (a)

Rim, Y. Machiavellianism and decisions involving risk. *British Journal of Social and Clinical Psychology,* 1966, **5**, 30–36. (b)

Schachter, S. Deviation, rejection, and communication. *Journal of Abnormal and Social Psychology,* 1951, **46**, 190–207.

Schein, E. H. *Organization psychology.* Englewood Cliffs, N.J.: Prentice-Hall, 1965.

Secord, P. F. and Backman, C. W. *Social psychology.* New York: McGraw-Hill, 1964.

Sherif, M. A study of some social factors in perception. *Archives of Psychology,* 1935, No. 187.

Sherif, M. *The psychology of social norms.* New York: Harper, 1936.

Stoner, J. A. Risky and cautious shifts in group decisions: The influence of widely held values. *Journal of Experimental Social Psychology,* 1968, **4**, 442–59.

Teger, A. I. and Pruitt, D. G. Components of group risk taking. *Journal of Experimental Social Psychology,* 1967, **3**, 189–205.

Teger, A. I., Pruitt, D. G., St. Jean, R., and Haaland, G. A. A reexamination of the familiarization hypothesis in group risk taking. *Journal of Experimental Social Psychology,* 1970, **6**, 346–50.

Vidmar, N. Group composition and the risky shift. *Journal of Experimental Psychology,* 1970, **6**, 153–66.

Wallach, M. A. and Kogan, N. The roles of information, discussion, and consensus in group risk taking. *Journal of Experimental Social Psychology,* 1965, **1**, 1–19.

Wallach, M. A., Kogan, N., and Bem, D. J. Group influence on individual risk taking. *Journal of Abnormal and Social Psychology,* 1962, **65**, 75–86.

Wallach, M. A., Kogan, N., and Bem, D. J. Diffusion of responsibility and level of risk taking in groups. *Journal of Abnormal and Social Psychology,* 1964, **68**, 263–74.

Wallach, M. A., Kogan, N., and Burt, R. B. Can group members recognize the effects of group discussion upon risk taking? *Journal of Experimental Social Psychology,* 1965, **1**, 379–95.

Wallach, M. A., Kogan, N., and Burt, R. B. Group risk taking and field dependence-independence of group members. *Sociometry,* 1967, **30**, 323–38.

Wallach, M. A., Kogan, N., and Burt, R. B. Are risk takers more persuasive than conservatives in group discussion? *Journal of Experimental Social Psychology,* 1968, **4**, 76–88.

Wallach. M. A. and Mabli, J. Information versus conformity in the effects of group discussion on risk taking. *Journal of Personality and Social Psychology,* 1970, **14**, 149–56.

Wallach, M. A. and Wing, C. W., Jr. Is risk a value? *Journal of Personality and Social Psychology,* 1968, **9**, 101–06.

Willems, E. P. Risk is a value. *Psychological Reports,* 1969, **24**, 81–82.

Willems, E. P. and Clark, R. D., III. Dependency of risky shift on instructions: A replication. *Psychological Reports,* 1969, **25**, 811–14.

Willems, E. P. and Clark, R. D., III. Shift toward risk and heterogeneity of groups. *Journal of Experimental Social Psychology,* 1971, **7**, 304–12.

Zander, A. and Medow, H. Individual and group levels of aspiration. *Human Relations,* 1963, **16**, 89–105.

40. ASSETS AND LIABILITIES IN GROUP PROBLEM SOLVING: THE NEED FOR AN INTEGRATIVE FUNCTION*

Norman R. F. Maier†

Research on group problem solving reveals that the group has both advantages and disadvantages over individual problem solving. If the potentials for group problem solving can be exploited and if its deficiencies can be avoided, it follows that group problem solving can attain a level of proficiency not ordinarily achieved. The requirement for achieving this level of group performance seems to hinge on developing a style of discussion leadership which maximizes the group's assets and minimizes its liabilities. Since members possess the essential ingredients for the solutions, the deficiencies that appear in group solutions reside in the processes by which group solutions develop. These processes can determine whether the group functions effectively or ineffectively. The critical factor in a group's potential is organization and integration. With training, a leader can supply these functions and serve as

* *Psychological Review,* Vol. 74, No. 4 (July 1967), pp. 239–49.

† Department of Psychology, University of Michigan.

the group's central nervous system, thus permitting the group to emerge as a highly efficient entity.[1]

A number of investigations have raised the question of whether group problem solving is superior, inferior, or equal to individual problem solving. Evidence can be cited in support of each position so that the answer to this question remains ambiguous. Rather than pursue this generalized approach to the question, it seems more fruitful to explore the forces that influence problem solving under the two conditions (see reviews by Hoffman, 1965; Kelley & Thibaut, 1954). It is hoped that a better recognition of these forces will permit clarification of the varied dimensions of the problem solving process, especially in groups.

The forces operating in such groups include some that are assets, some that are liabilities, and some that can be either assets or liabilities, depending upon the skills of the members, especially those of the discussion leader. Let us examine these three sets of forces.

GROUP ASSETS

Greater Sum Total of Knowledge and Information

There is more information in a group than in any of its members. Thus problems that require the utilization of knowledge should give groups an advantage over individuals. Even if one member of the group (e.g., the leader) knows much more than anyone else, the limited unique knowledge of lesser-informed individuals could serve to fill in some gaps in knowledge. For example, a skilled machinist might contribute to an engineer's problem solving and an ordinary workman might supply information on how a new machine might be received by workers.

Greater Number of Approaches to a Problem

It has been shown that individuals get into ruts in their thinking (Duncker, 1945; Maier, 1930; Wertheimer, 1959). Many obstacles stand in the way of achieving a goal, and a solution must circumvent these. The individual is handicapped in that he tends to persist in his approach and thus fails to find another approach that might solve the problem in a simpler manner. Individuals in a group have the same failing, but the approaches in which they are persisting may be different. For example, one researcher may try to prevent the spread of a disease by making man immune to the germ, another by finding and destroying the carrier of the germ, and still another by altering the environment so as to kill the germ before it reaches man. There is no way of determining which approach will best achieve the desired goal, but undue persistence in any one will stifle new discoveries. Since group members do not have identical approaches, each can contribute by knocking others out of ruts in thinking.

Participation in Problem Solving Increases Acceptance

Many problems require solutions that depend upon the support of others to be effective. Insofar as group problem solving permits participation and influence, it follows that more individuals accept solutions when a group solves the problem than when one person solves it. When one individual solves a problem he still has the task of persuading others. It follows, therefore, that when groups solve such problems, a greater number of persons accept and feel responsible for making the solution work. A low-quality solution that has good acceptance can be more effective than a higher-quality solution that lacks acceptance.

Better Comprehension of the Decision

Decisions made by an individual, which are to be carried out by others, must be communicated from the decision-maker to the decision-executors. Thus individual problem solving often requires an additional stage—that of relaying the decision reached. Failures in this communication process detract from the merits of the decision and can even cause its failure or create a problem of greater magnitude than the initial problem that was solved. Many organizational problems can be traced to inadequate communication of decisions made by superiors and transmitted to subordinates, who have the task of implementing the decision.

The chances for communication failures are greatly reduced when the individuals who must work together in executing the decision have participated in making it. They not only understand the solution because they saw it develop, but they are also aware of the several other alternatives that were considered and the reasons why they were discarded. The common assumption that decisions supplied by superiors are arbitrarily reached therefore disappears. A full knowledge of goals, obstacles, alternatives, and factual information is essential to communication,

[1] The research reported in the following reading was supported by Grant No. MH-02704 from the United States Public Health Service. Grateful acknowledgment is made for the constructive criticism of Melba Colgrove, Junie Janzen, Mara Julius, and James Thurber.

and this communication is maximized when the total problem-solving process is shared.

GROUP LIABILITIES

Social Pressure

Social pressure is a major force making for conformity. The desire to be a good group member and to be accepted tends to silence disagreement and favors consensus. Majority opinions tend to be accepted regardless of whether or not their objective quality is logically and scientifically sound. Problems requiring solutions based upon facts, regardless of feelings and wishes, can suffer in group problem-solving situations.

It has been shown (Maier & Solem, 1952) that minority opinions in leaderless groups have little influence on the solution reached, even when these opinions are the correct ones. Reaching agreement in a group often is confused with finding the right answer, and it is for this reason that the dimensions of a decision's acceptance and its objective quality must be distinguished (Maier, 1963).

Valence of Solutions

When leaderless groups (made up of three or four persons) engage in problem solving, they propose a variety of solutions. Each solution may receive both critical and supportive comments, as well as descriptive and explorative comments from other participants. If the number of negative and positive comments for each solution are algebraically summed, each may be given a valence index (Hoffman & Maier, 1964). The first solution that receives a positive valence value of 15 tends to be adopted to the satisfaction of all participants about 85 percent of the time, regardless of its quality. Higher quality solutions introduced after the critical value for one of the solutions has been reached have little chance of achieving real consideration. Once some degree of consensus is reached, the jelling process seems to proceed rather rapidly.

The critical valence value of 15 appears not to be greatly altered by the nature of the problem or the exact size of the group. Rather, it seems to designate a turning point between the idea-getting process and the decision-making process (idea evaluation). A solution's valence index is not a measure of the number of persons supporting the solution, since a vocal minority can build up a solution's valence by actively pushing it. In this sense, valence becomes an influence in addition to social pressure in determining an outcome.

Since a solution's valence is independent of its objective quality, this group factor becomes an important liability in group problem solving, even when the value of a decision depends upon objective criteria (facts and logic). It becomes a means whereby skilled manipulators can have more influence over the group process than their proportion of membership deserves.

Individual Domination

In most leaderless groups a dominant individual emerges and captures more than his share of influence on the outcome. He can achieve this end through a greater degree of participation (valence), persuasive ability, or stubborn persistence (fatiguing the opposition). None of these factors is related to problem-solving ability, so that the best problem solver in the group may not have the influence to upgrade the quality of the group's solution (which he would have had if left to solve the problem by himself).

Hoffman and Maier (1967) found that the mere fact of appointing a leader causes this person to dominate a discussion. Thus, regardless of his problem-solving ability a leader tends to exert a major influence on the outcome of a discussion.

Conflicting Secondary Goal: Winning the Argument

When groups are confronted with a problem, the initial goal is to obtain a solution. However, the appearance of several alternatives causes individuals to have preferences and once these emerge the desire to support a position is created. Converting those with neutral viewpoints now enters into the problem-solving process. More and more the goal becomes that of winning the decision rather than finding the best solution. This new goal is unrelated to the quality of the problem's solution and therefore can result in lowering the quality of the decision (Hoffman & Maier, 1966).

FACTORS THAT SERVE AS ASSETS OR LIABILITIES, DEPENDING LARGELY UPON THE SKILL OF THE DISCUSSION LEADER

Disagreement

The fact that discussion may lead to disagreement can serve either to create hard feelings among members or lead to a resolution of conflict and hence to an innovative solution (Hoffman, 1961; Hoffman,

Harburg, & Maier, 1962; Hoffman & Maier, 1961; Maier, 1958, 1963; Maier & Hoffman, 1965). The first of these outcomes of disagreement is a liability, especially with regard to the acceptance of solutions; while the second is an asset, particularly where innovation is desired. A leader can treat disagreement as undesirable and thereby reduce the probability of both hard feelings and innovation, or he can maximize disagreement and risk hard feelings in his attempts to achieve innovation. The skill of a leader requires his ability to create a climate for disagreement which will permit innovation without risking hard feelings. The leader's perception of disagreement is one of the critical factors in this skill area (Maier & Hoffman, 1965). Others involve permissiveness (Maier, 1953), delaying the reaching of a solution (Maier & Hoffman, 1960b; Maier & Solem, 1962), techniques for processing information and opinions (Maier, 1963; Maier & Hoffman, 1960a; Maier & Maier, 1957), and techniques for separating idea-getting from idea-evaluation (Maier, 1960, 1963; Osborn, 1953).

Conflicting Interests versus Mutual Interests

Disagreement in discussion may take many forms. Often participants disagree with one another with regard to solutions, but when issues are explored one finds that conflicting solutions are designed to solve different problems. Before one can rightly expect agreement on a solution, there should be agreement on the nature of the problem. Even before this, there should be agreement on the goal, as well as on the various obstacles that prevent the goal from being reached. Once distinctions are made between goals, obstacles, and solutions (which represent ways of overcoming obstacles), one finds increased opportunities for cooperative problem solving and less conflict (Hoffman & Maier, 1959; Maier, 1960, 1963; Maier & Solem, 1962; Solem, 1965).

Often there is also disagreement regarding whether the objective of a solution is to achieve quality or acceptance (Maier & Hoffman, 1964b), and frequently a stated problem reveals a complex of separate problems, each having separate solutions so that a search for a single solution is impossible (Maier, 1963). Communications often are inadequate because the discussion is not synchronized and each person is engaged in discussing a different aspect. Organizing discussion to synchronize the exploration of different aspects of the problem and to follow a systematic procedure increases solution quality (Maier & Hoffman, 1960a; Maier & Maier, 1957). The leadership function of influencing discussion procedure is quite distinct from the function of evaluating or contributing ideas (Maier, 1950, 1953).

When the discussion leader aids in the separation of the several aspects of the problem-solving process and delays the solution-mindedness of the group (Maier, 1958, 1963; Maier & Solem, 1962), both solution quality and acceptance improve; when he hinders or fails to facilitate the isolation of these varied processes, he risks a deterioration in the group process (Solem, 1965). His skill thus determines whether a discussion drifts toward conflicting interests or whether mutual interests are located. Cooperative problem solving can only occur after the mutual interests have been established and it is surprising how often they can be found when the discussion leader makes this his task (Maier, 1952, 1963; Maier & Hayes, 1962).

Risk Taking

Groups are more willing than individuals to reach decisions involving risks (Wallach & Kogan, 1965; Wallach, Kogan, & Bem, 1962). Taking risks is a factor in acceptance of change, but change may either represent a gain or a loss. The best guard against the latter outcome seems to be primarily a matter of a decision's quality. In a group situation this depends upon the leader's skill in utilizing the factors that represent group assets and avoiding those that make for liabilities.

Time Requirements

In general, more time is required for a group to reach a decision than for a single individual to reach one. Insofar as some problems require quick decisions, individual decisions are favored. In other situations acceptance and quality are requirements, but excessive time without sufficient returns also represents a loss. On the other hand, discussion can resolve conflicts, whereas reaching consensus has limited value (Wallach & Kogan, 1965). The practice of hastening a meeting can prevent full discussion, but failure to move a discussion forward can lead to boredom and fatigue-type solutions, in which members agree merely to get out of the meeting. The effective utilization of discussion time (a delicate balance between permissiveness and control on the part of the leader), therefore, is needed to make the time factor an asset rather than a liability. Unskilled leaders tend to be too concerned with reaching a solution and therefore terminate a discussion before the group potential is achieved (Maier & Hoffman, 1960b).

Who Changes

In reaching consensus or agreement, some members of a group must change. Persuasive forces do not operate in individual problem solving in the same way they operate in a group situation; hence, the changing of someone's mind is not an issue. In group situations, however, who changes can be an asset or a liability. If persons with the most constructive views are induced to change the end-product suffers; whereas if persons with the least constructive points of view change the end-product is upgraded. The leader can upgrade the quality of a decision because his position permits him to protect the person with a minority view and increase his opportunity to influence the majority position. This protection is a constructive factor because a minority viewpoint influences only when facts favor it (Maier, 1950, 1952; Maier & Solem, 1952).

The leader also plays a constructive role insofar as he can facilitate communications and thereby reduce misunderstandings (Maier, 1952; Solem, 1965). The leader has an adverse effect on the end-product when he suppresses minority views by holding a contrary position and when he uses his office to promote his own views (Maier & Hoffman, 1960b, 1962; Maier & Solem, 1952). In many problem-solving discussions the untrained leader plays a dominant role in influencing the outcome, and when he is more resistant to changing his views than are the other participants, the quality of the outcome tends to be lowered. This negative leader-influence was demonstrated by experiments in which untrained leaders were asked to obtain a second solution to a problem after they had obtained their first one (Maier & Hoffman, 1960a). It was found that the second solution tended to be superior to the first. Since the dominant individual had influenced the first solution, he had won his point and therefore ceased to dominate the subsequent discussion which led to the second solution. Acceptance of a solution also increases as the leader sees disagreement as idea-producing rather than as a source of difficulty or trouble (Maier & Hoffman, 1965). Leaders who see some of their participants as troublemakers obtain fewer innovative solutions and gain less acceptance of decisions made than leaders who see disagreeing members as persons with ideas.

THE LEADER'S ROLE FOR INTEGRATED GROUPS

Two Differing Types of Group Process

In observing group problem solving under various conditions it is rather easy to distinguish between cooperative problem-solving activity and persuasion or selling approaches. Problem-solving activity includes searching, trying out ideas on one another, listening to understand rather than to refute, making relatively short speeches, and reacting to differences in opinion as stimulating. The general pattern is one of rather complete participation, involvement, and interest. Persuasion activity includes the selling of opinions already formed, defending a position held, either not listening at all or listening in order to be able to refute, talking dominated by a few members, unfavorable reactions to disagreement, and a lack of involvement of some members. During problem solving the behavior observed seems to be that of members interacting as segments of a group. The interaction pattern is not between certain individual members, but with the group as a whole. Sometimes it is difficult to determine who should be credited with an idea. "It just developed," is a response often used to describe the solution reached. In contrast, discussions involving selling or persuasive behavior seem to consist of a series of interpersonal interactions with each individual retaining his identity. Such groups do not function as integrated units but as separate individuals, each with an agenda. In one situation the solution is unknown and is sought; in the other, several solutions exist and conflict occurs because commitments have been made.

The Starfish Analogy

The analysis of these two group processes suggests an analogy with the behavior of the rays of a starfish under two conditions: one with the nerve ring intact, the other with the nerve ring sectioned (Hamilton, 1922; Moore, 1924; Moore & Doudoroff, 1939; Schneirla & Maier, 1940). In the intact condition, locomotion and righting behavior reveal that the behavior of each ray is not merely a function of local stimulation. Locomotion and righting behavior reveal a degree of coordination and interdependence that is centrally controlled. However, when the nerve ring is sectioned, the behavior of one ray still can influence others, but internal coordination is lacking. For example, if one ray is stimulated, it may step forward, thereby exerting pressure on the sides of the other four rays. In response to these external pressures (tactile stimulation), these rays show stepping responses on the stimulated side so that locomotion successfully occurs without the aid of neural coordination. Thus integrated behavior can occur on the basis of external control. If, however, stimulation is applied to opposite rays, the specimen may be "locked" for a time, and in some species the conflicting locomotions may divide the animal, thus destroying it (Crozier, 1920; Moore & Doudoroff, 1939).

Each of the rays of the starfish can show stepping responses even when sectioned and removed from the animal. Thus each may be regarded as an individual. In a starfish with a sectioned nerve ring the five rays become members of a group. They can successfully work together for locomotion purposes by being controlled by the dominant ray. Thus if uniformity of action is desired, the group of five rays can sometimes be more effective than the individual ray in moving the group toward a source of stimulation. However, if "locking" or the division of the organism occurs, the group action becomes less effective than individual action. External control, through the influence of a dominant ray, therefore can lead to adaptive behavior for the starfish as a whole, but it can also result in a conflict that destroys the organism. Something more than external influence is needed.

In the animal with an intact nerve ring, the function of the rays is coordinated by the nerve ring. With this type of internal organization the group is always superior to that of the individual actions. When the rays function as a part of an organized unit, rather than as a group that is physically together, they become a higher type of organization—a single intact organism. This is accomplished by the nerve ring, which in itself does not do the behaving. Rather, it receives and processes the data which the rays relay to it. Through this central organization, the responses of the rays become part of a larger pattern so that together they constitute a single coordinated total response rather than a group of individual responses.

The Leader as the Group's Central Nervous System

If we now examine what goes on in a discussion group we find that members can problem-solve as individuals, they can influence others by external pushes and pulls, or they can function as a group with varying degrees of unity. In order for the latter function to be maximized, however, something must be introduced to serve the function of the nerve ring. In our conceptualization of group problem solving and group decision (Maier, 1963), we see this as the function of the leader. Thus the leader does not serve as a dominant ray and produce the solution. Rather, his function is to receive information, facilitate communications between the individuals, relay messages, and integrate the incoming responses so that a single unified response occurs.

Solutions that are the product of good group discussions often come as surprises to discussion leaders. One of these is unexpected generosity. If there is a weak member, this member is given less to do, in much the same way as an organism adapts to an injured limb and alters the function of other limbs to keep locomotion on course. Experimental evidence supports the point that group decisions award special consideration to needy members of groups (Hoffman & Maier, 1959). Group decisions in industrial groups often give smaller assignments to the less gifted (Maier, 1952). A leader could not effectually impose such differential treatment on group members without being charged with discriminatory practices.

Another unique aspect of group discussion is the way fairness is resolved. In a simulated problem situation involving the problem of how to introduce a new truck into a group of drivers, the typical group solution involves a trading of trucks so that several or all members stand to profit. If the leader makes the decision the number of persons who profit is often confined to one (Maier & Hoffman, 1962; Maier & Zerfoss, 1952). In industrial practice, supervisors assign a new truck to an individual member of a crew after careful evaluation of needs. This practice results in dissatisfaction, with the charge of *unfair* being leveled at him. Despite these repeated attempts to do justice, supervisors in the telephone industry never hit upon the notion of a general reallocation of trucks, a solution that crews invariably reach when the decision is theirs to make.

In experiments involving the introduction of change, the use of group discussion tends to lead to decisions that resolve differences (Maier, 1952, 1953; Maier & Hoffman, 1961, 1964a, 1964b). Such decisions tend to be different from decisions reached by individuals because of the very fact that disagreement is common in group problem solving and rare in individual problem solving. The process of resolving difference in a constructive setting causes the exploration of additional areas and leads to solutions that are integrative rather than compromises.

Finally, group solutions tend to be tailored to fit the interests and personalities of the participants; thus group solutions to problems involving fairness, fears, facesaving, etc., tend to vary from one group to another. An outsider cannot process these variables because they are not subject to logical treatment.

If we think of the leader as serving a function in the group different from that of its membership, we might be able to create a group that can function as an intact organism. For a leader, such functions as rejecting or promoting ideas according to his personal needs are out of bounds. He must be receptive to information contributed, accept contributions without evaluating them (posting contributions on a chalk board to keep them alive), summarize information to facilitate integration, stimulate exploratory behavior, create awareness of problems of one member by others, and detect when the group is ready to resolve differences and agree to a unified solution.

Since higher organisms have more than a nerve ring and can store information, a leader might appropriately supply information, but according to our model of a leader's role, he must clearly distinguish between supplying information and promoting a solution. If his knowledge indicates the desirability of a particular solution, sharing this knowledge might lead the group to find this solution, but the solution should be the group's discovery. A leader's contributions do not receive the same treatment as those of a member of the group. Whether he likes it or not, his position is different. According to our conception of the leader's contribution to discussion, his role not only differs in influence, but gives him an entirely different function. He is to serve much as the nerve ring in the starfish and to further refine this function so as to make it a higher type of nerve ring.

This model of a leader's role in group process has served as a guide for many of our studies in group problem solving. It is not our claim that this will lead to the best possible group function under all conditions. In sharing it we hope to indicate the nature of our guidelines in exploring group leadership as a function quite different and apart from group membership. Thus the model serves as a stimulant for research problems and as a guide for our analyses of leadership skills and principles.

CONCLUSIONS

On the basis of our analysis, it follows that the comparison of the merits of group versus individual problem solving depends on the nature of the problem, the goal to be achieved (high quality solution, highly accepted solution, effective communication and understanding of the solution, innovation, a quickly reached solution, or satisfaction), and the skill of the discussion leader. If liabilities inherent in groups are avoided, assets capitalized upon, and conditions that can serve either favorable or unfavorable outcomes are effectively used, it follows that groups have a potential which in many instances can exceed that of a superior individual functioning alone, even with respect to creativity.

This goal was nicely stated by Thibaut and Kelley (1961) when they

> wonder whether it may not be possible for a rather small, intimate group to establish a problem solving process that capitalizes upon the total pool of information and provides for great interstimulation of ideas without any loss of innovative creativity due to social restraints [p. 268].

In order to accomplish this high level of achievement, however, a leader is needed who plays a role quite different from that of the members. His role is analogous to that of the nerve ring in the starfish which permits the rays to execute a unified response. If the leader can contribute the integrative requirement, group problem solving may emerge as a unique type of group function. This type of approach to group processes places the leader in a particular role in which he must cease to contribute, avoid evaluation, and refrain from thinking about solutions or group *products.* Instead he must concentrate on the group *process,* listen in order to understand rather than to appraise or refute, assume responsibility for accurate communication between members, be sensitive to unexpressed feelings, protect minority points of view, keep the discussion moving, and develop skills in summarizing.

REFERENCES

Crozier, W. J. Notes on some problems of adaptation. *Biological Bulletin,* 1920, **39,** 116–29.

Duncker, K. On problem solving, *Psychological Monographs,* 1945, 58 (5, Whole No. 270).

Hamilton, W. F. Coordination in the starfish. III. The righting reaction as a phase of locomotion (righting and locomotion). *Journal of Comparative Psychology,* 1922, **2,** 81–94.

Hoffman, L. R. Conditions for creative problem solving. *Journal of Psychology,* 1961, **52,** 429–44.

Hoffman, L. R. Group problem solving. In L. Berkowitz (ed.), *Advances in experimental social psychology,* Vol. 2. New York: Academic Press, 1965, pp. 99–132.

Hoffman, L. R., Harburg, E., and Maier, N. R. F. Differences and disagreement as factors in creative group problem solving. *Journal of Abnormal and Social Psychology,* 1962, **64,** 206–14.

Hoffman, L. R. and Maier, N. R. F. The use of group decision to resolve a problem of fairness. *Personnel Psychology,* 1959, **12,** 545–59.

Hoffman, L. R. and Maier, N. R. F. Quality and acceptance of problem solutions by members of homogeneous and heterogeneous groups. *Journal of Abnormal and Social Psychology,* 1961, **62,** 401–07.

Hoffman, L. R. and Maier, N. R. F. Valence in the adoption of solutions by problem-solving groups: Concept, method, and results. *Journal of Abnormal and Social Psychology,* 1964, **69,** 264–71.

Hoffman, L. R. and Maier, N. R. F. Valence in the adoption of solutions by problem-solving groups: II. Quality and acceptance as goals of leaders and members. Unpublished manuscript, 1967 (Mimeo).

Kelley, H. H. and Thibaut, J. W. Experimental studies of group problem solving and process. In G. Lindzey (ed.), *Handbook of social psychology*. Cambridge. Mass.: Addison Wesley, 1954, pp. 735–85.

Maier, N. R. F. Reasoning in humans. I. On direction. *Journal of Comparative Psychology*, 1930, **10**, 115–43.

Maier, N. R. F. The quality of group decisions as influenced by the discussion leader. *Human Relations*, 1950, **3**, 155–74.

Maier, N. R. F. *Principles of human relations*. New York: Wiley, 1952.

Maier, N. R. F. An experimental test of the effect of training on discussion leadership. *Human Relations*, 1953, **6**, 161–73.

Maier, N. R. F. *The appraisal interview*. New York: Wiley, 1958.

Maier, N. R. F. Screening solutions to upgrade quality: A new approach to problem solving under conditions of uncertainty. *Journal of Psychology*, 1960, **49**, 217–31.

Maier, N. R. F. *Problem solving discussions and conferences: Leadership methods and skills*. New York: McGraw-Hill, 1963.

Maier, N. R. F. and Hayes, J. J. *Creative management*. New York: Wiley, 1962.

Maier, N. R. F. and Hoffman, L. R. Using trained "developmental" discussion leaders to improve further the quality of group decisions. *Journal of Applied Psychology*, 1960, **44**, 247–51. (a)

Maier, N. R. F. and Hoffman, L. R. Quality of first and second solutions in group problem solving. *Journal of Applied Psychology*, 1960, **44**, 278–83. (b)

Maier, N. R. F. and Hoffman, L. R. Organization and creative problem solving. *Journal of Applied Psychology*, 1961, **45**, 277–80.

Maier, N. R. F. and Hoffman, L. R. Group decision in England and the United States. *Personnel Psychology*, 1962, **15**, 75–87.

Maier, N. R. F. and Hoffman, L. R. Financial incentives and group decision in motivating change. *Journal of Social Psychology*, 1964, **64**, 369–78. (a)

Maier, N. R. F. and Hoffman, L. R. Types of problems confronting managers. *Personnel Psychology*, 1964, **17**, 261–69. (b)

Maier, N. R. F. and Hoffman, L. R. Acceptance and quality of solutions as related to leaders' attitudes toward disagreement in group problem solving. *Journal of Applied Behavioral Science*, 1965, **1**, 373–86.

Maier, N. R. F. and Maier, R. A. An experimental test of the effects of "developmental" vs. "free" discussions on the quality of group decisions. *Journal of Applied Psychology*, 1957, **41**, 320–23.

Maier, N. R. F. and Solem, A. R. The contribution of a discussion leader to the quality of group thinking: The effective use of minority opinions. *Human Relations*, 1952, **5**, 277–88.

Maier, N. R. F. and Solem, A. R. Improving solutions by turning choice situations into problems. *Personnel Psychology*, 1962, **15**, 151–57.

Maier, N. R. F. and Zerfoss, L. R. MRP: A technique for training large groups of supervisors and its potential use in social research. *Human Relations*, 1952, **5**, 177–86.

Moore, A. R. The nervous mechanism of coordination in the crinoid *Antedon rosaceus*. *Journal of Genetic Psychology*, 1924, **6**, 281–88.

Moore, A. R. and Doudoroff, M. Injury, recovery and function in an aganglionic central nervous system. *Journal of Comparative Psychology*, 1939, **28**, 313–28.

Osborn, A. F. *Applied imagination*. New York: Scribner's, 1953.

Schneirla, T. C. and Maier, N. R. F. Concerning the status of the starfish. *Journal of Comparative Psychology*, 1940, **30**, 103–10.

Solem, A. R. 1965: Almost anything I can do, we can do better. *Personnel Administration*, 1965, 28, 6–16

Thibaut, J. W. and Kelley, H. H. *The social psychology of groups*. New York: Wiley, 1961.

Wallach, M. A. and Kogan, N. The roles of information, discussion and consensus in group risk taking. *Journal of Experimental Social Psychology*, 1965, **1**, 1–19.

Wallach, M. A., Kogan, N., and Bem, D. J. Group influence on individual risk taking. *Journal of Abnormal and Social Psychology*, 1962, **65**, 75–86.

Wertheimer, M. *Productive thinking*. New York: Harper, 1959.

Section B

LEADERSHIP

Neither a description nor an explanation of group behavior would be complete without a consideration of leadership phenomena. Consequently, we now turn to a detailed examination of leadership processes and of the factors which may contribute to one's leadership effectiveness.

Vonnegut illustrates some of the assumptions about human needs and abilities that can underlie the adoption and assessment of various styles of leader behavior. The manner of management within an organization reflects the assumptions made by the organization's managers regarding both human motivation and the basic premises of organized activity.

Hollander and Julian set the stage for our analysis by providing an overview of the contemporary trends in the conceptualization and study of leadership. They critically review earlier conceptualizations which emphasized either the traits of the leader *or* situational factors, and then describe some trends toward a more satisfactory analysis. Among other things, they note a renewed interest in the concept of power and a tendency to view leadership as a two-way social influence process in which both the follower's behavior and the leader's behavior is shaped over a period of time. Hollander and Julian believe that it is more fruitful to think of leadership effectiveness in terms of group output *and* conditions prevailing within the group. They imply that if the two-way influence process has been mutually rewarding, group performance, member satisfaction, and the leader's influence potential will have been strengthened. They emphasize that the leader can be a major determinant of group performance and group stability by virtue of his goal-setting behavior, his expertise in the major group activity, and his ability and interest in shaping the behavior of group members. However, the typical conception of leadership as one person directing the behavior of others is too simplistic.

Bowers and Seashore also note the shift in research emphasis from a search for universal leadership traits to a search for leader behaviors that make a difference in the performance and satisfaction of followers. They suggest that leadership is comprised of aggregates of separate behaviors which may be grouped in a variety of ways and which are believed to be instrumental in controlling the behavior of others. They compare a number of classification schemes arising from studies conducted at The Ohio State University and the University of Michigan, and offer a four-factor classification of leader behaviors which may be related to organizational effectiveness. They further describe a study in which perceptions of leader supportive behavior, interaction facilitation behavior, goal emphasis, and work facilitation behavior were found to be related, though in complex ways, to group effectiveness and member satisfaction.

Yukl points out that few consistent relationships between measures of how a leader behaves and subordinate behavior have been found. He attributes this failure to the lack of clarity in the classes of leader behavior which have been proposed and to the failure to consider situational variables as determinants of leadership effectiveness. He reviews the Ohio State studies in which two leader behavior dimensions—consideration and initiating structure—have been investigated, and proposes an additional leadership factor called decision centralization.[1] He goes on to propose a multiple linkage model of leader effectiveness which incorporates situational variables which are assumed to interact with leader behaviors in determining the outcome. Yukl compares his model to Fiedler's contingency model of leadership effectiveness to which we now turn.

In the early 1960s, Fiedler introduced a contingency model of leadership effectiveness in which it was postulated that group performance is determined by leadership style in interaction with situational favorableness. The measure of leadership style is assumed to be an index of some underlying trait which leads some individuals to become relationship oriented (high LPC persons) or task oriented (low LPC persons) in stressful circumstances. Situational favorableness has been operationalized in different ways, but generally it is postulated that the situation is most favorable when subordinates respect and trust the leader, when the group task is highly structured and when the leader has control over significant positive and negative reinforcers. Fiedler reviews a number of studies conducted both before and after the model was formulated and concludes that field studies provide strong support for the validity of the model while experimental laboratory studies do not. As Fiedler notes, Graen and his colleagues feel that their experiments designed specifically to test the contingency model do not support it, but Fiedler criticizes those studies on methodological grounds.[2]

---

[1] Edwin A. Fleishman has provided an interesting account of the development of the Ohio State Measures of initiating structure and consideration. Furthermore, he outlines 20 years of use of these measures in relation to several indices of organizational effectiveness; grievances, turnovers and proficiency ratings, etc., as well as interpersonal processes such as empathy, sociometric structures and others. Fleishman also specifies several areas needing additional research. See Edwin A. Fleishman. Twenty years of consideration and structure, presentation at the Southern Illinois University Centennial Event Symposium, "Contemporary Development in the Study of Leadership," Carbondale, Illinois, April 29–30, 1971.

[2] The contingency theory has been criticized as not being supported by post facto evidence; that is, data collected after the formulation of the theory and intended as explicit tests of the theory (see G. Graen, K. Alvares, J. B. Orris, and J. A. Martella, Contingency model of leadership effectiveness: Antecedent and evidential results, *Psychological Bulletin,* 1970, *74,* 285–96). It has also been argued that experimental results do not support the theory as well as field studies; see G. Graen, J. B. Orris, and V. M. Alvares, Contingency model of leadership effectiveness: Some experimental results, *Journal of Applied Psychology,* 1971, *55,* 196–201. This study has, in turn, been criticized on methodological grounds; see F. E. Fiedler, Note on the methodology of the Graen, Orris, and Alvares studies testing the contingency model, *Journal of Applied Psychology,* 1971, *55,* 202–04. For a study offering partial support of the contingency model in the *classroom setting,* see Robert C. Hardy, Effect of leadership style on the performance of small classroom groups: A test of the contin-

House proposes a path-goal theory of leadership effectiveness in an attempt to reconcile some inconsistencies found in studies of leader consideration and initiating structure behavior. Drawing upon expectancy ideas, he postulates that the motivation to work is a function of the value placed on reinforcing consequences, those intrinsic to the task as well as those mediated by others, and the subjective probability that those outcomes will occur given task behavior of which the individual feels he is capable. House describes a series of general propositions in which he postulates that the leader may motivate subordinates by increasing their outcomes for a work-goal achievement, by clarifying path-goal relationships, and by reducing obstacles and providing needed resources such as tools, materials, and technical expertise. House goes on to list and test a number of hypotheses which specify the circumstances in which leader consideration and initiation of structure may lead to subordinate satisfaction and performance. On balance, House's theory offers some promise of explaining some of the troublesome inconsistencies in the leadership literature. It also contains the valuable suggestion, long past due, that initiation of structure and consideration behavior should be considered as behavioral strategies that should vary with the circumstances rather than as unchanging "styles" which are universally effective. However, we need to examine the assumption, implicit in the theory, that there is a one-to-one relationship between what leaders do to the environment and how that environment is perceived by the subordinate. For example, it is not at all clear how the leader's manipulation of rewards influences either the subjective value which the subordinate places on those rewards or his estimates of path instrumentalities. Finally, the assumption that a given class of leader behaviors causes subordinate behavior is a troublesome one especially when the casual assumption is based upon analysis of relationships between leader behaviors *as perceived by subordinates* and some index of subordinate behavior.

Lowin and Craig also ask why it is that the literature on leadership styles moves so readily from correlational data to casual inferences and prescriptions for leader behaviors without considering the obvious alternatives. After all, an organizational leader's rewards are at least partially contingent upon the progress of his group, and there are several views of interpersonal interaction which would predict that leadership style (behavior) should be sensitive to subordinate performance. Lowin and Craig systematically manipulated the performance of a subordinate and noted the consequences in terms of closeness of supervision, initiating structure, and consideration behaviors. (Like Yukl they found that conceptualizations of leader styles were so vague that it was difficult to class a given leader reaction as an instance of a given style.) They found that supervisors of a low-performing subordinate practiced closer surveillance, more often insisted that the subordinate follow prescribed methods, and showed less consideration for the subordinate than supervisors of high-performing subordinates. They suggest that the casual relationship which they demonstrated may be at least as important as the opposite one which is usually assumed. At the very minimum, they provide support for an earlier assertion that leadership should be thought of as a reciprocal influence process in which both the leader's behavior and that of his subordinates is shaped over a period of time. We may take a picture of it at any point in time but that picture may not tell us very much about the process.

---

gency model, *Journal of Personality and Social Psychology,* 1971, *19,* 367–574.

For two papers dealing with the practical and applied implications of the contingency model, see F. E. Fielder, Engineer the job to fit the manager, *Harvard Business Review,* 1965, *43,* 115–22; and F. E. Fielder, On the death and transfiguration of leadership training, invited address to Divisions 8, 14, and 19, American Psychological Association, September 3, 1971.

41. BICYCLES FOR AFGHANISTAN*

Kurt Vonnegut, Jr.

"Christ, back in Chicago, we don't make bicycles any more. It's all human relations now. The eggheads sit around trying to figure out new ways for everybody to be happy. Nobody can get fired, no matter what; and if someones does accidentally make a bicycle, the union accuses us of cruel and inhuman practices and the government confiscates the bicycle for back taxes and gives it to a blind man in Afghanistan."

"And you think things will be better in San Lorenzo?"

"I know damn well they will be. The people down there are poor enough and scared enough and ignorant enough to have some common sense!"

42. CONTEMPORARY TRENDS IN THE ANALYSIS OF LEADERSHIP PROCESSES*

Edwin P. Hollander and James W. Julian†

The history of leadership research is a fitful one. Certainly as much, and perhaps more than other social phenomena, conceptions and inquiry about leadership have shifted about. The psychological study of leadership in this century began with a primary focus on the personality characteristics which made a person a leader. But the yield from this approach was fairly meager and often confused, as Stogdill (1948) and Mann (1959) among others documented in their surveys of this literature. In the 1930s, Kurt Lewin and his co-workers (Lewin, Lippitt, & White, 1939) turned attention to the "social climates" created by several styles of leadership, that is, authoritarian, democratic, or laissez-faire. Together with developments in the sociometric study of leader-follower relations (e.g., Jennings, 1943), this work marked a significant break with the past.

Two residues left by Lewin's approach fed importantly into later efforts, even with the limited nature of the original study. One was the concern with "leader style," which still persists, especially in the work on administrative or managerial leadership (see e.g., McGregor, 1960, 1966; Preston & Heintz, 1949). The other was the movement toward a view of the differential contexts of leadership, ultimately evolving into the situational approach which took firm hold of the field by the 1950s (cf. Gouldner, 1950).

For the most part, the situational movement was spurred by the growing recognition that there were specialized demands made upon leadership, depending upon the nature of the group task and other aspects of the situation. Clearly, a deficiency in the older approach was its acceptance of "leader" as a relatively homogeneous role, independent of the variations in leader-follower relationships across situations. The disordered state in which the trait approach left the study of leadership was amply revealed by Stogdill in his 1948 survey, which marked a point of departure for the developing situational emphasis. The publication in 1949 of Hemphill's *Situational Factors in Leadership* contributed a further push in this direction.

The main focus of the situational approach was the study of leaders in different settings, defined especially in terms of different group tasks and group structure. Mainly, though not entirely, through laboratory experimentation, such matters as the continuity in leadership across situations with variable tasks was studied (e.g., Carter, Haythorn, Meirowitz, & Lanzetta, 1951; Carter & Nixon, 1949; Gibb, 1947). The findings of this research substantially supported the contention that who became a leader depended in some degree upon the nature of the task. With this movement, however, there came a corresponding deemphasis on the personality characteristics of leaders or other group members. Though a number of studies systematically placed people in groups on the basis of their scores on certain personality dimensions (e.g., Berkowitz, 1956; Haythorn,

---

* Taken from Chapter 42 "Bicycles for Afghanistan," *Cat's Cradle* (New York: Holt, Rinehart & Winston, Inc., 1963), p. 66. (New York: Dell Publishing Company, Inc. © 1963 by Kurt Vonnegut, Jr.).

* *Psychological Bulletin,* Vol. 71, No. 5 (1969), pp. 387–97.

The preparation of this paper was facilitated by the support of a program of research under ONR Contract 4679 from the group Psychology Branch, Office of Naval Research.

† State University of New York at Buffalo.

Couch, Haefner, Langham, & Carter, 1956; Scodel & Mussen, 1953; Shaw, 1955), more typically laboratory experimentation tended to disregard personality variables. In McGrath and Altman's (1966) review of small-group research, for example, they reported that of some 250 studies reviewed, only 16 employed such measures as variables of study. Thus, in little more than a decade, the pendulum swung very much away from the leader as the star attraction.

Within the present era, characterized by a greater sensitivity to the social processes of interaction and exchange, it becomes clearer that the two research emphases represented by the trait and situational approaches afforded a far too glib view of reality. Indeed, in a true sense, neither approach ever represented its own philosophical underpinning very well, and each resulted in a caricature. The purpose here is to attempt a rectification of the distortion that these traditions represented, and to point up the increasing signs of movement toward a fuller analysis of leadership as a social influence process, and not as a fixed state of being.

AN OVERVIEW

By way of beginning, it seems useful to make a number of observations to serve as an overview. First, several general points which grow out of current research and thought on leadership are established. Thereafter, some of the directions in which these developments appear to be heading are indicated, as well as those areas which require further attention.

One overriding impression conveyed by surveying the literature of the 1960s, in contrast to the preceding two decades, is the redirection of interest in leadership toward processes such as power and authority relationships (e.g., Blau, 1964; Emerson, 1962; Janda, 1960; Raven, 1965). The tendency now is to attach far greater significance to the interrelationship between the leader, the followers, and the situation (see, e.g., Fielder, 1964, 1965, 1967; Hollander, 1964; Hollander & Julian, 1968; Steiner, 1964). In consequence, the problem of studying leadership and understanding these relationships is recognized as a more formidable one than was earlier supposed (cf. Cartwright & Zander, 1968). Several of the particulars which signalize this changing emphasis may be summarized under four points, as follows:

1. An early element of confusion in the study of *leadership* was the failure to distinguish it as a process from the *leader* as a person who occupies a central role in that process. Leadership constitutes an influence relationship between two, or usually more, persons who depend upon one another for the attainment of certain mutual goals within a group situation. This situation not only involves the task but also comprises the group's size, structure, resources, and history, among other variables.

2. This relationship between leader and led is built *over time*, and involves an exchange or *transaction* between leaders and followers in which the leader both gives something and gets something. The leader provides a *resource* in terms of adequate role behavior directed toward the group's goal attainment, and in return receives greater influence associated with status, recognition, and esteem. These contribute to his "legitimacy" in making influence assertions, and in having them accepted.

3. There are differential tasks or functions attached to being a leader. While the image of the leader frequently follows Hemphill's (1961) view of one who "initiates structure," the leader is expected to function too as a mediator within the group, as a group spokesman outside it, and very often also as the decision maker who sets goals and priorities. Personality characteristics which may fit a person to be a leader are determined by the perceptions held by followers, in the sense of the particular role expectancies and satisfactions, rather than by the traits measured via personality scale scores.

4. Despite the persisting view that leadership traits do not generalize across situations, leader effectiveness can and should be studied as it bears on the group's achievement of desired outputs (see Katz & Kahn, 1966). An approach to the study of leader effectiveness as a feature of the group's success, in system terms, offers a clear alternative to the older concern with what the leader did do or did not do.

A richer, more interactive conception of leadership processes would entertain these considerations as points of departure for further study. Some evidence for a trend toward this development is considered in what follows.

WHITHER THE "SITUATIONAL APPROACH"?

What was the essential thrust of the situational approach, after all? Mainly, it was to recognize that the qualities of the leader were variously elicited, valued, and reacted to as a function of differential group settings and their demands. Hemphill (1949a) capped the point in saying "there are no absolute leaders, since successful leadership must always take into account the specific requirements imposed by the nature of the group which is to be led, requirements as diverse in nature and degree as are the organizations in which persons band together [p. 225]."

Though leadership events were seen as outcomes of a relationship that implicates the leader, the led, and their shared situation, studies conducted within the situational approach, usually left the *process* of leadership unattended. Much of the time, leaders were viewed in positional terms, with an emphasis on the outcome of their influence assertions. Comparatively little attention was directed to followers, especially in terms of the phenomenon of emergent leadership (cf. Hollander, 1961). With a few exceptions, such as the work of McGregor (see 1966) and others (e.g., Slater & Bennis, 1964), the leader's maintenance of his position was emphasized at the expense of understanding the attainment of it through a process of influence.

But even more importantly, the situational view made it appear that the leader and the situation were quite separate. Though they may be separable for analytic purposes, they also impinge on one another in the perceptions of followers. Thus, the leader, from the follower's vantage point, is an element in the situation, and one who shapes it as well. As an active agent of influence he communicates to other group members by his words and his actions, implying demands which are reacted to in turn. In exercising influence, therefore, the leader may set the stage and create expectations regarding what he should do and what he will do. Rather than standing apart from the leader, the situation perceived to exist may be his creation.

It is now possible to see that the trait and situational approaches merely emphasize parts of a process which are by no means separable. One kind of melding of the trait and situational approaches, for example, is found in the work of Fiedler. His essential point, sustained by an extensive program of research (see 1958, 1964, 1965, 1967), is that the leader's effectiveness in the group depends upon the structural properties of the group and the situation, including interpersonal perceptions of both leader and led. He finds, for example, that the willingness of group members to be influenced by the leader is conditioned by leader characteristics, but that the quality and direction of this influence is contingent on the group relations and task structure (1967). This work will be discussed further in due course.

Another kind of evidence about the importance to group performance of the leader's construction of the situation is seen in recent research on conflict. Using a role-playing test situation involving four-person groups, Maier and Hoffman (1965) found that conflict is turned to productive or nonproductive ends, depending on the attitude of the discussion leader. Where the leader perceived conflict in terms of "problem subordinates," the quality of the decision reached in these discussion groups was distinctly inferior to that reached under circumstances in which the discussion leader perceived disagreements as the source for ideas and innovation. In those circumstances, innovative solutions increased markedly.

A leader, therefore, sets the basis for relationships within the group, and thereby can affect outcomes. As Hemphill (1961) suggested, the leader initiates structure. But more than just structure in a concrete sense, he affects the process which occurs within that structure. Along with other neglected aspects of process in the study of leadership is the goal-setting activity of the leader. Its importance appears considerable, though few studies give it attention. In one of these, involving discussion groups, Burke (1966) found that the leader's failure to provide goal orientations within the group led to antagonism, tension, and absenteeism. This effect was most acute when there was clear agreement within the group regarding who was to act as the leader. Though such expectations about the leader undoubtedly are pervasive in groups studied in research on leadership, they are noted only infrequently.

LEGITIMACY AND SOCIAL EXCHANGE IN LEADERSHIP

Among the more substantial features of the leader's role is his perceived legitimacy—how he attains it and sustains it. One way to understand the process by which the leader's role is legitimated is to view it as an exchange of rewards operating to signalize the acceptance of his position and influence.

In social exchange terms, the person in the role of leader who fulfills expectations and achieves group goals provides rewards for others which are reciprocated in the form of status, esteem, and heightened influence. Because leadership embodies a two-way influence relationship, recipients of influence assertions may respond by asserting influence in return, that is, by making demands on the leader. The very sustenance of the relationship depends upon some yielding to influence on both sides. As Homans (1961) put it, "Influence over others is purchased at the price of allowing one's self to be influenced by others [p. 286]." To be influential, authority depends upon esteem, he said. By granting esteem itself, or symbolic manifestations of it, one may in turn activate leadership, in terms of a person taking on the leader role.

The elicitation of leader behavior is now a demonstrable phenomenon in various experimental settings. In one definitive study conducted by Pepinsky, Hemphill, and Shevitz (1958), subjects who were low on leader activity were led to behave far more actively in that role by the group's evident support for their assertions. Alternatively, other subjects known to be high on leader activity earlier were affected in precisely the opposite way by the group's evident disagreement with their statements. In simplest terms, an exchange occurs between the group and the target person. The group provides reinforcement which in turn elicits favored behaviors. In other terms, the reinforcement of a person's influence assertions substantiates his position of authority.

Other, more recent, work suggested that even the use of lights as reinforcers exerts a significant effect on the target person's proportion of talking time as well as his perceived leadership status (Bavelas, Hastorf, Gross, & Kite, 1965; Zdep & Oakes, 1967). Thus, the lights not only produced a heightening of leader acts, but also created the impression of greater influence with the implication of legitimacy as well.

In a similar vein, Rudraswamy (1964) conducted a study in which some subjects within a group were led to believe they had higher status. Not only did they attempt significantly more leadership acts than others in their group, but they even outdistanced those subjects who were given more relevant information about the task itself.

It is also clear that agreement about who should lead has the effect in groups of increasing the probability of leader acts (e.g., Banta & Nelson, 1964). Relatedly, in a study of five-man groups involving changed as against unchanged leadership, Pryer, Flint, and Bass (1962) found that group effectiveness was enhanced by early agreement on who should lead.

When a basis is provided for legitimately making influence assertions, it is usually found that individuals will tend to act as leaders. This, of course, does not deny the existence of individual differences in the propensity for acting, once these conditions prevail. In a recent study by Gordon and Medland (1965), they found that positive peer ratings on leadership in army squads was consistently related to a measure of "aspiration to lead." Similarly, research findings on discussion groups (e.g., Riecken, 1958) indicated that the more vocal members obtain greater reinforcement, and hence experience the extension of legitimacy.

The "idiosyncrasy credit" concept (Hollander, 1958) suggests that a person's potential to be influential arises out of the positive dispositions others hold toward him. In simplest terms, competence in helping the group achieve its goals, and early conformity to its normative expectations for members, provide the potential for acting as a leader and being perceived as such. Then, assertions of influence which were not tolerated before are more likely to be acceptable. This concept applies in an especially important way to leadership succession, since it affords the basis for understanding how a new leader becomes legitimized in the perceptions of his peers. Further work on succession phenomena appears, in general, to be another area of fruitful study. There are many intriguing issues here, such as the question of the relative importance in legitimacy of factors such as "knowledge" and "office," in Max Weber's terms, which deserve further consideration (see, e.g., Evan & Zelditch, 1961).

THE PERCEPTION OF LEADERSHIP FUNCTIONS WITHIN GROUP STRUCTURE

A major deficiency in the older trait approach was its conception of "traits" within the framework of classic personality typologies. Personality measures were applied to leaders, often in profusion, without reference either to the varying nature of leadership roles or the functions they were to fulfill. As Mann's (1959) review revealed, such measures indeed do yield inconsistent relationships among leaders, variously defined. To take a common instance, dominance and extroversion are sometimes related positively to status as the leader, but mainly are neither related positively nor negatively to this status. On the other hand, Stogdill (1948) reported that such characteristics as "originality," "initiative," and "adaptability" have a low but positive relationship with leader status.

Granting that some essentially personality-type variables are more often found among those designated as leaders than among those designated as nonleaders, there can be no dismissing the widespread failure to treat the characteristics of the leader as they are perceived—and, what is more, as they are perceived as *relevant*—by other group members within a given setting. As Hunt (1965) and Secord and Backman (1961) pointed out, traits are viewed relative to the interpersonal context in which they occur. In short, followers hold expectations regarding what the leader ought to be doing here and now, and not absolutely.

One probable source for the disparate findings concerning qualities of the leader is the existence of differential expectations concerning the functions the leader is to perform. In simplest terms, there are various leadership roles. Without nearly exhausting the roster, it helps to realize that the leader in various time-space settings may be a task director, mediator, or spokesman, as well as a decision maker who, as Bavelas (1960) put it, "reduces uncertainty."

Whether in the laboratory or the field, studies of the perceptions of the leader's functions often have depended upon a sociometric approach (cf. Hollander, 1954). Thus, Clifford and Cohen (1964) used a sociometric device to study leadership roles in a summer camp, with 79 boys and girls, ranging in age from 8 to 13 years. Over a period of 4 weeks, they had nine elections by secret ballot asking the youngsters to indicate how the others would fit into various roles, including such things as planner, banquet chairman, swimming captain, and so forth. Their results indicated that the perceived attributes of campers were tied variously to their election for different leader roles. In line with the earlier point about the interpersonal context of leader traits, these researchers say, "the problem should be rephrased in terms of personality variables required in a leader role in a specific situation, which is in turn a function of the follower's perceptions [p. 64]."

Apart from personality traits, one prevailing expectation which does yield consistent findings across situations is that the leader's competence in a major group activity should be high. Dubno (1965), for example, reported that groups are more satisfied when leaders are demonstrably competent in a central function and do most of the work associated with that function. This is seen, too, in an experiment with five-man discussion groups, from which Marak (1964) found that the rewards associated with the leader's ability on a task led to greater perceived as well as actual influence. In general, the greater influence of a leader perceived to be more competent was verified experimentally by Dittes and Kelley (1956) and by Hollander (1960), among others.

Another leader attribute which evidently determines the responsiveness of followers is his perceived motivation regarding the group and its task. This was seen in Rosen, Levinger, and Lippitt's (1961) finding that helpfulness was rated as the most important characteristic leading to high influence potential among adolescent boys. In a more recent study of the role dimensions of leader-follower relations, Julian and Hollander (1966) found that, aside from the significance of task competence, the leader's "interest in group members" and "interest in group activity" were significantly related to group members' willingness to have a leader continue in that position. This accords with the finding of a field study by Nelson (1964) among 72 men who spent 12 months together in the Antarctic. While those men most liked as leaders had characteristics highly similar to those who were most liked as followers, Nelson reported that perceived motivation was the major factor which distinguished the two. Hollander (1958) considered this as one critical factor determining the leader's ability to retain status, even though nonconforming. In Nelson's study, the highly liked leaders were seen significantly more to be motivated highly toward the group in line with his hypothesis that "a critical expectation held of the leader, if he is to maintain esteem, is that he display strong motivation to belong to the group [p. 165]."

A study by Kirkhart (1963) investigated group leadership among Negro college students as a function of their identification with their minority group. In terms of follower expectations, he found that those selected most frequently by their peers for leadership roles, in both the "internal system" and the "external system" activities of the group, scored higher on a questionnaire expressing Negro identification. This quality of being an examplar of salient group characteristics was noted long ago by Brown (1936) as a feature of leadership. Its relationship to processes of identification with the leader is discussed shortly.

SOURCE AND NATURE OF LEADER AUTHORITY

The structural properties of groups affect the processes which occur within them. In leadership, the source of the leader's authority constitutes a significant element of structure. Yet, experimentation on leadership has given little attention to this variable, apart from some promising earlier work by Carter et al. (1951) with appointed and emergent leaders, and the previously mentioned work by Lewin and his associates on the style of the leader and its consequences to the group's social climate (Lewin et al., 1939; Preston & Heintz, 1949). More recently, Cohen and Bennis (1961) demonstrated that where groups could elect their leaders, the continuity of leadership was better maintained than where their leaders were appointed. In research on the productivity of groups, Goldman and Fraas (1965) found that differences occured among four conditions of leader selection, including election and appointment.

With four-man discussion groups, Julian, Hollander, and Regula (1969) employed a multifactor design to study three variables: the source of a leader's authority, in either election or appointment; his competence, in terms of perceived capability on the task; and his subsequent task success. Their main dependent measure was the members' acceptance of the leader as a spokesman for the group. The findings of this experiment indicated that the latter two variables were significantly related to this acceptance, but that these relationships were differentially affected by whether the leader was appointed or elected. The shape of the three-way interaction suggested that election, rather than making the leader more secure, made him more vulnerable to censure if he were either initially perceived to be incompetent or subsequently failed to secure a successful outcome as spokesman for the group. While this finding alone does not sustain a generalization that the appointed leader necessarily is more firmly entrenched, it does support the conclusion that the leader's source of authority is perceived and reacted to as a relevant element in the leadership process.

Other work on a differentiation of the leader's role, through the social structure, was conducted by Anderson and Fiedler (1964). In their experiment with four-man discussion groups, half the groups had leaders who were told to serve as a "chairman" in a participatory way, and the other groups had leaders who were told to serve as an "officer in charge" in a supervisory way. They found that the nature of the leadership process was affected markedly by this distinction, thus paralleling the main findings of Preston and Heintz (1949). In general, the more participatory leaders were significantly more influential and made more of a contribution to the group's performance. But, more to the point, the relationship between leader attributes, such as intelligence and group performance, was significant for certain tasks under the participatory condition, though not for any of the tasks under the supervisory condition. The conclusion that Anderson and Fiedler reached, therefore, is that the characteristics of a leader, including intelligence and other personality attributes, become more salient and more highly relevant to group achievement under conditions of participation by the leader, as against circumstances where a highly formal role structure prevails.

EFFECTIVENESS OF THE LEADER

By now it is clear that an entire interpersonal system is implicated in answering the question of the leader's effectiveness. The leader is not effective merely by being influential, without regard to the processes at work and the ends achieved. Stressing this point, Selznick (1957) said that, "far more than the capacity to mobilize personal support . . . (or) the maintenance of equilibrium through the routine solution of everyday problems," the leader's function is "to define the ends of group existence, to design an enterprise distinctively adapted to these ends, and to see that the design becomes a living reality [p. 37]."

As Katz and Kahn (1966) observed, any group operates with a set of resources to produce certain outputs. Within this system, an interchange of inputs for outputs occurs, and this is facilitated by leadership functions which, among other things, direct the enterprise. The leader's contribution and its consequences vary with system demands, in terms of what Selznick referred to as "distinctive competence." Taken by itself, therefore, the typical conception of leadership as one person directing others can be misleading, as already indicated. Though the leader provides a valued resource, the group's resources are not the leader's alone. Together, such resources provide the basis for functions fulfilled in the successful attainment of group goals, or, in other terms, group outputs.

Given the fact that a group must work within the set of available resources, its effectiveness is gauged in several ways. Stogdill (1959), for one, distinguished these in terms of the group's performance, integration, and member satisfaction as group outputs of a leadership process involving the use of the group's resources. Thus, the leader and his characteristics constitute a set of resources contributing to the effective utilization of other resources. A person who occupies the central role of leader has the task of contributing to this enterprise, within the circumstances broadly confronting the group.

One prominent exemplification of the system's demands and constraints on the leader's effectiveness is seen in Fiedler's "contingency model" (1964, 1965, 1967). He predicted varying levels of effectiveness for different *combinations* of leader and situational characteristics. Thus, depending upon the leader's orientation toward his co-workers, in the context of three situational variables—the quality of leader-member liking, the degree of task structure, and the position power of the leader—he finds distinct variations in this effectiveness.

In a recent test of his model, Fiedler (1966) conducted an experiment to compare the performance of 96 three-man groups that were culturally and linguistically homogeneous or heterogeneous. Some operated under powerful and others under weak leadership positions on three types of tasks varying in structure and requirements for verbal interaction. Despite the communication difficulties and different backgrounds, heterogeneous groups performed about as well on the nonverbal task as did the homogeneous groups. Groups with petty officers as leaders (powerful) did about as well as the groups with recruits as leaders (weak). The main finding of the experiment was support for the hypothesis from the contingency model that the specific leadership orientation required for effectiveness is contingent on the favorableness of the group-task situation. Partial support for this hypothesis came also from a study by Shaw and Blum (1966) in which they manipulated some of the same variables with five-person groups, and with three tasks selected to vary along a dimension reflecting different levels of favorability for the leader. Their results indicated that the directive leader was more effective than the nondirective leader only when the group-task situation was highly favorable for the leader, but not otherwise.

IDENTIFICATION WITH THE LEADER

For any leader, the factors of favorability and effectiveness depend upon the perceptions of followers. Their identification with him implicates significant psychological ties which may affect materially his ability to be influential. Yet the study of identification is passé in leadership research. Though there is a recurring theme in the literature of social science, harking back to Weber (see 1947), about the so-called "charismatic leader," this quality has a history of imprecise usage; furthermore, its tie with identification processes is by no means clear. Putting the study of the sources and consequences of identification with the leader on a stronger footing seems overdue and entirely feasible.

Several lines of work in social psychology appear to converge on identification processes. The distinction made by Kelman (1961) regarding identification, internalization, and compliance, for example, has obvious relevance to the relationship between the leader and his followers. This typology might be applied to the further investigation of leadership processes. The work of Sears (1960) and of Bandura and Walters (1963), concerning the identification of children with adult models, also has implications for such study.

One point which is clear, though the dynamics require far more attention, is that the followers' identification with their leader can provide them with social reality, in the sense of a shared outlook An illustration of this is seen in work on the social psychology of political leadership by Hollander (see 1963). In two phases, separated by an interval of 8 years, he studied Republicans in 1954 who had voted for President Eisenhower in 1952 and who would or would not vote for him again in 1954; and then in 1962, he studied Democrats who had voted for President Kennedy in 1960 and who would or would not vote for him again in 1962. He found that continuing loyalty to the President of one's party, among these respondents, was significantly associated with their views on issues and conditions and with their votes for the party in a midterm congressional-senatorial election. The defectors showed a significant shift in the precise opposite direction, both in their attitudes and in their voting behavior. In both periods, the ideology of loyalists was highly consistent with the leader's position. In the economic realm, for example, even where actual well-being varied considerably among loyalists, this identification with the President yielded highly similar attitudes regarding the favorability of the economic picture facing the nation.

With appropriate concern for rectifying the balance, there may be virtue in reopening for study Freud's (1922) contention that the leader of a group represents a common "ego ideal" in whom members share an identification and an ideology. Laboratory experimentation on groups offers little basis for studying such identification in light of the ephemeral, ad hoc basis for the creation of such groups. In fact, a disproportionate amount of our current knowledge about leadership in social psychology comes from experiments which are methodologically sophisticated but bear only a pale resemblance to the leadership enterprise that engages people in persisting relationships.

There also is the problem of accommodating the notion of identification within prevailing conceptions of leader-follower transactions and social exchange. But that is not an insurmountable difficulty with an expansion of the reward concept to include, for instance, the value of social reality. In any case, as investigators move increasingly from the laboratory to studies in more naturalistic settings, one of the significant qualities that may make a difference in leadership functioning is precisely this prospect for identification.

SOME CONCLUSIONS AND IMPLICATIONS

The present selective review and discussion touches upon a range of potential issues for the further study of leadership. The discussion is by no means exhaustive in providing details beyond noting suggestive developments. It is evident, however, that a new set of conceptions about leadership is beginning to emerge after a period of relative quiescence.

In providing a bridge to future research here, these newer, general ideas are underscored in a suggestive way. The methodologies they demand represent a challenge to imaginative skill, especially toward greater refinements in the conduct of field experiments and field studies which provide a look at the broader system of leadership relationships. Then, too, there is a need to consider the two-way nature of the influence process, with greater attention paid to the expectations of followers within the system. As reiterated here, the key to an understanding of leadership rests in seeing it as an influence process, involving an implicit exchange relationship over time.

No less important as a general point is the need for a greater recognition of the system represented by the group and its enterprise. This recognition provides a vehicle by which to surmount the misleading dichotomy of the leader and the situation which so long has prevailed. By adopting a systems approach, the leader, the led, and the situation defined broadly, are seen as interdependent inputs variously engaged toward the production of desired outputs.

Some release is needed from the highly static, positional view of leadership if we are to analyze its processes. A focus on leadership maintenance has weighted the balance against a more thorough probe of emerging leadership and succession phenomena. Investigators should be more aware of their choice and the differential implications, as between emerging and ongoing leadership. In this regard, the significance of the legitimacy of leadership, its sources, and effects requires greater attention in future investigations.

In studying the effectiveness of the leader, more emphasis should be placed on the outcomes for the total system, including the fulfillment of expectations held by followers. The long-standing overconcern with outcome, often stated only in terms of the leader's ability to influence, should yield to a richer conception of relationships geared to mutual goals. Not irrelevantly, the perception of the leader held by followers, including their identification with him, needs closer scrutiny. In this way, one may approach a recognition of stylistic elements allowing given persons to be effective leaders.

Finally, it seems plain that research on task-oriented groups must attend more to the organizational frameworks within which these groups are imbedded. Whether these frameworks are industrial, educational, governmental, or whatever, they are implicated in such crucial matters as goal-setting, legitimacy of authority, and leader succession. Though not always explicit, it is the organizational context which recruits and engages members in particular kinds of tasks, role relationships, and the rewards of participation. This context deserves more explicitness in attempts at understanding leadership processes.

REFERENCES

Anderson, L. R. and Fiedler, F. E. The effect of participatory and supervisory leadership on group creativity. *Journal of Applied Psycholgy,* 1964, **48**, 227–36.

Bandura, A. and Walters, R. H. *Social learning and personality development.* New York: Holt, Rinehart & Winston, 1963.

Banta, T. J. and Nelson, C. Experimental analysis of resource location in problem-solving groups. *Sociometry,* 1964, **27**, 488–501.

Bavelas, A. Leadership: Man and function. *Administrative Science Quarterly,* 1960, **4**, 491–98.

Bavelas, A., Hastorf, A. H., Gross, A. E., and Kite, W. R. Experiments on the alteration of group structure. *Journal of Experimental Social Psychology,* 1965, **1**, 55–70.

Berkowitz, L. Personality and group position. *Sociometry,* 1956, **19**, 210–22.

Blau, P. *Exchange and power in social life.* New York: Wiley, 1964.

Brown, J. F. *Psychology and the social order.* New York: McGraw-Hill, 1936.

Burke, P. J. Authority relations and descriptive behavior in small discussion groups. *Sociometry,* 1966, **29**, 237–50.

Carter, L. F., Haythorn, W., Meirowitz, B., and Lanzetta, J. The relation of categorizations and ratings in the observation of group behavior. *Human Relations,* 1951, **4**, 239–53.

Carter. L. F. and Nixon, M. An investigation of the relationship between four criteria of leadership ability for three different tasks. *Journal of Psychology,* 1949, **27**, 245–61.

Cartwright, D. C. and Zander, A. (eds.) *Group dynamics: Research and theory.* (3d ed.) New York: Harper & Row, 1968.

Clifford, C. and Cohen, T. S. The relationship between leadership and personality attributes perceived by followers. *Journal of Social Psychology,* 1964, **64**, 57–64.

Cohen, A. M. and Bennis, W. G. Continuity of leadership in communication networks. *Human Relations,* 1961, **14**, 351–67.

Dittes, J. E. and Kelley, H. H. Effects of different conditions of acceptance upon conformity to group norms. *Journal of Abnormal and Social Psychology,* 1956, **53**, 100–7.

Dubno, P. Leadership, group effectiveness, and speed of decision. *Journal of Social Psychology,* 1965, **65**, 351–60.

Emerson, R. M. Power-dependence relations. *American Sociological Review,* 1962, **27**, 31–41.

Evan, W. M. and Zelditch, M. A laboratory experiment on bureaucratic authority. *American Sociological Review,* 1961, **26**, 883–93.

Fiedler, F. E. *Leader attitudes and group effectiveness.* Urbana: University of Illinois Press, 1958.

Fiedler, F. E. A contingency model of leadership effectiveness. In L. Berkowitz (ed.), *Advances in experimental social psychology.* Vol. 1. New York: Academic Press, 1964.

Fiedler, F. E. The contingency model: A theory of leadership effectiveness. In H. Proshansky & B. Seidenberg (eds.), *Basic studies in social psychology.* New York: Holt, Rinehart & Winston, 1965.

Fiedler, F. E. The effect of leadership and cultural heterogeneity on group performance: A test of a contingency model. *Journal of Experimental Social Psychology,* 1966, **2**, 237–64.

Fiedler, F. E. *A theory of leadership effectiveness.* New York: McGraw-Hill, 1967.

Freud, S. *Group psychology and the analysis of the ego.* London and Vienna: International Psychoanalytic Press, 1922.

Gibb, C. A. The principles and traits of leadership. *Journal of Abnormal and Social Psychology,* 1947, **42**, 267–84.

Goldman, M. and Frass, L. A. The effects of leader selection on group performance. *Sociometry,* 1965, **28**, 82–88.

Gordon, L. V. and Medland, F. F. Leadership aspiration and leadership ability. *Psychological Reports,* 1965, **17**, 388–90.

Gouldner, A. W. (ed.) *Studies in leadership.* New York: Harper, 1950.

Haythorn, W., Couch, A., Haifner, D., Langham, P. and Carter, L. F. The effects of varying combinations of authoritarian and equalitarian leaders and followers. *Journal of Abnormal and Social Psychology,* 1956, **53**, 210–19.

Hemphill, J. K. The leader and his group. *Educational Research Bulletin,* 1949, **28**, 225–29, 245–46.

Hemphill, J. K. *Situational factors in leadership.* Columbus: Ohio State University, Bureau of Educational Research, 1949. (b)

Hemphill, J. K. Why people attempt to lead. In L. Petrullo and B. M. Bass (eds.), *Leadership and interpersonal behavior.* New York: Holt, Rinehart & Winston, 1961.

Hollander, E. P. Authoritarianism and leadership choice in a military setting. *Journal of Abnormal and Social Psychology,* 1954, **49**, 365–70.

Hollander, E. P. Conformity, status, and idosyncrasy credit. *Psychological Review,* 1958, **65**, 117–27.

Hollander, E. P. Competence and conformity in the acceptance of influence. *Journal of Abnormal and Social Psychology,* 1960, **61**, 365–69.

Hollander, E. P. Emergent leadership and social influence. In L. Petrullo & B. M. Bass (eds.), *Leadership and interpersonal behavior.* New York: Holt, Rinehart & Winston, 1961.

Hollander, E. P. The "pull" of international issues in the 1962 election. In S. B. Withey (Chm.), Voter attitudes and the war-peace issue. Symposium presented at the American Psychological Association Philadelphia, August, 1963.

Hollander, E. P. *Leaders, groups, and influence.* New York: Oxford University Press, 1964.

Hollander, E. P. and Julian, J. W. Leadership. In E. F. Borgatta and W. W. Lambert (eds.), *Handbook of personality theory and research.* Chicago: Rand McNally, 1968.

Homans, G. C. *Social Behavior: Its elementary forms.* New York: Harcourt, Brace & World, 1961.

Hunt, J. McV. Traditional personality theory in the light of recent evidence. *American Scientist,* 1965, **53**, 80–96.

Janda, K. F. Towards the explication of the concept of leadership in terms of the concept of power. *Human Relations,* 1960, **13**, 345–63.

Jennings, H. H. *Leadership and isolation.* New York: Longmans, 1943.

Julian, J. W. and Hollander, E. P. A study of some role dimensions of leader-follower relations. Technical Report No. 3, April 1966, State University of New York at Buffalo, Department of Psychology, Contract 4679, Office of Naval Research.

Julian, J. W., Hollander, E. P., and Regula, C. R. Endorsement of the group spokesman as a function of his source of authority, competence, and success. *Journal of Personality and Social Psychology,* 1969, **11**, 42–49.

Katz, D. and Kahn, R. *The social psychology of organizations.* New York: Wiley, 1966.

Kelman, H. C. Processes of opinion change. *Public Opinion Quarterly,* 1961, **25**, 57–78.

Kirkhart, R. O. Minority group identification and group leadership. *Journal of Social Psychology,* 1963, **59**, 111-17.

Lewin, K., Lipitt, R., and White, R. K. Patterns of aggressive behavior in experimentally created "social climates." *Journal of Social Psychology,* 1939, **10**, 271–99.

Maier, N. R. and Hoffman, L. R. Acceptance and quality of solutions as related to leader's attitudes toward disagreement in group problem solving. *Journal of Applied Behavioral Science,* 1965, **1**, 373–86.

Mann, R. D. A review of the relationships between personality and performance in small groups. *Psychological Bulletin,* 1959, **56**, 241–70.

Marak, G. E. The evolution of leadership structure. *Sociometry,* 1964, **27**, 174–82.

McGrath, J. E. and Altman, I. *Small group research: A critique and synthesis of the field.* New York: Holt, Rinehart & Winston, 1966.

McGregor, D. *The human side of enterprise.* New York: McGraw-Hill, 1960.

McGregor, D. *Leadership and motivation.* (Essays edited by W. G. Bennis & E. H. Schein) Cambridge, Mass.: M.I.T. Press, 1966.

Nelson, P. D. Similarities and differences among leaders and followers. *Journal of Social Psychology,* 1964, **63**, 161–67.

Pepinsky, P. N., Hemphill, J. K., and Shevitz, R. N. Attempts to lead, group productivity, and morale under conditions of acceptance and rejection. *Journal of Abnormal and Social Psychology,* 1958, **57**, 47–54.

Preston, M. G., and Heintz, R. K. Effects of participatory versus supervisory leadership on group judgment. *Journal of Abnormal and Social Psychology,* 1949, **44**, 345–55.

Pryer, M. W., Flint, A. W., and Bass, B. M. Group effectiveness and consistency of leadership. *Sociometry,* 1962, **25**, 391–97.

Raven, B. Social influence and power. In I. D. Steiner & M. Fishbein (eds.), *Current studies in social psychology.* New York: Holt, Rinehart & Winston, 1965.

Riecken, H. W. The effect of talkativeness on ability to influence group solutions to problems. *Sociometry,* 1958, **21**, 309–21.

Rosen, S., Levinger, G., and Lippitt, R. Perceived sources of social power. *Journal of Abnormal and Social Psychology,* 1961, **62**, 439–41.

Rudraswamy, V. An investigation of the relationship between perceptions of status and leadership attempts.

Journal of the Indian Academy of Applied Psychology, 1964, 1, 12–19.

Scodel, A. and Mussen, P. Social perception of authoritarians and nonauthoritarians. *Journal of Abnormal and Social Psychology*, 1953, 48, 181–84.

Sears, R. R. The 1958 summer research project on identification. *Journal of Nursery Education*, 1960, 16, (2).

Secord, P. F. and Backman, C. W. Personality theory and the problem of stability and change in individual behavior: An interpersonal approach. *Psychological Review*, 1961, 68, 21–33.

Selznick, P. *Leadership in administration.* Evanston: Row, Peterson, 1957.

Shaw, M. E. A comparison to two types of leadership in various communication nets. *Journal of Abnormal and Social Psychology*, 1955, 50, 127–34.

Shaw, M. E. and Blum, J. M. Effects of leadership style upon group performance as a function of task structure. *Journal of Personality and Social Psychology*, 1966, 3, 238–42.

Slater, P. E. and Bennis, W. G. Democracy is inevitable. *Harvard Business Review*, 1964, 42,(2), 51–59.

Steiner, I. Group dynamics. *Annual review of psychology*, 1964, 15, 421–46.

Stogdill, R. M. Personal factors associated with leadership: A survey of the literature. *Journal of Psychology*, 1948, 25, 35–71.

Stogdill, R. M. *Individual behavior and group achievement.* New York: Oxford University Press, 1959.

Weber, M. *The theory of social and economic organization.* (Trans. and ed. by T. Parsons & A. M. Henderson.) New York: Oxford University Press, 1947.

Zdep. S. M. and Oakes, W. I. Reinforcement of leadership behavior in group discussion. *Journal of Experimental Psychology*, 1967, 3, 310–20.

43. PREDICTING ORGANIZATIONAL EFFECTIVENESS WITH A FOUR-FACTOR THEORY OF LEADERSHIP*

***David G. Bowers and Stanley E. Seashore*†**

Recent research in the area of leadership seems to point to the existence of four basic dimensions of leadership: support, interaction facilitation, goal emphasis, and work facilitation. Data from a recent study of 40 agencies of one of the leading life insurance companies are used to evaluate the impact of both supervisory and peer leadership upon outcomes of satisfaction and factorial performance measures.

Results from the study suggest that this conceptual model is useful and that leadership's relation to organizational outcomes may best be studied when both leadership and effectiveness are multidimensional. Both peer and supervisory leadership measures relate to outcomes. In most instances, the ability to predict is enhanced by taking simultaneous account of certain nonleadership variables.

For centuries writers have been intrigued by the idea of specifying predictable relationships between what an organization's leader does and how the organization fares. In our own time, behavioral science has looked extensively at this question, yet incongruities and contradictory or unrelated findings seem to crowd the literature. It is the intent in this paper to locate and integrate the consistencies, to explore some neglected issues, and, finally, to generate and use a network of variables for predicting outcomes of organizational effectiveness.

Leadership has been studied informally by observing the lives of great men and formally by attempting to identify the personality traits of acknowledged leaders through assessment techniques. Review of the research literature from these studies, however, reveals few consistent findings.[1] Since the Second World War, research emphasis has shifted from a search for personality traits to a search for behavior that makes a difference in the performance or satisfaction of the followers. The conceptual scheme to be outlined here is an example of this approach.

In this paper, the primary concern is with leadership in business or industrial enterprises, usually termed "supervision" or "management," although most of the constructs of leadership to be used here apply equally well to social groups, clubs, and voluntary associations.

Work situations in business organizations in a technologically advanced society typically involve a

* *Administrative Science Quarterly*, Vol. 11, No. 2 (1966), pp. 238-63.

† Both of the Institute for Social Research, University of Michigan.

David G. Bowers is program associate at the Center for Research on the Utilization of Scientific Knowledge, The University of Michigan.

Stanley E. Seashore is professor of psychology and assistant director of the Institute for Social Research, The University of Michigan.

[1] C. A. Gibb, Leadership, in G. Lindzey, *Handbook of social psychology* (Cambridge, Mass.: Addison-Wesley Publishing Co., Inc., 1954), II, pp. 877-917; R. M. Stogdill, Personal factors associated with leadership: A survey of the literature, *Journal of Psychology*, Vol. 25 (1948), pp. 35-71.

comparatively small number of persons who receive direction from one person. This is the basic unit of industrial society and has been called the "organizational family."[2] In this modern organizational family, there is usually task interdependence and there is frequently social interdependence as well. The ideal is that of a group of people working effectively together toward the accomplishment of some common aim.

This paper presents a review of the conceptual structure resulting from several programs of research in leadership practices, followed by a reconceptualization that attempts to take into consideration all of these earlier findings. In an attempt to assess the usefulness of the reconceptualization, it is then applied to leadership and effectiveness data from a recent study.

DIMENSIONS OF LEADERSHIP

It seems useful at the outset to isolate on a common-sense basis certain attributes of "leadership." First, the concept of leadership is meaningful only in the context of two or more people. Second, leadership consists of behavior; more specifically, it is behavior by one member of a group toward another member or members of the group, which advances some joint aim. Not all organizationally useful behavior in a work group is leadership; leadership behavior must be distinguished from the performance of noninterpersonal tasks that advance the goals of the organization. On a common-sense basis, then, leadership is organizationally useful behavior by one member of an organizational family toward another member or members of that same organizational family.

Defined in this manner, leadership amounts to a large aggregation of separate behaviors, which may be grouped or classified in a great variety of ways. Several classification systems from previous research have achieved considerable prominence, and are briefly described here.

Ohio State Leadership Studies

In 1945, the Bureau of Business Research at Ohio State University undertook the construction of an instrument for describing leadership. From extended conversations and discussions among staff members who represented various disciplines, a list of nine dimensions or categories of leadership behavior were postulated. Descriptive statements were then written and assigned to one or another of the nine dimensions, and after further refinement, 150 of these were selected as representing these nine dimensions and were incorporated into the Leader Behavior Description Questionnaire.

Two factor analyses attempted to simplify its conceptual framework further. Hemphill and Coons[3] intercorrelated and factor-analyzed group mean scores for 11 dimensions for a sample composed largely of educational groups,[4] and obtained three orthogonal factors.

1. ***Maintenance of Membership Character.*** Behavior of a leader which allows him to be considered a "good fellow" by his subordinates; behavior which is socially agreeable to group members.

2. ***Objective Attainment Behavior.*** Behavior related to the output of the group; for example, taking positive action in establishing goals or objectives, structuring group activities in a way that members may work toward an objective, or serving as a representative of group accomplishment in relation to outside groups, agencies, forces, and so on.

3. ***Group Interaction Facilitation Behavior.*** Behavior that structures communication among group members, encouraging pleasant group atmosphere, and reducing conflicts among members.

Halpin and Winer[5] made an analysis using data collected from air-force crews, revising the original measuring instrument to adapt it to the respondent group. Only 130 items were used, with appropriate rewording, and the number of dimensions was reduced to eight. Treatment of the data indicated that five of the eight were sufficient for describing the entire roster, and the correlation of the 130 items with these five dimensions was regarded as a matrix of oblique factor loadings. These item loadings were then factor analyzed and the results rotated, producing four orthogonal factors.

1. ***Consideration.*** Behavior indicative of friendship, mutual trust, respect, and warmth.

2. ***Initiating Structure.*** Behavior that organizes and defines relationships or roles, and establishes well-defined patterns of organization, channels of communication, and ways of getting jobs done.

---

[2] F. C. Mann, Toward an understanding of the leadership role in formal organization, in R. Dubin, G. C. Homans, F. C. Mann, and D. C. Miller, *Leadership and productivity* (San Francisco, Calif.: Chandler Publishing Company, 1965), pp. 68–103.

[3] J. K. Hemphill and A. E. Coons, Development of the leader behavior description questionnaire, in R. M. Stogdill and A. E. Coons (eds.), *Leader behavior: its description and measurement* (Research Monograph No. 88, Columbus, Ohio: Bureau of Business Research, the Ohio State University, 1957), pp. 6–38.

[4] The 11 dimensions were made up of the original 9, one of which (communication) had been subdivided, plus an overall leadership evaluation.

[5] A. W. Halpin and J. Winer, A factorial study of the leader behavior description questionnaire, in R. M. Stogdill and A. E. Coons, *Leader behavior,* pp. 39–51.

3. ***Production Emphasis.*** Behavior which makes up a manner of motivating the group to greater activity by emphasizing the mission or job to be done.

4. ***Sensitivity (Social Awareness).*** Sensitivity of the leader to, and his awareness of, social interrelationships and pressures inside or outside the group.

The Halpin and Winer analysis has been the more widely known and used. Because the investigators dropped the third and fourth factors as accounting for too little common variance, "consideration" and "initiating structure" have become to some extent identified as "the Ohio State" dimensions of leadership.

Early Survey Research Center Studies

Concurrent with the Ohio State studies was a similar program of research in human relations at the University of Michigan Survey Research Center. Approaching the problem of leadership or supervisory style by locating clusters of characteristics which *(a)* correlated positively among themselves and *(b)* correlated with criteria of effectiveness, this program developed two concepts called "employee orientation" and "production orientation."[6]

Employee orientation is described as behavior by a supervisor, which indicates that he feels that the "human relations" aspect of the job is quite important; and that he considers the employees as human beings of intrinsic importance, takes an interest in them, and accepts their individuality and personal needs. Production orientation stresses production and the technical aspects of the job, with employees as means for getting work done; it seems to combine the Ohio State dimensions of initiating structure and production emphasis. Originally conceived to be opposite poles of the same continuum, employee orientation and production orientation were later reconceptualized,[7] on the basis of further data, as representing independent dimensions.

Katz and Kahn,[8] writing from a greater accumulation of findings, presented another conceptual scheme, with four dimensions of leadership.

1. ***Differentiation of Supervisory Role.*** Behavior by a leader that reflects greater emphasis upon activities of planning and performing specialized skilled tasks; spending a greater proportion of time in actual supervision, rather than performing the men's own tasks himself or absorption in impersonal paperwork.

2. ***Closeness of Supervision.*** Behavior that delegates authority, checks upon subordinates less frequently, provides more general, less frequent instructions about the work, makes greater allowance for individuals to perform in their own ways and at their own paces.

3. ***Employee Orientation.*** Behavior that gives major emphasis to a supportive personal relationship, and that reflects a personal interest in subordinates; being more understanding, less punitive, easy to talk to, and willing to help groom employees for advancement.

4. ***Group Relationships.*** Behavior by the leader that results in group cohesiveness, pride by subordinates in their work group, a feeling of membership in the group, and mutual help on the part of those subordinates.

Differentiation of supervisory role corresponds in part to what the Ohio State studies refer to as initiating structure or objective attainment behavior, and clearly derives from the earlier concept of production orientation. Closeness of supervision, on the other hand, has something in common with maintenance of membership character, consideration, and employee orientation, but also with objective attainment behavior, initiating structure, and production orientation. Employee orientation clearly corresponds to the earlier concept by the same name, while group relationships is to some extent similar to the interaction facilitation behavior and social sensitivity of the Ohio State studies.

In still another conceptualization, combining theory with review of empirical data, Kahn[9] postulated four supervisory functions.

1. ***Providing Direct Need Satisfaction.*** Behavior by a leader not conditional upon behavior of the employee, which provides direct satisfaction of the employee's ego and affiliative needs.

2. ***Structuring the Path to Goal Attainment.*** Behavior that cues subordinates toward filling personal needs through attaining organizational goals.

3. ***Enabling Goal Achievement.*** Behavior that removes barriers to goal attainment, such as eliminating bottlenecks, or planning.

4. ***Modifying Employee Goals.*** Behavior that influences the actual personal goals of subordinates in organizationally useful directions.

Direct need satisfaction clearly resembles con-

[6] D. Katz, N. Maccoby, and Nancy C. Morse, *Productivity, supervision, and morale in an office situation* (Detroit, Mich.: Darel Press, Inc., 1950); D. Katz, N. Maccoby, G. Gurin, and Lucretia G. Floor, *Productivity, supervision, and morale among railroad workers* (Ann Arbor, Mich.: Survey Research Center, 1951).

[7] R. L. Kahn, The prediction of productivity, *Journal of Social Issues,* Vol. 12 (1956), pp. 41–49.

[8] D. Katz and R. L. Kahn, Human organization and worker motivation, in L. R. Tripp (ed.), *Industrial productivity* (Madison, Wis.: Industrial Relations Research Association, 1951), 146–71.

[9] R. L. Kahn, Human relations on the shop floor, in E. M. Hugh-Jones (ed.), *Human relations and modern management* (Amsterdam, Holland: North-Holland Publishing Co., 1958), pp. 43–74.

sideration and employee orientation; enabling goal achievement seems similar to initiating structure or objective attainment behavior; structuring the path to goal attainment and modifying employee goals are probably closer to the Ohio State production emphasis factor.

Studies at the Research Center for Group Dynamics

Cartwright and Zander,[10] at the Research Center for Group Dynamics, on the basis of accumulated findings, described leadership in terms of two sets of group functions.

1. ***Group Maintenance Functions.*** Behavior that keeps interpersonal relations pleasant, resolves disputes, provides encouragement, gives the minority a chance to be heard, stimulates self-direction, and increases interdependence among members.

2. ***Goal Achievement Functions.*** Behavior that initiates action, keeps members' attention on the goal, develops a procedural plan, evaluates the quality of work done, and makes expert information available.

These descriptive terms clearly refer to broader constructs than consideration or initiating structure. Group maintenance functions, for example, include what has been termed consideration, maintenance of membership character, or employee orientation, but they also include functions concerned with relationships among group members not in formal authority positions. This concept is in some ways similar to group interaction facilitation behavior in the Ohio State factor analysis of Hemphill and Coons.[11] Goal achievement functions seem to encompass what the Ohio State studies referred to as initiating structure and production emphasis or objective attainment behavior, and what early Survey Research Center studies called production orientation.

Mann's Three Skills

In subsequent work at the Survey Research Center built upon earlier findings, a recent classification, proposed by several writers and developed and operationalized by Floyd Mann,[12] treats leadership in terms of a trilogy of skills required of supervisors or managers. Although behaviors requiring particular skills and those skills themselves are not necessarily perfectly parallel, it seems reasonable to assume at least an approximate correspondence between the two. The three skills are:

1. ***Human Relations Skill.*** Ability and judgment in working with and through people, including knowledge of principles of human behavior, interpersonal relations, and human motivation.

2. ***Technical Skill.*** Ability to use knowledge, methods, techniques, and equipment necessary for the performance of specific tasks.

3. ***Administrative Skill.*** Ability to understand and act according to the objectives of the total organization, rather than only on the basis of the goals and needs of one's own immediate group. It includes planning, organizing the work, assigning the right tasks to the right people, inspecting, following up, and coordinating the work.

Likert's New Patterns of Management

Rensis Likert of the University of Michigan Institute for Social Research, building upon many of the findings of the Survey Research Center and the Research Center for Group Dynamics as well as upon his own early work in the same area for the Life Insurance Agency Management Association, describes five conditions for effective supervisory behavior.

1. ***Principle of Supportive Relations.*** The leadership and other processes of the organization must be such as to ensure a maximum probability that in his interactions and his relationships with the organization, each member will, in the light of his background, values, and expectations, view the experience as supportive, and as one that builds and maintains his sense of personal worth and importance.[13]

2. ***Group Methods of Supervision.*** Management will make full use of the potential capacities of its human resources only when each person in an organization is a member of one or more effectively functioning work groups that have a high degree of group loyalty, effective skills of interaction, and high performance goals.[14]

3. ***High Performance Goals.*** If a high level of performance is to be achieved, it appears to be necessary for a supervisor to be employee-centered, and at the same time to have high performance goals and a contagious enthusiasm as to the importance of achieving these goals.[15]

4. ***Technical Knowledge.*** The (effective) leader has adequate competence to handle the technical

[10] D. Cartwright and A. Zander, *Group dynamics: Research and theory* (Evanston, Ill.: Row, Peterson & Co., 1960).

[11] Hemphill and Coons, Development of the leader behavior description questionnaire.

[12] Mann, Toward an understanding of the leadership role in formal organization.

[13] R. Likert, *New patterns of management* (New York: McGraw-Hill Book Co., 1961), p. 103.

[14] Ibid., p. 104.

[15] Ibid., p. 8.

problems faced by his group, or he sees that access to this technical knowledge is fully provided.[16]

5. *Coordinating, Scheduling, Planning.* The leader fully reflects and effectively represents the views, goals, values, and decisions of his group in those other groups where he is performing the function of linking his group to the rest of the organization. He brings to the group of which he is the leader the views, goals, and decisions of those other groups. In this way, he provides a linkage whereby communication and the exercise of influence can be performed in both directions.[17]

Comparison and Integration

These various research programs and writings make it clear that a great deal of conceptual content is held in common. In fact, four dimensions emerge from these studies, which seem to comprise the basic structure of what one may term "leadership":

1. *Support.* Behavior that enhances someone else's feeling of personal worth and importance.

2. *Interaction Facilitation.* Behavior that encourages members of the group to develop close, mutually satisfying relationships.

3. *Goal Emphasis.* Behavior that stimulates an enthusiasm for meeting the group's goal or achieving excellent performance.

4. Work Facilitation. Behavior that helps achieve goal attainment by such activities as scheduling, coordinating, planning, and by providing resources such as tools, materials, and technical knowledge.

This formulation is obviously very close, except in terminology, to that expressed by Rensis Likert and was, in fact, stimulated by it. Table 1 indicates how concepts from the various research programs relate to these four basic concepts of leadership. More important, however, is the fact that each of these four concepts appears, sometimes separately, sometimes in combination, in all but two (Katz *et al.*, 1950; Kahn, 1958) of the previous formulations listed. These four dimensions are not considered indivisible, but capable of further subdivision according to some regularity of occurrence in social situations or according to the conceptual preferences of investigators.

INDEPENDENCE OF LEADERSHIP AND POSITION

Traditional leadership research has focused upon the behavior of formally designated or recognized leaders. This is probably due, at least in part, to the historical influence of the hierarchical models of the church and the army. As a result, it has until recently been customary to study leadership either as an attribute of the person of someone who is authority-vested, or as an attribute of his behavior. More recently, attention has been paid to leadership in groups less formally structured, as illustrated by the work of Bass with leaderless group discussion, the work of Sherif, as well as some of the work of other researchers in the area of group dynamics.[18]

In the previous section, leadership was conceptualized in terms of four social-process functions, four kinds of behavior that must be present in work groups if they are to be effective. The performance of these functions was deliberately not limited to formally designated leaders. Instead, it was proposed that leadership, as described in terms of support, goal emphasis, work facilitation, and interaction facilitation, may be provided by anyone in a work group for anyone else in that work group. In this sense, leadership may be either "supervisory" or "mutual"; that is, a group's needs for support may be provided by a formally designated leader, by members for each other, or both; goals may be emphasized by the formal leader, by members to each other, or by both; and similarly for work facilitation and interaction facilitation.

This does not imply that formally designated leaders are unnecessary or superfluous, for there are both common-sense and theoretical reasons for believing that a formally acknowledged leader through his supervisory leadership behavior sets the pattern of the mutual leadership which subordinates supply each other.

LEADERSHIP AND ORGANIZATIONAL EFFECTIVENESS

Leadership in a work situation has been judged to be important because of its connection, to some extent assumed and to some extent demonstrated, to organizational effectiveness. Effectiveness, moreover, although it has been operationalized in a variety of ways, has often been assumed to be a unitary characteristic. These assumptions define a commonly accepted theorem that leadership (if not a unitary characteristic, then a limited roster of closely related ones) is always salutary in its effect and that it always enhances effectiveness.

The pattern of the typical leadership study has

[16] Ibid., p. 171.

[17] Ibid., p. 171.

[18] B. M. Bass, *Leadership, psychology, and organizational behavior* (New York: Harper & Bros., 1960); Cartwright and Zander, *Group dynamics;* M. and Carolyn W. Sherif, *An outline of social psychology* (New York: Harper & Bros., 1956).

TABLE 1 CORRESPONDENCE OF LEADERSHIP CONCEPTS OF DIFFERENT INVESTIGATORS

Bowers and Seashore (1964)	*Hemphill and Coons (1957)*	*Halpin and Winer (1957)*	*Katz et al. (1950)*	*Katz and Kahn (1951)*	*Kahn (1958)*	*Mann (1962)*	*Likert (1961)*	*Cartwright and Zander (1960)*
Support	Maintenance of membership character	Consideration	Employee orientation	Employee orientation Closeness of supervision	Providing direct need satisfaction	Human relations skills	Principle of supportive relationships	Group maintenance functions
Interaction facilitation	Group interaction facilitation behavior	Sensitivity		Group relationships			Group methods of supervision	
Goal emphasis	Objective attainment behavior	Production emphasis	Production orientation		Structuring path to goal attainment Modifying employee goals	Administrative skills	High-performance goals	Goal achievement functions
Work facilitation		Initiating structure		Differentiation of supervisory role Closeness of supervision	Enabling goal achievement	Technical skills	Technical knowledge, planning, scheduling	

been first, to select a criterion of effectiveness: sometimes a rating of overall effectiveness by superiors, at other times a questionnaire measure of "morale," on still other occasions a few measures such as output, absence, or accident rates. Next, an attempt is made to relate leadership to the criterion selected. When, in fact, a relationship is obtained, this is accepted. When no relationship or one opposite to that expected is obtained, the investigator often makes some statement referring to "error" or "further research."

It seems that a better strategy would be to obtain: *(a)* measures reflecting a theoretically meaningful conceptual structure of leadership; *(b)* an integrated set of systematically derived criteria; and *(c)* a treatment of these data, which takes account of the multiplicity of relationships and investigates the adequacy of leadership characteristics in predicting effectiveness variables.

In the present study an attempt is made to satisfy these conditions. A conceptual structure of leadership is developed, using empirical evidence. The four concepts of this structure are operationalized in terms of questionnaire items describing behavioral acts largely "loaded" on one or another of these constructs, and a systematically derived set of criteria of organizational effectiveness is obtained.

RESEARCH METHODS

Research Site

This study was conducted in 40 agencies of a leading life insurance company. These agencies are independently owned businesses, performing identical functions in their separate parts of the country. Only one or two hierarchical levels intervene between the regional manager, at the top of the hierarchy, and the sales agent at the bottom. The typical agency consists of an exclusive territory comprising a number of counties of a state or states. The regional manager ordinarily has headquarters in some principal city of his territory, and contracts with individuals to service the area as sales agents. He receives an "override" upon the commissions of policies sold by these agents, in addition to the full commissions from whatever policies he sells personally.

If geographical distance or volume of business is great enough, he may contract with individuals to serve as district managers. The district manager is given territorial rights for some subportion of the regional manager's territory, is permitted to contract agents to service the area, subject to the approval of the regional manager, and receives a portion of what would otherwise be the regional manager's override upon sales within his territory.

Although this is the usual arrangement, variations occur. Occasionally, for example, a territory will be so constituted as to prevent subdivision into districts. In these cases, the regional manager contracts directly with sales agents throughout his territory. In other cases, the territory is almost entirely urban, in which case the regional manager may substitute salaried or partially salaried supervisory personnel for district managers. In all cases, however, there are at least a regional manager and sales agents, and frequently, in addition, a district manager between these two parties.

In all, the company's field force comprises nearly 100 agencies. Of these, 40 were selected as being roughly representative of them all. Selection was made by company personnel, with an effort to select half of the 40 from the topmost part of the list of agencies ordered by performance, and the other half from among poorer performing agencies, omitting any having recent organizational disruption or change. Questionnaires were mailed out in April, 1961, to all contracted regional managers, district managers, sales agents, and supervisory personnel on full or part salary in these agencies; 83 percent were returned by June, 1961, for a total of 873 respondents.

Measurement

This report is concerned with 20 index measurements obtained through paper-and-pencil questionnaires, and seven factorial measures of agency performance obtained from company records. A short description of each questionnaire variable appears in Table 2. These measures reflect perceptions of behavior rather than behavior itself, and are therefore no different from any other method of quantifying behavior: all involve the measurement of behavior, by some person and some mechanism. Close familiarity by the recipients of the behavior—and whatever systematic bias this introduces—is here considered as more desirable than the lack of information and large random error that an outside observer would very probably introduce.

In addition to these questionnaire measurements, the company provided some 70 measures of agency performance, which were then factor analyzed,[19] resulting in seven orthogonal factors.

Factor I. Staff-Clientele Maturity. This factor reflects a difference in the kind of business produced by the agency attributable to the age and experience of the agent staff and the clientele that they reach. A high score reflects a high average premium per thousand, collected relatively infrequently, with very

[19] The factor analysis method used was that of a principal axes solution with varimax rotation.

TABLE 2 CONTENT OF VARIABLES USED

Area	Description of Questionnaire Variable
Leadership*	Importance of morale
Support	Willingness to make changes Friendliness Conversational ease Opinion acceptance
Goal emphasis	Importance of competitive position Extra work effort
Work facilitation	Stressing standard procedures Offering new approaches Checking works vs capacity Emphasis upon meeting deadlines
Satisfaction†	With company With fellow agents With income prospects With regional manager With office costs With job
Need for affiliation	Importance of being liked Importance of being accepted
Regional manager's expert power	Respect for regional manager's competence and good judgment
Classical business ideology‡	Extent of agreement with statements of value and belief about nature of "best" economic society
Rivalry among agents	Extent to which some agents are trying to advance at others' expense.

* Items in the leadership area were adapted from two sources: items used in the Ohio studies and those used in previous Survey Research Center studies.

† 11 items, 6 satisfaction areas.

‡ Items based upon conceptualization by F. X. Sutton, S. E. Harris, C. Kaysen, and J. Tobin, *American business creed* (Cambridge, Mass.: Harvard University Press, 1956).

little term insurance or graduated premium life insurance, a small proportion of the business from new or young agents, and greater profitability from business already on the books.

Factor II. Business Growth. This seems to indicate in fairly uncomplicated fashion the growth of business volume over the years immediately preceding the year of measurement.

Factor III. Business Costs. Although the principal loadings are on variables measuring the costs per unit of new business, some minor loadings occur on variables relating to costs of renewal business. This factor, therefore, seems to be a business-cost dimension.

Factor IV. Advanced Underwriting. This seems to be a factor measuring the extent to which there is emphasis by the agent staff upon advanced underwriting. High score on this factor reflects a large average face value per life and per policy, comparatively large premiums per collection, a fairly high ratio of cases rejected, very little prepayment, fairly high costs, and high profitability of new business. A low score, of course, reflects a reverse pattern.

Factor V. Business Volume. A fairly straightforward dimension measuring the dollar volume of new business done by the agency.

Factor VI. Manpower Turnover. A measure of the extent to which there was a change in personnel within the agency during 1959. This factor loads most heavily on the ratio of terminations plus appointments to manpower, and on the ratio of terminations alone to manpower.

Factor VII. Regional Manager's Personal Performance. This factor differs from those above by representing the performance of the regional manager, not of the agency as a whole. It seems to reflect the extent to which he is putting energy into agency maintenance and development, as against taking short-run gain. It is, perhaps, an age factor, related in some measure to the regional manager's distance from retirement.

Four of these factors are measures of performance in the usual sense; that is, a positive and a negative value can be placed at opposite ends of these continua: business growth, business costs, business volume, and manpower turnover. Factor I (staff-clientele maturity) and Factor IV (advanced underwriting) are descriptive, rather than evaluative,[20] and Factor VII is peculiar to only one person in the agency.

There are, therefore, within this study multiple-criteria measures, both of satisfaction, described earlier, and of performance. Although the use of multiple-criteria measures has become more common in recent years, it is still infrequent enough to make the study somewhat unique.

From the data that resulted, the following questions suggest themselves:

1. Are both mutual and supervisory leadership measures useful; that is, are there differential effects from the various leadership dimensions such that some criteria are associated with certain measures or combinations of measures and some with others?

2. In what way are mutual leadership measures related to supervisory measures?

3. How adequately may criteria of effectiveness be predicted from leadership measures as compared to other kinds of measures?

The reader should from the outset be reminded of several problems of the analysis. First, the analytic model used in this study assumes a particular causal directionality. Since the data are from a single period of time, this directionality cannot be proved. As an operating assumption, it must be either accepted or rejected by the reader, and the relationships otherwise interpreted by him. The assumption of managerial behavior as an organizational prime mover is, however, a common one. Second, since the model starts from assumptions about the nature of leadership, the analysis considers first the relationships of leadership characteristics to criteria of effectiveness. Third, since this is an attempt to locate possible precursors of effectiveness, the analysis then considers the relationship of nonleadership variables to effectiveness, paying serious attention only to those nonleadership variables that can reasonably be interpreted as causes of effectiveness. Fourth, not all of either leadership or nonleadership variables with statistically significant relationships are used to predict effectiveness measures; only the one or two of each category that is most highly correlated.

[20] It should be noted that these factors are interpreted by the authors on the basis of a single set of data. Data from other periods or other firms, as well as interpretations by life insurance experts, might differ from those presented here.

RESULTS

Relation of Leadership to Effectiveness

Table 3 presents the correlation co-efficients of leadership measures with measures of satisfaction. Table 4 presents similar correlations of leadership measures to performance factors. These data indicate first, that the incidence of significant relationships of leadership to effectiveness is well above the chance level. Of 40 satisfaction-leadership coefficients, 30 are significant beyond the five percent level of confidence. Of 56 performance-leadership coefficients, 13 are significant beyond the five percent level of confidence. Second, the significant coefficients are not uniformly distributed throughout the matrix; instead, certain effectiveness criteria (e.g., satisfaction with income) and certain leadership measures (e.g., peer work facilitation) have many significant relationships, whereas others have few or none (e.g., performance factor VI). Third, significant coefficients are as often found in relation to peer as to managerial leadership characteristics.

For parsimony, the leadership characteristic with the largest coefficient in relation to each criterion measure is chosen as the analytic starting point in these matrices. To this is then added in turn each of the other significant leadership relationships by means of a two-predictor multiple-correlation technique. Because no r-to-z transformation of multiple correlation coefficients is possible, these cannot

TABLE 3 CORRELATION OF LEADERSHIP WITH SATISFACTIONS

	Satisfaction with				
Leadership Measure	*Company*	*Fellow Agents*	*Job*	*Income*	*Manager*
Peer:					
Support	0.03*	0.68	0.39	0.29*	0.47
Goal emphasis	0.37	0.77	0.26*	0.42	0.62
Work facilitation	0.29*	0.68	0.34	0.51	0.45
Interaction facilitation	0.31	0.72	0.30*	0.42	0.55
Manager:					
Support	0.31	0.65	0.35	0.45	0.86
Goal emphasis	0.11*	0.71	0.09*	0.43	0.31
Work facilitation	0.31	0.61	0.24*	0.36	0.41
Interaction facilitation	0.30*	0.67	0.10*	0.58	0.78

* All others significant beyond 0.05 level of confidence, 2-tail.

TABLE 4 CORRELATION OF LEADERSHIP WITH PERFORMANCE FACTORS

Leadership Measure	Performance Factor I	III	III	IV	V	VI	VII
Peer:							
Support	0.26	−0.02	−0.27	−0.21	0.23	−0.12	0.27
Goal emphasis	0.49*	−0.05	−0.45*	−0.27	0.15	0.04	0.04
Work facilitation	0.33*	0.14	−0.41*	−0.41*	0.18	0.00	0.04
Interaction facilitation	0.44*	−0.13	−0.44*	−0.24	0.11	0.14	0.05
Manager:							
Support	0.28	−0.24	−0.26	−0.12	0.25	0.16	0.10
Goal emphasis	0.31*	0.11	−0.27	−0.18	0.41*	0.03	−0.19
Work facilitation	0.43*	0.13	−0.37*	−0.33*	0.21	0.16	−0.12
Interaction facilitation	0.42*	−0.29	−0.30	−0.21	0.13	0.20	0.01

* Significant beyond 0.05 level of confidence, 2-tail.

TABLE 5 IMPROVEMENT OF PREDICTION OF CRITERIA OF EFFECTIVENESS BY ADDITION OF OTHER SIGNIFICANTLY RELATED LEADERSHIP CHARACTERISTICS

Effectiveness Measure	Best Predictor	Other Measures Improving Prediction
Satisfaction with		
Company	Peer goal emphasis	None
Fellow agents	Peer goal emphasis	None
Job	Peer support	None
Income	Manager interaction facilitation	Per goal emphasis
Manager	Manager support	None
Factors*		
I Staff clientele maturity	Peer goal emphasis	Peer work facilitation
III Business costs	Peer goal emphasis	None
IV Advanced underwriting	Peer work facilitation	None
V Business volume	Manager goal emphasis	None

* Performance Factors II, VI, and VII showed no significant relationships to leadership characteristics.

be compared with the original *r* value; therefore, seven correlation points are arbitrarily set as the criterion of significant improvement in prediction.[21]

It is apparent from Table 5, that, with two exceptions, adding other leadership characteristics that display somewhat smaller, but significant, correlations does not improve prediction. It is also apparent that peer goal emphasis plays a central role in this analysis: it is either the best predictor, or a significant additive, in five of the twelve cases.

Relation of Peer to Managerial Leadership

Before assessing the adequacy of leadership as a predictor of effectiveness, it seems advisable to answer the question posed earlier about the relationship between peer and managerial leadership. Table 6 presents the intercorrelation; all 16 coefficients in the table are statistically significant, indicating therefore that there is a close relationship between all managerial characteristics, on the one hand, and all peer characteristics on the other. Following the same method as that used for effectiveness, it appears that the best predictor of peer support is managerial support; of peer goal emphasis, managerial interaction facilitation; of peer work facilitation, managerial work facilitation, and of peer interaction facilitation, managerial interaction facilitation. With one exception, therefore, the best predictor of the peer characteristic is its managerial opposite number. Table 7 indicates that three predictions are improved by related managerial characteristics.

Assuming causation, one may say that if a manager wishes to increase the extent to which his subordinates support one another, he must increase his own support and his own emphasis upon goals. If he wishes to increase the extent to which his subordinates emphasize goals to one another, he must first increase his own facilitation of interaction and his emphasis upon goals. By increasing his facilitation of the work, he will increase the extent to which his subordinates do likewise, and if, in addition, he increases his facilitation of interaction, his subordinates will in turn facilitate interaction among themselves.

These data appear to confirm that there is in fact

[21] The actual multiple correlation values require much space and are therefore omitted here. Copies of these tables of multiple correlation coefficients may be obtained upon request from the authors.

TABLE 6 INTERCORRELATION OF MANAGERIAL AND PEER LEADERSHIP VARIABLES*

	Peer Leadership Characteristics			
Managerial Variables	*Support*	*Goal Emphasis*	*Work Facilitation*	*Interaction Facilitation*
Support	0.59	0.67	0.52	0.58
Goal emphasis	0.54	0.65	0.72	0.59
Work facilitation	0.49	0.63	0.82	0.66
Interaction facilitation	0.55	0.71	0.62	0.74

* All coefficients significant beyond 0.05 level of confidence, 2-tail.

TABLE 7 IMPROVEMENT OF PREDICTION OF PEER LEADERSHIP CHARACTERISTICS BY ADDITION OF OTHER MANAGERIAL LEADERSHIP CHARACTERISTICS

Peer Measure	*Managerial Best Predictor*	*Other Managerial Measures Improving Prediction*
Support	Support	Goal emphasis
Goal emphasis	Interaction facilitation	Goal emphasis
Work facilitation	Work facilitation	None
Interaction facilitation	Interaction facilitation	Work facilitation

TABLE 8 PREDICTION OF CRITERIA BY NONLEADERSHIP VARIABLES

Criterion	*Total No. of Significant Relations (N = 214)*	*No. of Significant Nonleadership Variables*	*No. of Significant Nonleadership Variables Exceeding Best Leadership Predictor*	*No. of Possible Causal Variables**
Satisfaction with				
Company	56	52	33	23
Job	39	36	11	8
Manager	66	44	1	1
Fellow agents	56	34	0	0
Income	60	43	2	2
Factors				
Factor I	22	15	1	1
Factor II	19	19	19	17
Factor III	50	39	9	6
Factor IV	26	23	12	6
Factor V	19	17	5	1
Factor VI	17	13	13	0
Factor VII	11	9	9	0

* Based upon the judgment of the research staff.

a significant and strong relationship between managerial and peer leadership characteristics. In general, the statement may be made that a forerunner of each peer variable is its managerial opposite number, and that substantial improvement is in most cases made by combining with this another managerial characteristic.

Adequacy of Prediction by Leadership Measures

Because this analysis has placed great emphasis on leadership constructs as predictors of organizational outcomes, it seems desirable to consider the extent to which prediction of these outcomes can be enhanced by the inclusion of nonleadership variables.[22] Table 8 summarizes the data on predictability of all criteria by nonleadership measurements. It seems from these data that some of the criteria may be much more successfully predicted using nonleadership variables than using leadership measures, that some others may be enhanced by using both, and that the predictability of still others is not improved by nonleadership characteristics.

The analysis at this point becomes somewhat

[22] Nonleadership variables comprised a large majority of the 214 items in the questionnaire.

complex, since relationships exist not only between leadership or nonleadership variables and criteria, but also among leadership and among nonleadership variables. In effect, therefore, the search for the best predictive model turns into a rather complicated examination of various chains and arrangements of constructs. To simplify this procedure, each criterion is presented separately, diagramming for each a plausible and statistically optimal "causal" schema.

Figure 1*a* presents the relationships of leadership and nonleadership variables to satisfaction with the company and with income. This diagram indicates that supportive managers make more satisfactory arrangements about the office expenses of their agents, and that these arrangements, in part, lead to greater satisfaction with the company as a whole. In addition, as managers facilitate the interaction of their agents, the goals of the company and needs or aspirations of the people who work for it come to be more compatible, which also leads to satisfaction with the company and with income.

Figure 1*b* presents a similar chain of relationships to satisfaction with the job itself. This diagram is interpreted to mean that as agents facilitate the work for each other, less time is spent by agents in paperwork for specific clients. When this happens, when agents behave more supportively toward each other, and when the agents are, on the whole, higher in need for affiliation, there is greater job satisfaction. Figure 1*c* presents relationships to two criteria:

FIGURE 1

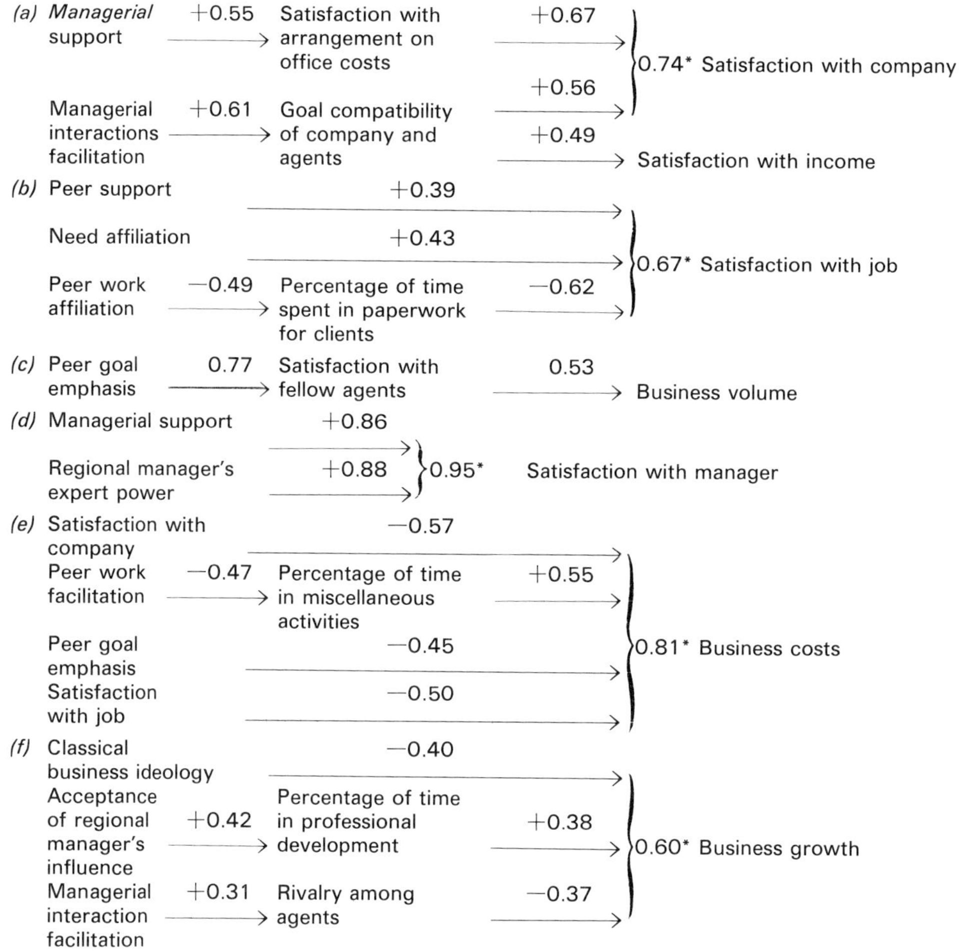

(a) *Managerial* support —(+0.55)→ Satisfaction with arrangement on office costs —(+0.67)→ }
Managerial interactions facilitation —(+0.61)→ Goal compatibility of company and agents —(+0.56)→ } 0.74* Satisfaction with company
Goal compatibility of company and agents —(+0.49)→ Satisfaction with income

(b) Peer support —(+0.39)→ }
Need affiliation —(+0.43)→ } 0.67* Satisfaction with job
Peer work affiliation —(−0.49)→ Percentage of time spent in paperwork for clients —(−0.62)→ }

(c) Peer goal emphasis —(0.77)→ Satisfaction with fellow agents —(0.53)→ Business volume

(d) Managerial support —(+0.86)→ }
Regional manager's expert power —(+0.88)→ } 0.95* Satisfaction with manager

(e) Satisfaction with company —(−0.57)→ }
Peer work facilitation —(−0.47)→ Percentage of time in miscellaneous activities —(+0.55)→ }
Peer goal emphasis —(−0.45)→ } 0.81* Business costs
Satisfaction with job —(−0.50)→ }

(f) Classical business ideology —(−0.40)→ }
Acceptance of regional manager's influence —(+0.42)→ Percentage of time in professional development —(+0.38)→ } 0.60* Business growth
Managerial interaction facilitation —(+0.31)→ Rivalry among agents —(−0.37)→ }

Predicted Measures: *(a)* Satisfaction with Company and with Income; *(b)* Satisfaction with Job; *(c)* Satisfaction with Fellow Agents; Business Volume; *(d)* Satisfaction with Manager; *(e)* Business Costs; *(f)* Business Growth

* Multiple correlation of variables listed against the effectiveness measure.

satisfaction with fellow agents and volume of business. When agents emphasize goals among themselves, they become more satisfied with each other; and when this condition exists, an agency does a greater volume of business. Figure 1*d* shows very succinctly that agents are satisfied with their manager if he is supportive and knowledgeable. Figure 1*e* presents relationships to business costs in diagram form. Earlier diagrams showed the network of relationships associated with satisfaction with the company and with the job; here, these two satisfaction states are associated with lower business costs. In addition, as agents facilitate the work for each other, they spend a smaller proportion of their time in miscellaneous activities. When this occurs, and when agents emphasize goals to one another, costs are also lower.

Figure 1*f* diagrams relationships to business growth. The relationships presented in this diagram are less reliable than those presented in earlier figures. They are, as a group, somewhat smaller in size than those found in relation to other criteria already described. With this caution in mind, however, they can be interpreted as follows: business growth is high when the agent force does *not* hold a classical business ideology; when regional managers, by accepting the opinions and ideas of their agents, encourage professional development; and when managers reduce rivalries among agents by encouraging their interaction. Far from stressing growth attained by competitive effort, this paradigm presents a picture of growth through cooperative professionalism.

Two additional performance measures of effectiveness present one significant, reasonable "causal" relationship each: staff-clientele maturity is greater when agents have a higher level of aspiration, and more advanced underwriting occurs when agents have a higher level of education. Although significant correlations were presented earlier in relation to these two factors, the reasonable interpretation of them is that the leadership measures are either effects or coordinates, not causes, of these descriptive rather than evaluative performance factors.

That no reasonable, significant relationships to manpower turnover are to be found is extremely puzzling. In most investigations of the effect of social psychological variables upon organizational behavior, it is assumed that performance measures which are more "person" than "production" oriented will show the highest relationships to questionnaire measurements. In the present case this assumption is not supported. No variations of analysis that were attempted produced any noticeable change. An attempt was made to assess curvilinear correlations, but no improvement over linear correlation resulted. It was also thought that the factorial measure of turnover might be too complicated and that a simpler measure of proportion of terminations might be more productive. This also produced no noticeable effect. Apparently, manpower turnover in this particular company or industry is related to forces in the individual, the environment, or perhaps the organizational situation not tapped by the questionnaire measurement used.

It is not surprising that no correlations are found with the regional manager's personal performance. It is, as explained earlier, the weakest factor, and differs from the other factors in being descriptive of a single individual rather than of the agency as a whole. It may well be affected more by variables such as the regional manager's distance from retirement than by factors assessed here.

DISCUSSION AND CONCLUSIONS

To what extent have the data demonstrated the usefulness of the conceptualization presented at the beginning of this article? It seems reasonable to state the following:

1. Seven of the eight leadership characteristics outlined above in fact play some part in the predictive model generated from the data; only peer interaction facilitation seems to play no unique role.
2. Both managerial and peer leadership characteristics seem important.
3. There are plausible relationships of managerial to peer leadership characteristics.
4. The model is not a simple one of managerial leadership leading to peer leadership, which in turn leads to outcomes separately; instead, different aspects of performance are associated with different leadership characteristics, and, in some cases, satisfaction outcomes seem related to performance outcomes.
5. Some effectiveness measures are related to causal factors other than those tapped in this instrument.
6. The ability to predict outcomes with the variables selected varies from 0.95 to 0.00.
7. The role of leadership characteristics in this prediction varies in importance from strong, direct relationships in some cases (e.g., satisfaction with manager) to indirect relationships (e.g., business volume) to no relationship (e.g., advanced underwriting).
8. Leadership, as conceived and operationalized here, is not adequate alone to predict effectiveness; instead, additional and, in some cases, intervening constructs must be included to improve prediction. These "other" constructs are of several distinct types:

a. *Leadership-Related.* Regional manager's expert power, regional manager's influence acceptance, and rivalry among agents.
b. *Work Patterns.* Percentage of time in miscellaneous activities, in paperwork for clients, in professional development.
c. *Personal and Motivational.* Education, level of aspiration, need for affiliation, goal compatibility of individual and organization, and classical business ideology.

44. TOWARD A BEHAVIORAL THEORY OF LEADERSHIP*

Gary Yukl†

Despite over two decades of extensive leadership research, the relation of leader behavior to subordinate productivity and satisfaction with the leader is still not very clear. The apparent absence of consistent relationships in the research literature (Sales, 1966; Korman, 1966; Lowin, 1968) may be due in part to several related problems. First, there is a great deal of semantic confusion regarding the conceptual and operational definition of leadership behavior. Over the years there has been a proliferation of leader behavior terms, and the same term is often defined differently from one study to the next. Secondly, a great deal of empirical data has been collected, but a theoretical framework which adequately explains causal relationships and identifies limiting conditions has not yet emerged. Finally, the research has often failed to include intermediate and situational variables which are necessary in order to understand how a leader's actions can affect his subordinates' productivity.

The purpose of this article is to begin the development of a theory which explains how leader behavior, situational variables, and intermediate variables interact to determine subordinate productivity and satisfaction with the leader. In the first section of the article, a system of three distinct and generally applicable leader behavior dimensions will be proposed. In the next two sections, these leadership dimensions will be used to develop a discrepancy model of subordinate satisfaction and a multiple linkage model of leader effectiveness. Finally, the extent to which the research literature supports these behavioral models will be evaluated.

CLASSIFICATION OF LEADER BEHAVIOR

Consideration and Initiating Structure

Some early investigators began with a list of very specific leadership activities (e.g., "inspection," "write reports," "hear complaints") and attempted to determine how performance of these activities or the amount of time allocated to them related to leader success. Since the number of specific leader activities that are possible is nearly endless, several Ohio State University psychologists attempted to find a few general behavior dimensions which would apply to all types of leaders. Factor analyses of leadership behavior questionnaires were carried out, and two orthogonal factors were found (Hemphill & Coons, 1957; Halpin & Winer, 1957). These factors were called Consideration and Initiating Structure. Consideration refers to the degree to which a leader acts in a warm and supportive manner and shows concern and respect for his subordinates. Initiating Structure refers to the degree to which a leader defines and structures his own role and those of his subordinates toward goal attainment.

The principal method for measuring these variables has been the use of either the Leader Behavior Description Questionnaire (Hemphill & Coons, 1957) or the Supervisory Behavior Description Questionnaire (Fleishman, 1957a). These questionnaires are administered to a leader's subordinates. A related questionnaire, called the Leadership Opinion Questionnaire (Fleishman, 1957b), is administered to the leader himself. This questionnaire is considered to be a measure of leader attitudes rather than leader behavior. Occasionally other observers, such as peers or superiors, are the source of leader behavior descriptions, and in some studies Consideration and Initiating Structure are experimentally manipulated by having leaders play predetermined roles.

* Reprinted from *Organizational Behavior and Human Performance,* Vol. 6, No. 4 (July 1971), pp. 414–40.

The author is grateful to Ken Wexley and Alexis Anikeeff for their helpful comments.

† Baruch College, City University of New York.

Decision-Centralization

A somewhat different approach to the classification of leaders was initiated by Lewin's (1944) theoretical typology of democratic, autocratic, and laissez-faire leaders. Studies following in this tradition have usually focused on the relative degree of leader and subordinate influence over the group's decisions. The various decision-making procedures used by a leader, such as delegation, joint decision-making, consultation, and autocratic decision-making, can be ordered along a continuum ranging from high subordinate influence to complete leader influence. Although a leader will usually allow more subordinate participation and influence for some decisions than for others, the average degree of participation can be computed for any specified set of typical decisions. Heller and Yukl (1969) have used the term "Decision-Centralization" to refer to this average. A high Decision-Centralization score means a low amount of subordinate participation. Naturally, a leader is capable of voluntarily sharing decision-making with his subordinates only to the extent that he has authority to make decisions.

Most methods that have been used to measure participation can also be regarded as a measure of Decision-Centralization. Participation and Decision-Centralization have been measured by subordinate ratings of their perceived autonomy or influence in decision-making, by subordinate responses to a questionnaire concerning the leader's decision behavior, and by leader responses to a decision behavior questionnaire. In some studies the leader's actual decision-making behavior has been experimentally manipulated. The term Decision-Centralization was introduced for two reasons. First, this term emphasizes the behavior of the leader rather than the behavior of the subordinates. Second, the definition of Decision-Centralization explicitly encompasses a greater variety of leader decision procedures than does the typical definition of participation (Heller & Yukl, 1969).[1]

Reconciling the Two Approaches to Leader Behavior Classification

Is Decision-Centralization equivalent to Consideration and Initiating Structure, or is it a distinct leadership dimension? The degree to which the three dimensions are independent depends upon the precise definitions given them. Since the definitions vary from study to study, it is not surprising that there is some disagreement regarding the relation between these dimensions. For example, Lowin (1968) has suggested that Initiating Structure is conceptually similar to autocratic supervision, Sales (1966) has suggested that "employee orientation" (which includes high Consideration) is usually associated with democratic leadership, and Newport (1962) has suggested that Consideration and Initiating Structure are similar, respectively, to democratic and autocratic leadership. On the other hand, Gomberg (1965), McMurray (1958), Schoenfield (1959), and Stanton (1962) have claimed that high Consideration and autocratic leadership are not incompatible, or in other words, that Consideration and Decision-Centralization are separate dimensions.

There are several sound theoretical arguments for treating Decision-Centralization as a separate dimension of leader behavior. Let us look first at the relation between Consideration and Decision-Centralization. The Consideration scale in the Ohio State questionnaires includes several items pertaining to the decision-making participation of subordinates, and Consideration is sometimes defined as including the sharing of decision-making with subordinates. However, one can argue that this sharing is only considerate of subordinates when they clearly desire participation, and the desire for participation can vary substantially from person to person and from situation to situation. Inclusion of participation items in a Consideration scale results in scores which are not comparable across persons unless first adjusted for differences in participation preferences. It is more practical to define Consideration as simply the degree to which a leader's behavior expresses a positive attitude rather than an indifferent or negative attitude toward subordinates. When defined in this manner, Consideration can be regarded as conceptually distinct from Decision-Centralization. In general, a high Consideration leader is friendly, supportive, and considerate; a low Consideration leader is hostile, punitive, and inconsiderate. A leader who acts indifferent and aloof is between these extremes but is closer to the low end of the continuum. The specific behaviors used in scaling Consideration should be generally applicable to all types of leadership situations.

What about the relation between Decision-Centralization and Initiating Structure? Although Initiating Structure is defined broadly as task-oriented behavior, it appears to include at least three types of task behavior: (1) Behavior indicating the leader's concern about productivity (e.g., goal-oriented comments to subordinates, and use of various rewards and punishments to encourage productivity), (2)

[1] Despite my preference for the term Decision-Centralization, the more familiar term participation will usually be used when discussing the direction of correlations in order to avoid confusion.

behavior insuring that necessary task decisions are made, and (3) behavior insuring that these decisions and directives from higher levels in the organization are carried out (e.g., training and supervision). Note that this definition does not specify who will actually make the decisions. The task orientation of the leader does not appear to be very closely related to the amount of influence he will allow subordinates in the making of task or maintenance decisions. Even very autocratic leaders can differ considerably with respect to their task orientation and concern about group performance. Therefore, it seems reasonable to treat Initiating Structure and Decision-Centralization as separate dimensions of leader behavior.

The empirical evidence on the relation of Decision-Centralization to Consideration and Initiating Structure is scanty, and the research which will be cited should be regarded as suggestive rather than conclusive. Most of these studies use the Consideration scale of the Leader Behavior Description Questionnaire, which includes some participation items. Naturally these items increase the likelihood of finding a significant correlation between Consideration and Decision-Centralization.

In a study of 67 second-line supervisors in three companies, this author found a low but significant correlation ($r = -.24$; $p < .05$) between Consideration and Decision-Centralization. Decision-Centralization was measured by means of leader responses on the decision procedure questionnaire (Form C) described in Heller and Yukl (1969). There was no significant correlation between Decision-Centralization and Initiating Structure.

Other evidence is provided by analyses of a more recent version of the Leader Behavior Description Questionnaire, which has ten new subscales in addition to the original scales for Consideration and Initiating Structure. One of the new scales, called "Tolerance of Member Freedom," can be regarded as a measure of participation or Decision-Centralization. Stogdill, Goode, and Day (1962, 1963, 1964) administered this questionnaire to "subordinates" of corporation presidents, labor union presidents, community leaders, and ministers. The correlations between Consideration and Tolerance of Member Freedom for the four samples, respectively, were .41, .42, .40, and .49. For a sample of office supervisors rated by female subordinates on this questionnaire, the correlation was .50 (Beer, 1966).[2] Decision-Centralization and Initiating Structure were not significantly correlated in any of the five samples just described.

Argyle, Gardner, and Cioffi (1957) analyzed the relation among leadership dimensions as measured by questionnaires administered to managers in England. Democratic (vs. authoritarian) leadership correlated .41 with nonpunitive (vs. punitive) leadership. Democratic leadership was not significantly correlated with pressure for production, a component of Initiating Structure.

If we remember to reverse the sign of the correlation when necessary in order to correct for the fact that high participation equals low Decision-Centralization, then it is obvious that the results of these studies are remarkedly consistent. Decision-Centralization and Initiating Structure appear to be independent dimensions. Decision-Centralization and Consideration should probably be regarded as oblique rather than orthogonal dimensions. That is, there will tend to be a low to moderate negative correlation between them, but some leaders will have high scores on both dimensions ("benevolent autocrat") and some leaders will have low scores on both dimensions ("malevolent democrat").

A DISCREPANCY MODEL OF SUBORDINATE SATISFACTION WITH THE LEADER

In this section, a discrepancy model of satisfaction will be used to explain the relation of the three leadership dimensions to subordinate satisfaction with the leader. Discrepancy or subtraction models of job satisfaction have been proposed by a number of psychologists (Morse, 1953; Schaffer, 1953; Rosen & Rosen, 1955; Ross & Zander, 1957; Porter, 1962; Katzell, 1964; Locke, 1969). In a discrepancy model, satisfaction is a function of the difference between a person's preferences and his actual experience. The less the discrepancy between preferences and experience, the greater the satisfaction. This hypothesis has received some support in the studies cited above, but the evidence is by no means conclusive. In some versions of the discrepancy model there is a second hypothesis which states that the amount of dissatisfaction with a given discrepancy also depends upon the importance of the needs affecting the preference level. If importance varies from person to person, the discrepancy scores cannot be compared unless first adjusted for importance. Whether such a correction is necessary, and if so, how it should be made appears to be a matter of growing controversy.

Although the discrepancy model appears to be applicable to the analysis of subordinates' satisfaction with their leader, only a few studies have used it for this purpose. In two of these studies (Foa, 1957; Greer, 1961), leadership variables other than Consideration, Initiating Structure, and Decision-Cen-

[2] Significance levels for the correlations were not given, but judging from the sample sizes, they should all be significant at the .05 level or better.

tralization were used. No studies were found which included subordinate preferences for Consideration and Initiating Structure as a moderating variable. The results from studies which have included subordinate preferences for participation in decision-making tend to be consistent with the discrepancy model.

According to the proposed discrepancy model, the shape of the curve relating leader behavior to subordinate satisfaction will vary somewhat depending upon a subordinate's preference level. A preference level will be defined tentatively as a range of leader behavior acceptable to subordinates rather than as a single point on a behavior continuum. Figure 1 shows the theoretical curves for a low, medium, and high preference level. The curves represent the relation for a single subordinate. When the preference levels of group members are relatively homogeneous, the relation between leader behavior and average group satisfaction with their leader will yield a curve similar to that for an individual. However, the more variable the preferences are in a group, the less likely it is that any significant relation will be found between leader behavior and average group satisfaction.

FIGURE 1 THE RELATION BETWEEN LEADER BEHAVIOR AND SUBORDINATE SATISFACTION FOR A LOW, MEDIUM, AND HIGH PREFERENCE LEVEL (PL)

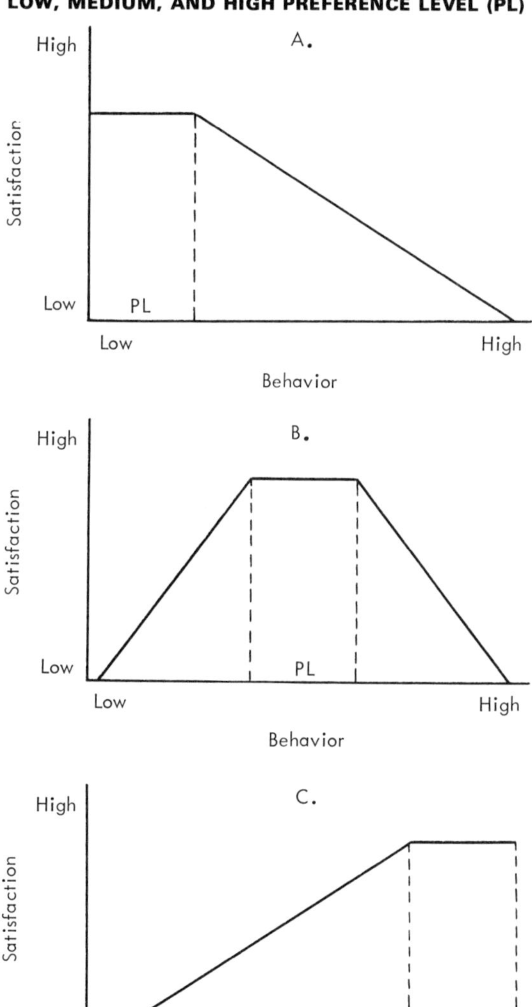

FIGURE 2 A DISCREPANCY MODEL OF SUBORDINATE SATISFACTION WITH THE LEADER

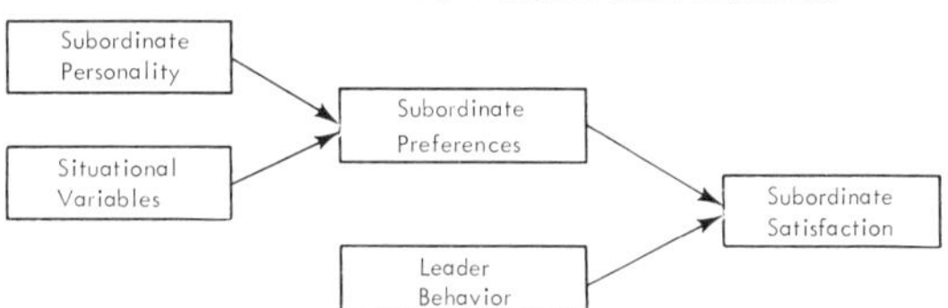

Subordinate preference levels are determined both by subordinate personality and by situational variables (see Figure 2). Preferences can be expected to vary more for Initiating Structure and Decision-Centralization than for Consideration. Except for a few masochists, it is probably safe to assume that subordinates will desire a high degree of considerate behavior by their leaders. As a result, the function relating Consideration and subordinate satisfaction should resemble curve C in Figure 1.

Preference levels for Decision-Centralization, i.e., the subordinate's desire for participation in decision-making, may be partially determined by two personality traits: Authoritarianism (Vroom, 1959) and "need for independence" (Trow, 1957; Ross & Zander, 1957; Vroom, 1959; Beer, 1966, p. 51; French, Kay, & Meyer, 1966). Although none of these investigators assessed the relation between a personality measure and expressed behavior preferences, they did find that personality had the expected moderating effect upon the relation between Decision-Centralization and subordinate satisfaction. However, it should be noted that Tosi (1970) was not able to replicate the results of the study by Vroom (1959). The measurement of subordinate preferences in future replications may aid in clearing up the contradition between these two studies.

The major situational determinant of the preference level for participation in making a decision is probably the importance of that decision for the subordinate (Maier, 1965, p. 165). When a decision is very important to subordinates, they are likely to prefer as much influence as possible (e.g., joint de-

FIGURE 3 A MULTIPLE LINKAGE MODEL OF LEADER EFFECTIVENESS

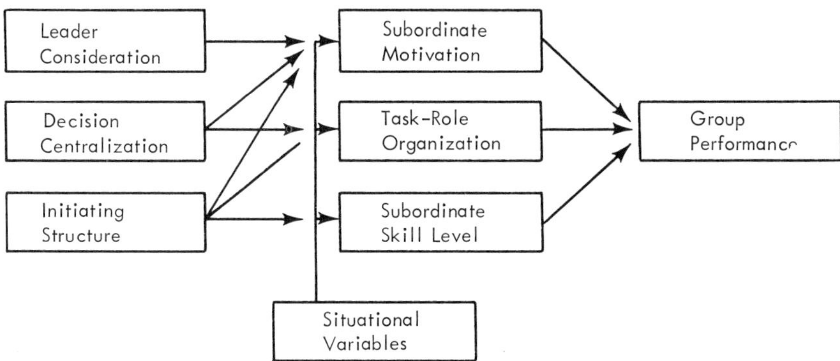

cision-making or delegation). When decisions do not involve matters of importance, consultation or even autocratic decision-making is more likely to be preferred. Of course, the more that subordinates trust their leader to make a decision favorable to them, the less need they will feel to participate in order to protect their interests. Also, when the subordinates are committed to group goal attainment or survival and the task or environment favors centralized decision-making (e.g., a crisis), then they are likely to expect the leader to make most of the decisions (Mulder & Stemerding, 1963).

Preference levels for Initiating Structure are partially determined by the subordinates' commitment to group goals and their perception of the amount of structuring that is necessary to help the group attain these goals. Subordinates who are indifferent about or hostile toward the goal of maximum productivity are likely to prefer a leader who is not very task oriented in his behavior.

Summary of the Discrepancy Model

The major features of the proposed discrepancy model can be summarized in terms of the following hypotheses:

Hyp 1: Subordinate satisfaction with the leader is a function of the discrepancy between actual leader behavior and the behavior preferences of subordinates.

Hyp 2: Subordinate preferences are determined by the combined effect of subordinate personality and situational variables.

Hyp 3: Subordinates usually prefer a high degree of leader Consideration, and this preference level results in a positive relation between Consideration and subordinate satisfaction.

The discrepancy model in its present form is only a static model representing one-way causality at one point in time. No attempt has been made to include additional complexities such as the effects of leader behavior on subordinate preferences. For example, a leader who gradually allows greater subordinate participation may find that the subordinates' preference for decision-making increases over time. Nor does the model explicitly deal with such other determinants of subordinate satisfaction with the leader as his intelligence or the feedback effects from successful or unsuccessful group performance. Finally, the influence of various components of the model on leader behavior has also been ignored. For example, subordinate preferences represent one of several sources of role expectations for the leader, and these role expectations interact with other situational variables and leader personality to determine his behavior.

A MULTIPLE LINKAGE MODEL OF LEADER EFFECTIVENESS

When a leader is dependent upon his subordinates to do the work, subordinate performance is unlikely to improve unless the leader can increase one or more of the following three intermediate variables: (1) Subordinate task motivation (i.e., effort devoted to their tasks), (2) subordinate task skills, and (3) Task-Role Organization (i.e., the technical quality of task decisions).[3] Consideration, Initiating Structure, Decision-Centralization, and various situational variables interact in their effects on these intermediate variables. The intermediate variables interact in turn to determine group performance (see Figure 3).

[3]The leader can also improve productivity by obtaining necessary information, resources, and cooperation from other organization members and outside agencies, but this involves leader behavior outside the context of the work group.

Consideration, Initiating Structure, and Subordinate Motivation

Consideration and Initiating Structure interact in their effect upon subordinate task motivation. Subordinate task motivation will be highest when the leader is high on both Consideration and Initiating Structure. The ordering of the other combinations is less certain, because the interaction appears to be highly complex and irregular. If leaders were subgrouped according to their Initiating Structure scores, for high structuring leaders there would probably be a positive relation between Consideration and subordinate task motivation. For low structuring leaders, there is some reason to suspect that the relation between Consideration and subordinate motivation is described by an inverted U-shaped curve. In other words, subordinate task motivation can be adversely affected when the low structuring leader is either very supportive and friendly or very hostile and punitive.

There are at least two hypotheses for explaining the interaction between Consideration and Initiating Structure, and it is not yet clear if either or both are correct. From instrumentality theory (Vroom, 1964, p. 220; Galbraith & Cummings, 1967), comes the hypothesis that a leader can improve subordinate performance by being highly considerate to subordinates who make an effort to perform well, while withholding Consideration from subordinates who show little task motivation. In effect, considerate behavior is a reward which is contingent upon the display of certain task-motivated behavior by subordinates.

The "identification" hypothesis proposes that subordinate motivation is a response to previous leader Consideration rather than an attempt to obtain future Consideration. As Consideration increases, subordinate attitudes toward the leader become more favorable and his influence over the subordinates increases correspondingly. In effect, the considerate leader has greater "referent power" (French & Raven, 1959). However, in order for subordinate loyalty to be translated into task motivation, it is necessary for the leader to communicate a concern for productivity. If the leader is highly considerate but does not stress productivity, the subordinates are likely to feel that they can safely neglect their tasks.

If a leader actually becomes hostile and punitive, it is likely that subordinate task motivation will be adversely affected, regardless of the level of Initiating Structure. Punitive leadership can lead to counter-aggression by subordinates in the form of slowdowns and subtle sabotage (Day & Hamblin, 1964).

Decision-Centralization and Subordinate Motivation

Although there is some direct evidence that subordinate participation can result in increased task motivation (Baumgartel, 1956), the nature and relative importance of the psychological processes accounting for the relation and the prerequisite conditions for their occurrence are not yet clear. A number of explanations for the effect of participation on subordinate motivation have been proposed during the last two decades.

Probably the most important of the proposed processes is the possibility that subordinates become "ego-involved" with a decision which they have helped to make. When subordinates identify with a decision, they become motivated to help make the decision successful, if only to maintain a favorable self-concept. However, there may be several limiting conditions for this causal sequence (Strauss, 1964; Vroom, 1964; Lowin, 1968). It is possible that there is some minimal amount of individual influence, actual or perceived, which is necessary before identification will occur. As a group gets larger, the influence of each member over a decision will necessarily decline; thus the size of the group may be one limiting factor. Also, it is not clear whether a person who supports a proposal that is rejected will become committed to the proposal finally selected by the group. Another prerequisite may be the subordinate's perception that the decision process is a test of his decision ability and those skills of his which are used in implementing the decision. In the case where subordinates participate in making decisions unrelated to their tasks, there is no reason to assume that any increased commitment to these decisions will generalize to task decisions. Finally, if responsibility for making decisions is thrust upon subordinates who do not want it or who see it as the legitimate role of the leader, then these subordinates may fail to identify with the decisions (French, Israel, & As, 1960).

Another explanation of the relation between Decision-Centralization and task motivation is that participation facilitates reduction of subordinate resistance to change (Coch & French, 1948). One way this could occur is through direct persuasion. Since the leader is usually not aware of all the subordinates' fears and doubts regarding a proposed change, consultation provides him with an opportunity to uncover these fears and to persuade subordinates that the change will be beneficial rather than harmful. When a leader's proposal involves features which clearly are detrimental to subordinates, mere persuasion is not likely to win their support. However, consultation or joint decision-making provides the opportunity for bargaining and agreement on a compromise proposal which the subordinates can support (Strauss, 1964).

When the leader allows his subordinates to make a group decision, the interaction dynamics of the group are yet another possible source of increased task motivation. If the work group is cohesive, its members are subject to direct social pressure to conform to group norms (Schachter, Willerman, Festinger, & Hyman, 1961; Berkowitz, 1954; Seashore, 1954). In addition, the work group may function as a "reference group" for its members (Newcomb, 1965, p. 109). Subordinates who have positive attitudes toward their work group will tend to support group norms, including group decisions made in a legitimate manner. This tendency for member attitudes and behavior to be consistent with reference group norms will occur even in the absence of direct social pressure.

Of course, increased commitment to carry out decisions is not conceptually equivalent to increased task motivation. Subordinates can make task decisions which in effect restrict output or resist change. Subordinate attitudes toward the leader and the organization constitute an important situational variable which moderates the effect of participation upon task motivation. If relations between the leader and the subordinates are very poor, or the subordinates are in opposition to the goal of maximum group performance, then participation in decisions involving production goals, standards, quotas, etc., is not likely to result in increased subordinate task motivation (Strauss, 1964). Since Consideration is an important determinant of subordinate attitudes toward the leader, participation is more likely to be effective if combined with high Consideration than if combined with low Consideration.

Leader Behavior and Subordinate Task Skill

The second way in which leaders can increase group performance is to increase the ability of subordinates to perform their individual tasks. A number of studies (reviewed in Vroom, 1964, p. 197) support Maier's (1965) hypothesis that performance is a function of a person's Motivation × Ability. According to this hypothesis, even highly motivated subordinates will not perform well if they lack the necessary knowledge or skills to carry out their assignments. Therefore, one way for a leader to improve group performance is to correct deficiencies in subordinates task skills and knowledge by means of on-the-job instruction and improved downward communication of task-relevant information. Instruction and communication of this nature are, by definition, elements of Initiating Structure. A more complex analysis of the relation between Initiating Structure and subordinate task skill was beyond the scope of this article.

The Nature of Task-Role Organization

Task-Role Organization refers to how efficiently the skill resources of subordinates are utilized to perform the group's formal tasks. Adequacy of Task-Role Organization depends upon how well job assignment decisons and work method decisions are made. The making of job assignment decisions is usually referred to in industrial psychology as "placement" or "classification." When the jobs of each subordinate are identical and subordinates work independently of each other, it doesn't matter what subordinates are assigned to what jobs. However, when jobs are highly specialized, each job has different skill requirements, and skill differences among subordinates are substantial, then job assignments are an important type of task decision. If work assignments are not made carefully, the skills of some workers will not be fully utilized, while other workers will be placed in jobs which they cannot perform adequately. Furthermore, if the jobs are interdependent, bottlenecks will occur at various points in the flow of work.

Work method decisions are important whenever a task can be performed in many different ways, and some ways are better than others. Work methods and procedures can be designed with the available skills of a particular work group in mind, but it is common practice in industrial engineering to ignore individual differences and develop methods which maximize the efficiency of the typical worker. Decisions about work procedures are not always the responsibility of the leader. In some organizations, work methods are designed by staff specialists or are rigidly prescribed by company or union regulations.

Task-Role Organization was included in the multiple linkage model to account for any variability in group productivity which is not attributable to subordinate motivation, subordinate ability, or to extraneous events such as an improvement in the flow of material inputs, a breakdown in equipment, etc. The identification of Task-Role Organization as a separate variable is analogous to Maier's (1965) distinction between the quality of a decision and group acceptance of the decision. Although Task-Role Organization is an important conceptual component of the multiple linkage model, measurement of this variable is likely to prove troublesome. Any measure of Task-Role Organization will be highly specific to a given set of tasks and subordinates. Within a specific situation, one could attempt to scale the adequacy of job assignment decisions by evaluating the match between job requirements and subordinate skills for all possible combinations of job assignments. Adequacy of work method decisions could be evaluated in several ways. In some situations, the accumulated knowledge of industrial engineering specialists may permit the subjective ranking of various possible work procedures according to their relative efficiency. When objective measures of group performance (e.g., quantity or quality of output, labor time, errors) are available to use as a criterion of efficiency, then alternative work methods may be experimentally compared. However, it may be difficult to hold task motivation constant, even within a single work group, because job design can affect the intrinsic motivation of workers as well as their efficiency.

Initiating Structure, Decision-Centralization, and Task-Role Organization

Both Initiating Structure and Decision-Centralization appear to be related to Task-Role Organization. By definition, a leader who is high in Initiating Structure will attempt to improve the efficiency of his group. However, simply engaging in structuring behavior does not guarantee that Task-Role Organization will improve. The leader's success depends upon his organizing skills, technical knowledge, and the extent to which he taps the knowledge of his subordinates by allowing them some degree of participation in making task decisions. The relation between Decision-Centralization and Task-Role Organization is moderated by the relative amount of leader and subordinate organizing skills and task knowledge. When the leader is very capable in this respect but the subordinates lack the appropriate talents, then there will be a negative relation between participation and Task-Role Organization. When the subordinates have more relevant knowledge and organizing talent than the leader, we would expect a positive relation between participation and Task-Role Organization. We have already seen that Decision-Centralization can affect the task motivation of subordinates as well as the quality of task decisions. This means that in the situation where there is a negative relation between participation and Task-Role Organization, there may also be a positive relation between participation and subordinate motivation. When such a trade-off dilemma occurs, some intermediate degree of Decision-Centralization will probably be optimal with respect to group performance.

In some situations, the quality of task decisions involves a time dimension. That is, the effectiveness of decisions depends in part upon how quickly they are made (Strauss, 1964; Lowin, 1968). Autocratic decision-making is faster than other decision procedures because little communication with subordinates is necessary. Therefore, participation is likely to be negatively related to group performance when rapid decision-making is required. The magnitude of this negative relation will be greatest when the leader already has the necessary knowledge and ability to make good decisions, the subordinates are motivated by the urgency of the situation, and the task group is very large.

Summary of the Multiple Linkage Model

The major features of the multiple linkage model of leadership effectiveness can be summarized by means of the following hypotheses:

Hyp 1: Group productivity is a function of the interaction among subordinate task motivation, subordinate task skills, and Task-Role Organization for the group.

Hyp 2: Initiating Structure and Consideration interact in the determination of subordinate task motivation. Task motivation is highest when the leader is high on both behavior variables.

Hyp 3: Decision-Centralization is negatively correlated with subordinate task motivation (i.e., high participation causes high motivation) when subordinate relations with the leader are favorable, the decisions are relevant to subordinate tasks, and subordinates perceive their participation to be a test of valued abilities.

Hyp 4: Initiating Structure interacts with Decision-Centralization in the determination of Task-Role Organization. The relationship is moderated by the level and distribution of task knowledge and planning ability in the group.

Hyp 5: Initiating Structure is positively related to the level of subordinate task skill.

REVIEW OF RELATED RESEARCH

Most studies of the relation between leader behavior and subordinate satisfaction with the leader have not measured subordinate preferences or the personality and situational variables which determine these preferences. Most studies of the relation between leader behavior and group productivity have not included measures of the intermediate and situational variables in the proposed linkage model. The approach typical of most leadership research has been to look for a linear relation between leader behavior and one of the criterion variables. Nevertheless, previous research does provide some direct and some indirect evidence for evaluating the proposed models.

In the following sections of this article, relevant leadership research will be reviewed. The review will include studies dealing with variables which are reasonably similar to those in the proposed discrepancy and linkage models. However, it should be emphasized that in many of these studies, the operational measurement of a variable only approximates the conceptual definition presented in this article. Studies using scales which can be regarded as a measure of leader attitudes (e.g., LPC scale, F scale, Leadership Opinion Questionnaire) rather than leader behavior were not included. Also excluded were studies of general vs. close supervision. This leadership dimension, as usually defined, confounds Decision-Centralization with Initiating Structure. Finally, the review does not include studies of emergent leaders in informal groups, studies using children, studies involving an entire organization rather than individual work groups or departments, and studies in which leader behavior is obviously confounded with organizational variables such as the incentive system.

Consideration and Satisfaction

In seven studies of the relation between Consideration and subordinate satisfaction with their leader, Consideration was measured by means of subordinate responses on leader behavior description questionnaires. In five of these studies (Halpin, 1957; Halpin & Winer, 1957; Nealey & Blood, 1968; Yukl, 1969a; Anderson, 1966) there was a strong positive relation between Consideration and subordinate satisfaction. In the remaining two studies (Fleishman & Harris, 1962; Skinner, 1969) there was a significant curvilinear relation between Consideration and two objective measures which reflect subordinate satisfaction, namely turnover and grievances. The curve describing the relation corresponded roughly to curve C in Figure 1. If subordinate preferences were homogeneous, this curve would represent supporting evidence for the concept of a zone of indifference within which leader behavior does not affect subordinate satisfaction. Below this indifference zone, the relation between Consideration and satisfaction was positive.

In research reported in Likert (1961, p. 17), aspects of Consideration such as "supervisor takes an interest in me and understands my problems" and "supervisor thinks of employees as human beings rather than as persons to get the work done," were related to favorable attitudes on job-related matters. In two laboratory experiments (Day & Hamblin, 1964; Misumi & Shirakashi, 1966) punitive leader behavior (i.e., low Consideration) was associated with low subordinate satisfaction. In another laboratory experiment, Lowin et al. (1969) found a significant positive relation between subordinates' satisfaction and their ratings of leader Consideration, but the difference in satisfaction between high and low Consideration conditions, although in the right direction, was not significant.

Only two studies were found in which a positive relation between Consideration and subordinate satisfaction with the leader did not occur. In a study by Argyle, Gardner, and Cioffi (1958), leader self-reports of punitive behavior did not correlate significantly with subordinate turnover and absences. Pelz (1952) found an interaction between the degree to which a leader acts as a representative of his subordinates when dealing with higher management (one form of Consideration) and the leader's upward influence in the organization. For leaders with little upward influence, subordinates were less satisfied when the leader "went to bat" for them than when he did not go to bat. Presumably the leader representation raised expectations which he could not fulfill, thereby frustrating subordinates. In terms of the discrepancy model, the subordinates' preferences for leader representation are probably lower when it repeatedly causes frustration. Whether the negative effects of unsuccessful representation can completely cancel out the positive effects of other considerate behavior by the leader is not clear. It does not seem likely.

In summary, the research literature indicates that in most situations, considerate leaders will have more satisfied subordinates. Although none of the investigators included subordinate preferences in their analysis, the results are consistent with the discrepancy model if we can make the relatively safe assumption that most subordinates prefer considerate leaders.

Initiating Structure and Satisfaction

A consistent linear relation between Initiating Structure and subordinate satisfaction was not found, even within sets of studies using comparable measures. Unfortunately, none of the studies reviewed included subordinate preferences. Baumgartel (1956), Halpin and Winer (1957), Argyle *et al.* (1958), Misumi and Shirakashi (1966), Lowin et al. (1969), Anderson (1966), and Likert (1961, pp. 16–18) failed to find a significant relation. Halpin (1957) and Yukl (1969a) found positive correlations. Vroom and Mann (1960) found a significant negative correlation between pressure for production and job satisfaction for delivery truck drivers but not for loaders. Nealey and Blood (1968) found a negative correlation between Initiating Structure and subordinate satisfaction for second-level supervisors and a positive correlation for first-level supervisors.

Only three studies were found which examined the possibility of a curvilinear relation between

Initiating Structure and subordinate satisfaction. Likert (1955) found that the relation between pressure for productivity and subordinate satisfaction took the form of an inverted U-shaped curve which is similar to curve B in Figure 1. Fleishman and Harris (1962) and Skinner (1969) found a curvilinear relation between Initiating Structure and both turnover and grievances. Although subordinate preferences were not measured, the relationships in these studies were roughly comparable to curve A in Figure 1.

Fleishman and Harris also tested for an interaction between Initiating Structure and Consideration. The results of their analysis suggest that Consideration has a greater effect upon subordinate satisfaction than does Initiating Structure. High Consideration leaders could increase Initiating Structure with little accompanying increase in turnover or grievances. Fleishman and Harris provide two possible explanations for this interaction. One explanation is that considerate leaders are more likely to deal with any dissatisfaction caused by high structuring behavior before the dissatisfaction results in official grievances or withdrawal (i.e., turnover). Another explanation is that Consideration affects the way subordinates perceive structuring behavior. In terms of the discrepancy model, subordinates of highly considerate leaders are more likely to have a higher preference level for Initiating Structure because they do not perceive leader structuring as threatening and restrictive.

Decision-Centralization and Satisfaction

Six studies were found which examined the correlation between subordinate satisfaction and participation as perceived either by the leaders or by the subordinates (Baumgartel, 1956; Argyle *et al.*, 1958; Vroom, 1959; Bachman, Smith, & Slesinger, 1966; Yukl, 1969a; Tosi, 1970). In each of these studies, evidence was found to support a positive relation between participation and subordinate satisfaction, although within some of the studies, a significant relation was not obtained for every subsample or for every alternative measure of the variables. A significant positive relation was also found in each of five studies in which participation was experimentally manipulated (Coch & French, 1948; Shaw, 1955, Morse & Reimer, 1956; Solem, 1958, Maier & Hoffman, 1962). The results of these studies are generally consistent with the discrepancy model if one can assume that the subordinates preferred a substantial degree of participation.

In those cases where a significant relation between participation and subordinate satisfaction was not found, there was usually some reason to expect that the subordinates preferred a moderate or low amount of participation. In the study by Vroom (1959), a positive correlation occurred for subordinates with a high need for independence but not for subordinates with a low need for independence. Bass (1965, pp. 169–170) and French *et al.* (1960) found that subordinate participation did not result in more favorable attitudes toward a leader unless the subordinates perceived the decision-making as a legitimate part of their role. Further evidence for the moderating effect of subordinate preferences can be found in a study by Baumgartel (1956) and in two unpublished studies (Jacobson, 1953; Tannenbaum, 1954) which were reported in Likert (1961, pp. 92–93). In the Tennenbaum study, some subordinates reacted adversely to a sudden substantial increase in participation. Finally, Morse (1953, p. 64) found that, regardless of whether workers made some decisions or none, they reported more intrinsic job satisfaction when the amount of decision-making equalled the amount desired than when they were not allowed to make as many decisions as they desired. Although intrinsic job satisfaction is conceptually distinct from satisfaction with the leader, these two variables are probably highly correlated when the leader determines how much responsibility a subordinate has for making task decisions.

Consideration, Initiating Structure, and Productivity

Considering the complexity of the interaction between Consideration and Initiating Structure, it is not surprising that research on the relation between Consideration and productivity does not yield consistent results. In the large majority of studies there was either a significant positive relation (Katz, Maccoby, Gurin, & Floor, 1951; Argyle *et al.*, 1958; Besco & Lawshe, 1959; Schachter *et al.*, 1961; Kay, Meyer, & French, 1965) or there was no significant linear relation (Bass, 1957; Halpin, 1957; Rambo; 1958; Day & Hamblin, 1964; Anderson, 1966; Nealey & Blood, 1968; Rowland & Scott, 1968). Lowin et al. (1969) found a positive relation for objectively manipulated Consideration in an experiment but not for subordinate ratings of Consideration. A significant negative relation was found by Halpin and Winer (1957) for aircraft commanders and by Fleishman, Harris, and Burtt (1955, p. 80) for foremen of production departments but not for nonproduction departments. In both of these studies, productivity was measured by superior ratings, and the highest ratings went to leaders low on Consideration but high on Initiating Structure. It is possible that the ratings were influenced more by the raters' task-oriented stereotype of the ideal leader than by actual group performance.

Turning to research on the relation between Initiating Structure and productivity, we again find mixed results. In a number of studies a significant positive relation was reported (Fleishman *et al.*, 1955; Likert, 1955; Halpin & Winer, 1957; Maier & Maier, 1957; Besco & Lawshe, 1959; Anderson, 1966; Nealey & Blood, 1968). For some subsamples in three of these studies, and for leaders studied by Argyle *et al.* (1958), Bass (1957), Halpin (1957), Rambo (1958), and Lowin et al. (1969), a significant relation was not found. In no case was a significant negative relation reported.

It is unfortunate that so few investigators measured intermediate variables or tested for an interaction between Consideration and Initiating Structure. However, the few studies which are directly relevant to the proposed linkage model do provide supporting evidence. In a laboratory experiment in Japan, Misumi and Shirakashi (1966) found that leaders who were both task oriented and considerate in their behavior had the most productive groups. Halpin (1957) found that aircraft commanders were rated highest in effectiveness when they were above the mean on both Consideration and Initiating Structure. Hemphill (1957) obtained the same results for the relation between the behavior of department chairmen in a Liberal Arts College and faculty ratings of how well the department was administered. Fleishman and Simmons (1970) translated the Supervisory Behavior Description into Hebrew and administered this questionnaire to the superiors of Israeli foremen. Proficiency ratings for the foremen were also obtained from their superiors. Once again, the foremen with the best ratings tended to be high on both Consideration and Initiating Structure. Patchen (1962) found that personal production norms (i.e., task motivation) of workers were highest when the leader encouraged proficiency as well as "going to bat" for them. These production norms were related in turn to actual group production. Finally, although he didn't measure Consideration, Baumgartel (1956) found a significant positive relation between subordinate motivation and the concern of research laboratory directors for goal attainment (i.e., Initiating Structure).

Decision-Centralization and Productivity

Seventeen studies were found which examined the relation between Decision-Centralization and group productivity. A significant positive relation between participation and productivity was found by Bachman *et al.* (1966), Coch and French (1948), Fleishman (1965), French (1950), French, Kay, and Meyer (1966), Lawrence and Smith (1955), Likert (1961, p. 20), Mann and Dent (1954), McCurdy and Eber (1953), Meltzer (1956), and Vroom (1959). Argyle et al. (1958) found a positive relation only for departments without piece rates, suggesting that the organizational incentive system, a situational variable, interacts with Decision-Centralization in determining the subordinates' task motivation. Tosi (1970), French *et al.* (1960), and McCurdy and Lambert (1952) failed to find a significant relation between participation and productivity. In two other studies (Shaw, 1955; Morse & Reimer, 1956) a significant negative relation was found. Several of these studies demonstrate that various situational variables can moderate the effects of leader decision behavior on group performance. Nevertheless, the high percentage of studies reporting a positive relation is an indication that some degree of participation leads to an increase in group performance in most situations. However, this generalization is *not* equivalent to concluding "the more participation there is, the greater will be group productivity." For a particular group, there is probably some optimal pattern of decision-making which will consist of various amounts of delegation, joint decision-making, consultation, and autocratic decision-making (Heller & Yukl, 1969). The optimal pattern is likely to involve some intermediate amount of subordinate influence, rather than the greatest possible amount.

DISCUSSION

The Multiple Linkage Model and Fiedler's Contingency Model

A considerable number of leadership studies have been conducted by Fred Fiedler and his associates at the University of Illinois (Fiedler, 1967). Fiedler has developed a theory of leadership effectiveness to explain the results of this research. According to Fiedler's theory, group performance is a function of the interaction between the leader's "esteem for his least preferred co-worker" (LPC) and there situational variables: task structure, leader—member relations, and the position power of the leader. Leaders with low LPC scores have the most productive groups when the leadership situation, in terms of the three situational variables, is either very favorable or very unfavorable. Leaders with high LPC scores are more effective when the situation is intermediate in favorableness. Although Fiedler provides a behavioral explanation for these hypothesized relations, most of his studies did not measure leader behavior. The few studies which have attempted to identify the behavioral correlates of LPC scores have not yielded consistent results (Sample & Wilson, 1965; Fiedler, 1967, p. 53; Nealey & Blood, 1968; Yukl, 1970; Gruenfeld, Rance, & Weissenberg, 1969; Reilly, 1969). Thus, it is not possible at this time to determine whether Fiedler's model is compatible with the proposed linkage model. Both theories are generally supported by their own separate bodies of empirical research. Reconciliation of the two approaches will probably require additional research which includes variables from both theories.

Direction for Future Research

The theoretical framework and the literature review presented earlier point out some empirical gaps which badly need filling. The central feature of the linkage model is the set of intermediate variables. A leader can do little to improve group productivity unless he can alter one or more of these variables. Yet the mediating role of these variables, their relation to each other, and their interaction in the determination of productivity have seldom been investigated in leadership studies. Future research should be more comprehensive in scope. Leader behavior variables, intermediate variables, situational variables, subordinate preferences, criterion variables (i.e., satisfaction and productivity), and relevant leader traits should all be included. Situational variables other than those discussed in this article also need to be investigated. Likely candidates are the organizational limiting conditions for participation suggested by Lowin (1968) and Strauss (1964), the structural variables found to be associated with leader decision behavior by Heller and Yukl (1969), the situational variables in Fiedler's model, the situational variables cluster-analyzed by Yukl (1969b), and Woodward's (1965) system for classifying production technology. Finally, the way in which the three behavior dimensions interact in determining the intermediate variables should be investigated. If possible, the leader behavior variables should be experimentally manipulated in order to avoid the measurement problems associated with leader behavior descriptions by subordinates.

The analysis of leader effectiveness has utilized leader behavior variables which maintain a basic continuity with traditional conceptualization and research. However, in speculating about future research, it is appropriate to evaluate the continued usefulness of these broadly defined behavior dimensions. It is obvious that Consideration and Initiating Structure are composed of relatively diverse elements, while Decision-Centralization is an average based on many different types of decisions. In order to improve the predictive power of the model, it may be necessary to identify which components of the behavior variables are the most important determinants of each intermediate variable.

The discrepancy model and the multiple linkage model provide only the skeleton of a static leadership theory which purposely ignores the additional complexities of feedback loops and circular causality. Much additional research and revision will be necessary to transform the skeleton into a full-fledged dynamic model which permits accurate predictions about leader effectiveness in formal task groups.

REFERENCES

Anderson, L. R. Leader behavior, member attitudes, and task performance of intercultural discussion groups. *Journal of Social Psychology,* 1966, **69**, 305-19.

Argyle, M., Gardner, G., and Cioffi, F. The measurement of supervisory methods *Human Relations,* 1957, **10**, 295-313.

Argyle, M., Gardner G., & Cioffi, F. Supervisory methods related to productivity, absenteeism, and labor turnover. *Human Relations,* 1958, **11**, 23-40.

Bachman, J. G., Smith, C. G., and Slesinger, J. A. Control, performance, and satisfaction: An analysis of structure and individual effects. *Journal of Personality and Social Psychology,* 1966, **4**, 127-36.

Bass, B. M. Leadership opinions and related characteristics of salesmen and sales managers. In R. M. Stogdill and A. E. Coons (eds.), *Leader behavior: Its description and measurement.* Columbus: Bureau of Business Research, Ohio State University, 1957.

Bass, B. M. *Organizational psychology.* Boston: Allyn & Bacon, 1965.

Baumgartel, H. Leadership, motivations, and attitudes in research laboratories. *Journal of Social Issues,* 1956, **12**, (2), 24-31.

Beer, M. *Leadership, employee needs, and motivation.* Columbus: Bureau of Business Research, Ohio State University, Monograph No. 129, 1966.

Berkowitz, L. Group Standards, cohesiveness, and productivity. *Human Relations,* 1954, **7**, 509-19.

Besco, R. O. and Lawshe, C. H. Foreman leadership as perceived by supervisor and subordinate. *Personnel Psychology,* 1959, **12**, 573-82.

Coch, L. and French, J. R. P. Overcoming resistance to change. *Human Relations,* 1948, **1**, 512-32.

Day, R. C. and Hamblin, R. L. Some effects of close and punitive styles of supervision. *American Journal of Sociology,* 1964, **16**, 499-510.

Fiedler, F. E. *A theory of leadership effectiveness.* New York: McGraw-Hill, 1967.

Fleishman, E. A. A leader behavior description for industry. In R. M. Stogdill and A. E. Coons (eds.), *Leader behavior:*

Its description and measurement. Columbus: Bureau of Business Research, Ohio State University, 1957. (a).

Fleishman, E. A. The Leadership Opinion Questionnaire. In R. M. Stogdill and A. E. Coons (eds.), *Leader behavior: Its description and measurement.* Columbus: Bureau of Business Research, Ohio State University, 1957. (b).

Fleishman, E. A. Attitude versus skill factors in work group productivity. *Personnel Psychology,* 1965, **18**, 253–66.

Fleishman, E. A. and Harris, E. F. Patterns of leadership behavior related to employee grievances and turnover. *Personnel Psychology,* 1962, **15**, 43–56.

Fleishman, E. A., Harris, E. F., and Burtt, H. E. *Leadership and supervision in industry.* Columbus: Bureau of Educational Research, Ohio State University, Research monograph No. 33, 1955.

Fleishman, E. A. and Simmons, J. Relationship between leadership patterns and effectiveness ratings among Israeli foremen. *Personnel Psychology,* 1970, **23**, 169–72.

Foa, U. G. Relation of worker's expectations to satisfaction with his supervisor. *Personnel Psychology,* 1957, **10** 161-68.

French, J. R. P. Field experiments: Changing group productivity. In J. G. Miller (ed.), *Experiments in social process: A symposium on social psychology.* New York: McGraw-Hill, 1950.

French, J. R. P., Israel, J., and As, D. An experiment on participation in a Norwegian factory. *Human Relations,* 1960, **13**, 3–19.

French, J. R. P., Kay, E., and Meyer, H. Participation and the appraisal system. *Human Relations,* 1966, **19**, 3–20.

French, J. R. P. and Raven, B. The bases of social power. In D. Cartwright (ed.), *Studies in social power.* Ann Arbor: Institute for Social Research, University of Michigan, 1959.

Galbraith, J. and Cummings, L. L. An empirical investigation of the motivational determinants of task performance: Interactive effects between instrumentality-valence and motivation-ability. *Organizational Behavior and Human Performance,* 1967, **2**, 237–57.

Gomberg, W. The trouble with democratic management. *Transaction,* 1966, **3**, (5), 30–35.

Greer, F. L. Leader indulgence and group performance. *Psychological Monographs,* 1961, **75** (12, Whole No. 516).

Gruenfeld, L. W., Rance, D. E., and Weissenberg, P. The behavior of task-oriented (low LPC) and socially-oriented (high LPC) leaders under several conditions of social support. *Journal of Social Psychology,* 1969, **79**, 99–107.

Halpin, A. W. The leader behavior and effectiveness of aircraft commanders. In R. M. Stogdill and A. E. Coons (eds.), *Leader behavior: Its description and measurement.* Columbus: Bureau of Business Research, Ohio State University, 1957.

Halpin, A. W. and Winer, B. J. A factorial study of the leader behavior descriptions. In R. M. Stogdill and A. E. Coons (eds.), *Leader behavior: Its description and measurement.* Columbus: Bureau of Business Research, Ohio State University, 1957.

Heller, F. and Yukl, G. Participation, managerial decision-making, and situational variables. *Organizational Behavior and Human Performance,* 1969, **4**, 227–41.

Hemphill, J. K. Leader behavior associated with the administrative reputations of college departments. In R. M. Stogdill and A. E. Coons (eds.), *Leader behavior: Its description and measurement.* Columbus: Bureau of Business Research, Ohio State University, 1957.

Hemphill, J. K. and Coons, A. E. Development of the leader behavior description questionnaire. In R. M. Stogdill and A. E. Coons (eds.), *Leader behavior: Its description and measurement.* Columbus: Bureau of Business Research, Ohio State University, 1957.

Jacobson, J. M. Analysis of interpersonal relations in a formal organization. Unpublished doctoral dissertation, University of Michigan, 1953.

Katz, D., Maccoby, N., Gurin, G., and Floor, L. *Productivity, supervision, and morale among railroad workers.* Ann Arbor: Survey Research Center, University of Michigan, 1951.

Katzell, R. A. Personal values, job satisfaction, and job behavior. In H. Borrow (ed.), *Man in a World of Work.* Boston: Houghton-Mifflin, 1964.

Kay, E., Meyer, H. H., and French, J. R. P. Effects of threat in a performance appraisal interview. *Journal of Applied Psychology,* 1965, **49**, 311–17.

Korman, A. K. Consideration, initiating structure, and organizational criteria—A review. *Personal Psychology,* 1966, **19**, 349–62.

Lawrence, L. C. and Smith, P. C. Group decision and employee participation. *Journal of Applied Psychology,* 1955, **39**, 334–37.

Lewin, K. The dynamics of group action. *Educational Leadership,* 1944, **1**, 195–200.

Likert, R. Developing patterns in management. *Strengthening management for the new technology.* New York: American Management Association, 1955.

Likert, R. *New patterns of management.* New York: McGraw-Hill, 1961.

Locke, E. A. What is job satisfaction? *Organizational Behavior and Human Performance,* 1969, **4**, 309–36.

Lowin, A. Participative decision-making: A model, literature critique, and prescriptions for research. *Organizational Behavior and Human Performance,* 1968, **3**, 68–106.

Lowin, A., Hrapchak, W. J., and Kavanagh, M. J. Consideration and Initiating Structure: An experimental investigation of leadership traits. *Administrative Science Quarterly,* 1969, **14**, 238–53.

McCurdy, H. G. and Eber, H. W. Democratic vs. authoritarian: A further investigation of group problem-solving. *Journal of Personality,* 1953, **22**, 258–69.

McCurdy, H. G. and Lambert, W. E. The efficiency of small groups in the solution of problems requiring genuine co-operation. *Journal of Personality,* 1952, **20**, 478–94.

McMurray, R. N. The case for benevolent autocracy. *Harvard Business Review,* 1958, **36,** (1), 82–90.

Maier, N. R. F. *Psychology in industry.* (3d ed.) Boston: Houghton-Mifflin Co., 1965.

Maier, N. R. F. and Hoffman, L. R. Group decision in England and the United States. *Personnel Psychology,* 1962, **15,** 75–87.

Maier, N. R. F. and Maier, R. A. An experimental test of the effects of "developmental" vs. "free" discussions on the quality of group decisions. *Journal of Applied Psychology,* 1957, **41,** 320–23.

Mann, F. C. and Dent, J. The supervisor: Member of two organizational families. *Harvard Business Review,* 1954, **32,** (6) 103–12.

Meltzer, L. Scientific productivity in organizational settings. *Journal of Social Issues,* 1956, **12,** (2), 32–40.

Misumi, J. and Shirakashi, S. An experimental study of the effects of supervisory behavior on productivity and morale in a hierarchical organization. *Human Relations,* 1966 **19,** 297–307.

Morse, N. *Satisfaction in the white-collar job.* Ann Arbor: Institute for Social Research, University of Michigan, 1953.

Morse, N. C. and Reimer, E. The experimental change of a major organizational variable. *Journal of Abnormal and Social Psychology.* 1956, **52,** 120–29.

Mulder, M. and Stemerding, A. Threat, attraction to group and strong leadership: A laboratory experiment in a natural setting. *Human Relations,* 1963, **16,** 317–34.

Nealey, S. M. and Blood, M. R. Leadership performance of nursing supervisors at two organizational levels. *Journal of Applied Psychology,* 1968, **52,** 414–22.

Newcomb, T. H., Turner, R. H., and Converse, P. E. *Social psychology.* New York: Holt, Rinehart, & Winston, 1965.

Newport, G. A study of attitudes and leadership behavior. *Personnel Administration,* 1962, **25** (5), 42–46.

Patchen, M. Supervisory methods and group performance norms. *Administrative Science Quarterly,* 1962, **7,** 275–94.

Pelz, D. C. Influence: A key to effective leadership in the first-line supervisor. *Personnel,* 1952, **29,** 209–17.

Porter, L. W. Job attitudes in management: I. Perceived deficiencies in need fulfillment as a function of job level. *Journal of Applied Psychology,* 1962, **46,** 375–84.

Rambo, W. W. The construction and analysis of a leadership behavior rating form. *Journal of Applied Psychology,* 1958, **42,** 409–15.

Reilly, A. J. The effects of different leadership styles on group performance: A field experiment. Paper presented at the American Psychological Association Convention, Washington, D.C., September 1, 1969.

Rosen, R. A. H. and Rosen, R. A. A. Suggested modification in job satisfaction surveys. *Personnel Psychology,* 1955, **8,** 303–14.

Ross, I. C. and Zander, A. Need satisfactions and employee turnover. *Personnel Psychology,* 1957, **10,** 327–38.

Rowland, K. M. and Scott, W. E. Psychological attributes of effective leadership in a formal organization. *Personnel Psychology,* 1968, **21,** 365–78.

Sales, S. M. Supervisory style and productivity: Review and theory. *Personnel Psychology,* 1966, **19,** 275–86.

Sample, J. A. and Wilson, T. R. Leader behavior, group productivity, and rating of least preferred coworker. *Journal of Personality and Social Psychology,* 1965, **1,** 266–70.

Schachter, S., Willerman, B., Festinger, L., and Hyman, R. Emotional disruption and industrial productivity. *Journal of Applied Psychology,* 1961, **45,** 201–13.

Schaffer, R. H. Job satisfaction as related to need satisfaction in work. *Psychological Monograph,* 1953, **67,** (14, Whole No. 364).

Schoenfeld, E. Authoritarian management: A reviving concept. *Personnel,* 1959, **36,** 21–24.

Seashore, S. *Group cohesiveness in the industrial work group.* Ann Arbor: Institute for Social Research, University of Michigan, 1954.

Shaw, M. E. A comparison of two types of leadership in various communication nets. *Journal of Abnormal and Social Psychology,* 1955, **50,** 127–34.

Skinner, E. W. Relationships between leadership behavior patterns and organizational-situational variables. *Personnel Psychology,* 1969, **22,** 489–94.

Solem, A. R. An evaluation of two attitudinal approaches to delegation. *Journal of Applied Psychology,* 1958, **42,** 36–39.

Stanton, E. S. Which approach to management—democratic, authoritarian, or . . .? *Personnel Administration,* 1962, **25** (2), 44–47.

Stogdill, R. M., Goode, O. S., and Day, D. R. New leader behavior description subscales. *Journal of Psychology,* 1962, **54,** 259–69.

Stogdill, R. M., Goode, O. S., and Day, D. R. The leader behavior of corporation presidents. *Personal Psychology,* 1963, **16,** 127–32.

Stogdill, R. M., Goode, O. S., and Day, D. R. The leader behavior of presidents of labor unions. *Personnel Psychology,* 1964, **17,** 49–57.

Strauss, G. Some notes on power equalization. In H. J. Leavitt (ed.), *The social science of organizations: Four perspectives.* Englewood Cliffs, New Jersey: Prentice-Hall, 1964.

Tannenbaum, A. S. The relationship between personality and group structure. Unpublished doctoral dissertation. Syracuse University, 1954.

Tosi, H. A re-examination of personality as a determinant of the effects of participation. *Personnel Psychology,* 1970, **23,** 91–99.

Trow, D. B. Autonomy and job satisfaction in task-oriented groups. *Journal of Abnormal and Social Psychology,* 1957, **54,** 204–9.

Vroom, V. H. Some personality determinants of the effects of participation. *Journal of Abnormal and Social Psychology,* 1959, **59,** 322–27.

Vroom, V.H. *Work and Motivation.* New York: John Wiley & Sons, 1964.

Vroom, V. H. and Mann, F. C. Leader authoritarianism and employee attitudes. *Personnel Psychology,* 1960, **13,** 125–140.

Woodward, J. *Industrial organization:* Theory and practice. London: Oxford University Press, 1965.

Yukl, G. A. Conceptions and consequences of leader behavior. Paper presented at the annual convention of the California State Psychological Association, Newport Beach, January, 1969. (a).

Yukl, G. A. A situation description questionnaire for leaders. *Educational and Psychological Measurement,* 1969, **29,** 515–18. (b).

Yukl, G. A. Leader LPC scores: Attitude dimensions and behavioral correlates. *Journal of Social Psychology,* 1970, **80,** 207–12.

45. VALIDATION AND EXTENSION OF THE CONTINGENCY MODEL OF LEADERSHIP EFFECTIVENESS: A REVIEW OF EMPIRICAL FINDINGS

***Fred E. Fiedler*†**

A contingency model of leadership effectiveness, described in a theoretical paper 7 years ago (Fiedler, 1964), has stimulated numerous studies in the area testing the model as well as attacking it in a recent issue of this journal (Graen, Alvares, Orris, & Martella, 1970). The present paper reviews 25 investigations purporting to test or extend the model.

The contingency model postulates that the performance of interacting groups is contingent upon the interaction of leadership style and situational favorableness. It has been suspected for some time that group effectiveness depends on attributes of the leader as well as of the situation (e.g., Tannenbaum & Schmidt, 1958; Terman, 1904). The question in leadership theory has been, What kind of leadership style for what kind of situation? The contingency model specifies that the so-called "task-oriented" leaders perform more effectively in very favorable and very unfavorable situations, while "relationship-oriented" leaders perform more effectively in situations intermediate in favorableness. The theory operationalizes leadership style as well as situational favorableness and, therefore, lends itself to empirical testing.

This study first defines the main terms of the theory, and briefly reviews the findings on which the model is based. It then presents *(a)* validation evidence relevant to the model's prediction of group performance in real-life studies and laboratory experiments; *(b)* extensions of the model to a more broadly defined hypothesis; and *(c)* an analysis of results bearing upon the reclassification and prediction of performance of coacting groups.

Definitions

The main terms of the theory—*leadership style, situational favorableness,* and *leadership* or *group effectiveness*—are briefly described below, as are the definitions of *interacting* and *coacting* groups.

Interacting Groups. These are groups in which the members work cooperatively and interdependently on a common task. The contributions of individual members of these groups cannot, therefore, readily be isolated, and the members, for this reason, are typically rewarded or penalized as a group. In contrast, in *coacting* groups members perform their tasks in relative independence of one another, as for example, members of bowling teams, men in piecework production or in training situations in which each participant typically receives an individual score or evaluation at the end of training.

Leadership Style. The predictor measure used in studies of the contingency model is the least preferred co-worker (LPC) score. This score is obtained by first asking an individual to think of all co-workers he has ever had. He is then asked to describe the one person with whom he has been least able to work well, that is, the person he least prefers as a coworker. This need not be someone with whom he works at the time. The description is made on 8-point, bipolar adjective scales, for instance,

---

* *Psychological Bulletin,* Vol. 76, No. 2 (1971), pp. 128–48.

This review was prepared under Contract N00014-67-A-0103-0012 with the Office of Naval Research and the University of Washington, Seattle (Fred E. Fiedler, Principal Investigator). Research was supported in part by Contract N00014-67-A-0103-0013 with the Advanced Research Projects Agency of the Office of Naval Research.

† University of Washington, Department of Psychology.

I am indebted to my colleagues, Anthony Biglan, Uriel Foa, Terence R. Mitchell, and Gerald Oncken for their invaluable criticisms and suggestions for the successive manuscripts.

friendly	8	7	6	5	4	3	2	1	unfriendly
cooperative	8	7	6	5	4	3	2	1	uncooperative

As a rule, 16 to 24 items have been used in LPC scales. The LPC score is obtained by summing the item values, giving a value of 8 to the favorable pole of each scale. Thus, a high score indicates that the subject has described his least preferred co-worker in relatively favorable terms, that is, with an average item value in the neighborhood of 5 on the 8-point scale. A low score means that the least preferred co-worker is described in a very negative, rejecting manner, that is, an LPC score of about 2 (Fiedler, 1967a, p. 43). It should also be noted that the low LPC person describes his least preferred co-worker in a uniformly, hence undifferentiated or stereotyped manner as "all bad." The high LPC person's description has a considerably greater item variance (a standard deviation of 1.43 for the high versus .43 for the low LPC person).

The score has been difficult to interpret. While labels of relationship-oriented versus task-oriented have been given to high versus low LPC persons, the terms are somewhat misleading. First, only in situations which are unfavorable (that is, stressful, anxiety arousing, giving the leader little control) do we find leader behaviors which correspond to these terms (Fiedler, 1967a). Second, Mitchell (1970) has found evidence that high LPC leaders tend to be cognitively more complex in their thinking about groups, while low LPC leaders tend to give more stereotyped cognitively simple responses. Similar results (i.e., a correlation of .35) have been reported by Schroder and his co-workers (H. Schroder, personal communication, 1969).

Thus, the LPC score must be seen as a measure which at least in part reflects the cognitive complexity of the individual and which in part reflects the motivational system that evokes relationship-oriented and task-oriented behaviors from high versus low LPC persons in situations which are unfavorable for them as leaders.

Situational Favorableness. The variable that moderates the relationship between LPC and group performance is the situational favorableness dimension. It is conceptually defined as the degree to which the situation itself provides the leader with potential power and influence over the group's behavior. Situational favorableness appears to be quite important in affecting a wide range of group phenomena, as well as interpersonal behaviors. It seems likely that this dimension may have far-reaching significance in other personality research, as well as in social psychological investigations.

Situational favorableness has been operationalized in a number of ways which are discussed later. The original work on the contingency model presented one method based on three component dimensions that affect the degree to which the situation provides the leader with potential power and influence. These are leader-member relations, task structure, and position power. The hypothesis was that *(a)* it is "easier" to be a leader of a group that respects and accepts its leader, or in which the leader feels accepted, than in a group that distrusts and rejects its leader. Likewise *(b)*, it is considered easier to be a leader of a group that has a highly structured, clearly outlined task than of a group that has a vague, unstructured, nebulous task; *(c)* it is easier to be a leader when the position is vested with power (when the leader has the power to hire and fire, promote and transfer, give raises or lower salaries) than it is to be a leader who enjoys little or no power over his members: It is easier to be a general manager than the chairman of a volunteer group.

Leader-member relations were considered to be the most important of these situational factors, and subsequent studies have supported this supposition (Fishbein, Landy, & Hatch, 1969; Mitchell, 1969). Detailed instructions for obtaining measures of leader-member relations, task structure, and position power have been described. Leader-member relations can be measured by means of sociometric preference ratings or by a group atmosphere scale which is similar in form and content to LPC, but asks the subject to rate his group as a whole. Scales for rating task structure and position power are described in Fiedler (1967a, pp. 24, 28, 269, 281–291).

We could then classify group situations by means of the three dimensions. For this purpose, all groups were classified as falling above or below the median on each dimension. This led to an eight-celled classification system which can be depicted as an eight-celled cube (Figure 1). Each of the eight cells or "octants" can be scaled in terms of how much power and influence a leader might have in such a situation. Obviously, a liked and accepted leader who has a clear-cut task as well as power over the fate of his members (Octant I) will have a very favorable situation. Conversely, a distrusted chairman of a volunteer group with a vague problem-solving or

FIGURE 1 A MODEL FOR THE CLASSIFICATION OF GROUP TASK SITUATIONS

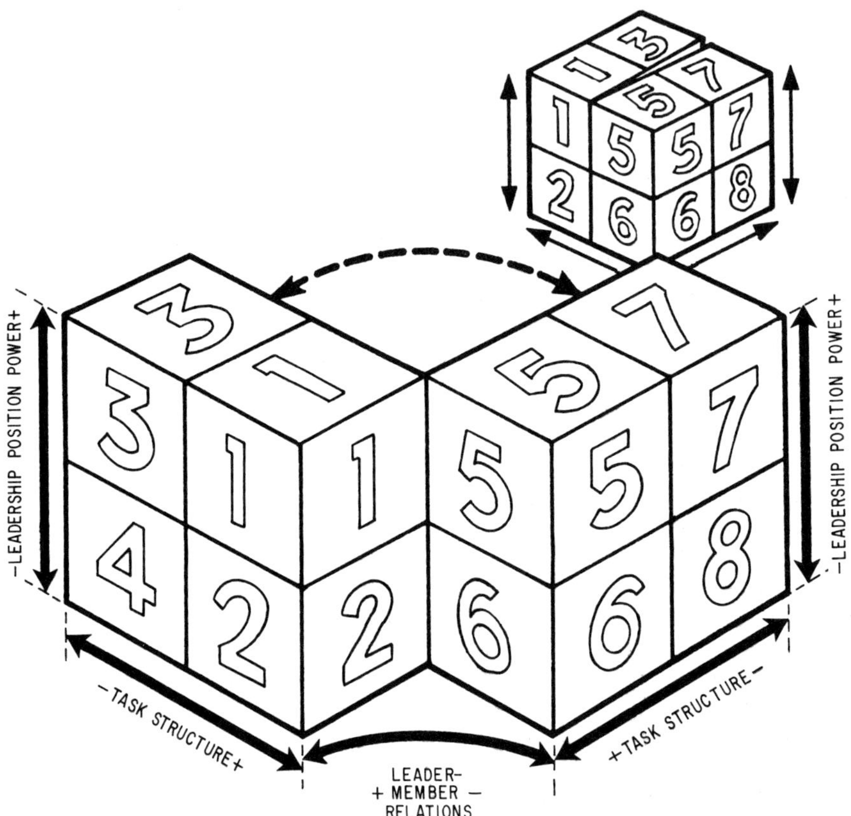

Reproduced with permission from *The Harvard Business Review,* September-October 1965, p. 117.

policy-making task (Octant VIII) will be in a very unfavorable situation to exert power. Other octants fall between these two extremes.

Leadership Effectiveness. The performance of the leader is here defined in terms of the major assignment of the group; that is, the leader's effectiveness is measured on the basis of the group's performance of its major assigned task. While such other aspects of group behavior as morale, member satisfaction, or personal growth might be important concomitants of group effectiveness, they are here not considered to be the primary criterion, but rather contributors to performance. In other words, we evaluate the performance of an orchestra conductor not by his ability as a musicologist or the happiness of his musicians, but by how well his orchestra plays. Whether happy musicians play better than unhappy musicians, or whether the man who is a great musicologist is a better conductor is an important research question in its own right. The major question asked here is the relationship of leadership style (specifically LPC) and group or organizational effectiveness.

Previous Results

Interacting groups from 15 studies, antedating 1963, were classified according to their situational favorableness, and the correlation between leader LPC and performance was then computed for each set of grgups. The correlations between the leader's LPC score and the group's effectiveness measures, when plotted against situational favorableness, generated a bow-shaped distribution indicating that the low LPC leaders performed more effectively than high LPC leaders in very favorable and very unfavorable situations; high LPC leaders performed more effectively in situations intermediate in favorableness (see Figure 2).

We here review the validation evidence that has accumulated since publication of the model in 1964. Before specifically reporting any of the studies, it should be stressed that the group classification system was viewed "as a very convenient starting point for presenting the empirical results which we have obtained in our research on interacting groups [Fiedler, 1967a, p. 34]." Improved methods for mea-

FIGURE 2 CORRELATIONS BETWEEN LEADERSHIP, LPC SCALES, AND GROUP EFFECTIVENESS PLOTTED FOR EACH CELL OR OCTANT OF THE SITUATIONAL FAVORABLENESS DIMENSION FOR STUDIES OF INTERACTING GROUPS CONDUCTED PRIOR TO 1963

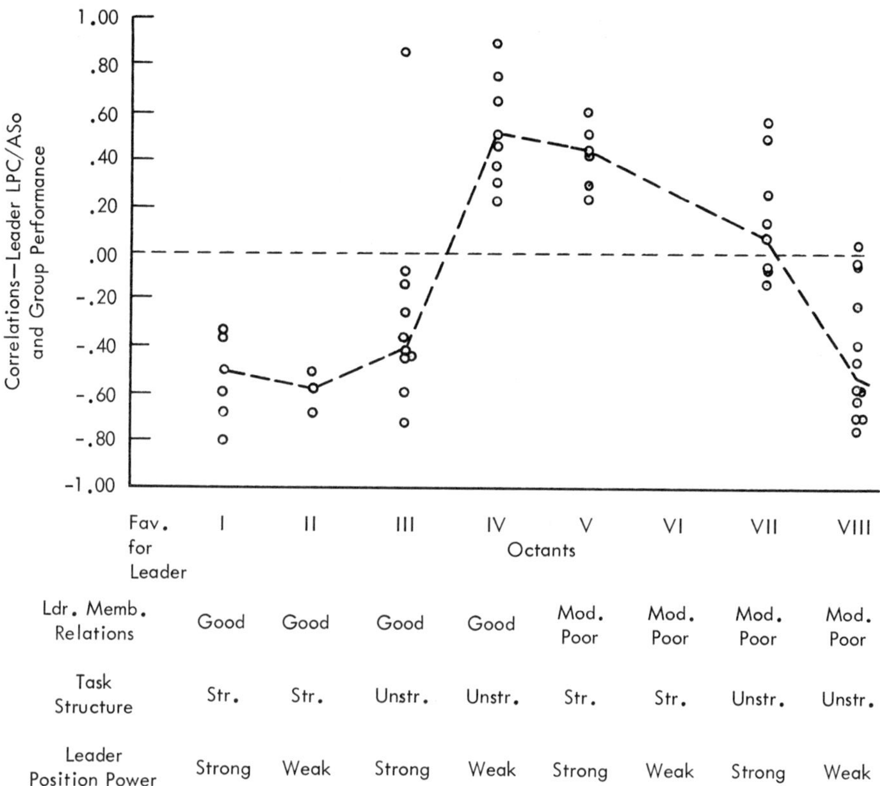

suring situational favorableness were expected to be developed in time. The three component dimensions did, however, turn out to be a very convenient method for testing the model since operationalized measures were available.

VALIDATION EVIDENCE OF THE CONTINGENCY MODEL

Classification of Studies

A number of studies designed to test the model have been conducted by various independent investigators as well as by the writer and his associates. Some of these investigators, by design, and others, by oversight, have not followed the methodology originally described. Different operationalizations of situational favorableness were used in some studies, while others extended the model to coacting groups (e.g., Hill, 1969; Hunt, 1967), and some used leadership style measures unrelated to LPC (Shaw & Blum, 1966). These differences in methodology and divergencies from the model are, of course, quite appropriate and desirable. However, studies that do not conform to the explicit methodology of the earlier work cannot be used as exact tests of the model.

This divergence in method presents difficulties only where the investigator and this reviewer disagree on the appropriateness of a study for testing the contingency model, or where the methodology is inadequate to test the model. This problem has here been handled as follows:

1. Four independent judges carefully read the definition of interacting and coacting groups, and the definitions of the various sub-dimensions of the situational favorableness dimension presented by Fiedler (1967a).

2. The judges were then given all studies that purported to test the contingency model. They were asked to read the entire methodology section in the case of shorter investigations, and relevant sections of very extensive studies. They were not asked to read the results. Using the scales described by Fiedler (1967a) the judges classified each study in terms of the group situation into which it should be classified.

3. Groups were included among the validation studies of interacting groups if three of the four judges could agree that the groups were interacting,

and if at least three of the judges agreed into which octant the groups should be classified.

Because of the nature of the pre-1963 research on which the original analysis was based, all groups in Octant I, II, and V were from field studies of natural groups and organizations, and all but one set of groups in Octants III, IV, VII, and VIII were from laboratory experiments using ad hoc groups. It is very difficult to reproduce certain effects commonly found in natural groups under experimental conditions. These include, for example, high leader position power, high stress, and very poor leader-member relations. For this reason, the model can be more meaningfully evaluated as a predictor if natural groups and ad hoc groups in laboratory experiments are considered separately, as well as together.

Field Studies

The Hunt Studies. The first field study to test the contingency model was conducted by Hunt (1967) in three different organizations, namely, a large physical science research laboratory, a chain of supermarkets, and a heavy machinery plant. In each case Hunt obtained group atmosphere scores from managers and foremen, and ratings of position power and task structure from management personnel at higher levels in the hierarchy. Higher management of the research laboratory and in the manufacturing plant also provided performance ratings, while objective criteria based on an index of sales per employee man-hour was derived for managers of meat markets.

The position power of all managers and foremen was judged to be high. Task structure was rated to be high for developmental research and for meat market managers, and low for managers of basic research groups and for general foremen of the heavy machinery plant. The correlations obtained for each of these groups, by octant, are presented in Table 1. (Hunt's results on coacting groups are presented in a later section.)

Electronics Firm. A second set of real-life groups was investigated by Hill (1969). The research was conducted in a large electronics firm. The study dealt with supervisors of engineering teams and with instructors of assembly groups. Assembly-line instructors were rated by Hill's judges as having structured tasks and low position power, while supervisors of engineering groups were rated as having unstructured tasks and high position power. Leader-member relations were measured by supervisors' group atmosphere scores, trichotomized, with the upper third considered to have good leader-member relations, and the lower third considered to have poor leader-member relations.

The correlation for nine assembly instructors' teams with high group atmosphere (Octant II) was −.10, and for the nine teams with low group atmosphere (Octant IV), −.24. The correlation between eight engineering supervisors' LPC and performance for high group atmosphere (Octant III) was −.29, and for eight supervisors with low group atmosphere groups (Octant VII), it was .62.

Public Health Teams: I. Fiedler, O'Brien, and Ilgen (1969) conducted a study of public health volunteers in Honduras during the summer of 1966. The sample consisted of 225 teenagers who were assigned to teams in Honduras to operate public health clinics and to perform community development work in outlying towns and villages. Formal leaders were not assigned. The teams informal leaders were identified at the end of the volunteer period on the basis of sociometric questionnaire responses. The task of these groups, namely, to run a public health clinic and, time permitting, to perform some community development work, was fairly well-specified by the sponsoring organization. Problems arose when the villagers and the town officials failed to cooperate and when the population was unsupportive or hostile. Under these conditions the volunteers experienced considerable stress, often verbalized as "feeling at a loss about what to do." Under these stressful conditions, the team members were more or less on their own in trying to cope with the problems they encountered. All judges who eval-

TABLE 1 TEST OF THE CONTINGENCY MODEL IN HUNT'S STUDIES

	Octants			
Sample	*I*	*III*	*V*	*VII*
Research chemists: basic research		.60 (6)		.30 (5)
Research chemists: development	−.67 (7)			
Meat markets	−.51 (10)		.21 (11)	
General foremen: heavy manufacturing		−.80 (5)		−.30 (5)

Note.—Numbers in parentheses indicate number of cases.

TABLE 2 CORRELATIONS BETWEEN LEADER LPC SCORES AND RATES: TEAM PERFORMANCE IN TWO STUDIES (1966, 1968) OF PUBLIC HEALTH VOLUNTEER TEAMS

Situation				*1966*		*1968*		
Group Atmosphere	*Task Structure*	*Position Power*	*Octant*	*Correlation*	*n*	*Correlation*	*n*	*Median*
High	High	Low	II	−.21	13	−.46	7	−.33
High	Low	Low	IV	.00	15	.47	9	.23
Low	High	Low	VI	.67*	9	−.45	8	.11
Low	Low	Low	VIII	−.51	12	−.14	7	−.32

* $p < .05$.

uated the study agreed that the position power of the leader was low, and three of four judges considered the task to be relatively structured in the stress-free condition, but unstructured in the situation in which village support was absent.

The informal leader's group atmosphere scores were used to measure the leader-member relations. Groups operating in cooperative or favorable villages could then be classified as falling into Octants II or VI, depending on the leader's group atmosphere score; groups in uncooperative, unfavorable villages could be classified as falling into Octants IV or VIII, again dependicg on the leader's group atmosphere scores.

Public Health Teams: II. A second study, practically identical in procedure, was conducted in the same organization (but with different volunteers) 2 years later by O'Brien, Fiedler, and Hewett.[1] One major difference in training was that most volunteers had received a culture training program developed for use of the project. This program made the situation somewhat more favorable since it provided some information that enabled the volunteers to understand and to communicate more effectively with their host nationals. A study of the effects of this program on adjustment and performance, conducted in 1967, provided evidence that individuals who had received "culture assimilator" training had adjusted and performed more effectively abroad than those who had not.

The correlations between leader LPC and performance ratings of the headquarters staffs are presented in Table 2 for both studies. The median correlations for these groups support the model (correlations for Octant VI were not predicted). The patterns of the 1966 and 1968 correlations both form a bow-shaped pattern, but the positive correlation was found in Octant VI in the 1966 group, but in Octant IV in the 1968 group.

[1] G. E., O'Brien, F. E. Fiedler, and T. Hewett, The effects of programmed culture training upon the performance of volunteer medical teams in Central America. Urbana, Ill.: Group Effectiveness Research Laboratory, University of Illinois, 1969.

Unclassifiable Field Studies

A number of other studies designed to test the contingency model cannot be included in the present analysis because the judges rating the published research could not agree on the classification of the groups. Thus, a major study by Butterfield (1968) attempted to compare five theories of leadership, namely, four theories developed at the University of Michigan and the contingency model. The study was conducted in an administrative unit of a federal agency. The sample of groups was not clearly described. References to groups indicated, however, that "the various work units were engaged in rather different functions ranging from delivering mail to performing financial audits . . . [p. 61]," and measures of effectiveness such as "typed papers, delivered mail, dispatched automobiles, coding systems . . . [Appendix B]." These descriptions led all four judges to the conclusion that a number of groups must have been coacting (e.g., messenger services, typing pools, motor pool dispatchers, etc.). Equally important, however, Butterfield's measure of leader-member relations consisted of only two questionnaire items, one of which dealt with how much annoyance an employee feels with the manager. The important leader-member relations dimension was, therefore, not adequately represented in Butterfield's study.

A field study by Kretzschmar and Luecke (1969) dealt with 67 managers in business administrations of four industrial companies in Germany. In contrast to other studies, all measures of task structure, leader-members relations, and position power were based on supervisors' own ratings. In addition, supervisors also rated their own effectiveness. Our studies have shown that leaders' evaluations of their own performance typically do not correlate with objective measures, and these methodological differences made it impossible to compare this study with others in the group.

The field studies which can be used to test the contingency model are, then, those by Hunt (1967), by Hill (1969), by Fiedler et al. (1969), and by

TABLE 3 CORRELATIONS BETWEEN LEADER LPC SCORES AND GROUP PERFORMANCE SCORES OBTAINED IN STRUCTURED AND UNSTRUCTURED TASKS OF THE BELGIAN NAVY STUDY

Homogeneous Groups						Heterocultural Groups					
Octant	GA	TS	PP	Correlations*		Octant	GA	TS	PP	Correlations*	
I	+	+	+	−.72	−.77	IX	+	+	+	.03	.77
II	+	+	−	.37	.50	X	+	+	−	.77	−.53
III	+	−	+	−.16	−.54	XI	+	−	+	.20	−.26
IV	+	−	−	.08	.13	XII	+	−	−	−.89	.70
V	−	+	+	.16	.03	XIII	−	+	+	.08	−.19
VI	−	+	−	.07	.14	XIV	−	+	−	.53	−.90
VII	−	−	+	.26	−.27	XV	−	−	−	−.37	.08
VIII	−	−	−	−.37	.60	XVI	−	−	−	−.36	−.60

Note.—GA = group atmosphere, TS = task structure, PP = position power.
* Two correlations were obtained per cell corresponding to the order of presentation ($n = 6$).

O'Brien et al. (see Footnote 1). These results are now discussed, along with those obtained in laboratory studies.

Laboratory and Field Experiments

The contingency model was based on field studies in Octants I, II, and V, and on controlled experiments in Octants III, IV, VII, and VIII. Since that time a number of field and laboratory experiments have attempted to test the predictions of the model in all octants.

The Belgian Navy Study. This was a large field experiment conducted in cooperation with the Belgian naval forces. The study involved 96 three-man teams which were experimentally assembled so that 48 teams would be culturally homogeneous (all French or all Dutch speaking) and 48 teams were heterogeneous (the leader from one language sector and the members from the other). In 48 teams the leader was a petty officer who had high position power, while the other 48 teams were headed by a recruit who had low position power. The groups were given four different tasks, one of which was coacting (teaching men to assemble an automatic pistol). The coacting task and one of the two structured tasks could not be reliably scored, and only one structured and one unstructured task were, therefore, suitable for more intensive analysis.[2] Leader-member relations were assessed on the basis of group climate scores obtained from leaders after each of the task sessions.

Since the contingency model, presented in 1964, was based on culturally homogeneous groups, that is, groups in which all members had the same mother tongue, only these will be used for validation purposes at this time. Table 3 presents the correlations between leader LPC scores and group performance scores. Two correlation coefficients, each with $n = 6$, were computed since the tasks were presented in counterbalanced order. As can be seen, the findings do not support the contingency model which postulates a curvilinear relationship.

A post facto analysis of the data suggested that the laboratory manipulations had not been adequate for the purpose of creating a sufficiently unfavorable situation for the leader. The homogeneous groups probably did not develop really poor leader-member relations, and there was also a question whether the supposedly structured task (requiring the group to find the shortest route for a ship which had to cover 12 ports) was sufficiently structured. The task, basically a topological puzzle, requires problem solving, and subsequent studies have shown this type task to be intermediate in structure. A bow-shaped relationship similar to that of the contingency model did emerge when heterocultural groups were included in the analysis to intensify the situational difficulty for the leader. Heterocultural groups are, of course, much more difficult to handle, and leaders reported significantly higher anxiety and greater tension in heterogenous groups than in homogeneous groups. This effect was, however, not predicted.

The Japanese Student Study. Shima (1968) tested the contingency model in Japan, using two Guilford[3] tests, namely, the Unusual Uses Test considered to be moderately structured, and an "integration" task which required groups to invent a story using 10 unrelated words. All Subjects were high school students, and these were assembled into 32 groups. The leaders were elected by the group members, and the group's relations with the leaders were,

[2] The Graen et al. review (1970) included all three interacting tasks in the analysis of evidential results of the contingency model. However, it was clearly pointed out by the present writer (1967a, p. 161) that the first structured task was methodologically inadequate: 9 groups obtained perfect scores and 62 groups made a total of 189 erroes by not following instructions. The first task was, therefore, quite unsatisfactory and could not very well have yielded anything but random results.

[3] J. P. Guilford, R. M. Berger, and P. R. Christiansen, A factor analytic study of planning I: Hypothesis and description of tests. Los Angeles, Calif.: Psychological Laboratory, University of Southern California, 1954.

therefore, assumed to be good. However, the judges rating this study disagreed with Shima's classification of position power. Since the leader was elected and, therefore, had obtained his position from his fellow students, and since the groups were ad hoc, the judges rated position power in this study as being low. Based on the assumption that leader position power was low, the groups would be classified as falling into Octants II and IV. The corresponding correlations were $-.26$ ($n = 16$) and .71 ($n = 16$, $p < .05$), thus supporting the model.

Church Leadership Groups. Mitchell (1969) conducted a small study of group performance as part of a leadership training workshop to determine the relationship between cognitive complexity and LPC. The participants were members of Unitarian churches who attended a leadership workshop. Each of the groups performed two of four tasks, one structured, and one unstructured. The tasks consisted of finding the shortest route for *(a)* a school bus and *(b)* a cross-country road race. The two unstructured tasks were to write a position paper on the church's stand on *(c)* legalizing abortion and *(d)* a "Black Caucus" within the Unitarian-Universalist church. Leader position power was low.

Mitchell (1969) originally computed correlations for groups with poor as well as with good leader-member relations, and these correlations were included in the Graen et al. (1970) critique. The Mitchell study was not, however, designed as a test of the model, and an analysis of the data showed that only 2 of the 64 group sessions in this study had group atmosphere scores below 55, a score which is roughly at the median of group atmosphere scores for similar studies. As pointed out before, a finding of this type is neither unusual nor unexpected in ad hoc groups. Most researchers, testing the model, have, therefore, tried to increase the difference between groups with high and low group atmosphere scores by using only the upper and lower thirds of the distribution, whenever this was possible. In light of the high group atmosphere scores in the Mitchell study, all groups were classified as falling into Octants II and IV depending upon task structure. The resulting rank-order correlations for Octant II were .24 and .17 ($n = 16$), and for Octant IV, .43 and .38 ($n = 16$).

Executive Development Workshop. An almost identical study was conducted by Fiedler as part of an executive development program. Here again, all but one of the group atmosphere scores were above the usual cutting score, and all groups were classified as having high group atmosphere. The groups were given a relatively structured task and an unstructured task (i.e., routing a truck convoy and writing a recruiting statement inviting college students to become junior executives). All leaders were rated as having low position power, and thus all groups fell into Octants II and IV. The correlations were .34 and .51 for the structured and unstructured tasks, respectively ($ns = 11$). (See also the section reviewing results on groups in training which might apply to the church leadership and the executive development workshop studies.)

West Point Cadets. Skrzypek[4] recently completed a study of 32 four-man groups composed of cadets at West Point. Leaders were chosen from among a pool of 400 men whose LPC scores fell either one standard deviation above or below the mean. Members were assigned at random. Unlike other laboratory studies, which used postsession questionnaires, leader-member relations in this study were determined a priori on the basis of previously obtained sociometric ratings that identified well-accepted and not-accepted leaders among the cadets. Position power was varied by informing the group that the leader in the high positon power would be evaluating each of his group members at the conclusion of the tasks and that these evaluations would become part of the individual's leadership score (a very important aspect of West Point's system). The leaders in the low position power were instructed to act as chairmen, and the group was told that the members as a group would be evaluated on their performance.

Each group performed one structured task and one unstructured task in counterbalanced order. The structured task consisted of drawing a plan for barracks and a military-post area to scale. The unstructured task required the groups to design a program which would educate enlisted men in overseas assignments on world politics and maintain their interest throughout their tour.

The results were as follows for each of the eight octants: Octant I, -43; Octant II, $-.32$; Octant III, .10; Octant IV, .35; Octant V, .28; Octant VI, 13; Octant VII, .08; Octant VIII, $-.33$. Thus, while none of the correlations reached the .05 level of significance, all but the correlation for Octant III were in the predicted direction.

Nonclassifiable Studies.

Student Nurses. A study by Reilly[5] was excluded because the judges could not agree with one another or with the investigator on the position power of the

[4] G. J. Skrzypek, The relationship of leadership style to task structure, position power, and leader-member relations. West Point, N.Y.: United States Military Academy, 1969.

[5] A. J. Reilly, The effects of different leadership styles on group performance: A field experiment. Ames, Ia.: Industrial Relations Center, Iowa State University, 1968.

leaders. Reilly studied groups composed of nurses who were given successively structured and unstructured discussion problems. Whether the leader actually had high position power was questioned because the leader was a fellow student, and her additional responsibilities were limited: They consisted of making certain arrangements for the groups as well as assigning 20% of the grade each student would obtain. This study is discussed in a later section, since it may also be classified as a training study.

Experimental Change of Position Power. A second nonclassifiable study was conducted by Nealey and Shiflett (S. Nealey, personal communication, 1969) who attempted experimentally to induce a change of situational favorableness from Octant III to Octant IV and vice versa. The groups were assembled on the basis of LPC and intelligence scores. The experimental manipulation, changing the groups, did not succeed although the study prior to the experimental manipulation yielded relations between LPC and group performance.

Here again, the judges did not agree on whether the leader's position was, in fact, strong, since in the appropriate experimental condition the leader's position power was established basically by instructing the leader to role play a person with a powerful or weak position power.

Graen, Orris, and Alvares (1971) described two laboratory experiments which were specifically designed to test the contingency model. These studies also constituted the main basis for a recent article in this journal by Graen et al. (1970), which questioned the adequacy of the model.

Graen et al. (1971) used 78 and 96 male college students randomly assembled into 52 and 64 three-man groups, respectively. Each group worked on two tasks. The students were paid for their participation, and one person in each three-man group was chosen at random to serve as the leader during the first task. Another member of the same group served as leader during the second task.

Each of the groups was given one structured and one unstructured task in counterbalanced order. Using an 8-point scale for assessing task structure (Fiedler, 1967a, p. 25ff) Graen et al. (1971) chose two structured and two unstructured tasks. Position power was varied by giving the leaders of one set of groups

> superior formal status relative to the members . . . special information about the task, and . . . the highest decision-making authority and responsibility. In the weak leader condition, the leader role was one of discussion leader without special information and with decision-making authority and responsibility close to that of the members. Each group worked on both tasks under only one of the two power conditions. The task sequence was randomized within power conditions [Graen et al., 1971, p. 198].

Group atmosphere scores were obtained after each task session, and the groups were divided into those whose group atmosphere scores had fallen above and below the median for the entire set. Groups were then assigned to the appropriate cell of the contingency model by dichotomizing the three situational variables of position power, task structure, and group atmosphere. The results of the two experiments are given in Table 4.

Graen and his associates claim that their two studies followed as closely as possible the prescriptions of the contingency model and research methodology used in its development. Because their results were nonsignificant, the authors concluded that their studies, therefore, "cast doubt on the plausibility of the contingency model [Graen et al., 1971, p. 201]."

Nonsignificant results obviously can occur for any number of reasons, including inadequate experimental design. A study that attacks a theory, therefore, must not only be methodologically sound (especially if it does not support an alternative hypothesis), but it must also guard against the possibility of obtaining nonsignificant and randomly distributed data because of inappropriate or marginal experimental manipulations.

A methodological critique in the *Journal of Applied Psychology* (Fiedler, 1971) pointed to various weaknesses in the manipulation of three independent variables in the Graen et al. (1971) experimental design. The manipulations were inadequate and make the studies inappropriate for inclusion in the present analysis. A summary of the inadequacies is presented below. The discussion is based on data in the original Graen et al. (1971) paper as well as sub-

TABLE 4 CORRELATIONS BETWEEN LEADER LPC AND PERFORMANCE IN THE GRAEN ET AL. STUDIES

	Octant							
Experiment	*I*	*II*	*III*	*IV*	*V*	*VI*	*VII*	*VIII*
1.	.47*	−.41	.46*	.33	.25	−.39	.43	−.33
2.	−.13	.18*	.02*	−.08*	−.52*	−.43	.45	.44*

* Correlations in a direction counter to the hypothesis of the model.

sequent data included in a rejoinder to the methodological critique of their studies.

1. *Task Structure.* Task structure was assessed by means of a rating scale with scores ranging from a maximum of 8.0 to a minimum of 1.0 (Fiedler, 1967a). The average task structure scores of the studies on which the original contingency model paper was based averaged 7.39 for the structured and 3.15 for the unstructured tasks. In contrast, the scores in the Graen et al. (1971) studies were 5.85 and 5.45 for the two structured tasks, and 3.69 and 3.60 for the two unstructured tasks. The scores for the structured task were, therefore, less than 1 scale point above the cutting score of 5.0, and the differences between structured and unstructured tasks were only 2.17 and 1.85 scale points. This clearly represents a very weak manipulation as compared with the differences of 4.24 in the original tasks.

While it may be argued that the task structure scores in some of the original studies were similar to those in the Graen et al. studies, an experiment which seeks to disconfirm a theory should not use marginal manipulations in testing the null hypothesis.

2. *Position Power.* Graen et al. (1971) manipulated this variable by giving the randomly chosen leader "superior formal status" and "special information about the task," and delegating to him "the highest decision-making authority and responsibility." This was done here by talking directly to the leader in the presence of the members, presenting written task instructions to the leader only, "maintaining body orientation and eye contact with the leader," and giving an official timing device to the leader. In the weak position power condition, the formal status of the leader was not reinforced, verbal instructions were addressed to the group, written instructions were given to no one in particular, and the timing device was placed in the center of the table.

A number of reasons suggest that this power manipulation is inadequate. First of all, it is difficult to believe that the particular experimenter behaviors—like looking the leader in the eye, and giving the leader of an ad hoc group a timing device and written instructions—are sufficiently powerful manipulations to do all the things the authors expected to accomplish. Position power is conceptualized as providing the leader with some real power to give rewards and sanctions. In other words, the leader must have some fate control over his members. It is very difficult to give high position power to a leader in any laboratory situation. Where this was done successfully, it was usually accomplished by using individuals who had some formal position power outside the laboratory. Thus, the Belgian Navy study (Fiedler, 1966) compared petty officers with recruit leaders; a study of ROTC cadets by Meuwese and Fiedler (Fiedler, 1967a) and a study of West Point cadets by Skrzpek (see Footnote 4) used cadet officers who held higher rank than their members. Moreover, Graen et al. (1971) demoted the leader appointed for the first task session to member status in the second session and made another member of the same group the leader in the second session. This procedure is likely to dilute the formal leadership power.

Graen et al. (1971) subsequently reported data on perceived leader influence in support of their claim that the position power manipulation actually had been effective. Cell means of perceived influence ratings are reported in Table 5.

Thus, the difference in means over octants in Experiment 2 was only .16. A t test comparing the perceived influence ratings in the strong and weak position power conditions was 1.746, which is not significant. As can be seen, some of the weak position power octants had means which were higher than some of the supposedly high position power octants. Specifically, two of the "weak" octants had mean scores of 5.38, while two of the "strong" octants in the first experiment had mean scores of only 5.14. The position power manipulation in Experiment 2 appears, therefore, not to have been effective.

3. *Distribution of LPC Scores.* Leaders were as-

TABLE 5 CELL MEANS OF PERCEIVED INFLUENCE RATINGS IN GRAEN ET AL. STUDY

Condition	*Octant*				X
	Experiment 1				
Strong position power	5.83	6.17	5.14	5.14	5.57
Weak position power	4.33	4.83	3.24	4.86	4.32
M_{diff}					1.25
	Experiment 2				
Strong position power	5.75	5.63	6.13	3.50	5.29
Weak position power	5.38	5.00	5.38	4.75	5.13
M_{diff}					.16

signed at random and LPC scores were obtained after the three-man groups had been assembled. This procedure does not properly assure that leader LPC scores within each octant will have similar means and distributions. It is obvious that a meaningful test of the contingency model cannot be obtained if, for example, all groups within one octant have leaders with high LPC scores, while all groups in another octant have leaders with very low scores. An appropriate test is an analysis of variance to determine whether the means of various octants are reasonably similar; if so, the *F* test will be nonsignificant.

Data provided by Graen et al. (1971) show that the means of LPC scores within the various octants ranged from 84.7 to 42.7 in the first experiment and from 77.3 to 52.9 in the second experiment. A one-way analysis of variance was performed for each study with the eight octants as cells in the design. The *F* ratio for the second study was not significant (1.17), indicating that the various octants did not differ in mean LPC. The F ratio for the first study was, however, 3.10, which is significant at the .01 level and indicates that the distribution of leader LPC scores differed markedly from octant to octant. In other words, some octants, (e.g., Octant IV) contained few, if any, low LPC leaders, while others (e.g., Octant V) contained few, if any, high LPC leaders.

Since the position power manipulation in addition to the weak task structure manipulations in Experiment 2 and the LPC score distributions in Experiment 1 were inadequate for testing the contingency model, neither experiment was included in the validation analysis.

Summary of Results

Table 6, which summarizes all correlations from acceptable studies, shows that the median correlations for six of the seven octants are in the predicted direction (Octant VI was not predicted). Of these, the joint probabilities of the correlations in Octants I, III, and IV are significant below the .05 level. Also, 34 of the 45 correlations are in the predicted direction, a finding significant at the .01 level by binomial test. It should be noted that the number of correlations in the predicted direction would be significant at the .01 level by binomial test even if we included the two Graen et al. (1970, 1971) experiments. These results permit the conclusion that we are not dealing with random effects: Group performance appears to be contingent upon leadership style and situational favorableness.

On the other hand, 5 of the 10 correlations obtained in Octant II are in the positive rather than in the negative direction. These counter-expectational positive correlations, although found only in this octant, throw considerable doubt on the overall generality of the relationship predicted in the Fiedler

TABLE 6 SUMMARY OF FIELD AND LABORATORY STUDIES TESTING THE CONTINGENCY MODEL

Study	Octants I	II	III	IV	V	VI	VII	VIII
Field Studies								
Hunt (1967)	−.64		−.80		.21		.30	
	−.51		.60				−.30	
Hill (1969)*		−.10	−.29			−.24	.62	
Fiedler et al. (1969)		−.21		.00		.67†		−.51
O'Brien et al. (1969)		−.46		.47		−.45		.14
Laboratory Experiments								
Belgian Navy	−.72	.37	−.16	.08	.16	.07	.26	−.37
	−.77	.50	−.54	.13	.03	.14	−.27	.60
Shima (1968)*		−.26		.71†				
Mitchell (1969)		.24		.43				
		.17		.38				
Fiedler exec.		.34		.51				
Skrzypek*	−.43	−.32	.10	.35	.28	.13	.08	−.33
Median								
All studies	−.64	.17	−.22	.38	.22	.10	.26	−.35
Field studies	−.57	−.21	−.29	.23	.21	−.24	.30	−.33
Laboratory experiments	−.72	.24	−.16	.38	.16	.13	.08	−.33
Median correlations of Fiedler's original studies (1964)	−.52	−.58	−.33	.47	.42		.05	−.43

Note.—Number of correlations in the expected direction (exclusive of Octant VI, for which no prediction had been made) = 34; number of correlations opposite to expected direction = 11; *p* by binomial test = .01.

* Studies not conducted by the writer or his associates.

† $p < .05$.

1964 paper. It is, therefore, essential that we examine the relations in greater detail.

It will be recalled that in the 1964 study, data for Octants I, II, and V came from field studies, while the data for Octants III, IV, VII, and VIII came, with but one exception, from laboratory studies. Field and laboratory results should, therefore, be examined separately.

Field Studies. The median correlations for field studies are quite similar to those predicted in the Fiedler 1964 paper. All of the medians are in the predicted direction, and 13 of the 15 predicted correlations are in the expected direction, which is significant at the .05 level. The curve, based on relatively few studies, is not as regular as that obtained in 1964. Octant VI was not predicted. The predicted median correlation of .05 in Octant VII which we based on 12 correlations in the 1964 study, now is shown with a median correlation of .30, based on three correlation coefficients. Overall, considering the small number of studies and the small number of cases within each of these studies, the results seem rather remarkably consistent with the 1964 data, suggesting that the model is valid for the prediction of leadership performance under field conditions.

Experiments and Laboratory Studies. Only the Belgian Navy, the West Point, and Graen et al. (1971) studies provided data for all predicted octants. It is, therefore, hazardous to draw more than tentative conclusions for any octants but II and IV for which sufficient data are available. Data for Octants I and IV tended to support the prediction of the contingency model, while they did so only directionally in Octants III, V, VII, and VIII. The data clearly indicate that the model does not adequately predict leadership performance in Octant II of laboratory studies. On the other hand, 22 of the 29 predicted correlation coefficients were in the expected direction, which is significant at the .01 level for binomial tests.

A number of possible explanations for the nonpredicted results suggest themselves. The most parsimonious and obvious of these might simply be that it is difficult to manipulate leadership variables in laboratory experiments, and some important aspects of real-life situations do not permit themselves to be readily built into the laboratory.

EXTENSIONS OF THE CONTINGENCY MODEL

A number of studies have tested the more general hypothesis that the situational favorableness affects the relationship between leadership style and performance. Some of these studies tested groups in situations ranging from the very favorable to the very unfavorable; other studies considered groups falling on only two points on the situational favorableness continuum. The various group situations were categorized as being favorable, intermediate, or unfavorable situations by two or more judges. However, since the degree of situational favorableness in some of these investigations was not operationally specified in advance, the rejection of the null hypotheses becomes correspondingly more hazardous in these cases. This is especially so in studies in which the statistical relations do not reach the commonly accepted level of significance. On the other hand, it is difficult to obtain a large sample of groups or organizations in any one study; and it is essential, therefore, that we consider the cumulative evidence from different investigations.

Experimental Variation in Leadership Behavior. Shaw and Blum (1966) instructed nine leaders to act in a highly controlling and directive manner, while a second set of 9 leaders was told to be permissive and passive. The groups were given three tasks in counterbalanced order, and the tasks varied in degree of structure. Permissive, passive leaders performed more effectively in the two relatively unstructured tasks (roughly Octant IV), the directive leaders, as predicted by the investigators, performed more effectively in the highly structured tasks (roughly Octant II). These results conform to the general expectations of the model.

Objectification of Situational Favorableness by Structural Role Theory. O'Brien (1969) measured situational favorableness objectively by applying methods of structural role theory (Oeser & Harary, 1962, 1964). O'Brien assumed that a situation would be more favorable to the leader the greater the number of paths he had to the task structure. The more readily and directly the leader could influence task performance, the greater his influence and control of task-relevant group behavior.

The structural role theory deals with relations among three elements, namely, persons, positions, and tasks. Relations among the first indicate the interpersonal relationships, relations among the positions indicate authority relations, and relations among the tasks indicate allocations and task sequences. O'Brien assembled groups on the basis of personal compatibility depending upon the members' similarity or dissimilarity in scores on Schutz' FIRO scale (1958). The group task consisted of constructing models from spheres and sticks according to a given pattern. Position and task allocation were manipulated by determining the means by which the leader could interact in the task performance. A coefficient of situational favorableness could then be computed which, in oversimplified form, expressed the leader's paths to the task structure as a ratio of all possible paths. The higher the ratio, the more favorable the leader's position power.

The results of O'Brien's study, based on the correlation between leader LPC and the number of models produced, showed the predicted relationships. For 16 groups with high situational favorableness the correlation was −.08; for 16 groups with intermediate favorableness it was .77 (significant at .01); and for 32 groups with low situational favorableness the correlation was −.13.

Heterocultural American and Indian Groups. Anderson (1966) conducted a laboratory experiment which used graduate students from India as well as from the United States. These groups consisted of one American leader, one American group member, and one Indian group member. The tasks required the groups to negotiate an agreement on hiring practices between an Indian village and an American company, and to compose two different stories based on the same TAT card. Half the leaders had high LPC, and half had low LPC scores. Of these, half were instructed to be as considerate as possible in their leadership behavior, while the other half were told to structure the situation as firmly as possible.

Anderson performed a post hoc analysis that scaled the situations on the basis of favorableness. This scaling suggested that the TAT tasks were more favorable than the hiring problem (which required negotiation) and that the considerate condition would be more favorable than the structuring condition. This ordering of situations was supported by leader responses to questions about their anxiety and tension in each of these conditions.

The correlations for the four tasks in order of favorableness (TAT-considerate. TAT-structuring, negotiation-considerate, negotiation-structuring) were −.50, .21, −.22, and −.12, thus suggesting a curvilinear relationship between LPC-performance correlations and situational favorableness ($ns = 8$).

Chemical Processing Companies. Lawrence and Lorsch (1967) compared the performance of six chemical processing companies, each of which had four subsystems: production, sales, applied research, and basic research. Each subsystem was under the direction of a senior management official, either at the vice-presidential level or immediately below. The structure of these subsystem tasks was rated by a number of judges. Fundamental research was rated as lowest in structure, while production was rated as highest. This reviewer correlated the manager's LPC and rated performance from the Lawrence and Lorsch data. The results follow the expectation that a low LPC manager would perform better on structured tasks, while a high LPC manager would perform better in unstructured situations. The correlations, in order of rated structure, were for production, −.50; sales, −.31; applied research, −.10; and fundamental research, .66. ($ns = 6$).

Since these results were obtained without reference to leader-member relations, they suggest that the leader-member relations dimension might be relatively less important at higher levels of the organization. This seems reasonable since the manager at the third and higher levels usually has very few direct contacts with production workers at the non-supervisory levels, and relatively few contacts with first-line supervisors.

Psychiatric Nursing Organization. Nealey and Blood (1968) investigated the psychiatric nursing service of a large Veterans Administration hospital. LPC scores were obtained from supervisors at the first and second levels of the organization, namely, head nurses in charge of a ward, and "unit supervisors" in charge of one of the hospital's six large units, which are both quite comparable as to structure and function. Performance of wards and of units was judged by management personnel at the level above the head nurse and the unit supervisor, respectively.

The most important difference between the job of the head nurse and that of the unit supervisor for purposes of the present analysis appears to be the structure of her subordinates' tasks. The work of the psychiatric aide is relatively structured since there are fairly specific guidelines available on the management of psychiatric patients and ward personnel. The job of the unit supervisor, or more precisely, the work of the head nurses she supervises, requires considerably more policy and decision making, and it is correspondingly less structured. Nealey and Blood correlated the LPC scores of these nursing supervisors with rated performance. In a very similar study, Nealey and Owen (1970) about 18 months later recomputed these correlations on 25 head nurses, 15 of whom had participated in the first study. The correlations between head-nurse LPC and performance for the first and second studies were −.22 ($n = 21$) and −.50 ($n = 25$, $p < .05$), and for unit supervisors tested in the first study, .79 ($n = 8$, $p < .01$). Thus, as in the Lawrence and Lorsch study, the structure of the supervisory task strongly moderates the direction of the relationship between LPC and organizational performance.

Stress as an Index of Situational Favorableness. A study by Fiedler and Barron (cited in Fiedler, 1967a) investigated the relationship between leader LPC and creative group performance under varying conditions of stress. Fifty-four three-man teams composed of ROTC cadets participated in this study under relatively stress-free conditions, intragroup conflict, and relatively severe external stress. Within each of these stress conditions the groups were divided into those with high, medium, and low leader group-atmosphere scores. The resulting LPC-performance relations were then plotted against stressfulness of the situation and resulted in a bow-shaped curve with low LPC leaders performing better than high LPC leaders in relatively stress-free and stress-conditions, and high LPC leaders performing better in situations of intermediate stress.

Summary of Studies Testing the Contingency Theory. The results presented in this section are, in one respect, quite weak, and in another, quite strong. The investigations do not permit an exact test of a theory since the methodology, the criteria, and the subject populations vary from study to study. At the same time, these studies provide consistent cumulative evidence that the correlation between leadership style and group performance is moderated by the situational favorableness dimension even though this dimension is operationalized in a wide variety of ways. Thus, the Shaw and Blum experiment, the Lawrence and Lorsch investigation, as well as the Nealey and Blood and the Nealey and Owen studies show that the structure of the task is important in determining the direction of the correlation between LPC and group performance. The Fiedler and Barron (Fiedler, 1967a) study used stress as an index of situational favorableness. The O'Brien experiment presented an ingenious new metric of situational favorableness based on structural role theory, and the results of his study yielded relations in the expected direction with one of the correlations highly significant. Finally, the Anderson (1966) experiment, based on post hoc analysis of the data, also yielded data that tended to show an interaction of task and leadership style. Thus, notwithstanding the diversity of the studies, there is clear evidence that identified situational components determine, in part, the type of leadership style that a particular group requires for effective performance.

EXTENSION OF THE MODEL TO COACTING GROUPS

A number of field studies have attempted to investigate the relation of leader LPC scores to the performance of coacting groups and organizations (Fiedler, 1967b). The number of studies reported is now sufficient so that a review of the findings appears appropriate.

Task Groups and Organizations

Craft Shops and Grocery Markets. Two organizations studied by Hunt (1967) were coacting. These were craft shops in the physical science laboratory and grocery departments of chain stores. Both of these types of organizations performed coacting tasks that were highly structured. In both organizations the leader's position power was high. Performance of craft shops was assessed by ratings, while grocery departments were evaluated on the basis of an objective measure of number of man-hours over total sales volume.

The correlations for six workshops with high, and five with low group atmosphere scores (comparable to Octants I and V), were, respectively, −.48 and .90 ($p < .05$), those for 13 supermarkets with high group atmosphere, −.06, and those with low group atmosphere, .49.

Hospital Departments. Hill's (1969) study included various departments in a hospital, including the nursing service, the controller's department, dietetics, housekeeping, stores, central supply, and maintenance. All were rated to be coacting, and all supervisory personnel were rated as having high position power. The nursing service was rated by Hill as having an unstructured task, while other departments were rated as having structured tasks. Classifying the groups on the basis of the contingency

TABLE 7 SUMMARY OF LPC-GROUP PERFORMANCE CORRELATIONS OF STUDIES EXTENDING THE CONTINGENCY HYPOTHESIS

Study and Date	Favorable			Intermediate			Unfavorable		
O'Brien (1969)	−.08			.77*				−.13	
Anderson (1966)	−.50		.21		−.22			.12	
Lawrence & Lorsch (1967)*	−.50	−.10	−.13	.66					
Nealey & Blood (1968)	−.22			.79*					
Nealey & Owen (1970)	−.50*								
Fiedler & Barron†									
Task I	−.42	−.56	−.32	.67	−.08	−.01	−.53	−.72	.18
Task II	−.71	−.59	.69	.41	−.15	−.20	−.47	−.61	−.14
Median		−.37			.20			−.30	

Note.—The location of the correlation coefficient in the table indicates degree of judged favorableness of the leadership situation. The farther to the left, the more favorable the situation.

* Study not conducted by writer or his associates.

† In Fiedler (1967a).

model classification would make the nursing service fall into Octants III and VII and other departments into Octants I and V, depending on the leader's group atmosphere score. The correlations for the Octant I and V groups were $-.21$ ($n = 8$) and $.52$ ($n = 8$) and for the Octant III and VII groups (nursing) $-.32$ ($n = 7$) and $.87$ ($n = 7$, $p < .05$).

Telephone Offices. Bates (1967) conducted a study of telephone supervisors in two offices of the Bell Telephone Company. The total sample consisted of 112 operators working in 13 groups. Of these employees, 21 were first-line supervisors who provided LPC and group atmosphere scores. The task was rated as highly structured, and the position power as high. These groups would then fall into Octants I and V.

Bates obtained two criterion scores, a "quality index" reflecting the accuracy and courtesy with which the operators handle calls as well as the accuracy in billing calls. A second index, called the "load factor," reflects the average number of calls handled by an office. Three telephone executives who were independently interviewed agreed that the quality index is the more important and that offices rarely performed below the minimum load factor. Since the quality and load indexes were negatively correlated ($-.43$), only the quality index was here considered. Bates divided his groups into six with relatively high group atmosphere and seven with low group atmosphere scores. The corresponding correlations between supervisors' LPC scores and quality indexes were $-.77$ and $.75$.

School Principals. McNamara (1967) investigated the effectiveness of elementary school principals in 32 elementary schools of the Edmonton, Alberta, school system. The schools were relatively small in size, some containing as few as six teachers. Although McNamara spoke of his schools as interacting, all four judges classified the schools as coacting. Their reason was that there is relatively little interaction among teachers in the performance of their instructional duties, nor is it likely that the principal's job demands that he share his administrative duties with his staff or teachers. The principal's position power was rated as being high.

The effectiveness of schools was judged by five members of the school system's administrative staff. Leader-member relations were indexed by group atmosphere scores, with the upper third of the schools and the lower third of the schools used, and the middle third deleted from the sample.

The correlation between principal's LPC and performance in high group atmosphere schools (Octant I) was $-.48$ ($n = 11$), while that in low group atmosphere schools (Octant V) was $.31$ ($n = 12$).

Training Situations

Naval Aviation Cadets. Fiedler and Hutchins (Fiedler, 1967a) conducted a study of aviation cadets (including some commissioned officers in flight training) and their instructors. The student pilots were in the advanced course which concentrated on formation flying, a rather anxiety-arousing phase of training. The cadets were assigned to "flights" of eight men, and each flight was under the direction of an instructor team. The performance of the men in each flight was evaluated by instructors regularly assigned to another squadron of the training base.

Two samples of 16 instructors were tested, using their groups' performance scores as criterion of leadership (Octants I and V). The correlation of head instructors' LPC scores and performance of their flights was .45 and .17. Fiedler (1967a) also obtained correlations between the sociometrically chosen men, that is, informal leaders with very little position power. Since all were sociometrically chosen, all had good leader-member relations. The correlation between the LPC scores of 22 leaders and performance ratings was .55 ($p < .02$) and .28 for *n*s of 22 and 15. The lower correlations in the second set of teams may be due to the smaller range and standard deviation of performance scores in the second sample of teams.

Management Trainees. A study by Seifert (1969) used 14 management training groups in Germany. These groups, each consisting of 25 to 30 participants, remained together for almost 1 year. Similar to the naval aviation cadet study, each group had a team of instructors and a head instructor. Each group also had an informal leader, designated as spokesman of the group, but having very little position power. Similar to the naval aviation cadets, Seifert reported that the men were under considerable pressure and anxiety lest they fail. (Although Seifert treated these groups as interacting, all four judges considered the Seifert study one of coacting groups.) Effectiveness was rated by instructors and was based on several scales of motivational and performance characteristics of the men.

Correlations between the LPC of head instructors and performance was .56 for those with high group atmosphere and $-.20$ for those with low group atmosphere scores. The correlation between spokesmen's LPC and performance scores was .45, regardless of group atmosphere.

Student Nurses. A study by Reilly, mentioned above (see Footnote 5), was designed to test the contingency model. However, the judges rating Reilly's method were divided on the leader's position power. The study involved the assembly of 14 groups of stu-

TABLE 8 CORRELATIONAL SUMMARY OF STUDIES EXTENDING THE CONTINGENCY MODEL TO COACTING TASK AND TRAINING GROUPS

	Octants							
Group	*I*	*II*	*III*	*IV*	*V*	*VI*	*VII*	*VIII*
Task groups								
Craft shops	—.48				.90*			
Groceries	—.06				.49			
Hospital departments*	—.21		—.32		.52		.87	
Telephone offices	—.77				.75			
School principals*	—.48				.31			
Median	—.48		—.32		.52		.87	
Training groups								
Naval aviation								
Chief instructors	.45							
	.17							
Informal leaders			.55					
			.28					
Management trainees*								
Head instructors	.56					—.20		
Informal leaders	.45		.45					
Student nurses*			.63					
Medians	.45		.50			—.20		

* Studies not conducted by writer or his associates.

dent nurses with each group required to complete 10 sets of discussion problems and examination questions posed by the faculty of the school over the course of the year. Some of these problems were highly structured; that is, there was an answer or a solution available. Other problems were highly unstructured; that is, the group had to discuss a case or an ethical issue for which no definite answer was available. Reilly reported a correlation of .63 between leader LPC and group performance, irrespective of leader group atmosphere scores.

The leader had responsibility for arranging the sessions and seeing that the group's solutions were typed and handed in to the faculty. She also had the responsibility to assign 20% of each of her fellow students' grades. Leaving aside for the moment the question of position power on which our judges disagreed, or that these groups may well have been interacting in most tasks, the more important point might well be that the Reilly study, as well as the naval aviation cadet study by Fiedler and Hutchins (Fiedler, 1967a) and the Seifert study of German management trainees, is distinguished by having as its purpose the training of the group members rather than the performance of some task that results in an output beneficial to the organization.[6] In all of the studies, the exercise was designed to be beneficial to the individual group member. There might well be a psychological difference in leading a group for the purpose of benefiting the members and leading a group for the purpose of benefiting the organization. Our data suggest that this may be the case.[7]

Summary of Results from Coacting Groups. As we suggested in the discussion of the Reilly (see Footnote 5) study, the results obtained from studies of coacting groups can best be discussed by separating results from task groups and results from training groups (Table 8).

The results from task groups are highly consistent in showing that groups or organizations with structured tasks and high leader position power perform more effectively under low LPC leaders when the group climate is rated as favorable, and more effectively under high LPC leaders when the group climate is unfavorable. Classifying coacting groups in the same manner as interacting groups indicates that the correlations are quite similar in the two octants for which data are available, namely, Octants I and V.

Hill, in his study of a hospital, classified the supervising nurses' job as unstructured. The correlation for Octant III is in the predicted direction, and the correlation for Octant VII, while much higher than would be expected for this octant, is not incompatible with data from interacting groups.

The data on coacting *task* groups suggest that the

[6] An earlier unpublished study of classroom performance by Marse (1958) showed negative correlations of —.70 ($n = 6$) and —.36 ($n = 12$) for physics and rhetoric section instructors at the University of Illinois where rated student performance was the criterion. In that study, however, the class members never interacted in groups as part of their training. Whether this is an important determining factor remains to be seen.

[7] Note, however, that a school principal's group membership consists primarily of teachers and clerical staff, not of students.

distinction between interacting and coacting task groups might be unnecessary, while the distinction between *task* groups and *training* groups might be essential. The latter appear to follow quite dissimilar rules.

The Seifert (1969), the Fiedler and Hutchins (Fiedler, 1967a), and Reilly (see Footnote 5) studies suggest that groups in training might constitute a valid subclassification for leadership studies, a classification that needs to be intensively examined further. The possibility should be considered that this set of studies might also include those by Mitchell (1969) and Fiedler which used participants in leadership workshops.

Recent Empirical Findings from Research on Leadership Training. Despite intensive efforts, research has failed to show that leadership experience or leadership training systematically improve organizational performance (Campbell et al., 1970). These disappointing results can be deduced from the contingency model. Specifically, we can interpret leadership experience and training as improving situational favorableness (e.g., human relations training is supposed to improve leader-member relations, technical training would make the task appear more structured). Training and experience should then differentially affect the performance of high and low LPC leaders. The contingency model would then predict that training for intermediate situations will improve the performance of high LPC leaders—but *decrease* that of low LPC leaders. Likewise, training and experience for favorable and unfavorable situations will improve performance of low LPC leaders—but *decrease* performance of high LPC leaders. These results have now been obtained in several studies and further support the contingency model (Fiedler, in press).

SUMMARY

A review of studies testing and extending the contingency model evaluated the model's predictive power in field and laboratory situations and in coacting task and training groups.

The model seems to predict leadership performance in field situations, but not completely in laboratory situations. The major discrepancy between the model and the field studies on the one hand, and the laboratory studies on the other, was in Octant II, where the model predicted negative correlations, while the laboratory studies showed predominately positive correlations between LPC and group performance. This discrepancy, if it is not due to chance, may well bring to light important aspects of leadership interactions that are not usually reproduced in laboratory situations.

A series of studies, extending the theory, was reviewed. Taken as a group, these studies provide strong evidence that the situational favorableness dimension does indeed moderate the relationship between leadership style and group performance, and that it therefore provides an important clue to our understanding of leadership phenomena.

Finally, studies of coacting groups and organizations suggested that we differentiate between groups that exist primarily for the benefit of the organization—that is, the typical task groups—and groups that exist for the benefit of the individual—groups of trainees. Coacting task groups appear to follow the predictions of the contingency model, at least for Octants I and V. Data from groups-in-training showed consistently positive relations between leader LPC and group performance measures in Octants I and III, and only one small negative correlation in Octant VI. These findings suggest a new approach to the classification of coacting groups and training groups which might lead to a better understanding of managerial performance in task and training organizations.

REFERENCES

Anderson, L. R. Leader behavior, member attitudes, and task performance of intercultural discussion groups. *Journal of Social Psychology*, 1966, **69**, 305–19.

Bates, P. A. Leadership performance at two managerial levels in the telephone company. Unpublished bachelor's thesis, University of Illinois, 1967.

Butterfield, D. A. An integrative approach to the study of leadership effectiveness in organizations. Unpublished doctoral dissertation, University of Michigan, 1968.

Campbell, J. P., Dunnette, M. D., Lawler, E. E., and Weick, K. E. *Managerial behavior, performance, and effectiveness.* New York: McGraw-Hill, 1970.

Fiedler, F. E. A contingency model of leadership effectiveness. In L. Berkowitz (ed.), *Advances in experimental social psychology.* New York: Academic Press, 1964.

Fiedler, F. E. The effect of leadership and cultural heterogeneity on group performance: A test of the Contingency Model. *Journal of Experimental Social Psychology*, 1966, **2**, 237–64.

Fiedler, F. E. *A theory of leadership effectiveness.* New York: McGraw-Hill, 1967. (a)

Fiedler, F. E. Führungsstil und Leistung koagierender Gruppen, *Zeitschrift fur experimentelle und angewandte Psychologie*, 1967, *14*, 200-17. (b)

Fiedler, F. E. Note on the methodology of the Graen, Orris, and Alvares studies testing the contingency model. *Journal of Applied Psychology*, 1971, **55**, 202–04.

Fiedler, F. E. *Leadership.* (A module for the General Learning Press, in press.)

Fiedler, F. E., O'Brien, G. E., and Ilgen, D. R. The effect of leadership style upon the performance and adjustment of volunteer teams operating in a stressful foreign environment. *Human Relations,* 1969, **22**, 503–14.

Fishbein, M., Landy, E., and Hatch, G. Consideration of two assumptions underlying Fiedler's Contingency Model for the prediction of leadership effectiveness. *American Journal of Psychology,* 1969, **4**, 457–73.

Graen, G., Alvares, K., Orris, J. B., and Martella, J. A. Contingency model of leadership effectiveness: Antecedent and evidential results. *Psychological Bulletin,* 1970, **74**, 285–96.

Graen, G., Orris, J. B., and Alvares, V. M. Contingency model of leadership effectiveness: Some experimental results. *Journal of Applied Psychology,* 1971, **55**, 196–201.

Hill, W. The validation and extension of Fiedler's theory of leadership effectiveness. *Academy of Management Journal,* 1969, March, 33–47.

Hunt, J. G. Fiedler's leadership contingency model: An empirical test in three organizations. *Organizational Behavior and Human Performance,* 1967, **2**, 290–308.

Kretzschmar, V. and Luecke, H. E. Zum Fiedlerschen Kontingenzmodell Effektiver Fuhrung. *Arbeit und Leistung,* 1969, **23**, 53–55.

Lawrence, P. and Lorsch, J. Differentiation and integration in complex organizations. *Administrative Science Quarterly,* June 1967, **12**, 1–47.

Marse, J. E. Assumed similarity between opposites and the performance of leadership functions. Unpublished master's thesis, University of Illinois, 1958.

McNarmara, V. D. A descriptive-analytic study of directive-permissive variation in the leader behavior of elementary school principals. Unpublished master's thesis, University of Alberta, 1967.

Mitchell, T. R. Leader complexity, leadership style, and group performance. Unpublished doctoral dissertation, University of Illinois, 1969.

Mitchell, T. R. Leader complexity and leadership style. *Journal of Personality and Social Psychology,* 1970, **16**, 166–74.

Nealey, S. M. and Blood, M. Leadership performance of nursing supervisors at two organizational levels. *Journal of Applied Psychology,* 1968, **52**, 414–22.

Nealey, S. M. and Owen, T. M. A multitrait-multi-method analysis of predictors and criteria of nursing performance. *Organizational Behavior and Human Performance,* 1970, **5**, 348–65.

O'Brien, G. E. Group structure and the measurement of potential leader influence. *Australian Journal of Psychology,* 1969, **21**, 277–89.

Oeser, O. A. and Harary, F. A mathematical model for structural role theory I. *Human Relations,* 1962, **15**, 89–109.

Oeser, O. A. and Harary, F. A mathematical model for structural role theory II. *Human Relations,* 1964, **17**, 3–17.

Schutz, W. C. *FIRO: A Three-dimensional theory of interpersonal behavior.* New York: Holt, Rinehart & Winston, 1958.

Seifert, K. H. Untersuchungen zur Frage der Fuhrungseffektivität. *Psychologie und Praxis,* 1969, **13**, 49–64.

Shaw, M. E. and Blum, J. M. Effects of leadership style upon group performance as a function of task structure. *Journal of Personality and Social Psychology,* 1966, **3**, 238–42.

Shima, H. The relationship between the leader's modes of interpersonal cognition and the performance of the group. *Japanese Psychological Research,* 1968, **10**, 13–30.

Tannenbaum, R. and Schmidt, W. H. How to choose a leadership pattern, *Harvard Business Review,* 1958, **36**, 95–101.

Terman, L. M. A preliminary study of the psychology and pedagogy of leadership. *Pedagogical Seminary,* 1904, **11**, 413–51.

46. A PATH GOAL THEORY OF LEADER EFFECTIVENESS*

***Robert J. House*†**

INTRODUCTION

Two major behavioral dimensions that have emerged from leadership reseach are those which sociologists have termed instrumental and social-emotional, or expressive, leadership behavior. Psychologists who have studied leadership have independently discovered these dimensions (Korman, 1966). The terms most frequently used to describe these behaviors are initiating structure and consideration. Leader initiating structure is used to describe the degree to which the leader initiates psychological structure for subordinates by doing such things as assigning particular tasks, specifying procedures to be followed, clarifying his expectations of subordinates, and scheduling work to be done. This dimension of leader behavior describes leaders who are similar to those prescribed by classical manage-

* Reprinted from *Administrative Science Quarterly,* Vol. 16, No. 3 (September 1971), pp. 321–38. Copyright © 1971 by Cornell University.

† University of Toronto.

ment theorists, that is, leaders who plan, organize, direct, and control. Leader consideration is used to describe the degree to which the leader creates a supportive environment of psychological support, warmth, friendliness, and helpfulness by doing such things as being friendly and approachable, looking out for the personal welfare of the group, doing little things for subordinates, and giving advance notice of change.

Research has indicated that leaders who initiate structure for subordinates are generally rated highly by superiors and have higher producing work groups than leaders who are low on initiating structure; and that leaders who are considerate of subordinates have more satisfied employees (Filley & House, 1969); however the evidence with respect to the relationship between initiating structure and satisfaction of subordinates is very mixed. Several studies have shown that initiating structure is frequently resented by unskilled and semiskilled employees and is a source of dissatisfaction (Filley & House, 1969), grievances, and turnover (Fleishman & Harris, 1962). However, employees in large groups have been found either to prefer initiating structure more or to dislike it less than employees in smaller groups (Hemphill, 1950, Mass, 1950; Vroom & Mann, 1960). And, Oaklander and Fleishman (1964) found initiating structure to be negatively correlated with intergroup conflict. Recent studies have shown that among high-level employees, initiating structure is positively related to satisfaction (House *et al.*, 1971a, 1971b), performance (House *et al.*, 1971b), and perceptions of organizational effectiveness, but negatively related to role conflict and ambiguity (Rizzo *et al.*, 1970).

This paper presents a theory of leader behavior that attempts to reconcile and integrate the conflicting results of previous studies under a set of general propositions from which they could have been deduced, and reports three studies designed to test eight hypotheses derived from the theory.[1]

THEORETICAL BACKGROUND

The theory advanced here is derived from the path-goal hypothesis advanced by Georgopoulos *et al.* (1957), and from previous research supporting the broad class of expectancy theory of motivation (Atkinson, 1958; Vroom, 1964; Porter & Lawler, 1967; Galbraith & Cummings, 1967; Graen, 1969; Lawler, 1968). The central concept of expectancy theories is that the force on an individual to engage in a specific behavior is a function of (1) his expectations that the behavior will result in a specific outcome; and (2) the sum of the valences, that is, personal utilities or satisfactions, that he derives from the outcome. The research findings indicate that the function is a nonlinear, monotonically increasing product of expectations and valences. Thus, according to this theory of motivation, an individual chooses the behaviors he engages in on the basis of (1) the valences he perceives to be associated with the outcomes of the behavior under consideration; and (2) his subjective estimate of the probability that his behavior will indeed result in the outcomes. Vroom (1964) formalized one perspective of expectancy motivation theory mathematically, and Galbraith and Cummings (1967) extended his formulation by pointing out that some of the valences associated with a specific behavior are intrinsic to the behavior itself and some are the extrinsic consequences of that behavior. To the extent that behavior is intrinsically valent it is also intrinsically motivational because the behavior is highly instrumental to the outcome of satisfaction. A person will be motivated to engage in such behavior because his expectancy that satisfaction will follow is nearly unity. That is, if the outcomes were contingent on an external rewarder—any significant other—the expectancy would be less that unity because the behavior might not be observed or recognized by the rewarder. However, when the reward is essentially self-administering, expectancy approaches unity.

The theory may be further extended and broken down into parts that have specific relevance for leadership using the concept of path instrumentality advanced by Evans (1968: 14): "This is the cognition of the degree to which following a particular path (behavior) will lead to a particular outcome, it is akin to (but not identical to) the concept of 'expectancy' introduced by Vroom." Evans (1968) has also advanced an extension of Vroom's (1964) theory and a path-goal theory of leadership. His theory is different from the one presented here in that its predictions are not contingent on situational variables, and it is not an attempt to account for the conflicting findings just reviewed.

According to the formulation advanced here, the individual makes probability estimates with respect to two linking points connecting behavior with its outcomes, and subjectively places values on the outcomes. The magnitude of these probability esti-

[1] This paper is based on a presentation made at the Southern Illinois University Symposium on Contemporary Development in the Study of Leadership in Carbondale on April 30, 1971. The author is indebted to Larry L. Cummings for his critical comments and suggestions which resulted in significant improvement of an earlier version of this paper, and to Thomas H. Stone for his editorial suggestions which helped clarify the discussion of the probabilities associated with intrinsically motivated behavior.

mates indicates the degree of path instrumentality of his behavior for work-goal accomplishment and valence. This formulation can be expressed in the following formula:

$$M = IV_b + P_1 \left[IV_a + \sum_{i=1}^{n} (P_{2i}EV_i) \right] \qquad i = 1, \ldots, n,$$

where:

M = motivation to work;
IV_b = intrinsic valence associated with goal-directed behavior;
IV_a = intrinsic valence associated with work-goal accomplishment;
EV_i = extrinsic valences associated with work-goal accomplishment;
P_1 = path instrumentality of behavior for work-goal attainment;
P_{2i} = path instrumentalities of work goal for extrinsic valences.

In work situations the individual estimates the path instrumentality, P_1, of his behavior for the accomplishment of some work goal. Here he considers such factors as his ability to behave in an appropriate and effective manner as well as the barriers to work-goal accomplishment in the environment, and the support he will receive from others to accomplish the work goal. In addition, he estimates the path instrumentality, P_2, of the work goal for attaining personal outcomes that have valence for him. For example, he estimates the probability that his superiors will recognize his goal accomplishment and reward him accordingly. He also considers, and places subjective values on the intrinsic valence associated with the behavior required to achieve the work goal, IV_b, the intrinsic valence associated with the achievement of the work goal, IV_a, and the extrinsic valences associated with the personal outcomes that he accrues as a result of achieveing the work goal, EV_i.

The behavior of the leader is clearly relevant to all of the independent variables in this formulation. The leader, at least in part, determines what extrinsic rewards should be associated with work-goal accomplishment, EV_i. For example, he has some influence over the extent to which work-goal accomplishment will be recognized as a contribution and whether it will be rewarded with financial increases, promotion, assignment of more interesting tasks or opportunities for personal growth and development. Consequently, he influences the magnitude of the sum of the personal outcomes available. Second, the leader, through his interaction with the subordinate, can increase the subordinate's path instrumentality concerning the rewards forth-coming as a result of work-goal accomplishment, P_2. If he is consistent in his decision making with respect to recognizing and rewarding work-goal achievement, he will clarify the linkage between work-goal achievement and rewards. Thus, if he consistently rewards achievement, this will most probably increase the subordinate's path instrumentality, P_2, for valent personal outcomes. Third, through his own behavior he can provide support for the subordinate's efforts and thereby influence the probability that this effort will result in work-goal achievement, that is P_1. Fourth, the leader influences the intrinsic valences associated with goal accomplishment, IV_a, by the way he delegates and assigns tasks to subordinates, which determines the amount of influence the subordinate has in goal setting and the amount of control he is allowed in the task-directed effort. The greater the sub-ordinate's opportunity to influence the goal and exercise control, the more intrinsically valent the work-goal accomplishment. Finally, the leader can increase the net intrinsic valence associated with goal-directed behavior, IV_b, by reducing frustrating barriers, being supportive in times of stress, permitting involvement in a wide variety of tasks, and being considerate of subordinate's needs.

PROPOSITIONS

The above interpretation of motivation theory as applied to leadership suggests the following general propositions:

1. The motivation functions of a leader are to increase the net positive valences associated with work-goal attainment, increase the net positive valences associated with the path—behavior—to work-goal attainment, and increase the subordinate's path instrumentality with respect to work-goal attainment for personal outcomes and the behavior required for work-goal attainment. This statement assumes that when the subordinate is working under ambiguous path-goal relationships, his subjective probability estimates that his behavior will affect the valences he receives are less than the objective probabilities that his behavior will affect the valences he receives. When this assumption does not hold, that is, when under conditions of role ambiguity, his subjective probability estimates exceed the objective probabilities, then clarification of path-goal relationships will result in reduced motivation.

Stated less formally, the motivational functions of the leader consist of increasing personal pay-offs to subordinates for work-goal attainment, and making the path to these pay-offs easier to travel by clarifying it, reducing road blocks and pitfalls, and increasing the opportunities for personal satisfaction en route. The function of making the path easier and more satisfying to follow has been dealt with only implicitly in the leadership literature and, as will be shown, has significant implications for leader's behavior.

2. In increasing path instrumentality by clarifying path-goal relationships, the leader's behavior will have positive motivational effects to the extent that it reduces role ambiguity or makes possible the exercise of externally imposed controls. Reduction of role ambiguity results in increased motivation because role ambiguity is both negatively valent to subordinates (Rizzo *et al.*, 1970), and because it is usually associated with low path instrumentality. Externally imposed controls are motivational because they make possible the allocation of valences contingent on desirable behavior. Externally imposed control results in improved performance only to the extent that the rewards that are under the control of the leader are positively valent to the subordinates; punishments that are under the control of the leader are negatively valent to the subordinates; rewards and punishments are contingent on performance; and the contingency is clearly perceived by the subordinates. Whether performance motivated by external controls is satisfying to the subordinate depends on his unconscious needs, conscious values, and perceptions of equity in the exchange of effort for rewards.

3. Where leader attempts to clarify path-goal relationships are redundant with existing conditions, that is, where path-goal relationships are apparent because of the routine of the tasks or objective system-fixed controls, attempts by the leader to clarify path-goal relationships will result in increased externally imposed control and will be seen by subordinates as redundant. Although such control may increase performance, it will also result in decreased satisfaction.

4. Leader behavior directed at need satisfaction of subordinates will result in increased performance to the extent that such satisfaction increases the net positive valence associated with goal-directed effort.

HYPOTHESES

From the above general propositions, several specific hypotheses concerning leader consideration, initiating structure, closeness of supervision, hierarchical influence, and authoritarianism can be derived. These hypotheses are consistent with empirical findings and thus illustrate how these prior findings could have been deduced from the general propositions of the theory. These hypotheses do not constitute an exhaustive list of relationships between the variables, but rather, serve to illustrate how the general propositions can be operationalized.

1. Leader initiating structure increases the path instrumentality for subordinates whose roles have nonroutine task demands by decreasing role ambiguity (Rizzo et al., 1970).

2. Informal leaders high in structure influence positively the subjective probabilities other group members assign to positively valent outcomes (Rim, 1965).

3. Leader initiating structure and consideration will have differential effects, depending on whether the task is satisfying or unsatisfying to the subordinate, and whether the task-role demands are clear or ambiguous.

The more satisfying the task, the less positive the relationship between consideration and subordinate satisfaction and performance (Fleishman, 1971: 13–14). These correlations will vary from insignificant to positive, depending on task satisfaction. For unsatisfying tasks, consideration will tend to offset dissatisfaction associated with the task; for satisfying tasks, consideration will be less important.

The less satisfying the task the more negative will be the relationship between structure and satisfaction and the more positive will be the relationship between structure and performance (Fleishman, 1971: 19–20). For unsatisfying tasks, structure will be viewed as an imposition of external control and, therefore, dissatisfying, but will also be required to motivate subordinate effort toward goal achievement (Fleishman, 1971: 19–20).

The more ambiguous the task the more positive the relationship between leader initiating structure and subordinate satisfaction and performance. Structure serves to reduce role ambiguity and clarify path-goal relationships for ambiguous tasks but is viewed as unnecessary and redundant for nonambiguous tasks.

When task demands are self-evident due to a high degree of routinization, or where roles are clearly defined by such factors as mechanization, legal constraints, contracts, professional ethics, or group norms, initiating structure will not result in role clarification and will be unsatisfying to subordinates.

4. Where the follower's tasks are varied and interdependent and where teamwork norms are not developed within the group, initiating structure and close supervision will regulate and clarify path-goal relationships. Therefore, structure and close supervision will result in increased coordination, satisfaction, and performance (Patchen, 1962; Mass, 1950; Hemphill, 1950; Fleishman, 1971: 26).

5. Where tasks are interdependent, varied, and ambiguous, consideration will result in social sup-

port, friendliness among group members, increased cohesiveness, and team effort. These social outcomes will be positively valent to the members and thus increase the net sum of the positive valences associated with interdependent jobs requiring cooperation and team spirit (Oaklander & Fleishman, 1964; Fleishman, 1971: 13–14).

6. Where tasks and/or environment are frustrating and stress inducing, consideration will result in increased social support for followers and thus reduce negative valence associated with task-oriented behavior (Fiedler, 1967; Rim, 1965; Fleishman, 1971; 12–13).

7. Where stress is from sources external to the work unit and tasks are ambiguous, structure will result in increased ego protection, security, and satisfaction (Oaklander & Fleishman, 1964). In this instance, structure serves as an umbrella which protects followers from externally imposed stress.

8. Among hierarchically dependent employees under leaders with high upward influence, consideration will be positively related to satisfaction and performance of subordinates (Pelz, 1952). Among independent employees, or under leaders with low upward influence, consideration will have a lower positive relationship to subordinate satisfaction and performance (Wager, 1965; House et al., 1971a; 1971b). Leader influence permits the leader to have more control over rewards for subordinates and thereby permits the leader to make subordinate valences contingent on performance and to make the outcomes of work-goal attainment more valent or less valent.

9. Under conditions of authoritarian or punitive leadership, both leader initiating structure and leader hierarchical influence will be negatively related to subordinate satisfaction. Under such conditions, both structure and influence will be seen as bases of authoritarian power by subordinates.

RECONCILIATION OF PRIOR FINDINGS

The usefulness of the theory can be illustrated by showing how it can be applied to reconcile what appear to be conflicting results of prior research cited earlier.

Fleishman and Harris (1962) found that when the leader's consideration toward subordinates' needs was used as a moderating variable—that is, when separate correlations are computed for high-considerate, medium-considerate, and low-considerate leaders—the relationship between leader structure and grievances and turnover varied. Specifically they found that there was no relationship between structure and grievances or turnover for highly considerate leaders; but for leaders with low consideration, the relationship was positive and significant.

House et al. (1971b) attempted to conduct a replication of the findings of Fleishman and Harris (1962), using the same scales for the predictor and moderator variables and eight measures of satisfaction with subordinate role expectations as criterion variables. The populations studied were salaried engineers, scientists, and technicians in three large research, design and development organizations. Unexpectedly, the data not only failed to replicate Fleishman and Harris' (1962) findings but suggested their opposite. Specifically it was found that leader initiating structure had a significant linear—unmoderated—positive relationship to half the satisfaction measures in two of the three companies, and significant positive correlations, $> .36$, $p < .05$, with satisfaction with the company management in all three companies studied. Furthermore, in one company under conditions of high leader consideration, leader initiating structure had significant positive curvilinear relationships to measures of satisfaction with job freedom, advancement, security, and family attitudes toward the respondent's job, with the eta correlation ranging from .36 to .50.

In a subsequent study of 192 nontechnical corporate office employees of a chemical manufacturing company, House et al. (1970) failed to replicate the findings of Fleishman and Harris (1962) and showed significant positive relationships between leader initiating structure and six measures of satisfaction.

The following three hypotheses derived from the theory serve to reconcile these findings.

Leader initiating structure can be hypothesized to clarify path-goal relationships for higher occupational level jobs which are frequently ambiguously defined. Such clarification reduces role ambiguity and increases the employee's perceived instrumentality of effort toward goal attainment. That is, it increases his subjective probability estimates that his efforts will result in goal attainment. Thus, the path-goal theory advanced here offers an explanation for the positive correlations between leader initiating structure and satisfaction among the high occupational level groups studied by House et al. (1970, 1971a, 1971b). The theory also explains the negative relationships found at lower occupational levels by Fleishman and Harris (1962). If it can be assumed that lower level jobs are generally more routine, that their path-goal relationships are usually self-evident, and that the job itself is frequently not intrinsically satisfying, then it can be hypothesized that leader initiating structure would be viewed by subordinates as an imposition of external control that does little to clarify path-goal relationships and is viewed by subordinates as being directed at keeping them working at unsatisfying activities. Although such control is likely to increase productivity by preventing soldiering, work restriction, or slowdowns, it is also a source of dissatisfaction to employees.

Another hypothesis derived from path-goal theory explains the findings concerning the moderating effect of consideration in some studies and not in others. Where the path is not viewed as satisfying, that is, for lower level jobs, it can be hypothesized that consideration serves as a source of extrinsic social satisfaction and support to the employee, thus making the path easier to travel. Consequently, for Fleishman and Harris' (1962) blue-collar workers, leader consideration moderated the unsatisfying effects of leader structure; whereas, for higher level jobs, where the path was intrinsically satisfying, the need for such support was lower and consequently consideration would be expected to have little or no moderating effect on the relationship between initiating structure and satisfaction.

Similarly in the International Harvester study reviewed by Fleishman (1971: 19–20), high leader initiating structure was found to be related to foremen ratings of proficiency, but also higher grievances; high leader consideration was found to be related to lower proficiency ratings, a tendency more pronounced in production than in other departments. The specific variable that was subsequently discovered to account for the differential relations across departments was pressure for output. If it can be assumed that the tasks in the production departments were less satisfying, then it follows that under conditions of high pressure for output, leader initiating structure would be viewed as an externally imposed form of control. Such control would be more acceptable to higher managers, but resented by the subordinates on whom it was imposed. Leader consideration is more likely to serve as a stress reducer as tasks become more unsatisfying and pressure for output increases. Thus the differential relationship found across types of departments can be explained in terms of differences in task satisfaction, that is, path valence and pressure for production differences. This explanation is directly deducible from the path-goal theory presented here and again illustrates the ability of the theory to accommodate and explain otherwise confusing empiric findings.

Three studies were conducted in which eight hypotheses specifically derived from the theory were tested, and three of these hypotheses were retested.

STUDY NUMBER 1

Method

The first study was based on an analysis of data collected as part of a larger ongoing research project. The scale means, standard deviations, and intercorrelations were reported by Rizzo et al. (1970).

Sample. The sample for the study consisted of 199 office employees of a heavy equipment manufacturing company. All respondents were salaried and performed either professional, administrative, or somewhat administrative-clerical tasks. The sample was randomly selected and constituted 35 percent of the total population of salaried employees at the corporate offices and main plant of the company, excluding first-level production foremen.

Hypotheses. The following hypotheses were tested:

Hypothesis 1. Leader initiating structure will be positively related to subordinate satisfaction.

TABLE 1 ZERO-ORDER AND PARTIAL CORRELATIONS BETWEEN LEADER INITIATING STRUCTURE AND SUBORDINATE SATISFACTION WITH AND WITHOUT AMBIGUITY HELD CONSTANT

Variables	*Zero-Order Correlations*	*Correlations with Role Ambiguity Held Constant*	*Reliabilities*
Satisfaction with			
Advancement opportunity. . .	.20†	.09	.83
Job autonomy.	.10	—.05	.82
Intrinsic job rewards	.17*	.03	.92
Job security	.03	—.06	.70
Pay	.05	—.01	.86
Recognition.	.16*	—.06	.85
Social environment	.21†	.04	.78
Role ambiguity	—.41†		.78
Initiating structure.			.65
$N = 199$			

$^{*}p \leq .05$.
$^{\dagger}p \leq .01$.

Hypothesis 2. Leader initiating structure will be negatively related to subordinate role ambiguity.

Hypothesis 3. The variance in role ambiguity will account for the relationship between leader initiating structure and subordinate satisfaction.

The rationale for these hypotheses is as follows. Since the sample consisted primarily of employees doing quasi-administrative work, it seemed likely that much of their time would be devoted to ambiguously defined tasks, for which the path to goal achievement was not clear; consequently, initiating structure by the leader would be expected to reduce ambiguity and therefore increase the clarity of path-goal relationships and increase satisfaction.

Measures. The scales used were the leader-initiating-structure scale taken from the Ohio State Leader Behavior Description Questionnaire (Stogdill, 1965) and measures of satisfaction and role ambiguity derived by factor analysis and developed specifically for the larger research project from which these data were taken.

In the satisfaction and role-ambiguity scales, the respondents were asked to indicate the degree to which descriptive statements were true or false on a 7-point scale ranging from 1, very false, to 7, very true. One sample item for each of the satisfaction scales follows:

Satisfaction category

Advancement opportunity
Job autonomy
Intrinsic job rewards
Job security
Pay
Recognition
Social environment

Sample item

Chances for advancing at a reasonable rate
The opportunity for independent thought
The feeling of worthwhile accomplishment at work
Chances of keeping this job as long as I want it
The pay I receive for my work
The awareness that others have of my performance when I perform well
The dignity with which I am treated

The items in the role ambiguity scales were:

I feel certain about how much authority I have.
Clear, planned goals and objectives for my job.
I know that I have divided my time properly.
I know what my responsibilities are.
I know exactly what is expected of me.
Explanation is clear of what has to be done.

Scale Validities. The leader initiating structure scale was shown by Halpin (1957) to have concurrent criteria validity and by Stogdill (1969) to have experimental criteria validity. The role ambiguity measure has been construct validated (Rizzo *et al.*, 1970) against measures of organization practices, leader behavior, and satisfaction. Although not validated, the reliabilities of the satisfaction measure are moderately high and adequate for research purposes. The reliabilities for all measures are reported in Table 1.

Statistical Procedure. Hypotheses 1 and 2 were tested by simple product-moment correlations; hypothesis 3 by comparing the zero-order correlations between structure and satisfaction with partial correlations between the same variables, with role ambiguity held constant.

Findings

The results of the analysis, reported in Table 1, indicate support of all the hypotheses. Four of the relationships between initiating structure and satisfaction are significant, as is the relationship between structure and role ambiguity. It can also be seen that when the effect of role ambiguity is partialled out, the four significant correlations are no longer significant.

The zero-order correlations, while significant and in the hypothesized direction, are very low, but not inconsistent with the theoretical interpretation, since a significant proportion of the sample were probably doing relatively routine work and for which the path-goal relationships were relatively clear regardless of the amount of structure initiated by the leader.

Conclusion

Although the above findings support all three hypotheses, inability to control for the characteristics of the sample studied and the magnitude of the correlations require the interpretation that the theory is not disconfirmed, but only weakly tested and supported. A more sensitive test of the same hypotheses would require careful selection of a sample of employees known to be performing primarily ambiguous but also satisfying tasks.

STUDY NUMBER 2

Method

The second study tested hypotheses about the moderating effect of task characteristics on the relationships between leader initiating structure and consideration, and subordinate satisfaction and performance.

How often are you required to perform tasks which previously had not been part of your job responsibility?
5. very often 4. often 3. sometimes 2. occasionally 1. rarely
How often do you see projects through to completion?
1. rarely 2. occasionally 3. sometimes 4. often 5. very often
To what extent do you set objectives, goals and procedures for your job rather than following directions or established procedures?
5. very large 4. large 3. somewhat 2. little 1. almost never
To what extent do you participate in decisions concerning the methods to be used in performing your job?
1. almost never 2. occasionally 3. frequently 4. usually 5. almost always
To what extent are you able to allocate a portion of your time to tasks related to corporate objectives but not specifically assigned to you?
5. very large 4. large 3. sometimes 2. little 1. almost never

Sample. The sample was that used by House *et al.* (1970); however, two additional measures were used to stratify the population according to task autonomy and job scope, thus permitting tests of specific hypotheses derived from the theory.

Hypotheses. The following hypotheses were tested:

Hypothesis 1. Job autonomy will have a positive moderating effect on the relationship between leader initiating structure and subordinate job satisfaction; that is the relationship will be stronger under high job autonomy than under low job autonomy. This hypothesis was based on the expectation that for autonomous tasks the role demands are likely to be more ambiguous than for nonautonomous tasks. Thus, under autonomous tasks, leader structure will serve to reduce role ambiguity, clarify path-goal relationships, and thereby increase satisfaction.

Hypothesis 2. Job autonomy will have a negative moderating effect on the relationship between leader initiating structure and subordinate performance; that is, for nonautonomous jobs the relationship will be stronger than for autonomous jobs.

This hypothesis is based on the expectation that for nonautonomous tasks, role demands are more likely to be dissatisfying, so that initiating structure will control behavior and ensure higher performance. For subordinates with autonomous jobs, initiating structure will be irrelevant to performance, since the subordinate is less dependent on the leader for resources, assistance, or guidance.

Hypothesis 3. Job autonomy will have a negative moderating effect on the relationship between leader consideration and subordinate satisfaction; that is, the relationship will be weaker for autonomous jobs than for nonautonomous jobs.

Hypothesis 4. Job autonomy will have a negative moderating effect on the relationship between leader consideration and subordinate performance.

Hypotheses 3 and 4 are based on the assumption that under high job autonomy, the role demands are more likely to be satisfying and, consequently, leader behavior will be less relevant to the needs or performance of subordinates than under low job autonomy.

Hypothesis 5. Job scope will have a negative moderating effect on the relationship between leader consideration and subordinate satisfaction and performance; that is, the wider the variety of tasks performed by subordinates, the weaker the correlations between leader consideration and subordinate satisfaction and performance.

This hypothesis is based on the assumption that a wide variety of tasks is more likely to be satisfying and, therefore, subordinates with varied tasks have less need for social support, that is, consideration from their leaders; whereas for highly routine jobs, leader consideration is a source of support to the employee, thus making the path easier to travel.

Measures. The measures used were the leader-consideration and initiating-structure scales taken from the Ohio State questionnaire, the Ohio State job-description scale and job-expectation scales (Stogdill, 1965), multimethod-multitrait ratings of individual performance, a job-scope and a task-autonomy scale.

The job-scope scale developed by Wigdor (1969), consisted of five questions designed to measure the extent to which the subject performs various tasks, sees projects through to completion, and determines job objectives and methods. The questions are at the top of this page.

The task-autonomy scale also developed by Wigdor (1969) consisted of 16 items intended to reflect the degree to which the respondent was able to perform his job without depending upon his superior or others for financial resources, nonfinancial resources, and directions; independently scheduled and planned his activities; and innovated independently of others. Three sample questions and response choices follow:

To what extent are you able to act independently of your superior in performing your job function?
1. hardly ever 2. seldom 3. occasionally 4. frequently 5. almost always
When someone else in the company requests you to perform a task for them, how frequently do you seek advice from your superiors?
1. almost always 2. very often 3. often 4. occasionally 5. rarely
To what extent are you able to schedule and plan your task requirements independent of others in the organization?
1. hardly ever 2. seldom 3. occasionally 4. frequently 5. almost always

The job-description questionnaire essentially measured employees' attitudes toward the company and its management. Factor analysis by Stogdill (1965) of a previous satisfaction scale yielded a single factor with high loadings for the 12 items of the job-description questionnaire, which were related to satisfaction with the company, management, and with recognition.

The job-expectation questionnaire measured employee satisfaction with role expectation with respect to work, advancement, the prestige of the respondent's job as compared with the jobs of others, pay, freedom, family attitudes toward the respondent's job, and job security. Respondents were asked to indicate the degree to which each characteristic of the job met their expectations. Each class of expectation was measured by averaging the scores of the questions.

In the present study the items pertaining to advancement, pay, and prestige expectations were combined to provide a single measure—extrinsic job satisfaction.

The performance scale used for this study was a multitrait-multirater scale. Lawler (1968: 370), in a review of methods for measuring performance, indicated that the multitrait-multirater method provides many of the advantages of both the more objective and more subjective measures, and added: "Moreover, with this approach it is possible to assess the criterion by determining its convergent and discriminant validity, and it is not necessary to depend on an objective indicator such as sales or profits that may miss the essence of the job."

The index of performance was the average of the ratings given the subject when rated by one peer and one superior. The obvious constraint in the choice of the raters was that they had to be familiar with the aspects of the individual's performance that they were to rate, otherwise, the ratings tend to be affected by the halo tendency (Bescoe & Lawshe, 1959). To ensure the choice of knowledgeable raters, the subject was asked to indicate the names of his superiors and two peers who knew his performance best. The choice of which superior and which peer ratings was used was made randomly by the investigator.

Scale Validities and Reliabilities. Kuder Richardson reliabilities for the leader consideration and leader initiating structure scales, corrected with the Spearman-Brown prophesy formula, were .86 and .90 respectively.

The job-autonomy scale was validated by Wigdor (1969) on two samples assumed to be significantly different on job autonomy because of their occupational level. Wigdor (1969) found that the scale discriminated, as predicted, between a sample of 33 corporate vice presidents and a sample of white-collar trainees and secretaries. The difference in the distribution of the two samples were in the predicted direction and significant at the .0001 level, Mann-Whitney $U = 801$, $Z = 6.10$. A similar result was found when 18 college professors with tenure were used in place of the vice presidents, $p < .0001$; $U = 421$; $Z = 4.97$. This scale had a .90 reliability for the present sample.

The job-scope scale was also validated by Wigdor (1969) who compared 30 employees at a high organizational level making a wide variety of decisions and performing a large number of functions, with 30 employees who were low on these characteristics, and found a difference in responses significant at the .0001 level, Mann-Whitney $U = 861$, $Z = 6.08$, in the hypothesized direction. This scale has a .70 reliability for the present sample.

The satisfaction scales were based on factor analyses reported by Stogdill (1965). Although no validity data are available, the reliabilities of these scales are moderately high and adequate for research purposes. Reliabilities of all multiple-item scales are given in Table 2.

The performance measures were tested for convergent and discriminant validity according to the criteria suggested by Campbell and Fiske (1959). Of the following criteria, the first shows convergent validity and the rest discriminant validity.

1. There should be high and significant interrater agreement, that is, correlation, among measures of the same traits.

2. The correlations among two ratings of a single trait should be greater than the correlation between any one rating of that trait and any other trait rated by the other rater.

TABLE 2 CORRELATIONS BETWEEN LEADER INITIATING STRUCTURE AND SUBORDINATE SATISFACTION AND PERFORMANCE MODERATED BY JOB AUTONOMY

	Study Number 2				
	Job Autonomy			Differences in Correlations—	
Variables	Low (N = 61)	Medium (N = 68)	High (N = 62)	Low versus High Group	Reliabilities
Satisfaction with					
Company and management . . .	35†	45†	47†		.90
Intrinsic job rewards	30	16	20		.64
Extrinsic job rewards.	11	26*	51†	.01	.72
Family attitude toward job	—9	14	15*		.72
Security	14	17	25*		.61
Job freedom.	37†	7	36†		.70
Average satisfaction	19	21	33		
Performance ratings					
Quality	33†	22	6		
Ability	34†	8	12		
Effort.	43†	20	20		
Initiative	46†	13	27*		
Ability without guidance	36†	27*	23		
Quantity.	55†	17	18	.05	
Average performance	47	18	18		

* $p \leq .05$.
† $p \leq .01$.

3. The correlation between two ratings of a single trait should be greater than the correlation between any one rating of that trait and any other trait rated by the same rater.

4. There should be the same pattern of trait interrelationships in all the multitrait triangles of the multirater-multitrait correlation matrix.

The validity tests, using Spearman rank-order correlations, are summarized in Table 3.

The sample used to test the validity of the performance ratings consisted of a subsample of 172 subjects of the 192 used to test the hypotheses. The subsample of 172 consists of all subjects for whom self-, superior, and peer ratings were obtained. As can be seen from Table 3, for study number 2, the superior-peer correlations indicated substantially higher convergent and discriminant validity than the self-superior or the self-peer correlations. For this reason the self-ratings were discarded and the superior and peer ratings for each subject were averaged to arrive at a measure of performance for this study.

All ratings meet the requirement of convergent validity and the third test of discriminant validity. Four of the six ratings meet the first requirement of discriminant validity and two were marginally significant ($p = .055$), but none of the ratings meet the second. Sign tests were used for the first two tests of discriminant validity, and the W coefficient of concordance for the third. These tests were first used for this purpose by Evans (1969) and are explained by Siegel (1956). There is also indicated a high level of halo. The W test of concordance indicated that this halo was common among all four multitrait triangles of the multittrait-multirater matrix, thus indicating not only interrater agreement on individual scales but also a similarity of rater response sets, that is, halo. These findings suggest that any tests of the hypotheses based on these performance scales are susceptible to a type one error; that is, an error in which data might result in rejecting a true hypothesis because the measure of the dependent variable, performance, included a large halo and had only moderate-to-low discriminant validity. Thus, use of the average of peer-superior ratings constitute conservative tests of the hypotheses.

Statistical Procedure. The sample was divided into respondents with low-, medium-, and high-task autonomy. The medium group consisted of the third closest to the mean of the total population and included all tied subjects at the borderlines. Correlations were computed for the relationship between leader consideration and subordinate satisfaction and performance. The same procedure was repeated using job scope as the moderating variable.

Findings

Table 2, showing the findings relevant to hypothesis 1, indicates that the average correlation and four of the individual correlations between initiating structure and satisfaction increase monotonically with increases in job autonomy, and that the

TABLE 3 SUMMARY OF TESTS OF CONVERGENT AND DISCRIMINANT VALIDITY FOR MEASURES OF PERFORMANCE

Study Number 2 N = *172*

Ratings	*1*	*2*	*3*	*4*	*5*	*6*
Peer-superior ratings						
Convergent validity, p = ...	.01	.01	.01	.01	.01	.01
Discriminant validity						
Test 1, p = ...	.001	.055	.001	.001	.055	.001
Test 2, p = ...	N.S.	N.S.	N.S.	N.S.	N.S.	N.S.
Test 3, overall test, = .80 $x^2 = 44.8$ $p \leq .001$						
Peer-self ratings						
Convergent validity, p = ...	.025	N.S.	.01	.05	N.S.	.05
Discriminant validity						
Test 1, p = ...	.001	N.S.	.055	N.S.	N.S.	N.S.
Test 2, p = ...	N.S.	N.S.	N.S.	N.S.	N.S.	N.S.
Test 3, overall test, $w = .55$ $x^2 = 30.8$ $p \leq .01$						
Self-superior ratings						
Convergent validity, p = ...	.01	.05	.01	.025	.10	.025
Discriminant validity						
Test 1, p = ...	.001	N.S.	.055	N.S.	N.S.	N.S.
Test 2, p = ...	N.S.	N.S.	N.S.	N.S.	N.S.	N.S.
Test 3, overall test, $w = 56$ $x^2 = 31.4$ $p \leq .01$						

Study Number 3 N = *122*

Ratings	*1*	*2*	*3*	*4*	*5*	*6*
Peer-superior ratings						
Convergent validity, p = ...	.01	.01	.01	.01	.01	.01
Discriminant validity,						
Test 1, p = ...	N.S.	N.S.	N.S.	N.S.	N.S.	N.S.
Test 2, p = ...	0.55	.828	.001	.01	.001	.172
Test 3, overall test, $w = 61$ $x^2 = 34.1$ $p \leq .01$						

correlation between extrinsic job satisfaction and initiating structure is significantly higher for groups with high autonomy than for groups with low or medium autonomy. These findings, while in the predicted direction for four of the classes of satisfaction and for the average correlations, are only clearly and strongly supportive, that is, differences in correlations are large and significant for hypothesis 1, with respect to extrinsic satisfaction.

Table 2 also presents the findings relevant to hypothesis 2. Again, the average of the correlations between leader initiating structure and subordinate performance decrease in the predicted direction from .47 for the low-autonomy group to .18 for the medium- and high-autonomy groups. Three of the correlations decrease monotonically in the predicted direction and all 6 of the correlations in the low-autonomy group are significant at the .01 level, whereas only one in the high-autonomy group is significant. Finally, the correlation between initiating structure and quantity of subordinate performance is significantly higher for the low-autonomy group than for either the medium- or high-autonomy group.

Table 4 presents the findings relevant to hypotheses 3 and 4. For hypothesis 3, while none of the correlations between leader consideration and subordinate satisfaction in the group with low job autonomy are significantly higher than those in the groups with medium or high autonomy, both the average correlations and three of the individual correlations decrease monotonically in the predicted direction.

For hypothesis 4, four of the correlations between leader consideration and subordinate performance are significantly higher for the low-autonomy group than for the medium- or the high-autonomy group. All six correlations in the low-autonomy group are significant at the .01 level, while none are significant in the medium- or high-autonomy groups, and the average of the correlations decreases monotoni-

TABLE 4 RANK-ORDER CORRELATIONS BETWEEN LEADER CONSIDERATION AND SUBORDINATE SATISFACTION AND PERFORMANCE MODERATED BY JOB AUTONOMY AND JOB SCOPE—STUDY NUMBER 2

	Job Autonomy					Job Scope				
				Differences in Correlations					Differences in Correlations	
Variables	*Low* (N = 59)	*Medium* (N = 74)	*High* (N = 59)	*Low versus Medium Group*	*Low versus High Group*	*Low* (N = 51)	*Medium* (N = 86)	*High* (N = 55)	*Low versus Medium Group*	*High versus Low Group*
Satisfaction with										
Company	56†	46†	48†			58†	53†	34†		
Intrinsic job rewards	35†	30†	4			37*	24*	34†		
Extrinsic job rewards	34†	29*	38†			43†	31†	28*		
Family attitude toward job	20	18	4			14	16	18		
Security	26†	16	17			13	20	31†		
Job freedom	50†	39†	32†			58†	36†	33†		
Average satisfaction	37	30	23			36†	30	30		
Performance ratings										
Quality	34†	18	9			51†	9	13	.01	
Ability	36†	6	2			32*	9	−4	.05	
Effort	46†	11	14	.01		60†	0	17	.01	
Initiative	43†	9	18	.01		62†	4	9	.01	.01
Ability without guidance	39†	26	2		.05	49†	4	14	.01	
Quantity	51†	5	0		.01	55†	3	7	.01	.01
Average performance	42†	11	8	.01		52	2	9		.05

* $p \leq .05$.
† $p \leq .01$.

cally from .42 to .11 to .08 with increases in job autonomy.

Table 4 also presents the findings relevant to hypothesis 5. The differences in the correlations between leader consideration and subordinate satisfaction are neither significant nor consistently in the hypothesized direction. Evidently, consideration has a pervasive effect and when not controlled for subordinate autonomy the relationship between leader consideration and subordinate satisfaction remains constant, regardless of subordinate job scope. However, the moderating effect of job scope on the relationship between leader consideration and performance is rather profound. The average correlation decreases from .52 for the low job-scope group to .02 and .09 for the medium and high job-scope groups respectively. Five of the six correlations between leader consideration and performance in the low job-scope group are significantly higher than their respective correlations in the medium or high job-scope groups. Finally, all of the correlations in the low job-scope group are significant while none in either the medium or high job-scope groups are.

Conclusion

Although the tests were conservative because of measurement error in the performance ratings, that is halo, the findings from this study provide rather strong support for the hypotheses derived from the theory.

STUDY NUMBER 3

Method

This study consisted of replications of hypotheses 3, 4 and 5 of study number 2. The data for this study were collected as part of a larger study. Unfortunately, the leader-initiating-structure scale was not included in the larger study, thus precluding the possibility of replicating hypotheses 6 and 7.

Sample. The sample for this study consisted of 122 employees, that is, 97 percent of the employees of a chemical manufacturing plant. Those not included were absent on the day the questionnaire was administered, so that the final sample consisted of 13 managers, 8 technicians, 2 secretaries, and 99 hourly production workers. The sample was not divided by occupational level because this would have restricted the variance in task autonomy and job scope and would have precluded a test of the hypotheses.

Scale Validity and Reliabilty. The scales used in this study are the same as those used in study number 2, with the exclusion of the initiating-structure scale.

The performance measures were based on multitrait-multirater scales completed by the subject's peers and immediate superiors, with tests of discriminant and convergent validity based on those subjects for whom peer and superior ratings were available. The same statistical tests were applied to these data as were applied to the performance data in the second study. As shown in Table 3, the results of these tests are very similar to those of Lawler (1966) and the results of the second study. Specifically, all of the peer-superior correlations met the requirement of convergent validity. Four of the correlations met the second test of discriminant validity and the overall pattern of concordance was significant at the .01 level. As in the second study, the ratings had a large amount of halo, which accounted for the failure to pass the first test of discriminant validity. The reliabilities for the job-scope, job-autonomy, and consideration scales were .64, .88, and .87 respectively.

Statistical Procedure. The sample was divided into approximately equal thirds on the basis of scores on job scope and job autonomy, using the same procedure as described in study number 2. The medium group was slightly larger because borderline ties were placed in this group. For each group, correlations were computed for the relationships between leader consideration and subordinate satisfaction and performance.

Findings

From Table 5 it can be seen that the correlations between consideration and satisfaction with intrinsic job rewards decreases from .61 to .24 to .10 for those in jobs with low, medium, and high autonomy, and that the correlation for the low-autonomy group is significantly less than for the high-autonomy group. Other differences between groups appear to be negligible. Thus, hypothesis 3 is replicated only with respect to intrinsic job satisfaction, and hypothesis 4 is not supported.

Table 5 also presents the data relevant to hypothesis 5. The average correlations between consideration and satisfaction decrease from .38 to .24 to .18 for the groups with low, medium and high job scope. Two of the correlations for low job scope are significantly higher than their respective correlations for the groups with medium or high job scope.

The average correlations between leader consideration and performance decrease from .33 to .18 to −.04 as predicted. Two of the correlations with low job scope are significantly higher than their correlations with the groups with high job scope.

TABLE 5 RANK-ORDER CORRELATIONS BETWEEN LEADER CONSIDERATION AND SUBORDINATE SATISFACTION AND PERFORMANCE MODERATED BY JOB AUTONOMY AND JOB SCOPE—STUDY NUMBER 3

	Job Autonomy				*Job Scope*					
				Differences in Correlations				*Differences in Correlations*		
Variables	*Low* (N = *36)*	*Medium* (N = *41)*	*High* (N = *40)*	*High versus Low Group*	*Low* (N = *39)*	*Medium* (N = *46)*	*High* (N = *37)*	*Low versus Medium Group*	*Low versus High Group*	*Reliabilities*
Satisfaction with										
Company	58	54†	65†		.18	.23	.00			.84
Intrinsic job rewards	61†	24	10	.05	.58†	.50†	.44†			.64
Extrinsic job rewards	50†	24	43†		.50†	.32*	.07		.01	.79
Family attitude toward job . . .	34*	17	23		.15	.16	.27			.72
Security	7	13	31*		.22	.19	.09			.61
Job freedom	60†	33†	44†		.60†	.08	.38*	.01		.70
Average satisfaction	45	28	36		.38	.24	.19			
Performance ratings										
Quality	—17	—1	7		.49†	.19	—.03			
Ability	—7	—7	—21		.28	.07	—.01			
Effort	0	—8	—5		.39†	.23	—.03			
Initiative	—39†	—18	—23		.32†	.23	—.09		.01	
Ability without guidance	—24	21	11		.18	.20	.21			
Quantity	—5	—22	—3		.36†	.20	.11			
Average performance	—15	—6	—6		.33	.18	.04			

* $p \leq .05$.
† $p \leq .01$.

Conclusion

The findings about the moderating effect of job scope replicated the findings of the second study and thus provide rather strong support for the hypothesis. However, the findings about the moderating effect of job autonomy only partially replicated those of the second study, possibly because the population for the third study consisted primarily of blue-collar workers who were probably quite dependent on their superiors, even when they scored in the upper third of the job-autonomy scale. The job-autonomy scale means for the sample in the second study were 2.9, 3.4, and 4.0 for the low, medium, and high groups and 2.6, 3.3, and 3.8, respectively, for the third study. The finding that consideration has a significant and positive relationship to satisfaction for groups with both low and high job autonomy is consistent with the interpretation that all respondents were probably dependent on their superiors for satisfaction, regardless of their response to the job-autonomy scale. Thus, this study provides moderate support for the hypothesis with respect to the influence of job scope and ambiguous results with respect to the influence of job autonomy.

CONCLUSION

The theory advanced here has been shown to reconcile apparently conflicting findings from previous research. It has also been shown to provide an integrated explanation of the results of findings about authoritarianism in leader hierarchical influence, closeness of supervision, initiating structure, and consideration.

The theory was tested by correlational tests of 8 hypotheses derived from general propositions. The tests are somewhat weak in that the theoretical constructs, such as intrinsic task satisfaction and ambiguity of task-role demands, were inferred from situational measures of task autonomy and job scope and from occupational characteristics of the populations studied. These inferences make the tests susceptible to the error of rejecting a valid hypothesis, so that the tests are conservative ones. A further limitation is inherent in cross-sectional survey research, which can rule out invalid hypotheses, but cannot establish causal relationships among the variables.

The findings, when viewed collectively, generally support the theory. Among high-occupational groups, leader initiating structure was generally positively related to subordinate satisfaction and performance. This relationship was accounted for in terms of variance in subordinate role ambiguity, which was shown to have a negative correlation with initiating structure. The relationships between leader structure and subordinate role ambiguity, and satisfaction, although significant and in the theoretically predicted direction, were quite low, probably because it was not possible to control for contaminating variables that would be expected to suppress these relationships. The relationships between initiating structure and consideration, and subordinate satisfaction and performance varied significantly and widely in the directions predicted when moderated by job scope. When moderated by task autonomy the theoretical predictions were supported by one sample and not supported by another which raised a question about the appropriateness of task autonomy as an indicator of ambiguity of task-role demands and satisfaction among blue-collar workers as well as a question about the validity of the general proposition from which the hypothesis was derived.

On balance, the ability of the theory to reconcile and integrate earlier findings, together with moderate-to-strong support, for seven of the eight hypotheses tested, two of which were replicated in a second study, suggests that the theory shows promise and warrants further testing with more direct measurement of the theoretical constructs using experimental as well as correlational methods.

REFERENCES

Atkinson, J. W. Towards experimental analysis of human motivation in terms of motives, expectancies, and incentives. In J. W. Atkinson (ed.), *Motives in Fantasy, Action and Society.* New York: Van Nostrand, 1958.

Bescoe, Robert O. and Lawshe, C. H. Foreman leadership as perceived by superiors and subordinates. *Personnel Psychology,* 1959, **12**, 573–82.

Campbell, Donald T. and Fiske, Donald W. Convergent and discriminant validation by the multitrait, multimethod matrix. *Psychological Bulletin,* 1959, **56**, 81–105.

Evans, Martin G. The effects of supervisory behavior upon worker perception of their path-goal relationships. Doctoral dissertation, Yale University, 1968.

Evans, Martin G. Convergent and discriminant validities of the Cornell job descriptive index and a measure of goal attainment. *Journal of Applied Psychology,* 1969, **55**, 102–06.

Fiedler, Fred E. *A theory of leadership effectiveness.* New York: McGraw-Hill, 1967.

Filley, Alan C. and House, Robert J. *Managerial process and organizational behavior.* Glenview, Ill.: Scott Foresman, 1969.

Fleishman, Edwin A. Twenty years of consideration and structure. In *Symposium on contemporary development in the study of leadership.* Carbondale: Southern Illinois University, 1971, in press.

Fleishman, Edwin A. and Harris, Edwin F. Patterns of leadership behavior related to employee grievances and turnover. *Personnel Psychology,* 1962, **15**, 43–56.

Galbraith, Jay and Cummings, Larry L. An empirical investigation of the motivational determinants of past performance: Interactive effects between instrumentality, valence, motivation and ability. *Organizational Behavior and Human Performance* 1967, **2**, 237–57.

Georgopoulous, Basil S., Mahoney, Gerald M., and Jones, Nyle W., Jr. A path-goal approach to productivity. *Journal of Applied Psychology,* 1957, **41**, 345–53.

Graen, George. Instrumental theory of work motivation: Some empirical results and suggested modifications. *Journal of Applied Psychology,* 1969, **53**, 1–25.

Halpin, Andrew W. The leader behavior and effectiveness of aircraft commanders. In Ralph H. Stogdill and A. E. Coons (eds.), *Leader behavior: Its description and measurement.* Ohio State University, Bureau of Business Research, 1957.

Hemphill, John K. Relations between the size of the group and the behavior of superior leaders. *Journal of Abnormal and Social Psychology,* 1950, **32**, 11–12.

House, Robert J., Filley, Alan C., and Gujarati, Domo N. Leadership style, hierarchical influence and the satisfaction of subordinate role expectations: A test of Likert's influence proposition. *Journal of Applied Psychology,* 1971 in press. (a)

House, Robert J., Filley, Alan C., and Kerr, Steven. Relation of leader consideration and initiating structure to R and D subordinate satisfaction. *Administrative Science Quarterly,* 1971 **16**, 19–30. (b)

House, Robert J., Wigdor, Lawrence A., and Shulz, Kenneth. Leader behavior, psychological participation, employee satisfaction and performance: An extension of prior investigations and a motivation theory interpretation. In W. M. Frey (ed.), *Proceedings Seventh Annual Conference of Eastern Academy of Management,* Amherst: University of Massachusetts, 1970, pp. 179–95.

Korman, Abraham K. Consideration, initiating structure and organizational criteria—A review. *Personnel Psychology,* 1966, **19**, 349–61.

Lawler, Edward E. III. Ability as a moderator of the relationship between job attitudes and job performance. *Personnel Psychology,* 1966, **19**, 153–64.

Lawler, Edward E. III. A correlation-causal analysis of the relationship between expectancy attitudes and job performance. *Journal of Applied Psychology,* 1968, **52**, 462–68.

Mass, H. S. Personal and group factors in leader's social perception. *Journal of Abnormal and Social Psychology,* 1950, **45**, 54–63.

Oaklander, Harold and Fleishman, Edwin A. Patterns of leadership related to organizational stress in hospital settings. *Administrative Science Quarterly,* 1964, **8**, 520–32.

Patchen, Marvin. Supervisory methods and group performance norms. *Administrative Science Quarterly,* 1962, **7**, 275–94.

Pelz, Donald C. Influence: A key to effective leadership in the first-line supervisor. *Personnel,* 1952, 29: 209–21.

Porter, Lyman and Lawler, Edward E. III. *Managerial attitudes and performance.* Homewood, Ill.: Irwin Dorsey, 1967.

Rim, Y. Leadership attitudes and decisions involving risk. *Personnel Psychology,* 1965, **18**, 423–30.

Rizzo, John R., House, Robert J., and Lirtzman, Sidney E. Role conflict and ambiguity in complex organizations. *Administrative Science Quarterly,* 1970, **15**, 150–53.

Siegel, Sidney. *Nonparametric statistics.* New York: McGraw-Hill, 1956.

Stogdill, Ralph M. *Manual for the Leader Behavior Description Questionnaire.* Columbus: Ohio State University of Business Research, 1965.

Vroom, Victor H. *Work and motivation.* New York: Wiley, 1964.

Vroom, Victor and Mann, Floyd. Leader authoritarianism and employee attitudes. *Personnel Psychology,* 1960, **13**, 125–39.

Wager, Wesley L. Leadership style, influence and supervisory role obligations. *Administrative Science Quarterly,* 1965, **9**, 391–420.

Wigdor, Larry. Effectiveness of various management and organization characteristics on employee satisfaction and performance as a function of employees need for independence. Doctoral dissertation, Bernard M. Baruch College, City University of New York, 1969.

47. THE INFLUENCE OF LEVEL OF PERFORMANCE ON MANAGERIAL STYLE: AN EXPERIMENTAL OBJECT-LESSON IN THE AMBIGUITY OF CORRELATIONAL DATA*

***Aaron Lowin and James R. Craig*†**

With few exceptions, observational studies purporting to identify managerial styles (leadership styles in a formal system) which enhance or impair subordinate performance can as easily be interpreted as picturing the reverse effect of performance *on* managerial style[1] (Carey, 1967, p. 415; Korman, 1966; Vroom, 1964, p. 215). This is, of course, the classic criticism of observational research. There are several reasons why this issue bears further inquiry. *(a)* The latter causal sequence is undoubtedly to some extent a valid one. It is difficult to conceive of a competent manager whose behavior is utterly insensitive to the performance level of his subordinates. How is the manager to guide his subordinates' actions, if not by his own behavior? *(b)* There are data available (Jackson, 1953) which suggest that managerial style does indeed alter with the setting in which the manager finds himself; differential productivity of subordinates between settings may account for part of that variability (Bem, 1967). Yet, observational studies are not necessarily insensitive to causality (Campbell & Stanley, 1963; Lipset, Lazarsfeld, Barton, & Linz, 1954), and Farris (1966) has recently employed a canonical correlation technique to evaluate the relative weights of the two proceesses: Subordinate productivity = Managerial style. The data clearly indicate that the effect of productivity on style, in at least Farris' setting, is more important than is the reverse process. *(c)* If one considers the immense amount of organized speculation and observational research which has been concerned with "leadership," which is today being expended, and which will certainly be brought to bear in the future —and the varied backgrounds of the researchers or their leader—subjects (business, church, community affairs, education, government and politics, military, sports . . .), then the importance of the topic and of this critical issue must be appreciated.

The significance of such criticism of the myriad observational studies of "leadership" must, in the end, be gauged by empirical evidence.[2] We are, therefore, reporting here a laboratory demonstration of the extent to which managerial style can be affected by subordinate productivity.

It would not be terribly enlightening to report merely the finding that supervisors of substandard productivity subordinates show high levels of monitoring and guidance. They probably do.[3] But there are dimensions of managerial style which are not so patently related to productivity. It is because these dimensions are common in the leadership literature that data indicating they are sensitive to productivity would be of value. The study below reports data not only on *(a) closeness of supervision* (a measure of monitoring and guidance), but also on *(b) initiating structure* (defined *here* as the extent to which the supervisor presses for organizational goal and subgoal attainment, especially in his strict adherence to the detailed behavior prescriptions set for his subordi-

---

**Organizational Behavior and Human Performance,* Vol. 3 (1968), pp. 440–58.

We are grateful to Mike Kavanagh and Pete Pruessing for their roles as "Charlie," and for their assistance in planning the study and analyzing data. The study was supported by a grant from the General Electric Foundation.

†Iowa State University and Western Kentucky University, respectively.

[1] The *content* of such studies is not an issue here. For summaries, see, for example, Fleishman and Harris (1962), Fleishman, Harris, and Burt (1955), Likert (1961), or Vroom (1964, Chs. 5, 8).

[2] In the volume *Assessment of Men* (OSS Staff, 1948) there is a report of an experimental situation in which *S* attempted to supervise two subordinates, who, being confederates of *E,* thoroughly obfuscated and annoyed *S.* As the task was intended to evaluate *S's* temperament and leadership qualities, and as no control groups were provided for, the data cannot be used for our present purposes. Considerable variance in reactions to this rather structured situation was, however, evident (pp. 111–113). (See also footnote 3.)

[3] Indeed, it seems so direct and trivial to predict that subordinate productivity would affect managerial style that the reader may well question the need for the research or for this report. The authors feel that there are several reasons why this issue deserves attention. *(a)* However intuitively obvious, the above proposition is not necessarily valid. If managerial style and subordinate performance are pictured in systemic equilibrium, then the manager of the sub-standard subordinate may perhaps be found to show little monitoring or guidance (for those managers who do show these behaviors have either successfully affected their subordinates or have left the system). But as the present study *manipulates* productivity in an unselected population of managers, the equilibrium analysis is inappropriate. *(b)* Intuition is no substitute for empirical inquiry, at least as regards the present issue. Absurd as it may seem, we know of no published definitive demonstration of the argument we have posed (the Farris, 1966, and OSS Staff, 1948 reports are, however, relevant). An empirical theory of organizational behavior presupposes some data, thus the present report. *(c)* If the argument we propose is, indeed, such a trivial one, then why is it that the vast literature on managerial style moves so readily from correlational data to causal inferences and prescriptive advice without adequately considering the "obvious" alternatives? A demonstration such as we propose here would have didactic value as an object lesson in the interpretation of data.

nate, even if the prescriptions and the alternative behaviors attempted by the subordinate would, in the end, achieve the identical larger goal in much the same manner), and *(c) consideration for subordinate* (defined here as concern for the needs and desires of the subordinate on job-*irrelevant* activities).[4] If we can show that each of these aspects of managerial style is sensitive to subordinate productivity, then our above criticism of the direction of causality may indeed be a serious one.

However valuable such a demonstration would be for leadership or organizational research, or as a contribution to methodology, our discussion to this point remains only a reaction to analyses reported by others, and lacks a theoretical thrust in its own right. But there are available several broad views of interpersonal interaction, all of which predict that managerial style should be sensitive to subordinate performance. By suggesting the very alternative analysis we have presented above, these approaches substantiate what might otherwise be considered only a petty and pedantic critique of someone else's labors. A functional view of attitudes (Katz & Stotland, 1959; Newcomb, 1950, Ch. 4; Peak, 1955; Rosenberg, 1956) would argue that positive attitudes develop toward objects which are instrumental for motive attainment. This analysis may readily be extended to the manager-subordinate situation in a formal organization (Lowin, 1968). The reward system in such an organization makes the outcomes to the manager heavily contingent on the performance of his subordinates. The more valuable to the organization the actions of the subordinate, the greater the eventual desired outcomes to the manager, the more positive the manager's attitude toward the subordinate. Any of the several analyses of games and instrumental interaction (e.g., Homans, 1961; Thibaut & Kelley, 1959) generally argue that persons whose actions cause another to be rewarded are positively cathected by the other. Adams' Theory of Equity (1963, 1965) would predict that, in an exchange, a person (manager) who perceives that another (subordinate) is contributing a great deal to some situation (the organization) will try to increase the number of desirable outcomes that person equitably receives from the situation. A Heider (1958)—or Newcomb (1959)—type cognitive consistency model of interpersonal attraction would argue that a shared orientation toward some common object (manager desires high productivity, subordinate is highly productive) would elicit positive affect by the one actor (manager) toward the other. These theoretical orientations allow us to make the following predictions for the stylistic dimensions of *initiating structure* and *consideration for subordinate.* The manager of a highly productive subordinate will be the more inclined to allow his subordinate to do as he (the subordinate) wishes, both in regard to job-relevant activities (low initiating structure) and job-irrelevant ones (an aspect of high consideration). In addition, such a manager will show positive affect toward his subordinate (another aspect of high consideration).

The two facets of the total above analysis complement each other nicely. The predictions for *closeness of supervision* may be directly derived from the demands placed on the manager by his occupancy of the organization role. But this approach does not of itself predict managerial *initiating structure* or *consideration* style, for these stylistic dimensions are not central to the prescribed role behavior of the proper manager. But the more theoretical interpersonal affect analysis, which says little with regard to proper role behavior (thus making no predictions about *closeness of supervision*) is able to predict for *initiating structure* and *consideration.* Combining the two we expect that, as compared with competent subordinates, managers of incompetent subordinates will show closer supervision, more initiating structure, and less consideration.

[4]Although these operational definitions are not the ones conventionally employed for *closeness of supervision* (defined for example, in Kahn & Katz, 1953) or *initiating structure* and *consideration* (see Fleishman & Peters, 1962), we feel they properly capture essential qualities of the concepts. In any event, the present study is primarily concerned with the *general* issue of the effects of productivity on managerial style, and not especially with *specific* criticism of any particular approach Therefore, it is not crucial that our operational definitions of the style dimensions we purport to examine render absolute justice to those dimensions described by others. (It is an interesting fact that the style literature is so vague as to make it all but impossible to obtain adequate agreement on just what a particular style "label" does and does not represent. Ambiguity in the literature makes it difficult to prescribe for an experimental confederate the behaviors appropriate to some style the researcher wishes to simulate, and it is equally difficult to get judges to agree on their ratings of a given behavior or given style dimension.) Although we propose to measure three style dimensions, we can make no priori claim for their mutual statistical independence.

METHOD

Subjects who truly believed they had been hired for supervisory positions in an office were systematically observed reacting to a series of carefully programmed probes by a competent (HI comp) or incompetent (LO comp) subordinate (actually a confederate *(C)* of the experimenter *(E).* The *S* then completed a 14-item "confidential evaluation" post-situation questionnaire (PSQ) on the subordinate. Finally, the experiment was revealed, and *S* was debriefed and paid for his time at the agreed rate. This radical deception, in which *S* applied for and was supposedly hired for a real job, was reluctantly undertaken because it was strongly felt that extrapolation from data of Ss who were cognizant of their participation in research to "the real world" would, in this instance, be systematically deficient.

Male Ss were recruited with an ambiguous school newspaper ad which offered a part-time temporary job for college men, or by a letter to persons who had registered with the school student employment office. Responding, S telephoned "Dr. Egbert Souse," who described the position as that of office supervisor for a group of Job Corpsmen who were engaged in secretarial work for a conference of high school teachers of English, to be held during the summer. S's duties were to be entirely supervisory; he was himself not expected to do any secretarial work. S was promised $2.50 per hour. A two-hour appointment was made for S to meet with Dr. Souse and to apply for the job. It was emphasized that, as he was not the only applicant, S should in no way alter his other plans (or job prospects) on the assumption that he would be hired for the present position. The 155 mail solicitations resulted in close to 85 inquiries, the first 44 of which were processed. The ad generated 14 replies, of which the first 8 were processed.

The following sequence of events took place when S arrived (programmed times italicized in parentheses). *(0–20)* E introduced himself as Dr. Souse, welcomed S, and described the situation. The program Dr. Souse represented would be conducting a teacher development conference and, in anticipation, was hiring an office staff. The nature of the project required Souse to hire Job Corps people as secretarial help, and he was in need of a supervisor for his office staff of Corpsmen. One Corpsman, Charlie *(C)*, was already at work in an adjoining office; others would be starting work in a few days. Charlie was now typing letters to high school officials to solicit nominations for the English teachers' conference participants. E asked S to complete a job application, examined the application and, after appropriate comments, offered the job to S. E answered S's questions. S (always) accepted the job. Stating that he must attend a conference for the next hour-and-a-half, E asked whether S was available to supervise Charlie and keep an eye on things. S (always) agreed. E called in Charlie and introduced S to C. After handing E a set of letters and envelopes he had supposedly already completed, C left. E scanned the letters and commented on the quantity and quality (see below), asked S to check the letters and prepare them for E's signature, then left. C and S were now alone in two separate rooms of one office complex.

At the times indicated below C entered S's office and delivered certain verbatim probes. C then returned to his own office and recorded S's responses, as verbatim as possible. C also kept as complete a record of other events as possible. A considerable number of events spontaneously initiated by S usually occurred.[5] The probes are reported below in temporal order within the managerial style dimension they were intended to elicit.

Probes to Evaluate Effectiveness of HI-LO Manipulation

(57) C brought in some cards or envelopes he was supposed to be working on. "Hey—about how many letters a day do I have to do anyway?" (Pause) "I mean I never did this before. How am I doing?" (Pause) "Am I doing enough?" (Pause) "How do they look?"

Six PSQ items also tapped manipulation effectiveness.

Probes for Closeness of Supervision

(47) Immediately after address probe (below): "I can't find my cigarettes. Do you mind if I go down to the snack-bar for some cigarettes and take myself a coffee-break while I'm there? I'm tired." If S consents: "How much time can I have? 10 minutes? 15? 20?" C suddenly "found" his cigarettes, and returned to his office.

(85) C brought in some cards or envelopes he was supposed to be working on. "I'm finished doing the first batch of these. Man, there are still a lot of them to do yet. I guess I'll take a break now and read a magazine." C sat down and ignored any hint to leave. C resisted first order to leave: "Why? I did the work." C remained seated until E returned *(100)* unless order to leave was repeated.

---

[5] The variety of these events made it impossible to adequately systematically record and code each with the rich detail it deserved, or to communicate them here. In the present study, C's probes and S's direct replies accounted for perhaps only 10–15% of the elapsed time. Unlike experiments in which the confederate is given an extensive and closely programmed script with which he is to occupy a good portion of the S's time, and where extra-script comments by S are largely ignored, we deliberately sought to limit the probes which allow S one of two or three responses, and increase instead the behavioral initiative of S. The record of these events is, from a rigorous point of view, tainted. C, who was thoroughly cognizant of the fact that he was to minimize his component of interaction and act neutrally for the rest was, however, aware of S's condition. There was no point in trying to keep C unaware, since the character of S's comments to C immediately identified the condition. There is, therefore, the possibility that C subtly elicited desirable responses from S. This possibility is less troublesome if the analysis is based as completely as possible on gross observations which are not easily subject to subtle shaping, and which can be analyzed objectively. For the most part we have relied on such data for the present report, and it is hoped that the quantity and variety of the data given in Tables 1 and 2 adequately support the conclusions. The additional evidence accumulated but ignored here nicely rounds out the picture of S as evidencing a coherent style with regard to C, and not so many truncated reactions to as many probes.

C also recorded the number and length of spontaneous supervisory visits *S* made to *C*'s office.

Two PSQ items tapped *S*'s opinion as to the degree of closeness of supervision appropriate for *C*.

Probes for Initiating Structure

(35) *C* brought in some completed letters and envelopes. "Do you want all the letters typed first, then all the envelopes, or do you mind if I type a letter, then an envelope, then a letter. . . ? The last way is easier and I like to do it that way. But Mr. Souse told me to do it the other way." If *S* chose Souse's way: "Look, there really isn't any difference, and I can do it better my way. Do you mind if I do it my way instead?"

(47) *C* brought in envelope with address typed with each line staggered to the right of the previous line, and on which there was a hand-written comment: "Charlie do it this way." *C* had been typing envelopes with a constant margin for all lines. "Mr. Souse told me to type the addresses this way (shows sample), but it is a lot easier to do them the way I've been doing them. Which way should I do them?"

(68) *C* entered. "I'm all out of paper. Mr. Souse is supposed to be getting some more. Should I keep on typing the envelopes, like Mr. Souse said—or can I start sorting these cards" (pointing to some IBM cards.) "I'll have to do the cards sooner or later, and I'd like to get started."

Four PSQ items tapped *S*'s willingness to share or delegate responsibility with *C*.

Probes for Consideration

(42) *C* entered. "It's all right if I make a personal long-distance phone call, isn't it? I don't think Mr. Souse minds." (If *S* consented, *C* faked a call.)

(47) At end of coffee-break probe (if break was sanctioned, and before finding cigarettes): "Would you like me to bring you a cup of coffee?"

(57) Immediately after closeness of supervision probe: "I'm still kind of new around here. I just moved into town. Do you know any girls I could call up for a date?" After reply: "Any good places around, where a guy could spend some time, or maybe pick up some girls?"

(85) As an afterthought, after *C* sits down during closeness of supervision probe: "Hey, if you want to read one of these (magazines), help yourself." *C* proceeded to read a *Playboy*, and offered *S* three others he brought in (one "girlie" magazine, one hot-rod, one sports).

C also recorded the number and length of spontaneous non-supervisory visits *S* made to *C*'s office. Although not included in the original plan, these data were recorded for most *Ss* for, after the first few, it became clear that such visits were, for the most part, social pleasantries.

Two PSQ items tapped *S*'s perception of *C*'s friendliness (on the assumption that perceived friendliness would foster reciprocal behavior by *S*, and as a measure of the affective link from *S* to *C*).

Additional Data

(100) *E* returned: "Well, how did it go?" (pause) "What do you think of Charlie?" (pause) In a secretive voice: "You know, Charlie is with us for a trial period. If he really isn't good enough, we can ask the Job Corps people to take him back and send us someone else. He's sort of on probation. Do you think we should keep him or send him back?" (pause) "I have to let the Job Corps know tomorrow what we want to do with Charlie. He's been here two days, and that's the trial period. But I've been out of the office for so long that I don't really know what he's doing, and how well he's doing it. (Showing *S* the PSQ) They sent me this form to fill out, about his probationary period. Why don't you fill it out, instead of me. After all, you are really his immediate supervisor." The PSQ was headed "Federal Job Corps Training Program, Clerical Division . . . Confidential report on trial employment period . . . To employer: this is a confidential report. Please complete it as it will allow us to evaluate the further training needs and present abilities of the Job Corpsman you are presently employing. . . . Note: this form must be completed by the employee's immediate supervisor. It is essential that all your replies be absolutely frank."

Finally, *E* disclosed the study and intensively debriefed *S*. After *S* was paid, it was ascertained whether *S* had indeed been taken in, had earlier heard of the study, and would be agreeable to *E*'s utilizing *S*'s data. Of 52 *Ss* run after pretesting, four admitted strong suspicions about the nature of the setting (their data were eliminated). Using Aronson's (1966) suggestion for inducing *S* not to reveal the study we found that none of 51 *Ss* questioned admitted hearing of the study from someone else. On the whole, *S*'s reactions to *E*'s disclosure were gratifyingly pleasant, and about two-thirds apparently seemed amused about the "candid camera" nature of the setting and their own reactions, interested in the nature of the project, and more than willing to forgive *E* his trangression. The remaining *Ss* reacted in a more neutral and surface manner; one *S* angrily refused payment and left with his PSQ before the debriefing could be completed.

Manipulation of Subordinate Competence

Competence was controlled by simultaneously varying the productivity and quality of the letters and envelopes *C* had presumably typed. The HI comp *C* presented 11 two-page letters to *E* at time = *17*, 3 to *S* at *35*, and 3 to *S* at *57*. The LO comp *C* presented 7 one-page letters at *17*, 2 at *35*, 2 at *57*. Similar numbers of envelopes were delivered with the letters. To free *C* from the disagreeable task of having to type continuously for two hours for each *S*, a tape recording of typing sounds was utilized. The recorder was run at high or low speed to reinforce the manipulation.

The HI comp letters and envelopes contained only a half-dozen errors, all of which were minor. In sharp contrast, the LO comp letters each contained an average of six errors, many of which were gross and entirely inexcusible. These included shift in margins, omissions in lines, spacing and paragraph indentations, inappropriate or missing capitalization and punctuation, multiple misspellings, mistyped or improper salutations, etc. The envelopes were similarly disfigured. The letters were designed so that on identifying only a fraction of the errors, any college student should recognize them to pose a serious threat of embarrassment to the sending organization, the high school English teacher development conference, for which *S* was working.

In order to compress the process by which *S* gradually learned of *C*'s skills, *E* thumbed through the materials *C* handed him at time = *17* (before *E* left) and commented as follows to *S:* (HI comp condition) "Well, Charlie seems to have done a lot more than I expected him to. He's apparently quite fast. And there don't seem to be very many errors at all. He's a good typist." (LO comp condition) "Well, Charlie doesn't seem to have done very much at all. He's only got this much done, and he's been at it for several hours now. He's a slow typist. And there seem to be quite a few errors here, quite a few. He may not be that good a typist."

Other than for the direct and powerful manipulations of productivity and quality, the balance of the experiment was held constant across conditions. We were hoping that the perception of a Job Corpsman was sufficiently ambiguous to allow these limited manipulations to shape the situational Gestalt (see footnote 5).

In order to shorten the duration of the study, *E* worked with two *C*'s (*C*1, *C*2) in separate buildings. Final cell *N*'s (excluding the four suspicious *S*s) were: C1, 13 HI and 12 LO, C2, 11 HI and 12 LO. Subject allocation was randomly determined with the two constraints that *(a)* near-equal cell *N*'s (2 conditions $\times$ 2 *C*s design) should result and *(b)* an irregular supply of stimulus materials (hand-typed letters and envelopes) forced a run of 12 HI, then 11 LO *S*s at the beginning of the study.

RESULTS AND DISCUSSION

The data we will consider consist of PSQ item means (Table 1) and coded observations (Table 2). All PSQ items consisted of 5-, 6- or 8-point scale structured questions, and the raw data required no subjective judgments. But subjective judgments were necessary for the observational records made by *C*. (Note that *C* logged behaviors and verbatim comments, but did not code these while recording the raw data.) Three coders (*E*, *C*1, and A.L.) jointly and blindly examined a random sample of 10 recorded observations for each observation item, in order to establish coding criteria. Each coder then coded an observational item (across all *S*s, and without knowledge of *S*'s condition or of any of *S*'s other data) until all items were processed. Intercoder disagreement was resolved by conference. For each *S*-item unit, there could be as many as three disagreements between the three orders. Overall, cross-coder comparisons reflected agreement on from 75 to 90% of the judgments, depending on the particular observational item being considered.

Before examining the dependent variables, it is useful to evaluate the adequacy of the manipulations. Items 1–6 of Table 1 and 1–6 of Table 2 were intended for this purpose. The data conclusively argue that the HI-LO manipulation left a clear and powerful impression. Of the 24 planned comparisons (12 items evaluated for *C*1 and *C*2), all fall as predicted ($p_{Ho} < .001$).[6] The forcefulness of the manipulations can be appreciated if one considers that, having been instructed to do so by *E*, most of the *S*s spent 20–40 minutes of the 80 they were supposedly supervising *C* engaged in proofreading *C*'s letters. Especially in the LO condition *S* found himself faced unambigu-

[6]This report does not include item-by-item statistical tests. Such tests evaluate the probable adequacy of the null hypothesis in accounting for the findings. The data of Table 1 are so pervasive as to preclude the need for such evaluations. Even though the data of Table 2 often suffer from low Ns (see footnote a to Table 2) the data are still so consistent across items as to obviate the need for statistical analyses. We report instead the probability that C or more of PC planned comparisons could emerge in the predicted direction under the null hypothesis. This strategy is exceedingly conservative in that it ignores the scalar qualities of all the Table 1 data and some of the Table 2 data, and the extent of the observed differences (compare the cell differences in the data of Table 1 with the maximum item ranges reported in the Note to the Table). This mode of analysis requires that we report *all* differences anticipated prior to examining the data, and no post hoc analyses. Such is the case.

TABLE 1 MEANS OF PSQ ITEMS

Item	Confederate			
	C1		C2	
	HI Comp	LO Comp	HI Comp	LO Comp
Number of cases (N)	13	12	11	11[a]
Tests of manipulation				
1. How competent do you think this employee is?	2.23	3.66	2.54	3.57
2. How much further training could this employee still benefit from?	2.08	3.58	2.55	3.36
3. What is your opinion of the training he has received to date?	1.92	3.66	2.00	3.36
4. How would you grade this person's competence?	2.15	3.75	2.27	3.80[b]
5. How is his *productivity* rate?	2.38	5.00	2.18	5.00
6. How is the *quality* of the work he does?	1.85	5.16	2.18	4.55
Closeness of supervision				
7. As his supervisor, what is the best way of handling him?	2.62	3.16	2.55	3.45
8. He appears to need _______ type of supervision	2.46	4.08	2.64	3.82
Initiating structure				
9. As his supervisor, how do you feel about his taking responsibility for his work?	2.54	4.00	2.64	3.36
10. Would you prefer he did his jobs the way you want them done, or the way he thinks they ought to be done?	3.08	3.25	3.09	3.73
11. Most of the time, when he makes a suggestion, is it a good one or a bad one?	1.85	2.75	2.91	2.28
12. When he does things his own way, they are usually	2.23	3.83	2.27	4.00
Consideration				
13. Is he personable and friendly?	2.46	3.83	2.27	3.91
14. Is he the sort of person you might become personal friends with?	3.00	6.17	3.64	5.09

Note — Scale range was from 1 to 5 for all items except 1–6 for items 5 and 6, 1–8 for items 13 and 14. Predictions are always HI < LO.

[a] Twelve *S*s observed, but one refused to turn in his PSQ.

[b] *N* = 10 as one *S* left this item blank.

TABLE 2 Ns OR MEANS FOR OBSERVATIONAL DATA

Observation (Time in Parentheses)		Confederate			
		C1		C2	
		HI Comp	LO Comp	HI Comp	LO Comp
No. of *S*s in condition[a]		13	12	11	12
Tests of manipulation					
1. How am I doing? (57)	Fine	13	1	10	—
	Poor	—	8	—	7
2. Am I doing enough? (57)	Yes	13	4	7	—
	Don't know	—	3	1	5
	No	—	3	—	—
3. How do they look? (57)	Few errors, good	13	1	11	—
	Many errors, poor	—	11	—	10
4. Well, how did it go? (100)	*C* is incompetent	—	9	—	8
	C is improving	—	1	—	—
	C is competent	11	—	8	1

TABLE 2 *(Continued)*

Observation (Time in Parentheses)		Confederate C1 HI Comp	Confederate C1 LO Comp	Confederate C2 HI Comp	Confederate C2 LO Comp
5. What do you think about Charlie? (100)	Competent	13	—	7	—
	Improving	—	1	—	1
	Incompetent	—	9	—	7
	S is ambivalent	—	—	—	2
6. Should we keep Charlie? (100)	Yes	9	1	10	—
	Non-committal	4	2	1	4
	No	—	9	—	8
Closeness of supervision					
7. *S* authorizes coffee-break demand (47)	Yes	11	7	9	8
	No	2	5	2	4
8. Time permitted for coffee-break, for those allowing the break (47)	10 mins or less	3	5	5	5
	over 10 mins	7	2	4	3
9. *S* reminds *C* of his errors (57)	Yes	3	10	—	3
	No	10	2	11	6
10. *S* criticizes *C* for taking unauthorized work-break in *S*'s office (85)	Yes	1	4	4	9
	No	10	6	6	3
11. *S orders C* to end his unauthorized work-break and return to work, in emotional, commanding or threatening tone, or with physical contact (85)		1	2	1	6
12. *S* enters *C*'s office for supervisory purposes	Yes	4	11	9	10
	No	9	1	2	2
13. Average no. of such visits, for those *Ss* doing so		1.0	2.0	1.67	4.10
14. Average length of such visit, mins[b]		1.00 ($N=3$)	4.45 ($N=4$)	1.44 ($N=8$)	1.93 (N = 10)
Initiating structure					
15. Type letters and envelopes (35)	*C*'s way	12	11	9	6
	Souse's way	1	0	2	6
16. Type addresses (47)	*C*'s way	12	5	5	—
	Souse's way	1	6	6	12
17. Sort cards (*C*'s desire) vs. type envelopes (Souse's desire)	*C*'s way	7	2	8	4
	Souse's way	6	10	3	8
Consideration					
18. Personal long-distance phone call (42)	Permitted	5	2	4	1
	Not permitted	8	10	7	10
19. *S* accepts *C*'s offer of a cup of coffee (47)	Yes	1	1	—	—
	No	9	6	9	8
20. *S* implies he can or will help *C* get girls' names for dates, or leaves topic open (57)	Yes	3	2	4	3
	No	10	10	7	9
21. Average number of entertainment locations *S* suggests to *C* (57)		2.00	1.33	1.73	1.00 ($N=2$)
22. *S* accepts *C*'s offer of a magazine (85)	Yes	4	2	3	1
	No	8	8	4	6
23. *S* enters *C*'s office for non-supervisory purposes	Yes	7	1	2	2
	No	6	11	9	10
24. Average number of such visits for those *Ss* doing so.		.85	.08	.18	.17
25. Average length of such visit, mins.[b]		2.95 ($N=4$)	7.00 ($N=1$)	1.5 ($N=2$)	1.5 ($N=2$)

[a]Several of these items were deliberately intended to draw *S* into a quasi-free-response situation which would not necessarily force one of two or three responses. As a result, a considerable number of irrelevant replies were often received, and the cell Ns associated with the relevant replies fell short of the number of *Ss* in that cell.

[b]Data reported for all *Ss* where it is available. Data was not recorded during the first third of the study, and situational constraints often kept *C* from taking or recording the data.

ously with the prospect of having to supervise someone who was probably the world's worst typist and who was, unaccountably, now typing for a university program to improve the competence of teachers of English. Most of the LOs "red-pencilled" C's letters to an extent which clearly implied that the letter could not possibly be sent out as is, or even corrected, and that it was to be retyped (thus forcing the early run of HI Ss while more LO materials were prepared). Many Ss said as much to C or E. More interesting, as observed by C during the course of the experiment and by E when he first returned, many of the LOs were clearly emotionally aroused, if not upset, by what could logically only be the performance of their subordinate. This may be interpreted as evidence for a gradually evolving negative attitude toward his subordinate by the supervisor.

Closeness of Supervision

The data are shown as items 7–8 in Table 1 and 7–14 in Table 2. The Ss clearly prescribe closer supervision for LOs than for HIs (Table 1) and follow their prescription by their actions (Table 2). The 20 independent planned comparisons all support the predictions ($p_{Ho} < .001$). As indicated in our introductory paragraphs, it is not surprising to find that S monitors and controls C, and feeds back to C information on C's performance. Perhaps more interesting is the evidence in Table 2 that closeness of supervision generalized to other aspects of work-relevant activities. Typically, S pressed C not to take a work-break (items 7, 10) and to end his work-break quickly (items 8, 11) more under LO competence. Likewise, more Ss spontaneously entered C's office for supervisory purposes (item 12), made more visits per person (item 13) and remained there longer (item 14) under LO. To be sure, these visits were in part taken up with direct criticism of C's letters, but they often extended to other job-relevant matters. Especially in the LO condition, S occasionally undertook to instruct C in the use of the typewriter and in the proper positioning of the original copy on the desk, checked to make sure C had been supplied with all the necessary paraphernalia of the typist, checked on the originals from which C was typing, examined the list of names and addresses to which letters were being sent. Not only did S usually suggest C speed up his work, but occasionally S suggested C slow down (to reduce errors) or take a break (to reduce fatigue).

Initiating Structure

The findings for initiating structure, items 9–12, Table 1 and 15–17, Table 2, similarly confirm our predictions. Twelve of 14 planned comparisons emerge in the predicted direction ($p_{Ho} < .007$; disconfirmations are: Table 1, item 11, *C2*, and Table 2, item 15, *C1*). The typical LO S thinks little of potential contributions made by C, prefers C to do things the way they are prescribed, and sees C as irresponsible (Table 1). Table 2 reflects situations in which S would have found it difficult to rationally argue that the prescribed method was better than C's. It is, of course, possible to argue that S chose the prescribed method because, as he was inexperienced with the operation, prudence would dictate he not change anything of his own accord. But this analysis fails to account for the *differential* acceptance of C's suggestions in the two conditions. In many instances S openly remarked to C that there would appear to be no real difference between the methods, yet then proceeded to pass arbitrary judgment on C's suggestion. The differential acceptance of C's suggestion in the two conditions was probably due not only to the possible hidden advantage of one method over another (as a function of the generalized perceived competence of C), but also to S's disinclination to accept any of the LO C suggestions at face value, when the choice between the two alternatives was quite arbitrary. The latter behavior suggests that affective, as well as cognitive, factors may be operative.

Consideration

Under this label we are considering all those actions which link S with C but which are more or less job-irrelevant. Perhaps most direct are the two questionnaire items about perceived friendliness (items 13–14, Table 1), for they tap S's affective link to C. Clearly, the predictions are supported. Here too the observational data (items 18–25, Table 2) back the questionnaire. Twelve of 16 planned comparisons of Table 2 fall in the expected direction (exceptions: items 19 and 25, both Cs). The four disconfirmations can easily be reconciled. As there was virtually no variance on item 19, no analysis of the variance can be made. The paucity of subjects for whom data was recorded for item 25 easily accounts for that poor data. But even including the latter items, 16 of 20 planned comparisons support the analysis ($p_{Ho} < .006$).

It should be recognized that many of the items of Table 2 are suggestive of stylistic dimensions other than the one with which they have been somewhat arbitrarily identified. It is possible to view items 1–3 as probing closeness of supervision, or 10–11 as initiating structure. More importantly, most of the #1–17 items at least indirectly imply an affective component in S's reaction to C. The affective component can similarly be interpreted from the questionnaire items (Table 1). It may, perhaps, be possible to consider affect as that aspect of supervisory behavior which unifies the otherwise diverse facets of his actions vis-a-vis a subordinate. At the very least, this analysis suggests that while leadership behavior may be portrayed as multidimensional in character, the dimensions may share a common affective orientation.

One should comment, also, on the apparent main and interaction effects of competence with confederate and location (Table 1, item 14; Table 2, items 9–13, 15, 16, 20, 24). We have delayed discussion of this point because there is no immediate relevance of such effects for the main issues of the study. But, clearly, the manager-subordinate relationship is shaped by characteristics of the subordinate other than competence (as narrowly conceived in the present study). For instance, the subordinate's behavior vis-à-vis his manager likely governs and directs the manner in which affectively loaded actions by the manager are undertaken. Insofar as the present study attempted to standardize *C*'s behavior, the *C*1–*C*2 differences suggest that the script was less than perfect. Nevertheless, the main and interaction *C*1-*C*2 effects fail to upset the central findings, for the HI-LO differences were obtained, to at least some extent, by each *C*.

With the few exceptions noted above, all the data support the predictions that subordinate performance would affect his manager's closeness of supervision, initiating structure and consideration. Indeed, the negative data lend additional confidence to the conclusion for, when 54 predictions are made, several type-II errors should be expected. Several of the six non-confirmations may be of this sort. (A "perfect" set of findings would in this respect be suspect.) The data strongly confirm Farris' (1966) finding that organizational behaviors are quite sensitive to prior organizational effectiveness. In like manner, this study lends strong support to the criticism of much observational data as not indicative of causal relationships, at least in organizational research. The extent and quality of the present findings suggest that the causal direction often ignored may be at least as important as the opposite one usually indicated. Our theoretical and empirical concern with the affective aspects of the manager's behavior may prove a useful concept in further analyses of leadership phenomena.

The present study nicely illustrates the interacting role of field and laboratory research. This project was in part motivated by Farris' (1966) field data; a field experiment is now indicated in order to validate this laboratory study under more relevant conditions.

REFERENCES

Adams, J. S. Toward an understanding of inequity. *Journal of Abnormal and Social Psychology,* 1963, **67**, 422–36.

Adams, J. S. Inequity in social exchange. In L. Berkowitz (ed.), *Advances in experimental social psychology,* Vol. 2. New York: Academic Press, 1965, Pp. 267–99.

Aronson, E. Avoidance of inter-subject communication. *Psychological Reports,* 1966, **19**, 238.

Bem, D. J. Self-perception: The dependent variable of human performance. *Organizational Behavior and Human Performance,* 1967, **2**, 105–21.

Campbell, D. T. and Stanley, J. C. *Experimental and quasi-experimental designs for research.* Chicago: Rand McNally, 1963.

Carey, A. The Hawthorne studies: A radical criticism. *American Sociological Review,* 1967, **32**, 408–16.

Farris, G. F. *A causal analysis of scientific performance.* Doctoral dissertation. University of Michigan, 1966. (Abstract.)

Fleishman, E. A. and Harris, E. F. Patterns of leadership behavior related to employee grievances and turnover. *Personnel Psychology,* 1962, **15**, 43–56.

Fleishman, E. A., Harris, E. F., and Burtt, H. E. *Leadership and supervision in industry.* Columbus: Ohio State University Press, 1955.

Fleishman, E. A. and Peters, D. A. Interpersonal values, leadership attitudes, and managerial success. *Personnel Psychology,* 1962, **15**, 127–43.

Heider, F. *The psychology of interpersonal relations.* New York: Wiley, 1958.

Homans, G. C., *Social behavior: Its elementary forms.* New York: Harcourt, Brace & World, 1961.

Jackson, J. M. The effect of changing the leadership of small work groups. *Human Relations,* 1953, **6**, 25–44.

Kahn, R. L. and Katz, D. Leadership practices in relation to productivity and morale. In D. Cartwright and A. Zander (eds.), *Group Dynamics* (2d ed.). Evanston: Row, Peterson, 1960. Pp. 554–70.

Katz, D. and Stotland, E. A preliminary statement to a theory of attitude structure and change. In S. Koch (ed.), *Psychology: A study of a science,* Vol. 3. New York: McGraw-Hill, 1959. Pp. 423–75.

Korman, A. K. "Consideration," "initiating structure," and organizational criteria—A review. *Personnel Psychology,* 1966, **19**, 349–61.

Likert, R. *New patterns of management.* New York: McGraw-Hill, 1961.

Lipset, S. M., Lazarsfeld, P. F., Barton, A. H., and Linz, J. The psychology of voting: An analysis of political behavior. In G. Lindzey (ed.), *Handbook of social psychology,* Vol. II. Reading, Mass.: Addison-Wesley, 1954. Pp. 1124–75.

Lowin, A. Participative decision-making: A model, literature critique and prescriptions for research. *Organizational Behavior and Human Performance,* 1968, **3**, 68–106.

Newcomb, T. M. *Social psychology,* New York: Dryden, 1950.

Newcomb, T. M. Individual systems of orientation. In S. Koch (ed.), *Psychology: A study of a science,* Vol. 3. New York: McGraw-Hill, 1959, Pp. 384–422.

OSS (Office of Strategic Services) Assessment Staff. *Assessment of men.* New York: Rinehart, 1948.

Peak, Helen. Attitude and motivation. In M. R. Jones (ed.), *Nebraska symposium on motivation,* 1955. Lincoln: University of Nebraska Press, 1955. Pp. 149–188.

Rosenberg, M. J. Cognitive structure and attitudinal affect. *Journal of Abnormal and Social Psychology,* 1956, **53**, 367–72.

Thibaut, J. W. and Kelley, H. H. *The social psychology of groups.* New York: Wiley, 1959.

Vroom, V. H. *Work and motivation.* New York: Wiley, 1964.

chapter 5

BEHAVIORAL DIRECTION AND CHANGE STRATEGIES

In the previous two chapters we have examined the processes through which an organization activates and directs its members. We have also focused on the functions that group and leadership processes play in these activities. We are now faced with an ongoing organization with the behavior of its members directed toward many institutional as well as individual goals. Furthermore, the system is continually evolving over time and seeking to simultaneously maintain reasonable internal stability and sensitivity to the need for change.

Thus, the readings in this chapter concern four basic processes in organizational behavior; namely, direction, control, conflict, and change. The direction and control of human behavior in the pursuit of organizational objectives is our first focus. Direction and control are conceived as processes of monitoring and, where feasible, measuring the behavioral outcomes, comparing these measurements against desired ends and desired processes, and adjusting either the inputs into the organization or the processes and structure of the organization in order to attain more desirable outcomes. This last step in the control process moves us to a consideration of the conflicts thereby potentially created within organizations and to the change strategies and tactics utilized by organizations to prevent, utilize and/or overcome such resultants.

Section A

BEHAVIORAL DIRECTION AND CONTROL

In this part of Chapter 5, we focus specifically on the control concepts and tactics available to management of an organization in its attempts to monitor and maintain reasonable behavioral stability in the pursuit of organizational objectives.

We begin with Peabody's broad conceptualization of the kinds of authority talked about in the literature of organization theory. This classification scheme provides us with a general, conceptual introduction into the specific strategies and tactics of control usually found in organizations.

In classical organization theory, control has been thought of as a nonexpandable process; that is, if a superior delegates authority to a subordinate, thereby allowing him to exert greater control over his own methods of work, the gain in control by the subordinate is offset by an equal loss of control by the superior. Tannenbaum, on the basis of empirical data generated in several organizations, questions this proposition. He finds that in many cases both the subordinates and the superior may simultaneously perceive an increase in influence and control over the situation. Tannenbaum's work suggests some of the conditions under which such increases in the total influence reservoir of the organization can be generated.

Certainly one of the primary control mechanisms in all goal-seeking organizations is the system by which monetary values are placed on the assets of the organization and on the utilization of those assets. Until very recently, few attempts had been made to explicitly value the human resources of an organization. Many social scientists have argued that organizations, because they had no method for directly assessing the value of their human assets, tended to engage in actions which actually depleted those assets or, at least, did not increase their value over time. Brummet, Pyle, and Flamholtz argue that such a system of human resource accounting is desirable and practical. They describe the behavioral and economic principles involved in such a system and provide an illustration of such a system in action.

Control within organizations is not exclusively vertical; lateral or horizontal control and coordination are also necessary for effectiveness. Furthermore, questions of organizational control frequently focus on the relations among *units or departments* within an organization rather than upon individual relations exclusively. Hickson, Hinings, Lee, Schneck, and Pennings argue that differential power among organizational units is central to the question of organizational control and direction. Drawing upon the works of March, J. D. Thompson, and Lawrence and Lorsch, they argue that all organizational units face contingencies and constraints which limit their ability to control themselves, and that all units face interdependence with other units. Power then becomes a question of unequal dependencies among units. In order to attain and maintain control an organizational subunit will seek power relative to other subunits through three strategies: (1) absorb or cope with some of the uncertainty faced by the other unit, (2) reduce its substitutability relative to that of other units, and (3) increase its centrality in the work flow of the organization.

However the various strategies for maintaining control and direction of both individuals and subunits within the organization frequently generate interpersonal and interunit conflict and can also create rigid structural and psychological frameworks which are difficult to change. We will focus on these two phenomena of conflict and change in the next section.

48. PERCEPTIONS OF ORGANIZATIONAL AUTHORITY: A COMPARATIVE ANALYSIS*

***Robert L. Peabody*†**

This paper argues that the bases of formal authority—legitimacy and position—need to be distinguished from sources of functional authority—technical competence and human relations skills—which support and often compete with formal authority. Four analytical types of authority relations are developed from the literature and the examination of superior-subordinate relationships among 76 of the 77 members of three public service organizations. In all three organizations, but particularly among welfare workers, considerable importance was attributed to legitimacy and position as bases of authority. Police officers, however, singled out authority of person more frequently than either authority inherent in position or authority derived from superiors. Welfare organization members attached more importance to legitimacy and position than to technical competence and experience as sources of authority. School employees stressed professional competence as a base of authority much more than either police officers or welfare workers.

* *Administrative Science Quarterly*, Vol. 6, No. 4 (1962), pp. 463–82.

† Department of Political Science, Johns Hopkins University.

Authority relations are an integral component of organizational behavior. Clarification of the concept of authority would seem to be essential to the development of systematic organization theory.[1] Despite numerous attempts at conceptual clarification and a growing body of empirical inquiries focusing on or-

[1] This article is based on the author's doctoral dissertation at Stanford University entitled "Authority in Organizations: A Comparative Study" (1960). The research was financed in part by a grant from the Stanford University Committee on Research in Public Affairs. Further revision was made possible by a Brookings Institution Research Fellowship for 1960–61. For helpful comments on earlier versions of this paper I am indebted to Heinz Eulau and Robert A. Walker of Stanford University, James D. Thompson of the University of Pittsburgh, and F. P. Kilpatrick, Milton Cummings, and M. Kent Jennings of the Brookings Institution.

ganization behavior, Herbert A. Simon could conclude in 1957 that "there is no consensus today in the management literature as to how the term 'authority' should be used."[2] For Simon, the source of the difficulty lay in the failure of many writers to distinguish between "(1) a specification of the set of behaviors to which they wish to apply the term 'authority'; and (2) a specification of the circumstances under which such behaviors will be exhibited."[3] The first problem, one of definition, or the way in which the term "authority" will be used, continues to plague students of administration.[4] There seems to be considerable agreement, however, on an important facet of the second problem, namely, identification of the bases of authority that facilitate its acceptance. This paper briefly summarizes this apparent consensus in the literature and reports some tentative findings developed from an exploratory study of authority relations in three public service agencies: a branch office of.a county welfare department, a municipal policie department, and a suburban elementary school.

THE BASES OF AUTHORITY

This study is focused upon the organizational authority in its several forms. Although authority is initially based on formal position, legitimacy, and the sanctions inherent in office, its acceptance is conditioned by several additional factors. In analyzing such related phenomena as professional competence, experience, and leadership, which modify and condition the exercise of formal authority, several different approaches could be taken. Some sociologists, for example Robert K. Bierstedt, would clearly distinguish between authority, competence, and leadership, reserving the label "authority" for hierarchical status relationships between incumbents of formal positions in organizations.[5] Other students of administration, notably Herbert A. Simon and Robert V. Presthus, would broaden the meaning of authority to include additional bases beyond formal position and the sanctions inherent in office.[6] Everyday usage of the word and much of the interview data of this inquiry seem to support the more inclusive interpretations of Simon and Presthus. However, the development of a science of administration may necessitate either a restriction of the term "authority" to a more precise technical meaning or an abandonment of the term for purposes of rigorous theory building.[7] Which of these two usages of the term is finally adopted is not as important as making clear the implications of each. The bases of *formal* authority—legitimacy, position, and the sanctions inherent in office—need to be distinguished from the sources of *functional* authority, most notably, professional competence, experience, and human relations skills, which support or complete with formal authority.[8]

Rather than attempt an exhaustive review of the literature, five contributors to the study of authority

[2]*Administrative behavior* (2d ed.; New York, 1957), pp. xxxiv–xxxv. For criticism of Simon's "operational definition" of authority and Simon's rejoinder, see Edward C. Banfield, The decision-making schema, *Public Administration Review,* Vol. 17 (1957), pp. 278–85, and Simon, The decision-making schema: A reply, *Public Administration Review,* Vol. 18 (1958), pp. 60–63.

[3]*Administrative behavior,* p. xxxv.

[4]For a more recent unsuccessful attempt at an operational definition, see Daniel J. Duffy, Authority considered from an operational point of view, *Journal of the Academy of Management,* Vol. 2 (Dec. 1959), pp. 167–75. For a more traditional viewpoint of authority, see Merten J. Mandeville, The nature of authority, *Journal of the Academy of Management,* Vol. 3 (Aug. 1960), pp. 107–18. While numerous definitions of authority occur in the literature of administration and organization theory, a review of these writings reveals considerable variation, vagueness, and ambiguity. For extended comment, see the author's review of the literature of organizational authority (cited in note 1) and a closely parallel review of leadership theories by Warren G. Bennis, Leadership theory and administrative behavior: The problem of authority, *Administrative Science Quarterly,* Vol. 4 (1959), pp. 259–301.

[5]The problem of authority, Morroe Berger, Theodore Abel, and C. H. Page (eds..), *Freedom and control in modern society* (New York, 1954), pp. 67–81. In an earlier paper, Bierstedt defined authority as "institutional power," which appears to be a concept of authority somewhat broader than formal status relationships (An analysis of social power, *American Sociological Review,* Vol. 15 [1950], p. 736.)

[6]Simon, Authority, in C. M. Arensberg, et al., *Research in industrial human relations* (New York, 1957), pp. 104–6; Herbert A. Simon, D. W. Smithburg, and V. A. Thompson, *Public administration* (New York, 1950), pp. 189–201; Presthus, Authority in organizations, *Public Administration Review,* Vol. 20 (1960), pp. 86–91.

[7]In the initial stages of scientific inquiry, descriptions as well as generalizations are stated in the vocabulary of everyday language. The growth of a scientific discipline, however, always brings with it the development of a system of specialized, more or less abstract, concepts and of a corresponding technical terminology. See Carl G. Hempel, Fundamentals of concept formation in empirical science, *International Encylopedia of Unified Science* (Chicago, 1952), II, No. 7, p. 1.

[8]In general, functional authority supports formal authority. In a given superior-subordinate relationship, it is the superior's lack of functional authority or the subordinate's possession of greater competence, experience, or personal skills which tends to undermine formal authority. Competition may also occur between incumbents of equal formal rank, but different task or specialist orientations, as for example between the controller and the merchandise manager of a department store. Finally, competition between functional and formal authority may occur where hierarchical channels are ambiguous, a condition frequently characteristic of staff-line relationships. Cf. Victor A. Thompson's Distinction between hierarchical and nonhierarchical authority, hierarchy, specialization, and organizational conflict, *Administrative Science Quarterly,* Vol. 5 (1961), p. 499. See also Melville Dalton, Conflicts between staff and line managerial officers, *American Sociological Review,* Vol. 15 (1950), pp. 342–51; O. Glenn Stahl, The network of authority, *Public Administration Review,* Vol. 18 (1958), pp. ii–iv; O. Glenn Stahl, More on the network of authority, *Public Administration Review,* Vol. 20 (1960), pp. 35–37; Robert T. Golembiewski, Toward the new organization theories: Some notes on "Staff," *Midwest Journal of Political Science,* Vol. 5 (1961), pp. 237–59.

TABLE 1 THE BASES OF AUTHORITY

	Formal Authority		Functional Authority	
	Legitimacy	*Position*	*Competence*	*Person*
Weber*	Legal Legal order	 Hierarchical office	Rational authority Technical knowledge, experience	Traditional authority Charismatic authority
Urwick†		Formal, conferred by the organization	Technical, implicit in special knowledge or skill	Personal, conferred by seniority or popularity
Simon‡.	Authority of legitimacy, social approval	Authority of sanctions	Authority of confidence (technical competence)	Techniques of *persuasion* (as distinct from authority
Bennis§.		Role incumbency	Knowledge of performance criteria	Knowledge of the human aspect of administration
Presthus¶	Generalized deference toward authority	Formal role or position	Technical expertise	Rapport with subordinates, ability to mediate individual needs

* Max Weber, *The theory of social and economic organization,* A. M. Henderson and Talcott Parsons (trans.), Talcott Parsons (ed.) (New York, 1947), pp. 328, 339.

† L. Urwick, *The elements of administration* (London, 1944), p. 42.

‡ Herbert A. Simon, Authority, in Conrad M. Arensberg. *et al.* (eds.), *Research in industrial human relations* (New York, 1957), pp. 104–6; H. A. Simon. D. W. Smithburg, V. A. Thompson, *Public administration* (New York, 1950), pp. 189–201.

§ Warren G. Bennis, Leadership theory and administrative behavior: The problem of authority, *Administrative Science Quarterly,* Vol. 4 (1959), pp. 288–89.

¶ Robert V. Presthus, Authority in organizations, *Public Administration Review,* Vol. 20 (1960), pp. 88–91.

relations in organizations—Max Weber, Lyndall F. Urwick, Herbert A. Simon, Warren G. Bennis, and Robert V. Presthus—will be singled out as illustrative of a growing consensus as to the importance of several bases of authority which condition its acceptance. While not all these social scientists have placed emphasis on the same sources of authority and while they have frequently used different words to convey similar meanings, the essential points of agreement can be classified under four broad categories: (1) authority of legitimacy; (2) authority of position, including the sanctions inherent in position; (3) authority of competence, including both technical skills and experience, and (4) authority of person, including leadership and human relations skills (see Table 1).

Authority of Legitimacy

Unlike the related concepts of power and influence, the concept of authority has implicit in it the notion of legitimacy or ethical sanctification. Philosophers have long struggled with the complex and continuing problems of political authority, couched in the language of social contract theories and doctrines of political obligation.[9] The employment relationship, evolving out of the relationship between master and servant, has frequently been phrased in the same language.[10] Those in authority have the *right* to demand obedience; those subject to authority have the *duty* to obey.[11] Max Weber, whose influence permeates almost all studies of bureaucracy, classifies the types of authority "according to the kind of claim to legitimacy typically made by each."[12] While both traditional authority and charismatic authority are owed to a *person,* the chief or charismatic leader, "in the case of legal authority, obedience is owed to the legally established impersonal order."[13] As Parsons and Gouldner have pointed out, Weber sets forth but does not elaborate on several additional bases of legal-rational authority, for example, hierarchical office and technical knowledge and experience.[14] Other writers, most notably Simon and Presthus, have further developed these concepts of the underlying bases of authority. While Simon uses "authority of legitimacy" in the narrower sense utilized here, Presthus extends the concept of "legiti-

[9] See, for example, Carl J. Friedrich (ed.), *Authority* (Cambridge, Mass., 1958), or Bertram de Jouvenel, *Sovereignty* (Chicago, 1957).

[10] Reinhard Bendix, *Work and authority in industry* (New York, 1956).

[11] Simon, Smithburg, and Thompson, *Public Administration* p. 180.

[12] *The theory of social and economic organization,* A. M. Henderson and Talcott Parsons (trans.), Talcott Parsons (ed.) (New York, 1947), p. 325.

[13] Ibid., p. 328.

[14] Parsons, in ibid., n. 4, pp. 58–60; Gouldner, Organizational analysis, in Robert K. Merton, Leonard Broom, and Leonard S. Cottrell, Jr. (eds.), *Sociology today* (New York, 1959), pp. 400–23.

mation" to include all processes by which authority is accepted, reserving the concept of a "generalized deference to authority" (which in turn reflects the process of individual socialization), for this narrower sense of ethical sanctification.[15] For Simon, it is through the indirect mechanism of social approval from the particular reference group that the motive of legitimacy obtains its greatest force.[16] But whether used in the broad or narrow sense, authority of legitimacy is inextricably fused in reality with a second source or base frequently discussed in the literature, that is, authority of position.

Authority of Position

As Robert K. Merton restates Weber's classic treatment of authority based on hierarchical office: "Authority, the power of control which derives from an acknowledged status, inheres in the office and not in the particular person who performs the official role."[17] That is to say, when a person becomes a member of an organization he is already predisposed to accept orders given to him by persons acknowledged to be his superiors by their position in the formal organizational chart. As March and Simon make this point:

> In joining the organization [the employee] accepts an authority relation; i.e., he agrees that within some limits (defined both explicitly and implicitly by the terms of his employment contract) he will accept as the premises of his behavior orders and instructions supplied to him by the organization.[18]

Although their language has been different, writers such as Urwick, Bennis, and Presthus all have had reference to much the same thing when they discussed formal authority, role incumbency, and formal position.

Simon among others, has given the authority of position an extended interpretation in his discussion of the authority of rewards and sanctions inherent in office. His assertions that "the most important sanctions of managers over workers in industrial organizations are *(a)* power to hire and fire, *(b)* power to promote and demote, and *(c)* incentive rewards," are equally true of public organizations.[19] Both participants in a superior-subordinate relationship are aware of the disparities in sanctions which support the relationship. However, while the subordinate is subject to the commands of the superior, the superior is dependent on the subordinate to get the job done. The supervisor engages in periodic ratings of his workers, ratings which affect promotion, pay raises, and even the chances of keeping the job. But if subordinates take no initiative, solve no problems for themselves, do everything the superior asks them, but *no more,* the superior will soon be faced with the impossible task of trying to do every job in the organization by himself.[20] On the other hand, as long as subordinates know that a superior controls ultimate sanctions to compel obedience if his orders are resisted, authority cannot be defined solely in terms of acceptance or consent.[21] But even this advantage possessed by the superior is not without its costs. As Peter M. Blau points out, the continued use of sanctions, or threat of their use, will in the long run undermine authority. "This is the dilemma of bureaucratic authority: it rests on the power of sanction but is weakened by frequent resort to sanctions in operations."[22] One consequence of this relationship of mutual dependency with disparate sanctions is that the superior must broaden the base of his authority if he is to secure the active cooperation of his subordinates in order to achieve organizational goals. Formal authority flowing from legitimacy and organizational status almost invariably must be supported by authority based on professional competence and human relations skills.

Authority of Competence

While the authority of competence is not limited to formal hierarchical relationships, and indeed frequently cuts across the formal channels of communications, possession of experience and appropriate technical skills by the superior obviously greatly enhances the acceptance of his formal authority by his subordinates. In general, authority based on technical knowledge and authority based on experience are closely related, although distinctions can be made between these two subtypes of the authority of competence. Familiarity with certain operations can only be gained from day-to-day confrontation of problems. What may be a crisis for the beginner is routine to the old hand. Technical knowledge, in contrast with experience, is more apt to come from professional training, for example, specialized graduate education. Indeed, when promotional opportunities

---

[15] Presthus, Authority in organizations., n. 8, p. 88.

[16] Authority, p. 106.

[17] *Social theory and social structure* (rev. ed.; Glencoe, 1957), p. 195.

[18] *Organizations* (New York, 1958), p. 90.

[19] Authority, p. 104.

[20] Harold J. Leavitt, *Managerial psychology* (Chicago, 1958), pp. 150–51.

[21] Robert V. Presthus, Toward a theory of organizational behavior. *Administrative Science Quarterly,* Vol. 3 (1958), p. 57.

[22] *Bureaucracy in modern society* (New York, 1956), pp. 76–77.

arise, seniority may frequently compete with technical proficiency; therefore the prerequisites for most supervisory positions stress both professional training and experience.

There remains, however, a more fundamental ambivalence regarding bases of authority in organizations. As Gouldner asserts, "one of the deepest tensions in modern organization, often expressed as a conflict between the line and staff groups, derives from the divergence of . . . two bases of authority" —authority legitimized by incumbency in office and authority based on professional competence.[23] Not only do subunits of organizations differ as to the importance attached to these two bases of authority, but different kinds of organizations,[24] over different time periods,[25] and within different cultures[26] also seem to emphasize one or the other of these bases of authority. While a number of writers have commented upon an increasing tendency toward reliance on professional competence with an attending decline in the perceived legitimacy of hierarchical authority, evidence suggests that the strategic location and influence of those in hierarchical roles often enables them to resist specialist claims. As Victor A. Thompson shows, control of the organization's distribution system remains in hierarchical hands:

> Above what might be considered a market minimum, the satisfactions which the organization has to offer are distributed according to hierarchical rank. They include, in addition to money, deference, power, interesting activities and associations, conveniences, etc. Because these goods are distributed according to status rank, and access to any rank is controlled by . . . hierarchical position, these positions acquire great power . . .[27]

The tension between positional and specialist authority, which appears to be endemic in hierarchical organizations, may sometimes be mediated by a fourth basis of authority, authority of person.

[23] Organizational analysis, p. 414. See Thompson, Distinction between hierarchical and nonhierarchal authority, . . . for an extended analysis of conflict arising from growing inconsistencies between specialist and hierarchical roles.

[24] James D. Thompson and Frederick L. Bates, Technology, organization, and administration, *Administrative Science Quarterly,* Vol. 2 (1957), pp. 332–34; Amitai Etzioni, Authority, structure and organizational effectiveness, *Administrative Science Quarterly,* Vol. 4 (1959), pp. 43–67.

[25] Morris Janowitz, Changing patterns of organizational authority: The military establishment, *Administrative Science Quarterly,* Vol. 3 (1959), pp. 473–93; Bendix, *Work and authority in industry.*

[26] Walter B. Miller, Two concepts of authority, *American Anthropologist,* Vol. 57 (1955), pp. 271–89; Stephen A. Richardson, Organizational contrasts on British and American ships, *Administrative Science Quarterly,* Vol. 1 (1956), pp. 189–207; Elliot Jaques, *The changing culture of a factory* (London, 1951), p. 254; Heinz Hartmann, *Authority and organization in German management* (Princeton, 1959), pp. 5–7.

[27] *Modern organization* (New York, 1961), p. 65.

Authority of Person

Authority based on legitimacy, position, and competence can be analytically distinguished from the authority of person. Such a distinction takes a number of forms in the literature. As already suggested, Weber makes use of the distinction between authority based on office and authority based on personal attributes to differentiate the first of his three pure types of authority—legal-rational authority (itself containing seeds of other bases of authority) from his second and third types—traditional and charismatic authority.[28] Both Henri Fayol and Chester Barnard make similar distinctions between what Fayol referred to as "official authority" and "personal authority" and what Barnard described as "authority of position" and "authority of leadership."[29] A number of social scientists, including Bierstedt, Blau, Gibbs, Selznick, and Urwick, have made analytical distinctions between authority and leadership.[30] The focus in this study is not so much on personal or informal leader-follower relations, but rather on the *fusion* of leadership skills—be it charisma or routinized human relations skills—in a person who *also* occupies a position of authority; not on leadership as personal quality, but on leadership as an organizational function.[31] Thus, as Bennis, Presthus, and others have suggested, "the knowledge of the human aspect of administration," "the ability to mediate individual needs," and the possession of certain leadership traits by a superior enhance the frequency and extent of acceptance of formal authority on the part of his subordinates.[32]

Before reporting some results from an empirical inquiry of authority relations which seem to support a fourfold typology of authority, several assumptions underlying the selection of field setting, working hypotheses, and methodology of this study should be made explicit.

FIELD SETTING AND METHODOLOGY

Three local public service organizations were selected as the field setting in which working hy-

[28] Weber, *Social theory and social structure,* p. 328.

[29] Fayol, *General and industrial management,* Constance Storrs, (trans).(London, 1949) pp. 19–21; Barnard, *The functions of the executive* (Cambridge, Mass., 1937), p. 173.

[30] Bierstedt, An analysis of social power, pp. 70–71; Peter M. Blau, *The dynamics of bureaucracy* (Chicago, 1955), p. 178; Cecil A. Gibbs, Leadership, in Gardiner Lindzey (ed.), *Handbook of social psychology* (Reading, Mass., 1954), Vol. II, 882; Philip Selznick, *Leadership in administration* (Evanston, Ill., 1957), p. 24; L. F. Urwick, *Leadership in the twentieth century* (New York, 1957), p. 37.

[31] Alex Bavelas, Leadership: Man and function, *Administrative Science Quarterly,* Vol. 4 (1960), p. 491.

[32] Bennis, Leadership theory and administrative behavior, pp. 283–87; Presthus, Authority in organizations, p. 91.

potheses relating these analytical types of authority could be explored. Before stating these hypotheses more explicitly, several characteristics of the organizational environment, size, and hierarchy need to be set forth. These three organizations—a branch office of a large county welfare department, a police department in a council-manager city of some 25,000 population, and an elementary school in a suburban school district—share roughly the same broad cultural setting in that all three public agencies are located within a ten-mile radius of one another and operate from overlapping or analogous political, social, and economic bases. The welfare office with 23 members, the police department with 33 members, and the elementary school with 21 members, were roughly comparable in size. The hierarchical structure of the police department consisted of five formal ranks (chief, lieutenant, sergeants-inspectors, patrolmen, and dispatchers-clerical staff), the welfare office had four (district director, supervisors, social workers, and clerical staff), and the elementary school had three (principal, teacher, and supporting staff).

The police department was selected as an organization that, at least outwardly, seemed to epitomize reliance on authority of position as exemplified by such characteristics as clear-cut distinctions between ranks and within ranks, the wearing of uniforms, and the use of strict sanctions for disciplinary purposes. In contrast, it was expected that school teachers and social welfare workers would, at least in theory, place greater emphasis on professional standards with a consequent diffusion of authority throughout the hierarchical structure. A further index of the differing emphasis on hierarchy in the three organizations was the ratio of supervisory personnel to rank-and-file workers, ranging from one to five in the police department, one to six in the welfare department, and one to seventeen in the elementary school.[33]

In attempting to relate the four analytical types of authority based on legitimacy, position, competence, and person, the most appropriate index to authority of position was obvious, namely, the incumbent's occupancy of formal office, including job title, in the organization. For the purposes of this study it was assumed that authority of legitimacy would be attributed to position until further inquiry revealed otherwise. Given this assumption, several working hypotheses relating authority of competence and authority of person to this composite authority of position were advanced:

1. Authority of position is strongest when supported by both authority of competence and authority of person.
   1.1 If the immediate superior or superiors are not perceived as a source of professional advice and assistance (authority of competence), then authority of position is weakened.
   1.2 If the immediate superior or superiors are not perceived as good leaders in the organization (authority of person), then authority of position is weakened.
2. Conversely, if the immediate superior or superiors are perceived neither as a source of professional advice nor as good leaders, then the absence of these bases of authority will result in a breakdown of authority of position and the loss of authority of legitimacy attributed to that position.

An eighteen-question interview schedule was designed to investigate related perceptions of authority in organizations.[34] Formal interviews were held with 76 of the 77 members of the three organizations. Interviews ranged from twenty minutes to over three hours, averaging about an hour in length. The information gained from the use of a structured interview schedule was supplemented by customary research materials, including informal discussions, the observation of routine and crisis operations within the organizations, and the analysis of manuals, charts, procedures, policy statements, personnel records, and newspaper accounts. In addition, some twenty relatively unstructured interviews were held with key administrative and staff personnel in the parent organizations: the county manager's office and central office of the welfare department; the city manager's office; and the central office of the school district.

The limitations of the exploratory approach adopted here should be clearly noted, however. This research was not aimed at describing total organizational behavior, nor was it designed to test hypotheses consisting of causal relationships between clearly defined and carefully controlled variables. A research design having minimization of bias and maximization of the reliability of the evidence as its principal objectives seemed premature.[35]

---

[33] The school principal shared supervisory responsibilities with central office personnel over the office secretary, custodian, and school nurse (part-time).

[34] Responses to the following two questions were used as indices of authority of competence and authority of person, respectively:

"14. When you need some professional advice or assistance, where do you get it?
 (14a) In particular, what persons do you go to?
 (14b) Why do you go to him (or her, or them)?
 (14c) If he (or she, or they) doesn't have the answer, then who do you go to?"

"17. More specifically, who do you think is a good leader in [name of organization]?"

Question 17 followed a question about the qualities or traits making for a "good leader" in the particular organization.

[35] Claire Selltiz, Marie Jahodo, Morton Deutsch, and Stuart W. Cook, *Research methods in social relations* (rev. ed.; New York, 1959), p. 50.

TABLE 2 PERCEPTIONS OF THE BASES OF AUTHORITY IN THREE PUBLIC SERVICE ORGANIZATIONS

Bases of Authority	Police Department (N = 33)	Welfare Office (N = 23)	Elementary School (N = 20)
Authority of legitimacy	%*	%*	%*
Generalized legitimacy	12	9	10
Law, state legislation, city ordinances, the state, county, city	15	17	15
Administrative codes, rules, regulations, manuals	0	17	0
Governing boards, policies of board	0	0	10
Authority of position			
Top *external* executive or executives, organization as a whole†	0	17	15
Top *internal* executive, ranking officers, administration as a whole‡	27	13	30
Immediate supervisor	9	39	0§
Inherent in position or job characteristics	30	26	15
Authority of competence:			
Professional or technical competence, experience	15	22	45
Authority of person:			
Personal characteristics or way in which authority is exercised	42	13	15
Other sources	6	4	0
No source specified	18	22	15

* Percentages total more than 100 percent because some respondents indicated more than one base of authority.

† The category of "top *external* executive" included the chief executives of the parent organization, for example, the county manager, director of public welfare, city manager, and school superintendent.

‡ The category of "top *internal* executive" included the police chief, the district director, and the principal.

§ Coded as "top *internal* executive" in the case of the elementary school.

Instead, maximum flexibility permitting the broadest consideration of as many different aspects of authority relations as possible seemed preferable. No claims are made as to the representativeness of the three organizations under study; therefore, generalizations are hazardous. Only in a limited sense can the interview data be construed as any sort of "proof" of the working hypotheses which guided this study. A final note of caution should be sounded about cultural and temporal qualifications. The field phase of this study was carried out in several adjacent suburban community settings in one western state in the United States during a five-month period from late November, 1959, to early April, 1960. This, then, was an exploratory study aimed at clarifying the concept of organizational authority, illustrating some of the bases which condition its acceptance, and establishing guidelines for further investigation.

EMPIRICAL RESULTS

What are the underlying bases of authority which facilitate its acceptance in organizations? Four types of authority based on legitimacy, position, competence, and person have been abstracted from the literature of administration and organization theory. While these analytical distinctions seem to facilitate understanding of complex organizational relations, do members of organizations also perceive these as important bases of authority?[36]

In response to the question, "What does authority mean to you?"[37] all but about one-fifth of the members in each of the three organizations specified one

[36] The constructs of the social sciences are, so to speak, constructs of the second degree, namely, constructs of the constructs made by actors on the social scene, whose behavior the social scientist has to observe and to explain in accordance with the procedural rules of his science" (Alfred Schutz, Concept and theory formation in the social sciences, *Journal of Philosophy,* Vol. 51 [1954], p. 267).

[37] Question 5, which was primarily designed to elicit perceptions of internal authority, was preceded by a brief introduction:

"5. In the study of organizations one hears a lot about 'authority' and 'responsibility'. Now these are pretty broad terms, but I'm interested in trying to pin down the meaning of some of these words. What is your definition of these words? What does authority mean to you?

After the respondent replied to this open-ended question, he was asked to compare his authority with that of other positions in the organization, by way of the following two questions:

"5a) In comparison with other positions in [name of organization] would you say you had
—a great deal of authority
—somewhat above average authority
—an average amount of authority
—somewhat below average authority
no authority at all.

5b) What leads you to say that?"

or more sources from which authority sprang. A summary of these reported bases of authority is presented in Table 2. The various sources of authority were classified according to the four analytical types developed from the literature. Despite the diversity of responses, which was characteristic of all three organizations, the tendency to localize the source of authority in the top internal executive, immediate supervisor, or the worker's own position, was particularly apparent. Representative excerpts from the interviews, some of which convey more than one source in a single response, illustrate the more specific classifications.

A number of members emphasized legitimacy or called more specific attention to legislation, manuals, or governmental institutions as bases of authority:

When I work any place I feel that whatever they want, I give 'em. It's as simple as that. Whoever the boss is . . . [shrugs shoulders].

Authority to me is something you're bound to obey. It's something that I respect.

A lot of authority is in the manual—it's the law.

Authority as far as I'm concerned is the rights we have as a policeman to do certain things. There is a certain authority given to us by the courts, by the state government . . .

Several comments illustrate the many references to authority inherent in the position or in the persons occupying certain ranking positions:

The person with the rank has the final say. Whether you agree with him or not you go along with him.

My understanding of authority is that it is more or less part of a job, something which you have to accomplish, particularly as a supervisor or a director.

Authority in reference to the ranking officers, the sergeants, the lieutenant, the chief? It's a sign or symbol to the average patrolman or average citizen that the man is in authority. He has, how would you put it? . . . a little more power than the average patrolman within the police department.

Authority is mostly our supervisor and grade-II supervisor.

Others emphasized professional competence or experience as the source of authority:

I have the final word in licensing. There is no written law as to what a good foster home or what a bad foster home is, except as we have defined it in our experience and knowledge. We have the authority to deny the license entirely. And it's based on this knowledge and experience rather than the manual.

Well, my authority is completely within my classroom, and I'm given a great deal of authority there. And I'm appreciative of this. I'm given a complete reign. I can use my own philosophy, mainly because it's the philosophy of the district. With a good teacher, that's O.K. With a bad teacher, it's not.

The source of authority was also seen to depend on the way authority was exercised and certain underlying personal traits:

Authority in general? Oh, I don't know. I've never objected to people having authority over me, if I felt they were competent. They don't have to be an intellectual or sharp-looking, but they should at least be on an equal with me as far as mental and physical ability. If not, I'd object to it. I had some bosses back home, which I didn't go for. I still did the work. Maybe not as hard and not as efficiently, but I did it.

Authority is based on someone to lead . . . so a person in authority would have to be a leader. He would have to have the ability to command and other traits of leadership. My favorite one is this: "They should back up their men." I hate a person who says out in front of everyone, "You did that wrong." He should stick up for his men.

Finally, authority might be seen as coming from other sources as mundane as a uniform—"Actually, I have no authority to the other men, but the police uniform gives you a certain authority out in the public"—or from such "ultimate" sources as the social worker who saw authority as "God-given," or the police officer who expressed the view that authority was derived from "the people as a whole."

Some Tentative Generalizations

In Table 2 we saw that authority of position was emphasized in the police department, particularly the authority delegated from the chief of police or incorporated in all ranking officers of the organization. In an organization where formal rank—epitomized by uniforms, insignia, and militarylike courtesy—plays such an important part in day-to-day activity, it could hardly be otherwise. The amount of authority attributed to sergeants and inspectors (theoretically of the same rank) varied extensively, but each of these officers was well aware that he had more formal authority than a patrolman, if less than the lieutenant or police chief. What was somewhat surprising, however, was the importance attached to authority of person. Not only were human relations skills singled out more frequently than any other basis of authority, but police officers placed much greater emphasis on the possession of such skills than did social workers or elementary school teachers. In part, of course, this was a reflection of the type of activity that differentiates these jobs as well as the kind of person attracted to them. These findings also seem to support Janowitz's conclusions that in militarylike establishments, skill in interpersonal relations rather than technical competency is emphasized as the basis of authority.[38] As younger,

[38] Changing patterns of organizational authority, p. 492.

career-oriented police officers with college training in police administration replace older, "small-town cops," the importance attached to authority of competence in this police department will probably increase.

Another unexpected finding was the extent to which social workers, in contrast to police officers and elementary school teachers, singled out authority of position. Approximately 40 percent of the 23 members of the public welfare branch office mentioned their immediate supervisor as a source of authority. Authority inherent in their own position was the second most frequently mentioned basis of authority, followed by authority of competence (Table 2). In part, the social workers' emphasis on the authority of their immediate supervisor reflected the matriarchal role assumed by one of the three line supervisors, an older woman who had played an instrumental role in creating the branch office and who felt responsible for its entire operation. Workers who rejected her authority or served under other supervisors, were more likely to mention the authority implicit in their jobs, or to cite administrative manuals or regulations. The relatively low degree of importance attributed to authority of competence may have been a function of the lack of graduate professional training characteristic of all but three members of the staff.

Perhaps the most striking contrast between these three public service agencies was the relative importance attached to authority of professional competence in the elementary school. Almost half of the 20-member school staff singled out this basis as compared with 22 percent of the welfare workers and only 15 percent of the police officers. In part, this was related to the fact that 75 percent of the school staff had had graduate training, including nine teachers with the equivalent of master's degrees or beyond. Furthermore, all school staff members except the secretary and the custodian belonged to two or more professional organizations, as compared with about half the members of the police department and about one-quarter of the welfare workers who belonged to one or more professional organizations. While the principal of this school played a more passive "democratic" leadership role than either the police chief or the district director his position or the school administration as a whole was the next most frequently mentioned source of authority in the school. The diffusion of authority which seemed to characterize this school may be the dominant pattern of authority relations in such highly professionalized organizations as research institutions, psychiatric and medical clinics, and universities.[39]

[39] Etzioni, Authority structure and organizational effectiveness, p. 67.

Earlier in this paper it was suggested that functional authority based on technical and human relations skills might serve to bolster formal authority based on legitimacy and position. In the course of these interviews with public service employees, however, numerous examples were cited which seem to suggest a basic ambivalence, if not an inherent conflict, between these different bases of authority. Approximately 40 percent of the members in each of these three organizations responded to a question on whether or not they ever received conflicting instructions from above with either a concrete example of authority of competence taking precedence over authority of position, or acknowledged the supremacy of authority based on technical skills within certain spheres of their work.[40] The following quotation from an interview with a veteran patrolman illustrates a situation in which authority based on technical knowledge supersedes a higher ranking officer's authority of position:

> Last Tuesday a man came out of the . . . Bar with another man chasing him, carrying a rifle. He fired three shots and then left. The guy being shot at told us the story. I picked up a .22 short shell on the property. The [ranking officer] came out and said, "Make it up as a 417." That's displaying a weapon in a rude and unlawful manner. It's only a misdemeanor. It would have meant I couldn't have arrested him, and yet he fired three shots at somebody. That's assault with a deadly weapon at a minimum, a felony. They should throw the book at that guy! A misdemeanor? Ridiculous. And I told the [ranking officer] so. I finally got him to change it to my way, and finally a day later I did arrest the man.

A more typical reaction to conflicting instructions from above in the police department and the welfare office, and to a lesser extent in the elementary school, was acquiescence to authority of position, particularly among the less experienced members.

SUMMARY

A survey of the bases of authority posited by five contributors to organizational theory—Weber, Urwick, Simon, Bennis, and Presthus—reveals considerable consensus, despite different terminology. From writings of these and other social scientists, four analytical types of authority relations have been developed: (1) authority of legitimacy, (2) authority

[40] This question was worded as follows:

"7. Do you ever get instructions from above which seem to conflict with what you as [job title] feel you should do?
   7a) (If yes) Can you give me an example?
   (If no) If you did get such instructions, what would you do?
   7b) What did you do then?
   7c) How does this work out?"

of position, (3) authority of competence, and (4) authority of person. This typology also seems to be useful for ordering perceptions of authority by 76 members of three public service agencies: a branch office of a county welfare department, a municipal police department, and a suburban elementary school. Interactions between superiors and subordinates contain elements of all four types of authority, although the relative importance of each would seem to vary from person to person as well as from organization to organization. While the interview data must be interpreted with caution, the following generalizations can be derived from this study of the bases of authority in these three organizations. Over one-third of the members of all three organizations, particularly welfare department employees, emphasized legitimacy and position as important bases of authority. In addition, police officers stressed authority of person, while school employees emphasized authority of competence. Authority relations need to be examined in a number of different types of organizations within one culture and in several cultural settings at different periods in order to develop generalizations as to what types of authority lead to what consequences for different kinds of organizations under a variety of stable and crisis situations.

49. CONTROL IN ORGANIZATIONS: INDIVIDUAL ADJUSTMENT AND ORGANIZATIONAL PERFORMANCE*

Arnold S. Tannenbaum†

This analysis focuses upon the control aspects of organizations. Organizations are characterized as orderly arrangements of individual human interactions, in which control is an essential ingredient. A major assumption is that the total amount of control or influence in an organization is not a constant, fixed amount but that it may vary. Increasing the influence of one group (e.g., the workers) in an organization does not necessarily imply decreasing that of others (e.g., supervisors and managers). Some evidence is presented to suggest that increased control exercised by all levels of the organization hierarchy is associated with increased organizational effectiveness. A relatively high level of total control may reflect increased participation and mutual influence throughout the organization and a greater degree of integration of all members. This is likely to result in the enhancement of ego-involvement, identification, motivation, and job satisfaction of members. Some of the psychological costs of increased control and responsibility on the part of workers and management are noted.

Man's life in contemporary society can be characterized largely as one of organizational memberships. Man commits a major portion of his waking hours to participation in at least one—and more often several—social organizations. His motivation, aspirations, his general way of life, are tied inextricably to the organizations of which he is a part—and even to some of which he is not.

Organizations are of vital interest to the sociologist and the psychologist because one finds within them an important juncture between the individual and the collectivity. Out of this juncture comes much in our pattern of living that has been the subject of both eulogy and derogation. That man derives a great deal from organizational membership leaves little to be argued; that he often pays heavily for the benefits of organizational membership seems an argument equally compelling. At the heart of this exchange lies the process of control.

Characterizing an organization in terms of its patterns of control is to describe an essential and universal aspect of organization, an aspect of organizational environment which every member must face and to which he must adjust. Organization implies control. A social organization is an ordered arrangement of individual human interactions. Control processes help circumscribe idiosyncratic behaviors and keep them conformant with the rational plan of the organization. Organizations require a certain amount of conformity as well as the integration of diverse activities. It is the function of control to bring about conformance to organizational requirements and achievement of the ultimate goals of the organization. The coordination and order created out of the diverse interest and potentially diffuse behaviors of members is largely a function of control. It is at this point that many of the problems of organizational functioning and of individual adjustment arise.

Control is an inevitable correlate of organization. But it is more than this. It is concerned with aspects

* *Administrative Science Quarterly,* Vol. 7, No. 2 (1962), pp. 236–57.

† Survey Research Center, Institute for Social Research, University of Michigan.

of social life that are of the utmost importance to all persons. It is concerned with the questions of choice and freedom, with individual expression, with problems of the common will and the common weal. It is related not only to what goes on within the organization but also with what the organization does in its external relations. It touches on the questions of democracy and autocracy, centralization and decentralization, "flat" and "tall" organizational structures, close versus general supervision, workers' councils and joint management.

The problems of control and conformity in organizations contribute to a serious dilemma. Organization provides order—a condition necessary for man to produce abundantly and live securely. Abundance and security in turn create opportunities and choice—conditions which form the basis for human freedom. Yet social order itself requires conformity and imposes limitations. Furthermore, the responsibility for creating and sustaining order tends to be distributed unevenly within organizations. Often it is the few who decide about the kind of order to which the many must conform. But regardless of how order is created, it requires the conformity of all or nearly all to organizational norms.

The magnitude of this problem as it applies to our economic institutions has been indicated by Berle and Means:

> To the dozen or so men who are in control there is room for . . . [individual] initiative. For the tens of thousands and even hundreds of thousands of workers and of owners in a single enterprise, [individual] initiative no longer exists. Their activity is group activity on a scale so large that the individual, except he be in a position of control, has dropped into relative insignificance.[1]

And the *trend*, according to Barnard, is in the direction of greater concentration of control in the hands of fewer persons:

> There has been a greater and greater acceleration of centralization in this country, not merely in government, and not merely in the organization of great corporations, but also a great concentration on the part of labor unions and other organizations. There has been a social disintegration going along with this material development, and this formulation of organization activities implies payment of a price, the amount of which we are not yet able to assess.[2]

This, perhaps, is one of the more crucial problems of social morality which we face in the age of massive organization, although the problem is not an entirely new one. We see it in Rousseau's *Social contract*, Freud's *Civilization and its discontents*, Huxley's *Brave new world*, Whyte's *Organization man*. And social and administrative scientists have become increasingly interested in this question, as indicated by the work by F. Allport, Argyris, Likert, McGregor, and Worthy. As a result, social researchers have applied themselves to the study of the problems of control, individual adjustment, and organizational performance, and a body of facts and hypotheses is growing. We would like to review some of these, drawing heavily upon the work done at the Institute for Social Research at the University of Michigan.[3]

SOME DEFINITIONS

Control has been variously defined, and different terms (e.g., power, authority, influence) are sometimes used synonymously with it. Its original application in business organizations derives from the French usage meaning to check. It is now commonly used in a broader and perhaps looser sense synonymously with the notions of influence, authority, and power. We shall use it here in this broader way to refer to any process in which a person or group of persons or organization of persons determines, i.e., intentionally affects, what another person or group or organization will do.

Control, of course, may operate very specifically, as, for example, a foreman's specifying how a subordinate will do a particular job. Or it may operate more generally, as for example, the determination of organizational policies or actions. Control may be mutual, individuals in a group each having some control over what others will do; or it may be unilateral, one individual controlling and the others controlled. We ascribe power to an individual to the extent that he is in a position to exercise control. Authority refers to the right to exercise control. If by freedom we mean the extent to which an individual determines his own behavior, being controlled can be seen in general to relate inversely to freedom. The more an individual's behavior is determined by others (i.e., is controlled), the less an individual is free to determine his own course of action.

IMPLICATIONS FOR INDIVIDUAL ADJUSTMENT

The elementary importance of control to people can be seen in the fact that every act of control has

[1] A. A. Berle, Jr. and G. C. Means, The control of the modern corporation, in R. Merton et al. (eds.), *Reader in bureaucracy* (Glencoe, 1952).

[2] C. I. Barnard, Organization and management, as quoted in *Harvard Business Review*, Vol. 29 (1951), p. 70.

[3] This article was made possible by funds granted by the Carnegie Corporation of New York. The statements made and views expressed are the responsibility of the author. I would like to thank Robert Kahn, Rensis Likert, Stanley Seashore, and Clagett Smith for their helpful suggestions.

two implications: pragmatic and symbolic. Pragmatically, control implies something about *what* an individual must or must not do, the restriction to which he is subject, and the areas of choice or freedom which he has—whether, for example, a worker is transferred to a new machine or stays on the old, whether he is classified into a $1.75 or a $2.00 wage category, whether he is free to talk, smoke, rest, slow down, or speed up while on the job. These pragmatic implications are often of vital importance to the controlled individual as well as to the individual exercising power.

Control also has a special psychological meaning or significance to the individuals involved. It may imply superiority, inferiority, dominance, submission, guidance, help, criticism, reprimand. It may imply (as some students of control argue) something about the manliness and virility of the individuals involved. The exercise of control, in other words, is charged emotionally.[4]

Emotional reactions to control may be explained, in part, by the predispositions which individuals develop early in life to types of authority relations. The infant's behavior is controlled by persons upon whom he is highly dependent, and the process of socialization involves the imposition of controls by parents, teachers, and other authority figures. In the development of a pattern of responses to control during this process of socialization, control takes on emotional meaning.

A great deal of research has been done regarding predisposition to varying patterns of control. Tests have been devised, for example, to measure authoritarianism, egalitarianism, need for independence, need for power. Research employing some of these measures suggests that individuals' reactions to patterns of organizational control may differ according to personality.

This is illustrated by an experiment in a large clerical organization in which about two hundred female clerks were given greater responsibility to make decisions about some of the rules that affected their work groups. They were able to make decisions affecting work assignments, vacation schedules, length of recess, overtime, and other matters. These decisions previously had been made by persons at higher levels. Most of the clerks reacted favorably to this experimental program. A small number, however, did not. Among these were a relatively high proportion of clerks whose personalities were not suited to the type of authority relations brought into play by this experimental program. These preferred to be submissive, depend on others, obey rules, and follow directions.[5] Similar results were found among male workers in an industrial service organization. Workers who received low scores on measures of authoritarianism were more likely to react favorably to supervisors who were judged to use participative methods (asking workers' advice, trying to involve them in decision making) than workers with high scores. Furthermore for workers with low scores, those who judged their supervisors to use participative methods were generally higher in productivity than those who did not judge their supervisors so.[6]

Preferences for different kinds of authority relations may develop out of early childhood experiences. They may also represent reactions to certain contemporaneous circumstances. Research on the authoritarian personality, for example, suggests that individuals who suffer anxiety because of a failure in their work may tend to prefer more structured authority relations. A study of high-producing and low-producing insurance salesmen suggests the tenability of this idea. Productivity varied widely for these agents. An agent might show high productivity during one period and low productivity during another. Those who were low producers tended to suffer some anxiety. They also indicated "a desire for interpersonal interaction where the status of a man's position was the basis for communication, where orders were to go through 'the chain of command,' where decisions 'must be made by the District Manager,' and where 'those in control' of the situation were to act 'aloof,' and/or 'be friendly but not too intimate.'"[7] The more successful, less threatened salesmen preferred more permissive, informal authority relations—no communication barriers because of status and no reporting through the chain of command.

Emotional reactions to authority relations may develop because authority, control, or power represents, as we have pointed out, an important social

[4]The criticism which labor groups have sometimes hurled at human relations research in industry is in large measure a criticism concerning the emphasis which this research has placed on the psychological or symbolic rather than the pragmatic aspect of control. The human relations approach, the argument goes, is not so much concerned with *what* decisions are made by management nor with the implications of these decisions for the welfare of the workers, but rather with *how* these decisions might be conveyed to workers so as to facilitate their acceptance. See, for example, Deep therapy on the assembly line, *Ammunition,* Vol. 7 (1949), pp. 47–51.

[5]A. S. Tannenbaum, One man's meat, *Adult Leadership,* Vol. 3 (1955), pp. 22–23; A. S. Tannenbaum and F. H. Allport, Personality structure and group structure: An interpretative study of their relationship through an event-structure hypothesis, *Journal of Abnormal and Social Psychology,* Vol. 58 (1956), pp. 272–80.

[6]V. Vroom, *Some personality determinants of the effects of participation* (Englewood Cliffs, N.J., 1960).

[7]L. G. Wispe and K. E. Lloyd, Some situational and psychological determinants of the desire for structured interpersonal relations, *Journal of Abnormal and Social Psychology,* Vol. 51 (1955), pp. 57–60.

symbol. Power, for example, is often understood as synonymous with prestige, status, social eminence, or superiority. Indeed, it is often correlated with these criteria of success. Persons obviously are perceived and treated differently according to their power. The man with power is often looked up to and treated with respect. Equally important, individuals can be expected to evaluate themselves in this way. An individual's self-concept is very likely affected by his power in the organizations and other social situations in which he takes part. The emotional effects of authority, as they bear on the way organization members may perceive authority and nonauthority figures, is illustrated by an experiment in which Navy recruits described the physical appearances of men, some of whom wore first-class petty officer's uniforms and others of whom wore recruit uniforms. The men being judged as petty officers and those being judged as recruits were well matched in physical appearance. Differences existed, however, in their uniforms—the kind and number of stripes on their arms and whether or not they wore canvas leggings. The recruits viewed these persons through a series of lenses which distorted their appearance to varying degrees. However, a greater tendency to resist this distortion occurred in the perception of the "petty officer." Rank may create an emotional set which affects how the men holding this rank appear to those who do not.[8]

While individual differences may exist in preferences for types of authority relations, organization members generally prefer exercising influence to being powerless. Studies repeatedly show that workers and supervisors are much more likely to feel that they have too little authority in their work than too much. It is the rare individual indeed who thinks he has too much. Several thousands of workers in a large number of organizations (including one Norwegian factory) were asked to describe how much control various groups in their work places exercised and how much they *should* exercise. In all the organizations studied the "average" worker reported, as might be expected, that managerial personnel exercised more control than did the workers as a group. In response to another question, workers reported that managerial groups *should* exercise more control than the workers. However, in 98 percent of these organizations, workers felt that the workers did not have as much control as they should.[9] It is interesting to contrast these results with responses to the same questions addressed to supervisory personnel. None of the supervisory groups questioned felt that *workers* should exercise more control than they did.

For whatever reasons, power is desired. This desirability may be attributed to the gratification which individuals may derive simply by knowing that they are in control—from the psychological satisfactions which come from exercising control. Or it may derive from the pragmatic implications of power—being able to affect the work situation in ways favorable to one's personal interests, as the individual sees them.

A concern for the rewards which accompany power results in a serious oversimplification, however, unless one considers also some of the correlates of power which are sources of serious tension and frustration. Among these are the added feelings of responsibility for, commitment to, and effort on behalf of the organization. Power can be an important stimulant, pushing the individual toward a greater and greater share of the work load of the organization. Furthermore, in so far as control may imply weighty decisions, decisions affecting the welfare of people as well as the destiny of the organization itself, exercising control can be burdensome.

Individuals who are not able to exercise control are, in general, less satisfied with their work situations than those who have some power, but their dissatisfaction often has the quality of apathy and disinvolvement. For the individual in control, added dimensions of personality come into play contributing to the energies which he puts into his work and to the problems he may encounter. The man who exercises control gives more of himself to the organization. He is likely to be more identified, more loyal, more active, on behalf of the organization. A recent national survey suggests that individuals in positions of control and responsibility in industrial and business organizations are more "ego involved" in their work. Managerial personnel, for example, derive not only greater satisfactions from their jobs, but also greater frustrations.[10] The responsibility which devolves upon persons in control creates a sense of personal involvement and concern over the success or failure of the decisions made. These individuals have a personal stake in the outcome of decisions taken. This can be a satisfying, even an exhilarating experience, but it can also lead to sleepless nights.

This mixed blessing which power sometimes represents is illustrated by the experiment in the large clerical organization described in which about two

[8] W. J. Wittreich and K. B. Radcliffe, Jr., Differences in the perception of an authority figure and a non-authority figure by Navy recruits, *Journal of Abnormal and Social Psychology*, Vol. 53 (1956), pp. 383–84.

[9] In the Norwegian plant the question was phrased in terms of control over the setting of piece-rate standards. Not only did the workers indicate that they should exercise more control than they did, but that they should exercise more control than managerial groups.

[10] G. Gurin, J. Veroff and Sheila Feld, *Americans view their mental health: A nationwide interview study* (New York, 1960).

TABLE 1 CHANGES IN CLERK'S ATTITUDES FOLLOWING DELEGATION OF CONTROL TO CLERKS IN WORK GROUPS

Clerk's Job Attitudes	*Mean Changes in Attitudes**
Feeling of responsibility for getting work done on time	+0.15
Feeling of self-actualization	+0.14
Average satisfaction with supervisor	+0.15
Satisfaction with company	+0.17
Satisfaction with control	+0.35
Satisfaction with accomplishment at end of work day	−0.27
Clerk's satisfaction with her present level in company	−0.42

*All of the differences are statistically significant at the 0.05 level or better.

hundred clerks were given greater responsibility to make decisions about their work conditions. In general, morale increased as a result of the change in control. Clerks felt more satisfied with the company, with supervision, with their work in general. They were, in large measure, favorable toward the increased control which they were able to exercise. Despite the general increase in satisfaction, however, the clerks felt less of a sense of accomplishment at the end of the work day. They were also less satisfied with their present level in the organization (see Table 1). In acquiring an increased feeling of responsibility for the work through the added control which they were able to exercise, the clerks no doubt developed standards of achievement which were harder to satisfy.

A similar result was found in a study by Mann and Hoffman comparing a newly automated electrical power plant with a less highly automated one.[11] Workers in the new plant exercised more control and experienced greater responsibility than those in the older plant, according to the responses of the workers in the two plants. The men in the new plant made important decisions about the work and had significant influence on their supervisors concerning their work place. They also reported greater satisfaction with their immediate supervisor, with the amount of information they received about plant operations, and with plant management in general. Despite this generally heightened state of morale, however, workers in the newly automated plant more often reported that their work made them feel "jumpy" or nervous and that they were tense and on edge when equipment was being started up or shut down. (Yet workers in the *old* plant reported slightly more danger in their work.) These may be some of the costs to the workers of their increased power and responsibility.

Certain kinds of psychosomatic ailments are known to be relatively frequent among individuals in positions of control and responsibility in organizations. Research in this country and abroad provides added documentation for this generally recognized fact. French reported a greater prevalence of psychosomatic disorders of varying kinds among supervisors than among workers in a large Midwest plant.[12] Vertin found the frequency of ulcers increases at ascending levels of the hierarchy in a large Dutch company.[13] "Uneasy lies the head that wears the crown," always seemed to make good sense. To the extent that power and responsibility are distributed widely among organization members, however, a number of heads may lie uneasy.

CONTROL AND PERFORMANCE

Variations in control patterns within organizations have important—and in some cases quite predictable—effects on the reactions, satisfactions and frustrations, feelings of tension, self-actualization, or well-being of members. They also have implications for the performance of the work group and for the organization as a whole.

This can be seen in the plight of the first-line supervisor who sometimes finds himself in the anomalous position of being a leader without power. The first-line supervisor is often referred to as the man in the middle. He is often caught, as an innocent bystander, in a serious cross fire. In effect he may be a messenger transmitting orders from above. On the one hand, he must bear the brunt of resistance and expressed grievances from below and, on the other, must suffer criticism from above for the failure of his subordinates to conform to expectations. The seriousness of this situation is compounded by the fact that orders coming from above are often formed without the advantage of adequate knowledge of conditions at lower levels. The powerless supervisor lacks effective means of gaining the confidence of his men, of understanding their views, and of transmitting this important intelligence up the hierarchy. The orders

[11] F. C. Mann and L. R. Hoffman, *Automation and the worker: A study of social change in power plants* (New York, 1960).

[12] R. P. French, Jr., The effects of the industrial environment on mental health: A theoretical approach, (paper presented at the meetings of the American Psychological Association, 1960).

[13] Ibid.

which he is responsible for relaying, then, are often the least likely to gain full acceptance, thus making his position all the more untenable and that of his subordinates all the more difficult. The powerless leader can do little in the hierarchy on behalf of his subordinates or himself and is relatively helpless in the face of many serious problems which confront him and his work group. This is illustrated by the research of Pelz, who shows that unless the supervisor is influential with his own superiors, "good" supervisory practice on his part is not likely to make much difference to subordinates. Subordinates are more likely to react favorably to "good" and adversely to "bad" supervisory practices *if* the supervisor is influential in the company.[14]

TOTAL AMOUNT OF CONTROL IN AN ORGANIZATION

Many administrators seem to face a serious problem in their understanding of supervisory-subordinate relations. They often assume that the amount of control exercised by members of a group or organization is a fixed quantity and that increasing the power of one individual automatically decreases that of others. There is good reason, however, to question this conclusion. The total amount of control exercised in a group or organization can increase, and the various participants can acquire a share of this augmented power. Conversely, the total amount of control may decrease, and all may share the loss. This is illustrated in everyday social situations—friendships, marital relations, as well as supervisory-subordinate interactions. One can easily picture the laissez-faire leader who exercises little control over his subordinates and who may at the same time be indifferent to their wishes. He neither influences nor is influenced by his men. A second supervisor interacts and communicates often, welcomes opinions, and elicits influence attempts. Suggestions which subordinates offer make a difference to him and his subordinates are responsive, in turn, to his requests. To the extent that this may contribute to effective performance—and we have reason to believe that it does if the supervisor also has influence with his manager—the group itself will be more powerful or influential. The manager under these circumstances is more likely to delegate additional areas of decision making to the group, and he, in turn, will respect and be responsive to the group's decisions. To the extent that the organizational hierarchy, from top to bottom, is characterized in these terms, we have a more highly integrated, tightly knit social system. We have, in the terms of Rensis Likert, a more substantial "interaction-influence system."[15]

The importance of the notion of "total amount of control" and of the "interaction-influence system" is illustrated in an analysis by Likert of data collected in thirty-one geographically separated departments of a large industrial service organization.[16] Each of the departments did essentially the same work, and careful records of department productivity were kept by the company. Nonsupervisory employees were asked the following question in a written questionnaire: "In general, how much say or influence do you feel each of the following groups has on what goes on in your department?" Answers were checked on a five-point scale from "little or no influence" to "a very great deal of influence." Employees answered this question relative to the following groups within their departments: the department manager, the supervisors, the men. Likert then divided the 31 departments into three groups according to their level of productivity. Figure 1 shows the average responses of the departments to the question for the third highest in productivity and for the third lowest in productivity.

According to these employees, not only did they have more influence as a group within the high-producing departments, but so did the supervisors and managers. Likert's analysis of these departments suggests that the social systems differed in the high- and low-producing departments. The former was characterized by a higher total amount of control, by a greater degree of mutual influence. "The high-performing managers have actually increased the size of the 'influence pie' by means of the leadership processes which they use. They listen more to their men, are more interested in their men's ideas, and have more confidence and trust in their men."[17] There was a greater give-and-take and supportiveness by superiors, a higher level of effective communication upward, downward, and sideward. This all contributed to a greater sensitivity and receptivity on the part of each organization member to the influence of others—superiors relative to subordinates and subordinates relative to superiors. There was in all cases a higher level of mutual influence and control and a more likely integration of the interests of workers, supervisors, and managers. Under these circumstances, the high level of influence

---

[14] D. C. Pelz, Influence: A key to effective leadership in the first-line supervisor, *Personnel,* Vol. 9 (1952), pp. 3–11.

[15] R. Likert, *New patterns of management* (New York, 1961).

[16] R. Likert, Influence and national sovereignty, in J. C. Peatman and E. L. Hartley (eds.), *Festschrift for Gardner Murphy* (New York, 1960).

[17] Ibid.

FIGURE 1 CONTROL CURVES OF HIGH- AND LOW-PRODUCING DEPARTMENTS

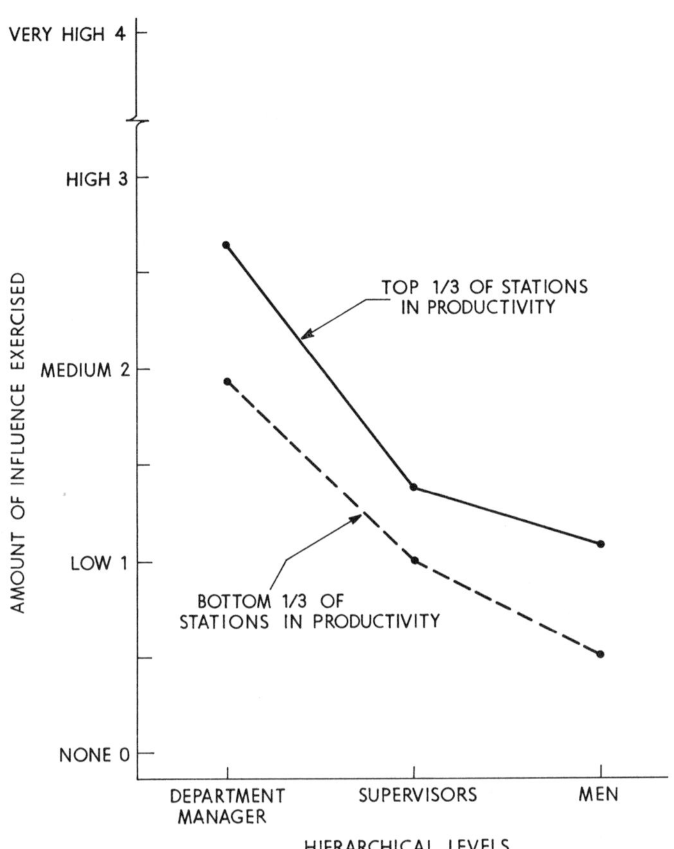

among workers was not a threat to managerial personnel. On the contrary, it was part of a process leading to more effective organizational performance.[18]

It is interesting to see that similar findings occur in several other types of organizations. In a study of four labor unions, for example, we found that the two more effective, active, and powerful unions had the highest total amount of control exercised by members and officers.[19] The most powerful of the four unions had a relatively influential membership—but the leaders (the president, executive board, and bargaining committee) were by no means uninfluential. In this union, members and leaders were relatively more active. They attended more meetings, took part in discussions at meetings, communicated informally about union affairs, and heard and considered the feeling and ideas of others. Members and leaders influenced each other and in the process created effective concerted action. This union "keeps management on its toes" as the personnel manager at the plant philosophically pointed out. In the least effective union, however, the members were relatively uninfluential in union affairs, and so were the leaders. A kind of laissez-faire atmosphere prevailed. Members were not integrated and not tied together by bonds of interaction and influence. They were not really part of an organization system. The ineffectiveness of this union was illustrated by the comments of a union field representative: "If the company wanted to take advantage, they could make the people live hard here." An old-timer of the local expressed his disillusionment: "We feel that it is not what it used to be . . . Nothing happens to grievances. You can't find out what happens to them—they get lost. . . . The [bargaining] committee doesn't fight anymore." The differences between the most powerful and least powerful union in their distributions of control as reported by members is shown

[18] Ibid.

[19] A. S. Tannenbaum and R. L. Kahn, *Participation in union locals* (Evanston, Ill., 1958); A. S. Tannenbaum, Control structure and union functions, *American Journal of Sociology,* Vol. 61 (1956), pp. 536–45.

FIGURE 2 CONTROL CURVES OF EFFECTIVE AND INEFFECTIVE UNIONS

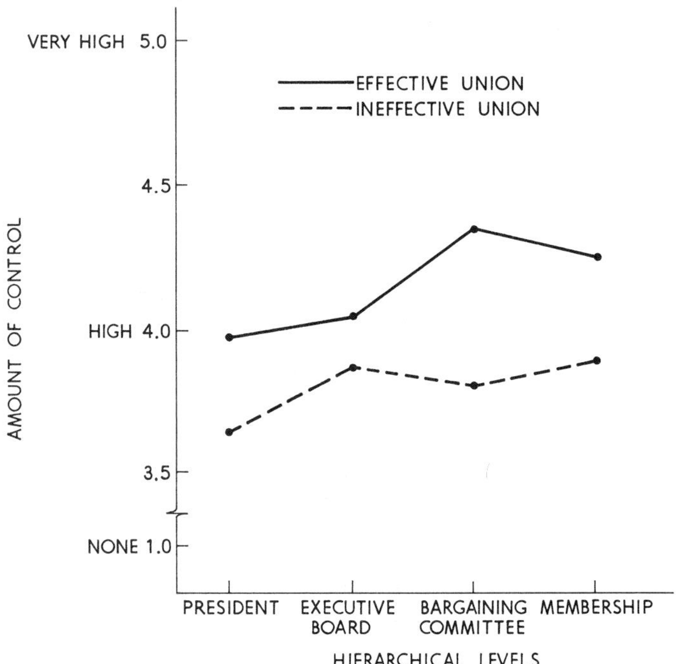

in Figure 2. Although the wording of the question in this study is somewhat different from that of the industrial service organization study discussed, the implications are very similar.[20]

Mann and Hoffman applied a similar methodology in studing some of the effects of automation in a power plant. They illustrated, through a comparison of a new, highly automated plant with an older, less automated one, how changes in technology might affect the social structure of a plant, including its patterns of control, worker responsibility, and level of morale.[21] Fewer employees operated the new plant, although the ratio of non-supervisory to supervisory personnel was about the same. The jobs in the new plant required more knowledge and responsibility of the workers, and, as Table 2 illustrates, the patterns of control in the two plants differed too. According to the workers (and the supervisors were in essential agreement), the new plant was characterized by more control than the old.

The difference between the plants is particularly interesting at the foreman level. In the new plant, foreman were judged to have more influence than the men; in the old, less. Nor was the more powerful supervisor considered a threat to the workers in the new plant. Despite—or should we say, because of—the greater influence of foremen together with that of the men, the men reported less often that their foreman treated them like inferiors, that he was a "driver" of men, that he was "bossy," or that he said one thing and did another. They reported more often

TABLE 2 AMOUNT OF INFLUENCE EXERCISED BY THREE LEVELS AS PERCEIVED BY THE MEN IN TWO PLANTS*

Level	*Old Plant*	*New Plant*
Men.	2.64	3.12†
Foremen.	2.42	3.51†
Front office.	4.56	4.48

*F. C. Mann and L. R. Hoffman, *Automation and the worker: A study of social change in power plants* (New York, 1960), p. 57; by permission of the publisher, Holt, Rinehart & Winston, Inc. The following questions were employed:

Question: "In general, how much do you and the other men of your work group have to say about how things are done?"

Responses: 5—"Our foreman gives us a great deal of say in how things are done." . . . 1—"Our foreman gives us hardly any say at all in how things are done."

Question: "In general, how much do you think the foremen have to say about how things are done in this plant?"

Responses: 5—"They have a great deal to say." . . . 1—"They have very little or no say at all."

Question: "In general, how much say do you think the men in the front office of this plant have in how things are done in this plant?"

Responses: 5—"They have a great deal to say in how things are done in this plant." . . . 1—"They have very little or no say at all in how things are done in this plant."

†Differences significant beyond the 0.001 level of confidence.

[20] Question in union study: "In general, how much do you think the president [membership, plant bargaining committee, executive board] has to say about how things are decided in this local?" Responses ranged on a five-point scale from "a great deal of say" to "no say at all."

[21] Mann and Hoffman, *Automation and the worker.*

that the foreman tried to get ideas from the work group, that he was a warm and friendly person, that he would "go to bat" for the men and that he was a "leader" of men. When all the responses are taken into consideration, 66 percent of the men in the new plant and 36 in the old report that they are very satisfied with their immediate supervisor. The new plant is more tightly integrated social (as well as physical) system. Workers feel more a part of a work group and feel free to call on others in the work group for help with job problems. There is a higher degree of interdependence between foremen and men and to some extent among the men themselves. The foremen in the plant have more influence than their counterparts in the old—and so do the men.

Results from an unpublished study of forty insurance agencies show the same direction. D. Bowers and S. Seashore compared 20 insurance agencies high in sales volume with twenty agencies low in volume. In the high-producing agencies, the general agents, the district agents, and the sales agents as a group were all reported to have more influence in their agencies than were their counterparts in the low-producing agencies.

The clerical experiment discussed previously yielded similar results. The increased control which the clerks reported was not accompanied by a corresponding decrease in the control attributed to supervisory and managerial personnel. The total amount of control reported by clerks increased, accompanied by a more effective social system. Not only did morale increase in this group, but so did motivation and productivity.[22]

Interestingly, the kinds of relationships suggested by these data apply in a voluntary organization too, as indicated by research in over one hundred geographically separate local Leagues of Women Voters.[23] The effectivness of each local league was rated by a group of judges in the national office, and a sample of the members and leaders in each was then asked several questions relating to control within their organizations. The results indicate that members in effective leagues exercised more control than did their counterparts in ineffective leagues, but leaders did not exercise less. A greater total amount of control was ascribed to effective leagues than to ineffective ones.

While these results from a variety of organizations seem to suggest an important hypothesis connecting the total amount of control and organizational performance, our research findings are not completely consistent on this point. A recent study of thirty automobile dealerships, for example, did not reveal any relationship between criteria of effectiveness (including growth in sales during the past year) and the total amount of control within the dealership as reported by salesmen. The automobile sales agency may present a somewhat different social structure in which "individual enterprise" and competitive behavior among salesmen is more at a premium. We do not know what the effect would be if agencies were structured more like the typical business organization with greater emphasis on coordination and cooperative effort. The total amount of control might be greater under these conditions, and this variable might prove, under these circumstances, to have important implications for effective performance.

CONCLUSION

American management is dollar cost conscious. Many managers are also aware of the costs of organized productive effort which cannot be calculated immediately in terms of dollars and cents. These are the human costs of organization, costs paid by members and ultimately by society as a whole. Nor are they to be calculated simply in terms of the dissatisfactions which industrial man faces. They may be paid in terms of the shaping of his very personality. The evidence on this is not very clear, but we have reason to believe that adult personality may change as a result of persistent conditions in the environment. The nature of man's experiences in an organization can affect his general mentality and outlook on life. In the clerical experiment described above we saw evidence of slight changes in personality after a year's exposure of clerks to different patterns of control. These changes were in the direction of increasing "fit" between the worker's personality and the nature of the control structure.[24] Notorious "brain washing" methods represent the ultimate in the process of institutionalized personality change, and we see illustrated in the fiction of Orwell and Huxley the psychological bludgeoning of individual personality into a perfect fit to the institutions of a "hypothetical" society of the future. As Huxley puts it, "Round pegs in square holes tend to have danger-

[22] Productivity also increased in a contrasting experimental group within the company under conditions of lowering the amount of control exercised by clerks. Here, however, clerk morale, loyalty, and motivation decreased. Considerable tension was felt in this group, and it gave the appearance of high instability. There is serious doubt that this type of system could sustain itself as well as the other for an extended period under conditions which prevail in American society. See R. Likert, Measuring organizational performance, *Harvard Business Review,* Vol. 36 (1958), pp. 41–50, and *New patterns of management* (New York, 1961), chs. v, vi.

[23] A. S. Tannenbaum, Control and effectiveness in a voluntary organization, *American Journal of Sociology,* Vol. 67 (1961), pp. 33–47.

[24] A. S. Tannenbaum, Personality change as a result of an experimental change of environmental conditions, *Journal of Abnormal and Social Psychology,* Vol. 55 (1957), pp. 404–6.

ous thoughts about the social system and to infect others with their discontent."[25] Organizations cannot often tolerate deviants, and there are pressures, sometimes subtle, on deviants to change.

Organizations in a democratic society present a seeming dilemma. As Geoffrey Vickers puts it,

> We are forever oscillating between two alternatives which seem mutually exclusive—on the one hand, collective efficiency won at the price of individual freedom; on the other, individual freedom equally frustrated by collective anarchy. Those who believe in a middle way which is more than a compromise do so in the faith that human beings are capable or can become capable of social organization which is both individually satisfying and colletively effective; and they have plenty of evidence for their faith. On the other hand, our knowledge of the laws involved is still rudimentary.[26]

Middle ways are sprouting up around the globe today. The work council systems in Yugoslavia, in Germany, France, Belgium, England, though differing radically in character and effectiveness are, within their respective cultures, experiments in the middle way. We have our Scanlon plans, profit-sharing and suggestion schemes, as well as varying degrees of participative management. However, our knowledge of the effects of these systems is, as Vickers says, rudimentary.

If the clues provided by our research so far are substantiated, the middle way will have to take into account the important facts about control: how control is distributed within an organization, and how much it all amounts to. Patterns of control—as they are perceived by organization members, at least—are tied significantly to the performance of the organization and to the adjustments and satisfactions of members. If our research leads are correct, the more significant improvements in the human side of enterprise are going to come through changes in the way organizations are controlled, and particularly through changes in the size of the "influence pie." This middle way leans on the assumption that influential workers do not imply uninfluential supervisors or managers. This is a relatively novel assumption for many managers who have been weaned on the all-or-none law of power: one either leads or is led, is strong or is weak, controls or is controlled. Disraeli was no less influential a leader, however, for having questioned this when he said, "I follow the people. Am I not their leader?" And, managers who in their behavior question the all-or-none principle do not seem less influential for it.

Our middle way assumes further that the worker, or supervisor, or manager, who exercises some influence over matters of interest to him in the work situation, acquires a sense of self-respect which the powerless individual may lack. He can also elicit the respect and high regard of others. This is the key to good human relations. Supervisory training alone cannot achieve this any more than good intentions in bad organization can achieve it. The pattern of control in an organization, however, has a direct and profound effect on the organization's human relations climate. Workers who have some sense of control in the organizations we have studied, are, in general, more, not less, positively disposed toward their supervisors and managers. And their managers are more positively disposed toward them.

We assume further, with some support from research, that increasing and distributing the exercise of control more broadly in an organization helps to distribute an important sense of involvement in the organization. Members become more ego involved. Aspects of personality which ordinarily do not find expression now contribute to the motivation of the members. The organization provides members with a fuller range of experiences. In doing this, however, it creates its own dilemmas, similar in some respects to those described by Vickers.

A first dilemma concerns the increased control to which the influential organization members may become subject. While he controls more, he is not controlled less. The loyalty and identification which he feels for the organization lead him to accept organizational requirements and to conform to organizational norms which he might not otherwise do. We find evidence of this in the behavior of members of the effective union with high total control. Their behaviors were more uniform than were those of members in the ineffective laissez-faire union.[27] Norms and pressures toward conformity existed in the effective union which were lacking in the ineffective one. Members in the effective union pay for the increased control which they exercise (and for the effectiveness of their organization) not only in terms of the greater effort that they put into union activities, but also by their greater sensitivity and accession to controls within the union. An analysis in the thirty-one departments of the industrial service organization described revealed a similar phenomenon. Norms, measured in terms of uniformity in the behavior of workers, were more apparent in the departments having high total control than in those having low control. In these "better" departments, influence by the men as a group was greater, morale was more favorable, productive effort was higher,

[25] A. Huxley, *Brave new world* (New York, 1953), p. xvi.

[26] "Control stability and choice," reprinted in *General Systems, Yearbook of the Society for General Systems,* Vol. 2 (1957), pp. 1–8.

[27] Tannenbaum and Kahn, *Participation in union locals;* Tannenbaum, Control structure and union functions.

and so was uniformity.[28] The exercise of control did not spare the controller from being controlled. The contrary may be true in effective organizations with high total control, where influence tends to be reciprocal.

A second dilemma arises out of the increased involvement and motivation that are likely to accompany the exercise of control. While we see greater opportunity for human satisfaction in the middle way, the result is not simple felicity. Whenever man is highly motivated he may experience the pangs of failure, as well as the joys of success. He will know some of the satisfactions which come from a challenge met and a responsibility fulfilled. He may also feel frustration from the development of goals which are not easily reached.

50. HUMAN RESOURCE ACCOUNTING IN INDUSTRY*

R. Lee Brummet, William C. Pyle, and Eric G. Flamholtz†

INVESTMENTS IN THE BUSINESS ENTERPRISE

Investments are expenditures made for the purpose of providing future benefits beyond the current accounting period. If a firm purchases a new plant with an expected useful life of fifty years, it is treated as an investment on the corporate balance sheet, and is depreciated over its useful life. If the structure should be destroyed or become obsolete, it would lose its service potential and be written off the books as a loss which would be reflected as an offset against earnings on the company's statement of income.

Firms also make investment in *human* assets. Costs are incurred in recruiting, hiring, training, and developing people as individual employees and as members of viable interacting organizational groups. Furthermore, investments are made in building favorable relationships with *external* human resources such as customers, suppliers, and creditors. Although such expenditures are made to develop future service potential, conventional accounting practice assigns such costs to the "expense" classification, which, by definition, assumes that they have no value to the firm beyond the current accounting year.

For this reason human assets neither appear on a corporate balance sheet, nor are changes in these assets reflected on the statement of corporate income. Thus, conventional accounting statements may conceal significant changes in the condition of the firm's unrecognized human assets. In fact, conventional accounting statements may spuriously reflect *favorable* performance when human resources are actually being liquidated.[1] If people are treated abusively in an effort to generate more production, short term profits may be derived through liquidation of the firm's organizational assets. If product quality is reduced, immediate gains may be made at the expense of customer loyalty assets.

A need exists, therefore, to develop an organizational accounting or information system which will reflect the current condition of and changes in the firm's human assets. Some accountants have recnized such a need, but measurement difficulties pose problems for them. As early as 1922, William A. Paton observed:

> In the business enterprise, a well-organized and loyal personnel may be a more important "asset" than a stock of merchandise. . . . At present there seems to be no way of measuring such factors in terms of the dollar; hence, they cannot be recognized as specific economic assets. But let us, accordingly, admit the serious limitations of the conventional balance sheet as a statement of financial condition.[2]

IMPORTANCE OF HUMAN RESOURCES

Why have industry and the accounting profession steadfastly neglected accounting for human resources? Aside from the measurement difficulties, the answer may be found, partly, in the perpetuation of accounting practices which trace their origins to an early period in our industrial history when human resource investments were relatively low. In more recent years, however, those occupational classifications exhibiting the highest rates of growth, such as

[28] C. G. Smith, O. Ari, and A. S. Tannenbaum, The relationship of patterns of control to norms in a service organization (unpublished report, 1962).

* *Personnel Administration,* Vol. 32, No. 4 (July-August 1969), pp. 34–46.

† R. Lee Brummet is on the faculty at the University of North Carolina. William C. Pyle directs human resources accounting site research for the University of Michigan. In 1966 Pyle initiated the first human resource accounting project in conjunction with the R. G. Barry Corporation. Eric G. Flamholtz is on the faculty at the Graduate School of Business, Columbia University.

[1] Rensis Likert, *The human organization: Its management and value* (New York: McGraw-Hill, 1967), pp. 101–15.

[2] W. A. Paton, *Accounting theory* (New York: The Ronald Press, 1922), pp. 486–87.

FIGURE 1 THE PROCESS OF RESOURCE MANAGEMENT

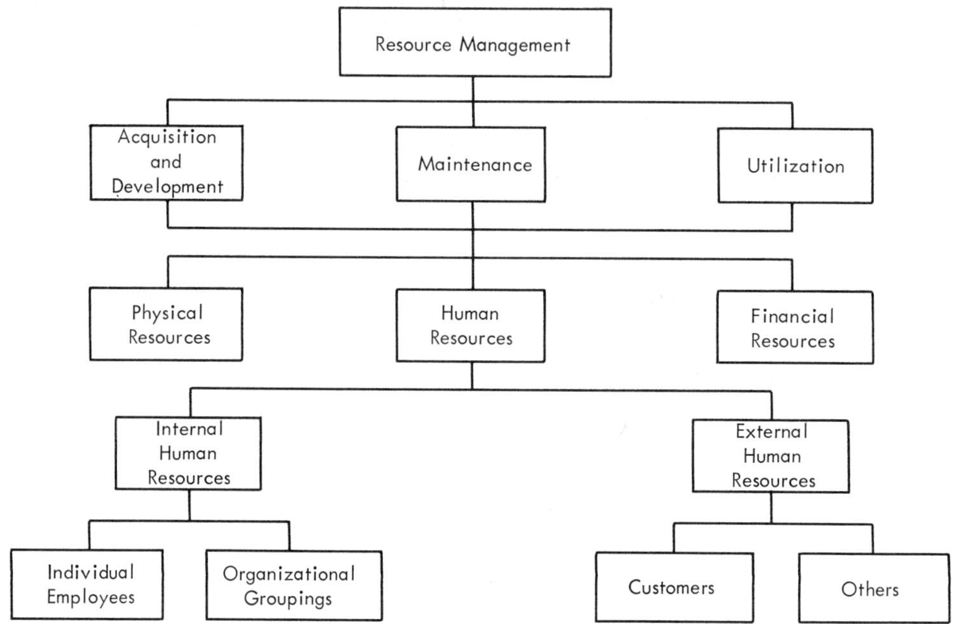

managerial and technical groupings, are those which require the greatest investment in human resources.[3] In addition, rising organizational complexity has created new demands for developing more sophisticated interaction capabilities and skills within industry.[4] These and other factors, coupled with persistent shortages in highly skilled occupational groupings increase the need for information relevant to the management of human resources.

RESOURCE MANAGEMENT NEEDS

Although oversimplified, management may be viewed as a process of *acquisition and development, maintenance,* and *utilization* of a "resource mix" to achieve organizational objectives, as suggested in Figure 1. Accounting and information systems contribute to this process by identifying, measuring, and communicating economic information to permit informed judgments and decisions in the management of the resource mix. Management needs information regarding: (1) resource acquisition and development, (2) resource maintenance or condition, and (3) resource utilization.

Resource Acquisition and Development Information Needs. Organizations acquire a wide variety of resources to achieve their purposes. Investments are undertaken in those resources which offer the greatest potential returns to the enterprise given an acceptable degree of risk. Calculation of resource acquisition and development costs is necessary, therefore, not only for investment planning, but also as a base for determining differential returns which accrue to those investments. The *resource acquisition and development information needs* reflect themselves along two dimensions; (1) the need for measurement of *outlay costs* when assets are actually acquired, and (2) the need for estimating the *replacement cost* of these investments in the event they should expire.

Resource Utilization Information. Once .new capabilities, levels of competency, and other "system the objective of creating new capabilities, levels of competency, types of behavior, forms of organization, and other conditions which will facilitate achieving organizational objectives. An information need exists, therefore, to ascertain the degree to which investments in resources actually produce and sustain the desired new capabilities, levels of competency, types of behavior, and forms or organization.

Resource Utilization Information. Once new capabilities, levels of competency, and other "system states" are achieved, *resource utilization information* needs become more salient. Management should know the degree to which changes in resource conditions or "system states" are translated into organiza-

[3] U.S. Bureau of the Census, *Historical statistics of the United States, colonial times to 1957* (Washington, D.C., 1960), pp. 74–75, 202–14.

[4] Likert, *The human organization,* pp. 156–60.

tional performance. The answer to this question is reflected in the rate of return on the investments which created the new "system state" or resource condition.

Conventional Accounting and Information Needs. Conventional accounting or information systems answer these three basic information needs for *non-human resources.* Measurement of investment in plant and equipment fulfills the "acquisition information need." Over time, these assets are depreciated, and new investments are recorded. The current "book values" of such investments reflect, at least in theory, the "resource condition" of the organization's physical assets. Finally, "utilization information needs" are supplied in the form of return on investment calculations.

Unfortunately, conventional accounting systems do not answer these three basic information needs for human assets. The objective of our research effort, therefore, is to develop a body of human resource accounting theory and techniques which will, at least in part, alleviate these information deficiencies.

HUMAN RESOURCE ACCOUNTING MODEL

The development of human resource accounting in the business enterprise derives from the pioneering work of Rensis Likert and his colleagues at the University of Michigan's Institute for Social Research. For more than two decades, their research studies have revealed that relationships exist between certain variable constructs and organizational performance. *"Causal variables,"* such as organizational structure and patterns of management behavior have been shown to affect *"intervening variables"* such as employee loyalties, attitudes, perceptions, and motivations, which in turn have been shown to affect *"end-result variables"* such as productivity, costs, and earnings.[5] Furthermore, research by Likert and Seashore indicates that time lags of two years or more often exist between changes in the "causal variables" and resultant changes in the "end-result variables."[6]

As seen in Figure 2, Likert's three variable models have been adopted into a human resource accounting model with the addition of two variable constructs —*"Investment variables"* and *"return on investment variables."* Why have these new variable classifications been added? All business firms wish to improve organizational performance. In doing so, however, a more crucial question is, *how much* will performance be improved and *what will it cost.* When a firm invests in new capital equipment, the costs of various alternatives are estimated for each along with projected rates of return. For example, one piece of equipment may cost $75,000 and have an estimated rate of return of 20 percent, while another may cost $100,000 with a return estimate of 15 percent.

An important objective of our research is to extend capital budgeting concepts to the firm's human resources. If the company invests $50,000 in a new training program, what is the anticipated return? If the firm invests $75,000 in an organizational development program, what return will accrue to that investment?

HUMAN RESOURCE VARIABLES AND INFORMATION NEEDS

Investment Variables. Investments in both human and non-human assets are recorded in dollar units and are measured to fulfill the *"resource acquisition and development information"* needs of management through identification of investment *outlay costs* and *replacement costs.* Conventional accounting practice now identifies *non-human* resource investments, at least on an outlay cost basis. In January 1968, a human resource accounting system was operationalized at the R. G. Barry Corporation to measure "individual employee" investments. Development work is now in progress to provide a system for identifying "organizational investments."

"Causal Variables." These are independent variables which management may alter to affect the course of developments within the organization. These variables include the type and condition of plant and equipment, and the type and level of employee competency, managerial behavior, organizational structure, and related factors. As suggested by the arrows in Figure 2, the state of the "individual employee causal variables" is more likely to *directly* affect the "end-result variables" (e.g., productivity, costs, and product quality) than the "organizational causal variables," whose effects tend to pass through a series of "intervening variables," which will be discussed shortly.

"Causal variables" are measured to supply the "resource maintenance or condition information" needs of management. Both dollar and socio-psychological based measurements may be employed to reflect the condition of the "causal variables." Conventional accounting practice now provides "non-human causal variable" data in the form of asset

[5] Ibid.

[6] R. Likert and S. Seashore, Making cost control work, *Harvard Business Review,* November-December 1963, pp. 96–108.

FIGURE 2 A HUMAN RESOURCE ACCOUNTING MODEL (WITH EXAMPLES OF VARIABLES)

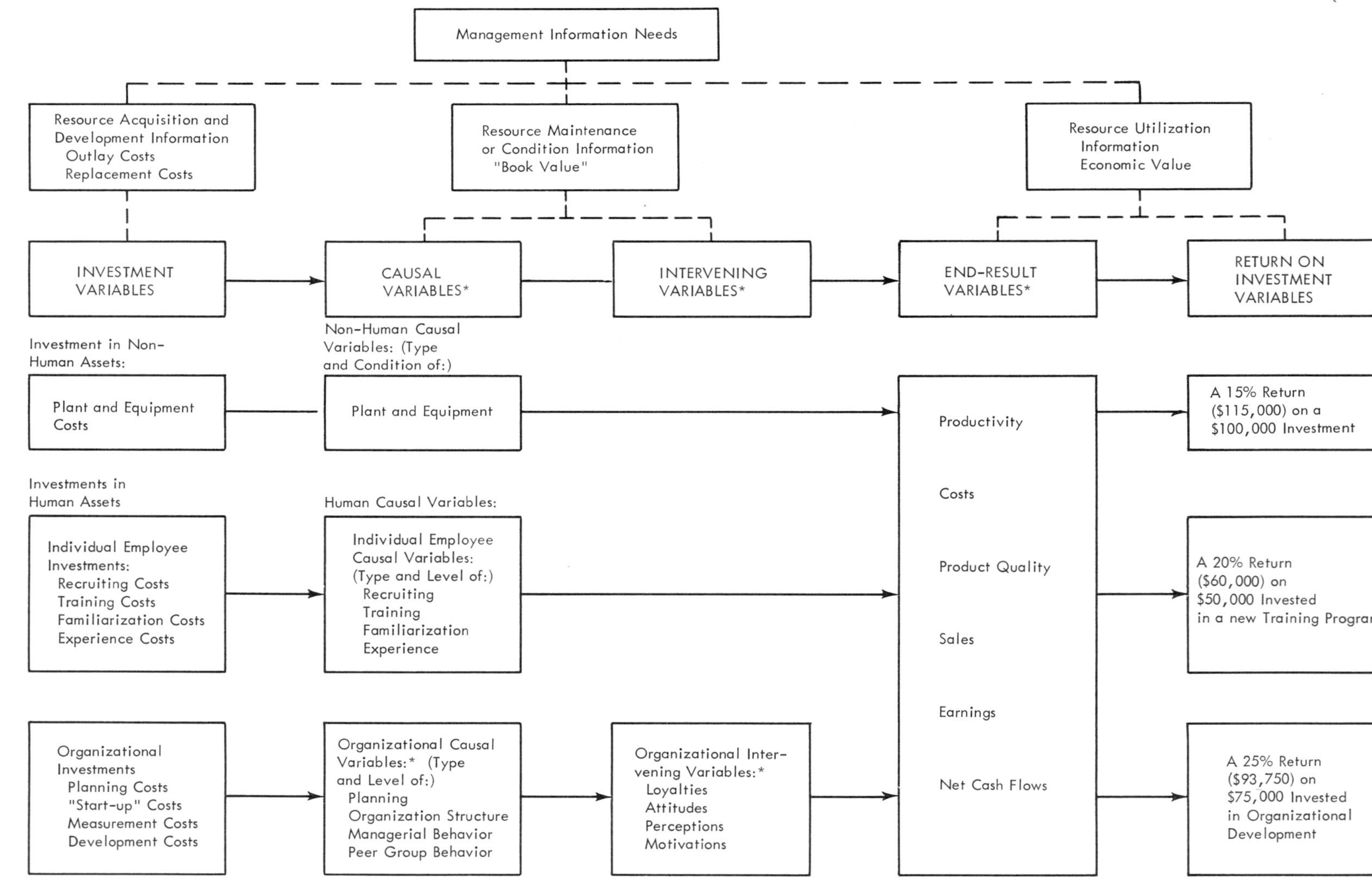

book values which, at least in theory, reflect the current state of those assets. A similar system for measuring "individual employee causal variables" has been implemented at the R. G. Barry Corporation. Questionnaire survey techniques developed by the Institute for Social Research are being employed to measure "organizational causal variables."

Intervening Variables. As stated above, the effect of "organizational causal variables" may not be directly reflected in the "end-result variables." Time lags of two years or more have been observed between changes in these "causal variables" and resultant changes in the "end-result variables." The effects of changes in "organizational causal variables" have been traced through a series of *"intervening variables,"* which include employee loyalties, attitudes, perceptions, and motivations.

"Intervening variables" are not measured in dollar units, but in terms of a scaling of perceptions derived from a socio-psychological questionnaire. Measurements of the "intervening variables" are directed toward the "resource maintenance or condition information" needs of the organization.

End-result Variables. These are dependent variables which reflect the achievements of the organization. The particular "end-result variables" for a given enterprise are a function of performance objectives which have been defined by that organization. These may include the level of productivity, costs, product quality, sales, earnings, net cash flows, employee health and satisfaction, and related factors.

"End-result variables" are normally measured in monetary terms, but they may also be reflected in socio-psychological units, as in the case of employee satisfaction. Changes in "end-result variables" may be associated with variations in "investment," "causal," and "intervening" variables through multiple correlation analyses of data collected in each of the variable classifications over an extended period of time. In this fashion, "end-result variables" may be expressed in the form of *"return on investment variables"* where a particular change in the "end-result variables" can be significantly associated with a particular "investment variable" change. For example, if $75,000 were invested in an organizational development program, and a $93,750 change in predetermined "end-result variables" was observed, a return of 25 percent would be realized on the investment. Such analyses may be employed to improve the allocation of organizational resources by indicating which investment patterns should be increased, reduced, or maintained at their current level.

Ultimately, it may be possible to place a current valuation on the firm's human resources through a process of discounting estimates of future "end-result variables," using time lags and relationships which have been observed among the variable classifications. The results of this valuation can be cross-checked against the unexpired costs which are recorded in the human asset accounts.

HUMAN RESOURCE ACCOUNTING OBJECTIVES

The ultimate objective of the research is to develop an integrated accounting function which fulfills basic information needs with respect to physical, financial, and human resources both internal and external to the organization. As an intermediate objective, we are concentrating on the development of an *internal human resource* accounting capability. This research effort divides itself into three functions: (1) *the development of a human resource accounting system oriented to basic managerial information needs,* (2) *the development and refinement of managerial applications of human resource accounting, and* (3) *the analysis of the behavioral impact of human resource accounting on people.* These objectives are being pursued in a five-year inter-company research program which has been initiated by the University of Michigan's Institute for Social Research and Graduate School of Business Administration in cooperation with several corporations.

Research at the R. G. Barry Corporation. Since October 1966, the University of Michigan has been engaged, along with the management of the R. G. Barry Corporation, in development of what is believed to be the first human resource accounting system. The Barry Corporation's 1,300 employees manufacture a variety of personal comfort items including foam-cushioned slippers, chair pads, robes, and other leisure wear, which are marketed in department stores and other retail outlets under brand names such as Angel Treds, Dearfoams, Kush-ons, and Gustave. The corporate headquarters and four production facilities are in Columbus, Ohio. Several other plants, warehouses, and sales offices are located across the country. The firm has expanded from a sales volume of about $5½ million in 1962 to approximately $20 million in 1968.

Implementation of a Human Resource Accounting System. The first phase of a human resource accounting system became operational at the R. G. Barry Corporation during January 1968. This system measures investments which are undertaken in the firm's some 96 members of management, on both *outlay cost* and *replacement cost* bases. An account structure applicable to organizational investments is now being developed. The Barry Corporation is now in the process of extending human resources accounting to other occupational classifications in the firm, In the future, a system will be developed for its cus-

FIGURE 3 MODEL OF AN OUTLAY COST MEASUREMENT SYSTEM

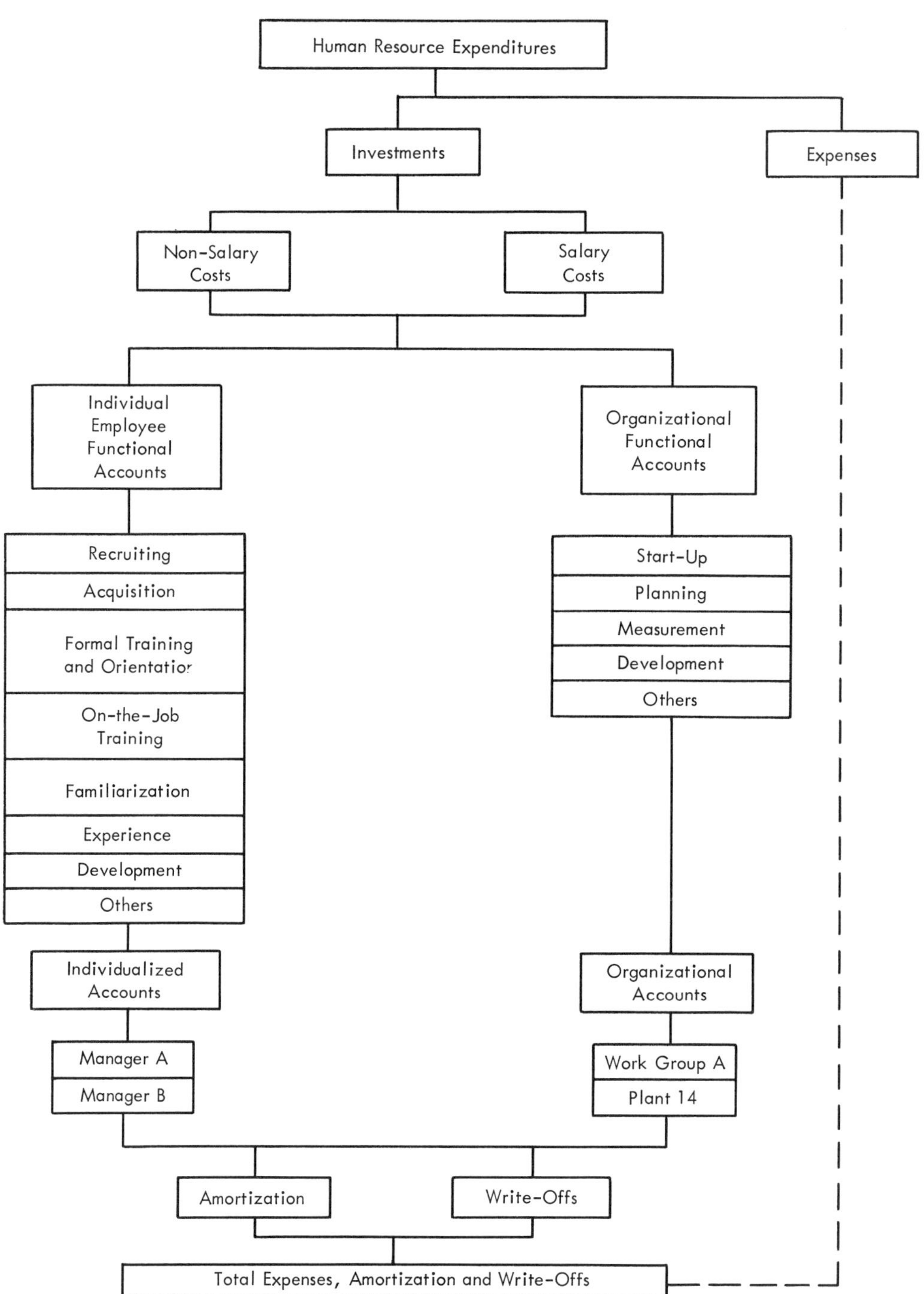

tomer resources. A model of an outlay cost measurement system for employees is presented in Figure 3.

HISTORICAL AND REPLACEMENT INVESTMENTS MEASURED

An Outlay Cost Measurement System. Investments in human resources may be measured in terms of outlay costs. *Outlay costs* are sacrifices incurred by the firm in the form of out-of-pocket expenditures associated with a particular human resource investment. These are measured in terms of *non-salary* and *salary* costs. Examples of the former include travel costs in support of recruiting or training, and tuition charges for management development programs. The latter would include employee salary allocations during an investment period. For example, if an executive attends a two-week management seminar, his salary for this time period should be viewed as part of the investment, in addition to the tuition and travel costs. Similarly, if during the first year of tenure with a firm, 30 percent of a new manageer's time is devoted to familiarization with company policy, precedents, organization structure, interaction patterns, and the like, 30 percent of his salary should be recorded as an outlay cost associated with the familiarization investment.

At the R. G. Barry Corporation, instruments have been designed to measure investments undertaken in *individual managers* for each of the functional accounts indicated in Figure 3. To qualify as assets, specific expenditures must meet the test of offering service potential beyond the current accounting period in relation to long term written corporate objectives. Charges to the functional accounts are also entered in "individualized accounts" for each manager. With a few modifications the individual manager account structure will also be applied to other occupational groupings within the firm. However, it is not contemplated that "individualized accounts" will be developed for factory and clerical personnel.

Procedures have also been designed to record investment expirations. Asset accounts are amortized on two bases: (1) *maximum life* and (2) *expected life.* Functional investments are separately identified in each manager's account and are amortized according to the *maximum life* of each investment type. For example, recruiting and acquisition costs provide benefits to the firm so long as an employee remains with the organization. The *maximum life* of this investment would be the mandatory retirement age less the employee's age when hired. If *maximum life* were relied on exclusively for amortization, asset accounts would be overstated since employees frequently leave the firm prior to the mandatory retirement age. To assure a more realistic statement of assets, maximum life amortization periods[7] are adjusted to expected life by application of weighted probabilities which reflect a particular individual's likelihood of remaining until mandatory retirement based upon his age, tenure, organizational level, marital status, job satisfaction, and related factors. *Expected life* periods are employed in the amortization of the functional accounts.

The choice between these two bases is essentially a choice between relevance and verifiability. "Maximum life" provides a highly verifiable base, but it is less relevant than "expected life." "Expected life" may, to some degree, be influenced by job satisfaction as well as many other factors. For this reason, a firm may wish to obtain a range of estimates. To be more conservative, "expected life" is employed to calculate the investments shown on the firm's balance sheet and an adjustment to net income based upon changes occurring in those investments. Other estimates may be more useful for planning purposes.

Specific measurement instruments have been designed to record human asset losses resulting from turnover, obsolescence, and health deteriorations. Turnover is immediately identifiable; however, obsolescence is much more elusive. For this reason individual employee asset accounts are reviewed quarterly for obsolescence by each supervisor. Review also occurs when an employee is transferred to a new position. Accounts are also adjusted for known health deteriorations in proportion to the seriousness of the impairment as reflected in actuarial data.

As suggested in Figure 3, an outlay cost measurement system designed to record *organizational investments* is now being developed at the R. G. Barry Corporation. Investments are undertaken in human resources *over and above* those made in *individual employees as individuals.* Organizational "start-up" costs are reflected in heavy individual employee investments and in production below standard during the initial period when the organization is building and developing group interaction patterns for the first time. Additional investments are also made in the form of organizational planning. Furthermore, periodic measurement of organizational causal and intervening variables are in themselves investments in the organization when they lead to development activities which improve the functioning of the enterprise as an interacting system. Finally, investments are undertaken in the organization which cannot be readily traced to individual employees. A portion of

[7] Where relationships between the level of job satisfaction and expected tenure can be identified, turnover losses may be calculated in dollar terms and predicted for varying levels of job satisfaction, as a function of measured changes in causal and intervening variables.

the operating costs of the personnel department, company library, health service, safety department, and similar departments may be traced to activities which offer long term benefits to the organization.

Charges made to the "organizational functional accounts" will also be allocated to appropriate entities such as work groups, plants, divisions, or the enterprise as a whole. In addition, a capability is being developed to reflect expirations which occur in these accounts. Many "organizational investments" differ *in kind* from "individual employee investments" which lose their usefulness to the firm when a particular individual leaves the firm. For example, benefits could be derived indefinitely from costs incurred in molding the organization into a system of effective interacting groups despite a moderate level of individual employee turnover within the system. This suggests the possibility that some organizational investments may be non-depreciable.

This would not, however, preclude the possibility of expirations. If for example, an enterprise invests $50,000 in an organizational development program which succeeds in improving employee attitudes and motivations by a measurable amount, subsequent deterioration in those attitudes and motivations could justify a write-off of the original investment.

A Replacement Cost Measurement System. The outlay cost system described above is designed to record human resource investments, obsolescence, and losses as they are actually incurred. These data, however, only partially fulfill the "resource information" needs of the organization. For planning purposes, the *positional replacement cost* of human resources becomes more salient. Positional replacement costs are the outlay costs (recruiting, training, etc.) which would be incurred if an incumbent should leave his position. The human resource accounting system which has been installed at the R. G. Barry Corporation has the capability of supplying average positional replacement cost data for each manager. These positional replacement cost data reflect annual adjustments for price level changes. The system also records "compositional" investment changes since some investments undertaken in the past will not be repeated and, conversely, others not made in the past will be undertaken in the future. For these and other reasons, positional replacement cost may be less than, equal to, or greater than historical outlay cost.

Appropriate Measurement Units. As noted above, "investment variables" are measured exclusively in dollar or socio-psychologically based units. However, "causal variables" may be measured in either dollars or socio-psychological terms. For example, the current condition of the firm's plant and equipment (a "causal variable") should be reflected at its current book value, although other indicators can also be employed. Similarly, the *current condition* of the company's "individual employee investments" (a "causal variable") should be reflected at the book values recorded in the functional asset accounts discussed above. However, other indicators are being developed as cross-checks. Socio-psychological survey questions are now being used to measure employee perceptions of the current condition of "individual employee causal variables" such as the quality of recruiting and training. Trends in these data are being compared with trends in the individual employee asset account balances. These socio-psychological data may suggest more realistic amortization procedures for individual employee investments." The current condition of "organizational causal variables" may also be reflected in the current book value of "organizational investments," recorded in dollar units. However, socio-psychological survey instruments may prove more valid since managerial behavior (a "causal variable") may be altered independently of cost outlays.

"Intervening variable" measurements have been undertaken at the R. G. Barry Corporation and additional surveys are planned. However, an accumulation of several years' data will be required before meaningful "return on investment variables" may be calculated.

HUMAN RESOURCE ACCOUNTING APPLIED

Human resource accounting system applications are oriented toward fulfilling the three basic organizational information needs: (1) resource acquisition and development information, (2) resource maintenance or condition information and (3) resource utilization information. Inasmuch as the human resource accounting system at the R. G. Barry Corporation is in an early stage of development, its potential applications can only be stated in tentative terms at this time.

It is contemplated that the system will generate two types of data: (1) information which is integrated with conventional accounting statements and (2) information which is presented independently of these statements.

Human Resource Data Integrated and Conventional Financial Reports. One of the first reports generated by the system is a *balance sheet* indicating the firm's investment in human resources. The corporate *income statement* is also affected to the degree that there is a net change in the firm's investment in human resources during the reporting

FIGURE 4 BALANCE SHEET

Assets	Dec. 31, 1967	Dec. 31, 1968
Current Assets (cash, etc.)	$ 1,000,000	$ 1,500,000
Plant and Equipment	8,000,000	8,000,000
Investment in Individual Employees (recruiting, training, development, etc.)	750,000	850,000
Organizational Investments (start-up, planning, development, etc.)	900,000	700,000
Total Assets	$10,650,000	$11,050,000
Equities		
Liabilities	$ 2,000,000	$ 2,000,000
Owner's Equity:		
Stock	6,000,000	6,000,000
Retained Earnings (including investment in human resources)	2,650,000	3,050,000
Total Equities	$10,650,000	$11,050,000

INCOME STATEMENT
Year Ending December 31, 1968

Sales		$2,000,000
Expenses		1,500,000
Net Income		$ 500,000
Adjustment for change in investment in human resources		
—Individual employee adjustment	+$100,000	
—Organizational adjustment	—$200,000	—100,000
Adjusted Net Income		$ 400,000

period. This situation is illustrated in Figure 4. The two balance sheets indicate that a hypothetical company experienced a *net increase* in its investment in *individual employees* during the period. This change, taken by itself, would result in a positive adjustment to the firm's net income[8] of $100,000. However, this firm also experienced a *net decline* in its organizational investments during the period. (This could result, for example, from a plant being closed in one location with operations being moved to another state.) This change, taken by itself, would result in a negative net income adjustment of $200,000. When the two changes are taken together, a negative adjustment of $100,000 is reflected in the firm's net income.

Data generated by the human resource accounting system at the R. G. Barry Corporation indicate that the replacement investment of their some 96 managers is approximately $1,000,000, while the current "book value" is about $600,000. The firm invests around $3,000 in a first line supervisor and upwards of $30,000 in a member of top management.

Other Human Resource Accouting Reports. A variety of additional reports are now being generated by a human resource accounting system. Periodic comparative data for different work groups, plants, and divisions contrast human resource investment changes during reporting periods. Turnover losses are also being quantified and analyzed according to such factors as employee job satisfaction, age, occupation, tenure and the like. Special purpose reports are also being prepared to evaluate various organizational alternatives which require investments in human resources. To increase production capacity, for example, should a firm expand its existing plant or construct a new facility? For each alternative these reports indicate projected new investments, write-offs, and the effect on net cash flows. Once a particular alternative is chosen, actual investment, write-offs and cash flows may then be contrasted against projections. As patterns of return on investments in human resources become apparent, the firm will learn which investment types should be increased, reduced, or maintained at their current level.

The ultimate success of any accounting system is determined by its impact on the behavior of people. Where the goals of employees and the organization are reasonably consistent, data may be employed as a problem solving tool to achieve organizational objectives. However, the social science literature is replete with evidence of the distortions which may be introduced into an information system when in-

[8] The net income that would be indicated without a human resource accounting system.

dividual and organizational goals are not congruent.[9] For this reason, an integral part of human resource accounting research will focus on determining the behavioral impact of an operational human resource accounting system on employees. Socio-psychological survey instruments supplemented by personal interviews will be employed to assess the impact. These data will, in turn, be used to design organization development activities which will facilitate installation and sustained operation of the human resource accounting system.

CONCLUSIONS

Human resource accounting is now in an early stage, and a host of problems remain to be resolved before a fully developed system can become operational. However, the initial results are encouraging as many beneficial results are being derived prior to full scale operation. Investments in human resources may be determined at a relatively early stage. The techniques developed to measure these assets may also be employed in extended organizational and manpower planning which underlie and sustain corporate growth. Even before return on investment data become available, measurement of trends and rates of change in "causal" and "intervening" variable data may suggest new behaviors and investment routes which will improve organizational effectiveness.

51. A STRATEGIC CONTINGENCIES' THEORY OF INTRAORGANIZATIONAL POWER*

***D. J. Hickson, C. R. Hinings, C. A. Lee, R. E. Schneck,* and *J. M. Pennings*†**

Typically, research designs have treated power as the independent variable. Power has been used in community studies to explain decisions on community programs, on resource allocation, and on voting behavior: in small groups it has been used to explain decision making; and it has been used in studies of work organizations to explain morale and alienation. But within work organizations, power itself has not been explained. This paper sets forth a theoretical explanation of power as the dependent variable with the aim of developing empirically testable hypotheses that will explain differential power among subunits in complex work organizations.[1]

The problems of studying power are well known from the cogent reviews by March (1955, 1966) and Wrong (1968). These problems led March (1966: 70) to ask if power was just a term used to mask our ignorance, and to conclude pessimistically that the power of the concept of power "depends on the kind of system we are confronting."

Part of March's (1966) pessimism can be attributed to the problems inherent in community studies. When the unit of analysis is the community, the governmental, political, economic, recreational, and other units which make up the community do not necessarily interact and may even be oriented outside the supposed boundaries of the community. However, the subunits of a work organization are mutually related in the interdependent activities of a single identifiable social system. The perspective of the present paper is due in particular to the encouraging studies of subunits by Lawrence and Lorsch (1967a, 1967b), and begins with their (1967a: 3) definition of an organization as "a system of interrelated behaviors of people who are performing a task that has been differentiated into several distinct subsystems."

Previous studies of power in work organizations have tended to focus on the individual and to neglect subunit or departmental power. This neglect led Perrow (1970: 84) to state: "Part of the problem, I suspect, stems from the persistent attempt to define power in terms of individuals and as a social-psycho-

---

[9] C. Argyris, Human problems with budgets. *Harvard Business Review,* January-February 1953, pp. 97–110; W. F. Whyte *Money and motivation* (New York: Harper & Row, 1955)

* *Administrative Science Quarterly,* Vol., No. (19), 216–29.

†David J. Hickson is Ralph Yablon professor of behavioural studies, organizational analysis research unit, University of Bradford Management Centre, England; Christopher R. Hinings is a senior lecturer in sociology, industrial administration research unit, University of Aston-in-Birmingham, England; Charles A. Lee and Rodney E. Schneck are professors in the faculty of business administration and commerce, University of Alberta, Canada; and Johannes M. Pennings is an instructor and doctoral student at the institute for social research, University of Michigan.

[1] This research was carried out at the Organizational Behavior Research Unit, Faculty of Business Administration and Commerce, University of Alberta, with the support of Canada Council Grants numbers 67-0253 and 69-0714.

logical phenomenon. . . . Even sociological studies tend to measure power by asking about an individual. . . . I am not at all clear about the matter, but I think the term takes on different meanings when the unit, or power-holder, is a *formal group* in an *open system* with *multiple goals,* and the system is assumed to reflect a political-domination model of organization, rather than only a cooperative model. . . . The fact that after a cursory search I can find only a single study that asks survey questions regarding the power of functional *groups* strikes me as odd. Have we conceptualized power in such a way as to exclude this well-known phenomenon?"

The concept of power used here follows Emerson (1962) and takes power as a property of the social relationship, not of the actor. Since the context of the relationship is a formal organization, this approach moves away from an overpersonalized conceptualization and operationalization of power toward structural sources. Such an approach has been taken only briefly by Dubin (1963) in his discussion of power, and incidentally by Lawrence and Lorsch (1967b) when reporting power data. Most research has focused on the vertical superior-subordinate relationship, as in a multitude of leadership studies. This approach is exemplified by the extensive work of Tannenbaum (1968) and his colleagues, in which the distribution of perceived power was displayed on control graphs. The focus was on the vertical differentiation of perceived power, that is the exercise of power by managers who by changing their behavior could vary the distribution and the total amount of perceived power.

By contrast, when organizations are conceived as interdepartmental systems, the division of labor becomes the ultimate source of intraorganizational power, and power is explained by variables that are elements of each subunit's task, its functioning, and its links with the activities of other subunits. Insofar as this approach differs from previous studies by treating power as the dependent variable, by taking subunits of work organizations as the subjects of analysis, and by attempting a multivariate explanation, it may avoid some of the previous pitfalls.

ELEMENTS OF A THEORY

Thompson (1967: 13) took from Cyert and March (1963) a viewpoint which he hailed as a newer tradition: "A newer tradition enables us to conceive of the organization as an open system, indeterminate and faced with uncertainty, but subject to criteria of rationality and hence needing certainty . . . we suggest that organizations cope with uncertainty by creating certain parts specifically to deal with it, specializing other parts in operating under conditions of certainty, or near certainty."

Thus organizations are coneived of as interdepartmental systems in which a major task element is coping with uncertainty. The task is divided and allotted to the subsystems, the division of labor creating an interdependency among them. Imbalance of this reciprocal interdependence (Thompson, 1967) among the parts gives rise to power relations. The essence of an organization is limitation of the autonomy of all its members or parts, since all are subject to power from the others; for subunits, unlike individuals, are not free to make a decision to participate, as March and Simon (1958) put it, nor to decide whether or not to come together in political relationships. They must. They exist to do so. Crozier (1964: 47) stressed in his discussion of power "the necessity for the members of the different groups to live together; the fact that each group's privileges depend to quite a large extent on the existence of other group's privileges." The groups use differential power to function within the system rather than to destroy it.

If dependency in a social relation is the reverse of power (Emerson, 1962), then the crucial unanswered question in organizations is: what factors function to vary dependency, and so to vary power? Emerson (1962: 32) proposed that "the dependence of actor A upon actor B is (1) directly proportional to A's motivational investment in goals mediated by B, and (2) inversely proportional to the availability of those goals to A outside of the A–B relation." In organizations, subunit B will have more power than other subunits to the extent that (1) B has the capacity to fulfill the requirements of the other subunits and (2) B monopolizes this ability. If a central problem facing modern organizations is uncertainty, then B's power in the organization will be partially determined by the extent to which B copes with uncertainties for other subunits, and by the extent to which B's coping activities are available elsewhere.

Thus, intraorganizational dependency can be associated with two contributing variables: (1) the degree to which a subunit copes with uncertainty for other subunits, and (2) the extent to which a subunit's coping activities are substitutable. But if coping with uncertainty, and substitutability, are to be in some way related to power, there is a necessary assumption of some degree of task interconnection among subunits. By definition, organization requires a minimum link. Therefore, a third variable, centrality, refers to the varying degree above such a minimum with which the activities of a subunit are linked with those of other subunits.

Before these three variables can be combined in a theory of power, it is necessary to examine their definition and possible operationalization, and to define power in this context.

Power

Hinings et al. (1967: 62) compared power to concepts such as bureaucracy or alienation or social class, which are difficult to understand because they tend to be treated as "large-scale unitary concepts." Their many meanings need disentangling. With the concept of power, this has not yet been accomplished (Cartwright, 1965), but two conceptualizations are commonly employed: (1) power as coercion, and (2) power as determination of behavior.

Power as coercive force was a comparatively early conceptualization among sociologists (Weber, 1947; Bierstedt, 1950). Later, Blau (1964) emphasized the imposition of will despite resistance.

However, coercion is only one among the several bases of power listed by French and Raven (1959) and applied across organizations by Etzioni (1961); that is, coercion is a means of power, but is not an adequate definition of power. If the direction of dependence in a relationship is determined by an imbalance of power bases, power itself has to be defined separately from these bases. Adopting Dahl's (1957) concept of power, as many others have done (March, 1955; Bennis et al., 1958; Emerson, 1962; Harsanyi, 1962; Van Doorn, 1962; Dahlstrom, 1966; Wrong, 1968; Tannenbaum, 1968; Luhmann, 1969), power is defined as the determination of the behavior of one social unit by another.

If power is the determination of A's behavior by B, irrespective of whether one, any, or all the types of bases are involved, then authority will here be regarded as that part of power which is legitimate or normatively expected by some selection of role definers. Authority may be either more or less than power. For subunits it might be represented by the formally specified range of activities they are officially required to undertake and, therefore, to decide upon.

Discrepancies between authority and power may reflect time lag. Perrow (1970) explored the discrepancy between respondent's perceptions of power and of what power should be. Perhaps views on a preferred power distribution precede changes in the exercise of power, which in turn precede changes in expectations of power, that is in its legitimate authority content. Perhaps today's authority hierarchy is partly a fossilized impression of yesterday's power ranking. However this may be, it is certainly desirable to include in any research not only data on perceived power and on preferred power, but also on positional power, or authority, and on participation, or exercised power (Clark [ed.], 1968).

Kaplan (1964) succinctly described three dimensions of power. The weight of power is defined in terms of the degree to which B affects the probability of A behaving in a certain way, that is, determination of behavior in the sense adopted here. The other dimensions are domain and scope. Domain is the number of A's, persons or collectivities, whose behavior is determined; scope is the range of behaviors of each A that are determined. For subunit power within an organization, domain might be the number of other subunits affected by the issues, scope the range of decision issues affected, and weight the degree to which a given subunit affects the decision process on the issues. In published research such distinctions are rarely made. Power consists of the sweeping undifferentiated perceptions of respondents when asked to rank individuals or classes of persons, such as supervisors, on influence. Yet at the same time the complexity of power in organizations is recognized. If it is taken for granted that, say, marketing has most to do with sales matters, that accounting has most to do with finance matters, supervisors with supervisory matters, and so on, then the validity of forcing respondents to generalize single opinions across an unstated range of possibilities is questionable.

To avoid these generalized opinions, data collected over a range of decision topics or issues are desirable. Such issues should in principle include all recognized problem areas in the organization, in each of which more than one subunit is involved. Examples might be marketing strategies, obtaining equipment, personnel training, and capital budgeting.

Some suggested subvariables and indicators of power and of the independent variables are summarized in Table 1. These are intended to include both individual perceptions of power in the form of questionnaire responses and data of a somewhat less subjective kind on participation in decision processes and on formal position in the organization.

It is now possible to examine coping with uncertainty, substitutability and centrality.

Uncertainty and Coping with Uncertainty

Uncertainty may be defined as a lack of information about future events, so that alternatives and their outcomes are unpredictable. Organizations deal with environmentally derived uncertainties in the sources and composition of inputs, with uncertainties in the processing of throughputs, and again with environmental uncertainties in the disposal of outputs. They must have means to deal with these uncertainties for adequate task performance. Such ability is here called coping.

In his study of the French tobacco manufacturing industry, Crozier (1964: 164) suggested that power

TABLE 1 VARIABLES AND OPERATIONALIZABLE SUBVARIABLES

Power (weight, domain, scope)
Positional power (authority)
Participation power
Perceived power
Preferred power
Uncertainty
Variability of organizational inputs
Feedback on subunit performance;
Speed
Specificity
Structuring of subunit activities
Coping with uncertainty, classified as:
By prevention (forestalling uncertainty)
By information (forecasting)
By absorption (action after the event)
Substitutability
Availability of alternatives
Replaceability of personnel
Centrality
Pervasiveness of workflows
Immediacy of workflows

is related to "the kind of uncertainty upon which depends the life of the organization." March and Simon (1958) had earlier made the same point, and Perrow (1961) had discussed the shifting domination of different groups in organizations following the shifting uncertainties of resources and the routinization of skills. From studies of industrial firms, Perrow (1970) tentatively thought that power might be due to uncertainty absorption, as March and Simon (1958) call it. Lawrence and Lorsch (1967b) found that marketing had more influence than production in both container-manufacturing and food-processing firms, apparently because of its involvement in (uncertain) innovation and with customers.

Crozier (1964) proposed a strategic model of organizations as systems in which groups strive for power, but his discussion did not clarify how uncertainty could relate positively to power. Uncertainty itself does not give power: coping gives power. If organizations allocate to their various subunits task areas that vary in uncertainty, then those subunits that cope most effectively with the most uncertainty should have most power within the organization, since coping by a subunit reduces the impact of uncertainty on other activities in the organization, a shock absorber function. Coping may be by prevention, for example, a subunit prevents sales fluctuations by securing firm orders; or by information, for example, a subunit forecasts sales fluctuations; or by absorption, for example, a drop in sales is swiftly countered by novel selling methods (Table 1). By coping, the subunit provides pseudo certainty for the other subunits by controlling what are otherwise contingencies for other activities. This coping confers power through the dependencies created.

Thus organizations do not necessarily aim to avoid uncertainty nor to reduce its absolute level, as Cyert and March (1963) appear to have assumed, but to cope with it. If a subunit can cope, the level of uncertainty encountered can be increased by moving into fresh sectors of the environment, attempting fresh outputs, or utilizing fresh technologies.

Operationally, raw uncertainty and coping will be difficult to disentangle, though theoretically the distinctions are clear. For all units, uncertainty is in the raw situation which would exist without the activities of the other relevant subunits, for example, the uncertainty that would face production units if the sales subunit were not there to forecast and/or to obtain a smooth flow of orders. Uncertainty might be indicated by the variability of those inputs to the organization which are taken by the subunit. For instance, a production subunit may face variability in raw materials and engineering may face variability in equipment performance. Lawrence and Lorsch (1967a) attempted categorizations of this kind. In addition, they (1967a: 14) gave a lead with "the time span of definitive feedback from the environment." This time span might be treated as a secondary indicator of uncertainty, making the assumption that the less the feedback to a subunit on the results of what it is doing, and the less specific the feedback, the more likely the subunit is to be working in a vague, unknown, unpredictable task area. Both speed and specificity of feedback are suggested variables in Table 1.

Furthermore, the copious literature on bureaucratic or mechanistic structures versus more organic and less defined structures could be taken to imply that routinized or highly structured subunits, for example, as conceptualized and measured by Pugh *et al.* (1968), will have stable homogeneous activities and be less likely to face uncertainty. This assumption would require empirical testing before structuring of activities could be used as an indicator of uncertainty, but it is tentatively included in Table 1.

In principle, coping with uncertainty might be directly measured by the difference between the uncertainty of those inputs taken by a subunit and the certainty with which it performs its activities nonetheless. This would indicate the degree of shock absorption.

The relation of coping with uncertainty to power can be expressed by the following hypothesis:

Hypothesis 1. The more a subunit copes with uncertainty, the greater its power within the organization.

The hypothesis is in a form which ignores any effects of centrality and substitutability.

Substitutability

Concepts relating to the availability of alternatives pervade the literature on power. In economics theory the degree of competition is taken as a measure of the extent to which alternatives are available from other organizations, it being implied that the power of an organization over other organizations and customers is a function of the amount of competition present. The same point was the second part of Emerson's (1962) power-dependency scheme in social relations, and the second requirement or determinant in Blau's (1964) model of a power relationship.

Yet only Mechanic (1962) and Dubin (1957, 1963) have discussed such concepts as explanations of organizational power. Mechanic's (1962: 358) hypothesis 4 stated: "Other factors remaining constant, a person difficult to replace will have greater power than a person easily replaceable." Dubin (1957) stressed the very similar notion of exclusiveness, which as developed later (Dubin, 1963: 21), means that: "For any given level of functional importance in an organization, the power residing in a functionary is inversely proportional to the number of other functionaries in the organization capable of performing the function." Supporting this empirically, Lipset *et al.* (1956) suggested that oligarchy may occur in trade unions because of the official's monopoly of political and negotiating skills.

The concept being used is represented here by the term substitutability, which can, for subunits, be defined as the ability of the organization to obtain alternative performance for the activities of a subunit, and can be stated as a hypothesis for predicting the power of a subunit as follows:

Hypothesis 2. The lower the substitutability of the activities of a subunit, the greater its power within the organization.

Thus a purchasing department would have its power reduced if all of its activities could be done by hired materials agents, as would a personnel department if it were partially substituted by selection consultants or by line managers finding their staff themselves. Similarly, a department may hold on to power by retaining information the release of which would enable others to do what it does.

The obvious problem in operationalization is establishing that alternative means of performing activities exist, and if they do, whether they could feasibly be used. Even if agents or consultants exist locally, or if corporation headquarters could provide services, would it really be practicable for the organization to dispense with its own subunit? Much easier to obtain are data on replaceability of subunit personnel such as length of training required for new recruits and ease of hiring, which can be regarded as secondary indicators of the substitutability of a subunit, as indicated in Table 1.

Centrality

Given a view of organizations as systems of interdependent roles and activities, then the centrality of a subunit is the degree to which its activities are interlinked into the system. By definition, no subunit of an organization can score zero centrality. Without a minimum of centrality, coping with uncertainty and substitutability cannot affect power; above the minimum, additional increments of centrality further differentiate subunit power. It is the degree to which the subunit is an interdependent component, as Thompson (1967: 54) put it, distinguishing between pooled, sequential, and reciprocal interdependence patterns. Blau and Scott (1962) made an analogous distinction between parallel and interdependent specialization. Woodward (1965: 126) also introduced a concept of this kind into her discussion of the critical function in each of unit, large batch and mass, and process production: "there seemed to be one function that was central and critical in that it had the greatest effect on success and survival."

Within the overall concept of centrality, there are inconsistencies which indicate that more than one constitutive concept is being used. At the present stage of conceptualization their identification must be very tentative. First, there is the idea that the activities of a subunit are central if they are connected with many other activities in the organization. This workflow pervasiveness may be defined as the degree to which the workflows of a subunit connect with the workflows of other subunits. It describes the extent of task interactions between subunits, and for all subunits in an organization it would be operationalized as the flowchart of a complete systems analysis. For example, the integrative subsystems studied by Lawrence and Lorsch (1967a: 30), "whose members had the function of integrating the sales-research and the production-research subsystems" and which had structural and cultural characteristics intermediate between them, were presumably high on workflow pervasiveness because everything they did connected with the workflows of these several other subsystems. Research subsystems, however, may have been low on this variable if they fed work only to a single integrative, or production, subsystem.

Secondly, the activities of a subunit are central if

they are essential in the sense that their cessation would quickly and substantially impede the primary workflow of the organization. This workflow immediacy is defined as the speed and severity with which the workflows of a subunit affect the final outputs of the organization. Zald (1962) and Clark (1956) used a similar idea when they explained differential power among institution staff and education faculty by the close relation of their activities to organization goals.

The pervasiveness and immediacy of the workflows of a subunit are not necessarily closely related, and may empirically show a low correlation. A finance department may well have pervasive connections with all other subunits through the budgeting system, but if its activities ceased it would be some time before the effects were felt in, say, the production output of a factory; a production department controlling a stage midway in the sequence of an automated process, however, could have high workflow immediacy though not high pervasiveness.

The two main centrality hypotheses can therefore be stated as follows:

Hypothesis 3a. The higher the pervasiveness of the workflows of a subunit, the greater its power within the organization.

Hypothesis 3b. The higher the immediacy of the workflows of a subunit, the greater its power within the organization.

CONTROL OF CONTINGENCIES

Hypotheses relating power to coping with uncertainty, substitutability, and the subvariables of centrality have been stated in a simple single-variable form. Yet it follows from the view of subunits as interdependent parts of organizational systems that the hypotheses in this form are misleading. While each hypothesis may be empirically upheld, it is also hypothesized that this cannot be so without some values of both the other main independent variables. For example, when a marketing department copes with a volatile market by forecasting and by switching sales staff around to ensure stable orders, it acquires power only because the forecast and the orders are linked to the workflow of production, which depends on them. But even then power would be limited by the availability of a successful local marketing agency which could be hired by the organization, and the fact that salesmen were low skilled and easily replaceable.

To explain this interrelationship, the concept of control of contingencies is introduced. It represents organizational interdependence; subunits control contingencies for one another's activities and draw power from the dependencies thereby created. As a hypothesis:

Hypothesis 4. The more contingencies are controlled by a subunit, the greater its power within the organization.

A contingency is a requirement of the activities of one subunit which is affected by the activities of another subunit. What makes such a contingency strategic, in the sense that it is related to power, can be deduced from the preceding hypotheses. The independent variables are each necessary but not sufficient conditions for control of strategic contingencies, but together they determine the variation in interdependence between subunits. Thus contingencies controlled by a subunit as a consequence of its coping with uncertainty do not become strategic, that is, affect power, in the organization without some (unknown) values of substitutability and centrality. A strategic contingencies theory of power is therefore proposed and is illustrated by the diagram in Figure 1.

In terms of exchange theory, as developed by Blau (1964), subunits can be seen to be exchanging control of strategic contingencies one for the other under the normative regulation of an encompassing social system, and acquiring power in the system through the exchange. The research task is to elucidate what combinations of values of the independent variables summarized in hypotheses 1–3 allow hypothesis 4 to hold. Ultimately and ideally the aim would be to discover not merely the weightings of each in the total effect upon power, but how these variables should be operationally interrelated to obtain the best predictions. More of one and less of another may leave the resulting power unchanged. Suppose an engineering subunit has power because it quickly absorbs uncertainty by repairing breakdowns which interfere with the different workflows for each of several organization outputs. It is moderately central and nonsubstitutable. A change in organization policy bringing in a new technology with a single workflow leading to a single output would raise engineering's centrality, since a single breakdown would immediately stop everything, but simultaneously the uncertainty might be reduced by a maintenance program which all but eliminates the possibility of such an occurrence.

Though three main factors are hypothesized, which must change if power is to change, it is not assumed that all subunits will act in accord with the theory to increase their power. This has to be demonstrated. There is the obvious possibility of a cumulative reaction in which a subunit's power is used to preserve or increase the uncertainty it can cope with, or its centrality, or to prevent substitution, thereby

FIGURE 1 THE STRATEGIC CONTINGENCIES THEORY AND ROUTINIZATION

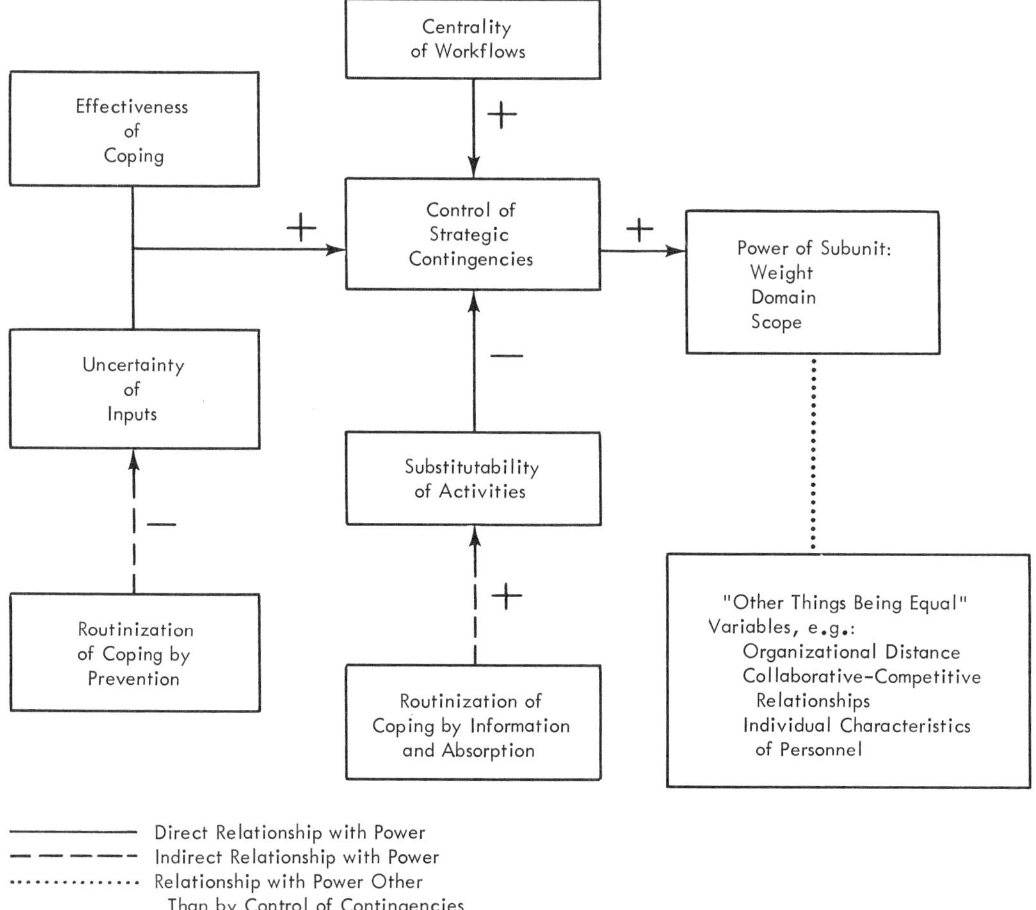

increasing its power, and so on. Nor is it argued that power or authority are intentionally allocated in terms of the theory, although the theory is open to such an inference.

Routinization

Most studies that refer to uncertainty contrast is with routinization, the prior prescription of recurrent task activities. Crozier (1964) held that the power of the maintenance personnel in the tobacco plants was due to all other tasks being routinized. A relative decline in the power of general medical personnel in hospitals during this century is thought to be due to the routinization of some tasks, which previously presented uncertainties which could be coped with only by a physician, and the transfer of these tasks to relatively routinized subunits, such as inoculation programs, mass X-ray facilities, and so on (Perrow, 1965; Gordon & Becker, 1964). Crozier (1964: 165) crystallized the presumed effects of routinization; "But the expert's success is constantly self-defeating. The rationalization process gives him power, but the end results of rationalization curtail his power. As soon as a field is well covered, as soon as the first intuitions and innovations can be translated into rules and programs, the expert's power disappears."

The strategic contingencies' theory as developed in Figure 1 clarifies this. It suggests that research has been hampered by a confusion of two kinds of routinization, both of which are negatively related to power but in different ways. Routinization may be *(a)* of coping by prevention, which prevents the occurrence of uncertainty; and *(b)* of coping by information or absorption which define how the uncertainty which does occur shall be coped with.

Preventive routinization reduces or removes the uncertainty itself, for example, planned maintenance, which maintenance in Crozier's (1964) tobacco factories would have resisted; inoculation or X-ray programs; and long-term supply contracts, so that the sales staff no longer have to contend with unstable demand. Such routinization removes the opportunity for power, and it is this which is self-defeating (Crozier, 1964: 165) if the expert takes his techniques to a point when they begin not only to cope but to routinely diminish the uncertainty coped with. Thus reducing the uncertainty is not the same as reducing the impact of uncertainty. According to the hypothesis, a sales department which transmits steady orders despite a volatile market has high power; a sales department which reduces the uncertainty itself by long-term tied contracts has low power.

Routinization of coping by information and absorption is embodied in job descriptions and task instructions prescribing how to obtain information and to respond to uncertainty. For maintenance personnel, it lays down how to repair the machine; for physicians, it lays down a standard procedure for examining patients and sequences of remedies for each diagnosis. How does this affect power, since it does not eliminate the uncertainty itself, as preventive routinization does? What it does is increase substitutability. The means of coping become more visible and possible substitutes more obvious, even if those substitutes are unskilled personnel from another subunit who can follow a standard procedure but could not have acquired the previously unexpressed skills.

There is probably some link between the two kinds of routinization. Once preventive routinization is accomplished, other coping routinization more easily follows, as indeed it follows any reduction of uncertainty.

STUDIES OF SUBUNIT POWER

Testing of Hypotheses on Earlier Work

The utility of the strategic contingencies theory should be tested on published work, but it is difficult to do this adequately, since most studies stress only one possibility. For example, Crozier (1964) and Thompson (1967) stressed uncertainty, Dubin (1963) stressed exclusiveness of function, and Woodward (1965) spoke of the critical function.

The difficulty is also due to the lack of data. For example, among several studies in which inferences about environmental uncertainty are drawn, only Lawrence and Lorsch (1967b) presented data. They combine executive's questionnaire responses on departmental clarity of job requirements, time span of definitive feedback on departmental success in performance, and uncertainty of cause and effect in the department's functional area.

Lawrence and Lorsch (1967b: 127) found that in two food-processing organizations, research was most influential, then marketing, excluding the field selling unit, and then production. However, influence, or perceived power as it is called here, was rated on the single issue of product innovation and not across a range of issues as suggested earlier in this paper; validity therefore rests on the assumption of equal potential involvement of each function in this one issue. Would research still be most influential if the issues included equipment purchase, or capital budgeting, or personnel training? Even so, on influence over product innovation, an uncertainty hypothesis could be said to fit neatly, since the subunits were ordered on perceived uncertainty of subenvironment exactly as they were on influence.

But uncertainty alone would not explain power in the other firms studied. Although in six plastics firms, coordinating sections or integrating units were perceived as having more influence than functional subunits because "integration itself was the most problematic job" (Lawrence & Lorsch 1967b: 62), it was also a central job in terms of workflow pervasiveness.

Furthermore, in two container manufacturing organizations, although the market subenvironment was seen as the least uncertain, the sales subunit was perceived as the most influential (Lawrence & Lorsch 1967b: 111). An explanation must be sought in the contingencies that the sales subunit controls for production and for research. In this industry, outputs must fit varying customer requirements for containers. Scheduling for production departments and design problems for research departments are therefore completely subject to the contingencies of orders brought in by the sales department. Sales has not only the opportunity to cope with such uncertainty as may exist over customer requirements, it is highly central; for its activities connect it directly to both the other departments—workflow pervasiveness—and if it ceased work production of containers would stop—workflow immediacy. The effects of centrality are probably bolstered by non-substitutability, since the sales subunit develops a necessary particularized knowledge of customer requirements. Production and research are, therefore, comparatively powerless in face of the strategic contingencies controlled by the sales subunit.

In short, only a sensitive balancing of all three factors can explain the patterns of contingencies from which power strategically flows.

This is plain also in Crozier's (1964) insightful study of small French tobacco-manufacturing plants. Crozier (1964: 109) had the impression that the maintenance engineers were powerful because "machine stoppages are the only major happenings that cannot be predicted"; therefore the engineers had (Crozier, 1964: 154) "control over the last source of uncertainty remaining in a completely routinized organizational system." But this is not enough for power. Had it been possible to contract maintenance work to consulting engineers, for example, then programs of preventive maintenance might have been introduced, and preventive routinization would have removed much of the uncertainty. However, it is likely that union agreements ensured that the plant engineers were nonsubstitutable. In addition, in these small organizations without specialist control and service departments, the maintenance section's work linked it to all production subunits, that is, to almost every other subunit in the plant. So workflow pervasiveness was high, as was workflow immediacy, since cessation of maintenance activities would quickly have stopped tobacco outputs. The control of strategic contingencies which gave power to the engineers has to be explained on all counts and not by uncertainty alone.

Crozier's (1964) study is a warning against the facile inference that a power distribution fitting the strategic contingencies theory is necessarily efficient, or rational, or functional for an organization; for the power of the engineers to thwart the introduction of programmed maintenance was presumably neither efficient, rational, nor functional.

A challenge to the analysis made is presented by Goldner's (1970) description of a case where there was programmed maintenance and yet the maintenance section held power over production. Goldner (1970) attributed the power of the maintenance subunit to knowing how to install and operate such programs, to coping with breakdowns as in the Crozier (1964) cases, and to knowing how to cope with a critical problem of parts supplies. The strategic contingencies theory accords with his interpretation so long as knowing how to install a program takes effect as coping with uncertainty and not yet as preventive routinization which stops breakdowns. This is where an unknown time element enters to allow for changes in the variables specified and in any associated variables not yet defined. For a time, knowing the answer to an uncertainty does confer power, but the analyses of routinization derived from the theory, as shown in Figure 1, suggests that if this becomes successful preventive routinization, it takes a negative effect upon power. The net result for power in Goldner's (1970) case would then be from the interplay of the opposed effects of activities some of which are preventively routinized, thus decreasing power, and some of which continue to be nonroutine, thus increasing power.

On the other hand, Goldner's (1970) description of the powerful industrial relations subunit in the same plant clearly supports the strategic contingencies theory by showing that coping with uncertainty, centrality, and substitutability had the effect predicted here. The industrial relations subunit exploited uncertainty over the supply and cost of personnel, which arose from possible strikes and pay increases, by (Goldner, 1970: 104) "use of the union as an outside threat." It coped effectively by its nonroutinized knowledge of union officials and of contract interpretation; and its activities were centrally linked to those of other subunits by the necessity for uniform practice on wages and employment. Industrial relations staff developed nonsubstitutable interpersonal and bargaining skills.

There are no means of assessing whether the univariate stress on uncertainty in the handful of other relevant studies is justified. Perrow (1970) explained the greater perceived power of sales as against production, finance, and research, in most of 12 industrial firms, by the concept of uncertainty absorption (March & Simon, 1958). Sales was strategic with respect to the environment. Is the one case where it came second to production the only case where it was also substitutable? Or not central?

White (1961) and Landsberger (1961) both suggested that power shifts over periods of time to follow the locus of uncertainty. Both studied engineering factories. From the histories of three firms, Landsberger (1961) deduced that when money was scarce and uncertain, accounting was powerful; when raw materials were short, purchasing was powerful; and, conversely, when demand was insatiable sales were weakened. In the Tennessee Valley Authority, a nonmanufacturing organization, Selznick (1949) attributed the eventual power of the agricultural relations department to its ability to cope with the uncertain environmental threat represented by the Farm Bureau.

Yet while these earlier studies emphasized uncertainty in one way or another, others called attention to substitutability and probably also to centrality. Again the implication is that contingencies are not strategically controlled without some combination of all three basic variables. For example, the engineers described by Strauss (1962, 1964) appeared to have more power than purchasing agents because the latter were substitutable, that is, the engineers can set specifications for what was to be bought even though the purchasing agents considered this their own responsibility. Thompson (1956: 300) attributed variations in perceived power within and between two U.S. Air Force wings to the changing "technical requirements of operations," which may have indicated changing centralities and substitutabilities.

In the absence of data, consideration of further different kinds of organization must remain pure speculation, for example, the power of surgical units in hospitals, the power of buyers in stores, the power of science faculties in universities.

Other Variables Affecting Power

In order that it can be testable, the strategic contingencies theory errs on the side of simplicity. Any theory must start with a finite number of variables and presume continual development by their alteration or deletion, or by the addition of new variables. As stated, the theory uses only those variables hypothesized to affect power by their contribution to the control of contingencies exercised by a subunit. Other possible explanations of power are not considered. This in itself is an assumption of the greater explanatory force of the theory. Blalock (1961: 8) put the problem clearly: "The dilemma of the scientist is to select models that are at the same time simple enough to permit him to think with the aid of the model but also sufficiently realistic that the simplifications required do not lead to predictions that are highly inaccurate."

In recognition of this, Figure 1 includes several "other things being equal" variables as they are called, that may affect power, but are assumed to do so in other ways than by control of contingencies. One such range of possible relevant variables is qualities of interdepartmental relationships, such as competitiveness versus collaborativeness (Dutton & Walton, 1966). Does the power exercised relate to the style of the relationship through which the power runs? Another possibility is pinpointed by Stymne (1968: 88): "A unit's influence has its roots partly in its strategical importance to the company and partly in nonfunctional circumstances such as tradition, or control over someone in top management through, for example, family relationship." The tradition is the status which may accrue to a particular function because chief executives have typically reached the top through it. Many case studies highlight the personal links of subunits with top personnel (Dalton, 1959; Gouldner, 1955). The notion might be entitled the organizational distance of the subunit, a variant of social distance.

Finally, but perhaps most important, individual differences must be accepted, that is, differences in the intelligence, skills, ages, sexes, or personality factors such as dominance, assertiveness, and risk-taking propensity, of personnel in the various subunits.

CONCLUSION

The concept of work organizations as interdepartmental systems leads to a strategic contingencies theory explaining differential subunit power by dependence on contingencies ensuing from varying combinations of coping with uncertainty, substitutability, and centrality. It should be stressed that the theory is not in any sense static. As the goals, outputs, technologies, and markets of organizations change so, for each subunit, the values of the independent variables change, and patterns of power change.

Many problems are unresolved. For example, does the theory implicitly assume perfect knowledge by each subunit of the contingencies inherent for it in the activities of the others? Does a workflow of information affect power differently to a workflow of things? But with the encouragement of the improved analysis given of the few existing studies, data can be collected and analyzed, hopefully in ways which will afford a direct test.

REFERENCES

Bennis, Warren G., Berkowitz, N., Affinito, M., and Malone, M. Authority, power and the ability to influence. *Human Relations,* 1958, **11**, 143–56.

Bierstedt, Robert. An analysis of social power. *American Sociological Review,* 1950, **15**, 730–36.

Blalock, Hubert M. *Causal inferences in nonexperimental research.* Chapel Hill, N.C.: University of North Carolina Press, 1961.

Blau, Peter. *Exchange and power in social life.* New York: Wiley, 1964.

Blau, Peter, and Scott, W. Richard. *Formal organizations: A comparative approach.* London: Routledge and Kegan Paul, 1962.

Cartwright, Darwin. Influence, leadership, control. In James G. March (ed.), *Handbook of organizations.* Chicago: Rand McNally, 1965, pp. 1–47.

Clark, Burton R. Organizational adaptation and precarious values: A case study. *American Sociological Review,* 1956, **21**, 327–36.

Clark, Terry N. (ed.). *Community structure and decision-making: Comparative analyses.* San Francisco: Chandler, 1968.

Crozier, Michel. *The bureaucratic phenomenon.* London: Tavistock, 1964

Cyert, Richard M. and March, James G. *A behavioral theory of the firm.* Englewood Cliffs, N. J. : Prentice-Hall, 1963.

Dahl, Robert A. The concept of power. *Behavorial Science,* 1957, **2**, 201–15.

Dahlstrom, E. Exchange, influence, and power. *Acta Sociologica,* 1966, **9**, 237–84.

Dalton, Melville. *Men who manage.* New York: Wiley, 1959.

Dubin, Robert. Power and union-management relations. *Administrative Science Quarterly,* 1957, **2**: 60–81.

Dubin, Robert. Power, function, and organization. *Pacific Sociological Review,* 1963, **6**, 16–24.

Dutton, John M. and Walton, Richard E. Interdepartmental conflict and cooperation: Two contrasting studies. *Human Organization,* 1966, **25**, 207–20.

Emerson, R. E. Power-dependence relations. *American Sociological Review,* 1962, **27**, 31–41.

Etzioni, Amitai. *A comparative analysis of complex organizations.* New York: Free Press, 1961.

French, John R. P. and Raven, Bertram. The bases of social power. In D. Cartwright (ed.), *Studies in social power.* Ann Arbor: University of Michigan, 1959, pp. 150–67.

Goldner, Fred H. The division of labor: process and power. In Mayer N. Zald (ed.), *Power in organizations.* Nashville: Vanderbilt University Press, 1970, pp. 97–143.

Gordon, Gerald and Becker, Selwyn. Changes in medical practice bring shifts in the patterns of power. *The Modern Hospital,* 1964 (February), 89–91, 154–56.

Gouldner, Alvin W. *Wildcat strike,* London: Routledge, 1955.

Harsanyi, John C. Measurement of social power, opportunity costs, and the theory of two-person bargaining games. *Behavioral Science,* 1962, **7**, 67–80.

Hinings, Christopher R., Pugh, Derek S., Hickson, David J., and Turner, Christopher. An approach to the study of bureaucracy. *Sociology,* 1967, **1**, 61–72.

Kaplan, Abraham. Power in perspective. In Robert L. Kahn and Elise Boulding (eds.), *Power and conflict in organizations.* London: Tavistock, 1964, pp. 11–32.

Landsberger, Henry A. The horizontal dimension in bureaucracy. *Administrative Science Quarterly,* 1961, **6**, 299–332.

Lawrence, Paul R. and Lorsch, Jay W. Differentiation and integration in complex organizations. *Administrative Science Quarterly,* 1967, **12**, 1–47. (a)

Lawrence, Paul R. and Lorsch, Jaw W. Organization and environment, Cambridge, Mass.: Division of Research, Graduate School of Business Administration, Harvard University, 1967. (b)

Lipset, Seymour M., Trow, Martin A., and Coleman, James A. *Union democracy.* Glencoe, Ill.: Free Press, 1956.

Luhmann, Niklaus. Klassiche theorie der macht. *Zeitschrift fur Politik,* 1969, **16**, 149–70.

March, James G. An introduction to the theory and measurement of influence. *American Political Science Review,* 1955, **49**, 431–50.

March, James G. The power of power. In David Easton (ed.), *Varieties of political theory.* Englewood Cliffs. N.J.: Prentice-Hall, 1966, pp. 39–70.

March, James G. and Simon, Herbert A. *Organizations,* New York: Wiley, 1958.

Mechanic, David. Sources of power of lower participants in complex organizations. *Administrative Science Quarterly,* 1962 7, 349–64.

Perrow, Charles. The analysis of goals in complex organizations. *American Sociological Reveiw,* 1961, **26**, 854–66.

Perrow, Charles. Hospitals: Technology, structure, and goals. In James G. March (ed.), *Handbook of organizations.* Chicago: Rand McNally, 1965, pp. 910–71.

Perrow, Charles. Departmental power and perspectives in industrial firms. In Mayer N. Zald (ed.), *Power in organizations.* Nashville, Tenn.: Vanderbilt University Press, 1970, pp. 59–89.

Pugh, Derek S., Hickson, David J., Hinings, Christopher R., and Turner, Christopher. Dimensions of organization structure. *Administrative Science Quarterly,* 1968, **13**, 65–105.

Selznick, Philip. *T.V.A. and the grass roots.* Berkeley: University of California Press, 1949.

Strauss, George. Tactics of lateral relationship: the purchasing agent. *Administrative Science Quarterly,* 1962, **7**, 161–86.

Strauss, George. Work-flow frictions, interfunctional rivalry, and professionalism. *Human Organization,* 1964, **23**, 137–50.

Stymne, Bengt. Interdepartmental communication and intraorganizational strain. *Acta Sociologica,* 1968, **11**, 82–100.

Tannenbaum, Arnold S. *Control in organizations.* New York: McGraw-Hill, 1968.

Thompson, James D. Authority and power in "identical" organizations. *American Journal of Sociology,* 1956, **62**, 290–301.

Thompson, James D. *Organizations in action.* New York: McGraw-Hill, 1967.

Van Doorn, Jaques A. A. Sociology and the problem of power. *Sociologica Neerlandica,* 1962, **1**, 3–47.

Weber, Max. *The theory of social and economic organization.* Glencoe, Ill.: Free Press, 1947.

White, Harrison. Management conflict and sociometric structure. *American Journal of Sociology,* 1961, **67**, 185–99.

Woodward, Joan. *Industrial organization: Theory and practice.* London: Oxford University Press, 1965.

Wrong, Dennis H. Some problems in defining social power. *American Journal of Sociology,* 1968, **73**, 673–681.

Zald, Mayer N. Organizational control structures in five correctional institutions. *American Journal of Sociology,* 1962, **68**, 335–45.

Section B

BEHAVIORAL CONFLICT AND CHANGE

As we noted in the previous section, as organizations attempt to direct and control the activities of their participants strains and tensions may arise among these participants and among subunits, and rigidities may develop within the organization causing low adaptability and flexibility. In addition, most organizations seem to be facing external environments of ever-increasing complexity and turbulence. Thus, two increasingly important concepts in organizational behavior are examined in this section: (1) the nature and management of conflict and (2) change within and of organizations.

Walton and Dutton examine the determinants, processes, and several consequences of interunit conflict among subunits of an organization. They specify nine major antecedents of interunit conflict: mutual task dependence, asymmetrics in task dependencies, differentiated performance criteria and rewards, organizational differentiation, participant dissatisfaction with their roles, role ambiguity, dependence on common resources among units, communication obstacles, and several personal traits and skills. Walton and Dutton do not imply that all conflicts within organization are necessarily dysfunctional, but they do suggest several structural and interpersonal strategies for more effectively managing interunit conflict.

We then shift our focus to behavioral change. One of the most significant and lasting contributions to the literature of change processes has been made by the group dynamic theorists. In a classic article, Dorwin Cartwright explores the relevance of several areas of findings and theory in group dynamics for the change process in formal organizations.

One of the most dramatic and publicized strategies for individual and organizational change is frequently referred to as T-group or sensitivity training. Campbell and Dunnette review the published literature describing the nature of such change efforts. In addition, their review focuses on the evaluation of such training efforts in terms of their specific, measured impact on various indices of leadership and organizational effectiveness.

Bennis broadens our examination of change by taking a theoretical overview of behavioral science contributions to planned organizational change. He also describes several applied programs utilized by organizations in their change attempts. Implicit in Bennis' ideas is the emergence of the professional executive as a *change agent* responsible for facilitating the continual adjustment of organizational structures and processes.

B. F. Skinner extends our focus on change to include the cultural or societal level. The technologies for cultural design and change suggested by Skinner draw heavily upon some of the materials covered in Chapter 1 under learning and conditioning. We have, in a sense, come full circle. We have extended our view to incorporate the macrocultural level; yet we do this through the application of basic psychological processes.[1]

---

[1] For a more journalistic account of Skinner's theory and findings as well as a review of the philosophical basis of his position, the reader should see "Skinner's Utopia: Panacea, or Path to Hell?" *Time,* Vol. 98, No. 12 (September 20, 1971), pp. 55–61. For a much extended view of Skinner's thoughts regarding the design of culture, see B. F. Skinner *Walden Two* (1948) and his *Beyond Freedom and Dignity* (1971).

52. THE MANAGEMENT OF INTERDEPARTMENTAL CONFLICT: A MODEL AND REVIEW*

Richard E. Walton **and** ***John M. Dutton*** †

Horizontal interactions are seldom shown on the organizational chart, but transactions along this dimension are often at least as important as vertical interactions (Simpson, 1959; Landsberger, 1961; Burns & Stalker, 1961). This paper presents a general model of interdepartmental conflict and its management, together with a review of the relevant literature.[1] The model includes five sets of related variables: antecedents to conflict, attributes of the lateral relationship, management of the interface, consequences of the relationship, and responses of higher executives. Figure 1 shows the general relationship among these sets of variables.

The general model is postulated as applicable to all lateral relations between any two organizational units (departments, divisions, sections, and so on) that engage in any type of transaction, including joint decision making, exchanging information, providing expertise or advice, and auditing or inspecting.

---

* Reprinted from *Administrative Science Quarterly,* Vol. 14, No. 1 (March 1969), pp. 73–84.

† Graduate School of Business Administration, Harvard University and University of South Florida, respectively.

[1] This research was supported by a grant from the McKinsey Foundation for Management Research, Inc.

ANTECEDENTS TO INTERUNIT CONFLICT AND COLLABORATION

Manifest conflict results largely from factors which originate outside the particular lateral relationship under consideration or which antedate the relationship. Hypotheses and models that use external factors to predict lateral relations have been advanced by March and Simon (1958), Thompson (1961), Caplow (1964), Lawrence and Lorsch (1967a, 1967b) and Pondy (1967). The present model describes nine major types of antecedents: mutual dependence, asymmetries, rewards, organizational differentiation, role dissatisfaction, ambiguities, common resources, communication obstacles, and personal skills and traits.

Mutual Task Dependence

Mutual task dependence is the key variable in the relevance of the interunit conflict model in general and the impact of the postulated conflict antecedents in particular. Task dependence is the extent to which two units depend upon each other for assistance, information, compliance, or other coordinative acts in the performance of their re-

FIGURE 1 GENERAL MODEL OF INTERUNIT CONFLICT

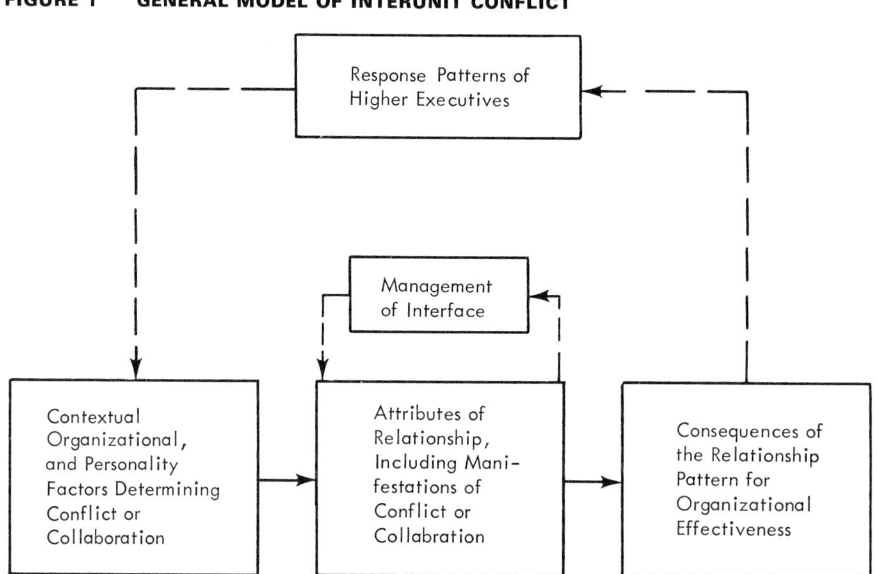

spective tasks. It is assumed here that dependence is mutual and can range from low to high. Asymmetry in the interdependence is treated later.

According to Miller (1959), the more performance of one unit depends on the performance of all other units, the more likely is the system to perform without external control. Other studies, however, Dutton and Walton (1966), for example, indicate that task interdependence not only provides an incentive for collaboration, but also presents an occasion for conflict and the means for bargaining over interdepartmental issues. A related factor, task overload, has similarly mixed potential for conflict and collaboration. Overload conditions may intensify the problem of scarce resources and lead to bargaining; may increase tension, frustration, and aggression; and may decrease the time available for the social interactions that would enable the units to contain their conflict. On the other hand, overload may place a premium on mutual assistance. The net directional effects of high task interdependence and overload are therefore uncertain.

Other implications of the extent of mutual task dependence are more predictable. High task interdependence and overload tend to heighten the intensity of either interunit antagonisms or friendliness, increase the magnitude of the consequences of unit conflict for organizational performance, and contribute to the difficulty of changing an ongoing pattern.

Task-related Asymmetries

Symmetrical interdependence and symmetrical patterns of initiation between units promote collaboration; asymmetrical interdependence leads to conflict. For example, in a study by Dalton (1959), a staff group resented the asymmetries in their relationship with line groups. The staff group had to understand the problems of the line groups, had to get along with them, promote their ideas, and justify their existence; but none of these relations were reciprocal requirements imposed on the line groups. Strauss (1962) reported that asymmetrical high dependence of purchasing agents on another group led them to make more attempts to influence the terms of requisitions they received and thereby force interaction to flow both ways.

The adverse effects of asymmetrical conditions are sometimes related to the fact that one unit has little incentive to coordinate. The more dependent unit may try to increase the incentive of the more independent unit to cooperate by interfering with their task performance. The assumption is that once the independent unit is made aware of their need for the cooperation of the dependent unit (i.e., to desist from interfering acts), they will behave more cooperatively (supply the assistance necessary). This tactic may indeed achieve its purpose, and the conflict-interfering acts may cease; but frequently interference elicits a retaliatory response.

Conflict is also produced by differences in the way units are ranked along various dimensions of organizational status, namely direction of initiation of action, prestige, power, and knowledge. Seiler (1963) studied in an organization in which it was generally agreed that research had more prestige than engineering and engineering had more prestige than production. When the sequential pattern of initiation and influence followed this status ordering, it was accepted. However, where a lower-status industrial engineering group needed to direct the higher-status research group to carry out routine tests, the result was a breakdown in relationships between the departments.

Inconsistency between the distribution of knowledge among departments and the lateral influence patterns are also a source of conflict. Lawrence and Lorsch (1967a) advanced the idea that the more the influence of each unit is consistent with key competitive factors, the more effectively will interunit issues be resolved. They noted that in container firms, customer delivery and product quality were crucial for competitive success; therefore, sales and production were required to have the most influence in the resolution of interunit conflict. By contrast, in the food industry, where market expertise and food science were essential, sales and research were required to be the more influential. Landsberger (1961) also found that the locus of power among three plants in the same industry was attacked by their different market positions.

Zald (1962) in a study of correctional institutions offered a power-balance proposition about the effect of relative power: assuming task interdependence and divergent values among three units (teachers, cottage parents, and social service workers), conflict is most likely to occur between units that are unable to control the situation and those perceived as being in control. He found that the patterns of conflict among these three units were generally consistent with predictions based on this power-balance hypothesis.

Performance Criteria and Rewards

Interunit conflict results when each of the interdependent departments has responsibility for only one side of a dilemma embedded in organizational tasks. Dutton and Walton (1966) noted that the preference of production units for long, economical runs conflicted with the preference of sales units for quick delivery to good customers. Dalton (1959) observed that staff units valued change, because that was one way they proved their worth; whereas line units valued stability, because change reflected unfavorably upon them or inconvenienced them. Also, staff units were strongly committed to preserving the integrity of control and rule systems, whereas line personnel believed they could be more effective by flexible reinterpretation of control and incentive schemes, and by ignoring many discipline and safety violations. A study by Strauss (1962) showed that engineers preferred to order brand items, whereas purchasing agents sought specifications suitable for several vendors. Similar instances abound. Landsberger (1961) postulated several basic dilemmas which probably underlie many interdepartmental differences: flexibility versus stability; criteria for short-run versus long-run performance; emphasis on measurable results versus attention to intangible results; maximizing organizational goals versus responding to other societal needs.

Although the dilemmas may be inherent in the total task, the reward system designed by management can serve either to sharpen or to blunt their divisive effective: the more the evaluations and rewards of higher management emphasize the separate performance of each department rather than their combined performance, the more conflict.

Close, one-to-one supervisory styles have generally been assumed to promote more conflict among peers than general supervision in which the superior also deals with subordinates as a group (Likert 1961). One might speculate that group supervisory patterns are taken to indicate emphasis on group rather than individual performance criteria; and that group patterns allow the supervisor to observe the process and to reward cooperative acts.

Organizational Differentiation

Litwak (1961) postulated that uniform tasks require a bureaucratic type of organization, characterized by impersonality of relations, prior specification of job authority, emphasis on hierarchical authority, separation of policy and administration, and emphasis on general rules and specialization; whereas nonuniform tasks require a human-relations organization with the contrasting characteristics. In contemporary society, most large-scale organizations have to deal with both uniform and nonuniform tasks, and must combine these contradictory forms of social relations into a professional model. Litwak regards the inclusions of these contradictory forms as a source of organizational conflict.

Lawrence and Lorsch (1967a) emphasized the effects of differentiation. Where each unit (such as research, sales, or production) performs a different type of task and copes with a different segment of the environment, the units will develop significant internal differences. Such units may differ from each other *(a)* in the degree of structure, that is, tightness of rules, narrowness of span of supervisory control, frequency and specificity of performance review; and in the orientation of its members; *(b)* toward the environment, such as, new scientific knowledge versus customer problems and market opportunities versus costs of raw materials and processing; *(c)* toward time, such as planning time perspective; and *(d)* toward other people, such as, openness and permissiveness of interpersonal relationships. Lawrence and Lorsch measured these differences in six plastics organizations with the results shown in Table 1.

Lawrence and Lorsch believe this fourfold differentiation is largely a response to the degree of uncertainty in the environments of the different departments. They use a notion of optimum degree of differentiation, which depends upon the task environments. Thus, either overdifferentiation or underdifferentiation has implications for the coordinative processes. Although greater differentiation apparently results in more *potential* for conflict, these authors do not assume that more manifest conflict will automatically result. In their study of six plastics organizations, the degree of integration did not, in fact, vary strictly with the degree of differentiation.

TABLE 1 DIFFERENCES RELATED TO ENVIRONMENT OF DEPARTMENTS.*

Departments	*Orientation toward Environment*	*Orientation toward Time*	*Degree of Formality in Departmental Structure*	*Permissiveness versus Directiveness in Orientation toward Others*
Applied research	Techno-economic	Long	Medium	Medium
Sales	Market	Short	High	Low
Production	Techno-economic	Short	High	High

* After Lawrence and Lorsch (1967).

Role Dissatisfaction

Role dissatisfaction, stemming from a variety of sources, can be a source of conflict. Blocking status aspirations in purchasing agents (Strauss, 1962) and in staff members (Dalton, 1959) led to conflict with other units. In these cases, professionals felt they lacked recognition and opportunities for advancement. Similarly, White (1961) stated that members might feel that the growth of their units and its external status did not meet their needs, and therefore might enter another unit or withdraw from contacts which were painful reminders of the lack of status. Where one unit informally reports on the activities of another unit, resentment can occur, as with staff units reporting to management on production irregularities (Dalton, 1959). Argyris (1964) and Dalton (1959) both argued that role dissatisfaction and conflict followed where one unit with the same or less status set standards for another.

Where there is role dissatisfaction, ambiguities in the definition of work responsibilities further increase the likelihood of interunit conflict. Landsberger (1961) pointed out that ambiguities tempted the dissatisfied unit to engage in offensive maneuvers so as to improve its lot, and thus induced other units to engage in defensive maneuvers.

Role dissatisfaction and ambiguity are related to more basic organizational variables, including growth rate, organizational level, and hierarchical differences. Organizational growth appears to have offsetting consequences. Slower rates of organizational growth and of opportunities for promotion increase role dissatisfaction, but are also accompanied by fewer ambiguities. Interfaces higher in the organization are more likely to be marked by conflict to redefine departmental responsibilities. At the higher levels, jurisdictional boundaries are less clear (Pondy, 1967), and the participants perceive more opportunity to achieve some restructuring. Steep and heavily emphasized hierarchical differences in status, power, and rewards were seen by Thompson (1961) as responsible for some lateral conflict, because these factors tended to activate and to legitimate individual aspiration for increased status and power and tended to lead to increased upward orientation toward the desires of one's superiors, rather than to problem orientation and increased horizontal coordination.

Ambiguities

In addition to its interaction with role dissatisfaction, ambiguity contributes to interunit conflict in several other ways. Difficulty in assigning credit or blame between two departments increases the likelihood of conflict between units. Dalton (1959) attributed part of the staff-line conflict he observed to the fact that although improvements required collaboration between line and staff units, it was later difficult to assess the contribution of each unit. Similarly, disputes resulted between production and sales units, when it could not be determined which department made a mistake (Dutton & Walton, 1966).

Low routinization and uncertainty of means to goals increase the potential for interunit conflict. This proposition is supported by Zald (1962) in his study of interunit conflict in five correctional institutions. Similarly, ambiguity in the criteria used to evaluate the performance of a unit may also create tension, frustration, and conflict (Kahn, Wolfe, *et al.*, 1964). Organization planning, which includes clarity of rule definition, correlated positively with measures of lateral coordination and problem solving in a study of ten hospitals by Georgopoulos and Mann (1962).

Dependence on Common Resources

Conflict potential exists when two units depend upon a common pool of scarce organizational resources, such as, physical space, equipment, manpower, operating funds, capital funds, central staff resources, and centralized services (e.g., typing and drafting). If the two units have interdependent tasks, the competition for scarce resources will tend to decrease interunit problem solving and coordination. Also, if competition for scarce resources is not mediated by some third unit and they must agree on their allocation, they will come into direct conflict.

Communication Obstacles

Semantic difficulties can impede communications essential for cooperation. Strauss (1964) observed that differences in training of purchasing agents and engineers contributed to their conflicts. March and Simon (1958) stated that organizational channeling of information introduced bias.

Common experience reduces communication barriers and provides common referents. Miller (1959) proposed that the less units know about each other's job, the less collaboration and that lack of knowledge can lead to unreasonable interunit demands through ignorance. Cozer (1956) argued that accommodation is especially dependent on knowledge of the power of the other unit.

Personal Skills and Traits

Walton and McKersie (1965), reviewing experimental studies, found that certain personality attributes, such as high authoritarianism, high dogmatism, and low self-esteem, increased conflict behavior. Kahn *et al.* (1964: 256) found that in objective role conflict persons who scored lower on neurotic anxiety scales tended to depart more from "cordial, congenial, trusting, respecting, and understanding relations," and introverts tended to lose their confidence, trust, and respect for work associates more than extroverts.

Most interunit relationships are mixed-motive situations, which require high behavioral flexibility to manage optimally. A person with a narrower range of behavioral skills is less likely to exploit the integrative potential fully in an interunit relationship. He may either engage in bargaining to the exclusion of collaborative problem solving, or withdraw or become passive (Walton & McKersie, 1966). Dalton (1959) and Thompson (1960) found that personal dissimilarities, such as, background, values, education, age, social patterns lowered the probability of interpersonal rapport between unit representatives, and in turn decreased the amount of collaboration between their respective units. Personal status incongruities between departmental representatives, that is, the degree to which they differed in rank orderings in various status dimensions (such as length of service, age, education, ethnicity, esteem in eyes of superiors, pay and so on) increase the tendency for conflict (Dutton & Walton, 1966).

Personal satisfaction with the internal climate of one's unit decreases the likelihood that a member will initiate interunit conflict. Seiler (1963) observed that in one firm, constructive handling of interdepartmental differences occurred in part because the members of each department derived social satisfaction from their work associates, had high job interest and good opportunities for promotions, and were not in conflict with each other.

INTERDEPARTMENTAL RELATIONSHIP

Tactics of Conflict and Indicators of Collaboration

The literature on interdepartmental relations has been most vivid in its description of manifest conflict and collaboration processes. Dalton (1959) observed that staff units were encouraged by top management to monitor and report on the activities of line units, and the line units retaliated by resisting the ideas of the staff units and discouraging their promotions. He also observed power struggles between line units and documented the conflict tactics of coalitions, distortion of information, and misappropriation of resources.

Strauss (1962) observed the tactics of purchasing agents who wished to increase their authority and influence over decisions shared with engineering and production. The purchasing agents made restrictive rules for the other units, evaded their rules, relied on personal contacts and persuasion to subvert the other units, and altered organization structure.

Focusing on positive relations, Georgopoulos and Mann (1962) used coordination as their broadest concept, which included "the extent to which the various interdependent parts of an organization function each according to the needs and requirements of the other parts of the total system. In a study of ten hospitals, they found that over-all coordination correlated positively with *(a)* shared expectations, *(b)* absence of intraorganizational tension, *(c)* awareness of problems and solving of problems, and *(d)* ease of communication.

System Characteristics of an Interunit Relationship

Attempting to incorporate aspects of the approaches just described, Walton (1966) developed a theory which also explains the system dynamics of conflict and collaboration in the interunit relationship. Three components of the relationship are considered: *(a)* exchange of information in the joint decision process, *(b)* structure of interunit interactions and decision making, and *(c)* attitudes toward the other unit. Two opposite types of relationships, "integrative" and "distributive," are postulated as frequently encountered systems of interunit behavior (see Table 2). This particular model now appears to be most applicable to lateral relations where the dominant transaction at the interface is joint decision making; where there is relative symmetry in interdependency; and where the transactions required are relatively frequent and important.

In the most general sense, the chain of assumptions underlying Walton's systems theory of lateral relationships (and explaining the distributive syndrome, in particular) is as follows: First, an antecedent, say goal competition between participants engaged in joint decision making, induces the units to engage in concealment and distortion tactics in their exchange of information, such that joint decision

TABLE 2 COMPONENTS AND CHARACTERISTICS OF CONTRASTING TYPES OF LATERAL RELATIONSHIPS*

	Type of Lateral Relationship	
Component	*Integrative*	*Distributive*
Form of joint decision process	Problem solving: free exchange of information, conscientious accuracy in transmitting information	Bargaining: careful rationing, and deliberate distortion of information.
Structure of interaction and framework of decision.	Flexible, informal, open	Rigid, formal, circumscribed.
Attitudes toward other unit.	Positive attitudes: trust, friendliness, inclusion of other unit.	Negative attitudes: suspicion, hostility, dissociation from other unit.

*After Walton (1966)

making takes on the character of bargaining. Second, in order to ration and distort information effectively and systematically, a unit will attempt to place limitations on the interactions and other behavior of their counterpart in order to make them more predictable and keep them within certain boundaries. Third, the way information is handled (concealment, distortion, etc.) and the way interactions are patterned (circumscribed, rigid, etc.) results in suspicion and hostility. Furthermore, these negative attitudes have a feedback effect which tend to reinforce the same interaction structure and information-handling pattern.

Regardless of the antecedents, the theory hypothesizes that the conflict relationship will become fixed as a result of: the tendency to generalize a conflictful orientation to the many areas of interunit decision making, the self-reinforcing nature of the various elements of a relationship pattern, the reciprocal nature of a conflictful orientation between units, and the tendency toward socialization and institutionalization of these orientations within a unit.

The individual propositions contained in the model are generally supported by a review of the relevant literature in experimental social psychology (Walton, 1966). The hypothesized variation of attributes of a relationship are also generally supported by a comparative field study of production-sales relationships in six plants (Walton, Dutton, & Fitch, 1966). The hypothesized dominant cause-effect relationships among process, structure, and attitude are anecdotally supported in a comparison of two plants (Dutton & Walton, 1966).

The theory suggests that the total lateral relationship is influenced or determined by contextual factors operating first upon the way the parties exchange information, with the effects on interaction structure and interunit trust as subsequent reactions. However, although the process of exchanging information may be the most frequent determinant, it is not exclusively the point of entry in the lateral relationship. For instance, personality and status may first influence attitudes such as trust and friendliness in which case the pattern of information exchange and interaction structure are a secondary reaction.

MANAGEMENT OF THE INTERFACE

The relationship between units is largely a function of the conflict potential inherent in the factors already discussed; but it is also subject to control by the participants, their effectiveness depending upon how much conscious effort they invest in management of the interface and the appropriateness of the techniques they use.

Interface conflict will be managed best where the attention devoted to interface management corresponds to the degree of differentiation between departments. Lawrence and Lorsch (1967a) compared integrative devices used by three high-performing organizations selected from industries with high, medium, and low differentiation. The most differentiated firm had the most elaborate array of interface management techniques, including a separate integrative department with the primary purpose of coordinating the basic functional units, permanent teams consisting of representatives of members from functional units together with the integrative department, direct contact across hierarchies at all levels, procedures for appeal to a common superior, and a coordination system involving written communications. As expected, when all three organizations were compared, the same rank order obtained for the differentiation scores as for the degree of elaboration of integrative devices. Explicit conflict-resolution mechanisms can be overelaborate, however. For example, a formal coordinative unit was used between slightly differentiated units in a *low*-performing unit. Lawrence and Lorsch concluded that the units were not sufficiently differentiated to justify the coordinative unit, and the result was that the superfluous unit added noise to the system, actually decreasing coordination.

In their comparison of six plastics firms, Lawrence and Lorsch found that three factors promoted effective resolution of interdepartmental conflict and thus high organizational performance. First, where there is a separate coordinating person or unit, the coordinating unit will be most effective if its degree of structure and the goal, time, and interpersonal orientations of its personnel are intermediate between those of the units linked. Second, where there is a separate coordinating unit, conflict resolution will be more effective if its personnel have relatively high influence based on perceived expertise, and if they are evaluated and rewarded on over-all performance measures embracing the activities of the several departments. Third, interunit cooperation will be more effectively achieved and over-all organizational performance will be higher to the extent that managers openly confront differences rather than smooth them over or force decisions. The more subtle aspects of confrontation are discussed by Schmidt and Tannenbaum (1960) and Walton (1968), who analyze the advantages and risks of confronting differences, the timing and skill required, as well as the conditions under which confrontation is most appropriate.

Seiler (1963) also observed techniques for management of interunit conflict. A department may keep its own records, so as to reduce requests for information and thus avoid distasteful contact; a junior member may be assigned as the liaison person, where his presence will not arouse status conflict; and inventories may be introduced to reduce scheduling interdependence.

CONSEQUENCES OF INTERUNIT CONFLICT

The manifest characteristics of interunit conflict include: a competitive orientation, bargaining and restrictions on information, circumscribed interaction patterns, and antagonistic feelings. To determine whether the conflict has an adverse effect on organizational performance, one must assess the consequences of these characteristics. Whether a competitive orientations is in fact energizing or debilitating for members of the unit will depend in part on the personalities of the participants. For some, competition is motivating and arouses energies not otherwise available for organizational tasks; for others conflict is a major threat. Whether competitive energy will contribute to over-all performance depends upon whether a unit can improve its performance without interfering with the performance of another unit.

Another factor governing the motivational effect of conflict is the degree of symmetry in tactics between units. Crozier (1961) reported that managers who were not able to retaliate when conflict was initiated responded by withdrawing commitment from their job. Seiler (1963) postulated that internal social stability, value sharing between units, and a legitimate authority hierarchy between units were important in influencing whether interunit competition would result in destructive conflict.

According to Strauss (1964), the competitive orientation that accompanies conflict behavior may also contribute to a system of checks and balances, increase the availability of new ideas to compete with established ones, and decrease the type of collusion among middle managers, deprives higher-level top management of information.

It seems reasonable to assume that the more important the interdependence, the more a restriction on interunit information becomes damaging. When a lateral relationship involves joint decision making, each unit can bias the decisions in its own favor by controlling information relevant to these decisions. Even minor concealment or distortion can be of great importance, if the decisions are key ones.

The structural attributes of a conflictful relationship are not necessarily variable in the lateral relationship, as for example, the number of liaison contacts between departments, which may be specified by higher authorities. Whether a structural attribute has a positive or an adverse effect on over-all performance depends on factors other than structure. For example, in a conflictful pattern more problems are referred to the superiors. On the one hand, referral may overload a superior; on the other, a superior may find himself more informed about operations and subordinates. Similarly, referral of problems requiring new policy may also be organizationally useful. Also, the inability of a decision-making pair to change decision rules or apply them flexibly may result in decisions that are not innovative. However, given the larger network of task relationships in which the pair is embedded, the inflexibility may produce a degree of predictability, which is valuable for some other reason.

Channeling all interunit interactions through a few liaison persons in a conflict syndrome often reduces over-all performance; for where other persons are either affected by an interunit decision or have potentially relevant information or opinions, ignoring their contribution decreases the quality of the decisions and lowers the commitment to decisions.

Apart from their influence on the quality of decisions, the attributes of an interunit relationship may impinge upon coordinative activities. For example, a tendency to avoid contact can result in implementation that lacks coordination. The seriousness of the effect of conflict in decreasing the rate of interaction between the units therefore depends in part upon how much coordination is required to implement joint decisions.

Conflict relationships involve sterotyping and include *attitudes* of low friendliness, low trust and low respect. Such attitudes indirectly affect performance. For example, low trust limits the flow of relevant task information and decreases coordinative interactions. Furthermore, some persons experience psychological strain when other persons dislike or distrust them. Dalton (1959: 95) reported that staff men were shocked by the need to engage in conflict that required them to use their interpersonal skills as much as their academic skills. The stress of this interpersonal or intergroup climate may result in higher turnover or withdrawal from interdepartmental relations.

A positive by-product of interunit rivalry is more unit cohesion, which contributes to cooperation within the unit. Each unit may become more receptive to directives from their own hierarchy; but sometimes the centralization of control within the unit causes frustration in subordinates (Seiler, 1963). Competition may serve as a useful training device. Managers' insight into how the respective goals of interdependent units contribute to over-all goals may be sharpened. Negotiating and policy-making skills of prospective top managers may be increased, and tolerance of unavoidable conflict may be developed.

Some of the postulated relationships between attributes of a conflictful syndrome and consequences for over-all performance are shown in Table 3. Each of the relationships is subject to limiting conditions, some of which were noted earlier. The point being made is that conclusions about the effect of a generally competitive or conflictful relationship can only be made on the basis of an analysis of the specific components of the pattern together with an analysis of the task. Comparative field data are needed to evaluate the validity of the concept of an optimum degree of competitiveness and rivalry. The optimum might be expected to vary, depending upon the type of interunit interdependence, the type of work of each unit, and the personalities of unit representatives.

TABLE 3 CONSEQUENCES OF INTERUNIT CONFLICT

Attributes of Conflictful Lateral Relationships	*Illustrative Consequences*
Competition in general	Motivates or debilitates Provides checks and balances
Concealment and distortion	Lowers quality of decisions
Channeled interunit contacts	Enhances stability in the system
Rigidity, formality in decision procedures	Lowers adaptability to change
Appeals to superiors for decisions	Provides more contact for superiors May increase or decrease quality of decisions
Decreased rate of interunit interaction	Hinders coordination and implementation of tasks
Low trust, suspicion, hostility	Psychological strain and turnover of personnel or decrease in individual performance.

RESPONSES OF HIGHER EXECUTIVES

Response Tendencies of Executives

The response of executives refers to how superiors react to information about subordinate organizational units; that is, to low performance and attributes of the interunit relationship itself. Here "low performance" means inadequate productivity, low adaptability, or inability of the units to conserve their human and other resources.

A manager's response is a combination of his habitual patterns, emotional reactions, and deliberate responses. This idiosyncratic element in the system of interunit conflict shown in Figure 1 is a major problem in developing a general explanatory or predictive model of the total system. For the same reason, however, it is an opportunity for improving the interunit relationship. Several automatic responses to low performance can be noted for illustration. If the joint performance of two units is considered inadequate, higher executives may place particular emphasis on observable, short-run measures of performance for each subunit. Thus, poor performance, whatever its source, may lead to the very rewards, controls, and styles of supervision here shown to be antecedents to conflict. If the relationships hypothesized are valid, reinforcing feedback will lead to more interunit conflict and still lower performance. White (1961) reported that higher executives who were dissatisfied with the performance of subordinate units frequently responded by reorganizing the units. The feelings of status depreciation or power deprivation and the ambiguity which frequently follow a reorganization may increase the potential for conflict.

Executive Responses in Relation to Model

The model has implications both for determining what needs changing and for developing a strategy for achieving the change. Executive responses can either reinforce and intensify a conflict pattern, or create pressures to change it. Much depends upon how sophisticated a diagnostic model the manager uses. Ideally he would take into account all the valid implications of a model of the antecedents, dynamics, and consequences of conflict.

The Model as a Diagnostic Tool. Cause-and-effect relationships can be traced back through the model as follows:

1. Are there manifestations of conflict or low collaboration in the lateral relationship? If not, this interunit conflict model is not relevant. If so, determine the particular aspects of the relationship processes that are impinging upon performance; for instance, distortion of information, infrequent interaction, and lack of mutual assistance.

2. Are these dysfunctional elements of the conflict process inherent in a competitive interunit relationship? If not, determine how the management activities at the interface are inadequate, and whether these can be modified by suggesting or requiring changes in them. If they are, determine what particular contextual variables are responsible for the competitive orientation; for example, scarce resources, competitive reward system, asymmetrical task interdependence, or personalities of key liaison personnel.

3. Which of the contextual factors that create the interunit conflict are not inherent in the technology or are not essential parts of the administrative apparatus? Determine which of these might be modified to have a significant influence on the relationship.

An exhaustive treatment of the factors which are instrumental in altering a conflictful interunit relationship and which executives can modify would review the entire model. Instead, only a few relevant executive responses that have been treated in the literature are considered.

Thompson (1960) identified three areas of executive response: First, "Within limits, administrative allocations (of rewards, status symbols, resources, etc.) determine the relative deprivation experienced by organizational members, and thereby control potential conflict inherent in modern technologies" (392). Second, "To the extent that recruitment and selection procedures limit or maintain it within manageable pattern, the organization can manage the potential conflict in latent role diversity" (394). By latent role diversity, Thompson means differences in socioeconomic status, ethnic background, and so on. Third, "By varying the distinctiveness of the organization, the proportion of members exposed, and the frequency and regularity of their exposure, the organization gains a measure of control over conflict stemming from potential reactions to competing pressures" (396). Here he is referring to organizational conflict induced by ideas or pressures from the organization's environment.

Landsberger (1961) states that horizontal differences in authority can be more strongly supported by organizational logic, and need be less dependent on arbitrary fiat than vertical authority. On the other hand, differences in lateral authority are less obvious and are less likely to be stated explicitly, and therefore tend toward conflict. Consequently, one executive response is to make explicit rules allocating final authority for decisions on interunit activities, so as to depersonalize the order. A related response is for higher executives to develop rules to cover an increasing proportion of interunit transactions, and thereby confine decisions to exceptional situations, a practice noted by both Brown (1960) and Landsberger (1961).

Pondy (1967) refers to other devices which are not only available to those who manage the interface, but which can also be included in the executive response repertory: reducing dependence on common resources, transfer pricing between units, loosening schedules, or introducing buffer inventories. Litwak (1961) suggests many "mechanisms or segregation," used to reduce the conflict generated by contradictory social forms which modern organizations must incorporate, including stricter role separation between those for whom affect and those for whom strict objectivity is important; physical separation, such as moving the research facility away from the production facility; and transferral occupations, such as engineers who maintain involvement with a product from research to production stages.

Implications of the Model for Change of Strategy. Ideally, higher executives would develop a strategy for modifying the level of interunit conflict and collaboration which not only acts on the problem diagnosed, but also takes into account the self-perpetuating characteristics of conflict relationships. The analysis of the dynamics of lateral relationship not only underscored the self-reinforcing tendencies of conflictful processes of information exchange, interaction patterns, and attitudes between units; it is also stressed the reciprocal and regenerative tendencies of conflictful approaches to the interface.

These self-reinforcing, regenerative and reciprocal tendencies lead to persistence of a conflict process; therefore, higher management needs to engage in activities designed to replace existing patterns. Blake, Shephard and Mouton (1964), and Walton (1968) have outlined theories and techniques of third-party consulting interventions. The underlying assumption is that the units must find a new culture in which to view and understand each other. Various techniques of re-education can be used to change intergroup perceptions based on stereotypes, misunderstanding the intention of others, and past history of hostile relations. Thus, whether higher executives conclude that basic contextual factors or techniques for interface management need to be modified, change effort will be effective only if it includes some interventions which help change the existing pattern.

CONCLUSIONS

Several features of the model of interunit conflict deserve emphasis: First, no a priori assumption is made that interunit conflict should be reduced. Second, the model recognizes a large number of potential determinants of conflict and conflict-reinforcement syndromes. Third, the model incorporates contextual and structural factors emphasized by sociologists and economists, as well as interpersonal interaction phenomena studied by social psychologists. These approaches are integrated in the explanatory model and in the action implications of the model. Fourth, the model of the internal dynamics of the relationship particularly throws light on the problems of unfreezing the existing patterns. Fifth, the ability to manage interunit conflict is shown to require sophistication in executive response.

REFERENCES

Argyris, Chris. *Integrating the individual and the organization.* New York: Wiley, 1964.

Blake, R. R., Shephard, H. A., and Mouton, J. S. *Intergroup conflict in organizations.* Ann Arbor: Foundation for Research on Human Behavior, 1964.

Brown, Wilfred. *Explorations in management.* London: Tavistock, 1960.

Burns, T. and Stalker, G. M. *The management of innovation.* London: Tavistock, 1961.

Caplow, T. *Principles of organization.* New York: Harcourt, Brace and World, 1964.

Cozer, L. A. *The functions of social conflict.* Glencoe, Illinois: Free Press, 1956.

Crozier, Michel. Human relations at the management level in a bureaucratic system of organization. *Human Organization,* 1961, **20**, 51–64.

Dalton, M. *Men who manage.* New York: Wiley, 1959.

Dutton, J. M. and Walton, R. E. Interdepartmental conflict and cooperation: two contrasting studies. *Human Organization,* 1966, **25**, 207–20.

Georgopoulos, B. and Mann, F. *The community general hospital.* New York: Macmillan, 1962.

Kahn, R. L., Wolfe, D. M., Quinn, R. P., Snoek, J. D., and Rosenthal, R. A. *Organizational stress: Studies in role conflict and ambiguity.* New York: Wiley, 1964.

Landsberger, H. A. The horizontal dimension in a bureaucracy. *Administrative Science Quarterly,* 1961, **6**, 298–333.

Lawrence, P. R. and Lorsch, J. W. *Organization and environment.* Boston: Division of Research, Graduate School of Business Administration, Harvard University, 1967. (a)

Lawrence, P. R. and Lorsch, J. W. Differentiation and integration in complex organizations. *Administrative Science Quarterly,* 1967, **12**: 1–47. (b)

Likert, R. *New patterns of management.* New York: McGraw-Hill, 1961.

Litwak, E. Models of bureaucracy which permit conflict. *American Journal of Sociology,* 1961, **67**, 177–84.

March, J. G. and Simon, H. A. *Organizations.* New York: Wiley, 1958.

Miller, E. J. Technology, territory and time. *Human Relations,* 1959, **12**, 243–72.

Pondy, L. R. Organizational conflict: Concepts and models. *Administrative Science Quarterly,* 1967, **12**, 296–320.

Schmidt, W. and Tannenbaum, R. The management of differences. *Harvard Business Review,* **38** (November-December 1960), 107–15.

Seiler, J. A. Diagnosing interdepartmental conflict. *Harvard Business Review,* **41** (September–October 1963), 121–32.

Simpson, R. L. Vertical and horizontal communication in formal organization. *Administrative Science Quarterly,* 1959, **4**, 188–96.

Strauss, G. Tactics of lateral relationship: the purchasing agent. *Administrative Science Quarterly,* 1962, **7**, 161–86.

Strauss, G. Work-flow frictions, interfunctional rivalry, and professionalism: A case study of purchasing agents. *Human Organization,* 1964, **23**, 137–49.

Thompson, J. D. Organizational management of conflict. *Administrative Science Quarterly,* 1960, **4**: 389–409.

Thompson, V. A. *Modern organization.* New York: Alfred A. Knopf, 1961.

Walton, R. E. Theory of conflict in lateral organizational relationships. In J. R. Lawrence (ed.), *Operational research and the social sciences.* London: Tavistock, 1966. Pp. 409–28.

Walton, R. E. Interpersonal confrontation and basic third-party roles. *Journal of Applied Behavioral Sciences,* 1968 **4**, 20–31.

Walton, R. E., Dutton, J. M., and Fitch, H. G. A study of conflict in the process, structure, and attitudes of lateral relationships. In Haberstroh and Rubenstein (eds.), *Some theories of organization.* (rev. ed.) Homewood, Illinois: Irwin, 1966. Pp. 444–65.

Walton, R. E. and McKersie, R. B. *A behavioral theory of labor negotiations.* New York: McGraw-Hill, 1965.

Walton, R. E. and McKersie, R. B. Behavioral dilemmas in mixed-motive decision making. *Behavioral Science,* 1966, **11**, 370–84.

White, J. Management conflict and social structure. *American Journal of Sociology,* 1961, **67**, 185–91.

Zald, M. N. Power balance and staff conflict in correctional institutions. *Administrative Science* Quarterly, 1962, **7**, 22–49.

53. ACHIEVING CHANGE IN PEOPLE: SOME APPLICATIONS OF GROUP DYNAMICS THEORY*

***Dorwin Cartwright*†**

I

We hear all around us today the assertion that the problems of the twentieth century are problems of human relations. The survival of civilization, it is said, will depend upon man's ability to create social inventions capable of harnessing, for society's constructive use, the vast physical energies now at man's disposal. Or, to put the matter more simply, we must learn how to change the way in which people behave toward one another. In broad outline, the specifications for a good society are clear, but a serious technical problem remains: How can we change people so that they neither restrict the freedom nor limit the potentialities for growth of others; so that they accept and respect people of different religion, nationality, color, or political opinion; so that nations can exist in a world without war, and so that the fruits of our technological advances can bring economic well-being and freedom from disease to all the people of the world? Although few people would disagree with these objectives when stated abstractly, when we become more specific, differences of opinion quickly arise. How is change to be produced? Who is to do it? Who is to be changed? These questions permit no ready answers.

Before we consider in detail these questions of social technology, let us clear away some semantic obstacles. The word "change" produces emotional reactions. It is not a neutral word. To many people it is threatening. It conjures up visions of a revolutionary, a dissatisfied idealist, a trouble-maker, a malcontent. Nicer words referring to the process of changing people are education, training, orientation, guidance, indoctrination, therapy. We are more ready to have others "educate" us than to have them "change" us. We, ourselves, feel less guilty in "training" others than in "changing" them. Why this emotional response? What makes the two kinds of words have such different meanings? I believe that a large part of the difference lies in the fact that the safer words (like education or therapy) carry the implicit assurance that the only changes produced will be good ones, acceptable within a currently held value system. The cold, unmodified word "change," on the contrary, promises no respect for values; it might even tamper with values themselves. Perhaps for this very reason it will foster straight thinking if we use the word "change" and thus force ourselves to struggle directly and self-consciously with the problems of value that are involved. Words like education, training, or therapy, by the very fact that they are not so disturbing, may close our eyes to the fact that they too inevitably involve values.

Another advantage of using the word "change" rather than other related words is that it does not restrict our thinking to a limited set of aspects of people that are legitimate targets of change. Anyone familiar with the history of education knows that there has been endless controversy over what it is about people that "education" properly attempts to modify. Some educators have viewed education simply as imparting knowledge, others mainly as providing skills for doing things, still others as producing healthy "attitudes," and some have aspired to instill a way of life. Or if we choose to use a word like "therapy," we can hardly claim that we refer to a more clearly defined realm of change. Furthermore, one can become inextricably entangled in distinctions and vested interests by attempting to distinguish sharply between, let us say, the domain of education and that of therapy. If we are to try to take a broader view and to develop some basic principles that promise to apply to all types of modifications in people, we had better use a word like "change" to keep our thinking general enough.

The proposal that social technology may be employed to solve the problems of society suggests that social science may be applied in ways not different from those used in the physical sciences. Does social science, in fact, have any practically useful knowledge which may be brought to bear significantly on society's most urgent problems? What scientifically based principles are there for guiding programs of social change: In this paper we shall restrict our considerations to certain parts of a relatively new branch of social science known as "group dynamics." We shall examine some of the applications for social action which stem from research in this field of scientific investigation.

---

* *Human Relations,* Vol. IV, No. 4 (1951), pp. 381–92.

This paper is based on a lecture delivered at Wayne University, Detroit, in the Leo M. Franklin Lecture Series, 1950–51.

† Research Center for Group Dynamics, University of Michigan.

What is "group dynamics"? Perhaps it will be most useful to start by looking at the derivation of the word "dynamics." It comes from a Greek word meaning force. In careful usage of the phrase, "group dynamics" refers to the forces operating in groups. The investigation of group dynamics, then, consists of a study of these forces: what gives rise to them, what conditions modify them, what consequences they have, etc. The practical application of group dynamics (or the technology of group dynamics) consists of the utilization of knowledge about these forces for the achievement of some purpose. In keeping with this definition, then, it is clear that group dynamics, as a realm of investigation, is not particularly novel, nor is it the exclusive property of any person or institution. It goes back at least to the outstanding work of men like Simmel, Freud, and Cooley.

Although interest in groups has a long and respectable history, the past 15 years have witnessed a new flowering of activity in this field. Today, research centers in several countries are carrying out substantial programs of research designed to reveal the nature of groups and of their functioning. The phrase "group dynamics" has come into common usage during this time and intense efforts have been devoted to the development of the field, both as a branch of social science and as a form of social technology.

In this development the name of Kurt Lewin has been outstanding. As a consequence of his work in the field of individual psychology and from his analysis of the nature of the pressing problems of the contemporary world, Lewin became convinced of society's urgent need for a *scientific approach* to the understanding of the dynamics of groups. In 1945 he established the Research Center for Group Dynamics to meet this need. Since that date the Center has been devoting its efforts to improving our scientific understanding of groups through laboratory experimentation, field studies, and the use of techniques of action research. It has also attempted in various ways to help get the findings of social science more widely used by social management. Much of what I have to say in this paper is drawn from the experiences of this Center in its brief existence of a little more than five years (2).

II

For various reasons we have found that much of our work has been devoted to an attempt to gain a better understanding of the ways in which people change their behavior or resist efforts by others to have them do so. Whether we set for ourselves the practical goal of improving behavior or whether we take on the intellectual task of understanding why people do what they do, we have to investigate processes of communication, influence, social pressure—in short, problems of change.

In this work we have encountered great frustration. The problems have been most difficult to solve. Looking back over our experience, I have become convinced that no small part of the trouble has resulted from an irresistible tendency to conceive of our problems in terms of the individual. We live in an individualistic culture. We value the individual highly, and rightly so. But I am inclined to believe that our political and social concern for the individual has narrowed our thinking as social scientists so much that we have not been able to state our research problems properly. Perhaps we have taken the individual as the unit of observation and study when some larger unit would have been more appropriate. Let us look at a few examples.

Consider first some matters having to do with the mental health of an individual. We can all agree, I believe, that an important mark of a healthy personality is that the individual's self-esteem has not been undermined. But on what does self-esteem depend? From research on this problem we have discovered that, among other things, repeated experiences of failure or traumatic failures on matters of central importance serve to undermine one's self-esteem. We also know that whether a person experiences success or failure as a result of some undertaking depends upon the level of aspiration which he has set for himself. Now, if we try to discover how the level of aspiration gets set, we are immediately involved in the person's relationships to groups. The groups to which he belongs set standards for his behavior which he must accept if he is to remain in the group. If his capacities do not allow him to reach these standards, he experiences failure, he withdraws or is rejected by the group and his self-esteem suffers a shock.

Suppose, then, that we accept a task of therapy, of rebuilding his self-esteem. It would appear plausible from our analysis of the problem that we should attempt to work with variables of the same sort that produced the difficulty, that is to work with him either in the groups to which he now belongs or to introduce him into new groups which are selected for the purpose and to work upon his relationships to groups as such. From the point of view of preventive mental health, we might even attempt to train the groups in our communities—classes in schools, work groups in business, families, unions, religious and cultural groups—to make use of practices better designed to protect the self-esteem of their members.

Consider a second example. A teacher finds that in her class she has a number of troublemakers, full of aggression. She wants to know why these children are so aggressive and what can be done about it. A foreman in a factory has the same kind of problem with some of his workers. He wants the same kind of help. The solution most tempting to both the teacher and the foreman often is to transfer the worst troublemakers to someone else, or if facilities are available, to refer them for counselling. But is the problem really of such a nature that it can be solved by removing the troublemaker from the situation or by working on his individual motivations and emotional life? What leads does research give us? The evidence indicates, of course, that there are many causes of aggressiveness in people, but one aspect of the problem has become increasingly clear in recent years. If we observe carefully the amount of aggressive behavior and the number of troublemakers to be found in a large collection of groups, we find that these characteristics can vary tremendously from group to group even when the different groups are composed essentially of the same kinds of people. In the now classic experiments of Lewin, Lippitt, and White (7) on the effects of different styles of leadership, it was found that the same group of children displayed markedly different levels of aggressive behavior when under different styles of leadership. Moreover, when individual children were transferred from one group to another, their levels of aggressiveness shifted to conform to the atmosphere of the new group. Efforts to account for one child's aggressiveness under one style of leadership merely in terms of his personality traits could hardly succeed under these conditions. This is not to say that a person's behavior is entirely to be accounted for by the atmosphere and structure of the immediate group, but it is remarkable to what an extent a strong, cohesive group can control aspects of a member's behavior traditionally thought to be expressive of enduring personality traits. Recognition of this fact rephrases the problem of how to change such behavior. It directs us to a study of the sources of the influence of the group on its members.

Let us take an example from a different field. What can we learn from efforts to change people by mass media and mass persuasion? In those rare instances when educators, propagandists, advertisers, and others who want to influence large numbers of people, have bothered to make an objective evaluation of the enduring changes produced by their efforts, they have been able to demonstrate only the most negligible effects (1). The inefficiency of attempts to influence the public by mass media would be scandalous if there were agreement that it was important or even desirable to have such influences strongly exerted. In fact, it is no exaggeration to say that all of the research and experience of generations has not improved the efficiency of lectures or other means of mass influence to any noticeable degree. Something must be wrong with our theories of learning, motivation, and social psychology.

Within very recent years some research data have been accumulating which may give us a clue to the solution of our problem. In one series of experiments directed by Lewin, it was found that a method of group decision, in which the group as a whole made a decision to have its members change their behavior, was from two to ten times as effective in producing actual change as was a lecture presenting exhortation to change (6). We have yet to learn precisely what produces these differences of effectiveness, but it is clear that by introducing group forces into the situation a whole new level of influence has been achieved.

The experience has been essentially the same when people have attempted to increase the productivity of individuals in work settings. Traditional conceptions of how to increase the output of workers have stressed the individual: select the right man for the job; simplify the job for him; train him in the skills required; motivate him by economic incentives; make it clear to whom he reports; keep the lines of authority and responsibility simple and straight. But even when all these conditions are fully met we are finding that productivity is far below full potential. There is even good reason to conclude that this individualistic conception of the determinants of productivity actually fosters negative consequences. The individual, now isolated and subjected to the demands of the organization through the commands of his boss, finds that he must create with his fellow employees informal groups, not shown on any table of organization, in order to protect himself from arbitrary control of his life, from the boredom produced by the endless repetition of mechanically sanitary and routine operations, and from the impoverishment of his emotional and social life brought about by the frustration of his basic needs for social interaction, participation, and acceptance in a stable group. Recent experiments have demonstrated clearly that the productivity of work groups can be greatly increased by methods of work organization and supervision which give more responsibility to work groups, which allow for fuller participation im important decisions, and which make stable groups the firm basis for support of the individual's social needs (3). I am convinced that future research will also demonstrate that people working under such conditions become more mature and creative individuals in their homes, in community life, and as citizens.

As a final example, let us examine the experience of efforts to train people in workshops, institutes, and special training courses. Such efforts are common in various areas of social welfare, intergroup relations, political affairs, industry, and adult education generally. It is an unfortunate fact that objective evaluation of the effects of such training efforts has only rarely been undertaken, but there is evidence for those who will look that the actual change in behavior produced is most disappointing. A workshop not infrequently develops keen interest among the participants, high morale and enthusiasm, and a firm resolve on the part of many to apply all the wonderful insights back home. But what happens back home? The trainee discovers that his colleagues don't share his enthusiasm. He learns that the task of changing others' expectations and ways of doing things is discouragingly difficult. He senses, perhaps not very clearly, that it would make all the difference in the world if only there were a few other people sharing his enthusiasm and insights with whom he could plan activities, evaluate consequences of efforts, and from whom he could gain emotional and motivational support. The approach to training which conceives of its task as being merely that of changing the individual probably produces frustration, demoralization, and disillusionment in as large a measure as it accomplishes more positive results.

A few years ago the Research Center for Group Dynamics undertook to shed light on this problem by investigating the operation of a workshop for training leaders in intercultural relations (8). In a project, directed by Lippitt, we set out to compare systematically the different effects of the workshop upon trainees who came as isolated individuals in contrast to those who came as teams. Since one of the problems in the field of intercultural relations is that of getting people of good will to be more active in community efforts to improve intergroup relations, one goal of the training workshop was to increase the activity of the trainess in such community affairs. We found that before the workshop there was no difference in the activity level of the people who were to be trained as isolates and of those who were to be trained as teams. Six months after the workshop, however, those who had been trained as isolates were only slightly more active than before the workshop whereas those who had been members of strong training teams were now much more active. We do not have clear evidence on the point, but we would be quite certain that the maintenance of heightened activity over a long period of time would also be much better for members of teams. For the isolates the effect of the workshop had the characteristic of a "shot in the arm" while for the team member it produced a more enduring change because the team provided continuous support and reinforcement for its members.

III

What conclusions may we draw from these examples? What principles of achieving change in people can we see emerging? To begin with the most general proposition, we may state that the behavior, attitudes, beliefs, and values of the individual are all firmly grounded in the groups to which he belongs. How aggressive or cooperative a person is, how much self-respect and self-confidence he has, how energetic and productive his work is, what he aspires to, what he believes to be true and good, whom he loves or hates, and what beliefs and prejudices he holds—all these characteristics are highly determined by the individual's group memberships. In a real sense, they are properties of groups and of the relationships between people. Whether they change or resist change will, therefore, be greatly influenced by the nature of these groups. Attempts to change them must be concerned with the dynamics of groups.

In examining more specifically how groups enter into the process of change, we find it useful to view groups in at least three different ways. In the first view, the group is seen as a source of influence over its members. Efforts to change behavior can be supported or blocked by pressures on members stemming from the group. To make constructive use of these pressures the group must be used *as a medium of change.* In the second view, the group itself becomes the *target of change.* To change the behavior of individuals it may be necessary to change the standards of the group, its style of leadership, its emotional atmosphere, or its stratification into cliques and hierarchies. Even though the goal may be to change the behavior of *individuals,* the target of change becomes the group. In the third view, it is recognized that many changes of behavior can be brought about only by the organized efforts of groups *as agents of change.* A committee to combat intolerance, a labor union, an employers association, a citizens group to increase the pay of teachers—any action group will be more or less effective depending upon the way it is organized, the satisfaction it provides to its members, the degree to which its goals are clear, and a host of other properties of the group.

An adequate social technology of change, then, requires at the very least a scientific understanding of groups viewed in each of these ways. We shall consider here only the first two aspects of the problem: the group as a medium of change and as a target of change.

The Group as a Medium of Change

Principle No. 1. If the group is to be used effectively as a medium of change, those people who are to be changed and those who are to exert influence for change must have a strong sense of belonging to the same group.

Kurt Lewin described this principle well: "The normal gap between teacher and student, doctor and patient, social worker and public, can . . . be a real obstacle to acceptance of the advocated conduct." In other words, in spite of whatever status differences there might be between them, the teacher and the student have to feel as members of one group in matters involving their sense of values. The chances for reeducation seem to be increased whenever a strong we-feeling is created (5). Recent experiments by Preston and Heintz have demonstrated greater changes of opinions among members of discussion groups operating with participatory leadership than among those with supervisory leadership (12). The implications of this principle for classroom teaching are far-reaching. The same may be said of supervision in the factory, army, or hospital.

Principle No. 2. The more attractive the group is to its members the greater is the influence that the group can exert on its members.

This principle has been extensively documented by Festinger and his coworkers (4). They have been able to show in a variety of settings that in more cohesive groups there is a greater readiness of members to attempt to influence others, a greater readiness to be influenced by others, and stronger pressures toward conformity when conformity is a relevant matter for the group. Important for the practitioner wanting to make use of this principle is, of course, the question of how to increase the attractiveness of groups. This is a question with many answers. Suffice it to say that a group is more attractive the more it satisfies the needs of its members. We have been able to demonstrate experimentally an increase in group cohesiveness by increasing the liking of members for each other as persons, by increasing the perceived importance of the group goal, and by increasing the prestige of the group among other groups. Experienced group workers could add many other ways to this list.

Principle No. 3. In attempts to change attitudes, values, or behavior, the more relevant they are to the basis of attraction to the group, the greater will be the influence that the group can exert upon them.

I believe this principle gives a clue to some otherwise puzzling phenomena. How does it happen that a group, like a labor union, seems to be able to exert such strong discipline over its members in some matters (let us say in dealings with management), while it seems unable to exert nearly the same influence in other matters (let us say in political action)? If we examine why it is that members are attracted to the group, I believe we will find that a particular reason for belonging seems more related to some of the group's activities than to others. If a man joins a union mainly to keep his job and to improve his working conditions, he may be largely uninfluenced by the union's attempt to modify his attitudes toward national and international affairs. Groups differ tremendously in the range of matters that are relevant to them and hence over which they have influence. Much of the inefficiency of adult education could be reduced if more attention were paid to the need that influence attempts be appropriate to the groups in which they are made.

Principle No. 4. The greater the prestige of a group member in the eyes of the other members, the greater the influence he can exert.

Polansky, Lippitt, and Redl (11) have demonstrated this principle with great care and methodological ingenuity in a series of studies in children's summer camps. From a practical point of view it must be emphasized that the things giving prestige to a member may not be those characteristics most prized by the official management of the group. The most prestige-carrying member of a Sunday school class may not possess the characteristics most similar to the minister of the church. The teacher's pet may be a poor source of influence within a class. This principle is the basis for the common observation that the official leader and the actual leader of a group are often not the same individual.

Principle No. 5. Efforts to change individuals or subparts of a group which, if successful, would have the result of making them deviate from the norms of the group will encounter strong resistance.

During the past few years a great deal of evidence has been accumulated showing the tremendous pressures which groups can exert upon members to conform to the group's norms. The price of deviation in most groups is rejection or even expulsion. If the member really wants to belong and be accepted, he cannot withstand this type of pressure. It is for this reason that efforts to change people by taking them from the group and giving them special training so often have disappointing results. This principle also accounts for the finding that people thus trained sometimes display increased tension, aggressiveness toward the group, or a tendency to form cults or cliques with others who have shared their training.

These five principles concerning the group as a medium of change would appear to have readiest application to groups created for the purpose of producing changes in people. They provide certain specifications for building effective training or therapy groups. They also point, however, to a difficulty in producing change in people in that they show how resistant an individual is to changing in any way contrary to group pressures and expectations. In order to achieve many kinds of changes in people, therefore, it is necessary to deal with the group as a target of change.

The Group as a Target of Change

Principle No. 6. Strong pressure for changes in the group can be established by creating a shared perception by members of the need for change, thus making the source of pressure for change lie within the group.

Marrow and French (9) reports a dramatic case study which illustrates this principle quite well. A manufacturing concern had a policy against hiring women over 30 because it was believed that they were slower, more difficult to train, and more likely to be absent. The staff psychologist was able to present to management evidence that this belief was clearly unwarranted at least within their own company. The psychologist's facts, however, were rejected and ignored as a basis for action because they violated accepted beliefs. It was claimed that they went against the direct experience of the foremen. Then the psychologist hit upon a plan for achieving change which differed drastically from the usual one of argument, persuasion, and pressure. He proposed that management conduct its own analysis of the situation. With his help management collected all the facts which they believed were relevant to the problem. When the results were in they were now their own facts rather than those of some "outside" expert. Policy was immediately changed without further resistance. The important point here is that facts are not enough. The facts must be the accepted property of the group if they are to become an effective basis for change. There seems to be all the difference in the world in changes actually carried out between those cases in which a consulting firm is hired to do a study and present a report and those in which technical experts are asked to collaborate with the group in doing its own study.

Principle No. 7. Information relating to the need for change, plans for change, and consequences of change must be shared by all relevant people in the group.

Another way of stating this principle is to say that change of a group ordinarily requires the opening of communication channels. Newcomb (10) has shown how one of the first consequences of mistrust and hostility is the avoidance of communicating openly and freely about the things producing the tension. If you look closely at a pathological group (that is, one that has trouble making decisions or effecting coordinated efforts of its members), you will certainly find strong restraints in that group against communicating vital information among its members. Until these restraints are removed there can be little hope for any real and lasting changes in the group's functioning. In passing it should be pointed out that the removal of barriers to communication will ordinarily be accompanied by a sudden increase in the communication of hostility. The group may appear to be falling apart, and it will certainly be a painful experience to many of the members. This pain and the fear that things are getting out of hand often stop the process of change once begun.

Principle No. 8. Changes in one part of a group produce strain in other related parts which can be reduced only by eliminating the change or by bringing about readjustments in the related parts.

It is a common practice to undertake improvements in group functioning by providing training programs for certain classes of people in the organization. A training program for foremen, for nurses, for teachers, or for group workers is established. If the content of the training is relevant for organizational change, it must of necessity deal with the relationships these people have with other subgroups. If nurses in a hospital change their behavior significantly, it will affect their relations both with the patients and with the doctors. It is unrealistic to assume that both these groups will remain indifferent to any significant changes in this respect. In hierarchical structures this process is most clear. Lippitt has proposed on the basis of research and experience that in such organizations attempts at change should always involve three levels, one being the major target of change and the other two being the one above and the one below.

IV

These eight principles represent a few of the basic propositions emerging from research in group dynamics. Since research is constantly going on and since it is the very nature of research to revise and reformulate our conceptions, we may be sure that these principles will have to be modified and improved as time goes by. In the meantime they may serve as guides in our endeavors to develop a scientifically based technology of social management.

In social technology, just as in physical technology, invention plays a crucial role. In both fields progress consists of the creation of new mechanisms for the accomplishment of certain goals. In both fields inventions arise in response to practical needs and are to be evaluated by how effectively they satisfy these needs. The relation of invention to scientific development is indirect but important. Inventions cannot proceed too far ahead of basic scientific development, nor should they be allowed to fall too far behind. They will be more effective the more they make good use of known principles of science, and they often make new developments in science possible. On the other hand, they are in no sense logical derivations from scientific principles.

I have taken this brief excursion into the theory of invention in order to make a final point. To many people "group dynamics" is known only for the social inventions which have developed in recent years in work with groups. Group dynamics is often thought of as certain techniques to be used with groups. Role playing, buzz groups, process observers, post-meeting reaction sheets, and feedback of group observations are devices popularly associated with the phrase "group dynamics." I trust I have been able to show that group dynamics is more than a collection of gadgets. It certainly aspires to be a science as well as a technology.

This is not to underplay the importance of these inventions nor of the function of inventing. As inventions they are all mechanisms designed to help accomplish important goals. How effective they are will depend upon how skilfully they are used and how appropriate they are to the purposes to which they are put. Careful evaluative research must be the ultimate judge of their usefulness in comparison with alternative inventions. I believe that the principles enumerated in this paper indicate some of the specifications that social inventions in this field must meet.

REFERENCES

1. Cartwright, D. Some principles of mass persuasion: Selected findings of research on the sale of United States war bonds. *Human Relations,* 1949, **2**(3), 253–67.
2. Cartwright, D. *The research center for group dynamics: A report of five years' activities and a view of future needs.* Ann Arbor: Institute for Social Research, 1950.
3. Coch, L. and French, J. T. P., Jr. Overcoming resistance to change. *Human Relations,* 1948, **1**(4), 512–32.
4. Festinger, L., et al. *Theory and experiment in social communication: Collected papers.* Ann Arbor: Institute for Social Research, 1950.
5. Lewin, K. *Resolving social conflicts,* p. 67. New York: Harper & Bros., 1948.
6. Lewin, K. *Field theory in social science,* pp. 229–36. New York: Harper & Bros., 1951.
7. Lewin, K., Lippitt, R., and White, R. K. Patterns of aggressive behavior in experimentally created "social climates." *Journal of Social Psychology,* 1939, **10**, 271–99.
8. Lippitt, R. *Training in Community Relations.* New York: Harper & Bros., 1949.
9. Marrow, A. J. and French, J. R. P., Jr. Changing a stereotype in industry. *Journal of Social Issues,* 1945, **1**(3), 33–37.
10. Newcomb, T. M. Autistic hostility and social reality. *Human Relations,* 1947, **1**(1), 69–86.
11. Polansky, N., Lippitt, R., and Redl, F. An investigation of behavioral contagion in groups. *Human Relations,* 1950, **3**(4), 319–48.
12. Preston, M. G. and Heintz, R. K. Effects of participatory vs. supervisory leadership on group judgment. *Journal of Abnormal and Social Psychology,* 1949, **44**, 345–55.

54. EFFECTIVENESS OF T-GROUP EXPERIENCES IN MANAGERIAL TRAINING AND DEVELOPMENT*

***John P. Campbell* and *Marvin D. Dunnette*†**

Research studies relating T-group experiences to the behavior of individuals in organizations are reviewed in depth. Attention is also devoted to summarizing the stated objectives of the method and its technological elements. In addition, speculation is offered about the nature and viability of implicit assumptions underlying T-group training. Examination of the research literature leads to the conclusion that while T-group training seems to produce observable changes in behavior, the utility of these changes for the performance of individuals in their organizational roles remains to be demonstrated. It is also evident that more research has been devoted to T-group training than to any other single management-development technique; however, the problems of observation and measurement are considerably more difficult in T-group research than in most other areas.[1]

* *Psychological Bulletin,* Vol. 70, No. 2 (August 1968), pp. 73–104. © 1968 by the American Psychological Association, Inc.

† University of Minnesota.

[1] This investigation was supported in part by the National Institute of Mental Health, United States Public Health Service (Research Grant 5 R01 MH 08563-04), and in part by a be-

The following short episode taken from a management-development session illustrates many of the features of an educational technique referred to as the T-group method of sensitivity training. When integrated with other techniques such as lectures and group problem-solving exercises, the complete program is usually relabeled "laboratory education."

> At the fifth meeting the group's feelings about its own progress became the initial focus of discussion. The "talkers" participated as usual, conversation shifting rapidly from one point to another. Dissatisfaction was mounting, expressed through loud, snide remarks by some and through apathy by others.
>
> George Franklin appeared particularly disturbed. Finally pounding the table, he exclaimed, "I don't know what is going on here! I should be paid for listening to this drivel? I'm getting just a bit sick of wasting my time here. If the profs don't put out—I quit!" George was pleased; he was angry, and he had said so. As he sat back in his chair, he felt he had the group behind him. He felt he had the guts to say what most of the others were thinking! Some members of the group applauded loudly, but others showed obvious disapproval. They wondered why George was excited over so insignificant an issue, why he hadn't done something constructive rather than just sounding off as usual. Why, they wondered, did he say their comments were "drivel"?
>
> George Franklin became the focus of discussion. "What do you mean, George, by saying this nonsense?" "What do you expect, a neat set of rules to meet all your problems?" George was getting uncomfortable. These were questions difficult for him to answer. Gradually he began to realize that a large part of the group disagreed with him; then he began to wonder why. He was learning something about people he hadn't known before. ". . . How does it feel, George, to have people disagree with you when you thought you had them behind you? . . ."
>
> Bob White was first annoyed with George and now with the discussion. He was getting tense, a bit shaky perhaps. Bob didn't like anybody to get a raw deal, and he felt that George was getting it. At first Bob tried to minimize George's outburst, and then he suggested that the group get on to the real issues; but the group continued to focus on George. Finally Bob said, "Why don't you leave George alone and stop picking on him. We're not getting anywhere this way."
>
> With the help of the leaders, the group focused on Bob. "What do you mean, 'picking' on him?" "Why, Bob, have you tried to change the discussion?" "Why are you so protective of George?" Bob began to realize that the group wanted to focus on George; he also saw that George didn't think he was being picked on, but felt he was learning something about himself and how others reacted to him. "Why do I always get upset," Bob began to wonder, "when people start to look at each other? Why do I feel sort of sick when people get angry at each other?" . . . Now Bob was learning something about how people saw him, while gaining some insight into his own behavior (Tannenbaum, Weschler, & Massarik, 1961, p. 123].

havioral science research grant to the second author from the General Electric Foundation.

There is little doubt that T-groups have become a popular management-development device (House, 1967). The National Training Laboratories (NTL) and the Western Training Laboratories conduct programs for several hundred managers and executives each year (National Training Laboratories, 1967), a number of consulting firms have made this type of training a standard part of their repertoire, and many colleges and universities incorporate T-groups as part of the curriculum in business education, public administration, education, or psychology. In addition, a number of university institutes such as Boston University's Human Relations Center and UCLA's Institute of Industrial Relations conduct T-groups for business personnel. There are also instances, and here a trend is impossible to document, of line managers being trained to conduct T-groups as an ongoing part of their organization's management-development program. It seems accurate to say that a T-group is within easy reach of almost any manager.

This paper is devoted to an analysis and appraisal of the application of this technique to problems of managerial development. The focus is on the published literature surrounding the topic and not upon the authors' personal experiences. The authors are academic psychologists interested in organizational behavior and not T-group or laboratory-education practitioners.

In brief, this paper attempts to: *(a)* identify and summarize the crucial elements of the T-group method, *(b)* call attention to some of the difficulties in researching both the dynamics and the effects of the method, and *(c)* summarize in some detail the research evidence bearing on the utility of T-groups for training and development purposes.

It is acknowledged at the outset that no single explicitly defined set of experiences can be labeled the laboratory method. There are many variations, or "training designs," depending upon the characteristics of certain parameters. However, at the heart of most efforts is a common core of experience known as the T-group, usually regarded as the crucial part of the program (Bradford, Gibb, & Benne, 1964, p. 2; Schein & Bennis, 1965; p. 15). It is this common core which receives most of the attention from practitioners, researchers, and critics and which is the focus of this review.[2]

[2]See also the "debate" between Argyris and Odiorne reported in the *Training Directors Journal,* Vol. 17, No. 10 (1963), pp. 4–37.

FORM AND NATURE OF THE T-GROUP METHOD

Two elements used to distinguish the T-group from other training methods are the learning goals involved and the processes used to accomplish these goals. Advocates of T grouping tend to focus on goals at two different levels (Buchanan, 1965; Schein & Bennis, 1965). Flowing from certain scientific and democratic values are several meta-goals, or goals which exist on a very general level. Schein and Bennis mentioned five, which they asserted to be the ultimate aims of all T-group training: *(a)* a spirit of inquiry or a willingness to hypothesize and experiment with one's role in the world; *(b)* an "expanded interpersonal consciousness" or an increased awareness of more things about more people; *(c)* an increased authenticity in interpersonal relations or simply feeling freer to be oneself and not feeling compelled to play a role; *(d)* an ability to act in a collaborative and interdependent manner with peers, superiors, and subordinates rather than in authoritative or hierarchical terms; and *(e)* an ability to resolve conflict situations through problem solving rather than through horse trading, coercion, or power manipulation.

According to Schein and Bennis (1965), these metagoals are seldom articulated, but are implicit in the functioning of most T groups. A number of more proximate objectives usually are made explicit and are regarded by most authors as the direct outcomes of a properly functioning T-group. It is true that not *all* practitioners would agree that *all* T-groups try to accomplish *all* of these aims, but they are sufficiently common to most discussions of the T-group method that the authors feel relatively few qualms in listing them as the direct or proximate outcomes desired. The list is drawn from a variety of sources (Argyris, 1964; Bradford et al., 1964; Buchanan, 1965; Miles, 1960; Schein & Bennis, 1965; Tannenbaum et al., 1961):

1. Increased self-insight or self-awareness concerning one's own behavior and its meaning in a social context. This refers to the common aim of learning how others see and interpret one's behavior and gaining insight into why one acts in certain ways in different situations.

2. Increased sensitivity to the behavior of others. This goal is closely linked with the above. It refers first, to the development of an increased awareness of the full range of communicative stimuli emitted by other persons (voice inflections, facial expressions, bodily positions, and other contextual factors, in addition to the actual choice of words) and second, to the development of the ability to infer accurately the emotional or noncognitive bases for interpersonal communications. This goal is very similar to the concept of empathy as it is used by clinical and counseling psychologists, that is, the ability to infer correctly what another person is feeling.

3. Increased awareness and understanding of the types of processes that facilitate or inhibit group functioning and the interactions between different groups—specifically, why do some members participate actively while others retire to the background? Why do subgroups form and wage war against each other? How and why are pecking orders established? Why do different groups, who may actually share the same goals, sometimes create seeming insoluable conflict situations?

4. Heightened diagnostic skill in social, interpersonal, and intergroup situations. Achievement of the first three objectives should provide an individual with a set of explanatory concepts to be used in diagnosing conflict situations, reasons for poor communication, and the like.

5. Increased action skill. Although very similar to No. 4, it was mentioned separately by Miles (1960) and refers to a person's ability to intervene successfully in inter- or intragroup situations so as to increase member satisfactions, effectiveness, or output. The goal of increased action skill is toward intervention at the interpersonal rather than simply the technological level.

6. Learning how to learn. This does not refer to an individual's cognitive approach to the world, but rather to his ability to analyze continually his own interpersonal behavior for the purpose of helping himself and others achieve more effective and satisfying interpersonal relationships.

Differential emphasis among the above objectives constitutes one of the most important dimensions for distinguishing among variations in T groups. Some groups tend to emphasize the individual's goals of fostering self-awareness and sensitivity. Others orient toward the more organizational objectives of understanding interaction phenomena and intergroup processes (Buchanan, 1965) with the ultimate aim of improving organizational effectiveness. The evolution of different forms of T-groups designed to achieve these two major emphases is discussed at length by Benne (1964) and Schein and Bennis (1965).

What processes and structural elements does the T-group use to achieve these goals? The technology of any given group depends, in part, on the goals held to be paramount, but the thrust of the literature emphasizes a common core of experiences around which specialized variations may be developed.

Thus, the T-group learning experience has as its focal point the small, unstructured, face-to-face group, usually consisting of 10–15 people. Typically, no activities or topics for discussion are planned. A trainer is usually present, but he does not accept, in fact he overtly rejects, any leadership role. The participants are to discuss themselves and the way they portray themselves in the group. In the language of T-grouping, the focus is on the "here and now," that is, on behavior emitted in the group rather than behavior involving past experiences or future problems. The here and now includes the feelings and emotions experienced by the group members. In fact, the cognitive aspects of problems are ancillary to this affect-laden orientation. Focusing on the here and now is facilitated by the trainer's abdication of the leadership role and his lack of responsiveness to the status symbols brought to the group by the participants (e.g., company position, education, family background, etc.). Frequently, the trainer merely specifies the length of time the group will be meeting and that the major concern is with seeking to understand one's own and others' behaviors. He then falls silent or otherwise refuses further guidance.

The vacuum is often filled by feelings of frustration, expressions of hostility, and eventual attempts by some members to impose an organized, and usually hierarchical (leaders, committees, etc.), structure on the group. These initial attempts to assume a leadership role are usually resented by other members, and, either spontaneously or because of the trainer's intervention, they begin to consider why the self-appointed leader has tried to force his will on the group. If events follow their proper course, the behavior of the other group members also becomes a basis for discussion such that every participant has an opportunity to learn how his own within-group behavior is perceived. This process is illustrated by the episode quoted at the beginning of the present paper. More complete narrative accounts of what goes on in a T-group are given by Klaw (1961), Weschler and Reisel (1959), and Kuriloff and Atkins (1966).

Given the unstructured group as the vehicle and the behavior emitted in the group as the principal topic of conversation, the success of the venture depends on the crucial process of feedback. Thus, the participants must be able to inform each other how their behavior is being seen and interpreted and to describe the kinds of feelings generated. This is the primary process by which the delegates "learn." They must receive articulate and meaningful feedback about their own behavior, including their own feedback attempts (feedback on feedback) and their efforts to interpret group processes. (E.g., did the other group members think Individual X was correct when he observed that Y and Z were forming a clique because they both felt rejected?)

For the feedback process to contribute to the goals of the training, at least two additional elements are believed necessary. First, a certain amount of anxiety or tension must be generated, particularly in the early part of the group's life. Anxiety supposedly results when an individual discovers how deficient his previous role-bound methods of interacting are for successful functioning in this new type of group situation.

A possible explanation for this type of anxiety generation flows from some of the stimulus-response formulations of Dollard and Miller (1950). Almost every individual has an established self-image protected by a number of defense mechanisms. Such mechanisms have become resistant to change because of their repeated association with the reinforcing properties of anxiety reduction; that is, they protect the self-image from threat. Thus, in the T-group when an individual's usual mode of interacting is thwarted and his defense mechanisms are made a direct topic of conversation, considerable anxiety results. Such anxiety then constitutes a force for new learning because, if the group experience is a successful one, new methods of anxiety reduction will be learned. If the T-group is successful, these methods will be more in line with the goals of the training and will have more utility for the individual in coping with his environment than his old methods which may indeed have been dysfunctional. Thus, anxiety serves the purpose of shaking up or jarring loose the participant from his preconceived notions and habitual forms of interacting so that feedback may have its maximum effect. Without such "unfreezing," feedback may be ineffectual (Schein, 1964).

The second element necessary for assuring effective feedback is what Schein and Bennis (1965) referred to as a climate of "psychological safety" and Bradford et al. (1964) called "permissiveness." That is, no matter what an individual does in a group or what he reveals about himself, the group must act in a supportive and nonevaluative way. Each individual must feel that it is safe to expose his feelings, drop his defenses, and try out new ways of interacting. Such an atmosphere has its obvious counterpart in any constructive clinical or therapeutic relationship.

The role of the trainer also constitutes a dominant technological element bearing on the group's effectiveness for giving feedback and promoting psychological support. The trainer serves as a model for the participants to imitate; that is, he absorbs feelings of hostility and frustration without becoming defensive, provides feedback for others, expresses his own feelings openly and honestly, and is strongly supportive of the expression of feelings in others. In short, he exhibits for consideration the very processes deemed necessary for maximum learning to occur.

However, in the so-called "instrumented" T-group (Berzon & Solomon, 1966; Blake & Mouton, 1962) there may be no trainer. The function of a behavior model is accomplished by a series of questionnaires requiring the participants to rate themselves and each other on how supportive they are, how freely they express feelings, and how skillfully they give feedback.

Another structural ingredient of the T-group method bearing on the accomplishment of its goals is the organizational affiliation of the participants. So-called "stranger" groups (such as the groups conducted by the NTL) are composed of individuals from a number of different organizations and seem to emphasize self-insight and sensitivity as the primary goals. In contrast, "family" groups are composed of individuals drawn from a vertical slice of a particular unit of an organization, and, for them, goals relevant to group processes and intergroup interaction in the organization are more salient (Tannenbaum et al. 1961). Other types of group composition are possible. Members may be drawn from a horizontal slice of the organization or they may constitute an intact work group (Schein & Bennis, 1965). Organizational development rather than just individual development is paramount for these latter types of groups.

SOME ASSUMPTIONS

The training technology just described seems to make a number of assumptions, both explicitly and implicitly. The authors offer the following list for consideration:

1. A substantial number of group members, when confronted with others' behaviors and feelings in an atmosphere of psychological safety, can produce articulate and constructive feedback.

2. A significant number of the group members can agree on the major aspects of a particular individual's behavior exhibited in the group situation. Certainly a complete consensus is not to be expected, but neither must the feedback go off in all directions. A certain degree of communality is necessary if the feedback is to be helpful for the individual.

3. Feedback is relatively complete and deals with significant aspects of the individual's behavior.

4. The behavior emitted in the group is sufficiently representative of behavior outside the group so that learning occurring within the group will carry over or transfer.

5. Psychological safety can be achieved relatively quickly (in the matter of a few hours) among either complete strangers or among associates who have had varying types and degrees of interpersonal interaction.

6. Almost everyone initially lacks interpersonal competence; that is, individuals tend to have distorted self-images, faulty perceptions, and poor communication skills.

7. Anxiety facilitates new learning.

8. Finally, transfer of training occurs between the cultural island and the "back home" situation.

Little can be said about the validity of such assumptions since they involve extremely complex processes with as yet only a very thin research context. However, a few points seem relevant. The first four assumptions must be substantially met if the T group is to achieve the goals regarding self-insight, sensitivity, and understanding of group process; each of these assumptions places severe demands on individual abilities in observing and communicating. Maslow (1965) suggested that because of the skills demanded of individuals in this type of learning situation perhaps only a very small percentage of the population can hope to benefit. Further, a consideration of these four assumptions points up a potentially troublesome paradox underlying the T-group method —their close resemblance to the major T-group objectives themselves. That is, it appears that some of the interpersonal skills most important for accomplishing the T-group's objectives are also the very skills constituting the major learning goals of the method.

Thus, some critical issues that must be resolved concern how rapidly such observational and communicative skills can be developed, whether or not a few relatively skilled participants can "carry" the rest of the group for the time necessary for others to develop minimal capability, and, finally, the degree to which *all* members profit from the group experience even if they initially differ greatly in these interpersonal abilities.

Assumption 5 is also related to the above. People must certainly differ greatly in their ability to accept the guarantee of psychological safety. To the extent that the feeling of safety cannot be achieved—and quickly—the prime basic ingredient for this form of learning is absent. Its importance cannot be overemphasized, nor can the difficulty of its being accomplished.

It would be informative to have normative data about Assumption 6; however, this encompasses certain definitional and measurement problems that will be touched on later. It should be noted that if Assumption 6 is strongly supported the demands of Assumptions 1 through 4 for "quick learning" become even more severe.

Assumption 7 also raises a number of difficult questions. The bulk of the evidence bearing on the relationship of anxiety and learning has been obtained from animal studies or from experiments using human subjects and relatively simple psychomotor tasks (Deese, 1958; Kimble, 1961). No firm generalizations have emerged from these investigations except that the relationship is a complex one and dependent on various parameters such as relative level of anxiety, motivational state prior to learning, complexity of the task, and a number of others. On the other hand, for complex human learning of the academic variety, Skinner (1953) argued that a complete absence of anxiety is desirable. In sum, the previous literature on the topic is equivocal.

Although no data directly relevant to the role of anxiety in inducing interpersonal learning are available, it might be informative to review Solomon's (1964) insightful analysis of the probable effects of punishment on learning. Based on his and others' research, Solomon theorized that learning as a consequence of punishment occurs in a two-stage process: First, a conditioned emotional reaction must be established to temporarily suppress the unwanted behavior. Second, and most important, responses incompatible with the punished response must then be reinforced and established; only in this way can one guard against the rapid extinction of the conditioned emotional reaction and the corresponding reappearance of the unwanted behavior. In the context of the T-group, this means that "punishment" in the form of anxiety arousal must be accompanied by the reinforcement and shaping of responses incompatible with those responsible for originally inducing the anxiety. In a sense this is what the T-group tries to do; however, it seems reasonable to ask whether or not the usual T-group is sufficiently structured to assure the sophisticated control of stimuli and reinforcement configurations necessary in the two-stage process suggested by Solomon. Given the variability in contingencies that this lack of structure probably produces, some possible alternative outcomes might be either simply that no permanent learning occurs of that some of the negative side effects are incurred. The reality of their occurrence in other learning situations is well documented by Yates (1962).

The authors are not arguing that such negative outcomes are almost certain to occur. No empirical data exist on which to base such an argument. However, research results in other learning contexts suggest it is a potential danger for the T-group situation that should not be ignored.

PROBLEMS FACING T-GROUP RESEARCH

Before reviewing research results, the authors shall comment on some of the problems faced by investigators who wish to conduct research on the T-group and its effects. Many of these difficulties are certainly not peculiar to the T-group, but it is believed that T-group research faces certain unique problems which severely constrain any effort to explicate the effects of the method.

One of the major difficulties mentioned by Schein and Bennis (1965) is the lack of an explicit theory of learning for use in specifying the relation between learning experiences and learning outcomes. Nine individuals presented their formulations of the T-group change process in Bradford *et al.* (1964), and all were very different. Schein and Bennis attributed this diversity of theory to the wide range of learning outcomes seen as possible. Outcomes may include increased awareness, increased knowledge, changes in values, changes in attitudes, changes in motivation, or changes in actual behavior. Organizing all these into a single coherent system specifying relationships between training elements and learning outcomes is difficult indeed—probably more difficult for laboratory education than for other training methods. Presently, it is unclear what kinds of outcomes to expect from any specific T-group effort.

A second problem, not unique to T-groups, is the ever-present question of transfer of learning from the training group to the individual's life outside the group. More specifically, does what is learned in a T-group transfer to the organizational setting? According to its practitioners, a crucial aspect of the T-group is the creation of anxiety and the open expression of feelings in an atmosphere of psychological safety. Schein and Bennis (1965) speculated that the conditions which facilitate the necessary climate of safety are: *(a)* a T-group which meets for a relatively long time in an isolated environment; *(b)* a heterogeneous group which will probably not meet again and which thus does not constitute such a threatening audience; *(c)* continual reinforcement by the staff that the laboratory culture is supportive, nonevaluative, nonthreatening, and, therefore, "different" than the world back home; and *(d)* an attitude on the part of the participants that the T-group is something of a temporary "game" to be played with relative abandon because it is not "for keeps." As Schein and Bennis recognized, all these conditions heighten the differences between the work group and the T group and would seem to work against transfer to the work situation. Groups conducted closer to the work situation, involving people from the same organization or subunit, and incorporating particular organizational problems for discussion may enhance the probability of transfer, but they may also lessen the probability of achieving many of the goals of a T-group. Many of the supporting elements seen as facilitating open expression of feeling, accurate feedback, and psychological safety have been removed.

Assuming that transfer does occur, the problem of observing and measuring it remains. The measurement problem involves two major steps: *(a)* assessing what changes have occurred over the course of the training, and *(b)* determining how such changes are manifested in the organizational setting. For example, do people really become more sensitive to the feelings of others during the course of the T-group, and are they then also more sensitive to the feelings of others on the job? Both these questions must be examined empirically.

The measurement problems involved in assessing the cognitive, attitudinal, and behavioral effects sought by the T-group experience are considerable. All the difficulties cannot be elaborated here nor can all potential areas of interpersonal change be discussed separately, but the magnitude of the problem can be illustrated by giving brief attention to the many difficulties involved in measuring interpersonal awareness. This factor has been chosen because nearly all T-groups strive, either explicitly or implicitly, toward increasing members' empathy, interpersonal sensitivity, or interpersonal accuracy as a first and crucial step on the road toward developing improved interpersonal competence. T-group advocates forcefully and rightly call attention to the important role played by interpersonal perception in getting to know and learning to work constructively with other people. They make it the key to developing mature and understanding interaction in nearly all human relationships. As a consequence, the central focus of T-group training is to increase the level of accuracy with which persons discern the attributes, attitudes, opinions, feelings, and reactions of others in their social and work environments.

Any assessment or measurement of what goes on in T-group training must first cope with the problems involved in measuring this elusive phenomenon called interpersonal sensitivity. The problems are many, and they have already been well documented by Cronbach (1955), Gage and Cronbach (1955), Cline (1964), and H. C. Smith (1966). The major difficulty grows out of the plethora of strategies available to anyone who seeks to discern accurately the attributes, feelings, and reactions of others.

First, he may truly know each and every person in his environment *perfectly* and be able to make ideographic behavioral predictions for each one. This is probably the metagoal of most T-group training, but few would claim that it is realistically possible. A somewhat easier way of increasing the interpersonal accuracy of T-group participants might be by training them in the "art" of forming accurate stereotypes about people in general or about persons belonging to various subgroups in society. That is, one strategy for accomplishing a modicum of interpersonal accuracy is simply to know the base rates of particular behavior patterns, reactions, and feelings typically shown by different subgroups. The authors believe that most T-group advocates might be distressed if they were charged with seeking to develop accurate stereotypes instead of helping participants to "know" each and every person in their environment. Nonetheless, prediction of base rates has repeatedly been shown to be one of the most likely avenues for successfully predicting the responses of other persons.

Another strategy yielding accurate predictions for some persons is the "assumed similarity strategy" or, for want of a better name *projective sensitivity.* Here, an effective and accurate interpersonal perceiver might be "sensitive" in the sense that he can accurately identify that subset of persons whose reactions, feelings, and attitudes are similar to his own. Then, simply by projecting his own feelings and behavior tendencies onto them, he can accomplish the desirable goal of "knowing others" in his environment. In this case, the successful T-group will be one that manages to make persons more similar to one another in their behavioral tendencies, attitudes, opinions, feelings, and reactions or that teaches people to recognize individuals who are like themselves. However, this latter strategy is rather narrow and would appear to have limited utility for the development of interpersonal perceptual accuracy. T-group advocates might also be distressed if they were charged with training for conformity, but here again, assumed similarity (or projective sensitivity) has been repeatedly shown to be an important component of accurate interpersonal perception (Cronbach, 1955; H. C. Smith, 1966).

Many other strategies for accomplishing accurate interpersonal prediction could be mentioned. Some may be artifactual (such as "accuracy" related to pervasive response sets—e.g., social desirability), and others may be illusory (such as the unwillingness of a perceiver to "go out on a limb" or to deviate from the average in predicting for others).

The major purpose here is simply to emphasize that interpersonal sensitivity is not only an elusive, but also a highly complex phenomenon. Persons involved in a T-group training program may indeed become more "sensitive," but the nature and underlying strategies of the sensitivities developed may differ widely from person to person and from program to program. Unless the various components and strategies involved in interpersonal sensitivity are taken into account during the design of measuring instruments and during the design and implementation of research investigations, little new knowledge concerning T-group training effects or the likelihood of transferring skills back to the work setting will accrue. So far (as will be seen in subsequent sections), most investigators have not attempted to cope with the serious measurement and design problems inherent in this area.

A REVIEW OF THE EMPIRICAL LITERATURE

Three reviews (Buchanan, 1965; House, 1967; Stock, 1964) of the T-group literature have previously appeared. Each has incorporated a somewhat different emphasis, either in type and breadth of studies reviewed or in conclusions drawn from the results. Stock (1964) devoted attention to investigations of how individuals behave in a T-group, the relationship between personality and perceptions of other group members, the perceptions of the group by its members, the relationship of group composition to the course of group development, and the relationship of group composition to subgroup structure, group anxiety level, and member satisfaction. She also gave some attention to the role of the trainer and the impact of a T-group on individual learning, but no studies were reviewed relative to the development of people in their organizational roles or to the complex question of transfer of learning. In sum, Stock's principal emphasis was on the behavior of individuals in the group setting rather than on the influence of T-group training on members' behavior in their organizations. In contrast, House (1967) and Buchanan (1965) discussed a sampling of studies aimed at evaluating the T-group as a development technique; however, their treatment and conclusions differed somewhat from those in the present paper. The range of their citations was a bit narrower, and they tended to be more positive in their conclusions.

The present review is focused primarily on studies of the usefulness of the T-group technique for influencing the behavior of people in organizations. That is, of principal interest here is the relationship of T-group training to appropriate criterion measures. In addition, studies bearing on the viability of the assumptions underlying the method and investigations showing how successful the technique has been in capitalizing on the essential features of its technology have also been included. For example, investigations of the utility of interpersonal feedback in a group or studies of the effects of different trainer styles are relevant. The authors have also tried to limit citations to studies employing subjects who have some sort of management or supervisory responsibility. However, in the interest of including all potentially relevant research, the authors have also reviewed studies using students in business administration or related fields that imply an interest in management or administrative careers.

The discussion is organized according to the type and quality of criteria used. Martin's (1957) distinction between internal and external measures of training effects has been adopted. *Internal criteria* are measures linked directly to the content and processes of the training program, but which have no direct linkage to actual job behavior or to the goals of the organization. Examples of internal criteria include measures of attitude change, performance in simulated problem-solving situations, and opinions of trainees concerning what they thought they had learned. Obviously, changes in internal criteria need imply no necessary change in job behavior; for example, a change in attitudes toward employees may or may not be accompanied by different behavioral patterns back on the job.

External criteria are those linked directly with job behavior. Superior, subordinate, or peer ratings, unit production, or unit turnover are examples of external criteria that have been used. Nether of these two classes of criteria is regarded as more important than the other. It will subsequently be argued that a thorough knowledge of both is essential for a full understanding of training effects. The relationship between internal and external criteria is the essence of the problem of transfer to the organizational setting.

EXTERNAL CRITERIA

Studies by Boyd and Elliss (1962), Bunker (1965), and Miles (1965) are the three research efforts most frequently cited in support of the ability of the T-group experience to change job behavior. Valiquet (1964) carried out a similar study. All four investigations used a "perceived change" measure as the basic external criterion. This measure is an open-ended question asking a superior, subordinate, or peer of the subject to report any changes in the subject's behavior in the job situation during some specified period of time. The specific question used in the Bunker (1965), Miles (1965), and Valiquet (1964) studies is as follows:

Over a period of time people may change in the ways they work with other people. Do you believe that the person you are describing has changed his/her behavior in working with people over the last year as compared with the previous year in any specific ways? If YES, please describe:

Estimates of change were usually obtained from several (three to seven) observers for each subject. In the Boyd and Elliss (1962) study, the observers were interviewed by the researchers, while in the other three studies, data were obtained by including the above question in a mailed questionnaire. Observers were not asked to judge the positive or negative aspects of the behavior changes, but merely to describe those which had occurred. In all four studies the perceived-change data were obtained several months after completion of training.

All studies used at least one control group, and in the Bunker, Miles, and Valiquet studies they were chosen in a similar, but unusual, fashion. Controls were matched with experimental subjects by asking each person in the experimental group to nominate a "control" individual who was in a similar organizational position and who had never participated in a T group. It is not clear from the report how the control subjects were chosen in the Boyd and Elliss study.

Subjects in the Miles (1965) and Bunker (1965) studies were participants in NTL programs. Miles used 34 high school principals as an experimental group and two groups of principals as controls. One "matched" group of 29 was chosen via the nomination procedure, and a second group of 148 was randomly selected from a national listing. Responses to the perceived-change measure were solicited from six to eight associates of each experimental and control subject and from the subjects themselves approximately eight months after the training. Returns were obtained from an average of five observers per subject.

Two other external criterion measures also were used: the Leadership Behavior Description Questionnaire (LBDQ—Stogdill & Coons, 1957), which was completed by observers, and the Group Participation Scale, a peer-nomination form originally developed by Pepinsky, Siegel, and Van Alta (1952) as a counseling criterion measure. Data from both these instruments were collected before and after the training for one half of the experimental group and the matched-pair control group. To check any Treatment × Measurement interaction effects, data for the second half of the experimental group were collected post-training only. There were no interactions.

A large number of other measures were also included in the study. Ratings of various training behaviors (internal criteria) were obtained from trainers, peers, and the participants themselves. These ratings were analyzed via the multitrait, multimethod (Campbell & Fiske, 1959) technique and subsequently collapsed into an overall "trainee effectiveness" score. More importantly, five measures of the individual's organizational situation were obtained: *(a)* security, as measured by length of tenure in present job; *(b)* power, as measured by the number of teachers in the participant's school; *(c)* autonomy, as measured by length of time between required reports to the immediate superior; *(d)* perceived power, as measured by a Likert-type scale; and *(e)* perceived adequacy of organizational functioning, as measured by a Likert-type scale. In addition, a number of personality measures were administered, including items intended to assess ego strength, flexibility, and self-insight. The participants were also asked to rate their "desire for change" before starting the training.

No significant results were found with the LBDQ or the Group Participation Scale, and the personality measures were not predictive of anything. However, results obtained with the perceived-change measure were statistically significant. The observers reported perceived behavioral changes for 30 percent of the experimentals, 10 percent of the matched controls, and 12 percent of the randomly selected controls. The corresponding percentages for self-reported changes are 82 percent, 33 percent, and 21 percent for the three groups. The participants tended to report considerably more changes than the observers. An informal content analysis was carried out, and Miles (1965) concluded that the nature of the changes reported included increased sensitivity to others, heightened equalitarian attitudes, greater communication and leadership skills, and patterns of increased consideration and relaxed attitudes in their jobs. No details are given as to how the content analysis was performed.

With certain exceptions, most of the other relationships were not significant. One of the exceptions was a correlation of 0.55 between the perceived-change measure and trainer ratings of amount of change during the T-group. Also, two of the situational variables, security and power, correlated 0.30 and 0.32 with the perceived-change measure; that is, more changes in job behavior tended to be observed for the high school principals with longer tenure and more subordinates.

Bunker's (1965) experimental group included 229 people from six different laboratories conducted at the NTL during 1960 and 1961. The participants were presumably rather heterogeneous, but a substantial proportion had leadership or managerial responsibilities. The matching-by-nomination procedure yielded 112 control subjects. Perceptions of behavior change were obtained from each experimental and control subject and from five to seven associates of each subject approximately a year after the training period. The 229 experimentals and 112 controls represented return rates of approximately 75 percent and 67 percent. Eighty-four percent of the observers returned questionnaires.

Bunker presented a list of 15 inductively derived categories that were used for content analyzing the perceived-change data. The 15 categories were grouped within three major classes labeled: *(a)* overt operational changes, that is, communication, relational facility, risk taking, increased interdependence, functional flexibility, self-control; *(b)* inferred changes in insight and attitudes, that is, awareness of human behavior, sensitivity to group behavior, sensitivity to others' feelings, acceptance of other people, tolerance of new information, self-confidence, comfort, insight into self and role; and *(c)* global judgments, really a catchall for changes with no specific referent. No details were given concerning how this classification scheme was developed. However, an agreement rate of 90 percent was reported when trained independent judges used the categories to classify the responses. Eleven of the 15 subcategories yielded statistically significant differences between experimental and control groups with the trained group showing greater change in each category. The greatest differences (ranging up to 20–25 percent) were in areas related to increased openness, receptivity, tolerance of differences, increased operational skill in interpersonal relationships, and improved understanding of self and others. Again, about one third (ranging up to 40 percent) of the members of the experimental group were reported to have changed in comparison with 15–20 percent in the control group. Categories showing no differences between the groups reflected such things as effective initiation of action, assertiveness, and self-confidence. However, Bunker (1965) emphasized that changes among the trainees differed greatly from person to person and that actually there was "no standard learning outcome and no stereotyped ideal toward which conformity is induced [p. 42]."

Both the Boyd and Elliss (1962) study and Valiquet's (1964) investigation used managerial personnel from a single organization. Boyd and Ellis employed an experimental group of 42 managers selected from three different T-groups conducted during 1961 at a large Canadian public utility. Their two control groups consisted of 12 control individuals who received no training and 10 managers who received a conventional human-relations training program employing lectures and conference techniques. Perceived changes were collected by interviewing each manager's superior, two of his peers, and two of his subordinates. The percentages of observers reporting changes for the laboratory-trained group, the conventionally trained group, and the no-training group were 65 percent, 51 percent, and 34 percent, respectively. The percentage of subjects showing changes "substantially" agreed upon by two or more observers was 64 percent for the experimental group and 23 percent for the two control groups taken together. All the above differences are statistically significant. For all subjects a total of 351 statements of perceived change was reported, but only 137 changes were agreed upon by two or more observers. Of 22 reported changes judged to be unfavorable (e.g., an increase in irritability or loss of tolerance) by the researchers, 20 were attributed to members of the laboratory-trained group. The observers were also asked to *Q* sort a deck of 80 statements describing different kinds of job-behavior changes. No significant differences were found with this instrument. In their conclusions, Boyd and Elliss emphasized the great heterogeneity among the trainees in their behavioral outcomes. They also argued that no particular pattern could be regarded as a typical training outcome.

Valiquet (1964) randomly selected 60 participants from an ongoing laboratory type training program conducted in certain divisions of a large multiproduct corporation. The program was a continuing one and included T-group meetings at various management levels and follow-up meetings designed to promote the effective use of interpersonal skills for solving current organizational problems and planning future activities. Difficulties encountered in choosing an appropriate control group coupled with a low rate of response to the questionnaire resulted in a serious loss of subjects. Final results were available for 34 trained subjects and only 15 matched control-group subjects. On the average about five observers were nominated by each experimental and control subject. The change categories developed by Bunker were used to content analyze the descriptions obtained from each observer. Statistically significant differences were obtained between experimentals and controls on total number of changes observed, total changes agreed upon by two or more observers, and total number of changes reported by the subjects themselves. Results by category were much the same as in the Bunker study except that differences were greater in this study for the categories of "risk taking" and "functional flexibility," defined as the ability to accept change and to be an effective group member. Valiquet believes these differences occurred because the program involved inplant training conducted with co-workers, and the trainers were from within the firm, thereby facilitating the transfer of actual behavior to the work situation.

The above investigations, primarily the first three, seem to form the backbone of the evidence used to support the utility of the T-group method for the development of individuals in organizations. Certain summary statements can be made. In all the studies, between two and three times as many "changes" were reported for the experimental groups as for the control groups. In absolute terms about 30–40 percent of the trained individuals were reported as exhibiting some sort of perceptible change. The percentage was somewhat higher in the Boyd and Elliss (1962) study where the observer opinions were gathered by means of an interview rather than by questionnaire. Within the limits of the method, the types of perceived changes which seemed to discriminate best between experimentals and controls have to do with increased sensitivity, more open communication, and increased flexibility in role behavior.

The studies suffer from a number of obvious methodological limitations: The observers responding to the criterion measures apparently knew whether or not the individual they were describing had been through T-group training. Several of the authors suggested that the effects of such contamination were probably not serious, arguing that the variance in the types of changes was always greater for the experimental groups than for the control groups and that the proportion of changes verified by more than one observer was always higher for the trained group. Such arguments may or may not soothe the stomach-aches of those who worry about this type of bias. There is a second potential source of error in that the multiple describers for each subject were nominated by the subject and probably had varying degrees of interaction with each other. It is not known to what extent the observers might have discussed the fact that they had been asked to describe a particular individual and thus contaminated each other's observations. Also, no before measures were used, and the estimation of change depended solely on recollection by the observers. The pervasive influence of perceiver bias on what is remembered and reported is a well-documented phenomenon in psychological research. Further, it is difficult even to speculate how the above potential biases might interact with the practice of having individuals in the experimental groups suggest subjects for the control group who in turn nominate their own observers. A suggestion of such a troublesome interaction is reported in the Valiquet (1964) study. The group of subjects for whom the least changes were reported had originally nominated a significantly higher percentage of peers as describers, rather than superiors or subordinates.

Moreover, it is important to remember that the kinds of changes reported in these four studies have no direct or established connection with job effectiveness. Even if an individual does actually exhibit more "sensitivity" or "functional flexibility" on the job, one still knows nothing about how these constructs may be related to performance effectiveness. The relationship between such measures and job effectiveness constitutes an additional research question which has yet to be examined.

Underwood (1965) did ask observers to rate behavior changes according to their effects on job performance, but his study used fewer subjects and describers than those discussed above. Fifteen volunteers from a group of 30 supervisors who had participated in 30 hours of inplant T-group training were assigned to the experimental group. The control group consisted of 15 supervisors who had not been in the course, but who were matched on department, organization level, and age with those in the experimental group. Each subject was asked to recruit one observer who was then given a sealed envelope containing instructions for observing and reporting on any behavioral changes in the subject's "characteristic behavior pattern." Thirty-six reports of behavior change were gathered over a 15-week period. Some observers made no reports; several made more than one.

Nine individuals in the experimental group were reported to have changed in some fashion versus seven in the control group; however, there were nearly two and a half times as many changes reported for the experimental group as for the control group. The changes were classified into three categories relating to interpersonal behavior, personal behavior, and nonpersonal behavior. The bulk (32 of 36) were classified in the first two categories. Although the frequencies are small, it is interesting to note that in the control group the ratio of changes judged to increase effectiveness to those judged to decrease effectiveness was 4:1, while in the experimental group the ratio was only 2:1. In other words, the suggestion is that while the T group produced more observable changes in its members' job behavior it also produced a higher percentage of unfavorable changes with respect to their rated effects on job effectiveness. This is the only study of its kind, and it is unfortunate that the *N*s are so small and the sources of observer bias so prevalent.

Finally, a study by Morton and Bass (1964) also dealt with perceived changes in job behavior. Conducted in an aerospace corporation, the study focused on a T-group-type program (referred to as an organizational training laboratory) for managers from different levels within the same department. Feedback was speeded by requiring written descriptions from the trainees as to what they were thinking and feeling. Three months after the training, the 107 managers who attended the laboratory were asked to report any critical job incident which had occurred since the training and which they considered a consequence of the laboratory. Replies listing 359 incidents were received from 97 of the original trainees, and almost all of the incidents were judged by the researchers to have a favorable influence on job behavior. Almost two thirds of the incidents dealt with personal improvement and improved working relationships. Unfortunately, the criterion measure relied on self-report by the trainees, and there were no attempts at experimental control.

N = 1 Studies

Another type of external criterion study might be labeled the $N=1$ (Dukes, 1965) investigation. Its distinguishing feature is that the criteria used to evaluate the effectiveness of the training consist of summary data reflecting the overall performance of the organization or organizational subunit. For example, changes in the firm's profit picture or changes in a subunit's turnover rate over the course of the training period might be used as criterion measures. Such a procedure is probably most appropriate for T-group and laboratory programs aimed at increasing organizational effectiveness by means of inplant training sessions and the incorporation of actual organizational problems as topics of discussion during the latter stages of the program. If only one organization is studied, N does indeed equal 1, and, in a statistical sense, there are zero degrees of freedom. Of course, basing observations on just one case precludes any estimation of sampling error. This is not to say that studies based on one observation have no use. Dukes (1965) has recently summarized several instances of interesting and fruitful $N=1$ studies in the history of psychology. For example, a sample of one is appropriate if the measure used to assess the dependent variable is highly reliable, and the variable itself shows little variation in the population. Perhaps a more frequent situation amenable to an $N=1$ strategy is when the research aim is to establish that a particular event is indeed possible. Thus, a particular study is used to reject a generalization. Another use of one observation studies is for the generation of hypotheses to guide future research. Unfortunately, none of the studies cited below serves any of the functions discussed in the Dukes paper.

The most frequently cited study relevant to T-group training was reported by Blake, Mouton, Barnes, and Greiner (1964). The training experience was the Management Grid program which progresses in several stages. Initially, a series of T-group-like sessions is conducted for the purpose of exploring interpersonal relationships among peers and giving managers feedback about their particular management styles. A certain amount of structure and theory is also introduced in an attempt to move individual managers toward what Blake and Mouton (1964) called the 9,9 style of management, a style roughly akin to a maximum concern for both interpersonal relations and production problems. Over the course of a year or more, other training phases consisting of group examination of authority relationships between management levels, practice in the resolution of intergroup conflict, and collaborative problem solving are implemented. The program is intended to involve all managerial personnel from a particular firm.

Blake et al. (1964) presented the first phases of the grid program to all 800 managers in a 4,000-employee division of a large petroleum corporation. A large number of evaluation criteria were used with some being applied both before and after training and others only after the program had been completed. The measures obtained after completion of the program were such things as perceived changes in work-group performance (e.g., "boss's work effort," "quality of group decisions," and "profit and loss consciousness"), perceived changes in working relationships, and a number of items concerning attitudes toward specific management values and techniques. The above data were gathered from approximately 600 managers, and each respondent also was asked to estimate the change in his perceptions from 1962 to 1963, the year that included the grid program. The before-and-after measures included indexes of net profit, controllable operating costs, unit production per employee, frequency of management meetings, management-promotion criteria, frequency of transfers, and relative success in solving a number of persistent organizational problems (e.g., high maintenance costs, high utility costs, plant safety, and management communication). The data concerning the effectiveness of problem solutions were quite subjective and largely anecdotal in nature.

In general, the results were interpreted positively. For example, over the course of the training program the firm experienced a considerable increase in profits and a decrease in costs. The investigators attributed 56 percent of the profit increase to noncontrollable factors, 31 percent to a reduction in manpower, and 13 percent (amounting to several million dollars) to improved operating procedures and higher productivity per man-hour. The substantial increase in productivity per employee was said to have been achieved without increased investment in plant and equipment. Other criterion changes cited were an increased frequency of meetings, increased transfers within the plant and to other parts of the organization, a higher frequency of promotion for young line managers as opposed to staff men with more tenure, and a greater degree of success in solving the organizational problems discussed above.

Besides these summary criteria, the individual measures of values and attitudes suggested a shift toward the attitudinal goals of the grid program, and the perceptual measures indicated a change toward the 9,9 style of managing. Recall, however, that these individual measures were obtained post-training only, and the respondent was asked to estimate the amount of change that had taken place over a year's time.

Studies by Blansfield (1962) and Buchanan (1964) are also of the $N = 1$ type. Both involved lengthy laboratory-type programs, but both are described rather sketchily. Blansfield deals almost entirely with anecdotal evidence about those organizational developments reflecting favorably on the training program. No objective data besides the percentage of favorable trainee opinions are reported. Buchanan's (1964) study (reported in Buchanan, 1965) points to a shift from centralized to decentralized decision making, increased cooperation among work units, and a substantial increase in profits as evidence for the utility of the development program.

The utility of these results is difficult to judge. Neither the Blansfield nor the Buchanan study is reported in sufficient detail to allow careful consideration. However, more important difficulties in interpreting $N = 1$ studies are illustrated in the Blake et al. (1964) report. For example, the index showing a rise in productivity per employee appeared to be the result of an almost constant level of output with an accompanying substantial decrease in the size of the work force during the 12-month period. The crucial question of whether or not total productivity would have fallen along with the size of the work force if the training program had not been functioning is an unanswerable one. In addition, a development program that relies heavily on group participation and team spirit must live constantly in the shadow of the Hawthorne effect. The specific theoretical content or technology of the program may make little difference.

Questionnaire Measures of Individual Perceptions

Most of the criterion measures used in these investigations are individual perceptions obtained by means of standardized questionnaires. In some cases it is stretching a point to classify them as external criteria. For example, a measure of job satisfaction may have little or no relationship to measures of job behavior, but it is still a job-centered rather than a training-centered measure. A number of other ambiguities will be evident.

Beer and Kleisath (1967) studied the effects of the laboratory phase of the Management Grid program on the 230 managerial and professional personnel in one corporate division. Several questionnaire measures of perceptions of organizational functioning were obtained before and approximately a year after the 1-week grid program.

One of these was composed of established subscales developed in previous research at Ohio State University and the University of Michigan. A total of 14 scales was included: representation of department to people outside, persuasiveness, initiating structure, consideration for subordinates, tolerance of freedom, assumption of leadership role, production emphasis, integration of group members, participation of subordinates in decision making, emphasis on group rather than individual discussion, degree of employee influence on work, responsibility delegated to subordinates, authority delegated to subordinates and the degree to which the supervisor perceives he delegates authority and responsibility. Since people from several levels had been through the grid program, all the subjects responded in terms of how they perceived their superiors' behavior.

Other questionnaire measures were used to assess changes in perceptions of group processes (integration, peer supportiveness of achievement, peer supportiveness of affiliation, and group norms), perceptions of intergroup processes (intergroup dependence, intergroup cooperation, and definition among departments), perceptions of communication patterns (informal, upward, downward, intergroup), job satisfaction (11 dimensions), and commitment to the organization. Voluntary turnover was also included as a criterion measure.

The questionnaires provided a total of 41 scales with which to assess perceptual changes, and the authors pointed out that 37 of these changed in the predicted direction. However, only 14 of the 37 were statistically significant, and a number of significant differences were quite small. The change in turnover is difficult to interpret in that the index decreased over the experimental period, but only back to the level it had been two years before. Turnover had increased prior to the implementation of the grid program.

In sum, the results of the study tend to be in the predicted directions, but not overwhelmingly so. Unfortunately, there are competing explanations. No control groups were used, and the grid cannot be isolated as the cause of the changes. Even if it were, the same criticism applies here as with the Blake et al. (1964) study regarding Hawthorne-type effects. Perhaps any kind of group human-relations program would produce similar outcomes.

Beer and Kleisath (1967) also reported that some of the results were in line with the objectives of later phases of the grid program which had not yet been implemented. This was interpreted as evidence for the pervasive effects of the initial phase of the grid. It could just as well be used as evidence for a pervasive Hawthorne effect.

Zand, Steele, and Zalkind (1967) studied 90 middle and top managers in a company employing 2,000 people. Two criterion measures were used. One consisted of a 42-item questionnaire designed to assess a manager's perceptions of his own behavior, his relations with his superior, the situation in his work group, the organizational climate, and the behavior norms in the company. No details were given as to how the instrument was constructed. The second criterion was an eight-item questionnaire originally developed by Haire, Ghiselli, and Porter (1966) to measure an individual's attitudes toward Theory X versus Theory Y (McGregor, 1960), a dichotomy roughly akin to authoritarian and directive management versus democratic and participative management.

The first questionnaire was administered before, immediately after, and one year after a one-week laboratory consisting of T-groups, lectures, and group exercises, while the Theory X-Theory Y measure was given before and one year after. Perceptions of trust of others, openness in communication, seeking help, and superior receptivity to others' ideas declined significantly immediately after post-training and then returned to pro-training levels on the one year follow-up. No changes were found on the Theory X-Theory Y measure. These results were interpreted as supportive of the laboratory program. The less favorable perceptions immediately after training were seen as reflecting the adoption of "more realistic" standards, and the return to former levels after one year represented perceptions of real behavior change, given the lower standards. Obviously, there are strong competing explanations which cannot be ruled out because of the lack of control.

The lack of change toward Theory Y was explained on the basis of the already strong orientation toward Theory Y for the managers in the sample. Almost all the initial item means were between 3.0 and 4.0 on a five-point scale.

One other finding deserves comment because of its unique interpretation. Individuals who were rated as most "involved" in the laboratory also tended to be rated as the most involved in follow-up activities back in the organization. Again this was seen as evidence for the ability of the laboratory to change behavior. However, it could also be interpreted as simply consistency of behavior. The training program may not have changed anything.

Some of the difficulties involved in using perceptual data as criteria are illustrated in a study reported by Taylor (1967). The primary criterion measures were 20 semantic differential scales used to describe the trainee, 25 pairs of statements defining scales for describing the trainee's work group, and the eight-item Likert scale for measuring the trainee's orientation toward Theory Y or Theory X (Haire et al., 1966).

All the measures were completed before and six months after a one-week T-group laboratory conducted for 32 managers in a single organization. Some of the measures were also administered one month after the T-group. An average of four associates of each subject also responded to the criterion measures with the aim of describing the participants' observed behavior. While the results tended to show a number of significant changes in the participants' own responses, corresponding changes were not observed by the trainees' associates. This general result was also true regarding the Theory Y-Theory X measure.

Friedlander (1968) used perceptual measures to evaluate the impact of still another kind of training group. Four work groups (total $N = 31$) from a large governmental research facility met in off-site locations for four to five days and tried to accomplish three objectives: *(a)* identify problems facing the work-group system, *(b)* develop solutions, and *(c)* plan implementation of the solutions. During the course of the sessions, interpersonal and intergroup processes affecting the work system were explored with the help of a trainer.

The questionnaire used to assess change was composed of six scales developed factor analytically (group problem-solving effectiveness, approach versus withdrawal from leader, degree of mutual influence, personal involvement, intragroup trust versus competitiveness, general evaluation of meetings). The item pool for the factor analysis originally was obtained from interview data, discussions with other groups, and a search of the literature. The questionnaire was administered to the four training groups and eight "comparison" groups before and six months after the group training sessions.

An analysis of covariance procedure was used to control for pretraining differences between trained and nontrained groups. While it was reasonable to predict post-training differences between the individuals in experimental and comparison groups on all the dimensions, the results were mixed. The subjects felt they had achieved greater participation, mutual influence, and problem-solving effectiveness. Somewhat paradoxically, however, there were no changes on the competitiveness or general evaluation dimensions. Friedlander (1968) interpreted the results as "complex" but generally in support of the utility of the training effort.

Buchanan and Brunstetter (1959) used trainees'

perceptions of how their work units changed as a measure of the effects of an intraorganizational laboratory program directed at organization development. All the managers in one large department ($N = 224$) were used as an experimental group, and all the managers in a second department ($N = 133$) constituted a control group. Three to seven months after the completion of the training, the participants were asked via a questionnaire to rate changes in the effectiveness of various functions occurring in their own subunits during the previous year. No before measure was used. On those functions judged by the researchers to be under the control of the manager, the experimental group reported a greater number of effective changes. Unfortunately, it is difficult to draw conclusions from the results of such a study. There is no way to estimate how comparable the two departments were before the training began. Also, the trainees were actually being asked to judge what kind of an effect they themselves had had on the department, since it was only through them that the training could have an impact.

While the questionnaire studies cited above have yielded a relatively vast amount of data, the results are quite mixed and are open to numerous alternative explanations. Statistically significant differences are not abundant, and even these tend to be quite small. Over it all hangs the constant threat of response biases that have no parallel in actual behavior change.

INTERNAL CRITERIA

A variety of internal criteria has been incorporated in studies varying widely in sophistication. Because of the larger number of studies in this category, they will be dealt with more briefly; however, this does not imply a lower opinion of such research. As noted above; an understanding of both types of criteria is essential.

Perceptions of Self

Several investigations have focused on the change in an individual's self-perception occurring during training. Such a criterion flows directly from one of the major aims of T-group training—increasing the clarity and accuracy of individuals' perceptions of their own behavior. Studies by Bass (1962a), Bennis, Burke, Cutter, Harrington, and Hoffman (1957), Burke and Bennis (1961), Clark and Culbert (1965), Gassner, Gold, and Snadowsky (1964), Grater (1959), and Stock (1964) are relevant. A number of these were designed to assess discrepancies between descriptions of "actual self," "ideal self," and "others" (either a specific or some generalized other) and to measure any changes in these discrepancies produced by the T-group experience.

Two such studies are the ones by Burke and Bennis (1961) and Gassner et al. (1964). Burke and Bennis asked 84 participants from six different NTL groups to use 19 bipolar, adjectival rating scales to describe three concepts: *(a)* "The way I actually am in this T-group," *(b)* "The way I would like to be in this T-group," and *(c)* "Each of the other people in this group." The series of ratings of others was used to develop a pooled (or average) description of each subject on each of the 19 scales. The rating scales were administered during the middle of the first week and readministered at the next-to-last session of the third week. Changes were in the direction of greater agreement between actual and ideal self-descriptions and toward subjects' seeing themselves more nearly as others described them. The changes were statistically significant on all rating scales for all groups combined, but not for each of the six groups. No control group was used.

The results by Gassner et al. (1964) illustrate the dangers of making inferences from studies without control groups. They conducted three experiments using undergraduate students at CCNY as subjects, and each of the experiments employed a control group which received no training. Sample sizes were 45–50 for the experimental groups and 25–30 for the controls. The principal measure was the Bills Index of Adjustment and Values (a checklist of 40 descriptive adjectives). It was completed by each subject for each of three sets: *(a)* "This is most characteristic of me," *(b)* "I would like this to be most characteristic of me," and *(c)* "Most CCNY students my age would like this to be characteristic of them." As in this previous study, members of the experimental groups reduced their discrepancies between actual and ideal self-descriptions. They also tended to see themselves as being more similar to the average student. However, the control groups showed similar changes, and there were no differences between the two groups on the postmeasures.

Although tangential to the present review because the training group was not really a T-group, a study by Grater (1959) also used the Bills Index of Adjustment and Values to obtain descriptions of "real self," "ideal self," and "average group member" before and after a 22-session leadership-training course. The trainer attempted to keep interpersonal evaluation to a minimum, and discussion of emotional reactions was avoided. The group discussion focused mostly on leadership problems the participants had faced in the past and, to a lesser degree, on behavior shown in the group situation. However, a climate of psychological safety was consciously emphasized. Even though this training experience lacked many of the elements of a T-group, results similar to those of Burke and Bennis (1961) were obtained. That is, self-perceived discrepancies between real self and ideal self were significantly reduced over the course of training (due primarily to changes in descriptions of the real self), and differences between descriptions of the ideal self and the average group member were reduced, but not significantly so.

However, even with a bona fide T-group, significant changes in the self-image are not always found. The Bennis et al. (1957) study was carried out on 12 business-administration students participating in a semester-long T-group, and changes in perceptions of actual self and ideal self were assessed by means of a 34-item inventory of possible role behaviors. The items were culled from a wide variety of sources and represented such role behaviors as, "tries hard to understand the contributions of others . . . ," "uses group setting to express nongroup oriented feelings . . . ," etc. The subjects rated each of the possible role behaviors on a seven-point scale according to how descriptive they felt it was of their real or ideal self. Over the course of the T-group, there was no significant change in the discrepancy between actual and ideal self-descriptions. However, the authors pointed out that the study was intended to be exploratory, and only 12 subjects were used.

A study by Stock (1964) serves to muddy the waters a bit more. On the basis of her own data, she suggested that individuals who change the most in terms of their self-percept actually become more variable and seem less sure of what kinds of people they really are. Again, however, no control group was employed.

Bass (1962a) asked 30 trainees participating in a 10-day T-group laboratory to describe their mood at five different times during the training period. They did this by indicating on a four-point scale how well each of 27 adjectives (previously selected to reflect nine different moods such as pleasantness, anxiety, etc.) fit their feelings. Four of nine mood factors showed statistically significant trends. Skepticism decreased, throughout the period, concentration increased initially and then declined, depression increased initially and then declined, and activation decreased, went up, and then came down again. Contrary to Bass' expectations, very little anxiety was expressed at any time, and it showed no significant trend either up or down over the period of the training.

In summary it seems relatively well established that the way in which an individual sees himself may indeed change during the course of a T-group. However, there is no firm evidence indicating that such changes are produced by T-group training as compared with other types of training, merely by the passage of time, or even by the simple expedient of retaking a self-descriptive inventory after a period of thinking about one's previous responses to the same inventory.

Interpersonal Sensitivity

Relative to a somewhat different type of criterion measure, a major aim of the T-group method is to increase skill and accuracy in interpersonal perception, in addition to increasing the clarity of self-perceptions. In spite of the complex measurement problems involved, several studies have attempted to assess how a T-group affects the accuracy of interpersonal perception.

In the Bennis et al. (1957) study cited above, a measure of "social sensitivity" was derived by first computing the discrepancy between an individual's prediction of another subject's response and the subject's actual response. For each individual the discrepancies were then summed over all the items and all the other group members. While there was a slight tendency for the accurate predictors to be predicted more accurately themselves, no changes occurred in this measure over the course of the T-group.

Gage and Exline (1953) also attempted to assess how well T-group participants could predict the questionnaire responses of the other group members. Two NTL groups of 15 and 18 persons, respectively, responded to a 50-item questionnaire before and after a three-week laboratory. The items were opinion statements concerning group processes, leadership styles, the scientific study of human relations, and so on. To control for the effects of taking the same items twice, two 50-item forms judged to be "equivalent" by the researchers were administered before and after. The subjects were asked to give their own opinions and also to predict how they thought the group as a whole would respond. An accuracy score for each person was obtained by correlating his predictions on each of the 50 items with the group's composite response on each of the items. Thus, each correlation, or accuracy index, was based on an N of 50. In addition to the accuracy measure, a "similarity" index was obtained by correlating the actual responses of each subject with the group response. The actual responses of the subjects were also correlated with their predictions of the group response to yield a measure of "assumed similarity." None of these three indexes changed significantly over the course of the training.

Lohman, Zenger, and Weschler (1959) gave the Gordon Personal Profile to 65 students at UCLA before and after their participation in semester-long courses using T-groups. The students filled out the inventory themselves and for how they thought the trainer did. There was a slight increase in the degree of agreement between students' predictions and the trainer's responses, but, as has been seen, this could be due to any number of different prediction strategies. Fortunately, Lohman et al. placed little emphasis on the finding. No change occurred in the students' self-descriptions. No control group was used, and no attempt was made to account for the effects of taking the same items twice. In sum, the studies incorporating a measure of how well an individual can predict the attitudes and values of others before and after T-group training have yielded largely negative results.

In his report of a laboratory program conducted by Argyris, Harrison (1962) found that T-group participants (19 middle and top managers) used a larger number of interpersonal terms in describing others than did 12 control-group managers selected from the same organizational levels. However, the trained managers did this only when they were describing individuals who had been in the T-group.

In a later study employing a larger sample ($N =$ 115) but no control group, Harrison (1966) used a modified version of Kelly's Role Construct Repertory Test to secure self-descriptions and descriptions of 10 associates before, three weeks after, and three months after participation in NTL training. The modified form of the Kelly test asks the describer to respond to triads of individuals by selecting a word or phrase that discriminates one member of the triad from the other two and then to give its opposite. The concepts used by the subjects were coded into two categories: *(a)* concrete-instrumental, and *(b)* inferential-expressive. The former included such bipolar terms as man-woman, has power-has little power, and knows his job-incompetent. Some examples from the latter category are: afraid of people-confident, tries to get personal-formal and correct, and warm-cold. Interrater agreement for coding terms was 94 percent and 83 percent of the bipolar terms used by the subjects were classified into one of the two categories, 29 percent as concrete-instrumental and 54 percent as inferential-expressive. In sharp contrast to the usual finding of an effect shortly after training with a subsequent drop.off over time, Harrison found significant increases in the frequency of subjects' use of interpersonal concepts to describe associates three months after training, but no short-term (three-week) differences.

Oshry and Harrison (1966) asked 46 middle managers to evaluate some possible causes of unresolved interpersonal work problems, and the resources available for dealing with them, before and after they participated in a two-week NTL program. The problems were actual situations faced by the subjects in their back home work situation. The subjects were given a standard set of 45 items which listed a number of antecedent causes and possible ways of dealing with such problems. According to Oshry and Harrison, the managers, after training, viewed their work as more "human" and less impersonal, and they saw more distinct connections between getting work done and the satisfaction of interpersonal needs than before training. Moreover, after training the managers tended more often to see themselves as the most significant cause or contributor to their own work problems, but they failed to see how these new views of problem causes could be translated into managerial action.

In a similar study, Bass (1962b) showed the film *Twelve Angry Men* to 34 executives before and after two weeks of T-group training. The subjects were asked to finish a series of incomplete sentences describing the behavior of the characters portrayed in the film. Bass concluded that the training resulted in participants becoming more sensitive to the interpersonal relationships exhibited in the film. Although no control group was used, two other groups of trainees were shown the film only after training in order to assess possible effects of seeing the film twice. All groups responded similarly on the post-training questionnaire, suggesting that the increased sensitivity to interpersonal relations was due to the training and not merely to seeing the film twice.

Stock (1964) discussed an unpublished study by Miles, Cohen, and Whitam in which participants were asked at various stages during T-group training to rank 10 statements describing the trainer's behavior and to complete a questionnaire about group interactions. Responses were compared to the trainer's diagnosis of the group's difficulties. Some change seemed to occur on a variable labeled "sensitivity to feelings," but other results were negligible or uninterpretable because no control group was available for comparison. Few details were given.

Finally, in another study without a control group, Clark and Culbert (1965) analyzed the content of nine college students' verbailzations when interviewed before and after participating in a T-group as part of a course requirement. Clark and Culbert concluded that four of the nine subjects were better perceivers of group processes at the end of the training than they had been at the beginning.

In contrast to the negative findings regarding perceptual accuracy scores, the six studies cited above establish fairly well that people who have been through a T-group describe other people and situations in more interpersonal terms. However, there is still the more important question of whether this finding actually represents increased sensitization to interpersonal events or merely the acquisition of a new vocabulary.

Attitude Change

Turning to another type of internal criterion, the authors were surprised to find relatively few studies relating T-group experiences to attitude changes. This is in contrast to recent reviews of other areas of management-development research (J. P. Campbell, 1966; Miner, 1965) which have shown a rather heavy reliance on attitude measures as criteria. P. B. Smith (1964), Schutz and Allen (1966), and Baumgartel and Goldstein (1967) used the Fundamental Interpersonal Relations Orientation-Behavior questionnaire (FIRO-B; Schutz, 1958) as the primary dependent variable to assess the impact of T-group training. FIRO-B includes a series of attitude items designed to measure six relatively homogeneous dimensions related to three major types of an individual's behavior in groups: control (i.e., attempting to influence the proceedings), inclusion (i.e., initiating contacts with others in a group), and affection (i.e., moving toward others in a close and personal way). The questionnaire contains a pair of scales for each behavior category: one to assess the respondent's own tendency or desire to show the behavior, and the other to assess how much he wants others in the group to show it.

Using only the four scales measuring attitudes toward affection and control, P. B. Smith (1964) obtained responses from 108 English managers and students before and after they had been trained in T-groups (11 groups in all) and compared them with responses obtained from a control group of 44 students (six groups in all) who merely took part in a series of discussions. The overall disparity between one's own behavioral tendencies and that desired in others decreased for the T-group trainees, but showed no change for those in the control group. The largest changes occurred for those who initially showed strong control and weak affection tendencies and who desired low control and high affection from others in the groups. These changes are consonant with the aims of the T-group method.

Schutz and Allen (1966) used FIRO-B to study possible attitude changes among 71 persons of widely varied backgrounds who participated in a Western Training Laboratories sensitivity program. Thirty students in an education class at the University of California (Berkeley) were used as a control group. FIRO-B was administered before training, immediately after the two-week session, and again by mail six months after the session had been completed. Correlations between pre- and posttest scores for the various FIRO-B scales were much lower for the experimental group than for the control group, indicating that the training induced greater changes in the attitudes measured by FIRO-B. The lowest correlations on all six scales (i.e., most change) were obtained between the pretest and six-month posttest scores obtained by the trainee group. This outcome reinforces Harrison's results showing that T-group effects may be manifested only after some time. Unfortunately, the investigators did not report the specific nature or direction of the changes occurring on the various scales of the FIRO-B.

Baumgartel and Goldstein (1967) also used FIRO-B as a criterion measure, in addition to the Allport-Vernon-Lindzey Study of Values (Allport, Vernon, & Lindzey, 1960). Subjects were 100 students (59 male, 41 female) in five sections of a semester-long human-relations course (including T-group experiences) conducted at the University of Kansas. The two criterion instruments were administered pre and post, and the results were analyzed for males versus females and for high-valued versus low-valued participants identified by peer nominations. The data for the latter dichotomy were gathered at the conclusion of the course. No control group was used. The researchers predicted changes in the direction of more expressed control, lower religious values, and higher political values—especially for the participants who were seen as high valued by their peers. Only the prediction for the religious scale was supported; however, there were a number of significant results not predicted by the investigators. Overall, there was a significant increase in wanted control and a significant decrease in wanted affection. Most of the changes could be attributed to the high-valued females and low-valued males. The statistical significance of these interactions was not subjected to a direct test; however, the implication is clear that taking account of individual differences is a necessity when evaluating the effects of such training experiences.

The Baumgartel and Goldstein (1967) study illustrates another serious difficulty in evaluating T-group research. In a large number of the studies cited in this review the training program presented the T-group in conjunction with other learning experiences such as reading assignments, lectures, simulated problem exercises, and the like. Thus, it is difficult to attribute any positive or negative results, unequivocally to the influence of the T-group, although this is often the implication given by investigators. The difficulty is compounded by descriptions of training programs which are usually so incomplete as to preclude any careful assessment of the role played by these other methods.

An attitude measure derived from the goals of the Management Grid program was used by Blake and Mouton (1966) to assess changes in union and management attitudes toward supervisory practices. Only the first phase (the part most analogous to a T-group) of the grid program was evaluated, and the researchers' attention was concentrated on changes in attitudes toward five "distinct" managerial styles: maximum concern for both production and people (9,9), minimum concern for both production and people (1,1), maximum concern for production and minimum concern for people (9,1), maximum concern for people and minimum concern for production (1,9), and a moderate but balanced concern for both production and people (5,5). The criterion measure consisted of 40 attitude items in a forced-choice format. Each item presented a pair of statements describing how subordinates could be used in a production setting to solve a problem in supervision. Each statement of the pair represented one of the five management styles, and each style was paired with every other style a total of four times. The respondent was instructed not to indicate which of the two alternatives he preferred, but rather to distribute a total of three points between the two alternatives according to his preference. The inventory was given before and after identical grid programs conducted for 33 management personnel and 23 union representatives, all of whom had management or staff responsibilities within the local. The analysis consisted of examining mean scores on all the alternatives pertaining to a particular management style. Significant differences in the predicted directions were obtained between the two groups on the pretest. Managers scored higher than union members on the styles with a high production orientation and lower on those with a low production orientation. No initial differences were found on the 5,5 style. Relative to the before and after comparisons, the managers tended to exhibit more shifts than the union personnel although both groups tended to move in the same direction. The management group increased on 9,9 (the largest difference), decreased on 5,5, and decreased on 1,9. The differences for the other two styles were not significant. Union members increased on 9,1 and decreased on 1,9.

While these results are encouraging, several problems remain. There were no comparison groups, and the strong possibility that any one of a number of other human-relations training methods would produce similar results cannot be entirely discounted. Also, the items appeared to be geared to the stated goals and content of the training program. Thus, the "correct" answer was apparent to the respondent, and a positive response bias may have been elicited which would account for the results.

Kernan (1964) used the Leadership Opinion Questionnaire (LOQ—Fleishman, Harris, & Burtt, 1955) to study possible attitude changes resulting from T-group training. The LOQ yields scores labeled "Consideration" and "Initiating Structure," corresponding roughly to a concern for employee human relations and a concern for getting the work out. It was administered before and after a three-day laboratory-training program conducted within a single organization. Experimental and control groups consisted of 40 and 20 engineering supervisors, respectively. No significant before-after differences were obtained for either group on either of the scales of the LOQ.

In contrast, significant before and after differences were found on the LOQ in the previously cited study by Beer and Kleisath (1967). Recall, however, that no control group was used.

Finally, Kassarjian (1965) attempted to assess changes in inner- versus other-directedness in four student and six adult extension T-groups ($N = 125$) and observed no significant differences. His criterion measure was a 36-item forced-choice inventory, which had yielded predicted relationships with other variables in previous research. The items, generated from Riesman's formulations (Riesman, Glazer, & Denny, 1950), yielded a test-retest reliability of 0.85 and on previous occasions had discriminated significantly (and in the expected direction) between foreign-born and native-born United States citizens, urban and rural groups, occupational categories, and age groups. In addition, the inventory yielded significant and expected correlations with the Allport-Vernon-Lindzey Study of Values. Control groups ($N = 55$) similar in composition to the experimental groups were also used, and no significant differences were observed.

Again, the scarcity of research relating laboratory education to attitude change is disappointing and rather hard to understand.

Personality Change

An internal criterion, which so far has yielded completely negative results, is the standardized personality measure. Massarik and Carlson (cited in Dunnette, 1962) administered the CPI (Gough, 1957) before and after a relatively long sensitivity-training course conducted with a group of students ($N = 70$) at UCLA. No significant changes were observed. Kernan (1964) also administered the *F* scale (Adorno, Frenkel-Brunswik, Levinson & Sanford, 1950) before and after the three-day T-group laboratory. Again, no significant differences were obtained between scores before and after training for the 40 engineering supervisors. However, as the authors of both these studies are quick to point out, changes in such basic personality variables may be just too much to expect from such a relatively short experience, even if the T-group is a "good" one.

Simulations

The last class of criteria to be considered is the situational test or artificial task which is intended to simulate job activities or job behavior. Performance in a business game or on a case problem is an example of this kind of dependent variable.

Bass (1967) used the Carnegie Institute of Technology Management Game (Cohen, Dill, Kuehn, & Winters, 1964) to study the effects of T-group training on the simulated managerial behavior of a number of University of Pittsburg graduate students in business administration. The Carnegie Tech game is extremely complex and is designed to simulate the activities of several firms in a multiproduct industry. A number of students compose each firm, and they must interact effectively if the company is to prosper. Nine T-groups (without trainers) met for 15 weeks. At the end of the 15 weeks three of the groups were divided into thirds and reformed into three new groups, three of the groups were split in half and reassembled, and three of the nine groups remained intact. The nine teams then competed with one another in the game. The splintered groups broke even or made a profit, but the intact groups lost an average of $5.37 million over the 15-week trial period even though the intact groups gave the most positive descriptions of their openness, communication, and cooperation. On the basis of his own subjective observation, Bass attributed the lower performance of the intact groups to their neglect of the management-control function. In his opinion, the members of the intact groups never bothered to ask each other if they were carrying out their respective assignments. These results are somewhat difficult to assimilate into an evaluation of the T-group experience *per se* since both the splinter and intact groups had identical training. However, the study does demonstrate the danger of assuming relatively straightforward transfer from the T-group to another setting.

Argyris (1965) used a case discussion as a situational task and then attempted to measure, via observational techniques, the changes in interpersonal competence over the course of a laboratory program conducted for executives in a university setting. On the basis of previous work, an extremely complex method for content analyzing sound tape recordings of group sessions was developed such that scores on various dimensions of interpersonal competence could be assigned to each individual. The dimensions were originally derived by rationally grouping discrete individual verbalizations and were given such labels as "owning up versus not owning up," "experimenting versus rejecting experimentation," "helping others to be open versus not helping others be open," etc. Certain logically defined group norms such as trust versus conformity are also scored. The dimensions are all bipolar, and rationally assigned integers carrying pluses and minuses are used to represent magnitude. Behaviors are also categorized according to their expression of cognitive ideas versus feelings, and the feelings component is given much greater weight. Case discussions were scored before and after the T-group experience, which was part of a six-week "living-in" executive development program. There were 57 managers in the experimental group and 56 in the control group. In general, the results were mixed and fell short of what the author considered to be success. As reflected in the content analysis, the norms which evolved in the experimental groups seemed to reflect greater overall competence than the controls. However, differences on the individual dimensions were much more difficult to interpret and seemed to offer no clear pattern. One frustrating aspect of the article is that the nature of the difference between the experimental and control groups is never actually described. Such an oversight was obviously unintentional, and the joint probability of such an error by both author and editor must be fantastically small; however, the effect is to leave the definition of experimental and control to the interpretive powers of the reader.

There are, of course, many other studies purporting to evaluate the effectiveness of laboratory training by using trainee opinion gathered at the conclusion of the training program. Almost without exception such studies are favorable. However, in the absense of at least a control group or before and after measures, such studies are not reviewed here.

INDIVIDUAL DIFFERENCES

So far research focused on the "average" effects of T-group or laboratory training has been considered. That is, the crucial question has been whether or not the training makes a difference for the group as a whole. Such a generalized interpretation may cover up important interactions between individual differences and training methods. Given a particular kind of outcome, certain kinds of people may benefit from T-group training while others may actually be harmed. The same reasoning may be applied to the interaction of differences in situational and organizational variables with the training experience. However, very few studies have investigated interactive effects.

The previously mentioned study by Bennis et al. (1957) used standardized personality measures to make differential predictions about the possible influences of T-group training. The personality measures included Cattell's 16 PF, the EPPS, and Harrington's Self-Sort Test. Schutz' FIRO-B was also administered. Relationships between these variables and the perceptual data were negligible.

Essentially negative results were also found by Steele (in press) who used the Sensation-Intuition (S-N) scale from the Myers-Briggs Type Indicator (Myers, 1962) to predict changes for 72 participants in an NTL program, 39 middle managers in a two-week Managerial Grid laboratory, and 45 students in a course employing a T-group. The S-N scale is conceptualized as measuring a preference for basic modes of perceiving or becoming aware of the world, with the sensation end of the scale corresponding to preferences for facts, realism, practicality, and thoroughness, while intuition represents preferences for multiple causation, abstractness, experimentation with stimuli, and a chance to generate individualistic ideas and association about stimuli.

The criteria were trainer ratings and a questionnaire consisting of seven open-ended items designed to measure interpersonal values by posing a hypothetical conflict situation and asking for a course of action. In general, the S-N scale was related to the value orientation of the participants and to their general style of group behavior, as rated by the trainer. However, it was not related to changes on any of these variables.

Still in the personality realm, Mathis (1958) developed an index of T-group trainability using a sentence-completion format. From the theories of group development formulated by Bion (1959) and Lewin (1947), he reasoned that the existence of intrapersonal conflicts and tendencies toward the open communication of both agression and affection would signify greater receptivity to the training, and the sentence-completion scale was scored to reflect these factors. The scale was then administered to 50 people at the beginning of a T-group, and the 10 highest and 10 lowest scorers were interviewed at the conclusion of the sessions. The individuals scoring high on the trainability index were rated higher on sensitivity, sophistication, and productivity. Again, it must be remembered that these ratings were based on what the subject said in an interview immediately following the T-group program. There was no control group and no interviews before training.

Finally, Harrison and Lubin (1965) divided 69 people in a 1962 Western Training Laboratories program into two categories based on their orientations toward people versus tasks expressed via a questionnaire. Judgments of learning during training were made by the trainers. The investigators concluded that while the person-oriented members were more expressive, warm, and comfortable the task- or work-oriented members learned the most over the course of the laboratory program. However, the authors did not report if the work-oriented participants were still judged to be less effective than the person-oriented individuals, in spite of what they had learned, or were equal or superior to the person-oriented group after training. They were only "observed" to exhibit more "change." The data are quite subjective.

T-GROUP TECHNOLOGY

Research concerning the relative contributions of specific technological features of the T-group is also sparse. For example, there are no systematic studies examining the influence of differences in trainer personality and/or style on the outcomes achieved by participants. Case reports and anecdotal evidence are all that exist.

Stock (1964) reported a number of studies focusing on differences in group composition as an independent variable; however, the dependent variable usually consisted of observations of the type of behavior going on in the group. No studies were found designed to relate differences in group composition to differences on either external or internal criterion measures. The authors do not mean to imply that descriptions of the behavior emitted in the group are not of considerable interest; they are simply not the focus of this review.

Feedback is one of the few T-group elements that has been examined empirically, but the evidence from two unpublished studies reported in Stock (1964) is equivocal. Both evaluated effectiveness of T-group feedback indirectly by observing the effects of providing additional feedback at the completion of the T-group experience. Large effects from additional feedback would imply that T-group feedback was not sufficient. Lippitt selected 14 pairs of individuals from two different T-groups. The members of each pair were described in similar fashion by the other members of their group. One person of each pair was told in a counseling interview what the other group members thought of him and how they would like him to change. Trained observers rated the behavior of all the T-group members before and after the additional feedback was given. Thirteen of the 14 counseled subjects changed in the desired direction, but only eight of the non-counseled individuals changed in the desired direction. This would appear to be negative evidence for the sufficiency of T-group feedback.

In contrast, Roberts, Schopler, Smith, and Gibb studied 26 small problem-solving groups composed of college students. Twelve of the groups had T-group experience and 14 had not. Half of the trained and untrained groups received only "feelings" oriented feedback, and the other half received only "task" oriented feedback. In general, the feelings-oriented feedback increased the efficiency and decreased the defensiveness of problem-solving behavior more in the untrained groups than in the trained groups. This was interpreted as positive evidence for the utility of T-group-type feedback.

A more recent study (French, Sherwood, & Bradford, 1966) also tends to argue for the insufficiency of T-group feedback. Twenty middle managers from a large organization participating in a two-week laboratory program were asked, at the outset, to rate themselves on 19 bipolar scales (e.g., reserved versus talkative). Each subject then chose the four scales on which he wanted to change most. All 19 scales were readministered five times over the two-week training period and again 10 months after the completion of training. The experimental manipulation consisted of four different levels of additional feedback ranging from Level A—being rated on one of the four salient scales by all other group members, being told the results of the rating, and discussing it with two other group members—through Levels B and C—which omitted discussion of the rating and feedback of the rating, respectively—to Level D—where the subject was asked to focus on one of the four scales, but other group members did not rate him nor was there any discussion of the scale. In a fifth condition (Level E) none of the four originally chosen scales was selected for attention and no feedback was given. Thus, for Level E, changes were measured on the 15 scales not originally chosen as important by an individual. Although it is not very clearly specified, the sample size for each treatment condition was apparently 20; that is, all the subjects received every treatment condition, but for a different scale. Feedback Levels A, B, and C produced greater changes in the self-ratings than Levels D and E for the selected scale, and this difference was statistically significant. This outcome (like Lippitt's results) may be interpreted as demonstrating the insufficiency of purely T-group feedback. But the results also seem rather obvious because they are based on self-ratings of "change" instead of behavior observations of others as in the Lippitt study.

Finally, some of the problems involved in the transfer of T-group skills back to the work role are illustrated in a quasi case study by Wagner (1965). A nine-member T-group composed of managers from different organizations played the UCLA Executive Decision Game No. 2 immediately following a four-day sensitivity-training laboratory. At the end of each business "quarter" the participants were asked to rate the adequacy of the group's decision processes and the extent to which various individuals helped or hindered decision making. During the first quarter of the game, considerable regression from T-group norms took place. After this was pointed out to the group members, they apparently overcompensated during the second quarter by becoming overly conscious of interpersonal factors. Only a second critique session in which regression and overcompensation were both discussed did the group seem to make efficient use of its T-group skills. Wagner freely pointed out the many qualifications that must be appended to conclusions drawn from such a study.

SUMMARY AND CONCLUSIONS

Argyris (1964) has commented that probably more research has been conducted on the effects of the T-group method than on any other specific management-development technique. A comparison of the present paper with a recent review of evaluation research on all types of management-development methods (J. P. Campbell, 1966) supports the validity of Argyris' statement. Thirty-seven of the 44 studies cited in the present review were focused on evaluating the outcomes of T-groups. Of these 37, the majority (23) used internal criteria. Based on the results of these studies, the following comments seem warranted:

1. The evidence, though limited, is reasonably convincing that T-group training does induce behavioral changes in the "back home" setting. This statement is based primarily on results from the first five studies reviewed. However, the subjective probability estimate of the truth of this generalization is not 1.00 because of the confounding elements already discussed, namely, the manner of choosing control groups, and the fact that most observers probably knew who had or had not received the T-group experience.

The $N = 1$ studies can contribute very little to any general conclusions. Their lack of control, zero degrees of freedom, and susceptibility to contaminating influences such as the Hawthorne effect cast considerable doubt on the utility of their results.

Given the fact of actual behavioral changes attributable to the T-group method, there remains the vexing problem of specifying the nature of these changes. Here the data are even less conclusive. Several researchers (e.g., Boyd & Elliss, 1962; Bunker, 1965) strongly resisted discussing the nature of any "typical" training effect; they implied that each trainee's pattern of change on various behavioral dimensions is unique. If this is true, the present lack of knowledge about how individual difference variables interact with training-program variables makes it nearly impossible for anyone to spell out ahead of time the outcomes to be expected from any given development program. That is, if training outcomes are truly unique and unpredictable, no basis exists for judging the potential worth of T-group training from an institutional or organizational point of view. Instead, its success or failure must be judged by each individual trainee in terms of his own personal goals.

However, in spite of this strong focus on uniqueness, it is true that group differences have been obtained which seem to be compatible with some of the major objectives of laboratory training.

Still another problem in evaluating the back home changes is that the perceived-change measures have not usually related observed changes to actual job effectiveness. Observers have been asked to report changes in behavior, not changes in performance. The only study to attack this problem directly was Underwood's (1965). His results lead to the suggestion that while laboratory training seems to produce more actual changes than the simple passage of time the relative proportion of changes detrimental to performance is also higher for the laboratory method.

2. Results with internal criteria are more numerous but even less conclusive. For example, evidence concerning changes in self-perceptions remains equivocal. It still cannot be said with any certainty whether T-groups lead to greater or lesser changes in self-perceptions than other types of group experience, the simple passage of time, or the mere act of filling out a self-description questionnaire.

The special problems of measuring changes in sensitivity and accuracy of interpersonal perception have already been touched upon. People who have been in a T-group do apparently use more interpersonally oriented words to describe certain situations, but this says nothing about their general level of "sensitivity" or the relative accuracy of their interpersonal perceptions.

Again, the authors lament the small number of studies using well-researched attitude measures and/or situational measures as criteria. If such criteria were more widely used, one might have a clearer idea of exactly what kinds of attitudes and skills are fostered by laboratory education. As it is, no conclusions can be drawn. The P. B. Smith (1964) and Schutz and Allen (1966) studies using FIRO-B are suggestive of positive effects, but the studies by Kernan (1964) and Beer and Kleisath (1967) using the LOQ yielded mixed results. Bass' (1967) use of a simulated exercise has rather negative implications.

NEEDED RESEARCH APPROACHES

Since the research results for both external and internal criteria tend to be equivocal, one might properly speculate on how research *should* proceed if one is to gain a better understanding of what the effects of T-group training are. Only with such an understanding can one judge the relative worth of T-group training as a personnel development technique. Hopefully, future research will take into account at least seven major considerations:

1. Researchers must devote more effort to specifying the behavioral outcomes they expect to observe as a result of T-group training. The specifications should include the kinds of situations in which the behavior will or will not be exhibited. The loophole of being able to explain either behavior change or lack of change as supportive of the training method must be avoided.

2. More measures of individual differences must be incorporated in future T-group studies. Quite simply, the question is, for what kinds of people are particular training effects observed? Initially, most current researchers seem to act as if laboratory training should have similar effects for everyone. However, this seems hardly likely, and considerably more effort must be expended toward mapping the relevant interactions with individual differences. Only then can investigators avoid the embarrassment of having to conclude that the effects of the learning experience were unpredictably "unique."

3. More attention must be given to interactions between organizational characteristics, leadership climates, organizational goals, and training outcomes and effects. Obviously, the things learned in a development program are not transferred to a vacuum.

4. The effects of T-group training should be compared more fully with the behavioral effects stemming from other training methods. Perhaps the same behavioral objectives can be realized at less cost to the individual and to the organization by using different methods. Research results specifying the conditions when T-group training should be used and when other methods should be used are needed.

5. A corollary to the above is the need to explore the *interaction* of T-group training and other learning experiences. This has immediate relevance because of the frequent practice of combining the T-group with other methods in a laboratory program. The only investigation dealing with such an interaction is Bunker's recent reanalysis of his original data obtained from the 1960 and 1961 Bethel laboratories (Bunker & Knowles, 1967). Between these two sets of summer programs, the total length of the laboratory was reduced from three to two weeks. However, the total time devoted to T-group sessions remained almost constant, while the cutback was at the expense of theory sessions, lectures, and problem exercises. Taking advantage of this built-in difference, Bunker and Knowles compared the per-

ceived-change scores (described earlier) for 52 people in the three-week laboratories and 101 people in the two-week laboratories. On both the total change score and the verified change score the three-week group was significantly superior to the two-week group. The two-week group fell about midway between the three-week group and the control group on the total change index. Bunker and Knowles argued that these results illustrate the necessity of providing additional transfer-facilitating experiences so as to take full advantage of the T-group's power. Adopting a different view, one might also argue that it is these other learning experiences which are producing the changes, not the T-group. Also, as Bunker and Knowles pointed out, there may have been systematic pretraining differences between the groups since there was no random assignment of subjects. Only further research can decide among these alternatives.

6. It is imperative that the relative contributions of various technological elements in the T-group method be more fully understood. It is surprising indeed that essentially no research has been done on the differential effects of changes in the trainer role, in spite of frequent allusions in the literature to the crucial role played in a T-group by the trainer's behavior. Questions concerning the optimal procedures for giving feedback, for enhancing feelings of psychological safety, and for stimulating individuals to try new behaviors should also be investigated. In addition, Schein and Bennis (1965, p. 312) pointed to the necessity of studying the effects of variation in such parameters as the total amount of time the participants spend in the T-group, how the total time is distributed, the degree of the laboratory's isolation, and the nature of the participant population. The array of variants in these technological features seems endless, but this should serve to stimulate rather than to inhibit research. At present, the development of new and different training designs seems to be based on a total lack of research evidence.

7. Finally, more effort should be directed toward forging the link between training-induced behavior changes and changes in job-performance effectiveness. Perceived-change measures as they have been used stop far short of this goal. In trying to define the link between job behavior and job effectiveness, researchers will need to make much more use of a wider variety of internal criterion measures flowing directly from the behavioral objectives of the T-group method.

Once again, one should emphasize that neither internal nor external measures are the more "important." Considerable research is needed on both; most important, the relationships between changes in internal criteria and changes in external criteria must be investigated thoroughly. For example, if a T-group produces a change in interpersonal sensitivity, will the change be accompanied by improved performance in certain job dimensions or will it not? Is a particular attitude change induced by the laboratory method related to an increase or decrease in job effectiveness or is it entirely independent of performance? These, and others like them, are the crucial "payoff" questions in this whole area of research. So far, the literature offers only one example of an effort to link these two classes of criteria. In a study already cited, Miles (1965) reported that judgments by trainers of the degree of learning shown by participants correlated 0.55 with the degree of change observed back in their job situations. However, the trainees' own judgments made at the conclusion of the training period were not related to the amount of change their observers reported. Such a finding suggests that self-insight was not achieved and was not, therefore, the mediator of the observed behavior changes.

To sum up, the assumption that T-group training has positive utility for organizations must necessarily rest on shaky ground. It has been neither confirmed nor disconfirmed. The authors wish to emphasize again that utility for the organization is not necessarily the same as utility for the individual.

It should also be strongly emphasized that many if not all the points leading to the above statement can be applied equally to other methods of management development. The entire field suffers from a lack of research attention. However, the objectives of the T-group method are considerably more far reaching than other techniques, and the types of behavior changes desired are, by their very nature, more difficult to observe and measure. These two features serve to place greater research demands on the T-group method than on other techniques dealing with more restricted, and perhaps less important, behavior domains. For the time being, the T group must remain a very interesting and challenging research area, which is where the energies of its proponents should be applied.

AN ADDENDUM

In the opinion of the present authors, one cannot come away from an examination of the T-group literature without a strong impression of its humanistic and sometimes existential flavor, even when the intended focus is the development of individuals in their organizational roles. This impression is fostered by a sometimes heavy reliance on anecdotal evidence (e.g., Argyris, 1962, 1964; Blake & Mouton, 1963; Foundation for Research on Human Behavior, 1960) by the emphasis often placed on purely personal development (Bugental & Tannenbaum, 1963), and by explicit attempts to conceptualize T-group learning in an existential framework (Hampden-Turner, 1966). To practitioners with this sort of bias, the present treatment of the research literature probably seems unduly mechanistic and sterile.

There are at least two possible replies to the perceived sterility of controlled systematic research. On the one hand, it is an unfortunate fact of scientific life that the reduction of ambiguity in behavioral data to tolerable levels demands systematic observations, measurement, and control. Often the unwanted result seems to be a dehumanization of the behavior being studied. That is, achieving unambiguous results may generate dependent variables that are somewhat removed from the original objectives of the development program and seem, thereby, to lack relevant content. This is not an unfamiliar problem in psychological research. As always, the constructive solution is to increase the effort and ingenuity devoted to developing criteria that are *both* meaningful and amenable to controlled observation and measurement. Such a solution must be found if T-group research is ever to contribute to an understanding of human behavior or eventually establish scientifically the utility of laboratory education as a training and development device. In this respect, people doing research on T-group effects deserve considerable encouragement and, because of the many difficulties involved, a great deal of sympathy.

On the other hand, negative feelings about the sterility of research results may reflect a rejection of both the scientific and organizational points of view. That is, it may be argued that the crucial factor in T-group training is how each *individual* feels at the end of the training program, and that investigating hypotheses concerning human behavior or assessing performance change is of little consequence. This view is quite legitimate so long as the T-group assumes a status similar to that enjoyed by other purely individual events such as aesthetic appreciation or recreational enjoyment—events from which each individual takes what he chooses. These are events to be experienced for their own sake, and the individual decides whether they are "life enhancing" or not.

The danger in all of this is that the scientific and existential orientations may not be kept distinct. Argyris (1967) and Bass (1967) argued strongly that the distinction has become blurred at a number of key points, to the detriment of laboratory education. The present authors' view is that a normative or scientific orientation definitely cannot be used to argue against an individual's positive feelings about his own experiences in a T-group, and it is hoped that any such connotation has been avoided. However, it is equally inappropriate to claim that a program has utility for accomplishing organizational goals and then to justify such a statement on existential grounds.[3]

REFERENCES

Adorno, T. W., Frenkel-Brunswik, E., Levinson, D. J., and Sanford, R. M. *The authoritarian personality.* New York: Harper, 1950.

Allport G. W., Vernon, P. E., and Lindzey, G. *Manual study of values.* 3d ed. Boston: Houghton-Mifflin, 1960.

Argyris, C. *Interpersonal competence and organizational behavior.* Homewood, Ill.: Irwin, 1962.

Argyris, C. T-groups for organizational effectiveness. *Harvard Business Review,* 1964, **42**(2), 60–74.

Argyris, C. Explorations in interpersonal competence—II. *Journal of Applied Behavioral Science,* 1965, **1**, 255–69.

Argyris, C. On the future of laboratory education. *Journal of Applied Behavioral Science,* 1967, **3**, 153–82.

Bass, B. M. Mood changes during a management training laboratory. *Journal of Applied Psychology,* 1962, **46**, 361–64. (a)

Bass, B. M. Reactions to *Twelve angry men* as a measure of sensitivity training. *Journal of Applied Psychology,* 1962, **46**, 120–24. (b)

Bass, B. M. The anarchist movement and the T-group. *Journal of Applied Behavioral Science,* 1967, **3**, 211–26.

Baumgartel, H. and Goldstein, J. W. Need and value shifts in college training groups. *Journal of Applied Behavioral Science,* 1967, **3**, 87–101.

Beer, M. and Kleisath, S. W. The effects of the Managerial Grid lab on organizational and leadership dimensions. In S. S. Zalkind (Chm.), Research on the impact of using different laboratory methods for interpersonal and organizational change. Symposium presented at the meeting of the American Psychological Association, Washington, D.C., September 1967.

Benne, K. D. History of the T-group in the laboratory setting. In L. D. Bradford, J. R. Gibb and K. D. Benne (eds.), *T-group theory and laboratory method.* New York: Wiley, 1964.

Bennis, W., Burke, R., Cutter, H., Harrington, H., and Hoffman, J. A note on some problems of measurement and prediction in a training group. *Group Psychotherapy,* 1957, **10**, 328–41.

Berzon, B. and Solomon, L. N. Research frontier: The self-directed therapeutic group—three studies. *Journal of Counseling Psychology,* 1966, **13**, 491–97.

Bion, W. R. *Experiences in groups.* New York: Basic Books, 1959.

Blake, R. R. and Mouton, J. S. The instrumented training

[3] For further discussion of these points the reader should consult the responses to the Argyris and Bass articles published in the *Journal of Applied Behavioral Science,* 1967, **2**(3).

laboratory. In I. R. Wechsler and E. H. Schein (eds.), *Issues in human relations training.* Washington, D.C.: National Training Laboratories—National Education Association, 1962.

Blake, R. R. and Mouton, J. S. Improving organizational problem solving through increasing the flow and utilization of new ideas. *Training Directors Journal,* 1963, **17**(9), 48–57.

Blake, R. R. and Mouton, J. S. *The management grid.* Houston: Gulf, 1964.

Blake, R. R. and Mouton, J. S. Some effects of Managerial Grid seminar training on union and management attitudes toward supervision. *Journal of Applied Behavioral Science,* 1966, **2**, 387–400.

Blake, R. R., Mouton, J. S., Barnes, L. B., and Greiner, L. E. Breakthrough in organization development. *Harvard Business Review,* 1964, **42**(6), 133–55.

Blansfield, M. G. Depth analysis of organizational life. *California Management Review,* 1962, **5**, 29–42.

Boyd, J. B. and Elliss, J. D. *Findings of research into senior management seminars.* Toronto: Hydro-Electric Power Commission of Ontario, 1962.

Bradford, L. P., Gibb, J. R., and Benne, K. D. *T-group theory and laboratory method.* New York: Wiley, 1964.

Buchanan, P. C. *Organizational development following major retrenchment.* New York: Yeshiva, 1964. (Mimeo)

Buchanan, P. C. Evaluating the effectiveness of laboratory training in industry. In *Explorations in human relations training and research.* No. 1. Washington, D.C.: National Training Laboratories—National Education Association, 1965.

Buchanan, P. C. and Brunstetter, P. H. A research approach to management development: II. *Journal of the American Society of Training Directors,* 1959, **13**, 18–27.

Bugental, J. R. T. and Tannenbaum, R. *Sensitivity training and being motivation.* Los Angeles: University of California, Institute of Industrial Relations, 1963.

Bunker, D. R. Individual applications of laboratory training. *Journal of Applied Behavioral Science,* 1965, **1**, 131–48.

Bunker, D. R. and Knowles, E. S. Comparison of behavioral changes resulting from human relations training laboratories of different lengths. *Journal of Applied Behavioral Science,* 1967, **2**, 505–24.

Burke, H. L. and Bennis, W. G. Changes in perception of self and others during human relations training. *Human Relations,* 1961, **14**, 165–82.

Campbell, D. T. and Fiske, D. W. Convergent and discriminant validation by the multi-trait, multi-method matrix. *Psychological Bulletin,* 1959, **56**, 81–105.

Campbell, J. P. *Management training: The development of managerial effectiveness.* Greensboro, N.C.: The Richardson Foundation, 1966.

Clark, J. V. and Culbert, S. A. Mutually therapeutic perception and self awareness in a T-group. *Journal of Applied Behavioral Science,* 1965, **1**, 180–94.

Cline, V. B. Interpersonal perception. In B. A. Maher (ed.), *Progress in experimental personality research.* New York: Academic Press, 1964.

Cohen, K. J., Dill, W. R., Kuehn, A. A., and Winters, P. R. *The Carnegie Tech Management Game: An experiment in business education.* Homewood, Ill.: Irwin, 1964.

Cronbach, L. J. Processes affecting scores on "understanding of others" and "assumed similarity." *Psychological Bulletin,* 1955, **52**, 177–93.

Deese, J. *The psychology of learning.* New York: McGraw-Hill, 1958.

Dollard, J. and Miller, N. E. *Personality and psychotherapy: An analysis in terms of learning, thinking, and culture.* New York: McGraw-Hill, 1950.

Dukes, W. F. $N = 1$. *Psychological Bulletin,* 1965, **64**, 74–79.

Dunnette, M. D. Personnel management. *Annual Review of Psychology,* 1962, **13**, 285–314.

Fleishman, E. A., Harris, F. F., and Burtt, H. E. *Leadership and supervision in industry.* Columbus: Ohio State University, Personnel Research Board, 1955.

Foundation for Research on Human Behavior. *An action research program for organization improvement.* Ann Arbor, Mich.: Author, 1960.

French, J. R. P., Jr., Sherwood, J. J., and Bradford, D. L. Changes in self-identity in a management training conference. *Journal of Applied Behavioral Science,* 1966, **2**, 210–18.

Friedlander, F. The impact of organizational training laboratories upon the effectiveness and interaction of ongoing work groups. *Personnel Psychology,* 1968, in press.

Gage, N. L. and Cronbach, L. J. Conceptual and methodological problems in interpersonal perception. *Psychological Review,* 1955, **62**, 411–22.

Gage, N. L. and Exline, R. V. Social perception and effectiveness in discussion groups. *Human Relations,* 1953, **6**, 381–96.

Gassner, S., Gold, J., and Snadowsky, A. M. Changes in the phenomenal field as a result of human relations training. *Journal of Psychology,* 1964, **58**, 33–41.

Gough, H. *California Psychological Inventory manual.* Palo Alto, Calif.: Consulting Psychologists Press, 1957.

Grater, M. Changes in self and other attitudes in a leadership training group. *Personnel and Guidance Journal,* 1959, **37**, 493–96.

Haire, M., Ghiselli, E. E., and Porter, L. W. *Managerial thinking.* New York: Wiley, 1966.

Hampden-Turner, C. H. An existential "learning theory" and the integration of T-group research. *Journal of Applied Behavioral Science,* 1966, **2**, 367–86.

Harrison, R. Import of the laboratory on perceptions of others by the experimental group. In C. Argyris, *Interpersonal competence and organizational behavior.* Homewood, Ill.: Irwin, 1962.

Harrison, R. Cognitive change and participation in a sensitivity training laboratory. *Journal of Consulting Psychology,* 1966, **30**, 517–20.

Harrison, R. and Lubin, B. Personal style, group composition and learning. *Journal of Applied Behavioral Science,* 1965, **1**, 286–301.

House, R. J. T-group education and leadership effectiveness: A review of the empirical literature and a critical evaluation. *Personnel Psychology,* 1967, **20**, 1–32.

Kassarjian, H. H. Social character and sensitivity training. *Journal of Applied Behavioral Science,* 1965, **1**, 433–40.

Kernan, J. P. Laboratory human relations training: Its effect on the "personality" of supervisory engineers. *Dissertation Abstracts,* 1964, **25**(1), 665–66.

Kimble, G. A. *Hilgard and Marquis' "Conditioning and learning."* 2d ed. New York: Appleton-Century-Crofts, 1961.

Klaw, S. Two weeks in a T-group. *Fortune,* 1961, **64**(8), 114–17.

Kuriloff, A. H. and Atkins, S. T-group for a work team. *Journal of Applied Behavioral Science,* 1966, **2**, 63–94.

Lewin, K. Group decision and social change. In T. Newcomb and E. Hartley (eds.), *Readings in social psychology.* New York: Holt, Rinehart & Winston, 1947.

Lohman, K., Zenger, J. H., and Weschler, I. R. Some perceptual changes during sensitivity training. *Journal of Educational Research,* 1959, **53**, 28–31.

Martin, H. O. The assessment of training. *Personnel Management,* 1957, **39**, 88–93.

Maslow, A. H. *Eupsychian management: A journal.* Homewood, Ill.: Irwin, 1965.

Mathis, A. G. "Trainability" as a function of individual valency pattern. In D. Stock and H. A. Thelen (eds.), *Emotional dynamics and group culture.* Washington, D.C.: National Training Laboratories—National Education Association, 1958.

McGregor, D. *The human side of enterprise.* New York: McGraw-Hill, 1960.

Miles, M. B. Human relations training: Processes and outcomes. *Journal of Counseling Psychology,* 1960, **7**, 301–6.

Miles, M. B. Changes during and following laboratory training: A clinical-experimental study. *Journal of Applied Behavioral Science,* 1965, **1**, 215–42.

Miner, J. B. *Studies in management education.* New York: Springer, 1965.

Morton, R. B. and Bass, B. M. The organizational training laboratory. *Journal of the American Society of Training Directors,* 1964, **18**(10), 2–15.

Myers, I. B. *Manual for the Myers-Briggs Type Indicator.* Princeton, N.J.: Educational Testing Service, 1962.

National Training Laboratories. *21st annual summer laboratories.* Washington, D.C.: Author, 1967.

Oshry, B. I. and Harrison, F. Transfer from here-and-now—to there-and-then: Changes in organizational problem diagnosis stemming from T-group training. *Journal of Applied Behavioral Science,* 1966, **2**, 185–98.

Pepinsky, H. B., Siegel, L., and Van Alta, E. L. The criterion in counseling: A group participation scale. *Journal of Abnormal and Social Psychology,* 1952, **47**, 415–19.

Riesman, D., Glazer, N., and Denny, R. *The lonely crowd.* New Haven: Yale University Press, 1950.

Schein, E. H. Management development as a process of influence. In H. J. Leavitt and L. R. Pondy (eds.), *Readings in management psychology.* Chicago: University of Chicago Press, 1964.

Schein, E. H. and Bennis, W. G. *Personal and organizational changes through group methods: The laboratory approach.* New York: Wiley, 1965.

Schutz, W. C. *FIRO: A three-dimensional theory of interpersonal behavior.* New York: Holt, Rinehart & Winston, 1958.

Schutz, W. C. and Allen, V. L. The effects of a T-group laboratory on interpersonal behavior. *Journal of Applied Behavioral Science,* 1966, **2**, 265–86.

Skinner, B. F. *Science and human behavior.* New York: Macmillan, 1953.

Smith, H. C. *Sensitivity to people.* New York: McGraw-Hill, 1966.

Smith, P. B. Attitude changes associated with training in human relations. *British Journal of Social and Clinical Psychology,* 1964, **3**, 104–13.

Solomon, R. L. Punishment. *American Psychologist,* 1964, **19**, 239–53.

Steele, F. I. Personality and the "laboratory style." *Journal of Applied Behavioral Science,* in press.

Stock, D. A survey of research on T-groups. In L. P. Bradford, J. R. Gibb and K. D., Benne (eds.), *T-group theory and laboratory method.* New York: Wiley, 1964.

Stogdill, R. M. and Coons, A. E. *Leader behavior: Its description and measurement.* (Business Res. Monogr. No. 88) Columbus: Ohio State University, Bureau of Business Research, 1957.

Tannenbaum, R., Weschler, I. R., and Massarik, F. *Leadership and organization: A behavioral science approach.* New York: McGraw-Hill, 1961.

Taylor, F. C. Effects of laboratory training upon persons and their work groups. In S. S. Zalkind (Chm.), Research on the impact of using different laboratory methods for interpersonal and organizational change. Symposium presented at the meeting of the American Psychological Association, Washington, D.C., September 1967.

Underwood, W. J. Evaluation of laboratory method training. *Training Directors Journal,* 1965, **19**(5), 34–40.

Valiquet, I. M. Contribution to the evaluation of a management development program. Unpublished master's thesis, Massachusetts Institute of Technology, 1964.

Wagner, A. B. The use of process analysis in business decision games. *Journal of Applied Behavioral Science,* 1965, **1**, 387–408.

Weschler, I. R. and Reisel, J. *Inside a sensitivity training group.* Los Angeles: University of California, Institute of Human Relations, 1959.

Yates, A. J. *Frustration and conflict.* New York: Wiley, 1962.

Zand, D. E., Steele, F. I., and Zalkind, S. S. The impact of an organizational development program on perceptions of interpersonal, group, and organizational functioning. In S. S. Zalkind (Chm.), Research on the impact of using different laboratory methods for interpersonal and organizational change. Symposium presented at the meeting of the American Psychological Association, Washington, D.C., September 1967.

55. THEORY AND METHOD IN APPLYING BEHAVIORAL SCIENCE TO PLANNED ORGANIZATIONAL CHANGE*

Warren G. Bennis†

Three assumptions underlie this paper:[1] (1) that the proportion of contemporary change that is planned or that issues from deliberate innovation is much higher than in former times; (2) that man's wisdom and mundane behavior are somewhat short of perfection insofar as they regulate the fate and selective adaptation of complex human organizations; (3) that behavioral scientists in increasing numbers are called upon to influence organizational functioning and effectiveness. The paper is concerned with the strategic, methodological, and conceptual issues brought about by the emergence of the action role of the behavioral scientist.

What we have witnessed in the past two or three decades has been called the "Rise of the Rational Spirit"—the belief that science can help to better the human condition (Merton & Lerner, 1951). The focus of this paper is on one indication of this trend: the emerging role for the behavioral scientist and, more specifically, the attempts by behavioral scientists to apply knowledge (primarily sociological and psychological) toward the improvement of human organizations.

THE EMERGENCE OF THE ACTION ROLE

Many signs and activities point toward an emerging action role for the behavioral scientist. The *manipulative standpoint,* as Lasswell calls it, is becoming distinguishable from the *contemplative standpoint* and is increasingly ascendant insofar as knowledge utilization is concerned.[2] Evidence can be found in the growing literature on planned change through the uses of the behavioral sciences (Bennis, Benne & Chin, 1961; Freeman, 1963; Zetterberg, 1962; Gibb & Lippitt, 1959; Leeds & Smith, 1963; Likert & Hayes, 1957; Glock, Lippitt, Flanagan, Wilson, Shartle, Wilson, Croker, & Page, 1960) and in such additions to the vocabulary of the behavioral scientist as action research, client system, change agent, clinical sociology, knowledge centers, social catalysts. The shift is also reflected in increased emphasis on application in annual meeting time of the professional associations or in the formation of a Center for Research on the Utilization of Scientific Knowledge within The University of Michigan's Institute for Social Research.

It is probably true that in the United States there is a more practical attitude toward knowledge than anywhere else. When Harrison Salisbury (1960) traveled over Europe he was impressed with the seeming disdain of European intellectuals for practical matters. Even in Russia he found little interest in the "merely useful." Salisbury saw only one great agricultural experiment station on the American model. In that case professors were working in the fields. They told him, "People call us Americans."

Not many American professors may be found working in the fields, but they can be found almost everywhere else: in factories, in the government, in underdeveloped countries, in mental hospitals, in educational systems. They are advising, counseling, researching, recruiting, developing, consulting, training. Americans may not have lost their deep ambivalence toward the intellectual, but it is clear that the academic intellectual has become *engagé* with spheres of action in greater numbers, with more diligence, and with higher aspirations than at any other time in history.

It may be useful to speculate about the reasons for the shift in the intellectual climate. Most important, but trickiest to identify, are those causative factors bound up in the warp and woof of "our times

* *Applied Behavioral Science,* Vol. 1, No. 4 (1965), 337–60.

† President, University of Cincinnati.

[1] Drawn from keynote address presented at International Conference on Operational Research and the Social Sciences, Cambridge, England, September 1964.

[2] For an excellent discussion of the "value" issues in this development, see A. Kaplan, *The conduct of inquiry.* San Francisco: Chandler, 1964, chap. 10; and K. D. Benne and G. Swanson, (eds.). Values and social issues. *Journal of Social Issues,* Vol. 6 (1960).

and age" that Professor Boring calls the *Zeitgeist.* The apparently growing disenchantment with the moral neutrality of the scientist may be due, in C. P. Snow's phrase, to the fact that "scientists cannot escape their own knowledge." In any event, though "impurity" is still implied, action research as distinguished from pure research does not carry the opprobrium it once did.

Perhaps the crucial reason for the shift in emphasis toward application is simply that we know more.[3] Since World War II we have obtained large bodies of research and diverse reports on application. We are today in a better position to assess results and potentialities of applied social science.

Finally, there is a fourth factor having to do with the fate and viability of human organization, particularly as it has been conceptualized as "bureaucracy." I use the term in its sociological, Weberian sense, not as a metaphor *à la* Kafka's *The Castle* connoting "red tape," impotency, inefficiency, despair. In the past three decades Weber's vision has been increasingly scrutinized and censured. Managers and practitioners, on the one hand, and organizational theorists and researchers on the other, are more and more dissatisfied with current practices of organizational behavior and are searching for new forms and patterns of organizing for work. A good deal of activity is being generated.

THE LACK OF A VIABLE THEORY OF SOCIAL CHANGE

Unfortunately, no viable theory of social change has been established. Indeed it is a curious fact about present theories that they are strangely silent on matters of *directing* and *implementing* change. What I particularly object to—and I include the "newer" theories of neo-conflict (Coser, 1956; Dahrendorf, 1961), neo-functionalism (Boskoff, 1964), and neo-revolutionary theories—is that they tend to explain the dynamic interaction of a system without providing one clue to the identification of strategic leverages for alteration. They are suitable for *observers* of social change, not for practitioners. They are theories of *change,* and not of *changing.*

It may be helpful to suggest quickly some of the prerequisites for a theory of changing. I am indebted here to my colleague Robert Chin (1961, 1963):

a) A theory of changing must include manipulable variables—accessible levers for influencing the direction, tempo, and quality of change and improvement.

b) The variables must not violate the client system's values.

c) The cost of usage cannot be prohibitive.

d) There must be provided a reliable basis of diagnosing the strength and weakness of conditions facing the client system.

e) Phases of intervention must be clear so that the change agent can develop estimates for termination of the relationship.

f) The theory must be communicable to the client system.

g) It must be possible to assess appropriateness of the theory for different client systems.

Such a theory does not now exist, and this probably explains why change agents appear to write like "theoretical orphans" and, more important, why so many change programs based on theories of social change have been indadquate. This need should be kept in mind as we look at models of knowledge utilization.

THE NOTION OF PLANNED CHANGE

Planned change can be viewed as a linkage between theory and practice, between knowledge and action. It plays this role by converting variables from the basic disciplines into strategic instrumentation and programs. Historically, the development of planned change can be seen as the resultant of two forces: complex problems requiring expert help and the growth and viability of the behavioral sciences. The term "behavioral sciences" itself is of post-World War II vintage coined by the more empirically minded to "safeguard" the social disciplines from the non-quantitative humanists and the depersonalized abstractions of the econometricists. The process of planned change involves a *change agent,* a *client system,* and the collaborative attempt to apply *valid knowledge* to the client's problems.[4]

Elsewhere I have attempted a typology of change efforts in which planned change is distinguished from other types of change in that it entails mutual goal setting, an equal power ratio (eventually), and deliberateness on both sides (Bennis et al 1961, p. 154).

It may further help in defining planned change to compare it with another type of deliberate change effort, Operations Research. I enter this with a humility bordering on fear and a rueful sense of kinship in our mutual incapacity to explain to one another the nature of our work. There are these similarities. Both are World War II products; both are problem-centered (though both have also provided inputs to

[3] For a recent inventory of scientific findings of the behavioral sciences, see B. Berelson and G. A. Steiner. *Human behavior.* New York: Harcourt, Brace & World, 1964.

[4] For a fuller discussion, see R. Lippitt, J. Watson, and B. Westley, *The dynamics of planned change.* New York: Harcourt, Brace & World, 1961; and Bennis *et al.* (1961).

the concepts and method of their parent disciplines).[5] Both emphasize improvement and to that extent are *normative* in their approach to problems. Both rely heavily on empirical science; both rely on a relationship of confidence and valid communication with clients; both emphasize a *systems* approach to problems—that is, both are aware of interdependence within the system as well as boundary maintenance with its environment; and both appear to be most effective when working with systems which are complex, rapidly changing, and probably science-based.

Perhaps the most crucial difference between OR and planned change has to do with the identification of strategic variables, that is, with those factors which appear to make a difference in the performance of the system. Planned change is concerned with such problems as (1) the identification of mission and values, (2) collaboration and conflict, (3) control and leadership, (4) resistance and adaptation to change, (5) utilization of human resources, (6) communication, (7) management development. OR practitioners tend to select economic or engineering variables which are more quantitative, measurable, and linked to profit and efficiency. Ackoff and Rivett (1963), for example, classify OR problems under (1) inventory, (2) allocation, (3) queuing, (4) sequencing, (5) routing, (6) replacement, (7) competition, (8) search.

A second major difference has to do with the perceived importance of the relationship with the client. In planned change, the quality and nature of the relationship are used as indicators for the measure of progress and as valid sources of data and diagnosis. Undoubtedly, the most successful OR practitioners operate with sensitivity toward their clients; but if one looks at what they *say* about their work, they are clearly less concerned with human interactions.

A third major difference is that the OR practitioner devotes a large portion of his time to research, to problem solving. The change agent tends to spend somewhat more time on implementation through counseling, training, management development schemes, and so forth. Fourth, planned-change agents tend to take less seriously the idea of the *system* in their approaches. Finally, the idea of an interdisciplinary teams, central to OR, does not seem to be a part of most planned-change programs.

One thing that emerges from this comparison is a realization of the complexity of modern organization. Look through the kaleidoscope one way, and a configuration of the economic and technological factors appears; tilt it, and what emerges is a pattern of internal human relations problems. It is on these last problems and their effects upon performance of the system that practitioners of planned organizational change tend to work.

A FOCUS OF CONVENIENCE

To develop what George Kelley refers to as a "focus of convenience" for planned organizational change, I want to make two key aspects clearer: the notions of "collaborative relationships" and of "valid knowledge." I see the outcome of planned-change efforts as depending to some considerable extent on the relationship between client and agent. To optimize a collaborative relationship, there need to be a "spirit of inquiry," with data publicly shared, and equal freedom to terminate the relationship and to influence the other.

As to valid knowledge, the criteria are based on the requirements for a viable applied behavioral science research—an applied behavioral science that:

a) Takes into consideration the behavior of persons operating within their specific institutional environments;
b) Is capable of accounting for the interrelated levels (person, group, role, organization) within the context of the social change;
c) Includes variables that the policy maker and practitioner can understand, manipulate, and evaluate;
d) Can allow selection of variables appropriate in terms of its own values, ethics, moralities;
e) Accepts the premise that groups and organizations as units are amenable to empirical and analytic treatment;
f) Takes into account external social processes of change as well as interpersonal aspects of the collaborative process;
g) Includes propositions susceptible to empirical test focusing on the dynamics of change.

These criteria must be construed as an arbitrary goal, not as an existing reality. To my knowledge, there is no program which fulfills these requirements fully. In this focus of convenience, I have arbitrarily selected change agents working on organizational dynamics partly because of my greater familiarity with their work but also because they seem to fulfill the criteria outlined to a greater extent than do other change agents. My choice of emphasis is also based on the belief that changes in the sphere of organizations—primarily industrial—in patterns of work and relationship, structure, technology, and administration promise some of the most significant changes in our society. Indeed it is my guess that industrial soci-

[5] For a brilliant exposition on the contributions of applied research to "pure" theory, see A. Gouldner. Theoretical requirements of the applied social sciences, in Bennis et al. (1961), pp. 83–95.

ety, at least in the United States, is more radical, innovative, and adventurous in adapting new ways of organizing than the government, the universities, and the labor unions, who appear rigid and stodgy in the face of rapid change. If space permitted, however, I would refer also to change agents working in a variety of fields—rural sociology, economics, anthropology—and in such settings as communities, hospitals, cultural-change programs.

Let us turn now to some of the "traditional" models of knowledge utilization.

EIGHT TYPES OF CHANGE PROGRAMS[6]

It is possible to identify eight types of change programs if we examine their strategic rationale: exposition and propagation, élite corps, human relations training, staff, scholarly consultations, circulation of ideas to the élite, developmental research, and action research.

I should like to look at each of these programs quickly and then refer to four biases which seem to me to weaken their impact.

Exposition and propagation, perhaps the most popular type of program, assumes that knowledge is power. It follows that the men who possess "Truth" will lead the world.

Elite corps programs grow from the realization that ideas by themselves do not constitute action and that a strategic *role* is a necessity for ideas to be implemented (e.g., through getting scientists into government as C. P. Snow suggests).

Human relations training programs are similar to the élite corps idea in the attempt to translate behavioral science concepts in such ways that they take on personal referents for the men in power positions.

Staff programs provide a source of intelligence within the client system, as in the work of social anthropologists advising military governors after World War II. The strategy of the staff idea is to observe, analyze, and to plan rationally (Myrdal, 1958).

Scholarly consultation, as defined by Zetterberg (1962), includes exploratory inquiry, scholarly understanding, confrontation, discovery of solutions, and scientific advice to client.

Circulation of ideas to the élite builds on the simple idea of influencing change by getting to the people with power or influence.

Developmental research has to do with seeing whether an idea can be brought to an engineering stage. Unlike Zetterberg's scholarly confrontation, it is directed toward a particular problem, not necessarily a client, and is concerned with implementation and program (I would wager that *little* developmental research is being done today in the behavioral sciences.)

Action research, the term coined by Kurt Lewin, undertakes to solve a problem for a client. It is identical to applied research generally except that in action research the roles of researcher and subject may change and reverse, the subjects becoming researchers engaging in action steps.

These eight programs, while differing in objectives, values, means of influence, and program implications, are similar in wanting to use knowledge to gain some socially desirable end. Each seems successful or promising; each has its supporters and its detractors. Intrinsic to them all, I believe, is some bias or flaw which probably weakens their full impact. Four biases are particularly visible.

Rationalistic Bias: No Implementation of Program

Most of the strategies rely almost totally on rationality. But knowledge *about* something does *not* lead automatically to intelligent action. Intelligent action requires commitment and programs as well as truth.

Technocratic Bias: No Spirit of Collaboration

Change typically involves risk and fear. Any significant change in human organization involves rearrangement of patterns of power, association, status, skills, and values. Some may benefit, others may lose. Thus change typically involves risk and fear. Yet change efforts sometimes are conducted as if there were no need to discuss and "work through" these fears and worries (e.g., F. W. Taylor's failure to consider the relationship between the engineer with the stopwatch and the worker, or Freud's early work when he considered it adequate to examine the unconscious of his patients and tell them what he learned—even to the extent on occasion of analyzing dreams by mail).

Individualist Bias: No organization Strategy Is Involved

This refers to strategies which rely on the individual while denying the organizational forces and roles surrounding him. There is, however, simply no guarantee that a wise individual who attains power will act wisely. It may be that *role corrupts*—both the role of power and the role of powerlessness. In any

[6] For a fuller exposition of these ideas, see my paper, A new role for the behavioral sciences: Effecting organizational change. *Administrative Science Quarterly,* Vol. 8 (1963), pp. 125–65.

event, there is no guarantee that placing certain types of people in management—or training them or psychoanalyzing them or making scientists of them—leads to more effective action. Scientists act like administrators when they gain power. And graduates of human relations training programs tend to act like non-alumni shortly after their return to their organizational base.

The staff idea, proposed by Myrdal, is limited by the unresolved tensions in the staff-line dilemma noted by students of organizational behavior and by the conflicts derived from the role of the intellectual working in bureaucratic structures. The élite strategy has serious drawbacks, primarily because it focuses on the individual and not the organization.

Insight Bias: No Manipulability

My major quarrel here is not with the formulation: insight leads to change, though this can be challenged, but with the lack of provision of variables accessible to control. It is not obvious that insight leads directly to sophistication in rearranging social systems or making strategic organizational interventions. Insight provides the relevant variables for planned change as far as personal manipulation goes, but the question remains: How can that lead directly to the manipulation of external factors?

THE ELEMENTS OF PLANNED ORGANIZATIONAL CHANGE

In the October 7, 1963, edition of the *New York Times,* a classified ad announced a search for change agents. It read:

> What's a change agent? A result-oriented individual able to accurately and quickly resolve complex tangible and intangible problems. Energy and ambition necessary for success . . .

The change agents I have in mind need more than "energy and ambition." They are *professionals* who, for the most part, hold doctorates in the behavioral sciences. They are not a very homogeneous group, but they do have some similarities.

They are alike in that they take for granted the *centrality of work* in our culture to men and women in highly organized instrumental settings; in their concern with improvement, development, and measurement of *organizational effectiveness;* in their *preoccupation with people* and the process of human interaction; in their interest in changing the relationships, perceptions, and values of *existing personnel.* They may be members of the client system, arguring that inside knowledge is needed, or external agents, arguing that perspective, detachment, and energy from outside are needed. They intervene at different structural points in the organization and at different times.

Though each change agent has in mind a set of unique goals based on his own theoretical position and competencies as well as the needs of the client system, there are some general aims. In a paradigm developed by Chris Argyris (1962), bureaucratic values tend to stress the rational, task aspects of work and to ignore the basic human factors which, if ignored, tend to reduce task competence. Managers brought up under this system of values are badly cast to play the intricate human roles now required of them. Their ineptitude and anxieties lead to systems of discord and defense which interfere with the problem-solving capacity of the organization.

Generally speaking, the normative goals of change agents derive from this paradigm. They include: improving interpersonal competence of managers; effecting a change in values so that human factors and feelings come to be considered legitimate; developing increased understanding among and within working groups to reduce tensions; developing "team management"; developing better methods of "conflict resolution" than suppression, denial, and the use of unprincipled power; viewing the organization as an organic system of relationships marked by mutual trust, interdependence, multigroup membership, shared responsibility, and conflict resolution through training or problem solving.

PROGRAMS FOR IMPLEMENTING PLANNED ORGANIZATIONAL CHANGE

Discussion here will focus on three broad types of change programs that seem to be most widely used, frequently in some combination: training, consultation, and research.

Training

Training is an inadequate word in this context, as its dictionary meaning denotes "drill" and "exercise." I refer to what has been called laboratory training, sensitivity or group dynamics training, and most commonly, T-Group training.[7] The idea originated in Bethel, Maine, under the guidance of Leland Bradford, Kenneth Benne, and Ronald Lippitt, with ini-

[7] For a popular account of laboratory training, see C. Argyris, T-groups for organizational effectiveness, *Harvard Business Review,* Vol. 42 (1964), pp. 60–74. For a theoretical background, see L. P. Bradford, J. R. Gibb, and K. D. Benne (eds.), *T-group theory and laboratory method.* New York: Wiley, 1964; and E. H. Schein and W. G. Bennis, *Personal and organizational change via group methods.* New York: Wiley, 1965.

tial influence from the late Kurt Lewin. The T-Group has evolved since 1947 into one of the main instruments for organizational change. Bradford has played a central role in this development as director of the National Training Laboratories. Growth has been facilitated through the active participation of a number of university-based behavioral scientists and practitioners. Tavistock Institute has played a similar role in England and recently a group of European scientists set up a counterpart to the National Training Laboratories.

The main objective at first was *personal change* or *self-insight.* Since the fifties the emphasis has shifted to *organizational development,* a more precise date being 1958, when the Esso Company inaugurated a series of laboratories at refineries over the country under the leadership of Blake and Shepard (Shepard, 1960).

Briefly, laboratory training unfolds in an unstructured group setting where participants examine their interpersonal relationships. By examining data generated by themselves, members attempt to understand the dynamics of group behavior, e.g., decision processes, leadership and influence, norms, roles, communication distortions, effects of authority on behavioral patterns, coping mechanisms. T-Group composition is itself a strategic issue. Thus the organization may send an executive to a "stranger laboratory" which fills a "seeding" function; "cousin laboratories" may be conducted for persons of similar rank and occupational responsibilities within the company but from different functional groups; "diagonal slices" may be composed of persons of different rank but not in the same work group or in direct relationship; and "family laboratories" may be conducted for functional groups. The more the training groups approach a "family," the more the total organization is affected.

Consulting

The change agent *qua* consultant, perhaps best exemplified in the work of the Tavistock Institute, operates in a manner very like the practicing physician or psychoanalyst: that is, he starts from the chief "presenting symptom" of the client, articulates it in such a way that causal and underlying mechanisms of the problem are understood, and then takes remedial action. Heavy emphasis is placed on the strategy of *role model* because the main instrument is the change agent himself. Sofer (1961) reveals this when he suggests that psychotherapy or some form of clinical experience is necessary preparation for the change agent. Argyris, as consultant, confronts the group with their behavior toward him as an analogue of their behavior *vis-a-vis* their own subordinates.

If the role of the consultant sounds ambiguous and vague, this probably reflects reality. Certainly in the consultant approach the processes of change and the change agent's interventions are less systematic and less programmed than in training or applied research programs. A word about the latter.

Applied Research

I refer here to research in which the results are used systematically as an *intervention.* Most methods of research application collect information and report it. Generally, the relationship ends there. In the survey-feedback approach, as developed primarily by Floyd Mann (1957) and his associates at The University of Michigan's Institute for Social Research, this is only the beginning. Data are reported in "feedback" meetings where subjects become clients and have a chance to review the findings, test them against their own experience, and even ask the researchers to test some of their hypotheses. Instead of being submitted "in triplicate" and probably ignored, research results serve to activate involvement and participation in the planning, collection, analysis, and interpretation of more data.

Richard Beckhard, too, utilizes data as the first step in his work as change agent (in press). In his procedure the data are collected through formal, nonstructured interviews which he then codes by themes about the managerial activities of the client for discussion at an off-site meeting with the subjects.

It should be stressed that most planned-change inductions involve all three processes—training, consulting, researching—and that both agent and client play a variety of roles. The final shape of the change agent's role is not as yet clear, and it is hazardous to report exactly what change agents do on the basis of their reports. Many factors, of course, determine the particular intervention the change agent may choose: cost, time, degree of collaboration required, state of target system, and so on.

STRATEGIC MODELS EMPLOYED BY CHANGE AGENTS

More often than not, change agents fail to report their strategy or to make it explicit. It may be useful to look at two quite different models that are available: one developed by Robert Blake in his "Managerial Grid" system, and one with which I was associated at an Esso refinery and which Chris Argyris evaluated some years later.

Blake has developed a change program based on his analytic framework of managerial styles (Blake, Mouton, Barnes & Greiner, 1964). Figure 1 shows the grid for locating types of managerial strategies.

FIGURE 1 THE MANAGERIAL GRID

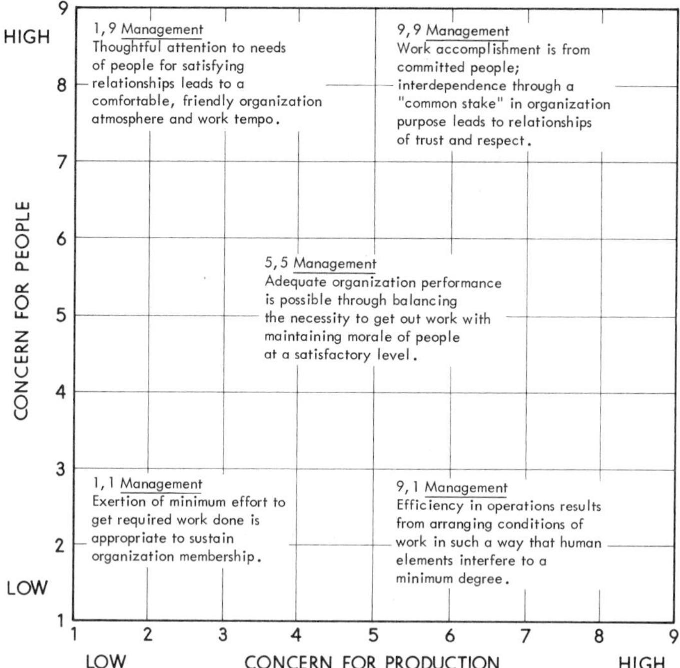

1,9 Management
Thoughtful attention to needs of people for satisfying relationships leads to a comfortable, friendly organization atmosphere and work tempo.
9,9 Management
Work accomplishment is from committed people; interdependence through a "common stake" in organization purpose leads to relationships of trust and respect.
5,5 Management
Adequate organization performance is possible through balancing the necessity to get out work with maintaining morale of people at a satisfactory level.
1,1 Management
Exertion of minimum effort to get required work done is appropriate to sustain organization membership.
9,1 Management
Efficiency in operations results from arranging conditions of work in such a way that human elements interfere to a minimum degree.
HIGH
LOW
CONCERN FOR PEOPLE
1 2 3 4 5 6 7 8 9
LOW
CONCERN FOR PRODUCTION
HIGH

Blake and his colleagues attempt to change the organization in the direction of "team management" (9,9 or high concern for people and high concern for production). Based on experience with 15 different factories, the Blake strategy specifies six phases: off-site laboratory for "diagonal slice" of personnel; off-site program focused on team training for "family" groups; training in the plant location designed to achieve better integration between functional groups; goal-setting sessions for groups of 10 to 12 managers.

Blake and his colleagues estimate that these four phases may require two years or longer. The next two, implementing plans and stabilizing changes, may require an additional two years.

Figure 2 (Argyris, 1960) presents another strategy: a change program used in a large oil company to improve the functioning of one of its smaller refineries. A new manager was named and sent to a T-Group training session to gain awareness of the human problems in the refinery. The Headquarters Organizational Development staff then conducted a diagnosis through a survey and interview of the managerial staff (70) and a sample of hourly employees (40/350). About that time the author was brought in to help the headquarters staff and the new manager.

It was decided that a laboratory program of T-Groups might be effective but premature, with the result that weekly seminars that focused on new developments in human relations were held with top management (about 20). A one-week laboratory training program followed for all supervisors in diagonal slices, and then another re-evaluation of needs was undertaken. Some structural innovations were suggested and implemented. During the last phase of the program (not shown in the figure), the Scanlon Plan was adapted and installed (incidentally, for the first time in a "process" industry and for the first time that a union agreed to the Plan without a bonus automatically guaranteed).

Though it cannot be said with any assurance that these two strategies are typical, it may be helpful to identify certain features: *(a) length of time* (Blake estimates five years; the refinery program took two years up to the Scanlon Plan); *(b) variety of programs* utilized (research, consulting, training, teaching, planning); *(c) necessity of cooperation* with top management and the parent organization; *(d)* approaching the organization *as a system* rather than as a collection of individuals; *(e) phasing program* from individual to group to intergroup to overall organization; *(f)* intellectual *and* emotional content.

POWER AND THE ROLE OF THE CHANGE AGENT

How and why do people and organizations change, and what is the nature and source of the power exerted by the change agent? We have to make inferences because change agents themselves tend to be silent on this. It is not *coercive power,* for

FIGURE 2 A CHANGE PROGRAM

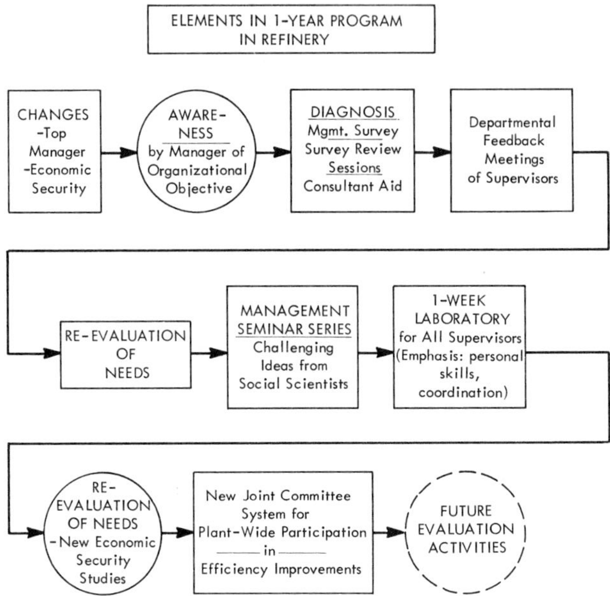

the change agent generally does not have the ability to reward or punish. Moreover, he would prefer, at least intellectually, not to wield power at variance with his normative goals. Further, there is some evidence that coercive power is less durable than are other kinds of power, except under conditions of viligant surveillance.

Traditional power? Almost certainly not. The change agent is, in fact, continually working without legitimization. *Expert power?* Possibly some, but it is doubtful whether his knowledge is considered "expert" enough—in the sense that an engineer or doctor or lawyer is seen as expert. *Referent* or *identification power?* Aparently so. Sofer, for example, attributes some influence to the client system's ability and desire to emulate the change agent. Still, this will vary from a considerable degree to not at all.

This leaves us with *value power* as the likeliest candidate of the possible sources of power. Most change agents do emit cues to a consistent value system. These values are based on Western civilization's notion of a scientific humanism: concern for our fellow man, experimentalism, openness and honesty, flexibility, cooperation, democracy. If what I have said about power is correct, it is significant (at least in the United States) that this set of values seems to be potent in influencing top management circles.

CHARACTERISTICS OF CLIENT SYSTEM

For the most part, the client systems appear to be subsystems of relatively large-scale international operations who find themselves in increasingly competitive situations, in rapidly changing environments, subjected to what have been called "galloping variables." Often the enterprise was founded through an innovation or monopolistic advantage which is thought to be in jeopardy.

Then there is some tension—some discrepancy between the ideal and the actual—which seems to activate the change program.

Finally, there is some faith in the idea that an intermediate proportion of organizational effectiveness is determined by social and psychological factors and that improvement here, however vague or immeasurable, may improve organizational effectiveness.

THE MEASUREMENT OF EFFECTS

Until very recently, change agents, if they did any evaluation research at all, concentrated almost exclusively on attitudinal and subjective factors. Even so-called "hard" behavioral variables, like absentee rates, sickness and accident rates, personnel turnover, and so forth, were rarely investigated. Relating change programs to harder criteria, like productivity and economic and cost factors, was rarely attempted and never, to my knowledge, successful.

And again, the research that was conducted—even on the attitudinal measures—was far from conclusive. Roger Harrison attempted an evaluation study of Argyris' work and found that while there was a significant improvement in the individual executive's interpersonal ability compared with a control group, there was no significant "transfer" of this acuity to the real-life organizational setting. In short, there was a fairly rapid "fade-out" of effects obtained in T-Group training upon return to the organization (Harrison, 1962). This study also shows that new tensions were generated between those individuals who attended the training program and those who did not—an example of the lack of a *systems* approach. Shepard's evaluation on the Esso organization shows that the impact of laboratory training was greatest on personal and interpersonal learnings, but "slightly more helpful than useless" in changing the organization.

More recently, though, some studies have been undertaken which measure more meaningful, less subjective variables of organizational effectiveness. Blake, Mouton, Barnes, and Greiner (1964), for example, conducted an evaluation study of their work in a very large (4,000 employees) petrochemical plant. Not only did they find significant changes in the values, morale, and interpersonal behavior of the employees, but significant improvements in productivity, profits, and cost reduction. David (in press), a change agent working on a program that attempts to facilitate a large and complicated merger, attributed the following effects to the programs: increased productivity, reduced turnover and absenteeism, in addition to a significant improvement in the area of attitudes and subjective feelings.

While these new research approaches show genuine promise, much more has to be done. The research effort has somehow to equal all the energy that goes into developing the planned-change programs themselves.

SOME CRITICISMS AND QUALIFICATIONS

The work of the change agents reported here is new and occurs without the benefit of methodological and strategic precedents. The role of the change agent is also new, its final shape not fully emerged. Thus it has both the advantage of freedom from the constraints facing most men of knowledge, and suffers from lack of guidelines and structure. Let us touch quickly on problems and criticisms facing the change agents.

PLANNED CHANGE AND ORGANIZATIONAL EFFECTIVENESS

I can identify six dimensions of organizational effectiveness: legal, political, economic, technological, social, and personal. There is a good deal of fuzziness as to which of these change agents hope to affect, and the data are inconclusive. Argyris, who is the most explicit about the relationship between performance and interpersonal competence, is still hoping to develop good measures to establish a positive relationship. The connection has to be made, or the field will have to change its normative goal of constructing not only a *better* world but a more *effective* one.

A QUESTION OF VALUES

The values espoused indicate a way of *behaving and feeling;* for example, they emphasize openness rather than secrecy, collaboration rather than dependence or rebellion, cooperation rather than competition, consensus rather than individual rules, rewards based on self-control rather than externally induced rewards, team leadership rather than a one-to-one relationship with the boss, authentic relationships rather than those based on political maneuvering.

Are they natural? Desirable? Functional? What then happens to status or power drives? What about those individuals who have a low need for participation and/or high need for structure and dependence? And what about those personal needs which seem to be incompatible with these images of man, such as a high need for aggression and a low need for affiliation? In short, what about those needs which can be best realized through bureaucratic systems? Or benevolent autocracies? Are these individuals to be changed or to yield and comply?

The problem of values deserves discussion. One of the obstacles is the emotional and value overtones which interfere with rational dialogue. More often than not, one is plunged into a polarized debate which converts ideas into ideology and inquiry into dogma. So we hear of "Theory X versus Theory Y," personality versus organization, democratic versus autocratic, task versus maintenance, human relations versus scientific management, and on and on.

Surely life is more complicated than these dualities suggest, and surely they must imply a continuum—not simply extremes.

LACK OF SYSTEMS APPROACH

Up to this point, I have used the term "organizational change" rather loosely. In Argyris' case, for example, organizational change refers to a change in values of 11 top executives, a change which was not necessarily of an enduring kind and apparently brought about some conflict with other interfaces. In most other cases of planned organizational change, the change induction was limited to a small, élite group. Only in the work of Blake and some others can we confidently talk about organizational change

—in a systems way; his program includes the training of the entire management organization, and at several locations he has carried this step to include wage earners.

Sometimes the changes brought about simply "fade out" because there are no carefully worked out procedures to ensure coordination with other interacting parts of the system. In other cases, the changes have "backfired" and have had to be terminated because of their conflict with interface units. In any case, a good deal more has to be learned about the interlocking and stabilizing changes so that the total system is affected.

SOME GENERALIZATIONS

It may be useful, as peroration, to state in the most tentative manner some generalizations. They are derived, for the most part, from the foregoing discussion and anchored in experience and, wherever possible, in research and theory.

First, a forecast: I suspect that we will see an increase in the number of planned-change programs along the lines discussed here—toward *less* bureaucratic and *more* participative, "open system" and adaptive structures. Given the present pronounced rate of change, the growing reliance on science for the success of the industrial enterprise, the growing number of professionals joining these enterprises, and the "turbulent contextual environment" facing the firm, we can expect increasing demand for social inventions to revise traditional notions of organized effort.

As far as adopting and acceptance go, we already know a good deal.[8] *Adoption* requires that the *type* of change should be proven quality, easily demonstrable in its effects, and with information easily available. Its cost and accessibility to control by the client system as well as its value accord have to be carefully considered.

Acceptance also depends on the relationship between the change agent and the client system: the more profound and anxiety-producing the change, the more collaborative and closer relationship required. In addition, we can predict that an anticipated change will be resisted to the degree that the client system possesses little or incorrect knowledge about the change, has relatively little trust in the source of the change, and has comparatively low influence in controlling the nature and direction of the change.

What we know least about is *implementation*—a process which includes the creation of understanding and commitment toward a particular change and devices whereby it can become integral to the client systems' operations. I will try to summarize the necessary elements in implementation:

a) The *client system* should have as much understanding of the change and its consequences, as much influence in developing and controlling the fate of the change, and as much trust in the initiator of the change as is possible.

b) The *change effort* should be perceived as being as self-motivated and voluntary as possible. This can be effected through the legitimization and reinforcement of the change by the top management group and by the significant reference groups adjacent to the client system. It is also made possible by providing the utmost in true volition.

c) The *change program* must include emotional and value as well as cognitive (informational) elements for successful implementation. It is doubtful that relying solely on rational persuasion (expert power) is sufficient. Most organizations possess the knowledge to cure their ills; the rub is utilization.

d) The *change agent* can be crucial in reducing the resistance to change. As long as the change agent acts congruently with the principles of the program and as long as the client has a chance to test competence and motives (his own and the change agent's), the agent should be able to provide the psychological support so necessary during the risky phases of change. As I have stressed again and again, the quality of the client-agent relationship is pivotal to the success of the change program.

[8] See in particular, E. Rogers. *The diffusion of innovations.* New York: Free Press, 1962; and M. Miles (ed.). *Innovation in education.* New York: Bureau of Publications, Teachers College, Columbia University, 1964.

REFERENCES

Ackoff, R. L. and Rivett, P. *A manager's guide to operations research.* New York: Wiley 1963, p. 34.

Argyris, C. *Organization development: An inquiry into the Esso approach.* New Haven, Conn.: Yale University, 1960.

Argyris, C. *Interpersonal competence and organizational effectiveness.* Homewood, Ill.: Dorsey, 1962, p. 43.

Beckhard, R. An organization improvement program in a decentralized organization. In D. Zand (ed.), *Organization development: Theory and practice,* in press.

Bennis, W. G., Benne, K. D., and Chin, R. (eds.) *The planning of change.* New York: Holt, Rinehart & Winston, 1961.

Blake, R. R., Mouton, Jane S., Barnes, L. B., and Greiner, L. E. Breakthrough in organization development.

Boskoff, A. Funcational analysis as a source of a theoretical repertory and research tasks in the study of social change. In G. K. Zollschan and W. Hirsch, *Explorations in social change.* Boston: Houghton Mifflin, 1964.

Chin, R. The utility of system models and developmental models for practitioners. In W. G. Bennis, K. D. Benne, and R. Chin (eds.), *The planning of change.* New York: Holt, Rinehart & Winston, 1961, pp. 201–14.

Chin, R. Models and ideas about changing. Paper read at Symposium on Acceptance of New Ideas, University of Nebraska, November, 1963.

Coser, L. *The functions of social conflict.* New York: Free Press, 1956.

Dahrendorf, R. Toward a theory of social conflict. In W. G. Bennis, K. D. Benne, and R. Chin (eds.), *The planning of change.* New York: Holt, Rinehart & Winston, 1961, pp. 445–51.

David, G. The Weldon study: An organization change program based upon change in management philosophy. In D. Zand (ed.), *Organization development: Theory and practice,* in press.

Freeman, H. E. The strategy of social policy research. *The social welfare forum,* 1963, 143–60.

Gibb, J. R. and Lippitt, R. (eds.) Consulting with groups and organizations. *Journal of Social Issues,* 1959, **15.**

Glock, C. Y., Lippitt, R., Flanagan, J. C., Wilson, E. C., Shartle, C. L., Wilson, M. L., Croker, G. W., and Page, H. E. *Case studies in bringing behavioral science into use.* Stanford, Calif.: Inst. Commun. Res., 1960.

Harrison, R. In C. Argyris, *Interpersonal competence and organizational effectiveness.* Homewood, Ill.: Dorsey, 1962, Chap. 11.

Leeds, R. and Smith, T. (eds.) *Using social science knowledge in business and industry.* Homewood, Ill.: Irwin, 1963.

Likert, R. and Hayes, S. P., Jr. (eds.) *Some applications of behavioral research.* Paris: UNESCO, 1957.

Mann, F. Studying and creating change: A means to understanding social organization. *Research in industrial relations.* Ann Arbor, Mich.: Industrial Relations Research Association, 1957, Publication No. 17.

Merton, R. K. and Lerner, D. Social scientists and research policy. In D. Lerner and H. D. Lasswell (eds.), *The policy sciences: Recent developments in scope and method.* Stanford, Calif.: Stanford University Press, 1951.

Myrdal, G. *Value in social theory.* New York: Harper, 1958, p. 29.

Parsons, R. T. Evolutionary universals in society. *American Sociological Review,* 1964, **29**, 339–57.

Salisbury, H. E. *To Moscow and beyond.* New York: Harper, 1960, p. 136.

Shepard, H. Three management programs and the theory behind them. In *An action research program for organization improvement.* Ann Arbor, Mich.: Foundation for Research on Human Behavior, 1960.

Sofer, C. *The organization from within.* London: Tavistock, 1961.

Zetterberg, H. L. *Social theory and social practice.* Totowa, N.J.: Bedminster, 1962.

56. CONTINGENCIES OF REINFORCEMENT IN THE DESIGN OF A CULTURE*

***B. F. Skinner*†**

Excessive eating, excessive procreation, and excessive pugnacity, according to Professor Skinner, are the results of reinforcement patterns which once had survival value and so were selected for in the process of evolution. In our day of abundance, overpopulation, and war, these reinforcement patterns are a threat. The dangers of overindulgence in food, sex, aggression, and related behaviors have been dealt with by three traditional methods. The author proposes a fourth method based on contingent reinforcement.[1]

The world in which man lives has been changing much faster than man himself. In a few hundred generations, highly beneficial characteristics of the human body have become troublesome. One of these is the extent to which human behavior is strengthened by certain kinds of reinforcing consequences.

It was once important, for example, that men should learn to identify nutritious food and remember where they found it, that they should learn and remember how to catch fish and kill game and cultivate plants, and that they should eat as much as possible whenever food was available. Those who were most powerfully reinforced by certain kinds of oral stimulation were most likely to do all this and to survive—hence man's extraordinary susceptibility to reinforcement by sugar and other foodstuffs, a sensitivity which, under modern conditions of agriculture and food storage, leads to dangerous overeating.

A similar process of selection presumably explains the reinforcing power of sexual contact. At a time when the human race was periodically decimated by pestilence, famine, and war and steadily attenuated by endemic ills and an unsanitary and dangerous environment, it was important that procreative behavior should be maximized. Those

* *Behavioral Science,* 1966, pp. 159–66.

† Department of Psychology, Harvard University.

[1] Lecture given at the Walter Reed Army Medical Center under the auspices of the Washington School of Psychiatry, March 26, 1965. Preparation of the manuscript has been supported by Grant K6-MH-21,775 of the National Institute of Mental Health of the U.S. Public Health Service, and by the Human Ecology Fund.

for whom sexual reinforcement was most powerful should have continued to copulate most frequently. The breeders selected by sexual competition must have been not only the most powerful and skillful members of the species but those for whom sexual contact was most reinforcing. In a safer environment the same susceptibility leads to serious overpopulation with its attendant ills.

The principle also holds for aggressive behavior. At a time when men were often plundered and killed, by animals and other men, it was important that any behavior which harmed or frightened predators should be quickly learned and long sustained. Those who were most strongly reinforced by evidences of damage to others should have been most likely to survive. Now, under better forms of government, supported by ethical and moral practices which protect person and property, the reinforcing power of successful aggression leads to personal illness, neurotic and otherwise, and to war—if not total destruction.

Such discrepancies between man's sensitivity to reinforcement and the contribution which the reinforced behaviors make to his current welfare raise an important problem in the design of a culture. How are we to keep from overeating, from overpopulating the world, and from destroying each other? How can we make sure that these properties of the human organism, once necessary for survival, shall not now prove lethal?

THREE TRADITIONAL SOLUTIONS

One solution to the problem might be called the voluptuary or sybaritic. Reinforcement is maximized while the unfortunate consequences are either disregarded—on the principle of eat, drink, and be merry for tomorrow we die—or prevented. Romans avoided some of the consequences of overeating, as an occasional neurotic may do today, by using the vomitorium. A modern solution is nonnutritious food. Artificial sweeteners have an effect on the tongue similar to that of ripe fruit, and we can now be reinforced for eating things which have fewer harmful effects. The sybaritic solution to the problem of sexual reinforcement is either irresponsible intercourse or the prevention of consequences through contraception or nonprocreative forms of sex. Aggressive behavior is enjoyed without respect to the consequences in the donnybrook. Some consequences are avoided by being aggressive towards animals, as in bearbaiting and other blood sports, or vicariously aggressive toward both men and animals, as in the Roman circus or in modern body sports and games. (Broadcasters of professional football and prize fights often use special microphones to pick up the thud of body against body.)

It is not difficult to promote the sybaritic solution. Men readily subscribe to a way of life in which primary reinforcers are abundant, for the simple reason that subscribing is a form of behavior susceptible to reinforcement. In such a world one may most effectively pursue happiness (or, to use a less frivolous expression, fulfill one's nature), and the pursuit is easily rationalized: "Nothing but the best, the richest and fullest experience possible, is good enough for man." In these forms, however, the pursuit of happiness is either dangerously irresponsible or deliberately nonproductive and wasteful. Satiation may release a man for productive behavior, but in a relatively unproductive condition.

A second solution might be called, with strict attention to etymology, the puritanical. Reinforcement is offset by punishment. Gluttony, lust, and violence are classified as bad or wrong (and punished by the ethical group), as illegal (and punished by the government), as sinful (and punished by religious authorities), or as maladjusted (and punished by those therapists who use punishment). The puritanical solution is never easy to "sell," and it is not always successful. Punishment does not merely cancel reinforcement; it leads to a struggle for self-control which is often violent and time consuming. Whether one is wrestling with the devil or a cruel superego, there are neurotic by-products. It is possible that punishment sometimes successfully "represses" behavior and the human energies can then be redirected into science, art, and literature, but the metaphor of redirection of energy raises a question to which we must return. In any event the puritanical solution has many unwanted by-products, and we may well explore other ways of generating the acceptable behaviors attributed to it.

A third solution is to bring the body up to date. Reinforcing effects could conceivably be made commensurate with current requirements for survival. Genetic changes could be accelerated through selective breeding or possibly through direct action on the germ plasm, but certain chemical or surgical measures are at the moment more feasible. The appetite-suppressing drugs now available often have undesirable side effects, but a drug which would make food less reinforcing and therefore weaken food-reinforced behavior would be widely used. The possibility is not being overlooked by drug manufacturers. Drugs to reduce the effects of sexual reinforcement—such as those said to be used, whether effectively or not, by penal institutions and the armed services—may not be in great demand, but they would have their uses and might prove surprisingly popular. The semistarvation recommended in some religious regimens as a means of weakening sexual behavior presumably acts through chemical changes. The chemical control of aggressive behavior—by tranquilizers—is already well advanced.

A physiological reduction in sensitivity to reinforcement is not likely to be acceptable to the sybarite. Curiously enough, the puritan would also find it objectionable because certain admirable forms of self-control would not be exhibited. Paraphrasing La Rochefoucauld, we might say that we should not give a man credit for being tranquil if his aggressive inclinations have been suppressed by a tranquilizer. A practical difficulty at the moment is that measures of this sort are not specific and probably undercut desirable reinforcing effects.

A FOURTH SOLUTION

A more direct solution is suggested by the experimental analysis of behavior. One may deal with problems generated by a powerful reinforcer simply by changing the contingencies of reinforcement. An environment may be designed in which reinforcers which ordinarily generate unwanted behavior simply do not do so. The solution seems reasonable enough when the reinforcers are of no special significance. A student once defended the use of punishment with the following story. A young mother had come to call on his family, bringing her five-year-old son. The boy immediately climbed onto the piano bench and began to pound the keys. Conversation was almost impossible and the visit a failure. The student argued for the puritanical solution: He would have punished the child—rather violently, he implied. He was overlooking the nature of pianos. For more than 200 years talented and skillful men have worked to create a device which will powerfully reinforce the behavior of pressing keys. (The piano is, indeed, an "eighty-eight lever box." It exists solely to reinforce the pressing of levers—or the encouraging of others to press them.) The child's behavior simply testified to the success of the piano industry. It is bad design to bring child and piano together and then punish the behavior which naturally follows.

A comparable solution is not so obvious when the reinforcers have strong biological significance because the problem is misunderstood. We do not say that a child possesses a basic need to play the piano. It is obvious that the behavior has arisen from a history of reinforcement. In the case of food, sex, and violence, however, traditional formulations have emphasized supposed internal needs or drives. A man who cannot keep from overeating suffers from strong internal stimulation which he easily mistakes for the cause (rather than a collateral effect) of his uncontrollable behavior, and which he tries to reduce in order to solve his problem. He cannot go directly to the inner stimulation, but only to some of the conditions responsible for it—conditions which, as he puts it, "make him feel hungry." These happen also to be conditions which "make him eat." The easiest way to reduce both the internal stimulation and the strength of the behavior is simply to eat, but that does not solve the problem. In concentrating on other ways of changing needs or drives, we overlook a solution to the behavioral problem.

What a man must control to avoid the troublesome consequences of oral reinforcement is the behavior reinforced. He must stop buying and eating candy bars, ordering and eating extra pieces of cake, eating at odd times of the day, and so on. It is not some inner state called hunger but overeating which presents a problem. The behavior can be weakened by making sure that it is not reinforced. In an environment in which only simple foods have been available a man eats sensibly—not because he must, but because no other behavior has ever been strengthened. The normal environment is of a very different sort. In an affluent society most people are prodigiously reinforced with food. Susceptibility to reinforcement leads men to specialize in raising particularly delicious foods and to process and cook them in ways which make them as reinforcing as possible. Overanxious parents offer especially delicious food to encourage children to eat. Powerful reinforcers (called "candy") are used to obtain favors, to allay emotional disturbances, and to strengthen personal relations. It is as if the environment had been designed to build the very behaviors which later prove troublesome. The child it produces has no greater "need for food" than one for whom food has never been particularly reinforcing.

Similarly, it is not some "sexuality" or "sex drive" which has troublesome consequences but sexual behavior itself, much of which can be traced to contingencies of reinforcement. The conditions under which a young person is first sexually reinforced determine the extent as well as the form of later sexual activity. Nor is the problem of aggression raised by a "death instinct" or "a fundamental drive in human beings to hurt one another" (Menninger, 1964), but rather by an environment in which human beings are reinforced when they hurt one another. To say that there is "something suicidal in man that makes him enjoy war" is to reverse the causal order; man's capacity to enjoy war leads to a form of suicide. In a world in which a child seldom if ever successfully attacks others, agressive behavior is not strong. But the world is usually quite different. Either through simple neglect or in the belief that innate needs must be expressed, children are allowed and even encouraged to attack each other in various ways. Aggressive behavior is condoned in activities proposed as "a moral equivalent of war." It may be that wars have been won on the playing fields of Eton, but they have also been started there, for a playing field is an arena for the reinforcement of aggressive action, and the behaviors there reinforced will sooner or later cause trouble.

The distinction between need and reinforcement is clarified by a current problem. Many of those who are trying to stop smoking cigarettes will testify to a basic drive or need as powerful as those of hunger, sex, and aggression. (For those who have a genuine drug addiction, smoking is reinforced in part by the alleviation of withdrawal symptoms, but most smokers can shift to nicotine-free cigarettes without too much trouble. They are still unable to control the powerful repertoire of responses which compose smoking). It is clear that the troublesome pattern of behavior—"the cigarette habit"—can be traced, not to a need, but to a history of reinforcement because there was no problem before the discovery of tobacco or before the invention of the cigarette as an especially reinforcing form in which tobacco may be smoked. Whatever their other needs may have been, our ancestors had no need to smoke cigarettes, and no one has the need today if, like them, he has never been reinforced for smoking.

The problem of cigarette smoking has been approached in the other ways we have examined. Some advertising appeals to the irresponsible sybarite: Buy the cigarette that tastes good and inhale like a man. Other sybaritic smokers try to avoid the consequences; the filter is the contraceptive of the tobacco industry. The puritanical solution has also been tried. Cigarettes may be treated so that the smoker is automatically punished by nausea. Natural aversive consequences—a rough throat, a hoarse voice, a cigarette cough, or serious illness—may be made more punishing. The American Cancer Society has tried to condition aversive consequences with a film, in color, showing the removal of a cancerous lung. As is often the case with the puritanical solution, aversive stimuli are indeed conditioned—they are felt as "guilt"—but smoking is not greatly reduced. A true nicotine addiction might be controlled by taking nicotine or a similar drug in other ways, but a drug which would be closer to the chemical solution promised by anti-appetite, anti-sex, and anti-agression drugs would specifically reduce the effect of other reinforcers in smoking. All these measures are much more difficult than controlling the contingencies of reinforcement.

(That there is no need to smoke cigarettes may be denied by those who argue that it is actually composed of several other kinds of needs, all of them present in nonsmokers. But this is simply to say that cigarette smoking is reinforced by several distinguishable effects—by odor, taste, oral stimulation, vasoconstriction in the lungs, "something to do with the hands," appearing to resemble admired figures, and so on. A non-smoker has not come under the control of a particular combination of these reinforcers. If any one should cause trouble on its own or in some other combination, it could be analyzed in the same way.)

MAKING CONTINGENCIES LESS EFFECTIVE

The problems raised by man's extraordinary sensitivity to reinforcement by food, sexual contact, and aggressive damage cannot be solved, as the example of cigarette smoking might suggest, simply by removing these things from the environment. It would be impossible to change the world that much, and in any case the reinforcers serve useful functions. (One important function is simply to encourage support for a culture. A way of life in which food, sex, and aggression were kept to a bare minimum would not strongly reinforce those who adopted it nor discourage defections from it.) The problem is not to eliminate reinforcers but to moderate their effects. Several possible methods are suggested by recent work in the experimental analysis of behavior. The mere frequency with which a reinforcer occurs is much less important than the contingencies of which it is a part.

We can minimize some unwanted consequences by preventing the discovery of reinforcing effects. The first step in "hooking" a potential heroin addict is to give him heroin. The reinforcer is not at first contingent on any particular form of behavior; but when its effect has been felt (and, particularly, when withdrawal symptoms have developed), it can be made contingent on paying for the drug. Addiction is prevented simply by making sure that the effect is never felt. The reinforcing effects of alcohol, caffeine, and nicotine must be discovered in a similar way, and methods of preventing addiction take the same form. The process underlies the practice of giving free samples in food markets; customers are induced to eat small quantities of a new food so that larger quantities may be made contingent on surrendering money. Similar practices are to be found in sexual seduction and in teaching the pleasures of violence.

Reinforcers are made effective in other ways. Stimuli are conditioned so that they become reinforcing; aversive properties are weakened through adaptation so that reinforcing properties emerge with greater power (a "taste" is thus acquired); and so on. Processes of this sort have played their part in man's slow discovery of reinforcing things. It has been, perhaps, a history of the discovery of human potentialities, but among these we must recognize the potentiality for getting into trouble. In any case, the processes which makes things reinforcing need to be closely scrutinized.

The excessive consummation which leads to overweight, overpopulation, and war is only one result of man's sensitivity to reinforcement. Another, often equally troublesome, is an exhausting preoccupation with behavior which is only infrequently consummated. A single reinforcement may generate and miantain a great deal of behavior when it comes at the end of a sequence or chain of responses. Chains of indefinite length are constructed in the laboratory by conditioning intermediate reinforcers. Teachers and others use the same method for many practical purposes. We may assume that something of the sort has occurred whenever we observe long chains. The dedicated horticulturalist is ultimately reinforced, say, by a final perfect bloom, but all the behavior leading up to it is not thereby explained; intermediate stages in progressing toward a final bloom must in some way have become reinforcing. In order for early man to have discovered agriculture, certain early stages of cultivation must first have been reinforced by accident or at least under conditions irrelevant to the eventual achievement.

The reinforcers we are considering generate many sequences of this sort with troublesome results. Ultimate reinforcement is often ridiculously out of proportion to the activity it sustains. Many hours of careful labor on the part of a cook lead at last to brief stimulation from a delicious food. A good wine reinforces months or years of dedicated care. Brief sexual reinforcement follows a protracted campaign of seduction (see, for example, Choderlos de Laclos's *Les liaisons dangereuses* or Kierkegaard's *The Seducer.*) The campaign of the dedicated aggressor, domestic or international, is often similarly protracted and suggests a long history in which a chain has been built up. Problems of this sort can be solved simply by breaking up the conditions under which long chains are formed.

Another kind of exhausting preoccupation is due to intermittent reinforcement. A single form of response is repeated again and again, often at a very high rate, even though only infrequently reinforced. Activities such as reading magazines and books, going to the theatre, and watching television are reinforced on so-called "interval" schedules. So-called "ratio" schedules are exemplified by piece-rate pay in industry and by gambling systems and devices. (Ratio schedules are so powerful that their use is often restricted or controlled by law.) Large quantities of behavior are generated by such schedules only when they have been carefully programmed. Reinforcement is at first relatively frequent, but the behavior remains strong as the frequency is reduced. Thus, a television program grows less and less reinforcing as the writer runs out of themes or as the viewer no longer finds the same themes interesting, but one who has followed a program from the beginning may continue to watch it long after reinforcements have become quite rare. The dishonest gambler prepares his victim by steadily "stretching" the mean ratio in a variable ratio schedule. Eventually the victim continues to play during a very long period without reinforcement.

There are many natural systems which "stretch" ratios. As addiction develops, the addict must take more and more of a drug (and presumably work harder and harder to get it) to achieve a given effect. To the extent that novelty is important, all reinforcers grow less effective with time. The gourmet is less often reinforced as familiar foods begin to cloy. The ratio schedule of sexual reinforcement is automatically stretched by satiation. The enormities suffered by the unfortunate Justine in de Sade's story suggest that her many persecutors were being reinforced on ratio schedules severely strained by both aging and sexual exhaustion. Frank Harris has suggested, in his biography of Oscar Wilde (1916), that the word "lead" in "lead us not into temptation" is an unconscious recognition of the progression through which more and more troublesome forms of behavior are approached. Unwanted consequences are averted in all such cases by breaking up the programs through which infrequent reinforcement comes to sustain large quantities of behavior.

ARRANGING USEFUL CONTINGENCIES

We are usually interested—for example, in education—in getting the greatest possible effect from weak reinforcers in short supply. The problem here is just the reverse—we are to minimize the effect of reinforcers which are all too abundant and powerful. Hence, instead of systematically building up long chains of responses, we prevent their formation, and instead of constructing programs which make strained schedules effective we break them up. We can use the same procedures in the more familiar direction, however, in another solution to our problem. Reinforcers can be made contingent on productive behavior to which they were not originally related. Soldiers have often been induced to fight skillfully and energetically by arranging that victory will be followed by the opportunity to plunder, rape, and slaughter. It has always been particularly easy for the barbarian to mount an attack on a more advanced civilization which emphasizes the delectations of food and sex. It has been said, for example, that the wines of Italy (and presumably her well-groomed and beautiful women) made Rome particularly vulnerable. All governments make aggressive damage to an enemy especially reinforcing to their soldiers with stories of atrocities. Religious visions of another world have been made reinforcing in the same modes. Many of the offerings to the gods portrayed in Egyptian temples are edible, and Greek and Roman gods were distinguished by their taste for ambrosia and nectar, although less advanced civilizations have looked forward only to a happy hunting ground. Sex has its place in the Muslem heaven where men may expect to enjoy the attention of beautiful virgin Huris, and some theologians have argued that one of the attractions of the Christian heaven is the spectacle of sinners being tormented in hell—a spectacle which, as portrayed for example in the *Inferno,* competes successfully with the Roman circus at its most violent.

Marriage is often described as a system in which unlimited sexual contact with a selected partner is contingent on nonsexual behavior useful to the culture—such as supporting and managing a household and family and, following St. Paul's famous principle, foresaking sexual activity elsewhere. Women have often raised moral standards with practices which were merely carred to an extreme by Lysistrata. Educators use the basic reinforcers rather timidly. Erasmus (1529) advocated cherries and cakes in place of the cane in teaching children Greek and Latin, but he was the exception rather than the rule. Homosexual reinforcement was explicit in Greek education, however, and a sadistic or masochistic violence has supported corporal punishment and competitive arrangements among students down to modern times. Economic transactions characteristically involve food, sex, and aggression since money as a generalized reinforcer derives much of its power when exchanged for them. In the nineteenth century it was expected that wages would be exchanged primarily for food, and charity was opposed on the grounds that the industrial system needed a hungry labor force. Better working conditions have made other reinforcers effective, but many of them are still related to sex and aggression.

Our reinforcers have, of course, a special place in art, music, and literature. Their place in science is not always obvious. Max Weber has argued, indeed, that the scientist is a product of the puritanical solution—profiting, for example, from the scrupulous or meticulous concern for exact detail generated by aversive consequences (the etymologies of *scrupulous* and *meticulous* show punitive origins). Feuer (1963) has recently shown, however, that almost all outstanding men in science have followed a "hedonist ethic."

A solution to our problem in which food, sex, and aggression are made contingent on useful forms of behavior to which they are not naturally related has much to recommend it. It should be acceptable to the sybarite because he will not lack reinforcement. It should also assuage the puritan, not only because objectionable consequences which seem to call for punishment have been attenuated but because a man must work for the reinforcers he receives. It should not require any change in human behavior through chemical, surgical, or even genetic means, since a natural sensitivity to reinforcement is now useful rather than troublesome.

The solution has not yet been satisfactorily worked out, however. The contingencies of positive reinforcement arranged by governmental and religious agencies are primitive, and the agencies continue to lean heavily on the puritanical solution. Wage systems only rarely make effective use of positive reinforcement. In practice, wages simply establish a standard from which the worker can be cut off by being discharged. The control is aversive and the results unsatisfactory for both the employers (since not much is done) and the employee (since work is still work). Education is still largely aversive; most students study mainly in order to avoid the consequences of not studying. In short, some of the most powerful forces in human behavior are not being effectively used.

And for good reason. We are only beginning to understand how reinforcement works. The important things in life seem to be food, sex, and many other pleasant, enjoyable, and satisfying stimuli. These are the things which define happiness. They are the "good" things which contribute to the greatest good of the greatest number. They characterize human purpose, for they are among the things men live *for.* When we design a better world, either utopian or theological, we make sure that there will be an abundant supply of them. We thus go directly to the reinforcers and are no doubt reinforced for doing so. We overlook a much more important consideration—the ways in which these wonderful things are contingent on behavior.

The concept of drive or need is particularly at fault here. We neglect contingencies of reinforcement because we seek solutions to all our problems in the satisfaction of needs. "To each according to his need" is the avowed goal of both an affluent society and a welfare state. (The principle is scriptural. St. Augustine discussed it long before St. Karl.) If those who seem to have everything are still not happy, we are forced to conclude that there must be less obvious needs which are unsatisfied. Men must have spiritual as well as material needs—they must need someone or something beyond themselves to believe in, and so on—and it is because these needs are unfulfilled that life seems so often empty and man so often rootless. This desperate move to preserve the concept of need is unnecessary because a much more interesting and fruitful design is possible.

Men are happy in an environment in which active, productive, and creative behavior is reinforced in effective ways. The trouble with both affluent and welfare societies is that reinforcers are not contingent on particular forms of behavior. Men are not reinforced for doing anything and hence they do nothing. This is the "contentment" of the Arcadian idyll and of the retired businessman. It may represent a satisfaction of needs, but it raises other problems. Those who have nothing important to do fall prey to trivial reinforcers. When effectively scheduled, even weak reinforcers generate strong, compulsive, repetitive behavior which ultimately proves aversive. Only when we stop using reinforcers to allay needs can we begin to use them to "fulfill man's nature" in a much more important sense.

Contingencies of reinforcement are far more important than the reinforcers they incorporate, but they are much less obvious. Only very recently, and then only under rigorous experimental conditions, have the extraordinary effects of contingencies been observed. Perhaps this explains why it has not been possible to design effective contingencies simply with the help of common sense or of practical skill in handling people or even with the help of principles derived from scientific field observations of behavior. The experimental analysis of behavior thus has a very special relevance to the design of cultures. Only through the active prosecution of such an analysis, and the courageous application of its results to daily life, will it be possible to design those contingencies of reinforcement which will generate and maintain the most subtle and complex behavior of which men are capable.

REFERENCES

Erasmus. *The liberal education of children.* 1529. Cited by Curtis, S. J. and Boultwood, M. E. A. *A short history of educational ideas.* London: University Tutorial Press, 1953, p. 129.

Feuer, Lewis S. *The scientific intellectual.* New York: Basic Books, 1963.

Harris, Frank. *Oscar Wilde, his life and confessions.* New York, 1916.

Menninger, Karl. Quoted in *Boston Globe,* December 13, 1964.